*To Beth, Chris, Holly, Jon, Nancy, Piotr, and Susan*

*—M.C.C.*

*To Joan, Christopher, Jon, and Anne*

*—D.W.*

# Brief Contents

## PART FOUR GOVERNMENT IN OPERATION

# Contents

# PART TWO POLITICS AND PEOPLE

## PART THREE THE POLICYMAKERS

## PART FOUR GOVERNMENT IN OPERATION

# Preface

There is, without doubt, no better experience than revising a college text in government and politics to remind one of the astonishing pace of change within the American political system.

This revised 2006 election update of *Democracy Under Pressure* reflects that rapid pace of change both at home and abroad. Since the publication of the tenth edition two years ago, the nation has experienced increasing public concerrn about the war in Iraq, the rising toll of American troops killed and wounded in that conflict, and the escalating sectarian violence there; Hurricane Katrina, and the failed response of the federal government to the disaster; more cases of corruption and ethical lapses in Congress; the appointment of a new chief justice at the Supreme Court; the start of a new prescription drug benefit for seniors; the war between Israel and the militants of Hezbollah in Lebanon; and an underground nuclear test by North Korea, together with the continuing worry that Iran may be secretly building nuclear weapons.

Many of the events that occurred in the last two years affected the outcome of the congressional elections of November 2006, in which the Democrats won control of the United States Senate and the House of Representatives. Those midterm elections are reported and analyzed in this new, updated edition.

So much has happened in America in less than a decade—the horrors of the 9/11 terrorist attacks on New York and Washington, the war and continuing conflict in Afghanistan, the creation of a new cabinet department for homeland security, the debate over the war in Iraq and whether and when American troops might leave, the election of President George W. Bush to a second term in the White House by a sharply divided electorate, the capture of Saddam Hussein, the threat of terrorism, and economic problems. All of these developments are discussed in this 2006 election update, along with other important changes in American politics and government.

Even before 9/11, the changes in American society and in the political landscape were remarkable. America had moved into a new century, survived the impeachment and acquittal of President William Jefferson Clinton, and elected a new president in 2000 only after a 36-day postelection trauma finally settled by the U.S. Supreme Court. America had also experienced something like a digital revolution, as the use of the Internet increased exponentially, and cell phones, laptop computers, wi-fi technology, and e-mail became a normal part of the lives of millions of Americans.

The nation's political tides changed as well with the election and reelection of George W. Bush as president. The election of Bill Clinton in 1992 had marked an end to 12 years of Republican rule in the White House. But American political parties are resilient; in 2000, after Clinton's two terms as president, the GOP returned to power. Then came the attacks of 9/11 and Bush's re-election in 2004. As in previous editions, a detailed, in-depth analysis of the voting patterns in the 2004 presidential and the 2006 congressional elections appears in Chapter 11, "Voting Behavior and Elections."

The presidential race in 2004 took place against a background of an uncertain economy and the loss of jobs, especially in the industrial heartland; a weakened dollar; and a huge federal deficit. A few years earlier, many people, including retirees, had invested in great numbers in stocks and mutual funds. Many had seen their savings dwindle or disappear when the market slid sharply downward. Americans were concerned as well about the state of the nation's public schools. As the 2004 election had demonstrated—9/11 and the continuing threat of terrorist attacks remained a concern to many voters.

All of these shifting currents are discussed in this edition, along with a revised and updated examination of the power of the news media, trends in the decisions of the Supreme Court, the debate over the future of Social Security, the controversy over the USA Patriot Act, and important demographic shifts in the population.

As America moved further into the 21st century, the world had changed as well. International terrorism clearly posed a new threat to peace and security at home and abroad. With the collapse of the Soviet Union in 1991, the peril of a nuclear holocaust had seemed to recede, but nuclear proliferation remained a major danger to world peace as more nations acquired weapons of mass destruction.

These and many other issues, both domestic and international, are explored in this edition, including the use of television and the Internet in political campaigns; the role of professional campaign managers; and how "soft money," although banned by the McCain-Feingold campaign finance law of 2002, continued to flow into the political arena through "527 organizations."

More than three decades have passed since *Democracy Under Pressure* first made its appearance. And what extraordinary years they have been: the end of the long war in Vietnam; the Watergate trauma and impeachment inquiry; the resignation and pardon of the president of the United States; the energy crisis; the Carter years; the seizure of American hostages in Iran and in Lebanon; the election and reelection of Ronald Reagan, a conservative Republican president pledged to increasing the nation's military strength while cutting a broad range of social programs; the Iran-contra affair; the first President Bush's one-term presidency; his triumph in the Persian Gulf War, forcing Iraq's Saddam Hussein to withdraw from Kuwait; the failed coup attempt against Soviet president Mikhail S. Gorbachev, and, only four months later, Gorbachev's resignation and the end of the Soviet Union—and with it, the end of the Cold War; the rise of Boris N. Yeltsin and then Vladimir Putin as the leader of Russia; that country's first free presidential elections and subsequent restrictions on the press and political activity; the turmoil and continuing search for peace in the Middle East; the assassination of Israel's prime minister, Yitzhak Rabin; the advent of domestic terrorism in the United States, with the bombing of the federal building in Oklahoma City; the Clinton scandals, his impeachment, trial, and acquittal; the dramatic economic expansion and prosperity at home, followed by recession and economic difficulties; the 9/11 terrorist attack on America; the wars in Afghanistan and Iraq; the reelection of George W. Bush; and the death of Palestinian leader Yasir Arafat; and the underground nuclear test by North Korea.

## The Tenth Edition 2006 Election Update

This tenth edition election update of *Democracy Under Pressure* has been revised not only to reflect many of these kaleidoscopic events, but also to focus on the broader trends in and newer interpretations of the American political system.

As in the past, the making of public policy is discussed throughout the book (and particularly in Part Three, "The Policymakers"), and a section introducing the student to policy analysis is included in Chapter 1. This introduction to the policy process follows, in logical progression, the discussion of the concept of a political system.

There are many new features, boxes, and websites incorporated in this edition, as well as extensive additional resources available to instructors and students. The appendix includes the Constitution, the Declaration of Independence, two essays from *The Federalist,* and a list of the presidents of the United States and the votes they received. The glossary has been revised and expanded for this edition.

Near the start of each chapter, we have included a key question designed to stimulate critical thinking on the part of the student. In addition, other basic questions to consider about the workings of the American political system are posed near the beginning of each chapter. The book does not, in every case, provide ready answers to those questions, but it raises them for the student's consideration and, if desired, for classroom discussion.

Many new topics and events are also explored in this edition. We discuss and explain the Supreme Court's 2004 and 2006 decisions restricting the Bush administration's power over enemy combatants and detainees and congressional action to allow military trials of detainees to go forward. Included as well are the Court's ruling in the University of Michigan affirmative action cases, and other significant Supreme Court decisions, including the Court's reaffirmation of its historic 1966 *Miranda* decision protecting the rights of criminal suspects. We have also expanded and updated our discussion of capital punishment, and the growing reevaluation of the death penalty.

In addition, we have revised and updated our discussion of the many barriers women still face in American society, and of the bias experienced by many minority groups, including African Americans, Hispanic Americans, Asian Americans, gays and lesbians, and disabled persons. We have covered as well the recall of the governor of California and the election of his successor.

Our chapter on the media and politics includes a revised discussion of the multibillion-dollar mergers among the media giants, and the potential impact on society, and a new case study of the leak of the identity of a CIA officer and its investigation. The chapter on political parties reflects how national conventions have to an even greater extent become scripted, controlled, made-for-television events now that the spring primaries in effect choose the nominees long before the conventions ratify them.

The examination of the 2004 presidential campaign contains new data on money and politics, and the power of television commercials—with examples, including the impact of the negative "Swift Boat Veterans for Truth" ads on the Kerry campaign.

Finally, in the complete, hardcover version of the book, we have revised and expanded the discussion of foreign policy to examine the importance of terrorism, globalization, the role of the United Nations and its peacekeeping missions, the expansion of NATO, the renewed violence in the Middle East, and global issues including overpopulation, famine, disease, and ethnic and religious conflicts.

## Goals of the Book

As the title of this book indicates, the authors recognize that the American political system is under pressure, that its ability to cope with the problems facing the nation is being questioned by many individuals and groups in our society. In such a time, we continue to believe it useful to provide a book that focuses not only on the very considerable achievements of the American system of government but on its shortcomings too—a book that focuses on the reality as well as the rhetoric of American democracy. We have tried to do this in a textbook designed for today. To emphasize this theme, we have included a new box series, "Myth vs. Reality," in several chapters. We have also greatly expanded the series of boxes on comparative government.

In writing this book, we set three goals. First, we believe that a textbook should be lively and stimulating to read. So we have attempted to provide a text that is as clear and readable as possible without sacrificing scholarship or content.

Second, although we present American governmental and political institutions in their historical context, we have sought to relate politics and government to contemporary issues. At the same time, we have tried to relate those contemporary issues to larger concepts.

Third, as we have indicated, we have attempted to focus on the gaps, where they exist, between American myths and American realities and the political system's promise and its performance. Students and other citizens may not be disillusioned with the principles of American democracy, but they do ask that the political system practice those principles.

In examining the structure and processes of American politics and government, we have tried to ask: How is the political system supposed to work? How does it actually work? What might be done to make it work better? At the same time, the book emphasizes the importance of each individual citizen for the quality of American society and American government. It emphasizes how one person can make a difference, and a box in each chapter reflects that lesson. The text provides examples of participation in the political process by students and other citizens. It examines the responsibilities as well as the rights of citizens in a democracy.

## Acknowledgments

The authors deeply appreciate the assistance of the many people who helped to produce the tenth edition. We must begin with the incomparable Laura Milner, our director of research, who provided superb and tireless research and editorial assistance throughout every phase of the preparation of the revised manuscript for this tenth edition and the 2006 election update. Her contribution was invaluable, her Internet and computer skills essential to our task, and her dedication and talent both unflagging and wondrous.

For the tenth edition, we are grateful as well for the editorial assistance we received from Professor Harvey L. Schantz, of the State University of New York, Plattsburgh.

We also wish to thank our research assistants for previous editions: Norma W. Batchelder and Thomas A. Horne for the first edition (1971), Freda F. Solomon for the second edition (1974), Nancy D. Beers for the third edition (1977), M. J. Rusk-Pierce for the fourth edition (1981), Jessica Tolmach for the fifth edition (1985), Robin G. Colucci for the sixth edition (1989), Kristin Kenney Williams for the seventh edition (1993) and the eighth edition (1997), and Sarah J. Albertini, for the ninth edition (2001).

We wish to express our appreciation as well to Graham Fetterman, Alexandra Evans, and Elizabeth Evans, who kept our reference files up-to-date for this edition; to G. Evans Witt, CEO of the Princeton Survey Research Center; to Matthew C. Price of Texas A&M University, Kingsville; to Justin C. Shaberly, John Quinn Kerrigan, William Rankin, and Conor A. Reidy, who provided assistance on the ninth edition; to Geoffrey D. Gray, who helped us on several chapters of the eighth edition; and to John Fox Sullivan, president and publisher of the *National Journal.*

We are grateful as well to the many people who gave us the benefit of their advice and assistance along the way. That list is long, and it includes Frederick L. Holborn of the School of Advanced International Studies, The Johns Hopkins University; Dean John R. Kramer of the Tulane University School of Law; Herbert E. Alexander, former director of the Citizens' Research Foundation; Roger H. Davidson of the University of California, Santa Barbara; Walter J. Oleszek of the Congressional Research Service of the Library of Congress; Harry Balfe of Montclair State College; Richard C. Wald, senior vice president, ABC News; Richard M. Scammon, director of the Elections Research Center; Jane E. Kirtley, former executive director of the Reporters Committee for Freedom of the Press; Jonathan W. Wise, Christopher J. Wise, Francis J. Lorson, chief deputy clerk, and Daniel Long of the Office of the Reporter, U.S. Supreme Court; Tony Albertini, of Mediavest; Rich Bond, of The Johns Hopkins University; Philip Robbins, of the George Washington University; as well as the many scholars, colleagues, and others whose help was acknowledged in earlier editions and to whom we remain indebted.

A number of professors who are specialists on various aspects of American politics also offered us invaluable chapter-by-chapter comments on the ninth edition that helped us to plan the tenth edition: They include Rebecca Britton, University of California-Davis; Jim Cox, Georgia Perimeter College; Joyce Gelb, The City College of New York; Forest Grieves, University of Montana; Scott Heffner, De Anza College; Alfred R. Light, St. Thomas University; Thomas R. Marshall, University of Texas at Arlington; and David Robinson, University of Houston–Downtown.

We are grateful also to professors who helped guide the revision of this update edition: John Bertalan, Hillsborough Community College; Richard Chesteen, University of Tennessee–Martin; Jeff Fox, Fort Lewis College; Joseph Gaziano, Lewis University; Thomas R. Hunter, University of West Georgia; Judson Jeffries, Purdue University; Melody Massih, Colorado Mountain College; Allen Meyer, Mesa Community College; and Kenneth Quinnell, Central Florida Community College–Citrus.

The comments of all these reviewers were consistently helpful. At the same time, responsibility for the final text, including any errors or shortcomings, is ours.

Finally, we wish to express our thanks to the staff of Thomson Higher Education, beginning with Carolyn O. Merrill, executive editor, who supervised this 2006 election update, and Stacey Sims, our outstanding and talented developmental editor. P. J. Boardman, vice president and editor-in-chief for humanities; Clark Baxter, publisher; Janise Fry, marketing manager; Paul Wells, senior project manager, editorial production; Rebecca Green, assistant editor; Patrick Rheaume, editorial assistant; and Kassie Tosiello, marketing assistant. For the tenth edition, we would also like to acknowledge the contribution of David C. Tatom, who as executive editor in political science oversaw the tenth edition and the previous three editions and whose support and counsel for this project were invaluable.

We also wish to thank the dedicated team at Newgen–Austin, including Mary Keith Trawick, production services coordinator for the 2006 election update; and, for the tenth edition, Gretchen Otto, production coordinator; Alison Rainey, project editor; and Jessie Dolch, copy editor.

We shall always owe a special debt of gratitude to the late William A. Pullin, senior editor, who first proposed this book project to us and gave it his continued support; to Virginia Joyner, our manuscript editor for the first two editions; to Harry Rinehart, designer for the first four editions; to Joanne D. Daniels, editor for the third and fourth editions; to Drake Bush, our editor for the fifth and sixth editions; to Margie Rogers, our manuscript editor for the sixth edition; to Bill M. Barnett, senior vice president at Harcourt; and to Kathryn M. Stewart, the senior project editor on the ninth edition. For the tenth edition and this 2006 election update, we are grateful as well to Linda L. Rill, who researched many of the photographs and cartoons, and to executive art director Maria Epes, who applied her creative talents to integrate the whole—type and graphics—into a result that captures in visual form the spirit and purpose of our examination of *Democracy Under Pressure.*

*Milton C. Cummings, Jr.*
*David Wise*

# ABOUT THE AUTHORS

MILTON C. CUMMINGS, JR. is an award-winning educator who received his undergraduate degree from Swarthmore College in Pennsylvania. After two years of graduate study in England, where he was a Rhodes scholar at Oxford University, he earned a Ph.D. in political science from Harvard University.

Professor Cummings worked for six years at the Brookings Institution in Washington, D.C., where he did research and writing on American government and politics. He then joined the political science faculty at Johns Hopkins University in Baltimore, Maryland, where he is currently professor emeritus. For 15 years, he also served as a consultant for NBC News, specializing in the network's television coverage of U.S. congressional elections. He is also a member of the Research Advisory Council of the Center for Arts and Culture.

At Johns Hopkins, Professor Cummings has been honored with numerous awards. These include the George Owen Teaching Award, the Edward H. Griffin Award, and several other citations for outstanding teaching. He has also received fellowships and grants for research from the Social Science Research Council, the National Science Foundation, the Ford Foundation, and the Guggenheim Foundation.

Professor Cummings is the author or editor of an extensive number of scholarly articles and books, including *The Image of the Federal Service; Congressmen and the Electorate; The Patron State: Government and the Arts in Europe, North America, and Japan;* and, of course, *Democracy Under Pressure.*

DAVID WISE is a political writer based in Washington, D.C. He is the author or coauthor of 10 books on government and politics and is a leading writer on intelligence, espionage, and government secrecy. His articles have appeared in the *New York Times Magazine, Vanity Fair,* and many other major publications.

He is the former chief of the Washington bureau of the *New York Herald Tribune* and was a regular weekly commentator on CNN for six years.

A native New Yorker and graduate of Columbia College, he joined the *Herald Tribune* in 1951 and served as the newspaper's White House correspondent before becoming chief of the Washington bureau. He is a former Fellow of the Woodrow Wilson International Center for Scholars in Washington, D.C., and for two years he lectured in political science at the University of California at Santa Barbara.

His recent book, *Spy: The Inside Story of How the FBI's Robert Hanssen Betrayed America* (Random House, 2002), received high praise from reviewers. He is also the author of *Nightmover: How Aldrich Ames Sold the CIA to the KGB for $4.6 Million,* which was excerpted in *Time* magazine. He is coauthor of *The Invisible Government,* a number-one best seller about the Central Intelligence Agency that has been widely credited with bringing about a reappraisal of the role of the CIA in a democratic society.

He has received several awards, including, in 1974, the George Polk Memorial Award for his book *The Politics of Lying.*

# Democracy Under Pressure

*An Introduction to the American Political System*

"All the News That's Fit to Print"

# The New York Times

**Late Edition**

New York: **Today,** rainy, windy, hig 59. **Tonight,** rain ends, some clearin low 54. **Tomorrow,** partly cloudy ar very mild, high 68. **Yesterday,** high 5 low 47. Weather map is on Page A1

VOL. CLVI . . No. 53,757 + Copyright © 2006 The New York Times NEW YORK, WEDNESDAY, NOVEMBER 8, 2006 ONE DOLLA

# DEMOCRATS TAKE HOUSE

## *WHITE HOUSE CONCEDES DEFEAT; SENATE IS TIGHT; SPITZER IN ROUT; MENENDEZ AND LIEBERMAN WIN*

### THE '06 ELECTION

**THE REGION**

**Menendez Wins Handily; Comeback for Lieberman**

Senator Joseph I. Lieberman made a comeback in Connecticut, winning re-election as an independent three months after losing the Democratic primary and despite his support for the Iraq war. Antiwar sentiment appeared to play a greater role in New Jersey, where the Democratic incumbent, Bob Menendez, above, defeated his Republican challenger, Thomas H. Kean Jr. PAGE P8

**THE HOUSE**

**New Faces in Congress**

Chris Murphy, a 33-year-old Democrat, defeated the longest-serving representative in Connecticut history, Nancy L. Johnson. Mr. Murphy had criticized Mrs. Johnson, a 12-term Republican, for her support for the war in Iraq. In upstate New York, another antiwar Democrat, John Hall, above, a founding member of the band Orleans, ousted a six-term Republican, Sue Kelly. PAGE P2

**COMPTROLLER**

**Hevesi Hangs On**

Alan G. Hevesi, a Democrat, was re-elected as New York State comptroller, despite accusations that have led to governmental and criminal inquiries. Even with his victory over J. Christopher Callaghan, Mr. Hevesi, above, faces doubts about his future after using a state employee to chauffeur his wife. PAGE P14

**GOVERNORS**

**A First in Massachusetts**

Deval Patrick, the Justice Department's top civil rights lawyer under President Bill Clinton, was elected governor of Massachusetts — the state's first black governor and only the second in the nation since Reconstruction. Republicans also lost the governorship in Ohio, where Representative Ted Strickland, a Democrat, defeated Secretary of State J. Kenneth Blackwell. PAGE P1

**BALLOT QUESTIONS**

**No to an Abortion Ban**

Voters in South Dakota rejected the most sweeping abortion ban proposed in the nation in more than a decade, an effort to challenge Roe v. Wade. Michigan voters approved a measure barring affirmative action by public institutions in education, employment or contracting. PAGE P8

### ONLINE

- *For the latest results of House, Senate and regional races.*
- *News and analysis from the New York Times political staff.*
- *Interactive graphics to highlight who will control the next Congress.*

Doug Mills/The New York Times

Democrats, including Representative Nancy Pelosi, celebrated victories from coast to coast.

Ruth Fremson/The New York Times

Senator Joseph I. Lieberman thanked supporters.

Chang W. Lee/The New York Times

Eliot Spitzer enjoying his victory in Manhattan.

## *12-Year Run Over, Balance May Rest on Virginia Race*

By ADAM NAGOURNEY

Democrats seized control of the House of Representatives and defeated at least three Republican senators yesterday, riding a wave of voter discontent with President Bush and the war in Iraq.

Democrats were still short of the six seats they need to win the Senate. But with Missouri going Democratic early this morning and Montana within reach, control of the Senate increasingly seemed to hinge on the outcome in Virginia, where the two candidates were virtually tied.

The Democratic victory in the House — overcoming a legendarily efficient White House political machine — represented a dramatic turnaround in the fortunes of the Democratic Party and signaled a sea change in the political dynamics in Washington after a dozen years in which Republicans controlled Congress for all but a brief period.

No less significant for the long-term political fortunes of their party, Democrats won at least six governors' seats now held by Republicans — most notably in Ohio, a state that has been at the center of the past two presidential elections.

By early this morning, Democrats had picked up at least 25 House seats held by Republicans, far more than the 15 seats they needed to win control, knocking off Republican incumbents from New Hampshire to Indiana. Among the faces that will be absent from the halls of Congress next year are some high-profile and long-serving soldiers of the Republican Party, including Representatives Charles Bass of New Hampshire, Clay Shaw Jr. of Florida, J.D. Ha worth of Arizona, Jim Ryun of Ka sas and Nancy L. Johnson of Co necticut.

The Republicans lost nearly all th seats that had been touched by sca dals this year, including the seat v cated by Representative Mark F ley, who quit after sending sexuall suggestive messages to male tee age pages, and by Tom DeLay Texas, the former Republican m jority leader who resigned after b ing indicted on charges of conspirin to violate Texas election laws.

The departing Republican sen tors included Mike DeWine of Ohi Rick Santorum of Pennsylvania an Lincoln Chafee of Rhode Island.

Karl Rove, the president's top p litical strategist, informed the pres dent that the House was lost around 11 p.m., the White House sai

"His reaction was, he was disa pointed in the results in the House said Tony Fratto, a White Hous spokesman. "But he's eager to wor with both parties on his prioriti over the next two years. He's got a agenda of important issues he wan to work on, and he's going to wor with both parties."

Mr. Bush called a news conferen for this afternoon at the White Hous Mr. Fratto said that Mr. Bush wou call the new Democratic Congre sional leaders today, including Re resentative Nancy Pelosi of Califo nia, likely to be the next Hous

*Continued on Page P3*

**NEWS ANALYSIS**

## *A Loud Message for Bush*

By ROBIN TONER

Everything is different now for President Bush. The era of one-party Republican rule in Washington ended with a crash in yesterday's midterm elections, putting a proudly unyielding president on notice that the voters want change, especially on the war in Iraq.

Mr. Bush now confronts the first Democratic majority in the House in 12 years and a significantly bigger Democratic caucus in the Senate that were largely elected on the promise to act as a strong check on his administration. Almost any major initiative in his final two years in office will now, like it or not, have to be bipartisan to some degree.

For six years, Mr. Bush has often governed, and almost always campaigned, with his attention focused on his conservative base. But yesterday's voting showed the limits of those politics, as practiced — and many thought perfected — by Mr. Bush and his chief political adviser, Karl Rove.

In the bellwether states of Ohio and Pennsylvania, two Republican senators, both members of the legendary freshman class of 1994, were defeated by large margins. Across the Northeast, Republican moderates were barely surviving or, like Senator Lincoln Chafee of Rhode Island, falling to Democrats who had argued that they were simply too close to a conservative president.

Most critically, perhaps, Republicans lost the political center on the Iraq war, according to national exit polls. Voters who identified themselves as independents broke strongly for the Democrats, the exit polls showed, as did those who described themselves as moderates.

Senator Olympia J. Snowe, a Maine Republican who was re-elected yesterday, said that with the election's results, the administration's Iraq policy "has to change."

"It absolutely has to change," Ms. Snowe said. "And that message should have been conveyed by the administration much sooner."

*Continued on Page P2*

Lawrence Jackson/Associated Pr

President Bush arriving at th White House yesterday.

## *For Democrats, Time to Savor Victory at Last*

By JEFF ZELENY and KATE ZERNIKE

Democrats, at least in this millennium, have not been accustomed to much celebration.

So after they won control of the House last night — precisely 12 years after the Republican revolution touched off the first in a sequence of punishing elections — there was a momentary paralysis at the victory parties. It quickly passed, however, as the Democrats reveled in the glow of winning control of the House even while nervously watching Senate returns trickle in.

From a hotel ballroom in the shadow of the Capitol in Washington to statehouses to private vote-watching gatherings across the United States, Democrats celebrated their victories.

Yet even as they savored a still-unfolding success story, they tested their ability to stick to a basic principle of their agreed upon game plan: no gloating allowed.

"The news has arrived!" declared Representative Rahm Emanuel of Illinois, who was a prime engineer of the party's comeback. "You have

## Clinton and Democrats Sweep Top Contests in New York State

By PATRICK HEALY

Eliot Spitzer, the state attorney general who crusaded against Wall Street corruption, was elected governor of New York yesterday in a historic Democratic sweep of statewide offices, which included a huge victory by Senator Hillary Rodham Clinton that positions her for a possible presidential bid in 2008.

Rounding out the party's triumph were Andrew M. Cuomo, who mounted a political comeback to succeed Mr. Spitzer and restore his family name as a force in New York politics, and State Comptroller Alan G. Hevesi, who won re-election despite his potentially illegal use of state workers to chauffeur his ailing wife at taxpayer expense.

Mr. Spitzer scored a record percentage for a governor's race, beating Gov. Mario M. Cuomo's 64.6 percent in 1986. Senator Clinton won a fifth of the vote of Republicans and a quarter of conservatives, according to exit polls — a show of strength that makes a White House bid more possible, said some of her advisers, who expect deliberations about 2008 to turn serious soon.

The Democratic landslide turned Republicans out of the governor's office after 12 years under George E. Pataki. It also left Republicans in control of only the State Senate, and the Spitzer camp confident that it had a mandate to reform a chronically dysfunctional state government.

Republican leaders, taken aback by the breadth of their defeat, were already talking about party rebuilding yesterday, perhaps centered on a brewing revolt in the suburbs over high property taxes.

With more than 90 percent of the ballots counted, Mr. Spitzer had 70 percent of the vote over the Republican candidate, former Assemblyman John Faso, who had 29. Senator Clinton led her opponent, John Spencer, by 67 to 31 percent. Mr. Cuomo

*Continued on Page P15*

INSIDE

# Chapter 1

# Government and People

THE MIDTERM CONGRESSIONAL elections of 2006 were enveloped in far more drama—and political importance—than usually occurs in a year when there is no presidential contest.

To many voters, the congressional elections were, in a sense, a referendum on the presidency of George W. Bush. Across America, as the leaves turned to the burnished colors of autumn, the candidates of both parties were intensely aware of the president's record and his weak standing in the polls. Some Republican candidates distanced themselves from Bush. They did not welcome him to campaign alongside them in their districts, fearing that his low approval ratings might do them more harm than good.

Public opinion polls indicated that the war in Iraq was central to voters' concerns. American casualties had passed the 2,700 mark a little more than a month before the election, and the roadside explosive devices, suicide car bombs, and carnage as Sunni and Shiite groups fought each other were a daily horror show on the evening news and the Internet. A scandal that broke in late September added to the Republicans' woes when it was disclosed that Mark Foley, a Republican congressman from Florida, had sent sexually explicit e-mails to underage House pages.

On Election Day, the Democrats won control of both the House and the Senate for the first time in 12 years. Riding a nationwide tide—much of it driven by disillusion with the war in Iraq—the Democrats gained six seats in the Senate, to win control, 51–49. Many races were extremely close, and the outcome in Virginia, which decided control of the Senate, was not known for two days. In the House, the Democrats gained thirty-one seats, for a new lineup of 233 Democrats to 202 Republicans. The Democrats moved swiftly to choose the new House Speaker, Representative Nancy Pelosi of California.

The results meant that in his last two years in office President Bush would face a Congress controlled by the opposition party—and able to investigate the administration and Republican scandals in the months leading up to the 2008 presidential election.

In the months before the 2006 elections, other factors appeared to work to the advantage of the Democrats. More than 1700 people had died and hundreds of thousands were made homeless by Hurricane Katrina, which struck New Orleans and the Gulf Coast in 2005; Bush had announced, "I am responsible" for the slow and inadequate reaction to the disaster by the federal government.[1]

And the public had a low opinion of the Republican-controlled Congress. A Gallup Poll in September 2006 reported that 63 percent of those questioned did not approve "of the way Congress is handling its job."[2] Nor was corruption in Congress confined to the Foley scandal; the activities of lobbyist Jack Abramoff cast a cloud over other members and led to a federal investigation.

Gasoline prices had topped $3 a gallon in August, dismaying motorists. Although the prices at the pump had dropped suddenly in the weeks before the election, gas remained more than $2 a gallon on average, still higher than when Bush was elected for a second term as president two years earlier.

That contest in 2004 also took place against a backdrop of war in Iraq and the continuing threat of terrorism at home. Bush, the Republican president, had successfully persuaded the voters that he was the best person to defend the nation against terrorists; in his campaign speeches, he frequently referred to the attacks on America by al Qaeda on September 11, 2001.

© Ron Sachs/Corbis

On May 1, 2003, President George W. Bush landed on the aircraft carrier U.S.S. *Abraham Lincoln* . . .

© 2003 AP/Wide World Photos

. . . and in front of a "Mission Accomplished" banner announced that "major combat operations in Iraq have ended." Four years later, however, American troops were still battling insurgents there.

## From the Frontline in Iraq: A Soldier's Goodbye

Excerpt of a letter from Army Pfc. Jesse A. Givens, 34, of Springfield, Missouri. Private Givens was killed May 1, 2003, when his tank fell into the Euphrates River after the bank on which he was parked gave way. This letter was written to be delivered to his family if he died. Melissa is his wife, Dakota his 6-year-old stepson, and Bean the name he used for his son, Carson, who was born May 29.

My family,

I never thought that I would be writing a letter like this. I really don't know where to start. I've been getting bad feelings, though and, well, if you are reading this. . . .

The happiest moments in my life all deal with my little family. I will always have with me the small moments we all shared. The moments when you quit taking life so serious and smiled. The sounds of a beautiful boy's laughter or the simple nudge of a baby unborn. You will never know how complete you have made me. You saved me from loneliness and taught me how to think beyond myself. You taught me how to live and to love. You opened my eyes to a world I never dreamed existed.

Dakota . . . you taught me how to care until it hurts, you taught me how to smile again. You taught me that life isn't so serious and sometimes you just have to play. You have a big, beautiful heart. Through life you need to keep it open and follow it. Never be afraid to be yourself. I will always be there in our park when you dream so we can play. I love you, and hope someday you will understand why I didn't come home. Please be proud of me.

Bean, I never got to see you but I know in my heart you are beautiful. I know you will be strong and big-hearted like your mom and brother. I will always have with me the feel of the soft nudges on your mom's belly, and the joy I felt when I found out you were on your way. I love you, Bean.

Melissa, I have never been as blessed as the day I met you. You are my angel, soulmate, wife, lover and best friend. I am sorry. I did not want to have to write this letter. There is so much more I need to say, so much more I need to share. A lifetime's worth. I married you for a million lifetimes. That's how long I will be with you. Please keep my babies safe. Please find it in your heart to forgive me for leaving you alone. . . . Teach our babies to live life to the fullest, tell yourself to do the same.

I will always be there with you, Melissa. I will always want you, need you and love you, in my heart, my mind and my soul. Do me a favor, after you tuck the children in. Give them hugs and kisses from me. Go outside and look at the stars and count them. Don't forget to smile.

Love Always,
Your husband,
Jess

—From the *New York Times*, p. A23, November 11, 2003

Senator John Kerry of Massachusetts, the Democratic candidate, was a decorated Navy officer in the Vietnam War who had first come to national attention as a young veteran speaking out against that war. He argued that his military service and experience in Congress would enable him to protect the national security, create jobs, and revive a sputtering economy.

Bush was reelected, with 286 electoral votes to 251 for John Kerry. Bush carried 31 states. Kerry won 19 states plus the District of Columbia. Bush also won the popular vote, 62,040,610 to 59,028,439 for Kerry.

Bush had justified the war against Iraq on the grounds that "regime change" in that Middle Eastern country was a necessary step in the fight against terrorism. In the months before the war began in March 2003, Bush, supported by estimates of the Central Intelligence Agency, claimed that Iraq possessed weapons of mass destruction—both biological and chemical weapons—and might soon have nuclear weapons. Iraq and its brutal dictator, Saddam Hussein, Bush maintained, were therefore a threat to America's national security.

Both Bush and his national security adviser, Condoleezza Rice, invoked images of a "mushroom cloud," a nuclear attack that might be unleashed at any moment on the United States. "The first time we may be completely certain he has a—nuclear weapons is when, God forbids, he uses one," Bush told the United Nations the following month.[3]

The president spelled out a new strategy of preemptive war, under which the United States, when faced with "imminent danger," would, "if necessary, act preemptively."[4]

At first, the war seemed to be over quickly; in three weeks, American forces were in Baghdad, the Iraqi capital, pulling down the statue of Saddam Hussein. On May 1, 2003, President Bush in a flight suit famously landed on the aircraft carrier U.S.S. *Abraham Lincoln* off San Diego and announced—in front of a banner that read "Mission Accomplished"—that "major combat operations in Iraq have ended."

But in the aftermath of the U.S. invasion, no weapons of mass destruction were found in Iraq. And American troops were being killed almost every day by roadside bombs and rocket-propelled grenades.

In April 2004, for the first time, public support for the war dropped below 50 percent.[5] Critics of the adminis-

U.S. marines in combat in Baghdad, Iraq

A second jetliner hijacked by terrorists about to crash into the south tower of the World Trade Center in New York City, September 11, 2001



tration questioned whether Iraq had become a "quagmire" comparable to the Vietnam War of the 1960s.

Although the critics contended that the conflict in Iraq was a diversion from the war on terrorism, President Bush argued that his decision to invade Iraq flowed directly from the 9/11 attacks on America.

The terrorists had struck on a perfect September day. The cloudless skies over New York and Washington were bright blue, the sun sparkling. Then, at 8:46 a.m. on September 11, 2001, a Boeing 767 jetliner slammed into the north tower of the World Trade Center in lower Manhattan.

It seemed like a terrible accident until 17 minutes later when a second jetliner, also heavily laden with fuel, struck the south tower. The world watched in horror on television as smoke billowed from the towers and a number of people, trapped by flames on the high floors, leaped to their deaths.

In Washington at 9:37 a.m. a third airliner crashed into the Pentagon. In New York at 9:58 a.m. the south tower of the Trade Center collapsed.

At 10:03 a.m. a fourth jetliner, apparently with the White House as its target, crashed in western Pennsylvania after courageous passengers struggled with the hijackers. Then at 10:28 a.m., the north tower of the Trade Center collapsed. Almost 3,000 people died, including office workers unable to escape from the two towers, hundreds of firefighters, dozens of police, all the passengers and crew members of the four airliners, and the terrorists who had seized control of the planes.

In 1 hour and 40 minutes, America was changed forever. Nineteen hijackers of Middle Eastern origin, 15 from Saudi Arabia, had carried out the suicide attack on America. Many observers compared it to the Japanese attack on Pearl Harbor on December 7, 1941, that led the United States to enter the Second World War.

The attack on 9/11 had an enormous and far-reaching effect on America's government and politics, on its foreign and military policies, and on the economy. Few aspects of American life were untouched by the terrible events of those few minutes in September.

In big ways and small, America would never be the same. The change was felt all the way from airline pas-

October 7, 2001: Terrorist leader Osama bin Laden, in a videotaped broadcast, praised the September 11 attacks on New York and Washington.

September 11, 2001: Firefighters raise an American flag where the World Trade Center's twin towers once stood.

sengers being asked to remove their shoes so screeners could check for hidden weapons or explosives, to the creation of a vast new cabinet agency, the Department of Homeland Security.

For the first time, ordinary Americans realized how vulnerable the nation and its infrastructure were to terrorist acts. Its cities, airports, bridges, tunnels, dams, power plants, communications, transportation, and computer networks—all were potential targets.

Osama bin Laden, a wealthy Saudi terrorist, and his al Qaeda network were quickly pinpointed by Washington as the leader and the organization responsible for the attacks of 9/11. Nine days later, President Bush stood before a joint session of Congress and launched the "war on terror."

Any nation "that continues to harbor or support terrorism" would be regarded as a hostile regime, he warned. He denounced the Taliban rulers of Afghanistan, the country where bin Laden and his training camps were based. He was careful to target "Islamic extremism" as the enemy, not Muslims or Arabs in general. He demanded that Afghanistan surrender bin Laden. He also announced the appointment of Pennsylvania governor Tom Ridge to head a new White House Office of Homeland Security, which became a cabinet department in January 2003.

Only 10 months before the 9/11 attacks, Bush, a Republican, had won a disputed presidential election with fewer popular votes than his Democratic rival, Al Gore. When Bush was the governor of Texas, he had little experience in foreign policy, and as a candidate, and even later as president, he was lampooned by cartoonists and on the television show *Saturday Night Live* as frivolous and less than brilliant. But that night after the attack on

September 20, 2001: President George W. Bush addresses a joint session of Congress to launch a "war on terror."

Nancy Pelosi, the California Democrat, was slated to be the House Speaker after her party won control of the House in 2006. She is all smiles as she watches the election returns on November 7, 2006.



America, in his speech to Congress, he seemed to step into the mantle of the presidency for the first time. He spoke forcefully and well. His approval ratings soared, and it would be almost a year before Democrats dared to criticize his leadership. For a time, at least, the country, angry and reeling from the attacks, united behind the president and his war on terrorism.

Even as Bush spoke, U.S. forces were moving into the region around Afghanistan. By early October 2001, American bombers and cruise missiles were pounding that country. Later that month, American special forces, joined by the anti-Taliban Northern Alliance, were fighting inside Afghanistan. By mid-November Kabul, the capital, fell. In December, U.S. warplanes bombed a complex of caves near Tora Bora, in the mountains of eastern Afghanistan where bin Laden was thought to be hiding. By December 16, the war was largely over. Many of the Taliban leaders and al Qaeda fighters were reported to have fled over the border into Pakistan. Hundreds of al Qaeda prisoners were captured during the war, but Osama bin Laden was not among them.

President Bush and other senior officials warned, however, that the battle against terrorism would continue and might lead to the deployment of American forces to other countries where terrorists were active. And a little over a year later, U.S. troops invaded Iraq. A series of color-coded threat warnings by the Department of Homeland Security reminded Americans of the continuing risk of more attacks against targets in the United States. Some critics assailed the color-coded warnings as too general and too vague to be useful to the public.

By the 2006 midterm election, the political landscape had changed dramatically. Only six years earlier, the world had seemed a very different and less dangerous place.

In 2000, America began a new century as the strongest democracy on the planet. On November 7, its citizens went to the polls to choose a new president of the United States and a new Congress to lead the nation into the future.

But as the dawn broke the next morning, America was stunned to learn that the contest was not over. There was no clear winner because the crucial result in Florida hung in the balance. Nationwide, Vice President Al Gore was ahead of Texas Governor George W. Bush in the popular vote by a thin margin, but Bush was slightly ahead in Florida, where the state's 25 electoral votes would determine who became the next president. Teams of lawyers descended on the Sunshine State, the Democrats demanding a hand recount in four largely Democratic counties.

Florida's highest court ordered a partial vote recount. But the Bush campaign appealed to the U.S. Supreme Court, which halted the recount. Then in a historic decision on December 12, a bitterly divided U.S. Supreme Court ruled 5–4 for Bush, declaring that because the recount lacked uniform standards it was unconstitutional.

Finally, it was official: George W. Bush was the next president of the United States. Bush carried 30 states with 271 electoral votes; Gore won 20 states and the District of Columbia with 267 electoral votes. In the popular vote, however, Gore ran ahead of Bush, 51,003,894 to 50,459,211. Ralph Nader, the Green Party candidate, received 2,834,410 votes, but because he did not carry any state, he won no electoral votes. Pat Buchanan, the Reform Party candidate, won 446,743 votes and, like Nader, won no electoral votes.

The Republicans held on to their majority in the House, but the Senate was equally divided, with 50 Republicans and 50 Democrats. Only seven months later, however, in May 2001, Senator James M. Jeffords of Ver-

Protesters outside the Supreme Court as Bush appealed the Florida recount in the disputed 2000 election



mont left the Republican Party and became an independent, giving the Democrats control of the Senate by one vote until the 2002 midterm election, when Republicans regained control of the Senate and maintained their majority in the House.

Before Bush's election in 2000, the Democrats had captured the White House for eight years under Bill Clinton, who was elected in 1992 and again in 1996. Two years later, however, the House impeached the president, accusing him of lying to a federal grand jury about his affair with a young White House intern, Monica Lewinsky, and obstructing justice. Tried by the Senate early in 1999, Clinton was found not guilty by a vote that fell well short of the two-thirds needed to convict. But the many months of scandal had tarnished the president's reputation.

The New York Times

CLINTON ACQUITTED DECISIVELY: NO MAJORITY FOR EITHER CHARGE

President Says He Is Sorry And Seeks Reconciliation

CENSURE IS BARRED

The Fallout Of the Trial

'Senators, How Say You?'

"The House impeached the president. . . . Clinton was found not guilty."



Nevertheless, and despite his personal difficulties, Clinton's approval rating as president remained remarkably high. Voters seemed willing to distinguish between his personal foibles and his performance in office. As a candidate for president in 1992, Clinton had promised to end the unpopular federal welfare program, and in 1996 he signed a Republican-sponsored bill to restructure the program. He had eliminated the federal budget deficit and transformed it into a huge surplus. And he had presided over an unprecedented period of economic expansion.

Clinton and his successor, George W. Bush, led the United States during a time of change. The Cold War that had held the world hostage since the end of the Second World War had ended in 1991 when the Soviet Union, the Communist superpower, collapsed. The threat of nuclear war between the United States and Russia, which still possessed nuclear missiles,

© David Brauchli/Reuters/Corbis

November 1989: The Berlin Wall comes down.

had diminished, but other nations had become nuclear powers, notably India, Pakistan, and North Korea. As a result, the world was not free of the danger of a nuclear conflict. And the risks faced during the years of the Cold War were replaced by the newer peril of terrorist attacks. Political leaders in the United States and other Western countries worried that terrorists might acquire nuclear, biological, or chemical weapons.

At home, millions of Americans, many more than in the past, had invested in the stock market, especially in mutual funds. But by the fall of 2000 a number of major Internet companies had suffered financial setbacks. The "dot-com" firms that had appeared so glamorous only months earlier suddenly seemed a mirage. In the wake of 9/11 the Dow Jones industrial average and the NASDAQ index dropped sharply, and in the months that followed many small investors lost some or all of the savings they had counted on for their retirement.

Investor confidence was shaken even further by a series of corporate and accounting scandals. First, Enron, a giant Texas-based energy trader, collapsed and the previously respected accounting firm, Arthur Andersen, Enron's outside auditor, was convicted of obstruction of justice. Other major corporations were revealed to have engaged in questionable practices to inflate earnings, especially the giant telecommunications firm WorldCom, which had concealed more than $7 billion in expenses. By midsummer of 2002, the corporate scandals had contributed to a steep slide in the stock market. The market recovered somewhat in 2003, but remained volatile in 2004.

Even aside from the scandals, the American corporate culture had undergone vast changes. The traditional belief that workers or managers could toil loyally for one company for all of their careers, and be rewarded with a gold watch and a dependable pension, was proving to be no longer true. Many workers found that their 401(k) retirement plans, heavily invested in stocks, had shrunk disastrously.

Despite economic gains in some industries, there were continuing economic problems as well. In several areas of the country, smokestack industries had declined sharply, resulting in dislocation and hardship for the blue-collar workers who were laid off or dismissed in the steel, automobile, and other plants. Many white-collar employees found themselves out of work as well, sometimes as a result of corporate mergers and dot-com failures, but increasingly because jobs had migrated overseas, to China, South Asia, and Latin America, where American firms paid much lower wages to foreign workers.

Globalization—the increasingly interconnected worldwide economy—and trade competition from Asia and other industrialized nations meant that the United States was no longer assured of economic preeminence in the world. Opponents of globalization protested that

© AP/Wide World Photos

A dot-com company takes to the skies to advertise.

The American Past

## GEORGE WASHINGTON: HIS HIGH MIGHTINESS?

When the framers of the Constitution met in Philadelphia in 1787, one of the momentous tasks they faced was to design the executive branch of the government and decide what to call the leader of the new nation:

> During the sessions of the convention, the subject of the presidency caused much disquiet. Persistent rumors were current outside the convention that the establishment of a monarchy was under consideration. The common form of the rumor was that the Bishop of Osnaburgh, the second son of George III, was to be invited to become King of the United States. . . . There were several of the delegates, conspicuous among whom was [Edmund] Randolph, who distrusted a single executive as savoring of monarchy, and who favored an executive body of three or more. But the convention decided in favor of a single person. . . . It seems to have been generally accepted . . . that Washington would be the first president of the United States. In 1787 Washington was at the very height of his popularity and so great was the trust in him that no fear was felt regarding the inauguration of the new office. . . . After the new government was installed, the title which Washington himself was said to have preferred as the most fitting one for his position was "His High Mightiness, the President of the United States and Protector of their Liberties."

—Adapted from Max Farrand, *The Framing of the Constitution of the United States*

it led to the exploitation of cheap labor in poor countries and damaged the environment.

Racial divisions, despite outward progress, continued to exist in America. In several cities, for example, what appeared to be racially motivated shootings had cost innocent lives.

Even before September 11, 2001, terrorism, both homegrown and foreign, had come to America. In New York City, Islamic terrorists bombed the World Trade Center in 1993, killing six people and injuring more than 1,000. On April 19, 1995, the federal building in Oklahoma City was destroyed by a truck bomb, killing 168 people. Two Americans, Timothy McVeigh and Terry Nichols, who had served in the same Army unit, were convicted for that crime, and McVeigh was executed.

Former Enron CEO Kenneth Lay surrenders to authorities in 2004. He was found guilty of conspiracy and fraud, but his conviction was vacated when he died before he could be sentenced.

Armed militia groups, although small in number, were deeply suspicious of government. Some of these groups were identified with white supremacist views and spouted hatred over the Internet.

America was grappling as well with a host of domestic challenges, including the rising costs of health care, the uncertain quality of public education, and the interlocking problems of crime, drugs, poverty, and homelessness—problems often particularly acute in the inner cities.

There were other changes in the shape of American politics. Congress in 2002 passed a new campaign finance law that sought to curb the hundreds of millions of dollars of unregulated "soft money" flowing into both major parties from corporations, unions, and wealthy donors. The new law banned contributions of soft money to national political parties and placed restrictions on the use of such funds to broadcast "issue ads" in federal elections. Predictably, however, political parties and candidates were scrambling to find new ways to use soft money.

Special interest groups, often well financed and supporting a single issue, had become powerful actors in the nation's politics. Often such groups contributed to political candidates through political action committees (PACs), which had grown in number and influence even though a few candidates declined to accept PAC money. Other trends were visible: to some, the nation's political parties appeared to be declining in importance, and public confidence in the institutions of government was relatively low.

Well before the wars in Afghanistan and Iraq, in the post–Cold War era, the United States found itself called upon to intervene in local or regional conflicts or for humanitarian purposes. In the early 1990s, President Clin-

Floodwaters in New Orleans after Hurricane Katrina struck

ton sent American troops to Haiti and Bosnia. In 1999, through the NATO alliance, U.S. warplanes bombed Yugoslavia repeatedly for more than two months after that country's armed forces had invaded Kosovo. As president, Clinton several times brokered attempts to achieve peace between Israel and the Palestinians in the volatile Middle East. President George W. Bush also found himself drawn into diplomatic efforts to bring peace in the region after Israel, responding to repeated suicide bombings of civilians, sent troops and tanks into Palestinian towns.

American influence and military power, while still enormous, did not always seem capable of achieving long-range goals. The first President Bush had dispatched half a million troops to the Persian Gulf; in the brief war fought early in 1991, the American military forced Iraq's dictator, Saddam Hussein, to withdraw from Kuwait. But for 12 more years, Saddam remained in power in Iraq.

In 2003, President George W. Bush, the son of the 41st president, sent the American military into Iraq; U.S. forces toppled Saddam's government, then hunted down and captured the brutal dictator. But Iraq, fragmented into rival ethnic and religious groups, remained in turmoil in 2006, with American and allied troops under steady attack by well-armed insurgents. It remained unclear whether America's enormous military might could ultimately succeed in imposing democracy at the point of a gun. Iraqis may have disliked Saddam, who ruled by fear, but many were also resentful of an occupying power.

Since the 1960s, America had passed through a long and extraordinarily turbulent period of assassination,

2004: Iraqi Sunni Muslim insurgents celebrate their attack on a U.S. convoy near Fallujah, Iraq.

civil unrest, war, abuse of presidential power, and economic hardship. The murder of President John F. Kennedy in 1963 had been followed by explosions of anger in the black areas of the nation's cities, the assassination of Dr. Martin Luther King and Robert F. Kennedy, eight years of war in Vietnam, the Watergate scandal—when burglars working for the Republican president's reelection campaign broke into Democratic Party headquarters—and the resulting resignation and pardon of Richard Nixon. Then came the seizure in Iran of American hostages, periodic inflation, high unemployment, economic recession, and the Iran-contra scandal—in which President Ronald Reagan's administration sought to trade American arms for hostages in the Middle East. This was followed by the Persian Gulf War, the impeachment of President Clinton, and the September 11 terrorist attacks.

The swirling currents of these events brought change not only to America but to the way Americans perceived their government and their political system. Many voters professed to see little difference between the major parties, and expressed little faith in politicians.

Even before the Reagan years, many liberals and conservatives alike had questioned the effectiveness of government solutions to some social problems. Five decades earlier, President Franklin D. Roosevelt had ushered in an era of great social reform through federal government programs. John F. Kennedy and Lyndon B. Johnson had followed in his path. But many of the programs of Johnson's "Great Society" had not worked as their architects had envisioned, and in 1980 Reagan successfully assailed the "bureaucracy" and the government in Washington.

There were continuing signs of change. In 1984, Geraldine Ferraro was the Democratic candidate for vice president, the first woman to be nominated for that office by a major political party. In 1996 many people,

white and black, had hoped that former general Colin Powell, an African American, would run for president. In 2000, Joseph I. Lieberman became the first person of Jewish faith to be named to a major party presidential ticket. By that year, more women, more African Ameri-

© Bob Strong/ Reuters/Corbis

Senator Joseph I. Lieberman, the first person of Jewish faith named to a major-party presidential ticket, responds to cheers at the 2000 Democratic National Convention.

## The Reciprocal Nature of Democratic Power

In July 1945 a small group of scientists stood atop a hill near Alamogordo, New Mexico, and watched the first atomic bomb explode in the desert. At that instant the traditional power of government to alter the lives of people took on a terrifying new dimension. With the onset of the nuclear age and the later development of intercontinental ballistic missiles (ICBMs), people lived less than 30 minutes away from possible destruction. That is all the time it would take for ICBMs to reach their targets, destroying whole cities and perhaps entire nations. As already noted, with the collapse of the Soviet Union in 1991 and the end of the Cold War, these concerns diminished considerably, but they have not disappeared. Many of the missiles were still in their silos in the United States, Russia, and China. Several other powers possessed nuclear weapons, and a number of smaller countries were trying to acquire them. By 2004, North Korea was reported to have perhaps as many as eight nuclear bombs. The threat of a nuclear war between India and Pakistan remained.

At the height of the Cold War, when America and the Soviet Union faced each other as hostile superpowers, the president of the United States was often described as a person with his finger "on the nuclear but-

cans, and more Hispanics had been elected to Congress and sat in the cabinet and on the Supreme Court.

Beyond the policies of any particular president, broader questions were raised by the problems the nation had experienced over the past several decades.

Key Question

A key question may be asked: ***After more than 200 years, was the American political system capable of meeting the social and economic needs of the people and preserving the national security?***

There are many other questions to consider. How has the continuing threat of terrorism changed the quality of life in the post-9/11 United States? Were the nation's institutions gridlocked and too slow to change with the times? Could America's industries maintain a high level of employment and still remain competitive with other nations? At the same time, could Americans preserve the environment? In a multicultural society, with minority groups increasing in numbers, could Americans learn to overcome racial divisions and live in harmony? Was the American democracy still workable, even though it had been subjected to unusual pressures?

These and other questions will be explored in this book, but first it might be useful to examine the general relationship between people and government in a democratic system.

© Dennis Brack/Black Star/Stockphoto.com

ton." The existence of such chilling terminology, and of nuclear weapons, reflects the increasingly complex, technological, computerized nature of the world in which Americans live. As the country has changed through the development of science, technology, and industrialization, government has changed along with it. Government has expanded and grown more complex; it is called on to perform more and more tasks.

## The Impact of Government on People

Obviously, government can affect the lives of students or other citizens by sending them overseas to fight in a war in which they may be killed. Less obvious, perhaps, are the ways in which government pervades most aspects of daily life, sometimes down to minute details. For example, the federal government regulates the amount of windshield that the wipers on a car must cover and even the speed of the windshield wipers. (At the fast setting, wipers must go "at least 45 cycles per minute.")[6]

***for more information about federal highways, see: http://www.fhwa.dot.gov***

College students driving to class (perhaps over a highway built largely with federal funds) are expected to observe local traffic regulations. They may have to put a coin in a city parking meter. The classroom in which they sit may have been constructed with a federal grant. Possibly they are attending college with the aid of federal loans or grants. In fiscal year 2003, for example, the government awarded $59.3 billion to assist more than 6 million college undergraduates and graduate students.[7]

Clearly government's impact is real and far-reaching. Americans often must pay three levels of taxes—local, state, and federal. They attend public schools and perhaps public colleges. They draw unemployment insurance, welfare benefits, Medicare, and Social Security. They must either obey the laws, or pay the penalty of a fine or imprisonment if they break them and are caught and convicted. Their savings accounts and home mortgages are guaranteed by the federal government. Their taxes support the armed forces and police, fire, health, and sanitation departments. To hunt, fish, marry, drive, fly, or build they must have a government license. From birth certificate to death certificate, government accompanies individuals along the way. Even after they die, the government is not through with them. Estate taxes may be collected and wills probated in the courts.[8]

***for more information about Social Security, see: http://www.ssa.gov***

© Peter Marlow/Magnum Photos

In the United States, "government" is extraordinarily complicated. There are federal, state, and local layers of government, metropolitan areas, commissions, authorities, boards and councils, and quasi-governmental bodies. Many of the units of government overlap. And all affect the lives of individuals.

## The Impact of People on Government

Just as government affects people, people affect government. The American system of government is based on the concept that power flows from the people to the government. Thomas Jefferson expressed this eloquently when he wrote in the Declaration of Independence that "to secure these rights, Governments are instituted among men, deriving their just powers from the consent of the governed." Abraham Lincoln expressed the same thought in his Gettysburg Address, speaking of "government of the people, by the people, for the people."

These are ideals, statements embodying the principles of democracy. As we note at many points in this book, the principles do not always mesh with the practices. Yet, it remains true that if government in the United States has real and often awesome powers over people, at the same time people—both individuals and the mass of citizens together—can have considerable power over the government.

The reciprocal nature of democratic power is a basic element of the American political system. As V. O. Key,

George Tames/The New York Times Photo Archives

Jr., the distinguished Harvard political scientist, put it: "The power relationship is reciprocal, and the subject may affect the ruler more profoundly than the ruler affects the subject."[9] There are several ways that people influence government.

**Voting** The first and most important power of the people in America is the right to vote in free elections to choose those who govern. At regular intervals, the people may, in the classic phrase of Horace Greeley, the 19th-century journalist and politician, "turn the rascals out." The fact that a president, member of Congress, governor, mayor, or school board member may want to stand for reelection influences his or her performance in office. The knowledge of officials that they serve at the pleasure of the voters usually tends to make those officials sensitive to public opinion.

But isn't one person's vote insignificant when millions are cast? Not necessarily. That the individual's vote does matter even in a nation as big as the United States has been illustrated many times in close presidential elections—including in 2000 when George W. Bush carried Florida by a mere 537 votes and was awarded the election.

Presidents are elected by electoral votes, but these are normally cast by the electors in each state for the candidate who wins the most popular votes in the state. Each state has a number of electors and electoral votes equal to its number of senators and representatives in Congress. (See the description of the electoral college in Chapter 11.) In 1960 a shift from John F. Kennedy to Richard M. Nixon of only 9,421 voters in Illinois and Missouri would have prevented either candidate from gaining a majority in the electoral college. In 1968 and 1976, shifts of relatively small numbers of voters in a few states would have changed the outcomes of the presidential elections in those years. In 2000, a shift in Florida of 269 votes from George W. Bush to Gore would have given that state, and the presidency, to the Democratic candidate.

**Party Activity** Political parties are basic to the American system of government because they provide a vehicle for competition and choice. Without that, "free elections" would be meaningless. For the most part the two-party system has predominated in the United States. Since candidates for public office, even at the presidential level, are usually selected by their parties, people can influence government, and the choice of who governs, by participating in party activities. Whether political campaigns offer meaningful alternatives on the issues depends in part on who is nominated. And that in turn may be influenced by how many people are politically active. Political participation can take many forms, from ringing doorbells to running for local party committees or for public office.

*for more information about the two major political parties, see: http://www.democrats.org and http://www.gop.com*

**Public Opinion** Candidates and elected officials are sensitive to what the public is thinking. This has been particularly true since the Second World War, when sophisticated methods of political polling and statistical analysis were developed. But citizens do not have to wait

© Kristin Kenney Williams

around to be polled. They can make their opinions felt in a variety of ways: by voting and participating in political activities, talking to other people, writing or sending e-mails or faxes to their representatives in Congress, telephoning the members of their city council, writing to their newspapers, or testifying at public hearings. Even by reading the newspapers and watching television news broadcasts (or by not doing those things), people may indirectly influence government. A citizen who carefully follows public issues in the news media and magazines of opinion may help to influence government, since a government is less likely to attempt to mislead when it knows it is dealing with an informed public.

**Interest Groups** When people belong to groups that share common attitudes and make these views felt, or when they organize such groups, they may be influencing government. These private associations, or interest groups, may be business and professional organizations, unions, racial and religious groups, or organizations of groups such as farmers or veterans. An interest group does not have to be an organized body. Students, for example, constitute a highly vocal interest group, even when they do not belong to a formal student organization.

**Direct Action** At various times in American history, people have sought to influence government by civil disobedience and sometimes by militant or violent action. In the late 1960s and early 1970s, for example, some civil rights leaders and student activists practiced "the politics of confrontation." The idea of direct and often disruptive action to achieve political ends appeared to have grown in part out of the civil rights movement (beginning with peaceful "sit-ins" to desegregate lunch counters in the South) and in part out of the organized opposition to the war in Vietnam. Demonstrations, marches, sit-ins, campus strikes, picketing, and protest characterized those years.

With the end of the war in Vietnam, this type of direct political action diminished considerably, but it has by no means disappeared. In the early 1990s, pro-life groups sought to prevent women from having abortions by blocking access to clinics. (This tactic was prohibited by a federal law enacted in 1994.) Protesters in Seattle disrupted meetings of the World Trade Organization in 1999, to advocate greater protection for the environment and workers. In 2000, thousands of people participated in the Million Mom March in Washington to call for stronger gun control laws. In the spring of 2004, hundreds of thousands of people gathered on the mall in the capital for the March for Women's Lives, a rally to support the right of women to choose to have an abortion.

Over the years, farmers have demonstrated in Washington for government assistance, and antiabortion groups, peace activists, gay men and women, and others have held rallies on the mall in the nation's capital to focus attention on their goals.

## What Is Government?

The words "government," "politics," "power," and "democracy" ought to be clearly defined. The difficulty is that political scientists, philosophers, and kings have never been able to agree entirely on the meanings of these terms.

Kathy Brownell

The ancient Greek philosopher Plato and his pupil Aristotle speculated on their meaning, and the process has continued up to the present day. Bearing in mind that no universal or perfect definitions exist, we can still discuss the words and arrive at a general concept of what they mean.

## Government

Even in a primitive society, some form of government exists. A tribal chief emerges with authority over others and makes decisions, perhaps in consultation with the elders of the tribe. The tribal leader is governing.

**Government,** then, even in a modern industrial state, can be defined on a simple level as the individuals, institutions, and processes that make the rules for society and possess the power to enforce them. But rules for what? To take an example, if private developers wish to acquire a wildlife preserve for commercial use, and environmental groups protest, government may be called on to settle the dispute. In short, government makes rules to decide who gets what of valued things in a society.* It attempts to resolve conflicts among individuals and groups.

David Easton, a political scientist at the University of Chicago, has written:

> Even in the smallest and simplest society someone must intervene in the name of society, with its authority behind him, to decide how differences over valued things are to be resolved. This authoritative allocation of values is a minimum prerequisite of any society. . . . Every society provides some mechanisms, however rudimentary they may be, for authoritatively resolving differences about the ends that are to be pursued, that is, for deciding who is to get what there is of the desirable things.[10]

Easton's concept has come to be broadly accepted by many scholars today. In highly developed societies the principal mechanism for resolving differences is government. Government makes binding rules for society that determine the distribution of valued things.

## Politics

Benjamin Disraeli, the 19th-century British prime minister and novelist, wrote in *Endymion* that "politics are the possession and distribution of power."

Disraeli's definition of politics comes very close to our definition of government. Disraeli was ahead of his time, for many political scientists today would agree in general with his definition, and they would add that there is little difference between politics and government.

For example, V. O. Key, Jr., equated politics with "the process and practice of ruling" and the "workings of governments generally, their impact on the governed, their manner of operation, the means by which governors attain and retain authority."[11] In other words, **politics** may be defined as the pursuit and exercise of power.

Such a definition might be confusing to those Americans who tend to look at politics as the pursuit of power, and government as the exercise of power. The conventional notion is that people engage in politics to get elected. But, in fact, those who govern are constantly making political decisions. It is very difficult to say where government ends and politics begins. The two terms overlap and intertwine, even if their meanings are not precisely the same.*

## Power

**Power** is the possession of control over others. People have sought for centuries to understand the basis of power, why it exists, and how it is maintained. Authority over others is a tenuous business, as many a deposed South American dictator can attest.

A century ago, Boss Tweed, the leader of Tammany Hall, the Democratic Party machine in New York City, reportedly expressed a simple, cynical philosophy: "The way to have power is to take it." But once acquired, power must be defended against others who desire it. For seven years Nikita Khrushchev appeared to be the unquestioned ruler of the Soviet Union. One day in October 1964, he was summoned back to Moscow from his Black Sea vacation retreat and informed by his colleagues in the Presidium of the Communist Party that he was no longer premier of the Soviet Union. It was reported that those who deposed him changed all the confidential government and party telephone numbers in Moscow so that Khrushchev could not attempt to rally support among elements still loyal to him.[12] Khrushchev was helpless, cut off from the tremendous power that was his only 24 hours before.

The coup against Khrushchev had its echo more than 25 years later when a group of hard-liners in the Kremlin tried to overthrow Mikhail Gorbachev in August 1991 while the Soviet leader was vacationing—again at a dacha on the Black Sea. The coup failed, thanks to the intervention of Russia's president, Boris Yeltsin, who mounted a tank to defy the coup plotters. But

---

*A definition close to that suggested by the title of Harold D. Lasswell's *Politics: Who Gets What, When, How* (New York: McGraw-Hill, 1936).

*Of course, the word "politics" can also refer to a process that occurs in a wide variety of nongovernmental settings—in fact, in every form of social organization where different people, with competing goals and differing objectives, interact. Thus, one sometimes speaks of politics in the local PTA, the politics of a garden club, or the politics in the newsroom of a campus newspaper. In this book, however, we are talking about politics as it is more commonly understood, in its governmental setting.

William Marcy Tweed, the New York City political leader known as Boss Tweed

four months later, Gorbachev resigned, the Soviet Union broke up, and Yeltsin emerged as the most influential leader of the former Soviet republics.

It is a truism that power often destroys those who hold it. Lord Acton, the 19th-century British peer and historian, said that "power tends to corrupt and absolute power corrupts absolutely." The 18th-century French philosopher Montesquieu expressed a similar idea in *The Spirit of the Laws:* "Every man who has power is impelled to abuse it."

As Key has observed, power is not something that can be "poured into a keg, stored, and drawn upon as the need arises."[13] Power, Key notes, is relational—that is, it involves the interactions between the person who exercises power and those affected by that exercise of power.

If people, even in a primitive state, find it necessary to accept rulers who can authoritatively decide who gets what, then it follows that those who govern possess and exercise power in part because of their position. In other words, power follows office. To some extent, we accept the power exercised over us by others because we recognize the need to be governed.

## Democracy

**Democracy** is a word that comes from two Greek roots, *demos,* "the populace," and *kratia,* "rule"—taken together, "rule by the people."

The Greeks used the term to describe the government of Athens and other Greek city-states that flourished in the 5th century B.C. In his famous *Funeral Oration,* Pericles, the Athenian statesman, declared: "Our constitution is named a democracy, because it is in the hands not of the few, but of the many." To the ancient Greeks, therefore, democracy meant government by the mass of people, as distinguished from rule by those with special rank or status.

All governments make decisions about the distribution of valued things. As was noted earlier, in a democratic government, power, in theory, flows from the people as a whole. This is one of the ideals on which the American democracy was founded. But the United States is too big for every citizen to take part in the delib-

"Then we agree! We're doing the best job that can be done considering that the country's ungovernable."

Pfc. Lynndie England holds a leash around the neck of a naked Iraqi in a photo that became a symbol of the prisoner abuse scandal that damaged America's image.

erations of government, as in ancient Athens, so the distinction is sometimes made that America is a representative democracy, rather than a direct one. Leaders are elected to speak for and represent the people. Thus, the United States can also be described as a **republic,** a form of government in which the people are sovereign but their power is exercised by their elected representatives.

Government by the people also carries with it the notion of **majority rule,** a concept of government by the people in which everyone is free to vote, but normally whoever gets the most votes wins the election and represents all the people, including those who voted for the losing candidate. But in a system that is truly democratic, minority rights and views are also recognized and protected.

Every schoolchild knows the phrase from the Declaration of Independence: "We hold these truths to be self-evident, that all men are created equal." The concept of **equality**—that all people are of equal worth, even if not of equal ability—is also basic to American democracy. So are basic rights such as freedom of speech, press, religion, and assembly; the right to vote; and the right to dissent from majority opinion. The idea of individual dignity and the importance of each individual is another concept basic to American democracy. And, American government is constitutional—the power of government is limited by a framework of fundamental written law. Under such a government—in theory—the police power of the state should not be used illegally to punish individuals or to repress dissent.

These are the ideals, noble, even beautiful, in their conception. But, this is not always what really happens. African Americans and other minorities are still struggling for full equality; the police sometimes have their own views on freedom of assembly; and the government has sometimes committed abuses in the name of national security. In the mid-1970s, for example, congressional investigations disclosed widespread violations of the constitutional rights of individuals by federal intelligence agencies. In the 1980s, the Iran-contra scandal revealed that officials in the White House had acted outside the law in the pursuit of foreign policy objectives. In 2004, shocking photographs were published that revealed how the American military had abused prisoners in Iraq, a nation to which the United States had promised to bring freedom, justice, and human rights.

American democracy is far from perfect. "This is a great country," President John F. Kennedy once declared, "but it must be greater."[14] All citizens have to judge for themselves how far America falls short of fulfilling the principles on which it was founded. Nevertheless, the ideals endure; the goals are there if not always the reality.

## The Concept of a Political System

In today's electronic world, most people have listened to a stereo. Suppose for a moment that a visitor from outer space dropped in and asked you to describe a stereo system. You might say, "This is a compact disc player. I'm putting this CD in the little drawer that slides back in. This thing with all the knobs and buttons is an amplifier, and these big boxes over here are what we call speakers." Perhaps you might take the trouble to describe the details of each component at some length. At the end of your elaborate explanation, the visitor from space would still not know what a stereo was.

A better way to describe the compact disc player and the other components would be to explain that it is a system for the reproduction of sound, consisting of several parts, each of which performs a separate function and relates to the others. Having said that, you might turn on the power and play some music. Now the visitor would understand.

### A Dynamic Approach

In the same way, it is possible either to describe people, government, politics, and power as isolated, static elements, or to look at them as interacting elements in a political system. The concept of a political system may provide a useful framework, or approach, for understanding the total subject matter of this book. Just as in the case of the stereo system, a political system consists of several parts that relate to one another, each of which performs a separate, vital function. If we think in terms of a system, we visualize all the pieces in motion, acting and interacting, dynamic rather than static. In other words,

Fred R. Conrad/The New York Times

something is happening—just as when the compact disc is playing.

As David Easton says, "We can try to understand political life by viewing each of its aspects piecemeal," or we can "view political life as a system of interrelated activities."[15] One of the problems of trying to look at a political system is that government and politics do not exist in a vacuum—they are embedded in, and closely related to, many other activities in a society. But it is possible to separate political activity from other kinds of activity, at least for purposes of study.

Just as the CD player is part of a stereo system for the reproduction of sound, a political system also operates for a purpose: It makes the binding, authoritative decisions for society about who gets what.

## Inputs, Outputs, and Feedback

We may carry the analogy of a stereo system and a political system even further. A sound system has inputs, outputs, and sometimes a loud whistling noise called feedback. Those are precisely the same terms political scientists use when talking about a political system.

The **inputs** of a political system are of two kinds: the demands upon, and supports for, the system. **Demands,** as the word indicates, are what people and groups want from the political system, whether it be health care for the aged, loans for college students, equal opportunity for minorities, or higher subsidies for farmers. **Supports** are the attitudes and actions of people that sustain and buttress the system at all levels and allow it to continue

© 2002 AP/Wide World Photos

The National Organization for the Reform of Marijuana Laws (NORML) launched an ad campaign asking New York City to stop arresting and jailing marijuana smokers.

to work. They include everything from the patriotism drilled into schoolchildren to public backing for specific government policies.

The **outputs** of a political system are chiefly the binding decisions it makes, whether in the form of laws, regulations, or judicial decisions. Often such decisions reward one segment of society at the expense of another. The millionaire on New York's Park Avenue may be heavily taxed to clothe inner-city children on the South Side of Chicago. Or he or she may benefit from a tax loophole enacted by Congress. The freeway that runs through a poor urban neighborhood may speed white commuters from the suburbs but dislocate black residents of the inner city. These decisions are "redistributive" measures in that something of value is reallocated by the political system. Sometimes even a decision not to act is an output of a political system. By preserving an existing policy, one group may be rewarded while another group is not.

**Feedback** in a political system describes the response of the rest of society to the decisions made by the authorities. When those reactions are communicated back to the authorities, they may lead to a fresh round of decisions and new public responses.

The concept of a political system is simply a way of looking at political activity. It is an approach, an analytical tool, rather than a general theory of the type developed to explain the workings of scientific phenomena. It enables us to examine not only the formal structure of political and governmental institutions, but also how these institutions actually work.

## PUBLIC POLICYMAKING

There is a tendency in the study of American politics and government to concentrate on the institutions of government, such as the presidency, Congress, and the courts, and on the role of political parties, campaigns, and voters.

The analysis of public policy is another way of looking at government and politics. Instead of examining only institutions, policy analysis looks at what the institutions do.

A **policy** is a course of action decided upon by a government—or by any organization, group, or individual—that usually involves a choice among competing alternatives. When policies are shaped by government officials, the result is called **public policy.**

The analysis of public policy, therefore, focuses on how choices are arrived at and how public policy is made. It also focuses on what happens afterward. How well or badly is a policy carried out? What is its impact in its own policy area? And what effect does it have in other policy areas?

As Robert L. Lineberry has put it, policy analysts "focus, in systems language, on the outputs of the political system and their impact on the political, social, and economic environment."[16]

As Lineberry and other scholars have pointed out, if a problem does not get on the public agenda—the subjects that government policymakers try to deal with—no policy or output will be framed to deal with the problem. For example, some people feel marijuana should be legalized, but unless a federal or state government acts, its possession and sale remain illegal.

But what happens when an issue does get on the public agenda and results in the creation of a public policy? Sometimes nothing. In 1964 President Lyndon Johnson declared his "war on poverty." A major federal program was launched to try to deal with the problem. But more than three decades later, poverty in America had not been eradicated.

In other words, programs do not always work as intended. "Bills are passed, White House Rose Garden ceremonies held, and gift pens passed around by the president. At that point, when attention has waned, when the television cameras are gone and the reporters no longer present, the other face of policy emerges."[17] This second face of policy analysis, as Lineberry has suggested, is concerned with implementation, impact, and distribution.

**Implementation** is the action, or actions, taken by government to carry out a policy. "When policy is pronounced, the implementation process begins. What happens in it may, over the long run, have far more impact . . . than the intentions of the policy's framers."[18]

© AP/Wide World Photos

Government "redistributive" policies don't always work—a homeless family in California.

The impact of a policy can be measured in terms of its consequences, both in its immediate policy area and in other areas. For example, a government decision to combat inflation by tightening credit and raising interest rates may adversely affect the stock market if investors fear that companies will not be able to borrow enough money to invest in and expand their businesses.

**Distribution** is what occurs when government adopts a public policy that provides, or distributes, benefits to people or groups. Sometimes distribution involves who wins and who loses from a given public policy. When the government builds post offices or maintains national parks, its policies are distributive, and people assume that everyone benefits. But a **redistributive policy** takes something away from one person and gives it to someone else. A Medicaid program that uses taxes collected from more affluent members of society to assist the poor would be an example of such a policy. It is here in the area of redistributive policies that many of the major political battles are fought.

Public policies and policymaking are discussed throughout this book and are the subject, in particular, of Part Four, "Government in Operation."

## Democratic Government and a Changing Society

A political system relates to people, and the size of the population affects the outputs of the system. Of equal importance is the qualitative nature of the population: who they are, where they live, how they work, how they spend, how they move about. How the political system works, in other words, is affected to some extent by the surrounding social, economic, and cultural framework. As society changes, the responses of government are likely to change. Government reacts to basic alterations in the nature of a society; it tries to tailor programs and decision making to meet changing needs and demands. Population changes are also important politically; for example, the 2000 census data confirmed that the American population balance had continued to shift from the Northeast to the South and West. As a result, some southern and western states gained more seats in Congress in 2002.

### 300 Million Americans

In 2000 federal census-takers fanned out across America, counting the population as the Constitution requires every 10 years. When they were done more than 281 million people had been counted—a total that had increased to more than 300 million by October 2006. The Census Bureau predicted that by 2010 the total population may reach 308 million and could rise to about 420 million by 2050.[19]

According to one study of population patterns in the United States, if the projections of some experts were realized, "we would have close to one billion people in the United States one hundred years from now."[20] Although the authors of the study added that birth control and other factors made it unlikely that such a staggering total will be reached by that time, they estimated that the United States could not support a population of a billion without people pushing one another into the oceans.

How the nation has expanded from a population of about 4 million in 1790, and what the future may hold, can be charted with Census Bureau statistics and projections to 2050, as shown in Table 1-1. This dramatic increase in numbers of people—the "population explosion"—is taking place around the world. It raises questions that governments must ponder. Will there be enough food to eat? Enough room to live? Enough oil and water and other natural resources to meet humanity's future needs? Will the environment be destroyed?

***for more information about Census Bureau statistics, see: http://www.census.gov***

### America in the 21st Century

WASHINGTON, Mar. 13—Fueled by immigration and higher birth rates among Hispanic women, the United States is undergoing a profound demographic shift, and by the middle of the [21st] century only about half of the population will be non-Hispanic whites, the Census Bureau predicted today.

By 2050, the bureau said, immigration patterns and differences in birth rates, combined with an overall slowdown in growth of the country's population, will produce a United States in which 53 percent of the people will be non-Hispanic whites, down from 74 percent today.

In contrast, Hispanic people will make up 24.5 percent of the population, up from the current 10.2 percent, and Asians will make up 8.2 percent, an increase from the current 3.3 percent. The percentage of the black population will remain relatively stable, rising to about 13.6 percent by the year 2050 from the current 12 percent.

The population as a whole will rise to about 394 million from 262 million, an increase of 50 percent, the bureau said.

—From "Census Sees a Profound Ethnic Shift," by Steven A. Holmes, from the *New York Times*, March 14, 1996. 

## TABLE 1-1

### Profile of the U.S. Population, 1790–2050

| | Population (in millions) | | | | | | | | | | |
|---|---|---|---|---|---|---|---|---|---|---|---|
| | Actual | | | | | | | | Projected | | |
| | 1790 | 1870 | 1920 | 1960 | 1970 | 1980 | 1990 | 2000 | 2010 | 2020 | 2050 |
| Total population | 4 | 39 | 106 | 179 | 203 | 226 | 249 | 282 | 308 | 335 | 419 |
| Urban | —* | 10 | 54 | 125 | 149 | 167 | 187 | NA | NA | NA | NA |
| Rural | 4 | 29 | 52 | 54 | 54 | 60 | 62 | NA | NA | NA | NA |
| Nonwhite | 1 | 5 | 11 | 20 | 25 | 32 | 40 | 54 | 64 | 75 | 117 |
| White | 3 | 34 | 95 | 159 | 178 | 195 | 208 | 228 | 244 | 260 | 302 |
| Median age (years) | NA | 20 | 25 | 30 | 28 | 30 | 33 | 36 | 37 | 38 | 39 |
| Primary and secondary school enrollment | NA | 7 | 23 | 42 | 53 | 45 | 46 | 53 | 56† | NA | NA |
| College enrollment | NA | —* | 0.6 | 3 | 7 | 10 | 13 | 15 | 18† | NA | NA |

*Less than 200,000.
†Projection for 2013.
NA: Not available.
SOURCES: U.S. Bureau of the Census, and National Center for Education Statistics, Department of Education. Population figures rounded.

An interesting profile of the American public can be sketched with statistics, as presented in Table 1-2, that answer the question "Who are we?" A portrait of national origins can also be drawn. The great successive waves of immigration placed a stamp of diversity on America; even third- and fourth-generation Americans may think of themselves as "Irish" or "Italian."

The 2000 census indicated that the ancestry groups of Americans included the following: German, 15.2 percent; Irish, 10.8 percent; English, 8.7 percent; African American, 12.9 percent; Hispanic, 12.5 percent; Italian, 5.6 percent; French, 3.0 percent; Polish, 3.2 percent;

## TABLE 1-2

### Who Are We?*

149.1 million females
144.5 million males
20 million under 5 years
36.3 million 65 and over
236 million white
57.5 million nonwhite
125.9 million married
35.6 million divorced or widowed
215.7 million old enough to vote
17.6 million in college
54.9 million in primary and secondary schools
139.2 million employed
69 million homeowners

*Data for 2004.
SOURCE: U.S. Bureau of the Census, *Statistical Abstract of the United States: 2006*, pp. 13, 15, 18, 49, 141, 263, 387, 631.

© Robert W. Ginn/PhotoEdit

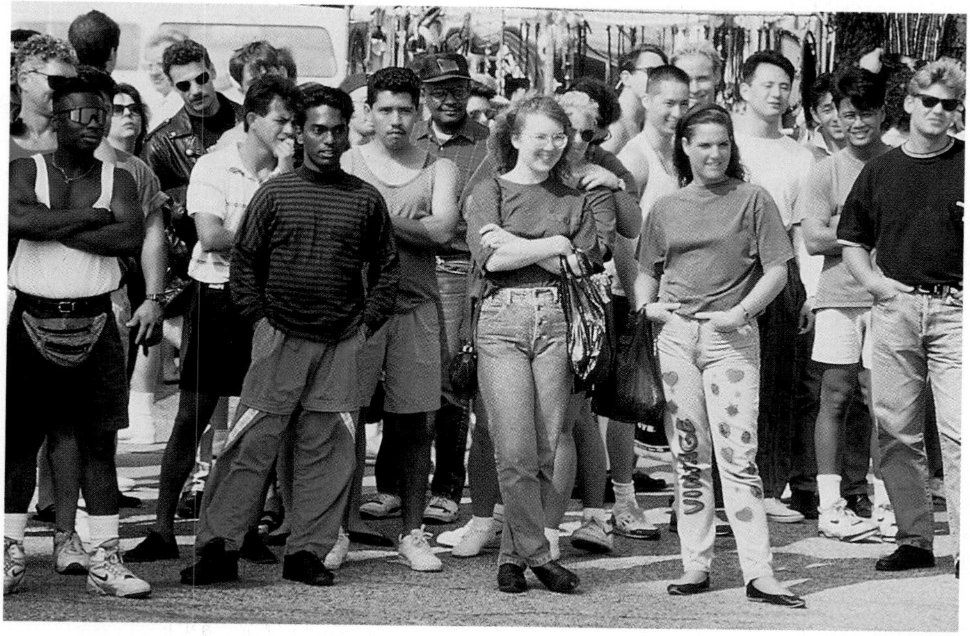
© David Young-Wolff/PhotoEdit

Venice Beach, California: a changing population

Asian American, 4.2 percent; Dutch, 1.6 percent; Scottish, 1.7 percent; and Native American, 0.3 percent.[21] America is also a nation of 64.6 million Protestants, 58 million Catholics, 4.1 million Muslims, 5.6 million Jews, and 1 million Hindus.[22]

Sometimes, prevailing notions about America's population are incorrect. For example, America is often thought to be a nation of white Anglo-Saxon Protestants. That group is influential in many areas of American national life. But as the national origin figures indicate, a majority of Americans stem from other than Anglo-Saxon stock.[23] By midcentury, according to Census Bureau projections, the combined Hispanic, black, Asian American, and American Indian population will outnumber the white population.[24]

Although the accent in America is on youth, the median age of Americans is not 18 or 21 but about 37 and likely to go up because people are living longer.

## The Mobile Society

A political system reacts not only to shifts in population totals but also to the movement of people geographically, socially, and economically. For example, farm population declined from 30.5 million in 1930 to 3.0 million in 2000.[25] As the nation changed from a predominantly rural to an urban society (see Table 1-1), the political importance of the "farm bloc" decreased.

Americans move about a great deal. According to the Census Bureau, about 14 percent of Americans change their residence each year. In 1964 California surpassed New York as the most populous state in the Union. As a result, presidential candidates in some years spend more time than they used to campaigning in California. And in four of the past 10 presidential election years (1968, 1972, 1980, and 1984), two Californians, Richard Nixon and Ronald Reagan, were elected or reelected president.

During and after the Second World War, as blacks migrated to northern cities, many whites in the central cities moved to the suburbs. All these shifts and changing population patterns affect the American political system. The migration of millions of African American citizens to northern cities resulted in the election of black mayors in several large cities by the mid-1970s and in the election of more African American members of Congress. And the population shift from the cities to the suburbs increased the political power of suburbia. More members of Congress and state legislators now represent suburban areas than in the past, because lawmakers' districts are apportioned according to population.

## Technological, Economic, and Social Change

In addition to the population explosion, America has experienced a knowledge explosion. Science and technology, the astonishing growth of the Internet, computers, cell phones, and high-speed communications are reshaping society. Americans have split the atom and traveled to the moon and back. We listen for signals from other galaxies in outer space and explore the inner space of the human brain. There appear to be no limits to technological potential—except the inability of human beings to control their own nature.

Technological change is soon reflected within the political system. Consider for a moment a single innovation of the electronic age: television. Prior to the Second World War, television did not exist for the mass

*Making a Difference*

## AMERICAN INDIANS: A FEDERAL OFFICIAL SPEAKS OUT

In September 2000, for the first time in the nation's history, a high-ranking government official apologized for the nation's brutal treatment of the first Americans. Kevin Gover, head of the Bureau of Indian Affairs, told President Clinton's staff that he was going to do it, and the White House did not object:

> The head of the Bureau of Indian Affairs apologized yesterday for the agency's "legacy of racism and inhumanity" that included massacres, forced relocations of tribes and attempts to wipe out Indian languages and cultures.
>
> "By accepting this legacy, we accept also the moral responsibility of putting things right," Kevin Gover, a Pawnee Indian, said in an emotional speech marking the agency's 175th anniversary.
>
> Gover said he was apologizing on behalf of the BIA, not the federal government as a whole. Still, he is the highest-ranking U.S. official ever to make such a statement regarding the treatment of Indians. The audience of about 300 tribal leaders, BIA employees and federal officials stood and cheered as a teary-eyed Gover finished the speech. . . .
>
> Gover recited a litany of wrongs the BIA had inflicted on Indians. . . . Estimates vary, but the agency is believed responsible for hundreds of thousands of deaths.
>
> "This agency participated in the ethnic cleansing that befell the western tribes," Gover said.
>
> After the BIA became part of the Interior Department in 1849, Gover said, children were brutalized in BIA-run boarding schools and Indian languages and religious practices were banned.
>
> "Poverty, ignorance and disease have been the product of this agency's work," Gover said.
>
> Now, 90 percent of the BIA's 10,000 employees are Indian and the agency has changed into an advocate for tribal governments.
>
> —Adapted from Matt Kelley, Associated Press, in the *Washington Post,* September 9, 2000

of Americans. Today, political candidates spend hundreds of millions of dollars to purchase television time. Presidential nominees may deplore the "packaging" of political candidates by Madison Avenue, but they hire advertising agencies to do just that. Commercials are produced and presidents and candidates sold in the manner of detergents.

A considerable amount of electronic-age technology is the by-product of defense research and development. In his farewell address to the nation in 1961, President Dwight D. Eisenhower, although himself a career soldier, warned of the dangers to liberty and democracy of the **military-industrial complex,** a term now often used to describe the economic and political ties between

Sony's pet robot dog

## The World of the Future: Virtual Assistants and Space Colonies?

Researchers at George Washington University have forecast possible technological breakthroughs in the 21st century, and one expert listed some of the likely changes to come in the first decade and beyond:

- *Fuel-Cell Powered Automobiles.* Today's hybrid cars, which use various combinations of small internal combustion engines and batteries, are simply an intermediate step to an advanced automobile powered by fuel cells. Fuel cells chemically combine hydrogen and oxygen to produce electricity and simple by-products, mainly small amounts of water.
- *Virtual Assistants* . . . to help you solve . . . problems—in just about the same way a real assistant would. We envision the virtual assistant as a very smart program stored on your PC or portable device that monitors all e-mails, faxes, messages, computer files, and phone calls in order to "learn" all about you and your work. In time, your VA would gain the knowledge to take over routine tasks, such as writing a letter, retrieving a file, making a phone call. . . .
- *Smart, Mobile Robots.* The robots in factories today will seem primitive compared with the next generation, which will be able to sense their environment, make complex decisions, and learn how to improve their behavior. . . . Authorities working in this field think robots will soon perform more sophisticated factory work, run errands, do household chores, and assist the handicapped.
- *Advanced Transportation Systems.* Individual vehicles will be replaced by transportation systems: magnetic levitation trains, gliding on a cushion of air at 300 mph and connecting major cities; automated superhighways that take over steering, speed, and braking as cars caravan at 70 mph; and intelligent networks of roadways that monitor traffic flow and direct smart cars toward the least congested routes.
- *Computing with Light.* Scientists estimate that today's computer technology will reach its limit in a decade or so as chip circuits shrink to one molecule wide and can miniaturize no further. What then? . . . Optical computers will be more powerful because they use light—the fastest known force in the universe—rather than electricity.
- *The Coming Biogenetic Payoff.* The enormous investment poured into the biogenetic revolution—1,300 biotech companies employing 100,000 people in the United States alone—is likely to mature and produce unprecedented benefits in a decade or two. Genetic engineering is fraught with risk and social prohibitions, of course. But parents are likely to select major characteristics of their children in about 2012, cloned organs should be used to replace defective ones in about 2020, and genetic therapy is likely to cure most inherited diseases in 2025.
- *Colonizing Our Solar System and Beyond.* We are likely to colonize our solar system over the next few decades. NASA plans several Mars projects, and the George Washington panel thinks humans will land on the planet about 2022. . . . However, human travel beyond our solar system will probably have to wait until the middle of the 21st century. The nearest star system is four light-years away from Earth.

—Adapted from William E. Halal,
*The Futurist,* July 1, 2000

© Yoshikazu Tsuno/AFP/Getty Images

General Motors' concept of a fuel cell–electric car

the military establishment and the defense-aerospace industry. What Eisenhower feared was that the Pentagon and the defense contractors who produce weapons for the military would gain "unwarranted influence" in the political system.

A few years later, economist John Kenneth Galbraith argued that there already existed a "close fusion of the industrial system with the state," and in time "the line between the two will disappear." As a result of the technological revolution, Galbraith contended, a few hundred huge corporations were shaping the goals of society as a whole.[26]

But government, too, exercises great power in the modern industrial state. Government is expected to help prevent either periodic economic recession or depression. Although economists argue over the best methods of managing the economy, they generally agree that the government has the major responsibility in promoting prosperity and full employment.

The past four decades also have been a time of rapid social change in America. At almost every level, wherever one looks, the change is visible—in manners and morals, in civil rights, in the theater, in literature, and in the arts. The change could be seen as well in the contin-

uing emphasis on a youth-oriented culture, and at the same time, the growing concern over problems of the elderly, whose ranks are increasing in numbers. As a result, the political system was paying more attention to health care and retirement security for senior citizens.

These social changes have been accompanied by new political concerns. Today, large numbers of people are disturbed about the pollution of the natural environment that has resulted from technological advance. Many American cities are blanketed in smog despite new laws. Some rivers are cleaner as a result of environmental legislation, but many are polluted by industrial and human waste. Across the land, toxic wastes have endangered communities, even forcing the relocation of an entire town, Times Beach, Missouri, in 1983. Pesticides are killing the wildlife in America.[27] Oil spills, from tankers and offshore drilling, and medical waste have fouled beaches. The gasoline engine and power plants and other industries pour smoke and chemicals into the atmosphere. Problems such as acid rain and global warming transcend national boundaries.

Concern about the environment is not only a matter of aesthetics, of preserving the natural beauty of the land. Air and water pollution damage health and upset the delicate balance of nature, the total relationship between human beings and their environment. They raise serious questions about whether humanity will be able to survive the damage it is inflicting on the earth that sustains all life. (We examine the problem of environmental pollution in more detail in Chapter 18.)

The long-range problem of energy resources for the future and the potential threat to the world's oil supply posed by conflict in the Middle East underscore the fact that environmental problems are, in the end, also political problems. They pose for America questions of priorities and values. For example, will people ever be willing to use their cars less or buy smaller cars to conserve energy and reduce pollution? For years, the enormous popularity of gas-guzzling sport utility vehicles (SUVs) suggested otherwise. Only in the spring and summer of 2004, after gasoline prices soared—and again in the summer of 2006, when gas exceeded $3 a gallon—were some consumers attracted to vehicles with better fuel economy. Do voters favor relaxation of environmental standards to increase the supply of oil and other energy sources? Or to preserve jobs at the expense of endangered species? The environment and energy needs have created conflicting choices for individual citizens, for political leaders, and for society as a whole.

There were many other areas of conflict and change. Back in the 1960s, for example, to any white American who cared to listen, the message of the times was clear: Black Americans would wait no longer to obtain the equality and freedom that are the rights of everyone under the American political system. This was the message preached peacefully by Dr. Martin Luther King, Jr., and expressed violently in the burning black neighborhoods of the nation's cities.

Yet the biggest test of the political system may still lie ahead, in how America adjusts to a population that is becoming increasingly more racially and ethnically diverse. America is no longer just a white society; it is brown and black and other hues. But what, it may be asked, lies at the end of the rainbow? Harmony and understanding, or conflict?

It is not possible to discuss or even list in a few pages all the social, economic, and cultural factors that are influencing the American political system today. Suggested here are simply some of the major changes, currents, and conflicts that have placed enormous pressures on American democracy. In later chapters, these will be taken up in more detail.

## The Consent of the Governed

One of the characteristics of a viable political system is that it adapts to change. More than 200 years after its creation, the ability of the American political system to adapt to relentless change, and to cope with recurring political crises, was being tested.

The Vietnam War and the Watergate scandal were followed by a new atmosphere of questioning of presidential power by the public and by Congress. That kind of questioning is appropriate in a democracy. President Kennedy declared, in a speech at Amherst College less than a month before his death in 1963, that "men who create power make an indispensable contribution to the Nation's greatness, but the men who question power make a contribution just as indispensable."[28]

© AP/Wide World Photos

© 2003 AP/Wide World Photos

Gas-guzzling SUVs have been popular.

The divisions in American society that had been caused by the war in Vietnam, and the strains placed upon the political system by the trauma of Watergate, the Iran-contra scandal, the impeachment of President Clinton, the 2001 terrorist attacks, and the war in Iraq, underscored and renewed a basic truth. The American political system rests on the consent of the governed, but that consent, to be freely given, required that the nation's political leaders earn and merit the trust of the people. In the 21st century, such a bond of trust appeared to offer the best hope for the survival in America of democracy, a system that Winston S. Churchill once described as "the worst form of government except all those other forms that have been tried from time to time."[29]

## KEY TERMS

government, p. 18
politics, p. 18
power, p. 18
democracy, p. 19
republic, p. 20
majority rule, p. 20
equality, p. 20
inputs, p. 21
demands, p. 21
supports, p. 21
outputs, p. 22
feedback, p. 22
policy, p. 22
public policy, p. 22
implementation, p. 22
distribution, p. 23
redistributive policy, p. 23
military-industrial complex, p. 26

## SUGGESTED WEBSITES

**http://www.census.gov**
*The Census Bureau*
The Census Bureau's website offers users the decennial censuses of the U.S. population, five-year censuses of state and local governments, and current demographic reports about how Americans live and work.

**http://www.fedstats.gov**
*FedStats*
The Federal Interagency Council on Statistical Policy maintains this website, which allows users to look up any topic and then be linked to the relevant government agencies. Provides contact information for the agencies and links to statistical data by subject.

**http://www.firstgov.gov**
*FirstGov*
Serves as a single point of entry to every service and department of the federal government. FirstGov is maintained by the U.S. General Services Administration.

**http://www.whitehouse.gov**
*The White House*
The official website of the White House. Offers presidential speeches, press conferences, interviews, and other documents. Provides links to the personal home pages of the president, the First Lady, and the vice president. Also contains links to the websites of departments that make up the cabinet, independent agencies that report to the president, and special presidential commissions.

## SUGGESTED READING

Brown, D. Clayton. *Globalization and America since 1945** (Scholarly Resources, 2003). A useful description of the process of globalization. The author traces its roots to efforts by the United States after 1945 to reach trade agreements and win the Cold War. Discusses the impact of technology, immigration, culture, and terrorism. The author approves of globalization, but criticizes some of its consequences.

Easton, David. *The Political System: An Inquiry into the State of Political Science,* 2nd edition (University of Chicago Press, 1981). (Originally published in 1953.) The first edition was an early statement of the systems approach to the study of politics developed by Easton. See also his *A Framework for Political Analysis* (University of Chicago Press, 1979), and *A Systems Analysis of Political Life* (University of Chicago Press, 1979).

Finer, S. E. *The History of Government from the Earliest Times** (Oxford University Press, 1999). A remarkably comprehensive survey of the varying forms of government that have been established throughout human history, and the efforts that societies have made to control their political institutions. Covers forms of government from ancient Sumeria to the time of the French Revolution.

Frantzich, Stephen E. *Studying in Washington: A Guide to Academic Internships in the Nation's Capitol,* 5th edition* (American Political Science Association, 2002). A pamphlet on undergraduate internships in Washington, D.C. Includes a list of many university programs. The authors discuss how to obtain an internship, and housing opportunities in Washington.

Grossman, Lawrence K. *The Electronic Republic: Reshaping Democracy in the Information Age** (Penguin, 1996). A useful examination of the growing impact of communications technology on the political process in the United States. The author explores the potential benefits and hazards that emerging media, such as the Internet, hold for American democracy.

Key, V. O., Jr. *Public Opinion and American Democracy* (Philadelphia Book Company, 1961). An important work in which findings about public opinion and mass attitudes toward politics are analyzed in terms of their consequences for the actual workings of government.

Lineberry, Robert L. *American Public Policy: What Government Does and What Difference It Makes* (Harper & Row, 1978). A concise analysis of the making of public policy, its implementation, and its impact. Provides a useful introduction to policy analysis, illustrated by specific case studies.

Roberts, Sam. *Who We Are Now: The Changing Face of America in the Twenty-First Century* (Time Books/Henry Holt & Company, 2004). A fascinating picture of recent and probable future changes in the makeup of the U.S. population. The author draws heavily on data from the 2000 Census and emphasizes the major changes in America's population that took place between 1990 and 2000.

Schattschneider, Elmer E. *The Semisovereign People** (Harcourt Brace College Publishers, 1975). (Originally published in 1960.) A lively and revealing analysis of the role of American interest groups and political parties in bringing public demands to bear on political officials.

Schneiderman, Jill S., ed. *The Earth Around Us: Maintaining a Livable Planet* (Perseus Books, 2003). A wide-ranging collection of essays by 31 scientists, who discuss the environmental challenges facing the world's citizens now and in the coming years. The essays in this volume were written in tribute to Rachel Carson, who many years ago wrote a highly influential book, *The Sea around Us.*

Scott, John. *Power** (Polity Press, 2001). A detailed and careful analysis of the concept of power in its political context. The author draws a fundamental distinction between relations based on force and manipulation, and relations that are based on persuasion. Topics covered include the behavior of political elites, political pressure and protest, and bureaucratic power. Relations on both the international and interpersonal levels are also discussed.

Tocqueville, Alexis de. *Democracy in America,* 2 vols.* Phillips Bradley, ed. (Knopf, 1945). (Available in many editions.) A classic analysis of American political and social life as seen through the eyes of a 19th-century French observer.

Wills, Garry. *A Necessary Evil: A History of American Distrust of Government** (Simon and Schuster, 2002). An insightful analysis of the deeply rooted American tradition of distrust of the national government and its institutions. The author examines the consequences of that distrust for the American political system.

Wilson, Edward O. *The Diversity of Life** (Norton, 1999). A wide-ranging survey of the development of life on earth over the last 4 billion years. Emphasizes the dangers that currently threaten to reduce the number of living species, and argues that it is important to maintain biodiversity.

*Available in paperback edition.

# Chapter 2

# The Constitutional Framework

EVERY EVENING in Washington an unusual ceremony takes place in the great rotunda of the National Archives. There, beneath the gold eagles in the ornate hall, are displayed the Declaration of Independence, the Constitution, and the Bill of Rights. The faded parchments are sealed under pressure in protective gold-plated titanium-and-glass cases containing a mixture of argon and helium and a small amount of water vapor for preservation.

When the last visitor has left the building, a guard activates a mechanism, and with a great whirring noise, the documents in their cases glide slowly into a high-security, fireproof vault behind the display area. The vault clangs shut and the documents are safely put to bed for the night. The whole eerie process takes less than a minute.

*for more information about the National Archives & Records Administration see:*
*http://www.archives.gov*

Ideas, of course, cannot be preserved in a vault, but documents can. The documents, and the mystique that surrounds them, are part of what Daniel J. Boorstin called the "search for symbols."[1] The quest for national identity, in which such symbols play a role, is a continuing process in America.

But the Constitution is much more than a symbol. The Constitution established the basic structure of the American government and a written set of rules to control the conduct of that government; in its own words, the Constitution is "the supreme Law of the Land." As one scholar has noted, "A constitution . . . is not ordinary law, but rather an embodiment of fundamental principles, higher law, law above law."[2] The United States was, in fact, the first nation to have a written constitution. It is a charter that has been continually adapted to new problems, principally through amendment and judicial interpretation by the Supreme Court, changes that often reflect the prevailing political climate.

Yet, the American political system is sometimes attacked for what its critics see as a failure to respond to urgent national problems, such as education, health care, crime, urban decay, poverty, and racial tensions. Nor are the nation's problems only social and economic; some are political and constitutional. The growth of presidential power in the 20th century at times placed great strains on the system of constitutional government. In the 1980s, the Iran-contra affair revealed that a secret foreign policy had been conducted from the White House under President Ronald Reagan, a policy that circumvented laws enacted by Congress. And twice in the 20th century, presidents were the target of impeachment efforts. In 1998 President Bill Clinton was impeached by the House of Representatives after an independent counsel reported he had lied under oath about his sexual involvement with a White House intern. He was tried by the Senate, but not convicted, and he was not removed from office. In 1974, the Watergate scandal resulted in the resignation of President Richard Nixon, under threat of impeachment for abuses of power.

Key Question In this chapter we will explore a key question: ***Is the constitutional framework constructed in 1787 sufficiently flexible to meet the needs of a complex, urban society in the 21st century?***

For example, even though the Constitution is reinterpreted by the Supreme Court to meet changed conditions, does that process take place fast enough? Why, for example, did it take nearly 100 years after the Civil War for the Supreme Court to apply the Constitution to outlaw racial segregation in public schools? Or why did 131 years pass after the nation was founded before the Constitution recognized the right of women to vote?

As we explore the origins and the meaning of the Constitution, there are other questions to consider: Who were the framers of the Constitution? What political ideas influenced them? Were they rich men merely interested in protecting their own economic positions? What political bargains were struck by the framers? Why does the United States have a federal system of government, and what does that mean? How did the Supreme Court acquire its power to interpret the Constitution? How does the Constitution affect people's lives today?

# The Constitution and the Declaration of Independence

## The Constitution Today

In the summer of 2003, the Supreme Court handed down a landmark decision that upheld the principle of affirmative action, that is, preference for minority students seeking admission to colleges and graduate schools. The Court's decision in two cases involving the University of Michigan endorsed the goal of racial diversity to achieve equality in American society.[3]

The cases began in the mid-1990s when three white students applied to the university, were turned down, and sued on the grounds that less-qualified minority students had been admitted. Barbara Grutter, who had applied to UM's law school, was rejected although she had a grade point average of 3.8 and a score of 161 on the Law School Admission Test (LSAT). She argued that minority students with lower grades and test scores had been admitted, violating the equal protection provision of the Constitution and the Civil Rights Act of 1964.

The university, in its law school admission policies, considered race as one factor among many in its decisions. Justice Sandra Day O'Connor, writing for the 5–4 majority, sided with the university. "Today," she wrote, "we hold that the law school has a compelling interest in attaining a diverse student body." She went on to explain the various ways in which the nation benefited from racial diversity in business, the government, and the military. In *Grutter* v. *Bollinger,* the university won a major victory.

***for more information about the Constitution see:***
***http://www.gpoaccess.gov/constitution/browse.html***

However, in a companion case, the Supreme Court made it clear that universities could not use quotas, in this case a point system based in part on race, to achieve diversity. Two white students, Jennifer Gratz and Patrick Hamacher, were turned down as undergraduates at Michigan. By a vote of 6–3, the Court in *Gratz* v. *Bollinger* invalidated the university's affirmative action program that automatically gave minority students 20 points of the 100 needed for admission. But taken together, the two decisions meant that colleges and universities could continue to give preference to black, Hispanic, Native American, and other minorities as long as applicants were evaluated individually.

Barbara Grutter, 49 by the time the Court ruled, never earned a law degree. Jennifer Gratz and Patrick Hamacher went on to graduate from other colleges. But the Supreme Court's rulings renewed affirmative action as a valid goal for America, and its twin decisions might affect millions of students for years to come.

In the Michigan disputes, three students had taken their cases all the way to the Supreme Court. The decisions had a direct impact on college campuses and admissions policies. In both instances, the Supreme Court wrote new chapters in the continuing battle over affirmative action. These cases arose and were decided within the framework of the Constitution.

The Constitution directly affects many other facets of American life and politics. When in 1954 the Supreme Court outlawed officially supported segregation in the public schools, it did so on the grounds that "separate-but-equal" schools violated the Constitution.[4]

© 2003 AP/Wide World Photos

2003: Affirmative action supporters at the University of Michigan

Abortion is another controversial political issue affected by Supreme Court rulings. In 1973, in *Roe* v. *Wade*, the Supreme Court ruled that state laws restricting abortions during the first three months of pregnancy were unconstitutional.[5] (The Court's rulings on abortion are discussed in more detail on pp. 147–150.)

As these examples illustrate, constitutional government affects the quality of American society here and now, today and tomorrow. Yet it is a story that has been unfolding for more than two centuries; it began, as much as anywhere, in the city of Philadelphia in June 1776.

## We Hold These Truths . . .

Early in May 1776, Thomas Jefferson rode down the mountain on horseback from Monticello, his Virginia home, and headed north to take his seat in the Continental Congress at Philadelphia. It had been just over a year since the guns blazed at Lexington and Concord, but the 13 American colonies, although at war, were still under the jurisdiction of the British crown.

Independence was in the air, however, nourished by the words of an Englishman only recently arrived in America. His name was Thomas Paine, and his pamphlet, *Common Sense,* attacked George III, the British monarch, as the "Royal Brute." Paine's fiery words stirred the colonies.

***for more information about the Continental Congress and Constitutional Convention see:***
***http://memory.loc.gov/ammem/bdsds/bdsdhome.html***

On June 7 Richard Henry Lee, one of Jefferson's fellow delegates from Virginia, introduced a resolution declaring that the colonies "are, and of right ought to be, free and independent States." Four days later, after impassioned debate, the Continental Congress appointed a committee of five, including Jefferson, to "prepare a declaration."

At age 33, Jefferson was already known, in the words of John Adams of Massachusetts, as a man with a "peculiar felicity of expression," and the task of writing the Declaration fell to him. Jefferson completed his draft in about two weeks. Sitting in the second-floor parlor of the house of Jacob Graff, Jr., a German bricklayer, Jefferson composed some of the most enduring words in the English language. His draft, edited somewhat by Benjamin Franklin and John Adams, was submitted on June 28.

On July 2 the Continental Congress approved Richard Henry Lee's resolution declaring the colonies free of allegiance to the crown. The Declaration of Independence is not the official act by which Congress severed its ties with Britain. Lee's resolution did that. Rather, the Declaration "was intended as a formal justification of an act already accomplished."[6]

For two days Congress debated Jefferson's draft, making changes and deletions that Jefferson found painful. No matter; what emerged has withstood the test of time:

> We hold these Truths to be self-evident, that all Men are created equal, that they are endowed by their Creator with certain unalienable Rights, that among these are Life, Liberty, and the pursuit of Happi-

© Bettmann/Corbis

Thomas Jefferson

The American Past

## THOMAS JEFFERSON BECOMES PRESIDENT

At four o'clock the morning of March 4, 1801, a humiliated President Adams left Washington, D.C., to avoid seeing his successor's inauguration. Shortly before noon, President-elect Thomas Jefferson, a month shy of fifty-eight years old, stepped out of Conrad and McMunn's boardinghouse on New Jersey Avenue at C Street and joined an escort of officers of the Alexandria, Virginia, militia and stepped off briskly through the muddy streets of the still-unfinished federal city escorted by District of Columbia marshals and congressmen. Walking to the Capitol, he shunned the splendor of Washington's and Adams's inaugural parades in ceremonial carriages. He wore no elegant suit, no sword as his predecessors had. The *Alexandria Times* reported that "his dress was, as usual, that of a plain citizen without any distinctive badge of office." . . . Jefferson hiked up Capitol Hill, where he had insisted the Capitol be built on higher ground than the President's House to symbolize the preeminence of the people. He acknowledged the cheers of Republicans lining his route. Arriving at the unfinished Capitol, Jefferson strode confidently between ranks of Alexandria riflemen who presented arms as he entered the only finished room, the Senate Chamber. . . . In a single sentence, he declared his program as president: "Peace, commerce and honest friendship with all nations, entangling alliances with none."

—William Sterne Randall, *Thomas Jefferson: A Life*

ness—That to secure these Rights, Governments are instituted among Men, deriving their just Powers from the Consent of the Governed, that whenever any Form of Government becomes destructive of these Ends, it is the Right of the People to alter or to abolish it, and to institute new Government. . . .

The Continental Congress approved the Declaration on July 4 and ordered that it be "authenticated and printed." Although the fact is sometimes overlooked, Jefferson and his colleagues produced and signed a treasonable document. They were literally pledging their lives.

Dr. Benjamin Rush of Philadelphia, one of the signers, asked John Adams many years later: "Do you recollect . . . the pensive and awful silence which pervaded the house when we were called up, one after another, to the table of the President of Congress to subscribe what was believed by many at that time to be our own death warrants?"[7]

The solemnity of the moment was breached only once. It is said that Benjamin Harrison of Virginia, whom Adams once described as "an indolent and luxurious heavy gentleman of no use in Congress or committee," turned to Elbridge Gerry of Massachusetts, a skinny, worried-looking colleague, and cackled: "I shall have a great advantage over you, Mr. Gerry, when we are all hung for what we are now doing. From the size and weight of my body I shall die in a few minutes, but from the lightness of your body you will dance in the air an hour or two before you are dead."[8]

### WHAT WAS EDITED OUT OF THE DECLARATION OF INDEPENDENCE?

Jefferson's draft of the Declaration of Independence originally included an attack on slavery, and sought to blame that "execrable commerce" on King George III. But the Continental Congress cut the passage out of the final document in deference to the wishes of South Carolina and Georgia, and, Jefferson suspected, those Northerners who profited from carrying slaves in their ships. Had the passage remained in, the Declaration would have included these words:

> He has waged cruel war against human nature itself, violating its most sacred rights of life & liberty in the persons of a distant people who never offended him, captivating & carrying them into slavery in another hemisphere, or to incur miserable death in their transportation thither. This piratical warfare, the opprobrium of infidel powers, is the warfare of the Christian king of Great Britain. Determined to keep open a market where Men should be bought & sold . . . suppressing every legislative attempt to prohibit or to restrain this execrable commerce . . . he is now exciting those very people to rise in arms among us, and to purchase that liberty of which he has deprived them, by murdering the people upon whom he also obtruded.

—Carl L. Becker, *The Declaration of Independence*

## THE POLITICAL FOUNDATIONS

Although Jefferson later said he had "turned to neither book nor pamphlet" in writing the Declaration of Independence, he was certainly influenced by the philosophy of John Locke (1632–1704) and others, by his British heritage with its traditional concern for individual rights, and by the colonial political experience itself.

## The Influence of John Locke

John Locke advanced the philosophy of **natural rights,** the belief that all people possess certain basic rights that may not be abridged by government. Locke's concept of natural rights was political gospel to most educated Americans in the late 18th century. Jefferson absorbed Locke's writings, and some of the English philosopher's words and phrases—such as "a long train of abuses"—emerged verbatim in the Declaration.

Locke reasoned that human beings were "born free" and possessed certain natural rights when they lived in a state of nature before governments were formed. People contracted among themselves to form a society to protect those rights. All people, Locke believed, were free, equal, and independent, and no one could be "subjected to the political power of another, without his own consent."[9] These dangerous ideas—dangerous in an age of the divine right of kings—are directly reflected in the language of the Declaration of Independence, written nearly a century later.

## The English Heritage

The irony of the American Revolution is that the colonists, for the most part, rebelled because they felt they were being deprived of their rights as English citizens. Many of the ideas of the Declaration of Independence, written in 1776, the Constitution, framed in 1787, and the Bill of Rights, added to the Constitution in 1791, evolved from this English heritage. The political and intellectual antecedents of the American system of government included such British legal milestones as the **Magna Carta,** the document issued by King John at Runnymede in 1215, in which the nobles confirmed that the power of the king was not absolute; the Habeas Corpus Act (1679); and the Bill of Rights (1689).

***for more information about the Magna Carta see:***
***http://www.archives.gov/exhibit_hall/featured_documents/magna_carta/index.html***

From England also came a system of **common law,** the cumulative body of law as expressed in judicial decisions and custom rather than by statute. The men who framed America's government were influenced by the writings of Sir Edward Coke, the great British jurist and champion of common law against the power of the king, and Sir William Blackstone, the Oxford law professor whose *Commentaries on the Laws of England* (1765–1769) is still an important historical work.

But if the ideas embodied in the American system of government are to be found largely in the nation's English heritage, it is also true that American institutions developed to a great extent from colonial foundations. The roots of much of today's governmental structure can be found in the colonial charters.

## The Colonial Experience

Even before they landed at Plymouth in 1620, the Pilgrims—a group of English Puritans who had separated from the Church of England—drew up the Mayflower Compact. The Pilgrims had sailed from Holland intending to settle in the area that is now New York City, but landed instead just north of Cape Cod. In the cabin of the *Mayflower,* 41 men signed the compact, declaring that "we . . . solemnly & mutualy in the presence of God, and one of another, covenant & combine our selves togeather into a civill body politick."

Smithsonian Institution

Jefferson composed the first draft of the Declaration of Independence on this portable writing desk.

The Mayflower Compact, as Samuel Eliot Morison noted, "is justly regarded as a key document in American history. It proves the determination of the small group of English emigrants to live under a rule of law, based on the consent of the people, and to set up their own civil government."[10]

A year earlier at Jamestown, Virginia, a group of settlers had established the first representative assembly in the New World. In 1639, Puritans from the Massachusetts Bay Colony and another group from London framed America's first written constitution, the Fundamental Orders of Connecticut. The Massachusetts Body of Liberties (1641) embodied traditional English rights, such as trial by jury and due process of law (later incorporated into the Constitution and the Bill of Rights).

The political forms established by the Puritans contributed to the formation of representative institutions. Beyond that, Puritanism shaped the American mind and left its indelible stamp on the American character. The English Puritans who came to America were influenced by the teachings of John Calvin, the 16th-century French theologian of the Protestant Reformation. Theirs was a stern code of hard work, sobriety, and intense religious zeal. Even today, with rapidly changing, increasingly liberal sexual and moral codes, traces of America's Puritan heritage remain.

**The Colonial Governments** The 13 original colonies, some formed as commercial ventures, others as religious havens, all had written charters that set forth their form of government and the rights of the colonists. All had governors (the executive branch), legislatures, and a judiciary.

The eight **royal colonies** were New Hampshire, New York, New Jersey, Virginia, North Carolina, South Carolina, Georgia, and Massachusetts. They were controlled by the king through governors appointed by him. Laws passed by their legislatures were subject to approval of the crown. In the three **proprietary colonies**—Maryland, Delaware, and Pennsylvania—the proprietors (who had obtained their patents from the king) named the governors, subject to the approval of the crown; laws (except in Maryland) also required the crown's approval. Only in the two **charter colonies** of Rhode Island and Connecticut was there genuine self-government. There, freely elected legislatures chose the governors, and laws could not be vetoed by the king.

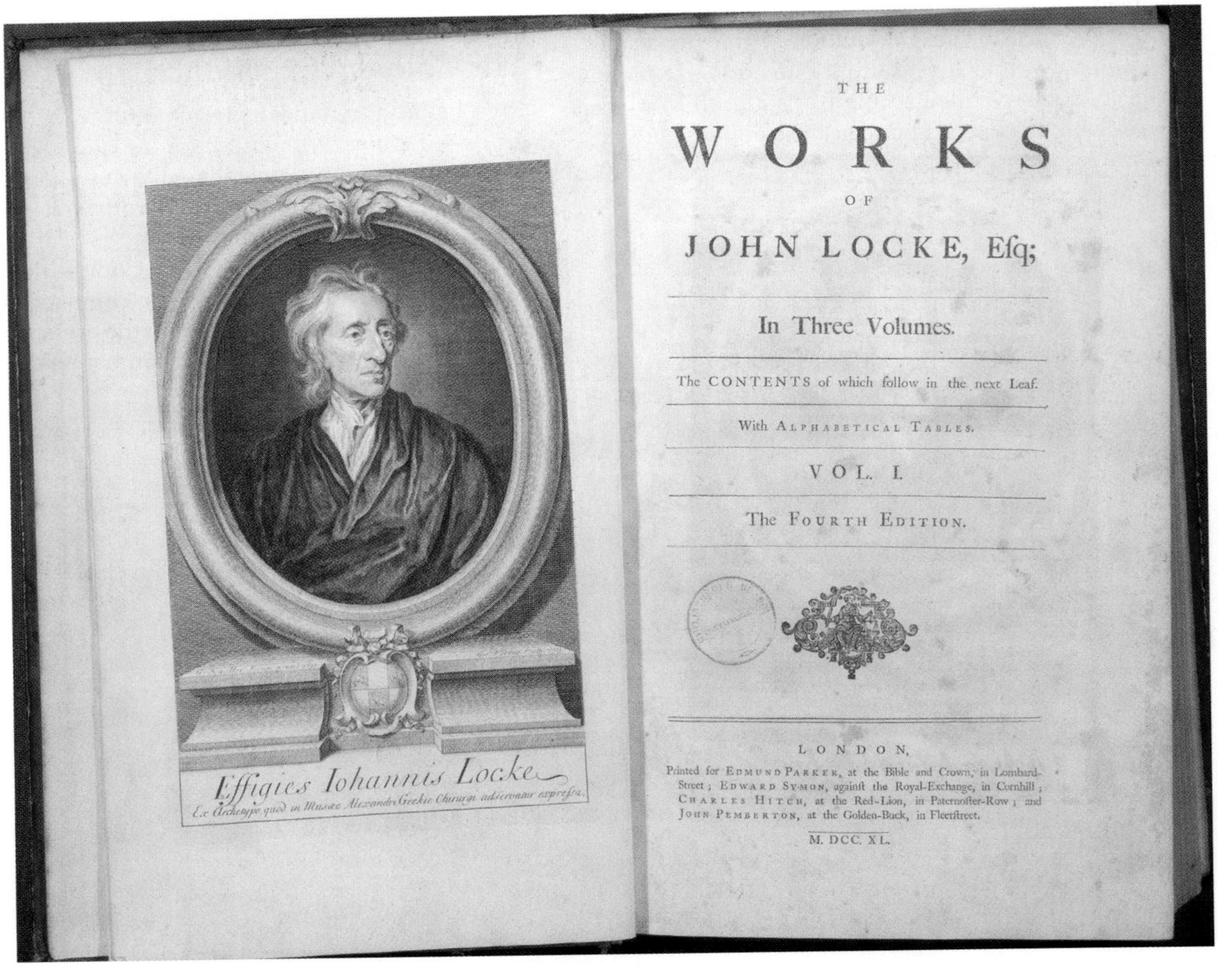


© Archivo Iconografico S.A./Corbis

John Locke's philosophy was reflected in the Declaration of Independence.

Before they landed at Plymouth in 1620, the Pilgrims drew up the Mayflower Compact to establish a government under the rule of law.

Except for Pennsylvania, which had a **unicameral legislature,** a legislative body with only one house, the colonial legislatures had two houses. The members of the upper house were appointed by the crown or proprietor except in Rhode Island and Connecticut. Members of the lower house were elected by the colonists. Appeals from the colonial courts could usually be taken to the Privy Council in London.

## The Paradox of Colonial Democracy

Democracy, in the modern sense, did not exist in colonial America. For example, by the 1700s every colony had some type of property qualification for voting. Women and blacks were not considered part of the electorate. In 1765, of the 1,850,000 estimated population of the colonies, 400,000 were blacks, almost all of them slaves. Consequently, "whatever political democracy did exist was a democracy of white, male property owners." [11]

In addition, many white people were indentured servants during the colonial period. These were English, Scotch-Irish, and western Europeans, including many convicts, who sold their labor for four to seven years in return for passage across the sea.

Even aside from slavery and indentured servitude, there was little social democracy. A tailor in York County, Virginia, in 1674 was punished for racing a horse because "it was contrary to law for a labourer to make a race, being a sport only for gentlemen." [12] In colonial New York, the aristocracy "ruled with condescension and lived in splendor." [13]

Nine of the 13 colonies had an established, official state church. Although the colonists had in many cases fled Europe to find religious freedom, they were often themselves intolerant of religious dissent. The Massachusetts Bay Colony executed four Quakers who had returned there after being banished for their religious convictions. In Virginia the penalty for breaking the Sabbath

The Magna Carta

## Comparing Governments

### HAIL BRITANNIA! BUT IT'S DIFFERENT

Although the new American government created at Philadelphia in 1787 had many features rooted in the British system and legal tradition, the government of Great Britain is significantly different from that of the United States.

Britain is both a parliamentary democracy and a constitutional monarchy. It has no single, formal written constitution like that of the United States. Britain's constitution consists of acts of Parliament, court decisions, traditions, and customs. The hereditary monarch is the head of state, but the powers of the king or queen are largely ceremonial. Real power resides not in Buckingham Palace, but with the prime minister, who is the leader of the majority party in Parliament. The ministers who comprise the British cabinet are normally chosen by the prime minister from the majority party members elected to Parliament.

Britain's Parliament is the legislative branch, and it is made up of two houses: the House of Commons, whose members are elected to terms of up to five years, and the House of Lords. Under reforms adopted by the Labor government in 1999, members of the House of Lords no longer inherit their posts, as was true for some 800 years, but most are now appointed for life. In the United States presidential elections take place every four years in November, but the British prime minister may call for general elections at any time. Britain's judicial branch is headed by a supreme court, but unlike the U.S. Supreme Court, the British high court has no power of judicial review.

Britain has had a predominantly two-party system for most of the past three centuries. The Conservative (Tory) Party and the Labour Party have been the two strongest parties competing for power in modern times.

© AP/Wide World Photos

Queen Elizabeth II opens Parliament.

for the third time was death.[14] And although the colonial press and pamphleteers developed into a powerful force for liberty, the first newspaper to appear in America, *Publick Occurrences,* was immediately suppressed.[15]

Yet, despite their shortcomings, the colonial governments provided an institutional foundation for what was to come. Certain elements were already visible: separation of powers, constitutional government through written charters, bicameral legislatures, elections, and judicial appeal to London, which foreshadowed the role of the Supreme Court. Equally important, in their relationship with England the colonies became accustomed to the idea of sharing powers with a central government, the basis of the federal system today. It was, in Clinton Rossiter's apt phrase, the "seedtime of the republic."

## THE AMERICAN REVOLUTION

"The Revolution," John Adams wrote in 1818, "was effected before the war commenced. The Revolution was in the minds and hearts of the people."[16]

And, in time, the revolt against the British crown brought enormous social and political change, resulting in a new nation based on the idea of freedom and equality. As one constitutional scholar has argued, "That revolution did more than legally create the United States; it transformed American society."[17]

### A Growing Sense of Injury

In the eyes of the crown, the American colonies existed chiefly for the economic support of England. Economic conflicts with the mother country, as well as political and social factors, impelled the colonies to revolt.

The British had routed the French from North America and provided military protection to the colonies; England in turn demanded that its subjects in America pay part of the cost. At the same time, the colonies were expected to subordinate themselves to the British economy; ideally they would remain agricultural, develop no industry of their own, and serve as a captive market for British goods.

The colonists had no representatives in the British Parliament. They resented and disputed the right of London to raise revenue in America. Whether or not James Otis, the Boston patriot, actually cried, "Taxation without representation is tyranny!"—and there is reason to think he did not—the words reflected popular sentiment in the colonies.*

A series of laws designed to give the mother country a tight grip on trade, to restrict colonial exports, and to

*Otis supposedly uttered his famous line in a speech to the Massachusetts Superior Court in 1761. But as Daniel J. Boorstin points out, the line does not appear in the original notes of the speech taken by John Adams. See Boorstin, *The Americans: The National Experience,* pp. 309, 360–361.

British tax stamps

protect producers in England proved to be the economic stepping stones to revolution. In 1772 Samuel Adams of Massachusetts formed the Committees of Correspondence to unite the colonies against Great Britain. This network provided an invaluable political communications link for the colonies; letters, reports, and decisions of one town or colony could be relayed to the next.

The committees resolved to hold the First Continental Congress, which met in Philadelphia in September 1774. The war began in April 1775. The Second Continental Congress met the following month, and by June 1776 Thomas Jefferson was busily writing in the second-floor parlor of the bricklayer's house in Philadelphia.

## The Articles of Confederation (1781–1789)

The Declaration of Independence had proclaimed the colonies "free and independent states." During the war all the colonies adopted new constitutions or at least changed their old charters to eliminate references to the British crown. Seven of the new constitutions contained a bill of rights, but all restricted suffrage in one way or another. All provided for three branches of government, but their dominant features were strong legislatures and weak executives. Governors were elected by the people or by legislatures, and their powers were reduced. For the first time, the colonies began to refer to themselves as "states."

When Richard Henry Lee offered his resolution for independence in June 1776, he also proposed that "a plan of confederation" be prepared for the colonies. (A **confederation** is a group of independent states or nations that come together for a common purpose and whose central authority is usually limited to defense and foreign relations.) The plan was drawn up by a committee and approved by the Continental Congress in November 1777, a month before George Washington withdrew with his troops for the long, hard winter at Valley Forge. The **Articles of Confederation** (1781–1789) were the written framework for the government of the original 13 states before the Constitution was adopted. The Articles were ratified by the individual states by March 1, 1781, and so were already in effect when the war ended with the surrender of Cornwallis at Yorktown that October. The formal end to hostilities came with the conclusion of the Peace of Paris in February 1783.

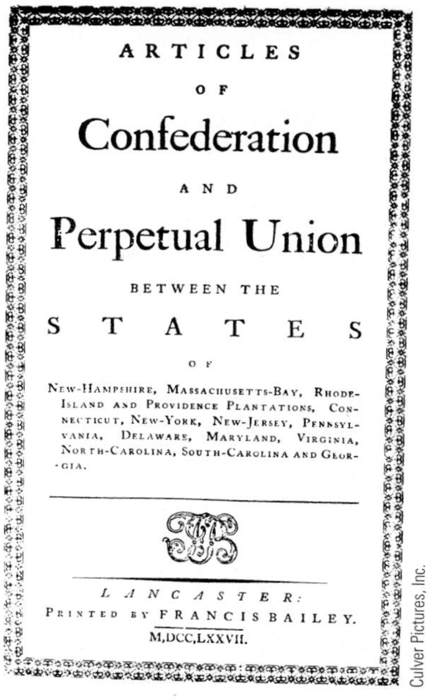

ARTICLES OF Confederation AND Perpetual Union BETWEEN THE STATES OF NEW-HAMPSHIRE, MASSACHUSETTS-BAY, RHODE-ISLAND AND PROVIDENCE PLANTATIONS, CONNECTICUT, NEW-YORK, NEW-JERSEY, PENNSYLVANIA, DELAWARE, MARYLAND, VIRGINIA, NORTH-CAROLINA, SOUTH-CAROLINA AND GEORGIA.

LANCASTER: PRINTED BY FRANCIS BAILEY. M,DCC,LXXVII.

But the Articles of Confederation created a national government that was weak and dominated by the states. The Articles really established a "league of friendship" among the states, rather than a national government. No executive branch, no president, no "White House" existed. Instead, Congress, given power to establish executive departments, created five: foreign affairs, finance, navy, war, and post office. Congress had power to declare war, conduct foreign policy, make treaties, ask for—but not demand—revenues from the states, borrow and coin money, equip the navy, and appoint senior officers of the army, which was made up of the state militias. Congress was unicameral, and each state, regardless of size, had only one vote. The most important actions by Congress required the consent of at least nine states. There was no national system of courts.

Although these were not inconsiderable powers, the most significant fact about the government created under the Articles was its weakness. Congress, for example, had no power to levy taxes or regulate commerce—the colonies had seen enough of these powers under English rule. Above all, Congress could not enforce even the limited powers it had. The functioning of government under the Articles depended entirely on the goodwill of the states. Because unanimous agreement of the states was required to amend the Articles, but in practice could never be obtained, there was no practical way to increase the powers of the government; the Articles were never amended.

By 1783 the American states had achieved their independence not only from Great Britain but also from each other. They had won their freedom, but they had been unable to form a nation. Yet the Articles did represent the idea of some form of national government, for under them, "Congress waged war, made peace, and kept alive the idea of union when it was at its lowest ebb."[18] As historian Merrill Jensen emphasized, the Articles "laid foundations for the administration of a central government which were to be expanded but not essentially altered in function for generations to come."[19]

# Toward a More Perfect Union

## The Background

Under the inadequate government of the Articles of Confederation, the states came close to losing the peace they had won in war. They quarreled among themselves over boundary lines and tariffs. For example, New Jersey farmers had to pay heavy fees to cross the Hudson River to sell their vegetables in New York. With no strong national government to conduct foreign policy, some states even entered into negotiations with foreign powers. General Washington worried that Kentucky might join Spain.[20] There was real concern over possible military intervention by European powers.

By 1786 severe economic depression had left many farmers angry and hungry. Debtor groups demanded that state governments issue paper money. The unrest among farmers and the poor alarmed the upper classes. They feared, in today's terms, a revolution of the left. These political and economic factors, combined with fear of overseas intervention, generated pressure for the creation of a new national government.

Alexander Hamilton

Virginia, at the urging of James Madison, had invited all the states to discuss commercial problems at a meeting to be held at Annapolis, Maryland, in September 1786. The Annapolis conference was disappointing. Representatives of only five states turned up. But one of those delegates was Alexander Hamilton, a brilliant 31-year-old New York attorney who was one of a small group of men pushing for a convention to create a stronger government. There had been talk of such a meeting since 1780, when Hamilton wrote to a friend listing the "defects of our present system."[21]

At Annapolis, Hamilton and Madison persuaded the delegates to call on the states to hold a constitutional convention in Philadelphia in May 1787. In the interim a significant event took place. Late in 1786, angry farmers in western Massachusetts, unable to pay their mortgages or taxes, rallied around Daniel Shays, who had served as a captain in the American Revolution. They were seeking to stop the Massachusetts courts from foreclosing the mortgages on their farms. Armed with pitchforks, the farmers marched on the Springfield arsenal to get weapons. They were defeated by the militia. Fourteen ringleaders were sentenced to death, but all were pardoned or released after serving short prison terms. Daniel Shays escaped to Vermont.

Shays's Rebellion, coming on the eve of the Philadelphia Convention, had a tremendous effect on public opinion. Aristocrats and merchants were thoroughly alarmed at the threat of "mob rule." The British were amused at the American lack of capacity for self-government. The revolt was an important factor in creating the climate for a new beginning at Philadelphia.

## The Philadelphia Convention

On February 21, 1787, Congress grudgingly approved the proposed Philadelphia Convention "for the sole and express purpose of revising the Articles of Confedera-

Shays's Rebellion: The aristocrats and merchants were alarmed.

© Bettmann/Corbis

George Washington

The Granger Collection, New York

tion." Beginning in May, the delegates met and, disregarding Congress's cautious mandate, worked what has been called a "miracle at Philadelphia."[22]

**The Delegates** Because the story of how a nation was born is in large part a story of people, it might be useful to focus briefly on some of the more prominent delegates who gathered at Philadelphia. First was George Washington, who had commanded the armed forces during the Revolution. A national hero, a man of immense prestige, Washington was probably the only figure who could have successfully presided over the coming struggle in the convention. When Washington arrived in Philadelphia, a crowd gathered and bells rang out. He immediately paid a call on Benjamin Franklin, internationally famous as a scientist, diplomat, and statesman. Then 81 and suffering from gout, Franklin arrived at the sessions in a sedan chair borne by four convicts from the Walnut Street jail. Alexander Hamilton was there as a delegate from New York, but he took surprisingly little part in the important decisions of the convention. From Virginia came James Madison, often called the "Father of the Constitution," who had long advocated a new national government. A tireless notetaker, Madison kept a record of the debates. Without him there would have been no detailed account of the most important political convention in the nation's history.

Gouverneur Morris of Pennsylvania, a colorful man who stumped about on a wooden leg, shatters the image of the delegates as stuffy patriarchs. His wit offended some, but his pen was responsible for the literary style and polish of the final draft of the Constitution. From Massachusetts came Elbridge Gerry and Rufus King, a lawyer with a gift for debating; from South Carolina, John Rutledge, a leading figure of the revolutionary period and later a justice of the Supreme Court; General Charles Cotesworth Pinckney, Oxford-educated war hero and aristocrat; and his second cousin, Charles Pinckney, an ardent nationalist.

Twelve states sent delegates to Philadelphia. Only Rhode Island boycotted the convention; an agrarian party of farmers and debtors controlled the Rhode Island state legislature and feared that a strong national government would limit the party's power. Of the 55 men who gathered at Philadelphia in the Pennsylvania State House (now Independence Hall), 8 had signed the Declaration of Independence, 7 had been chief executives of their states, 33 were lawyers, 8 were businessmen, 6 were planters, and 3 were physicians. About half were college graduates.[23] The delegates, in sum, were generally men of wealth and influence; the Constitution was not drafted by small farmers, artisans, or laborers. And in an era when political power was exercised by men, there were no women delegates.

It was a relatively young convention. Jonathan Day-

The Granger Collection, New York

Gouverneur Morris

© The Corcoran Galley of Art/Corbis

Benjamin Franklin

ton of New Jersey, at 26, was the youngest delegate. Alexander Hamilton was 32. Charles Pinckney was 29. James Madison was 36. The average age of the delegates was just over 43. (At 81, Franklin pulled the average up.)

**The Setting** The convention of 1787 had many of the earmarks of a modern national political convention but for one factor: To preserve their freedom of debate, the delegates worked in strictest secrecy. The press and public were not allowed in the room. In other respects the setting would be a familiar one today: The weather was intolerably hot and the speeches interminable. And just as in a modern convention, a plush tavern and inn, the Indian Queen, soon became a sort of informal headquarters.

Philadelphia was not a pleasant place 200 years ago. It was a crowded city of open sewers, foul smells, and rotting animal carcasses. The clatter of wagon wheels on the rough cobblestones was so bad that, when the sessions got under way, at the request of the delegates the city spread a load of gravel outside the hall to muffle the noise.

The convention opened on May 14, 1787, but it was not until May 25 that a quorum of delegates from seven states was reached. The delegates gathered in the East Room of the State House, the same chamber where the Declaration of Independence had been signed 11 years before. "Delegates sat at tables covered in green baize—sat and sweated, once the summer sun was up. By noon the air was lifeless, with windows shut for privacy, or intolerable with flies when they were open."[24] For almost four months the stuffy East Room was to be home.

## The Great Compromise

On May 29 Edmund Randolph, the 33-year-old governor of Virginia, took the floor to present 15 resolutions that stunned the convention. The resolutions, which Madison strongly influenced and helped to draft, went far beyond mere revision of the Articles—they proposed an entirely new national government under a constitution. Randolph was moving swiftly to make the **Virginia Plan,** as the proposals are known, the main business of the convention.

As John P. Roche has noted, the Virginia Plan "was a political masterstroke. Its consequence was that once business got underway, the framework of discussion was established on Madison's terms. There was no interminable argument over agenda; instead the delegates took the Virginia Resolutions—'just for the purposes of discussion'—as their point of departure."[25] The Virginia Plan called for

1. A two-house legislature, the lower house chosen by the people and the upper house chosen by the lower. The legislature would have the power to annul any state laws that it found unconstitutional.
2. A "national executive"—the makeup was not specified, so there might have been more than one president under the plan—to be elected by the legislature.
3. A national judiciary to be chosen by the legislature.

The convention debated the Virginia Plan for two weeks. As the debate wore on, the delegates from the smaller states became increasingly alarmed. It had not taken them long to conclude that the more heavily populated states would control the government under the Virginia Plan. "The Virginia Plan," one writer has contended, "would mean nothing less than a second American revolution."[26]

On June 15, William Paterson of New Jersey, a lawyer, "a squat man with a bulbous nose, a receding chin and traces of his native Ireland in his voice,"[27] rose to offer an alternative plan. He argued that the convention had no power to deprive the smaller states of the equality they enjoyed under the Articles of Confederation. Paterson proposed what became known as the **New Jersey Plan,** which called for

1. Continuation of the Articles of Confederation, including one vote for each state represented in the legislature. Congress would be strengthened so that it could impose taxes and regulate trade, and acts of Congress would become the "supreme law" of the states.
2. An executive of more than one person to be elected by Congress.
3. A Supreme Court, to be appointed by the executive.

The Paterson plan would have merely amended the Articles. The government would have continued as a weak confederation of sovereign states. But many of the delegates at Philadelphia were determined to construct a strong national government, and for this reason the Paterson plan was soon brushed aside. As both the weather and tempers grew warmer, the convention swung back to consideration of the Virginia Plan. But little progress was made.

The fact was that the convention was in danger of breaking up. Alexander Hamilton and the New York delegates, as well as some delegates from other states, left

Philadelphia to return home. "I almost despair," Washington, presiding over the deadlock, wrote to Hamilton in New York.

The impasse over the makeup of Congress was broken on July 16 when the convention adopted the **Great Compromise,** often called the **Connecticut Compromise** because it had been proposed by Roger Sherman of that state. As adopted after much debate, the Connecticut Compromise called for

1. A House of Representatives apportioned by the number of free inhabitants in each state plus three-fifths of the slaves.
2. A Senate, or upper house, consisting of two members from each state, elected by the state legislatures.

The plan broke the deadlock because it protected the small states by guaranteeing that each state would have an equal vote in the Senate. Only in the House, where representation was to be based on population, would the larger states have an advantage.

Catherine Drinker Bowen has suggested that the delegates might never have reached agreement "had not the heat broken." On Monday, July 16, the day the compromise was approved, "Philadelphia was cool after a month of torment; on Friday, a breeze had come in from the northwest. Over the weekend, members could rest and enjoy themselves."[28]

With the controversy of large states versus small states resolved by this compromise, the convention named a committee to draft a constitution. Then the convention adjourned for 11 days, and General Washington went fishing.

> **AN AMERICAN KING**
>
> Charles Pinckney rose . . . to urge a "vigorous executive." He did not say a "President of the United States." It took the Convention a long while to come around to President. Always they referred to a chief executive or a national executive, whether plural or single. James Wilson followed Pinckney by moving that the executive consist of a single person; Pinckney seconded him. A sudden silence followed. "A considerable pause," Madison wrote. . . . A single executive! There was menace in the words, some saw monarchy in them. True enough, nine states had each its single executive—a governor or president—but everywhere the local legislature was supreme, looked on as the voice of the people which could control a governor any day. But a single executive for the national government conjured up visions from the past—royal governors who could not be restrained, a crown, ermine, a scepter!
>
> —Catherine Drinker Bowen, *Miracle at Philadelphia*

On August 6 the convention resumed its work. The committee brought in a draft constitution that called for a "congress," made up of a house of representatives and a senate; a "supreme court"; and a "president of the United States of America."

The broad outline of the Constitution as it is today was finally clear. But much work remained:

> And so the men of Philadelphia persevered through the hot [summer] days, filling out the details now that the grand design had been set in the Connecticut Compromise, sawing boards to make them fit, as Benjamin Franklin said. Some of the boards required much sanding and smoothing, as the delegates thrashed out irksome but vital aspects of the relations between the national and state governments, the enumerated powers of Congress, the jurisdiction of the courts, the reach of impeachment, the amending clause, and procedures for ratifying the Constitution itself. . . . They deliberated as if the eyes of the world were on them.[29]

## The Other Compromises

As debate continued, the convention made other significant compromises. Underlying the agreement to count three-fifths of all slaves in apportioning membership of the House of Representatives was a deep-seated conflict between the mercantile North and the agrarian South, where the economy was based on slave labor. Of the 55 delegates to the convention, at least 25 owned slaves.[30] The men of the North argued that if slaves were to be counted in determining representation in the House, then they must be counted for tax purposes as well. In the end, the South agreed.

The slave trade itself was the subject of another complicated compromise. On August 22 George Mason of Virginia attacked "the infernal traffic" and its evil effect on both individuals and the nation. Slavery, he said, would "bring the judgment of heaven on a Country. As nations can not be rewarded or punished in the next world they must in this. By an inevitable chain of causes & effects providence punishes national sins, by national calamities."[31]

Charles Cotesworth Pinckney of South Carolina warned that his state would not join the Union if the slave trade were prohibited. The issue was settled by an agreement that Congress could not ban the slave trade until 1808. This compromise is contained in Article I of the Constitution, which obliquely refers to slaves as "other persons."*

In yet another compromise, Southerners won certain trade concessions. They were worried, with reason,

*Acting on President Jefferson's recommendation, Congress did outlaw importation of slaves in 1808. But the illegal slave trade flourished up to the Civil War. Perhaps 250,000 slaves were illegally imported to America between 1808 and 1860. The slavery issue was not settled until the end of the Civil War and the ratification on December 18, 1865, of the Thirteenth Amendment, which declared that "neither slavery nor involuntary servitude, except as a punishment for crime whereof the party shall have been duly convicted, shall exist within the United States."

Sohm, Chromosohm/Stock Connection/PictureQuest

that a northern majority in Congress might pass legislation unfavorable to southern economic interests. Because the South relied almost entirely on exports of its agricultural products, it fought for, and won, an agreement forbidding the imposition of export taxes. Even today, the United States is one of the few nations that cannot tax its exports.

## We the People

On September 8 a Committee of Style and Arrangement was named to polish the final draft. Fortunately it included Gouverneur Morris. Morris, probably aided by James Wilson,[32] drafted the final version, adding a new preamble that rivals Jefferson's eloquence in the Declaration of Independence:

> We the People of the United States, in Order to form a more perfect Union, establish Justice, insure domestic Tranquility, provide for the common defence, promote the general Welfare, and secure the Blessings of Liberty to ourselves and our Posterity, do ordain and establish this Constitution for the United States of America.

On September 17 the long task was finished. The day was cool, and the trace of autumn in the air must have reminded the delegates of how long they had labored. Thirty-nine men signed the Constitution that afternoon. Benjamin Franklin had to be helped forward to the table, and it is said that he wept when he signed. According to Madison's notes, while the last members were signing, Franklin observed that often, as he pondered the outcome during the changing moods of the convention, he had looked at the sun painted on the back of Washington's chair and wondered whether it was rising or setting. "But now at length I have the happiness to know," Franklin declared, "that it is a rising and not a setting sun."[33]

## The Constitutional Framework

The Constitution was not perfect, but it represented a practical accommodation among conflicting sections and interests achieved at a political convention. And the central fact of the Constitution is that it created the potential for a strong national government where none had existed before, and provided the written framework to control the power and operation of that government. (See Figure 2-1.)

### A Republic—If You Can Keep It

When the delegates to the Constitutional Convention at Philadelphia ended their long and difficult task in September of 1787, it is said that a lady approached Benjamin Franklin and asked:

> "Well, Doctor, what have we got—a republic or a monarchy?"
>
> "A republic," was the reply, "if you can keep it."

—Adapted from "Debates in the Federal Convention in 1787," in *Documents Illustrative of the Formation of the Union of the American States*

**The Federal System** The structure of the government created by the Constitution is deceptively simple at first glance, yet endlessly intricate. Article VI declares that the laws passed by Congress "shall be the supreme Law of the Land." This important **supremacy clause** means that federal laws are supreme over any conflicting state laws. But the states also exercise control within their borders over a wide range of activities.

The Constitution thus brought into being a **federal system,** also known as **federalism,** in which the constitutional powers and functions of government are shared by the national government and the states. Although in the United States a strong national government has evolved over two centuries as the dominant partner, the states retain significant powers of their own. The system of federalism is discussed in detail in Chapter 3.

**The National Government** The Constitution divided the national government into three branches—legislative, executive, and judicial. It created a government, therefore, based on the principles of **separation of powers** and **checks and balances.** Separation of powers means that each of the three branches is constitutionally equal to and independent of the others. Checks and balances means that power is divided among the three constitutionally equal branches of government in the hope of preventing any single branch from becoming too powerful. (In fact, however, the 20th century saw the presidency become the most powerful branch of the federal government, at least in foreign affairs.)

In creating a government based on these ideas, the framers were influenced by the French political philosopher Baron de Montesquieu (1689–1755). In *The Spirit of the Laws,* published in 1748, Montesquieu advocated a separation of powers into legislative, judicial, and executive branches. "When the legislative and executive powers are united in the same person, or in the same body of magistrates, there can be no liberty," he wrote.[34]

Yet the term "separation of powers" is somewhat misleading. Although the Constitution established institutional checks and separated powers, the United States is also a government of shared powers. The branches of the government are separated, but their powers and functions are fused or overlapping. The Constitution provided many ways in which the three branches would interact. For example, although Congress makes the laws, the president submits legislation to it, and he may convene Congress in special session. The president also may veto bills that Congress passes. Clearly, the president is involved in the legislative function.

Similarly, Congress is involved in the executive process in its watchdog role and through its power to create federal executive agencies and to advise on and consent to the appointment of high-level federal officials. Because Congress appropriates money to run the federal government, it may delve deeply, through its committees, into the operations of executive agencies.

Through the process of **judicial review,** the courts decide whether the laws passed by Congress or actions taken by the president—or laws and actions at any level of local or state government—are constitutional. (See Chapter 15 for a detailed discussion of judicial review.)

FIGURE 2-1

**The Government of the United States**

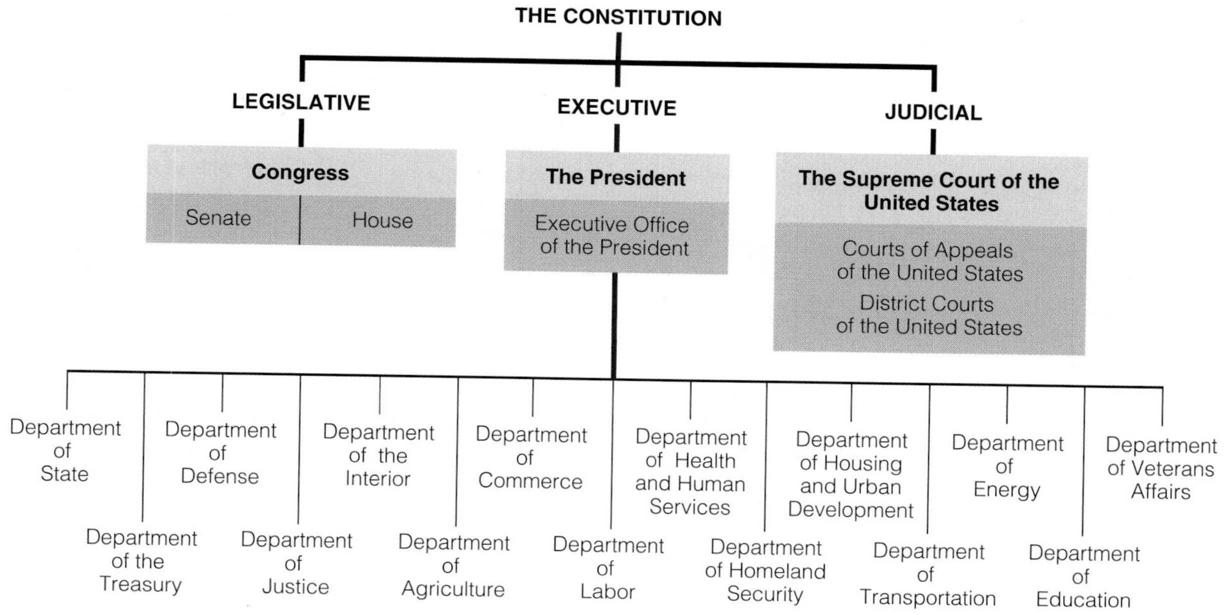

## THE CONSTITUTION: JEFFERSON'S VIEW

In questions of power, then, let no more be heard of confidence in man, but bind him down from mischief by the chains of the Constitution.

—Thomas Jefferson, 1798,
in Paul Leicester Ford, ed.,
*The Works of Thomas Jefferson*

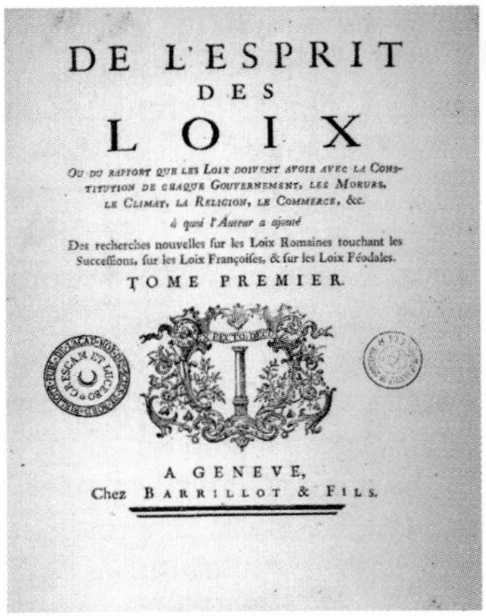
DE L'ESPRIT
DES
LOIX
OU DU RAPPORT QUE LES LOIX DOIVENT AVOIR AVEC LA CONSTITUTION DE CHAQUE GOUVERNEMENT, LES MOEURS, LE CLIMAT, LA RELIGION, LE COMMERCE, &c.
à quoi l'Auteur a ajouté
Des recherches nouvelles sur les Loix Romaines touchant les Successions, sur les Loix Françoises, & sur les Loix Féodales.
TOME PREMIER.
A GENEVE,
Chez BARRILLOT & FILS.

In *The Spirit of the Laws* [*De L'Esprit des Loix*], published in 1748, the French political philosopher Baron de Montesquieu advocated separation of powers.

The Granger Collection, New York

The decisions of the Supreme Court, and other courts, are an important example of the outputs of the political system because these decisions often determine who gets what in American society. President Woodrow Wilson called the Supreme Court "a kind of Constitutional Convention in continuous session."[35] The president participates in the judicial process through his power to nominate federal judges, including members of the Supreme Court. And Congress can pass laws to overrule Supreme Court decisions.

The notion of three separate-but-equal branches of government was eroded by the pressures of the 20th century. In the past, American presidents have at varying times exercised great powers, as Lincoln did during the Civil War. But in modern times, power, especially military-diplomatic power, has been largely concentrated in the hands of the president. The power of Congress to declare war, for example, has greatly diminished in importance since the Second World War. And in a nuclear attack the president obviously would have no time to consult Congress. But even in the case of protracted conflicts, such as in Korea (1950–1953) and Vietnam (1964–1973), Congress never did declare war. Nor did it do so in 2003 when U.S. troops invaded Iraq.

In other areas as well, the lines between the three branches of government have become blurred. Today, for example, the complex task of managing the economy has been delegated in part to independent regulatory commissions and agencies that do not fall neatly into any of the three categories—legislative, executive, and judicial—envisioned under the Constitution and in fact exhibit features of all three.

In sum, although the three branches of government are based on separated powers, they also share powers. And among the three branches (as among human beings) there is a never-ending tug-of-war for dominance, a process that Alpheus T. Mason has called "institutionalized tension."[36]

**The "Great Silences" of the Constitution** Some issues were so difficult and potentially divisive that the framers did not attempt to settle them at all. Because they were trying to construct a political document that stated general principles, they chose to avoid some sensitive problems.

The framers compromised over the vital moral and political issue of whether to abolish the importation of slaves while forming "a more perfect union"; the underlying question of whether to abolish slavery itself was not faced at Philadelphia. Five southern states might not have ratified the Constitution if the framers had abolished the slave trade in 1787. The delegates compromised in order to achieve enough unity to form a new nation, but America paid a high moral and political price. The question of slavery, avoided at Philadelphia, led in time to a bloody civil war. And today, three centuries later, African American men and women are still struggling for the full freedom and equality denied to them by the framers.

The framers also made no explicit statement in the Constitution defining the full scope of the powers of the national government. The history of the Supreme Court is the history of whether the Constitution is to be loosely or strictly interpreted.

Even the Supreme Court's power of judicial review is nowhere expressly provided for in the Constitution (although some scholars argue it is conferred in general terms). "Without some body to act as umpire," Archibald Cox has written, "the several parts must inevitably fall to squabbling and the enterprise launched at Philadelphia break up on the reefs. Yet the Constitution nowhere specifically and explicitly stated who, if anyone, was to have the final word."[37] The power of judicial review, which allows the Supreme Court to declare whether acts of Congress are constitutional, was exercised in several early opinions, but it was not firmly set forth and established until 1803, when the Court ruled in the case of ***Marbury* v. *Madison.***[38] Chief Justice John Marshall, in his historic opinion, argued that because the Constitution was clearly "superior" to an act of Congress, "It is emphatically the province and duty of the judicial department to say what the law is. . . . A law repugnant to the Constitution is void."

The Constitution says nothing whatever about how candidates for office shall be chosen. The development

## The Constitution: "Defective from the Start"

In May 1987, as the nationwide celebration of the 200th anniversary of the Constitution approached, Supreme Court Justice Thurgood Marshall broke dramatically with the almost universal acclaim the document had been receiving:

> Marshall [urged] Americans not to go overboard in praising a document that sanctioned slavery and denied women the right to vote.
>
> Marshall, [then] the Court's only black justice, said the Constitution was "defective from the start, requiring several amendments, a civil war and momentous social transformation to attain the system of constitutional government, and its respect for the individual freedoms and human rights, we hold as fundamental today." . . .
>
> The preamble's first three words, "we the people," Marshall said, did not include "the majority of American citizens," women and blacks.
>
> —*Washington Post,* May 7, 1987

of political parties, nominating conventions, and primaries all occurred without any formal constitutional provision for them.

Similarly, the cabinet is not specifically established in the Constitution but has evolved through custom, beginning during Washington's first administration. As Richard F. Fenno, Jr., has noted, the cabinet is "an extralegal creation," limited in power as an institution by the very fact that it has no basis in law.[39]

**Motives of the Framers** Were the framers of the Constitution selfless patriots who thrust aside all personal interests to save America? Or were they primarily rich men who were afraid of radicals like Daniel Shays? In short, did they form a strong government to protect themselves and their property, or did they act from nobler motives?

The debate has raged among scholars. Early in the 20th century, the historian Charles A. Beard analyzed in great detail the economic holdings of the framers and concluded that they acted to protect their personal financial interests. The Constitution, said Beard, was "an economic document drawn with superb skill by men whose property interests were immediately at stake."[40]

Later scholars, reacting to Beard, reached opposite conclusions. Forrest McDonald has asserted that of the 55 delegates, "a dozen at the outside, clearly acted according to the dictates of their personal economic interests." He concluded that an "economic interpretation of the Constitution does not work."[41] Similarly, Robert E. Brown has argued it would be unfair to the framers to assume that "property or personal gain was their only motive."[42]

John Marshall

**Was It Democratic?** The argument is sometimes advanced that the Constitution was framed to guard against popular democracy and unchecked majority rule. "The evils we experience flow from the excess of democracy," Elbridge Gerry of Massachusetts told the convention.*

The word "democracy" today generally has a favorable, affirmative meaning, but to the framers of the Constitution, it was a term of derision. "Remember," John Adams warned, "democracy never lasts long. It soon wastes, exhausts, and murders itself. There never was a democracy yet that did not commit suicide."[43] The framers preferred the word "republic" to describe what today would be called a democracy.[44]

From a contemporary viewpoint some of the provisions of the Constitution appear highly undemocratic. For example, slavery was permitted to flourish. In addition, because the Constitution leaves voting qualifications to the states, persons without property, women, and many African Americans were long disenfranchised. Until the passage of the Seventeenth Amendment in 1913, senators were elected by state legislatures. The framers had deliberately avoided direct election of senators, for the Senate was seen as a check on the multitudes. Madison assured the convention that the Senate would proceed "with more coolness, with more system, and with more wisdom, than the popular branch." And, of course, the Constitution interposed an electoral college between the voters and the presidency.

But to stress only these aspects of the Constitution would be to overlook the basically representative structure of the government it created—particularly in

---

*Bowen, *Miracle at Philadelphia,* p. 45. Elbridge Gerry, Edmund Randolph, and George Mason were the only three framers who refused to sign the Constitution. Much later, Gerry gave his name to a famous but controversial practice. While he was governor of Massachusetts in 1812, the legislature carved up Essex County to give maximum advantage to his party. One of the districts resembled a salamander. From then on, the practice of redrawing voting districts to favor the party in power became known as "gerrymandering." (See Chapter 11.)

The Granger Collection, New York

An 1812 cartoon depicts gerrymandering of voting districts in Massachusetts.

comparison with other governments that existed in 1787—and the revolutionary heritage of the framers. The Constitution perhaps originally reflected considerable distrust of popular rule, but it established a balanced institutional framework within which democracy could evolve.

## The Fight over Ratification

When the convention had finished its work, a successful outcome was by no means certain. The political contest over ratification of the Constitution lasted for more than two and a half years, from September 1787 until May 29, 1790, when Rhode Island finally joined the Union. But the Constitution went into effect in June 1788 when nine states had ratified it.

The Articles of Confederation had required that any amendment be approved by Congress and the legislatures of all 13 states. No such unanimity could ever be achieved. In effect, this created a box from which the framers could not climb out. So they chose another route—they simply ignored the box and built an entirely new structure. Defending the convention's action, Madison reminded his countrymen of the right of the people, proclaimed in the Declaration of Independence, to alter or abolish their government in ways "most likely to effect their safety and happiness."[45]

Article VII of the Constitution states that "ratification of the Conventions of nine States shall be sufficient for the Establishment of this Constitution." Why conventions and not legislatures? Because the Constitution took power away from the states, the framers reasoned that the state legislatures might not approve it. Second, if the Constitution were approved by popularly elected conventions, it would give the new government a broad base of legitimacy.

The great debate over ratification soon divided the participants into two camps: the **Antifederalists,** who opposed ratification of the Constitution, and the **Federalists,** who supported ratification. Although the debate was vigorous, relatively few people actually participated in the ratification process. The voters could not vote for or against the Constitution. Their choice was confined to selecting delegates to the state ratifying conventions. Only an estimated 160,000 people voted for delegates to the ratifying conventions, out of a total population of about 4 million.

Some historians tend to pay more attention to the Federalists—because they won—but those opposed to the Constitution had a strong case. The convention, after all, had met in complete secrecy, in a "Dark Conclave," as the Philadelphia *Independent Gazetteer* called it. What is more, the Constitution, as its opponents argued, was extralegal. The framers had clearly exceeded their mandate from Congress to revise the Articles of Confederation. Above all, the Constitution included no bill of rights to protect individual liberties against the power of the proposed new national government.

The Federalists argued that the states faced anarchy unless they united under a powerful central government. The omission of a bill of rights was difficult to justify, however. The question had not been raised until near the end of the Philadelphia Convention, and the weary delegates were not inclined to open a new debate. Furthermore, many delegates felt that a bill of rights would be superfluous since eight states already had bills of rights. Hamilton argued that "the Constitution is itself . . . a Bill of Rights."[46]

But during the struggle over ratification, the Antifederalists warned that without a bill of rights in the new Constitution, individuals in the states would have no protection against a strong central government. Ultimately, as the price of winning support in the state conventions, the Federalists had to promise to enact a bill of rights as the first order of business under a new government.

Richard Henry Lee's *Letters from the Federal Farmer* was among the most effective of the various Antifederalist attacks circulated among the states. In New York, Hamilton, Madison, and John Jay, writing as "Publius," published more than 80 letters in the press defending the Constitution. Together in book form they are known today as *The Federalist,* the classic work explaining and defending the Constitution.

By January 9, 1788, a little more than three months after the Philadelphia Convention, five states had ratified the Constitution: Delaware, Pennsylvania, New Jersey, Georgia, and Connecticut. Massachusetts, a key and doubtful state, ratified next, thanks to the efforts of Sam Adams and John Hancock. Maryland and South Carolina followed suit, and on June 21, 1788, New Hampshire became the ninth state to ratify.

The Constitution was now in effect, but Virginia and New York were still to be heard from. Without these two powerful states, no union could succeed. Washington, Madison, and Edmund Randolph, who finally decided to support the Constitution that he had not signed, helped to swing Virginia into the Federalist camp four days later. In part because of *The Federalist* papers, New York ratified on July 26 by a narrow margin of three votes. North Carolina finally ratified in 1789 and Rhode Island in 1790. (See Table 2-1.) By that time George Washington was already serving as president of the United States of America.

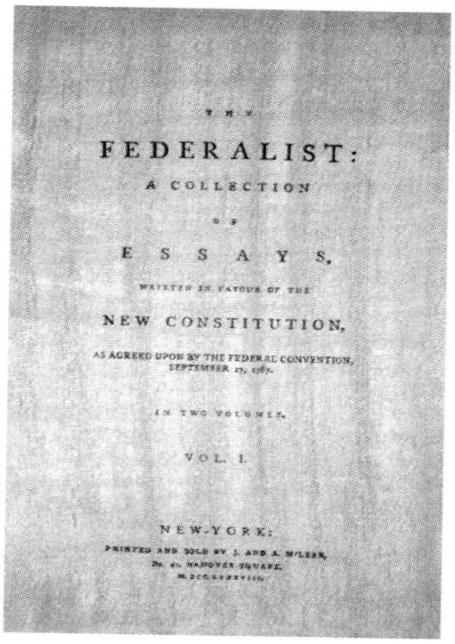


The Granger Collection, New York

*The Federalist* essays defended the Constitution.

## America: A Case Study in Nation Building

"The United States was the first major colony successfully to revolt against colonial rule," Seymour Martin Lipset has written. "In this sense, it was the first 'new nation.'"[47]

The Declaration of Independence and the success of the American Revolution influenced the philosophers and political leaders of the French Revolution. Jefferson's words were translated into many languages, influencing liberals during the 19th century in Germany, Italy, and South America. Even today, the ideas expressed in the Declaration of Independence have relevance in a world in which millions of people are still groping toward political freedom.

### Problems of a New Nation

The turmoil that has accompanied the growth of the new countries of Africa and Asia demonstrates that independence does not necessarily bring political maturity and peace. From Vietnam to Zimbabwe, as colonialism has given way to the forces of nationalism, political independence often has been accompanied by political instability and war. The same has proved true in some of the countries of Eastern Europe, notably Yugoslavia, after the collapse of the Soviet Union and its communist system in 1991. Yet America had a successful revolution. And despite the Civil War, two world wars, the Great Depression, periodic inflation and unemployment, the Vietnam War, Watergate, the impeachment of two presidents, and other issues that have confronted the nation, it has survived. How did the revolutionary leaders of America carve out an enduring new nation where none had existed before? The process was slow and difficult. As Lipset has observed:

> A backward glance into our own past should destroy the notion that the United States proceeded easily toward the establishment of democratic political institutions . . . it was touch and go whether the com-

**TABLE 2-1**

**The Ratification of the Constitution**

| State | Date | Vote in the Ratifying Convention |
|---|---|---|
| Delaware | December 7, 1787 | Unanimous |
| Pennsylvania | December 12, 1787 | 46–32 |
| New Jersey | December 18, 1787 | Unanimous |
| Georgia | January 2, 1788 | Unanimous |
| Connecticut | January 9, 1788 | 128–40 |
| Massachusetts | February 6, 1788 | 187–168 |
| Maryland | April 28, 1788 | 63–11 |
| South Carolina | May 23, 1788 | 149–73 |
| New Hampshire | June 21, 1788 | 57–47 |
| Virginia | June 25, 1788 | 89–79 |
| New York | July 26, 1788 | 30–27 |
| North Carolina | November 21, 1789 | 194–77 |
| Rhode Island | May 29, 1790 | 34–32 |

> plex balance of forces would swing in the direction of a one- or two-party system, or even whether the nation would survive as an entity. It took time to institutionalize values, beliefs, and practices, and there were many incidents that revealed how fragile the commitments to democracy and nationhood really were.[48]

The United States, in other words, went through growing pains similar to those of the new nations of Africa and Asia today. If some contemporary new nations have encountered difficulty in establishing political freedom and democratic procedures, so did America. For example, the Federalists under President John Adams wanted no organized political opposition and used the Alien and Sedition Acts, passed in 1798, to suppress their opponents. At least 70 people were jailed and fined under the Sedition Act, which made almost any criticism of the government, the president, or Congress a crime. The historical development of the American nation—with all its crises and problems—remains relevant to the emerging nations in today's world.

## The Constitution: A Document "Intended to Endure . . ."

The Constitution, Chief Justice Marshall said in *McCulloch* v. *Maryland,* was "intended to endure for ages to come, and consequently to be adapted to the various crises of human affairs."[49] This opinion, delivered in 1819, embodied the principle of loose or **flexible construction** of the Constitution—the concept that the Constitution must be interpreted flexibly to meet changing conditions.

The members of the Supreme Court have generally reflected the times in which they have lived. Successive Supreme Courts have read very different meaning into the language of the Constitution. But the Court is not the only branch of the government that interprets the Constitution. So does Congress when it passes laws. So does the president when he makes decisions and takes actions. In addition, through 2004, the Constitution has been amended 27 times. The inputs of the American political system have resulted in a continual process of constitutional change. (The Constitution follows the last chapter of this book.)

### What It Says

**The Legislative Branch** Article I of the Constitution vests all legislative powers "in a Congress of the United States, which shall consist of a Senate and House of Representatives." This article spells out the qualifications and method of election of members of the House and Senate. It gives power of impeachment to the House but provides that the Senate shall try impeachment cases. That power has rarely been used; two presidents, Andrew Johnson, in 1868, and Bill Clinton, in 1998, were impeached by the House; both were tried by the Senate, but neither was removed from office. A third president, Richard M. Nixon, resigned in 1974 in the face of threatened impeachment. Article I also empowers the vice president to preside over the Senate with no vote, except in the case of a tie.

Article I provides that all tax legislation must originate in the House. It allows the president to sign or veto a bill and Congress to override his veto by a two-thirds vote of both houses.

Section 8 of this article gives Congress the power to tax, provide for the "general welfare" of the United States, borrow money, regulate commerce (the commerce clause), naturalize citizens, coin money, punish counterfeiters, establish a post office and a copyright and patents system, create lower courts, declare war, maintain armed forces, suppress insurrections and repel invasions, govern the District of Columbia, and make all "necessary and proper laws" (sometimes called the **elastic clause**) to carry out the powers of the Constitution.

Section 9 provides certain basic protections for citizens against acts of Congress. For example, it says that the writ of habeas corpus shall not be suspended unless required by the public safety in cases of rebellion or invasion. One of the most important guarantees of individual liberty, the writ is designed to protect against illegal imprisonment. It requires that a person who is detained be brought before a judge for investigation so that the court may literally, in the Latin meaning, "have the body."

Article I also prohibits Congress or the states from passing a **bill of attainder**—legislation aimed at a particular individual—or an **ex post facto law,** imposing punishment for an act that was not illegal when committed. It provides that only Congress may appropriate money drawn from the Treasury, a provision that is the single most important check on presidential power. The article also outlaws titles of nobility in America.

**The Executive Branch** Article II states, "The executive Power shall be vested in a President of the United States of America." The framers did not provide for direct popular election of the president. Rather, they established the **electoral college,** with each state having as many electors as it had representatives and senators. The electors were to choose the president and vice president. Alexander Hamilton argued that by this means the presidency would be filled by "characters preeminent for ability and virtue." The electors, he thought, being "a small number of persons, selected by their fellow-citizens from the general mass, will be most likely to possess the information and discernment requisite."[50]

Under the Constitution, the person with the greatest number of electoral votes would be president and the one with the next highest number would be vice president. The election of 1800 was thrown into the House of Representatives because Jefferson and Aaron Burr, although members of the same party, each received the same number of electoral votes. On the 36th ballot, the House chose Jefferson as president. Afterward, the electoral system was modified by the Twelfth Amendment to provide that electors must vote separately for president and vice president.

The rise of political parties meant that in time the electoral college became largely a rubber stamp. As it works today, the voters in each state choose between slates of electors who usually run under a party label. All the electoral votes of a state normally go to the candidate who wins the popular vote in that state; electors on the winning slate routinely vote for their party's candidates for president and vice president. But the electors do not have to obey the will of the voters. For a variety of reasons (discussed in Chapter 11), there sometimes has been pressure to modify or abolish the electoral college system. However, a proposed constitutional amendment to provide for direct, popular election of the president failed to pass the Senate in 1970 and again in 1979.

The Constitution makes the president commander in chief of the armed forces. It also gives the president the right to make treaties "with the Advice and Consent" of two-thirds of a quorum of the Senate; to appoint ambassadors, judges, and other high officials, subject to Senate approval; and to summon Congress into special session.

**The Judiciary** Article III states, "The judicial Power of the United States, shall be vested in one supreme Court, and in such inferior Courts" as Congress may establish. It also provides for trial by jury. The Supreme Court's vital right of judicial review of acts of Congress stems from both the supremacy clause of the Constitution (see below) and Article III, which asserts that the judicial power applies to "all Cases . . . arising under this Constitution."

**Other Provisions** Article IV governs the relations among the states and between the states and the federal government. Article V provides methods for amending the Constitution and for ratifying these amendments. Article VI states that the Constitution, laws, and treaties of the United States "shall be the supreme Law of the Land." This, as noted earlier, is the powerful **supremacy clause** by which laws of Congress prevail over any conflicting state laws. Article VII declares that the Constitution would go into effect when ratified by conventions in nine states.

## The Amendment Process

The framers knew that the Constitution might have to be changed to meet future conditions. It had, after all, been created because of the need for change. So they provided two methods of proposing amendments: by a two-thirds vote of both houses of Congress or by a national convention called by Congress at the request of legislatures in two-thirds of the states. (See Figure 2-2.)

Once proposed, an amendment does not take effect unless ratified, either by the legislatures of three-fourths of the states or by special ratifying conventions in three-fourths of the states.

No amendment has ever been proposed by the convention method. In the 1970s, there were calls for a convention to propose an amendment to require a balanced federal budget. President Jimmy Carter cautioned that such a conclave would be "completely uncontrollable." Some political leaders and legal scholars warned that a constitutional convention might run wild and make sweeping changes in the structure of the federal government because no precedent existed for setting an agenda of such a convention. The effort to persuade the states to call a convention failed. Nevertheless, the Constitution

"The executive Power shall be vested in a President of the United States of America."

**FIGURE 2-2**

**Amending the Constitution**

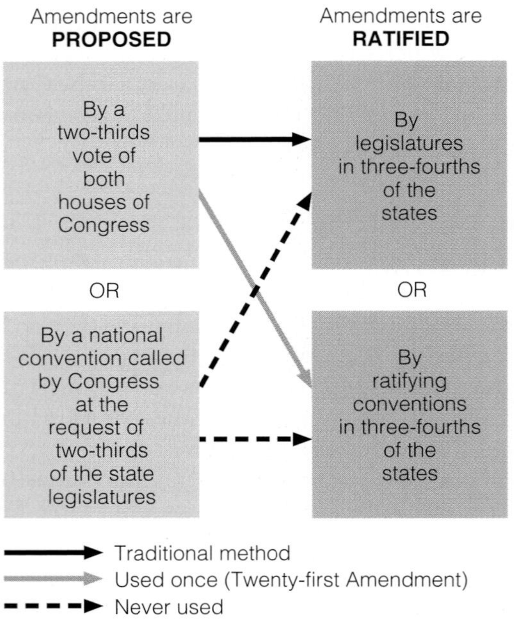


clearly permits a convention if two-thirds of the state legislatures request it.

Of the 27 amendments ratified by the year 2006, only the Twenty-first Amendment, repealing Prohibition, was ratified by state conventions; the rest were ratified by state legislatures. Some of the amendments add to the Constitution; others supersede or revise the original language of the Constitution.

## The Bill of Rights

The amendments to the Constitution fall into three major time periods. The first 12, ratified between 1791 and 1804, were remedial amendments designed to perfect the original instrument. The next three grew out of the great upheaval of the Civil War and were designed to deal with the new position of blacks as free men and women. Amendments in the third group were all passed during the 20th century and deal with a wide range of subjects, in part reflecting more recent pressures toward change in American society.

The first 10 amendments comprise the **Bill of Rights.** (Some scholars regard only the first eight or nine amendments as the Bill of Rights.) The first 10 amendments were passed by the 1st Congress in 1789 and went into effect when ratified by three-fourths of the states on December 15, 1791. (The Bill of Rights is discussed in detail in Chapter 4.)

The provisions of the first four amendments are: (First Amendment) freedom of religion, speech, press, assembly, and petition; (Second Amendment) the right to bear arms; (Third Amendment) protection against quartering of soldiers in private homes; and (Fourth Amendment) protection against unreasonable search and seizure of people, homes, papers, and effects and provision for search warrants.

The Fifth Amendment provides that no person can be compelled "to be a witness against himself" or to stand trial twice for the same crime. It also lists other rights of accused persons, including that of indictment by a grand jury for major crimes and the general provision that no person shall "be deprived of life, liberty, or property, without due process of law." In addition, the amendment provides that the government cannot take private property "for public use without just compensation" to the owners, a principle known as **eminent domain.**

The Sixth Amendment calls for a speedy and public trial by jury in criminal cases and sets forth other protections, including the right to have a lawyer.

The Seventh Amendment provides for jury trial in civil cases, and the Eighth Amendment bars excessive bail or fines and cruel and unusual punishment. The Ninth Amendment provides that the enumeration of certain rights in the Constitution shall not deny other rights retained by the people, and the Tenth Amendment reserves to the states, or to the people, powers not delegated to the federal government.

These 10 amendments were designed to protect Americans against the power of the federal government. Nothing in the Constitution specifically provides that state governments also must abide by the provisions of the Bill of Rights. But in interpreting the Fourteenth Amendment, ratified in 1868 after the Civil War, the Supreme Court in the 20th century gradually extended the protection of almost all of the Bill of Rights to apply to the states.

## The Later Amendments

The Eleventh Amendment (1795)[51] was added to protect the states from being hauled into federal court by a citizen of another state or by a foreign citizen. In *Chisholm* v. *Georgia,*[52] the Supreme Court had ruled for two South Carolina citizens who had sued the state of Georgia on behalf of a British creditor to recover confiscated property.

**FREEDOM TO DISSENT**

If there is any principle of the Constitution that more imperatively calls for attachment than any other it is the principle of free thought, not free thought for those who agree with us but freedom for the thought we hate.

—Justice Oliver Wendell Holmes, dissenting in *United States* v. *Schwimmer* (1929)

## Myth vs. Reality

# INNOCENT UNTIL PROVEN GUILTY?

Most Americans probably believe that the presumption of innocence—the principle that a criminal defendant is innocent until proven guilty beyond a reasonable doubt—is written in the Constitution.

Wrong. It isn't. Although a bedrock principle of Anglo-Saxon law for centuries, with roots even traceable to ancient Rome, the idea that a person is innocent until proven guilty appears nowhere in the language of the U.S. Constitution.

The Supreme Court, however, has held in several cases that the "due process clause" of the Constitution requires the presumption that a criminal defendant is innocent until proven guilty beyond a reasonable doubt. For example, as far back as 1895, in *Coffin* v. *United States,* 156 U.S. 432, the Court declared in a bank fraud case: "The principle that there is a presumption of innocence in favor of the accused is the undoubted law, axiomatic and elementary, and its enforcement lies at the foundation of the administration of our criminal law."

More recently, in *In re Winship,* 397 U.S. 358 (1970), the Court reaffirmed the principle in the case of Samuel Winship, a 12-year-old boy who stole $112 from a woman's purse in New York: "we explicitly hold that the Due Process Clause protects the accused against conviction except upon proof beyond a reasonable doubt."

Thus, the concept of innocent until proven guilty beyond a reasonable doubt does *not* appear in the Constitution, but the Supreme Court has made plain that it is the law of the land.

The Twelfth Amendment (1804), as already discussed, was adopted after the deadlocked election of 1800. It provided that presidential electors vote separately for president and vice president.

The next three amendments resulted from the Civil War. The Thirteenth Amendment (1865) forbids slavery. It also outlaws involuntary servitude in the United States and its territories except as punishment for a crime. Its purpose was to free the slaves and complete the abolition of slavery in America. Lincoln's Emancipation Proclamation, which was issued during the war, applied only to areas in rebellion and under Confederate control and therefore did not actually free any slaves.

The Fourteenth Amendment (1868) was adopted to make the former slaves citizens. But it has had other unintended and far-reaching effects. The amendment says that no state "shall abridge the privileges or immunities of citizens"; nor "deprive any person of life, liberty, or property, without due process of law"; nor deny anyone "the equal protection of the laws." The famous "due process" clause of the amendment has been used by the Supreme Court to protect the rights of individuals against the police power of the state in a broad spectrum of cases. The "equal protection of the laws" provision was the basis for the landmark 1954 Supreme Court decision outlawing segregation in public schools.

The Fifteenth Amendment (1870) barred the federal and state governments from denying any citizen the right to vote because of race, color, or previous condition of servitude. It did not, however, prevent some states from disenfranchising blacks by means of restrictive voting requirements, such as literacy tests.

Forty-three years elapsed after the adoption of the Fifteenth Amendment before another was ratified. The Sixteenth Amendment (1913) allowed Congress to pass a graduated individual income tax, in theory based on ability to pay. The tax has been, of course, the largest source of federal revenue.

The Seventeenth Amendment (1913) provided for direct election of senators by the people, instead of by state legislatures.

The Eighteenth Amendment (1919) established Prohibition by outlawing the manufacture, sale, or transportation of alcoholic beverages. It provides a classic instance of a government output doomed to failure because ultimately the input of popular support was lacking. Prohibition led to the era of bathtub gin, "flappers," speakeasies, and bootlegging. It was marked by widespread defiance of the law by otherwise law-abiding citizens and by the rise of organized crime, which quickly moved to meet public demand for illicit liquor. Partly as a result of Prohibition, organized crime remains entrenched in America today, exercising political influence in some areas of the country. Prohibition was repealed in 1933.

The Nineteenth Amendment (1920) guaranteed women the right to vote. Women in many states could vote even before the amendment was proposed, but it provided a constitutional basis for this major expansion of the electorate. Even so, it may seem surprising today that women's suffrage was not constitutionally adopted until 1920, in time for that year's presidential election.

Under the Twentieth (or "lame duck") Amendment (1933), the terms of the president and vice president begin on January 20 and the terms of members of Congress on January 3. Before that time a president and members of Congress defeated in November would continue in office for four months until March 4 (formerly the date of presidential inaugurations). Injured by the voters, the defeated incumbents sat like "lame ducks."[53] The amendment also provides alternatives in case of the death of the president-elect before Inauguration Day or in case no president has been chosen.

© Bettmann/Corbis

Federal agents destroying barrels of beer during Prohibition.

The Twenty-first Amendment (1933) repealed Prohibition but permitted states to remain "dry" if they so desired.

The Twenty-second Amendment (1951) limits presidents to a maximum of two elected terms. It was proposed after President Franklin D. Roosevelt had won a fourth term in 1944. Before Roosevelt, through hallowed tradition established by George Washington, no president had been elected more than twice.

The Twenty-third Amendment (1961) gives citizens of the District of Columbia the right to vote in presidential elections; they did so for the first time in 1964. When the amendment was adopted, the nation's capital had a population of 800,000—larger than that of 13 of the states.

The Twenty-fourth Amendment (1964) abolished the poll tax as a prerequisite for voting in federal elections or primaries. It applied only to five southern states that still imposed such a tax, originally a device to keep blacks (and in some cases poor whites) from voting.

The Twenty-fifth Amendment (1967) was spurred by President Dwight D. Eisenhower's 1955 heart attack and by the murder of President John F. Kennedy in Dallas on November 22, 1963. It defines the circumstances in which a vice president may take over the leadership of the country in case of the mental or physical illness or disability of the president. It also requires the president to nominate a vice president, subject to majority approval of Congress, when that office becomes vacant for any reason.*

*The amendment was used for the first time in October 1973 when President Richard Nixon nominated House Republican leader Gerald R. Ford to replace Vice President Spiro T. Agnew, who had resigned. Congress confirmed Ford in December. When Nixon resigned in August 1974, Ford became president, again under the amendment. The amendment was used a third time when President Ford that same month nominated Nelson A. Rockefeller of New York to be vice president. Congress confirmed Rockefeller in December 1974.

The Twenty-sixth Amendment (1971) gave people 18 years of age or older the right to vote in all elections—federal, state, and local. The amendment was proposed by Congress in March 1971 and ratified in June. As a result, 1972 was the first presidential election year in which people aged 18 through 20 were able to vote in elections at every level of government.

The Twenty-seventh Amendment (1992) prohibited any Congress from voting itself a pay raise. The amendment was first submitted to the states in 1789, but very few ratified it. By the early 1990s, spurred by a student at the University of Texas, and by public indigna-

### "Lame Duck": The Origin of the Species

How did the phrase "lame duck" quack its way into American politics? The term is used to describe an elected official who has been defeated, or by law cannot run again, or plans to retire and whose power may therefore be diminished. The phrase apparently originated as slang on the London stock exchange, where it was used to describe a stock jobber or broker who could not make good his losses and would "waddle out of the alley like a lame duck." Abraham Lincoln is sometimes credited with introducing the phrase in America. When a defeated senator called on Lincoln and asked for a job as commissioner of Indian affairs, Lincoln was quoted as saying afterward, "I usually find that a Senator or Representative out of business is a sort of lame duck."

The Granger Collection, New York

The Nineteenth Amendment, ratified in 1920, guarantees women the right to vote.

tion over congressional pay raises and perquisites, many states acted to approve the amendment. Although some scholars questioned the validity of the amendment, arguing that the states had taken too long to act—203 years—it was ratified in 1992. (See "Making a Difference" box, p. 59.) Since 1919, Congress has set deadlines, usually seven years, for states to ratify proposed amendments, but it did not do so in this case.

Several other constitutional amendments have been suggested in recent years. In 1995, for example, the Republican majority in the House passed a proposed constitutional amendment to balance the federal budget, a proposal that was an important part of the party's "Contract with America." However, the measure failed to pass the Republican-controlled Senate. In 1995, Congress turned down another proposed constitutional amendment to limit the terms of its members to 12 years.

A proposed amendment designed to guarantee equal rights for women was approved by Congress in 1972 and sent to the states for ratification. It was proposed to nullify the many state laws that discriminated against women in jobs, business, marriage, and other areas. After an initial burst of support, the Equal Rights Amendment (ERA) ran into increasing difficulty and failed to pass. Although later reintroduced, it was defeated again in 1983.

In 1982 foes of legalized abortion introduced a proposed amendment to the Constitution that would allow states to prohibit abortions. The "pro-life" amendment was designed to overturn the 1973 Supreme Court ruling that legalized abortions. The proposed amendment was defeated in the Senate in 1983.

In 1984, the Senate rejected a proposed constitutional amendment, supported by President Ronald Reagan, to permit organized, spoken prayers in the public schools. The Senate also voted down a proposed constitutional amendment to allow silent prayer in the public schools.

Presidents Reagan, Bush, and Clinton repeatedly urged Congress to enact a constitutional amendment to give presidents the power to veto parts of appropriations bills passed by Congress. The Constitution does not provide for such a line-item veto. In 1996, Congress passed and President Clinton signed legislation to give the president a limited line-item veto over appropriations bills. Two years later, however, the Supreme Court declared the law unconstitutional.[54]

In 2004, President George W. Bush proposed a constitutional amendment to prohibit gay marriages. The amendment, defining marriage as a union between a man and a woman, failed to pass.

## A Document for the Living . . .

At 4 p.m. in Philadelphia on September 17, 1987—the moment when, 200 years earlier, the delegates had finished signing their names to the Constitution—former chief justice Warren E. Burger rang a replica of the Liberty Bell. It was a signal for bells to ring throughout Philadelphia, in the capitals of the 50 states, and in U.S. diplomatic missions around the world.

Philadelphia was bedecked with balloons, flags, and parade floats for the bicentennial celebration. Tall ships sailed the Delaware River. President Reagan spoke at In-

Smithsonian Institution

The assassination of President John F. Kennedy, November 22, 1963

dependence Hall, recalling the convention 200 years before. "In a very real sense it was then, in 1787, that the revolution truly began," he said.

What Alexander Hamilton called "the American drama" had begun its third century. The world of the framers had changed beyond measure. At the outset of this chapter we posed the key question of whether the constitutional framework constructed more than two centuries ago allows for change at a sufficiently rapid pace to meet today's needs. That question lies at the heart of the ongoing political struggle in America. Competing groups can be expected to give different answers to the question. For example, the power of the government to regulate industry in order to protect the environment has expanded greatly under the Constitution. But loggers in Oregon who fear their jobs are threatened by the law protecting the spotted owl may have a different view of that expansion of government power than environmental activists may have. Nevertheless, the process of constitutional change had been foreseen long ago.

"The Constitution belongs to the living and not to the dead," Thomas Jefferson wrote. He added:

## Making a Difference

# A STUDENT GETS THE CONSTITUTION AMENDED

In 1789, it bothered James Madison that under the new Constitution he had helped to create, members of Congress could vote to increase their own salaries. They would, he warned, be able "without control to put their hand into the public coffers, to take out money to put in their pockets." Madison proposed a constitutional amendment requiring that any congressional pay raise take effect only after a new Congress had been elected. The proposed amendment was sent to the states as part of the original Bill of Rights. There it languished; after a century, only seven states had ratified it.

Enter Gregory D. Watson, a student of government at the University of Texas in Austin, who came across the amendment in 1982 while researching a paper. Watson made passage of Madison's amendment a personal crusade, and under his prodding, beginning in the mid-eighties, one state legislature after another ratified the proposal. Finally, on May 7, 1992, Michigan became the 38th state to ratify, providing the necessary three-fourths of the states.

. . . [S]ix days later the archivist of the United States pronounced the Twenty-seventh Amendment part of the Constitution. By that time Gregory Watson was an aide to a Democratic state legislator in Texas. "I always knew in my heart of hearts that this day would come," he said.

—Adapted from the *New York Times*, May 8, 1992

---

Some men look at constitutions with sanctimonious reverence and deem them like the ark of the covenant, too sacred to be touched. They ascribe to the men of the preceding age a wisdom more than human, and suppose what they did to be beyond amendment. . . . Laws and institutions must go hand in hand with the progress of the human mind. . . . As new discoveries are made, new truths disclosed, and manners and opinions change . . . institutions must advance also, and keep pace with the times.[55]

Through a variety of ways, including amendments and judicial review, the oldest written national constitution in the world remains the vital framework of the American political system. But are constitutional principles enough? Today, many Americans—women and members of minority groups, for example—continue to ask that the nation's institutions fulfill the promise of its ideals, and that principles be translated into reality. Constitutional democracy was born at Philadelphia, but, in a real sense, the work was only begun.

---

## CHAPTER HIGHLIGHTS

- The Constitution and the Bill of Rights provide the basic framework of American government. The Constitution established the structure of the government and a written set of rules to control the conduct of the government.
- The Declaration of Independence, approved by the Continental Congress on July 4, 1776, proclaimed that "all men are created equal" and that government derived its just powers from "the consent of the governed."
- Before the Constitution was framed, a weak central government had been established under the Articles of Confederation.
- During the Constitutional Convention of 1787, the Virginia Plan and the New Jersey Plan were debated. The Great Compromise, also called the Connecticut Compromise, was finally adopted as an alternative.
- The Great Compromise provided for a House of Representatives based on the population of each state, and a Senate with two members from each state—a solution that satisfied both the large and the small states.
- The convention also compromised over the slavery issue by delaying a ban on the importation of slaves until 1808 and by counting three-fifths of all slaves in apportioning the House of Representatives.
- The Constitution divided the national government into three branches: legislative, executive, and judicial. The government is based on the principles of separation of powers and checks and balances, even though in practice many powers and functions overlap and are shared.
- The Constitution also created a federal system, or federalism, in which the powers and functions of government are shared by the national government and the states. Although in the United States a strong national government has evolved over two centuries as the dominant partner, the states retain significant powers of their own.
- The Constitution was ratified in 1788, but only after a long debate and political struggle between the Federalists and the Antifederalists.
- In 1791 the states ratified a Bill of Rights intended to protect individuals from the power of the federal government. These first 10 amendments to the Constitution included provisions for freedom of religion, speech,

press, assembly, and petition; the right to bear arms; protection against unreasonable search and seizure; the right to due process of law and protection against self-incrimination and double jeopardy; the right to a speedy and public trial by jury in criminal cases; and protection against cruel and unusual punishment.

- Through 2006, the Constitution had been amended 27 times.
- The Supreme Court interprets the Constitution. By exercising judicial review, the Supreme Court decides whether laws passed by Congress or actions taken by the executive branch—or laws and actions at any level of local, state, and federal government—are constitutional.

## KEY TERMS

natural rights, p. 37
Magna Carta, p. 37
common law, p. 37
royal colonies, p. 38
proprietary colonies, p. 38
charter colonies, p. 38
unicameral legislature, p. 39
confederation, p. 41
Articles of Confederation, p. 41
Virginia Plan, p. 44
New Jersey Plan, p. 44
Great Compromise, p. 45
Connecticut Compromise, p. 45
supremacy clause, p. 47
federal system, p. 47
federalism, p. 47
separation of powers, p. 47
checks and balances, p. 47
judicial review, p. 47
*Marbury* v. *Madison,* p. 48
Antifederalists, p. 50
Federalists, p. 50
flexible construction, p. 52
elastic clause, p. 52
bill of attainder, p. 52
ex post facto law, p. 52
electoral college, p. 52
Bill of Rights, p. 54
eminent domain, p. 54

## SUGGESTED WEBSITES

**http://supct.law.cornell.edu/supct/**
*Cornell Law School—Legal Information Institute Website*
Offers material about cases presented to the U.S. Supreme Court and, whenever possible, the full text of decisions, including concurring and dissenting opinions.

**http://www.findlaw.com**
*FindLaw*
FindLaw is a Web portal focused on law and government, providing access to a comprehensive and fast-growing online library of legal resources for anyone with an interest in the law.

**http://lcweb2.loc.gov/ammem/mcchtml/corhome.html**
*Manuscript Division of the U.S. Library of Congress*
A collection of selected documents celebrating the first 100 years of the Manuscript Division of the Library of Congress.

**http://www.oyez.org/oyez/frontpage**
*The Oyez Project*
Offers synopses and texts of U.S. Supreme Court decisions. Some arguments and decisions are available in Real Audio. Also has a "tour" of the Supreme Court and biographies of current and past justices.

**http://thomas.loc.gov**
*Thomas—Legislative Information on the Internet*
A comprehensive guide to the current status in Congress of a bill, resolution, or amendment. Includes bills and issues that various congressional committees and subcommittees are considering. The site also includes links to the websites of members of Congress.

**http://www.supremecourtus.gov**
*The United States Supreme Court*
The official website of the U.S. Supreme Court. Opened in April 2000. Contains the full text of the Court's decisions the same day they are released, as well as the Court's calendar, dockets, rules, a visitor's guide, and other information about the Court.

In addition to the Supreme Court's official website, other websites offer comprehensive coverage of Supreme Court decisions, as well as other information about the Court:

**http://www.ushda.org**
*U.S. Historical Documents Archive*
A list of important documents in U.S. history.

## SUGGESTED READING

Bailyn, Bernard. *The Ideological Origins of the American Revolution,* 25th anniversary edition* (Belknap Press, 1992). A revealing analysis of the ideas and concepts that were developed by the American colonists and led to their declaration of independence from Great Britain. Bailyn argues that the colonists' political ideas grew out of their experience in America but could also be widely applied in other countries and other times.

Banning, Lance. *The Sacred Fire of Liberty: James Madison and the Founding of the Federal Republic** (Cornell University Press, 1998). A challenging study of the development of the political thought of James Madison from 1780 to 1792. Argues that although Madison supported the creation of a stronger national government in 1787, he was also greatly interested in maintaining effective popular control of that new government.

Casper, Gerhard. *Separating Power: Essays on the Founding Period** (Harvard University Press, 1997). Casper contends that the framers of the Constitution failed to develop fully their principles of constitutional government. As a result, when courts and scholars attempt to interpret the Constitution by turning to the "original intent" of the framers, they may be doomed to failure.

Corwin, Edward S., et al., eds. *The Constitution of the United States of America, Analysis and Interpretation* (U.S. Government Printing Office, 1964). An exposition of the Constitution. See also Corwin, revised by Harold W. Chase and Craig R. Ducat, *The Constitution and What It Means Today,* 14th edition (Princeton University Press, 1978).

Dahl, Robert A. *How Democratic Is the American Constitution?* 2nd edition* (Yale University Press, 2003). An eminent political scientist focuses attention on undemocratic features of the U.S. Constitution. Dahl emphasizes the allocation of two Senators to each state despite their unequal populations, the electoral college, the policy-making role of an unelected Supreme Court, and the winner-take-all elections for Congress and state legislatures. He is generally pessimistic about achieving a more democratic constitutional system in the United States.

Earle, Edward Mead, ed. *The Federalist* (Random House, Modern Library). A classic collection of essays written by Alexander Hamilton, James Madison, and John Jay, prominent supporters of the proposed Constitution during the struggle over ratification. The Federalist papers were published in the press under the pseudonym "Publius"; they remain an important exposition of the federal government's structure.

Ellis, Joseph J. *Founding Brothers: The Revolutionary Generation** (Vintage Books, 2002). This award-winning historical study focuses on key political leaders and issues in the 1790s, and the impact on the early development of American politics. The author pays particular attention to Jefferson, Adams, Washington, Madison, Franklin, Hamilton, and Burr, as well as crucial personal and political relationships among these leaders of the revolutionary generation. Political issues covered include slavery, relations with Britain and France, the selection of a site for the national capitol, and the assumption of state debts.

Farrand, Max. *The Framing of the Constitution of the United States** (Yale University Press, 1913). A good general account of the Constitutional Convention by the scholar who compiled in four volumes the basic documentary sources on the convention proceedings.

Kelly, Alfred H., Belz, Herman, and Harbison, Winfred A. *The American Constitution: Its Origins and Development,* 7th edition* (Norton, 1991). A good general history of American constitutional development beginning with the colonial period.

Ketcham, Ralph. *Framed for Posterity: The Enduring Philosophy of the Constitution* (University Press of Kansas, 1993). A thoughtful and incisive study of the principles embodied in the Constitution. Ketcham concludes that the Constitution reflects general, durable ideas that can be applied by the courts to the problems of today.

Lipset, Seymour Martin. *The First New Nation* (Transaction Publishers, 2003). An important historical and sociological study of America that seeks to trace the relationship between a nation's values and the development of stable political institutions. Compares the early American experience with that of emerging nations in the 20th century.

Maier, Pauline. *American Scripture: Making the Declaration of Independence** (Knopf, 1997). A fascinating account of how the Declaration of Independence came to be written and reinterpreted by subsequent generations of Americans. Initially, the Declaration of Independence was a justification for rebellion; by the time of Lincoln's Gettysburg Address, through emphasis on the document's proposition that "all men are created equal," it had become a fundamental ideal of the American nation.

Rossiter, Clinton. *1787: The Grand Convention* (Norton, 1987). (Originally published in 1966.) A very readable account of the Philadelphia convention, the battle for ratification of the Constitution, and the first years of the new republic. Includes observations on the personal characteristics and objectives of the framers of the Constitution.

Storing, Herbert J. *What the Anti-Federalists Were For** (University of Chicago Press, 2001). A detailed analysis of the position of the Antifederalists in the struggle over the ratification of the Constitution. Traces how the views of the Antifederalists helped to bring about the enactment of the Bill of Rights.

Wood, Gordon S. *The Creation of the American Republic** (University of North Carolina Press, 1998). A comprehensive analysis of the development of political attitudes and thought in America before the constitutional convention convened in Philadelphia in 1787.

Wood, Gordon S. *The Radicalism of the American Revolution** (Knopf, 1992). A detailed examination of the social, economic, and political forces that led to the creation of democracy in America. Wood argues that the American Revolution was as radical as any in history if measured in terms of the great social changes it produced.

*Available in paperback edition.

SPEED
LIMIT
75

# Chapter 3

# THE FEDERAL SYSTEM

IN COLORADO, Montana, Nevada, South Dakota, and half a dozen other states, it is legal to tool along the interstate at 75 miles an hour. In California and Texas, the speed limit is 70. But in New York, New Hampshire, Maryland, and many other states the speed limit is 65. In Hawaii, doing more than 55 can result in a ticket.

Why should there be so many different speed limits in different states? After all, the United States is one country and Congress makes laws that apply to all Americans.

In the case of the varying speed limits, Congress in 1995 did in fact pass a law—but it allowed the states to make their own rules. Under the law, signed by President Clinton, the 50 states were free to set their own speed limits on the nation's highways. The 55-mile-per-hour limit that had prevailed on many highways for more than two decades was no longer a federal requirement.

Many states passed new laws that increased speed limits to 70 miles per hour or more. Almost immediately, a solid bloc of 10 western states increased their legal speeds to 70 or 75. A total of 26 states had raised their limits within six months after the new law went into effect, and by 2006 a total of 31 states had limits of 70 or 75 on some of their roads.[1]

The 55-mile-per-hour limit had originally been set in 1974 to save gasoline during an oil embargo imposed by the Arab states. When Congress set the national limit, it had barred the release of any federal highway construction funds to states with a higher speed limit. Because of this provision, every state maintained a maximum speed limit of 55.

In western states, however, with wide-open spaces and straight stretches of highway, many motorists chafed under the lower speed limits. But the insurance industry and safety and environmental groups were opposed to higher speeds, arguing that increasing speed limits would mean 6,400 highway deaths a year in addition to the 41,000 annual fatalities that occurred under the slower speed limits.[2] Some studies have shown that more people are killed at higher speeds.

In 1995, in addition to repealing the 55-mile-per-hour limit, Congress also removed the penalties that had been imposed on states that did not require motorcycle drivers to wear helmets. On the other hand, the new law required so-called zero tolerance for younger drivers who drink alcohol; it would withhold a portion of federal highway money for states that did not classify minors as driving while intoxicated if their blood alcohol level was 0.02 percent or higher.

How is it that the government in Washington, D.C., could require or repeal speed limits or other highway rules for the 50 states? The answer can be found in the structure of government in the United States. The controversy over speed limits, and the response by Congress and the president in 1995, illustrated a basic fact about government in America: The United States has a federal system of government, in which power is constitutionally shared by a national government and 50 state governments. Within the states, of course, are thousands of local governments—and schools are controlled by localities and independent school districts, operating within standards set by the states.

The constitutional sharing of power by a national government and regional units of government (states, in the case of the United States) characterizes and defines a **federal system,** or **federalism.** The terms "federalism" and "the federal system" are used interchangeably to describe this basic structure of government in the United States. (These terms should not be confused with "the federal government," which simply refers to the national government in Washington.)

In the American federal system each level of government is able to make certain decisions that the other level cannot. For example, only the president can conduct America's relations with other nations; but only a governor, in some states, has the power to reprieve a prisoner on that state's death row.

To say that power in America is shared by the national and state governments may, at first glance, seem merely to be stating the obvious. Yet no principle of American government has been disputed more than federalism. Should that be doubted, one need only recall that more than 600,000 people died during the Civil War settling problems of federalism.

Not every country has a federal system. For example, France has a **unitary system of government.** The nation is divided into administrative units called departments, uniformly administered from Paris. Educational and other policies are set by the central government, even though in recent years France has sought to decentralize a number of government functions. (See Figure 3-1.)

Although the national government in Washington exercises great power, it also shares power with the states. The states, in turn, exercise certain exclusive powers. And, at times, the federal system of government created by the Constitution leads to significant conflict.

The rioting that erupted in the streets of Los Angeles in April 1992 provided a dramatic example of that fact. The disorders were triggered when a jury that included no black members in a state court in California acquitted four white police officers in the savage beating of Rodney King, a black motorist. Police in Los Angeles were slow to respond and failed to restore order, so the governor called out the California National Guard. When that, too, appeared inadequate to restore order, the president placed the National Guard under federal authority and dispatched thousands of federal agents and armed troops to the nation's second-largest city. All three layers of government—local, state, and national—were drawn

FIGURE 3-1

**Federal and Unitary Systems of Government Compared**

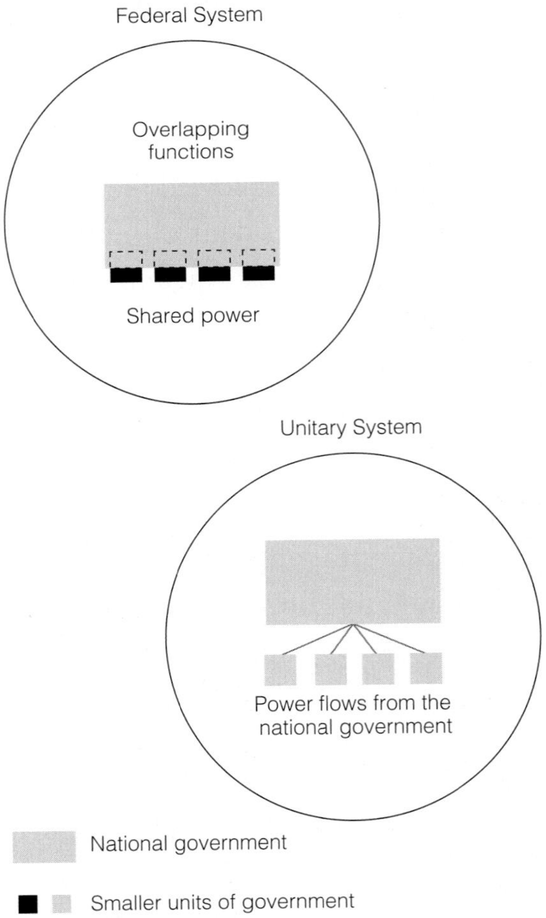

## Comparing Governments

### THE FRENCH GOVERNMENT DECIDES: YOU'VE GOT COURRIEL?

In 2003, the French government banned the use of the word "e-mail" in government documents, ministries, publications, or websites. France's government officially replaced the word "e-mail" with "Courriel," a merging of the words "courier electronic" [mail electronic], in an attempt to prevent more English words from seeping into the French language. The French government has this power because France has a unitary system of government.

For example, it used to be said that the French minister of education could, by glancing at the clock in his office, tell at any given moment what book was being read by every schoolchild in France. The tale may be a bit exaggerated, but no official in Washington could even begin to perform the same feat.

—Adapted from USAToday.com, July 18, 2003

into, and reacted to, the crisis. And all three layers would have to play a role in any long-term solutions to the problems of the nation's inner cities.

The question of how power is to be shared in the federal system is central to the political process in the United States. It is a subject of continuing political debate. It has been reflected in many important decisions of the Supreme Court. The migrant worker in the lettuce fields of California, the West Virginia coal miner, the spouse seeking a Nevada divorce, the murder suspect fighting extradition—these people do not think of their problems in terms of the federal system. Yet the relationship among national, state, and local governments vitally touches their lives. To a considerable extent, federalism affects who wins and who loses as a result of government decisions in American society. It affects the outputs of the political system.

© John Barr

Los Angeles, 1992

Federalism is one answer to the problem of how to govern a complex nation. Although there are all sorts of institutional arrangements in the 192 nations of the world, governments tend to be either centralized and unitary, or federated. In the 20th century, federalism became a popular style of government. By 1964, one study concluded, "well over half the land mass of the world was ruled by governments that with some justification, however slight, described themselves as federalisms."[3] The list of federal systems includes Switzerland, Canada, Australia, Mexico, India, and Germany.[4] Unitary systems, in which all power is vested in a central government, include France, Israel, and South Africa.

Key Question In this chapter we will explore a key question: ***How does federalism work in the United States?*** There are a number of other, related questions to consider. For example: Who benefits and who loses under the federal system? Does federalism restrict progress in solving national problems? Do the advantages of federalism outweigh the price of fragmented government? Why does the United States have a federal system? What are the problems it has created? What are the consequences of federalism in American politics? In the performance of the states?

## FEDERALISM: THE PROS AND CONS

What are the arguments for and against a federal system? (See Table 3-1.) Federalism permits diversity. Since problems and circumstances vary from one community to another, the argument can be made that a number of governments dealing directly with local problems, and accountable to local voters, may perform better than a single, remote bureaucracy. State governments, by this reasoning, may have a better idea than the national government of how to cope with local problems.

Another argument advanced for a federal system of

**TABLE 3-1**

### The Federal System

Scholars and political leaders alike have debated the relative merits and drawbacks of federalism since the founding of the republic. Here are some of the major arguments that have been made:

**Advantages**

Permits diversity and diffusion of power
Local governments can handle local problems better.
More access points for political participation
Protects individual rights against concentrated government power
Fosters experimentation and innovation
Suits a large country with a diverse population

**Disadvantages**

Makes national unity difficult to achieve and maintain
State governments may resist national policies.
May permit economic inequality and racial discrimination
Law enforcement and justice are uneven.
Smaller units may lack expertise and money.
May promote local dominance by special interests

government is that it allows more levels of government, more points of access to the government, and as a result, more opportunities for political participation. A system in which there are multiple points of access to government may offer advantages to individuals or groups seeking benefits from the political system. Americans may vote at frequent intervals for mayors, town council and school board members, governors, other state officials, and, at the national level, members of the House of Representatives and senators elected from the states.

Some analysts also argue that because power is diffused and fragmented among many different units in a federal system, there is better protection for individual rights than in a highly centralized government. Concentrated power is dangerous, supporters of federalism often maintain.

Advocates of a federal system also stress that the existence of many units of government allows for more experimentation and innovation in solving problems. For example, new social programs are sometimes originated in one state and then adopted in another, or even nationally. Many of the social programs of Franklin D. Roosevelt's New Deal were copied from some of the states, a pattern that was repeated during the 1960s and 1970s. During the Reagan era, when the federal government was trying to cut back spending for social programs, a number of states took the lead in education, economic development, and other important areas. Again in the early 1990s, many states redesigned their welfare programs before the federal government acted to restructure the national welfare system.

In addition, advocates of federalism argue that it is well suited to the United States, a nation covering a large geographic area with a highly diversified population of more than 300 million people.

But critics contend that a federal system also has distinct disadvantages. Federalism may serve as a mask for privilege and economic or racial discrimination.[5] In the past, at least, in some areas of the South and in other sections of the country, the federal system permitted state and local governments to repress blacks. Inequalities may occur when special interests exercise considerable influence on the politics and economy of a state or locality. West Virginia has often been cited as an example. Although the nation's second-leading coal producer, it has long been a relatively poor state, a fact sometimes attributed to its heavy dependence on a single industry. Along with abandoned strip mines, pockets of poverty scar the hillsides; in 2005 West Virginia ranked 47th in the nation in per capita income.[6]

Although the energy shortage of the 1970s increased the price of coal and brought greater prosperity to the state, industry pressures tended to keep taxes low. That in turn affected West Virginia's ability to provide social services for its residents.

Critics also argue that under the federal system, local or special interests—for example, the automobile indus-

### WASHINGTON: COLOR-BLIND IN A BLIZZARD?

While a trivial matter, one example indicates the difficulty of keeping too many strings tied to the center nail, of seeking too much uniformity, or setting one pattern for all of the diverse nation. The state of Wyoming had a slight hassle with the U.S. Bureau of Public Roads over the color of paint to be used to mark the sides and center line of Wyoming highways. Wyoming had painted a solid yellow line to mark the shoulder of the road and an intermittent yellow line for the center. The Bureau of Public Roads said the lines must be standardized with the rest of the country, which meant white lines except in the no-passing stretches. After much haggling Wyoming inevitably gave in, but with a parting comment: "Let them come out here and find one of their white lines during one of our blizzards." The highway engineers had found that in the blowing blizzards of Wyoming's winters, drivers could see yellow lines, but not white ones. In this encounter they learned that yellow lines could not be seen from Washington.

—Terry Sanford, *Storm over the States*

try, oil companies, or in the past, the white power structure in the Deep South—have often been able to frustrate efforts to solve national problems like segregated public schools, poverty, pollution, and energy needs. The same local officials whose understanding of local problems is often cited as a benefit of federalism may be in a position to thwart national policies. Government that is "closer to the people" may not serve all the people equally. Nor is it necessarily the case that local governments can solve problems more efficiently; they may lack the national government's skill and money. In fact, because the federal government collects most of the taxes in America, it can be argued that the system of federalism has often left cities and states unable to pay for local services.

Other arguments are sometimes made against a federal system: Its very diversity may make it difficult to achieve and maintain national unity; it can be more difficult and costly to make a complex system work; and law enforcement and justice may be administered unevenly.

The relations between the states and the federal government are thus a source of continuing conflict and controversy in the American political system.

## The Checkerboard of Governments

Americans sometimes complain that they are being squeezed by high taxes on at least three levels of government—national, state, and local. Depending on where they live, they may be confronted by a bewildering checkerboard of overlapping governments and local districts. One study of the federal system found that a resident of Park Forest, Illinois, paid taxes to 11 governmental units, starting with the United States of America and ending with the South Cook County Mosquito Abatement District.[7] Moreover, states have different laws and rules for dealing with such matters as taxation, criminal justice, education, marriage, and licensing of professions and businesses.

The Census Bureau has counted a total of 87,576 governments in the United States: 3,034 counties; 19,429 municipalities; 16,504 townships; 13,506 school districts; 35,052 special districts (for natural resources, fire protection, housing development, and other services); 50 states; and one national government.[8]

But knowing how many governments exist in America tells little about how the federal system operates—how the various levels of government relate to one another. One way to visualize the system as a whole was suggested by Morton Grodzins:

> The federal system is not accurately symbolized by a neat layer cake of three distinct and separate planes. A far more realistic symbol is that of the marble cake. Wherever you slice through it you reveal an inseparable mixture of differently colored ingredients. There is no neat horizontal stratification. Vertical and diagonal lines almost obliterate the horizontal ones, and in some places there are unexpected whirls and an imperceptible merging of colors, so that it is difficult to tell where one ends and the other begins. So it is with federal, state, and local responsibilities in the chaotic marble cake of American government.[9]

### Cooperation—and Tension

Is the American federal system essentially cooperative—or is it competitive? In fact, federalism can be seen both as a rivalry between the states and Washington and as a partnership. A system of 87,576 governments could not operate without a substantial measure of cooperation, but a great tension is built into the system as well.

In 1975, for example, New York City was in deep financial trouble; there was a real possibility that the city would default on its bonds. The administration of President Gerald R. Ford at first declined to help. The New York *Daily News* ran a page-one banner headline: "FORD TO CITY: DROP DEAD." Ford eventually relented, and Congress passed a bill providing billions in federal loan guarantees for the city. Ultimately, the federal government, and New York State, did not permit the nation's biggest metropolis to go broke, but the political struggle over aid to New York City was protracted and bitter.

There have been other dramatic examples of tension within the federal system. Several times in the 1950s and 1960s the president of the United States deployed armed federal troops in states experiencing civil disorders. In 1957 President Dwight D. Eisenhower sent troops into Little Rock, Arkansas, to enforce court-ordered integration of the previously all-white Central High School.

In the fall of 1962 two men were killed on the campus of the University of Mississippi at Oxford during rioting over the admission of James H. Meredith, a black stu-

**Federalism: It Doesn't Always Work**

BOOTHBAY HARBOR, MAINE (AP)—A seal that lay wounded on a beach for 14 hours because of a dispute between state and federal officials died early today. The animal, which had been shot in the stomach, died at the laboratory of the State Department of Sea and Shore Fisheries. State wardens said they couldn't aid the seal because a new federal law placed jurisdiction for marine mammals with the U.S. Marine Fisheries Service.

At the Newagen Inn, a resort near where the seal was beached . . . guests tried to get help, but failed. . . . Several of the guests placed a towel under the seal and then kept placing water on the towel to keep the seal moist. . . . The harbor seals killed in Maine this summer were probably shot by fishermen who complain that the seals tear holes in their nets.

—Adapted from the *Washington Post*

"A great tension is built into the system . . . ": federal troops on guard at Central High School in Little Rock, Arkansas, September 1957

© Bettmann/Corbis

dent. President John F. Kennedy deployed 16,000 federal troops in Mississippi to enroll Meredith and protect him as he attended classes. In June 1963 Governor George Wallace carried out a campaign pledge to "stand in the schoolhouse door" to try to prevent two black students from entering the University of Alabama. Wallace backed down after President Kennedy federalized the state's National Guard to enforce the order of a federal court.

In 1967, President Lyndon B. Johnson dispatched 4,700 federal paratroopers to quell racial disorders in Detroit; and in 1992, the first President Bush sent 4,500 troops and 1,000 federal law enforcement agents to Los Angeles after rioting broke out there. In 2005, four days after Hurricane Katrina had flooded New Orleans, President George W. Bush sent troops from the 82nd Airborne division to the city to help keep order and prevent looting. They were the vanguard of a total of 22,000 federal troops dispatched in response to the disaster.

Although presidents tend to use the rhetoric of cooperation when they talk about federal-state relations, there is clearly an underlying tension among competing levels of government. Sometimes the tensions arise from social issues, as in the armed confrontations over racial desegregation. Often, as in the case of the bailout of New York City, they are rooted in disagreements over how tax revenues should be shared or used.

Political and ideological tensions arise as well—between those who look to the federal government to solve major national social and economic problems, and those who tend to see the government in Washington as a threat to individual liberty and initiative and regard the states as a bulwark against expanding federal power.

## The Changing Federal Framework

The federal system has been viewed differently at various times. During much of the 19th century and until 1937, although the states and the national government cooperated in several areas—such as the construction of dams and the housing of prisoners—the concept of **dual federalism** prevailed. In this view, the federal government and the states were seen as competing power centers. During this era, the Supreme Court saw itself as an umpire between two competing power centers—the states and the federal government—each with its own responsibilities.

This orthodox view of the federal system prevailed until the New Deal of Franklin D. Roosevelt. During the 1930s the Roosevelt administration responded to the Great Depression with a series of laws establishing social-welfare and public works programs. In 1937 the Supreme Court began holding more of these programs constitutional. With the federal government thrust into a position of expanded power, a new view of federalism emerged, that of **cooperative federalism.** In this view, the various levels of government are seen as related parts of a single governmental system, characterized more by cooperation and shared functions than by conflict and competition. For example, the federal government provides most of the money to build major highways, but the program is administered by state and local governments. Some scholars have argued that, historically, the American federal system has always been characterized by such shared functions at the federal, state, and local levels.[10]

One student of the federal system, Michael D. Reagan, has suggested that it no longer makes sense to think of federalism "as a wall separating the national and state levels of government." Rather, he maintains, extensive federal financial aid to the states created "a nationally dominated system of shared power and shared functions."[11]

President Johnson used the term **creative federalism** to describe his own view of the relationship between Washington and the states. During his administration, Congress enacted Great Society legislation that further

*Making a Difference*

## THE SUPREME COURT RULES FOR BRENDA ROE

After Congress transferred the federal welfare program to the states in 1996, a woman who preferred to be known as "Brenda Roe," to preserve her privacy, moved her family from Oklahoma, where they had received $300 a month in welfare benefits, to California, where the family qualified for $600 a month.

But there was a catch: To discourage people from moving to California to receive higher benefits, the state had passed a law limiting benefits for new residents; for one year they could collect only the same amount they had received in their previous state.

Brenda Roe and other families in the same boat sued the state of California.

The case went all the way to the Supreme Court, where the justices heard arguments early in 1999. It was the first major high court test of the nation's welfare reform law.

In oral arguments, California said its program kept down costs and ensured that the state would not become a magnet for poor families. But Justice Ruth Bader Ginsburg suggested the policy violated a fundamental principle "that is the genius of the United States . . . that people can pick their states and states can't pick their people."

On May 17, 1999, the Supreme Court ruled in the case of *Saenz* v. *Roe.* It held, 7–2, that states may not limit welfare benefits for new residents, and it struck down the California law.

"Citizens of the United States, whether rich or poor, have the right to choose to be citizens of the state wherein they reside," Justice John Paul Stevens wrote for the Court. "The states, however, do not have any right to select their citizens."

The former Oklahoma woman who called herself Brenda Roe had, with the help of the U.S. Supreme Court, won her constitutional right to be treated like other citizens of the state of California. And her victory won those same equal rights for many other needy families struggling to make ends meet.

—Adapted from the *Washington Post,* January 14 and May 18, 1999

expanded the role of the federal government. President Nixon launched what he termed the **new federalism,** designed to return federal tax money to state and local governments.

In recent years yet another concept, that of **regulatory federalism,** has emerged as a new description of the changing pattern of federal-state relations. Under this concept, beginning in the 1960s, the federal government has set requirements for the states through federal laws and regulations dealing with the environment and a broad range of other concerns. The federal programs are then implemented by state and local governments. (The concept of regulatory federalism is discussed in greater detail later in this chapter.)

For example, the Clean Air Act of 1970 set federal air quality standards for the whole country and required states that wished to regulate air quality to draft plans to enforce the federal standards. To a lesser extent, similar requirements were contained in the 1990 amendments to the act.

1963: Alabama governor George C. Wallace tries to prevent two black students from entering the University of Alabama.

© UPI/Bettman/Corbis

1935: President Franklin D. Roosevelt signs the Social Security Act.

During the 1980s, President Reagan sought unsuccessfully to shift to the states welfare and other social programs costing billions of dollars. Political scientist Donald F. Kettl has contended that Reagan's promise to relax federal rules and return more power to state governments was in reality "a Trojan horse . . . to disguise budget cuts." Reagan, he concluded, left the federal system "even more entangled in regulation and the problems that accompany it."[12]

The relationship between Washington and the states became an intense political issue again during the Clinton administration after the Republicans came to power in Congress following the 1994 elections. The Republican-controlled Congress sought, wherever possible, to shift power away from Washington to the states.

In 1996, Congress passed and President Clinton signed a law that ended Aid to Families with Dependent Children (AFDC), the largest federal welfare program, which assisted poor families. The law turned the program over to the states and compelled states that receive federal funds to require recipients in state welfare programs to find work within two years. Under the law, the federal government provides block grants to help finance state welfare programs.

Because regulatory federalism resulted in federal laws that required states to meet certain standards, but often provided no money to help the states comply, many governors and other state and local officials complained that such "unfunded mandates" were placing them under severe financial strain. Laws imposing standards on the states, the governors argued, should be accompanied by the necessary funds.

One often-cited example of the problem is the city of Columbus, Ohio, which faced costs of $1 billion to comply with the Clean Water Act and the Safe Drinking Water Act. Health officials in Columbus estimated the federal laws would cost each household an additional $685 a year throughout the 1990s. New York City officials estimated that it would cost $1.3 billion to modify elevators in subways to accommodate disabled persons under federal law, again with no help from the federal government.

To try to remedy the problems created by federal requirements imposed on the states, Congress in 1995 passed, and President Clinton signed, the Unfunded Mandates Reform Act. The law required Congress normally to fund mandates placed on the states. The law,

© Jeff Greenberg/PhotoEdit

Smog in Houston: a target of regulatory federalism

however, applied only to new mandates and not to such past legislation as the Clean Air Act.

Controversy arose again during the administration of George W. Bush. This time, the battleground was education. When he ran for election in 2000, Bush promised he would insist on stringent performance standards for the nation's public schools. With his support, Congress in 2002 passed the No Child Left Behind Act, with the goal of insuring that all students were proficient in reading and math within a decade and a half. The bill expanded the role of the federal government in education by requiring states to give reading and math tests to students in the third to eighth grades. It also provided some federal funds for tutoring students in schools designated as "failing." But many states argued that the law's strict requirements for standardized tests would place unfair financial burdens on the states and would label schools as failing even if only a small group of students underperformed. What the administration hoped would become a showcase for its education policies became ensnared in the pitfalls of federalism. In 2005, Utah rejected the federal act; the state legislature passed a law giving Utah's education standards priority over the federal requirements.

Many of the changes over the decades in the patterns and language of federalism reflect the fact that the United States has to a great extent become a national society. People may demand more power for the states and localities, but they also often look to Washington to solve problems. Today, for example, most people expect the federal government—not their mayor or town council members—to deal with large-scale periodic economic difficulties, such as inflation and unemployment. But the need for solutions to major national problems has not resolved the larger question of how to make a federal system work. As one study viewed the problem:

> The basic dilemma . . . is how to achieve goals and objectives that are established by the national government, through the action of other governments, state and local, that are legally independent and politically may be hostile. Those state and local governments are subject to no federal discipline except through the granting or denial of federal aid. And that is not very useful, because to deny the funds is in effect to veto the national objective itself.[13]

## The Historical Basis of Federalism

### "A Middle Ground"

In April 1787, a month before the Constitutional Convention opened at Philadelphia, James Madison set forth his thoughts on the structure of a new government in a letter addressed to George Washington.

Madison argued that while the states could not each be completely independent, the creation of "one simple republic" would be "unattainable." Madison wrote: "I have sought for a middle ground which may at once support a due supremacy of the national authority, and not exclude the local authorities wherever they can be subordinately useful." [14]

Essentially, Madison had forecast the balanced structure that emerged from a compromise five months later.

President Bush praises his No Child Left Behind education program. Democrats criticized the law and many states complained that it was underfunded.

## No Child Left Behind?

SALT LAKE CITY, Feb. 20—It was 8 p.m., and Ken Meyer was smiling gamely from a gloomy high school stage at an audience of disgruntled teachers and parents to whom he had been introduced as "a bigwig from Washington," come to Utah to explain President Bush's centerpiece education law.

A former math teacher was at a microphone, arguing that it would cost $1 billion for the state to carry out the law's requirements, while the federal government gives Utah only about $100 million.

"That's like sending a child for $10 worth of groceries and giving him just $1 to buy them," the former teacher said.

"Let me correct that," Mr. Meyer interrupted wearily, wading in as if with a fire extinguisher, spraying official statistics on behalf of the Department of Education, where he is a deputy assistant secretary. "Believe me, I've traveled to 40 states to talk about this law, and I've done the math. It's very well funded."

As he campaigns for re-election, President Bush hopes to capitalize on the law, known as No Child Left Behind, as one of the pillars of his domestic agenda. But the Democratic presidential candidates have made it a frequent target of criticism and ridicule. . . .

More than a dozen . . . states have passed or introduced laws or resolutions challenging the federal law or commissioning studies of the costs of carrying it out.

Last month, the Republican-controlled Virginia House of Delegates passed a resolution, 98 to 1, urging Congress to exempt Virginia from the law. That vote came after Rod Paige, the education secretary, and other administration officials met with Virginia lawmakers, said James H. Dillard II, chairman of the House Education Committee.

"Six of us met with Paige," Mr. Dillard, a Republican, said. "He looked us in the eye and said, 'It's fully funded.' We looked him back in the eye and said, 'We don't think so.'"

"We got platitudes and stonewalls, but no corrective action," he said.

—From "Bush Education Officials Find New Law a Tough Sell," by Sam Dillon, from the *New York Times*, February 22, 2004. 

The bargain struck at Philadelphia in 1787 was a federal bargain. The Constitutional Convention created the concept of the American federal system, with its sharing of power by the states and the national government. The delegates to the convention agreed to give up some of the states' independence in order to achieve enough unity to create a nation. Yet America probably got a federal system of government because no stronger national government would have been acceptable to the framers or to the states.

There are a number of reasons why a stronger central government would have been unacceptable. First, public opinion in the states almost certainly would not have permitted adoption of a unitary form of government. Loyalty to the states was strong. The Articles of Confederation showed just about how far people had been willing to go in the direction of a central government prior to 1787—which was not very far. The diversity of the American people, regional interests, even the state of technology—transportation was slow and great distances separated the colonies—all militated against the establishment of a central government stronger than the one framed at Philadelphia. Finally, federalism was seen as an effective device for limiting national power by distributing authority between the states and the national government.

### A Tool for Nation Building

The collapse of European colonial empires since the Second World War confronted successful rebels in Africa and Asia with an urgent problem: how to organize their new nations. William H. Riker has suggested that large emerging nations face two alternatives: They can unite under a central government, in which case they have "merely exchanged one imperial master for a lesser one"; or they can join "in some kind of federation, which preserves at least the semblance of political self-control." He added, "In this sense, federalism is the main alternative to empire as a technique of aggregating large areas under one government."[15]

The framework of federalism in the United States first permitted a disunited people to find a basis for political union, and then allowed room for the development of a sense of national identity. As a result, "The United States of America" is not only the name of a country—to an extent, it is also a description of its formal governmental structure.

## The Constitutional Basis of Federalism

### Federal Powers: Enumerated, Implied, Inherent, and Concurrent

The Constitution established the framework for the American federal system. Certain **enumerated powers** are specifically granted to the three branches of the federal government under the Constitution. Congress, for example, has the power to coin money; the president is commander in chief of the armed forces.

In addition, the Supreme Court has held that the national government also has broad **implied powers** that flow from its enumerated powers and the "elastic clause" of the Constitution, which gives Congress power to make all laws "necessary and proper" to carry out its enumerated powers. For example, the right of the United States to establish a national banking system is an implied power flowing from its enumerated power to collect taxes and regulate commerce.[16]

The Supreme Court also has held that the national government has **inherent powers** that it may exercise simply because it exists as a government. One of the most important inherent powers is the right to conduct foreign relations. Because the United States does not exist in a vacuum, it must, as a practical matter, deal with other countries, even though the Constitution does not spell this out. The Court made clear in the *Curtiss-Wright* case that the "war power" of the U.S. government is an inherent power. It said, "The power to declare and wage war, to conclude peace, to make treaties, to maintain diplomatic relations with other sovereignties, if they had never been mentioned in the Constitution, would have vested in the federal government as necessary concomitants of nationality."[17]

Finally, the federal government and the states also have certain **concurrent powers,** which they exercise independently. The power to tax, for example, is enjoyed by both the federal and state governments. Of course, a state cannot exercise a power that belongs only to the federal government under the Constitution, nor can a state take actions that conflict with federal law.

These various powers are complex concepts. They developed slowly as the nation grew and found it necessary to adapt the Constitution to changing conditions.

## The Supreme Court as Umpire

The Supreme Court serves as an arbiter in questions of state versus national power. The federal system could not function efficiently without an umpire.

The Court's attitude has changed radically over the decades; sometimes the Court has supported states' rights, and sometimes it has supported expanded federal power. But in every period, the Court has served as a major arena in which important conflicts are settled within the federal framework.

***McCulloch* v. *Maryland*** The most important of these Supreme Court decisions was that of Chief Justice John Marshall in *McCulloch* v. *Maryland* in 1819. His ruling established the doctrine of implied powers and gave the federal government sanction to take giant steps beyond the literal language of the Constitution.

James W. McCulloch might otherwise not have gone down in American history. But as it happened he was cashier of the Baltimore branch of the National Bank of the United States, which had been established by Congress. The National Bank had failed to prevent a business panic and economic depression in 1819, and some of its branches were managed by what can only be termed crooks. As a result, several states, including Maryland, tried to force the banks out of their states. Maryland slapped an annual tax of $15,000 on the National Bank. McCulloch refused to pay, setting the stage for the great courtroom battle of the day. Daniel Webster argued for the bank, and Luther Martin, attorney general of Maryland, for his state.

The first question answered by Marshall in his opinion for a unanimous Court was the basic question of whether Congress had power to incorporate a bank. Marshall laid down a classic definition of national sovereignty and broad constitutional construction: "The government of the Union . . . is emphatically and truly a government of the people. In form and substance it

© AP/Wide World Photos

"Congress . . . has the power to coin money."

© Bettmann/Corbis

Chief Justice John Marshall: "Let the end be legitimate."

The American Past

## THE STORM OVER *MCCULLOCH V. MARYLAND*

Chief Justice John Marshall secured his place in history with his landmark decision in *McCulloch* v. *Maryland* in 1819. The unanimous ruling by the Supreme Court established the supremacy of the federal government over the states. At the time, however, Marshall was harshly attacked for his opinion:

> As soon as [Marshall's critics] recovered from their surprise and dismay, they opened fire from their heaviest batteries upon Marshall and the National Judiciary. The way was prepared for them by a preliminary bombardment in the *Weekly Register* of Hezekiah Niles.
>
> This periodical had now become the most widely read and influential publication in the country. . . . In the first issue of the *Register,* after Marshall's opinion was delivered, Niles began an attack upon it that was to spread all over the land. "A deadly blow has been struck at the sovereignty of the states, and from a quarter so far removed from the people as to be hardly accessible to public opinion," he wrote. . . . On March 30, [1819] Spencer Roane opened fire in . . . the *Enquirer*. . . . His first article is fair and moderate. . . . In his second article Roane grows vehement, even fiery, and finally exclaims that Virginia "never will employ force to support her doctrines till other measures have entirely failed." . . . No sooner had copies of the *Enquirer* . . . reached Kentucky than the Republicans of that State declared war on Marshall. . . . Marshall's principles, said the Kentucky correspondent, "must raise an alarm throughout our widely extended empire. . . . The people must rouse from the lap of Delilah and prepare to meet the Philistines. . . . No mind can compass the extent of the encroachments upon State and individual rights which may take place under the principles of this decision."
>
> —Albert J. Beveridge, *The Life of John Marshall*

emanates from them. Its powers are granted by them, and are to be exercised directly on them, and for their benefit."[18]

Marshall conceded that the Constitution divided sovereignty between the states and the national government but said that "the government of the Union, though limited in its powers, is supreme within its sphere of action." Although the power to charter a bank was not among the enumerated powers of Congress in the Constitution, he said, it could be inferred from the "necessary and proper" clause. In short, Congress had "implied powers." Even the Tenth Amendment, reserving certain powers to the states or the people, Marshall argued, did not prohibit the exercise of these implied powers.

"Let the end be legitimate," Marshall wrote, "let it be within the scope of the Constitution, and all means which are appropriate, which are plainly adapted to that end, which are not prohibited, but consist with the letter and spirit of the Constitution, are constitutional." Congress, Marshall said, had the right to legislate with a "vast mass of incidental powers which must be involved in the Constitution, if that instrument be not a splendid bauble."

On the second question of whether Maryland had the right to tax the National Bank, Marshall ruled against the state, for "the power to tax involves the power to destroy." No state, he said, possessed that right because this implied that the federal government depended on the will of the states. Marshall ruled the Maryland law unconstitutional.

Thus, at an early stage in the nation's history, Marshall established the key concepts of implied powers, broad construction of the Constitution, and national supremacy. More than 100 years would pass before these powers were exercised fully, but the decision laid the basis for the future growth of national power.

## The Division of Federal and State Power

Under the Tenth Amendment, "The powers not delegated to the United States by the Constitution, nor prohibited by it to the States, are reserved to the States respectively, or to the people."

At first glance, this amendment might seem to limit the federal government to powers specifically enumerated and "delegated" to the federal government by the Constitution. But in deciding *McCulloch* v. *Maryland,* Chief Justice Marshall emphasized that the Tenth Amendment (unlike the Articles of Confederation) does not use the word "expressly" before the word "delegated."

This omission was not accidental. In 1789, during the debate on the first 10 amendments, James Madison and others blocked the attempt of states' rights advocates to limit federal powers to those "expressly" delegated.[19] During the debate, Madison objected to insertion of the key word "because it was impossible to confine a Government to the exercise of express powers; there must necessarily be admitted powers by implication, unless the Constitution descended to recount every minutia."[20]

The Supreme Court that followed the Marshall Court took a much narrower view of the powers of the federal government. Under Roger B. Taney, who served as chief justice from 1836 to 1864, the Court invoked the Tenth Amendment to protect the powers of the states. And in 1871 the Supreme Court ruled that the amendment meant that the federal government could not tax the salaries of state officials, a decision the Court later overruled.[21]

For two decades after the First World War, the Court invoked the Tenth Amendment to invalidate a series of federal laws dealing with child labor and regulating industry and agriculture. And in 1935 the Court cited the amendment in declaring unconstitutional the National Industrial Recovery Act, a major piece of New Deal legislation designed to reduce unemployment.[22]

But in the watershed year of 1937, the Court swung around and upheld the Social Security program and the National Labor Relations Act as valid exercises of federal power.[23] And in 1941 it specifically rejected the argument that the Constitution in any way limited the power of the federal government to regulate interstate commerce. The decision upheld the Fair Labor Standards Act. Speaking for the Court, Chief Justice Harlan Fiske Stone called the Tenth Amendment "a truism that all is retained which has not been surrendered."[24]

Thus, more than 120 years after *McCulloch* v. *Maryland,* the Supreme Court swung back to John Marshall's view of the Constitution as an instrument that gave the federal government broad powers over the states and the nation. In the years that followed, however, the Supreme Court zig-zagged again. In 1976, the Court struck down a federal law extending federal minimum-wage and maximum-hour provisions to 3.4 million state and municipal workers.[25] But in 1983 the Court ruled that a federal law prohibiting age discrimination in employment protected Bill Crump, a supervisor for the Wyoming Game and Fish Department, who had been forced to retire at age 55.[26]

© AP/Wide World Photos

After the First World War the Supreme Court struck down laws dealing with child labor. Here, children toil as coal miners in Pennsylvania.

In 1985, the Supreme Court reversed its 1976 decision by holding, 5–4, that federal minimum-wage standards covered public transit workers.[27] The landmark case, *Garcia* v. *San Antonio Metropolitan Transit Authority,* confirmed the federal government's power to regulate the states.

A decade later, the pendulum swung in a completely opposite direction, when the Supreme Court sharply limited the power of the federal government to intervene in state and local law enforcement.[28] The decision restricted the power of Congress, established in the Constitution, to regulate interstate commerce. Congress, the Court ruled 5–4, had exceeded its authority when it passed a law making it a federal crime to carry a gun within 1,000 feet of a school.

The decision struck down the Gun-Free School Zones Act of 1990. Now the Court had begun to reverse the trend of its decisions supporting federal power that had begun in 1937. Beginning in the mid-1990s, the

## SCHOOLS AND GUNS: THE SUPREME COURT OVERRULES CONGRESS

WASHINGTON, Apr. 26—Following are excerpts from the Supreme Court's decision today in *United States* v. *Lopez,* declaring unconstitutional a Federal law banning the possession of guns near schools. Chief Justice William H. Rehnquist wrote the majority opinion:

> Under the theories that the Government presents in support of [the Gun-Free School Zones Act of 1990], it is difficult to perceive any limitation on federal power, even in areas such as criminal law enforcement or education where States historically have been sovereign. . . .
>
> For instance, if Congress can, pursuant to its Commerce Clause power, regulate activities that adversely affect the learning environment, then . . . it also can regulate the educational process directly. Congress could determine that a school's curriculum has a "significant" effect on the extent of classroom learning. As a result, Congress could mandate a Federal curriculum for local elementary and secondary schools. . . .
>
> We do not doubt that Congress has authority under the Commerce Clause to regulate numerous commercial activities that substantially affect interstate commerce and also affect the educational process. That authority, though broad, does not include the authority to regulate each and every aspect of local schools.

—From "Excerpts of Opinions on Gun Ban Near Schools," from the *New York Times,* April 27, 1995. Copyright © 1995 by The New York Times Co. Reprinted with permission.

Culver Pictures, Inc.

In 1935, the Supreme Court struck down the NRA, a New Deal agency created to combat unemployment.

Court, under Chief Justice William H. Rehnquist, handed down a series of decisions greatly strengthening states' rights against the power of the federal government.

In 1996, for example, the Supreme Court ruled that Congress could not require the states to negotiate over gambling casinos with American Indian tribes.[29] In rapid succession, the Court invalidated a key section of the Brady gun control law that had required local sheriffs to check the backgrounds of gun buyers;[30] declared states immune from lawsuits by their employees for violation of federal labor laws;[31] and, despite its earlier ruling for Bill Crump, the Wyoming game and fish supervisor, it held that states could not, after all, be sued by their employees under the federal age discrimination law.[32] And it struck down a key provision of the Violence against Women Act of 1994, holding that Congress had exceeded its powers under the Constitution when it passed that law.[33]

The trend continued in 2002 when the Supreme Court expanded state power by ruling that states did not have to answer private complaints before federal agencies.[34] The case arose when a cruise line complained to the Federal Maritime Commission that the port of Charleston, South Carolina, had denied a berth to one of its ships, the *Tropic Sea.* The Court's 5–4 ruling expanded the scope of the Eleventh Amendment to the Constitution, which bars private lawsuits against the states.

Many advocates of increasing the power of the states continue to rely on the Tenth Amendment as the constitutional foundation for their argument. In general, they see the Constitution as the result of a compact among the states. It may also be argued, however, that the national government represents the people, and that sovereignty rests not with the states but with "we the people," who created the Constitution and approved it.

© AP/Wide World Photos

The Supreme Court invalidated a federal law banning guns within 1,000 feet of a school.

© AP/Wide World Photos

Christy Brzonkala reported that she was raped by two football players at her college. The Supreme Court ruled she could not sue them in federal court.

**Restrictions on the States** The **supremacy clause** of the Constitution (Article VI, Paragraph 2) makes it clear that the Constitution, and the laws and treaties of the United States made under it, are "the supreme Law of the Land" and prevail over any conflicting state constitutions or laws.

In addition, the Constitution places many restrictions on the states: They are forbidden to make treaties, coin money, pass bills of attainder or ex post facto laws, impair contracts, grant titles of nobility, tax imports or exports, keep troops or warships in peacetime, engage in war (unless invaded), or make interstate compacts without congressional approval. Much of the Bill of Rights, as interpreted by the Supreme Court, and the Fourteenth and Fifteenth Amendments place additional restrictions on the states.

Local governments derive their powers from the states and are subject to the same constitutional restrictions as are the states. If a state cannot do something, neither can a locality, since "in a strictly legal sense . . . all local governments in the United States are creatures of their respective states."[35]

Although the Constitution is supreme, under the American federal system, it should be noted again, each level of government possesses certain powers to make decisions that other levels cannot.

**Federal Obligations to the States** The Constitution (in Article IV) defines the relations of the federal government to the states. For example, the United States must guarantee to every state "a republican form of government." In addition, the federal government must protect the states against invasion and against domestic violence on request of the governor or legislature. Presidents have on several occasions intervened in the states with force either at the invitation of, or over the objections of, the governor.

Congress may admit new states to the Union, but the Constitution does not spell out any ground rules for their admission. In practice, when a territory has desired statehood, it has applied to Congress, which has passed an "enabling act" allowing the people of the territory to frame a constitution. If Congress approved the constitution, it passed a joint resolution recognizing the new state. (If in the future Congress should admit another state, it could follow this procedure or could adopt a new one.) As the frontier expanded westward, Congress steadily admitted new states until 1912, when New Mexico and Arizona, the last contiguous continental territories, became states. The 48 states became 50 in 1959 with the admission of Alaska and Hawaii—the only states of the Union that do not border on another state.

**Interstate Relations** Article IV of the Constitution also requires the states to observe certain rules in their dealings with one another.

First, states are required to give "full faith and credit" to the laws, records, and court decisions of another state. In practice, this simply means, for example, that a judgment obtained in a state court in a civil (not a criminal) case must be recognized by the courts of another state. If, for example, a person in New York loses a lawsuit and moves to California to avoid paying the judgment, the courts there will enforce the New York decision.

Sometimes, however, states fail to meet their obligations to one another. For example, a couple legally married in one state might not be legally married in another. In the famed *Williams* v. *North Carolina* cases[36]—the dispute went up to the Supreme Court twice—a man and a woman left their respective spouses in North Car-

Hawaii celebrated statehood in 1959.

olina, went to Nevada, got six-week divorces, and married each other. When they returned home, the state of North Carolina successfully prosecuted them for bigamy, convictions that were upheld when the case reached the Supreme Court the second time.

The situation had at least improved somewhat since an earlier landmark case, *Haddock* v. *Haddock*.[37] In the words of one constitutional scholar: "The upshot [of that Supreme Court decision] was a situation in which a man and a woman, when both were in Connecticut, were divorced; when both were in New York, were married; and when the one was in Connecticut and the other in New York, the former was divorced and the latter married."[38]

Second, the Constitution provides that the citizens of each state are entitled to "all privileges and immunities" of citizens in other states. As interpreted by the Supreme Court, this hazy provision has come to mean, in principle, that one state may not discriminate against citizens of another. But in practice, states do discriminate against people who are not legal residents. For example, a state university often charges higher tuition fees to out-of-state students. For fishing and hunting licenses, nonresidents of a state must often pay much higher fees than residents pay.

Finally, the Constitution provides for the return of fugitives who flee across state lines to escape justice. A state may request the governor of another state to return fugitives, and normally the governor will comply with such a request. But in several instances in the past, northern governors refused to surrender blacks who had escaped from chain gangs or prisons in the South.

One famous example arose in the Scottsboro cases, which began in 1931 when nine black youths were pulled off a freight train in Alabama by a white mob and accused, on the basis of very flimsy evidence, of raping two young white women. There was considerable doubt that the crime had even been committed. In 1932, the Supreme Court reversed death sentences imposed on seven of the defendants, ruling that they had been denied adequate counsel,[39] but all drew long prison terms. Three years later, the Supreme Court again reversed the death sentences of two of the defendants because blacks had been excluded from the jury.[40] In 1948 one defendant, Haywood Patterson, escaped from an Alabama prison and fled north. He was later arrested in Detroit by the FBI, and the state of Alabama demanded his return. Governor G. Mennen Williams of Michigan refused to send him back to Alabama.*

***for more information about the Scottsboro cases, see: http://www.law.umkc.edu/faculty/projects/FTrials/scottsboro/SB_HRrep.html***

**Interstate Compacts** The Constitution permits the states to make agreements with one another with the approval of Congress. These interstate compacts were of minor importance until the 20th century, but the spread of metropolitan areas—and metropolitan problems—across state borders and the increasing complexity of modern life have brought new significance to the agreements.

The Port Authority of New York and New Jersey was created by an interstate compact between the two states and approved by Congress in 1921. The powerful and quasi-independent authority operates, among other

* Patterson was convicted in 1951 of stabbing a man in a barroom brawl, sent to prison for manslaughter, and died there soon afterward. The other Scottsboro prisoners were freed on parole by 1950. Clarence Norris, believed to be the last survivor of the nine original defendants, was finally pardoned by the state of Alabama in 1976.

The states set their own marriage rules. In 2004 California's supreme court invalidated almost 4,000 same-sex marriages that had been performed in San Francisco.

© UPI/Bettmann/Corbis

Alabama, 1933: The defendants in the controversial Scottsboro case received long prison terms.

things, John F. Kennedy International Airport and La Guardia Airport in New York and Newark Airport in New Jersey. It also controls and runs the bridges and tunnels leading into Manhattan, and the world's largest bus terminal, near Times Square. Air and water pollution, pest control, toll bridges, and transportation are matters on which states have entered into agreements with one another, with varying degrees of success. A state often enters into several interstate compacts that deal with these and other regional concerns.

## The Growth of Strong National Government

The late Senator Everett McKinley Dirksen of Illinois, a legislator noted for his Shakespearean delivery and dramatic flair, once predicted sadly that the way things were going, "The only people interested in state boundaries will be Rand McNally."[41]

This may be an exaggerated view of trends in the American federal system—especially in the light of the series of recent Supreme Court decisions favoring the states—but Dirksen's remark reflected the fact that, overall, the national government has gained increased power in relation to the states. The formal structure of American government has changed very little since 1787, but the balance of power within the system has changed markedly.

### The Rise of Big Government

A century ago, the federal government did not provide Social Security, medical insurance for millions of citizens, vast aid to public and private education, or billions of dollars in welfare payments to the states. Nor did it have independent regulatory agencies to watch over various segments of the economy.

As American society has grown more complex, as population has surged, the national government's managerial task has enlarged. People demand more services and government has grown bigger in the process. Seven cabinet departments—Housing and Urban Development, Transportation, Energy, Health and Human Services, Education, Veterans Affairs, and Homeland Security—have been created since 1965.

The power to tax and spend for the general welfare is a function of the national government that expanded enormously in the 20th century. The government's role in the regulation of interstate and foreign commerce has also increased.

Much of the growth of big government and of federal social-welfare programs took place under Democratic presidents, during the New Deal in the 1930s and during Lyndon Johnson's Great Society in the 1960s. Although conservatives attacked these programs as "handouts" that create dependence on government, the major programs were so well established that the two Republican presidents elected in the 1980s were not

A dinner party in Dallas . . .

. . . and a homeless family in California.

able to abolish them. President Reagan, for example, came into office in 1981 determined to make substantial cuts in federal spending in the field of social welfare. He had repeatedly pledged to do so in his campaign for the presidency.

And during the Reagan administration there were indeed billions of dollars of reductions in domestic spending—in social-welfare and food programs designed to assist the poor as well as in a broad range of other programs aimed at helping low-income families, including Medicaid, housing subsidies, and student loans. Together, these spending cuts came to be known popularly as "the Reagan revolution." But federal spending actually increased in many of the programs that the Reagan administration claimed it had cut. In most cases, the "cuts" were reductions in what might have been spent.

Nevertheless, the Reagan program did have a measurable impact on government spending and on the outputs of the political system. The budget cuts "landed heavily on the poor and near poor. Education and training, community development, welfare, nutrition, housing assistance and other antipoverty programs suffered most."[42]

And the rich got richer. According to one survey of incomes by the Congressional Budget Office, for the 2.5 million people in the top 1 percent in America, incomes rose by about 75 percent between 1980 and 1990, to an average of more than $500,000 a year.[43]

After the Republicans captured Congress in 1994 there were new attempts, led by House Speaker Newt Gingrich, to dismantle or modify social programs and to shift control over them to the states. That effort achieved a major goal in 1996, when Congress passed and President Clinton signed the legislation shifting the federal welfare program to the states.

These political struggles revolved around the basic question of how power should be shared or divided in the federal system. The role of the federal government, particularly in the field of social-welfare programs, will undoubtedly continue to be debated in America. Although a particular administration or Congress may reduce the share of the pie allocated to social programs, the pie itself—the federal budget—keeps growing. Even as the states take on more responsibilities, many Americans still tend to look to the national government to solve national problems.

### Big Government and Foreign Policy

The responsibility of the federal government for the conduct of foreign affairs has increased the size of the national government. In fiscal 2005, for example, the budget request for national defense was more than $423 billion, a substantial 18 percent of the total federal budget.[44] The State Department, the Central Intelligence Agency, the National Security Agency, the Department of Homeland Security, and related agencies have expanded along with the Pentagon.

With the collapse of the Soviet Union in 1991, the military threat to the United States diminished dramatically, but the U.S. defense budget remained high. Defense industries and military bases provided jobs for many Americans and enjoyed strong support in Congress, where members are sensitive to the concerns of their districts. Partly as a result, the so-called "peace dividend"—the funds allocated to national defense that might be spent on domestic needs because of the end of the Cold War—seemed elusive. And in the aftermath of the 9/11 terrorist attacks on America, the wars in Afghanistan and Iraq added many billions of dollars to federal spending for national defense.

## The Impact of Federalism on Government and Politics

America's government institutions and its political system developed within a framework of federalism, and they reflect that fact. Federalism has also placed its stamp

DOD/Woodfin Camp & Associates

"The defense budget remained high. . . ." An Air Force F-117 stealth fighter plane

on a broad range of informal activities in American society, including the operations of many private groups.

## Federalism and Government

The nature of representation in Congress reflects the impact of federalism. Each state, no matter how small, has two senators who represent the constituents of their state. Members of the House represent districts within the states, but they also constitute an informal delegation from their states. Senators and representatives, when elected, must reside in the states they represent. In the event of a deadlock in the electoral college, the House of Representatives votes by state to select the president, with each state having one vote.

Federalism also affects the court system. State and local courts exist side by side with federal courts in the United States and handle the vast majority of cases. But even the federal district courts and circuit courts are organized along geographic lines that take into account state boundaries. And, under the custom of "senatorial courtesy," before the president appoints a federal district or circuit court judge, the White House privately submits the name to the senators representing the home state of the nominee. If the state has a senator from the same party as the president, and that senator objects, the name is usually dropped.[45]

Many powerful interest groups are in a sense federations of state associations and groups. This is true, for example, of the American Medical Association, the American Bar Association, and to some extent the American Federation of Labor–Congress of Industrial Organizations (AFL-CIO).

## Federalism and American Politics

When Senator John Kerry of Massachusetts sought the Democratic presidential nomination in 2004, he came from behind in the Iowa caucuses in January, defeating Senator John Edwards of North Carolina, his closest rival, and former governor Howard Dean of Vermont. A week later, Kerry went on to win the New Hampshire primary, and he was assured of the nomination when he won nine of 10 states on "Super Tuesday" in March.

Today, as a rule, the victory of a national political candidate is achieved long before it is ratified by the delegates in a noisy convention hall in the heat of July or August. Often, the candidate's eventual triumph gains its first momentum in the snows of New Hampshire in January or February. And other key primary states also may play an important role.

As the primary contests illustrate dramatically, federalism affects party politics in the United States. National political parties are organized along federal lines. The United States has no national party system such as that in Britain, for example. Rather, a federation of 50 state parties is precariously held together by a national committee between presidential nominating conventions.

The governorships in the 50 states are political prizes. As a result, 50 centers of political power in the states compete with the locus of national power in Washington.

***for more information about the National Governors Association, see: http://www.nga.org***

To a party out of power nationally, the existence of state political machinery takes on special importance.

© 2004 AP/Wide World Photos

"Key states . . . may play an important role." John Kerry's victory in the Iowa caucuses helped him win the Democratic presidential nomination in 2004.

State governors meeting in Washington in 2004. Often a strong governor emerges as a presidential contender.

By building up state parties and demonstrating leadership ability on the state level, the "out party" may consolidate its position and prepare for the next national election. Often a strong governor or a former governor will emerge as a contender for the party's presidential nomination.

Although state political parties constitute basic political units in the United States, state political systems vary greatly. In some states, such as New York, there is lively competition between Democrats and Republicans. Other states have often been dominated by one party. The makeup of the electorate in the states may differ from that of the nation as a whole. For example, proportionately, there are fewer Democrats in Kansas and Nebraska than in the national electorate.

State governments also vary in what they do and in the quality of their performance. How good are the schools in a state? Does the state have effective programs for health services, prisons, welfare, law enforcement, and pollution control? As anyone who has driven across America knows, some states just look (and are) wealthier; they have better state roads, for example. Some have adopted innovative social programs that have led the way for other states and the federal government.

**Policy Outcomes in the States** Inasmuch as state governments do vary in quality, does the nature of a political system in a state affect the types of public policies adopted in the state? In other words, does the politics of a state make a difference in the lives of the people of that state?

Political scientists have done a good deal of research on this question, and their answers have varied. One analysis suggested that states with active two-party com-

## Toga! Toga! From Animal House to the Statehouse

WASHINGTON, July 25—In a scene straight out of *Animal House,* the Massachusetts House of Representatives mixed the low art of late-night partying with the serious business of writing the government's budget for the coming year. They guzzled beer and snoozed in back offices. They chanted "Toga! Toga!" on the House floor, according to witnesses, while staffers took turns voting in the place of members missing from the chamber.

Amid the rowdiness that closed out this year's annual budget deliberations, the House quietly tucked into a spending bill language that would gut an ethics law enacted years earlier.

Such frat-house antics might not be typical in the gilded chambers of America's state legislatures, but attempts to weaken ethics laws that govern the conduct of legislators are becoming commonplace. In recent years, lawmakers in at least a dozen states have dismantled the strongest provisions of ethics laws or prevented passage of new, tougher ones. They have stranded ethics-related bills in committees, driven truck-size loopholes through disclosure laws already on the books, and chipped away at the power of watchdog agencies.

The result: The measures for holding some state lawmakers accountable are eroding at a time when the influence of legislatures is growing.

—Robert Moore, *The Public I, An Investigative Report of the Center for Public Integrity,* 1999 petition were more likely to enact broad social-welfare programs because both parties would compete for the votes of a state's "have-nots."[46]

Later studies found that socioeconomic factors (whether a state was rich or poor in per capita income), rather than political factors, seemed to account for most of the differences in state welfare expenditures and for differences in spending, taxing, and services among the states.[47] But another study concluded that if taxing and spending in a state were measured in terms of their redistributive impact—who gets what and who pays for it—then the politics of the state was considerably more important than its economics. Lower socioeconomic groups did fare better, for example, in states with certain political characteristics, such as higher levels of political participation.[48] Additional studies have suggested that other variables, besides politics and economics, may affect the policies of a state government. Religion, demographic factors, and in particular the actions of bureaucrats and the organization of a state government's bureaucracy may all play important roles.[49]

The fact that America has a federal system directly affects people's lives because the quality of the services provided by the states in which people live varies greatly. Not only the structure and performance of government but the whole political process is federalized.

© Larry Downing/Reuters/Landov

## Federalism Today

*The Budget of the United States Government, Fiscal Year 2007* is a 2,000-page, green-covered volume $4\frac{1}{2}$ inches thick and bigger than a telephone book. To the nonexpert, it seems a bewildering mass of statistics and gobbledygook, filled with phrases such as "object classification" and "unobligated balance expiring."

***for more information about the U.S. government budget, see: http://www.gpoaccess.gov/usbudget/index.html***

Buried in the budget's somewhat mysterious statistics are figures that add up to a substantial total of federal aid to state and local governments. For fiscal 2007, the amount was estimated at $459 billion.[50] The following figures show the sharp increase in federal aid to state and local governments since 1950:

1950: $2.3 billion
1960: $7.0 billion
1970: $24.1 billion
1980: $91.4 billion
1990: $135.3 billion
1995: $225.0 billion
2001: $317.2 billion
2005: $426.2 billion
2007 (est.): $459 billion

Any analysis of American government must take into account the huge sums of money flowing from people and corporations in the states to Washington in the form of taxes and back out again in the form of federal aid. It is here that federalism moves from the realm of theory into practical meaning in terms of dollars and cents.

The federal government channels money to states and local communities in three ways:

**Categorical grants** are earmarked for specific purposes only, such as Medicaid, pollution control, schools, or hospitals, for example.

**Block grants** are for general use in a broad area, such as community development.

**General purpose grants,** the smallest category, may be used by states and localities mostly as they wish.

By far the largest amount of federal aid comes in the form of categorical grants. Block grants rank next, and then general purpose aid. After the Republicans won control of Congress in 1994, they tried to shift money away from categorical grants and into block grants that would give the states substantially more power in deciding how to spend the money. One example was the 1996 law revamping the welfare system; it ended federal "entitlements" to poor families with children and instead

"It's too bad you can't get federal matching funds, whatever they are."

turned money over to the states in the form of block grants.

## Categorical Grants

In fiscal 2007, as in previous years, the great bulk of federal aid to states and local communities came in the form of categorical grants. A categorical grant is "money paid or furnished to state or local governments to be used for specific purposes"[51] in ways spelled out by law or administrative regulations. There are hundreds of such separate grant programs administered by various federal agencies. Not surprisingly, many state and local officials have complained that the maze of federal grants creates a burdensome amount of paperwork for them.

Typical categorical grants have been in the fields of education, pollution control, highways, conservation, and recreation. The Medicaid and Food Stamp programs are examples of two very large categorical grants.

The federal government distributes most aid under formulas that take into account the needs of the states; for example, grants for education are based on the number of low-income children, and grants for social services are based on population. To be eligible for federal aid, the state and local governments must sometimes meet matching requirements. That is, Washington requires the recipients to put up some of their own funds in order to get the federal money. When local governments and states match federal money, they sometimes do so according to a formula that takes into account their ability to pay. Under the formula, poor states pay less than rich states. For most programs, however, all states pay the same matching share.

It is in the administration of federal grants that the gears of national, state, and local governments mesh or collide. Federal fiscal aid is the primary means by which local, state, and federal governments interrelate. In dealing with such programs as education or welfare services, mayors, governors, and lesser officials communicate with one another and with administrators and legislators in Washington. Because of these aid programs, the lines of the federal system crisscross, linking various levels of government that must cope with common problems from pollution to poverty.

The result is both cooperation and conflict. For example, cities and states collaborate in a wide range of programs such as law enforcement and highway planning. But as a group, mayors tend to distrust state governments; they argue that the states are receiving too large a share of federal revenues at a time when the cities are desperate for funds.

## Block Grants

In addition to categorical grants, since the 1960s aid to the states and local communities has also flowed from Washington in the form of block grants. These grants are used "within a broad functional area largely at the recipient's discretion."[52] Among the major block grants typically included in the federal budget are programs for community development, social services, health care, employment and training, and education.

## Where the Money Goes

How was the estimated $459 billion total in federal aid to the states spent in fiscal 2007? Federal budget estimates show that almost all of it was allocated to eight major categories: health; income security; education, training, employment, and social services; transportation; community and regional renewal; natural resources and the environment; general government; and agriculture, in that order. (Figure 3-2 and Table 3-2 show where the money goes.)

**Fiscal Headaches in the Federal System** As state and local authorities have argued, state and local spending has increased at an even faster rate than federal spending. Yet the federal government collects 81 percent of the most important "growth" tax—the income tax, four times as much as states collect from income taxes.[53] These revenues from federal individual and corporate income taxes directly reflect economic growth, providing the federal government with increased tax receipts when the economy expands. By contrast, local governments rely mainly on real estate taxes, and state governments depend heavily on sales taxes; both of these sources of revenue tend to grow less rapidly than the economy as a whole. Although more states were taxing personal income by 2004, seven states still did not.*

* States with no state income tax in 2004 were Alaska, Florida, Nevada, South Dakota, Texas, Washington, and Wyoming. New Hampshire and Tennessee tax only interest and dividends.

FIGURE 3-2

**Federal Grants to State and Local Governments, 1980–2007**

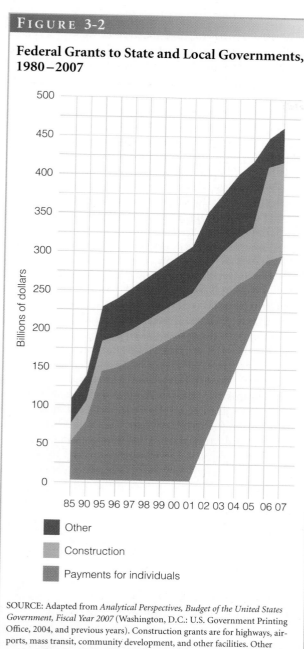

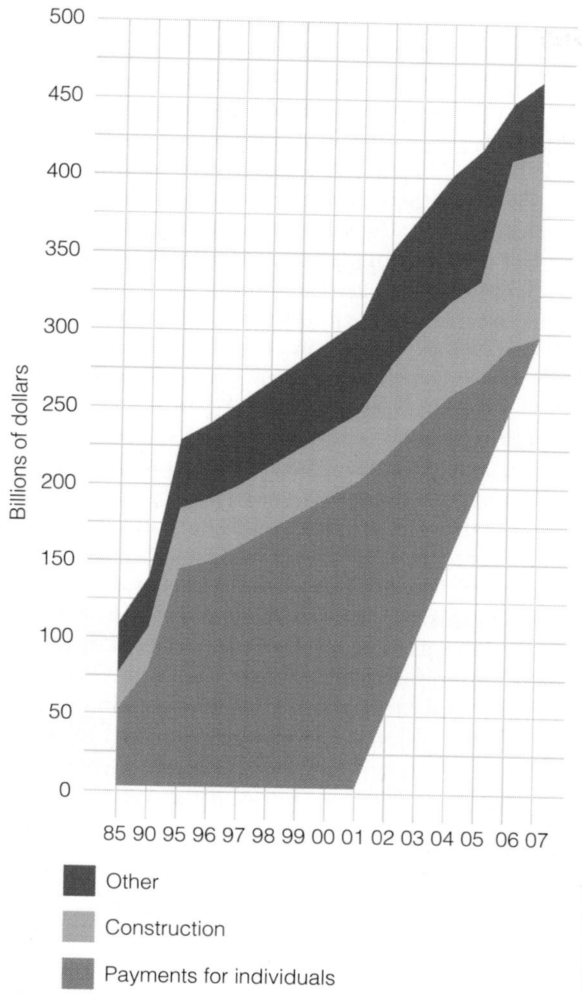


SOURCE: Adapted from *Analytical Perspectives, Budget of the United States Government, Fiscal Year 2007* (Washington, D.C.: U.S. Government Printing Office, 2004, and previous years). Construction grants are for highways, airports, mass transit, community development, and other facilities. Other grants are for education, training, employment, and social services. Figures for fiscal year 2007 are estimated.

## Regulatory Federalism

Beginning in the 1960s and continuing to the present, a series of federal laws have imposed strict standards on state and local governments. The Clean Water Act, for example, required cities to spend nearly $120 billion to build wastewater treatment plants. As discussed earlier in this chapter, the growth of such federal programs aimed at, or implemented by, state and local governments has been termed regulatory federalism.[54]

Legislation with this kind of impact on state and local governments includes the 1964 Civil Rights Act, the 1965 Highway Beautification Act, the 1970 Occupational Safety and Health Act, as well as many other laws dealing with clean air and water, endangered species, education, employment, and persons with disabilities.

Some of these laws apply directly to the states or local governments. The Equal Employment Opportunity Act of 1972, for example, bars job discrimination by states or localities on the basis of race, religion, sex, and national origin.

Other laws cut across all federal programs. The 1964 Civil Rights Act, for instance, prohibits discrimination under any program that receives federal money. Other laws "cross over" and impose rules in one area of government activity to influence policy in another; the 1995 law withholding federal highway funds for states that fail to impose "zero tolerance" alcohol standards for younger drivers is one such example. And finally, some laws, such as the Clean Air Act of 1970 and its later amendments, set standards for the states.

Many of these federal laws were passed to meet national goals, such as providing cleaner air and water. And often, those goals were supported by states and communities. But the complex federal requirements contained in these laws, and the extensive paperwork that goes with them, have given rise to intergovernmental tensions and to a continuing debate over the nature of regulatory federalism.

# THE FUTURE OF FEDERALISM

Clearly, the shape of relations among Washington, the statehouses, and city halls has changed considerably over time and continues to be characterized by both conflict and cooperation. But new ideas have been introduced into the mix. The state of Minnesota, for example, has dramatically modified state and local fiscal relations. Minnesota revamped its system of school aid to ensure equal funds for students throughout the state, regardless of the wealth of the school districts where they lived.

By the mid-1990s two-thirds of the states and the District of Columbia had adopted a "circuit breaker" system of property tax relief for low-income homeowners and for the aged. People in these categories, below certain income ceilings, were guaranteed property tax reductions.

The vast problems of metropolitan areas provide one of the greatest challenges to the American federal system. Some efforts have been made at new approaches. For example, increasing attention has been paid to solving problems on a metropolitan areawide basis. Many communities, especially in urban areas, have ignored traditional political jurisdictional lines to pool their efforts in attacking common problems (such as pollution) that respect no political boundaries, and in planning to take advantage of federal grants. Some federal legislation

## TABLE 3-2

**Where the Money Goes: Federal Grants to State and Local Governments, by Function, 2007 (in billions of dollars)**

| Percent | Category | Total | Major Items |
|---|---|---|---|
| 47.2 | Health | $216.5 | Medical assistance |
| 20.7 | Income security | 95.0 | Unemployment compensation, retirement, and welfare-to-work |
| 12.6 | Education, training, employment, and social services | 57.9 | Aid to elementary and secondary schools, job training, and foster care |
| 11.2 | Transportation | 51.5 | Highways |
| 4.7 | Community and regional renewal | 21.8 | Housing and urban development |
| 1.3 | Natural resources and environment | 5.9 | Construction of sewage treatment plants |
| 0.9 | General government | 4.1 | Collection of taxes |
| 0.2 | Agriculture | 0.7 | Crop insurance; animal and plant health programs |
| 0.2 | Other | 0.9 | National defense, energy, veterans' benefits, and administration of justice |
| Total 100 | | $459.0 | |

SOURCE: Adapted from *Analytical Perspectives, Budget of the United States Government, Fiscal Year 2007* (Washington, D.C: U.S. Government Printing Office, 2006), p. 108. Figures and percentages are estimated and rounded.

has been designed to assist and encourage areawide solutions to urban problems.

Yet serious dislocations and new problems of regulatory federalism continue to plague the federal system. Many critics of the federal structure question whether states are willing or able to meet their responsibilities. By contrast, defenders of the states have noted that most of the successful programs of the New Deal "had been anticipated, by experiment and practice, on the state level or by private institutions."[55]

In the 1990s, when the pendulum swung against such programs, the states were once again ahead of Congress. In 1995, as Congress and the president deadlocked over welfare reform, many states, including Wisconsin, California, and Michigan, were already testing new programs that required most welfare recipients to work or that limited the length of time that benefits were paid. In 1996, President Clinton endorsed the Wisconsin plan. Soon after, he signed the law turning over the largest federal welfare program to the states.

The booming economy of the 1990s was dramatically reflected in the states, virtually all of which were en-

Environmental Protection Agency workers measuring toxic waste in Denver

© AP/Wide World Photos

LaTanya Brown's life changed when she enrolled in a welfare-to-work program in Hampton, Virginia. She landed a job as a pharmacy technician.

joying strong financial health. By 1998, a majority of the states had cut a total of $7 billion in taxes, more than at any time in the past, despite a projected loss of tax revenues from the sale of goods over the Internet.[56] The economic expansion that had brought unprecedented prosperity to many Americans did not last indefinitely, however. By 2002, the nation's economic woes had placed the states in dire fiscal straits; from coast to coast, the states were forced to cut back on services, particularly in the fields of health care and education. By 2005, however, after four lean years, many states once again were enjoying large budget surpluses, the result of increased tax revenues and reduced spending. With the fiscal windfall, many states restored programs for education, health, transportation, and other areas.

There were substantial underlying tensions and conflicts in the federal system, even as the Supreme Court grappled with the proper balance of power between the states and the national government.

The problems that confront America in the 21st century continue to raise the fundamental question of whether a federal system born in compromise more than two centuries ago can adapt itself to the needs of a technological, urban society in an age of onrushing change.

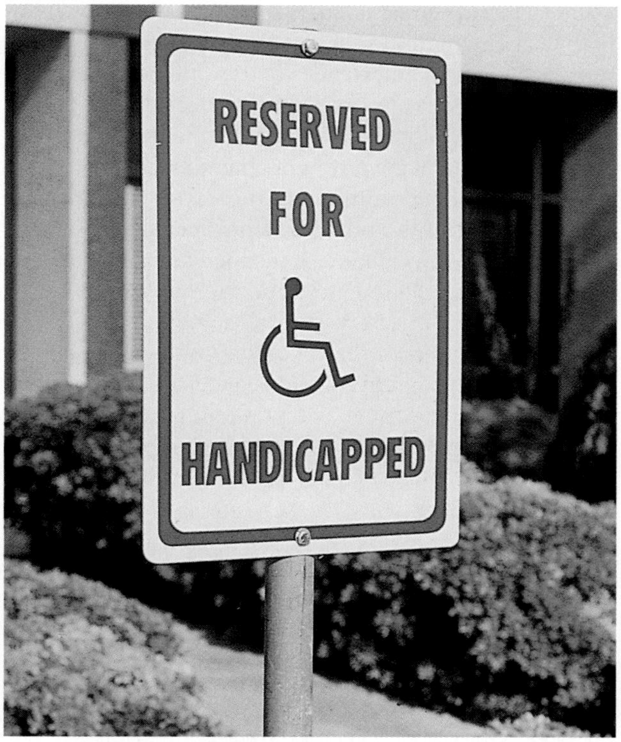


© Bob Daemmrich/Stock, Boston

## CHAPTER HIGHLIGHTS

- The United States has a federal system of government, in which power is constitutionally shared by a national government and 50 state governments.
- The terms "federalism" and "the federal system" are used interchangeably to describe this basic structure of government in the United States.
- The federal system has been viewed differently at various times. Until 1937 the concept of dual federalism prevailed—the federal government and the states were seen as competing power centers, with the Supreme Court as referee.
- Then, as the federal government's power expanded, the concept of cooperative federalism emerged, with the various levels of government seen as related parts of a single governmental system, characterized more by cooperation and shared functions than by conflict and competition.
- In recent years the concept of regulatory federal-

ism has emerged to describe how the federal government sets requirements for the states through federal laws and regulations.

- The Constitution established the framework for the American federal system. Certain enumerated powers are specifically granted to the three branches of the federal government under the Constitution.
- The Supreme Court has held that the national government also has broad implied powers that flow from its enumerated powers and the "elastic clause" of the Constitution, which gives Congress power to make all laws "necessary and proper" to carry out its enumerated powers.
- The Supreme Court also has held that the national government has inherent powers that it may exercise simply because it exists as a government.
- The federal government and the states also have certain concurrent powers, which they exercise independently.
- The supremacy clause of the Constitution (Article VI, Paragraph 2) makes it clear that the Constitution, and the laws and treaties of the United States made under it, are "the supreme Law of the Land" and prevail over any conflicting state constitutions or laws.
- The federal government channels money to states and local communities in three ways: categorical grants, block grants, and general purpose grants.

## KEY TERMS

federal system, p. 64
federalism, p. 64
unitary system of government, p. 64
dual federalism, p. 68
cooperative federalism, p. 68
creative federalism, p. 68
new federalism, p. 69
regulatory federalism, p. 69
enumerated powers, p. 72
implied powers, p. 73
inherent powers, p. 73
concurrent powers, p. 73
supremacy clause, p. 77
categorical grants, p. 83
block grants, p. 83
general purpose grants, p. 83

## SUGGESTED WEBSITES

**http://www.closeup.org/federal.htm**
*Close Up Foundation on Federalism*
A nonprofit, nonpartisan citizenship education organization that offers a time line of federalism and provides links to historical documents, outside analyses, government websites, and media resources.

**http://www.jamesmadison.org**
*The James Madison Institute*
A public policy research organization dedicated to the principles of federalism. The site offers access to its quarterly publication, *The Journal of the James Madison Institute*, the monthly newsletter "The Messenger," and excerpts from current books and studies.

**http://www.whitehouse.gov/omb**
*The Office of Management and Budget*
The Office of Management and Budget (OMB) controls the administration of the federal budget. OMB's site includes links to the current and previous budgets, OMB bulletins, legislative information, and other budget information.

**http://www.vote-smart.org/index.htm**
*Project Vote Smart*
A nonprofit, nonpartisan website that provides a database about thousands of elected officials and candidates for president, Congress, governor, state legislatures, and county and local offices. The site also includes public statements made by officials, a variety of information about the voting process, and links to government agencies, parties, and organizations. The information can also be accessed through the organization's toll-free hotline at 1-888-VOTE-SMART. The federalism section offers historical background on federalism and philosophical perspectives on this topic.

**http://www.thisnation.com/federalism.html**
*This Nation*
Provides resources and historical documents related to American government and politics and includes a link to a discussion of federalism.

## SUGGESTED READING

Beer, Samuel H. *To Make a Nation: The Rediscovery of American Federalism** (The Belknap Press of Harvard University Press, 1993). An illuminating study of the various theories of federalism that have been advocated in America. The author emphasizes the practical consequences those theories have had for American politics and government.

Conlan, Timothy. *From New Federalism to Devolution: Twenty-five Years of Intergovernmental Reform** (The Brookings Institution, 1998). An account of three waves of reform efforts, from 1969 to 1995, aimed at limiting the power of the national government and shifting many of its responsibilities to the states.

Derthick, Martha. *Keeping the Compound Republic: Essays on American Federalism** (The Brookings Institution, 2001). A leading scholar of federalism examines intergovernmental relations from a number of perspectives, including the roles of the states, Congress, and the Supreme Court, as well as the impact of the Progressive era and the New Deal. Policy areas examined include income support, tobacco, and social security. The author finds that the national government has become more dominant in the federal system, and that the 1960s was a crucial period for this centralizing trend.

Donahue, John. *Disunited States* (Basic Books, 1997). An examination of the push for the decentralization of governmental power, and the transferring of certain programs from the federal government to the states. The author argues that there are many functions that Washington can perform more effectively than state governments.

Elazar, Daniel J. *American Federalism: A View from the States,* 3rd edition (Harper & Row, 1984). A good general treatment of American federalism. The book emphasizes some of the problems and areas of controversy in contemporary intergovernmental relationships, and traces the historical roots of cooperation and shared functions among the various layers of government in the federal system.

Grodzins, Morton. *The American System** (Transaction Publishers, 1984). (Edited by Daniel J. Elazar.) A comprehensive analysis of American federalism by a leading authority on the subject.

Hovey, Harold A. *The Devolution Revolution: Can the States Afford Devolution?** (The Century Foundation, 1998). An analysis of the effort to shift programs away from the national government to the states, and the economic constraints which states face in meeting those new responsibilities.

Kincaid, John. *American Federalism: The Third Century* (The Annals of the American Academy of Political and Social Science, Vol. 509, May 1990). A valuable survey of trends in the American federal system. Stresses the complicated relationships among the national government, state governments, and local governments in the United States.

Noonan, John T., Jr. *Narrowing the Nation's Power: The Supreme Court Sides with the States** (University of California Press, 2002). This book is a critical review of how the Supreme Court has reduced the power of Congress and has favored the states. The author discusses recent Supreme Court decisions that sought to limit congressional lawmaking by relying on the concept of sovereign immunity of the states and the Eleventh Amendment.

Peterson, Paul E. *The Price of Federalism** (The Brookings Institution, 1995). A thoughtful assessment of how the federal system actually worked in the United States in the 1990s. The author evaluates both the strengths and the weaknesses of contemporary American federalism.

Reagan, Michael D., and Sanzone, John G. *The New Federalism,* 2nd edition* (Oxford University Press, 1981). An excellent study of the pattern of federalism in the United States. The book questions traditional definitions of a federal system and examines the development of federal grants-in-aid, the limited ability of state governments to finance public services, and the dominant role of the federal government in the American federal system.

Riker, William H. *Federalism: Origin, Operation, Significance* (Little, Brown, 1964). An historical and comparative analysis of federalism. Riker examines with great clarity the conditions that give rise to federalism and maintain it. He is sharply critical of certain aspects of American federalism and argues that historically it permitted the oppression of blacks.

Walker, David B. *The Rebirth of Federalism,* 2nd edition* (CQ Press, 1999). A detailed analysis of the conflicting tendencies—some toward a state-centered system and some toward a nation-centered system—that could be found in the United States in the 1990s. The author proposes an "agenda for reform," which includes reallocating some programs and responsibilities among the different levels of government.

Wheare, K. C. *Federal Government,* 4th edition (Greenwood Press, 1980). (Originally published in 1963.) A perceptive comparative analysis of federal governmental systems. Based primarily on a comprehensive examination of the workings of federalism in Australia, Canada, Switzerland, and the United States.

Winston, Pamela. *Welfare Policymaking in the States: The Devil in Devolution** (Georgetown University Press, 2002). A careful analysis of the legislative politics surrounding the welfare reform act of 1996, which transformed the program from a federal entitlement to a block grant program providing more discretion to the state governments. The author examines the legislative process in Congress, as well as interest group influences and participation in welfare policymaking in several state legislatures.

Zimmerman, Joseph F. *Interstate Relations: The Neglected Dimension of Federalism** (Praeger, 1996). A useful examination of the evolving relationship between states, from preconstitutional trade disputes to their contemporary struggle against the centralization of power.

*Available in paperback edition.

Swimsuit
swimsuit calendar 2000
NEC
AGFA

# Chapter 4

# Civil Liberties and Citizenship

IN THE 21ST CENTURY, the Internet has brought enormous changes in the lives of millions of people. The growth of the global electronic network has meant that anyone with a computer or a handheld device can be connected to the world. A high school student in Colorado on a wireless laptop can access a database in London; a lobster boat captain in Maine can chat with a rancher in Australia.

The world suddenly has become a much smaller place. The Internet has brought a revolution in the way people acquire information, purchase goods and services online, invest, and communicate with one another through e-mail and chat rooms. But the enormous flow of data from satellites and across fiber-optic cables into people's homes has created problems that the framers of the Constitution could not have foreseen.

For the Internet is more than a vast electronic shopping mall; it is also a powerful medium of communication. The First Amendment to the Constitution provides for freedom of speech and freedom of the press. But many parents of young children and other citizens object to the constant barrage of unwanted e-mail spam and the many websites offering sexual content. Does Congress have a responsibility to regulate the Internet in order to bar pornographic material? If it did so, would that not violate the freedom of speech protected by the First Amendment? And who would define what is pornography and what is an acceptable expression of human sexuality?

Concerned parents and religious conservatives have argued that even if consenting adults have a right to transmit or view such material, children do not. They have expressed dismay at images of bondage, bestiality, and child molesting freely transmitted across the Internet.

In 1996, Congress passed a telecommunications law containing penalties of up to $250,000 for transmitting material "indecent to minors" over computer networks available to children. Civil liberties groups immediately challenged the law, the Communications Decency Act, as an unconstitutional infringement on free speech.

In 1997, the Supreme Court struck down the law, 7–2, as unconstitutional, declaring that it was too vague and would restrict information available to adults in the name of protecting children.[1] It was a landmark decision because for the first time, the Supreme Court had ruled that the free speech provision of the First Amendment applied to cyberspace. Justice John Paul Stevens, who wrote the majority opinion, noted that under the law a parent "who sent his 17-year-old college freshman information on birth control via e-mail" could land in jail.[2]

The debate over whether and how to regulate "cyberporn" brought into sharp focus the complex problem of how fundamental constitutional rights can be preserved when they collide with other societal values. A father who believes strongly in free speech may still object if his 8-year-old daughter turns on her computer and sees a woman having sex with a horse.

Similar demands to censor the Internet arose in 1999 after two students in Littleton, Colorado, Eric Harris and Dylan Klebold, shot and killed 12 classmates and a teacher, wounded more than 30 other people, and then took their own lives at Columbine High School. Harris had spewed hatred and violence on his website and discussed the pipe bombs he had built and exploded. Some critics blamed the Internet—and violence in television, movies, and computer games—for inspiring the killings. But others argued that censorship would violate the First Amendment.

Key Question In this chapter we will explore a key question: ***In the American democracy, how should the rights of the individual be balanced against those of society as a whole?***

It is a question that often confronts the Supreme Court as well as the other branches of the government. In deciding cases under the Bill of Rights, the Supreme Court frequently has the difficult task of attempting to balance competing constitutional principles. The issues are complex. For example, should freedom of the press and freedom of expression be absolute rights under the First Amendment? What if free speech conflicts with the rights of others? Should prayer be allowed in public schools? What does the law say now about government wiretapping and "bugging"? What are the legal rights of student demonstrators? Can police search your home or car without a warrant? Will the Constitution's Bill of Rights be of any help to you if you are arrested by state or local police? These are some of the additional questions to consider in this chapter.

## Individual Freedom and Society

**Civil liberties** are the fundamental rights of a free society that are protected by the Bill of Rights. The Supreme Court's decisions in the area of civil liberties and individual rights often illustrate the tension between liberty and order in a democracy. Freedom is not absolute, for as Supreme Court Justice Oliver Wendell Holmes, Jr., once said, "The right to swing my fist ends where the other man's nose begins." But the proper balance between the rights of an individual and the rights of society as a whole can never be resolved to everyone's satisfaction. The rights of the individual should not always be viewed as competing with those of the community; the fullest freedom of expression for the individual also may serve the interests of society as a whole.

The 19th-century British philosopher John Stuart Mill advanced the classic argument for diversity of opinion in his treatise *On Liberty:* "Though the silenced opinion be an error, it may, and very commonly does, contain a portion of truth; and since the general or prevailing opinion on any subject is rarely or never the whole truth, it is only by the collision of adverse opinions that the remainder of the truth has any chance of being supplied."[3] In American society, the Supreme Court is the mechanism called upon to resolve conflicts between liberty and order, between the rights of the individual and the rights of the many. In doing so, the Court operates within the framework of what James Monroe called that "polar star, and great support of American liberty," the Bill of Rights.

## The Bill of Rights

The first 10 amendments to the Constitution constitute the **Bill of Rights.**[4] These vital protections were omitted from the Constitution as drafted in 1787. (See Chapter 2.) The supporters of the Constitution, it will be recalled, promised to pass a Bill of Rights in part so that they might win the struggle over ratification.

Although the Bill of Rights is the fundamental charter of American liberties, it is the Supreme Court that ultimately decides how those rights shall be defined and applied. The Supreme Court does not operate in a vacuum. Its nine justices are human beings and actors in the drama of their time. As former chief justice Earl Warren once declared, "Our judges are not monks or scientists, but participants in the living stream of our national life."[5] Individual liberties may depend not only on what the Court says in particular cases but on what the political system will tolerate in any given era.

Although the Bill of Rights was passed to guard against abuses by the new *federal* government, the Supreme Court has ruled over the years, case by case, that virtually all the safeguards of the Bill of Rights apply as well to *state* and *local* governments and agencies.

Alpheus T. Mason, a leading constitutional scholar, observed that the fundamental rights of a free society

Police search a California home.

gained "no greater moral sanctity" by being written into the Constitution, "but individuals could thereafter look to courts for their protection. Rights formerly natural became civil."[6]

## Freedom of Speech

"Congress shall make no law respecting an establishment of religion, or prohibiting the free exercise thereof; or abridging the freedom of speech, or of the press; or the right of the people peaceably to assemble, and to petition the Government for a redress of grievances."

These 45 words are the **First Amendment** of the Constitution. Along with due process of law and other constitutional protections, these words set forth basic American freedoms. As Justice Benjamin N. Cardozo once wrote, freedom of thought and of speech is "the matrix, the indispensable condition, of nearly every other form of freedom."[7]

Yet the courts have frequently placed limits on

### LIBERTY AND JUSTICE FOR ALL?

"The way they say it, it's as if there is liberty and justice, but there isn't."

Twelve-year-old Mary Frain, sitting pensively on a wooden rocker in her Jamaica, Queens, home, gave this explanation yesterday as one of her reasons for objecting to the daily Pledge of Allegiance to the flag in school.

The crank calls and angry letters have almost disappeared from the life of the introverted seventh grader who, with a classmate, Susan Keller, won a federal court decision on Dec. 10 permitting students in city schools to remain in their seats during the flag-saluting ceremony. Because of the pressure, Susan Keller soon transferred to another school. But Mary still refuses to stand in the morning when most of the children in her honors class at Junior High School 217 at 85th Avenue and 148th Street stand to recite the pledge.

At home, following a quick lunch, the youngster discussed the impact of the court case on her life.

"Like when we walked along the halls, the kids used to call us commies. We had phone calls. One was obscene. Some just laughed or breathed when you picked it up. But it's dying down now. . . ." Mary persisted, she said, because of strong objections to the wording of the pledge.

"Liberty and justice for all?" she said. "That's not true . . . for the blacks and poor whites. The poor have to live in cold miserable places. And it's obvious that blacks are oppressed."

The girl would compromise her position if the pledge were rephrased to be spoken as a "goal." "Like if when you say it you're making a vow to make it liberty and justice for all," she explained.

—*New York Times,* January 31, 1970

## Don't Tinker with the Bill of Rights

Mitch McConnell, a Republican senator from Kentucky, is a strong conservative on most issues. But he opposed a proposed constitutional amendment prohibiting flag desecration. The Senate rejected the amendment in 1995. Senator McConnell had these comments on the proposal to change the Constitution:

> It is hard to believe that burning a flag can be considered "speech." But a majority of the [Supreme] court has found this despicable behavior to be "political expression," protected by the First Amendment. So, advocates of a new constitutional amendment banning flag-burning argue that it's the only way we can protect the flag and punish flag-burners.
>
> Those who burn the flag deserve our contempt, but they should not provoke us to tamper with the First Amendment. After all, among the values the American flag symbolizes is free speech, even those ideas with which we disagree. While we revere the flag for the values and history it represents, we cannot worship the flag as an end unto itself. And we cannot coerce people to respect the flag in the manner in which we know it deserves to be respected. . . .
>
> As conservatives, we should be skeptical of tinkering with the Bill of Rights and restricting freedom even in the cause of patriotism.

—Mitch McConnell,
*Washington Post*, December 5, 1995

speech. Several types of expression do not enjoy constitutional immunity from government regulation. These include fraudulent advertising, obscenity (which courts have had vast difficulty in defining), child pornography, libel, and, in some cases, street oratory. The Supreme Court, for example, has ruled that police can arrest sidewalk speakers if they might incite a riot.[8] Three decades before that decision, Supreme Court Justice Oliver Wendell Holmes, Jr., had established the classic **clear and present danger test** to define the point at which speech loses First Amendment protection:

> The most stringent protection of free speech would not protect a man in falsely shouting fire in a theater and causing a panic. . . . The question in every case is whether the words used are used in such circumstances and are of such a nature as to create a clear and present danger that they will bring about the substantive evils that Congress has a right to prevent.[9]

In reconciling the requirement of free speech with other rights, the Supreme Court often has tried to draw a line between "expression" and "action." In 1968, David P. O'Brien had argued that when he burned his draft card to protest the Vietnam War, his action was "symbolic speech" protected by the Constitution. But the Court rejected this argument, 7–1. Chief Justice Warren, in his majority opinion, declared: "We cannot accept the view that an apparently limitless variety of conduct can be labeled 'speech.'"[10]

On the other hand, the Supreme Court has ruled that neither the states nor Congress may prohibit the burning of an American flag, even though many people find that form of free expression deeply offensive. At the 1984 Republican National Convention in Dallas, a protester, Gregory Lee Johnson, doused an American flag with kerosene and set it on fire while dozens of demonstrators chanted, "America, the red, white and blue, we spit on you." He was convicted of violating the Texas flag desecration law, fined $2,000, and sentenced to one year in prison. When the case reached the Supreme Court, the justices ruled, 5–4, that the Texas law and all federal and state laws protecting the flag violated the right of freedom of speech contained in the First Amendment to the Constitution.[11]

Justice William J. Brennan, Jr., writing for the majority, said, "If there is a bedrock principle underlying the First Amendment, it is that the Government may not prohibit the expression of an idea simply because society finds the idea itself offensive or disagreeable. . . ."

The American Past

## THE BILL OF RIGHTS: PRO AND CON

In the political struggle over ratification of the Constitution, the Antifederalists argued that the document was incomplete without an enumeration of the rights of the people:

> People, and very wisely too, like to be express and explicit about their essential rights, and not to be forced to claim them on the precarious . . . tenure of inferences and general principles . . . we discern certain rights, as the freedom of the press, and the trial by jury, which the people of England and of America of course believe to be sacred, and essential to their political happiness. . . .
>
> Perhaps it would be better to enumerate the particular essential rights the people are entitled to. . . . Freedom of the press is a fundamental right, and ought not to be restrained by any taxes, duties, or in any manner whatever. Why should not the people, in adopting a federal constitution, declare this.
>
> —Richard Henry Lee, *Letters from the Federal Farmer*

The Federalists argued that the Constitution as drafted protected the rights of individuals, making a bill of rights unnecessary:

> It has been several times truly remarked that bills of rights are, in their origin, stipulations between kings and their subjects, abridgments of prerogative in favor of privilege, reservations of rights not surrendered to the prince. . . . They have no application to constitutions. . . .
>
> I go further, and affirm that bills of rights . . . are not only unnecessary in the proposed Constitution, but would even be dangerous. They would contain various exceptions to powers not granted; and, on this very account, would afford a colorable pretext to claim more than were granted. For why declare that things shall not be done which there is no power to do? Why, for instance, should it be said that the liberty of the press shall not be restrained, when no power is given by which restrictions may be imposed?
>
> —Alexander Hamilton, *The Federalist,* No. 84

Culver Pictures, Inc.

Justice Oliver Wendell Holmes, Jr.

© Bob Kusel/SIPA

Protesters burning the flag in Chicago

Across the land, outraged citizens attacked the court for defending flag burners. Congress enacted a federal law barring flag-burning. But the Supreme Court, again by a vote of 5–4, struck down the federal law.[12] In 2006, an attempt to pass a proposed constitutional amendment to allow Congress to ban flag-burning failed by one vote in the Senate. Supporters said the amendment was needed to protect what many Americans regarded as a symbol of the nation. Critics charged that the amendment's sponsors had forced a vote to create an election-year issue in the hope that it would benefit conservative congressional candidates.

In an earlier case involving the flag, the Supreme

Court invalidated a Massachusetts law under which Valarie Goguen had been arrested and sentenced to six months in jail for wearing an American flag patch on the seat of his blue jeans.[13]

And the Court has ruled that public employees cannot be fired for exercising their constitutional right of free speech. Ardith McPherson, a clerk-typist for the county in Houston, Texas, heard of the 1981 assassination attempt against President Reagan. McPherson, an African American, speculated to a friend that the president might have been shot by a black person angered by the administration's cuts in welfare and social programs. She added: "If they go for him again, I hope they get him." A supervisor overheard the remark and McPherson was fired, although she said the comment was not serious. Justice Thurgood Marshall, writing for the Court majority, ruled that the remark was "political speech" for which, under the Constitution, Ardith McPherson could not be fired.[14]

In 1991, the Supreme Court struck down a New York State law that was designed to prevent criminals from profiting from books or movies about their crimes. The Court ruled that the law violated the First Amendment. The case concerned Henry Hill, a Mafia figure whose story was told in the book *Wiseguy* and the movie *GoodFellas*.[15]

In 1987 the Supreme Court ruled that the First Amendment protects the right of individuals "verbally to oppose or challenge police action."[16] On the other hand, the Supreme Court has ruled, in effect, that some rock music is too loud. In 1989, it upheld a New York City noise-control ordinance governing rock concerts in Central Park.[17]

**The First Amendment, Hate Crime Laws, and Campus Speech** In 2003, the Supreme Court ruled 6–3 that states could ban cross-burnings that are designed to intimidate. Such actions, the Court ruled, do not enjoy the protection of the First Amendment. The case arose when Barry E. Black, an imperial wizard of the Ku Klux Klan, was convicted for burning a 30-foot cross at a Klan rally in rural Virginia. Historically, members of the Klan, their faces covered in hooded white robes, burned crosses to intimidate and instill fear in blacks, in the South and elsewhere. (While upholding the principle that states can ban cross-burning, the Court overturned Virginia's law, and Black's conviction, on other grounds.)[18]

In an earlier decision in 1992 the Court unanimously ruled unconstitutional a St. Paul, Minnesota, hate crime law that banned speech or actions aimed at people because of their race, religion, or gender.[19] The case arose when a 17-year-old white high school dropout was arrested for burning a cross on the lawn of a black couple. The Court said the city law violated the First Amendment because it prohibited only certain kinds of speech on a selective basis.

The Supreme Court decision in the Minnesota case

Ku Klux Klan members burn the cross at a KKK rally.

had a noticeable impact on college campuses, where, in some cases, administrators had established speech codes prohibiting students from making racist or sexist remarks. The codes were created because many minority students felt threatened by hateful expressions and derogatory remarks and actions by some of their fellow students.

"I was shocked, hurt, and angry," Kenya Welch, a black senior at Clemson University, in South Carolina, told a Senate committee in 1992, as she described events on campus—a blackface homecoming skit, white students wearing Ku Klux Klan sheets for Halloween, and a group of white men who called her "nigger."[20] William Schendel, a gay student at Indiana University, said he was jeered every night by students screaming "Faggot!"[21]

In the wake of the Supreme Court's decision in the Minnesota case, the University of Wisconsin and several other colleges repealed their speech codes, but controversy continued on campuses over ways to deal with inflammatory speech directed at ethnic or other groups.

In 2000, the Supreme Court unanimously ruled that students at state universities and public colleges could be required to pay "activity fees" that are used to support campus groups whose views the students oppose.[22] Scott Southworth, an undergraduate at the University of Wisconsin, had objected to the $331.50 annual fee used to fund college publications and student groups. A conservative Christian, Southworth in particular protested the use of his money for the Lesbian, Gay, Bisexual & Transgender Campus Center; he also objected to the use of his fee to support 17 other groups, including Amnesty International and the National Organization for Women.[23] The university responded that students could not avoid activity fees any more than they could refuse to pay tu-

## Comparing Governments

### CHINA CRACKS DOWN ON THE FALUN GONG

Many of the nations of the world do not permit political dissent. Their citizens do not have the protection of a written provision, similar to the First Amendment of the U.S. Constitution, that allows freedom of speech and expression. In China in 1999, for example, the authorities dealt harshly with a group whose millions of members were regarded as a threat to the government:

> BEIJING, Dec. 26—Three men and a woman accused of being top leaders of the Falun Gong spiritual movement outlawed by the Chinese government last summer were given prison sentences today ranging up to 18 years.
>
> The severe sentences, issued by a Beijing court after a one-day trial, and their prominent announcement on national television tonight were clearly intended to show the authorities' determination to crush Falun Gong. Two of the sentences, for 18 years in one case and 16 years in another, were harsher than any given to leaders of . . . any other democracy advocate [in China] in the last several years.
>
> Promising good health and spiritual salvation, the Falun Gong movement gained millions of enthusiastic followers since its founding in 1992. It was officially condemned and outlawed as an "evil cult" in July after it held unauthorized demonstrations, including one by 10,000 people who surrounded the communist leaders' compound in Beijing in April.
>
> That silent demonstration, and the evident appeal of Falun Gong across society and even among members of the Communist Party, seems to have touched a raw nerve in the secretive leadership. . . .
>
> A dynamic offshoot of Chinese gigong, which is said to harness invisible forces to promote health and well-being, Falun Gong has been popular among retirees and middle-aged women, who gathered in urban parks to practice its slow, meditative exercises. But the membership of officials and party members was a sign of the broad appeal that so frightened the national leadership.
>
> —*New York Times,* December 27, 1999

ition because some courses might be taught "whose content they disapprove."

**The First Amendment and Student Rights** The Supreme Court has ruled that students do not lose their constitutional right of free expression simply because they are in school.

The case that brought about this decision arose during the Vietnam War, when the Court decided that a 13-year-old Iowa girl, Mary Beth Tinker, could not be suspended from her junior high school for wearing a black armband to class in protest against the war. "In our system," the Court held, "state-operated schools may not be enclaves of totalitarianism. School officials do not possess absolute authority over their students."[24] In winning the fight for her constitutional rights, Mary Beth Tinker had made a much broader point for all students in America, for the Court concluded: "It can hardly be argued that either students or teachers shed their constitutional rights to freedom of speech or expression at the schoolhouse gate."

But the Supreme Court also has made it clear that student rights to free expression are not unlimited. In 1983, Matthew Fraser, a 17-year-old high school student near Tacoma, Washington, gave a speech on behalf of a candidate for the student government. In it, he described his friend as "a man who is firm—he's firm in his pants . . . his character is firm . . . a man who will go to the very end, even the climax, for each and every one of you." The school suspended Matthew Fraser for disruptive conduct. In 1986, the Supreme Court ruled in favor of the school officials, holding, 7–2, that students may be suspended for using "vulgar and offensive" language.[25]

And in 1988, in a major decision on student rights, the Supreme Court upheld, 5–3, the power of school administrators to censor a high school newspaper, student plays, and other activities when part of classwork.[26] The case arose when a high school principal in Missouri removed from the student newspaper articles on teenage pregnancy and the effect of divorce on children. Justice William Brennan, in a sharp dissent, argued that the First Amendment did not permit school officials to act as "thought police."[27]

Scott Southworth

*Making a Difference*

## THE POWER OF THE FIRST AMENDMENT

On March 10, 1999, George Dohrmann, a sports reporter for the *St. Paul Pioneer Press,* wrote a story that began: "At least 20 men's basketball players at the University of Minnesota had research papers, take-home exams or other course work done for them during a five-year period." The article said that four former players had confirmed that the class work was prepared for them.

The story capped three months of interviews and fact-gathering. It appeared in the *Pioneer Press* on the eve of the Golden Gophers' appearance in the 1999 NCAA men's basketball tournament. The timing caused tremors throughout Minnesota and beyond. Gov. Jesse Ventura called the newspaper "despicable," and hundreds of readers canceled their subscriptions.

The university launched its own investigation, which led to the exit of coach Clem Haskins and the resignation of men's athletic director Mark Dienhart. Among other sanctions, the university cut back on men's basketball scholarships, restricted recruitment efforts, and returned money earned from the team's participation in three previous NCAA championship tournaments.

A year later, on April 10, 2000, cheers and champagne filled the *St. Paul Pioneer Press* newsroom as the newspaper learned that George Dohrmann had won the Pulitzer Prize, journalism's most coveted award.

After the announcement, Dohrmann wiped away tears as he was surrounded by his colleagues in the sixth-floor newsroom in downtown St. Paul.

"I'm a big believer that if you cover the college sports beat, you also cover the police blotter and the courtrooms," said Dohrmann. "This was my first run as the lead guy on something like this. [The editors] never laughed at me, never told me to shut up. They just trusted me and were totally supportive."

Mark Yudof, president of the University of Minnesota, called the award "deserved" and said Dohrmann's work was "a piece of outstanding investigative journalism."

"I used to teach the First Amendment," President Yudof said. "The story," he added, vindicated "the . . . power of the First Amendment."

—Adapted from the *St. Paul Pioneer Press,* April 11, 2000

The right of students to read books in the school library has been supported by the Supreme Court.[28] Steven Pico, a student at a high school in Levittown, Long Island, a suburb of New York City, sued the Island Trees school district when nine books, including Desmond Morris's *The Naked Ape,* were removed from the library shelves after objections by some members of the community. Despite the Court's decision, however, censorship of books in public schools, sometimes under pressure from conservative or liberal groups, has continued.[29]

**Preferred Freedoms and the Balancing Test** Different philosophies, often identified with particular justices, have emerged as the Supreme Court has struggled with problems of freedom of expression.

For example, Justices Hugo Black and William O. Douglas established themselves as advocates of the **absolute position.** Black argued that "there are 'absolutes' in our Bill of Rights"[30] that cannot be diluted by judicial decisions. He maintained, for instance, that obscenity and libel are forms of speech and therefore cannot be constitutionally limited. But a majority of the Court took the position that the rights of the First Amendment must be "balanced" against the competing needs of the community to preserve order and to preserve the state. This position was championed by Justice Felix Frankfurter and others. The majority of the Supreme Court has thus adhered to the **balancing test,** the view that First Amendment protections must be weighed against the competing needs of the community to preserve order and other rights.

In performing this delicate balancing act, however, some members of the Court have argued that the basic freedoms should take precedence over other needs. Thus, Justice Harlan Fiske Stone argued that the Constitution had placed freedom of speech and religion "in a preferred position."[31]

Despite these mixed views, the Supreme Court, while reluctant to narrow the scope of basic liberties, has generally not hesitated to balance such freedoms against other constitutional requirements.

## Freedom of the Press

Closely tied to free speech, and protected as well by the First Amendment, is freedom of the press. However, the courts do not always rule in favor of the press, despite the First Amendment. For example, the Supreme Court has sometimes required journalists to reveal sources, and some reporters have gone to jail rather than to obey court orders to do so. The Supreme Court has permitted individuals to sue the press for libel, recognized the right of privacy, banned the publication of "obscene" material, supported the right of public schools to censor student newspapers, and upheld the power of the government to regulate radio and television. Again, the Supreme Court has balanced the First Amendment's language protecting freedom of the press against the competing interests of society. The role of the press in the American political system is explored in depth in Chapter 8.

## Nude Dancing: The Supreme Court Requires a Bare Minimum

In 1991, and again in 2000, the Supreme Court decided by a vote of 5–4 that states could ban nude dancing. The first case, *Barnes* v. *Glen Theatre,* had been brought by the owners of the Kitty Kat Lounge in South Bend, Indiana. Following are excerpts from the majority opinion.

By William H. Rehnquist, the chief justice of the United States:

> Indiana's requirement that the dancers wear at least pasties and a G-string is modest, and the bare minimum necessary to achieve the state's purpose.

And by Justice Antonin Scalia, concurring:

> The purpose of Indiana's nudity law would be violated, I think, if 60,000 fully consenting adults crowded into the Hoosierdome to display their genitals to one another, even if there were not an offended innocent in the crowd.

In the second case, the owner of Kandyland, an adult establishment in Erie, Pennsylvania, filed suit against a city ordinance barring nude dancing. Justice Sandra Day O'Connor delivered the opinion of the Court:

> The ordinance prohibiting public nudity is aimed at combating crime and other negative secondary effects caused by the presence of adult entertainment establishments like Kandyland and not at suppressing the erotic message conveyed by this type of nude dancing. . . . The city council members, familiar with commercial downtown Erie, are the individuals who would likely have had first-hand knowledge of what took place at and around nude dancing establishments in Erie. . . .
>
> Even if Erie's public nudity ban has some minimal effect on the erotic message by muting that portion of the expression that occurs when the last stitch is dropped, the dancers at Kandyland and other such establishments are free to perform wearing pasties and G-strings.

—*Barnes* v. *Glen Theatre* (1991) and *City of Erie* v. *Pap's A.M.* (2000)

## Obscenity

Today, the Internet has thousands of websites devoted to pornography, showing endless varieties of sexual activity, in color. Most large American cities and many smaller communities have X-rated movie houses. Explicit videotapes can be rented or purchased for home viewing, and many hotels offer guests similar fare on pay-TV channels. In books, magazines, and films and on television, human sexuality is described and depicted in graphic terms.

All this seems a far cry from an earlier time, when the books of Edgar Rice Burroughs were almost removed from an elementary school library in Downey, California, because of persistent reports that Tarzan and Jane were unmarried. (When it was established that the jungle king and his mate were in fact husband and wife, the books were left on the shelves.)

Changing standards of public morality have resulted in freer acceptance of sex in art, literature, and motion pictures by some—but certainly not all—segments of the public. And in 1957 in the *Roth* case the Supreme Court held for the first time that "obscenity is not within the area of constitutionally protected speech or press."[32] Justice William J. Brennan, Jr., ruled for the Court that material that is "utterly without redeeming social importance" is not protected by the Constitution. Brennan went on to give his definition of obscene matter: "whether to the average person, applying contemporary community standards, the dominant theme of the material taken as a whole appeals to prurient interest."*

The Court, however, has had continued difficulty in defining obscenity. D. H. Lawrence, whose book *Lady Chatterley's Lover* was banned in the United States from 1928 until 1959, once said: "What is pornography to one man is the laughter of genius to another."[33]

Justice Potter Stewart, concurring in one Supreme Court decision, said he would not attempt to define hardcore pornography, "but I know it when I see it."[34]

The practical effect of these cases was to remove almost all restrictions on the content of books and movies as long as the slightest "social value" could be demonstrated. Then, in 1973, came the landmark case of *Miller* v. *California,* which set new standards for defining obscenity.[35] The case began when unsolicited mail arrived at a restaurant in Newport Beach, California. The envelope, the Court said, was "opened by the manager of the restaurant and his mother" and included an advertising brochure for a book titled *Sex Orgies Illustrated.*

In the *Miller* ruling, the Court set a new three-part test for judging works dealing with sexual conduct:

1. Whether the average person, "applying contemporary community standards," would find that the work, taken as a whole, "appeals to prurient interest."
2. Whether the work depicts "in a patently offensive way" sexual conduct prohibited by state law.
3. Whether the work as a whole "lacks serious literary, artistic, political, or scientific value."

**Webster's New International Dictionary* defines "prurient" as "itching, longing; uneasy with desire, or longing; or persons, having itching, morbid, or lascivious longings; or desire, curiosity, or propensity, lewd."

"No one could claim that Judge Walker doesn't approach these obscenity hearings with an open mind."



The Court seemed to rule, in effect, that local communities should be permitted to set their own standards. Chief Justice Warren E. Burger wrote: "It is neither realistic nor constitutionally sound to read the First Amendment as requiring that the people of Maine or Mississippi accept public depiction of conduct found tolerable in Las Vegas or New York City."[36] But in a series of subsequent decisions, the Supreme Court made it clear that there were limits to the right of communities to ban material as obscene.[37] The Court held that local juries did not have "unbridled discretion" under the *Miller* test to declare what was obscene.[38]

But the Supreme Court has also ruled that the First Amendment does not protect nude dancing; it decided in 1991 that states may prohibit such entertainment. The case had been brought by the owners of the Kitty Kat Lounge, an adult club in South Bend, Indiana, featuring live performances.[39]

Again in 2000, the Court reaffirmed that states and local communities may ban nude dancing and require dancers to wear "pasties and G-strings."[40] It upheld an Erie, Pennsylvania, ordinance that had been challenged by the owner of an establishment called Kandyland.

However, the Court struck down an attempt by Congress to ban the "dial-a-porn" industry, ruling that a part of a law barring "indecent" speech on the telephone was unconstitutional.[41] On the other hand, the Court upheld the conviction of William Hamling, who had published an illustrated version of the report of the President's Commission on Obscenity and Pornography.[42]

In 1982 the Supreme Court held that child pornography is not a category of speech protected by the Constitution. It ruled that works visually depicting sexual conduct by children could be banned by state law.[43] But in 2002, the Court overturned a federal law that made it a crime to create, distribute, or possess "virtual" child pornography that used computer-generated images rather than real children.[44] A year later, however, the Court upheld the Children's Internet Protection Act, which required libraries receiving federal money for Internet services to install software to prevent children and other patrons from viewing obscene or pornographic websites.[45]

In 1998 Congress passed yet another law, the Child Online Protection Act (COPA), that attempted to shield minors from Internet pornography. But the law was blocked by a legal challenge, and in 2004 the Supreme Court, ruling that filters might work better than the $50,000 fines the law provided, sent the case back to the lower courts for a trial on its constitutionality.[46] One study noted that the law, which applied only to websites in the United States, would hardly solve the problem; it found, for example, that 3 million adult sites originated from Niue, a Pacific island nation with a population of 2,100.[47]

The Court upheld a law passed by Congress allowing the National Endowment for the Arts to consider "general standards of decency and values of the American public" in giving taxpayer money to the arts.[48] Four performance artists, including Karen Finley, who was noted for smearing her nude body with chocolate, had challenged the law.

As these cases illustrate, the Supreme Court has swung back and forth over the years as it has tried to define and balance "obscenity" with the constitutional right of free expression.

***for more information about the National Endowment for the Arts, see: http://arts.endow.gov***

## Privacy

Although not specifically provided for in the Constitution, the "right" to privacy has been recognized to a considerable extent by the courts. Justice Louis Brandeis

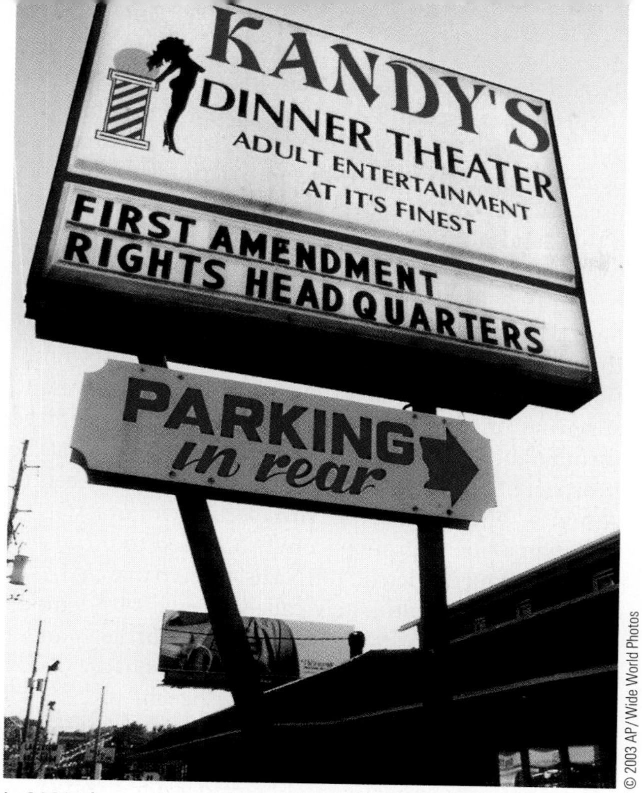



In 2000, the Supreme Court held that states and communities may ban nude dancing and require performers to wear "pasties and G-strings." A local ban had been challenged by Kandyland's owner; later, the club was sold and changed its name to Kandy's.

wrote that the makers of the Constitution sought to give Americans "the right to be let alone . . . the right most valued by civilized men."[49]

Today that right has been defined and protected by a series of Supreme Court decisions and by legislation. Nevertheless, in the age of the Internet, computerized data banks, and sophisticated surveillance techniques, the right of individuals to be free of intrusion into their privacy remains a subject of continuing concern and conflict. The government, corporations, credit firms, the press, insurance companies, schools, banks, and other institutions have all, to some degree, been accused of infringing on privacy. Because visitors to websites can be tracked and may be asked to provide personal information, privacy on the Internet has become a volatile issue.

The concept of a right of privacy was first given expression by the Supreme Court in the 1965 case of *Griswold* v. *Connecticut.*[50] The head of the state's Planned Parenthood League, along with a physician who was a professor at Yale Medical School, prescribed contraceptives and provided birth control information to married couples. They were convicted and fined under a state law prohibiting the use of contraceptives. In *Griswold,* however, the Supreme Court ruled that guarantees in the Bill of Rights cast "penumbras," or shadows, that may encompass other rights not specifically mentioned. "Various guarantees create zones of privacy," the Court said. The police must be kept out of the bedroom, the Court added, citing "a right of privacy older than the Bill of Rights."

In other cases, the Supreme Court, in the past, at least, has reiterated the right to privacy in very clear language. In the controversial case of *Roe* v. *Wade,* for example, the justices ruled that the concept of privacy included the right to a legal abortion. "The Constitution does not explicitly mention any right of privacy," the Court declared. But "the Court has recognized that a right of personal privacy, or a guarantee of certain areas or zones of privacy, does exist under the Constitution."[51]

In yet another decision, the Court ruled that Robert Eli Stanley, a Georgia resident, had the right to watch pornographic movies in his own home.[52] The case arose when police with a warrant searched Stanley's home for evidence of bookmaking activity, found three reels of 8-millimeter film, and viewed them on a projector in Stanley's living room.

Performance artist Karen Finley

### Privacy: The Secret Zone

Generally speaking, the concept of a right to privacy attempts to draw a line between the individual and the collective, between self and society. It seeks to assure the individual a zone in which to be an individual, not a member of the community. In that zone he can think his own thoughts, have his own secrets, live his own life, reveal only what he wants to the outside world. The right of privacy, in short, establishes an area excluded from the collective life, not governed by the rules of collective living. It is based upon premises of individualism, that the society exists to promote the worth and the dignity of the individual. It is contrary to the theories of total commitment to the state, to society, or to any part thereof.

—Thomas I. Emerson,
*The System of Freedom of Expression*

What if the right of the press to report the news under the First Amendment conflicts with the individual's right to be left alone? Sometimes the Supreme Court has sided with the individual, sometimes with the press.

After a construction worker in West Virginia died when a bridge collapsed, a Cleveland newspaper referred to his family as "hillbillies." The Court upheld a $60,000 judgment against the paper for invasion of privacy.[53] But in a Georgia case, the Court ruled in favor of a television station that broadcast the name of a young woman who had been raped and killed by six teenage boys. The victim's father sued the station, but the Court said his privacy had not been invaded because the broadcaster had obtained his daughter's name from public court records.[54]

Congress has passed a series of laws relating to personal privacy. The Privacy Act of 1974 gives individuals a degree of control over government files maintained about them. The Fair Credit Reporting Act (1970) regulates credit agencies, department stores, and banks. And the Family Education Rights and Privacy Act (1974) gives parents and students who are 18 years old or older or in college the right to see school records and instructional materials.[55]

## Freedom of Assembly

In addition to protecting free speech, the First Amendment protects the right of the people "peaceably to assemble." The Supreme Court has held this right to be "equally fundamental" to the right of free speech and free press.[56] It ruled in 1897 that a city can require a permit for the "use of public grounds."[57] But a city, in requiring licenses for parades, demonstrations, and sound trucks, must do so in the interest of controlling traffic and regulating the use of public streets and parks; it cannot—in theory—exercise its licensing power to suppress free speech.[58] The legitimate responsibility of public officials and police to control traffic or prevent a demonstration from growing into a riot is sometimes used as a device to suppress free speech because there is a thin, and not always readily distinguishable, line between crowd control and thought control.

In 1977 the heavily Jewish suburb of Skokie, Illinois, passed three ordinances designed to prevent a march by the American Nazi Party, an anti-Semitic group. Emotions ran high in Skokie, the home of several thousand survivors of Hitler's Nazi regime. Jews who had lived through the Holocaust were understandably angry at the prospect of homegrown Nazis marching in the streets of America. The American Civil Liberties Union (ACLU), although a liberal group strongly opposed to the Nazis, went into court to defend the Nazis' right to march. Leaders of the march ultimately called off plans to demonstrate in Skokie. In 1978 the Supreme Court let stand a lower court ruling that Skokie's ordinances had violated the constitutional guarantees of free speech.[59]

***for more information about the ACLU, see:***
***http://www.aclu.org***

But in 1995 the Supreme Court ruled, 9–0, that private sponsors of Boston's St. Patrick's Day parade had a constitutional right to exclude marchers who identified themselves as gay and lesbian.[60] The Court said that a parade, even though it takes place in a public place, is a form of private expression. As a result, the Court held the sponsors could not be forced by state law to include marchers who carried an unwanted message.

In 1983 the Supreme Court permitted people to picket and to display flags and signs on the sidewalk outside the Supreme Court itself. The case was brought by two protesters who had been asked to leave when they picketed the Court.[61]

## Freedom of Religion

In 2000, Michael A. Newdow, an emergency room physician in Sacramento, California, and an avowed atheist, objected when his daughter was forced to watch and listen as her classmates in elementary school pledged allegiance to one nation "under God." He filed a lawsuit in federal court.

In 2002 a federal appeals court in San Francisco struck down the pledge, concluding that the religious content violated the separation of church and state required by the First Amendment. Although the ruling was stayed pending an appeal, it caused a national uproar. President George W. Bush announced that "America is a nation . . . that values our relationship with an Almighty." Almost all members of the Senate and the House gathered to recite the pledge. Poll data indicated that most Americans supported the reference to God in the pledge. The two words, "under God" had been added to the language by Congress in 1954.

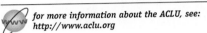

In 2004, the Supreme Court, by a vote of 8–0, overturned the lower court decision; as a result, the words "under God" remained in the pledge. The Court said that Newdow did not have legal standing to sue. Because the Court acted on procedural grounds, however, it left open the possibility that the constitutionality of the pledge might be challenged in the future.[62]

The controversy over the pledge of allegiance is only one example of the continuing conflict over religion and the meaning of the Constitution.

President Jefferson wrote in 1802 that the freedom of religion clause of the First Amendment was designed to build "a wall of separation between Church and State."[63] The wall still stands, but in several areas the Supreme Court has modified its contours.

Many of the American colonies were settled by groups seeking religious freedom but who were themselves intolerant of religious dissent. Gradually, however, religious tolerance increased. When the Bill of Rights was passed, its first words were: "Congress shall make no law respecting an establishment of religion, or prohibiting the free exercise thereof."

**The Free Exercise Clause** The **free exercise clause** of the First Amendment protects the right of individuals to worship or believe as they wish, or to hold no religious beliefs. It also means that people cannot be compelled by government to act contrary to their religious beliefs, unless religious conduct collides with valid laws. In that difficult area, the courts have had to try to resolve the conflict between the demands of religion and the demands of law.

For example, in a number of instances the Supreme Court has attempted to define the grounds that may be invoked by conscientious objectors to military service. Ever since the military draft began during the Civil War, the law has provided some form of exemption for those whose religious beliefs would not permit them to serve in the armed forces. In 1965 the Supreme Court ruled that a "sincere and meaningful" objection to war on religious grounds did not require a belief in a Supreme Being.[64]

Then, in June 1970, with the war in Vietnam still in progress, the Court extended this protection to people opposed to war for reasons of conscience. It ruled that Elliott Ashton Welsh II, a 29-year-old computer engineer from Los Angeles, could not be imprisoned for his refusal on ethical and moral grounds to serve in the armed forces. Welsh—and therefore other young Americans—the Court ruled, did not have to base his refusal on a belief in God. The government must exempt from military service, the Court declared, "all those whose consciences, spurred by deeply held moral, ethical, or religious beliefs, would give them no rest or peace if they allowed themselves to become part of an instrument of war."[65] The draft law, the Supreme Court added, did not require military service by "those who hold strong beliefs about our domestic and foreign affairs" and who objected to all wars[66] and not just to particular wars.[67]

April 2004: Hundreds of thousands of demonstrators assemble in Washington to support women's rights.

In a series of flag-salute cases, the Court initially ruled in 1940 that children of Jehovah's Witnesses could not be excused from saluting the American flag on religious grounds.[68] But three years later the Court reversed itself and decided in favor of Walter Barnett, also a member of the Jehovah's Witnesses, whose seven children had been expelled from West Virginia schools for refusing to salute the flag. Justice Robert H. Jackson, speaking for the Court, held that "the flag salute is a form of utterance" protected by the First Amendment. "If there is any fixed star in our constitutional constellation," Jackson said, "it is that no official, high or petty, can prescribe what shall be orthodox in politics, nationalism, religion or other matters of opinion."[69] Because the Court's decision rested on the free speech clause, it protects anyone who refuses to salute the flag for whatever reason.

Some religious practices have caused controversy. Although peyote, a variety of cactus containing the hallucinogenic drug mescaline, is a narcotic under California law, the California supreme court ruled that the state could not prohibit the religious use of the drug by the Navajo Indians.[70] In 1990, the U.S. Supreme Court upheld an Oregon law that banned the use of peyote in religious ceremonies.[71] Later, however, Oregon enacted a new law permitting the religious use of peyote. At the time of the Supreme Court's ruling, federal law and 24 states, many with large American Indian populations, did permit the sacramental use of peyote. In 2006, the Supreme Court, with John G. Roberts, the new Chief Justice, presiding, ruled unanimously that UDV, a small religious group in New Mexico, could continue to use hoasca hallucinogenic tea for religious purposes.[72] The tea, made from plants in the Amazon rainforest of Brazil, contains dimethyltryptamine, a mind-altering illegal drug. In his opinion for the Court, Roberts said that since the religious use of peyote was permitted, the government could not ban hoasca.

Not every religious practice is protected by the First

In 2004, the Supreme Court ruled that the phrase "under God" may remain in the pledge of allegiance.

Amendment, however. During the 19th century the Supreme Court outlawed polygamy.[73] Although George Reynolds proved that as a Mormon he was required to have more than one wife, the Supreme Court sustained his conviction. The Court ruled that religious conduct could not violate the law, adding, rather gruesomely: "Suppose one believed that human sacrifices were a necessary part of religious worship?"

The Supreme Court has, however, permitted animal sacrifice as part of a religion. In Florida, some 70,000 people practice Santería, an Afro-Cuban religion in which goats, chickens, sheep, pigeons, and turtles are killed. The city of Hialeah passed a law forbidding the practice. In 1993, the Supreme Court ruled unanimously that the ban was unconstitutional because it violated religious freedom.[74]

But the Supreme Court does not permit racial discrimination based on religious beliefs. It has denied tax-exempt status to schools that practice such discrimination.[75]

**The Establishment Clause** The **establishment clause** of the First Amendment means, in the words of Justice Hugo Black, that "neither a state nor the federal government can set up a church. Neither can pass laws that aid one religion, aid all religions, or prefer one religion over another."[76]

Despite the constitutional separation between church and state, religion has always been a significant factor in American life. Since 1865 U.S. coins have borne the motto "In God We Trust"; many presidential speeches end with a reference to the Almighty; public meetings often open with invocations and close with benedictions; and a chaplain opens the daily sessions of Congress.

In 1984 the Supreme Court narrowly upheld the right of cities to include the nativity scene as part of an official Christmas display.[77] In this and other cases, the Court has held that not every expression of religion in a public forum violates the First Amendment's establishment clause.

Yet hardly any subject generates more emotion than church-state relations. In 1962 the Supreme Court outlawed officially composed prayers in the public schools.[78] The initial school prayer case arose after the Board of Regents of New York State composed a "nondenominational" prayer that it recommended local school boards adopt.[79] The parents of 10 children in New Hyde Park, New York, objected and went to court. In ruling the prayer unconstitutional, Justice Hugo Black, speaking for the Court, declared that the First Amendment means "that in this country it is no part of the business of government to compose official prayers for any group of the American people to recite as part of a religious program carried on by government."[80] In 1963 the Court outlawed daily Bible reading and recitation of the Lord's Prayer in public schools.[81] These decisions by the Court brought down a tremendous storm of protest upon its marble pillars. Some school districts openly defied the rulings.

More controversy erupted in 2003 when Chief Justice Roy Moore of the Alabama supreme court refused to obey a federal court order to remove a two-and-a-half-ton monument inscribed with the Ten Commandments that he had placed in the state courthouse. Moore, defiant, was removed from office by a nine-member panel of his colleagues who said he had placed himself above the law. Two years later, the Supreme Court ruled that two Kentucky courthouses could not display copies of the Ten Commandments.[82] But the Court held that a statue inscribed with the Ten Commandments on the grounds of the Texas state capitol in Austin did not violate the Constitution.[83]

© Bill Gentile/SIPA

A Santería priest in Hialeah, Florida

A major constitutional argument over church-state relations centers on the question of whether, and to what extent, the government can aid church-related schools. Many students attend such schools. In 2004, for example, more than 2.5 million students, about 5 percent of the nation's 55 million schoolchildren, were enrolled in Roman Catholic schools.[84]

In 1947, in the celebrated *Everson* case, the Supreme Court ruled as constitutional a New Jersey law under which parents of both public and parochial students were reimbursed for the fares their children paid to get to school on public buses.[85] The payments, the Court held, did no more than "help parents get their children, regardless of their religion," safely to and from school.

In 1960 John F. Kennedy became the first Roman Catholic to be elected president. Politically, it would have been awkward for him to propose federal aid to church-supported schools, and he did not do so. In 1965, however, during President Lyndon Johnson's administration, Congress passed the first general bill authorizing federal aid to elementary and secondary schools. It provided aid, through the states, to children in both public and church-supported schools. By emphasizing assistance to children in low-income areas, it avoided much of the religious controversy that had surrounded previous attempts to pass an education bill.

More than two-thirds of the states enacted various kinds of aid to parochial schools, ranging from free lunches to driver education programs. In 1971, however, the Supreme Court declared unconstitutional certain state programs of direct aid to parochial schools.[86] But in 2000 the Court held that federal funds could be used to put computers and other "instructional equipment" in parochial school classrooms.[87]

And the Supreme Court has sometimes permitted religious-oriented extracurricular activities. In 1985, for example, Bridget Mergens, a senior at a high school in Omaha, Nebraska, was denied permission to organize a Christian Bible study group at the school. Mergens took her case to court. She contended that she had as much right to study the Bible before or after classes as to learn how to play chess or scuba dive, activities that other students enjoyed. The Supreme Court ruled, 8–1, for Mergens.[88]

But the Court has ruled that prayers may not be included in public school graduation ceremonies.[89] The Court also ruled that the constitutional separation of church and state did not permit prayer at high school football games, as had been allowed in a Texas school district.[90]

In 2002, the Court in a landmark 5–4 ruling upheld the use of public money for school vouchers to send children to religious and other private schools.[91] The decision approved the program in Cleveland, Ohio, where about 3,700 of the district's 75,000 children used vouchers of up to $2,250 to attend private schools. Almost all of the children were enrolled in religious schools.

For this reason, school vouchers remained a controversial issue. Advocates argued that vouchers would give low-income students the same opportunities as more affluent students. Opponents contended that vouchers violated the constitutional separation of church and state and would weaken the public school system by drawing the best students away and reducing budgets. The National Education Association, the teachers' union, led the opponents of vouchers. The Supreme Court ruling in the Cleveland case did not end the debate over "school choice" because the battle was likely to continue in the states and in local communities.

Although it has restricted aid to religious primary and secondary schools, the Supreme Court has approved some forms of government aid to church-related private colleges and universities.[92] And the Court has held that universities that disburse student activity fees must subsidize religious as well as secular groups.[93]

In deciding cases that relate to freedom of religion under the First Amendment, the Supreme Court has always faced a dilemma, because the two clauses of the

Parochial school children praying in classroom

© Joe Raedle/Newsmakers/Getty Images

The Supreme Court said "no": school prayer at a high school football game in Texas

amendment in a sense clash with each other. That is, in protecting the rights of a particular religious group to engage in the free exercise of its faith, the Court might be viewed as favoring a religion in violation of the establishment clause. Recognizing this dilemma, the Court has attempted to exercise what it has called a "benevolent neutrality" in order to protect freedom of religion without sponsorship of a particular faith.

## Loyalty and Security

Should those who would destroy the Bill of Rights enjoy its protection? This dilemma was at the heart of the public debate that began with the end of the Second World War. In this area two constitutional principles clashed: the right of the individual to freedom of expression and the government's responsibility to protect national security.

Today, years after the collapse of the Soviet Union in 1991, it might be hard for many Americans to understand the political atmosphere that prevailed in the United States more than half a century ago. The emergence of the Soviet Union as a rival power to the United States, the onset of the Cold War, and the division of the world during the 1950s into two armed nuclear camps created fear of communism at home and generated pressures to curb dissent and root out Communists or "radicals" from government posts.

Some political leaders, notably Senator Joseph R. McCarthy, a Wisconsin Republican, exploited public concern for political benefit. During the early 1950s McCarthy's freewheeling investigations of alleged Communists in the State Department and other agencies injured many innocent persons, destroyed careers, and created a widespread climate of fear in the federal government and in the nation. Few dared to raise their voices against him. When he attacked the Army in 1954, a series of public hearings exposed McCarthy's methods to the blinding light of television and led to his censure by the Senate later that year. After that, McCarthy lost influence; he died in 1957.

During the 1990s, with the end of the Cold War, documents became available to historians, both in the United States and in the former Soviet Union, that shed additional light on the identities of certain Soviet agents and sympathizers who had worked inside the government in Washington decades earlier. But in the view of most analysts and historians, the new information did not justify McCarthy's scattershot approach or the unfair accusations that his name has come to symbolize.

During the Cold War era, two opposing views crystallized in the Court and within American society. One view was that a nation, like an individual, has the right to self-preservation; it must take action against internal enemies, and it need not wait until the threat is carried out, for that may be too late. The other view was that the First Amendment guarantees free speech for everyone, that if Americans have confidence in the democratic system they need not fear other ideologies or the clash of ideas. A similar debate arose over the government's actions against suspected terrorists in the wake of the attacks of 9/11.

The effort to suppress dissent did not begin with "McCarthyism." As early as 1798, the Alien and Sedition Acts had provided a maximum fine of $2,000 and two years in prison for "malicious writing" against the government of President John Adams. The first person to be convicted under the acts was Matthew Lyon, a Vermont congressman whose "crime" was to accuse President Adams of "a continual grasp for power . . . an unbounded thirst for ridiculous pomp, foolish adulation and selfish avarice." After Jefferson became president in 1801, the various Alien and Sedition Acts were repealed or permitted to expire.

In 1940 Congress passed the Smith Act, which made it unlawful for any person to advocate overthrowing the government "by force or violence." In 1951 the Supreme Court upheld the constitutionality of the Smith Act and the conspiracy conviction of 11 Communist Party leaders.[94] In later decisions, however, the Supreme Court severely restricted the use of the act.[95]

After the outbreak of the Korean War, Congress passed the Internal Security Act of 1950, known as the McCarran Act. It required Communist "front" organizations to register with the attorney general. But the Court ruled that to require individual Communists to register would violate the Fifth Amendment.[96]

As time has shown, however, freedom of expression has varied sharply with the political climate; even a "fixed star" may be viewed through a very different telescope in each decade.

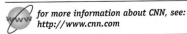

© Phillips/Black Star/Stockphoto.com

Senator Joseph R. McCarthy

## Due Process of Law

"The history of liberty," Justice Felix Frankfurter once wrote, "is largely the history of the observance of procedural safeguards."[97] A nation may have an enlightened system of government, but if the rights of individuals are abused, then the system falls short of its goals.

The Fifth and Fourteenth Amendments to the Constitution provide for **due process of law,** a phrase designed to protect the individual against the arbitrary power of the state. Sometimes the distinction is made between *substantive due process* (laws must be reasonable) and *procedural due process* (laws must be administered in a fair manner).

Until 1937 the Supreme Court used the concept of substantive due process to protect the "liberty" of businesses against regulation by Congress and the states. After 1937, the Court abandoned substantive due process as it upheld laws passed by Congress during the New Deal to regulate business. In so doing, the Court took the view that economic regulation was the responsibility of Congress and the state legislatures, not of the judicial branch. But in the area of civil rights, civil liberties, and privacy, the Court has continued to apply substantive due process.

**Searches and Seizures** Due process begins at home, for the right of individuals to "be secure in their persons, houses, papers, and effects, against unreasonable searches and seizures" is spelled out in the Fourth Amendment and marks a fundamental difference between a free and a totalitarian society.

The Fourth Amendment also provides important protections against the government. In the United States, as a general principle, police are not authorized to search a home without a search warrant signed by a judicial officer and issued on "probable cause" to believe that the materials to be seized are in the place to be searched.

In 1999, for example, the Supreme Court ruled unanimously in two cases that police who allowed journalists and television cameras into people's homes to witness and record searches or arrests violated the Fourth Amendment.[98] In one of these cases, police in Rockville, Maryland, accompanied by a *Washington Post* reporter and photographer, raided the home of the parents of a suspected parole violator. Police pinned the man's father to the floor with a gun to his head.[99] In a companion case, 21 armed officers and a TV crew from CNN descended on the Montana home of a 72-year-old man with emphysema who was suspected of poisoning eagles.[100] The Court's ruling did not end the popular television programs that show police making dramatic arrests because it did not apply to action that takes place on the streets or in other public places.

WWW ***for more information about CNN, see: http://www.cnn.com***

Until 1980, police could lawfully enter a home without a warrant to make a valid arrest, and they could conduct a limited search at the same time. But that year, the Supreme Court ruled that the Fourth Amendment prohibited police from entering a home without a warrant to make a routine arrest.[101] Police must obtain a warrant except in emergency circumstances, the Court held. Justice John Paul Stevens ruled, in effect, that a family's home is its castle: "The Fourth Amendment has drawn a firm line at the entrance to the house. Absent exigent circumstances, that threshold may not reasonably be crossed without a warrant."[102] The decision invalidated the laws of 23 states. Although police with a search warrant are required to knock and announce their presence before entering a house, the Supreme Court ruled in 2006 that if they failed to do so, the evidence seized could still be used in court.[103] Police do not have to knock and announce if there is a probability of violence or immediate destruction of evidence.[104] And the Supreme Court ruled unanimously that police who waited 15 to 20 seconds before battering down a drug suspect's door acted lawfully; a longer delay, the justices said, would allow time for someone to flush the drugs down the toilet.[105] "Police seeking a stolen piano may be able to spend more time" before battering down the door, Justice David H. Souter observed.[106]

In 1969 the Supreme Court ruled that police lacking a search warrant could not ransack a home in the course of making a lawful arrest but must confine their search to the suspect and the immediate surroundings.[107] The decision overturned the conviction of Ted Steven Chimel of California, who had been serving a five-years-to-life term for stealing rare coins—which police found after searching his home without a search warrant.

Although the Constitution is designed to protect against unreasonable government intrusion, the reality

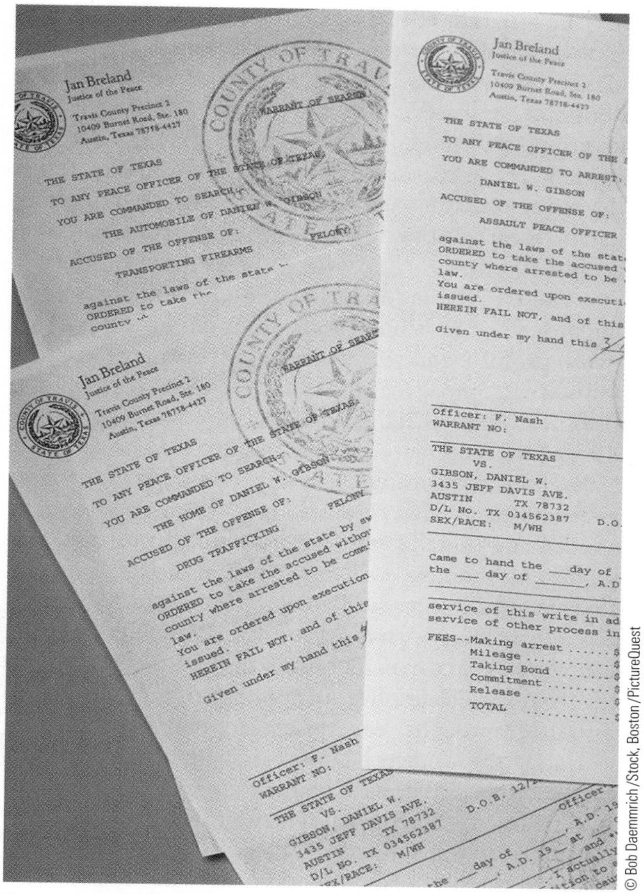

Search warrants issued in Travis County, Texas



## Alberta Spruill: A Botched Police Raid Claims a Life

A 57-year-old Harlem woman preparing to leave for her longtime city government job died of a heart attack yesterday morning after police officers broke down her door and threw a concussion grenade into her apartment, the police commissioner said. They were acting on what appeared to be bad information about guns and drugs in the apartment.

Commissioner Raymond W. Kelly apologized to the family of the woman, Alberta Spruill, and said he had ordered an investigation of the entire incident and suspended the use of the grenades, which are meant to stun and disorient people with a loud noise and a flash. . . .

Mr. Kelly said that the officers were executing what is known as a no-knock search warrant based on information provided by a drug dealer, who told the police that his supplier stored guns and drugs in Apartment 6F at 310 West 143rd Street.

The dealer had told the police that he had seen armed people in the apartment on three occasions and that there were dogs inside, Mr. Kelly said. But in the raid at 6:10 a.m., the officers found only Ms. Spruill, and realized the information was wrong.

The raid was carried out by a half-dozen officers from the Emergency Services Unit, which specializes in tactical entry. . . . They were joined by about six officers from the 25th Precinct. They broke through the door with a battering ram. Then they threw the small grenade.

In the minutes after the explosion, the terrified Ms. Spruill, who was dressed for work, was briefly handcuffed. . . . Ms. Spruill initially declined medical attention, although she told the captain that she had a heart condition. An ambulance was requested, and she went into cardiac arrest on the way to Harlem Hospital Center, where she died at 7:50 a.m.

—Adapted from the *New York Times,* May 17, 2003

may be different. Two innocent families in Collinsville, Illinois, found that out when federal narcotics agents kicked in the doors of their homes, terrorized them at gunpoint, and ransacked their houses in a drug raid based on false information. The agents had no search or arrest warrants. Subsequent investigations disclosed that dozens of other such raids, sometimes fatal to the victims, had been carried out by federal, state, and local narcotics agents.[108]

These violations of the Fourth Amendment rights of individuals are an unpleasant example of the gap between promise and performance in the American political system. Sometimes the outputs of the system violate the constitutional rights that distinguish the American democracy from authoritarian regimes. Although such episodes may be infrequent, they demonstrate that the system does not always function the way it was designed.

During the Nixon administration, it was disclosed that agents employed by the White House had burglarized the office of a psychiatrist who had treated Daniel Ellsberg, a former government official who leaked the Pentagon Papers, a secret history of the Vietnam War, to the news media. This was in addition to the illegal entry into the Democrats' Watergate headquarters by burglars working for President Nixon's campaign. It was also disclosed that Nixon himself had approved for a time a plan that included "surreptitious entry" into the homes or offices of people suspected by the government of being a threat to internal security—even though the president had been warned, in writing, that this was "clearly illegal" and "amounts to burglary." In 1975 the FBI admitted that it had conducted hundreds of illegal break-ins against dissident groups and individuals.[109]

Although the Bill of Rights was designed to guard against government misdeeds against individuals, public school students are not afforded the same Fourth Amendment protections as are other citizens. In one case a 14-year-old girl's purse was opened by a school official who found marijuana, a pipe, and letters indicating the student sold marijuana. The Court ruled that school officials do not need a warrant, only "reasonable grounds," to conduct a search.[110] In 1995 the Supreme Court held that public schools could require student athletes to submit to random drug testing. The Court said that students' rights under the Fourth Amendment were outweighed by a school's interest in deterring drug use. In 2002, the Supreme Court expanded its ruling to allow random drug testing of public school students engaged in a wide range of "competitive" activities, including cheerleading.[111]

Automobiles have less protection against search and seizure than do homes. Under Supreme Court rulings, police may search an automobile without a warrant if they have probable cause to believe it contains illegal articles, and they also may search any containers and packages found in such a car, even in a locked trunk.[112] "When a legitimate search is underway," the Court held, police could not be expected to make "nice distinctions . . . between glove compartments, upholstered seats, trunks and wrapped packages."[113] And police may search the personal belongings of passengers in a car whose driver is suspected of breaking the law, even though the passengers themselves are not suspected of a crime.[114]

Police who stop a car for a traffic violation may order the occupants to get out.[115] And police may search a car and its contents if they have lawfully arrested its occupants.[116] That case arose in New York State when Roger Belton and three friends were stopped by a state trooper for speeding. The officer smelled burnt marijuana and saw an envelope on the floor marked "Supergold." He arrested all four people and, while searching Belton's jacket, found cocaine. The Court ruled that the search was justified because it was limited to an area where a suspect might reach for a weapon or evidence. Police may stop drivers at roadside checkpoints to see whether they are intoxicated.[117] But police may not search a car merely because the driver was speeding.[118] The Supreme Court has ruled, however, that police can set up roadblocks and briefly stop motorists to ask whether they have knowledge of a crime.

Even when police are within their rights, the outcome may seem unreasonable, as occurred in one Texas case. Gail Atwater, a mother of two young children, was arrested in front of her children for driving without a seat belt, taken away in handcuffs, and spent time in jail before she was able to post a $310 bond for a misdemeanor with a maximum penalty of $50. The Supreme Court ruled in favor of the police.[119]

In the landmark case of *Terry* v. *Ohio,* the Supreme Court ruled that police may stop and frisk a suspect on the street without a warrant if they are reasonably suspicious that the person is armed or dangerous,[120] or if someone flees at the mere sight of the police.[121] And police may arrest someone in a public place without a warrant on probable cause that the person has committed a crime.[122] The overwhelming majority of arrests in the United States are, in fact, made without a warrant.

Cherished constitutional principles are usually established in cases involving criminals and other people who are not pillars of the community. In 1957 Cleveland police, with no search warrant, barged into the house of a woman named Dollree Mapp. They did not find the fugitive or the betting slips they were after but seized some "lewd and lascivious books and pictures." She was tried and convicted for possession of these items. But the Supreme Court ruled in 1961 that a state could not prosecute a person with unconstitutionally seized evidence, a decision that protected not only Dollree Mapp but every American.[123]

The Supreme Court had long held that the federal government could not use illegally seized evidence in court, a principle known as the **exclusionary rule.**[124] The Mapp case meant that the states, too, were subject to this rule. Over the years, however, the Court backed away from its earlier decisions, creating enough exceptions to the exclusionary rule that criminal defendants

Myth vs. Reality

## SEARCH AND SEIZURE: DO POLICE NEED A WARRANT?

Many Americans believe that under the Fourth Amendment of the Constitution, police cannot search their homes or offices without a warrant issued by a judge. That is normally the case. But is your personal property safe from a search that takes place without a court warrant, or from an unannounced search?

The truth is that there are multiple exceptions to the rule requiring a search warrant. Law enforcement authorities do not need a warrant for

- Searches that accompany arrests; police may conduct a full search of the arrested person's body or clothing
- Seizing evidence that is in plain view, when police are making an arrest or carrying out law enforcement responsibilities, even if that evidence is related to some other crime
- Consent searches, where a property owner or occupant agrees to a search
- Searches that are necessary for public safety or to prevent imminent danger to others
- Situations when destruction of evidence (weapons or contraband) may occur
- Searches under the 2001 USA Patriot Act; the law allows authorities to wiretap, search, and seize property and records without a warrant in foreign intelligence and terrorism investigations

However, your landlord may not give police the permission to search your apartment or house; even if you are behind on your rent or have been served an eviction notice. Most states have laws that allow landlords to enter and inspect apartments if they give the tenants one or two days' notice.

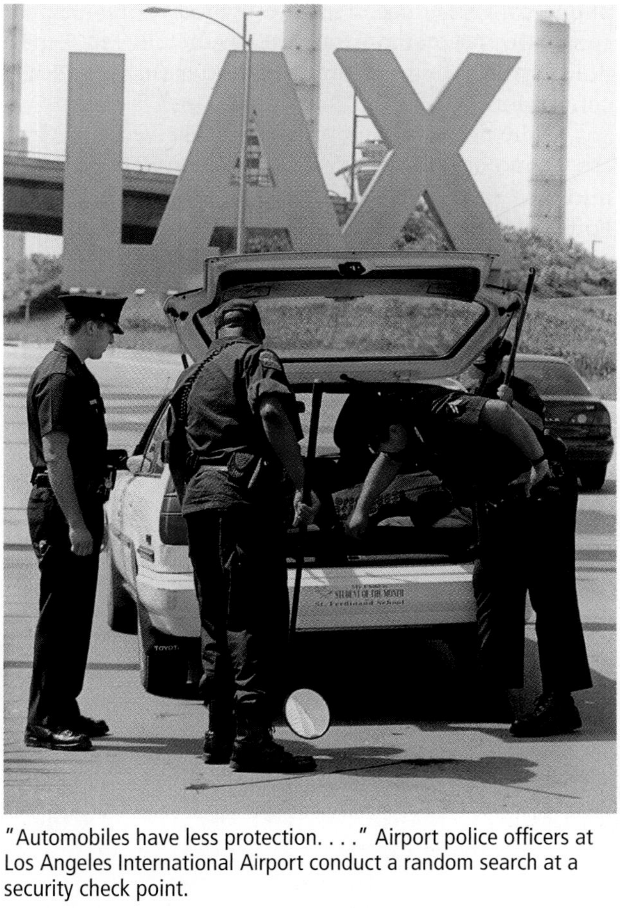


© 2004 AP/Wide World Photos

"Automobiles have less protection. . . ." Airport police officers at Los Angeles International Airport conduct a random search at a security check point.

could no longer count on it to protect them in every instance.

In a series of cases over several years, the Court under Chief Justice Burger substantially narrowed the exclusionary rule.[125] Justice William J. Brennan, Jr., warned in one dissent that the rule faced "slow strangulation."[126]

In another case the Court ruled that evidence obtained illegally may be admitted at a trial if the evidence would "inevitably" have been discovered lawfully.[127]

In 1984, the Supreme Court for the first time created a "good faith" exception to the rule, permitting courts to consider illegally seized evidence in some cases when police reasonably believed that their search was constitutional, even when their search warrants turned out to be flawed.[128] The Court's 6–3 decision was immediately hailed by conservatives, who contended that the exclusionary rule had interfered with law enforcement.

In still another case, after the fatal beating of a woman in Roxbury, Massachusetts, police searched the home of her friend Osborne Sheppard and found incriminating evidence, which was used to convict him of murder. Later, it turned out that police had used the wrong form in filling out the search warrant. The Supreme Court ruled against the defendant.[129] And in 1987 the Court held that evidence seized improperly as the result of "honest mistakes" by police may be used at trial.[130]

However, because courts still can and do suppress evidence seized illegally, police to some extent have become more cautious and careful in conducting searches. As a result, the exclusionary rule, however weakened, still serves to protect citizens against violations of the Fourth Amendment.

Sometimes Congress passes legislation that attempts to overturn or modify Supreme Court decisions. That

© Phil McCarten/PhotoEdit

happened in the case of police searches of newsrooms. In 1971 a group of antiwar demonstrators at Stanford University attacked police, and two were seriously injured. The university newspaper, the *Stanford Daily*, published photographs of the incident. The next day, armed with a warrant, police swooped down on the paper's newsroom and searched its photo labs, filing cabinets, desks, and wastepaper baskets. The Supreme Court ruled that the First Amendment does not bar newsroom searches for criminal evidence.[131]

---

WWW ***for more information about the Stanford Daily, see: http://stanforddaily.com***

---

Then in 1980 sheriff's deputies raided a television station newsroom in Boise, Idaho, searching for and seizing videotapes of a prison riot. The local prosecutor said he needed the tapes to identify the riot leaders. Reacting to these incidents, Congress enacted a law barring most such newsroom searches. The law, the Privacy Protection Act of 1980, ordinarily requires federal, state, and local authorities to use subpoenas, rather than searches, in seeking evidence from journalists, authors, scholars, and others who write for publication.

**The Uninvited Ear** In the technological age, the right of privacy has been threatened by highly sophisticated wiretapping and eavesdropping devices.

In Washington, D.C., practically anyone of importance assumes, or at least jokes, that his or her telephone is tapped. (One leading columnist would begin his telephone conversations: "Hello, everybody.") As a Senate committee has demonstrated, even the olive in a martini may be a "bug," a tiny transmitter that broadcasts conversations.

In the electronic age, privacy is a relative term. Modern technology has made possible government intrusion into the private lives of individuals, a threat that Justice Potter Stewart had called the "uninvited ear." Many prosecutors and law enforcement officials insist that wiretapping and electronic bugs are essential tools in cases in-

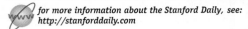

Police may stop and frisk suspects without a warrant. Here, members of an East Los Angeles street gang are searched for weapons.

© A. Ramey/Woodfin Camp & Associates

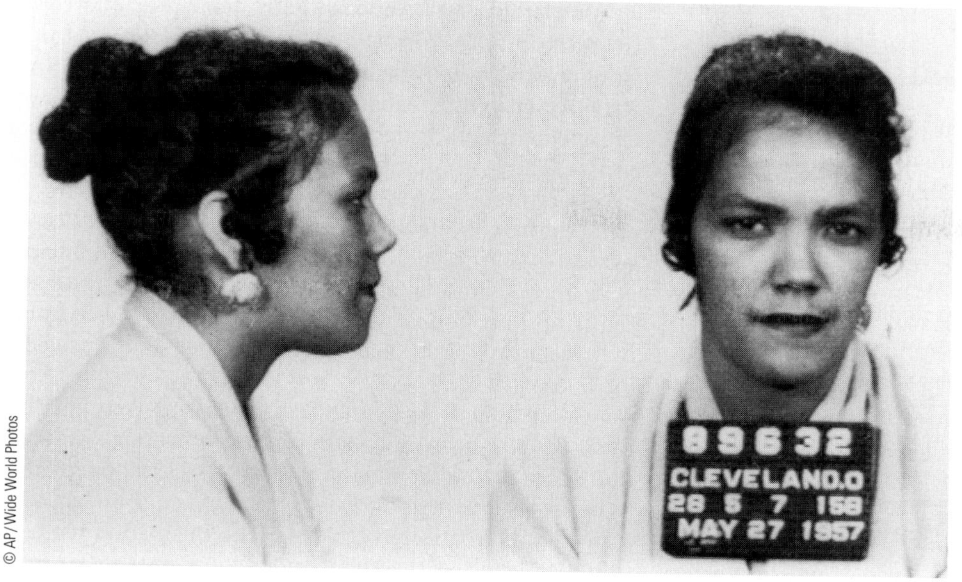




Dollree Mapp

volving terrorism, espionage, kidnapping, and organized crime. Other observers believe that such devices inevitably will be abused by government authorities and result in the violation of constitutional liberties.

Despite Justice Holmes's denunciation of wiretapping as "dirty business," the Supreme Court for almost 40 years (1928–1967) held that the practice did not violate the Fourth Amendment.[132] But the Federal Communications Act of 1934 outlawed wiretapping, and three years later the Supreme Court held that wiretap evidence could not be used in federal courts.[133] Finally, in 1967, the Court caught up with technology by ruling that a conversation was tangible and could be seized electronically. Thus, placing a bug or tap did not have to involve physical trespass to violate the Fourth Amendment, the Court ruled, and police therefore could not eavesdrop without a court warrant. The case involved Charles Katz, a Los Angeles gambler who made interstate telephone calls to bookmakers from a public phone booth to bet on college basketball games. Unknown to Katz, the FBI had taped a microphone to the top of his favorite phone booth on Sunset Boulevard. Because the FBI had no warrant, the Supreme Court held that Katz's constitutional rights had been violated and threw out his conviction.[134]

Technology creates continuing dilemmas for the Supreme Court's justices. Before the era of cell phones, cordless telephones came into widespread use in the 1980s; but conversations over those phones can often be overheard. Unbeknownst to the Scott Tyler family of Dixon, Iowa, their nearby neighbors, Sandra and Rich Berodt, were listening to their conversations, mistakenly concluded that they were dealing in cocaine, and called the sheriff's office. The Tylers' conversations were then taped, and based in part on what was overheard, Scott Tyler was charged with stealing $35,000 in merchandise from his company, convicted, and jailed for four months. The Tylers sued the Berodts for listening in on their conversations. But the Supreme Court let stand a lower court decision that the Tylers had no "reasonable expectation of privacy" when they used their cordless phone.[135] The Fourth Amendment may protect telephone booths, but it does not protect cordless phones.

When public concern over crime increases, so do pressures to use wiretaps and bugs. In the late 1960s "law and order" became a growing political issue. In 1968 Congress passed the Omnibus Crime Control and Safe Streets Act permitting court-authorized wiretapping and bugging by federal, state, and local authorities in a wide variety of cases, and the use of such evidence in trials.

In 1969, when the Nixon administration came to power, the Justice Department claimed it had the authority, even without court approval, to tap and bug domestic groups that it considered to be a threat to internal security. However, the Supreme Court ruled, in an 8–0 decision, that this highly controversial policy violated the Fourth Amendment of the Constitution.[136]

President Nixon, in an effort to plug news "leaks" and ostensibly to protect "national security," authorized FBI wiretaps of 17 White House aides, other officials, and news reporters. Warrantless wiretapping and bugging had taken place under other presidents as well, including Lyndon Johnson and John F. Kennedy. In 1978 Congress passed the Foreign Intelligence Surveillance Act (FISA), which, for the first time, required a court order even for wiretapping and bugging in national security investigations. The law also established a special court of seven judges, later increased to 11, to issue such

## The Constitution Protects Telephone Booths

The Fourth Amendment protects people, not places. . . . No less than an individual in a business office, in a friend's apartment, or in a taxicab, a person in a telephone booth may rely upon the protection of the Fourth Amendment.

One who occupies it, shuts the door behind him, and pays the toll that permits him to place a call, is surely entitled to assume that the words he utters into the mouthpiece will not be broadcast to the world.

—Justice Potter Stewart,
in *Katz* v. *United States* (1967)

warrants. The only exception in the law permits the government to eavesdrop on the communications of foreign powers without a warrant. The special court did not appear to be any great obstacle to government wiretapping, however. As of the end of 2002, the panel of rotating judges to whom requests come had approved 17,001 wiretapping applications and had rejected only one.[137] President George W. Bush in 2002 secretly ordered the warrantless wiretapping of international telephone calls and e-mails of hundreds of thousands of people in the United States, including Americans, in an attempt to track down terrorists.

In 1979 the Supreme Court held that a break-in by government agents to plant a court-authorized bug is constitutional; it said that Congress had not ruled out "covert entry" to carry out electronic surveillance.[138]

**Rights of the Accused** "Due process of law" may mean little to average Americans—unless and until they are arrested. This is because most of the important procedural safeguards provided by the Constitution, as interpreted by the Supreme Court, concern the rights of accused persons.

Before anyone may be brought to trial for a serious federal crime, there must be a grand jury **indictment,** a finding that enough evidence exists to warrant a criminal trial. The Constitution does not require states to use grand juries; in most state cases, in place of an indictment, to bring a person to trial officials file a **criminal information,** a statement presented to the court by a prosecutor charging a person with a crime. The Bill of Rights entitles suspects or defendants to be represented by a lawyer, to be informed of their legal rights and of the charges against them, to have a speedy and public trial by jury, to summon witnesses to testify in their behalf, to cross-examine prosecution witnesses, and to refuse to testify against themselves. In addition, they may not be held in excessive bail, or subjected to cruel and unusual punishment or to double jeopardy for the same offense. These rights are contained in the Fifth through Eighth Amendments.

In October 2001, only a month after the 9/11 terrorist attacks on the World Trade Center and the Pentagon, Congress overwhelmingly passed the controversial **USA Patriot Act,** greatly expanding the power of federal law enforcement authorities to move against suspected terrorists. The Bush administration defended the law as a necessary tool in the war on terrorism, but the law drew criticism from both civil liberties groups and some conservatives. Critics argued that the administration had gone too far and created a danger that constitutional rights and freedoms would be curtailed in the name of preserving them. The law was modified and renewed in 2006.

Soon after the 9/11 attacks, President George W. Bush issued an order creating military tribunals to try non-U.S. citizens who belonged to the Al Qaeda terrorist organization or who were suspected of engaging in, or assisting, international terrorists. The Bush administration also asserted the right under the Constitution to label some persons, including American citizens, as "enemy combatants" and hold them indefinitely, not necessarily with access to an attorney. In 2003 a federal appeals court ruled that President Bush could not continue to detain Jose Padilla, a U.S. citizen and suspected terrorist, without trial simply by labeling him an "enemy combatant." The government had claimed that Padilla was plotting to detonate a radioactive "dirty bomb" in the United States. In June 2004 the U.S. Supreme Court declined on procedural grounds to rule in the Padilla case but held that Yaser Hamdi, another American who had been seized in Afghanistan and detained as an "enemy combatant," was entitled to a hearing.[139] Both men were held in military custody for two years. Later the government moved to try Padilla in federal court.

After the 9/11 attacks, 660 men from some 40 foreign countries were held at the U.S. naval base at Guantanamo Bay, Cuba, for two years or more without formal charges or access to their families or lawyers. Most had been captured during the fighting in Afghanistan and Pakistan, and the government claimed the right to detain the men as military prisoners. In June 2004 the Supreme Court ruled that the Guantanamo prisoners had the right to challenge their detention in court.[140] At the same time, the Court upheld the president's power to declare U.S. citizens and other persons "enemy combatants" and to detain them. Then in 2006, in a sharp rebuke to the Bush Administration, the Supreme Court ruled that the Guantanamo tribunals violated both military law and the Geneva Convention.[141] Three months later, however, Congress passed a law allowing detainees to be tried by the military tribunals.

The rights of accused persons have often been the subject of interpretations by the Supreme Court. As far back as 1957, the Court had established the *Mallory* rule, requiring that a suspect in a federal case be arraigned without unnecessary delay.[142] Under Chief Justice Earl Warren, the Supreme Court, in a series of split decisions in the mid-1960s, greatly strengthened the rights of accused persons, particularly in the period immediately after arrest. It is in the station house that police traditionally try to extract a confession from suspects. It is also the very time during which accused people may be most disoriented, frightened, and uncertain of their rights. The Court came under severe political attack for these decisions, which many law enforcement authorities argued would hamper their ability to fight crime.

The Warren Court rulings came at a time of rising violence and unrest in America. Many citizens, worried about "law and order," focused their criticism on the Supreme Court and on the judicial system, which was often accused of "coddling" criminals. Supporters of the Warren Court decisions and of civil liberties argued that there is no better test of a democracy than the procedural safeguards it erects to protect accused people from the police power of the state.

A landmark case of the Warren era began in Chicago in 1960 when police arrested Danny Escobedo, a laborer suspected of murdering his brother-in-law. Under interrogation he asked to see his lawyer, but the request was refused. During the long night at police headquarters, Danny Escobedo confessed. In 1964, in a 5–4 decision, the Supreme Court reversed his conviction, freeing him after four and a half years in prison. The Court ruled that under the Sixth Amendment, a suspect is entitled to counsel even during police interrogation once "the process shifts from investigatory to accusatory."[143] Nor can the government use incriminating statements made by a suspect to an informer imprisoned with him or her before a trial; the Supreme Court has ruled that use of such evidence deprives the suspect of the right to have an attorney present.[144]

© Darul Uloom Islamic Institute/Getty Images

Jose Padilla, although a U.S. citizen, was held without trial as a suspected terrorist.

**The Battle over *Miranda*** In 1966, the Supreme Court, in the case of *Miranda* v. *Arizona,* required that suspects in police custody be advised of their rights before they are interrogated. These ***Miranda* warnings** ("You have the right to remain silent. . . . Anything you say may be used against you in a court of law. . . . You have the right to an attorney. . . .") became familiar to generations of television viewers of crime shows. The Supreme Court's decision greatly expanded the protection granted to suspects. In March 1963 Ernesto A. Miranda, an indigent 23-year-old man described by the Court as mentally disturbed, was arrested 10 days after the kidnapping and rape of an 18-year-old woman near Phoenix, Arizona. The woman picked Miranda out of a police lineup, and after two hours of interrogation—during which he was not told of his right to silence and a lawyer—he confessed. The Supreme Court struck down Miranda's conviction; in a controversial 5–4 decision, the Court ruled that the Fifth Amendment's protection against self-incrimination requires that suspects be clearly informed of their rights before they are asked any questions by police.

***for more information about Miranda warnings, see: http://www.courttv.com/news/2003/0825/miranda_ap.html***

Chief Justice Warren ruled for the narrow majority that statements made by accused people may not be used against them in court unless strict procedures are followed: "Prior to any questioning, the person must be warned that he has a right to remain silent, that any statement he does make may be used against him, and that he has a right to the presence of an attorney, either retained or appointed."[145] Although defendants may knowingly waive these rights, Warren ruled, they cannot be questioned further if at any point they ask to see a lawyer or indicate "in any manner" that they do not wish to be interrogated.

The chief justice, declaring that *Miranda* went to "the roots of our concepts of American criminal jurisprudence," argued eloquently that the "compelling atmosphere" of a "menacing police interrogation" was designed to intimidate suspects, break their will, and lead to an involuntary confession in violation of the Fifth Amendment. That is why, he concluded, "procedural safeguards" must be observed in the police station. In a strong dissent Justice John Harlan said the decision would lead to "a gradual disappearance of confessions as a legitimate tool of law enforcement." After the ruling,

## USA Patriot Act: Big Brother or a Tool against Terrorism?

Congress passed the controversial USA Patriot Act in the wake of the deadly 9/11 terrorist attacks on New York City and Washington, D.C. President George W. Bush and supporters called it a necessary tool to fight terrorists. Critics have claimed it goes too far and violates the basic constitutional rights of Americans.

What does the act say? The Patriot Act gives the government unprecedented powers to detain or investigate anyone it suspects is a terrorist or supports terrorist activities. It allows the government to

- Access e-mail, voice mail, and records of Internet activity without a warrant
- Greatly expand secret searches of private premises without a warrant
- Search private premises unannounced with a warrant, even in nonterrorism cases
- Gain access to bank, library, educational, and other personal records. As modified in 2006, a court order is needed to require libraries to yield the names of book borrowers.
- Enforce stricter standards for issuing visas to foreigners seeking to enter the United States
- Remove the statute of limitations—the legal time limit—on prosecuting terrorist crimes that result in murder
- Detain indefinitely noncitizens suspected of terrorism

Some communities passed resolutions in support of civil liberties and against the Patriot Act, urging local law enforcement to refuse requests from federal authorities under the Patriot Act. Most provisions of the act were made permanent in 2006.

many police began carrying "*Miranda* cards" to read suspects their rights.

With the election of President Nixon in 1968, the era of the Warren Court ended. In 1969 Nixon named a new chief justice, Warren Burger. Within four years, Nixon had appointed three more Supreme Court justices who were, as a group, generally more conservative than their predecessors. Particularly in the area of criminal justice, the pendulum gradually began to swing back from the liberal philosophy of the Warren Court.

In 1971 the Burger Court handed down a decision that greatly narrowed the scope of the *Miranda* ruling. The Court held that statements made by suspects without proper *Miranda* warnings could still be used to discredit their testimony at a trial.[146] In a series of later decisions, the Supreme Court retreated even farther from *Miranda.*[147] For example, it held that even after suspects exercise the right to remain silent about one crime, they still can be questioned about another.[148]

The Court also appeared to permit the use of subtle psychology on suspects unless police were aware that their actions or words were "reasonably likely" to make a suspect confess. The case arose when Thomas Innis, a murder suspect, led police to a hidden weapon after officers remarked that it would be too bad if a child "would pick up the gun and maybe kill herself." The Court said that this was not the sort of "interrogation" forbidden by *Miranda.*

And in 1984, in another retreat from *Miranda,* the Supreme Court held that where "public safety" is endangered, police can question suspects without advising them of their rights.

In 1985 President Reagan's attorney general, Edwin Meese III, publicly attacked the Supreme Court's *Miranda* decision as "infamous" and wrong.[149] And the Court, under Chief Justice William H. Rehnquist, whom President Reagan appointed in 1986, continued to narrow the scope of suspects' rights.[150]

Protesters outside the New York Stock Exchange demonstrate against the controversial USA Patriot Act.

© Arizona Republic

Ernesto Miranda after his arrest on parole violations

Ernesto Miranda was stabbed to death in a barroom quarrel in Phoenix, Arizona, on February 1, 1976. Fernando Rodriguez Zamora was arrested on a murder charge for allegedly handing the knife to the assailant, who fled. The police read Zamora his rights. They used a "*Miranda* card."

More than three decades after the *Miranda* ruling, a new controversy arose. In 1968, Congress had passed major crime legislation including a section that tried to overturn the Supreme Court's *Miranda* decision. Under this provision, Section 3501, statements by suspects might be admissible as evidence if a judge considered them voluntary, even without a *Miranda* warning. Congress has power to modify Supreme Court decisions that do not address a basic constitutional issue. However, Congress does not have power to overturn an interpretation of the Constitution by the Supreme Court; that can only be done by a constitutional amendment.

Little attention was paid to Section 3501 of the 1968 law until Paul Cassell, a conservative law professor at the University of Utah, began a crusade to challenge *Miranda.* Cassell maintained that many crimes went unpunished because suspects, once warned, declined to confess. He argued that the Supreme Court had not said the warnings set forth in *Miranda* were required by the Constitution and that the overlooked Section 3501 of the crime law had therefore invalidated the decision. As a test case, Cassell chose the interrogation by the FBI in 1997 of Charles Thomas Dickerson, who was suspected of robbing a bank in Alexandria, Virginia. Although he was warned of his rights, Dickerson claimed that the warning had been given after he confessed. In 1999, the Court of Appeals in Richmond, Virginia, the most conservative of the federal appeals courts, sided with Dickerson. The Supreme Court agreed to hear the case, and in 2000, in a landmark decision, the Supreme Court voted, 7–2, to reaffirm its 1966 *Miranda* ruling; it held that the warnings police must give to criminal defendants to advise them of their rights are in fact required by the Constitution.[151]

In its majority opinion, written by Chief Justice Rehnquist, the Court declared: "We hold that *Miranda,* being a constitutional decision of this court, may not be in effect overruled by an act of Congress, and we decline to overrule *Miranda* ourselves."

The Court added that "*Miranda* has become embedded in routine police practice to the point where the warnings have become part of our national culture." Those words were a significant reminder that in interpreting the Constitution, the Court considers not only legal arguments but the political currents and attitudes of the larger society of which it is so important a part.

**The Right to Counsel** The right of an indigent defendant to have a lawyer in a state court might seem basic, but in fact it was not established by the Supreme Court until 1963 in the celebrated case of *Gideon* v. *Wainwright.*[152]

Clarence Earl Gideon petitioned the Supreme Court in 1962 from the Florida State Prison at Raiford, where he was serving a five-year term for allegedly breaking into a poolroom in Panama City, Florida, and stealing some beer, wine, and coins from a cigarette machine and a jukebox. A drifter, a man whose life had had more than the normal share of disasters, Gideon nevertheless had one idea fixed firmly in his mind—that the Constitution of the United States entitled him to a fair trial. And this, he insisted in his petition, he had not received. Clarence Earl Gideon had not been provided with a lawyer by the court.

In 1942 the Supreme Court had ruled that the right of counsel was not a "fundamental right," essential to a fair trial in a state court, and that it was not guaranteed by the due process clause of the Fourteenth Amendment.[153] But in *Gideon,* two decades later, the Court changed its mind. Justice Black declared for the majority: A person "who is too poor to hire a lawyer cannot be assured a fair trial unless counsel is provided for him." A few months later, Gideon won a new trial, and this time—with the help of a lawyer—he was acquitted.

The landmark *Gideon* decision left open a question of vital importance to millions of poor persons arrested each year for misdemeanors and so-called petty offenses, crimes carrying maximum penalties of six months in jail. Because Gideon had been convicted of a felony, the decision in his case did not clarify whether defendants accused of lesser offenses also were entitled to free counsel. Then in 1972 the Supreme Court overruled the con-

Reading Miranda rights to a suspect in California

© Laima Druskis/Photo Researchers, Inc.

viction of Jon Richard Argersinger, a Tallahassee, Florida, gas station attendant who had not been offered an attorney when he pleaded guilty to carrying a concealed weapon, a misdemeanor.[154] The decision meant that no persons—unless they voluntarily give up their right to a lawyer—may be sentenced to jail for any offense, no matter how minor, unless they have been represented by an attorney at their trial.

It should be noted, of course, that the concept of due process is not limited under the Constitution to protecting the rights of criminal defendants. It applies, in varying degrees, in civil proceedings as well. In administrative actions related to welfare benefits, education, licensing, zoning, and many other areas, states and the federal government must observe due process. However, individuals or groups in such administrative proceedings and civil cases are not afforded the same strict protections of due process as are followed in a courtroom for defendants whose liberty is at stake. A local school board, for example, may hold a public hearing, but it is not obliged to follow the same rules as a court of law in a criminal case.

© Flip Schulke/Black Star/Stockphoto.com

Clarence Earl Gideon

## An Expanding Umbrella of Rights

The Bill of Rights was passed as a bulwark against the new federal government. It did not apply to the states. Congress, in fact, rejected a proposal by James Madison to prohibit the states from interfering with basic liberties.

Because America has a federal system of government, this created a paradox: The same constitutional rights established under the federal government were often meaningless within a state. It was as though the Bill of Rights were a ticket valid for travel on a high-speed train but no good for local commuting. Not until 1925 did the Supreme Court systematically begin to apply the Bill of Rights to the states. By 1970 the process was virtually complete. But even today, there is no written provision in the Constitution requiring the states to observe the Bill of Rights.

In 1833 the Supreme Court ruled in *Barron* v. *Baltimore* that the provisions of the Bill of Rights did not apply to the state governments and "this Court cannot so apply them."[155] Near the end of the Civil War, Congress passed the Fourteenth Amendment, which for the first time provided that "No State shall . . . deprive any person of life, liberty, or property, without due process of law." Did Congress thereby mean to "incorporate" the entire Bill of Rights into the Fourteenth Amendment and apply the Bill of Rights to the states? The argument never has been settled, but the point—thanks to the decisions of the Supreme Court—is rapidly becoming moot.

In the *Gitlow* case in 1925, the Court held that freedom of speech and press were among the "fundamental personal rights" protected by the Fourteenth Amendment from abridgment by the states.[156] The Court thus began a process of **selective incorporation** of the Bill of Rights by applying most of its provisions to the states under the Fourteenth Amendment. Two years later, the Court confirmed that freedom of speech was locked in under the Fourteenth Amendment.[157] In 1931 freedom of the press was specifically applied to the states.[158] In 1932, the Court partially incorporated the Sixth Amendment by requiring that a defendant in a capital case be represented by a lawyer.[159] Two years later, it applied freedom of religion to the states.[160] In 1937 freedom of assembly was held to apply to the states.[161]

Later that same year came the landmark incorporation decision of *Palko* v. *Connecticut.*[162] Frank Palko had been sentenced to life imprisonment for killing two police officers. Under an unusual Connecticut statute, the state could appeal and did; a new trial resulted in a death sentence. Palko appealed to the Supreme Court, contending that the second trial had placed him in double jeopardy, in violation of the Fifth Amendment. Justice Benjamin Cardozo ruled that the Fourteenth Amendment did require the states to abide by the Bill of Rights where the rights at stake were so fundamental that "neither liberty nor justice would exist if they were sacrificed." But, Cardozo added, although procedural rights such as immunity against double jeopardy were important, "they are not of the very essence of a scheme of ordered liberty," and therefore not binding to the states. The distinction was not helpful to Frank Palko; he was executed.

In 1947 the *Everson* case incorporated the principle of separation of church and state, and in 1961 *Mapp* established that the Fourth Amendment applied to the states. In 1962 the Court carried the Eighth Amendment's protection against cruel and unusual punishment to the states, and it further extended this protection in 1972 when it held that capital punishment as then administered constituted cruel and unusual punishment in violation of the Eighth Amendment.[163] In rapid succession, other rights were applied to the states: the Fifth Amendment's protection against self-incrimination;[164] and the Sixth Amendment's rights to counsel,[165] to a speedy trial,[166] to confrontation of an accused person by the witnesses against him or her,[167] to compulsory process for obtaining witnesses,[168] and to trial by jury in all serious criminal cases.[169]

In 1969, on Earl Warren's final day as chief justice, the Court, in *Benton* v. *Maryland,*[170] finally applied the Fifth Amendment's prohibition of double jeopardy to the states; it ruled that John Dalmer Benton should not have been tried twice for larceny. The Court thus overruled Justice Cardozo's decision in the *Palko* case.

The process of incorporation had in effect come full circle in the 32 years between *Palko* and *Benton.* Of the portions of the Bill of Rights that could apply to the states, almost every significant provision—with the exception of the Fifth Amendment's right to indictment by grand jury for major crimes—had been applied.* Thus, through the slow and shifting process of selective incorporation, the Supreme Court has brought the states almost entirely under the protective umbrella of the Bill of Rights.

## Balancing Liberty and Order

At a time when democracy is under pressure, when the American political system is being tested to determine whether it can meet the problems of an urbanized, complex, and changing society; the threat of terrorism; and the impact of economic globalization, the Bill of Rights is more important than ever.

The Bill of Rights and the Supreme Court remain a buffer between popular emotion and constitutional principle. For it is precisely in times of stress that fundamental liberties require the most protection. As Justice Robert H. Jackson put it so eloquently, freedom to differ over "things that do not matter much" is a "mere shadow" of freedom. "The test of its substance is the right to differ as to things that touch the heart of the existing order."[171]

Although the Supreme Court may at times have been more zealous than other institutions in protecting civil liberties, it is by no means insensitive to public pressure. As John P. Frank, a renowned lawyer and legal historian, noted: "The dominant lesson of our history . . . is that courts love liberty most when it is under pressure least."[172] It is not enough, therefore, to leave the protection of fundamental liberties to the courts. Public support for civil liberties is a vital factor in the preservation of those liberties.

It is in the field of civil liberties and civil rights that some of the most sensitive demands and supports (inputs) are fed into the political system. For example, in weighing the rights of defendants versus the suppression of crime by society, the federal government is making some highly important allocations of values (outputs). And in Supreme Court decisions on topics such as abortion, the rights of suspects, capital punishment, and school prayer, the public reaction (feedback) is formidable.

In applying the First Amendment and in balancing the claims of individual rights versus those of society, the Supreme Court generally moved during the 1960s in the direction of freer expression, reflecting the attitudes of a more permissive society. However, the Warren Court's decisions on the rights of defendants collided with a public alarmed about crime. In the 1970s, under Chief Jus-

*The Supreme Court, in *Hurtado* v. *California,* 110 U.S. 516 (1884), and later cases, declined to apply to the states the requirement of a grand jury indictment. Four other provisions of the Bill of Rights have not been incorporated to apply to the states—these have not been tested at the Supreme Court level. They are the right to a jury trial in civil cases where the amount in dispute exceeds $20 (Seventh Amendment); the ban on "excessive bail" and "fines" (Eighth Amendment); the right of the people "to keep and bear arms" (Second Amendment); and the ban on peacetime quartering of soldiers in private homes (Third Amendment). See Henry J. Abraham and Barbara A. Perry, *Freedom and the Court: Civil Rights and Liberties in the United States,* 7th ed. (New York: Oxford University Press, 1998), pp. 87–91.

© Porter Gifford

Naturalization ceremony, California

tice Warren Burger, the Court became more conservative. The Rehnquist Court in some, but by no means all, decisions expanded the rights of free expression and of the press even as it continued, in a number of instances, to limit the rights of criminal defendants. The Supreme Court under Chief Justice John G. Roberts continued to grapple with many of these same issues.

As always, the Court was charting new waters against a background of strong public sentiment. The delicate balance between liberty and order is constantly shifting, from issue to issue and from one decade to the next. Even with the Constitution as ballast, this will always be so.

## CITIZENSHIP

### Who Is a Citizen?

Although the Constitution as framed in 1787 uses the phrase "citizen of the United States," the term was not defined until the adoption of the Fourteenth Amendment in 1868. It provides the following: "All persons born or naturalized in the United States . . . are citizens of the United States and of the State wherein they reside."

The amendment rests on the principle of **jus soli** ("right of soil"), which confers citizenship by place of birth. Congress by law has also adopted the principle of **jus sanguinis** ("right of blood"), under which the citizenship of a child is determined by that of the parents. All persons born in the United States, except for the children of high-ranking foreign diplomats, are citizens. But in addition, children born abroad of American parents, or even of one American parent, may become citizens if they and their parents meet the complex and varying legal requirements.

An immigrant who wishes to become a citizen may become "naturalized" after living in the United States continuously for five years, or three years in the case of the spouse of a citizen. Applicants must be able to read, write, and speak English and demonstrate knowledge of the history, principles, and form of government of the United States. The oath of citizenship is administered by a federal judge, but the processing of applications for citizenship is handled by the U.S. Citizenship and Immigration Services (USCIS) of the Department of Homeland Security. Children younger than age 18 of naturalized citizens normally derive their American citizenship from their parents. Generally speaking, naturalized citizens enjoy the same rights as native-born Americans, although no naturalized citizen may be elected president or vice president.

### Loss of Citizenship

It is sometimes believed that people lose their citizenship if imprisoned for a year and a day, but this is not so; the laws of most of the 50 states deprive people convicted of certain crimes of the right to vote, but no state may deprive Americans, native-born or naturalized, of their citizenship. In general, the Supreme Court has barred congressional attempts to deprive natural-born Americans of their citizenship as punishment for crimes. For example, the Court has ruled that desertion from the armed forces during wartime is not grounds for deprivation of citizenship because that penalty would constitute "cruel and unusual punishment," forbidden by the Eighth Amendment,[173] and it struck down a law that provided automatic loss of citizenship for leaving the country in wartime to evade the draft.[174] As a result, the young men who went to live in Canada during the late 1960s to avoid military service in the Vietnam War did not lose their citizenship. In January 1977 President Jimmy Carter granted a blanket pardon to most Vietnam draft evaders.

The Supreme Court has held that naturalized citizens enjoy the same rights as native-born Americans.[175] It voided a law that said naturalized people lost their citizenship for living three years in their country of national origin.

And in 1967, in the landmark case of *Afroyim* v. *Rusk,* the Court ruled that Congress had no power to take away American citizenship unless it is freely renounced.[176] Specifically, the Court held that Beys Afroyim, a naturalized American, could not be deprived of citizenship for voting in an election in Israel.

## A Nation of Immigrants

In the 1920s, Congress imposed a "national origins" system of quotas to curb the wave of immigration that followed the First World War. Opponents of the national origins quota system argued that it was based on racial prejudice and designed to give preference to white, northern Europeans over immigrants from southern and eastern Europe. For example, in 1965, before the system was changed, of the quota for all countries of 150,000, 70 percent was allotted to three countries—Great Britain, Ireland, and Germany. Italy, where thousands of young people desired to come to the United States, had a quota of 5,666. India had a quota of 100, as did most of the Asian and African nations. (From 1917 until 1952, Chinese and almost all other Asians were completely excluded.)

The Immigration Act of 1965 abolished the national origins quota system and substituted a higher annual ceiling. The law also permitted a varying number of refugees to enter each year above that total.

By the mid-1980s, Congress was struggling to cope with problems created by the increasing flow of immigrants who entered the United States illegally, particularly from south of the border. In 1986 Congress passed a major immigration bill designed to reduce the flow of undocumented immigrants by punishing employers who knowingly hired them. The law also granted legal status to those who had arrived before January 1, 1982. The law did little to slow the tide of undocumented aliens, however. An estimated 11 million people live in the country illegally.[177] Some analysts put the figure much higher.

In 1990, Congress enacted a comprehensive revision of the immigration laws, setting a new annual ceiling of 675,000 immigrants beginning in 1995. The new law gave preference to relatives of U.S. citizens and was also designed to allow more Europeans to immigrate to America and to attract professionals, scientists, executives, and workers with special skills. It also eliminated the provisions of the McCarran-Walter Act of 1952 that had excluded people from entering the United States because of their political beliefs or ideology. In 1991, the State Department began a three-year lottery program to allow 40,000 immigrants annually from Ireland and other countries from which immigration had been reduced when the national origins system was abolished in 1965. Beginning in 1995, within the annual ceiling 55,000 immigrants have been admitted each year from Third World countries, also by lottery.

In addition, refugees may be admitted if they are granted political asylum. The Refugee Act of 1980 defined those who may claim political asylum as persons with "a well-founded fear of persecution" based on race, religion, nationality, or their political opinions.

Thousands of Cuban and Haitian refugees who streamed into Florida by boat in 1980 were admitted outside any quotas and given special status. Vietnamese "boat people" who escaped from Vietnam during the same period were admitted to the United States under the parole authority of the attorney general. By the 1990s, the policy had shifted and thousands of Haitian refugees who tried to escape their country by boat were forcibly turned back by the Coast Guard. Under a 1995 agreement with Cuba, the United States began returning Cuban refugees who were intercepted in the same manner on their hazardous journey toward Florida. But Cubans who managed to reach the United States were allowed to remain. And Cubans who could demonstrate a well-founded fear of persecution could be resettled to other countries rather than being forced to return home.

Not all immigrants seek to become citizens, of course. People living abroad can apply for an immigrant visa, and if approved they are granted legal permanent residence when they arrive in the United States. They then receive "green cards," alien registration cards, permitting them to work. Foreign students, certain undocumented immigrants, and temporary workers already in this country can also apply for legal permanent residence. There were almost 14 million legal permanent residents in the United States in 2005.[178]

The Supreme Court has considerably enlarged the rights of legal immigrants by providing them with access, equal to that of citizens, to welfare benefits, Medicaid, and the right to practice law (although not to state employment as troopers or teachers).[179] And the children of undocumented aliens have the same right to attend public schools as the children of citizens.[180]

By the mid-1990s, however, a political backlash had developed against immigrants who crossed the nation's borders and entered the United States illegally. The sentiment was particularly high in states such as California,

## A Mexican Woman's Story: "My Heart Broke"

TUCSON— It took years for Normaeli Gallardo, a single mother from Acapulco, to drum up the courage to join the growing stream of Mexican women illegally crossing the border on the promise of a job, in her case working in a Kansas meatpacking plant for $5.15 an hour.

First, she had to grapple with the idea of landing in an unfamiliar country, all alone, with no grasp of English and no place to live.

Then she had to imagine crossing the Arizona desert, where immigrants face heat exhaustion by day, frostbite by night and the cunning of the "coyotes"—smugglers who charge as much as $1,500 to guide people into the United States and who make a habit of robbing and sexually assaulting them.

And finally, Ms. Gallardo, 38, who earned $50 a week at an Acapulco hotel, had to contemplate life without her two vivacious daughters, Isabel, 7, and Fernanda, 5. That once unimaginable trade-off—leaving her children behind so they could one day leave poverty behind—had suddenly become her only option.

She simply did not earn enough money, she said. If she paid the electric bill, she fell behind on rent; if she paid the water bill, she could forget about new clothes for the children. . . . "My heart broke, my heart broke," said Ms. Gallardo . . . "but I had to give them a better life. I told them I would go and work, and we could buy a small plot of land and build a little house and have a dog."

Ms. Gallardo never made it to Kansas. . . . After walking eight hours at night and committing $500 to a coyote, she stumbled down a rocky hill near Tucson and broke her ankle. The coyote left her sitting on a nearby highway in the desert, where the Border Patrol eventually found her, took her to a local emergency room and deported her to Nogales, Mexico, the next day . . . She needed surgery on her ankle at a cost of 3,000 pesos, or seven weeks' salary. She also owes the friends who gave the coyote $500.

—*New York Times,* January 10, 2006

Texas, and Florida, which had a high influx of undocumented immigrants.

In California, the then Republican governor, Pete Wilson, found a responsive audience for his anti-immigration crusade. Wilson argued that the state was spending more than $3 billion a year on education, health care, and prisons for undocumented immigrants. He supported Proposition 187, a measure to deny government welfare and other benefits to people who were in the state illegally. The voters of California overwhelmingly approved the proposition in 1994. But in 1995 a federal district court declared the major provisions of Proposition 187 unconstitutional. The state, the court ruled, could not deny education, health, and welfare services to undocumented immigrants. To do so, the court reasoned, would amount to a state scheme to control immigration, a power granted to the federal government under the Constitution.

In 1999, Governor Gray Davis, Wilson's Democratic successor, agreed that certain remaining provisions of the proposition would not be implemented, and the court approved that decision. Supporters of Proposition 187 failed to place it on the ballot in 2000 as an amendment to the state's constitution. Davis was recalled by California voters in 2003, and supporters of the anti-immigration measure hoped that it might be revived un-

A highway sign on Interstate 5 near San Diego, California, warns motorists to watch out for undocumented immigrants darting across the road. Many have been killed at this spot at night.

## Leaving Cuba: The U.S. Government's "Wet Foot, Dry Foot" Policy

Many refugees from Cuba have perished trying to make the hazardous voyage by boat to Florida. If intercepted at sea by the U.S. Coast Guard, the refugees are turned back. Under an agreement with Cuba by the Clinton administration, if the Cubans make it to dry land, they may be permitted to remain and seek legal status after a year. For that reason, the rule became known as the "wet foot, dry foot" policy.

der the new governor, Arnold Schwarzenegger. After his inauguration, the former actor urged that illegal immigrants be denied driver's licenses unless adequate background and security checks were conducted.

In 2004 President George W. Bush proposed a plan to allow undocumented immigrants to work legally for a time in the United States (see Chapter 5). Congress did not approve the plan, but by 2006 the immigration issue had become the subject of a major political battle. In April hundreds of thousands of immigrants peacefully demonstrated on the mall in Washington and in cities across America to urge Congress to grant citizenship to those who had entered the country illegally. In the nation's capital, the crowd chanted, "Today we march; tomorrow, we vote."

Bush found himself pressured on one side by conservatives who favored tough controls along the border with Mexico to keep out illegal immigrants, on the other side by business groups that contended immigrants were needed to perform low-paying jobs that many Americans shunned. In response, Bush sought the middle ground; a month after the nationwide demonstrations, in a speech from the Oval Office, he proposed to send 6,000 National Guard troops to patrol the border, but renewed his call for a guest worker program and outlined a plan to allow illegal immigrants to gain legal status and, in time, to become citizens. In the aftermath of Bush's speech, however, Congress remained deadlocked over immigration but in September 2006 voted $1.2 billion for a 700-mile fence along the border with Mexico.

*for more information about immigration see: http://www.closeup.org/immigrat.htm*

## Change, Citizen Action, and Dissent

The Bill of Rights is really a list of promises by the government to the people. There is no similar list of constitutional obligations of the people to the government. Nevertheless, for a democracy to work, citizens must be willing to participate in the political process. When Americans work for a better environment, support political candidates, or speak out or organize on public issues, whether they dissent from established policy or support it, they are participating in the democratic process. Their opinions and actions are inputs to the political system. Freedom to dissent is an important aspect of democracy. In fact, it may be argued that one of the most important responsibilities Americans have is to exercise the rights protected by the Constitution, including those of free speech and dissent.

Voting in elections, participating in political party activity and community programs, forming and expressing political opinions, either singly or through groups—all are necessary to the workings of a healthy political system.

Many Americans, however, lament that the system is not responsive enough to their interests. They complain that politicians are only interested in getting reelected and lining their own pockets. Often, they are right. But sometimes those who feel this way fail to take as simple a step as registering to vote. Frequently, it does seem that the political system is slow to respond to pressures for change and that ordinary citizens have no way to express themselves to influence political leaders. Yet, at times, individual citizens have shown that it is not only possible to "fight City Hall" but, occasionally, to win.

In Los Angeles three decades ago, a social worker named John Serrano, the son of a Mexican shoemaker, was told by a principal to get his children out of the barrio of East Los Angeles and into a better school "if you want to give them a chance." Serrano took the advice and moved out to a suburb, but he did not forget the encounter. It seemed to him unjust that schools in a poor Mexican American neighborhood should be worse than those in wealthier neighborhoods. Serrano, with a group of other parents, went to court. The supreme court of the State of California ruled that John Serrano was right, that a system of financing public schools through local property taxes "invidiously discriminates" against the poor because it makes the quality of a child's schooling depend on where the child lives.

The implications of the California decision were dramatic. Over time, it has gradually led to a sweeping change in the way public schools are financed across America.

Except for Hawaii, where the state finances school costs, every state relies heavily on real estate taxes to pay for public schools. In the wake of the *Serrano* case, however, dozens of lawsuits were filed in other states to try to bring about a change. The effort received a temporary setback in 1973 when the U.S. Supreme Court ruled in a similar case in Texas.[181] The Court held, 5–4, that the Texas system did not violate the Fourteenth Amendment "merely because the burdens or benefits . . . fall unevenly

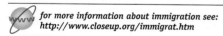

". . . tomorrow we vote." Thousands of immigrants demonstrated on the mall in Washington in 2006.



depending upon the relative wealth of the political subdivisions in which citizens live." Despite the Supreme Court's ruling, John Serrano's lawsuit had set in motion forces that could not be stopped. Many states adopted alternative methods of school financing as a result of the California decision. In 1989, for example, the Texas supreme court unanimously ruled that the state's system would have to be changed because of "glaring disparities" between rich and poor school districts.[182]

By 2003, more than two-thirds of the states had made progress closing the funding gaps for low-income districts.[183] In 43 states, state programs have been established to guarantee all pupils a minimum level of school funding.[184] The momentum for change and the pressures for equality of school district financing continued. In California, and in America, John Serrano had demonstrated that sometimes, at least, one citizen can make a difference.

## CHAPTER HIGHLIGHTS

- The Bill of Rights, the first 10 amendments to the Constitution, is the fundamental charter of American liberty.
- In a democratic society, freedom is not absolute. In the American political system, the Supreme Court is the mechanism called upon to resolve conflicts between liberty and order and between the rights of the individual and the rights of society. The Court operates within the framework of the Bill of Rights.
- The First Amendment is designed to protect freedom of religion, speech, press, assembly, and petition.
- The Supreme Court has limited the freedom of expression and freedom of the press in various ways. It has sometimes required journalists to reveal sources; permitted individuals to sue the press for libel; recognized the right of privacy; banned "obscene" material; and upheld the power of the government to regulate radio and television.
- The First Amendment has two clauses protecting freedom of religion. The free exercise clause protects the right of individuals to worship or believe as they wish, or to hold no religious beliefs. The establishment clause provides that "Congress shall make no law respecting an establishment of religion."
- The Fourth Amendment protects the right of individuals to "be secure in their persons, houses, papers, and effects, against unreasonable searches and seizures." In the United States, as a general principle,

police are not authorized to search a home without a search warrant signed by a judicial officer and issued on probable cause that the materials to be seized are in the place to be searched. But there are exceptions to the warrant requirement.

- The right of privacy, or what Justice Brandeis called "the right to be left alone," has been defined and protected by a series of Supreme Court decisions and legislation. In the 1973 case *Roe* v. *Wade,* the Court held that the concept of privacy included the right to a legal abortion.
- In the electronic age, the right of privacy has been threatened by sophisticated wiretapping and eavesdropping devices. However, Congress has passed laws requiring court warrants for electronic surveillance in domestic criminal cases and in national security cases.
- The Fifth and Fourteenth Amendments to the Constitution provide for "due process of law," a phrase designed to protect the individual against the arbitrary power of the state. The Bill of Rights entitles suspects or defendants to be represented by a lawyer, to be informed of the charges against them, to have a speedy and public trial by jury, to summon witnesses to testify in their behalf, to cross-examine prosecution witnesses, and to refuse to testify against themselves.
- The Fifth through Eighth Amendments also protect the accused from being held in excessive bail, or subjected to cruel and unusual punishment, or tried twice for the same offense.
- The rights of the accused were strengthened by the cases *Gideon* v. *Wainwright* (1963), *Escobedo* v. *Illinois* (1964), and *Miranda* v. *Arizona* (1966). *Miranda* held that suspects must be clearly informed of their rights—including the right to be silent and the right to a lawyer—before police can ask them any questions. In 2000, the Supreme Court, in *Dickerson* v. *United States,* rejected a challenge to the *Miranda* decision.
- The USA Patriot Act, passed after the 9/11 terrorist attacks and modified and renewed in 2006, expanded the power of the federal government to move against suspected terrorists. Critics, however, argued that it went too far and endangered constitutional rights.
- The Bill of Rights was passed as a safeguard against the new federal government. It did not apply to the states. But between 1925 and 1970, through the process of selective incorporation, the Supreme Court brought states and local governments almost entirely under the Bill of Rights.
- Under the Fourteenth Amendment, anyone born or naturalized in the United States is a citizen. The Supreme Court has held that Congress may not take away a person's citizenship unless it is freely renounced.

## KEY TERMS

civil liberties, p. 92
Bill of Rights, p. 92
First Amendment, p. 93
clear and present danger test, p. 94
absolute position, p. 98
balancing test, p. 98
free exercise clause, p. 103
establishment clause, p. 105
due process of law, p. 108
exclusionary rule, p. 112
indictment, p. 114
criminal information, p. 114
USA Patriot Act, p. 114
*Miranda* warnings, p. 116
selective incorporation, p. 119
jus soli, p. 120
jus sanguinis, p. 121

## SUGGESTED WEBSITES

**http://www.aclu.org**
*American Civil Liberties Union*
The ACLU is a nonpartisan, nonprofit public interest organization devoted exclusively to protecting the basic civil liberties of all Americans and extending them to groups that have traditionally been denied them. The ACLU seeks to do this in three ways—through litigation, legislation, and education.

**http://www.closeup.org**
*The Close Up Foundation*
The nation's largest nonprofit citizen education organization. Works to promote informed participation in the democratic process through educational programs for students.

**http://www.freedomforum.org**
*Freedom Forum*
A nonpartisan, international foundation dedicated to the freedoms covered by the First Amendment.

**http://www.judicialwatch.org**
*Judicial Watch*
A nonprofit foundation that supports conservative principles, acts as a watchdog over the government and the legal system, and attempts to expose corruption while promoting ethics in public life.

**http://www.nnirr.org**
*National Network for Immigrant and Refugee Rights*
The NNIRR is a national organization composed of local coalitions, activists, and immigrant, refugee, community, religious, civil rights, and labor organizations. The goals of NNIRR are to promote a just immigration and refugee policy in the United States and to defend and expand the rights of all immigrants and refugees.

**http://www.supremecourtus.gov**
*The United States Supreme Court*
The official website of the U.S. Supreme Court contains the full text of the Court's decisions the same day they are released, as well as the Court's calendar, dockets, rules, a visitors' guide, and other information about the Court.

**http://uscis.gov**
*The U.S. Citizenship and Immigration Services (USCIS)*
USCIS, a division of the Department of Homeland Security, oversees immigration to the United States. The USCIS also regulates permanent and temporary immigration to the United States. Additionally, it oversees the U.S. Border Patrol, which covers more than 8,000 miles of international boundaries.

**http://www.wlf.org**
*Washington Legal Foundation*
The WLF is an advocate for free enterprise principles, limited government, property rights, and reform of the civil and criminal justice system. The WLF tries to achieve its goals through litigation, publication of legal studies, and education.

## SUGGESTED READING

Abraham, Henry J., and Perry, Barbara A. *Freedom and the Court: Civil Rights and Liberties in the United States,* 8th edition* (University Press of Kansas, 2003). A detailed examination of the Bill of Rights. Analyzes how the Supreme Court, through decisions in specific cases, has gradually enlarged the area of constitutional freedom in the United States.

Berns, Walter. *Freedom, Virtue, and the First Amendment* (Greenwood Press, 1969). (Originally published in 1957.) A provocative analysis that takes sharp issue with some of the major court decisions designed to protect freedom of expression in the United States.

Blanchard, Margaret. *Revolutionary Sparks: Freedom of Expression in Modern America* (Oxford University Press, 1992). A broad historical overview of the evolution of free expression in the United States.

Fiss, Owen M. *The Irony of Free Speech* (Harvard University Press, 1996). The author, an eminent legal scholar, argues that unfettered freedom of speech can actually diminish liberty, and that certain types of expression—such as hate speech and pornography—should be restricted.

Hentoff, Nat. *The First Freedom: The Tumultuous History of Free Speech in America* (Delacorte Press, 1980). A lively, clearly written analysis of the history of the First Amendment. Contains a detailed discussion of leading Supreme Court cases involving free speech, freedom of the press, and freedom of religion.

Hentoff, Nat. *Living the Bill of Rights: How to Be an Authentic American** (University of California Press, 1999). A spirited argument in favor of maximum respect for individual liberties in public and private life, by a leading defender of civil liberties. According to Hentoff, unless Americans know and embrace the Bill of Rights, "the future of the nation as a strongly functioning constitutional democracy will be at risk."

Ivers, Gregg. *American Constitutional Law: Power and Politics, Volume 2: Civil Rights and Liberties** (Houghton Mifflin Company, 2002). A comprehensive civil liberties casebook. Focuses on first amendment freedoms, criminal justice, equal protection issues, privacy, and voting rights; and emphasizes the role of interest groups in the judicial process.

Kersch, Ken I. *Freedom of Speech: Rights and Liberties Under the Law* (ABC Clio, 2003). An analysis of the history and meaning of free speech in the United States. Includes an extended glossary and chronology, as well as excerpts from important documents about free speech.

Lewis, Anthony. *Make No Law: The Sullivan Case and the First Amendment** (Random House, 1991). A highly readable account of a landmark Supreme Court case on freedom of the press. The court's decision, in a 1960 libel suit brought by an Alabama official against the New York Times, redefined the boundaries of the First Amendment by allowing the press to report about public officials with much greater freedom.

Lewis, Anthony. *Gideon's Trumpet** (Random House, 1989). (Originally published in 1964.) A detailed and readable account of the Supreme Court case that established the right of a poor man to have a lawyer when charged with a serious criminal offense in a state court. Sheds light on the role of the Court in safeguarding the rights of defendants.

Mason, Alpheus T. *The Supreme Court: Palladium of Freedom** (University of Michigan Press, 1962). A concise discussion of the Supreme Court's place in the American political system by a distinguished scholar of constitutional law. Emphasizes the Bill of Rights and the Court's role in protecting minority views.

Matsuda, Mari J., Lawrence, Charles R., III, Delgado, Richard, and Crenshaw, Kimberlè Williams. *Words That Wound: Critical Race Theory, Assaultive Speech, and the First Amendment** (HarperCollins, 2003). A vigorous presentation of the case for measures such as "speech codes" to restrict hateful expression on American college campuses.

Mill, John Stuart. *On Liberty** (Broadview Press, 1999). (Originally published in 1859.) A classic examination of the problem of balancing individual rights and the rights of the community.

Savage, David. *The Supreme Court and Individual Rights*, 4th edition* (CQ Press, 2004). A useful survey of the impact of Supreme Court decisions on individual rights. Focuses on First Amendment rights and the guarantees of political participation, due process, and equal protection.

Tichenor, David J. *Dividing Lines: The Politics of Immigration Control in America** (Princeton University Press, 2002). A comprehensive analysis of U.S. immigration policy from 1776 to the 1990s. The author stresses that immigration policies have sometimes been expansive and at other times restrictive. He accounts for the variations by analyzing developments in Congress, the executive branch, and among interest groups.

White, G. Edward. *Justice Oliver Wendell Holmes: Law and the Inner Self* (Oxford University Press, 1993). A readable and absorbing biography, rich in historical detail and psychological insights, of the Supreme Court justice whom the author has called the "best known judge in American history."

*Available in paperback edition.

# Chapter 5

# The Struggle for Equal Rights

ON THE NIGHT of June 7, 1998, in Jasper, Texas, James Byrd, Jr., 49, was beaten, chained to a pickup truck by three men, and dragged 2 miles to his death. His head and arm were found a mile from the rest of his body. Four months later, in Laramie, Wyoming, Matthew Shepard, a 21-year-old college student, was badly beaten, tied to a fence on the prairie, and left for dead. He was found the next morning and taken to a hospital but died five days later.

Both crimes horrified the nation. In both cases, the victims were apparently singled out and killed because they were different. Byrd was an African American, and his murderers were white; two were white supremacists. Matthew Shepard was gay.

Although these are extreme examples of brutal crimes, many members of minority groups in America face discrimination—sometimes subtle, sometimes blatant—in their everyday lives. It is a truth well known to those who experience it, whether faced by the Hispanic newcomer struggling for a foothold in American society, or the woman executive who hits the "glass ceiling" that blocks her further ascent on the corporate ladder.

America is a multicultural society, made up of many groups with distinct ethnic, racial, and religious identities. Early in the 20th century there was a popular notion that immigrants should be rapidly assimilated into American society, into "the melting pot." Even that controversial concept, however, reflects a basic truth—that the United States is a land of astonishing diversity. Yet, the rights proclaimed in the Declaration of Independence and those set forth in the legal language of the Constitution are not enjoyed equally by all Americans. For many minority groups, the equality promised by these fundamental American charters has been an elusive goal rather than an achieved fact, a vision of a possible future rather than a description of the often bleak present.

Although progress has been made in reducing inequalities among diverse groups, there are continuing racial divisions in American society, as well as racial tensions, sometimes accompanied by violence. At times the images on television are horrifying, as when police in Los Angeles were captured on videotape clubbing an African American man whom they had stopped after a car chase. These images may not be typical, and they may even give a distorted picture of America to the world. But they are nonetheless real and cannot be ignored or wished away.

Despite the civil rights laws enacted by Congress in the 1960s and decisions of the Supreme Court, even today many of the more than 36.7 million African Americans do not enjoy full social and economic equality. Almost one out of four blacks in the United States is poor—by official definition of the federal government—as opposed to about one out of 12 whites.* Some African Americans, it is true, have made substantial economic gains in recent years. For example, half of black married couples earn $50,000 a year or more. But at the same time, the gap in income levels and living standards has widened between the growing African American middle class and the millions of blacks still below the poverty line. Economic gains registered by some African Americans were little comfort to the unemployed black youth in the inner city, or even to a middle-class black family seeking to move into a hostile white suburb.

In America today, the infant mortality rate for African American children is more than twice as high as it is for whites.[1] Among young black males, homicide is the leading cause of death.[2] Nearly one out of three African American men in their twenties is in prison, on parole, or on probation.[3] Black males have a 32 percent chance of serving time in prison at some point in their lives; white males have a 6 percent chance.[4]

In 2006 the rate of black unemployment was 8.9 percent, more than double that of whites.[5] And according to earlier census data, at $29,026, the median income of black families was less than two-thirds of the $46,900 median income of white families.[6]

This statistical portrait does not sketch in the daily indignities, the rebuffs, the humiliations, and the defeats that many African Americans may face. And despite substantial changes for the better in recent years, the African American citizen in many cases remains on the outside of American society, looking in. It is true that income, political power, education, and employment opportunities for African Americans have increased since the civil rights movement of the 1960s, especially for the black middle class. But William Julius Wilson and other scholars have suggested that, even with the gains of the civil rights movement, conditions have actually deteriorated for blacks in the inner cities.[7]

An African American still has a greater chance than a white American of being born in a poor neighborhood and of living in crowded, substandard housing. If an African American youth does not succumb to rats, crime, crack cocaine, heroin, drive-by shootings, gang warfare, acquired immune deficiency syndrome (AIDS), and other soul-destroying forces of the ghetto, perhaps he or she will obtain work when the economy is strong. But the work may be menial and low-paying. Black families may have to buy shoddy merchandise at high credit rates from neighborhood merchants. The food at the local chain supermarket—if any large chains operate branches in the neighborhood at all—may be of poorer quality and priced higher than the same items at the chain's branches in white neighborhoods. If an African American man or woman raises a family, the children may face the same bleak future, continuing the cycle of poverty and despair.

In some communities police engage in "racial profiling." In those localities black Americans have a greater chance of being stopped by police while driving or even walking down the street. Some African Americans speak

**FIGURE 5-1**

**Median Income of Selected Minorities in the United States, 2002**

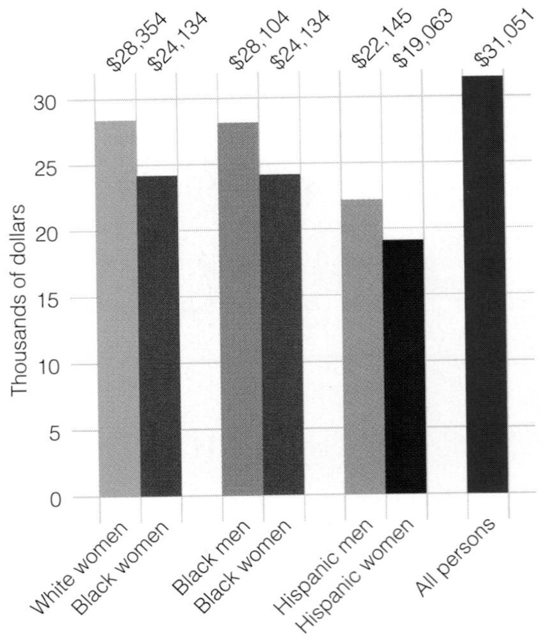


SOURCE: U.S. Bureau of the Census.

*The federal government has defined the poverty level for a family of four as an annual income of less than $18,392. Data from U.S. Bureau of the Census, Current Population Reports, *Poverty in the United States: 2002.*

© Chromosohm/Sohm/Photo Researchers, Inc.

Lettuce pickers, San Joaquin Valley, California

sardonically of a supposed crime only they may face: "driving while black."

Even if a black youth gets a job as a skilled worker, or goes to college and enters a profession, his or her troubles are not necessarily over. On moving to a white neighborhood, black families may encounter hostility and ostracism. In the best of economic circumstances, African American parents still must face the problem of explaining to their children the divisions in American society between white and black.

But it is not only African Americans who are struggling for equal rights in the United States. For the 2.8 million American Indians, the rhetoric of equality has a particularly ironic sound. Often living in poverty, with an unemployment rate on the reservations about eight times the national average, the first Americans are outcasts in a land that once was theirs.

By 2004 the nation's Hispanic community had become the largest minority group in the United States. Yet Hispanics are another major segment of the population that has been denied full equality in American society. The term "Hispanic" usually includes Mexican Americans—by far the largest group—as well as Puerto Ricans, Cubans, and persons of Central or South American or other Spanish origin. The Census Bureau has estimated that more than 40 million Hispanics live in the United States, including undocumented immigrants.[8] More than half of the total number of Hispanics—54.8 percent—were born in the United States.[9]

***for more information about the U.S. Census Bureau, see: http://www.census.gov***

## A Mississippi Memory

The earliest memory of my life is of an incident that occurred when I was three-and-a-half years old in Holly Springs, Mississippi. My father was registrar and professor of religion and philosophy at Rust College, a Negro Methodist institution there.

One hot summer day, my mother and I walked from the college campus to the town square, a distance of maybe half a mile. I remember it as clearly as though it were a few weeks ago. I held her finger tightly as we kicked up the red dust on the unpaved streets leading to the downtown area. When we reached the square she did her shopping, and we headed for home. Like any other three-and-a-half-year-old on a hot day, I got thirsty.

"Mother," I said, "I want a Coke." She replied that we could not get Cokes there and I would have to wait until we got home where there was lots of Coke in the icebox.

"But I want my Coke now," I insisted. She was just as insistent that we could not get a Coke now. "Do as I tell you," she said, "wait 'til we get home; you can have a Coke with plenty of ice."

"There's a little boy going into a store!" I exclaimed as I spied another child who was a little bigger than I. "I bet he's going to get a Coke." So I pulled my mother by the finger until we stood in front of what I recall as a drugstore looking through the closed screen doors. Surely enough, the other lad had climbed upon a stool at the counter and was already sipping a soft drink.

"But I told you you can't get a Coke in there," she said. "Why can't I?" I asked again. The answer was the same, "You just can't." I then inquired with complete puzzlement, "Well, why can he?" Her quiet answer thundered in my ears. "He's white."

We walked home in silence under the pitiless glare of the Mississippi sun. Once we were home she threw herself across the bed and wept. I walked out on the front porch and sat on the steps alone with my three-and-a-half-year-old thoughts.

—James Farmer, former national director of the Congress of Racial Equality (CORE), in *Esquire,* May 1969

"You'll just love the way he handles."



According to the Census Bureau, 20.6 million Mexican Americans lived in the United States. Although Mexican Americans make up a sizable population bloc in five southwestern states, they are underrepresented politically. Many are migrant workers living in abysmal conditions.

Puerto Ricans, all of whom are American citizens, form another important segment of the Hispanic community. Yet many of the approximately 3.8 million Americans of Puerto Rican background who live on the mainland suffer discrimination and poverty and are locked in the barrios, or slums, of the great cities.

Asian Americans have often been the targets of hostility and bias, sometimes by other ethnic groups. The more than 11.6 million Asian Americans are now the third-largest minority in the nation, ranking in size right after Hispanics and African Americans.[10]

The women's liberation movement that emerged as an important social and political force during the 1970s reflected the growing awareness that women, although constituting a majority of the population, were, in effect, another "minority group." Discrimination based on sex is built into many public and private institutions. Some indication of the problem may be seen in the gap in earnings between men and women. In 2004, for example, the median income of men was $40,798, while that of women was $31,223.[11]

Gay men and women, although gradually gaining acceptance in many American communities, still face formidable obstacles, ranging from subtle bias in the workplace to physical violence on the streets. Gay and lesbian voters, however, have become an important political force in a number of communities, and nationally.

The 51 million Americans with disabilities comprise another group whose rights, until recently, were often neglected. And many other minorities also have suffered discrimination. Jews have been widely accepted in many areas of American society but are still unwelcome in some private clubs, in the executive suites of some corporations, and in some residential areas. Until Al Gore chose Senator Joseph I. Lieberman as his vice-presidential running mate in the 2000 presidential campaign, no Jew had ever run for that office or for president as a major-party candidate. Prejudice against Catholics was a major issue in John F. Kennedy's 1960 presidential campaign. Italian Americans are often the victims of subtle discrimination because of the stereotype, reinforced by movies and television, that they are members of, or somehow linked to, organized crime. Arab Americans and Muslims—particularly in the wake of the 9/11 terrorist attacks—as well as other groups are victims of racial slurs and discrimination. And discrimination is not limited to ethnic or religious minorities. Older Americans may face discrimination when they seek employment or in other ways. Children and persons with AIDS also have sometimes been deprived of their rights.

All these inequalities cast a shadow over the ideals and the future of America. Racial polarization has been reflected in the nation's political issues and alignments. For example, as African Americans and other minority groups pressed for greater equality and opportunity, white blue-collar workers in many cases reacted with hostility. Blacks and Hispanics migrating outward from the inner city frequently moved into white ethnic neighborhoods. White factory or construction workers who had saved their money to buy modest houses in such neighborhoods often felt that their property values, their schools—and perhaps their jobs—were threatened by the newcomers. Ugly racial incidents sometimes resulted. Social tension and racial protests put continuing pressure on American institutions.

There is a great irony in all this, because, if present demographic trends continue, whites in the United States might become a minority sometime near the middle of the 21st century. By 2060, according to Census Bureau projections, it seems likely that the combined Hispanic, black, Asian American, and American Indian population will outnumber the white population.[12] When and if that happens, the struggle for minority rights will take on a rather different meaning.

By the 1990s, the use of the term "multiculturalism" among many scholars reflected the fact that America was made up of many different groups of diverse backgrounds and cultures. But as these groups vied for the political and economic power that had often been denied to them, critics raised the question of whether there might be serious disadvantages for America in all of this—a danger that the country might fragment into many separate ethnic groups and lose its national identity and unity. Nevertheless, in a society marked by diversity, the problems remained.

Key Question In this chapter we will explore a key question: ***Will the nation support programs that try to deal with some of the causes of racial inequality—poverty, hunger, discrimination, and unemployment—or will the public support substantial cuts in the government programs created to alleviate these problems?*** Underlying the political debate over social programs are deeper questions about the proper role, size, and reach of government.

A number of additional issues to consider arise in any discussion of civil rights. What steps has government taken to ensure the rights of minorities? What is the history of the struggle for equal rights in America? How did the civil rights movement of the 1960s evolve? How have government and private institutions contributed to discrimination? These are some of the problems we will explore in examining the continuing struggle for equality in America.

## Some Groups in Profile

### American Indians

Who is an American Indian? Because there is no accepted demographic definition, an American Indian is whoever tells the census-taker he or she is one. (In the 1990s, the term "Native American" was preferred by some individuals and tribal groups who found "Indian" objectionable.[13] As of 2004, however, the federal government still maintained a Bureau of Indian Affairs, and groups representing American Indians and Native Americans generally expressed no preference for one term over the other and regarded them as interchangeable.) According to the Census Bureau, 2.8 million American Indians, Aleuts, and Eskimos lived in the United States at the end of 2002.[14] (The Eskimos and Aleuts of Alaska are two culturally distinct groups and prefer the term "Alaska Natives.") An estimated 538,000 American Indians live on reservations or trust lands.[15]

*for more information about American Indians see:*
*http://www.census.gov/population/www/socdemo/race/indian.html*

American Indians are American citizens (Congress conferred citizenship on all Indians in 1924), and there is no requirement that Native Americans live on a reservation, an area of land "reserved" for their use and held in trust by the federal government. There are 309 reservations in 32 states, varying in size from California settlements of only a few acres to the 16-million-acre Navajo reservation spreading through Arizona, New Mexico, and Utah.

The federal government spends more than $11 billion a year on aid to American Indians.[16] But the Bureau of Indian Affairs does not have responsibility for assisting those who are living off the reservation, of whom almost one-third live in poverty.[17] And the plight of American Indians living on the reservation is little better.

Few reservations can support their populations; unemployment among Native Americans averages 50 percent on the reservations, and one quarter of American Indians and Alaska Natives live below the poverty level.[18] Many on the reservations live in shacks, adobe huts, even abandoned automobiles. Incidence of illness and disease is significantly higher among American Indians than among the white population. Unsanitary housing, unsafe water, and malnutrition all contribute to ill health among Native Americans. The suicide rate among Native Americans, primarily on reservations, is almost double that of all Americans.[19] Although the rate of deaths from alcoholism among American Indians has decreased, it is more than five times as high as the national average.[20] In recent years some American Indians have prospered by operating gambling casinos, but their wealth did not change the dismal conditions in which the majority lived.

The federal government has been deeply involved in the history of the white man's broken promises to the American Indians. Until 1871 the government treated Indian tribes as separate, sovereign nations. After that, the government stopped making treaties with the tribes and adopted a policy of breaking down the tribal structure. The Dawes Act of 1887 divided reservations into small allotments, but the land not distributed to individuals was put up for public sale. Between 1887 and 1934, some 90 million acres were removed from tribal hands in one way or another. When a 1934 federal law ended the prac-

**White America Keeps Its Promise**

They made us many promises, more than I can remember, but they never kept but one; they promised to take our land, and they took it.

—Anonymous American Indian

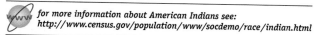

tice of breaking up the reservations, the tribes regained some of their vitality.

In 1953 Congress adopted a policy declaration designed to end the special trustee relationship between the federal government and American Indians. This policy of "forced termination" was almost unanimously opposed by American Indians, who feared that without federal protection their lands and cultural identity would vanish. Congress finally ended the policy in 1974 and gave Native American tribes control over federal programs on their reservations. In recent decades, a number of Indian tribes have had some success in receiving millions of dollars in compensation and recovering lands taken by the federal government.

© AP/Wide World Photos

"Some have prospered." Indian gambling casino near Albuquerque, New Mexico

But there were other grievances. Beset by poverty, disease, illiteracy, substandard housing, and the threat of forced cultural assimilation, American Indians felt they had long overdue claims on the American political system. Beginning in the 1960s, American Indians added their voices to the protests of other minorities. In 1972 several hundred Native Americans went to Washington and occupied the Bureau of Indian Affairs (BIA). The protesters arrived in a caravan they called "The Trail of Broken Treaties."

In 1973, 200 armed supporters of the American Indian Movement (AIM) seized the tiny village of Wounded Knee on the Pine Ridge Indian Reservation in South Dakota. The militants had chosen their target carefully and with a shrewd understanding of modern mass communications; Wounded Knee was the site of the massacre of at least 153 Sioux by the U.S. Army in 1890, and it was named in the title of a best-selling book published in 1970.[21] The occupation stirred national attention and attracted network television coverage.

© Dan Budnick/Woodfin Camp & Associates, Inc.

© John Running/Stock, Boston

The American Past

## SACAGAWEA: HONORING AN AMERICAN INDIAN WOMAN

In the year 2000, Sacagawea, the young American Indian woman who acted as interpreter for the Lewis and Clark expedition (1803–1806), was honored on the new one-dollar coin.

The daughter of a Shoshone Indian chief, Sacagawea was kidnapped by the Hidatsa Indians as a young girl. She became one of two wives to Toussaint Charbonneau, a French Canadian trader who won her in a bet with the Indians. When Charbonneau signed on with Meriwether Lewis and William Clark, Sacagawea, although just 15 years old and six months pregnant, was enlisted as interpreter. She was the only woman to accompany the 33 members of the permanent party to the Pacific Ocean and back.

In the late summer of 1805, the Americans were running low on food and were without fresh horses. With Sacagawea's help, they crossed the Continental Divide at Lemhi Pass. They then encountered a band of 60 Shoshone warriors who could have wiped them out easily, ending the expedition. But Sacagawea recognized their chief, Cameahwait, as her long-lost brother, and recognized another Shoshone, Jumping Fish, as a girl she had not seen since the kidnapping.

For her services on the expedition, Sacagawea was given nothing, though her husband received $500 and 320 acres of land. Six years after the expedition, Sacagawea gave birth to a daughter, Lisette. On December 23, 1812, Sacagawea died of an illness at age 25. Eight months after her death, William Clark legally adopted her two children.

On July 23, 1999, one dozen special 22-karat gold versions of the Sacagawea coin traveled aboard the space shuttle *Columbia* and were later donated to several museums. The captain of the spacecraft was Eileen Collins, the first woman to command a space shuttle.

In January 2000, the new dollar coins were sent to the Federal Reserve and began circulation.

—Adapted from the *New York Times,* October 26, 1999; PBS Online, "Lewis and Clark: The Journey of the Corps of Discovery"; and the U.S. Mint, "The Birth of the Golden Dollar Coin: A Timeline"

The golden dollar issued in 1999 honors Sacagawea, the young Shoshone Indian woman who acted as interpreter for Lewis and Clark.

For 70 days, U.S. marshals surrounded the village; two American Indian supporters were killed in exchanges of gunfire, and one federal agent was paralyzed. After more than two months, the militants surrendered under a peace agreement. The second battle of Wounded Knee was over, but the broader problems faced by American Indians remained.

### Hispanic Americans

Like Native Americans, many Americans of Hispanic origin must contend with the twin problems of discrimination and poverty. Of the total Hispanic American population of 40.4 million, almost 26 million are Mexican Americans. (See Figure 5-2.) Most Hispanic Americans live in five states of the South and West, where they are the largest minority group. (See Table 5-1.) California has the largest Hispanic and Mexican American population, followed by Texas. Other Hispanics are concentrated in New Mexico, Arizona, and Colorado.

The Second Battle of Wounded Knee, 1973

UPI/Bettmann/Corbis

According to one Census Bureau study, more than 21 percent of all Hispanics were living in poverty—compared with a national average of 12.1 percent. The median income for Hispanics was $33,103 a year.[22]

Unemployment was substantially higher than among the rest of the population. A little more than half of adult Mexican Americans had completed high school, much lower than the rate for the nation as a whole.[23]

Between 1943 and 1964, hundreds of thousands of Mexican migrant laborers entered the United States temporarily as farm workers under the *Bracero Program* enacted by Congress. Millions of others have entered the country illegally to join the ranks of the migrants.

Many migrants, whether legal or not, live and work under the most difficult conditions. They perform back-breaking stoop labor in the fields under the hot sun, risking injury from insecticides used to protect the crops. Often they must live in shacks without electricity or running water, their health endangered by open sewage and other unsanitary conditions. Migrant Mexican American workers have a life expectancy much shorter than the national average, and a much higher birth rate and infant mortality rate.

Farm workers are not covered by the National Labor Relations Act, and they have encountered great obstacles in organizing labor unions. In 1970 Cesar Chavez and his United Farm Workers (UFW) won a five-year strike against grape growers in central California. Chavez's effort, aided by a nationwide boycott of table grapes by consumers in sympathy with the strike, helped focus national attention on *La Causa,* as the grape workers called their movement, and on *La Raza,* the Mexican Americans themselves. In 1975 California passed legislation generally providing for farm workers the same rights held by union members in other industries. The landmark farm labor bill was a victory for Chavez.

During the 1960s, Chavez had emerged as an extraordinary figure, a quiet and determined man who became a symbol of the Chicanos (as many Mexican Americans called themselves). Chavez's childhood reads like a passage in John Steinbeck's Depression-era novel *The Grapes of Wrath.* His parents were Mexican migrant workers. Following the seasons, the family traveled back

**TABLE 5-1**

**Number of Hispanic Americans in the South and the West, 2000**

| State | Number of Hispanics |
|---|---|
| California | 10,974,413 |
| Texas | 6,672,582 |
| Arizona | 1,298,049 |
| New Mexico | 765,818 |
| Colorado | 735,515 |

SOURCE: U.S. Bureau of the Census.

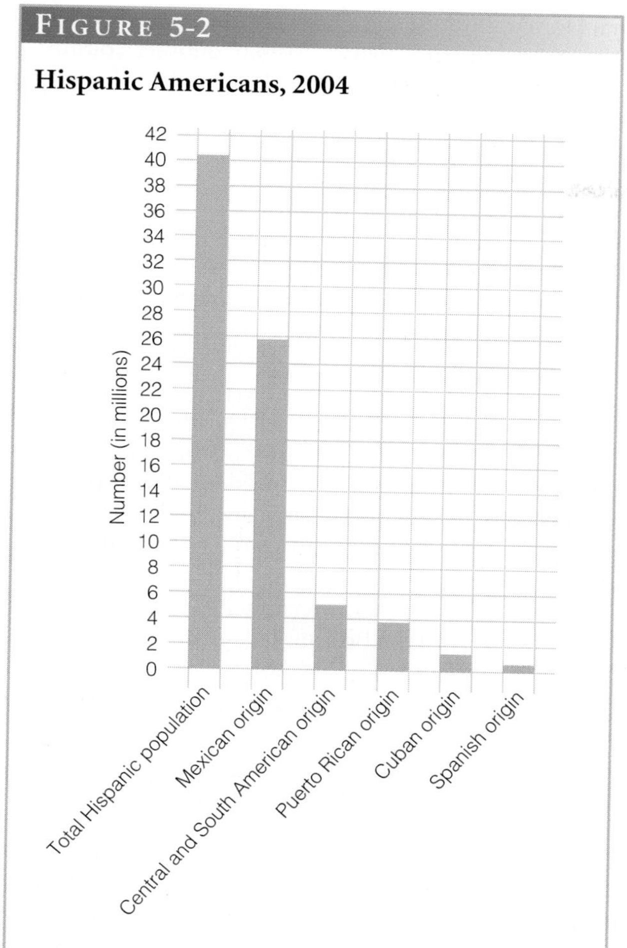

SOURCE: U.S. Bureau of the Census.

Undocumented immigrants crossing the border from Mexico

and forth between California's Imperial and San Joaquin Valleys. By the time Chavez finished the eighth grade he had attended 37 schools. Eventually the family settled in a poor neighborhood near San Jose called by its residents Sal Si Puedes ("get out if you can"). Chavez began organizing the UFW in 1962; within six years, the union had 17,000 members. Later, however, facing a variety of problems, Chavez and the UFW lost some of their power.

Cesar Chavez died in the spring of 1993. An estimated 25,000 farm workers and their supporters took part in the 3-mile funeral procession in Delano, in California's Central Valley. Chavez did not live to see it, but in 1996, after a struggle of nearly 18 years with lettuce growers in California's Salinas Valley, the UFW signed a contract with one of the nation's largest growers, Red Coach lettuce.

The percentage of Hispanics, including Mexican Americans, in the general population is not reflected in the makeup of Congress. In California, for example, where Hispanic Americans constitute about 32 percent of the population, only 17 percent, or nine of the 53 members, of the state's congressional delegation in 2004 were Hispanic Americans: Joe Baca, Xavier Becerra, Dennis Cardoza, Grace Flores Napolitano, Devin Nunes, Lucille Roybal-Allard, Linda Sanchez, Loretta Sanchez, and Hilda Solis.

Hispanics have joined the ranks of other minority groups fighting for full equality in American society. In 1986 Bob Martinez was elected as Florida's first governor of Hispanic descent. In 2001, President George W. Bush named an Hispanic American, Mel Martinez, as secretary of Housing and Urban Development. In 2006 there were 29 Hispanic members of the House. An Hispanic American, Bill Richardson, former secretary of energy for President Clinton, was the governor of New Mexico. In the nation, 4,624 Hispanics had been elected to public office.[24]

Mexican Americans and other Hispanics have registered additional political gains, electing mayors for the first time in Hartford, Connecticut; Austin, Texas; and Colorado Springs, Colorado. Many other cities, mainly in the Southwest, have Hispanic mayors, as has been true in Miami almost continuously since 1972. In addition, there has been a sizable increase in the number of Hispanic state legislators in the Southwest and in Califor-

© Arthur Schatz/Time Life Pictures/Getty Images

Cesar Chavez

nia, Florida, Illinois, and New York. But many Mexican Americans still felt isolated. "We are another country," said Miguel Garcia of East Los Angeles. "We have our own culture, our own language. We feel different from the rest of America."[25] Yet, when Hispanic Americans have organized politically, they often have made their voices heard. In Parlier, California, a small town near Fresno, the local council refused to appoint a Mexican American chief of police. In response, the Hispanic community organized, defeated three members of the council, and elected as mayor Andrew Benitez, a 22-year-old Mexican American.[26]

Hispanic voters have become a powerful force in elections on a national scale as well, courted by presidential, congressional, and gubernatorial candidates. In Florida, for example, a key state in presidential elections, political leaders woo Cuban Americans. Today, Hispanics are having an increasing impact on American culture and life in other ways—from baseball stars such as the Yankees' Alex Rodriguez, Mets pitcher Pedro Martinez, and David Ortiz of the Boston Red Sox to singer and actress Jennifer Lopez. In New York, Miami, Texas, and California, as well as other places, life in America has taken on a Latin beat.

**Undocumented Immigrants** Although the precise number of undocumented immigrants in the United States is not known, government and private demographers have estimated that as many as 11 million or more people are in the country illegally. (See Chapter 4, pp. 121–123.) The majority are Mexicans or other Latin

## "What Is the Worth of a Man?"

In 1979 Cesar Chavez led a strike by his United Farm Workers against the lettuce growers of California. On February 9, in the Imperial Valley, Rufino Contreras, a young lettuce worker taking part in the strike, was shot to death during a clash between pickets and nonunion workers. He left a widow and two young children. Two foremen and an equipment operator, all employees of the owner of the farm where Contreras died, were charged with murder, but the case was later dismissed.

Reporter Laurie Becklund of the *Los Angeles Times* attended the funeral and filed this account:

> CALEXICO—Rufino Contreras, the 27-year-old lettuce picker who was shot to death on Saturday, was buried here Wednesday morning after an outdoor mariachi funeral mass in which he was mourned as a martyr by more than 7000 United Farm Workers of America members and their families.
>
> "Rufino is not dead," UFW President Cesar Chavez said in his eulogy. "Wherever farm workers organize, stand up for their rights and strike for justice, Rufino Contreras is with them."
>
> Sitting in . . . the front row of a flower-filled shrine where the Mass was celebrated was Rosa Contreras, the young man's widow. . . . Clutching her 5-year-old son to her, she seemed oblivious to the labor leader's words.
>
> "Mis hijos," she said time after time, leaning her head back and moaning, tears running down her thin, youthful face. "My children, children of my heart. Where is their father; where are you, Fino?"
>
> "What is the worth of a man?" Chavez asked during his eulogy. "Rufino and his father and his brother together gave the company 20 years of their labor. . . ." The cries of Contreras's young widow could be heard throughout the eulogy. . . . She grabbed hold of [her son] and cried into his shoulder as if he were a man.
>
> Her other child, Nancy Berenice, 4, smiled when she saw her mother. She did not know she was supposed to cry.

—*Los Angeles Times*, February 15, 1979

New Mexico Governor Bill Richardson

Americans. The Census Bureau has estimated that about 68.5 percent of all undocumented persons are Hispanic.[27]

Some employers, particularly growers and farm owners in California and Texas, have hired undocumented workers as a source of cheap labor. Labor unions and some other groups, however, have argued that undocumented people in the United States undermine minimum wage, health, and safety laws and other benefits that American workers enjoy. The Supreme Court has ruled that states can bar the employment of people who are in the United States illegally.[28] But the Court declared unconstitutional a Texas law barring the children of undocumented people, most of them Mexicans, from attending public schools.[29] As noted in Chapter 4, in 1994 California voters approved Proposition 187, a measure to deny government welfare and other benefits to people in the state illegally, but a federal district court declared its major provisions unconstitutional.

In 1986, as discussed in Chapter 4, Congress passed a bill designed to reduce the flow of undocumented immigrants by punishing employers who knowingly hired them. The law has proved largely ineffective. Undocumented immigrants have continued to flow across the border, and many have obtained false identity papers, which are inexpensive and easily available.

In 2004, President George W. Bush proposed a plan to allow undocumented immigrants to work legally for three years, and to renew that status at least once for three more years. The temporary workers would have to show they had jobs, and their employers would have to certify that no American could be found for the job. Democrats criticized the plan as a political ploy to persuade Hispanics to vote for Bush in the 2004 presidential election. Conservatives attacked the proposal on the grounds that it would reward people who had entered the country illegally.

**Puerto Ricans** Puerto Rico has commonwealth status and Puerto Ricans are American citizens, with a nonvoting resident commissioner in the U.S. House of Representatives. The Constitution and most federal laws apply to its residents. As Americans, Puerto Ricans living on the island use U.S. currency, mail, and courts and may receive U.S. welfare benefits and food stamps. They pay

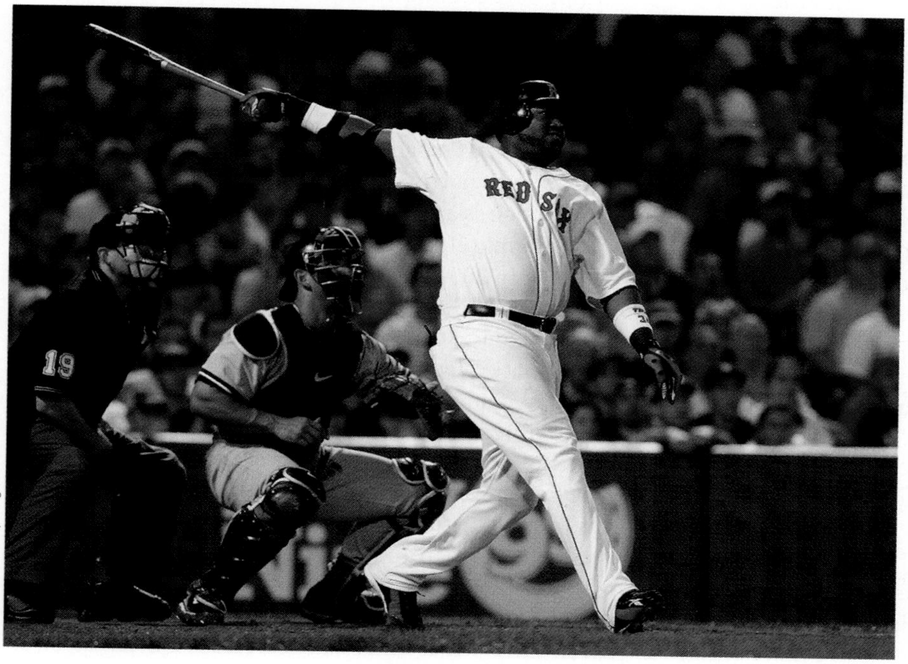


David Ortiz

© Jeff Christensen/Reuters/Corbis

Jennifer Lopez

## "A Message to Our People"

BELL GARDENS, CALIF., Dec. 29—The problem with Bell Gardens, a city official said not long ago, is that "we just have too many people."

With that in mind, the City Council passed a zoning ordinance last year to control population density. But the five-member City Council was all white, while almost 90 percent of the 42,000 people squeezed into the 2.5 square miles of this gritty industrial suburb were Hispanic. The residents, most of them recent arrivals from Mexico, saw the Council's move as an attempt to drive them from their low-cost homes. Several hundred existing housing units would be affected by the ordinance.

So the immigrant population of Bell Gardens rose up and seized political power, registering voters, drawing up petitions and ousting the white mayor and three other white City Council members in a special election earlier this month.

Local politicians were stunned. . . . "They didn't think we could do it," said Josefina Macias, a school attendance assistant who was a leader of the recall movement. "We've awakened the community. They were just asleep. This sends a message to our people everywhere that they can take hold of their government."

—*New York Times,* December 30, 1991

no federal taxes unless they move to the mainland. Islanders cannot vote in national elections, but in 1980, for the first time, they were able to vote in primaries to express their presidential preference and to select delegates to the Democratic and Republican national conventions. Puerto Ricans sing their own national anthem, have their own flag, and are Spanish-speaking.

Yet many of the island's residents who come to the mainland seeking a better life encounter not only a language barrier but economic and racial discrimination as well. Puerto Ricans who migrate to the mainland frequently settle in cities. If the newcomers find employment, it may be in unskilled, low-paying jobs in hotels, restaurants, and factories. Often forced to live in substandard housing, Puerto Ricans sometimes face hostility from inner-city blacks who regard them as an economic threat.

The population of Puerto Rico was more than 3.95 million in 2006; about 3.87 million more people of Puerto Rican origin lived in the continental United States.[30] About 800,000 lived in New York City, and there were large Puerto Rican communities in Chicago; Philadelphia; Newark, New Jersey; and Bridgeport and Hartford, Connecticut. The median income of Puerto Rican families was a little more than half that of other Americans, and the unemployment rate often much higher.

On the island itself, a continuing debate over Puerto Rico's political status has focused on three choices: continuing as a commonwealth, becoming a state, or gaining independence. The commonwealth status for Puerto Rico was established in 1952 under Luis Muñoz Marin's Popular Democratic Party. In 1967 a majority of voters in Puerto Rico voted to continue commonwealth status. The rival New Progressive Party favored statehood, but in 1993, by a narrow margin, Puerto Ricans again chose to have their island remain a commonwealth; in another referendum in 1998, statehood once more failed to win a majority. In 2001 Sila Calderon, the former mayor of San Juan, became the island's first female governor.

Few Puerto Ricans favor outright independence. One group that does, the Puerto Rican Armed Forces of National Liberation (FALN), was blamed for 130 bombings in the United States during the 1970s and 1980s that killed six people and wounded dozens of others. In 1979 President Carter freed four Puerto Rican nationalists who had served long prison terms after attempting to assassinate President Truman and shooting at members of Congress on the floor of the U.S. House of Representatives in 1950. In 1999, President Clinton granted clemency to 11 Puerto Rican nationalists who had served prison terms of al-

© 2003 AP/Wide World Photos

New York, 2003: cheering the Puerto Rican Day Parade

most 20 years but had not themselves been convicted of crimes that caused injuries or loss of life.

Like other minority groups, Puerto Ricans in the United States have evidenced growing cultural pride and political awareness in recent years. In several cities, Puerto Rican citizen groups have organized to work for such goals as better education and employment.

## Asian Americans

The estimated 12 million Asian Americans in 2004 made up a rapidly growing minority group in the United States. The number of Asian Americans more than doubled during the 1980s. By the 2000 census, Asian Americans constituted about 4 percent of the population and were the third largest minority, after Hispanics (about 13 percent) and African Americans (12 percent).[31]

In July 2000, Norman Y. Mineta, a former member of the House of Representatives from California's Silicon Valley, became the first Asian American to serve in the cabinet when President Clinton named him as secretary of commerce. Mineta, a Japanese American who served as a Democratic representative for 21 years, was sent to an internment camp as a boy during the Second World War. President George W. Bush named Mineta secretary of transportation and appointed Elaine L. Chao, a Chinese American born on Taiwan, as secretary of labor. Mineta resigned in 2006.

The largest group of Asian Americans were people of Chinese heritage, who composed more than 23 percent of the total, followed by Filipino Americans, Asian Indians, Vietnamese, Koreans, and Japanese. (See Table 5-2.)

© Darren McCollester/Getty Images

Elaine L. Chao, secretary of labor under President George W. Bush

**TABLE 5-2**

**Asian Americans in the United States, 2000**

| Asians or Pacific Islanders, by Group | Number | Percent |
|---|---|---|
| Chinese | 2,314,537 | 23.1 |
| Filipino | 1,850,314 | 18.4 |
| Asian Indian | 1,678,765 | 16.7 |
| Vietnamese | 1,122,528 | 11.2 |
| Korean | 1,076,872 | 10.7 |
| Japanese | 796,700 | 7.9 |
| Other Asian or Pacific Islander | 1,179,689 | 12.0 |
| Total | 10,019,405 | 100.0 |

SOURCE: U.S. Bureau of the Census.

California, the nation's most populous state, had 34 percent of all Asian Americans. The population of San Francisco is almost one-third Asian American. Although many people of Chinese, Japanese, and other Asian descent live in California and other western states, the Asian populations in New York and Texas have increased rapidly, resulting in some surprising statistics. For example, there were more Asian Americans in New York City (1.2 million) than in Hawaii (700,000).[32]

Among Asian nations, immigration from Vietnam, India, and South Korea has increased at a rapid rate. Although the stereotype of the Korean grocer or Asian retail store owner had some basis in fact, it was also true that Asian Americans included a successful professional class of scientists, engineers, and physicians. The increase in the numbers of Asian Americans has had a continuing political and cultural impact, not only in California, but in many other areas of the country as well.

For example, in the Silicon Valley city of Cupertino, California, where Asian Americans make up 44.8 percent of the city's population of 50,000, in 2004 nine of the 28 elected officials were Asian American, and a Chinese American had served as mayor.[33]

## Women

By 2006, four women were serving in the cabinet, Senator Hillary Rodham Clinton of New York was frequently talked about as a possible future Democratic presidential candidate, and Condoleezza Rice, a visible and high-ranking member of President George W. Bush's cabinet, was the secretary of state. One woman sat as associate justice of the U.S. Supreme Court, and 84 women, including 14 senators, were members of Congress. Nancy Pelosi was the House Democratic leader and the first woman to head her party in Congress.[34] Eight women were serving as governors, and more than 1,685 women were state legislators. Women served as generals in the armed forces and as astronauts exploring outer space.

None of this seems remarkable in today's world, and yet a few short decades ago, the path to these accomplishments was not open to most women. Sex discrimination is far from eradicated in American society. Although almost 51 percent of the nation's population are women, a much lower percentage of women are represented in government. For example, women make up less than 16 percent of Congress. And women still bump up against the invisible "glass ceiling" in much of the corporate world. But increasingly, women have achieved the rights, responsibilities, and power long denied to them by a male-dominated culture.

The organized effort to end sex discrimination in American society was generally known in its early years as women's liberation, or the women's movement. It drew support from many people of both sexes who were not actively engaged in the women's liberation movement but agreed with the objective of full equality for women.

Much of the progress that women have made in recent decades toward equal rights can be credited to the women's movement. The movement, which began in the 1970s, changed the way that Americans think and act about the role of women in the family and in society. Many women combined careers and child-rearing, and by the 1990s the two-income family in which both husband and wife worked was as common as it had been rare a few decades earlier.

In many arenas, the change in the role of women has been dramatic. When President Bush sent American military forces to invade Iraq in 2003, television viewers were not surprised to see women among the troops. One soldier, 19-year-old Jessica Lynch, of West Virginia, was in a unit caught in an attack that killed 11 Americans. Captured, then removed from an Iraqi hospital by American troops, she emerged as a female icon and a media celebrity with a lucrative book and film contract.

Only a little more than a decade earlier, however, the

© Oleg Popov/Reuters/Landov

President George W. Bush's secretary of state, Condoleezza Rice, had served before that as his national security adviser.

## SENECA FALLS: "ALL MEN AND WOMEN ARE CREATED EQUAL"

In 1848, Elizabeth Cady Stanton and Lucretia Mott invited approximately 100 men and women to Stanton's hometown of Seneca Falls, New York, for a meeting on women's rights. The Seneca Falls convention launched the women's suffrage movement in America.

"We are assembled to protest against a form of government existing without the consent of the governed," Stanton began, "to declare our right to be free as man is free, to be represented in the government which we are taxed to support, to have such disgraceful laws as give man the power to chastise and imprison his wife, to take the wages which she earns, the property which she inherits, and, in case of separation, the children of her love; laws which make her the mere dependent on his bounty . . . forever erased from our statute books. . . . We now demand our right to vote according to the declaration of the government under which we live."

Stanton's moving words spurred the convention to pass the Declaration of Sentiments, modeled after Jefferson's Declaration of Independence written 72 years earlier, but with one big difference: "We hold these truths to be self-evident; that all men *and women* are created equal. . . ." (italics added).

It was another 72 years before the Nineteenth Amendment, which gave women the right to vote, was ratified. Thus, 144 years after Jefferson's words were written, America finally accepted the principle that freedom was for everyone—both men and women.

presence of women in full camouflage gear was not taken for granted. In 1991, the United States was at war in the Persian Gulf. For the first time, the images that flashed across the television screens in American living rooms showed women as well as men risking their lives in that war. More than 35,000 women served in the Gulf War; 15 died, and two were taken prisoner.[35]

When that conflict began, women were officially barred from combat, even though, as a practical matter, they were exposed to the hazards of war. After the war ended, Congress voted to relax the restrictions somewhat by letting women in the Air Force and Navy fly combat missions. Although women were also assigned to combat support units in the Army, many women in the military, and civilians as well, objected to the more general Defense Department policy that barred the deployment of women in direct ground combat. In 2005, 202,949 women were on active duty in the military, making up almost 15 percent of the 1.4 million active-duty personnel in the armed services.[36]

The role of women in American politics has also changed rapidly. In 1984, Geraldine Ferraro, a 48-year-old member of Congress from New York, accepted the Democratic nomination for vice president at San Francisco. For the first time, a major party had selected a woman for the second highest office in the land. The convention had nominated Walter F. Mondale of Minnesota for president.

The Mondale-Ferraro ticket was defeated by Ronald Reagan and his vice president, George Bush. But today, women occupy high office in all three branches of the government. In 2006 a woman, Ruth Bader Ginsburg, sat on the Supreme Court, four women served in the cabinet, and there were 84 women in Congress. Women comprised almost 23 percent of state legislators and served as mayors in 197 larger cities.[37]

Yet the gains made by women on the political front could hardly conceal the many barriers they faced and the glaring economic inequalities between men and women. How many women were chief executive officers of the top 500 American corporations, for example? The answer in 2006 was only eleven.[38] The "glass ceiling" was not easily shattered.

© Stefan Zaklin/Reuters/Corbis

Private Jessica Lynch's hometown turns out to greet her.

Indra K. Nooyi became Pepsico's CEO in 2006.

Despite impressive advances, American women still struggle for equality in the marketplace. The median income of women is only 77 percent of that of men.[39] The stereotype of the female office worker as a secretary is all too real. In 2006, the 70.2 million working women in the United States made up 46 percent of the labor force—yet women held 79 percent of all administrative support and clerical jobs.[40] These statistics reflect the fact that many companies do not promote women to executive-level jobs. And even when women are hired in professional and executive positions, they earn considerably less than their male counterparts. (See Figure 5-3.) On the other hand, more women are entering the prestigious professions of law and medicine; beginning in the 1970s, the number of women graduating from medical and law schools rose dramatically, from 2,049 in 1970 to 25,964 in 2003.[41]

One of the most significant social developments of the past three decades has been the steady increase in the number of employed women, who since 1980 have outnumbered women at home. In 2002, 60 percent of adult American women were employed. (See Figure 5-4.) By comparison, in 1970, only about 41 percent held jobs outside the home.[42]

Clearly, and despite the continuing barriers, American women, if they so choose, are no longer limited to home, kitchen, and children (even though some television commercials persist in showing stereotyped women comparing laundry detergents and floor waxes). As Carol A. Whitehurst suggested, "Women, today, seldom think in terms of career versus marriage, but instead believe that they can successfully combine the two. As an increased number of women enter the labor force and the time spent on motherhood shortens, careers become more attractive to women, and old negative images of women with careers begin to decline."[43]

Women dividing their lives between career and home, however, may feel under pressure to excel in both. Still, many career women today are managing to spend more time at home with their children, by working part-time, for example. Others choose to leave the workforce entirely. At the same time, many men are taking more responsibility for child-rearing than has been the case in the past.

In June 1983 Sally K. Ride, a 32-year-old physicist from Encino, California, became the first American woman to travel in outer space. She was a crew member of the space shuttle *Challenger* on a successful six-day mission. In January 1986 astronaut Judith A. Resnick died tragically with five other astronauts and Christa McAuliffe, a New Hampshire schoolteacher, when the *Challenger* blew up shortly after launch. In 1992, Mae Jemison flew aboard the shuttle *Endeavour,* becoming the first African American woman in space. And in 1999, Eileen Collins, an Air Force lieutenant colonel, became the first woman to command a space shuttle mission. In February 2003, two more female astronauts, Laurel B. Clark and Kalpana Chawla, died when the space shuttle *Columbia,* with a crew of seven, disintegrated during reentry.

Despite the gains for women in some areas, the Constitution does not specifically guarantee equal rights for women. For more than a decade, the women's movement struggled but failed to pass a constitutional amendment to secure those rights.

In 1972, Congress proposed such an amendment to eliminate discrimination against women. The Equal Rights Amendment (ERA) said simply: "Equality of

FIGURE 5-3

**The Earnings Gap: Less Pay for Women**

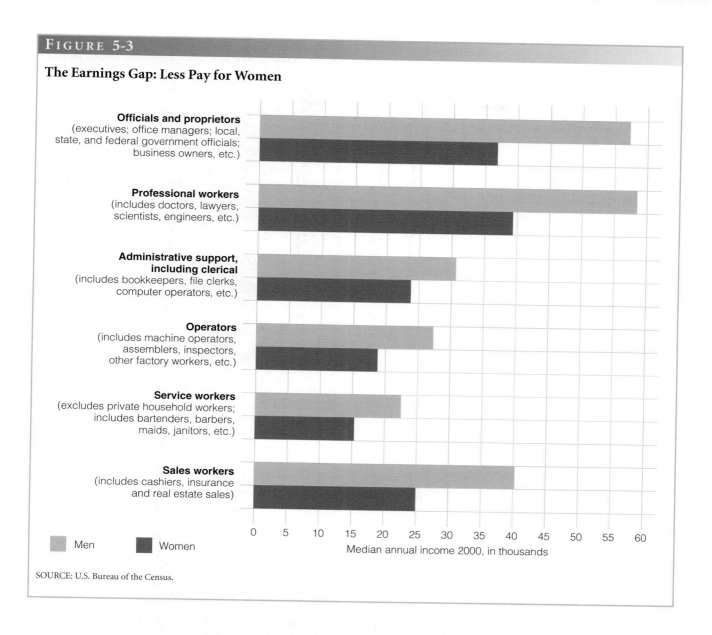

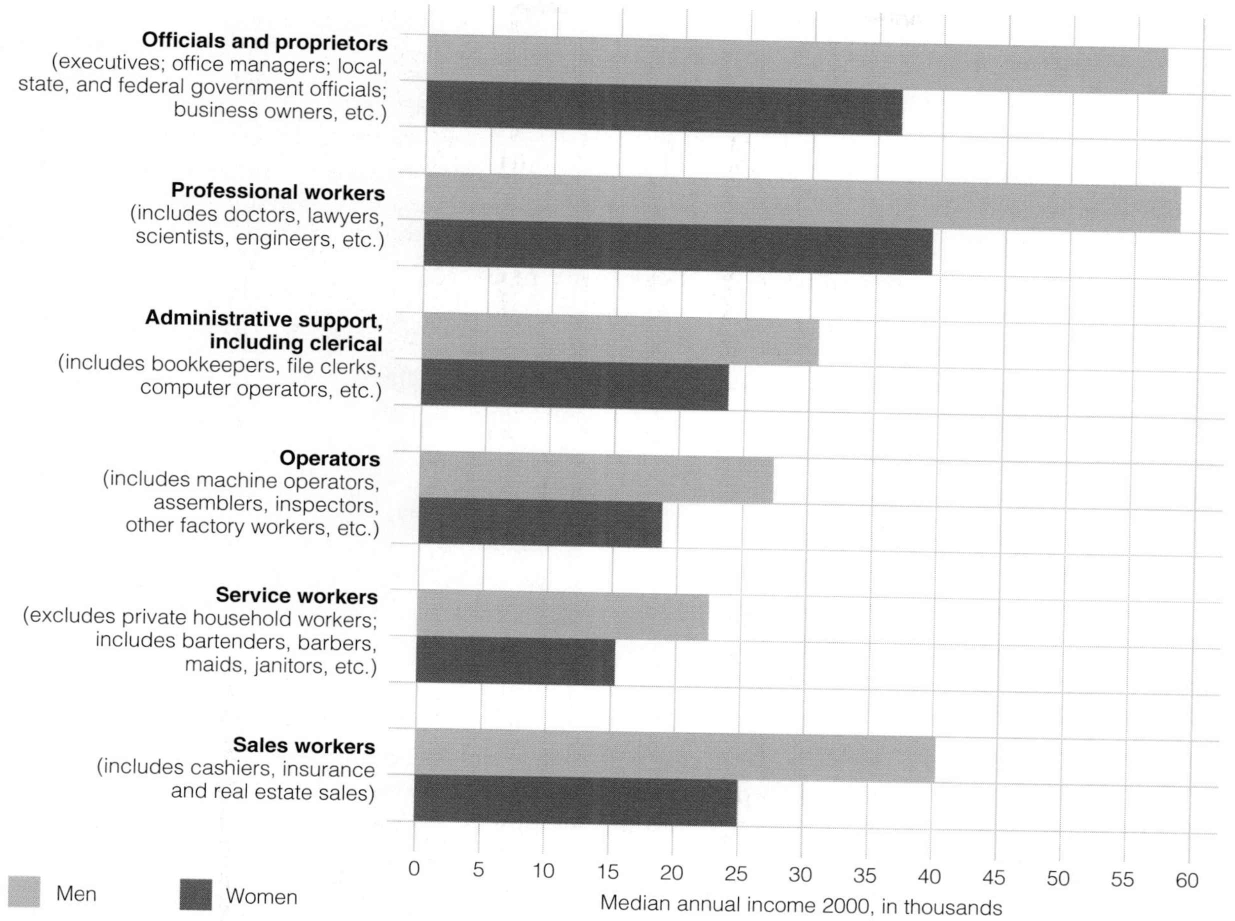


SOURCE: U.S. Bureau of the Census.

rights under the law shall not be denied or abridged by the United States or by any state on account of sex." The ERA was aimed at state laws that discriminate against women in such areas as marriage, property ownership, and employment.

The battle over the ERA represented a philosophical conflict between the more traditional concept of the role of women and the modern view of women as both liberated and fully equal. In 1982, the amendment fell three states short of the 38 necessary to win ratification. By 2004, however, 22 states had equal rights provisions in their constitutions.

In 1981 the Supreme Court ruled that the government may exclude women from the military draft and registration for it: "The Constitution requires that Congress treat similarly situated persons similarly, not that it engage in gestures of superficial equality."[44]

In 1972, Congress enacted a law barring discrimination because of a person's sex by schools and colleges that receive federal funds. As a result of the law, Title IX of the Education Amendments of 1972, many schools improved their athletic programs for women. When the Supreme Court ruled that the law applied only to specific departments or programs that received federal money, not to educational institutions as a whole, Congress in 1988, over President Reagan's veto, passed a law to undo the Supreme Court decision.[45] As a result, federal antidiscrimination laws once again applied to an entire institution if any department or program receives federal funds.

Laws benefiting women were to some extent a reflection of the growth of the women's movement. The movement, one study concluded, "has developed a sophisticated organizational structure and has established itself as a significant presence in national policy making."[46]

Two major groups represent women's rights: the National Women's Political Caucus and the National Or-

FIGURE 5-4

**How Many Women Work: The Percentage of Women Older than Age 16 in the Labor Force, 2006**

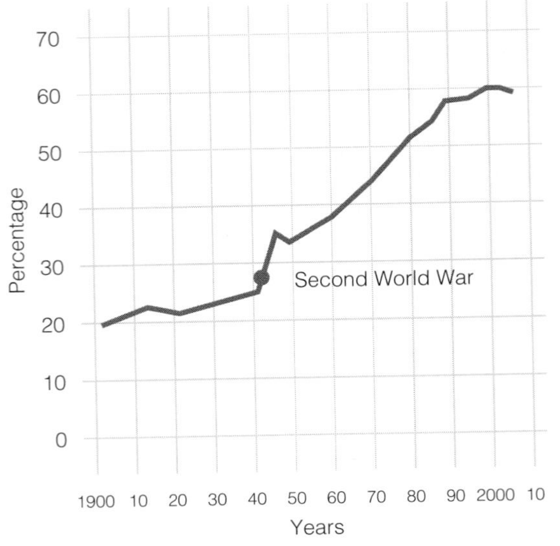


SOURCE: U.S. Bureau of the Census.

© Time Life Pictures/NASA/Getty Images

Mae Jemison, the first African American woman in space

ganization for Women (NOW). The National Women's Political Caucus, founded in 1971, has helped to increase the number of female delegates to the national party conventions as well as the total of women elected to public office. It emphasizes political goals, including the election and appointment of more women to public office. As noted, the number of women holding public office has increased noticeably since the women's movement began. Recent presidents have all named women to their cabinets. Yet, in the history of the United States through the year 2005, just 224 women had served in Congress, compared with 11,524 men.[47]

*for more information about the women's groups listed above, see: http://www.nwpc.org and http://www.now.org*

NOW, founded in 1966, shares some of the political aims of the National Women's Political Caucus but places more emphasis on other issues affecting women. NOW, with about 500,000 members, has worked to improve employment opportunities for women; has defended abortion, birth control, and reproductive rights for women; and has supported the reform of laws dealing with women. Its goals also include gaining equality for women, stopping violence against women, and ending discrimination based on sexual orientation, gender, or race.

Many issues sometimes seen as primarily affecting women are not really "women's issues" at all, but concern the entire society. One example is the issue of sexual harassment, which dramatically came to the attention of millions of Americans in the fall of 1991 when the Senate Judiciary Committee was considering the nomination to the Supreme Court of Judge Clarence Thomas. Anita Hill, a 35-year-old law professor at the University of Oklahoma and a former aide to Thomas, stunned the nation with her graphic testimony accusing Thomas of sexual harassment. According to Hill, Thomas spoke to her about pornographic materials, sex organs, and sexual acts and repeatedly asked to date her. Thomas denied all of Hill's charges, accused the committee of conducting a televised, "high-tech lynching," and was eventually confirmed by the panel and then by the full Senate, 52 to 48.

The hearings made many American men acutely aware of an issue that they had not taken seriously before. One poll published at the time reported that 38 percent of women felt they had been subjected to sexual harassment at work.[48] The Senate hearings appeared to have a political effect as well. Many women were outraged at the way several white male senators treated Hill. In the wake of the hearings, more women participated in the 1992 elections, both as campaign workers and as candidates.

In 1993, the Supreme Court ruled unanimously that a woman suing her employer for sexual harassment does not have to show that she suffered severe psychological injury in order to collect damages.[49] Teresa Harris, who worked for a trucking company in Nashville, Tennessee,. quit her job and sued the company, charging that her boss, Charles Hardy, called her a "dumb-ass woman," suggested they repair to a Holiday Inn "to negotiate your

© AP/Wide World Photos

raise," and asked female workers to retrieve coins from his front pants pocket. In her majority opinion, Justice Sandra Day O'Connor ruled for Harris, saying that the 1964 Civil Rights Act prohibited that kind of "hostile or abusive working environment."[50]

If women face sexual harassment in the workplace, it is also true that they may be subject to physical abuse at home. In one 1997 poll, 22 percent of women questioned—equal to 24 million women if projected to the adult female population—said that they had been physically abused by their husbands or partners.[51]

**Abortion** Probably no issue divides American society today as sharply as the controversy over abortion. For more than three decades, abortion has been a politically volatile social issue. On one side are pro-choice women and men who support the right of a woman to have an abortion to end a pregnancy. Many women feel that state regulation of pregnancies violates their right of privacy. Pro-choice groups, such as the Planned Parenthood Federation of America, argue that women have the right to control their reproductive systems and to make decisions about their own bodies.

On the other side are pro-life Americans—including many women—who strongly oppose abortion. Legalized abortion has been deplored by the Roman Catholic Church; many Americans feel abortions are a form of murder and violate the rights of what they consider to be unborn children. To an extent, therefore, the moral and legal arguments revolve around the question of when life begins. The antiabortion forces argue that life begins at the moment of conception, but that view has not been accepted by the pro-choice forces or by the U.S. Supreme Court.

In 1973 a Supreme Court decision gave dramatic evidence of the shifting social attitudes in America and the concerns of the women's movement. In the landmark case of *Roe* v. *Wade,* the Court ruled 7–2 that no state may interfere with a woman's right to have an abortion during the first three months of pregnancy.* The decision in effect struck down laws restricting abortion in 46 states. Reaffirming its decision in 1983, the Supreme Court invalidated various state laws designed to make it more difficult to obtain legal abortions.[52] Again in 1986 the Supreme Court narrowly reaffirmed *Roe* v. *Wade,* voting 5–4 to strike down a Pennsylvania law that discouraged abortions.[53] A year later, the Court invalidated an Illinois law that would have required teenagers to notify their parents before having abortions.[54]

The continued political opposition to legalized abortion, however, along with a decided conservative shift in the makeup of the Supreme Court, combined to create a climate in which the future of a woman's right to legal abortion was in doubt. In 1989, the Supreme Court in a Missouri case, *Webster* v. *Reproductive Health Services,* ruled 5–4 that states may impose sharp restrictions on abortions.[55] Although it stopped short of overturning *Roe* v. *Wade,* the Court held that states could regulate abortions at any stage of pregnancy, including the first three months. "For today, at least," Justice Harry A. Blackmun said in a dissent, "the law of abortion stands undisturbed. . . . But the signs are evident and very ominous, and a chill wind blows."[56]

Later Supreme Court decisions seemed to march in the same antiabortion direction. In 1990, the Court ruled in cases from Minnesota and Ohio that states may require teenage girls to notify both parents before having an abortion.[57]

In 1992, however, a narrowly divided Court reaffirmed, 5–4, the constitutional right to an abortion that it had first established in *Roe* v. *Wade.*[58] At the same time, it upheld parts of a Pennsylvania law that had imposed restrictions on abortion and had made it compulsory for minors to get the advance consent of one parent or a judge. Although the Court upheld most of the restrictions in the Pennsylvania law, it struck down a requirement that a woman notify her husband before having an abortion. The majority opinion held that "an entire generation" had come of age relying on the liberty of women to make reproductive choices. For the Court to overrule its own decision in *Roe* v. *Wade* under political pressure, the opinion said, would damage the public's confidence in the Court, the "legitimacy" on which the Court's power rests.[59]

---

* *Roe* v. *Wade,* 410 U.S. 113 (1973); *Doe* v. *Bolton,* 410 U.S. 179 (1973). In 1995, Norma McCorvey, the woman known as "Jane Roe," whose case led to the *Roe* v. *Wade* Supreme Court decision, announced that she had been baptized, had switched sides on the abortion issue, and had joined the antiabortion group Operation Rescue.

## THE REAL JANE ROE

Norma McCorvey, a slight, green-eyed carnival worker known as "Pixie" to her friends, became pregnant one night in 1969. McCorvey, then 21, did not want the baby. The product of a broken home in Dallas, she was a high school dropout, a bride and mother at 16, a divorcee within a year, a troubled and impoverished young woman who considered herself one of life's losers.

Her pregnancy set off a social revolution. Under the pseudonym of Jane Roe, her case, *Roe* v. *Wade*, became the landmark 1973 Supreme Court decision overturning antiabortion laws in Texas and in other states, one of the most controversial and hotly debated in history.

Few court decisions have had a more immediate impact on such a personal aspect of American life. According to the Alan Guttmacher Institute, a research affiliate of the Planned Parenthood Federation of America:

- An estimated 28 million legal abortions have been performed in the United States from 1973 to 1992.
- The number of abortions performed annually grew from 744,600 in 1973 to 1.3 million in 2003.

In 1995, Jane Roe announced a change of heart and left the abortion clinic where she had worked and became a volunteer for Operation Rescue, an antiabortion group.

—Adapted from the *Washington Post*, January 23, 1983; the Alan Guttmacher Institute, *Facts in Brief*, 1995; *Time*, August 21, 1995; and the Centers for Disease Control and Prevention, *National Vital Statistics Report*, October 31, 2003

In a separate opinion, Justice Blackmun joined the majority in upholding the essential principles of *Roe* v. *Wade*, the decision he had written almost two decades before. There had been little reason to hope that abortion rights would survive, he said. "But now, just when so many expected the darkness to fall, the flame has grown bright."[60]

The Supreme Court's 1973 guidelines in *Roe* v. *Wade* severely limited the power of a state government to regulate abortions. During the first three months, or first trimester, of a pregnancy, the decision was up to the woman and her physician. During the last six months, the state could regulate abortion procedures, but only during the last 10 weeks could a state ban abortions (except when abortion is necessary to preserve the life or health of the mother). The Court reasoned that a child born during the last 10 weeks of normal pregnancy is presumed to be capable of survival. In the wake of the Supreme Court's decision, the Centers for Disease Control and Prevention has estimated that about 1.3 million abortions are performed each year in the United States.[61]

In 2000, the Supreme Court decided one of the most controversial aspects of abortion rights when it struck down a Nebraska law that barred a procedure sometimes used in abortions in the second or third trimester of pregnancy.[62] Supporters of abortion rights called the procedure a "late-term" abortion; opponents called it "partial-birth" abortion because in the procedure the

## The Supreme Court Reaffirms *Roe*

On June 29, 1992, the last Monday of its term, the Supreme Court reaffirmed, 5–4, the essential principles of *Roe* v. *Wade*, its 1973 decision establishing the constitutional right of women to have abortions in the early stages of pregnancy. At the same time, the Court upheld most restrictions on abortion contained in a Pennsylvania law. Following are excerpts from the majority opinion:

> Our obligation is to define the liberty of all, not to mandate our own moral code. . . . These matters, involving the most intimate and personal choices a person may make in a lifetime, choices central to personal dignity and autonomy, are central to the liberty protected by the Fourteenth Amendment. At the heart of liberty is the right to define one's own concept of existence, of meaning, of the universe, and of the mystery of human life. . . .
>
> An entire generation has come of age free to assume Roe's concept of liberty in defining the capacity of women to act in society, and to make reproductive decisions. . . . A decision to overrule *Roe*'s essential holding under the existing circumstances would address error, if error there was, at the cost of both profound and unnecessary damage to the Court's legitimacy, and to the Nation's commitment to the rule of law. It is therefore imperative to adhere to the essence of *Roe*'s original decision, and we do so today.

—*Planned Parenthood of Southeastern Pennsylvania* v. *Casey,* 1992

fetus is drawn partially out of the uterus, the skull collapsed, and its contents suctioned. Opponents had made so-called partial-birth abortion a national political issue by widely publicizing the graphic details of the procedure in an effort to enlist public support against it.

Three years later, in November 2003, President George W. Bush signed legislation passed by the Republican-controlled Congress that banned "partial-birth" or late-term abortions. It was a major victory for foes of abortion. Opponents of the law immediately challenged it, and the measure did not take effect while the cases made their way through the courts. The law was declared unconstitutional by federal appeals courts in St. Louis and San Francisco, and in February 2006 the U.S. Supreme Court agreed to take up the issue.

As a result of the Supreme Court decision in *Roe* v. *Wade,* the National Right to Life Committee was formed. This committee and other pro-life groups became a powerful force in a number of political campaigns, where they opposed candidates who favor legalized abortion.

*Roe* v. *Wade* did not settle the question of who should pay for abortions. Congress in 1976 passed a controversial amendment sponsored by Representative Henry J. Hyde, an Illinois Republican. The Hyde amendment banned federal Medicaid payments for abortions, except in cases of rape or incest or when the mother's life was "endangered." The result was that poor women could no longer count on the government paying for abortions; Medicaid had been paying for an estimated 300,000 abortions a year.

In the meantime, antiabortion groups remained highly vocal and in some cases highly militant. In Wichita, Kansas, in 1991, pro-life activists of Operation Rescue attempted to block the entrances to abortion clinics. Antiabortion activists adopted the same strategy in several larger cities.

Soon, militancy turned to violence. There have been hundreds of incidents of bombings, arson, vandalism, and death threats directed at clinics where women can have their pregnancies terminated. In 1993, David Gunn, a doctor who worked for an abortion clinic in Pensacola, Florida, was shot three times in the back and

killed, the first physician to be murdered as a result of violence against abortion clinics. His assailant was sentenced to life in prison. In 1994, President Clinton signed a law barring antiabortion demonstrators from blocking access to clinics or threatening patients. But two months later, another doctor and his unarmed escort, a retired Air Force officer, were murdered outside another abortion clinic in Pensacola. Their killer was sentenced to death. And later that year, a gunman attacked two abortion clinics in Brookline, Massachusetts, killing two staff workers and wounding five other people. The gunman was sentenced to life and after two years in prison committed suicide.

But the killings did not end. In October 1998, Dr. Barnett Slepian was standing with his wife and son in the kitchen of his home in Amherst, New York, a suburb of Buffalo, when a sniper shot him fatally through an undraped window. Slepian had performed abortions at a Buffalo clinic despite several death threats. Authorities found a high-powered rifle buried in the woods behind the physician's home and linked it to James C. Kopp, an antiabortion extremist, who was tracked down in France and arrested three years later. Tried and convicted, he received a sentence of from 25 years to life in prison.

A gay couple weds in Massachusetts in 2004.

## Gay Rights

In November 2003, the highest court in Massachusetts ruled that gay couples have the right to marry. The state's constitution, the court said, "affirms the dignity and equality of all individuals. It forbids the creation of second-class citizens." The court ordered the state's legislature to change the law to carry out the decision.[63]

The ruling was highly controversial because a majority of Americans were opposed to gay marriages. A poll released at the time reported that 60 percent of the public disapproved of allowing gays to marry.[64] President George W. Bush, reacting to the ruling, declared: "Marriage is a sacred institution between a man and a woman."[65]

In February 2004 Bush proposed a constitutional amendment to prohibit gay marriages. He did so after

### Massachusetts Rules: A Victory for Gay Marriage

In November 2003 the Massachusetts Supreme Judicial Court ruled, 4–3, that gay couples have the right to marry under the state's constitution. It was the first time that a state's high court had ruled that same-sex couples could marry. Within days, the issue of gay marriage became a subject of controversy in the 2004 presidential election.

The Court held:

> The question before us is whether, consistent with the Massachusetts Constitution, the Commonwealth may deny the protections, benefits, and obligations conferred by civil marriage to two individuals of the same sex who wish to marry. We conclude that it may not. The Massachusetts Constitution affirms the dignity and equality of all individuals. It forbids the creation of second-class citizens.

The ruling said that the plaintiffs, seven gay and lesbian couples seeking marriage licenses, did not wish to undermine the institution of marriage. Many same-sex couples, the court noted, were raising children.

> It cannot be rational under our laws, and indeed it is not permitted, to penalize children by depriving them of state benefits because the state disapproves of their parents' sexual orientation. . . . If anything, extending civil marriages to same-sex couples reinforces the importance of marriage to individuals and communities. That same-sex couples are willing to embrace marriage's solemn obligations of exclusivity, mutual support and commitment to one another is a testament to the enduring place of marriage in our laws and in the human spirit.

—Excerpts from Massachusetts Supreme Judicial Court ruling, November 18, 2003

San Francisco allowed thousands of gay and lesbian couples to be married at City Hall in the wake of the Massachusetts decision. The California supreme court ruled the marriages invalid and the constitutional amendment did not pass, but the president's action pleased conservatives. In 2006, with the midterm congressional elections looming, conservatives—with Bush's support—tried again, but another proposed consitutional amendment to ban gay marriages failed.

By 2006, 41 states and the federal government had laws prohibiting gay marriage. A decade earlier, Congress passed the Defense of Marriage Act defining marriage as the union of a man and a woman and providing that no state would have to recognize a same-sex marriage performed in another state. But despite the act, the Constitution might require that a marriage legal in one state would have to be recognized nationwide. Ultimately, the courts would have to rule on the issue, unless an amendment to the Constitution was ratified to bar marriage between same-sex couples.

As a result of the Massachusetts ruling, gay and lesbian couples were married in that state, beginning in May 2004. The same-sex marriage ceremonies were the first ever to be performed in the United States. The Massachusetts decision came four years after the supreme court of Vermont ruled that gay couples are entitled to the same benefits and protections that the state grants to heterosexual married couples.[66] The Vermont court ruled that guaranteeing equal status for gay couples who seek "legal protection and security for their avowed commitment to an intimate and lasting relationship is simply, when all is said and done, . . . a recognition of our common humanity."[67] The state legislature in April 2000 approved a law allowing "civil unions." In Vermont, this meant that a gay or lesbian couple could be legally joined in a ceremony that creates a same-sex marriage in everything but name. California's domestic partnership law, effective in 2005, allows the courts to allocate assets if a gay couple breaks up. By then, four states and more than three dozen cities and counties had laws extending various rights and benefits to domestic partners.

A few months before the Massachusetts court recognized gay marriages, Gene Robinson of New Hampshire was elected as the first openly gay bishop of the Episcopal Church. The election caused controversy and debate among many of the 70 million members of the Anglican Communion worldwide.

According to a study by researchers at the University of Chicago, 2.8 percent of American men and 1.4 percent of American women identify themselves as homosexual or bisexual. In addition, 9.1 percent of men and 4.3 percent of women reported that they have had some homosexual experience.[68] The 2000 census counted 594,000 households with same-sex partners.[69] But estimates of the size of the gay population vary; although no one knows the size of the gay population in the United States, it is certainly in the millions.

Like other minority groups, gay men and lesbian women often have been discriminated against in jobs and other areas. Some of this stems from a long-standing general bias against gays by many individuals; in other cases, discrimination is fueled by the opposition of conservative or religious groups who feel that homosexuality violates moral or religious precepts.

According to poll data, 51 percent of the public have said they believe homosexual behavior is "morally wrong."[70] In recent years, however, changing public attitudes, the increased political power of gays, and the willingness of more gay men and women to express their sexual preferences openly—to "come out of the closet"

## Bush Responds to Massachusetts

Shortly after the Massachusetts high court's ruling that gay couples have the right to marry under the state's constitution, President George W. Bush promised to work with congressional leaders to defend the sanctity of marriage. In February 2004 Bush proposed an amendment to the U.S. Constitution to define marriage as between a man and a woman:

> After more than two centuries of American jurisprudence . . . a few judges and local authorities are presuming to change the most fundamental institution of civilization. Their actions have created confusion on an issue that requires clarity.
>
> If we are to prevent the meaning of marriage from being changed forever, our nation must enact a constitutional amendment to protect marriage in America. . . . The union of a man and woman is the most enduring human institution . . . honored and encouraged in all cultures and by every religious faith. Ages of experience have taught humanity that the commitment of a husband and wife to love and to serve one another promotes the welfare of children and the stability of society. Marriage cannot be severed from its cultural, religious, and natural roots without weakening the good influence of society.
>
> Today I call upon the Congress to promptly pass, and to send to the states for ratification, an amendment to our Constitution defining and protecting marriage as a union of man and woman as husband and wife. The amendment should fully protect marriage, while leaving the state legislatures free to make their own choices in defining legal arrangements other than marriage.

—Remarks by President George W. Bush, the White House, February 24, 2004

## Tammy Baldwin Makes History

Tammy Baldwin (D-Wis.) is one of the rare House freshmen who's already made her mark on American history.

The citizens of Madison, Wisconsin, made Baldwin the first openly gay person to win a seat in Congress. (Reps. Barney Frank [D-Mass.] and Jim Kolbe [R-Ariz.] told voters after they were already in office.) She is also the first woman Wisconsin has sent to the House of Representatives.

Unlike other firsts—the first African American, first Asian American—Baldwin does not have the luxury of flaunting her unique identity. Instead, she has to be a new kind of ground breaker, out to prove she can make what's special about her disappear.

She's aware some of her constituents fear she'll morph into a single-issue automaton, obsessed with pushing the gay rights agenda. As a state legislator she did support civil rights for gays and lesbians, but as one among many different issues. "They'll be able to watch what I do," Baldwin said. "I feel very comfortable they'll find I represent a broad cross section of values."

But she knows most of her constituents are not hanging rainbow flags on the porch and would not want to see their representative marching at gay pride events around the country. She knows, in other words, that, like much of America, many of Madison's citizens are uneasy with the fact that their congresswoman is gay. Her challenge is now to avoid triggering fears like the ones the men and women in a Madison focus group expressed, and slowly change the stereotype.

"It's pretty simple," Baldwin said. "The more people who have the opportunity to know and work with openly gay and lesbian people, the more acceptance and tolerance there will be."

—Adapted from the *Washington Post*, December 26, 1998, and Congresswoman Tammy Baldwin's biography at http://tammybaldwin.house.gov

—have given this minority a greater degree of visibility and acceptance in American society.

There has in fact been a pronounced shift in public attitudes. And the revulsion at violence directed at gays, such as the murder of Matthew Shepard, is shared even by many people who do not approve of the gay lifestyle.

A poll conducted by the Gallup organization in 2005 found that the vast majority of Americans—nine out of 10 people—favored equal job opportunities for gays and lesbians.[71] The same poll found that 52 percent of Americans thought that homosexual relations between consenting adults should be legal.

As a result of court decisions, legislative action, and changing public perceptions of homosexuals, many jurisdictions have protected gay rights. By 2003, some 242 communities—including New York, San Francisco, Boston, Detroit, Los Angeles, and Washington, D.C.—had passed local laws or taken executive action to protect gay rights in employment, housing, and other areas.[72]

It was much different a little more than a decade earlier. In 1986, the Supreme Court ruled 5–4 that the Constitution does not protect homosexual relations between consenting adults, even in the privacy of their homes.[73] The Court did so in upholding a Georgia law that prohibited oral or anal sex. The justices did not rule whether the same law could be applied to heterosexuals. The case arose when Michael Hardwick, a gay bartender in Atlanta, failed to pay a ticket for drinking in public. A police officer with a warrant was admitted to Hardwick's home and found Hardwick in his bedroom having sex with another man. Hardwick was arrested for violating the Georgia sodomy law.

Then in 2003, the Supreme Court reversed its 1986 decision and in a sweeping, landmark decision ruled 6–3 that states could not outlaw private sexual conduct.[74] The case was brought by two Houston men who were prosecuted under a Texas sodomy law for having sex in their own home. The statute, the Court ruled, violated the due process clause of the Fourteenth Amendment of the Constitution. Police had entered John G. Lawrence's apartment and saw him and another adult man, Tyron Garner, engaging in a consensual sexual act. Both were arrested and convicted of deviant sexual intercourse. Before the ruling, oral or anal intercourse between people of the opposite sex in Texas was not a crime; it was only a criminal act between persons of the same sex.

© Brian Snyder/Reuters/Landov

Gene Robinson of New Hampshire, the first gay bishop of the Episcopal church, is embraced by his partner, Mark Andrew.

On the other hand, in 2000, the Supreme Court ruled 5–4 that a private group, the Boy Scouts of America, had a constitutional right to ban gay members.[75] The Court held that the Boy Scouts believed gay conduct was "inconsistent with the values it seeks to instill in its youth members."[76] The case had been brought by James Dale, a gay scoutmaster in New Jersey who had been expelled by the Boy Scouts.

Congress has at times acted to protect the rights of gay people. It was the crisis over acquired immune deficiency syndrome (AIDS) that led to the first major congressional action benefiting gays. The disease devastated the homosexual community—although it was by no means limited to gays, since the human immunodeficiency virus (HIV) that causes AIDS could be transmitted not only by sexual contact between homosexuals but also by heterosexual sex, blood transfusions, needles used by drug addicts or others, and by infected pregnant mothers to their babies. Between 1981 and 2005, more than 900,000 people in the United States were reported to have contracted AIDS; of that cumulative total 529,113 had died.[77] More than 159,000 heterosexual AIDS cases had been reported, and it was estimated that 950,000 Americans were infected with HIV.[78] The AIDS and HIV cases in the United States were part of a worldwide epidemic of 38.6 billion people living with AIDS or HIV.

In October 1987, more than 200,000 gay men and women from across the nation gathered on the mall in Washington, the scene of many political protests. They carried signs that read "Get Ready for the Gay 90s," "Dyke from Ohio," and "Condoms, Not Condemnation." They had come to march for an end to discrimination against homosexuals and for more funds to fight AIDS.

Prodded by gay activists, in 1988 Congress passed its first comprehensive AIDS legislation. The $1 billion package included funds for research, new drugs, home health care for AIDS patients, and anonymous testing. Similar bills, with larger dollar amounts, were enacted in later years.

Under the Civil Service Reform Act of 1978, most federal agencies cannot discriminate against homosexuals in their hiring practices, but for many years the Federal Bureau of Investigation, the Central Intelligence Agency, and other "sensitive" government agencies could as a rule dismiss or refuse to hire gay people. In 1995, however, President Clinton signed an executive order prohibiting the denial of security clearances "solely on the basis of the sexual orientation of the employee." The order had a dramatic impact; in June 2000, a gay pride ceremony was held at CIA headquarters in Langley, Virginia, attended by some 100 gay employees of the intelligence agency and by workers from the National Security Agency, the nation's code-making and code-breaking agency, as well.[79]

The armed forces have exercised the right to dismiss or exclude homosexuals. In 1992, as a candidate for president, Bill Clinton pledged to end the ban on gay people in the military. After his election as president, however, strong opposition by the military and by Senator Sam Nunn of Georgia, then chairman of the Senate Armed Services Committee, forced Clinton to modify his stand. What emerged was a policy of "don't ask, don't tell." Under this policy, homosexuals were permitted to remain in the armed forces if they did not disclose their sexual orientation by statements or behavior.

In many cities and states, political leaders could ignore gay power only at their own peril. In San Francisco, with its large gay population, no mayor can be expected to win election without the support of members of the gay community. In New York, Denver, Houston, Austin, and Washington, D.C., gays have become an important political force. In 1980, a political action committee, the Human Rights Campaign, was formed to help elect officials who support gay rights.

***for more information about the Human Rights Campaign, see: http://www.hrc.org***

## Disabled Americans

According to the Census Bureau, there are an estimated 51 million Americans—almost one person in every five—with some kind of disability. Of that total, 32.5 million reported that their disabilities were severe.[80] Yet, until relatively recently, the millions of disabled Americans were a kind of invisible minority, their rights of equal treatment and equal access more often than not overlooked or neglected.

© Bob Daemmrich/The Image Works

## The Supreme Court Rules for George Lane—and Disabled Americans

George Lane, whose legs are paralyzed, had to crawl up two flights of stairs in the Polk County, Tennessee, courthouse in 1996 to face a traffic misdemeanor charge. Later, when he refused to crawl or be carried to court for a hearing, he was arrested and jailed.

Lane sued the state of Tennessee under the Americans with Disabilities Act, which requires public access to buildings for disabled persons. He was joined by five other plaintiffs, including Beverly Jones, a court stenographer, who said her use of a wheelchair prevented her from accepting work in many Tennessee courtrooms.

Although the Eleventh Amendment to the Constitution ordinarily bars citizens from suing the states, Congress has the power to allow such lawsuits. In 2004, the Supreme Court ruled, 5–4, that George Lane and other disabled persons who were denied access to courthouses could sue under the act. The Court struck down Tennessee's claim of constitutional immunity.

While the decision, in *Tennessee* v. *Lane,* was narrow in scope and covered only access to courthouses, it was a clear victory for George Lane and other disabled Americans, who can no longer be denied their day in court—with dignity.

A person in a wheelchair has as much need to enter a shopping mall or a restaurant as anyone else; but often no ramp has been available, and a set of stairs difficult or impossible to navigate blocks the way. In employment, transportation, access to other public facilities, and in other ways, the disabled have been disadvantaged.

In 1990, Congress acted to remove these everyday barriers for people with disabilities. The Americans with Disabilities Act, enacted in that year and signed into law by President George Bush, was the most significant antidiscrimination law since the 1964 Civil Rights Act.

The act defines a disabled person as anyone with "a physical or mental impairment that substantially limits one or more of the major life activities." The law, with provisions to take effect over a period of years, bans discrimination against such persons in employment, public accommodations, transportation, and telecommunications. Under the law, employers of more than 15 people cannot refuse to hire qualified disabled applicants. New buses, taxis, trains, hotels, restaurants, stores, schools, parks, museums, movie and other theaters, as well as auditoriums, doctors' offices, and health clubs must be accessible to disabled people. Banks must lower ATM machines to accommodate people in wheelchairs, and restaurants must provide menus in Braille for the blind or visually impaired. Public and other telephones, to the extent possible, must allow hearing- or voice-impaired people to place and receive calls. In every aspect, the law sought to accommodate the rights of disabled Americans far beyond what had ever been done before.

## Black and White: An American Dilemma

On March 3, 1991, officers of the Los Angeles Police Department cornered a 25-year-old motorist, Rodney G. King, after a wild automobile chase. Police said he had been speeding. As officers surrounded King, four of them beat him repeatedly with their metal batons and kicked him. He was clubbed more than 50 times and shocked with an electric stun gun as he lay near his car. Fifteen officers stood by and witnessed the savage beating but did not intervene.

Unknown to the police, a resident of a nearby apartment building turned on his video camera and recorded the scene. In millions of homes on television news broadcasts, and later in a courtroom in California, the videotape was played again and again. Rodney King's skull was fractured in at least nine places. He suffered many other injuries, including a shattered eye socket, a fractured cheekbone, and a broken leg.

Rodney King was black. The four officers who beat him were white. All four were later tried for assault with a deadly weapon and excessive use of force, and two were also charged with falsifying police reports. In their defense, the officers contended that King had aggressively resisted arrest. On April 29, 1992, all four were acquitted of state charges by a jury that included no blacks in suburban Simi Valley, the community where the trial was held.

Within a few hours of the verdict, the predominantly black area of South Central Los Angeles erupted in violent anger. Some people were dragged from their vehicles and beaten as television crews in helicopters videotaped the riots.* More than 3,700 fires were set, and many stores were looted. In three nights of destruction, more than 50 people died, most of them black and Hispanic, and more than 2,300 were injured. Close to 14,000 people were arrested.

The violence spread to other parts of Los Angeles and to other cities. Los Angeles Mayor Tom Bradley declared a curfew, and California Governor Pete Wilson called out the National Guard. The city of the angels was turned into a virtual war zone. A pall of dark smoke hung

*Millions of people saw a white truck driver, Reginald O. Denny, pulled from his truck and beaten. In 1993, Damian M. Williams, a black man, was sentenced to eight years in prison for felony mayhem in the attack on Denny.

Rob Crandall

Rodney King is beaten by Los Angeles police on the famous videotape.

over the city, closing all but one runway at Los Angeles International Airport. Freeways were clogged as thousands of frightened residents fled the city. Most businesses and offices shut down.

On the third day, President Bush sent in 1,000 federal law enforcement agents and ordered 4,500 federal troops to stand by; some later joined the National Guard in patrolling the streets. The president spoke to the nation on television, with a plea for racial harmony and a promise to restore law and order. Rodney King, whose terrible beating had begun it all, also went on television with an emotional plea for peace. "People," he said, "I just want to say, can we all get along? Can we get along?"[81]

Gradually, the violence diminished, but the scars remained.

The nation was shaken to the core by the terrible events in Los Angeles. Because the videotaped evidence had seemed clear, millions of people, black and white, were baffled by the jury's decision. President Bush said he had been "stunned" by the verdict. Few Americans condoned the violence, even if they understood the emotions that had fueled it. Some political leaders called for social programs to get at the root causes of poverty and hopelessness.

In Washington, the Justice Department began an investigation of the King beating. In 1993, two of the police officers were convicted in federal court of violating King's civil rights and sent to prison. The two other officers were acquitted. In 1994, a jury in Los Angeles ordered the city to pay Rodney King $3.8 million in damages in compensation for the beating.

If not for the damning videotape, would Americans have ever known about the attack on Rodney King? Obviously not. The fact that a motorist, even one who was breaking the law by speeding, could be treated this way by police in the nation's second-largest city shocked many white Americans. It might have come as less of a shock to those African Americans who had personal experience with the racial prejudice that still existed among individuals in many segments of American society, including, in some cases, the police.

The issue of police prejudice and of racial divisions among Americans arose dramatically again during the 1995 trial of O. J. Simpson, the former professional football star accused of murdering his ex-wife, Nicole Brown Simpson, and her friend, Ronald Goldman, in 1994 in the affluent Brentwood section of Los Angeles. During the trial, detective Mark Fuhrman testified that he found a "bloody glove" at Simpson's estate on the night of the murders that matched one at the crime scene, so his testimony was crucial to the prosecution's case. But it later developed that Fuhrman, in a series of taped interviews, had used racial epithets in speaking of African Americans, although he had denied this on the witness stand. He had also boasted of planting evidence in other cases. The disclosures were shocking, and race became a key part of the Simpson defense. When Simpson was acquitted, public attitudes reflected

Los Angeles riots, 1992

the continuing racial divisions in America. In a survey taken a few days before the jurors' decision, 77 percent of whites thought Simpson was guilty and 72 percent of blacks thought he was innocent.[82]

But violence, burning cities, and sensational trials divert attention from the everyday reality of prejudice faced by many members of minority groups. Perhaps no white man or woman can ever fully comprehend what it is like to be born with black skin in America. In his prophetic 1963 book *The Fire Next Time,* author James Baldwin wrote:

> Long before the Negro child perceives this difference, and even long before he understands it, he has begun to react to it, he has begun to be controlled by it.... He must be "good" not only in order to please his parents and not only to avoid being punished by them; behind their authority stands another, nameless and impersonal, infinitely harder to please, and bottomlessly cruel. And this filters into the child's consciousness through his parents' tone of voice as he is being exhorted, punished, or loved; in the sudden, uncontrollable note of fear heard in his mother's or his father's voice when he has strayed beyond some particular boundary. He does not know what the boundary is, and he can get no explanation of it.[83]

Another writer, Ralph Ellison, argued that the black adult was unseen by the white world. "I am an invisible man," he wrote. "I am a man of substance, of flesh and bone, fiber and liquids—and I might even be said to possess a mind. I am invisible, understand, simply because people refuse to see me."[84]

Ellison wrote those words in 1952. If African American men and women in America are visible today, it is because a revolution in civil rights has taken place since that time. Yet black Americans still have not been able to reach the goal of full equality in American society.

It is paradoxical, and tragic as well, that a nation founded on the principle that all people are created equal should have "a race problem." This is the paradox that the Swedish sociologist Gunnar Myrdal termed the "American Dilemma" in his classic study more than half a century ago.[85] "The American Dilemma," Myrdal wrote, ". . . is the ever-raging conflict between, on the one hand, the valuations preserved on the general plane which we shall call the 'American Creed,' where the American thinks, talks, and acts under the influence of high national and Christian precepts, and on the other hand . . . group prejudice against particular persons or types of people."[86]

Author Charles E. Silberman has argued that in one sense, "Myrdal was wrong. The tragedy of race relations in the United States is that there is no American Dilemma. White Americans are not torn and tortured by the conflict between their devotion to the American creed and their actual behavior.... What troubles them

## Making a Difference

### "THERE WAS DAYS I ATE BEANS"

OAKLAND, CALIF.—In 1987, real estate agent Oral Lee Brown walked into a class of first graders in a blighted neighborhood and made a promise: If the students stayed in school and graduated, Mrs. Brown would pay for their college.

This fall, she made good, sending 19 students off to the colleges of their choice. When Mrs. Brown, who was making about $45,000 a year selling working-class homes, offered to shepherd a group of first graders through college, "I almost fell through the floor," said Yolanda Peeks, then the principal of Brookfield Elementary.

Getting the group of kids into college took more than good intentions. There were monthly meetings with parents, weekly meetings with students, lunches on school playgrounds.

Sometimes there was trouble. The children of Brookfield went to class with all the problems of their neighborhood. On the tough streets of Oakland, drugs, gangs, and poverty take a lot of kids out of school.

"There's been times that I went home, put down my purse, went upstairs and got in bed and cried myself to sleep and said, 'I'm never going back,'" Mrs. Brown said. "I'd wake up the next morning and I was the first one there."

But how could one woman who makes $45,000 a year selling real estate pay for 19 college educations? Paying for the dream wasn't easy. Mrs. Brown, who is widowed and has two grown daughters, found $10,000 every year to put into a trust fund. "There was days I ate beans," she said. She also started a foundation that raised more money.

In four years she plans to attend 10 different college graduations. "When my babies walk across the stage," she said, "then they can just lay me down and let me die."

—Adapted from the Associated Press, November 16, 1999; and Roger O'Neil on *NBC Nightly News with Tom Brokaw,* December 23, 1999

is not that justice is being denied, but that when racial conflicts erupt their peace is . . . shattered and their business interrupted."[87]

The tension between black and white Americans is not only a problem for the African American still seeking a rightful place in society but also a problem for all citizens, a moral contradiction that strikes at the roots of American democracy. Two decades after Myrdal had summarized his views, and again in 1992, the "fire next time" predicted by James Baldwin visited American cities in the form of racial disorders, and social conflict remained a continuing threat to the nation's future.

By the 1980s a substantial black middle class had emerged in the United States, and black incomes were growing. But this created even deeper divisions among blacks. William Julius Wilson has suggested that economic class, rather than race, may have become more important in determining the status of blacks in America: "As the black middle class rides on the wave of political and social changes . . . the black underclass falls behind."[88] Other scholars have disagreed with Wilson's interpretation, arguing that the major problem black Americans face is that the nation "has historically oppressed black people because they are black."[89]

The unprecedented migration of blacks from the South to northern cities after the Second World War helped to create explosive ghetto conditions in those cities. And the poverty of the inner city continued to exist in the midst of what is, for many Americans, an affluent society. Blacks, Silberman noted, are "an economic as well as a racial minority." No matter how "assimilated" the black American is, because of his skin color "he cannot lose himself in the crowd. He remains . . . an alien in his own land."[90]

## The Historical Background

### The African American

Unlike most other immigrants, who came to these shores seeking freedom, African Americans came in slavery. Theirs was a forced immigration. While Irish Americans, Italian Americans, and other Americans might regard their forebears' country of national origin with pride, until the 1960s few black Americans identified with African culture. In part this was because black Americans absorbed the whites' concept of Africa as a land of jungles and savages. Only in recent years have substantial numbers of scholars explored the distinctive history and culture of West Africa.

It was there, south of the Sahara along the coast of West Africa, that most of the slaves brought to America were captured, to be transported across the sea under cruel conditions. The slaves, chained together and lying on their backs, were packed in layers between the decks in spaces that sometimes measured less than 2 feet. Often, only a third survived the voyage "and loss of half was not at all unusual."[91] It was not surprising that the slaves sometimes mutinied aboard ship.

No one knows precisely how many slaves were brought to North and South America and the West Indies between the 16th and the mid-19th centuries, but the figure has been estimated at 15 million. It easily may have been twice that.

## An African American Heritage

In the 1950s a white or black child reading an American history textbook scarcely would have realized that African Americans were a significant part of the American past. Beginning in the 1960s, however, interest in the cultural heritage of African Americans was accompanied by new studies of the role of blacks in the nation's history.

Perhaps the first person to fall in the American Revolution was a black man, Crispus Attucks. A 47-year-old runaway slave, later a sailor on whaling ships, he was among five men killed by British soldiers in the Boston Massacre of 1770, five years before the Revolutionary War began.[92] African Americans took part in the battles of Lexington, Concord, and Bunker Hill; they were with George Washington at Valley Forge. About 5,000 blacks served in the Continental Army. During the Civil War, 186,000 blacks served in the Union ranks, and blacks fought in later wars, including the First World War, the Second World War, Korea, Vietnam, the Gulf War, and Iraq.

Black explorers, soldiers, scientists, poets, writers, educators, public officials—the list of such men and women who made individual contributions is long and distinguished; moreover, blacks as a group have contributed to the culture of America and have participated in its historical development. Yet from the start, the role of African Americans was overlooked or neglected. "We hold these truths to be self-evident," the Declaration of Independence says, "that all men are created equal." But that soaring language was not meant to include the African American, who was recognized by the framers at Philadelphia as only "three-fifths" of a person. The American Dilemma, even as the republic began, was engraved in the new nation's Constitution but had scarcely touched its conscience.

## Dred Scott, Reconstruction, and "Jim Crow"

Citizens of a state automatically are citizens of the United States under the Constitution. Until after the Civil War, however, this in reality referred only to free white people. The citizenship status of free blacks—there were almost 100,000 in the early 1800s—remained a subject of political dispute. The Supreme Court ruled on the question in the famous ***Dred Scott* decision** of 1857.

Dred Scott was a slave who had lived in the North for four years. Antislavery forces sought to bring Scott's case before the Supreme Court on the grounds that his residence on free soil had made him a free man. To sue for freedom, Scott first had to prove he was a citizen. But Chief Justice Roger B. Taney ruled that Dred Scott and other black Americans "are not included, and were not intended to be included, under the word 'citizens' in the Constitution."[93]

It took a civil war and a constitutional amendment to reverse Taney's decision. In 1865, eight months after the surrender of Robert E. Lee's army at Appomattox, the states ratified the Thirteenth Amendment, abolishing slavery. The Fourteenth Amendment, ratified in 1868, reversed the *Dred Scott* decision by making citizens of the freed slaves. The Fifteenth Amendment, ratified in 1870, was designed to give former slaves the right to vote.

During the Reconstruction era (1863–1877), Congress passed a series of civil rights measures. Two laws enacted in 1870 make it a crime for police to violate a

A total of 186,000 African Americans served in the Union Army during the Civil War.

The Granger Collection, New York

Dred Scott

person's civil rights or for anyone to conspire to do so. The statutes were seldom invoked until the 1960s, when the federal government used them to prosecute and convict police in brutality cases in which local authorities had failed to act or the offenders had received light sentences. Of the laws passed during Reconstruction, the last, the Civil Rights Act of 1875, was the strongest. The law was aimed at providing equal public accommodations for blacks. But this postwar trend toward equality was short-lived. In the *Civil Rights Cases* of 1883, the Supreme Court struck down the 1875 Civil Rights Act, decreeing that the Fourteenth Amendment protected citizens from infringement of their rights by the states but not by private individuals. Discrimination by one citizen against another was a private affair, the Court held.

Thus, less than two decades after the Civil War, the Supreme Court had seriously weakened the Fourteenth Amendment and neutralized the efforts of Congress to pass civil rights laws to protect black citizens. The Court decisions were also a sign of what was to come.

After 1883 the atmosphere was ripe for the rise of segregation and of **Jim Crow laws** designed to segregate black and white Americans and give legal recognition to discrimination.*

**Segregation,** the separation of black and white Americans by race, became the new way of life in the South. Jim Crow laws were accompanied by hundreds of lynchings and terror for African Americans.†

### "You Shall Have Your Liberty . . . I Am a Soldier Now"

More than 185,000 African Americans volunteered to fight for the Union during the Civil War. One, Samuel Cabble, was a 21-year-old waiter who enlisted as a private in the 55th Massachusetts Infantry in 1863. That year, he wrote a letter to his wife:

> Dear wife I have enlisted the army. I am now in the state of Massachusetts but before this letter reaches you I will be in North Carolina and though great is the present national difficulties yet I look forward to a brighter day when I shall have the opportunity of seeing you in the full enjoyment of freedom. I would like to no [*sic*] if you are still in slavery if you are it will not be long before we shall have crushed the system that now oppresses you for in the course of three months you shall have your liberty. Great is the outpouring of the colored people that is now rallying with the hearts of lions against that very curse that has separated you and me. Yet we shall meet again and oh what a happy time that will be when this ungodly rebellion shall be put down and the curses of our land is trampled under our feet. I am a soldier now and I shall use my utmost endeavor to strike at the rebellion and the heart of this system that so long has kept us in chains . . . remain your own affectionate husband until death
>
> Samuel Cabble

—National Archives

## *Plessy* v. *Ferguson*

In 1896 the Supreme Court put its seal of approval on racial segregation in America. The great constitutional test of legal discrimination began on a June day in 1892, when Homer Adolph Plessy bought a ticket in New Orleans, boarded an East Louisiana Railroad train, and took his seat—in a coach reserved for whites. He was asked to move, but he refused and was arrested.

Plessy was chosen for this test by opponents of the state's Jim Crow railroad law, which required equal but separate accommodations for white and black passengers. The Supreme Court ruled in 1896 that the Louisiana statute did not violate the Fourteenth Amendment.

Yet *Plessy* v. *Ferguson* is remembered as well for the ringing dissent of a single justice, a former slaveholder from Kentucky, John Marshall Harlan. Shocked by the activities of the Ku Klux Klan, Harlan had become a champion of civil rights for blacks. And he declared: "Our Constitution is color-blind, and neither knows nor tolerates classes among citizens. . . . The thin disguise of 'equal' accommodations for passengers in railroad

* In 1832 Thomas D. "Daddy" Rice, a blackface minstrel, had introduced a song and dance about a slave named Jim Crow ("Weel a-bout and turn a-bout / And . . . jump Jim Crow"), and the term came to be applied to the antiblack laws of the 1890s.

† There were about 100 lynchings a year in the 1880s and 1890s; 161 lynchings took place in 1892.

© Carl Iwasaki/Time Life Pictures/Getty Images

Linda Carol Brown, denied admission to a white elementary school near her home, had to walk with her younger sister along the railroad tracks to attend a segregated school.

coaches will not mislead any one, nor atone for the wrong this day done."[94]

Despite Harlan's eloquent dissent, the doctrine of "separate but equal" remained the law of the land for 58 years, until 1954, when the Supreme Court finally ruled that it had no place in American life.

## The Case of Linda Carol Brown

In the city of Topeka, Kansas, more than half a century after *Plessy,* Oliver Brown, a black man and a welder by trade, was disturbed by the fact that his 8-year-old daughter, Linda Carol, attended an elementary school 21 blocks from her home. Only black students attended the school, for Topeka elementary schools were segregated by local option under state law. To go the 21 blocks to Monroe Elementary School, Linda Carol caught a school bus at 7:40 a.m. The difficulty was that the bus arrived at the school at 8:30 a.m., but the doors of the school did not open until 9 a.m. Often, this meant that children had to wait outside in the cold. To get home in the afternoon, she had to walk past the railroad tracks and cross a dangerous intersection. Oliver Brown tried to enroll his children at Sumner Elementary School, which was only seven blocks from the Brown home. He was unable to do so. Sumner was a school for white children. With the help of the National Association for the Advancement of Colored People (NAACP), Oliver Brown took his case to court.

## *Brown* v. *Board of Education*

On May 17, 1954, Chief Justice Earl Warren delivered the unanimous opinion of the Supreme Court in the case of ***Brown* v. *Board of Education of Topeka, Kansas,*** ruling that racial segregation in public schools violates the Fourteenth Amendment's requirement of equal protection of the laws for all people. The issue before the Supreme Court was very simple: The Fourteenth Amendment guarantees equal protection of the laws. The plaintiffs argued that segregated schools were not and could never be equal and were therefore unconstitutional.

Chief Justice Warren asked: "Does segregation of children in public schools solely on the basis of race, even though the physical facilities and other 'tangible' factors may be equal, deprive the children of the minority group of equal educational opportunities? We believe that it does." Such segregation of children, the chief justice added, "may affect their hearts and minds in a way unlikely ever to be undone. . . . We conclude that in the field of public education the doctrine 'separate but equal' has no place. Separate educational facilities are inherently unequal. Therefore, we hold that the plaintiffs . . . are, by reason of the segregation complained of, deprived of the equal protection of the laws guaranteed by the Fourteenth Amendment."[95]

The Supreme Court did not try in 1954 to enforce its decision. The Court, as Justice Robert Jackson pointed out, "is dependent upon the political branches for the execution of its mandates, for it has no physical force at its command."[96]

Much of the South reacted to *Brown* by adopting a policy of massive resistance. How, then, would the Court's ruling be implemented? A year later, in May 1955, the Supreme Court itself addressed the problem, unanimously ordering local school authorities to comply with the decision "with all deliberate speed."[97] But compliance was very slow, and in some instances there were direct armed confrontations between federal and state power.

## Little Rock, Oxford, and Alabama

In September 1957 nine black children attempted to enter the all-white Central High School in Little Rock, Arkansas, under a federal court order. Governor Orval Faubus called out the National Guard to block integration of the school, but the troops were withdrawn by direction of the court. The black students braved a screaming mob of whites. President Dwight Eisenhower reluctantly dispatched federal paratroopers to Little Rock to quell the violence. Central High was integrated.

Violence continued to flare in the South during the Kennedy administration. After James Meredith, a black student, enrolled in the University of Mississippi at Oxford in 1962, two men were killed and several injured in the rioting that occurred on the campus. President Kennedy dispatched federal marshals and ordered 16,000 troops to restore peace and protect Meredith. The following year, Alabama Governor George Wallace tried to block the enrollment of two black students at the University of Alabama at Tuscaloosa. Wallace backed down only after Kennedy federalized the Alabama National Guard.

## The School Decision: Aftermath

Fifteen years after the *Brown* decision, only 20 percent of black students in the South attended integrated public schools. Faced with continued defiance, the Supreme Court ruled unanimously in October 1969 that school districts must end segregation "at once" and operate integrated systems "now and hereafter."[98] Through federal court rulings and the efforts of the federal government in working with local school boards, the pattern gradually changed. But even as more schools became integrated, the question of public school desegregation, in the North as well as in the South, remained a volatile issue.

In Topeka, Kansas, where it had all begun, a federal judge in 1979 reopened the *Brown* case after a group of parents complained that, 25 years later, the city's schools were still segregated. Among the group of parents who filed the complaint was Linda Carol Brown, now the mother of two children in the Topeka public school system. In 1987 a federal district court ruled that the school district, although not totally integrated, was in compliance with the law.

## The Busing Controversy

In 1971, in a case that arose in Charlotte, North Carolina, the Supreme Court ruled unanimously that in some circumstances the Constitution required busing schoolchildren to schools outside their neighborhoods to achieve desegregation.[99] By the mid-1970s the familiar yellow school bus had become the symbol of a deeply divisive political and social issue in the United States. The Court did not require busing in every case. For example, it struck down plans to bus children to desegregate schools in some cities, while it upheld a busing plan in Boston, the scene of prolonged violence over busing in the mid-1970s.

Although millions of public school children rode school buses every weekday in the United States, many parents, both white and black, objected to busing to achieve desegregation. White parents often opposed the busing of their children into largely black, inner-city schools. A number of parents, black and white, objected to long bus rides into unfamiliar neighborhoods for their children.

As the issue continued to trouble the nation, some black educators argued that a high-quality education did not depend on busing and desegregation. Wilson Riles, the superintendent of education in California, rejected the idea "that a black child can't learn unless he is sitting next to a white child."[100]

In cities of the North, school segregation often has been the result not of law but of de facto segregation—residential patterns that created black neighborhoods and, along with them, black schools. The 1954 *Brown* decision did not deal with de facto segregation, but the issue was involved in a case in Denver that the Supreme Court decided in 1973.[101] The Court ruled that Denver had to desegregate its school system; the decision in effect warned the North that it, too, could not operate segregated schools.

In the 1990s, decisions of the Supreme Court and

© UPI/Bettmann/Corbis

© Bettmann/Corbis

Rosa Parks, in the front of the bus: Her courage made her a symbol of the civil rights movement.

lower federal courts made it easier for school districts to be released from desegregation orders and busing. More than four decades after the *Brown* decision, however, most minority students still attended segregated schools across the nation. One study found that 70 percent of the nation's black students and more than a third of Hispanic students attended predominantly minority schools.[102] It was clear in the years following *Brown* that racial problems were not confined to any one section of the nation.

## The Civil Rights Movement: Freedom Now

### The Montgomery Bus Boycott

On the evening of December 1, 1955, Rosa Parks, a 43-year-old seamstress, boarded a bus in Montgomery, Alabama, as she did every working day to return home from her job at a downtown department store. When half a dozen whites got on at a bus stop, the driver asked black passengers near the front of the bus to give up their seats to the whites and move to the rear. Three other black passengers got up; Rosa Parks did not. She was arrested and fined $10, but her quiet refusal launched a boycott of the bus line by a black population that had had enough. It was a remarkable year-long protest, and it catapulted to national fame the 27-year-old Baptist minister who led it. His name was Dr. Martin Luther King, Jr.

During the boycott, King went to jail and his home was bombed, but he won. The boycott ended in November 1956 as a result of a federal court injunction prohibiting segregation of buses in Montgomery. The victory set the pattern for other boycotts and for direct action throughout the South.

King, who led the civil rights movement and remained its symbolic head until his assassination in 1968, was an apostle of nonviolence, an eloquent man who attempted, with some success, to stir the American conscience. King grew up in comfortable middle-class surroundings in Atlanta, where his father was pastor of the Ebenezer Baptist Church. It was in Atlanta in 1957, following the Montgomery boycott, that King formed the Southern Christian Leadership Conference (SCLC) as a vehicle for his philosophy of nonviolent change, which had been influenced by the teachings of Gandhi.

Until then, the principal black organization in the United States had been the NAACP, which stressed legal action in the courts as the road to progress. It was a lawyer's approach, and it had won many important struggles. King's battleground was the streets rather than the courts, and he sought through nonviolent confrontation to dramatize the issue of civil rights for the nation and the world.

The civil rights movement came of age at a time when many blacks were growing impatient with the slow pace of "gradual" change. Their desire was for "freedom now"—rather than at some unspecified time in the future.

### Sit-Ins and Freedom Rides

In February 1960 four black college students in Greensboro, North Carolina, sat down at a lunch counter at Woolworth's and asked politely for cups of coffee. They were refused service. They continued to sit for the rest of the morning. They came back the next day, and the next. Soon other students, white and black, joined them. They were spattered with mustard and ketchup and spat upon and cursed by whites. But at Greensboro the sit-in movement was born.

It spread to seven other states. The new tactics were a success. Within six months, not only the Woolworth's in Greensboro but hundreds of lunch counters throughout the South were serving blacks. In 1961 the sit-in technique was adapted to test segregation on interstate buses and in bus terminals. Black and white "Freedom Riders" rode into Alabama, where they were beaten, slashed with chains, and stoned by whites. One bus was burned. But the Freedom Riders succeeded in publicizing the fact that segregation on interstate transportation, although outlawed by the Supreme Court, was still a reality.[103]

## Martin Luther King's Moral Theater

When the antiabortion mothers march around the Capitol, when the farmers jam the streets with their tractors, they are, consciously or otherwise, imitating the moral theater Martin Luther King staged for the mass audience of television. Sometimes it works, and often it doesn't, but a range of political strategies, now regarded as orthodox and acceptable, was considered outrageous [and] sometimes illegal when King introduced it.

—*Washington Post,* April 2, 1978

© AP/Wide World Photos

The police dogs of Birmingham, 1963

## Birmingham and the Dream

In the spring of 1963, Dr. King organized demonstrations against segregation in industrial Birmingham, Alabama. When arrests failed to stop the demonstrators, the authorities used high-pressure fire hoses, police dogs, and cattle prods. The demonstrators sang "We Shall Overcome" and continued to march. Photographs of police dogs attacking demonstrators on orders of Birmingham Police Commissioner Eugene "Bull" Connor went out on the news wires. Another photograph showed police kneeling on a black woman and pinning her to the sidewalk. The scenes outraged much of the nation and the world.

Late in August, King led a massive, peaceful "March on Washington for Jobs and Freedom." Some 200,000 Americans, black and white, jammed the mall between the Lincoln Memorial and the Washington Monument. The nationally televised, orderly demonstration had a powerful effect on the nation, but even more powerful were the words of Dr. King, who articulated the vision of what America could be and might become:

> I have a dream that one day this nation will rise up and live out the true meaning of its creed. . . . I have a dream . . . that my four little children will one day live in a nation where they will not be judged by the color of their skin but by the content of their character. . . . So let freedom ring. . . . From every mountainside, let freedom ring . . . to speed up that day when all of God's children, black and white men, Jews and Gentiles, Protestants and Catholics, will be able to join hands and sing in the words of that old Negro spiritual, "Free at last! Free at last! Thank God Almighty, we are free at last!" [104]

Eighteen days later in Birmingham, a bomb was thrown into the Sixteenth Street Baptist Church on a Sunday morning. Four black girls attending Bible class died in the explosion. But from the agony of Birmingham that summer, from the impressive march on Wash-

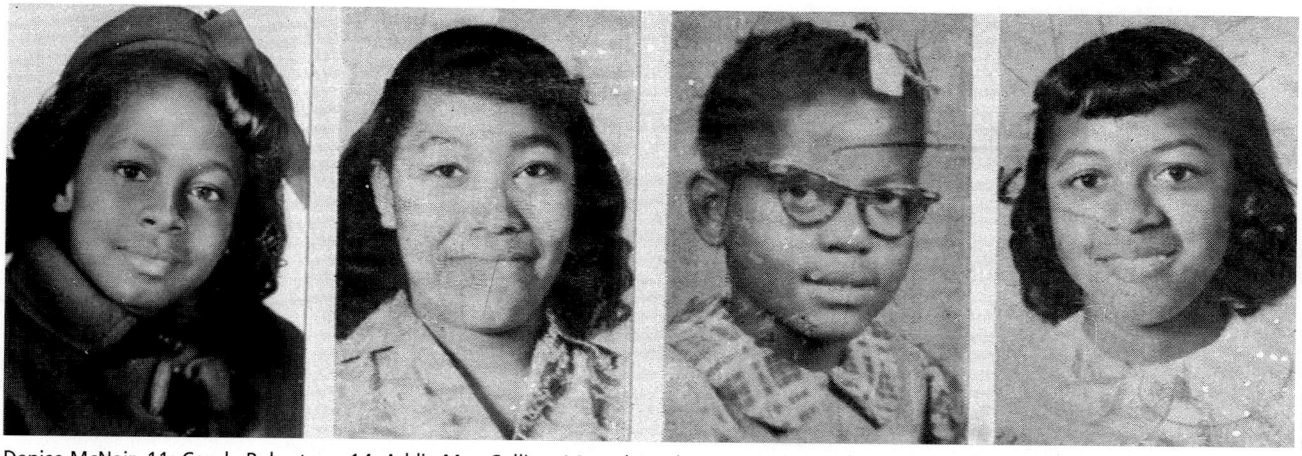

© AP/Wide World Photos

Denise McNair, 11; Carole Robertson, 14; Addie Mae Collins, 14; and Cynthia Dianne Wesley, 14, were all killed in the 1963 bombing of the Sixteenth Street Baptist Church in Birmingham, Alabama.

© AP/Wide World Photos

Dr. Martin Luther King, Jr., at the March on Washington, August 1963: "I have a dream. . . ."

ington, and from the powerful words of Dr. King, there emerged the strongest civil rights legislation since Reconstruction.

## The Legislative Breakthrough

During the Eisenhower administration, Congress had passed the Civil Rights Act of 1957, the first such legislation since 1875. It created the Commission on Civil Rights and strengthened the civil rights section of the Justice Department. However, the law proved to be of limited value in protecting civil rights.

> **"Lord, How Dare We Celebrate?"**
>
> ATLANTA, Jan. 17—The ceremony was to honor the achievements of the Rev. Martin Luther King Jr., but the Rev. Bernice King, the slain civil rights leader's youngest child, found no cause for joy.
>
> "Lord, how dare we celebrate?" she repeated as she recited chapter and verse of the nation's woes: 23 million Americans functionally illiterate, "more than 40 million Americans . . . without health care . . . young African-American boys . . . killing other young African-American boys over failed drug transactions. . . . Lord, how dare we celebrate?"
>
> —*Washington Post,* January 18, 1992

**The Civil Rights Act of 1964** In 1963 President Kennedy proposed a comprehensive civil rights bill. After Kennedy's assassination in November of that year, the House acted, but southerners in the Senate staged a 57-day filibuster. In June 1964 the Senate invoked cloture, a vote to cut off debate—the first time it had ever done so on a civil rights bill—and passed the measure. On July 2 President Lyndon Johnson signed the Civil Rights Act of 1964 into law. The principal provisions were designed to

1. Prohibit racial or religious discrimination in public accommodations that affect interstate commerce, including hotels, motels, restaurants, cafeterias, lunch counters, gas stations, movie houses, theaters, and sports arenas
2. Prohibit discrimination because of race, color, sex, religion, or national origin by employers or labor unions
3. Bar voting registrars from adopting different standards for white and black applicants
4. Permit the attorney general to bring suit to enforce desegregation of public accommodations, and allow individuals to sue for their rights under the act
5. Permit the executive branch of the federal government to halt the flow of funds to public or private programs that practice discrimination
6. Extend the life of the Civil Rights Commission, create a Community Relations Service to conciliate racial disputes, and an Equal Employment Opportunity Commission to enforce the fair employment section of the act

The 1964 act did not cover violence directed at black Americans or at civil rights workers, white or black. Two days after President Johnson signed the bill into law, the bodies of three young civil rights workers—two of them from the North—were found in a shallow grave near Philadelphia, Mississippi.* In a civil rights act passed in 1968, Congress provided criminal penalties for injuring or interfering with civil rights workers or any people exercising their civil rights; under the law, if the injury results in death, the maximum penalty is life imprisonment.

At the same time, Congress passed the Fair Housing Act, the first federal open housing law in the 20th century. It prohibited discrimination in the rental or sale of all privately owned single-family houses rented or sold through real estate agents or brokers.

**The Voting Rights Act of 1965** During the Reconstruction era, state governments in the South were controlled

* In 1967 seven men were convicted of conspiracy against the slain civil rights workers under an 1870 federal statute. Because the murders of the rights workers did not constitute a federal crime, the conspiracy statute was the only weapon available to the Justice Department. The seven, including an Imperial Wizard of the Ku Klux Klan and the deputy sheriff of Neshoba County, were given prison sentences ranging from three to 10 years.

## TABLE 5-3

### Voter Registration in the South before and after the Voting Rights Act of 1965

| Percent of Voting-Age Population Registered | | | | | | | | | |
|---|---|---|---|---|---|---|---|---|---|
| | 1964 | 1972 | 1980 | 1986 | 1992 | 1994 | 1996 | 2000 | 2004 |
| Black | 43.3 | 56.6 | 60.0 | 64.0 | 63.9 | 58.3 | 64.7 | 64.3 | 65.3 |
| White | 73.2 | 67.8 | 68.4 | 65.3 | 70.1 | 64.2 | 67.0 | 70.0 | 72.1 |

SOURCES: Congressional Quarterly; The Voting Rights Act: Ten Years After, Report of the U.S. Commission on Civil Rights (Washington, D.C.: U.S. Government Printing Office, 1975), p. 43; and U.S. Bureau of the Census.

by northern radical Republicans. After the white South regained control of its governments, particularly in the 1890s and thereafter, blacks were systematically denied the right to vote. What the Ku Klux Klan could not accomplish by intimidation, a broad range of other obstacles did. **Literacy tests,** designed to test a voter's ability to read and write, were rigged to keep black voters from the polls. Other barriers included the all-white primary (which rested on the theory, rejected by the Supreme Court in 1944, that political parties were private clubs), the **poll tax** (a tax on voting used to keep poor voters from participating in elections), and **gerrymandering** of election districts (redrawing lines to favor one party or group over another). All were attempts to keep black voters in the South from gaining political power and challenging or changing the existing order. In short, the Fifteenth Amendment was being systematically flouted.

Only 12 percent of blacks of voting age were registered in the 11 southern states in 1948. Although the figure rose substantially in later years, in the mid-1960s it was still far below the 73.2 percent white registration in the same states.[105] (See Table 5-3.)

In Dallas County, Alabama, in 1965 exactly 335 blacks out of a black population of 15,115 were registered to vote. Martin Luther King chose Selma, the county seat, as the place where he would dramatize the voting rights issue. Dr. King called for a 50-mile march from Selma to Montgomery, the state capital. State troopers acting under orders of Governor Wallace used tear gas, whips, and nightsticks to break up the march. President Johnson federalized the National Guard, and the march resumed under protection of the troops. Through the heat, the mud, and the rain, their ranks swelling in numbers and in pride, the marchers walked on until, joined by Dr. King, they reached the steps of the Alabama capitol building.

In the midst of the struggle that began in Selma, and before the marchers had finally reached Montgomery, President Johnson went on nationwide television to address a special joint session of Congress and to urge new legislation to assure black Americans the right to vote. Then, in a dramatic moment, the president from Texas invoked the song and the slogan of the civil rights movement. "And we shall overcome," he said slowly. Thunderous applause greeted the remark, and Congress responded to Johnson's appeal with a second landmark civil rights measure.

The Voting Rights Act of 1965, passed after the Senate once again imposed cloture to crush a filibuster, covered six southern states—Alabama, Georgia, Louisiana, Mississippi, South Carolina, and Virginia—as well as parts of North Carolina and three other states. The act suspended literacy tests in many areas covered by the law

March on Montgomery, Alabama, 1965

FIGURE 5-5

**Increase of Black Voter Registration in Seven Southern States Covered by the 1965 Voting Rights Act**

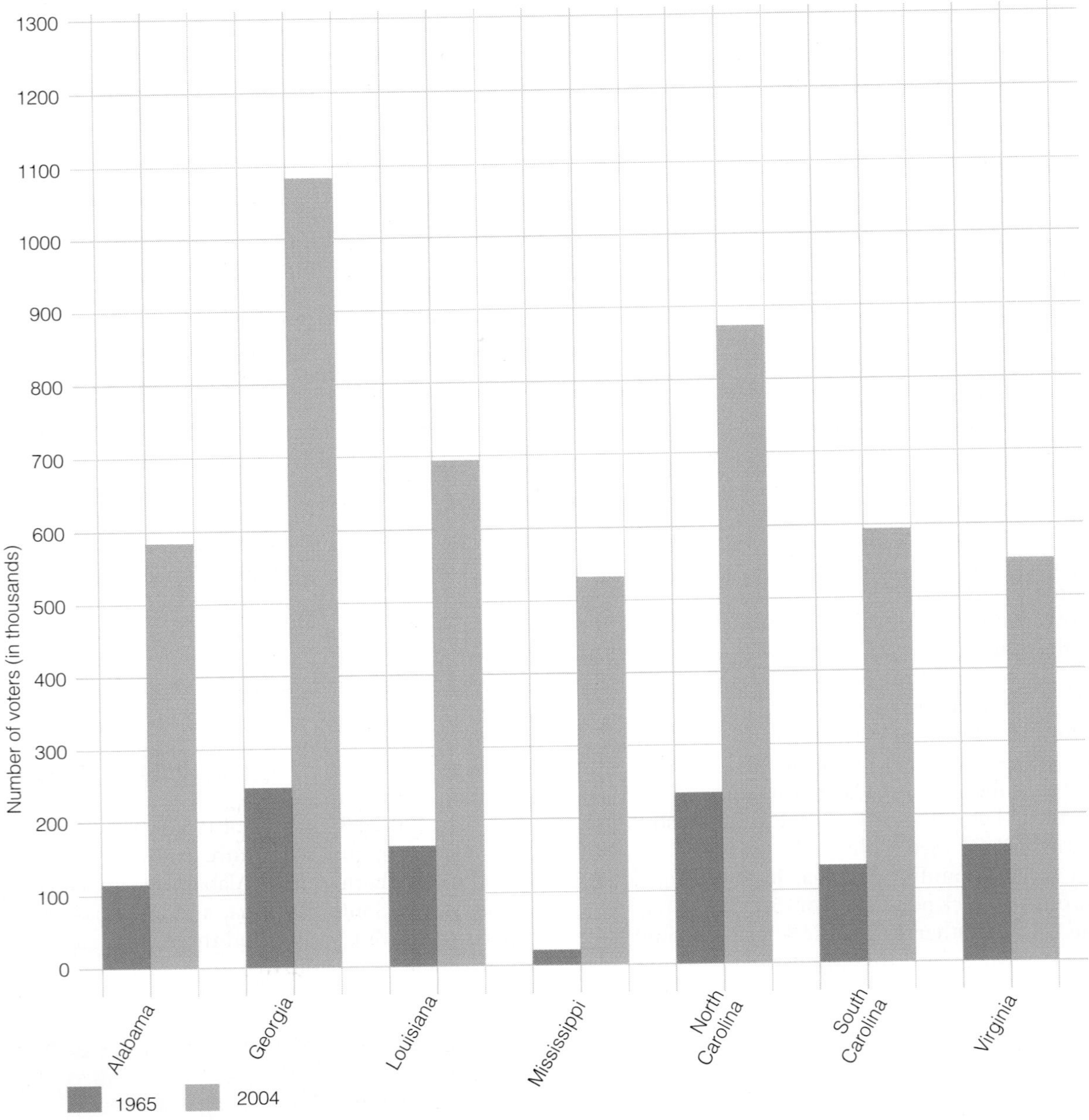


SOURCE: U.S. Bureau of the Census.

and provided for federal examiners to require enrollment of qualified voters in those areas and elsewhere.

The effect of the Voting Rights Act was immediate. Within two years, black registration increased by almost 1.3 million in the South. In Mississippi, black registration jumped from 6.7 percent of eligible voters to 59.8 percent.[106] Figure 5-5 shows increases in the number of registered black voters for seven southern states. At the same time, black registration drives in some southern states also spurred new white registration so that, in actual numbers, there were more new white voters in those states than new black voters.

In 1970 the Voting Rights Act (which would otherwise have expired that year) was extended for five years and its scope broadened to include areas of California, Oregon, and four New England states and parts of New York City. In 1975 Congress extended the act for seven more years and broadened its basic provisions to protect language and other minorities—Spanish-speaking Americans, American Indians, Asians, and Alaska Natives. The revised law covered about a dozen more states. Literacy and character tests were permanently banned throughout the nation. Then, in 1982, and again in 2006, Congress extended the Voting Rights Act for 25 years.

The Voting Rights Act encouraged blacks to run for office, and many did. By 1984, registration and turnout of black voters nationwide was a major theme of Rev. Jesse L. Jackson's campaign for the Democratic presidential nomination. Even before that, blacks in large numbers were registering to vote.

Only 4.4 million blacks had voted in 1966. In 1988, some 10.1 million blacks voted.[107] In 1996, the number of African American voters rose again, to 11.4 million.[108] In 2000, 12.9 million blacks voted, and in 2004, 14 million blacks voted.[109]

In the early 1990s, after prodding by the Justice Department, about two dozen majority-black congressional districts were drawn in the South to conform to the Voting Rights Act and to make possible the election of more African American representatives in Congress. Some of the districts were oddly shaped in order to achieve that goal. Although the redistricting resulted in the election of more blacks and Hispanics, the changes created a dilemma for the Supreme Court, which grappled with the question of whether the new districts were constitutional.

In 1993, the Supreme Court, in a 5–4 decision in a North Carolina case, ruled that districts drawn with "bizarre" shapes in order to separate voters on the basis of race may violate the equal protection clause of the Fourteenth Amendment.[110] The opinion, written by Justice Sandra Day O'Connor, created turmoil in the South. Federal district courts declared unconstitutional congressional districts in Texas, Louisiana, and Georgia. In 1995, the Supreme Court, by a 5–4 vote, struck down the Georgia redistricting plan.[111] A year later, the Court invalidated four predominantly black and Hispanic congressional districts as unconstitutional—three in Texas and one in North Carolina—because they were based on race.[112]

The Court's view in these cases was set forth in Justice Anthony M. Kennedy's majority opinion in the Georgia redistricting case. He wrote: "When the state assigns voters on the basis of race, it engages in the offensive and demeaning assumption that voters of a particular race, because of their race, think alike, share the same political interests, and will prefer the same candidates at the polls."

## The Urban Riots

Even as the major civil rights laws of the mid-1960s were taking effect, black protest in America entered a new phase. The great expectations aroused by the civil rights movement and legislative action by Congress had brought no visible change of status to the millions of blacks in the inner city. Frustration and poverty characterized the ghettos. Combined with summer heat and police incidents, the mixture proved volatile and tragic.

Los Angeles was sweltering in a heat wave on the night of August 11, 1965, when a white highway patrolman stopped a young black driver for speeding and arrested him. A crowd gathered, more police arrived, and trouble flared. By the time the police had left, the residents of Watts, the city's black ghetto, were in an angry mood. Two days after the incident, arson, looting, and shooting broke out. The Watts riot had begun. Cries of "burn, baby, burn!" filled the air. When it was all over, 34 people were dead, more than 1,000 had been injured, and $35 million in damage had been done.

The Watts explosion was the most dramatic event in a pattern of major violence that was to afflict dozens of American cities. After the assassination of Martin Luther King in April 1968, outbreaks occurred in Washington, D.C., and more than 100 other cities. More than 13,000 troops were dispatched to Washington, where rioters had set fires only a few blocks from the White House. For 12 days, armed soldiers occupied the capital of the United States.

During a major riot in Detroit in 1967, President Johnson went on nationwide television to plead for calm and to announce the appointment of a National Advisory Commission on Civil Disorders. The commission reported in March 1968:

> Our nation is moving toward two societies, one black, one white—separate and unequal. . . . Certain fundamental matters are clear. Of these the most fundamental is the racial attitude and behavior of white Americans toward black Americans. . . . Race prejudice has shaped our history decisively; it now threatens to affect our future. White racism is essentially responsible for the explosive mixture which has been accumulating in our cities since the end of World War II.[113]

To meet these problems, the commission recommended a national effort to eliminate racial barriers in employment, education, and housing and to create jobs. The commission's findings were controversial—many Americans disagreed with the emphasis on white racism as the primary cause of the urban riots. Few could disagree, however, with the gravity of the problems underscored by the explosions in the cities during the 1960s and in 1992.

## Black Power, Black Pride

During the late 1960s, advocates of direct, militant action had to a considerable extent drowned out the voices of moderate black leaders. Black Power advocates and members of the militant Black Panthers often found it easier to capture the attention of the public and the press than did the moderates. And the assassination of Martin

Luther King and other leaders committed to nonviolence weakened the position of the moderates.

Stokely Carmichael, a black leader who had popularized the phrase "Black Power," defined the term as "a call for black people in this country to unite, to recognize their heritage, to build a sense of community." [114] A common theme of Black Power was the need for African Americans to exercise political control of their communities. Economically, the term was tied to the creation of independent, black-owned and black-operated businesses. Spiritually, it meant racial pride; it also gave rise to slogans such as "Black is beautiful" and to an emphasis on "soul" and "soul brothers."

Black Panthers and police were killed in a series of shootings in several cities. The most widely publicized case took place in 1969, when Chicago police raided an apartment before dawn, allegedly in a search for weapons, and shot and killed Fred Hampton, chairman of the Illinois Black Panther party.[115]

Although militants had for a time commanded an audience, most black Americans sought full social and economic equality and dignity within the system rather than apart from it. Along with many white Americans, they still believed in Martin Luther King's dream.

In October 1995, Louis Farrakhan, the controversial leader of the Nation of Islam, organized the "Million Man March" that gathered on the mall in Washington to emphasize once again the themes of racial pride and responsibility. Because Farrakhan's rhetoric was often inflammatory and sometimes anti-Semitic, President Clinton distanced himself from Farrakhan. Many groups, including the NAACP, opposed the march because of its organizer. Despite these misgivings by opponents, several hundred thousand participants came together peacefully in Washington for the event.

## Affirmative Action: The Supreme Court Rules

The civil rights movement and the legislation enacted in the 1960s did not settle a larger constitutional question: Was **affirmative action**—programs of government, universities, and businesses, designed to favor minorities and remedy past discrimination—constitutional?

Supporters of affirmative action argue that black Americans, unlike other ethnic groups, have faced greater barriers to achieving equality. Studies have noted that other nationality groups, as members of the white majority, have been more easily assimilated into American society.

John F. Kennedy, in an executive order issued in 1961, was the first president to call for affirmative action by the government. The order prohibited discrimination by contractors who received federal money and instructed them to hire and promote members of minority groups.

The Civil Rights Act of 1964 barred discrimination by universities or others who received federal assistance. The act also outlawed discrimination by employers or unions. Many universities, employers, and unions went a step further and established affirmative action programs that gave preference in admissions or jobs to minorities. Merely guaranteeing minorities equal opportunity, it was argued, would not solve the problem, because members of such groups often would be at a disadvantage when competing with whites who had not suffered discrimination.

### *Bakke* and *Weber:* The Battle Is Joined

Opponents of affirmative action programs argued that the programs were a form of "reverse discrimination" against whites. Because the Fourteenth Amendment to the Constitution extended equal protection of the laws to everyone, and because the 1964 Civil Rights Act outlawed any form of discrimination, were programs unconstitutional if they favored a black or a Hispanic person over a white person?

As with many constitutional questions, these arguments and counterarguments eventually focused on the case of one person—a white man named Allan Paul Bakke. Bakke graduated from college in 1963 with an engineering degree and a 3.51 grade-point average. He joined the Marines, served in Vietnam, and later went to work on the moon program for the National Aeronautics and Space Administration (NASA). But what he wanted most was to be a doctor. Nights and weekends, he was a hospital volunteer.

In 1973 and 1974 Bakke applied to the medical school of the University of California at Davis. He did not get in. Davis had a special admissions program that reserved 16 out of 100 places in the medical school each year for minorities. In both years, minority students were admitted with much lower scores than Bakke's. Bakke sued. He contended that he had been excluded on the basis of his race in violation of the Constitution and the 1964 act.

In June 1978, the U.S. Supreme Court, by a vote of 5–4, ordered Bakke admitted to the medical school at Davis. At the same time, the Court upheld the right of universities to give preference to blacks and other minorities as long as they do not use rigid racial "quotas" such as the one used at Davis.

The majority based its decision not on the 1964 law but on the Fourteenth Amendment's guarantee of equal protection of the laws. Associate Justice Lewis F. Powell, Jr., who provided the swing vote in the case, delivered the majority opinion: "Preferring members of any one group for no reason other than race or ethnic origin is discrimination for its own sake. This the Constitution forbids." At the same time, Powell said, flexible admission programs, such as Harvard's, that "take race into account" but do not set a "fixed number of places" for minorities, were constitutional.[116]

© Bettmann/Corbis

Allan Paul Bakke on his first day of medical school at the University of California at Davis

In September, Bakke, by then 38, married, and the father of two young children, entered the medical school at Davis, California. He graduated in 1982 and became an anesthesiologist at a hospital in Minnesota.

The *Bakke* decision left unsettled the question of affirmative action in employment. But in 1979 the Supreme Court ruled in the case of Brian Weber, a blue-collar worker in a small town in Louisiana, who suddenly found himself in the vortex of a major constitutional test. Weber, a 32-year-old white man, was employed as a lab technician for the Kaiser Aluminum and Chemical Corporation.

Weber applied and was rejected for a training program that would lead to higher pay. The program set aside half the jobs for black workers. Several of the blacks selected had less seniority than Weber, who took his case to the Supreme Court and lost. The Court ruled 5–2 that the 1964 Civil Rights Act was designed to help minorities and did not prohibit private affirmative action programs.[117] In 1980 the Supreme Court also ruled that 10 percent of federal public works contracts could go to minority-owned business firms to remedy past discrimination.[118]

In 1987, in a broad endorsement of affirmative action, the Court ruled that employers may promote women and minorities ahead of white men, even when there is no evidence of prior discrimination.[119] It did so in the case of Diane Joyce, who had been a road repair worker in Santa Clara, California.

In 1995, however, in a Colorado highway construction case, the Supreme Court ruled that federal affirmative action programs must be "narrowly tailored" to be constitutional.[120] The Supreme Court often reflects the political environment of the times. In the wake of the Republican capture of Congress in 1994, the concept of affirmative action no longer enjoyed the same political support that it once had. The old arguments that such programs amounted to "reverse discrimination" against whites resurfaced, and affirmative action programs fell under increased pressure.

In California in 1995, the regents of the university system banned affirmative action in admissions. In 1996, California voters approved Proposition 209, which banned race or gender preferences in public hiring, contracting, and education. In 1999, as an alternative, Gray Davis, then the state's Democratic governor, initiated a program of admission to the University of California, starting in 2001, for the top 4 percent of graduates in each high school. Two years earlier, a similar law passed in Texas and supported by then governor George W. Bush guaranteed admission to the state university system of all students who graduated in the top 10 percent of their high school class.

In 1998, voters in the state of Washington banned state-sponsored affirmative action programs. Two years later, Florida governor Jeb Bush was defending his One Florida plan, modeled after the one in Texas, his brother's state, that guaranteed admission to a state university to the top 20 percent of high school graduates.

The future of affirmative action seemed uncertain until 2003, when the Supreme Court firmly upheld the principle of affirmative action for minority students seeking admission to colleges and universities.[121] As discussed in Chapter 2, the Court's decision in two cases involving the University of Michigan clearly endorsed the goal of affirmative action to achieve racial diversity and equality in American society.

## Equal Rights: A Balance Sheet

In 1995, millions of Americans, both white and black, were hoping that Colin L. Powell, the retired Army general who had been chairman of the Joint Chiefs of Staff, would seek the 1996 presidential nomination. Enthusiastic crowds turned out in cities from coast to coast as Powell traveled to promote his autobiography. When he announced soon afterward that he would not be a candidate for president in 1996, his supporters were deeply disappointed. But the fact that an African American, the son of poor immigrants from Jamaica, enjoyed such widespread support was a milestone in itself.

It proved as nothing else had that at long last, and despite the nation's troubled history of race relations, the color of a person's skin was no longer a barrier to seeking the highest office in the land. After George W. Bush was elected president in 2000, he named Powell secretary of state, the most prestigious post in the cabinet. Another African American, Roderick Paige, became secretary of education.

By 2006 there were 43 African Americans in Congress, and more than 9,000 others in elective offices throughout the nation. An African American, Condoleezza Rice, was secretary of state, and an African American, Clarence Thomas, sat on the Supreme Court. There were more than 500 black mayors, including those in large cities such as Detroit, New Orleans, Atlanta, and Washington, D.C.[122] The Rev. Jesse Jackson, a black, had twice run for the Democratic presidential nomination and gained the support of a substantial number of white voters. And Martin Luther King Day was a federal holiday observed on the third Monday in January in every state.

The American political system, in the civil rights legislation passed during the mid-1960s, had demonstrated its ability to respond to peaceful pressures for change. Black voters in the South, who came to the polls in increasing numbers, were better protected by federal law. Public accommodations were finally, by federal law, open to all Americans.

But these gains reflected only part of the picture. The urban ghettos still existed. Fewer than 2 percent of all elected officials were black. In jobs, housing, education, and income, the black man or woman still sat, figuratively, in the back of the bus.

Other minority groups as well were not sharing equally in the benefits of American society. Women earned only 77 cents for every dollar that men earned. Hispanic Americans and American Indians, as we have seen, lagged far behind society as a whole by every economic yardstick.

While inequalities remained between whites and blacks, there were some signs of change. The number of successful black-owned businesses had increased along with the size of the black middle class.

America today is a multicultural society, a land of diversity, and, often, conflict among groups. Some see danger in diversity, and a loss of national identity. The liberal historian Arthur M. Schlesinger, Jr., for example, has warned that the emphasis on ethnic differences may fragment the nation, dividing it into "separate ethnic and racial communities."[123]

Despite that danger, the need remained to remedy the persistent inequalities that mocked the ideals of American society. Although minorities had registered political and economic gains, serious racial divisions persisted, and substantial numbers of blacks, Hispanics, Asian Americans, American Indians, and other groups remained outside the mainstream of American affluence.

A century after the Civil War, many Americans were still struggling for equality and justice. In 1963, in an address to the nation about civil rights for blacks, President Kennedy declared: "This is not a sectional issue. . . . We are confronted primarily with a moral issue. It is as old as the scriptures and is as clear as the American Constitution." America, he said, "will not be fully free until all its citizens are free."[124]

How America responds to this moral issue in the 21st century might well decide its future. The continued struggle for equality for all Americans remains a great domestic challenge, testing the nation's political system and the minds and hearts of the American people.

## CHAPTER HIGHLIGHTS

- Many of the more than 36.7 million African Americans do not enjoy full social and economic equality. About one out of four blacks in the United States is poor—by official definition of the federal government—as opposed to about one out of 12 whites.
- American Indians are among the most disadvantaged of all minorities. Unemployment among American Indians on the reservations is high, life expectancy low. Many live in shacks, adobe huts, and abandoned automobiles.
- The nation's Hispanic community—which includes Mexican Americans, Central and South Americans, Puerto Ricans, people of Spanish origin, and Cubans—constitutes another group that struggles with discrimination and poverty. More than 21 percent of all Hispanics live in poverty—compared with a national average of 12.1 percent.
- Although the precise number of undocumented immigrants in the United States is not known, government and private demographers have estimated that as many as 11 million or more people are in the country illegally.
- The estimated 11.6 million Asian Americans in 2002 made up a rapidly growing minority group in the United States. By the mid-1990s, Asian Americans constituted the third-largest minority, after Hispanics and African Americans.
- Women, although constituting a majority of the population, are, in effect, another "minority group." Many women in the workplace still encounter an invisible "glass ceiling" that hinders their advancement to higher-level jobs. In 2004 the median income of men was $40,798 while that of women was $31,223. The median income of women is only 77 percent of that of men.

• The women's movement can be credited with much of the progress women have made toward equal rights in American society. More and more women combine careers and child-rearing; by the 1990s, the two-income family in which both husband and wife work was as common as it had been rare a few decades earlier.

• The number of women holding public office has increased substantially. By 2006, four women served in the cabinet, 84 women were members of Congress, eight women were state governors, and women comprised almost 23 percent of state legislators.

• In 1973, the Supreme Court ruled in *Roe* v. *Wade* that no state may interfere with a woman's right to have an abortion during the first three months of pregnancy. In 2003 President George W. Bush signed legislation passed by the Republican-controlled Congress that banned "partial-birth" or late-term abortions.

• The controversy over abortion has turned violent in recent years. A number of doctors who performed abortions have been murdered, and there have been hundreds of incidents of bombings, arson, vandalism, and death threats directed at clinics where women can have their pregnancies terminated.

• By 2003, some 242 communities—including New York, San Francisco, Boston, Detroit, Los Angeles, and Washington, D.C.—had passed local laws or taken executive action to protect gay rights in employment, housing, and other areas. In November 2003, the highest court in Massachusetts ruled that gay couples have the right to marry.

• Until relatively recently, the estimated 51 million Americans with disabilities were a kind of invisible minority, their rights of equal treatment and equal access more often than not overlooked or neglected. In 1990, Congress acted to remove these everyday barriers by passing the Americans with Disabilities Act, the most significant antidiscrimination law since the 1964 Civil Rights Act.

• Unlike most other immigrants who came to these shores seeking freedom, African Americans came as slaves. In the *Dred Scott* decision (1857), the Supreme Court ruled that blacks were not citizens under the Constitution. After the Civil War, the decision was reversed by the Fourteenth Amendment, which in 1868 made citizens of the freed slaves.

• The Supreme Court ruled in *Plessy* v. *Ferguson* (1896) that a state law requiring equal but separate accommodations for white and black railroad passengers did not violate the Fourteenth Amendment. This doctrine of "separate but equal" remained the law of the land until 1954, when Chief Justice Earl Warren delivered the unanimous decision of the Supreme Court in the historic school desegregation case of *Brown* v. *Board of Education of Topeka, Kansas.* The justices ruled that school segregation violated the Fourteenth Amendment's requirement of equal protection of the law for individuals.

• Dr. Martin Luther King, Jr., a black minister, led the civil rights movement that began in the 1950s. Largely in response to that movement, Congress enacted several important civil rights bills in the mid-1960s. The Civil Rights Act of 1964 prohibited racial or religious discrimination in public accommodations. The Voting Rights Act of 1965 suspended literacy tests in southern counties in which blacks were being denied the right to vote. The 1965 law was later amended to apply to other minorities as well, and to states in the North and West.

• Protests by minority groups in the inner cities of America have sometimes turned violent. The riots of the 1960s were repeated in Los Angeles in 1992 after an all-white jury acquitted four white police officers on trial for the beating of Rodney G. King, a black motorist.

• In the wake of the civil rights movement, affirmative action programs were established to give preference in university admissions or jobs to minorities. The programs were based on the theory that members of these groups were entitled to special preference because they were disadvantaged as a result of past discrimination. Opponents of affirmative action argued that such programs were a form of reverse discrimination against whites.

• By 2006, 43 African Americans served in Congress, and more than 9,000 others in elective offices throughout the nation. An African American sat on the Supreme Court. Condoleeza Rice, a black woman, was secretary of state. There were more than 500 black mayors, including those in several large cities. Blacks had registered some economic gains by the 1990s. However, the median income of black families was less than two-thirds of that of white families.

• Despite political and economic gains by African Americans, serious racial divisions persist, and substantial numbers of blacks, Hispanics, American Indians, and other groups remained outside the mainstream of American affluence.

## KEY TERMS

*Dred Scott* decision, p. 158
Jim Crow laws, p. 159
segregation, p. 159
*Brown* v. *Board of Education of Topeka, Kansas,* p. 160
literacy tests, p. 165
poll tax, p. 165
gerrymandering, p. 165
affirmative action, p. 168

## SUGGESTED WEBSITES

**http://www.all.org**
*American Life League*
A pro-life group that advocates the view that human life begins at conception. ALL is opposed to the use of birth control and believes that abortions should be prohibited in all cases, with no exceptions.

**http://www.cetel.org/res.html**
*Asian American Resources*
The Center for Educational Telecommunications (CET) lists Asian American websites that cover a wide variety of Asian American interests and concerns.

**http://www.census.gov/population/www/socdemo/race/indian.html**
*The Census Bureau, American Indian and Alaska Native Population*
The Census Bureau provides population estimates, social, economic, and tribal data for American Indians and Alaska Natives.

**http://www.hrc.org**
*Human Rights Campaign*
The Human Rights Campaign, the largest national lesbian and gay political organization, advocates equal rights for lesbians and gays. HRC lobbies on gay, lesbian, and AIDS issues; participates in election campaigns; and organizes volunteers.

**http://www.thekingcenter.com**
*The King Center*
Works to carry forward the legacy of Dr. Martin Luther King, Jr., through research, education, and training in the principles, philosophy, and methods of nonviolence.

**http://www.naral.org**
*National Abortion and Reproductive Rights Action League*
NARAL is a pro-choice group that advocates reproductive freedom for women through abortion or birth control. NARAL's activities include research and legal work, policy reports, public education campaigns, and leadership training for grass-roots activists.

**http://www.naacp.org**
*National Association for the Advancement of Colored People*
The NAACP is the oldest and largest civil rights organization in the United States. Its principal goal is to work for the political, educational, social, and economic equality of blacks and other minority groups in the United States.

**http://www.now.org**
*National Organization for Women*
NOW is the largest women's organization in the nation, with more than 500,000 contributing members. It seeks to protect the rights of women and end inequality based on sex. It engages in lobbying, grass-roots political organizing, and litigation.

**http://www.nod.org**
*National Organization on Disability*
NOD advocates the full and equal participation of America's 53 million people with disabilities in all aspects of life. It lists resources and links for people interested in disabilities or who are disabled.

## SUGGESTED READING


Baldwin, James. *The Fire Next Time* (Holt, Rinehart & Winston, 2000). (Originally published in 1963.) An examination of the status of blacks in America by a leading black writer. Baldwin argues for "total liberation" of blacks and maintains that blacks are the key to America's future.

Barker, Lucius J., Jones, Mack H., and Tate, Katherine. *African-Americans and the American Political System,* 4th edition* (Prentice Hall, 1998). A comprehensive analysis of how blacks have fared in the American political system. Includes discussions of how Congress, the courts, the presidency, and political parties have responded to the problems faced by African Americans.

Brown, Dee. *Bury My Heart at Wounded Knee,* 30th anniversary edition* (Owl Books, 2001). (Originally published in 1970.) A powerful, detailed, and highly readable account of how Native Americans were driven from their villages and hunting grounds, often brutally, by white Americans as the frontier was pushed westward. The book, which became a national best-seller, contains excellent descriptions of major American Indian chiefs and tribal leaders.

Carmichael, Stokely, and Hamilton, Charles V. *Black Power** (Random House, 1967). The political definition of Black Power. Carmichael, the black leader who popularized the term, and Hamilton, a political scientist, urged black Americans to seek community control and use other such political tools.

Clotfelter, Charles T. *After Brown: The Rise and Retreat of School Desegregation** (Princeton University Press, 2004). An assessment of school desegregation, measured as interracial contact, for the 50 years after the landmark 1954 case *Brown* v. *Board of Education.* The study found that interracial contact increased in all educational settings, public and private, including the college level. But the author feels that integration has not been fully achieved.

Edsall, Thomas Byrne, with Edsall, Mary D. *Chain Reaction: The Impact of Race, Rights, and Taxes on American Politics** (Norton, 1991). A study of the rise to power of the presidential wing of the Republican Party from 1968 to 1988. Argues that during this period the Republicans were able to forge a new coalition of voters, and to win five out of six presidential elections, by capitalizing on the twin issues of race and taxes.

Ellison, Ralph. *Invisible Man** (Spark Publishing Group, 2003). (Originally published in 1952.) In this novel a black writer describes the identity problem of blacks in a white society. The "invisible man" cannot be seen, Ellison argued, because whites refuse to acknowledge his existence.

Franklin, John Hope. *From Slavery to Freedom,* 8th edition* (McGraw-Hill, 2000). A classic study of black history in America written by a distinguished black historian.

Garcia, John A. *Latino Politics in America: Community, Culture, and Interests** (Rowman & Littlefield, 2003). A valuable analysis of the differences and shared characteristics within the Latino community. Topics covered include the demographic trends, political behaviors, and policy interests—including immigration—of this growing segment of the U.S. population.

Jordan, Winthrop D. *White over Black: American Attitudes Toward the Negro, 1550–1812** (University of North Carolina Press, 1995). (Originally published in 1968.) A detailed examination of the attitudes of whites toward blacks during the first two centuries of slavery in North America. The book draws extensively on newspaper accounts, speeches, pamphlets, letters, and court records of the day.

Martin, Janet M. *The Presidency and Women: Promise, Performance, and Illusion* (Texas A&M University Press, 2003). A comprehensive study of the role of women in five presidential administrations, Kennedy through Carter. The author finds that women's participation in government increased during these five administrations, and that official attention to issues of concern to women also went up.

McClain, Paula D., and Stewart, Joseph, Jr. *Can We All Get Along? Racial and Ethnic Minorities in American Politics,* 3rd edition (Westview Press, 2001). A useful and readable introduction to the experiences of primarily four ethnic groups in the United States (African Americans, Native Americans, Asian Americans, and Latinos), and their efforts to achieve full social, economic, and political representation within the American system.

McGlen, Nancy E., O'Connor, Karen, Van Assendelft, Laura, and Gunther-Canada, Wendy. *Women, Politics and American Society,* 4th edition* (Longman, 2004). An analysis of the changing roles of women in American society, and their growing political activity and influence.

Myrdal, Gunnar. *An American Dilemma: The Negro Problem and Modern Democracy** (Transaction, 1996). (Originally published in 1944.) A classic study of race relations in the United States until the time of the Second World War. Traces the history of blacks in America and stresses the gap between the American creed of equality for all and the actual treatment African Americans have received. This book, by an eminent Swedish sociologist, has had a major influence on American thought about race relations.

O'Connor, Karen. *No Neutral Ground: Abortion Politics in an Age of Absolutes** (Westview Press, 1996). A study of one of the most intractable policy issues. O'Connor examines the factors that have made abortion so politically incendiary and so resistant to political compromise.

Pincus, Fred L. *Reverse Discrimination: Dismantling the Myth* (Lynne Rienner Publishers, 2003). An examination of reverse discrimination and how it enters into discussions of affirmative action. The author, a supporter of affirmative action, minimizes the impact of reverse discrimination on white males.

Schlesinger, Arthur M., Jr. *The Disuniting of America: Reflections on a Multicultural Society,* 2nd revised edition* (Norton, 1998). An essay on America as a multicultural nation. The author argues that too much emphasis on the culture of separate ethnic groups will result in a fragmented society that loses its sense of national unity and American identity.

Sniderman, Paul M., and Piazza, Thomas. *The Scar of Race** (Harvard University Press, 1995). Drawing upon the results of several broad surveys, the authors conclude that the racial attitudes of white Americans have evolved since the 1960s, due in large part to the role of education in combating racism.

Thernstrom, Abigail, and Thernstrom, Stephen. *America in Black and White: One Nation, Indivisible** (Simon & Schuster, 1999). An impressive historical overview of the black struggle for equal rights in the 20th century. The authors credit the reforms accomplished by the civil rights movement as having had significant impact upon the quality of life for black Americans, but maintain that there is much yet to be accomplished to improve race relations in the United States.

Woodward, C. Vann. *The Strange Career of Jim Crow,* 2nd edition* (Oxford University Press, 2001). A classic study of the establishment and consequences of segregation laws in the South after the Civil War.

*Available in paperback edition.

THIS IS
MY
PATRIOTACT

# Chapter 6

# PUBLIC OPINION

WHEN MARIE ANTOINETTE, according to legend, responded to the bread shortage in France by remarking, "Let them eat cake," she was showing an unwise disregard for public opinion. In due course, her head was cut off on the guillotine.

After President Lyndon B. Johnson sent half a million men to fight in Vietnam, he discovered that public opinion had turned against him. In 1968, he announced that he would not run for president again and retired to his ranch in Texas.

When his successor, Richard Nixon, became entangled in the Watergate scandal, his popularity dropped almost 40 percentage points, the House Judiciary Committee voted to impeach him, and in 1974 he resigned.

*for more information about the House Committee on the Judiciary, see:*
*http://www.house.gov/judiciary*

In 1998, President Clinton wagged his finger at the TV cameras and denied that he had had "sexual relations" with White House intern Monica Lewinsky. It was a costly claim; months later he admitted that his relationship with the intern had been "inappropriate," and the salacious sexual details were recounted in great detail in a report by independent counsel Kenneth Starr. Clinton was impeached by the House of Representatives in December. Although acquitted by the Senate in February 1999, he never fully recovered the stature he had enjoyed before the scandal.[1]

Yet if the public recognized flaws in Clinton's character, public opinion also played a major role in saving him from being convicted in the Senate and removed from office. A Gallup poll taken during the trial reported that only 33 percent of the public wanted their senators to vote to convict the president; 64 percent favored a vote against conviction.[2]

Typically, the public's opinion of a president varies both with his performance and with external events. In 2001, for example, in the immediate aftermath of the September 11 terrorist attacks on New York and Washington, President George W. Bush's approval rating rose for a time to an extraordinary 90 percent.[3] The increase reflected a surge of public support for the leader of the nation at a perilous moment in the wake of his strong response to the attacks.

Two years later, with American soldiers being killed in Iraq almost every day and the economy lagging, his approval rating slid to a thin majority of 52 percent.[4] With the capture of Iraq's dictator Saddam Hussein on December 13, 2003, Bush's approval rating spiked to 63 percent. But two months later, with deadly attacks on U.S. troops continuing, and Democratic rivals assailing his record and capturing media attention in the early 2004 primary contests, Bush's approval rating slid downward again, dipping to 49 percent.[5] By the spring of 2006, amid growing U.S. casualties in Iraq, sectarian violence between Sunnis and Shiites, and public disenchantment with the war, Bush's approval rating had plummeted to 31 percent.[6]

All governments are based, to some extent, on public opinion. Even dictators must pay some attention to public opinion—if only in order to repress it. In a democracy, public opinion is often described as a controlling force. "Public opinion stands out, in the United States," the English statesman James Bryce wrote, "as the great source of power, the master of servants who tremble before it."[7] But in fact, the relationship of public opinion and government is elusive and difficult to define because political leaders help shape public opinion and are in turn influenced by it.

Key Question In this chapter we will explore a key question: ***What is the role of public opinion in the American democracy?***

Many related questions to consider grow out of this central question: Who is the public? What is public opinion? Does a person's opinion matter? Do political candidates and leaders manipulate public opinion? What role do the mass media play in the formation of public opinion? Should government leaders try to follow public opinion or their own judgment? What influence should, or does, public opinion have on government? On policymaking? The answers vary, for these are questions that continue to divide philosophers, politicians, pollsters, and political scientists.

## What Is Public Opinion?

Although people often speak about opinions held by "the public," the phrase is not very useful because there are few questions on which every citizen has an opinion. The concept of special publics was developed by political scientists "to describe those segments of the public with views about particular issues."[8] In short, there are many publics.

What is opinion and when does it become public opinion? People have opinions on many subjects—music, fashions, sports, television, and movies, for example. Sometimes such views are loosely referred to as "public opinion." For political scientists, however, only opinions about public matters constitute public opinion.

**Public opinion** may thus be defined as the expression of attitudes about government and politics.

Public opinion would mean little if it had no effect. Many political scientists, therefore, talk about public opinion as a process of interaction between the people and the government. V. O. Key, Jr., for example, defined public opinion as "those opinions held by private persons which governments find it prudent to heed."[9] Floyd Allport conceived of public opinion as enough people expressing themselves so strongly for or against something that their views are likely to affect government action.[10] And W. Lance Bennett has suggested that public opinion is situational, because the people who hold and express opinions are constantly changing, as do the issues and conditions to which the public responds.[11]

In the language of a political system (discussed in Chapter 1), public opinion can be thought of as one of the inputs of the system that may affect the outputs, or binding decisions, of the government. However, government officials try very hard to shape and manipulate public opinion to support their policies; to the extent that they succeed in this effort, public opinion also may be thought of as an output of the political system.

Private opinions become public—provided they are expressed—when they relate to government and politics. Not all privately held opinions about government and politics are expressed publicly, however; because of pressures to conform, people may sometimes find it more prudent to keep their views private.[12]

## How Public Opinion Is Formed

Walter Lippmann, in his classic study of public opinion, observed that each individual, in viewing distant events, tends to form a "picture inside his head of the world beyond his reach."[13] And, Lippmann noted, these mental snapshots do not always correspond with reality. How do individuals form their opinions about government and politics? As might be expected, the answer is as varied as the range of opinions people hold. The views of a 60-year-old white dairy farmer in Wisconsin may vary sharply from those of an African American youth in South Central Los Angeles. We know this instinctively. But why may their opinions differ? A person's political background, and such factors as the influence of family and schools, certainly play a part. So do such variables as age, social class, income, religion, sex, ethnic back-

© Akram Saleh/Getty Images

Iraq, 2006: After a car bomb explosion in a Shiite neighborhood of Baghdad

ground, geography, group membership, and political party preference.

## Political Socialization: The Family and the Schools

Over the years, a person acquires a set of political attitudes and forms opinions about political and social issues. In other words, a person undergoes **political socialization.**

The family may play a significant role in this process. In the view of Robert E. Lane, the family "incubates" political attitudes and opinions.[14] And the "crucial period" of a child's political, social, and psychological development is between the ages of 9 and 13.[15]

Through watching television programs, surfing the Internet, and various other ways, children acquire rudimentary ideas about politics at an early age. For example, 63 percent of fourth graders questioned in one study identified with a political party. Almost every one of the children interviewed thought of party affiliation as a family characteristic: "All I know is we're not Republicans."[16] Children may acquire not only party preferences by listening to their parents, but "an orientation toward politics" and a set of "basic values and outlooks, which in turn may affect the individual's views on political issues long after he has left the family fold."[17] Although children may later come to hold views different from those of their parents, party loyalty tends to be passed on from one generation to the next.

How then to explain the students who protested the Vietnam War on college campuses in the 1970s, even though in some cases their parents may have supported the war? The answer is that children, obviously, do not always follow the political leanings of their parents and may even come to hold completely opposite views. This should not be surprising. A family is a group, and its influence on political attitudes may tend to diminish as children grow older and come into contact with other groups.

A classic study of Bennington College students during the 1930s illustrates the point. Bennington had always been a very liberal college with a politically liberal faculty. During the Great Depression, however, "the families that could afford to send their daughters to an expensive private college tended to be conservative Republicans. The result was that women whose parents identified with the Republican party . . . were exposed to a faculty who were by and large Roosevelt Democrats. With each year of residence at the college, each successive class of students became more liberal and identified more strongly with Franklin D. Roosevelt than the class behind it."[18]

These and similar findings have led some political scientists to question the long-established emphasis on the family as the primary political influence on children. After studying a national sample of high school seniors, M. Kent Jennings and Richard G. Niemi concluded that the political "similarity between students and their parents was often modest."[19]

Elementary schools also play a part in the political socialization of children. Every country indoctrinates its schoolchildren with the basic values of its political system. American children salute the flag in school; sing patriotic songs, such as "America the Beautiful"; learn about George Washington's cherry tree (an invention of a literary charlatan named Parson Weems); and acquire some understanding of democracy and majority rule. In junior high or high school they are required to take "civics" courses.

But the extent of the influence of schools on opinion formation also has been questioned. The same study that found a divergence in views between parents and older children also reported that in high school, "Students gravitated toward the opinions of their friends

© Jerome Delay

A well-armed Georgia family

more so than toward those of their social studies teachers."[20] And today, the Internet and television have an enormous effect on how information is acquired and opinions are formed.

The political socialization of students continues in college—as the Bennington study suggests—and not only in the political science courses they may take. They also learn from the political environment on the campus. For example, in the 1960s and early 1970s, during the war in Vietnam, widespread student antiwar protests may have influenced the political opinions of other students who did not participate personally in the protest demonstrations.

While the gradual process of political socialization may have some general effect on the opinions people hold, a number of sociological and psychological factors also may have an influence on public opinion. Whether a person is young or old, rich or poor, farmer or city dweller, or Westerner or Southerner may affect the opinions he or she holds. This can be measured by taking almost any controversial public issue and analyzing the findings of public opinion polls. For example, when the Gallup poll asked people whether they approved of legalized gambling, the results varied with age. Nearly two-thirds, 63 percent, of adults approved, but only a little more than half, 52 percent, of young teenagers thought it was a good idea.[21]

In an earlier survey, only 32 percent of those interviewed said abortion should be legal in all circumstances, but among college graduates, 48 percent said abortion should always be legal.[22] In other words, a much higher proportion of college graduates favored legal abortion. On any issue—from legalizing marijuana to affirmative action—opinions often vary with such factors. Which factors are more important than others varies with the individual, and their relative significance is difficult to measure with precision. But a number can be identified.

## Social Class

Differences in social class, occupation, and income do appear to affect people's opinions on public matters. For example, one study indicates that people who identify with the working class are more likely to favor federal social-welfare programs than are people who identify with the middle class.[23]

Another survey found that community leaders were more tolerant of atheists and nonconformists than were people of lower social and economic status.[24] And income levels may affect opinions; a poll by Princeton Survey Research Associates showed that 79 percent of people with annual incomes less than $20,000 favored distributing condoms in high schools, a program adopted by some schools to prevent AIDS, compared with a lower proportion, 66 percent, of people with incomes above $50,000.[25]

One study of political learning suggests that children brought up in homes of lower economic status are taught to accept authority more readily than children reared in upper-class homes. This study found that upper-class children are therefore more likely to criticize political authority, they receive more political information from their parents, and they are more likely to become politically active.[26]

## Religion, Sex, and Ethnic Factors

Religion, sex, race, and ethnic background also may influence the opinions people hold. To appeal to voters from ethnic groups, political parties in New York and other large cities customarily run a "balanced ticket"—one that includes an Irish candidate, an Italian candidate, and a Jewish candidate. In a primary election for mayor of New York City years ago, the victorious Democratic candidate, Mario Procaccino, repeatedly emphasized that he was once an immigrant boy from Bisaccia, Italy. In a sentence that reached artistic perfection in its wide-ranging ethnic appeal, he told the crowds: "I couldn't get a job on Wall Street because my name was Procaccino and I was a Catholic, and my father was a shoemaker right in the heart of black Harlem."

Although Americans like to think they form their opinions without reference to race, creed, sex, or color, studies of their political behavior have demonstrated that this has not been the case in years past. For example, for a long time, many people said they would not vote for presidential candidates who were blacks, Jews, Catholics, women, or gays. (See Table 6-1.) In fact, no Catholic was

## TABLE 6-1

### How Race, Religion, and Sex Influence Voter Attitudes

*Nationwide surveys taken by the Gallup poll have shown that voter prejudice against blacks, Jews, Catholics, and women in politics has declined dramatically in recent years.*

Beginning in 1958, the Gallup poll asked voters whether they would vote for a black for president. Following are the answers received in selected years:

| | Yes (%) | No (%) | No Opinion (%) |
|---|---|---|---|
| 1958 | 38 | 53 | 9 |
| 1965 | 59 | 34 | 7 |
| 1969 | 67 | 23 | 10 |
| 1978 | 77 | 18 | 5 |
| 1983 | 77 | 16 | 7 |
| 1987 | 79 | 13 | 8 |
| 1997 | 93 | 4 | 3 |
| 1999 | 95 | 4 | 1 |
| 2003 | 92 | 6 | 2 |

Voters also were asked whether they would vote for a Jew for president. Following are the answers received in selected years:

| | Yes (%) | No (%) | No Opinion (%) |
|---|---|---|---|
| 1937 | 46 | 46 | 8 |
| 1958 | 62 | 28 | 10 |
| 1969 | 86 | 8 | 6 |
| 1978 | 82 | 12 | 6 |
| 1983 | 88 | 7 | 5 |
| 1987 | 89 | 6 | 5 |
| 1997 | NA* | NA | NA |
| 1999 | 92 | 6 | 2 |
| 2003 | 89 | 8 | 3 |

Voters also were asked whether they would vote for a Catholic for president. Following are the answers received in selected years:

| | Yes (%) | No (%) | No Opinion (%) |
|---|---|---|---|
| 1937 | 64 | 28 | 8 |
| 1958 | 68 | 25 | 7 |
| 1969 | 88 | 8 | 4 |
| 1978 | 91 | 4 | 5 |
| 1983 | 92 | 5 | 3 |
| 1987 | NA | NA | NA |
| 1997 | NA | NA | NA |
| 1999 | 94 | 4 | 2 |
| 2003 | 93 | 5 | 2 |

Voters also were asked whether they would vote for a woman for president. Following are the answers received in selected years:

| | Yes (%) | No (%) | No Opinion (%) |
|---|---|---|---|
| 1937 | 31 | 65 | 4 |
| 1958 | 52 | 44 | 4 |
| 1969 | 54 | 39 | 7 |
| 1978 | 76 | 19 | 5 |
| 1983 | 80 | 16 | 4 |
| 1987 | 82 | 12 | 6 |
| 1997 | NA | NA | NA |
| 1999 | 92 | 7 | 1 |
| 2003 | 87 | 12 | 1 |

*(continued)*

**TABLE 6-1**

## How Race, Religion, and Sex Influence Voter Attitudes *(continued)*

Voters also were asked whether they would vote for a homosexual for president. Following are the answers received:

| | Yes (%) | No (%) | No Opinion (%) |
|---|---|---|---|
| 1983 | 29 | 64 | 7 |
| 1987 | NA | NA | NA |
| 1997 | NA | NA | NA |
| 1999 | 59 | 37 | 4 |
| 2003 | NA | NA | NA |

*NA: Not available.

SOURCES: Adapted from *The Gallup Poll: Public Opinion 1935–1971,* vols. 1–3 (New York: Random House, 1972); *Gallup Opinion Index,* March 1976, p. 20, and November 1978, p. 26; *Gallup Report,* September 1983, pp. 9–14, and July 1987, no. 262, pp. 16–20; the Gallup Organization, *Poll Releases,* "Americans Today Much More Accepting of a Woman, Black, Catholic, or Jew as President," March 29, 1999, pp. 3–6; and *Gallup poll,* May 30–June 1, 2003.

elected president until 1960, when John F. Kennedy defeated Richard M. Nixon. But in public opinion polls today, Americans say they are much more willing to accept members of minority groups or women as political leaders.

There may be a gap, however, between how people say they will vote and their actual behavior in the voting booth. In 1988, for example, Jesse L. Jackson, an African American candidate, won several important Democratic presidential primaries and caucuses and demonstrated substantial strength among white voters. But many party leaders and voters said at the time that they felt a black person could not be elected president. Jackson did not receive the nomination.

By the mid-1990s, however, the hesitation about nominating a black candidate for the nation's highest office appeared to have diminished substantially. As noted in Chapter 5, former General Colin Powell, an African American, enjoyed enthusiastic support among many white and black voters when for several months he flirted with the possibility of entering the 1996 presidential race. By 2003, only 6 percent of Americans said they would not vote for a black presidential candidate; the overwhelming majority, 92 percent, said they would. (See Table 6-1.)

A voter's religious or ethnic background may affect party preference or political leanings. For example, in the 2004 presidential election, 52 percent of Catholics voted for President Bush, the Republican nominee, but only 47 percent voted for his Democratic opponent, John Kerry. Among Protestants the vote went a similar way: 59 percent for Bush to 40 percent for Kerry.[27] In another survey, Jewish and black voters questioned were more inclined to support government social-welfare programs than were other groups.[28]

Religious affiliation may also affect public opinion on specific issues—Jews may support aid to Israel, and Catholics may oppose the use of federal funds for abortions for the poor. Similarly, ethnic identification may help to shape public opinion on certain issues—Americans of Italian descent may be offended by the depiction of fictional gangsters with Italian names on publicly licensed television stations; American Muslims may feel unfairly discriminated against because of anger at Arabs after the 9/11 terrorist attacks.

### Geographic Factors

People's opinions are sometimes related to where they live. Democrats have traditionally been more numerous in the big cities of the North; Republicans have been

© Lou Dematteis/The Image Works

stronger in the Plains States, in most of the Rocky Mountain States, in rural areas, and in the suburbs. Yet sectional and geographic differences among Americans are often exaggerated; on some broad questions of foreign policy, for example, sectional variations are likely to be minimal. And, on many issues, differences in outlook between the cities and rural areas have replaced the old sectional divisions. Whether people come from an urban or rural background may be more significant today than their geographic roots.

## Group Influence

Although the shape of a person's opinions on public questions is initially influenced by the family, in later life other groups, friends, associates, and peers also influence individual views. In numerous experiments psychologists have discovered that people tend to go along with the decision of a group even when it contradicts accepted standards of morality and behavior. In a classic and controversial experiment at Yale University, Stanley Milgram placed subjects in groups of four, three of whom were secretly Milgram's assistants. The one unwitting subject was told to administer powerful electric shocks to the person serving as the "learner" in the experiment whenever the "learner" made an error in performing a laboratory task. In fact, no electricity was being administered, but the subject did not know that, and the "learner" shouted, moaned, and screamed as the supposed voltage became higher. The results were surprising: Egged on by their colleagues, 85 percent of the subjects administered shocks beyond what they believed would be 120 volts, and 17.5 percent went all the way to the maximum, a shock of 450 volts.[29]

On occasion, group influence may even prevent the expression of opinion. Almost everyone has been in a situation at one time or another in which he or she hesitates to express a political opinion because those listening might disagree or even be hostile. The author Mark Twain said he would expose to the world "only my trimmed and perfumed and carefully barbered public opinions and conceal carefully, cautiously, wisely, my private ones."[30] An individual who expresses an opinion is vulnerable because "social groups can punish him for failing to toe the line."[31] If a view seems too risky to express, an individual may keep it private. But if public opinion changes, a person may voice previously hidden feelings.[32]

Various types of groups may influence people. Groups whose views serve as guidelines to an individual's opinion are known as **reference groups.** There are two types of reference groups. Groups that people come into face-to-face contact with in everyday life—friends, office associates, or a social club—are known as **primary groups** because their influence is direct. **Secondary groups,** as the term implies, may be more remote. These are organizations or groups of people such as labor unions or fraternal, professional, or religious groups.

© Ray Ellis/Photo Researchers, Inc.

## Mass Media

In the television age, the images that flash into people's living rooms obviously have a major impact on public opinion. So do the Internet, newspapers, magazines, radio, and other media that bring news about government and politics to the public.

By the 2004 presidential year, the Internet had emerged as an even greater political force than in previous elections. For example, former Vermont governor Howard Dean was an early front-runner in what proved to be an unsuccessful quest for the Democratic presidential nomination. Dean raised $41 million almost entirely from small donations that his supporters made in response to fund-raising appeals on the Internet. Because he had raised so much money, he did not accept federal matching funds for his campaign in the party primaries.

Dean's website linked directly to his "blog," the first ever used by a presidential candidate. Dean's blog was an interactive Internet website that featured comments by Dean, his volunteers, and anyone else who cared to post one.

Talk radio, with its large audience, especially among more conservative voters, was credited by many observers with helping the Republican Party capture control of Congress in 1994. In 2004, many viewers watched televised events such as the closely fought presidential

Howard Dean was an early front-runner in the 2004 Democratic presidential primaries.

primary campaigns, the debates among the candidates, the national conventions, and the drama of Election Night on November 2. Political candidates appeared on televised talk shows, running the gamut from *Meet the Press* to Jay Leno and David Letterman. It is reasonable to assume that the opinions formed by many voters about these events were influenced by what they saw on television and absorbed through other media.

*for more information about the TV shows listed above, see:*
*http://www.msnbc.com/news/meetpress_front.asp;*
*http://www.nbc.com/tonightshow; and*
*http://www.cbs.com/lateshow*

Candidates who outspend their opponents to buy television time for commercials often enjoy an advantage. In 2004, as in previous recent presidential elections, voters were bombarded by political commercials. The broadcast and cable networks provided extensive coverage of the spring primaries, the party nominating conventions that began in July and August, the general election campaign, and the results flowing in from across the nation on Election Night. The impact of mass media on the formation of public opinion is discussed in greater detail in Chapter 8.

## Party Identification

In any campaign, voters are influenced by a candidate's personality and appearance and by the nature of the issues that arise. But how they vote and what they think

Senator John McCain, the Arizona Republican, attracted many independent voters during the 2000 presidential primaries.

about public issues may also be closely linked to their political party affiliation. Political scientists distinguish, therefore, among voters' views of candidates, voters' attitudes on issues, and voters' party identification.[33]

As an example of how party identification may relate to opinions, a Gallup poll reported that 21 percent of Republicans favored the legalization of marijuana, compared with 37 percent of Democrats and 44 percent of independents.[34] In a 1998 poll, 73 percent of Republicans but only 12 percent of Democrats approved of the decision of the House of Representatives to impeach President Clinton.[35]

There is evidence, however, that party ties are becoming somewhat less important; the number of Americans who consider themselves political independents has varied but gradually increased in recent decades. Despite the willingness of voters to cross party lines to support candidates they like, as many as two-thirds of all adult Americans identify with one of the two major parties.[36]

## The Qualities of Public Opinion

Public opinion has identifiable qualities. Like pictures, public opinions may be sharp or fuzzy, general or detailed—and they may fade. In analyzing the qualities of opinions, political scientists speak of direction, intensity, and stability.

There was a time when political scientists would describe people as being either "for" or "against" something. But after the Second World War, when public opinion polling evolved into a more exact science, pollsters and analysts discovered that simple "yes" or "no" answers sometimes masked wide gradations in opinion on a given subject. In other words, it is possible to measure opinions in *direction* along a scale.[37] Thus people speak of liberals and radicals as being "to the left" and conservatives "to the right," with moderates "in the center." If radical political opinions are thought of as being at one end of a line and conservative at the other end, the opinion of one individual may be located at a given point along the line.

"Grayson is a liberal in social matters, a conservative in economic matters, and a homicidal psychopath in political matters."

2004: Pro-choice supporters march past the White House to protest the Bush administration's policies on abortion.

One person may favor a government program of health care for everyone; another may prefer that federal health programs be limited to the aged, children, and the needy; and a third person may favor wholly private health care.

Public opinion varies in *intensity* as well as direction. A person may have moderate opinions or more deeply felt views. A farmer may be mildly in sympathy with attempts to reduce air pollution in urban areas. By contrast, a pro-life activist may hold very strong opinions against abortion. Robert E. Lane and David O. Sears have suggested that there may be "something congenial" about extreme views and intensity of opinion "which suggests a mutual support."[38] That is, people well to the left or right may hold their political opinions more fiercely than others.

Another quality of public opinion is its degree of *stability.* Opinions change—sometimes slowly, sometimes rapidly and unpredictably—in response to new events or personalities. For example, in the early 1990s public opinion about the first President Bush fluctuated widely, rising to great heights during the Persian Gulf War early in 1991 and then plunging downward when the economy faltered. He was defeated when he ran for reelection in 1992. These sharp variations in voter attitudes can be recorded with some degree of precision. Public opinion may be measured and its qualities analyzed. The measuring tool is the political poll.

## Political Polls

Today, virtually all presidential candidates rely on advice from a poll-taker. And on Election Day, even before the votes are counted, **exit polls** of citizens leaving the voting booth may prove a reliable indicator of the final result.

The data gathered by political polls are not always reliable, however. In 1948 the Gallup and Roper polls wrongly predicted that Governor Thomas E. Dewey of New York, the Republican candidate, would defeat President Harry S Truman.* Dewey lost. "I never paid any attention to polls myself," Truman later wrote in his typically direct style.[39]

The art of political polling has come a long way since 1948, and the margin of error has been greatly reduced. But polls may still be wrong or in conflict with one another. For example, several polls just before the 1988 New Hampshire presidential primary showed Republican George Bush, then the vice president, and Senator Bob Dole in a dead heat. But the final Gallup poll showed Dole ahead by 8 points. In the actual vote in New Hampshire, Bush defeated his rival by 9 percentage points, a 17-point error for Gallup.[40]

Even when polls are accurate, they may be so swiftly overtaken by events as to appear to be misleading. During the campaign for the Republican presidential nomination in 2000, polls reported George W. Bush and John McCain in a close race in the New Hampshire primary. But in the election in February McCain scored a sweeping victory, beating Bush 48 percent to 30 percent.[41]

*Truman was given just the letter "S" as a middle name. It was a compromise by his parents to honor his paternal grandfather, Anderson Shippe Truman, and his maternal grandfather, Solomon Young, both of whom had names beginning with that letter. Since the "S" was a name and not an initial, Truman himself usually did not include the period, but it is considered correct with or without the period.

1948: A victorious President Truman holds up an erroneous newspaper headline.

Despite some well-publicized errors, however, political polls are substantially accurate more often than not. For example, in the 2004 Democratic primaries, the polls, beginning in Iowa, accurately reflected Massachusetts Senator John F. Kerry's lead over his nearest rivals. Frequently, polls are useful as a guide to voter sentiment.

Politicians are convinced of their value. One Democratic senator described the heavy reliance on polls by the Clinton White House: "They just poll the daylights out of everything from every angle. . . . I've never been to the White House without hearing the staff and even the president talk about polls."[42]

Today, polls—before, during, and even after Election Day—are a standard part of political campaigns. In a presidential election year, millions of dollars are paid to the more than 200 polling organizations in the United States.*

## How Polls Work

A political polling organization may question only 600 or up to 1,000 people to measure public opinion on a given issue or to determine which candidate leads in a campaign. Many people find it difficult to accept the idea that public opinion in an entire nation may be measured from such a small sample. Behind some of the skepticism is the belief that each individual is unique, and that his or her thoughts cannot be so neatly categorized. If only 1,000 Americans are polled in a population of 294 million, each person questioned is, in effect,

*Major political polling organizations include the American Institute of Public Opinion (the Gallup poll), Louis Harris & Associates, Inc. (the Harris survey), the Princeton Survey Research Associates, and Zogby International, all of which publish their findings in newspapers and magazines. A number of pollsters also take private polls for political clients. In addition, there are many smaller state and regional polls, as well as polls conducted by newspapers and television networks.

### Counting the Beans

The federal government's Crop Reporting Board, later renamed the Agricultural Statistics Board, among its various duties must count the number of soybeans in America. It can't, so it takes a random sample. The results are closely guarded so that speculators in the commodities markets cannot profit from advance information. The following news story describes how the board works:

> WASHINGTON—The Agriculture Department's Crop Reporting Board . . . works primarily for the nation's farmers, who decide how much to plant, or breed, based on the board's predictions. . . .
>
> Across the United States, the board employs 3,500 part-time "enumerators," as they are called. . . . The enumerators might be assigned to estimate the soybean crop. They cannot count every bean, so instead they select random-sample plots and use probability tables, much the way opinion pollsters do, to predict a total. . . .
>
> For the soybean crop, enumerators in several states pick out sample plots three feet long and two rows wide. Then they get down on all fours and, yes, they count the beans. . . .
>
> The results of all those bean counts, top-secret totals that cannot be discussed on pain of going to jail, are sent to Washington, where they are locked into a safe at the Crop Reporting Board.
>
> —*New York Times,* February 20, 1984

## The American Past

# AND THE WINNER IS . . . HARRY TRUMAN

In 1948, President Harry S Truman, a Democrat, defeated Governor Thomas E. Dewey of New York, the Republican candidate, despite public opinion polls that reported Dewey far in the lead.

> The polls everywhere overwhelmingly provided reassurance that Dewey's strategy was right. Even in the farm belt both the Gallup and *Des Moines Register* polls indicated a Republican landslide. . . . In Cleveland Truman made a rollicking speech, comparing the current polls with the *Literary Digest* poll of 1936, which indicated that Roosevelt would lose to Landon, who in the end carried only Maine and Vermont. "These polls that the Republican candidate is putting out are like sleeping pills designed to lull the voters into sleeping on Election Day," Truman said. "You might call them sleeping polls. . . . My friends, we are going to win this election." . . .
>
> Truman went home to Independence. The final polls were published. The final columns on the election were written for the newspapers. . . . *Changing Times,* published by the Kiplinger organization, featured on its cover "What Dewey Will Do." Government would remain large and expensive under President Dewey, the *Wall Street Journal* reported. . . . The *New York Times* foresaw a Dewey victory with 345 electoral votes.
>
> In their final versions the Gallup poll gave Dewey an edge of 49.5 to 44.5 and the Crossley poll 51 to 42.
>
> By the time the polling places had closed in the East on Election Night Republican fat cats, the men in dinner jackets, the women in evening gowns and jewels, were waiting in line to get into the impending Dewey victory celebration in the ballroom of the Hotel Roosevelt in New York. . . . With three Secret Service men—James J. Rowley, chief of the White House detail, Henry Nicholson, and Frank J. Barry—Truman had slipped away by car and headed for The Elms, a hotel at Excelsior Springs, Missouri, thirty-two miles northeast of Kansas City. When he arrived he had a Turkish bath, then went up to his suite and dined alone on a ham sandwich and a glass of buttermilk. . . . Nationally, the result remained inconclusive [but] Truman still clung to a lead in the popular vote . . .
>
> By three or four in the morning bewilderment and disgust had fallen over the Roosevelt ballroom. . . . Dewey went to bed for a couple of hours of sleep. . . . The telephone rang in the Secret Service agents' suite in Excelsior Springs. . . . Illinois had gone for Truman. Rowley, Nicholson, and Barry could not resist telling the president. When they entered his room he woke up, squinting without his glasses. "That's it," he said when they gave him the word.
>
> "Now let's go back to sleep, and we'll go downtown tomorrow early and wait for the telegram from the other fellow," he said. On second thought he added: "Well, boys, we'll have one and then we'll all go to sleep." He got the bottle of bourbon off the dresser. "I'll pour the first one," he said.
>
> —Robert J. Donovan,
> *Conflict and Crisis: The Presidency of Harry S Truman 1945–1948*

"speaking for" 294,000 people. How, it may be asked, can the views of one individual represent the opinions of so many fellow citizens?

The answer lies in the mathematical law of probability. Toss a coin 1,000 times, and it will come up heads about 500 times. The same principle of probability is used by insurance companies in computing life expectancy. And it is used by poll-takers in measuring opinion. Because the group to be measured, known as the population or the **universe,** is usually too large to be polled individually on every issue, the poll-taker selects at random a sample of the population. The **random sample** is a group of people, chosen by poll-takers, that is representative of the universe being polled. A random sample is sometimes also called a probability sample.

But the random sample must be carefully chosen and must be representative of the universe being polled. When the *Literary Digest* polled owners of automobiles and telephones in 1936—a time when many Americans had neither—it was not sampling a representative group of Americans. As a result, its prediction that Franklin Roosevelt would lose the presidential election proved incorrect. If the sample is of sufficient size and properly selected at random, the law of probability will operate, and

"That's the worst set of opinions I've heard in my entire life."

BLONDIE by Young & Drake. © Reprinted with special permission of King Features Syndicate.

the results will usually be accurate within a 3 to 4 percent margin of error.

One way to conceptualize the principles involved in polling is to think of a huge jar of white marbles to which a smaller number of yellow marbles are added. Suppose the jar is thoroughly shaken so that all the marbles are completely mixed together. If a scoop is used to remove enough of the marbles, the sample should contain the same proportion of yellow to white marbles as exists in the entire jar.

Take another example. Suppose that one out of every four Americans has blue eyes. For the same reason that a flipped coin comes up heads half the time, or the same percentage of yellow marbles can be scooped from the jar each time, the probability is that a random sample will catch in its net the same percentage of blue-eyed people as exists in the whole population. Using this technique, the number of blue-eyed Americans can be estimated from a random sample. Similarly, the number of Americans who support abortion or who oppose capital punishment can be estimated from a random sample.

But a true random sample of the entire United States would be very difficult (and very expensive) to conduct. A survey researcher would, in theory, have to have a list of everyone in the population and then select at random the names of people to be questioned. To simplify the task, most polling organizations use **cluster sampling**—interviewing several people from the same neighborhood. As long as the geographic areas are chosen at random, the clustering will usually not result in an unacceptable margin of error.[43]

Poll-takers often combine the cluster technique with the selection, in a series of stages or steps, of geographic areas to be polled, with each unit selected becoming successively smaller. For example, in pinpointing the location for an interview, the pollster might start by selecting regions of the country, and then choose counties or other smaller areas at random within those regions. From there, still selecting at random, the researcher would scale down to a city, a neighborhood, a precinct, a block of houses, an apartment building, and then one apartment, where the actual interview would take place. The desirable size of the sample does not depend very much on the size of the population being measured, and beyond a certain point, increasing the number of people polled reduces the sampling error only slightly.

A less reliable method of polling is based on the **quota sample,** a method of polling in which interviewers are instructed to question members of a particular group in proportion to their percentage in the population as a whole. For example, an organization that wanted to test ethnic opinion would instruct its staff to interview blacks, Hispanics, Jews, Asians, Muslims and so on, in proportion to their percentage in the population as a whole. Under this method the interviewer has considerable discretion in the choice of persons selected to be questioned. The poll-taker might select only well-dressed or cooperative individuals, thus skewing the results. Therefore, quota sampling is less useful than random sampling as a method of measuring political opinion.

The method of selecting the sample is not the only factor that may affect the reliability of a poll. The way in which questions are phrased, the personality of the interviewer, and the manner in which poll data are interpreted may all affect the result.[44]

How the wording of a survey question may affect the results can easily be seen by comparing the data reported by two different polling organizations that ask questions on the same general subject. For example, in 2004 a *Time*/CNN poll asked, "Do you think the war with Iraq will have been worth it if weapons of mass destruction are never found, or don't you think it will have been worth it?" Fifty-three percent said the war was worth it, 41 percent said it was not, and 6 percent were not sure. But when a CBS News poll asked, "Do you think the result of the war with Iraq was worth the loss of American life and other costs of attacking Iraq, or not?" only 41 percent said the war was worth it, 50 percent said it was not, and 9 percent did not know.[45] In other words, there was 12 percent less support for the war when the question mentioned casualties.

Many voters do not make up their minds until just before an election, another factor that affects poll results. A CNN/*USA Today*/Gallup poll completed four days before the 2000 election showed 5 percent undecided—a fairly normal percentage in this flexible category.[46] How this undecided vote is interpreted and allocated can drastically affect the accuracy of a political poll.

There is another problem that increasingly plagues poll-takers. A lot of people don't want to be bothered to respond to surveys. A decade ago, typically half the people approached responded to polls. Today, the response rate, according to poll-takers, may fall as low as 20 percent in some cases. That means that perhaps eight out of 10 people interviewed may refuse to answer.[47]

Political polls do not necessarily predict the outcome of an election. A poll only measures opinion at the moment the survey is taken. It is a snapshot of the electorate at that instant, not necessarily a prediction of how voters may feel later. A poll taken a few days before an election, for example, will not always match the vote on Election Day.

An intriguing question often raised is whether there is a danger that political polls themselves may create a **bandwagon effect** and influence the outcome of an election. Do some voters or convention delegates, out of a desire to be with the winner, jump on the bandwagon of the candidate who is leading in the polls?

Whether or not a bandwagon effect really exists has been debated by political scientists for some time. For example, Bernard Hennessy found "little evidence" of such an effect, arguing that indifferent voters would not care who won or even remember poll results, and concerned voters would not cast their ballot for a candidate simply because of a poll.[48]

But other scholars have suggested that indeed there may be a bandwagon effect. As already noted, people often compare their views with the dominant public opinion before speaking out. Elisabeth Noelle-Neumann argues that there exists a "spiral process which prompts . . . individuals to perceive the changes in opinion and to follow suit."[49]

During some presidential elections, the television networks have been criticized for projecting the outcome before the voting booths had closed in California. The networks based their predictions either on mathematical projections of early returns or on exit polls. Critics of this practice argued that such early "calls" of an election would discourage some potential voters from bothering to cast their ballots at all.

In 1992 the networks agreed not to release exit polls to call a winner in a state until a majority of polling places had closed in that state. But exit polling led to mass confusion, and embarrassment for the networks, in the 2000 presidential election. On the basis of exit polls, on Election Night the TV networks initially called Florida for Gore. Then the networks awarded the state to Bush, only to retract that call hours later.

And holding back exit polls has proved difficult in the age of the Internet. During the key Michigan primary in February 2000, *Slate*, an online magazine, released numbers correctly predicting that John McCain would defeat George W. Bush. The magazine trumpeted the exit poll data under the headline, "Git Yer Early Exit Poll Numbers Here!"[50]

***for more information about* Slate*, see:***
***http://slate.msn.com***

In 2004, for exit polling and projections of winners, the television networks relied on a new National Elections Pool (NEP) made up of ABC, CBS, CNN, NBC, Fox, and the Associated Press. NEP was created after the problems in the 2000 election and a computer meltdown in the 2002 congressional elections by the previous network pool, the Voter News Service (VNS), which was dissolved and replaced by NEP.[51]

Polls may affect elections in other ways. For example, a candidate may need to make a strong early showing in the polls in order to attract and raise the money needed to campaign, and especially to buy television ads. Many contributors want to back a winner; favorable polls can help to bring in the dollars.

On the other hand, if the polls suggest that a candidate is running behind, supporters of that candidate may be more inclined to vote. Conversely, if the candidate's rating in the polls is high, some potential supporters may become complacent and stay home on Election Day. Such theories, based on present evidence, are debatable, but the possible effect of polls on voting is a subject that merits further exploration. In any event, polls today are a permanent part of the political landscape and an important tool of the "new politics."

## What Americans Believe

Do Americans agree on anything? Some people say that there is an underlying consensus in America, a basic agreement among its citizens on fundamental democratic values and processes, that permits democracy to flourish. Some political scientists speak of a nation's **political culture,** a set of fundamental beliefs about how government and politics should be conducted. Most Americans, for example, believe that—unlike in many other countries—the military in the United States should be subordinate to the elected civilian leaders. And Americans agree that whoever loses an election should leave office.

But the supposed underlying consensus in America often melts away on closer examination.

For example, Americans say they believe in fair play and justice, but they do not necessarily stick by those principles when their own interests are threatened. White homeowners may know that it is "fair" for a black family to buy the house next door, but they may oppose the sale if they believe that the value of their property would go down if the neighborhood becomes racially mixed.

On the whole, Americans seem to be pragmatic, ap-

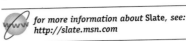

*Making a Difference*

## THE "PUSH-POLL" HADN'T COUNTED ON DONNA DUREN

Donna Duren, a resident of Spartanburg, South Carolina, heard only at the last minute that Senator John McCain of Arizona, who was then seeking the Republican presidential nomination, was in town. It was February 2000 and at the time, McCain was locked in a hard-fought primary battle in South Carolina with Texas Governor George W. Bush. Duren, an admirer of Senator McCain, rushed over to the auditorium on the campus of the University of South Carolina.

"He talked about teaching our children, at home and in the community, ethics and values and morals and integrity," she recalled. "That really touched a chord with me. I have a 14-year-old boy, Chris. Something in his speech moved me to speak.

"My son is interested in aviation and in Senator McCain's story, his tenacity in the Hanoi Hilton when he was a prisoner of war in Vietnam. He kind of idolizes Senator McCain. He saw him as a role model, a positive person to emulate."

The day before McCain's speech, someone who claimed to be conducting a poll had called the Duren household. Duren's son had answered the phone. Chris kept telling the caller that he was only 14, but the man continued to talk to him anyway, asking "questions" that unsettled Chris.

At the McCain rally the next day, Donna Duren got up. "I was so nervous. I never stood up before, I never participated in a town meeting. I got up and after a minute I realized the cameras were on me. I was so nervous."

She told McCain about the call to her son. "I don't know who called him. I don't know who's responsible. But he was so upset when he came upstairs and he said, 'Mom, someone told me that Senator McCain is a cheat and a liar and a fraud.' And he was almost in tears. I was so livid last night I couldn't sleep." Her complaint made the national news on television and was widely reported in the press.

Chris Duren had been the target of a "push-poll," a practice sometimes used in political campaigns. Under the guise of conducting an independent survey, a caller poses as a legitimate poll-taker, but asks "questions" that are really statements designed to smear or discredit the opposition candidate.

Questioned by reporters, George W. Bush denied any knowledge of the type of call described by Duren. "If anybody in my campaign has done that, they're going to be fired," he said.

Most voters had never heard the term "push-poll" before. Now, thanks to one courageous mother in South Carolina, millions of voters might be wary of such calls, and some candidates or their supporters might even hesitate to employ that tactic in the future. To an extent, at least, Donna Duren may have helped to change how political campaigns are conducted in America.

—Based on a telephone interview by the authors with Donna Duren, February 24, 2000

proaching each issue as it comes up and judging it on its merits. Most Americans, though, do not have a fixed, coherent set of political beliefs. People may have clear preferences on specific issues, but often their convictions are not interrelated. A voter who is liberal on one issue may be conservative on another. For example, one study found that a majority of Americans thought that "the Federal Government should act to meet public needs" in such fields as education, medical care, public housing, urban renewal, unemployment, and poverty.[52] But when the same Americans were asked questions about their general concepts of the proper role of government, they were "pronouncedly conservative." A clear majority agreed with this statement: "We should rely much more on individual initiative and not so much on governmental welfare programs."[53] On some issues, in short, Americans seem to have a split personality.

Why should Americans hold such seemingly contradictory opinions? One explanation may lie in the competing fundamental values of individualism and equality that observers such as Alexis de Tocqueville saw in America as far back as the early 19th century. The belief in "rugged individualism" may have caused some Americans to complain about "welfare chiselers." Yet, the belief in equality may explain why the same individuals may favor government social programs.[54]

Some political research has suggested that the pattern of beliefs in America is changing and that voters are becoming more aware of political issues and thinking about them more coherently. One study, *The Changing American Voter,* found "long-term tendencies of the public to move in one direction or another" on the issues.[55] Since the 1960s, the study found, voters have begun to evaluate candidates and parties more in terms of their issue positions, with this being reflected to some extent by how citizens vote. "The role of party has declined as a guide to the vote," the study reported. "And, as party has declined in importance, the role of issues appears to have risen."[56]

## POLITICAL PARTICIPATION

One way people can influence government is through the force of public opinion. An even more direct way people can make their opinions felt is by voting. Yet, one of the more surprising facts about America is that in

Not everybody votes: a polling place in Florida in 2000

© Dan Habib/Concord Monitor/Corbis

presidential elections, often only a little more than half the people of voting age—and sometimes less than half—bother to vote.

In 2004 the Census Bureau estimated that 215,694,000 Americans were old enough to vote. Of that total, 142,070,000 registered to vote. Of these, 125,736,000 actually cast ballots for president on Election Day, November 2. That means that 58.3 percent of the population of voting age actually voted.[57]

In off-year, nonpresidential elections, usually well under half of the voting-age population goes to the polls to vote for senators and representatives. In 1970, for example, 43.5 percent cast ballots for candidates for the House. In 1974 only 35.9 percent voted in House races. For 1978 the figure was down to 34.9 percent. It rose to 38.0 percent in 1982 and then dropped to 33.5 percent in 1986. There was no significant change in 1990, with 33.1 percent voting in House races. In 1994, 36 percent voted in House races. In 1998, the figure dropped to 32.9 percent. In 2002, voter turnout in House races rose somewhat, to 39.3 percent.[58] But this still meant that fewer than four out of 10 Americans of voting age bothered to cast their ballots.

These figures, not uncommon for American elections, raise important questions about the nature of "government by the people." "Every regime lives on a body of dogma, self-justification, glorification and propaganda about itself," E. E. Schattschneider wrote, continuing with:

> In the United States, this body of dogma and tradition centers about democracy. The hero of the system is the voter who is commonly described as the ultimate source of all authority. The fact that something like [one hundred] million adult Americans are so unresponsive to the regime that they do not trouble to vote is the single most truly remarkable fact about it. . . . What kind of system is this in which only a little more than half of us participate? Is the system actually what we have been brought up to think it is?[59]

Some people do not vote because they may feel the system holds no benefits for them, or because they feel there is no difference between the candidates. For some, therefore, not voting may be a form of protest. Others are nonvoters because they are apathetic about politics and political issues.

## Spinning Saddam and 9/11

Polls have shown that the majority of the public is often poorly informed about political issues, particularly in the area of foreign policy. But the opinions the public holds may be shaped and influenced by statements made by political leaders.

This was illustrated after U.S. forces invaded Iraq in 2003 and deposed that country's dictator, Saddam Hussein. A *Washington Post* poll taken in August of that year reported that almost seven in 10 Americans believed that Saddam was involved in the 9/11 terrorist attacks on New York and Washington two years earlier.

President George W. Bush and other administration officials had often cited the 9/11 attacks in justifying the decision to invade Iraq, which was repeatedly presented to the public as part of the "war on terror."

In September, Vice President Dick Cheney, when asked on NBC's *Meet the Press* whether there was a connection between Iraq and the 9/11 attacks, stated: "We don't know."

Less than a week later, however, President Bush announced that there was no connection between Saddam Hussein and the 9/11 attacks. But the seed had previously been planted in the mind of the public. Even after Saddam's capture in December 2003, a Gallup poll reported that 53 percent of the public still believed that Saddam Hussein was personally involved in the 9/11 attacks.

FIGURE 6-1

**Confidence in Institutions: Percentage of Americans Who Have a "Great Deal" or "Quite a Lot" of Confidence in Major U.S. Institutions**

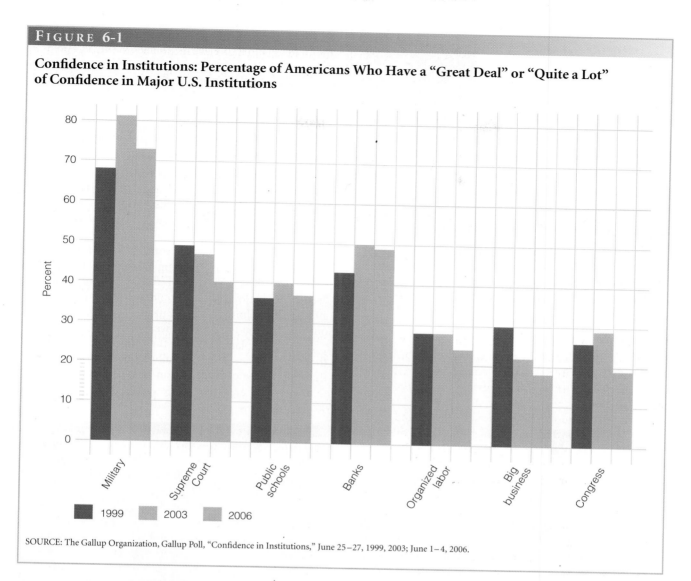

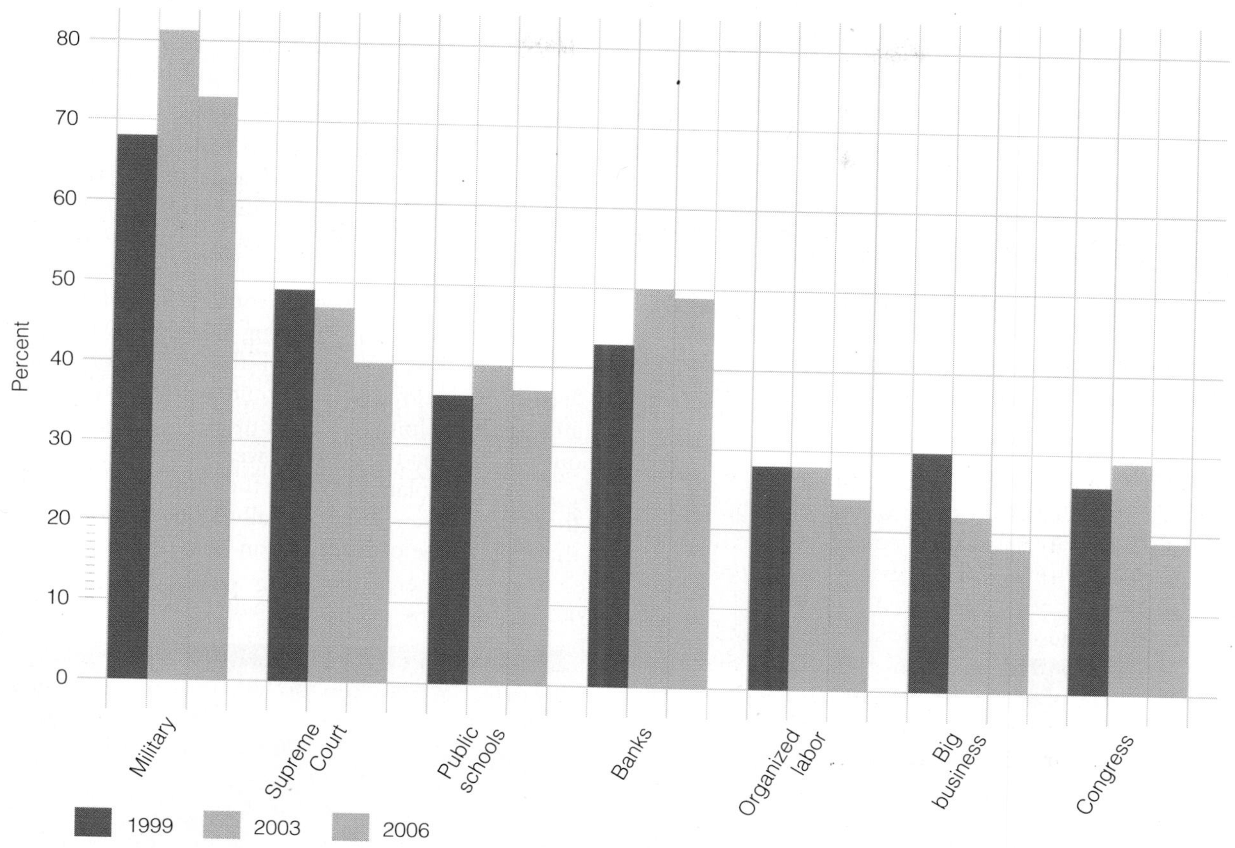


SOURCE: The Gallup Organization, Gallup Poll, "Confidence in Institutions," June 25–27, 1999, 2003; June 1–4, 2006.

Americans not only fail to participate fully in the political system, it has been argued, but they also are often poorly informed about government and many public issues. One study found only 26 percent of the American public to be well informed on specific questions dealing with international affairs (such as the identity of four major world leaders).[60]

Public knowledge about many specific questions concerning domestic politics is equally limited. A 2002 survey found that 23 percent of students in the nation's leading colleges and universities knew that James Madison was the "father of the Constitution," but 98 percent knew that Snoop Doggy Dogg (now known more often simply as Snoop Dogg) was a rap singer.[61] Another survey revealed that only half of people questioned knew that there are 100 U.S. senators or that the first 10 amendments to the Constitution are usually called the Bill of Rights.[62] Still another poll showed that four in 10 Americans could not name the vice president of the United States.[63]

***for more information on Gallup polls, see: http://www.gallup.com***

In a Gallup poll of college seniors, two-thirds thought that the words "government of the people, by the people, for the people shall not perish from the earth" appear in the U.S. Constitution, rather than in Lincoln's Gettysburg Address.[64]

Schattschneider concluded, "An amazingly large number of people do not seem to know very much about what is going on."[65] One effect of the lack of public knowledge is that government officials have wider latitude in making policy decisions, because they may assume that the public will neither know nor care very much about the results of those decisions. In other words, at least on some issues, bureaucrats who are confident of public ignorance or lack of interest may not worry about adverse reaction to their decisions—the outputs of the political system—or about possible feedback.

On the other hand, ignorance about political matters is not always the fault of the public. The government, in an effort to place its policies in the best possible light, sometimes issues misleading information or engages in outright deception.[66] For example, the Kennedy administration initially denied that CIA-supported exiles had invaded Cuba in 1961; the Johnson administration suppressed crucial information about events in the Tonkin Gulf in 1964; and in 1983 the Reagan White House denied that American military forces had invaded or planned to invade the Caribbean island of Grenada even as the troops prepared to land. Later, President Reagan ordered that his dealings with Iran, in an effort to trade arms for American hostages, be hidden from Congress and the public. And President Clinton misled the nation about his affair with a young White House intern. To build support for invading Iraq in 2003, President George W. Bush warned of the horror of a nuclear "mushroom cloud" that would result if that country attacked the United States. But after the war, it turned out that Iraq had no nuclear weapons.

Some scholars challenge the traditional assumption that many voters are politically ignorant. They suggest that the degree of information possessed by the public

© Bettmann/Corbis

The Johnson administration concealed doubts that this U.S. destroyer, the Turner Joy, had been attacked in the Tonkin Gulf on August 4, 1964. There was no attack, but reports that the ship and another destroyer, the Maddox, had come under fire were used to escalate the war in Vietnam.

© AP/Wide World Photos

Secret Service agents moments after the assassination attempt on President Reagan, March 30, 1981, Washington, D.C.

"Damn it, Turner, you were supposed to orchestrate public opinion!"

is "situational"—that is, it may vary from one election to another. For example, when differences between candidates are sharper, the public seems to absorb more information. "Voters can take stands, perceive party differences, and vote on the basis of them. But whether they do or not depends heavily on the candidate and the parties."[67]

## Violence and Politics

On the afternoon of March 30, 1981, as President Reagan left the Washington Hilton Hotel, John W. Hinckley, Jr., fired a .22-caliber revolver at him, seriously wounding the president and three other people. A Secret Service man pushed Reagan into his limousine, and he was taken to the hospital, where surgeons removed a bullet from his lung. Reagan recovered from his wounds. His 25-year-old assailant, tried and found not guilty by reason of insanity, was committed to a mental hospital for an indefinite period. (In 2003 a federal judge gave Hinckley the right to take unsupervised trips around Washington with his parents.)

As the television networks played and replayed the videotape of the moment when the president was shot, it seemed all too familiar. Assassination and violence have loomed over the political landscape several times in recent years.

Democracy operates on the premise that at least a substantial number of citizens will participate peacefully in the political system. The "consent of the governed" implies that public opinion plays a role in the political process. But if the system fails to respond to the demands placed upon it, or if participation is slow to bring change, individuals or groups may vent their anger against the system in violent ways. Or unbalanced people, acting out of personal frustration, may choose political targets.

Sometimes the violence is viewed as a form of political or social protest, such as the rioting that broke out in Los Angeles in April 1992 after a jury with no black members acquitted four white police officers in the beating of a black motorist, Rodney G. King. At other times, organized groups, such as the Weather Underground in the 1960s or the Puerto Rican nationalists, have engaged in bombings for stated political ends. And all too often in American history, deranged assassins have struck at political leaders.

The United States has had a violent past, for Americans have not always sought to bring about political change through lawful or peaceful means. The American Revolution, the Civil War, the settling of the frontier, racial lynchings, and the Ku Klux Klan are some examples. Clearly, assassination and violence are not new forms of American political behavior. Four presidents have been assassinated—Lincoln, Garfield, McKinley, and Kennedy—and serious attempts have been made against the lives of six others—Jackson, Theodore Roosevelt, Franklin Roosevelt, Truman, Ford, and Reagan. In addition, a Colorado man was convicted in 1995 of attempting to assassinate President Clinton after firing an assault

© 2004 AP/Wide World Photos

President George W. Bush speaks in Indiana in 2003 with a backdrop promoting the theme of his address.

rifle at the front of the White House from the sidewalk on Pennsylvania Avenue. This means that by 2004, an astonishing one-quarter of all American presidents had been murdered or targeted.

Political assassination and violence occurred with tragic frequency during the 1960s. The assassinations of President Kennedy in 1963; of his brother Robert Kennedy, a presidential candidate, in 1968; and of Dr. Martin Luther King, Jr., also in 1968, all dramatically affected the political process. So did racial violence in the cities.

The Warren Commission, the presidential panel that studied President Kennedy's assassination, concluded that the assassination had been carried out by Lee Harvey Oswald, who "acted alone," a finding challenged in many books and in the popular 1991 film *JFK* by those who contend that shots were fired by more than one person and that Kennedy was the victim of a conspiracy. Similar conspiracy theories circulated for many years after the assassination of President Lincoln in 1865. But most assassinations in American history appear to have been the acts of unbalanced individuals venting their rage and frustration on the national leader. Such purposeless acts differ in motivation from a planned assassination by conspirators or terrorists. Planned assassinations may be viewed as an attempt to go outside the political system. They are not a form of "participation" in the political system, but rather a rejection of that system.

As a presidential study panel reported, "Assassination, especially when the victim is a president, strikes at the heart of the democratic process. It enables one man to nullify the will of the people in a single, savage act. It touches the lives of all the people of the nation."[68]

## Mass Opinion in a Democracy

Suppose the president of the United States could push a button every morning and receive, along with the morning's toast and coffee, a printout summarizing the precise state of public opinion on a given spectrum of issues during the preceding 24 hours. And suppose the president tried to tailor the administration's policies to this computerized intelligence. Would that be good or bad?

Good, one person might respond. After all, democracy is supposed to be government "by the people," and if the government knows just what the people are thinking, the president can act in accordance with the popular will. Bad, another might answer. The president is elected to exercise his or her judgment and lead the nation, not follow the shifting winds of public opinion. After all, if the people are not satisfied with a president's leadership and decisions, they can elect a new one every four years.

Both arguments have merit. A president or a member of Congress usually tries to lead and shape public opinion and at the same time to follow it. No president can ignore public opinion during the four years between elections. But if our hypothetical president did try to rule according to computer printouts, it would soon become apparent that there was no way to please everybody. The president also would discover that if the policies suggested by the poll data failed to work, those policies and the president would soon become highly unpopular.

Nevertheless, modern political candidates and leaders are highly attuned to techniques for measuring and influencing public opinion. Ross Perot, a billionaire Texas businessman, made his fortune in the computer industry and was fascinated with the idea of using technology to interact with the voters. When he ran for president in 1992, Perot said that if elected he would not raise taxes unless electronic consultation with the public persuaded him that there was a "grass-roots consensus" to do so.[69]

Critics of "government by e-mail" argue that a president who merely responds to the public whim would have abdicated his leadership, and that electronic responses would come only from the more politically active citizens, a group that would not be representative of the entire electorate.

Political polls, Internet websites, television commercials, and professional campaign managers are all part of the efforts at mass persuasion used today. (These techniques are discussed in detail in Chapter 10.) Political leaders often try to "manage" public opinion or to manipulate it in their favor by using such techniques and by the conscious use of symbols.

For example, when a president addresses the nation on television during a military crisis, the dramatic format of the Oval Office of the White House and a nationwide television address are symbols of his power, designed to engender public support. When the president travels to make a speech, the presidential seal goes with him, and an aide unobtrusively hangs it on the rostrum just before the chief executive appears. Ronald Reagan, a veteran movie actor, used his polished skills as a performer to good advantage on television, both as a campaigner and as president. When President George W. Bush appeared in public and on television, he often spoke with a backdrop promoting the theme of his address, such as "Jobs and Growth," or "Strengthening Medicare." Sometimes the theme, such as the word "Opportunity," was repeated on the backdrop multiple times to drive the point home.

Public officials, political candidates, professional campaign consultants, media advisers, and government information officers customarily engage in political persuasion designed to influence or even manipulate the electorate. Indeed, as Dan Nimmo has suggested, "The political communicator not seeking to persuade others to his views is more rare than the whooping crane."[70]

Although leaders may court public opinion, it remains an elusive concept. The truth is that the role of public opinion in a democracy has always been difficult to define. The people, Walter Lippmann argued, "can elect the government. They can remove it. They can approve or disapprove its performance. But they cannot administer the government. They cannot themselves perform. . . . A mass cannot govern."[71]

Certainly, the public does not possess nearly as much information as the president, who daily receives a massive flow of intelligence from all over the globe to help him make decisions. The intelligence may be totally wrong, however, or a president may deliberately exaggerate it to justify a policy. And as E. E. Schattschneider pointed out, "nobody knows enough to run the government. Presidents, senators, governors, judges, professors, doctors of philosophy, editors, and the like are only a little less ignorant than the rest of us."[72]

It is reasonable to assume that presidents and legislators, because they hope to be reelected, do take public opinion into consideration in reaching major policy decisions—and smaller ones as well. In addition, they try to influence public opinion to win support for the decisions they have made.

Public opinion in a democracy, then, may be seen as a broad but flexible framework for policy making, setting certain limits within which government may act. As V. O. Key, Jr., has observed, "Unless mass views have some place in the shaping of policy, all the talk about democracy is nonsense."[73]

## CHAPTER HIGHLIGHTS

- Public opinion is the expression of attitudes about government and politics. All governments are based, to some extent, on public opinion.
- Political socialization is the process by which a person acquires a set of political attitudes and forms opinions about political and social issues.
- Many factors influence the opinions people hold. Among the most important are differences in social class, occupation, and income; religion, sex, race, and ethnic factors; sectional and geographic differences; and the views of reference groups. There are two kinds of reference groups: primary groups (such as friends, office associates, or a social club) and secondary groups (such as labor unions or fraternal, professional, or religious groups).
- Mass media—television, radio, newspapers, Internet websites and blogs, and other media—have a major impact on public opinion.
- The qualities of public opinion—direction, intensity, and stability—may be measured by political polls.
- Political polls, often useful as a guide to voter sentiment, are a standard part of political campaigns. They measure opinion by taking a random sample of a larger population, or universe. Because of the mathematical law of probability, the results of a poll usually reflect the opinions of the larger group. Although generally reliable, polls are sometimes wrong and do not necessarily predict the outcomes of elections.
- In presidential elections, often only a little more than half the people of voting age—and sometimes less than half—bother to vote. In off-year elections for Congress, usually well under half of the voting-age population votes.
- Americans have not always sought to express their opinions or to bring about political change through lawful or peaceful means. If the political system fails to respond to the demands placed on it, or if participation is slow to bring about change, individuals or groups may vent their anger against the system in violent ways.
- Modern political candidates and leaders are highly attuned to techniques for measuring and influencing public opinion. Political polls, television commercials, Internet websites, and professional campaign managers are all part of the efforts at mass persuasion used today.
- Public opinion in a democracy may be seen as a broad but flexible framework for policy making, setting certain limits within which government may act.

## KEY TERMS

public opinion, p. 176
political socialization, p. 177
reference groups, p. 181
primary groups, p. 181
secondary groups, p. 181
exit polls, p. 184
universe, p. 186
random sample, p. 186
cluster sampling, p. 187
quota sample, p. 187
bandwagon effect, p. 188
political culture, p. 188

## SUGGESTED WEBSITES

**http://www.gallup.com**
*The Gallup Organization*
Since 1935 the Gallup Organization has conducted surveys to measure public opinion on various issues. Its polls cover five subject areas: Politics and Elections, Business, Social Issues and Policy, Managing, and Lifestyle.

**http://www.headlinespot.com/opinion/polls/**
*Headline Spot Polls*
Has links to several polling sites that report public opinion on topics ranging from politics to everyday life.

**http://www.msnbc.com**
*MSNBC Opinions*
Provides opinion articles and transcripts of programs, and allows visitors to participate in MSNBC polls and to register their views on a bulletin board system (BBS) or through the MSNBC chat room.

**http://pollingreport.com**
An independent, nonpartisan resource on public opinion polls. The site organizes polls from multiple sources by category, such as the president, Congress, Election 2004, Iraq, and consumer confidence. It is updated whenever a new poll is released.

## SUGGESTED READING

Asher, Herbert B. *Polling the Public: What Every Citizen Should Know,* 6th edition* (CQ Press, 2004). The goal of this book is to help readers become informed consumers of public opinion polls by pointing out problems that are often found in each phase of the polling process. The author also discusses the roles that polls play in the political system.

Bennett, Linda, and Bennett, Stephen. *Living with Leviathan: Americans Coming to Terms with Big Government* (University of Kansas Press, 1990). A detailed examination of Americans' changing attitudes toward the expanding role of government in social and economic life.

Cantril, Albert H., and Cantril, Susan Davis. *Reading Mixed Signals: Ambivalence in American Public Opinion About Government** (Woodrow Wilson Center Press, 1999). An insightful study of the seemingly paradoxical attitudes toward government in the United States: Americans express distrust for government, and say that its size should be reduced, but when it comes to concrete issues, such as the environment, care for the elderly and young, and health care, they believe that government should be doing more.

Craig, Stephen C., and Bennett, Stephen E., eds. *After the Boom: The Politics of Generation X* (Rowman & Littlefield, 1997). A series of essays, including several by members of Generation X, examining the social and political thought and behavior of a younger segment of the population that will be increasingly important in the coming years.

DelliCarpini, Michael X., and Keeter, Scott. *What Americans Know About Politics and Why It Matters** (Yale University Press, 1997). A scholarly analysis, spanning half a century, of Americans' levels of political information. The authors conclude that whites and upper-income citizens are more likely to be politically informed, and argue that this has broad consequences for the distribution of political power.

Erikson, Robert S., MacKuen, Michael B., and Stimson, James A. *The Macro Polity** (Cambridge University Press, 2002). A major study of American public attitudes that analyzes trends in presidential approval ratings from 1952 to 1992, political party identification, the public's policy moods, and election outcomes. The authors look at the impact that public opinion about policy and election outcomes may have on policy formation.

Erikson, Robert S., and Tedin, Kent L. *American Public Opinion: Its Origins, Content and Impact,* 7th edition, update* (Pearson Education, 2005). A comprehensive introduction to the field of public opinion research and analysis. The authors examine influences upon public opinion, the process of opinion formation, and the importance of public opinion for democratic government.

Glynn, Carroll J., et al. *Public Opinion: Politics, Communication and Social Process,* 2nd edition* (Westview Press, 2004). A collection of readable essays on the formulation of mass opinion, its measurement, and its impact upon politicians and the political process.

Page, Benjamin I., and Shapiro, Robert Y. *The Rational Public: Fifty Years of Trends in Americans' Policy Preferences** (University of Chicago Press, 1994). A comprehensive analysis of Americans' political attitudes from the 1930s to the 1980s.

Shafer, Byron E., and Claggett, William J. M. *The Two Majorities: The Issue Context of Modern American Politics** (Johns Hopkins University Press, 1995). A detailed study of Americans' attitudes toward issues. The authors argue that on a cluster of economic and social insurance issues, the public prefers the Democratic Party's position; but on issues related to cultural values, civil liberties, and national defense, the public normally prefers the Republican Party's positions.

Stimson, James A. *Public Opinion in America: Moods, Cycles and Swings,* 2nd edition* (Westview Press, 1999). The author uses polling data to support the view that American public opinion goes through regular, cyclical fluctuations between conservatism and liberalism.

Traugott, Michael W., and Lavrakas, Paul J. *The Voter's Guide to Election Polls,* 3rd edition* (Rowman & Littlefield, 2004). A concise, readable guide for understanding public opinion polls. Examines how surveys are conducted, common problems facing pollsters, and the interpretation of survey results.

White, John Kenneth. *The Values Divide: American Politics and Culture in Transition** (Chatham House, 2003). Argues that divisions over cultural issues and lifestyle are the key conflict in contemporary politics. On most cultural issues, the author asserts, Democratic voters and leaders tend to take positions that are very different from those of Republicans. The author cites a wide variety of public opinion polls to develop his thesis.

Zaller, James. *The Nature and Origins of Mass Opinion** (Oxford University Press, 1992). An illuminating exploration of how citizens acquire political information, and how public opinion is formed.

*Available in paperback edition.

# Chapter 7

# Interest Groups

IN 2003, CONGRESS enacted a major overhaul of the Medicare program, adding a prescription drug benefit for the first time. The Medicare program, established in 1965, is designed to provide health care to older people through the social security system. The new drug benefit was controversial, and the pharmaceutical industry had a huge stake in the outcome of the legislative battle over the bill.

For example, analysts at a leading Wall Street firm, Goldman Sachs & Company, estimated that the new law could increase revenues of the drug companies by 9 percent, or about $13 billion a year—because more people would be able to buy drugs under the expanded Medicare program. At the same time, the pharmaceutical industry was strongly opposed to the importation of drugs from Canada, where the cost of medicines is as much as 75 percent lower than in the United States. Both the industry and the administration argued that drugs manufactured in the United States and then reimported might be unsafe because once leaving the country they were not subject to control by the U.S. Food and Drug Administration and might be counterfeit or diluted.

Not surprisingly, lobbyists for the pharmaceutical industry worked hard to shape the bill to their wishes. In the first half of the year, drug company lobbyists spent almost $38 million to influence legislation. And during the three years after the 2000 elections, the industry contributed $60 million in political donations.

Although polls indicated that an overwhelming majority of Americans supported legalizing the importation of drugs from Canada and Europe,

© Mark Meyer/Time Life Pictures/Getty Images

© Rhona Wise/EPA/Landov

Bush speaks to seniors in Florida about Medicare.

that provision—approved by a wide margin in the House—was dropped from the final version of the law passed by Congress and signed by President George W. Bush. The drug lobby had won its fight.

The industry's effort to influence the Medicare prescription drug bill was not unusual. Congress and the executive branch are the targets of similar lobbying efforts by all sorts of groups, not only industry and big corporations but also organizations representing older Americans, gun owners, labor unions, trial lawyers, teachers, and other special interests.

Key Question

The millions of dollars spent every year on influencing Congress and government officials in Washington raise a key question about the nature of democracy: ***Do the people really rule, through their elected officials and representatives? Or do powerful groups with deep pockets full of money control government policies and determine what laws get passed? Who is really in charge?***

## Who Governs?

Who governs in a democracy? Three answers are possible. It can be said that "the people" govern through political leaders nominated as candidates of political parties (or running as independents) and elected by the voters.

Another view is that a "power elite," a "power structure," or an "establishment" actually runs things. This was the view advanced more than four decades ago by sociologist C. Wright Mills in *The Power Elite.* Mills argued that a small group, "possessors of power, wealth and celebrity," occupies the key positions in American society.[1] This theory holds that elites rule, that power is held by the few and not by the masses. Many other social scientists have interpreted American society in terms of elite theory.[2] And "the establishment" is an expression that is sometimes used to describe elite power. Political writer Richard H. Rovere once described the "American Establishment" as a loose coalition of leaders of finance, business, the professions, and the universities, who hold power and influence in the United States regardless of what administration occupies the White House.[3]

Although elites do exist in almost every field of human activity, many scholars reject the concept that a single economic and social elite wields ultimate political power. In his classic study of community power in New Haven, Connecticut, Robert A. Dahl provided a third answer to the question of "Who governs?" He examined several specific public issues and traced the process by which decisions were made on those issues. He concluded that the city's economic and social "notables" did not run New Haven. Some individuals and groups were particularly influential in the making of one type of decision—educational policy, for example. But in other policy areas, different individuals and groups often played the most important role. The city was dominated by many sets of leaders: "It was, in short, a pluralist system."[4]

Other scholars have criticized Dahl's approach on the grounds that the wielders of power cannot always be identified by examining key decisions. For example, truly powerful people might prevent certain issues from ever reaching the public arena.[5] On such issues, those favoring the status quo are the winners because no decisions are made that might lead to change. In short, the power to set the agenda, to determine which public policy questions will be debated or even considered, may prove at least as important as the power to decide on the issues themselves.

Nevertheless, the pluralist character of American democracy is widely, although not universally, recognized. **Pluralism** is a system in which many conflicting groups within the community have access to government officials and compete with one another in an effort to influence policy decisions.

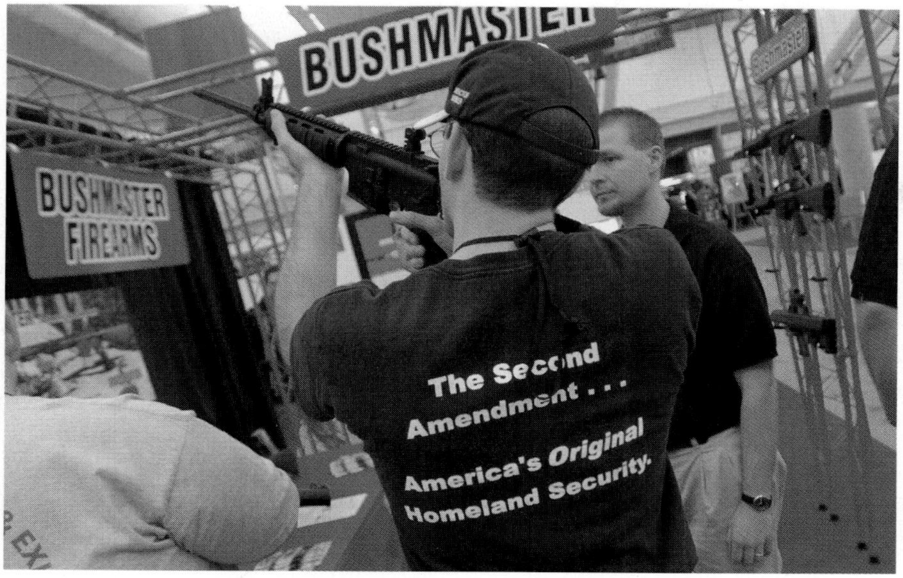




A gun enthusiast at the National Rifle Association's 2004 convention in Pittsburgh

Pluralism supposes that many individuals are active in groups and associations to advance their interests and that these multiple interests and memberships may overlap and often conflict. For example, the same person who favors new school construction as a member of the PTA may oppose higher taxes as a member of a neighborhood association. However, many groups have been badly underrepresented or left out of the pluralist system. Minorities, the poor, migrant workers, consumers, and others who do not belong to organized interest groups do not always fare well in a pluralist society. And many Americans do not join groups. Moreover, a case may be made that some interest groups can become too powerful; a classic example often cited is the National Rifle Association, which for years has opposed gun control legislation favored by a majority of Americans.

It has been argued that pluralism really consists of competing groups of elites, so that even a pluralist system falls far short of the classic democratic model. Some scholars who contend that America is ruled by the few are critical of elite power and argue that the political system must be opened up to give more people access to it. Other scholars claim that only elites are dedicated to democratic principles and that the masses of citizens have little allegiance to freedom, the right of dissent, First Amendment values, or equal opportunity. But this latter view diminishes the importance of the ordinary voter and citizen and reflects little confidence in representative democracy.

To an extent, the debate over whether America is an elite or pluralist democracy may pose the question in terms that are too rigid. As with most things, there is a mix. Elites do exercise power in and out of government, but competing groups also play an important role. And the voters retain the ultimate power of replacing elected leaders—from the school board member to the president of the United States.

## Interest Groups at Work

**Interest groups** are private groups that attempt to influence the government to respond to the shared attitudes of their members.

Public opinion, as noted in Chapter 6, is the expression of attitudes on public questions. When people organize to express attitudes held in common and to influence the government to respond to those attitudes, they become members of interest groups.

When one group wins, another may lose. David B. Truman has pointed out that interest groups may make "certain claims upon other groups in the society" by acting through "the institutions of government."[6]

Concern over the potential power of private groups is even older than the republic; James Madison warned of the "mischiefs of faction" in his famous essay, "*The*

### James Madison on Interest Groups

James Madison, one of the most influential figures in the shaping of the Constitution, worried about interest groups long before that term came into general use. More than 200 years ago, he wrote:

> By a faction, I understand a number of citizens, whether amounting to a majority or a minority of the whole, who are united and actuated by some common impulse of passion, or of interest, adverse to the rights of other citizens, or to the permanent and aggregate interests of the community.

—James Madison, *The Federalist,* No. 10, November 23, 1787

An antismoking interest group put up this billboard in Nashville, Tennessee.

© AP/Wide World Photos

*Federalist,* No. 10." But Madison also recognized that reconciling the competing interests of various groups was what legislation was all about, and "involves the spirit of party and faction in the necessary and ordinary operations of the government."[7] (The text of "*The Federalist,* No. 10," appears in the Appendix of this book, on pages A-13 to A-16.)

President Woodrow Wilson argued that government should act as a sort of referee among interest groups to protect the public. "The business of government," he said, "is to organize the common interest against the special interests."[8]

In the 19th century, political cartoonists were fond of drawing potbellied men in top hats and striped pants to represent Big Business. In the early 20th century, muckrakers—journalists such as Lincoln Steffens, who exposed business misconduct—assailed oil, steel, and railroad barons, calling them members of interest groups in league against the public welfare. Partly as a result of this muckraking tradition, many people tend to regard all interest groups as evil, business-dominated organizations plotting against the common good. And it is true that some powerful interest groups, employing well-paid lobbyists in Washington, often bring about legislation that benefits corporate America, sometimes at the expense of the broader public. But it is also true that today many other interest groups champion consumers, the environment, campaign finance reform, or other causes that benefit the public as a whole.

Many political scientists now consider interest groups a normal and vital part of the political process, conveyors of the demands and supports fed into the po-

An 1889 cartoon depicted fat-cat industrialists as the true bosses of the U.S. Senate.

© Corbis

litical system. In other words, interest groups provide many of the important inputs of the political system. Whether such groups are called "interest groups," "pressure groups," or "lobbies"—and there is some disagreement over which label is best—their purpose is much the same: to influence government policies and actions. The historian Clinton Rossiter has observed: "We call them 'interest groups' when we are feeling clinical, 'pressure groups' when we are feeling critical, and 'lobbies' when we are watching them at work in our fifty-one capitals."[9] These groups should not be confused with political parties, which also seek to influence government but by electing candidates to office. As noted in Chapter 1, the members of some interest groups—college students, for example—may not even be formally organized as a group.

## Who Belongs?

The tendency of Americans to come together in groups was noticed in the early 19th century by a remarkably perceptive French observer, Alexis de Tocqueville. "In no country of the world," he observed, "has the principle of association been more successfully used or applied to a greater multitude of objects than in America."[10]

There are more than 100,000 clubs and associations in the United States. Not everyone belongs to a group, however. In America, "more than one-third of the population has no formal group association."[11] And nearly half of those who do belong to groups are affiliated with social, fraternal, or church-connected organizations that may have little relation to politics.[12] Not all organizations are interested in influencing government, so only a minority of Americans belong to interest groups. One survey reported that only 31 percent of the population belonged to groups that sometimes take a stand on housing, better government, school problems, or other public issues.[13] That well over one-third of Americans belong to no groups at all raises basic questions about pluralist democracy that will be discussed later in this chapter.

## How They Operate

Although interest groups vary tremendously in size, goals, budget, and scope of interest, they often employ the same techniques to accomplish their objectives. The following examples illustrate some of these techniques.

Several years ago, the Federal Trade Commission proposed a set of rules designed to protect people who buy used cars. The rules would have required dealers to reveal to a buyer any major defects in a car. The nation's used-car dealers, led by the National Automobile Dealers Association, mounted a massive lobbying campaign in Congress to overturn the FTC proposal. According to Ralph Nader's Congress Watch, the auto dealers' group gave campaign contributions of $770,000 to members of the House.

***for more information about Ralph Nader's Congress Watch, see: http://www.citizen.org/congress***

Congress voted to kill the rules that would have helped car buyers know what they were buying. "This says a lot about the contamination of the political arena by campaign contributions," said Representative Toby Moffett, Democrat of Connecticut.[14] Another opponent of the congressional action, Representative Barbara A. Mikulski, a Maryland Democrat who was later elected to the Senate, said the rules would have protected car buyers from gypsy dealers such as "Happy Harry and Smiling Sam." She added: "People should know if they're getting a car in reasonable condition or a four-wheel-drive lemon."[15]

It was a blatant but effective case of lobbying by an industry group. It won, and the consumers lost.

But if the used-car dealers triumphed, it was consumers who won in another battle a few years later, in New York State, when beer prices rose as much as 31 percent. The reason: Brewers ordered their distributors to carve out exclusive territories and avoid competition with other distributors—competition that would have meant lower prices. In Washington, senators who had received substantial contributions from the beer industry introduced legislation to exempt such practices nationwide from provisions of the federal antitrust laws. Consumer activists, working with the states, defeated the measure, saving the nation's beer drinkers from higher prices, if not from larger waistlines.[16]

**Lobbying** One of the most powerful techniques of interest groups is **lobbying,** communication with legislators or other government officials to try to influence their decisions. Originally, the term "lobby-agent" was used to describe someone who waited in the lobbies of government buildings to buttonhole lawmakers. The term "lobbying" dates back to the 1600s in England,

### Seven Rules for the Successful Lobbyist

From extensive comments by lobbyists and their targets, Lester W. Milbrath drew up the following list of guidelines for Washington's lobbyists:

1. Be pleasant and non-offensive
2. Convince the official that it is important for him to listen
3. Be well prepared and well informed
4. Be personally convinced
5. Be succinct, well organized, and direct
6. Use the soft sell
7. Leave a short written summary of the case

—Lester W. Milbrath, *The Washington Lobbyists*

where the large antechamber near the floor of the House of Commons was called the "lobby." In the United States, the term first came into use in the New York state capital at Albany and was being used in Washington by the early 1830s.

The term "Washington lobbyist" is not always complimentary. Lobbyists and the interest groups they represent are often the target of attacks by political candidates during campaigns. But lobbying is not necessarily harmful, or incompatible with democracy, because groups, no less than individuals, have a right to express their views.

Although the word "lobbying" is often applied to mean direct contact with lawmakers, in its broadest sense lobbying is not confined to efforts to influence the legislative branch. Lobbyists also seek to influence officials of the executive branch, regulatory agencies, and sometimes the courts. And lobbyists spend much of their time monitoring events in Washington in order to alert their clients to government actions or plans that may affect them.

One way that lobbyists influence officials is simple: They get to know them. By paying visits to members of Congress and government officials; by attending hearings of congressional committees, government agencies, and regulatory commissions; and by forming friendships with staff members and bureaucrats, lobbyists make their presence felt. Lester Milbrath found that more than half the Washington lobbyists thought the personal presentation of viewpoints was the most effective way of reaching members of Congress.[17] Senators and representatives are busy people; often the lobbyists' chief value is that in support of their arguments they present carefully researched background material that may help a member of Congress decide how to vote on a complex bill. The material lobbyists provide may also find its way into the language of a bill.

How lobbyists are viewed often depends on whose interests are at stake. When reporters asked President Harry S Truman whether he would oppose lobbyists who worked for his programs, he replied with a twinkle: "We probably wouldn't call those people lobbyists. We would call them citizens appearing in the public interest."[18]

**Money: The Lobbyist's Tool** A few years ago, some 50 of the nation's top lobbyists posed for a group photograph in *Washingtonian* magazine, a glossy publication widely read in the capital. The photograph accompanied an article titled "Show Me the Money!"[19]

The phrase might well be the motto for one of the most affluent groups in Washington: the lobbyists and lawyers who represent large corporations and industry groups and other clients seeking to influence the government. Lobbyists and their firms are paid millions of dollars a year, and in turn, they contribute generously to political candidates and parties.

Some years ago, one of the capital's most publicized lobbyists, Michael K. Deaver, a former White House deputy chief of staff under President Reagan, got into trouble when he appeared on the cover of *Time* magazine. Deaver had set up his own lobbying firm in Washington when he left the White House. The cover photograph of Deaver showed him telephoning someone from his richly appointed limousine, alongside the headlines "Who's This Man Calling?" and "Influence Peddling in Washington."[20] Foreign governments, defense contractors, corporations, and others seeking access to the center of power flocked to hire Deaver at fees ranging into millions of dollars.

Federal law prohibits former government employees from appearing before their former agencies to represent clients for one year after leaving government service. Deaver was convicted of lying to Congress and to a grand jury about his lobbying. He was fined $100,000 and sentenced to three years' probation. It did not seem to inhibit his continued success as a lobbyist.

### "Money Does Talk"—The Tab for Washington Lobbying: $1.42 Billion

WASHINGTON, July 28—The capital of the United States is a city with no real industry except for politics and influence, and so huge sums of money are paid to lobbyists trying to influence politicians. Last year $1.42 billion was spent in that endeavor, a research group said today.

That total was a 13 percent increase over the $1.26 billion that lobbyists were paid in 1997, said the group, the Center for Responsive Politics. If all the money had been spent on Capitol Hill, it would have worked out to $2.7 million earmarked to persuading each of the 535 lawmakers on a host of issues, the center said.

Of course, not all was spent on Capitol Hill; much was spent trying to persuade various regulatory agencies and other offices of the executive branch, the center's communications director, Paul Hendrie, pointed out.

The $1.42 billion was paid to lobbyists by airplane manufacturers, bankers, doctors and lawyers, drug companies, hospitals, universities, Indian tribes—in short, by just about any person or any institution that has business before the Federal Government.

"There's certainly nothing inherently illegitimate about any of these interests' having their voices heard," Mr. Hendrie emphasized. "We don't think so, either," said Tom McMahon, a spokesman for Cassidy & Associates, which took in $19.9 million in fees last year. . . .

Still, Mr. Hendrie said, the huge sums spent on lobbying are cause for concern. "People who don't have the money to spend are not going to speak with as loud a voice," he said. "Money does talk."

—David Stout, the *New York Times,* July 29, 1999

More recently, Jack Abramoff—until his downfall in 2006—was one of Washington's most powerful lobbyists, hobnobbing with members of Congress, wining and dining key lawmakers, and hosting some of them on expensive foreign junkets. To entertain the legislators, he owned four skyboxes at Washington's sports arena and two restaurants on Capitol Hill. He helped his associates land government positions so they could in turn help him.

## Washington Lobbyists: The Top 10

The *National Journal,* a weekly political report, compiled this list of the nation's top 10 lobbying firms, and law firms that lobby, ranked according to revenue.

1. Patton Boggs
2. Akin, Gump, Strauss, Hauer, & Feld
3. Cassidy & Associates
4. Van Scoyoc Associates
5. Dutko Worldwide
6. Barbour Griffith & Rogers
7. Williams & Jensen
8. DLA Piper Rudnick Gray Cary
9. Hogan & Hartson
10. Quinn Gillespie & Associates

—*National Journal,* March 25, 2006, based on data for 2005

He convinced half a dozen Indian tribes that by paying him millions of dollars, they could influence Congress on legislation affecting their gambling casinos. Abramoff funneled the payments, totaling $82 million, through his public relations partner Michael Scanlon, a former press secretary to Tom DeLay, the Texas Republican who was the powerful House majority leader. Since PR fees need not be disclosed, the ploy kept the millions in payments hidden from public view.

In 2003 Abramoff's empire started to spiral out of control. Rival lobbyists were starting to talk, as reports circulated that Scanlon had paid for a $5 million beach house in cash. The *Washington Post* ran a story on the millions Abramoff and Scanlon were receiving from the Indian tribes.

At the same time, a fleet of casino boats in Florida that Abramoff had purchased went bankrupt. A state grand jury investigated a multimillion-dollar fraudulent wire transfer used by Abramoff to acquire the boats and the gangland-style murder of the man who had sold the fleet to Abramoff and his partner. In 2004 the Justice Department launched its own investigation of Abramoff.

The scandal spread and threatened to cause political and legal problems for several members of Congress and government officials linked to Abramoff. The lobbyist's close ties to Tom DeLay cast a cloud over the House leader. Delay was forced to step down from his leadership post after he was indicted in a separate case in Texas on charges of money laundering. Later, he announced he would not run for reelection in 2006.

Many officials who had received campaign contributions from Abramoff, including President Bush and House Speaker J. Dennis Hastert, hastened to give the money to charity. In 2006 Abramoff pleaded guilty to charges of fraud, tax evasion, and conspiracy to bribe public officials and agreed to testify against members of Congress and executive branch officials as part of the plea bargain. Scanlon pleaded guilty to conspiracy to de-

"If you still want to belong to an organization dedicated to killing Americans, there's always the tobacco lobby."

Tobacco industry executives testify to Congress. The industry spent millions on Washington lobbyists.

© AP/Wide World Photos

fraud the Indian tribes and agreed to testify about bribery and fraud in Washington and Florida. Abramoff also pleaded guilty in Florida to conspiracy and wire fraud in connection with the purchase of the gambling fleet. Nine months later, Representative Bob Ney, an Ohio Republican, agreed to plead guilty to accepting bribes from Abramoff to help the lobbyist and his clients and said he would not seek reelection.

Despite the Abramoff scandal, most lobbyists are not lawbreakers. Many law firms and lobbyists in Washington make big money legally representing corporations and interest groups to influence legislation. In 2006 one top lobbying law firm—Patton Boggs—reported that it had earned $36.9 million in fees the previous year.

Six years earlier, in 1997, the tobacco industry, beset by lawsuits by state attorneys general and private individuals, reached a multibillion-dollar settlement that required approval by Congress. Many antismoking activists opposed the deal as too favorable to Big Tobacco. In the first six months after the proposed settlement was negotiated, the tobacco giants spent $15.8 million to hire an astonishing 186 lobbyists to press their case with lawmakers and government regulators in Washington.[22] During the same six months, the tobacco industry gave $1.9 million to political party committees and $587,000 to candidates.[23]

When the Senate modified the settlement in 1998 in ways that the companies opposed, the industry turned against it. The number of lobbyists for the tobacco interests—now working against the legislation—increased dramatically, and the $368.5 billion tobacco deal collapsed. Later that year the industry and the states reached a much more limited settlement.

Although a great deal of lobbying is directed at Congress, sometimes even a president is lobbied. For example, during the Nixon administration, America's dairy industry wanted the price supports for milk raised. The dairy industry group agreed to contribute campaign funds to the president. In due course, the attorney for the largest of the milk cooperatives, the Associated Milk Producers, Inc. (AMPI), delivered a satchel containing $100,000 in cash to Nixon's lawyer. The milk producers met twice with the president in the White House and pledged to contribute $2 million to Nixon in the 1972 presidential campaign. The dairy industry won a large price increase.[24] With a satchel full of cash and a promise of $2 million, lobbyists for a powerful industry had directly influenced the president of the United States.[25]

The success of the dairy industry in winning price increases worth more than $300 million is a dramatic illustration of how lobbying by interest groups can affect—even reverse—public policy. In the policy-making process, interest groups play a key role. In this instance, an input of hard cash resulted in the output of higher prices that the milk industry wanted.

As this case demonstrated, money is often a useful tool for the lobbyist. The public often thinks of the lobbyist as someone who hands out money to buy the votes of legislators. That may happen. A direct bribe, however, is a violation of federal law. Under a 1962 statute, a person who bribes a member of Congress, or a member of Congress who takes "anything of value" in exchange for a vote, may be fined $20,000 and imprisoned up to 15 years. The language of the statute is broad enough to cover any kind of valuable favor, not just money. Bribery is illegal and risky, and there are better, legal ways to channel money to legislators. For example, lobbyists are expected to purchase tickets or whole tables of tickets to fund-raising dinners for political parties and candidates. And of course lobbyists and their clients can—and do—contribute to political campaigns.

Until Congress passed a law in 1995 to regulate the practice, lobbyists might, without regard to the cost, take a senator to lunch at an expensive restaurant in Washington, arrange a weekend on a yacht, or provide a free trip to a plush resort; Christmas might bring a legislator a

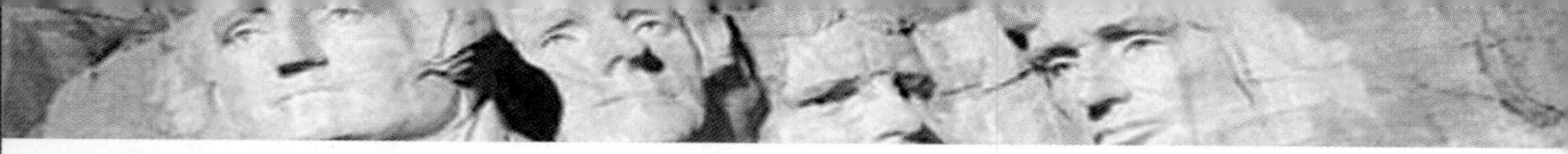

## The American Past

### "NO MAN IN PUBLIC OFFICE OWES THE PUBLIC ANYTHING"

A small class of men . . . arose at the time of our Civil War and suddenly swept into power.

The members of this new ruling class were generally, and quite aptly, called "barons," "kings," "empire builders," or even "emperors." They were aggressive men, as were the first feudal barons; sometimes they were lawless; in important crises, nearly all of them tended to act without moral principles. . . .

While busy carving up the country into baronies the captains of industry worked also with unremitting vigilance in the field of political action [penetrating] into the highest assemblies of the country: the Congress, the Senate, and even sometimes the President's cabinet. . . .

Instead of outright bribery, highly subtle methods of distributing rewards to political friends came into play. In the Pacific Railway Investigation of 1887, [Collis P.] Huntington stated candidly that he was opposed to giving politicians free liquor and cigars too open-handedly. And where [Thomas A.] Scott or [Jay] Gould gave free passes on all the railroads touching Washington, Huntington organized huge "junketing parties" on private trains at a cost of tens of thousands of dollars, by which politicians, their families and journalists might go on exhilarating excursions through his broad territories.

In time, all of the captains of industry found it greatly to their advantage to use the system of the hired "lobbyist," a type of professional public agent who had flourished from the earliest days of the republic, but who came to assume a tremendously important and confidential role in the last quarter of the nineteenth century. All the "interests," banks, railways, mines, steel, munitions and war materials, ended by having their specialized go-betweens or lobbies.

[On] May 8, 1890, a young Republican prosecuting attorney in Ohio, with the enthusiasm of an amateur, began a suit to annul the charter of the Standard Oil Company. At once Mark Hanna wrote him the letter which contained the famous line: "You have been in politics long enough to know that no man in public office owes the public anything."

—Adapted from Matthew Josephson, *The Robber Barons: The Great American Capitalists 1861–1901*

---

ham, a case of Scotch, or a pair of gold cuff links. The new law placed limits on these practices, but did not eliminate them; according to one report, at the Capital Grille, an expensive restaurant not far from the Capitol building, "lobbyists flaunt their clients and their expensive tastes with brass name plaques on private wine lockers."[26]

In the summer of 2000, a group of top lobbyists invested in, and opened, their own restaurant in Washington, complete with discreet private dining rooms for entertaining members of Congress. Appropriately, the restaurant was called the Caucus Room. But lunches, fine wines, and small favors are only relatively minor props in the drama of influencing lawmakers. Many members of Congress are practicing lawyers, insurance agents, bankers, and business executives. For example, in 2004, some 218 members—or about two-fifths—of the 109th Congress were lawyers. It is not difficult for interest groups with nationwide chapters and members to channel legal or insurance fees or bank loans to members of Congress. Unless such payments can be shown to be outright bribes, they are legal; in any event, they are difficult to trace.

For the most part, lobbyists for interest groups are able to exert influence by means of campaign contributions and fund-raising. The American Medical Association (AMA), representing more than 244,000 physicians, residents, and medical students, is an example of a highly active interest group that has spent millions of dollars opposing national health insurance and other medical legislation. The American Medical Association Political Action Committee (AMPAC), the AMA's political arm, contributed $2 million to congressional candidates in the 2004 election.

***for more information about the American Medical Association, see: http://www.ama-assn.org***

Many large interest groups are deeply involved in politics. For example, the AFL-CIO's Committee on Political Education (COPE) contributes money to candidates, runs voter-registration drives, publicly endorses candidates, publishes their voting records for union members, and often provides volunteers to assist in political campaigns. COPE contributed more than $486,000 to candidates for Congress in the 2004 election. Although ostensibly nonpartisan, COPE in fact has mainly aided Democrats, just as the AMA is Republican oriented.

As these examples illustrate, large amounts of money flow to political leaders and candidates from interest groups and corporations maneuvering to influence public policy. When George W. Bush, a former businessman in the oil industry, began his quest for the 2000 Republican presidential nomination, he received more than $1.42 million dollars from various oil and gas companies to support his campaign in the spring primaries. In contrast, Al Gore, his Democratic rival, received only $84,750 from those sources. Gore, on the other hand, got $806,690 from the entertainment industry during the same period, about $200,000 more than Hollywood gave to Bush.[27]

Despite their money and influence, Washington lobbyists do not always fit their popular image as glamorous figures who entertain powerful senators and dine at the best places. As most lobbyists are quick to point out, much of their work consists of solid research, long hours of committee hearings, and conversations with lawmakers in their offices. Whatever their technique, lobbyists—and their dollars—have a substantial influence on political decision making.

**Mass Propaganda and Grass-Roots Pressure** One of the ways in which interest groups try to influence public opinion in order to influence government is through mass-publicity campaigns. Using television, magazine, newspaper, and Internet advertising, as well as e-mails and direct mailings to the general public and specialized audiences, interest groups seek to create a favorable climate for their goals.

With the aid of a public relations firm, an interest group can use all the latest techniques of Madison Avenue. But it takes a great deal of money to influence public opinion enough to create a response from government, and only affluent interest groups can afford programs aimed at the manipulation of mass public opinion.[28]

A classic example of an apparently successful campaign by an affluent group was the publicity campaign of the American Automobile Association (AAA) against a bill that would have allowed bigger trucks on the nation's roads. The AAA ran newspaper advertisements showing a triple-trailer truck with a huge boar's head devouring the highway as John Q. Motorist sat helplessly by, trapped in a monstrous traffic jam. The ad urged that the bill be defeated for reasons of safety and "because of the irreparable damage bigger trucks will do to our highways and bridges." With the public alarmed and the nation's bridges in apparent danger of imminent collapse, Congress abandoned the trucking bill.[29]

MoveOn.org

Evangelical Christian groups have organized grass-roots pressure in political campaigns. Here Republican presidential candidate George W. Bush and wife, Laura, join hands at Bob Jones University in February 2000.

© AP / Wide World Photos

John Mead/Star File Photo

Pearl Jam in concert. Ticketmaster's Washington lobbyists called the tune.

*for more information about the American Automobile Association, see: http://www.aaa.com*

In addition to such mass-propaganda campaigns, many interest groups approach some members of the public directly to try to create various forms of grass-roots pressure that will affect government. To influence senators, for example, an interest group might persuade powerful bankers in the senators' states to telephone them in Washington. Lobbyists may ask close friends of the senators to get in touch with them. Or lobbyists may try to get great numbers of legislators' constituents to write, fax, or e-mail them.

Both mass propaganda and grass-roots pressure have been employed by highly organized evangelical Christian groups in political campaigns in recent years. In the 2000 Republican presidential primary race, for example, the support for George W. Bush by Pat Robertson and other evangelical Christians became a major campaign issue.

Liberal groups as well use grass-roots lobbying techniques. For example, MoveOn.org, which claims "1,700,000 online activists," worked in 2004 to try to defeat George W. Bush's reelection as president. Its website early that year urged that Congress censure Bush for "misleading statements that pushed the nation into war." It asked visitors to its website to contact their members of Congress and to donate money to the organization. MoveOn contributed $11 million to candidates in the 2004 congressional elections.[30]

Today, many interest groups use computerized mailing lists to contact their members and supporters; the National Rifle Association (NRA), an aggressive group opposed to gun control, reportedly can barrage Congress with a half-million letters on 72 hours' notice. The NRA has almost 4 million members, a budget of $200 million, and a full-time staff of about 500 people. In 2004, the NRA contributed over $1 million through its political victory fund to Senate and House candidates.[31]

Members of Congress are well aware that interest groups may be behind a sudden flood of letters, e-mails, or faxes on a pending bill. In addition, legislators know that because most people do not write letters to their representatives in Congress, the mail they receive reflects the feelings of only a small percentage of their constituents. One study showed that only 17 percent of the general public writes letters to members of Congress.[32] Nevertheless, grass-roots pressure remains a popular form of trying to influence government, in part because interest groups, never certain which techniques are the most effective, tend to try them all.

Today, with the enormous impact of the Internet, it is easier than ever for lobbyists to organize a seemingly grass-roots campaign in which citizens bombard their lawmakers with thousands of e-mails. When those computer messages bear the names of constituents, legislators are likely to pay attention.

## The Washington Lawyers: Access to the Powerful

Members of prestigious Washington law firms are among the capital's most effective lobbyists. Often, large corporations pay big fees to Washington lawyers, not only for their expert knowledge of how the bureaucracy works, but also for their political access and friends inside the government and in Congress.

Pearl Jam, the Seattle-based grunge band, found this out when it filed a complaint in 1994 with the Justice Department alleging that the Ticketmaster company had a monopoly on ticket sales in violation of federal antitrust laws. Other bands and consumer groups joined with Pearl Jam in an alliance designed to open up ticket sales and lower the prices. Ticketmaster fought back. It opened a Washington "government relations" office and hired not one but five powerful lobbyist, public relations, and law firms to represent it. A little more than a year later, the Justice Department announced that it had ended its antitrust investigation of Ticketmaster. It would not elaborate on its announcement. But Pearl Jam had lost.[33]

On more than one occasion, Washington lawyers have been able to orchestrate the passage of legislation designed to help their clients: "The lawyer's historic role was that of advising clients how to comply with the law. The Washington lawyer's present role is that of advising clients how to make laws, and to make the most of them."[34] Often, government lawyers leave to join Washington law firms, where they are highly paid to find the loopholes in the very laws they formerly enforced. This sort of "revolving door" is a common practice in the nation's capital.

For several decades until the 1990s, one of the most renowned of Washington lawyers was Clark M. Clifford, who served in the cabinet and as an adviser to Democratic presidents. Aware of his stature, bureaucrats and members of Congress tended to return his telephone calls, giving Clifford the kind of political clout that corporate clients want—and pay large fees to obtain. President Kennedy, who received a good deal of free advice from Clifford, once joked: "All he asked in return was that we advertise his law firm on the backs of one-dollar bills."[35]

### Who Lobbies for the Poor?

The poor are powerless because they are a minority of the population, are often difficult to organize, and are not even a homogeneous group with similar interests that could be organized into an effective pressure group. . . .

Although every citizen is urged to be active in the affairs of his community and nation, in actual practice participation is almost entirely limited to organized interest groups or lobbies who want something from government.

As a result, legislation tends to favor the interests of the organized: of businessmen, not consumers, even though the latter are a vast majority; of landlords, not tenants; doctors, not patients. . . . While the American political structure often satisfies the majority, it also creates outvoted minorities who can be tyrannized and repressed by majority rule, such as the poor and the black, students, migrant workers and many others.

—Herbert J. Gans, "We Won't End the Urban Crisis until We End Majority Rule," the *New York Times Magazine,* August 3, 1969

Much later in his career, however, Clifford encountered personal legal difficulties.[36]

## Public Interest Groups

Corporate lawyers and lobbyists have sometimes faced a new kind of opponent in recent years. Since the 1960s, public interest groups and public interest lawyers have also waged successful battles to influence public policy.

© Dennis Brack/IPN/Aurora Photos

Ralph Nader

© 2004 AP/Wide World Photos

## Washington Interest Groups: The Top 10

*Fortune* magazine ranks groups and associations that have the most power and political clout in Washington, based on a survey that returned responses by almost 400 people, including members of Congress, their senior staffs, lobbyists, and White House officials. Here are the top 10 on *Fortune*'s list:

1. National Rifle Association of America
2. AARP
3. National Federation of Independent Business
4. American Israel Public Affairs Committee
5. Association of Trial Lawyers
6. AFL-CIO
7. Chamber of Commerce of the United States of America
8. National Beer Wholesalers Association
9. National Association of Realtors
10. National Association of Manufacturers

—*Fortune,* May 28, 2001

John Rother, policy director of AARP, the nation's largest lobbying group

In the fields of the environment, consumer protection, health, minority rights, campaign finance reform, and many other areas, these public interest groups have brought class action and other lawsuits, lobbied Congress, and through the powerful weapon of publicity, added new issues to the government agenda.

One such public interest group is Common Cause, a national citizens' lobby with almost 300,000 members. Common Cause received major credit for passage of the election reform laws of the 1970s. But the laws proved ineffective, and Common Cause continued to do battle for campaign finance reform, including the major reform legislation enacted by Congress in 2002.

The best-known public interest lobbyist, Ralph Nader, heads a network of lawyers, lobbyists, and political analysts working in more than 20 organizations. Among the Nader-affiliated public interest groups are Public Citizen, an umbrella organization that includes Congress Watch, which concentrates on consumer affairs, the environment, transportation, congressional reform, and other legislation. Other Nader groups monitor nuclear power, medical care and food and drug safety, and auto safety. The Public Interest Research Groups (PIRGs) enlist students and other citizens in a variety of public interest and consumer projects. And the Freedom of Information Clearinghouse seeks to obtain government records under the Freedom of Information Act.

In addition to lobbying and working for consumers, the Nader organizations have produced a number of studies and books, including reports on land use, air pollution, corporate power, and many other subjects. Nader's activities are financed by foundations, income from

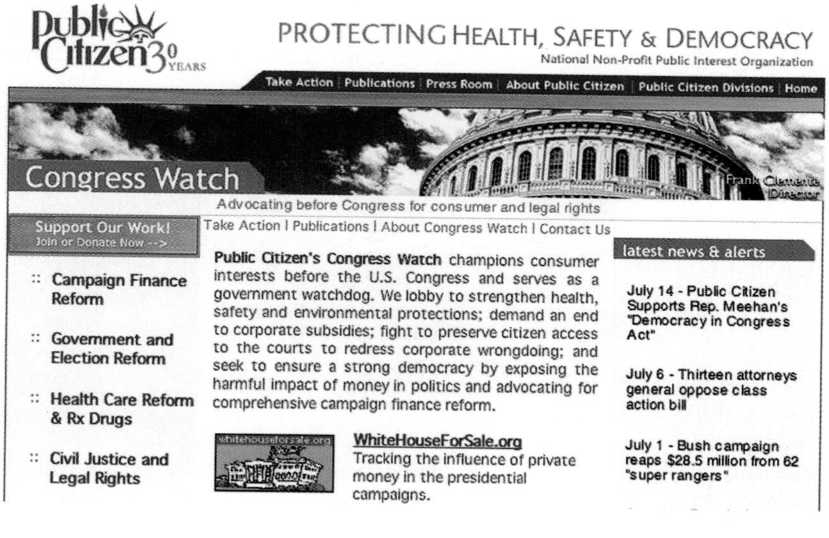




Web page of Congress Watch, part of Ralph Nader's Public Citizen

## Main Street Has Lobbyists, Too

If you are employed, active in community groups or just a functioning member of society, then you probably have at least a handful of lobbyists toiling on your behalf. . . .

Many of us became lobbyists unwittingly. For years we've been giving money to organizations that few would think of as pressure groups.

If you receive *Consumer Reports* magazine, for example, you are contributing money to Consumer's Union, which lobbies on banking, insurance and product safety laws.

Is your child farming with the National 4H Council? The council lobbies Congress and the Agriculture Department for additional dollars.

Do you have a daughter in the Girl Scouts, or have you bought any Girl Scout cookies lately? If so, you're subsidizing a group that has been fighting against taxing charitable contributions for years. . . . The YMCA has a lobbying group in Washington for its 14 million members as well. . . .

"When people think of lobbyists, they think of the back room cigar-chomper of 30 years ago," said Bob Smucker, vice president of Independent Sector, an umbrella group for public-interest groups. "The typical person giving to the American Cancer Society doesn't think he's giving to a lobbying group. But that's lobbying, too."

—*Washington Post,* July 10, 1995

© Vincent Dewitt/Stock, Boston/PictureQuest

The Girl Scouts lobby, too.

the sale of books, membership dues, contributions from the public, and Nader's own funds, earned in lecturing and writing.

In 2000, Nader ran as a presidential candidate on the Green Party ticket. Many Democrats contended that he siphoned enough votes in Florida and other key states to cost Al Gore the election. Mainstream Democrats were furious at Nader in 2004 when he announced he would run again, and did, this time as an independent.

After four decades as the nation's best-known public interest lobbyist, Nader and his organization are somewhat less powerful today, but if his political ambitions caused great controversy and criticism, it is also true that his record of accomplishment as an interest group leader and consumer advocate remains unchallenged.

### Single-Issue Groups

In recent years, single-issue interest groups have become significant actors in the political process. These groups concentrate on lobbying for or against a particular issue, often with devastating effect. The National Right to Life Committee and the National Rifle Association are examples of single-issue lobbies that have campaigned for such specific issues as ending legalized abortions and blocking gun control legislation. Beyond lobbying on the issues, such groups may also influence election results.

Sometimes, however, public opinion counters even the most effective single-issue lobbying groups. Early in 2000, President Clinton pushed hard for trigger locks to prevent children from firing guns, and for closing

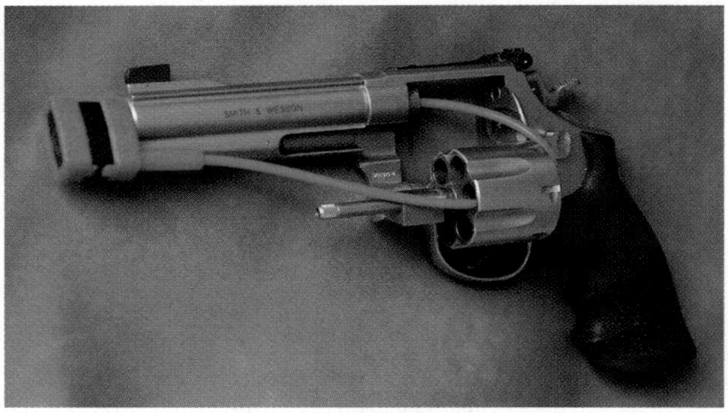

© AP/Wide World Photos

Smith & Wesson agreed to equip its guns with trigger locks. This revolver has a cable-type lock.

## "Shorter Than Their Shotguns": The NRA Starts Them Young

© Reuters New Media, Inc./Corbis

Thirty-one hunters in camouflage pants and orange vests gathered just after dawn on a recent Saturday morning at a state preserve . . . sipping from steaming cups, munching doughnuts and talking about barrel gauges and bird dogs.

It was a quintessential fall scene, except that the cups contained cocoa, not coffee, and these hunters were boys and girls, many just under 10 years old and some shorter than their shotguns. . . .

It was Take a Kid Pheasant Hunting Day, an event run since 1996 by the New Jersey Division of Fish, Game and Wildlife and partly paid for by the National Rifle Association Foundation, an arm of the gun lobby.

Shooting programs for children are nothing new; the N.R.A. and private clubs have had them for generations. . . . But the New Jersey pheasant shoot was an example of a newer and growing phenomenon: public wildlife agencies and the gun lobbies working hand in hand to promote hunting among children. . . .

New Jersey game officials say they are happy to accept the money.

—*New York Times,* November 17, 1999

the loophole that allowed sales of firearms at gun shows without requiring a background check of the purchaser. In a television commercial, Charlton Heston, the movie actor who was then president of the NRA, suggested Clinton was a liar for saying the organization opposed legislation to make Americans safer; and a high official of the NRA even asserted that the president did not mind "a certain level of killing to further his political agenda" because it might help the White House to gain public support for gun control.[37]

But the NRA's public relations barrage proved to be ill-timed. Less than a year earlier, a dozen students and a teacher had been shot to death at Columbine High School in Littleton, Colorado. The public was shocked by the killings—and in mid-March, Smith & Wesson, the nation's largest handgun manufacturer, agreed to equip its guns with trigger locks and hidden serial numbers, and to allow its dealers to take part only in gun shows where background checks were required for sales. True, Smith & Wesson acted in exchange for ending some lawsuits that had threatened to put it out of business, but the gunmaker's decision gave the appearance of bowing to public opinion and was immediately assailed by the NRA as a "sellout" and a "surrender."[38]

### Political Action Committees

Often, single-issue lobbies work through **political action committees,** or **PACs** (pronounced "packs"), which are sometimes independent organizations but are more often the political arms of corporations, labor unions, or interest groups established to contribute to candidates or to work for general political goals. (See Tables 7-1 and 7-2.)

WHAT DO I DO? THIS CONGRESSMAN SAYS HE ALREADY SOLD HIS SOUL TO A POLITICAL ACTION COMMITTEE.


Reprinted by special permission of United Feature Syndicate

## TABLE 7-1

### PACs: The Top 10

*These 10 political action committees gave the most to candidates in the 2004 congressional campaigns.*

| Political Action Committee | Amount Contributed (in millions) |
|---|---|
| National Association of Realtors Political Action Committee | $3.77 |
| Dealers Election Action Committee of the National Automobile Dealers Association (NADA) | $2.58 |
| International Brotherhood of Electrical Workers Committee on Political Education | $2.30 |
| National Beer Wholesalers Association Political Action Committee | $2.28 |
| Laborers' Political League–Laborers' International Union of NA | $2.24 |
| Build Political Action Committee of the National Association of Home Builders | $2.22 |
| Association of Trial Lawyers of America Political Action Committee | $2.17 |
| United Parcel Service Inc. Political Action Committee | $2.13 |
| American Medical Association Political Action Committee | $2.07 |
| UAW-V-CAP (United Automobile Workers Voluntary Community Action Program) | $2.06 |

SOURCE: Data provided by the Federal Election Commission, December 2004.

## TABLE 7-2

### PACs: The Top 10 Corporate PACs

*These 10 political action committees, created by various corporations, gave the most to candidates in the 2004 congressional campaigns.*

| Political Action Committee | Amount Contributed (in thousands) |
|---|---|
| United Parcel Service Inc. Political Action Committee | $2,139 |
| SBC Communications Inc. Employee Federal Political Action Committee (SBC EMPAC) | $1,787 |
| Wal-Mart Stores Inc. PAC for Responsible Government | $1,655 |
| Federal Express Political Action Committee | $1,475 |
| Employees of Northrop Grumman Corporation PAC | $1,179 |
| Lockheed Martin Employees' Political Action Committee | $1,156 |
| AFLAC Incorporated Political Action Committee (AFLACPAC) | $1,142 |
| Union Pacific Corporation Fund for Effective Government | $1,140 |
| Bank of America Corporation State and Federal Political Action Committee | $1,028 |
| General Electric Company Political Action Committee | $1,015 |

SOURCE: Data provided by the Federal Election Commission, through December 2004.

Several factors account for the growth of PACs. The Federal Election Campaign Act of 1974 permitted unions and corporations to establish political committees that could contribute up to $5,000 to each candidate in a primary or general election. The law was immediately challenged by Senator James Buckley of New York. In 1976, in the case of *Buckley* v. *Valeo,* the Supreme Court upheld many of the law's provisions. But the Court ruled unconstitutional a provision of the law that had placed limits on **independent expenditures,** funds spent for or against a candidate by committees not formally connected to the candidate's campaign.[39]

The Supreme Court's decision—and a 1975 ruling of the Federal Election Commission allowing the Sun Oil Company to set up a PAC—opened the way for vastly increased expenditures by PACs in political campaigns. These may range from outlays for bumper stickers and buttons to television spots endorsing a candidate. Even though direct contributions by a PAC to a federal candidate are still limited to $5,000 in each election, the number of political action committees is so large that PAC contributions totaled $289 million in the 2004 congressional campaigns.[40]

Supreme Court decisions also have encouraged corporate political activity. In 1978 the Court overturned a Massachusetts law that prohibited corporations from

## Making a Difference

### A WATCHDOG IN THE CORRIDORS OF POWER

Charles Lewis was asleep in a hotel room when the telephone rang at 8:15 a.m. If you're going to be awakened by a call that early when you're on vacation in Southern California, it ought to be good.

And it was: He had been granted $275,000 by the John D. and Catherine T. MacArthur Foundation as one of 29 MacArthur fellows.

Lewis runs a nonprofit, nonpartisan research organization that began as little more than a post office box in May 1990 but now occupies 4,400 square feet in downtown Washington, D.C. With a full-time staff of 24 and a $2 million annual budget, the center has carved out a prominent niche in Washington's watchdog subculture.

Lewis, soft-spoken and boyish, hardly looks the part of scourge of the lobbying world. A Delaware native, he did some part-time work for the home-state papers, then came to Washington to get a master's degree from the Johns Hopkins University School of Advanced International Studies.

Lewis came up with the idea for the Center for Public Integrity in 1989, during a long, ruminative pool game with Alejandro Benes, now the center's managing director. "I was basically frustrated," says Lewis, who was then a producer at *60 Minutes*, and who resembles the mild-mannered reporter Clark Kent. "I felt that the press had arrived on the scene late in a spate of scandals—Iran-contra, the savings-and-loan scandal. What if we were unfettered by time and space? What if you had your own journalistic utopia?"

The center's diverse portfolio has included investigations into airline safety, the Forest Service, and the chemical industry. Its first report, in 1990, disclosed that nearly half of White House trade officials since 1974 had registered—or their firms had registered—as representatives of foreign governments and corporations.

The center's 1996 book, *The Buying of the President*, was the first detailed history of the financial support behind the major presidential contenders. And in August 1996, a study by Lewis's group disclosed the use of White House sleep-overs as a perk for fat-cat donors. Much later, after the Democratic fund-raising scandal broke, the mainstream news media forced the White House to acknowledge that the Lincoln Bedroom was one of the top rewards for big contributors.

Perhaps the greatest thing about winning a MacArthur fellowship is that the award carries no restrictions or instructions. It's like getting lucky in Las Vegas.

"Everyone has given me their theory on what I should do with it," Lewis says.

Like take a sabbatical. Or go off somewhere and write fiction.

"But I'll probably do nothing dramatic or wild," he adds. "I'll probably pay off my bills and my child's tuition."

—Adapted from the *Washington Post*, June 2, 1998; the *New Yorker*, March 25, 1996; and the *National Journal*, March 13, 1993

spending money to influence the outcome of public referenda. The Court ruled that the state law violated the corporation's First Amendment rights.[41] In 1980 the Supreme Court ruled that a public utility could include statements on controversial political issues along with its monthly bills.[42]

A Harvard University study prepared for Congress identified other reasons for the growth of PACs. The study gave as one reason the changes in the federal election laws that have made it more difficult to raise campaign funds from individuals. And the study suggested that the decline in the power of political parties has forced candidates to turn to interest groups for money.[43]

Undoubtedly, the publicity given to PACs in recent years has encouraged the formation of even more such committees. Changes in the structure of Congress also may have contributed. In the 1970s Congress reduced the power of its committee chairs; as a result, power became fragmented among hundreds of subcommittees, each of which is cultivated by various lobbyists.

PACs often give contributions to committee chairpeople with specific legislative outcomes in mind. Interest groups clearly try to put their money where it will have the most influence. For example, in 2004 PACs representing the banking industry gave members of the House Banking Committee just over $3.3 million.[44]

One analysis of political spending suggested that PAC contributions follow an "investment pattern" aimed at strengthening the group's long-term influence with members of Congress.[45] That pattern is reflected in the top-heavy support by PACs for incumbents. In 2004, for example, members of the Congress received 79 percent of all PAC contributions, compared with only 7 percent received by challengers.[46]

In 1974 there were 608 PACs. By 2004 there were more than 4,400.[47] Beyond question, the explosive growth and influence of political action committees, often tied to single-issue lobbying, is having a significant, controversial, and sometimes disturbing influence on politics and policy in America.

## Regulating Interest Groups

Public concern over lobbying abuses led Congress, beginning early in the 20th century, to try to impose legal controls on interest groups. Not until 1946, however, did Congress pass a general bill that attempted to control lobbying.

The Federal Regulation of Lobbying Act of 1946 required individuals and groups to register with the clerk of the House and the secretary of the Senate if they solicit or collect money or any other thing of value "to be used principally to aid . . . the passage or defeat of any legislation by the Congress of the United States." In 1954 the Supreme Court narrowed the scope of the act by ruling that it applied only to lobbyists who communicated directly with members of Congress and not to grass-roots lobbying aimed at the public.[48] Because of this decision and the loose wording of the statute, many interest groups simply did not register on the grounds that lobbying was not their "principal purpose." Moreover, although the law contained penalties, it had no enforcement provision. As a result, there were few prosecutions after its enactment in 1946.

Estimates of the number of lobbyists in Washington vary greatly. In 2006 Washington Representatives, a directory of lobbyists and consultants, listed 11,500 active, registered lobbyists. The clerk of the House of Representatives listed 21,500 lobbyists in its database.[49] Some reports estimate that as many as 60,000 to 80,000 lobbyists are active in Washington.[50]

*for more information about the General Accounting Office, see: http://www.gao.gov*

In sum, the Lobbying Act did not effectively regulate lobbying of Congress. And, of course, it did not apply at all to lobbying of the executive branch or the independent regulatory commissions. Another loophole in an earlier law, the Foreign Agents Registration Act, exempted lawyers representing foreign clients. In the years that followed 1946, Congress periodically considered bills to strengthen the regulation of lobbying. Finally, in 1995, a new bill to regulate lobbyists passed both houses of Congress and was signed by President Clinton.

Under the law, lobbyists must register with the clerk of the House and the secretary of the Senate and report who their clients are, what agencies or branches of Congress were lobbied, and how much they were paid. In an effort to tighten the rules, the law defines lobbyists as people who spend at least 20 percent of their time in that activity. And under the law, most lawyers representing foreign clients are no longer exempt. Moreover, the law restricts gifts to lawmakers. Under the statute and rules adopted by Congress, senators, representatives, and employees of the legislative branch can accept only gifts worth less than $50, except for home-state products and foodstuffs, and minor items such as T-shirts. Yet despite the improvements and the increased disclosure requirements, there was a major loophole in the law: It did not apply to grass-roots lobbying, efforts by interest groups to generate phone calls, faxes, e-mails, and letters in support of, or in opposition to, a bill or program.

In the wake of the Abramoff scandal, Congress came under increased public pressure to pass ethics reform legislation, both to reduce the influence of lobbyists on lawmakers and to eliminate earmarks, funds set aside in appropriations bills or tax legislation for specific projects, locations, or institutions, often at the urging of lobbyists.

## Interest Groups and the Policy Process

The view persists in American politics that interest groups are undemocratic and that they work for narrow goals against the general welfare. Some do. But an interest group like Common Cause represents no narrow economic interest; it works on a wide spectrum of issues to promote its conception of "the public welfare." So have the organizations formed by consumer advocate Ralph Nader. It may be more realistic to view interest groups simply as one part of the total political process. Citizens have every right under the Constitution to organize to influence their government. Interest groups compete for the government's attention and action—but so do individual voters, political parties, and the press.

On many major issues, there are likely to be interest groups arrayed on opposite sides. Those who accept democratic pluralism and the politics of interest groups believe that out of these conflicting pressures some degree of balance may be achieved, at least much of the time.

Interest groups perform certain functions in the American political system that cannot be performed as well through the conventional structures of government, which are based largely on geographic representation.

The kind of representation that interest groups provide supplements the representation provided by Congress. Interest groups may also permit the resolution of intergroup conflicts. In collective bargaining, for example, differences between two powerful interest groups—management and labor—are resolved. Interest groups also perform a watchdog function; they can sound the alarm when new government policies threaten to injure the interests of their members. Finally, interest groups perform the function of initiating ideas; that is, they generate new ideas that may become government programs. So important are these functions, Lester Milbrath concluded, that "if we had no lobby groups and lobbyists we would probably have to invent them."[51]

Some very serious criticisms can be leveled at interest groups, however. Perhaps the most comprehensive criticism of interest-group politics was formulated by Theodore J. Lowi.[52] Lowi questions the assumption of many scholars and political leaders that the interest-group process in a pluralist society provides a desirable, or satisfactory, way for the government system to work. What are the effects of interest groups on public policy formation? Lowi argues that there is no assurance that the "pulling and hauling among competing interests" will result in policy decisions that are adequate to meet the social and political problems facing the United States. In Lowi's view, interest-group pluralism has not resulted in "strong, positive government" but in "impotent gov-

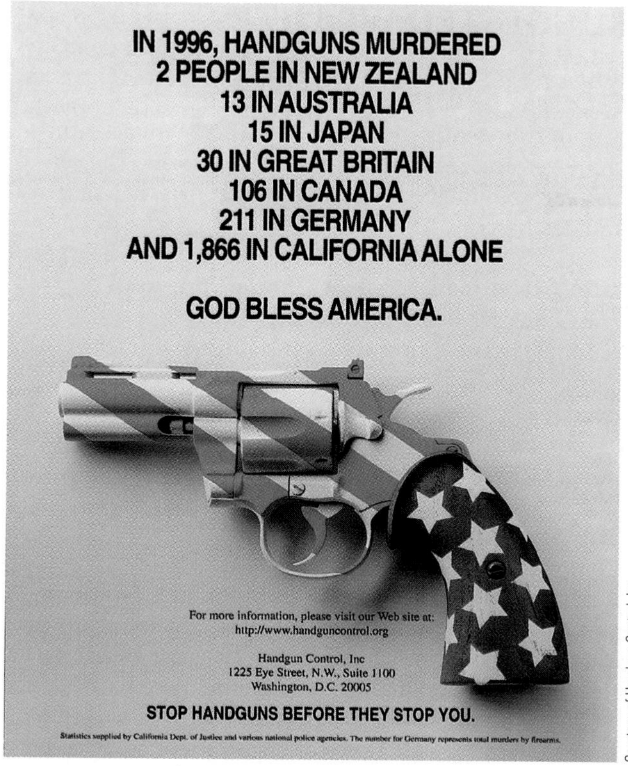

IN 1996, HANDGUNS MURDERED
2 PEOPLE IN NEW ZEALAND
13 IN AUSTRALIA
15 IN JAPAN
30 IN GREAT BRITAIN
106 IN CANADA
211 IN GERMANY
AND 1,866 IN CALIFORNIA ALONE
GOD BLESS AMERICA.
For more information, please visit our Web site at:
http://www.handguncontrol.org
Handgun Control, Inc
1225 Eye Street, N.W., Suite 1100
Washington, D.C. 20005
STOP HANDGUNS BEFORE THEY STOP YOU.
Statistics supplied by California Dept. of Justice and various national police agencies. The number for Germany represents total murders by firearms.


Courtesy of Handgun Control, Inc.

ernment" that can "neither plan nor achieve justice."[53] For example, if business groups succeed in weakening environmental legislation, the interests of the larger public may be diminished.

As we have seen, most Americans do not belong to interest groups. Those who do belong tend to come from the better-educated, middle- or upper-class backgrounds that produce citizens with a high degree of political motivation. "The flaw in the pluralist heaven," E. E. Schattschneider observed, "is that the heavenly chorus sings with a strong upper-class accent. Probably about 90 percent of the people cannot get into the pressure system."[54]

Some of the voter disenchantment with government and political candidates that was visible in recent presidential election years might be attributed, at least in part, to the feeling of many ordinary voters that they had been left out of the political system. And disadvantaged groups—the poor, inner-city blacks, Hispanics, migrant workers—often lack the money to organize to advance their interests. Interest-group politics, in other words, is biased against minorities and in favor of business organizations and other affluent groups.

The ordinary consumer is not as well represented in interest-group politics as are manufacturers. Americans who drive to work in a costly but possibly unsafe car, on tires that may be recalled, who swim at a beach polluted by oil or chemical effluents, who inhale pesticides and smog, and who eat food that might be contaminated and make them ill may be forgiven if they wonder what interest group represents them.

There are hundreds of business groups represented in Washington, but a much smaller number of consumer organizations. One reason is that the interest of consumers is so general that it does not lend itself to organized expression as readily as the narrower interest of a special group, such as physicians or truckers. And as Mancur Olson, Jr., pointed out, unless the number of individuals in a group is very small, or unless there is coercion or some special incentive to make individuals work together in their mutual interest, many people will not organize or act to achieve common or group interests through the political process.[55]

Even organized, active interest groups do not represent all they claim to represent. The leaders of an interest group tend to formulate policy positions for the group as a whole. Consequently, the public stance of an interest group often represents the views of an oligarchy rather than the views of the rank and file. The American Medical Association, for example, is more conservative than are many of its 250,000 members. Moreover, more than half of the nation's 690,000 physicians do not even belong to the AMA.

Despite all their flaws, interest groups do supplement formal channels of representation and allow for the expression of public opinion in an organized manner. But if American democracy is to become more responsive to the needs of its people, the nation's legislators must find new ways to heed the voice of ordinary citizens—consumers, the poor, minorities, and the powerless—groups that are much less likely to have a steel-and-glass office building and a team of registered lobbyists to speak for them in Washington.

## CHAPTER HIGHLIGHTS

- Interest groups are private groups that attempt to influence the government to respond to the shared attitudes of their members.
- Public opinion, as noted in Chapter 6, is the expression of attitudes on public questions. When people organize to express attitudes held in common and to influence the government to respond to those attitudes, they become members of interest groups.
- One of the most powerful techniques of interest groups is lobbying—communication with legislators or other government officials to try to influence their decisions.
- One of the ways in which interest groups try to influence public opinion in order to influence government is through mass-publicity campaigns. Using television, magazine, and newspaper and Internet advertis-

ing, as well as e-mails and direct mailings to the general public and specialized audiences, interest groups seek to create a favorable climate for their goals.

- In recent years, single-issue interest groups have become significant actors in the political process. These groups concentrate on lobbying for or against a particular issue.
- Often, single-issue lobbies work through political action committees (PACs), which are sometimes independent organizations but are more often the political arms of corporations, labor unions, or interest groups established to contribute to candidates or to work for general political goals.
- The Federal Regulation of Lobbying Act of 1946 required individuals and groups to register with the clerk of the House and the secretary of the Senate if they solicit or collect money or any other thing of value "to be used principally to aid . . . the passage or defeat of any legislation by the Congress of the United States." The law did not prove effective.
- In 1954 the Supreme Court narrowed the scope of the act by ruling that it applied only to lobbyists who communicated directly with members of Congress and not to grass-roots lobbying aimed at the public.
- In 1995, a new bill to regulate lobbyists passed both houses of Congress and was signed by President Clinton. Under the law, lobbyists must register with the clerk of the House and the secretary of the Senate. In an effort to tighten the rules, the new law defines lobbyists as people who spend at least 20 percent of their time in that activity.
- Interest groups perform certain functions in the American political system that cannot be performed as well through the conventional structures of government, which are based largely on geographic representation.
- Most Americans do not belong to interest groups. Those who do tend to come from the better-educated, middle- or upper-class backgrounds that produce citizens with a high degree of political motivation.
- Some of the voter disenchantment with government and political candidates that was visible in recent presidential election years might be attributed, at least in part, to the feeling of many ordinary voters that they had been left out of the political system. And disadvantaged groups often lack the money to organize to advance their interests. Interest-group politics, in other words, is biased against minorities and in favor of business organizations and other affluent groups.

## KEY TERMS

pluralism, p. 200
interest groups, p. 201
lobbying, p. 203
political action committees (PACs), p. 213
independent expenditures, p. 214

## SUGGESTED WEBSITES

**http://www.publicintegrity.org**
*The Center for Public Integrity*
A nonprofit center dedicated to government accountability, ethics, and campaign finance reform. The center's research includes investigative reports, newsletters, and databases.

**http://www.opensecrets.org/home/index.asp**
*The Center for Responsive Politics*
A nonpartisan, nonprofit organization that tracks money in politics and its effects on public policy and elections. Contains extensive data about lobbyists, soft money contributions, PACs, presidential and congressional races, and political donors.

**http://www.commoncause.org**
*Common Cause*
A nonprofit, nonpartisan organization that promotes government accountability. Provides a database of soft money contributions through the 2002 congressional elections to the Republican and Democratic Parties by donor name, donor location, or industry, as well as news about a wide range of government agencies and topics. After 2002, Congress banned soft money contributions.

**http://www.fec.gov**
*Federal Election Commission*
The branch of the federal government that oversees federal elections. Provides a citizens' guide to elections, including current rules for upcoming campaigns, how to support a candidate, and FEC publications.

**http://www.publiccitizen.org**
*Public Citizen*
Founded by Ralph Nader in 1971, Public Citizen calls itself "the consumer's eyes and ears in Washington." Its searchable database includes information about auto safety, congressional voting, and First Amendment issues, as well as the organization's publications.

## SUGGESTED READING

Baumgartner, Frank, and Leech, Beth L. *Basic Interests: The Importance of Groups in Politics and Political Science** (Princeton University Press, 1998). A scholarly survey of the important role that interest groups have played in the American political process, and as the subjects of research by political scientists.

Berry, Jeffrey M. *The Interest Group Society,* 3rd edition* (HarperCollins, 1997). An examination of the role of "factions" in American politics and society. Berry argues that interest groups are essential to democracy, and can play a positive role in American politics.

Berry, Jeffrey M. *Lobbying for the People* (Princeton University Press, 1977). A useful and readable analysis of the political and organizational behavior of public interest groups. Using case studies, Berry profiles in detail the activities and strategies of two public interest lobbying organizations.

Cigler, Allan J., and Loomis, Burdett A., eds. *Interest Group Politics,* 6th edition* (CQ Press, 2002). A wide-ranging and informative set of essays on interest-group behavior in the American political system.

Costain, Anne M., and McFarland, Andrew S., eds. *Social Movements and American Political Institutions** (Rowman & Littlefield, 1998). A useful collection of essays on a number of grass-roots movements in the United States, including Protestant fundamentalists, and coalitions advocating issues for women, protection of the environment, and civil rights.

Dahl, Robert A. *Who Governs?** (Yale University Press, 1961). An influential and detailed exploration of the nature of political power, based on a study of political decision making in New Haven, Connecticut. Dahl maintains that there is a pluralism of power—rather than a single "power elite"—in the United States.

Domhoff, G. William. *Who Rules America? Power and Politics,* 4th edition* (McGraw Hill, 2002). The author contends that the U.S. is dominated by an interlocking corporate community. This power elite, he argues, reaps great economic benefits, occupies key government positions, and wins most policy debates. Domhoff explicitly rejects the pluralist theory of power.

Green, John C., Rozell, Mark J., and Wilcox, Clyde, eds. *The Christian Right in American Politics: Marching to the Millennium** (Georgetown University Press, 2003). A study of the Christian Right in 13 states. The authors find that this movement has been most successful in elections in the South and least successful in the Pacific Coast states and New England. In general, the movement's electoral success has not been translated into the achievement of its policy goals.

Heinz, John P., Laumann, Edward O., Nelson, Robert L., and Salisbury, Robert H. *The Hollow Core: Private Interests in National Policymaking** (Harvard University Press, 1993). A comprehensive and important survey of interest-group activities in the nation's capital. The study draws upon a large number of personal interviews of both interest-group representatives and the government officials whom they attempt to influence.

Lowery, David, and Brasher, Holly. *Organized Interests and American Government** (McGraw Hill, 2004). A rigorous analysis of the behavior of interest groups. The authors discuss three broad models of interest group behaviors that have been developed by scholars.

Lowi, Theodore J. *The End of Liberalism: The Second Republic of the United States,* 2nd edition* (Norton, 1979). A stimulating analysis of the theory and practice of interest-group politics in the United States. Lowi is strongly critical of the consequences of the interest-group bargaining process as it has developed since the New Deal.

Mills, C. Wright. *The Power Elite** (Oxford University Press, 1956). One of the best-known statements of the view that there is a unified "power elite" in the United States. In Mills's view, wealth, prestige, and power in America are concentrated in the hands of a hierarchy of corporate, government, and military leaders.

Nownes, Anthony J. *Pressure and Power: Organized Interests in American Politics** (Houghton Mifflin, 2001) A useful description of interest groups and their role in politics, as well as an introduction to the relevant academic literature.

Olson, Mancur, Jr. *The Logic of Collective Action: Public Goods and the Theory of Groups,* revised edition (Harvard University Press, 1971). An important analysis of the role of groups in the American political process. Based on an application of economic analysis to the relationships between individual self-interest and group membership and activity. Examines the consequences these relationships have for politics.

Putnam, Robert. *Bowling Alone: The Collapse and Revival of American Community* (Simon & Schuster, 2000). An influential analysis of community in the United States. The author amasses a large body of research to support his contention that Americans are increasingly disconnected from social institutions, and that this isolation threatens to erode American civil society.

Truman, David B. *The Governmental Process,* 2nd edition* (Knopf, 1971). An influential study of interest groups in the United States. Develops and modifies a general theory of groups and applies it to American politics.

Walker, Jack L. *Mobilizing Interest Groups in America** (University of Michigan Press, 1991). A thoughtful and valuable analysis of the role of interest groups in the American political system.

*Available in paperback edition.

# Chapter 8

# The Media and Politics

IN THE SPRING OF 2004 investigative reporter Seymour M. Hersh and CBS's *60 Minutes II* broke the story of prisoner abuse in Iraq by American soldiers.

Hersh's article in *The New Yorker,* citing a secret Army report about the abuse, combined with the photographs aired on CBS, touched off a political storm. Soon, shocking photos of Iraqi prisoners were all over television, on the Internet, and on the front pages of newspapers in the United States and around the globe. The photos showed naked Iraqi prisoners cowering before snarling attack dogs, piled in a heap, handcuffed to prison bars, and subjected to sexual humiliation. One unforgettable image depicted Private Lynndie England holding a leash around the neck of a naked man on the floor.

Several of the U.S. soldiers involved were charged with various crimes, including dereliction of duty and maltreatment of detainees. Some of the defendants claimed they had been ordered by military intelligence to "soften up" the prisoners for interrogation, apparently in the belief that they might yield more information.

Congress launched an investigation of how far up the chain of command knowledge of, and responsibility for, the abuses went. Was it the work of a few sadistic, out-of-control soldiers, or a policy dictated or condoned by higher-ups? As the scandal grew, President Bush's approval rating fell to a new low of 41 percent.[1] There were calls for the resignation of Donald H. Rumsfeld, the secretary of defense.

For the Bush administration, the prisoner abuse scandal could hardly have come at a worse time, in the midst of a presidential election year. The public was growing restless over the continued violence against American forces in Iraq, with more soldiers killed almost daily. Contractors and other foreigners were targeted, kidnapped, and killed. Insurgents, led by a Shiite cleric, were fighting U.S. troops in several cities.

Inevitably, the scandal became caught up in the presidential campaign. As commander in chief, Bush was placed on the defensive.

A single news story in a magazine and on one television program had mushroomed into an enormous, worldwide scandal, damaging America's reputation and its claims of moral leadership and dedication to freedom and justice. Most of the American troops in Iraq were not torturing prisoners, but risking their lives to carry out their duties; some were building schools and providing medical care to Iraqis.

But the story of the abuse of prisoners, at the Abu Ghraib prison and other locations, was a shattering, unpleasant truth, uncovered by the news media in its indispensable role as a watchdog over government. The story was a dramatic example of the power of the press, of television, and of the intersection between media and politics. Because the prisoner abuse story was highly visual, the photographs and television images had an enormous impact on people everywhere.

As the story demonstrated once again, technology, especially television and the Internet, has changed the face of America and its politics. The framers of the Constitution and the Bill of Rights could not have conceived of instant mass communication via TV, let alone the development of the Internet. They could not have predicted a computer network linking the entire world.

Courtesy of The New Yorker/AFP/Getty Images

The press broke the story of the abuse of Iraqi prisoners by the U.S. military at the Abu Ghraib prison in Iraq.

But if the framers could not foresee the technological changes, they understood the importance of a free press in a democratic system.

As discussed in Chapter 4, however, freedom of the press and freedom of expression are not absolute. Under the Constitution, the Supreme Court has balanced those basic rights against competing needs of society. For example, the press can be sued for libel or for invasion of privacy, or it can be prosecuted if it publishes material deemed "obscene" by the courts. And television and radio are subject to regulation by the federal government.

Broadly defined, "the media" include TV, the Internet, newspapers, magazines, radio, wire services, books, and newsletters and other published material. Often, people use the term "the press" interchangeably with "the media" or "the news media." Sometimes, however, they may use the term "the press" more narrowly to refer only to newspapers. In our discussion, we use "the press" in its broadest meaning, to include both print and electronic media.

Key Question In this chapter, we will explore a key question: ***How do the press, the government, and politics interact in the American political system today?*** Other issues to consider flow from this basic question. For example: Why does the First Amendment of the Constitution protect a free press in America? Has the press grown too powerful? Has television distorted the political process, allowing the candidates with the most money to buy more commercials and win elections? Can government manipulate and manage the news to mislead the voters? Is the press biased? Can it be believed? Is tabloid journalism driving out responsible reporting? Many of these questions and related issues will be explored.

## A Protected Institution

The First Amendment to the Constitution protects the freedom of the press. It does so because the supporters of the Bill of Rights understood that the press must be free to report about the activities of the government, and, when necessary, to criticize those in power. By contrast, totalitarian systems are usually characterized by censorship and control of the press by the government.

The press plays a vital role in a democracy because it is the principal means by which the people learn about the actions and policies of the government. A democracy rests on the consent of the governed—but in order to give their consent in any meaningful way, the governed must be informed. And a free press remains the major source of information about government and politics. For example, in developing political opinions or in choosing among candidates, most voters rely on the news media—television, newspapers, the Internet, radio, magazines—for their information.

Perhaps no one has explained the special and constitutionally protected role of the press more eloquently than Supreme Court Justice Hugo Black in his opinion on the majority side in the famous Pentagon Papers case. He wrote: "The press was protected so that it could bare the secrets of government and inform the people."[2]

The press, in sum, provides a crucial link between the people and the government. It is the essential source of information that helps citizens to form opinions about government and politics and to decide how to cast their votes in elections.

As noted in Chapter 2, freedom of the press was not included in the original draft of the Constitution. But in order to win the struggle for ratification, the framers of the Constitution promised to add a Bill of Rights providing for freedom of the press, speech, religion, and assembly.

In a real sense, then, a free press, free expression, and freedom of thought were the price of nationhood. Having rid themselves of British rule, the new Americans insisted that these hard-won freedoms be spelled out in the basic law of the land, the Constitution. And they were.

William Randolph Hearst

Culver Pictures, Inc.

## The Development of the American Press

Until the 20th century, of course, the press consisted only of print media—newspapers, magazines, books, and pamphlets. The press moguls of the 19th and early 20th centuries—men like William Randolph Hearst, owner of the *New York Journal*, and Joseph Pulitzer, publisher of the *New York World*—had great influence on American society and on the government. Hearst beat the drums for a militant foreign policy and helped to whip up public opinion in favor of the Spanish-American War of 1898. Hearst sent the celebrated artist Frederic Remington to Cuba. Remington complained that there was no fighting and wanted to come home. Hearst cabled back: "You furnish the pictures and I'll furnish the war."[3] The *Journal* and the *World* outdid each other in reporting alleged Spanish atrocities in Cuba and demanding that the United States intervene. Their sensational reporting became known as "yellow journalism."*

,000 REWARD.—WHO DESTROYED THE MAINE?—$50,000 REW

NEW YORK JOURNAL

AND ADVERTISER.

DESTRUCTION OF THE WAR SHIP MAINE WAS THE WORK OF AN ENEM

$50,000!

$50,000 REWARD! For the Detection of the Perpetrator of the Maine Outrage!

Assistant Secretary Roosevelt Convinced the Explosion of the War Ship Was Not an Accident.

The Journal Offers $50,000 Reward for the Conviction of the Criminals Who Sent 258 American Sailors to Their Death. Naval Officers Unanimous That the Ship Was Destroyed on Purpose.

$50,000!

$50,000 REWARD! For the Detection of the Perpetrator of the Maine Outrage!

NAVAL OFFICERS THINK THE MAINE WAS DESTROYED BY A SPANISH MINE.

Hidden Mine or a Sunken Torpedo Believed to Have Been the Weapon Used Against the American Man-of-War---Officers and Men Tell Thrilling Stories of Being Blown Into the Air Amid a Mass of Shattered Steel and Exploding Shells---Survivors Brought to Key West Scout the Idea of Accident---Spanish Officials Protest Too Much---Our Cabinet Orders a Searching Inquiry---Journal Sends Divers to Havana to Report Upon the Condition of the Wreck. Was the Vessel Anchored Over a Mine?

Assistant Secretary of the Navy Theodore Roosevelt says he is convinced that the destruction of the Maine in Havana Harbor was not an accident.

The Journal offers a reward of $50,000 for exclusive evidence that will convict the person, persons or Government criminally responsible for the destruction of the American battleship and the death of 258 of its crew.

The suspicion that the Maine was deliberately blown up grows stronger every hour. Not a single fact to the contrary has been produced.

Captain Sigsbee, of the Maine, and Consul-General Lee both urge that public opinion be suspended until they have completed their investigation. ...ey are taking the course of tactful men who are convinced that there has been treachery.

Spanish Government officials are pressing forward all sorts of explanations of how it could have been an accident. The facts show that there was a ...port before the ship exploded, and that, had her magazine exploded, she would have sunk immediately.

Every naval expert in Washington says that if the Maine's magazine had exploded the whole vessel would have been blown to atoms.

The Granger Collection, New York

In the first decade of the 20th century, long before the modern term "investigative reporting" came into vogue, a group of writers, journalists, and critics known as **muckrakers** exposed corporate malfeasance and political corruption. They included Lincoln Steffens, who publicized municipal corruption; Ida Tarbell, who investigated the Standard Oil Company; and Upton Sinclair, whose novel *The Jungle* exposed unsanitary conditions in the meatpacking industry.

The 1920s brought radio into America's homes. For the first time, it allowed political leaders to speak directly to the voters. On March 12, 1933, President Franklin D. Roosevelt delivered the first of what became known as his "fireside chats" on radio, informing citizens that the banks—which had been closed to avoid a panic during the Depression—would reopen the next day.

In 1948, the Democratic National Convention at

*The phrase had its origin in the battle between the two papers over the rights to publish a popular comic strip known as "The Yellow Kid."

© Underwood & Underwood/Corbis

Franklin D. Roosevelt delivers a "fireside chat" in 1938.

Philadelphia that nominated Harry Truman for president was televised. Now, presidents could be seen as they spoke to their fellow Americans in their living rooms. Dwight D. Eisenhower allowed his presidential press conferences to be filmed, edited, and then released to the public. Then on January 25, 1961, John F. Kennedy held the first live, televised presidential news conference. Other presidents who followed him have done the same. Typically, presidents also use television to address the nation from the Oval Office in times of crisis.

By providing a direct visual link between political leaders and candidates and the voters, television changed the nature of American politics. Television has had an enormous impact, not only on the political process, but also on the shape and power of the media. With advertisers pouring millions into the TV networks to reach prime-time audiences, inevitably there were fewer advertising dollars invested in print journalism.

Although movies are not usually thought of as part of the news media, films are an important part of the nation's political culture and may sometimes have more influence than the press. Oliver Stone's movie *JFK* suggested that government complicity—and various dark conspiracies—were somehow behind the assassination of President Kennedy; although it did not pretend to be a factual documentary, it added fuel to the controversy. The film *A Civil Action* focused on corporate pollution. And *Erin Brockovich,* a huge box-office hit featuring Julia Roberts, dramatized the issue of groundwater contamination. In 2004, Michael Moore produced *Fahrenheit 9/11,* a controversial film that attacked and ridiculed President George W. Bush and drew large audiences in a presidential election year.

## The Internet

Just as television had altered the shape of American politics a half-century earlier, by the presidential elections of 2000 and 2004 the Internet had brought a dramatic new level of technological change to government and the political process. The White House and virtually every federal agency each had its own website, as did political candidates and parties.

The Internet had its origins in ARPANET, a computer network established in 1969 by the Defense Department to enable research scientists to communicate. In the early 1990s, Congress enacted legislation that expanded the government's computer network and opened it to commercial networks. In 1994, Netscape released its first browser (software to access the World Wide Web), and the following year, Microsoft released Internet Explorer, its own browser.

By 2004, about 204 million people (or 75 percent of the population with telephone lines) used the Internet in the United States, a number that had doubled in four

© UPI/Bettmann/Corbis

January 1961: President Kennedy in the first presidential press conference broadcast live on television

## Now Casting!: President of the United States

Television is at the root of much that ails politics today, Daniel Schorr, a veteran broadcaster, suggested in an interview published in 2002.

"Politicians have to play the game the way TV defines it"—a way that stresses imagery—and in the end, he said, "the country's the loser."

"The major part of a campaign is what you wear, what you look like," he said. "We're approaching the point where our candidates may as well come from central casting." Schorr said he believed that television's fundamental problems stem from being "a medium whose heart is really in Hollywood." In its scramble for ratings, he said, television has put conflict and entertainment, rather than substance, at the center of its news coverage, trivializing great issues in the process.

When he started in the business, Schorr said, he asked a producer what it took to be a success in TV. And the answer he got was, "If you can fake sincerity, you've got it made."

If Abraham Lincoln were to come on the scene today, Schorr added, "given his modesty and the fact he liked to speak in subdued tones . . . I would guess he would not get very far in politics. Most of our great early leaders wouldn't."

—Adapted from *AARP Bulletin*, "Is TV Turning Politics into a Game?" February 2002

years. Worldwide, 729.2 million people were connected to the Internet.[4]

As the Internet rapidly expanded, political information, census figures, poll data, the texts of speeches, legislation, Supreme Court decisions, and almost unlimited resources of all kinds became available at the click of a mouse button, part of a vast ocean of information that once could only be found in major libraries. Television networks, cable networks, and newspapers soon began posting breaking news on their websites, instantly accessible to anyone, anywhere in the world, with a computer or other electronic device linked to the Internet. News on the Internet was not limited to that posted by major networks and news organizations. Hundreds of Internet journalists and thousands of "bloggers" populated the Internet, as did a number of online magazines, of which *Salon* and *Slate* were the best known. To a great extent, the world had become a global electronic village.

"On the Internet, nobody knows you're a dog."

## Newspapers

A farmer in Nebraska and an attorney in Manhattan may both read newspapers, but the treatment of news about government and politics may be very different in the pages they read. The New York attorney probably reads the *New York Times,* which places heavy emphasis on national and international news gathered by its own correspondents. The Nebraskan may read a small-town daily that concentrates on crop reports, wheat prices, and local events and relies on the wire services for sketchy reports about national and world events.

There are a number of excellent newspapers in the United States. A partial list would include the *New York Times,* the *Washington Post,* the *Los Angeles Times,* the *Wall Street Journal,* the *Dallas Morning News,* the *Boston Globe,* the *Chicago Tribune,* the *Miami Herald,* and the *Baltimore Sun.* But for most Americans, who live outside the circulation area of such publications, the outstanding fact about their newspaper is often not its excellence but how limited is its coverage of national and world news.

***for more information about the newspapers listed above, see: http://www.nytimes.com; http://www.washingtonpost.com; http://www.latimes.com; www.wsj.com; http://www.dallasnews.com; http://www.boston.com/globe; http://www.chicagotribune.com; and http://www.baltimoresun.com***

The movement of Americans from the cities to the suburbs after the Second World War made it difficult for many newspapers, even prestigious ones in large cities, to hold on to their urban readers. The advent of CNN and cable television in the 1980s made further inroads on newspaper circulation. As a result of all these factors, the newspaper industry has been shrinking steadily.

In 1909 there were 2,600 dailies in the United States. By 1955 there were 1,785, by 1986 only 1,657, by 1994

The American Past

## MY LAI: A REPORTER UNCOVERS A MASSACRE

What happened at My Lai is now well known. C Company, First Battalion, Twentieth Infantry, Eleventh Brigade, America Division, entered the village of My Lai on March 16, 1968, and killed between ninety and 130 men, women, and children. Acting, the men said later, under orders from the platoon commander, Lieutenant William L. Calley, Jr., they gathered the villagers into groups and "wasted" them with automatic-weapons fire. Anyone who survived was then picked off. . . .

The army began a full-scale investigation on April 23, 1969, and in September, only days before he was due to be discharged from the army, Lieutenant Calley was charged with the murder of 109 "Oriental human beings." . . .

This fact was made public in a small item, of fewer than a hundred words, put out from Fort Benning, Georgia, by the Associated Press on September 6. The item did not say how many murders Calley had been charged with, and it gave no indication of the circumstances. It is not surprising, therefore, that not a single newspaper or broadcasting station called the AP to ask for more information. . . . That might have been the end of the matter had it not been for a free-lance reporter called Seymour Hersh.

Hersh, then aged thirty-two, had covered the Pentagon in 1966–67 for the Associated Press. . . . It took Hersh two days and twenty-five telephone calls to find out that the civilians numbered 109, and to sense that the story warranted a lot more effort and would require more money than he had. He telephoned Jim Boyd, of the Fund for Investigative Journalism, in Washington, and was promised $1,000. He then flew to Fort Benning and, after an amazing run-around, finally found Calley and on November 11 interviewed him at length. The problem now was where to publish the story. . . . Hersh turned to a little-known Washington agency, the Dispatch News Service, started only a few months earlier by his neighbor, David Obst, aged twenty-three. Obst telephoned some fifty newspapers, offering the story for $100 if it was used. Subsequently, thirty-six of the fifty—including *The Times* of London, the *San Francisco Chronicle,* the *Boston Globe,* and the *St. Louis Post-Dispatch*—ran the story. It was first printed on November 13. . . . Seymour Hersh won a Pulitzer Prize.

—Phillip Knightley, *The First Casualty*

© AP/ Wide World Photos

Pulitzer-prize winning journalist and author Seymour M. Hersh exposed the My Lai massacre.

only 1,538, by 1998 only 1,498, and by 2004 only 1,457. As a result, more and more cities have no competing newspapers—either there is only one daily newspaper or else all the papers are controlled by one owner. By 2000, only about a dozen cities had separately owned competing daily newspapers. New York City, for example, had eight major newspapers in 1948 and just three in 2006.[5]

The loss of newspapers has been accompanied by concentration in the hands of a few owners and the rise of newspaper groups or chains. For readers, the lack of competition may affect the nature of the stories that are published. For example, if a mayor is corrupt but enjoys the support of the city's single newspaper publisher, there is much less likelihood of an exposé than there would be if a rival newspaper existed.

On the other hand, as the number of newspapers has declined, the number of electronic information sources has increased. There were 1,744 television stations and 13,476 radio stations in the United States in 2004, almost double the number three decades earlier.[6] National Public Radio (NPR) provides a wide range of programming that often deals with political and social issues. As already noted, cable television programming has expanded dramatically. And millions of people have access to information on the Internet.

## Magazines

Citizens who feel that their local newspaper and broadcast outlets fail to provide them with enough news on public issues may, of course, subscribe to a weekly news-

## Newspapers: The Top 10

The *Columbia Journalism Review,* a publication of the Columbia University Graduate School of Journalism, ranks America's best newspapers:

| Paper Name | Ownership* |
|---|---|
| 1. *New York Times* | NY Times |
| 2. *Washington Post* | Washington Post |
| 3. *Wall Street Journal* | Dow Jones |
| 4. *Los Angeles Times* | Tribune |
| 5. *Dallas Morning News* | A. H. Belo |
| 6. *Chicago Tribune* | Tribune |
| 7. *Boston Globe* | NY Times |
| 8. *San Jose Mercury News* | Knight Ridder |
| 9. *St. Petersburg Times* | Independent |
| 10. *Baltimore Sun* | Tribune |

*Ownership as of 2004

—*Columbia Journalism Review,* December 1999

magazine. Only a small percentage of the population does so, however.

The circulation of *Time* is 4,112,311; *Newsweek* is 3,122,407; and *U.S. News & World Report* is 2,024,770. Smaller magazines that comment on public affairs have relatively tiny circulations and are usually struggling to survive. For example, as of 2003, the circulation of the *Atlantic Monthly* was 494,067; *Harper's* 228,955; *Mother Jones,* an alternative magazine often highly critical of the government, 227,192; *National Review,* a conservative journal, 155,584; and *The New Republic* 61,124.[7]

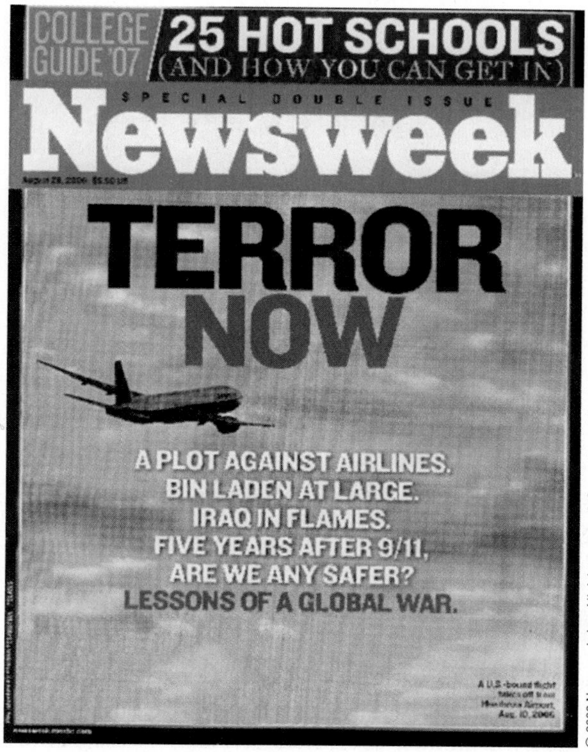




***for more information about the magazines listed above, see: http://www.time.com; http://www.newsweek.com; http://www.usnews.com; http://www.theatlantic.com; http://www.harpers.org; http://www.motherjones.com; http://www.nationalreview.com; and http://www.tnr.com***

## Who Owns the Media?

By 2006, the shape of the media had changed dramatically. One after another, like large fish gobbling up smaller ones—and sometimes the other way around—the giants of the media had joined in multibillion-dollar mergers.

The pace of change was breathtaking. As an example of the enormous impact of the Internet, early in 2000 America Online, with more than 20 million subscribers, bought Time Warner, becoming the world's biggest media company, with a market value of $342 billion. Time Warner had already bought CNN, the Cable News Network, four years earlier. Federal regulators approved the merger, which meant that AOL owned *Time* magazine, Warner Brothers, CNN, HBO, and Netscape. Like many of the "dot-coms," however, AOL lost billions of dollars and three years later, as a reflection of AOL's difficulties, the merged company reverted to its former name, Time Warner.

Only a few months before AOL bought Time Warner, Viacom—the company that owned Paramount Pictures, Blockbuster, MTV, and the book publisher Simon & Schuster—had bought CBS. NBC was already owned by General Electric; and in 1995 the Walt Disney Company purchased ABC, which meant that the three major networks were no longer independent but owned by giant corporations. GE expanded even further in 2004 when NBC merged with Vivendi Universal, owners of Universal Pictures and theme parks. In 2005, Viacom split into two corporations, but retained ownership of CBS

The mergers were also taking place in the print world. In 2000, for example, the *Chicago Tribune*'s parent company bought the *Los Angeles Times.* And cable and telecommunications companies were joining forces in the competition to bring high-speed Internet connections to consumers and businesses.

The extraordinary concentration of ownership raised questions about the independence and diversity of the American press. Would ABC be as quick to report the news if a story reflected adversely on Disney? Would NBC expose General Electric if one of its plants was a polluter? Would *Time* magazine be inclined to write anything unfavorable about AOL? Moreover, some analysts believed that the mergers would ultimately mean less competition, more entertainment, less news, and perhaps a tendency to be less responsive to the public. In the days when many big cities had more than one newspaper, for example, the competition often resulted in a greater flow of news to the readers. The giant media mergers could, in theory at least, also result in a few powerful corporate chiefs pushing their own political views, and reaching a huge audience.

Whatever the future impact of these mergers, the creation of mega-entertainment, information, television, and Internet giants was a reflection of the rapid change brought by the new technology.

## Television and the American Political System

With more than 248 million television sets in American homes, the potential for creating an informed public through TV is vast. But it is only a potential; the reality often falls short.

Entertainment is the economic heart of the television industry, and news and public affairs programs occupy only a small part of the broadcast day. True, the cable channel C-SPAN broadcasts the proceedings of the House and C-SPAN2 televises the Senate, CNN provides full coverage of important events, and public television often carries serious programming about political issues and public policy. But during prime time, the after-dinner hours when millions of Americans are home watching TV, sitcoms, sports, and so-called reality shows rule. Entertainment programs such as these draw the largest audiences. Advertisers want to sell cars, antacids, and deodorants, and they know that comedy, crime programs, and quiz shows are more likely to achieve that end than, say, a documentary about the high cost of health care.

The six major broadcast networks—CBS, NBC, ABC, Fox, UPN, and The WB—occupy a leading position in the industry. But in recent years CNN has taken its place alongside them, as has MSNBC. In the 1980s and 1990s, cable television grew rapidly, reaching more than 71 million homes in 2004, or 74 percent of all households with television.[8]

Even so, a substantial share of all television revenue goes to the six broadcast networks and the 115 TV stations they own. Almost $42 billion was spent on all television advertising in 2002.[9]

The networks sell popular packaged shows to affiliates across the nation and charge large fees for airing sponsors' commercials during prime time. The networks command huge fees to enable advertisers to reach large television audiences. In 2004, for example, NBC charged $2 million for 30 seconds of commercial time on the finale of *Friends,* a popular long-running sitcom watched by more than 52 million people on its last night.[10] For Super Bowl XXXVIII, in January 2004, CBS charged some advertisers a record $2.3 million for a 30-second commercial.[11]

Audience rating figures are the controlling statistics in the broadcast industry. As already noted, news programs are not as profitable as popular mass-entertainment shows. Still, television is not totally the mindless "wasteland" that one critic once called it.[12] The three older networks—CBS, NBC, and ABC—have evening television news programs that reach a combined total audience of almost 25 million people each night. (See Figure 8-1.) For many years, Tom Brokaw was the famil-

**FIGURE 8-1**

**Audiences Reached by Leading Media**

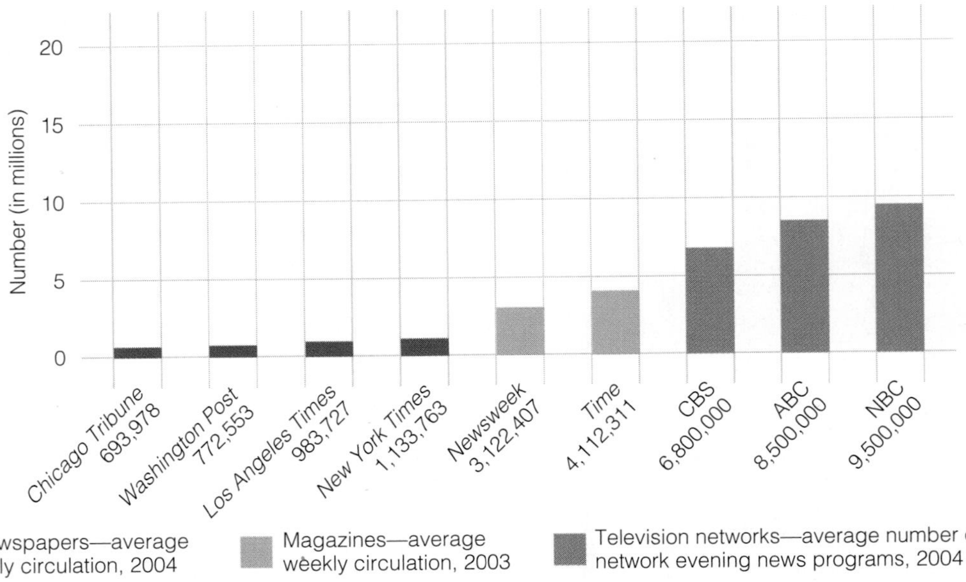


SOURCES: Audit Bureau of Circulations, average paid circulation for the six-month period ending March 31, 2004 (newspapers); December 31, 2003 (magazines); and May 2004 (network news, from <http://www.top5s.com/tvnews.htm>).

iar face as NBC's anchor on the *Nightly News;* Dan Rather was the anchor for CBS, and Peter Jennings for ABC. Then, in the space of less than a year, Brokaw retired as the NBC anchor, Rather stepped down as anchor of the *CBS Evening News,* and Peter Jennings died. In the wake of these changes, there was fierce competition among the networks to try to retain their viewers. CBS launched a massive advertising campaign to promote Katie Couric, former co-host of NBC's *Today Show,* as the new anchor of the *CBS Evening News*; by one estimate the TV commercials promoting her would have cost $10 million if bought by an outsider.[13] In addition to the evening news broadcasts, other news programs reach millions of viewers on CNN, which broadcasts news 24 hours a day; on the Public Broadcasting System (PBS); over C-SPAN; and on other cable and satellite systems.

© CNN/Getty Images

Magazine-style news programs, such as *60 Minutes, Dateline,* and *20/20,* have increased in number in recent years, and they sometimes broadcast stories about politics and government. In addition to news programs, Sunday panel shows such as *Meet the Press* and *Face the Nation* air political issues, and the commercial networks and public television broadcast a wide range of news documentaries. The networks and many local stations maintain their own news staffs.

Because television reaches millions of homes, news programs and live broadcasts of major events can have a strong influence on public opinion. Television may help to shape or change public opinion, or it may reinforce existing public attitudes.

The searing images in 2001 of the World Trade Center hit by airliners and then collapsing helped to build public support for the Bush administration's war on terrorism. Conversely, by the spring of 2004, news reports of the continuing attacks on American troops in Iraq and mounting casualties eroded support for Bush and became an election-year issue in the presidential campaign. In an earlier era, news reports and television pictures of the fighting in Vietnam brought that conflict into American living rooms night after night and were a major factor in swinging public opinion against the war.

During the war in the Persian Gulf in February 1991 and the unsuccessful coup against Soviet leader Mikhail Gorbachev in August of that year, not only the public but even high government officials relied on CNN to bring them minute-by-minute developments. Indeed, in a foreign policy crisis, CNN often brings the news to Washington faster than the government's secure communications channels. When American planes bombed Baghdad during the Iraq war in 2003, television viewers could see it happening on CNN and on the broadcast networks.

Television has a major impact during presidential election years, when viewers are bombarded with political commercials, many of them negative—attacking opponents—during the primary and general election campaigns. The commercials, even negative ones, do provide

© Alex Wong/Getty Images

2003: Vice President Dick Cheney appears on "Meet the Press."

© JP Filo/CBS Photo Archive via Getty Images

information to the voters, although the information is nearly always distorted in favor of the candidate who is paying for the TV ad. In addition, candidates vie to appear on televised talk shows, the networks' morning shows, and even the late-night entertainment programs.

Television provides extensive coverage of the primaries, the national conventions, and the campaigns. More than 40 million people, on average, have viewed one or more of the televised debates among the candidates in presidential election years. Television broadcasts of hearings and political debates, and the full coverage of the national conventions by cable and public TV, convey an immediacy and have an impact that no other medium can approach.

And candidates have often used television to try to defuse a threatened scandal in the midst of a campaign. Near the start of the 1992 presidential election year, for example, Gennifer Flowers, a former lounge singer, claimed in the *Star,* a supermarket tabloid, that she had engaged in a 12-year affair with Arkansas Governor Bill Clinton. In an appearance on *60 Minutes* with his wife, Hillary, Clinton denied Flowers's allegations but conceded marital "wrongdoing." Clinton's effective use of television helped to defuse an issue that for a time threatened to derail his presidential ambitions. Six years later, in a deposition in a civil lawsuit, Clinton reportedly acknowledged one sexual encounter with Flowers in 1977 when he was governor.[14] But by then, Clinton was in the White House.

So powerful is the medium of television that the candidate with the most money who is able to saturate the airwaves with political commercials may gain an advantage over a less well-financed opponent. But money, and TV time, is no guarantee of victory on Election Day. (The issue of money and television in political campaigns is discussed in detail in Chapter 10.)

## Television and Radio: A Limited Freedom

Radio and television do not enjoy as much freedom as other segments of the press, because, unlike newspapers, broadcast stations are licensed by the Federal Communications Commission (FCC). Although broadcast networks are not licensed, the stations they own and operate are.

***for more information about the Federal Communications Commission see: http://www.fcc.gov***

The FCC does not directly regulate news broadcasts, but stations are required to operate in "the public inter-

### Why Presidents Woo Local TV

WASHINGTON, Oct. 20—President Bush set off a round of media buzz last week when he took a pop at the national news media. "There's a sense that people in America aren't getting the truth," Mr. Bush said to a reporter for Hearst-Argyle Television, one of five back-to-back White House interviews he granted to regional broadcasters. "I'm mindful of the filters through which some news travels, and sometimes you have to go over the heads of the filter and speak directly to the people."

Mr. Bush's remarks generated newspaper articles, a report on ABC's "Nightline" and much comment about an administration that bypasses the White House press corps to push a cheery message onto local news media about the American occupation in Iraq. White House advisers readily say they consider the regional news outlets more hospitable and less judgmental, and a better place to sell their wares.

But as much as the interviews angered White House reporters, who have less access to Bush than they did his predecessors, the tactic is nearly as old as the presidency itself. Mr. Bush may be unique only in that he so openly acknowledged what he was up to.

"This goes back to at least the 19th century," said Bruce J. Schulman, a professor of history and American studies at Boston University. "Certainly every 20th century president has tried to go over the head of the national media directly to the people."

But Michael K. Deaver, Ronald Reagan's image maker, said that his attempt to cozy up to the regional news media met with mixed success. "In many ways, they were tougher," Mr. Deaver said. "The problem was, you always had some young reporter out there who was trying to get a Pulitzer or make a name for himself."

—Elisabeth Bumiller, "White House Letter: Trying to Bypass the Good News," *New York Times,* October 20, 2003, p. A12. Copyright © 2003 by The New York Times Co. Reprinted with permission.

est." For example, the Federal Communications Act requires broadcasters to provide **equal time** to all legally qualified political candidates. Under the rule, candidates must be given equal opportunity, if they can afford it, to buy air time for commercials if their opponents have run ads. However, the requirement does not apply to news broadcasts, interviews, and documentaries, nor does it mean that stations must include fringe candidates in televised presidential or other political debates, because debates are considered news.

Stations that ignore the FCC's rules could have their licenses revoked, although the commission has seldom exercised its power to do so. Potentially, however, the federal government has powerful leverage over the operations of the broadcasting industry.

For example, the FCC regulates how many television, cable, and radio stations a single company may own in addition to a newspaper. In 2003, the Republican-controlled FCC proposed new media ownership rules that would have allowed the television networks to own or buy more stations. A federal appeals court rejected the proposal and sent it back to the FCC, ruling that the commission had not justified the changes.

Why is the government able to regulate broadcasters but not the written press? The reason most often advanced is that the broadcast spectrum has a limited number of spaces and stations would overlap and interfere with one another if the government did not regulate them. As the Supreme Court has stated, "Unlike other modes of expression, radio (and television) is not available to all."[15] This scarcity theory has been criticized because, in fact, there are more broadcasting stations than newspapers in the United States. And later technology such as the rapid growth of cable television and satellite broadcasts has opened even more outlets to the public.[16] Indeed, in 1994 the Supreme Court, recognizing technological change, ruled that cable television is entitled to nearly the same constitutional protection as newspapers and magazines.[17] That is not true, however, for the broadcast networks.

The First Amendment clearly protects the written press. But the Constitution did not anticipate the invention of television. The result "is a major paradox: TV news, which has the greatest impact on the public, is the most vulnerable and least protected."[18]

In 1969 the Supreme Court specifically rejected the claim of the broadcasting industry that the free press provisions of the First Amendment protected it from government regulation of programs. The Court did so in upholding the FCC's "fairness doctrine"—later abolished—that at the time required radio and television broadcasters to present all sides of important public issues.[19] In 1987, the FCC abolished the fairness doctrine as an unconstitutional restriction on the First Amendment rights of broadcasters.

Although the Supreme Court has declined to extend full freedom of the press to broadcasters, it has held that the First Amendment protects the right of broadcasters to report news events.[20] In 1978, however, the Supreme Court ruled in the "seven dirty words" case that the government has the right to prohibit the broadcasting of "patently offensive" language.[21] That case began at 2 p.m. one afternoon in New York City when a station owned by the Pacifica Foundation broadcast a monologue by comedian George Carlin called "Filthy Words." In it, Carlin gave a detailed analysis of "the words you couldn't say on the public airwaves . . . the ones you definitely wouldn't say, ever." Soon after, a man wrote to the FCC complaining that he heard the broadcast while driving with his young son. The FCC reprimanded the station but later indicated it would permit such broadcasts only at times of the day "when children most likely" would not be listening or watching. It therefore prohibited "indecent speech" over the airwaves between 6 a.m. and 8 p.m.

By the 1996 presidential election year, violence and sex on television, in movies, and in popular music had become a much-debated social issue. Opinion polls showed many voters were concerned over this issue and fearful that the nation had lost its moral compass. Conservatives in particular argued that children and others

Television has less First Amendment protection than print media. . . . Here, TV satellite trucks are clustered outside the White House at the height of the Monica Lewinsky scandal.

© 2004 AP/Wide World Photos

Singers Janet Jackson and Justin Timberlake during the Superbowl XXXVIII halftime show that caused a record number of complaints to the FCC

exposed to a steady diet of TV violence might come to accept violent behavior as normal. In addition, critics contended that violence on television led to crime and violence in society. Many of these same arguments were voiced again after the killings at Columbine High School in Littleton, Colorado, in 1999.

Controversy over sexual content on the airwaves reached a crescendo in 2004. During halftime at the 2004 Superbowl, a brief glimpse of pop star Janet Jackson's bejeweled right breast caused a national furor and prompted the FCC to fine CBS $550,000 for "violation of the broadcast indecency standard." CBS had apologized to viewers for the incident but said it had no advance knowledge that it would happen. That same year the FCC fined radio host Howard Stern $495,000 for a broadcast in which he discussed various sexual practices in graphic detail. Clear Channel Communications, Stern's network, dropped his show. And the FCC sharply increased its fines of broadcasters for language it considered offensive to listeners.

In June 2004, Clear Channel agreed in a settlement with the FCC to pay the government a record-breaking fine of $1.75 million, releasing the company from all of the indecency charges filed against it, including complaints against Howard Stern.[22]

## The Press: Legal and Constitutional Issues

### Prior Restraint

The strong tradition of a free press in the United States rests on the principle, rooted in English common law, that normally there must be no governmental **prior restraint** of the press—the censoring of news stories by the government before publication. The Supreme Court dealt with this issue seven decades ago when it ruled that a Minneapolis weekly newspaper could not be suppressed because of articles attacking city officials as "corrupt" and "grafters."[23] The Court held that even "miscreant purveyors of scandal" were protected from prior restraint by the First Amendment. But the Court said that the press might be censored in advance by the government in "exceptional cases" relating to national security—during wartime, for example—and it gave as one illustration a news story that might report the sailing date of a troopship.[24]

© UPI/Bettmann/Corbis

The Pentagon Papers: A Washington Post printer reacts to the Supreme Court's decision.

In 1971 the federal government, claiming that national security was endangered, tried to stop the *New York Times* from continuing to publish a series based on a secret history of the Vietnam War—the so-called Pentagon Papers. For 15 days, the federal courts restrained publication. Finally, the Supreme Court ruled 6–3 that the *Times* and other newspapers that had been restrained were free to publish.[25] "In the First Amendment," Justice Black wrote in the Pentagon Papers case, "the Founding Fathers gave the free press the protection it must have to fulfill its essential role in our democracy. The press was to serve the governed, not the governors."[26]

The First Amendment to the Constitution, on its face, might indeed seem to prohibit the government from censoring an article in advance. But the Supreme Court, the ultimate arbiter of what the Constitution means, has always balanced the First Amendment against other social needs and other parts of the Constitution.

For example, in 1990, the Supreme Court made it clear that it will not, in every instance, prohibit censorship. It voted 7–2 to let stand a lower court order that barred CNN from broadcasting tape recordings of conversations between Manuel Antonio Noriega, Panama's deposed dictator, and his lawyer.[27]

Despite the outcome in the Pentagon Papers case, the larger issue remained unresolved. The press is protected by the First Amendment, but how far that protection extends is not clear. The periodic battles over content are but one facet of the continuing struggle between the press and the government in the American democracy.

As these cases show, freedom of the press is a relative term, applied differently by the Supreme Court at different times. For example, the Court has ruled unanimously that it is unconstitutional to compel a newspaper to provide free space for a political candidate to reply to editorial criticism.[28] The Court thereby rejected the argument that the First Amendment requires citizen "access" to newspapers to present differing viewpoints. But while the Court has usually protected the press under the First Amendment, it also has placed limitations on freedom of the press in several areas.

## Free Press and Fair Trial

When basic rights collide, the Supreme Court may be called upon to act as a referee. In recent years the Court has shown increasing concern over pretrial and courtroom publicity that may prejudice the fair trial of a defendant in a criminal case. The issue brings into direct conflict two basic principles of the Bill of Rights—the right of an accused person to have a fair trial and the right of freedom of the press.

In 1981 the Supreme Court ruled that states could permit trials to be televised. The use of television has continued to raise questions, however. Do cameras in the courtroom affect the right of a defendant to a fair trial? By 2004, 40 states allowed cameras in trial courts, and all 50 states allow appeals court proceedings to be televised. Television cameras are barred from most federal courts, however, including the Supreme Court. In the words of Supreme Court Justice David H. Souter, "The day you see a camera come into our courtroom, it's going to roll over my dead body."[29] Even in the states that allow cameras, judges can exercise their discretion to bar them. And in the wake of the much-televised O. J. Simpson murder trial, many judges did so.

The trial of the former football star, who was accused of killing his former wife and a young man, ended in his acquittal in 1995, as an enormous audience of 150 million people watched the verdict on television. The trial itself was carried live by CNN and Court TV and was covered extensively by the television networks, which often led their evening news broadcasts with the day's events in the Los Angeles courtroom. Comedian Jay Leno frequently commented on the trial on *The Tonight Show,* and as a regular feature he brought out "the dancing Itos," a black-robed male troupe whose members were made up to resemble the trial judge, Lance Ito. The lawyers for both sides became instant celebrities.

Critics of courtroom television have argued that television contributes to a circuslike atmosphere that may reduce the defendant's chance of getting a fair trial. They contend that lawyers play to the cameras, which may increase the length, and cost, of the trial. On the other hand, televised trials permit ordinary citizens, who may never have been in a courtroom, to learn how the legal system operates. And because trials must be open to the public, it can also be argued that television is merely an extension of that principle, bringing the courtroom proceedings to a larger audience.

Closely related to the controversy over cameras in the courtroom is the issue of pretrial publicity. In 1966 the Supreme Court reversed the conviction of Dr. Sam Sheppard, a Cleveland, Ohio, osteopath found guilty of bludgeoning his wife to death, ruling that the defendant's constitutional rights had been prejudiced by publicity

"Since you have already been convicted by the media, I imagine we can wrap this up pretty quickly."

Cameras in the courtroom: Can the defendant receive a fair trial?

© Todd Bigelow

that gave the trial the "atmosphere of a 'Roman holiday' for the news media."[30]

Similar excessive publicity influenced the 1966 decision of the Texas Court of Criminal Appeals to reverse the conviction of Jack Ruby for the murder of Lee Harvey Oswald, the accused assassin of President Kennedy. (However, before Ruby could be retried, he died of illness in January 1967.)

Sometimes, defense lawyers seek to avoid the effects of pretrial publicity by seeking a change of venue—requesting that a trial be moved to another city where the defendant's alleged crime was less publicized. Again, in the age of instant communication, that remedy may often be meaningless.

After a truck bomb blew up the federal building in Oklahoma City on the morning of April 19, 1995, killing 168 people, Timothy McVeigh was arrested as the prime suspect. In the hope of finding impartial jurors, his lawyers succeeded in having the trial moved from the scene of the tragedy to Denver. But in the television era it is unlikely that most people in Colorado were any less aware of the bombing than the citizens of Oklahoma, since the terrorist act was widely publicized in America and all over the world. McVeigh was convicted, sentenced to death, and executed.

Although the Supreme Court has recognized the dangers of excessive courtroom publicity, it ruled 7–1 in another case that trials must be open to the public and the press except in the most unusual circumstances. "We hold that the right to attend criminal trials is implicit in the guarantees of the First Amendment," the Court declared.[31]

## Confidentiality: Shielding Reporters and Their Sources

The right to have a fair trial often conflicts with the First Amendment in another important area—that of confidentiality for reporters and their news sources.

Journalists argue that they must offer confidential sources complete anonymity, particularly in the case of investigative reporting, when disclosure of the name of a source might lead to reprisals against that person. But what if a news reporter has information vital to the defense in a criminal trial, or which the government needs in order to prove its case? Do reporters have the "privilege" under the First Amendment of refusing to surrender such evidence? The Supreme Court has said no.

In a 1972 decision, the Court explored the question of whether reporters have the constitutional right to protect their sources. Specifically, the Court ruled that the First Amendment did not exempt news reporters from appearing and testifying before state and federal grand juries. The decision came in the case of Earl Caldwell, a reporter for the *New York Times,* and in two related cases.[32] Caldwell had declined to appear before a federal grand jury to testify about the Black Panthers in the San Francisco area. He argued that merely appearing would destroy his relationship of trust with his confidential news sources. But the Supreme Court said that the investigation by a grand jury of possible crimes was of greater importance to the public than the protection of news sources. The courts had generally taken this position even before the Supreme Court ruled. But some reporters have gone to jail rather than reveal their sources, and many members of the press feel that compelling reporters to testify abridges their First Amendment rights.[33]

© Bettmann/Corbis

*New York Times* reporter Earl Caldwell testifies to a House subcommittee.

By 2004, 31 states and the District of Columbia had

*Myth vs. Reality*

## DO AMERICANS REALLY BELIEVE IN FREEDOM OF THE PRESS?

Many people think of the First Amendment of the Constitution as the bedrock of American liberty, since it provides for the basic freedoms of speech, the press, religion, and assembly. After all, America fought a revolution to secure these rights.

The reality is rather different. For example, the public's support of the First Amendment's provision for freedom of the press varies with the times, and is always divided. When national security appears threatened, support for constitutional freedoms often diminishes. This was the case in the aftermath of the 9/11 terrorist attacks and the invasion of Iraq by U.S. forces.

A poll taken by the First Amendment Center at Vanderbilt University in 2003 reported the following:

- 43 percent believe the press has too much freedom to publish whatever it wants
- 44 percent disagree that newspapers should be allowed to freely criticize the U.S. military
- 41 percent favor increased government regulation of news media owned by just a few corporations
- 38 percent believe that the press is too aggressive in covering the war on terrorism
- 28 percent believe that newspapers should not be able to publish a story unless the government approves it
- 67 percent think the government should be able to review in advance stories from military combat areas

—"State of the First Amendment 2003"

passed **shield laws** designed to protect reporters from revealing their sources. But the degree of protection varies from state to state, and there are broad exceptions in libel cases or if a journalist is an eyewitness to a crime. As a result, reporters may face contempt of court charges if they refuse to name their sources when ordered to do so by a judge. Also, the shield laws do not cover freelance or Internet journalists, or authors of books. In 2001, Vanessa Leggett, a freelance Houston writer, was imprisoned for 168 days after refusing to disclose her sources. Because the shield laws provide only limited protection, a number of reporters have gone to jail rather than yield the names of the people who confided in them.

Congress has made periodic efforts to enact a federal immunity law for journalists. But many journalists preferred no legislation, arguing that a shield law, even though well intentioned, would violate the First Amendment by defining—and thus limiting—reporters' rights.

## Libel

A person defamed by a newspaper or other publication may be able to sue for libel and collect damages because the First Amendment does not protect this form of "free speech." Libel is a published or broadcast report that exposes a person to public contempt or injures the person's reputation. For example, some years ago a New York newspaper suggested that one Stanislaus Zbyszko, a wrestler, was built along the general lines of a gorilla. Near the article, it ran a picture of a particularly hideous-looking anthropoid. The New York State courts held this to be libelous.[34]

Truth has always been an absolute defense in libel cases. That is, if a publication can show that a story is true, the person claiming to have been libeled cannot recover damages. Under the *New York Times* rule, also known as the *Sullivan* rule, the Supreme Court has made

© AP Images/Pablo Martinez Monsivais

The First Amendment does not always shield news reporters. Judith Miller of the *New York Times* was jailed for 85 days for refusing to name . . .

© AP Images/J. Scott Applewhite

. . . I. Lewis "Scooter" Libby as her news source in a leak investigation.

## Reporters' Sources: The Justices Disagree

The issue in these cases is whether requiring newsmen to appear and testify before state or federal grand juries abridges the freedom of speech and press guaranteed by the First Amendment. We hold that it does not. . . .

Citizens generally are not constitutionally immune from grand jury subpoenas; and neither the First Amendment nor other constitutional provision protects the average citizen from disclosing to a grand jury information that he has received in confidence. . . .

We are asked . . . to grant newsmen a testimonial privilege that other citizens do not enjoy. This we decline to do.

—Justice Byron R. White in
*United States* v. *Caldwell* (1972)

The Court's crabbed view of the First Amendment reflects a disturbing insensitivity to the critical role of an independent press in our society. . . . The Court in these cases holds that a newsman has no First Amendment right to protect his sources when called before a grand jury. The Court thus invites state and federal authorities to undermine the historic independence of the press by attempting to annex the journalistic profession as an investigative arm of government.

—Justice Potter Stewart,
dissenting in *United States* v. *Caldwell*

it almost impossible to libel a public official unless the statement is made with "actual malice"—that is, "with knowledge that it was false or with reckless disregard of whether it was false or not."[35] Ruling against an Alabama official who had brought a libel suit against the *Times,* the Supreme Court held in 1964 that in a free society "debate on public issues should be uninhibited, robust and wide-open, and . . . may well include vehement . . . attacks on government officials."[36] Later Court decisions expanded the *New York Times* rule to include not only officials but "public figures" such as political candidates and people involved in events of general or public interest.[37]

But the Supreme Court has greatly narrowed its definition of a public figure. For example, the Court ruled in favor of Mrs. Russell A. Firestone and against *Time* magazine, which inaccurately reported that her husband had been granted a divorce on grounds of adultery (although the judge did note that some of her reported but unsubstantiated extramarital escapades "would have made Dr. Freud's hair curl"). Despite the extensive publicity surrounding the divorce, the Court ruled that Mrs. Firestone was not a public figure.[38]

The Supreme Court's position has left the press vulnerable to libel suits by people who might—or might not—be considered public figures. For example, the Court has ruled that a private person does not automatically become a public figure "just by becoming involved in . . . a matter that attracts public attention."[39]

In 1988, the Supreme Court overturned a $200,000 award to Jerry Falwell for "emotional distress," which the conservative television evangelist claimed he had suffered when *Hustler* magazine published a parody that portrayed Falwell as a drunk having sex with his mother in an outhouse. Although the Court found that the parody was "doubtless gross and repugnant in the eyes of most," it ruled that a public figure was not protected against satire or political cartoons, however "outrageous" or offensive.[40] On the other hand, the Supreme Court has held that expressions of opinion, such as those in a newspaper column, may be libelous if false and defamatory.[41]

Despite some victories by the press, the threat of libel actions has become a major problem for the news media, publishers, and writers. In a number of cases, juries have awarded multimillion-dollar damages to plaintiffs in libel cases. Most of these big awards were later overturned or reduced by the courts, but some First

© AP/Wide World Photos

Jerry Falwell: The Supreme Court ruled for *Hustler.*

Amendment students argue that large punitive damages and legal costs in libel cases inhibit press freedom.

Corporations have gone into court to battle the press on other legal grounds as well. In 1992, ABC television, using hidden cameras, broadcast a report charging that Food Lion, the supermarket chain, practiced unsanitary food-handling techniques and sold outdated and repackaged meat, fish, and chicken. ABC said that Food Lion ground expired beef with fresh beef and even applied barbecue sauce to the chicken to hide the rank smell. Two ABC employees had lied to get jobs with Food Lion for the network's inside report. A jury awarded Food Lion $5.5 million in damages, later reduced by an appeals court to a mere $2.[42] But the message to the media was clear; news organizations might pay a price if they engage in fraud even to expose shoddy practices.

Similarly, in 1998 the *Cincinnati Enquirer* paid $10 million to avoid a lawsuit by Chiquita Brands International after the newspaper accused the banana company of bribing foreign officials and carelessly using pesticides that harmed the health of hundreds of workers and others. The newspaper said it acted because its series of articles was apparently based on voice-mail messages stolen from Chiquita by the *Enquirer*'s reporter. Although the company denied the charges, the newspaper said it had no reason to believe the stories were fabricated.

## The Press and Terrorism

Well before the horrendous attacks on September 11, 2001, on the World Trade Center and the Pentagon, Americans learned that modern urban societies are tempting targets for terrorists. In 1993 Islamic terrorists carried out the first attack on the World Trade Center, a bombing that killed six people and injured more than 1,000. Other terrorists were arrested before they could carry out their plans to blow up bridges, tunnels, and the United Nations headquarters in Manhattan. As noted, in April 1995, Timothy McVeigh bombed the federal building in Oklahoma City, killing 168 people.

Some critics of the press have argued that giving widespread coverage to acts of terrorism, or to events such as the 1999 school shootings in Littleton, Colorado, plays into the hands of the perpetrators, who are seeking publicity for their violent acts. Another argument sometimes voiced is that press coverage can lead to "copycat" acts by others seeking the same notoriety for their deeds or for themselves. The press, however, has a responsibility to report major news events. It could hardly fail to do so in the case of acts of terrorism. The press, after all, is a mirror held up to society. It may sometimes influence events, but it also has the responsibility to report what happens.

At the same time, critics argue that the press does not always exercise restraint in situations where it might do so and still report the news. Is it really necessary, for example, for news helicopters to provide extensive live coverage of high-speed car chases or shootouts on Los Angeles freeways? To news directors making snap decisions under pressure, there are no easy answers to such questions.

A second, more difficult issue is whether the press should, in some instances, agree to the demands of terrorists in order to try to save human life. In 1995, two major newspapers faced this dilemma in the Unabomber case. For 17 years, an unknown terrorist had sent bombs through the mail. His devices killed three people and wounded 23 others. From his writings, it appeared that the person whom the FBI called the Unabomber—because his targets included universities and airlines—harbored a deep grudge against the effects of technology on society and against college graduates, scientists, and computer researchers. Then, in 1995, he offered to halt the killings if the *New York Times* or another national publication would print his 35,000-word essay. The *Washington Post,* in cooperation with the *Times,* did so.

© AP/Wide World Photos

Unabomber Theodore Kaczynski after his arrest by FBI agents in Montana, April 1996

## Comparing Governments

## LIBEL: A TOWN CALLED "SUE"

Because of the constitutional protection of freedom of the press and freedom of expression in the United States, it is often difficult to win a libel suit in American courts. This is especially true if the plaintiff is a public figure. Those who are judged to be public figures must not only prove they were defamed, but also that the offending material was published with knowledge that it was false, or with "reckless disregard" of whether it was false. It is a difficult standard of proof.

In Britain, by contrast, where there has historically been greater concern for preserving public reputations, and less protection for free expression, the burden of proof is not on the plaintiff making the accusation, but on the person being accused of libel. The statement in question is presumed to be false, and it is the legal responsibility of the defendant to prove it is true.

Because it is so much easier to win a libel suit in Britain, plaintiffs often choose to sue in British courts when they can, and London has come to be called "a town called Sue" by international media attorneys.

In her 1993 book *Denying the Holocaust: The Growing Assault on Truth and Memory,* Emory University professor Deborah Lipstadt, an American scholar, denounced British historian David Irving as "one of the most dangerous spokespersons for Holocaust denial," and called him a "Hitler partisan . . . a racist and an anti-semite." Irving, who has written admiringly of Hitler and denied the existence of gas chambers at Auschwitz, waited until the book was published in England, and then sued Lipstadt and her publisher, Penguin Books, for libel in the British courts. Under British libel law, it was Lipstadt's responsibility to show that the accusations she had made against Irving were true. After a trial that lasted five years, involved dozens of expert witnesses, and cost the defense over $3 million, the judge in the case ruled that Lipstadt had been justified in her characterizations of Irving, who had "deliberately misrepresented and manipulated historical evidence" regarding the Holocaust. Because Irving lost, he was required under British law to pay the defendant's legal expenses.

Ironically, it may have been Irving's ability to sue under Britain's plaintiff-friendly libel law which ultimately cost him what had remained of his reputation as a historian of Nazi Germany. "In the U.S., this would have been thrown out of court, but if it had been thrown out, Irving would have been able to say that he never got his day in court," said Ms. Lipstadt after the trial. "I thought, 'This British law is making me jump through hoops.' But he was the one who was stripped naked."

—*Washington Post,* April 12, 2000;
*New York Times,* July 22, 2000

Critics said that there was no assurance the Unabomber would keep his word and that the press had opened itself to blackmail by terrorists. A majority of the nation's editors, however, agreed with the decision to publish; they contended that with human lives at stake, there was little choice but to do so.

As it turned out, publication of the manifesto led to the arrest of the suspected Unabomber, Theodore J. Kaczynski. His brother, David, suspicious that some of his sibling's writings resembled the manifesto, notified the authorities. In April 1996, the FBI arrested Theodore Kaczynski at his remote mountain cabin in Montana. Inside, they found a bomb and bomb-making materials. He was tried, pleaded guilty, and was sentenced to life in prison.

## The Press and the Government

Like heavyweight boxers circling each other warily in the ring, the press and the government are adversaries who need each other.

The government often attempts to manipulate the press and to manage the news, to put a favorable "spin" on events. Officials have a vested interest in trying to influence what the press reports, in order to shape public opinion to support administration policies.

Although the press is powerful, so are political leaders. Presidents are well aware that their actions and words tend to dominate the news. They know that the press is obliged to report what they say and do and that the news that presidents generate has a strong influence on public opinion.

The press relies on the government as a crucial source of information. At the same time, the press serves a watchdog function. It is on the alert for stories about incompetence, waste, or outright corruption in the same government it cultivates for information.

To an extent, therefore, the press and government have a relationship that is at once adversarial and mutually dependent. Politicians want to get reelected, and they communicate with the voters for the most part through the press; the press in turn wants to report the news. Sometimes those two forces collide. Yet, each side needs the other. The public, in turn, relies on the press for its information about government, but is often critical of both. Out of the three-way interaction among the press, the government, and the voters, public opinion emerges and plays its key role in the political process.

### News Leaks and "Backgrounders"

Officials at every level of government frequently "leak" stories to the press, divulging information on condition that the officials remain anonymous. Sometimes a news leak has dramatic results. A leak to a syndicated columnist during the months before President George W. Bush launched the invasion of Iraq in 2003 led to a criminal investigation, the jailing of a *New York Times* reporter who refused to divulge her source, and the indictment of the chief of staff of the vice president of the United States. Following is the story of that leak.

**The Valerie Plame Affair: A Case Study** On January 28, 2003, President George W. Bush asserted in his State of the Union address that Iraq, according to the British government, had sought to acquire uranium from Africa. When highly enriched, uranium can be used to make nuclear weapons, and Bush cited the report to build his case for going to war in Iraq. But the report was false, based on what turned out to be forged documents supposedly from Niger.

Six months later, on July 6, 2003, former ambassador Joseph C. Wilson, in an op-ed piece in the *New York Times,* revealed he had investigated the Niger story for the CIA in 2002 and found it "highly doubtful." He could only conclude, Wilson added, "that some of the intelligence related to Iraq's nuclear weapons program was twisted to exaggerate the Iraqi threat." Wilson, who had been an ambassador in Africa, reported his findings to the government—well before the president's State of the Union speech. If his report was ignored because it did not fit the administration's game plan, Wilson wrote, an argument could be made "that we went to war under false pretenses."[43] His embarrassing disclosure infuriated officials in the White House.

Soon afterward, a high-level administration official leaked the name of Wilson's wife, Valerie Plame, a CIA officer, to conservative columnist Robert Novak, who revealed her identity in his column on July 14. Novak wrote that two "senior administration officials" told him that Wilson's wife had suggested sending Wilson to Niger to investigate the uranium story.[44] It seemed clear to many critics of the administration that the leak of Plame's name was a payback to Wilson for his article. It is a felony, however, if a government official learns the identity of an undercover CIA officer and intentionally discloses it. The FBI launched a criminal probe of the leak, questioning several White House aides. President George W. Bush was interviewed in the course of the investigation, although not under oath.

© Jonas Karlsson, represented by Walter Schupfer Management Corporation, and by kind permission of Ambassador Wilson, and Ron Beinner of *Vanity Fair.*

The FBI investigated the leak to a columnist of the name of Valerie Plame, a CIA officer, after her husband, Joseph Wilson, wrote an op-ed article that angered the Bush White House.

On July 17, *Time* reporter Matthew Cooper, in an article on the magazine's website, also reported that "government officials" had told *Time* that Valerie Plame was a CIA officer.[45]

In December 2003 the Justice Department appointed Patrick J. Fitzgerald, the U.S. attorney in Chicago, as a special counsel to investigate the leak. Fitzgerald sought to question several reporters in the case. In October 2004 a federal judge held Matthew Cooper in contempt and ordered him to jail for refusing to name his sources. Cooper avoided jail by testifying after Karl Rove, Bush's senior political adviser, waived their confidentiality agreement. Under subpoena, *Time* had turned over Cooper's internal notes to Fitzgerald, so there was little point in Cooper refusing to testify after that. He did testify, and said that in a telephone conversation, Rove, while not mentioning Plame by name, made it clear that she worked for "the CIA."[46]

Fitzgerald also sought to question Judith Miller, then a reporter for the *New York Times,* who had written stories suggesting that Iraq had weapons of mass destruction. Although Miller had not written about the Niger uranium issue, she refused a federal judge's order to testify to a grand jury. Rather than betray a source, Miller spent 85 days in jail. Finally, I. Lewis "Scooter" Libby, Vice President Cheney's chief of staff, wrote to Miller assuring her she was free to testify about their confidential conversations. Miller was released from jail on September 29, 2005, and testified to the grand jury about three conversations she had had with Libby. Although Libby did not reveal Plame's name, she said, he told her Wilson's wife worked at the CIA. And Miller's notes contained the name "Valerie Flame," a misspelling of the CIA officer's name.[47]

On October 28, 2005, Libby was indicted by the special counsel, accused of perjury, obstruction of justice, and making false statements. The indictment said Libby had lied about his conversations with Miller, Cooper, and Tim Russert of NBC. It said Libby claimed to have learned Plame's name from reporters, but in fact had been told about her by CIA and State Department officials. Libby resigned from his White House post the same day.[48] According to the indictment, Cheney's office was involved in a concerted effort to gather information about Wilson, and it was the vice president who told Libby about Plame's CIA employment weeks before the Novak column appeared.[49]

Libby's indictment still left a cloud hanging over Karl Rove, who had also discussed Wilson's wife with reporters. Not until June 2006 did the special counsel inform Rove that he would not be charged in the case.

On July 12, 2006, three years after his original column naming Plame, Novak finally told his readers that he had testified to Fitzgerald and the federal grand jury early in 2004, naming as his sources Karl Rove; Bill Harlow, a CIA public relations official; and a third official, whom Novak called his primary source and whose name he did not disclose in his column.[50] However, Richard Armitage, who at the time of the leak to Novak was the second-highest official of the state department, confirmed published reports that he was Novak's original source. Although Armitage was not himself regarded as a political operative, he learned about Wilson's wife from a State Department memo written after an inquiry by Cheney's chief of staff, Lewis Libby.[51]

Judith Miller's decision to go to jail rather than testify, until released by Libby to do so, in the end cost her her job at the *New York Times.* The intense publicity surrounding the case and her role in it focused renewed attention on the stories she had written that indicated Iraq had weapons of mass destruction, accounts that helped support the Bush administration's case for war. No such weapons were found, and Miller was criticized by her colleagues and the paper's editor. In November 2005, after 28 years at the Times, Miller departed.[52]

The disclosure of the name of Valerie Plame and the involvement of high-level White House officials is a classic example of how a news leak can have huge unintended consequences. The motives for leaks to the press vary greatly. For instance, a political leader may be launching a "trial balloon," an idea for a new policy or program, in order to test public reaction. If the reaction is unfavorable, the administration can deny the program was ever even contemplated. Or a story may be leaked to attack a political opponent in a campaign, to undermine or embarrass an opponent, or to increase public support and sympathy for a political leader. The military services have leaked "secrets" about other countries' weaponry to inflate their own budgets.

But another kind of leak, the unofficial leak at a lower level, often plagues presidents and other political leaders. In Washington, for example, presidents—infuriated by some disclosure or other in the press—have periodically called in the FBI to try to find the source of the leak. President Reagan once said he had "thought of the guillotine" for leakers. But the culprits are almost never uncovered.

During the lengthy investigation by Independent Counsel Kenneth Starr of President Clinton's relationship with Monica Lewinsky, a White House intern, the press reported continually on the progress of the probe, often quoting sources "close to" Starr. Later, Starr confirmed that he and an assistant had in fact briefed reporters from major news organizations.[53]

There is a great deal of hypocrisy surrounding the periodic outcries over leaks; the same officials who order lie detector tests for government employees to try to stop leaking of classified information may turn around and invite a correspondent to lunch to reveal similar information. And when high officials, including presidents, leave office, they often write books and, in effect, sell secrets to the public in their memoirs.

Although disclosures of information are often deplored by high officials, neither government nor the news media could really operate without the institution of the news leak. For the press, one astute observer commented, the leak is "its lifeline to unauthorized truth."[54]

When a leak takes place in a group setting, it is known as a "backgrounder." Officials in Washington often meet reporters to discuss government policies and plans with the mutual understanding that the information can be attributed only to unnamed "officials" or sometimes not attributed to any source at all.

Max Frankel, when he was chief of the Washington Bureau of the *New York Times,* filed an affidavit in the Pentagon Papers case explaining that officials and reporters "regularly make use of so-called classified, secret, and top secret information. . . . Without the use of 'se-

## Spinning the Media

*spin*—deliberate shading of news perception; attempted control of political reaction.

As a verb meaning "to whirl," spin dates back to Old English; by the 1950s, the verb also meant "to deceive," perhaps based on "to spin a yarn." . . . As a current noun, spin means "twist" or "interpretation." . . .

During the 1984 presidential campaign, spin entered the political lexicon with the phrase *spin doctor.* A *New York Times* editorial on October 21, 1984, commented on the televising of presidential debates:

> Tonight at about 9:30, seconds after the Reagan-Mondale debate ends, a bazaar will suddenly materialize in the press room. . . . A dozen men in good suits and women in silk dresses will circulate smoothly among the reporters, spouting confident opinions. They won't be just press agents trying to impart a favorable spin to a routine release. They'll be the Spin Doctors, senior advisors to the candidates.

Four days after its first print appearance, *spin doctor* was lowercased and defined by Elisabeth Bumiller in the *Washington Post:* "the advisers who talk to reporters and try to put their own spin, or analysis, on the story."

*Spin* terms have spun several derivatives, from *spin control* by *spin doctors* or *spinmeisters* who have formed a *spin patrol* operating in an area called *spin valley.*

—William Safire, *Safire's New Political Dictionary*

crets' . . . there could be no adequate diplomatic, military, and political reporting of the kind our people take for granted, either abroad or in Washington."

The *Times* correspondent cited several instances when he had been given secret information: "I remember President Johnson, standing beside me, waist-deep in his Texas swimming pool, recounting for more than an hour his conversation the day before . . . with Prime Minister Kosygin of the Soviet Union . . . for my 'background' information, and subsequent though not immediate use in print. . . . This is the coin of our business and of the officials with whom we regularly deal. . . . The government hides what it can . . . and the press pries out what it can. . . . Each side in this 'game' regularly 'wins' and 'loses' a round or two."[55]

## Investigative Reporting

Because the government is such a major source of news, the press is sometimes criticized for relying too much on press releases and "official sources," ranging all the way from the local police chief, to the mayor or governor, to the president's press secretary. The press has been faulted for becoming dependent on these sources instead of digging deeper.

But, especially over the past three decades, the press has shown that it often does dig deeply, investigating a wide range of alleged improprieties both inside the government and in the private sector. The importance of investigative reporting—which relies in part on confidentiality of sources—was dramatically illustrated during the Watergate affair, when reporters Bob Woodward and Carl Bernstein of the *Washington Post* uncovered many details of the break-in at Democratic Party headquarters by burglars employed by the president's campaign, and the cover-up of that crime by the Nixon administration.

Woodward's most celebrated source was known for decades only as "Deep Throat," his identity shielded by the reporter. In 2005 *Vanity Fair* magazine revealed that Deep Throat was Mark Felt, a former senior FBI official.[56] In 1980 Felt had been convicted of authorizing illegal break-ins in the search for members of the Weather Underground, a radical group; he was later pardoned by President Reagan. Once Felt told the magazine that he was Deep Throat, Woodward confirmed that the former FBI man was his source. One of the best-kept and longest-running secrets in Washington was finally unveiled.

In the wake of Watergate, Americans became much more aware of the role of investigative reporting. Although the practice has led to some abuses and considerable criticism, one Gallup poll reported that almost four out of five Americans, or 79 percent, favored investigative reporting, and only 18 percent disapproved.[47]

© Bettmann/Corbis

Woodward and Bernstein in the *Washington Post* newsroom, 1973

Making a Difference

## REPORTING RADIOACTIVE SECRETS

Few journalists look for important stories in seemingly boring places. Eileen Welsome, a reporter for the *Albuquerque Tribune,* possesses the relentless curiosity often deemed necessary for any journalist to achieve greatness. In 1987 that curiosity launched her, then an obscure reporter at a medium-sized New Mexico newspaper, on a quest that would pit her against the U.S. national security and medical power structures.

The story Welsome originally intended to pursue revolved around efforts by the U.S. Air Force to clean up hazardous waste sites throughout the nation. It could be important, sure, but pretty much routine. It was only while studying a dense government report on that topic that Welsome noticed an unexpected local angle: several dumps at Kirtland Air Force Base in Albuquerque.

Buried in those dumps, according to the report, were radioactive animal carcasses. Welsome just visited the base, read dry technical papers there for hours, and decided there was not enough material for a story. Just as she was about to leave, she noticed a footnote describing a human plutonium experiment.

"The information jolted me deeply," Welsome writes. "One minute I was reading about dogs that had been injected with large amounts of plutonium and had subsequently developed radiation sickness and tumors. Suddenly there was this reference to a human experiment. I wondered if the people had experienced the same agonizing deaths as the animals."

Nobody within the government or the medical world wanted to tell Welsome the names of the participants, or much else either, so she chipped away at the puzzle in stolen moments from her regular newspaper stories. She tracked down technical reports, talked to scientists, and used the Freedom of Information Act to ask the U.S. Department of Energy for documents.

As the information trickled in, Welsome learned that 18 people had been injected with plutonium. She started a file for each of the nameless 18 and developed a sketchy profile listing gender, race, date of birth, and the hospitals that originally admitted each person for treatment of a specific disease. These same hospitals administered the plutonium injections, perhaps without the full knowledge of the patients.

Years passed, and she continued to search. Many, perhaps most, beat and general assignment reporters would have given up in discouragement, worn down by the bureaucracy. Not Welsome.

Then Welsome decided to systematically review all the information she had collected in 1992. Two words on a page jumped out at her, words that had failed to register previously. The document said that a government scientist had written "to a physician in Italy, Texas, about contacting patient CAL-3."

"Italy, Texas" were the two words that provided a clue. Based on her painstakingly constructed profile, Welsome knew patient CAL-3 was an African American man who would be about 80 if still alive. She knew he had been injected with plutonium on July 18, 1947, in a San Francisco hospital where he was apparently being treated for bone cancer.

Looking at a Texas map, Welsome learned that Italy was a small town near Dallas. Welsome started by calling city hall, and she described the man to the clerk who answered the telephone. That would be Elmer Allen, the clerk said without hesitation. He had died a year ago. The clerk gave Welsome the telephone number of Allen's widow, still living in Italy.

Welsome traveled to Texas, talked to Allen's widow and daughter, and then started concentrating on the bigger story. The *Albuquerque Tribune* articles in November 1993 received little attention outside New Mexico until Secretary of Energy Hazel O'Leary held a news conference on December 7, 1993.

She expressed her shock at learning about the experimentation, then promised a new departmental policy of openness. President Bill Clinton followed up by directing other federal agencies to release information about the matter and by appointing an advisory committee on human radiation experiments.

In 1994, Eileen Welsome won the Pulitzer Prize for National Reporting for her articles about the Americans who had been used without their knowledge in the government's secret human plutonium experiments.

—Adapted from Steve Weinberg, "Persistence Pays Off," *IPI Report, The International Journalism Magazine,* First Quarter 2000

In recent years, magazine-style television programs on all the networks, modeled after CBS's *60 Minutes,* have broadcast aggressive investigative reports. Many newspapers have continued to publish such stories as well.

Press critics contend that in some cases, the news media carry investigative reporting too far, damaging reputations of corporations, officials, or other individuals in an overzealous effort to expose wrongdoing and win journalism prizes. Some of this criticism comes from officials who are themselves the target of press scrutiny.

But there have also been some instances of inaccurate investigative reporting. During the 2004 presidential election campaign, for example, CBS's *60 Minutes* aired documents that purported to show that President George W. Bush had received favorable treatment and disobeyed an order when he served in the Texas Air

National Guard. The documents were immediately attacked as fraudulent. CBS anchor Dan Rather, who had reported the story for *60 Minutes,* at first defended the account but then apologized on the air for a "mistake in judgment." Six months later, Rather stepped down as the network's news anchor, and a year later he left CBS in a contract dispute.

According to one study, two-thirds of the public think journalists "are too focused on the misdeeds and failings of public figures."[58] And almost as many members of the public, 60 percent, think that both national and local news media are "more adversarial than they should be."[59]

## Freedom of Information

Freedom of the press is diminished if the news media are unable to obtain information from official agencies of government. Beginning in 1955, Congressman John E. Moss, a California Democrat, pushed for legislation to force the federal government to make more information available to the press and public. As a result, the Freedom of Information Act (FOIA) was signed into law by President Johnson in 1966.

The **Freedom of Information Act** requires federal executive branch and regulatory agencies to make information available to journalists, scholars, and the public unless it falls into one of several confidential categories. Exempted from disclosure, for example, are national security information, personnel files, investigatory records, and the "internal" documents of an agency. The law provides that individuals can go into federal district court to force compliance by the government.

The law was strengthened in 1974 with a number of amendments. One permits federal courts to review whether documents withheld by the government on grounds of national security were properly classified in the first place; another provision requires the government to respond within 10 days to persons who make FOIA requests. But the responses are merely acknowledgments that a request has been received; the actual material may not be released for months or years—if at all. The law, however, has resulted in the release of considerable amounts of information to the public. Nonetheless, a House subcommittee noted that "foot dragging by the federal bureaucracy" had hindered the release of information under the act.[60] Often, federal agencies have refused to release meaningful information under the act unless citizens go into federal court and sue, an expensive and time-consuming process.

While encouraging a greater flow of government information to the public through the Freedom of Information Act, Congress also has responded to demands for tighter control over federal files on individuals. The Privacy Act of 1974 provides that the government may not make public its files about an individual—such as medical, financial, criminal, or employment records—without that person's written consent. The privacy law also generally gives citizens the right of access to information about themselves in government files.

Photo by thememoryhole.org via Getty Images

Coffins of U.S. soldiers killed in Iraq arrive at the Air Force base in Dover, Delaware. The White House did not want the photographs published.

At times, citizens and journalists have been able to use the Freedom of Information Act to pry loose information that the government would prefer to suppress. This happened during the war in Iraq that began in 2003. On the eve of the war, the Pentagon banned any news media coverage and photographs of the coffins of American war dead arriving at Dover Air Force Base in Delaware. But in the spring of 2004, with U.S. casualties continuing to mount, more than 300 photos of flag-draped caskets suddenly appeared on the Internet, and many were shown on television and published in newspapers. The photographs had been obtained by Russ Kick, a First Amendment advocate, who got them under FOIA—apparently through an error by the Defense Department—and posted them on his website, http://www.thememoryhole.org.

In the field of national security and foreign policy, government secrecy is supported by a formal security classification system. Under executive orders issued by every president since Truman in 1951, thousands of officials can stamp documents Top Secret, Secret, or Confidential if, in their judgment, disclosure would jeopardize national security. Under this system, millions of government documents are classified every year.

Beginning with President Kennedy, most presidents have issued executive orders providing that at least some secret documents be automatically declassified after a certain number of years.

In 1980 the Supreme Court ruled that CIA employees who sign secrecy agreements were not free to publish books about their experiences without prior agency approval.[61] The Court ruled that Frank W. Snepp, III, a former CIA officer in Vietnam, had to give the government the royalties earned from his book *Decent Interval*, even though it contained no classified information. The Court declined to consider Snepp's argument that the secrecy agreement he had signed violated his First Amendment rights.

## The Press as Target

Inevitably, a free press that investigates and reports on the government will itself become a target of government attacks. Because the press wields great power and influence in American politics, it has become a target for such attacks, not only by government officials but by many private citizens, organizations, and other critics.

In recent years, scandals at major newspapers and inaccurate reporting provided ample ammunition to the critics. First, the *New York Times*, generally regarded as the world's best and most respected newspaper, was shaken to its foundations by the disclosure in 2003 that one young reporter, Jayson Blair, 27, was making up stories out of thin air. Although there were complaints about Blair inside the *Times*, senior editors did not act to investigate. Blair resigned after a Texas newspaper questioned a story he had written about the family of Jessica Lynch, a soldier who had been captured and then freed during the Iraq war. As a result of the scandal, the top editor at the *Times*, Howell Raines, and his deputy, Gerald M. Boyd, the managing editor, resigned.

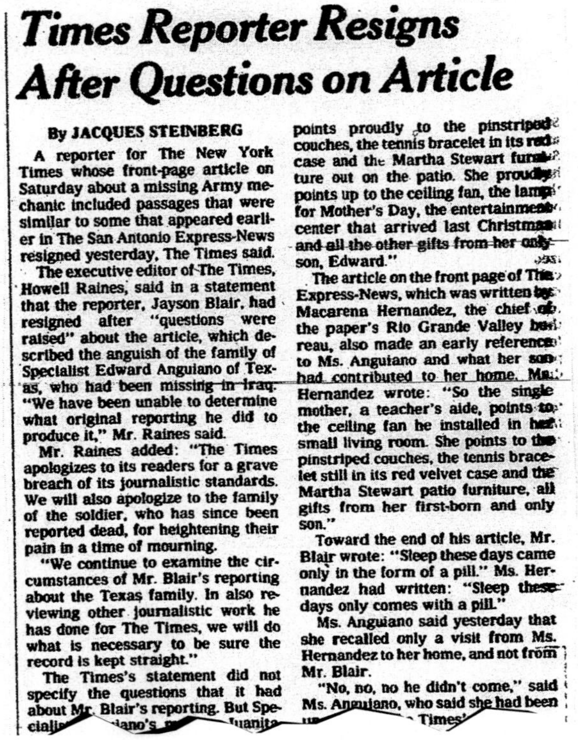

**Times Reporter Resigns After Questions on Article**

By JACQUES STEINBERG

A reporter for The New York Times whose front-page article on Saturday about a missing Army mechanic included passages that were similar to some that appeared earlier in The San Antonio Express-News resigned yesterday, The Times said.

The executive editor of The Times, Howell Raines, said in a statement that the reporter, Jayson Blair, had resigned after "questions were raised" about the article, which described the anguish of the family of Specialist Edward Anguiano of Texas, who had been missing in Iraq. "We have been unable to determine what original reporting he did to produce it," Mr. Raines said.

Mr. Raines added: "The Times apologizes to its readers for a grave breach of its journalistic standards. We will also apologize to the family of the soldier, who has since been reported dead, for heightening their pain in a time of mourning.

"We continue to examine the circumstances of Mr. Blair's reporting about the Texas family. In also reviewing other journalistic work he has done for The Times, we will do what is necessary to be sure the record is kept straight."

The Times's statement did not specify the questions that it had about Mr. Blair's reporting. But Specialis[illegible] ...ano's ... Juanita ...

points proudly to the pinstriped couches, the tennis bracelet in its red case and the Martha Stewart furniture out on the patio. She proudly points up to the ceiling fan, the lamp for Mother's Day, the entertainment center that arrived last Christmas and all the other gifts from her only son, Edward."

The article on the front page of The Express-News, which was written by Macarena Hernandez, the chief of the paper's Rio Grande Valley bureau, also made an early reference to Ms. Anguiano and what her son had contributed to her home. Ms. Hernandez wrote: "So the single mother, a teacher's aide, points to the ceiling fan he installed in her small living room. She points to the pinstriped couches, the tennis bracelet still in its red velvet case and the Martha Stewart patio furniture, all gifts from her first-born and only son."

Toward the end of his article, Mr. Blair wrote: "Sleep these days came only in the form of a pill." Ms. Hernandez had written: "Sleep these days only comes with a pill."

Ms. Anguiano said yesterday that she recalled only a visit from Ms. Hernandez to her home, and not from Mr. Blair.

"No, no, no he didn't come," said Ms. Anguiano, who said she had been ... Times' ...

*New York Times*, May 2, 2003, p. A30.

Then, in 2004, it was revealed that Jack Kelley, a star reporter for *USA Today*, the nation's largest newspaper with a circulation of more than 2 million, had fabricated stories and then conspired to mislead editors who investigated his work. Kelley had filed fictional accounts from the Middle East, Yugoslavia, Cuba, and other countries. Again, suspicions voiced by his colleagues were ignored, and the top editor, Karen Jurgensen, resigned in the wake of the scandal.

In May 2004 the *New York Times* published a statement by its editors admitting that the newspaper's coverage of the path to war in Iraq had not been as "rigorous as it should have been."[62] In publishing reports that Iraq had weapons of mass destruction, the *Times* said, it "fell for misinformation from exile groups," in particular from the group led by Ahmad Chalabi, the Iraqi National Congress, which had provided false reports from defectors. No such weapons were found after U.S. troops invaded Iraq.[63] Two months later, the *Washington Post* confessed to its readers that the newspaper should have given greater prominence before the war to stories that raised doubts about Iraq's supposed weapons of mass destruction.[64]

These shortcomings by the press did not begin with the war in Iraq. When a bomb went off in Atlanta during the summer Olympics in 1996, killing one person and injuring more than 100 others, Richard Jewell, a security guard at Olympic Park, fell under suspicion. Jewell had discovered the knapsack containing the device and had helped to move people away from the bomb, but his name was leaked to the press as a suspect. A media frenzy resulted, amid speculation that Jewell had planted the device in order to "discover" it so that his action might help him obtain a job in law enforcement. The FBI interrogated Jewell, who was finally and officially removed as a suspect three months later. He settled a threatened libel lawsuit against NBC for an undisclosed amount of money and sued the parent corporation of the *Atlanta Journal-Constitution* over the newspaper's coverage. The performance of both the FBI and the news media in the controversy was widely criticized.

In an earlier time, under President Nixon, criticism of the news media was encouraged by various government actions and by attacks on the press by high administration officials. In a celebrated speech in November 1969, Vice President Spiro T. Agnew assailed "a small band of network commentators and self-appointed ana-

© Stan Honda/AFP/Getty Images

Veteran CBS news anchor Dan Rather left the network in 2005.

lysts" who had discussed a televised address to the nation by President Nixon.[65] A week later, Agnew attacked the *Washington Post* and the *New York Times.*

Possibly some of these government pressures on the press were designed to divert public attention from the question of the government's own truthfulness; the Nixon administration in time became ensnared in scandals that led to the resignation of both Nixon and Agnew. At the same time, pressures on the press also seemed designed to persuade the news media to temper their criticism and present news about the government in a more favorable light.

During the Watergate episode, however, there was wide recognition of the fact that the press, and particularly the *Washington Post,* had played a significant role in uncovering the massive abuse of power by the Nixon White House. The disclosures by the press helped to shape public opinion and were one factor among many leading to Nixon's resignation as president.

As poll data show, the public has a low level of confidence in the accuracy of the press. (For example, see Table 8-1.)

Some of the animosity toward the press probably stems from the perception that it wields too much power. A Harris poll in 2002 reported that 72 percent of the public thought the press had "too much" power, and only 14 percent thought the press had "too little" power.[66] Asked by a Roper survey whether a president or the news media had more influence on events, 73 percent answered "the news media," and only 18 percent chose "the president."[67] And despite the First Amendment, 42 percent of respondents in one poll thought the press had "too much . . . freedom to do what it wants."[68]

A 2004 study of the press reported that only 49 percent of Americans think news organizations are "highly professional," a figure that declined from 72 percent between 1985 and 2002. Americans who think news organizations "generally get the facts straight" declined from 55 percent to 35 percent during the same period. And people who feel "news organizations try to cover up mistakes" increased from 13 percent to 67 percent.[69]

**Is the Press Biased?** Some critics contend that the press is biased, unfair, or inaccurate in its reporting of public issues. Some of this type of criticism stems from conservatives who feel the press is too "liberal." Even among the general public, only 15 percent of those ques-

## A Vice President Attacks the Press

In November of 1969 network analysts criticized an address by President Nixon in which the president defended his policy to end the Vietnam War. Ten days later, Vice President Spiro T. Agnew flew to Des Moines, Iowa, and delivered a famous speech blasting the news media:

> The purpose of my remarks tonight is to focus your attention on this little group of men who not only enjoy a right of instant rebuttal to every presidential address, but . . . wield a free hand in selecting, presenting and interpreting the great issues of our Nation [on the evening newscasts]. . . . These commentators and producers live and work in the geographical and intellectual confines of Washington, D.C., and New York City. . . . [They] draw their political and social views from the same sources. Worse, they talk constantly to one another, thereby providing artificial reinforcement to their shared viewpoints . . .
>
> The American people would rightly not tolerate this kind of concentration of power in government.
>
> Is it not fair and relevant to question its concentration in the hands of a tiny and closed fraternity of privileged men, elected by no one, and enjoying a monopoly sanctioned and licensed by government?
>
> The views of this fraternity do not represent the views of America.

—Quoted in John Anthony Maltese, *Spin Control: The White House Office of Communications and the Management of Presidential News*

## TABLE 8-1

### The Public Views the Press

Would you say that your overall opinion of [insert news category] is very favorable, mostly favorable, mostly unfavorable, or very unfavorable?

| | |
|---|---|
| Network TV: | Favorable: 68%<br>Unfavorable: 23%<br>Other: 9% |
| Daily Newspapers: | Favorable: 72%<br>Unfavorable: 18%<br>Other: 10% |
| Local Television News: | Favorable: 73%<br>Unfavorable: 20%<br>Other: 7% |
| Cable News: | Favorable: 67%<br>Unfavorable: 18%<br>Other: 15% |

How have you been getting most of your news?

Television: 74%
Newspaper: 44%
Internet: 24%
Radio: 22%
Magazine: 5%
Other: 3%

Do you think news organizations get the facts straight or do you think that their stories are often inaccurate?

Gets facts straight: 36%
Stories often inaccurate: 56%

Do you think news organizations are pretty independent, or are they often influenced by powerful people and organizations?

Independent: 21%
Influenced by powerful people and organizations: 73%
Don't know: 6%

Should journalists always reveal news sources?

Sometimes keep confidential: 76%
Always reveal: 19%
Don't know: 5%

SOURCE: The Pew Research Foundation for the People and The Press, "Public More Critical of Press, but Goodwill Persists," June 26, 2005, online at www.people-press.org.

tioned in one poll had a "great deal" of confidence in the press; 52 percent had "only some" confidence.[70] On the other hand, public confidence was low for many major institutions, including Congress, business, and organized labor.

A 2004 study found that 59 percent of the public thought the press biased.[71] On the other hand, the perception of political bias lies partly in the eye of the beholder; a Gallup poll taken during the Senate impeachment trial of President Clinton reported that 63 percent of Republicans thought the media was biased in favor of Clinton, but 48 percent of Democrats thought the press was biased against the president.[72]

© AP Images/Schwarz

In 2005, former FBI official Mark Felt was finally revealed as "Deep Throat," the *Washington Post*'s anonymous news source during the Watergate scandal.

What are the political views of members of the press? In one study, only 5 percent of the national press considered themselves "very liberal." Although 29 percent of the national press characterized themselves as "liberal," the majority—54 percent—called themselves "moderate." Seven percent of the national press described themselves as "conservative."[73]

Among talk radio hosts, however, a significantly higher number, 36 percent, described themselves as "conservative" or "very conservative."[74] Conservative talk radio hosts such as Rush Limbaugh have a large following, and at times their views have had considerable political impact.

One survey of political party identification among reporters showed that 44.4 percent identified themselves as Democrats, 34.4 percent as Republicans, and 16.3 percent as independents.[75]

Critics of the news media argue that bias in reporting is not simply a question of party identification among journalists; conservatives argue that the media are culturally liberal, in favor of gay rights, including same-sex marriages; against religion; pro-abortion; permissive about pornography; and closer to the views of liberal or moderate Supreme Court justices, rather than to conservatives such as Chief Justice William H. Rehnquist or Justices Clarence Thomas and Antonin Scalia.

Measuring the political or cultural views or party affiliations of members of the press, however, tells only part of the story. A more relevant question—the real

FIGURE 8-2

**The Politics of the Press: How Reporters and Broadcasters Describe Themselves**

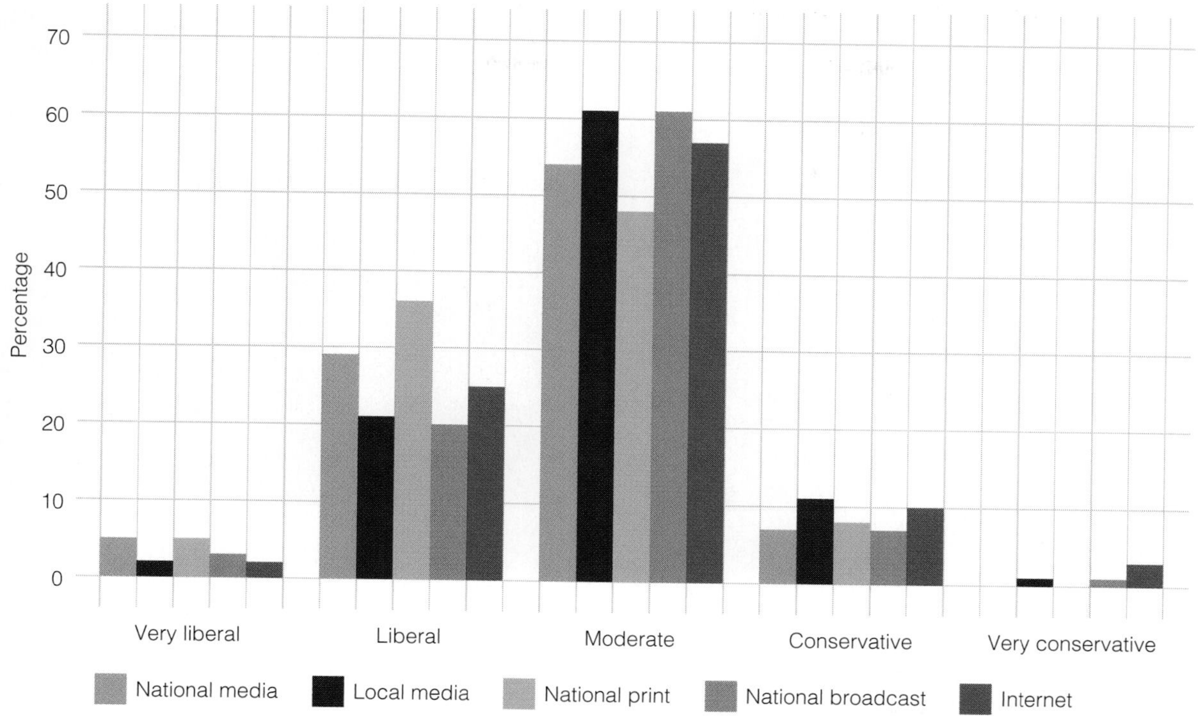


SOURCE: Adapted from The Pew Research Center for the People and the Press, *Survey of Journalists,* March 10–April 20, 2004.

test—is whether "news as reported to the public is biased."[76] The focus on the economic, social, and political background or personal beliefs of members of the press implies that reporters' politics will always necessarily be reflected in their stories. But members of the press, like doctors, social scientists, judges, and many other people, are daily called upon to make "objective" judgments. While complete "objectivity" may not be possible, most news reporters strive for accuracy even if they do not always achieve it.

And if reporters in Washington are biased in favor of Democrats, as conservatives often claim, it is difficult to explain why presidents Kennedy and Johnson, both Democrats, complained bitterly about their treatment

Michael Moore, liberal filmmaker and producer of *Fahrenheit 9/11,* debates Bill O'Reilly, conservative TV host of *The O'Reilly Factor.*

President Bush answers questions from reporters outside the White House.



in the press. The long-running Whitewater affair, a constant irritant to President Clinton, a Democrat, was first brought to public attention in 1992 by the *New York Times,* often considered the most prominent liberal paper in the country. In its editorials, the *Times* consistently accused both the president and his wife, Hillary, of delay in turning over documents to the independent prosecutor and to Congress and of evading questions about the scandal. And the press provided extensive coverage of Clinton's troubles over Monica Lewinsky and the charges by two other women, Kathleen Willey and Paula Jones, who claimed he had made improper sexual advances toward them.

Some critics of the press have suggested that the media failed to report the sexual indiscretions of President Kennedy because he was a Democrat and well liked by many reporters. However, in the 1960s, by common understanding, correspondents as a rule did not write about the private lives of public figures. It was another era. If a reporter wrote about Kennedy's affairs, his or her publisher in those years would almost certainly have declined to print the story. Moreover, there is a big difference between reporters being "aware" of a president's sexual liaisons, as many were, and being able to prove it. No responsible reporter would write a story based on mere rumor.

Times have changed; with the increased openness about sexual matters in society today, the press had no hesitation in reporting about the sexual activities of President Clinton. But there was another crucial difference; the two women made highly public charges against the president, and one, Paula Jones, sued him in federal court for sexual harassment. The Lewinsky affair was investigated by Independent Counsel Kenneth W. Starr, who filed a 445-page report containing explicit sexual details. These were legitimate, dramatic news stories, and the press reported them.

## Government Misinformation and the Press

Sometimes the government does not tell the truth to the press. It may mislead the press—and therefore the public—for a variety of reasons, such as to put a favorable "spin" on the news, to cover up wrongdoing, to conceal a foreign policy maneuver, or to protect a military or intelligence operation.

The Eisenhower administration lied when it denied at first that the CIA's U-2 spy plane had deliberately flown over the Soviet Union. The Kennedy administration falsely said it had not intervened in Cuba at the time of the Bay of Pigs invasion by CIA-supported exiles. Lyndon Johnson persuaded Congress to support the war in Vietnam by making public a misleading account of an attack on American warships in the Tonkin Gulf. Nixon lied about Watergate. Clinton lied about his affair with Monica Lewinsky. When the government puts out misleading information and that fact becomes known, it almost inevitably lowers public confidence in government. During the Johnson administration, the difference between the government's actions and its words became known as the "credibility gap."

During the 1990s there was concern among law enforcement authorities and the public about the apparent increase in the number of right-wing armed "militia" groups in the United States. The militias harbored a deep distrust of government, especially the federal government, which its members viewed as a threat to their safety and freedom. Whether this distrust of the government is related to the fact that the government has not always been truthful in its public statements is difficult to measure. But certainly suspicion of political leaders is fueled when they release information that is later revealed to be untrue or misleading. President George W. Bush's repeated claims that Iraq had weapons of mass destruction—the chief reason he gave to go to war—opened him to criticism when, more than a year later, no weapons had been found.

## The Press and the Military

Special problems arise when the press attempts to cover a war. Here, the desire of the news media for information may collide with the military's responsibility to protect the security of its troops and its battle plans. For example, the government imposed strict censorship of the press during the Second World War.

The military may also impose restrictions for another reason: to present its actions—and government policy—in the best possible light. During the Vietnam War, the military and the White House constantly reassured the public that the United States was winning the war. But a small group of reporters in Vietnam wrote stories that contradicted official policy and presented a much more realistic picture of the quagmire from which the United States eventually retreated.

Often, in military operations, the press in the past, at least, was confined to "pools," in which a few designated reporters were allowed to visit a particular area and then brief the rest of the press. This practice prevailed during the Persian Gulf War in 1991, when combat reporting was limited to small pools of correspondents whose movements were restricted and controlled by the military.

After the war, Secretary of State James Baker declared, perhaps only half in jest: "The Gulf War was quite a victory. But who could not be moved by the sight of that poor demoralized rabble—outwitted, outflanked, outmaneuvered by the U.S. military. But I think, given time, the press will bounce back."[77]

In the wake of the Gulf War, a new set of rules was drawn up in negotiations between the Pentagon and representatives of the press. The new regulations provided that pools would be used only when necessary and for brief periods. The Pentagon agreed to honor "open and independent reporting" in future wars.

And indeed, when American forces invaded Iraq in 2003, most television and print reporters were "embedded" with the troops, traveling with them as the units the correspondents were assigned to advanced on Baghdad. This had the advantage for viewers and readers of making available almost immediate, often dramatic images and stories from the front lines. On the other hand, critics of the practice noted that it made the correspondents appear to be almost an arm of the military and boosters for the war, perhaps too close in some instances to report with an independent and critical eye. The issue was whether embedded journalists were trading objectivity for access—and television footage.

Certainly the images were vivid. The embedded journalists used the latest digital technology to broadcast battles in real time, sometimes with grainy green video captured with night-vision photography. And the scenes of battle were not limited to those broadcast by journalists. Many soldiers used digital cameras to record images of combat. Even at war, a soldier could in some cases

October 2006: A U.S. general points to a map of Baghdad as he briefs the press on efforts to end sectarian violence in the Iraqi capital.

return to base and upload images via the Internet onto message boards and websites seen around the world.

## The Press in a Democratic Society

As we have seen, there are considerable pressures on the American press. The rapid expansion of television has resulted in a struggle for survival by many newspapers. The growth of cable TV, in turn, has placed economic pressures on the television networks. Media mergers have created economic giants and raised questions about the independence of news organizations subject to control by their corporate masters.

Exploding changes in technology and the growth and influence of the Internet have already had an effect on how news is gathered and presented to the public. The future will undoubtedly bring even more changes. Newspapers may be printed on home computers, to take one example, instead of being delivered to the front door; television sets as small as wristwatches may become as common as cellular phones. And those phones, originally used only for voice communication, are now often capable of surfing the Internet, reading e-mail, sending text messages, and taking digital photos. The whole future of the communications industry is one of rapid change.

The increased popularity of tabloid-style television news programs and talk shows has had a discernible impact on broadcast news. Television news has adapted to this trend by packaging information in ways designed to "entertain" viewers. And the news divisions of the TV networks are under constant pressure to cut back their budgets, as more money is poured into sitcoms and other light fare in the ratings battle for audience share.

The press is a business. Publishers and broadcasters may speak of their responsibility to inform the public and of their special role in the political system under the First Amendment. But they also keep a close eye on the bottom line. If they fail to make a profit, they may go under.

Despite its shortcomings—the lack of high-quality newspapers in many communities, for example—a free press in the United States is essential to the functioning of the American democracy and a vital link between the public and the government.

Public opinion is formed on the basis of what the news media present to the public. Democratic government rests broadly on public opinion and presupposes a fairly well-informed public. (The role of the press in political campaigns is discussed in Chapter 10, and the relationship between the president and the press is discussed in Chapter 13.)

Aside from its role of informing the general public, the American press, particularly the high-quality newspapers, magazines, and television news programs, does an excellent job of informing those who are politically aware—politicians, opinion leaders, political scientists, lawyers, journalists, college students, and any citizens who are interested in politics.

Nothing about democracy guarantees an alert, educated public. Like voting and other forms of political participation, knowledge of public affairs—the basis of intelligent public opinion—is largely up to the individual. Information about public affairs, however, is available to those who want it. It is gathered, published, broadcast, and posted online by the nation's free press, operating under the protection of the U.S. Constitution.

## CHAPTER HIGHLIGHTS

- The First Amendment to the Constitution protects the freedom of the press. It does so because the supporters of the Bill of Rights understood that the press must be free to report about the activities of the government and, when necessary, to criticize those in power.
- Freedom of the press and freedom of expression are not absolute. Under the Constitution, the Supreme Court has balanced these basic rights against competing needs of society.
- Broadly defined, "the media" include TV, the Internet, newspapers, magazines, radio, wire services, books, newsletters, and other published material. Often, as this book does, people use the term "the press" interchangeably with "the media" or "the news media."
- The press plays a vital role in a democracy because it is the principal means by which the people learn about the actions and policies of the government. A democracy rests on the consent of the governed, but in order to give their consent in any meaningful way, the governed must be informed.
- The press provides a crucial link between the people and the government. It is the essential source of information that helps citizens form opinions about government and politics and decide how to cast their votes in elections.
- Until the 20th century, the press consisted only of print media—newspapers, magazines, books, and pamphlets. The press moguls of the 19th and early 20th centuries had great influence on American society and on the government. Eventually, sensational reporting in their newspapers became known as "yellow journalism."
- In the first decade of the 20th century, long before the modern term "investigative reporting" came into vogue, a group of writers, journalists, and critics known as muckrakers exposed corporate malfeasance and political corruption.
- The 20th century brought radio into America's homes. For the first time, it allowed political leaders to speak directly to the voters.
- By providing a direct link between political leaders and candidates and voters, television changed the nature of American politics. Television had an enormous effect, not only on the political process, but also on the shape and power of the media. As advertisers poured millions into the TV networks to reach prime-time audiences, inevitably fewer advertising dollars were invested in print journalism.
- Just as television had altered the shape of American politics a half-century earlier, by the presidential elections of 2000 and 2004 the Internet had brought a dramatic new level of technological change to government and the political process. Political information, census figures, poll data, the text of speeches, legislation, Supreme Court decisions, and almost unlimited resources of all kinds became available at the click of a mouse button, part of a vast ocean of information that once could only be found in major libraries.
- By 2006 the shape of the media had changed dramatically. One after another, the giants of the media had joined in multibillion-dollar mergers. The concentration of ownership raised questions about the independence and diversity of the American press.
- Radio and television do not enjoy as much freedom as other segments of the press because, unlike newspapers, broadcast stations are licensed by the Federal Communications Commission. Although broadcast networks are not licensed, the stations they own and operate are. The law requires broadcasters to provide "equal time" to all legally qualified political candidates.
- In recent years the Supreme Court has shown increasing concern over pretrial and courtroom publicity that may prejudice the fair trial of a defendant in a criminal case. The right to a fair trial often conflicts with the First Amendment in another important area—that of confidentiality for reporters and their news sources. The Supreme Court has ruled that reporters must reveal the identity of their sources if the information is needed in a criminal case.
- A person defamed by a newspaper or other publication may be able to sue for libel and collect damages because the First Amendment does not protect this form of "free speech." Despite some victories by the press, the threat of libel actions has become a major problem for the news media, publishers, and writers.
- Some critics of the press argue that giving widespread coverage to acts of terrorism plays into the hands of the perpetrators, who are seeking publicity. Another argument sometimes voiced is that press coverage can lead to "copycat" acts by others seeking the same notoriety for their deeds or for themselves. The press, however, has a responsibility to report major news events.
- The government often attempts to manipulate the press and to manage the news, to put a favorable "spin" on events. It may even mislead the press—and therefore the public—for a variety of reasons. Officials have a vested interest in trying to influence what the press reports, in order to shape public opinion to support administration policies.
- The Freedom of Information Act requires federal executive branch and regulatory agencies to make information available to journalists and other people unless it falls into one of several confidential categories. Even so, it may take years before information is released under the act.
- Because the press wields great power and influence in American politics it has become a target of criticism. Some critics contend that the press is politically

biased. However, poll data suggest that more than half of the members of the national press consider themselves moderate, rather than liberal or conservative.

- Exploding changes in technology, and the growth and influence of the Internet, have already affected how news is gathered and presented to the public.

## KEY TERMS

muckrakers, p. 223
equal time, p. 231
prior restraint, p. 232
shield laws, p. 235
Freedom of Information Act, p. 243

## SUGGESTED WEBSITES

**http://www.cjr.org**
*Columbia Journalism Review*
The online version of the *Columbia Journalism Review,* a magazine that covers media issues. Resources on the website include lists of which corporations own the media; special reports on the issues involved in covering controversial topics such as AIDS, tobacco, mental health care, and money and politics; and links to other journalism websites.

**http://www.freedomforum.org**
*Freedom Forum*
A nonpartisan, international foundation that provides information about the freedoms covered by the First Amendment, including freedom of the press and freedom of speech.

**http://www.newseum.org**
*Newseum*
The Internet version of news museums in New York City, and planned for Washington, D.C. This website offers exhibits that focus on the past, present, and future of the news business.

**http://www.journalism.org**
*Project for Excellence in Journalism and the Committee of Concerned Journalists*
A consortium of reporters, editors, producers, publishers, owners, and academics. Visitors can read reports, studies, essays, and articles about the future of journalism.

**http://www.rcfp.org**
*The Reporters Committee for Freedom of the Press*
A nonprofit organization that provides legal assistance to journalists whose First Amendment rights are under attack. The committee publishes quarterly legal reviews and biweekly newsletters, and offers a 24-hour legal defense hotline for reporters.

## SUGGESTED READING

Barker, David C. *Rushed to Judgment: Talk Radio, Persuasion, and American Political Behavior** (Columbia University Press, 2002). A study of the impact of talk radio on public opinion, with a particular focus on Rush Limbaugh. The author concludes that Limbaugh has influenced his listeners on a range of issues, and that he has been able to generate strong opposition to specific politicians. In 2000, Limbaugh influenced his listeners to support George W. Bush over John McCain in the Republican primary.

Bennett, W. Lance, and Paletz, David L., eds. *Taken by Storm: The Media, Public Opinion, and U.S. Foreign Policy in the Gulf War** (University of Chicago Press, 1994). An illuminating series of essays by academic specialists and journalists analyzing the performance of the press and of the government during the Persian Gulf War.

Fallows, James. *Breaking the News: How the Media Undermine American Democracy** (Random House, 1997). A highly critical view of the press by a Washington writer. Fallows criticizes journalists for such practices as emphasizing political strategies and personalities over issues and for accepting large speaking fees from business and other interest groups.

Farnsworth, Stephen J., and Lichter, S. Robert. *The Nightly News Nightmare: Network Television's Coverage of U.S. Presidential Elections, 1988–2000** (Rowman & Littlefield, 2003). A research study that argues that between 1988 and 2000 the quality and quantity of television network news (ABC, CBS, NBC) declined. The authors criticize the networks for focusing on the "horse race" between candidates rather than on the substantive issues, and for coverage that the study finds generally negative and sometimes unfair or inaccurate.

Frankel, Max. *The Times of My Life: And My Life with the Times* (Dell Publishers, 2000). A fascinating autobiography by the reporter who became the executive editor of the *New York Times.* Provides revealing insights into the politics and conflicts inside the world's most prestigious newspaper.

Graber, Doris A. *Mass Media and American Politics,* 7th edition* (CQ Press, 2005). A comprehensive survey of the role of the mass media in American politics. Stresses the impact that the media have on citizens' attitudes and perceptions, and argues that the mass media are exerting a growing influence on social values and public policy.

Graber, Doris A., ed. *Media Power in Politics,* 5th edition* (CQ Press, 2006). A summary of the history of the mass media. Emphasizes the ability of the media to shape the political agenda.

Hersh, Seymour M. *My Lai 4: A Report on the Massacre and Its Aftermath* (Random House, 1970). A detailed reconstruction by a leading investigative journalist of the events that led to the murder of more than 100 civilians in a South Vietnam village by American troops in 1968. Hersh's account of the My Lai massacre earned him the 1970 Pulitzer Prize for international reporting.

Jamieson, Kathleen Hall, and Waldman, Paul. *The Press Effect: Politicians, Journalists, and the Stories that Shape the Political World* (Oxford University Press, 2003). A study that describes how the news media's overall approach to events, influences the content of news stories. The book focuses on three stories: The 2000 Bush-Gore presidential debates, election night 2000 and the subsequent 36 days before the outcome was settled, and 9/11 and its aftermath. The authors suggest ways in which the press can present news more effectively to the public.

Knightley, Phillip. *The First Casualty: The War Correspondent as Hero and Mythmaker from the Crimea to Iraq,* 3rd edition* (Johns Hopkins University Press, 2004). A lively examination, by a British author and journalist, of the major wars of the 19th and 20th centuries and the correspondents who covered them.

Maltese, John Anthony. *Spin Control: The White House Office of Communications and the Management of Presidential News,* 2nd edition (University of North Carolina Press, 1994). A detailed study of how the White House Office of Communications has attempted to control the public agenda by making presidential news. Contains examples from five presidential administrations, beginning with the presidency of Richard Nixon.

Sanford, Bruce. *Don't Shoot the Messenger: How Our Growing Hatred of the Media Threatens Free Speech for All of Us** (Harper Collins, 2001). A thoughtful analysis, by a respected First Amendment attorney, of the growing public distrust of the mass media. The author suggests that this public cynicism undermines the impact of journalists' efforts to expose corruption.

West, Darrell M. *The Rise and Fall of the Media Establishment** (Bedford/ St. Martin's Press, 2001). A short history of the U.S. press and politics that describes five broad periods: the partisan press (1790s to 1840s); the commercial media (1840s to 1920s); the objective media (1920s to 1970s); the interpretive media (1970s through 1980s); and the fragmented media (since the 1990s). The author argues that recent trends have weakened the role of the mainstream press.

*Available in paperback edition.

# Chapter 9

# Political Parties

IN 2006, as the midterm congressional elections approached, Democrats were hopeful of recapturing the House of Representatives, and also of making substantial gains in the Senate. The war in Iraq was marked by continued violence and suicide bombings; the job approval ratings of the Republican president, George W. Bush, were low; and gas prices remained high, even though they had dropped considerably by October. But well before the voters went to the polls, political leaders of both major parties were looking ahead to the presidential election of 2008. Under the Constitution, President George W. Bush, having served two terms, could not run again. Would Senator John McCain of Arizona emerge as the Republican nominee? Would the Democrats choose Senator Hillary Clinton of New York? Would the party turn to Barack Obama, the young, charismatic senator from Illinois? Might Senator John Kerry of Massachusetts, the party's nominee four years earlier, try again? It was too early to tell, but in 2008, as in most previous presidential years, the contest would likely be not only between candidates but also between the two major parties, the Republican Party and the Democratic Party.

When the Democrats' nominee, John Kerry, stood before the cheering national convention delegates in Boston in July 2004 and accepted their nomination with a pledge to fight terrorism "and restore trust and credibility to the White House,"[1] the party was energized and hopeful, but far from confident of victory in November. And indeed it was the Republican president, George W. Bush, who won the election that year.

Opinion polls before the convention showed that many voters felt they did not really know much about Kerry, despite his widely publicized combat as a decorated Navy lieutenant in Vietnam, his antiwar activism after that conflict—aspects of his past soon challenged by Bush partisans—and his 19 years in the U.S. Senate. Moreover, Kerry was opposing an incumbent president, George W. Bush, the Republican candidate, and in American election contests the occupant of the White House often has the advantage. He travels in Air Force One, the trappings and symbols of office follow him on the hustings, and he can take actions that dominate the nightly news.

Finally, Kerry, a tall, serious man whose appearance was frequently described as "Lincolnesque," was a political leader who sometimes seemed to have difficulty connecting with voters on a personal level. But Kerry surprised even his own supporters. At the convention, he delivered a vigorous, at times passionate speech that sketched his vision for America and assailed Bush. "I will be a commander in chief who will never mislead us into war," he said.[2] It was an obvious reference to Bush's claim that Iraq had weapons of mass destruction, requiring a U.S. invasion, although none had been found more than a year later. The convention also nominated Senator John Edwards of North Carolina, for vice president.

Despite Kerry's performance, in most polls he received very little of the "convention bounce"—the gain in the polls a candidate often enjoys after a national convention—that the Democrats had hoped to achieve.

One month later, it was the Republicans' turn to hold their national convention. The party chose New York City as the site in order to emphasize Bush's leadership after the 9/11 terrorist attacks on the World Trade Center and the Pentagon.

A series of speakers lashed out at Kerry, as the delegates, waving a sea of small American flags, repeatedly chanted "Four more years" and "USA." Vice President Dick Cheney was renominated and addressed the convention, and then on the climactic last night the president bounded onto a circular stage that had been constructed for him overnight so he would be surrounded by delegates.

In his acceptance speech, Bush repeatedly invoked 9/11 and the danger to America of terrorism. Future generations would look to New York, he said, "and they will say: Here buildings fell, and here a nation rose."[3]

Bush emerged from the convention with an 11-point "bounce" in the polls.[4] By the end of September, when the candidates met in their first televised debate, most polls still showed Bush running several points ahead of Kerry.

After elaborate negotiations, the Kerry and Bush camps agreed on a set of ground rules for three televised presidential debates proposed by the bipartisan Commission on Presidential Debates, and a fourth debate between the vice presidential candidates, Dick Cheney, the incumbent, and John Edwards, the Democratic challenger.

Despite the traditional advantages enjoyed by incumbents, there were statistical reasons for Bush and his political advisers to be concerned. By 2004, as had been true for many years in the past, more people in America called themselves Democrats than Republicans. But the gap between the parties had narrowed. In 2004, the Democrats enjoyed a modest 33 to 29 percent edge in party affiliation.[5] The number of people who identified themselves as Republicans had increased during the 1980s when the party controlled the White House. In addition, about a third of the voters called themselves independents.

Beyond the candidates' maneuvering over foreign policy, health care, and jobs, the 2004 campaign offered voters a choice between competing political philosophies. Although—as often happens—both major-party candidates tended to move toward the center during the election, there were still marked differences between the Democratic and Republican Parties and their nominees.

Key Question

In this chapter, we will explore a key question: ***Do political parties still perform a useful role in the American democratic system?*** A number of related questions may also be considered. Have the parties been eclipsed by powerful interest groups? Has the influence of television commercials and the money that pays for them become more important than party loyalties? Are political parties truly responsive and responsible instruments of democracy? Do they offer a genuine choice on the major issues facing the nation? Are parties elitist organizations controlled by a few leaders and closed to outsiders? Are national conventions—which have increasingly become carefully scripted television extravaganzas—still useful tools of representative government? In discussing the role, history, organization, and performance of American political parties, we will explore many of these questions.

## What Is a Party?

"As there are many roads to Rome and many ways to skin a cat," Frank J. Sorauf has written, "there are also many ways to look at a political party."[6] A political party is a group of men and women meeting in a small community in Connecticut to nominate a candidate for town council. It is a group of ward heelers in Chicago turning out to cheer at a political rally. It is the officials and supporters of the party in the 50 states. It is congressional leaders having a private breakfast at the White House with the president to discuss the administration's legislative proposals. It is the delegates to a national political convention exploding in a frenzy of noise, emotion, confetti, and balloons after their candidate for president accepts the nomination—even though in recent times, the convention's choice has been determined months earlier in the spring primaries. It is the party's national committee, chosen by the convention. It is the millions who vote on Election Day.

As Sorauf has concluded, the nature of a political party is somewhat in "the eye of the beholder."[7] There are the *voters,* a majority of whom consider themselves Democrats or Republicans; the *party leaders outside of government,* who frequently control the party machinery and sometimes have important power bases; the *party activists,* who ring doorbells, serve as delegates to county, state, and national conventions, and perform the day-to-day, grass-roots work of politics; and finally, the *party leaders in the government,* including the president, the leaders in Congress, and party leaders in state and local governments.

When someone speaks of "the Democratic Party" or "the Republican Party," that person may really mean any of these diverse elements—or all of them. Because a political party is made up of so many groups and individuals, it is difficult to define in a shorthand way. But, in very general terms, a **major political party** is a broadly based coalition that attempts to gain control of the government by winning elections in order to exercise power and reward its members.

Today, political parties are less powerful than in the past, as party allegiances among voters have declined and as competing groups—political action committees, professional campaign managers, and interest groups—have increasingly come to share many of the traditional roles of parties. Nevertheless, political parties continue to perform vital functions in the American political system.

The best way to look at political parties is not in terms of what they are, but in terms of what they do. One of the major problems of government is managing the transfer of power. In totalitarian governments, power, once seized, is seldom peacefully relinquished. Usually the change comes unexpectedly. A democracy, however, provides orderly institutional arrangements for the transfer of power.

In normal circumstances in the United States, a candidate for president, running as the nominee of a political party, is elected every four years and serves one or two terms. American political parties thus perform "an essential function in the management of succession to power."[8] They serve as a vehicle for choice, offering the electorate competing candidates for public office, and often, alternative policies. The element of choice is absolutely vital to democratic government. Where voters cannot choose, there is no democracy. The parties operate the machinery of choice: nominations, campaigns, and elections.

Within the framework of a political system (the concept discussed in Chapter 1), political parties help to mobilize the demands and supports that are fed into the system, and participate as well in the authoritative decision making, or outputs, of the government.

In a presidential election, the party in power traditionally defends its record and attacks its opponents, while the party out of power suggests that it is time for a change. That is exactly what happened in the 2004 presidential election between the two major-party candidates, President George W. Bush, who had been elected four years earlier, and Senator John Kerry, the Democratic challenger.

By seeking to mobilize mass opinion behind their slogans and policies, political parties channel public support for, or against, the administration in power. In so doing, they normally serve as an essential bridge between the people and the government. They provide a powerful means for the public's voice to be heard—and politicians must listen if they wish to survive in office. Parties thus help to hold officials accountable to the voters. They also help to recruit candidates for public office.

Because a political party consists of people expressing attitudes about government, it might seem to fit the definition of an interest group. But a political party runs candidates for public office. It is therefore much more comprehensive than an interest group. Instead of seeking only to influence government, often on a narrow range of issues, a major party attempts to win elections and gain control of the government.

The major political parties try to form "winning coalitions" by maneuvering "to create combinations powerful enough to govern."[9] In the process, they may serve to reconcile the interests of conflicting groups in society. The political party can fill the natural role of broker or mediator among interest groups, organized or not, because in order to win elections it usually tries to appeal broadly to many groups of voters.

*Myth vs. Reality*

## AMERICAN POLITICAL PARTIES: WHAT ARE THEY?

Everyone knows that there is a Republican Party and a Democratic Party in the United States that compete in elections for control of the White House and Congress. But exactly where are the parties to be found, and what are they?

That's easy, you might answer. Each has a headquarters and a staff in Washington, D.C. Well, not exactly. If you look in the telephone book for the nation's capital, you will not find the Democratic Party or the Republican Party listed. The Democratic National Committee had an office and phone number listed in 2004; the Republican National Committee was not listed. Nor does either party as such have a website, although both national committees do (http://www.democrats.org and http://www.rnc.org).

The fact that both major political parties are a bit elusive to track down reflects the now-you-see-them-now-you-don't reality of political parties in America. One could draw a neat organizational chart of a major political party, with the national chair and national committee at the top of the pyramid, and state and local party machinery arrayed below. The chart would be technically correct but highly misleading. In fact, the national party exists more on paper than in reality, in theory more than in fact.

The truth is that the national party is a broadly based, loose coalition of national political figures, state party leaders, staff workers, members of Congress, and other elected officials who come together every four years to support a presidential candidate. A political party tries to gain control of the government by winning elections in order to exercise power and reward its members.

But don't try to find it in the phone book.

---

Parties also play a key role in the governmental process. When the administration of President George W. Bush succeeded the Clinton administration in January 2001, Washington real estate agents were happy; it meant that Democrats would be selling their houses and Republicans would be buying them. After a presidential election, the White House staff, the cabinet, and the more important policymakers and officials of the various departments of the executive branch are for the most part appointed from the president's party. To the victors belong the White House limousines.

Political parties play a vital role in the legislative branch as well. The president appeals to party loyalty through the party's legislative leaders in order to get his programs through Congress (although he may face a Congress controlled by the opposition party, as President Clinton did after the 1994 congressional elections). And both major parties have "whips" in Congress—legislative leaders who are responsible for rounding up their party's members for important votes.

Because political parties are involved in the governmental process, they serve to link different parts of the government: The president communicates with party leaders in Congress; the two houses of Congress communicate in part through party leaders; and relationships among the national, state, and local governments depend to a considerable degree on ties among partisan officials and leaders.

In sum, political parties perform vital functions in the American political system. They (1) manage the transfer of power, (2) offer a choice of rival candidates and programs to the voters, (3) serve as a bridge between government and people by helping to hold elected officials accountable to the voters, (4) help to recruit candidates for office, (5) may serve to reconcile conflicting interests in society, (6) staff the government and help to run it, and (7) link various branches and levels of government.

## The Development of American Political Parties

The framers of the Constitution created the delicately balanced machinery of the federal government and provided for regular elections of a president and Congress, but they said not a word about political parties. The reason was simple: In the modern sense, they did not exist.

Yet James Madison, the "father of the Constitution," foresaw that Americans would group together in factions. In *The Federalist, No. 10,* he predicted that the task of regulating conflicting economic interests would involve "the spirit of party and faction in the necessary and ordinary operation of the government."

In his farewell address, George Washington warned against "the baneful effects of the spirit of party." His vice president, John Adams, had declared: "There is nothing I dread so much as the division of the Republic into two great parties, each under its leader."[10] Yet the American party system began to take just such a shape in the 1790s during Washington's administration.

### Federalists and Democratic-Republicans

The Federalist Party, organized by Alexander Hamilton, Washington's secretary of the treasury, was the first national political party in the United States. The Federalists stood for strong central government, and their appeal was to banking, commercial, and financial interests.

Thomas Jefferson built a rival coalition that be-

Photo by Steve Laschever/The Museum American Political Life, University of Hartford

These political buttons for George Washington were intended to be sewn on clothing.

came known as the Republican Party, or Democratic-Republicans, a name that tends to be confusing in tracing the origins of the American party system. Today's Democratic Party, the oldest political party in the world, claims the Democratic-Republican Party as its political and spiritual ancestor. Today's Republican Party invokes Abraham Lincoln, not Jefferson.

Jefferson's party was primarily an agrarian group of small farmers, debtors, southern planters, and frontiersmen. Being a practical politician, Jefferson sought to expand his coalition; in 1791 he made a famous trip to New York State, allegedly on a "butterfly hunting" expedition, but actually to form an alliance with Aaron Burr and the Sons of Tammany, the political organization that was to dominate New York City. In the partnership of rural America and the cities, the Democratic Party was born.

Ralph E. Becker Collection/Smithsonian Institution

Jefferson's triumph in the election of 1800 inaugurated a 28-year period of ascendancy by the Jeffersonian Democratic-Republicans. In fact, the Federalists never again tried for the presidency after 1816 when James Monroe, the Democratic-Republican candidate, was elected overwhelmingly. Monroe's victory launched the brief Era of Good Feelings, in which there was little partisan activity.

## Democrats and Whigs

By 1824 the Democratic-Republicans had split into several factions and the first phase of party government in the United States came to an end. The election in 1828 of Andrew Jackson, the hero of the War of 1812, opened a new era of two-party rivalry, this time between Democrats and Whigs. Jacksonian democracy soon came to symbolize popular rule and the aspirations of the common man.

The rival Whigs, led by Henry Clay, William Henry Harrison, and Daniel Webster, were a coalition of bankers, merchants, and southern planters held together precariously by their mutual distaste for Jacksonian democracy. The Whigs won two presidential elections between 1840 and 1854, and the two-party system flourished.[11]

As Clinton Rossiter has noted, "Out of the conflict

Indiana Historical Society

*The American Past*

## BALLOTS AND BARGAINS: THE REPUBLICAN CONVENTION OF 1860

The Republicans met in a huge box-like structure called the "Wigwam" in Chicago in May and drew up a platform opposing the extension of slavery . . . and upholding the Union. . . . The chief contenders for the Republican nomination were William H. Seward of New York and Abraham Lincoln of Illinois. . . .

Lincoln decided to stay in Springfield, Illinois, during the Chicago convention. . . . His managers went to Chicago with only Illinois in the bag, but did everything they could think of to build up support for their man in other state delegations. They hired two Chicagoans, whose shouts, it was said, could be heard above the howling of the most violent tempest on Lake Michigan, to lead the cheers whenever Lincoln's name was mentioned in the convention. They also packed the Wigwam with "Lincoln shouters." . . . "We are going to have Indiana for Old Abe, sure," said another just before the balloting. "How did you get it?" someone asked. "By the Lord," he was told, "we promised them everything they asked."

After nailing down Indiana, Lincoln's managers went after Pennsylvania, with fifty-six delegates ready to vote for Simon Cameron, a favorite son, on the first ballot, but open to other candidates after that. . . . Jesse Dubois telegraphed Lincoln to tell him they could win the Keystone State if they promised Cameron the Treasury Department. "I authorize no bargain," Lincoln wired back, "and will be bound by none." "Damn Lincoln!" exclaimed Dubois. "Lincoln ain't here," broke in [Judge David] Davis impatiently, ". . . we will go ahead as if we hadn't heard from him, and he must ratify it." . . . About midnight Joseph Medill ran into Judge Davis in a hotel lobby just after he left the Pennsylvania delegation. "How will they vote?" he asked. "Damned if we haven't gotten them," exulted Davis. "How did you get them?" asked Medill. "By paying the price," replied Davis and revealed they had agreed to make Cameron Secretary of the Treasury. Medill expressed some consternation. "Oh, what's the difference," cried Davis airily, "We are after a bigger thing than that; we want the Presidency, and the Treasury is not a great stake to pay for it." . . . Lincoln reluctantly made Cameron Secretary of War (not Treasury) after the election but he proved so incompetent he had to be replaced in a few months.

When Lincoln received the Republican nomination in Chicago, a friend of his at once wired the news to Springfield: "Abe, we did it. Glory to God!" The telegraph operator in Springfield wrote on a scrap of paper, "Mr. Lincoln, you are nominated on the third ballot," and gave it to a boy who ran to the office of the *State Journal* where Lincoln was awaiting the news with some friends. Lincoln took the message, read it aloud quietly, and, as his friends started cheering, put it in his vest pocket and said thoughtfully: "There's a little woman down at our house would like to hear this. I'll go down and tell her."

—Paul F. Boller, Jr., *Presidential Campaigns*

of Democrats and Whigs emerged the American political system—complete with such features as two major parties, a sprinkle of third parties, national nominating conventions, state and local bosses, patronage, popular campaigning, and the presidency as the focus of politics."[12]

Duke University Special Collections Library

During the 1850s, the increasingly divisive issue of slavery caused the Democratic Party to split between North and South. The Whigs, crushed by Democrat Franklin Pierce's landslide victory in 1852, were equally demoralized. The nation was about to be torn apart by civil war, and the major political parties, like the Union itself, were disintegrating.

### Democrats and Republicans

The Republican Party was born in 1854 as a party of protest against the extension of slavery into the territories. The Kansas-Nebraska Act, passed that year, permitted slavery to move westward with the frontier and aroused discontent in the North and West.

In February 1854, a group of Whigs, Free-Soilers, and antislavery Democrats gathered in a church at Ripon, Wisconsin, to recommend the creation of a new party to fight the further expansion of slavery.* The name "Republican Party" was suggested at the meeting.

* The party birthplace is also claimed by Jackson, Michigan, where the Republicans held their first state convention five months later.

Ralph E. Becker Collection/Smithsonian Institution

The political organization that resulted from the meeting replaced the Whigs as the rival party of the Democrats, but it was a new party and not merely the Whigs masquerading under another label.

The first Republican presidential candidate, John C. Fremont, the "Pathfinder of the Rockies," was unable to find the trail that led to the White House in the election of 1856. But in 1860 the Republicans nominated Abraham Lincoln. By that time, the Democratic Party was so badly divided over the issue of slavery that its northern and southern wings each nominated separate candidates for president. A fourth candidate ran as the nominee of the Constitutional Union Party. The four-way split enabled Lincoln to win with only 39.8 percent of the popular vote.

His election was a rare fusion of the man and the times. Lincoln preserved the Union; in the process, he ensured the future of the Republican Party. By rejecting slavery, the Republicans had automatically become a sectional party, representing the North and West. And at the time, North and West meant Union, emancipation, and victory. The Democrats and the South meant slavery, secession, and defeat. Having been on the losing side of the bloody and tragic Civil War, the Democrats were a long time in recovering; the party was trapped and tangled in the folds of the Confederate flag.

For 25 years after 1860, the Republicans consolidated their strength and ruled America, becoming known by the 1870s as the Grand Old Party, a term later shortened to GOP. But by 1876, the Democrats had recovered enough to give the Republicans a spirited, two-party competition for two decades. Twice, in 1884 and 1892, the Democrats elected Grover Cleveland as president.

America was changing. After the Civil War, the nation gradually became industrialized; railroad tracks pushed westward, spanning the continent; immigrants from Europe poured in. As the rail and steel barons amassed great fortunes, small farmers found themselves squeezed economically and outnumbered by industrial workers. Agrarian discontent was reflected in the rise of minor parties like the Grangers, the Greenbackers, and the Populists.

The Populists, or People's Party, were a protest party of western farmers. In 1892 their presidential candidate, James B. Weaver, showed surprising strength. By 1896 the spirit of populism had captured the Democratic Party, which nominated William Jennings Bryan for president. Bryan, running on a "free silver"* platform, lost to Republican William McKinley, who defended the gold standard and conservative fiscal policies. The election resulted in a major realignment of the parties, from which the Republicans emerged stronger than ever as a coalition of eastern business interests, urban workers, midwestern farmers, and New England Yankees.

Theodore Roosevelt held the coalition together while he was president from 1901 to 1909, but his attempt to move the Grand Old Party in a more progressive direction alarmed its conservative business wing. In 1912 the Republican Party split apart. The conservative wing renominated William Howard Taft, who had been Roosevelt's handpicked successor. The other wing, the Progressive ("Bull Moose") Party, nominated Roosevelt. The Republican split resulted in victory for Woodrow Wilson, the Democratic nominee.

Wilson's two terms proved to be a short Democratic interlude. A nation weary of the First World War chose

Ralph E. Becker Collection/Smithsonian Institution

*During the 1890s there was a populist call for the "free" or unlimited coinage of silver, which was seen as a remedy for the economic troubles of debtors and farmers who were suffering under tight monetary policies.

Stanley King Collection/Smithsonian Institution

Blank Archives/Getty Images

to "return to normalcy" in the 1920s with the Republican administrations of Warren G. Harding and Calvin Coolidge, two of the less distinguished presidents to occupy that office. Big Business dominated; it was the era of the Teapot Dome scandal, flappers, bathtub gin, and the Prohibition "speakeasy." In 1928 Republican Herbert Hoover defeated Al Smith, the first Roman Catholic nominee of a major party. A year later, the stock market crash and the onset of the Great Depression dealt the Republican Party a blow comparable to the effect of the Civil War on the Democrats.

The result of these events was the election of Franklin D. Roosevelt in 1932, the New Deal, and 20 years of uninterrupted Democratic rule under Roosevelt and his successor, Harry S Truman. Roosevelt put together a new, grand coalition composed of the South, the big cities of the North, labor, immigrants, blacks, and other minority groups.

In 1952, in the midst of the Korean War, the Republicans recaptured the presidency with General Dwight D. Eisenhower, a hero of the Second World War who led the allied invasion of Europe that defeated Nazi Germany. But the Eisenhower magic could not be transferred to Richard Nixon, who narrowly lost to John F. Kennedy in 1960. Kennedy's "New Frontier" seemingly opened a new era of Democratic supremacy—but he was assassinated in 1963. In 1964 Barry Goldwater, a conservative from Arizona, captured control of the GOP from its long-dominant and more liberal eastern, internationalist wing. The result was Republican disaster. Lyndon Johnson, who had succeeded to the presidency after Kennedy's death, was elected in his own right with 61.1 percent of the total vote—the greatest share of the popular vote in history.

But American political parties have extraordinary resilience: "Each one is a citadel that can withstand the impact of even the most disastrous national landslide and thus provide elements of obstinacy and stability in the two-party pattern."[13] The Republican Party survived the Goldwater debacle and regrouped around Richard Nixon in 1968. Lyndon Johnson, in the face of the Vietnam War and urban riots, did not choose to run for reelection. With the Democrats divided into at least three camps, Nixon triumphed, restoring the Republican Party to power and demonstrating anew the strength of the American two-party system. Nixon's landslide reelection victory in 1972 was soon overshadowed by the scandal of Watergate, the resignation of Vice President Spiro Agnew, and Nixon's own resignation in 1974 on the brink of impeachment.

Gerald R. Ford, the vice president, briefly became president but was defeated in 1976 by Jimmy Carter, the former governor of Georgia. Yet, only six years after Nixon's resignation, the Republican Party surged back to power in 1980, capturing the White House under Ronald Reagan and gaining control of the Senate for the first time in more than a quarter of a century. Reagan's landslide victory in 1984 consolidated Republican control of the presidency.

This ability of American political parties to survive adversity and rise again rests in part on the fact that many areas of the country and many congressional districts are dominated by one party; even when a party is defeated nationally, it will still have durable pockets of power across the nation. This remains true despite the spread of two-party politics to more states in recent years.

The Democrats recaptured control of the Senate in 1986. As a result, President George H. W. Bush, a Republican elected in 1988, faced a Congress with both houses controlled by the Democrats during his four years in office.

The election in 1992 of a Democratic president, Bill

Clinton, and a Democratic Congress brought to a close 12 years of Republican control of the White House. Only two years later, the Republicans captured both houses of Congress, demonstrating once again the ability of American political parties to regroup and return to power. Reelected in 1996, Clinton was impeached and acquitted, but his troubles, particularly the scandal over his sexual relationship with Monica Lewinsky, a young White House intern, helped to pave the way for the election of Bush's son, George W. Bush, in 2000.

## The Two-Party System

Under the two-party system that has prevailed during most of the nation's history, winning nomination by one of the two major parties is at least half the battle for some candidates. In areas where one party dominates, it is equivalent to election. Throughout most of the nation's history, two major political parties have been arrayed against each other. The Democrats, in one guise or another, have endured. During successive eras they have been challenged by the Federalists, the Whigs, and the Republicans. Minor or third parties have joined the struggle, with greater or lesser effect, but the main battle has been, historically, a two-party affair. As Allan P. Sindler has observed, "From 1828 to the present with few exceptions the two parties together have persistently polled upward of 90 percent of the national popular vote—that is, there has been little multi-partyism."[14]

In 1968 George Wallace formed the American Independent Party and ran for president outside the two-party framework. He received 13.5 percent of the popular vote. Although a substantial showing for a minor-party candidate, it was nowhere near enough to win.

In 1992, billionaire businessman Ross Perot ran as an independent and made the strongest showing of any candidate who was not a major-party nominee since Theodore Roosevelt ran as the head of the Progressive ("Bull Moose") Party in 1912. Perot financed most of his campaign with his own money. He got more than 19 million votes and was a major factor in the 1992 campaign, drawing votes from both Clinton and the first President Bush. About one in five voters chose Perot, the independent.

In 2000, the two major-party candidates received the overwhelming majority of the votes. There were other contenders, however, principally conservative Pat Buchanan, and Ralph Nader, whose Green Party enjoyed the support of many environmental and consumer-oriented activists. But Nader had no real chance to win the White House, and his critics charged that he had siphoned votes away from the Democratic ticket and contributed to the defeat of Vice President Al Gore, the Democratic nominee. Nader ran again in 2004, this time as an independent, over Democratic protests that he might draw votes away from John Kerry and thereby aid President George W. Bush. Nader also appeared as the candidate of the Reform Party on the ballot in seven states, including Florida, where it was widely believed that the votes he received in 2000 had helped Bush win that crucial state, and the presidency. But in 2004 Nader won less than 20 percent of the 2.8 million votes he received in 2000.

### The Roots of Dualism

In the states and in many local communities, one party may dominate, as the Democrats did for decades in the so-called Solid South and the Republicans did in Kansas. But on the whole, America has been a two-party nation. Why this should be so is a subject of mild dispute because there is no wholly satisfactory answer. Among the explanations that have been offered are the influence of tradition and history, the structure of the U.S. electoral system, and ideological patterns among the electorate.

**Tradition and History** The debate over ratification of the Constitution split the country into two groups. Dualism, therefore, is as old as the nation itself. And, once established, human institutions tend to perpetuate their original form. To some extent, Americans accept the two-party system because it has almost always been there.

Ralph E. Becker Collection/Smithsonian Institution

**The Electoral System** Many features of the American political system appear to be compatible with the existence of two major parties. In the United States, the single-member district system prevails in federal elections. For example, only one member of Congress may be elected from a congressional district, no matter how many candidates run—it is a case of winner-take-all. The same is true of a presidential election; normally in each state the candidate who receives the most popular votes wins all of the state's electoral votes. Under such a system, minor parties lacking a strong geographical base have little chance of poaching on the two-party preserve. They tend to lose and, having lost, to disappear. (By contrast, a system of proportional representation with multimember districts, as in Italy, encourages the existence of many parties by allotting seats to competing parties according to the percentage of votes that they win.)

The two parties that compete in the United States need not be the same in all areas of the country, however. In some states, historically, minor parties have competed successfully with one of the two major national parties. For example, in Minnesota during the 1920s and 1930s, the Farmer-Labor Party, not the Democratic Party, was the chief competitor of the Republican Party in state and congressional elections. Since a merger in 1944, the Democratic-Farmer-Labor Party has been the principal rival to the Republicans in Minnesota.

Other aspects of the electoral system also work against third parties. For example, state election laws often make it difficult for third parties to get on the ballot. The nation's basic political and legal structure, in other words, favors the two-party system.

**Patterns of Belief** A majority of voters stand somewhere near the middle ground on many issues of American politics. Ideological differences among Americans have normally not been strong enough to produce a broad range of established minor parties representing widely varying shades of political opinion, as is the case in many nations in western Europe.

## Democrats and Republicans: Is There a Difference?

As noted earlier, American presidential candidates generally try to make very broad-based appeals. Although there are usually more Democratic than Republican voters in America, neither party enjoys the support of a majority of the electorate, and both must therefore look outside their own ranks for victory. To put together a winning coalition, a presidential candidate usually appeals to the great mass of voters in the ideological center. As a result, in some elections it may appear that there is very little difference between the two major parties. Because both parties woo the same voters, it is not surprising that, to an extent, they look alike. But they have important differences as well.

A classic study of national convention delegates found that the opinions of Democratic and Republican leaders diverged sharply on many important issues—more so than differences of opinion among ordinary members of the two parties. What is more, the opinions of the leaders were found to conform to party images: Republican leaders identified with "business, free enterprise, and economic conservatism in general," and Democrats were friendly "toward labor and toward government regulation of the economy."[15]

Another survey of party leaders, conducted in 2004, also found pronounced differences between the attitudes of Democratic and Republican leaders. For example, among delegates to the 2004 Democratic National Convention, 77 percent agreed that the government is "enacting anti-terrorism laws that excessively restrict civil liberties." But among delegates to the Republican National Convention that year, only 15 percent agreed with that statement. Among Democratic delegates, 86 percent said the United States should have stayed out of Iraq instead of invading that country. But among delegates to the Republican National Convention, only 3 percent agreed with that statement. And 49 percent of Republican delegates said there should be no legal recognition of gay couples, compared with only 5 percent of Democratic delegates.[16]

## The Decline of Party Loyalties and Party Influence

The fading of party loyalties among many voters has been one of the most visible features of contemporary American politics. Beginning in 1974, about a third of the voters described themselves as independents. Only

"How would you like me to answer that question? As a member of my ethnic group, educational class, income group, or religious category?"

## Comparing Governments

## THE UNITED STATES AND ITALY: STABILITY OR CHOICE?

In the American "winner-take-all" political system, congressional candidates who receive the most votes in their district win the election. In practice, this has meant that, in nearly all elections, voters choose between the candidates of the only two parties with a real chance of winning office—the Republicans and the Democrats. With just two parties normally competing for power, it is inevitable that one or the other will gain majority control in each house of Congress, and one party has often controlled both.

Italy's multiparty system, by contrast, uses proportional representation, and Italian political parties are able to secure seats in the Parliament by winning just a small percentage of the vote. Italian voters are faced with a choice of more than a dozen political parties. With votes divided among so many parties, however, it is rare for any single party to win the majority required to establish a government in the parliamentary system. Instead, coalition governments are formed, consisting of several different parties joined in a single governing alliance.

But those coalitions are politically fragile, because they require the cooperation of parties that often have different agendas and constituencies. In fact, through mid-2000 there had been 54 such coalition governments in Italy in 53 years, an average life expectancy of only 11 months for each government.

On May 21, 2000, Italians held a national referendum in an attempt to reform the unstable system. The referendum was designed to move Italy closer to a two-party system. It called for the elimination of proportional representation. The measure was opposed by the smaller political parties, which feared they would disappear under the proposed new system.

Only a third of eligible voters cast their ballots, far less than the 50 percent turnout required for approval of the change in the system. The low turnout may have signaled the voters' frustration with Italian politics. The failure to win approval for a change in the electoral system means it is likely that Italy's political instability will continue.

—*Washington Post,* May 21, 2000; the International Foundation for Election Systems, online at <http://www.electionguide.org>; and news reports.

about two-thirds of the voters called themselves Republicans or Democrats.[17]

These figures have led some scholars to perceive a decline of parties in American politics. As Everett Carll Ladd, Jr., observed, "A growing section of the electorate has become relatively weakly tied to political parties and open to change in preference depending upon its reading of current performance."[18] As he also noted, "There has been a long-term decline of party allegiance."[19] Political scientist Martin P. Wattenberg has made the point even more strongly: "Once the central guiding forces in American electoral behavior, the parties are now perceived with almost complete indifference by a large proportion of the population."[20]

Of course, candidates and issues, not just party affiliations, influence voters. But the diminishing influence of parties is a significant change from the past. One observer, Austin Ranney, suggested that something approaching a "no-party system" has emerged in presidential politics.[21]

Various reasons have been suggested for the decline of party ties: a more educated electorate, less dependent on parties for guidance; an increase in "split-ticket" voting by people who may, for example, vote for a Republican candidate for president and a Democrat for governor; the increasing influence of television and the news media generally; and the breaking up of the old loyalties and alignments within the major parties.[22]

In addition, as already noted, political parties themselves have become less powerful. Other groups such as political action committees, professional campaign managers, and interest groups have taken over some of the functions of parties. Interest groups today provide much of the money that is used to finance election campaigns.

Moreover, urban political machines have declined. And candidates no longer rely on parties to run their campaigns to the extent that was true in the past. All the help that candidates once received from political parties and their workers, from ward captains and doorbell pushers to envelope stuffers, "they now can get from pollsters, the media, public relations people, volunteer workers, or even by 'renting a party' in the form of a campaign management firm."[23]

Despite what some see as the fading of party loyalties and influence, however, political parties in America have by no means become extinct. And even though the number of unaffiliated voters has increased, the combined total of Americans who call themselves Democrats or Republicans is still much greater than those who say they are independents.

### The Democrats

One way to perceive the differences between the two major parties is to examine their images. In the public's imagination, the "typical" Democrat lives in a big city in the North. He or she is a member of a minority or ethnic group—an African American, a Hispanic American, an Asian American, a Catholic, a Jew, a Pole, or an Italian, for example. The imaginary Democrat drinks beer, belongs to a labor union, works on an assembly line, goes bowling, and has a relatively low income.

Genus Republican's habitat, by contrast, is the hedge-trimmed suburbs. The imaginary Republican lives in a split-level house with a picture window and a white picket fence, commutes to the city, and belongs to a country club that has no members from minority groups. The male of the species is very likely a white Protestant. He drinks martinis and eats white bread. His wife drives a BMW. He owns his own company or is a corporate executive. He golfs on weekends. He is rich, or at least comfortable, equally at home in the boardroom or the locker room. That, at any rate, is the popular image.

Like any caricature, these portraits are greatly overdrawn and not necessarily accurate. For example, one study of shifts in the American electorate concluded that the Democrats' base "has changed somewhat from the New Deal era. . . . They have lost ground among some of their old constituencies, such as trade unionists, big-city whites, and Southern whites; while they have made up for such losses with gains among the upper-middle class." The study also suggested that the Republicans have "lost their grip on the American establishment, most notably among young men and women of relative privilege."[24] Republicans could no longer count on the automatic support of this affluent group; in the past several presidential elections, both parties battled for the support of young, upwardly mobile professionals with substantial incomes.

Still, the image of each party and of individual Democrats and Republicans, at least to an extent, mirrors reality: Studies have shown that the Democrats usually, although not always, enjoy greater voter support from labor, African Americans, Jews, ethnic minorities, young people, those who have not attended college and who have lower incomes, and those who live in the cities. Republicans are more likely to be white, suburban, Protestant, rural, wealthy, older, college educated, and professionals or business executives. In the words of one observer, "Republicans tend to see themselves as middle class, and Democrats are much more apt to consider themselves as working class."[25]

*for more information about the Democratic Party, see: http://www.democrats.org*

A number of these patterns are changing, however. For example, in the 1992 presidential election, "Catholics . . . a mainstay of earlier Democratic coalitions, continued . . . their long drift away from decisive Democratic loyalties."[26] This was particularly true among young white Catholics. One exit poll reported that 42 percent of white Catholics under age 30 identified themselves as Republicans.[27] And one-quarter of Hispanic Americans,

## TABLE 9-1

### Income and Party Identification

| Income | Democrats | Republicans | Independents |
|---|---|---|---|
| Less than $15,000 | 51% | 27% | 22% |
| $15,000–$25,000 | 40% | 20% | 40% |
| $25,000–$35,000 | 49% | 28% | 21% |
| $35,000–$50,000 | 32% | 44% | 24% |
| $50,000–$75,000 | 40% | 35% | 25% |
| $75,000 and over | 35% | 38% | 26% |

SOURCE: Zogby International, May 10, 2004. "In which party are you either registered to vote or do you consider yourself a member of—Democrat, Republican, independent/minor party, or Libertarian?"

usually thought to be a Democratic constituency, voted Republican.[28]

Nevertheless, whether a person identifies with the Democratic Party or the Republican Party may be related to socioeconomic factors. For example, one survey found that half of the people interviewed with low incomes considered themselves Democrats, but only about 27 percent of this group thought of themselves as Republicans. (See Table 9-1.)

Moreover, in some years the Republicans have suffered from a distinct "gender gap"—more women have tended to vote for Democrats than for Republicans. In 2000, for example, 53 percent of women but only 45 percent of men voted for Al Gore.[29]

And Democrats, political scientist Jo Freeman has argued, believe in "the inclusion of all relevant groups and viewpoints," while Republicans see themselves as "insiders who represent the core of American society and are the carriers of its fundamental values."[30] In 2004, for example, President George W. Bush, the Republican candidate, frequently invoked family values, patriotism, and religious faith, and supported a constitutional amendment to ban gay marriage. It was an appeal aimed at his Republican base, including conservatives and evangelical Christians.

Since 1932, in most presidential elections, the Dem-

Ralph E. Becker Collection/Smithsonian Institution

ocratic Party has, in spirit, been the party of Franklin D. Roosevelt. The vast social-welfare programs launched by the New Deal changed the face of America and gave the Democratic Party an identity that persisted for many years. Truman's "Fair Deal," Kennedy's "New Frontier," and Johnson's "Great Society" were all patterned on Roosevelt's New Deal. All sought to harness federal funds and federal energies to solve national problems. Bill Clinton, however, elected in 1992 as a self-described "New Democrat," moved to a more centrist position.

For decades the Democrats could count on the 11 states of the former Confederacy as a solid Democratic bloc. But no longer. Today, the South is a two-party battleground, and one in which the Republicans often have the upper hand. In 1972, for the first time, the southern states voted solidly for a Republican, Richard Nixon. In the South in 1980, Jimmy Carter, the Democratic nominee, carried only his home state of Georgia against his Republican opponent, Ronald Reagan. In 1984, Walter Mondale, the Democratic candidate for president, carried not a single state in the South, as happened again in 1988, when Massachusetts Governor Michael Dukakis was the Democratic nominee, and again in 2000 when Al Gore was the Democratic standard-bearer. Governor Bill Clinton of Arkansas, a Democrat and a southerner, carried only four southern states when he won the presidency in 1992 and when he was reelected in 1996. Between 1952 and 2000, every Republican presidential candidate won some or all of the southern electoral votes. (See Table 9-2.)

In political campaigns, Republicans like to label the Democrats as "spenders." On the whole, Democrats have been more willing to appropriate federal funds for social action. As a result of this political reality, the Democratic Party since 1933 has been the party of Social Security, the Tennessee Valley Authority, Medicare, and federal aid to education. It has, in short, often been the party of social innovation.

In addition to differences of substance, the two parties show perceptible differences in style. "I don't belong to any organized party," the humorist Will Rogers once quipped. "I'm a Democrat."[31] Democrats do tend to be uninhibited and occasionally raucous, fighting among themselves; Republicans are normally more sedate.

Of course, these differences do not always hold true. In 2004, for example, the Democrats gathered in Boston in unusual harmony to choose John Kerry, the junior senator from Massachusetts, who had already locked up the nomination with his victories in the Iowa caucuses and the spring primaries. In 1988, it was the Republican convention, thrown into turmoil by the controversy surrounding George Bush's choice of Senator Dan Quayle for vice president, that provided unexpected color and excitement. More often, however, it is the Democrats who brawl and squabble.

"A gathering of Democrats is more sweaty, disorderly, offhand, and rowdy than a gathering of Republicans," Clinton Rossiter has noted. "A gathering of Republicans is more respectable, sober, purposeful, and businesslike than a gathering of Democrats."[32] The Democratic donkey brays, snorts, kicks up its heels, balks, fusses, and is a very different animal in appearance, substance, and temperament from the Republican elephant. Today, of course, both parties' national conventions tend to be scripted and carefully manicured for television; in the era of the sound bite, the donkey and the elephant rarely bray or trumpet. As a result, the broadcast television networks gave only limited coverage to the national conventions in 2004.

## The Republicans

In describing the Republican Party, Theodore H. White wrote: "Two moods color its thinking. One is the old Protestant-Puritan ethic of the small towns of America. . . . The other is the philosophy of private enterprise, the sense that the individual, as man or corporation, can build swifter and better for common good than big

"Yes, son, we're Republicans."

TABLE 9-2

## The Growth of Republican Strength in the South, 1950–2004

| Year | U.S. Representatives | | U.S. Senators | | Governors | | States Voting for Presidential Nominee | |
|---|---|---|---|---|---|---|---|---|
| | D | R | D | R | D | R | D | R |
| 1950 | 103 | 2 | 22 | 0 | 11 | 0 | | |
| 1952 | 100 | 6 | 22 | 0 | 11 | 0 | 7 | 4 |
| 1954 | 99 | 7 | 22 | 0 | 11 | 0 | | |
| 1956 | 99 | 7 | 22 | 0 | 11 | 0 | 6 | 5 |
| 1958 | 99 | 7 | 22 | 0 | 11 | 0 | | |
| 1960 | 99 | 7 | 22 | 0 | 11 | 0 | 7 | 3* |
| 1962 | 95 | 11 | 21 | 1 | 11 | 0 | | |
| 1964 | 89 | 17 | 21 | 1 | 11 | 0 | 6 | 5 |
| 1966 | 83 | 23 | 19 | 3 | 9 | 2 | | |
| 1968 | 80 | 26 | 18 | 4 | 9 | 2 | 1 | 5† |
| 1970 | 79 | 27 | 16(1)‡ | 5 | 9 | 2 | | |
| 1972 | 74 | 34 | 14(1)‡ | 7 | 8 | 3 | 0 | 11 |
| 1974 | 81 | 27 | 15(1)‡ | 6 | 8 | 3 | | |
| 1976 | 82 | 26 | 16(1)‡ | 5 | 9 | 2 | 10 | 1 |
| 1978 | 77 | 31 | 15(1)‡ | 6 | 8 | 3 | | |
| 1980 | 69 | 39 | 11(1)‡ | 10 | 6 | 5 | 1 | 10 |
| 1982 | 82 | 34 | 11 | 11 | 9 | 2 | | |
| 1984 | 73 | 43 | 12 | 10 | 9 | 2 | 0 | 11 |
| 1986 | 77 | 39 | 16 | 6 | 6 | 5 | | |
| 1988 | 78 | 38 | 14 | 8 | 6 | 5 | 0 | 11 |
| 1990 | 77 | 39 | 15 | 7 | 8 | 3 | | |
| 1992 | 77 | 48 | 14 | 8 | 8 | 3 | 4 | 7 |
| 1994 | 61 | 64 | 9 | 13 | 5 | 6 | | |
| 1996 | 55 | 70 | 6 | 16 | 5 | 6 | 4 | 7 |
| 1998 | 54 | 71 | 8 | 14 | 4 | 7 | | |
| 2000 | 52 | 72(1)** | 9 | 13 | 5 | 6 | 0 | 11 |
| 2002 | 55 | 76 | 9 | 13 | 4 | 7 | | |
| 2004 | 49 | 82 | 4 | 18 | 4 | 7 | 0 | 11 |

Note: The 11 states of the South are Alabama, Arkansas, Florida, Georgia, Louisiana, Mississippi, North Carolina, South Carolina, Tennessee, Texas, and Virginia.
*The eight Mississippi electors voted for Harry Byrd.
**Virgil H. Goode, Jr., was elected in Virginia in 2000 as an Independent.
†George Wallace won five states on the American Independent ticket.
‡Harry Byrd, Jr., was elected in Virginia in 1970 and 1976 as an Independent.
SOURCES: House, governor, and president figures in Congressional Quarterly, *Politics in America 1945–1966* (Washington, D.C.: Congressional Quarterly Service, 1967), pp. 101, 123, 117–121. Senate figures in Richard Scammon, *America Votes 7* (Washington, D.C.: Governmental Affairs Institute, 1968), pp. 12, 31, 74, 82, 147, 205, 289, 357, 371, 379, 404. Data since 1968 from Congressional Quarterly, *Weekly Reports; The New York Times;* and *The Almanac of American Politics 2000* and *2004*. Additional data from www.congress.org and the National Governors Association.

government. From middle-class America the Republicans get their votes; from the executive leadership and from the families of the great enterprises they get their funds."[33]

Despite the success of the Republicans in five out of the six presidential elections between 1968 and 1988, since the New Deal the Republican Party has, in terms of party identification, usually enjoyed the support of only a minority of American voters. People who identify themselves as Democrats have, in recent decades, generally outnumbered people who say they are Republicans—although, as noted, by 2004 the Democratic advantage was relatively small. In the face of the party identification figures, the Republican Party's task has often been to broaden its popular appeal and turn its minority into a majority, or at least a plurality. The Republican Party won the presidency in 1980, 1984, and 1988 precisely because it was able to attract large numbers of Democrats and independents.

***for more information about the Republican Party, see: http://www.rnc.org***

The familiar Democratic charge that "the Republican Party is the party of Big Business" is partially accurate, just as it is true that, nationally, the Democrats have traditionally been the party of organized labor. The pref-

Courtesy of Bill Snead

erence of business for the Republican Party may be measured by analyzing campaign contributions. For example, in 2000, corporations and business executives contributed $221 million to the national Republican Party and a smaller amount, $160 million, to the Democratic Party.[34]

During the Eisenhower years, federal regulatory agencies were markedly friendly to the broadcasting networks, airlines, and other businesses they were supposedly regulating. It can be argued that "it does make a difference to the television industry, the railroads, or the stock exchanges whether Democrats or Republicans have a majority in the independent commissions."[35]

The Republicans have often had a split personality. The scar left when Theodore Roosevelt bolted the party in 1912 has never entirely healed; in modern times the battle of Republican conservatives (the political heirs of William Howard Taft) against Republican liberal-moderates (the heirs of Theodore Roosevelt) has continued, although in muted form during the strongly conservative Reagan years.

The struggle broke out in 1952 in the convention battle between Senator Robert A. Taft of Ohio (the son of President William Howard Taft) and General Eisenhower, who was backed by the eastern liberals. Then, in 1964, Goldwater and the conservative wing won control of the party from the eastern establishment led by Nelson Rockefeller.

Again in 1976 the split was reflected in the battle between President Ford and Ronald Reagan for the party's presidential nomination, the most serious challenge to a Republican president from within his own party since the revolt against William Howard Taft. Despite Ford's nomination in 1976, the right wing of the Republican Party remained a strong force within the GOP and recaptured the White House in 1980, with Ronald Reagan as its standard-bearer.

The traditional split surfaced again during the vote on the impeachment of President Clinton in 1999. Five moderate Republicans from the northeast broke ranks with their party to vote against both articles of impeachment.

Since the 1980s, the Republican Party has also often drawn support from conservative Christian religious groups. In 1988, a former television evangelist, Pat Robertson, challenged Vice President George Bush in the Republican primary elections. In 1996 the Christian Coalition, the most prominent of the religious right groups, supported Bob Dole, the Republican candidate.

Although fundamentalist religious groups varied in their methods and goals, they shared common social views and were "generally concerned with what is seen as the breakdown of family, community, religion, and traditional morality in American life. Abortion, . . . affirmative action, sexual permissiveness, drugs, prohibitions on school prayer, the secular curriculum in public schools, and many similar things are opposed on the grounds that they contribute to . . . social breakdown and moral decay."[36]

## Minor Parties and Independent Candidates

Minor parties have been active throughout most of the nation's history, from the Anti-Masons of the 1830s and the Barnburners of the 1840s, to the Know-Nothings[37] of the 1850s, the Greenbackers of the 1880s, the Populists of the 1890s, the Progressives of the 1920s, and the American Independents in 1968. (See Figure 9-1.)

In 1968 the third-party movement of Alabama's George Wallace scared major-party supporters because of the possibility that Wallace would carry enough states to prevent either major-party candidate from gaining a majority of electoral votes. Wallace would then have been in a position to bargain with his electoral votes, or to throw the outcome into the House of Representatives. (The electoral college machinery is discussed in Chapter 11.)

Although Wallace appeared on the ballot in every state, usually as the candidate of the American Independent Party, he carried only five southern states; his 46 electoral votes were not enough to deadlock the presidential election. His 13.5 percent of the popular vote was considerably less than the 21.1 percent received by the Know-Nothings in 1856, the 27.4 percent polled by Theodore Roosevelt's Progressive ("Bull Moose") Party in 1912, or the 16.6 percent received by Robert La Follette's Progressives in 1924. In 2000, Ralph Nader, running as the candidate of the Green Party, garnered 2.7 percent of the total vote.

In recent years, several candidates have run for the presidency as independents, without bothering to organize a third party. In 1992, Ross Perot invested an estimated $63.4 million of his own money in his independent campaign, which relied heavily on television. Although Perot's final share of the vote—19 percent—was very large, he did not carry a single state.

FIGURE 9-1

**Minor-Party and Independent Vote, 1880–2000, by Percentage of Total Vote**

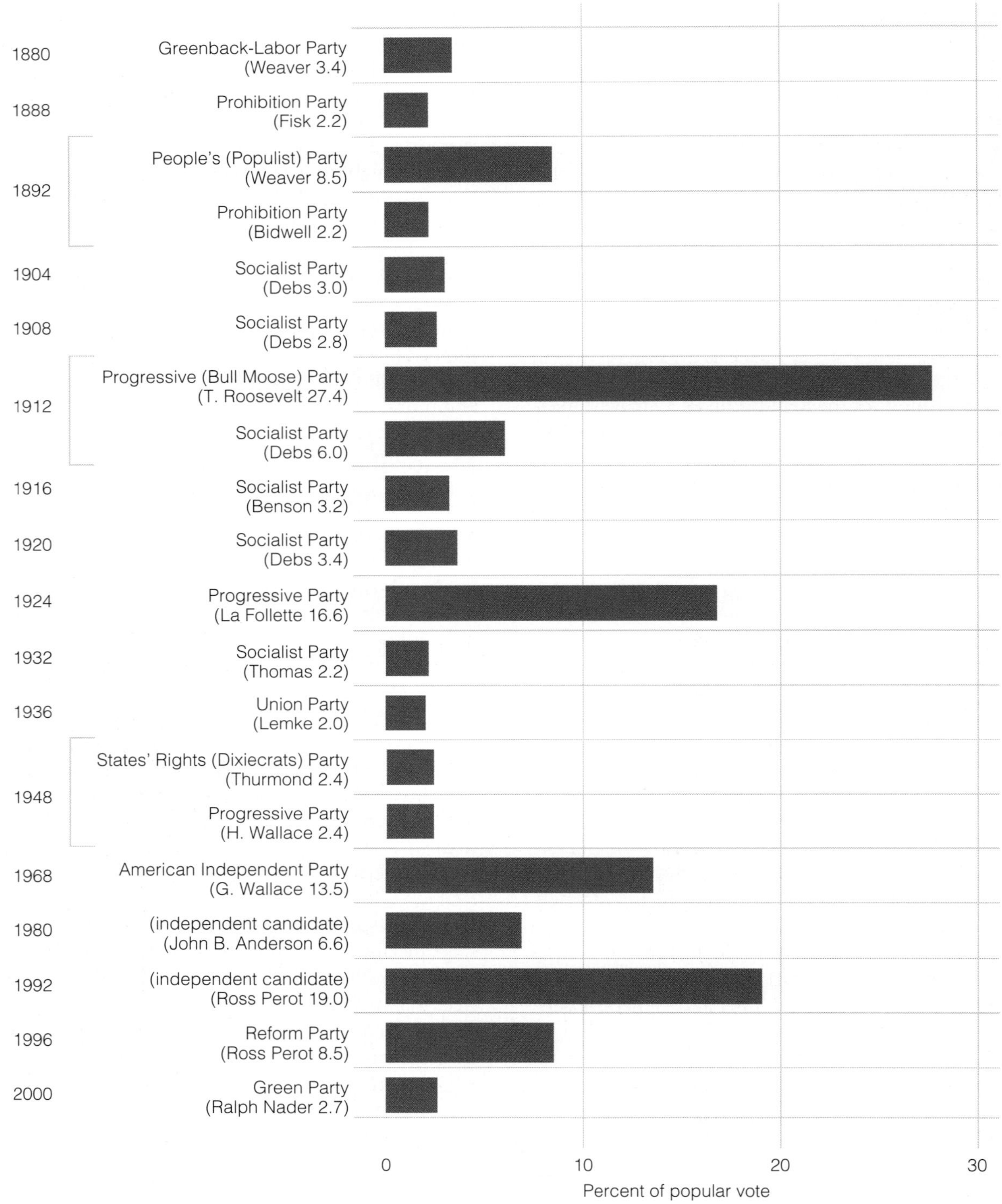


NOTE: Includes only those minor parties and independent candidates for president that polled 2 percent or more of the popular vote.

SOURCES: Neal R. Peirce, *The People's President* (New York: Simon & Schuster, 1968), pp. 305–307; Donald B. Cole, *Handbook of American History* (New York: Harcourt Brace Jovanovich, 1968), pp. 304–305; *Politics in America,* 4th ed. (Washington, D.C.: Congressional Quarterly, 1971), p. 91; *New York Times,* January 6, 1981, p. A14; *Washington Post,* November 5, 1992, p. A26; and *New York Times,* November 7, 1996, p. B5. Data for 2000 provided by the Federal Election Commission.

In 1980 independent candidate John B. Anderson, like Perot in 1992, did not carry a single state. But with 6.6 percent of the popular vote, Anderson did better than have many others, including Eugene McCarthy, who received less than 1 percent of the popular vote in 1976.

V. O. Key, Jr., has suggested that minor parties fall into two broad categories: "those formed to propagate a particular doctrine," and "transient third-party movements" that briefly appear on the American scene and then disappear. The Prohibition Party and the Socialist Party are examples of doctrinal parties that "have been kept alive over long periods by little bands of dedicated souls."[38] Among the transient third-party movements, Key perceived two types: parties of economic protest, such as the Populists, the Greenbackers, and the Progressives of 1924; and "secessionist parties" that have split off from one of the major parties, such as the Progressives in 1912 and the Dixiecrats in 1948.

Sometimes minor parties have a strong nativist streak. Just as the Wallace campaign played upon white fears of African Americans, more than a century ago the Know-Nothings, or Native American Party, exploited fear of Irish immigrants and other "foreigners." The party platform in 1856, when former president Millard Fillmore ran as the Know-Nothing candidate, warned: "Americans must rule America."

In certain states minor parties have gained a powerful position. The Liberal Party and the Conservative Party in New York have sometimes held the balance of power in elections in that state. Nationally, however, minor parties have never consistently enjoyed much power or influence. On some occasions they have influenced the policies of the major parties—as when Populism captured the Democratic Party in 1896.

"One of the persistent qualities of the American two-party system," one analyst concluded, "is the way in which one of the major parties moves almost instinctively to absorb (and thus be somewhat reshaped by) the most challenging third party of the time. In any case, it is a notable fact that no third party in America has ever risen to become a major party, and that no major party has ever fallen to become a third party."[39]

## Party Structure

American political parties are decentralized and only loosely organized. Rather than as a pyramid, with all

© Gary Hershorn/Reuters/Corbis

Boston, July 2004: John Kerry, the Democratic nominee for president, addresses delegates at the party's national convention.

© Robert Galbraith/Reuters/Landov

New York, September 2004: President George W. Bush and his wife, Laura, and Dick Cheney and his wife, Lynne, acknowledge the cheers of the delegates at the Republican National Convention.

power flowing from the top down, party structure "may be more accurately described as a system of layers of organization. Each successive layer—county or city, state, national—has an independent concern about elections in its geographical jurisdiction."[40]

## National Political Parties

Leadership of a national political party is somewhat like a sports trophy that a team may win and retain for a time but must eventually return so that it may be awarded to a new team. Thus, the first President Bush led the Republican Party in 1992, but after his defeat, he was obliged to give up control of the party machinery. Four years later, it belonged to Bob Dole. In 1992, Bill Clinton's capture of the Democratic presidential nomination and his election in November put the Democratic Party organization firmly in the hands of Clinton supporters.

On paper, the party's quadrennial **national convention** is the source of all authority within the party. The convention nominates the party's candidates for president and vice president; it writes a platform, settles disputes, writes rules, and elects the members of the national committee.

The **national chair,** the head of a national political party, is formally elected by the members of the national committee. In practice he or she is chosen or retained by the party's presidential nominee at the end of the national convention.

Between conventions, the **national committee** of each major political party is the governing body of the party. Members of the national committee are chosen in the states and formally elected by the party's national convention.

In the past, national committees have sometimes been little more than the permanent offices in Washington that house the national chair and the staff. More recently, the national committees of both parties have become more active between presidential elections. Between elections, the chief functions of the national committee staff are public relations, patronage, research, and fund-raising.

As a rule, presidential nominees either largely ignore the machinery of the national committee and build a personal organization to run their campaign, or they take over the national committee machinery and make it their own. In theory, the national chair's main job is to manage the presidential campaign; in practice, however, the candidate's real campaign manager is seldom the party chair.

Independent of the national committees, and serving as further evidence of the decentralization of American party politics, are the congressional leaders of each party, elected by their colleagues, and the congressional and senatorial campaign committees. Both major parties have campaign committees in the House and Senate; their members are chosen by party members in each branch of Congress. The congressional committees channel money, speakers, advice, and assistance to party members who are up for election.

In both the Republican and Democratic Parties, there is often a good deal of conflict between the party leaders in Congress and the leaders of the more presidentially oriented national party organization, a built-in tension often reflected in rivalry and jealousy between the congressional campaign committees and the national committee.

## State and Local Parties

Party organization and election laws vary tremendously in the states, with the result that one can find kaleidoscopic variety in almost any given phase of American politics below the national level. Just as the national party in power is controlled by the president, the state party is often dominated by the governor. In the case of some large northern industrial states, the mayor of a large city may wield considerable influence. On the other hand, the state party may be led by a party chair who is not obligated to, and was elected without, the support of the incumbent governor. And, of course, a state chair may head a party that is out of power and does not control the governor's office.[41] Some state party organizations are the fiefdom of a single party boss—either an elected official or a party leader outside government. But all-powerful party bosses exist less often today than in the past.

Political scientist David R. Mayhew has classified a number of states as having "traditional party organizations" that are independent, long entrenched, and highly organized; that seek to nominate candidates to a wide range of public offices; and that offer jobs and other tangible rewards to their followers. But he notes that within other state parties there is "persistent factionalism" in which two or more party organizations "commonly operate in the same party in the same city or county, normally competing against each other in primaries for a broad range of offices."[42]

Republicans or Democrats may consistently dominate within a state, or power may be divided between the two parties. But even within a party, there are great variations from state to state. The Democratic Party in Alabama is very different from its counterpart in Michigan. In both major parties, conservatives or moderates may control one state, liberals another. And these local differences tend to make American political parties decentralized, fragmented, and weak.

State politics often reflect geographic cleavages. In New York the Democratic Party traditionally controls New York City, while Republicans dominate "upstate," in areas outside the city. In Illinois the Democrats, strong in Chicago's Cook County, must often contend with a heavy downstate Republican vote. In Michigan, Democrats are strong in Detroit, but Republicans dominate many other areas of the state.

The state parties are bound together within the national political party by a mutual desire to have a "winner" at the head of the national ticket. Often, although not always, a strong presidential candidate will sweep state and local candidates into office on his coattails.

The layer of party organization below that of the national committees is the state committees. Like national committee members, members of the state committees are chosen in many different ways, including county conventions and direct primaries.

At the grass-roots of each major political party is a third layer of party organization, consisting of the county committees, county chairs, district leaders, precinct or ward captains, and party workers. The local party organization is held together in part by the paste of patronage—the rewarding of party faithfuls with government jobs. The old-style, big-city political machines depended almost entirely on patronage; even today a substantial portion of party workers may be found on town, city, and county payrolls.

Although big-city machines still exist, the cigar-chomping, derby-hatted political "boss" of the late 19th

### The Old Politics—Machine Style

George Washington (Boss) Plunkitt, a political leader in New York City at the turn of the 20th century, explained his philosophy for attracting votes:

> What holds your grip on your district is to go right down among the poor families and help them in the different ways they need help. I've got a regular system for this. If there's a fire in Ninth, Tenth, or Eleventh Avenue, for example, any hour of the day or night, I'm usually there with some of my election district captains as soon as the fire engines. If a family is burned out I don't ask whether they are Republicans or Democrats; and I don't refer them to the Charity Organization Society, which would investigate their case in a month or two and decide they were worthy of help about the time they are dead from starvation. I just get quarters for them, buy clothes for them if their clothes were burned up, and fix them up til they get things runnin' again. It's philanthropy, but it's politics, too—mighty good politics. Who can tell how many votes one of these fires brings me?

—Boss Plunkitt, in William L. Riordon, *Plunkitt of Tammany Hall*

Chicago's mayor Richard J. Daley, often described as the last of the big-city bosses

and early 20th centuries has in most areas enjoyed his last hurrah. At one time, Frank Hague, the Democratic boss of Jersey City, could blatantly declare: "I am the law." Edward J. Flynn, the boss of the Bronx, could rise to considerable power within the national Democratic Party. Carmine De Sapio, the leader of Tammany Hall, was able to dominate New York City politics in the 1950s. But as Frank J. Sorauf has suggested: "The defeat of Carmine De Sapio and the Tammany tiger by the reformers in the fall of 1961 may stand as one of the great turning points in American politics."[43]

Chicago's mayor Richard J. Daley, for many years a power in national Democratic politics, drew substantial support from the city's business community. He gave them what they wanted—"a new downtown area, an expressway, . . . confidence in the city's economic future"—and in the process made it almost impossible for Republican candidates to find any support among business leaders.[44] Daley, often described as the last of the big-city bosses, died in 1976.

The urban machines drew their power from the vast waves of immigrants to America's cities. The machines offered all sorts of help to these newcomers—from food baskets to city jobs. In return, all the boss demanded was the newcomer's vote. Each ward captain knew precisely how many votes he could deliver—the captain who did not would soon find that he was no longer a municipal inspector of sewers. Since the 1930s, Social Security, welfare payments, food stamps, unemployment benefits, and general prosperity have cut the ground out from under the city machines: The social services formerly provided by the party clubhouse now flow from the impersonal bureaucracy in Washington and from the states. And the establishment of the direct primary and internal party reforms have, in some cases, impaired the power of the bosses to control nominations.

However, the local party can still sometimes find a city job for a loyal worker, for "the power to hire is still an important power resource."[45] And urban machines can help the poor deal with complex city bureaucracies.[46] Or a city machine can award municipal construction contracts to party activists or financial contributors.

But people participate in politics at the grass-roots level today for a variety of reasons, not only for economic motives. The woman in Ohio who telephoned her neighbors and urged them to vote for George W. Bush in 2004 may have wanted to feel that, as a voter in a key battleground state, she was personally participating in the election of a president. The volunteers who rang doorbells for Kerry that year did so in many cases for the sheer excitement of being involved in a political campaign. The suburban man who serves as a precinct captain may be active in politics because he enjoys the added prestige that he acquires in the eyes of his neighbors. (He is the person who can get a new streetlight installed or the potholes filled in.) He may even be a party worker because he likes to attend the party's national convention as a delegate every four years.

Increasingly, two new kinds of activists are taking part in American politics at various levels, not only as delegates to national conventions. These are the issue activists—people committed to a particular issue, such as civil rights or women's rights—and activists who work in the organizations of political candidates. These new breeds are, to some extent at least, replacing the "ward heelers" and party regulars of yesteryear.

The number of political activists at any level is fairly small, however. Perhaps only about 10 percent of the population could be classified as "politically involved." (See Table 9-3.) If we apply the percentages shown in the table for 2000 to the 2000 voting-age population of 203,609,000, we find that in round numbers 18.3 million Americans spent money to help the campaign for one of the parties or candidates, 10.2 million attended political gatherings or functions, and 6.1 million did political work for parties or candidates.[47]

## The National Convention

Such is the influence of television on American politics that in 2004 both major-party national nominating con-

## TABLE 9-3

### Political Participation

| | 1968 | 1972 | 1976 | 1978 | 1980 | 1982 | 1984 | 1986 | 1988 | 1992 | 1996 | 2000 |
|---|---|---|---|---|---|---|---|---|---|---|---|---|
| Do you belong to any political club or organization? | 3% | * | * | * | 3% | 3% | 4% | * | 4% | * | * | * |
| Did you give any money or buy tickets or do anything to help the campaign for one of the parties or candidates? | 12% | 10% | 9% | 13% | 8% | * | 7% | 10% | 9% | 11% | 9% | 9% |
| Did you go to any political meetings, rallies, dinners, or things like that? | 14% | 9% | 6% | 10% | 8% | 9% | 4% | 7% | 7% | 8% | 6% | 5% |
| Did you do any other work for one of the parties or candidates? | 5% | 5% | 4% | 6% | 4% | 6% | 4% | 3% | 3% | 3% | 3% | 3% |
| Did you wear a campaign button or put a campaign bumper sticker on your car? | 15% | 14% | 8% | 9% | 7% | 8% | 9% | 7% | * | * | * | 10% |

*Data not available.

SOURCES: Survey Research Center/Center for Political Studies, University of Michigan, in William H. Flanigan and Nancy H. Zingale, *Political Behavior of the American Electorate,* 4th ed. (Boston: Allyn and Bacon, 1979), p. 163. Data for 1978 through 1982 and for campaign buttons and bumper stickers from the American National Election Studies, National Election Studies, Institute for Social Research, University of Michigan. Data for 1984 through 1996 from the Survey Research Center/Center for Political Studies/National Election Studies, in William H. Flanigan and Nancy H. Zingale, *Political Behavior of the American Electorate,* 8th ed. (Washington, D.C.: CQ Press, 1994), p. 13; and 9th ed., p. 16. Data for 2000 from the National Election Studies guide to political opinion and electoral behavior, online at <http://www.umich.edu/~nes/nesguide/gd-index.htm#6>.

ventions were carefully controlled, made-for-television entertainment, designed by professional TV producers to appeal to prime-time audiences. The national conventions were wired as well for Internet viewers. Some "bloggers," Web loggers who wrote online stories, were given access to the conventions as members of the press. Visitors to convention websites could select the main speakers on the podium or they could zoom in on the floor to see what was happening in a particular state delegation.

Gone are the days of gavel-to-gavel coverage by the major television networks, when the national conventions would often provide real drama as candidates for the presidential nomination vied for support of the delegates. Beginning in 1992, the networks cut back on their convention coverage. By 1996 and 2000, the major network broadcasts were limited on most nights to an hour or two of prime time. In 2004, the broadcast networks limited their coverage of the Democratic and Republican conventions to 10 to 11 p.m. (Eastern time) on only three of the four nights. Public television and the cable networks still provided much fuller coverage, and C-SPAN viewers could watch the proceedings gavel-to-gavel. The change was not solely the result of television, of course. The conventions themselves have, for the most part, become tame spectacles, emphasizing platitudes, balloons, and confetti.

As one political analyst has observed, "One of the

Three Texas delegates from El Paso show their support for John Kerry at the 2004 Democratic National Convention in Boston.

## Go Balloons! We Want More Balloons!

As John Kerry concluded his speech to the 2004 Democratic National Convention, the traditional balloon drop began. The presidential nominee, his running mate, John Edwards, and their families gathered onstage and waved to the cheering multitudes.

Then something went wrong.

The Democrats had hired two Boston balloon companies, as the official press release promised, to drop "100,000 air-filled, red, white, and blue bio-degradable balloons" from the ceiling of the Fleet Center. But not enough were wafting downward—at least not enough for Don Mischer, the convention producer, whose frantic voice was broadcast by mistake and heard by viewers watching CNN:

© Larry Downing/Reuters/Landov

> Go, balloons. I don't see anything happening. Go, balloons. Go, balloons. Go, balloons. Stand by, confetti. Keep coming, balloons. More balloons. Bring them. Balloons, balloons, balloons! More balloons. Tons of them. Bring them down. Let them all come. No confetti. No confetti yet. No confetti. All right. Go, balloons. Go, balloons. We're getting more balloons. All balloons. All balloons should be going. Come on, guys! Let's move it. Jesus. We need more balloons. I want all balloons to go. Go, confetti. Go, confetti. Go, confetti. I want more balloons. What's happening to the balloons? We need more balloons. We need all of them coming down. Go, balloons. Balloons. What's happening balloons? There's not enough coming down. All balloons! Why the hell is nothing falling? What the [expletive] are you guys doing up there? We want more balloons coming down. More balloons. More balloons.

CNN realized its error and anchor Judy Woodruff explained that Mischer's microphone had been left open by accident. Anchor Wolf Blitzer quickly changed the subject to comments about John Kerry's speech.

Later an official of the Democratic National Committee claimed there had been no malfunction and that balloons were timed to come down slowly, "making for a longer ending, which was nice."

—*USA Today,* July 30, 2004, and CNN transcripts

lessons of recent presidential elections is that national conventions are declining in importance as decision-making bodies. . . . National conventions no longer pick presidential nominees; they merely ratify the work of primaries and caucuses."[48] This is true because, as a rule, the preconvention campaigns and the primary elections are now decisive. By the time the conventions come along, the only battles are usually over the platform.

What the voters see of the conventions on TV is carefully managed, by both the parties and the networks. This is what Bill Greener, the manager of the 1996 Republican National Convention at San Diego, had to say about the constraints imposed on him by the television networks:

> We don't make the rules to the game. We are dealing with the rules. And the rules are: You get an hour and don't forget in that hour we have got our commercials to air and our station breaks, and don't forget that we need time to showcase our talent . . . and even before we think about going to the podium we have got to establish the presence of our anchor and our four floor correspondents, and don't forget that after that we are going to take a commercial break, and then we are going back to the anchor, and then we might take what you've got going at the podium. And that's just the way it is.[49]

Actually, the networks' rules are only part of the story. The political parties themselves now block out the convention proceedings down to the minute. For example, at the Republican convention in 1996, one account summarized the script of a segment this way: "Call to Order . . . from 05:00 to 05:01, followed by the Introduction of Colors . . . at 05:01 to 05:02, followed by the Presentation of the Colors by San Diego Joint Scouting Color Guard from 05:02 to 05:04 . . . ending applause from 05:21 to 05:24." Another event, running from 05:16 to 05:18, was described as "Ending Applause and Spotlight Sequentially on Each of Six American Dream Murals with Main Street Americans Moving to Positions Behind Podium."[50]

© Ralf-Finn Hestoft/Redux

© Robert Galbraith/Reuters/Landov

Nor are convention speakers always allowed to say what is on their minds. At the 2004 Democratic convention in Boston, for example, the Kerry campaign put out the word that speakers were to emphasize a positive, upbeat message and not to engage in "Bush-bashing." Only the Rev. Al Sharpton, who had been a candidate in the primaries, ignored the rule and let loose an old-fashioned stemwinder attacking President Bush by name to roars of approval from the delegates.

Despite the scripted nature of the conventions, television has brought American politics into the living room, and these events still provide a chance for millions of viewers to watch the candidates deliver their acceptance speeches. Some of the hoopla, speeches, and interviews at the presidential nominating conventions are still interesting even if they lack the drama of past years. And actually, viewers at home have a better and closer view of a national convention than the delegates. Network and cable television reporters roam the convention floor interviewing political leaders. In darkened rooms just off the convention floor, TV directors follow the action on glowing monitors. They bark crisp orders; the camera cuts to correspondents on the floor. The latest gossip, the newest rumor, is fed back to millions of American homes.

True, the television viewer will miss the sense of being in the convention hall, the actual feel of the crowd, the vast size of the amphitheater. On the other hand, viewers can sit back in the comfort of home and watch the Democrats and Republicans choose their candidates for the most powerful office in the world.

As noted, in most recent conventions the delegates have merely ratified what has been a foregone conclusion for weeks or months. Do the delegates have meaningful power and independent judgment, or are they robots legally bound to vote for the winner of their state's primary? Are some of them puppets taking orders from political bosses? Would it perhaps be better, after all, to watch a late movie? The answers to these questions depend entirely on what convention, what delegation, and which delegates one has in mind. Depending on the year and the circumstances, one can actually answer "yes" or "no" to each question. Although many of the convention proceedings draw a relatively small television audience, the acceptance speech by a presidential nominee, usually on the last night of the convention, normally draws a large audience of many millions of people.

© Shannon Stapleton/Reuters/Corbis

The national convention has been roundly denounced as a carnival and a bore, and vigorously defended as the most practical method of choosing political candidates in a democracy. It may be all three.

Today, Nelson W. Polsby has observed, "National conventions survive primarily as spectacle. . . . More and more conventions are designed as entertainment, although . . . they may still conduct business of great importance to the future of the party."[51]

Nevertheless, the national conventions of both major parties can play an important role in rallying voter support for their party's candidates. In 2004, for example, President George W. Bush came out of the Republican National Convention in New York with a "convention bounce" and momentum that placed his opponent, John Kerry, on the defensive for several weeks.

## Nominating a Presidential Candidate

National party conventions, today greatly diminished in importance, normally take place over four days in July or August. The convention city is often hot and overcrowded; delegates spend long hours waiting for elevators and attempting to do such ordinarily simple things as ordering breakfast in a hotel coffee shop or getting through to someone on the telephone. If there is competition for the nomination—and that has not been the case in recent years—rumors may fly of deals and of switches by key delegations. There are press conferences, television interviews, parades, bands, and other forms of confusion and diversion. Large corporations may set up hospitality suites, or provide cars for bigwigs, or throw lavish parties that double as fund-raisers for members of Congress attending the conventions.

The convention, on its first day, normally hears the report of its credentials committee, the body that decides which delegates will be seated. Sometimes, rival delegations claim to represent the party in a state, or one faction may charge irregularities in the selection of delegates. The credentials committee must decide these disputes, subject always to the approval of the convention. In the evening, or on the second night, the keynote speaker fills the air with the customary rhetoric. A good keynote speech stirs the delegates and sets the tone for the rest of the convention; it may also catapult the speaker into national prominence, possibly as a contender for the party's nomination in the future.

On the second day, as a rule, the party platform is debated and voted on. On the third day the nominations and balloting for the presidential nominee usually begin. Traditionally, a candidate's name is not mentioned until the very end of the nominating speech. ("I give you the next president of the United States, —— ———!") The name is a signal for a carefully planned, "spontaneous" demonstration on the floor, often employing professional demonstrators and organized to the split second by experts armed with noisemakers, walkie-talkies, and stopwatches.

Then the roll of states is called in alphabetical order for the balloting. In both parties, the candidate who wins a simple majority of the convention votes is nominated. In the past, when sometimes there were contests for the nomination, front-runners attempted to win on the first ballot. Today, however, delegates do not expect to vote more than once; 1952 was the last year in which a major-party presidential nomination was not settled on the first ballot.

It is the traditional privilege of the presidential nominee to select the vice presidential nominee.[52] The

© Mark Avery/Orange County Register/Corbis

convention nominates the vice presidential candidate, who delivers an acceptance speech.

On the fourth day the presidential candidate delivers his acceptance speech. The presidential and vice presidential candidates make their climactic appearance with their families before the cheering delegates and the television audience. This moment of high personal and political drama underscores the fact that a national convention also serves the function of a party pep rally, generating enthusiasm for the ticket and, in effect, kicking off the presidential campaign.

Beneath the hoopla and the ballyhoo of a national party convention, some serious business has taken place. At times, differences on issues within the party have been publicly aired. And a major political party has produced its nominees for the highest offices in the land.

## The Delegates

Who are the few thousand men and women formally entitled to select the presidential nominees of the two major parties? In general, they represent a cross section of the party, but a generally affluent cross section, since the cost of travel to a convention city, and of hotels and meals, is expensive. The delegates usually include governors; senators; members of Congress; mayors; state legislators; state party officials; candidates for local, state, and federal offices; and activists and contributors at the grass-roots level.

Delegates to national party conventions are chosen by a variety of methods. A majority of states select delegations in presidential primaries, in which voters in one or both parties select all or some convention delegates. In the remaining states, delegates are chosen by other methods, including state conventions, party caucuses, and state committees.

Because of reforms instituted by the Democratic Party, its 1972 national convention included for the first time substantial numbers of women, African Americans, youths, and Spanish-speaking delegates. Until that year, in some states, members of those groups were systematically excluded from Democratic Party delegations to national conventions. (See Table 9-4.) Both major parties apportion delegates under complicated formulas based on population and party strength within each state.

Delegates who are chosen by state and local party organizations are sometimes under the control of party leaders. But the growth of primaries and caucuses that choose delegates pledged to vote for a particular candidate has greatly reduced the power of party leaders to control national conventions. By 1980, however, many Democrats felt that grass-roots party reform had gone

TABLE 9-4

**Delegates, by Selected Groups, to the Democratic National Convention, 1968–2004**

| Year | Women | African Americans | Youth* |
|---|---|---|---|
| 1968 | 13% | 5.5% | 4% |
| 1972 | 38 | 15 | 21 |
| 1976 | 34 | 9 | 14.8 |
| 1980 | 49.9 | 14.9 | NA |
| 1984 | 50 | 18 | 8 |
| 1988 | 49 | 21 | 5 |
| 1992 | 49.7 | 17 | 4 |
| 1996 | 57 | 21 | 4† |
| 2000 | 58 | 19 | NA |
| 2004 | 50 | 20 | 7 |

*Ages 18 to 30.
†Ages 18 to 29.
SOURCES: *The Party Reformed,* Final Report of the Committee on Party Structure and Delegate Selection (Washington, D.C.: Democratic National Committee, July 7, 1972), pp. 7–8; *New York Times,* July 12, 1976, p. C5; 1980 data from Democratic National Committee; 1984 data from *New York Times,* July 15, 1984, p. 26; 1988 data from *Washington Post,* July 12, 1988, p. A27; 1992 data from *Washington Post,* July 12, 1992, p. A13, and the Democratic National Committee; 1996 data from *Washington Post,* August 25, 1996, p. M4; 2000 data from *New York Times,* August 14, 2000, p. A17. Data from 2004 from the *Boston Globe,* July 25, 2004, online at <http://www.boston.com>, and the *New York Times,* July 25, 2004, section 15, p. 1.

*Making a Difference*

## THE YOUNGEST DELEGATE AT LOS ANGELES

Some junior high school students aspire to be astronauts or rock stars. Thomas Santaniello wanted to be in politics. At the Democratic National Convention in Los Angeles in 2000, he achieved his dream.

At 17, Tom Santaniello was the youngest delegate at the Democratic convention. And he was not even old enough to vote.

"I've kind of been preparing for this since about the eighth grade," said the South Carolina delegate. Santaniello got involved in politics when he had to write a letter to a famous person for a junior high school English class. He wrote to Senator Ernest Hollings, Democrat of South Carolina, who responded, urging him to get involved in local politics.

Santaniello attended his first precinct caucus in his hometown of Spartanburg in 1996 and immersed himself in local Democratic Party politics. He took part in several campaigns, holding candidate signs on street corners and driving senior citizens to polling places.

But those chores were nothing like the personal campaign he undertook early in 2000. He began writing letters and making phone calls, urging Democrats to send a youth representative to the national convention.

The campaign paid off. Santaniello was one of two delegates elected from South Carolina's 4th Congressional District.

"A dream come true," he said.

After the convention, Santaniello heads to Furman University where he plans to major in—what else?—political science.

—Adapted from the Associated Press, August 15, 2000; and Gannett News Service, August 15, 2000

too far. A party commission recommended new rules designed to give party regulars—officeholders and party officials—more power to nominate a presidential candidate. At the party's national convention in 2000 at Los Angeles, for example, 13 percent of the delegates identified themselves as politicians, a number larger than any other group.[53]

And delegates may hold stronger views than rank-and-file party members. For example, 75 percent of delegates to the 2004 Democratic convention thought abortion should be generally available to those who want it, compared with 49 percent of Democratic voters; 44 percent of delegates favored gay marriage, compared with 36 percent of Democratic voters; and 93 percent of delegates thought the war in Iraq was not worth the loss of life and other costs, compared with 85 percent of Democratic voters.[54]

## From Smoke-Filled Rooms to the Television Age

The national nominating convention evolved slowly in American politics. Until 1824, nominations for president were made by party caucus in Congress. As a presidential aspirant that year, Andrew Jackson knew he did not have enough strength in the congressional caucus to gain the nomination; he was nominated instead by the Tennessee legislature. Jackson won the popular vote but

### The Smoke-Filled Room: "Harding Will Be Selected"

William Safire, in his authoritative political dictionary, tracked down the origin of a famous phrase in American politics, born at the 1920 Republican National Convention in Chicago:

> **smoke-filled room:** A place of political intrigue and chicanery, where candidates are selected by party bosses in cigar-chewing sessions. This sinister phrase is usually attributed to Harry Daugherty, an Ohio Republican who supported Senator Warren Harding for the party's presidential candidacy. Daugherty sensed that the two best-known candidates, General Leonard Wood and Governor Frank Lowden of Illinois, would start off with almost equal support. "The convention will be deadlocked," Daugherty is quoted as having said, "and after the other candidates have gone their limit, some twelve or fifteen men, worn out and bleary-eyed for lack of sleep, will sit down about two o'clock in the morning, around a table in a smoke-filled room in some hotel and decide the nomination. When that time comes, Harding will be selected."
>
> Daugherty later denied having said any such thing. . . . But William Allen White, editor of the *Emporia Gazette* and a respected Republican figure, corroborated the Daugherty prediction. A story filed at 5 a.m. on June 12, 1920, by Associated Press reporter Kirke Simpson, led off with the words "Harding of Ohio was chosen by a group of men in a smoke-filled room early today as Republican candidate for President."

—William Safire, *Safire's New Political Dictionary: The Definitive Guide to the New Language of Politics* no candidate received a majority of the electoral votes, and the selection of a president fell to the House of Representatives, which chose John Quincy Adams. Jackson's efforts, however, successfully dethroned "King Caucus"; for the election of 1832, presidential candidates of all political parties were nominated by national conventions for the first time.

The early conventions provided no surprises, but in 1844, on the eighth ballot, the Democrats chose James K. Polk, a **"dark horse"**—a term used to describe a candidate who is thought to have only an outside chance of gaining the nomination. Polk won the election and proved an able president. Polk's nomination "marked the coming of age of the convention as an institution capable of creating as well as of ratifying consensus within the party."[55]

The phrase "smoke-filled room," often used to describe the selection of a candidate by political bosses operating in secret, grew out of the 1920 GOP convention. There, a group of Republican leaders met in Suite 404 of Chicago's Blackstone Hotel and ended a convention stalemate by selecting Warren G. Harding of Marion, Ohio, who looked like a president but was otherwise a mediocre chief executive. Harding died in office in 1923, and his vice president, Calvin Coolidge of Vermont, succeeded to the presidency. A year later, in the historic Democratic National Convention of 1924, the delegates were deadlocked and split between supporters of Alfred E. Smith, the Roman Catholic governor of New York, and William Gibbs McAdoo of California, President Woodrow Wilson's secretary of the treasury and son-in-law. Finally, on the 103rd ballot, the convention nominated John W. Davis, a New York lawyer and former ambassador to Great Britain, as the Democratic standard-bearer. It was the longest convention ever held, but all to no avail. The Republicans nominated President Coolidge, a man of so few words that he was known as "Silent Cal," and the Progressive Party nominated Senator Robert M. "Fighting Bob" La Follette of Wisconsin. Coolidge, who was identified with prosperity, won.

Franklin D. Roosevelt led the field at the Democratic National Convention in 1932, but he was not nominated until the fourth ballot. In 1940, with the galleries chanting "We want Willkie," the Republicans nominated Wendell L. Willkie, a Wall Street lawyer and a true dark horse. The Taft-Eisenhower convention battle in 1952 reflected the greatest split in the Republican Party since 1912.

Since 1960, however, national conventions have filled more of a ratifying function than a selective one. The power of party leaders and bosses, which had been very strong in national conventions for more than a century, was ebbing. (See Table 9-5.)

As a result of the intense press coverage now given to presidential primaries and to preconvention campaigning, one or another candidate has tended to gain a clear lead in the minds of the public, in the political

© Rick Friedman/Corbis

polls, and often, within the rank and file of the party well before the convention. "News accounts of nominating campaigns play up the competition, reporting the campaign as if it were a game or a sporting event," one observer has noted. "The metaphor of choice is a horse race. The news focuses on favorites, dark horses, and also-rans, on candidates neck-and-neck, gaining ground, or running far behind."[56]

National conventions nominate candidates for president who go before the voters every four years. But most Americans do not participate in selecting the convention delegates who make this crucial choice. For example, in 2004, about 12.7 million people voted in the party primaries, or only about 8 percent of the population of voting age.[57] Moreover, a leading political scientist concluded that those who do vote in the presidential primaries are "quite unrepresentative" of the party identifiers who do not participate.[58] Even fewer people choose the delegates who are selected in ways other than the primaries. Most people, for example, have never attended a district or state party convention where delegates are chosen.

## The Future of the Convention System

From time to time various proposals have been made to revamp the national nominating convention or even re-

**TABLE 9-5**

**Development of the System for Nominating Presidential Candidates in the United States, 1790s–2004**

| Year | System Used to Nominate Presidential Candidates | Key Features | Consequences |
|---|---|---|---|
| 1790s–1824 | Congressional caucus | Presidential nominees are selected by a party's legislators in Congress. | Selection of the presidential nominee is controlled by the congressional wing of the party. |
| 1831–1908 | "Classic" convention system | Presidential nominees are selected by the party convention. Convention delegates are chosen by party leaders and party organizations. | Party leaders and "party bosses" retain maximum power to control nomination. |
| 1912–1968 | "Mixed" convention system | Some convention delegates are chosen in presidential primaries, where rank-and-file party members vote for delegates pledged to particular candidates. Most delegates are still chosen by party leaders and party organizations. | Convention still "decides." Party leaders and "party bosses" continue to be very influential. |
| 1972 to present | The age of presidential primaries | Most delegates are selected in presidential primaries. Delegates are pledged to particular candidates. | Decision is usually made before the convention meets. Convention no longer decides. |

place it with some presumably more representative or more dignified procedure. One of the proposals has been for a national presidential primary, in which the voters could directly choose the presidential candidates of the major parties.

The plan has some possible drawbacks, however. For example, critics have argued that if too many candidates enter the primary, no single candidate might receive a majority of the votes, forcing a runoff. In that case, the candidate who initially led the field might lose.[59] Moreover, a national presidential primary, held on a single day, might work against lesser-known candidates who may gain greater public recognition from a nominating process that is spread out over several months. And a national primary might further weaken American political parties by bypassing party organizations, while increasing the power of the news media to influence the electoral process.[60]

Nelson W. Polsby has suggested that political parties deserve a continuing role in the selection of presidential nominees, for "no better institutions have evolved to conduct nominating politics." Moreover, Polsby argued, political parties, because of their varied roles, are "crucial for the proper general functioning of the political system."[61]

In any event, the convention system, having survived since 1832, is not likely to disappear in the television age. Nor is it at all clear that the national convention should be replaced.

The conventions may no longer, as a rule, be an arena for political struggle, nor do they have the excitement of years past. But they still serve a purpose. They choose the nominees for president and vice president, they provide a forum for the voters to see the candidates in action as they deliver their acceptance speeches, they may unify the party, and they may also generate voter interest in the fall elections.

## POLITICAL PARTIES AND DEMOCRATIC GOVERNMENT

At best, Americans have always had a somewhat ambivalent attitude toward politics and politicians. "Politics," Clinton Rossiter noted, "is sin, and politicians, if not sinners, are pretty suspicious fellows."[62]

In 1952 General Eisenhower enjoyed the support of many voters who believed that he was "above politics" or "not a politician." The same was true of Ronald Reagan when he ran for governor of California for the first time in 1966, in a campaign that emphasized his nonprofessional political status.

Among many voters, the image of the politician as an unprincipled opportunist persists. The initial reac-

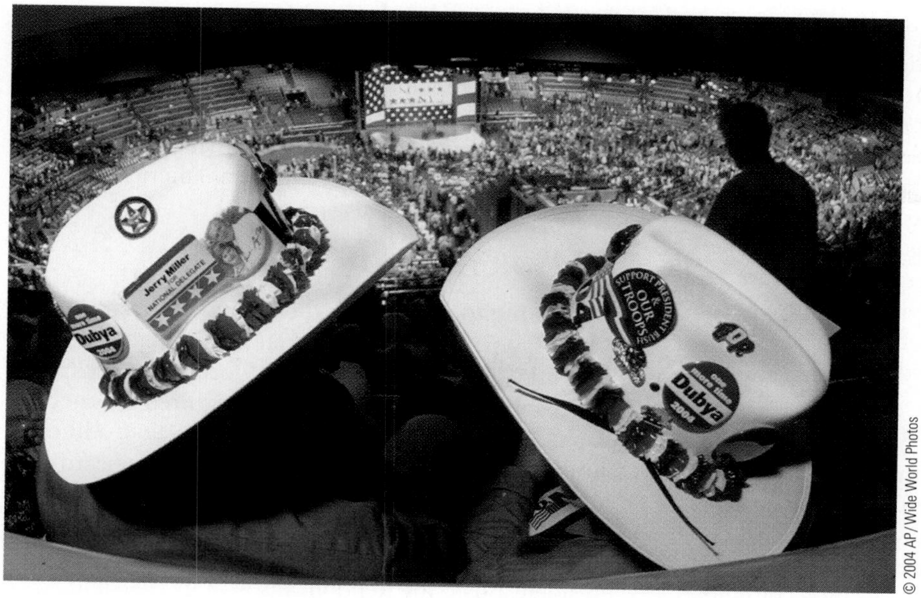


© 2004 AP/Wide World Photos

tion of many Americans to the Watergate scandal was not shock at the illegal acts committed by the Nixon administration but the view that "they all do it."

Because political parties are vital to the functioning of American democracy, it is somewhat paradoxical that politics and politicians—especially with their access to the image-making resources of Madison Avenue—do not enjoy greater prestige.

The truth about politics and its practitioners may lie somewhere between Aristotle's view that "the good of man" is the object of politics and the classic statement of Simon Cameron, the Republican boss of Pennsylvania, that "an honest politician is one who, when he is bought, will stay bought."[63]

Possibly, Americans would have a more generous view of the craft of politics if it were more widely understood that parties and democracy are mutually dependent. Competition among political parties is the essence of democracy. Political parties in America, as we have seen, provide a vehicle of political choice. They also manage the transfer of power, help to hold politicians accountable to the voters, recruit candidates, staff and link branches of the government, and may sometimes resolve social conflict.

The rest of the world also has a vital stake in the politics of American democracy; certainly the party nominee chosen by the electorate to be president has greater power than any other world leader. How an American president uses that power, including the nuclear weapons under his control, is of direct concern to all other nations, as well as to the voters at home.

The "brokerage" role of political parties in mediating among interest groups (whether such groups are organized or not) and in resolving social conflict is of tremendous importance in a democracy under pressure. Both major political parties try to form a broad base by appealing to diverse groups in society. As a result, when one party loses power and another wins the presidency, the change tends to be accepted, or at least tolerated, by the voters. At the same time, the party out of power plays a valuable role as the opposition party, offering alternative programs in Congress and serving as a rallying point for its followers. The "out party" keeps alive the possibility of change for another four years. In these ways parties help to keep conflict manageable, for if substantial numbers of voters violently opposed the election results, the political system could not work.

## A Choice, Not an Echo?

In his classic complaint about the similarity of American political parties, James Bryce concluded that "neither party has any principles, any distinctive tenets."[64] The similarities of American parties are often lamented, but, as noted earlier, there are significant differences as well.

Some of these differences can be measured by comparing contrasting party platforms in presidential elections. Most people pay little attention to party platforms. Although the conventional view is that platforms are "meaningless," Gerald M. Pomper has concluded that platforms in fact "are reasonably meaningful indications of the party's intentions" and serve to identify the parties with "certain policies."[65]

Moreover—as surprising as it might be to many people—in a majority of cases, Pomper concluded, political parties actually carry out the promises contained in their platforms. Analyzing 1,795 platform pledges over a 10-year period, Pomper determined that "almost two-thirds" of these promises were fulfilled.[66]

Although it is true that American parties are not

sharply ideological, it is also true that many American voters have not been sharply ideological. The argument is often made that major parties should offer a more pronounced choice on issues, not merely a choice between candidates; but it is by no means clear that extreme polarization of the parties on issues that divide American society is desirable. "The difference between Democrats and Republicans," Max Lerner has observed, "while it is more than the difference between Tweedledum and Tweedledee, is not such as to split the society itself or invite civil conflict. . . . The choices between the two are usually substantial choices but not desperate ones."[67]

### Are Parties Accountable to the Voters?

When Americans go to the polls, they do not elect parties; they elect officials who usually run as the candidates of political parties. By its very nature, the American political system holds these officials accountable to the voters while holding the parties only indirectly accountable.

The most frequent criticism of the American party system is that the parties are not "responsible" to the electorate, that there is no way to make them keep the promises outlined in their platforms, and that, in any event, they lack the internal discipline to whip their programs through Congress.[68]

In a parliamentary system of government, such as that in Great Britain, political parties are more closely linked to the popular will because the voters choose a majority party that is responsible for the conduct of both the executive and legislative branches of government. Because few critics of the American party system advocate parliamentary government for the United States, party accountability in America is likely to remain a matter of degree.

Many political scientists do not agree on the need for or desirability of greater party responsibility. For example, party cohesion strong enough to pass programs in Congress could only be achieved by reducing the importance and independence of individual legislators. But advocates of strong, responsible parties point to several ways that party responsibility can be strengthened, short of adopting the British system of parliamentary government—for example, attempting to achieve greater discipline within parties by rewarding cooperative members with campaign funds, and electing the chairs of congressional committees on the basis of party loyalty rather than seniority.

To an extent, however, a measure of party responsibility already exists. When American parties embark on courses of action that displease large numbers of voters, the voters may retaliate. The White House is not a permanent residence; a president who runs for reelection may be voted out of office, evidence that a measure of accountability is not wholly lacking in American politics.

## A Look Ahead

Attempting to predict the future of American political parties is a perilous business. Like life itself, politics is often unpredictable; those who had forecast the eclipse of the Republican Party in 1964 were required to watch the elephant ride into the White House in 1968. Although similar predictions of Republican doom were heard after Nixon's resignation over the Watergate scandal in 1974, the GOP with Ronald Reagan as its candidate won the presidential elections of 1980 and 1984. With the first President Bush, the Republicans won in 1988 and again in 2000 and 2004 with George W. Bush. The Democrats, whose prospects seemed bleak at the outset of the 1992 campaign, triumphed in November. Two years later, the Republicans, seemingly humbled by Bill Clinton's victory, won control of Congress.

One fact seems clear: Over a period of time, political parties must respond to the pressures for, or against, change, or pay the price of defeat. And it seems likely that minor parties of the right and left will periodically continue to arise. Possibly, more "nonparty" candidates will seek the presidency, as did Ross Perot in 1992. Yet, in one form or another, the two-party system has flourished since the beginning of the republic.

The increased importance of television and of preconvention campaigns makes the last-minute selection of an unknown candidate by a national convention far less likely than in the past. Candidates will probably continue to rely heavily on television, which can reach millions of people, while still continuing old-fashioned stump campaigning. Political commercials, "attack ads," and professional campaign managers who are skilled in media techniques now play a major role in campaigns. So too do political polls.

Political parties mirror the society in which they function. If government can be made more responsive to the public, political parties may play a vital part in that process, for they are uniquely situated to translate the hopes of the American people into action by the American government.

## CHAPTER HIGHLIGHTS

- A major political party is a broadly based coalition that attempts to gain control of the government by winning elections in order to exercise power and reward its members.
- In the United States, the two-party system has prevailed during most of the nation's history.
- Today, political parties are less powerful than in the past, as party allegiances among voters have declined and as competing groups—political action committees, professional campaign managers, and interest groups—have increasingly come to share many of the traditional roles of parties.
- Political parties perform vital functions in the American political system. They (1) manage the transfer of power, (2) offer a choice of rival candidates and programs to the voters, (3) serve as a bridge between government and people by helping to hold elected officials accountable to the voters, (4) help to recruit candidates for office, (5) may serve to reconcile conflicting interests in society, (6) staff the government and help to run it, and (7) link various branches and levels of government.
- The fading of party loyalties among many voters has been one of the most visible features of American politics in recent years. Beginning in 1974, about a third of the voters described themselves as independents. Only about two-thirds of the voters called themselves Republicans or Democrats.
- Various reasons have been suggested for the decline of party ties: a more educated electorate, less dependent on parties for guidance; an increase in "split-ticket" voting; the increasing importance of television and the news media; and the breaking up of old loyalties and alignments within the major parties.
- Studies have shown that the Democrats usually, although not always, enjoy greater voter support from labor, minorities, young people, those who have not attended college and who have lower incomes, and those who live in the cities. Republicans are more likely to be white, suburban, rural, wealthy, older, college educated, and professionals or business executives.
- There are also philosophical and ideological differences between the parties. Democrats tend to believe more in the ability of government to solve problems than do Republicans.
- Although presidential candidates are nominated by national political party conventions, in recent years the convention's choice has been determined months earlier by the results of the spring primaries. The increased importance of television and of preconvention campaigns makes the last-minute selection of an unknown candidate by a national convention far less likely than in the past.
- On paper, the party's quadrennial national convention is the source of all authority within the party. The convention nominates the party's candidates for president and vice president; it writes a platform, settles disputes, writes rules, and elects the members of the national committee.
- Over a period of time, political parties must respond to the pressures for, or against, change—or pay the price of defeat. And it seems likely that minor parties of the right and left will periodically continue to arise.

## KEY TERMS

major political party, p. 257
national convention, p. 272
national chair, p. 272
national committee, p. 272
dark horse, p. 281

## SUGGESTED WEBSITES

**http://www.democrats.org**
*Democratic Party*

**http://www.greenparty.org**
*Green Party*

**http://www.lp.org**
*Libertarian Party*

**http://www.vote-smart.org**
*Project Vote Smart*
A nonprofit, nonpartisan website that provides a database of information about elected officials and candidates, transcripts of speeches made by presidents, U.S. senators, U.S. representatives, and governors and information on voter registration for each state.

**http://www.reformparty.org**
*Reform Party*

**http://www.rnc.org or http://www.gop.com**
*Republican Party*

## SUGGESTED READING

Aldrich, John. *Why Parties? The Origin and Transformation of Political Parties in America** (University of Chicago Press, 1995). An insightful examination of the role of political parties. According to the author, parties fulfill three basic functions: they help organize the selection of candidates for public office, they mobilize the electorate, and they play a vital role in the policymaking process.

Bibby, John F., and Maisel, L. Sandy. *Two Parties—or More? The American Party System,* 2nd edition* (Westview Press, 2003). A comprehensive examination of third parties in U.S. presidential elections. The book discusses the causes of the two-party system that is dominant in the United States, as well as public dissatisfaction with two-party politics. The authors foresee a continuation of the two-party system, which they favor, and argue that the major parties should pursue the political center.

David, Paul T., Goldman, Ralph M., and Bain, Richard C. *The Politics of National Party Conventions,* revised edition (Rowman & Littlefield, 1984). A detailed examination of the historical development of national party conventions. Stresses the functions that the national conventions have performed in the American party system.

Duverger, Maurice. *Political Parties: Their Organization and Activity in the Modern State,* 3rd edition* (Methuen, 1964). An influential comparative analysis of political parties in a number of countries. Among other topics, Duverger, a French political scientist, examines the nature of party organization in different types of parties. He also explores the relationship between a country's electoral system and the type of party system that flourishes there.

Epstein, Leon D. *Political Parties in the American Mold,* reprint edition* (University of Wisconsin Press, 1989). A thoughtful analysis of the historical development and operation of political parties in America.

Epstein, Leon D. *Political Parties in Western Democracies,* reissue edition* (Transaction Publishers, 1993). A useful comparative study of political parties in various countries, with special emphasis on those in Great Britain and the United States. Examines the historical development of parties, recruitment of party leaders, and the contribution of the parties to governing.

Fiorina, Morris. *Divided Government,* 2nd edition, reissue* (Longman, 2003). A thoughtful analysis of a phenomenon that was once rare in American politics, but has become increasingly common.

Green, John C., and Farmer, Rick, eds. *The State of the Parties,* 5th edition* (Rowman & Littlefield, 2006). A readable and wide-ranging collection of essays on the evolving role of political parties in elections and governing.

Green, John C., and Herrnson, Paul S. eds. *Responsible Partisanship? The Evolution of American Political Parties Since 1950** (University Press of Kansas, 2002). An analysis of the development of the U.S. two-party system since the publication of the 1950 report, "Toward a More Responsible Party System," by the American Political Science Association. Two goals recommended in the report—increased party government in Congress and stronger national party organizations—have been at least partially achieved. But overall, the book suggests, "responsible party government" remains an elusive, and perhaps misguided, goal.

Hershey, Marjorie Randon. *Party Politics in America,* 12th edition* (Longman, 2006). A comprehensive analysis of American political parties. Examines party organization, the behavior of party supporters in the electorate, the role of parties in elections, and the impact of parties on government.

Keefe, William J., and Hetherington, Marc J. *Parties, Politics, and Public Policy in America,* 10th edition* (CQ Press, 2006). A useful introduction to the historical development, political functions, and current status of parties in the American political system.

Key, V. O., Jr. *Politics, Parties, and Pressure Groups,* 5th edition (Crowell, 1964). A comprehensive analysis of political parties and interest groups. Examines the nature of the American party system, party structure and procedures, the relations between parties and the voters, and the impact of parties on government.

Mayer, William G., ed. *The Making of the Presidential Candidates 2004** (Rowman & Littlefield, 2004). A comprehensive examination of the intricate process by which American presidential candidates are nominated.

Mayhew, David R. *Placing Parties in American Politics** (Princeton University Press, 1986). A thoughtful and detailed analysis of the American party structure on the state level. Points out that although some states have strong, unified party organizations, in other states parties are much weaker.

Polsby, Nelson W. *Consequences of Party Reform** (Oxford University Press, 1983). A study of reforms in the presidential nominating system and of changes in the way that campaigns and parties are financed. Analyzes the results of these reforms and evaluates proposals for further change.

Ranney, Austin. *Curing the Mischiefs of Faction: Party Reform in America* (University of California Press, 1975). A thoughtful analysis of the theory and practice of party reform in the United States. Emphasizes three main periods when major changes were made in American party institutions: 1820–1840, 1890–1920, and 1956–1974.

Wattenberg, Martin P. *The Decline of American Political Parties, 1952–1996** (Harvard University Press, 1998). A concise study of the diminishing importance of political parties and the growing impact of candidate images in American elections. Argues that voters have become indifferent to parties because of an increasing belief that parties no longer play a significant role in the governing process.

White, John Kenneth, and Shea, Daniel M. *New Party Politics: From Jefferson and Hamilton to the Information Age,* 2nd edition* (Thomson / Wadsworth, 2004). A comprehensive examination of political parties that describes how party organizations have adapted to their evolving environment, including most recently the use of new campaign technologies and the Internet.

*Available in paperback edition.

THE UNION AND THE CONSTITUTION FOREVER

# Chapter 10

# POLITICAL CAMPAIGNS AND CANDIDATES

AMERICANS WATCHING TELEVISION ONE NIGHT in 2004 saw an interesting commercial. It was not an advertisement for a detergent, a cruise line, or a breakfast cereal. Rather, it attacked Senator John Kerry, the Democratic candidate for president of the United States, and sought to sell the voters on the Republican candidate, President George W. Bush.

The spot opened with the president striding purposefully through the White House colonnade next to the Rose Garden, then sitting, deep in contemplation, in a darkened room. Against a black screen viewers saw the words: "John Kerry's Plan . . . Taxes At Least $900 billion." And then the next image, "John Kerry's plan . . . Weaken Fight Against Terrorists."

"I'm George W. Bush and I approve this message," the president said. An announcer began, "John Kerry's plan: . . . On the war on terror, weaken the Patriot Act used to arrest terrorists and protect America. And he wanted to delay defending America until the United Nations approved. John Kerry: Wrong on taxes. Wrong on defense." As the announcer spoke, the screen showed images of travelers before an airport departure monitor, a person in a chemical weapons suit, and a swarthy man, presumably supposed to suggest a terrorist, looking at the camera menacingly. (An Arab American group protested the negative stereotype; Bush advisers said the man in the commercial was not an Arab.)

In the war of the TV commercials, the Kerry camp lost no time in counterattacking. They immediately aired a commercial in which an announcer declared: "Once again, George Bush is misleading America. John Kerry has never called for a $900 billion tax increase . . . Doesn't America

© 2004 AP/Wide World Photos

Voice-over: "I'm George W. Bush, and I approve this message." An announcer says, "A president sets his agenda for America in the first 100 days. John Kerry's plan: to pay for new government spending, raise taxes by at least $900 billion. On the war on terror, weaken the Patriot Act used to arrest terrorists and protect America. And he wanted to delay defending America until the United Nations approved. John Kerry: Wrong on taxes. Wrong on defense."

deserve more from its president than misleading, negative ads?"

Democrats also assailed a commercial in which the Bush campaign used images of the World Trade Center in ruins after the 9/11 terrorist attacks, and firefighters carrying a flag-draped body. In addition, some members of the families of the victims protested the ads as inappropriate. The Bush campaign defended the images as defining moments of the Bush presidency and refused to pull the 9/11 ads.

The campaign was only weeks old when it turned even more acrimonious. A group financed by Bush contributors and supporters in Texas and calling itself "Swift Boat Veterans for Truth" ran TV ads seeking to discredit Kerry's service and decorations in the Vietnam War. Kerry struck back, calling the group "a front for the Bush campaign" and saying of the president, "he wants them to do his dirty work."[1] The White House insisted it was not responsible for the group's bitterly anti-Kerry commercials, but Bush declined specifically to condemn the ads. He said he opposed all commercials run by such groups, known as **527 organizations** for the section of the Internal Revenue Service code under which they must report their expenditures. The tax-exempt groups were created to exploit a loophole in the law regulating campaign finance.

During the presidential election campaign, both sides raised huge amounts of money, and both candidates and their supporters spent tens of millions of dollars on television ads, particularly targeting the so-called "battleground states" where the outcome was uncertain.

Most political TV ads are slippery creations, designed to bend facts to persuade the voters. Voters seldom have time or inclination to check up on the various charges and assertions that the ads present as facts.

Objectivity, however, is not the point of political commercials. They are designed to sell a product—

© 2004 AP/Wide World Photos

"Swift Boat Veterans for Truth" ran TV ads seeking to discredit Kerry's service and decorations in the Vietnam War.

© Kevin Winter/Getty Images

Democratic presidential candidate John Kerry rode a motorcycle onto the set of NBC's *Tonight Show* in 2004, earning applause from Jay Leno.

in this case a candidate—and get people to "buy" that product in the voting booth. In that sense, political commercials have the same goal as croaking frogs in a beer commercial or a Chihuahua selling tacos. And candidates believe that television spots are effective, or they would not spend a large portion of their total budget on commercials. "As a general rule, a campaign should spend 50 to 80 percent of its budget" on TV commercials, according to political consultants.[2]

Television commercials are an important aspect of modern political campaigns. Candidates at the presidential level and below now routinely advertise their wares in this fashion—or snipe at their opponents. For a moment, through the medium of television Bush's anti-Kerry message had been seen by millions of viewers.

Nor are commercials the only way that candidates use television to reach the voters. In 2004, as in past years, the presidential candidates appeared on television talk and entertainment shows. During the primaries, Al Sharpton hosted *Saturday Night Live.* Kerry, in a leather jacket, blue jeans, and riding boots, appeared on Jay Leno's show, driving onstage on a Harley. And Bush and Kerry and their wives appeared on the program of Dr. Phil, the TV psychologist.

In 2000, candidate George W. Bush planted a large kiss on Oprah Winfrey when he appeared on her program. It was a forum that allowed him to show off his sense of humor and considerable personal charm, and not incidentally to try to appeal to the millions of women who make up the largest portion of her audience.

During the 1992 presidential campaign, Bill Clinton, the Democratic candidate, wearing dark glasses and looking like one of the "Blues Brothers," played the saxophone one night on the *Arsenio Hall Show.*

The talk shows gave the presidential candidates a chance to clown around and show the voters their "human side." One might have trouble visualizing George Washington or John Adams on Oprah or Leno, but then, times and technology have changed.

It is not surprising in the television age that candidates for political office try to sell themselves and their ideas on TV. Once nominated, candidates must appeal to the voters. And television offers the surest means of reaching the largest number of people.

As a result, television has dramatically changed American political campaigns since 1948. The day is long past when a William McKinley could campaign from his front porch in Canton, Ohio. Today's candidates hire an advertising agency or a special team of consultants to prepare television spots—commercials that may air for 10 seconds or longer.

The candidates may debate their opponents on television, as the two major presidential rivals did in 1960, 1976, and every election since then. They may appear in carefully staged, televised question-and-answer sessions designed to display their warm personalities and firm grasp of the issues. Or they may buy an expensive half-hour of prime television time for a sincere talk to the American people.

As the candidates whirl around the country, their campaign appearances in each state are tailored for the statewide and local evening television news broadcasts,

2000: George W. Bush demonstrates his affection for Oprah Winfrey—and her large audience of women viewers—during the 2000 presidential campaign.

© AP/Wide World Photos

and, if possible, the nightly network news programs that reach a national audience. Their speeches on the campaign trail often include sound bites—colorful turns of phrase or sharp words for their rivals—that they hope will make the evening news. Television, in short, is an essential part of a modern political campaign.

In 2004, as they had four years earlier, the candidates for president and vice president also campaigned extensively on the Internet. All, including Ralph Nader, the independent candidate, offered websites that featured the latest speeches, news, and pronouncements of the presidential campaign. During the spring primaries, several candidates—notably former Vermont governor Howard Dean—used their websites to raise money and recruit volunteers.

For every candidate, between nomination and election there stands the campaign. In American politics, the campaign is the battleground of power. Victory may depend on how well the battle is fought, for often a third or more of the voters decide how to vote during the campaign.

Mostly because of the wide use of television, campaigns are expensive: In 2000 candidates for president and Congress spent almost $4 billion.[3] In 2004, campaign spending rose to an estimated $5 billion.[4]

Key Question In this chapter, we will explore a key question about political campaigns: ***In the era of electronic mass media, television commercials, and "image-makers," can the voters make a reasonable choice for themselves and for the nation?***

1992: Bill Clinton, the Democratic candidate for president, plays "Heartbreak Hotel" on the *Arsenio Hall Show.*

© 2000 AP/Wide World Photos

## Comparing Governments

### THE KREMLIN DOMINATES THE AIRWAVES

In the United States the Federal Communications Commission (FCC), a government agency, regulates radio and television. The FCC sets broadcast ownership limits to try to ensure diversity and competition in American media. The government does not control or own the media, however, and the First Amendment protects the freedom of the press.

Such is not the case in Russia where the government owns the stations:

> More than a dozen years after the collapse of the Soviet Union, what Russians see, especially on the news, remains subject to the only rating system that counts: the Kremlin's. One result has been abundant and invariably flattering portrayals of President Vladimir V. Putin that more and more are drawing unfavorable comparisons to Soviet broadcasts and prompting warnings that the state's control over the airwaves has become one of the most significant obstacles to a democratic society.
>
> "It's all propaganda," said Irina M. Khakamada, one of six candidates challenging Mr. Putin in the presidential election on March 14 and struggling to break into the only medium that reaches across Russia's vast expanses.
>
> On Russia's two largest channels, both government owned, and even on those with a lesser degree of state control, there is an uncritical deference to the nation's elected leader that would be unthinkable in Europe or the United States.
>
> "It's not our job to discuss and draw judgments about the actions of our president," said Mr. Antonov, a seasoned journalist and, he acknowledges, an ardent believer in Mr. Putin. . . . All of the national networks are now owned by the state or controlled by state corporations. The 20 highest-rated news programs in Russia all appear on three networks answerable directly or indirectly to the Kremlin.
>
> —"On Russian TV, Whatever Putin Wants, He Gets," by Steven Lee Meyers, *The New York Times,* February 17, 2004, p. A1. Copyright 2004, The New York Times Co.

There are other related questions to consider. Will the candidate with the best image—the most attractive appearance, the cleverest television advisers and consultants, the smoothest packaging—win the election? Political candidates do not always have equal financial and creative resources. Does the candidate with the most money always win? Should one candidate enjoy a financial advantage over another in a democracy? If not, what can be done about it? Do political polls influence the voters and affect the outcome of elections?

These questions have no easy answers. And yet, however imperfect campaigns may be, however raucous and divisive, they are a vital part of the American political system. Campaigns, in the words of the historian Henry Adams, are "the dance of democracy."[5]

© Jim Young/Reuters/Corbis

John Edwards and John Kerry in their first appearance as running mates

## How Campaigns Are Organized

Campaigns are organized chaos. On a national level, large numbers of people—professionals and volunteers—are thrown together for a relatively short period of time to mount an incredibly complex effort to elect a president. The candidate is rather like someone in the eye of a hurricane: jetting around the country—stumping, speechmaking, and handshaking—besieged by the crowds and camera crews, the press and the voters, local politicians and aides. The candidate may arise at 5 a.m. and not get to sleep until 2 a.m. the next morning, with a dozen cities and thousands of miles traversed in the interim. Physically exhausted, hands cut and bruised from the crowds, the candidate is expected to keep smiling throughout and to remain alert—ready to respond instantly to any new issue or crisis. In some remote cornfield of Iowa, a TV reporter may ask for comment on a sudden and complicated development in the Middle East.

The candidate worries that an inappropriate word or phrase might cost the election. An assassin may lurk in the hotel kitchen. The news media are ready to pounce

## The American Past

# TIPPECANOE AND TYLER TOO

Campaign songs, particularly in the 19th century, were an important way to appeal to the voters in the pretelevision age. Perhaps the most famous was the song that publicized "Tippecanoe and Tyler too," the slogan of the Whigs in the presidential election of 1840. William Henry Harrison, the Whig candidate, had defeated the Indians loyal to Chief Tecumseh in the Battle of Tippecanoe in the Indiana Territory in 1811. His vice presidential running mate was John Tyler. The Democrats renominated incumbent Martin Van Buren of New York as their presidential candidate—the "little Van" referred to in the Whig song, which was written by Alexander Coffman Ross, a jeweler and amateur clarinetist from Zanesville, Ohio. To the tune of a minstrel number, "Little Pigs," the song went like this:

> What's the cause of this commotion,
> Motion, motion, motion,
> Our country through?
> It is the ball a-rolling on,
> For Tippecanoe and Tyler too,
> For Tippecanoe and Tyler too,
> And with them we'll beat little Van,
> Van, Van is a used up man;
> And with them we'll beat little Van.

Harrison won the election, but he refused to wear a coat at his inauguration despite the cold and the stormy weather. He caught pneumonia and died a month later. Tyler became president.

—Irwin Silber, *Songs America Voted By*

Indiana Historical Society

on any mistake. In the jet age, the pressures on the candidate are constant and cruel.

The candidate, flying from one appearance to the next at 500 miles per hour, obviously must have an elaborate campaign organization with a headquarters staff to plan and coordinate the total effort. Ultimate success may depend on many variables—the candidate's charisma, smile and appearance, television makeup, advertising agency, and experience; the issues, the number of registered Democrats and Republicans, a sudden foreign policy crisis, an ill-advised remark, even the weather on Election Day. But not the least of these factors is the quality of the candidate's campaign organization.

A presidential candidate must have a campaign manager and a small group of top-level aides to give overall direction to the campaign. The candidate may

© Cornell Capa/Magnum Photos

## How to Win an Election: Republican Version

**Voter Canvass.** A volunteer often says something like this: "Hello, I'm (Name), a neighbor of yours, and I'm here to tell you about (Name), who's a candidate for (Office). He is running for office because he believes (Vision). Can (Name) count on your vote on Election Day, (Date)?"

The best time of day to canvass is when people are home. . . . Don't be afraid to walk during the dinner hour since it may be the only time to find people at home. Keep the visit short and cordial—apologize if you interrupt dinner. Never enter a person's home—you're not a salesman. When the person comes to the door, take a step back so you're less threatening to the voter. Notice children, if they're present; it makes a great impression and wins votes from parents. . . . Skip places that have dogs (Avoid potential bites!). Stick to sidewalks and driveways rather than cutting across lawns.

**Television.** If your event is outside, note the location of the sun before selecting the podium site. The sun should never be behind the speaker nor directly in the speaker's eyes. . . . Make-up is appropriate. Most women already wear make-up to avoid reflections; men should use a little light powder or pancake make-up, close to their natural skin tone, to minimize shine and hide any five o'clock shadow. . . . Avoid flashy, distracting clothing. Men should avoid plaids and narrowly striped shirts; women should avoid layers of jewelry and necklines with no place to anchor a clip microphone.

**Dealing with Reporters.** Contrary to many people's opinion, reporters are just like everybody else. . . . *Don't treat reporters like the enemy.* . . . Most reporters try to be fair. Our evaluation of what's fair or unfair is made through tinted glass: as Republican partisans we're not the most objective people ourselves. . . . *Don't feed the media material you know they won't use.* If you "cry wolf" too many times, the media will start to ignore you altogether. . . . Be honest and accurate. . . . Lying will get you in trouble. . . . If all else fails, respond with a simple "no comment." . . . Remember: NEVER TELL A REPORTER SOMETHING YOU DON'T WANT REPORTED. If the story is juicy enough, "off-the-record" has no meaning.

**Speeches.** *Greet the audience visually.* Walk like an Olympic athlete. . . . *Save and polish your applause lines.* Applause lines are like diamonds. Formed under pressure, cut and polished until they shine.

**Newspaper.** A coordinated letter-to-the-editor program, run by a volunteer, can be another effective way to communicate your message.

**Communications Basics.** *Don't feel compelled to respond to a reporter's exact question.* . . . The basic rule is: A reporter can ask any question he wants; you can answer any question you want. . . . Don't exaggerate resumé items. Every single item contained in a campaign biography must be the truth, the whole truth, and nothing but the truth. Failure to follow this rule will mean likely defeat.

**Phone Banks.** Cold-call prospecting is a telemarketing program which has been proven to produce a good list of prospective donors and at the same time make enough money to cover phone bank expenses. . . . The script you use will depend on whether you're calling as follow-up to a direct mail piece, making a cold-call prospect call, calling to enhance an event, or as a boiler-room operation.

**Graphics.** What guidelines should I follow when designing a logo? *Use credible colors.* Traditional campaign colors, such as dark blue, red, green and burgundy invoke trust. . . . Avoid using pink—it's too feminine.

**Fundraising.** It is important that the decoration chairman be well acquainted with novelty/florist /gift shops in the area, so that "freebies" can be arranged. . . . Flowers, as we all know, are not cheap. . . .

**Get-Out-the-Vote.** What activities can be implemented on Election Day?

1. *Victory Squads.* Victory squads are teams of volunteers who actually knock on the doors of favorable voters and urge them to vote. . . . Each team has a car and driver that can take the voter to the polls while a volunteer babysits or watches the house.
2. *Sign Waving.* In some states, it has become standard for volunteers (and sometimes candidates) to wave signs at key intersections to rouse interest. . . . Since there's no way to differentiate Republican cars from Democrat cars, it's best to do this activity in or around Republican areas. Be careful you don't cause accidents. Attractive young people may get the attention of drivers but can also be traffic hazards. . . .

To ensure an honest vote, you'll want to be sure only qualified voters cast their ballots on Election Day. . . . While most problems are with machine malfunctions, the practice of "voting dead people and vacant lots" is still all too prevalent. Therefore, it's important that Republican volunteers be visible in each precinct to help avoid voter fraud.

*What Should I [the Candidate] Do on Election Day?* Take time to have dinner with your family and friends. Election night has a habit of being the longest night of the year; rest and collect your thoughts. Prepare your remarks for a victory speech.

—Republican National Committee, *Campaign Encyclopedia*

## How to Win an Election: Democratic Version

**Campaign Planning.** You need to have a strategy in mind. . . . Creating a positive image, proving your candidate is a good person—often a necessary strategy element. Proving the opponent is a bad person, based on creating a negative image of the opponent.

**Campaign Message in the Plan.** Repeat, repeat, repeat. An average voter is bombarded with millions of pieces of information every day. The few dozen pieces of information you get through during the campaign must be consistent and reinforcing. . . . Remember: the image, like the message, is not just what comes out of the candidate's mouth. A candidate who does not pay child support will have a bad image and message about kids, no matter what he or she says about day care.

**Research.** In essence, opposition research—more appropriately thought of as *comparative research*—is the means by which you find the nuggets of information that support your campaign's message and bring the point home to voters.

**Educational History.** Verify the [opposition] candidate's degree and graduation date with the school registrar or alumni association; if possible, get his or her grade point average.

**Military Service & Draft Records.** Did the [opposition] candidate serve when and where he says he did? Did the candidate get any special treatment, or have a family member pull strings to get a deferment? What was his draft status during the Vietnam War?

**Country Club Memberships/Fraternal Organizations.** Does the club or group to which [the opposition] candidate belongs discriminate against women or minorities? Has it been involved in any scandals or lawsuits?

**Hobbies.** A candidate's love of golf, yachting, or polo might come to symbolize her elitism in a blue-collar community.

**Associates/Friends.** Is your opponent close with any known felons or other questionable characters? Find out about the company he keeps.

**Direct Mail.** Direct mail writers are always thirsty for spicy rhetoric and interesting statistics. Research that's a bit too hot for your press secretary to use may in fact make for great copy for a fundraising letter.

**Working with Reporters: On Background.** . . . if you spend any length of time talking to reporters, expect to get burned—expect it, shrug it off, and move on. It's happened to everybody and it will be forgotten by the next crisis.

**What to Outlet: Beyond Just Paper.** Websites, while now an essential campaign tool, should be tailored to the people likely to access them. In San Jose, California, where net penetration is high, it's worth spending time on a good, credible web site; but in areas where people can't even make a local call for Internet access, you might focus the bulk of your attention elsewhere. Beyond paper—and beyond the web—there are gimmicks. . . . In long campaigns, the press becomes fascinated with gimmicks. So don't call that musty room your research office: call it your rapid response war room (unnerving your opponents in the process). Don't write just a written report on ethical misdeeds—paste it up on the wall and call it the Wall of Shame.

**Budget.** Every day you learn something new about your expenses—your opponent has placed an early TV buy . . . your volunteers are eating pizza at an alarming rate.

**Candidate Rhythms.** Here's a basic but often forgotten point: Candidates are people, too. They have families and kids and likes and dislikes and certain rhythms that have to be recognized, unless you don't mind getting your head torn off several times a day by a candidate who's exhausted, missed his/her kid's big recital/birthday/ball game, etc.

**Thinking Visually.** One campaign sent their candidate to an urban development site, but the shot showed the candidate talking in front of a pornographic video store. Pay attention to what is immediately behind your candidate's head. It sounds silly, but that's the shot TV will use when the candidate is talking.

**Appropriate Furniture.** You can only sit on a crate for so long. Don't expect volunteers to submit to a torture test. Have enough chairs and tables (donated from unions, old campaigns or volunteers) for them to get the job done. . . .

**Election Day Legal Team.** Unfortunately, Republican voter intimidation operations have made Election Day legal teams a necessity. The Republican Party has a history of discouraging voting among traditional Democratic groups. The methods employed range from fake sample ballots, signs at polling places threatening arrest and armed guards at polling places, to simply allowing the machinery of election to break down. The campaign has to be prepared to contest Election Day problems in court.

—Democratic National Committee, campaign training manuals

hire a professional political consultant as well. There has to be someone in charge of fund-raising, for a national campaign costs millions of dollars; a media team to handle advertising and television; a press secretary; representatives to handle advance details of personal appearances; speechwriters; regional and state coordinators; and campaign aides who organize volunteers to support the candidate in their local communities. And the campaign staff must attempt to coordinate the work of national, state, and local party organizations so that there is a unified effort at all levels.

When a presidential candidate is victorious, key

staff members often move into the White House or into other high positions in the government. In 2000, when George W. Bush won the presidency, he appointed to his staff several of the aides who had worked in his campaign. Many came from Texas, where Bush had served as governor.

An incumbent president who runs for reelection normally enjoys certain advantages. The incumbent may benefit from the trappings of high office, and from the aura of the presidency that surrounds the chief executive. The president may award lucrative defense contracts to plants in key states that are needed to win reelection. In 2004, President George W. Bush funneled more than $12 billion in emergency aid mostly to Florida, a key battleground in the election contest, after that state was battered by four hurricanes in the midst of the campaign. With the elaborate communications systems available aboard Air Force One and everywhere else that a president moves, and with a huge White House staff, an incumbent almost inevitably has the logistical edge over a rival.

A president's campaign appearances, even more than the challenger's, are carefully planned. Several days before a presidential visit in a town or city, the Secret Service checks over locations for security, and the political advance staff determines the best way to display the crowds for the TV cameras, the most pleasing backdrops, and other details—all designed to maximize the political benefit to the chief executive.

Presidents running for reelection attempt to exploit many of the benefits of incumbency. In 1996, for example, President Clinton, running for reelection, journeyed to the United Nations in September to sign the Comprehensive Nuclear Test Ban Treaty aimed at barring all nuclear tests in the air, underground, at sea, or in outer space. Television and newspapers carried photos of Clinton signing the treaty and looking the part of a world statesman.

## Campaign Strategy

### Aiming for the Undecided

Studies have shown that many voters, more than half in recent decades, are committed to one candidate or another in advance of the campaign. Nevertheless, a large group of voters, often one-third or more, make their decision during the campaign. (See Table 10-1.)

Nelson W. Polsby and Aaron B. Wildavsky, in a study of presidential elections, contended that, for the majority of citizens in America, "campaigns do not function so much to change minds as to reinforce previous convictions."[6] Even so, when a third or more of the people make up their minds during a campaign, their votes may well determine the outcome. For example, if 100 million votes are cast in a presidential election, one-third, or 33 million votes, is a sizable bloc by any standard.

The undecided voters may hold the key to victory in close elections. Since some two-thirds of all American voters identify with one of the two major parties, political candidates try to preserve their party base—to hold

President George W. Bush works the crowd at La Crosse, Wisconsin, during the 2004 presidential race.

**TABLE 10-1**

**Presidential Elections: When the Voter Decides**

| Decided how to vote | 1956 | 1960 | 1964 | 1968 | 1972 | 1976 | 1980 | 1984 | 1988 | 1992 | 1996 | 2000 | 2004 |
|---|---|---|---|---|---|---|---|---|---|---|---|---|---|
| | Percentage | | | | | | | | | | | | |
| Knew all along | 45 | 25 | 18 | 21 | 33 | 20 | 20 | 30 | 15 | 19 | 27 | 12 | 33 |
| When candidate announced | 15 | 6 | 23 | 14 | 11 | 14 | 20 | 22 | 17 | 21 | 23 | 32 | 22 |
| During conventions | 19 | 31 | 25 | 24 | 18 | 21 | 18 | 18 | 29 | 14 | 13 | 10 | 14 |
| Post-convention | 12 | 26 | 21 | 19 | 24 | 22 | 15 | 17 | 22 | 22 | 17 | 23 | 15 |
| Last 2 weeks of campaign | 7 | 9 | 9 | 14 | 8 | 17 | 17 | 10 | 12 | 17 | 12 | 18 | 13 |
| Election Day | 2 | 3 | 4 | 7 | 5 | 7 | 9 | 4 | 5 | 8 | 7 | 5 | 2 |

SOURCE: Data provided by University of Michigan, Institute for Social Research, Center for Political Studies, American National Election Studies.

on to their natural constituency—while winning over voters from the other party, independents, and the undecided.

Although some poll data suggest that political campaigns do not influence the choice of a majority of voters, political analysts have concluded that campaigns may influence "a small but crucial proportion of the electorate. . . . Clearly, professional politicians drive themselves and their organizations toward influencing every undecided voter in the expectation that they are the key to providing, or maintaining, the winning margin."[7]

And a number of scholars have disagreed with the view that campaigns have minimal influence on voters. Dan Nimmo and Robert L. Savage have argued that "there is a close relationship between candidate images

Senator John Kerry, the Democratic presidential nominee, campaigns in Houston, Texas in 2004.

## Should You Be a Candidate?

Before the campaign can begin, there must be a candidate. And that job is not easy, as the following excerpt from a Republican Party manual suggests:

> The person who cannot answer virtually all of the following questions in the affirmative should not be running.
>
> 1. Does your family fully support your candidacy? Are they prepared to assume much more responsibility at home and put in extra time campaigning? Can they tolerate the verbal abuse you may receive and long hours you will spend away from home? Will your children accept and understand your frequent absence from home?
> 2. Can you afford to run? Can you expect enough contributions to keep out of serious personal debt? Is your business in good hands while you campaign? If you are employed, do you have a job to go back to in the event you lose?
> 3. Can your personal background stand intensive scrutiny? Are you fully prepared to have the public know about your debts, personal and organizational associations, past relationships with members of the opposite sex, family background, sources of income, health history, partners, etc.?
> 4. Are you strong enough physically and emotionally to stand up to the rigors of a tough campaign? Can your health tolerate long hours, poor food, erratic rest, continuing pressure, rejection and frustration? Most important, could your ego tolerate a loss if it should come?
>
> —"Candidate Recruitment," Republican National Committee campaign manual

and voting behavior."[8] They concluded that although candidates' images usually emerge early in a campaign and remain about the same, those images can and do change during campaigns. As examples, they cite John F. Kennedy in 1960 and Hubert Humphrey in 1968, whose images improved as their campaigns progressed.[9] In arguing that "campaigns make a difference," Nimmo and Savage emphasized that this is particularly true for independent voters, who are more likely than other voters to shift their impressions of the candidates during campaigns.[10]

Nimmo and others view political campaigns as "a process of communication" in which voters do not respond automatically on the basis of their socioeconomic backgrounds or party loyalties. Rather, Nimmo contends, voters tend to "construct" their own individual view of the campaign; they arrive at a decision by interpreting the symbols offered to them, often by drawing upon their own experience.[11]

Norman H. Nie, Sidney Verba, and John R. Petrocik argue in *The Changing American Voter* that campaigns may affect voting because "the public responds to the political stimuli offered it." The behavior of voters, they concluded, is influenced not only by psychological and sociological factors, "but also by the issues of the day and by the way in which candidates present those issues."[12]

An analysis by Walter DeVries and Lance Tarrance concluded that in many elections the outcome is determined by "ticket-splitters." They define a ticket-splitter as a voter likely "to be basically a Republican or Democrat, but one who occasionally splits off to vote for a candidate of another party."[13] To convince the ticket-splitters, DeVries and Tarrance contend, candidates must use campaigns to communicate their views on the issues.[14]

Strategists for the candidates "target" certain groups of voters. Some of these targets are geographic; for instance, a candidate may select specific states for special effort. In 2004, for example, both the Bush and Kerry campaigns spent large amounts of money to buy and air television commercials in so-called battleground states, such as Ohio, that were considered crucial to victory. Or, strategists may concentrate on specific categories of voters, such as white southerners, young voters, African Americans, Hispanics, or other demographic groups.

## Which Road to the White House?

Long before aspiring presidential candidates can get into a general-election campaign, they must, as a rule, enter the bruising arena of the primaries. In 2004, John Kerry was lagging behind his rivals until his dramatic victory in the Iowa caucuses, which launched him on the road to the Democratic nomination.[15]

However, the candidate who wins the most primaries does not necessarily gain the nomination. In 1984 Walter Mondale actually won fewer primaries than Senator Gary Hart of Colorado—11 to Hart's 16. But it was Mondale who got the party's nomination.

For relatively unknown political candidates, the primary route may prove an attractive means of demonstrating their strength and gaining nationwide exposure in the media. For example, Jimmy Carter was not widely known in 1976, and his primary election victories that year were essential to his successful campaign for the Democratic presidential nomination.

Even for a presidential aspirant who is far out in

© AP/Wide World Photos

"... the advantage of the incumbency." With the Grand Canyon as a backdrop and accompanied by Vice President Gore, President Clinton—running for reelection in 1996—signs a document setting aside canyon land in Utah as a national monument.

© The New Yorker Collection Weber from cartoonbank.com. All rights reserved.

"I'm going to do a flip-flop on Africa. Can you make it look good?"

front, entering the primaries is almost always necessary in order to win the nomination. Today, virtually all candidates feel compelled to take the primary route.

With preconvention campaigns so crucial, most candidates find it necessary to have a well-financed campaign organization already in operation long before the national convention. In recent presidential elections, the preconvention campaign organizations of major-party candidates have been hardly distinguishable in size from those of major-party nominees in a general election.

## Where and How to Campaign

Once nominated, candidates must decide how and where their precious time (and money) can be spent most profitably. Typically, candidates tend to spend more time campaigning in pivotal states such as Ohio, Pennsylvania, Michigan, and Florida. Their strategists know that the contest normally will be won or lost in the populous states with big electoral votes.

But the candidate who logs the most miles on the

© Craig Mitchelldyer/Getty Images

President Theodore Roosevelt campaigning

Harvard University Library/Theodore Roosevelt Collection

campaign trail may not harvest the most votes. In 1960 Richard Nixon pledged to become the first candidate to take his presidential campaign to all 50 states. He did so, but at great physical and political cost, as he lost to John F. Kennedy. By contrast, in 1968 Nixon moved at a relatively serene pace that preserved his physical energies. He concentrated on 10 populous battleground states, on those states in the South that might be captured from former Alabama governor George Wallace, who ran as a third-party candidate, and on the border states.[16] This time, Nixon won.

Television has, of course, influenced the pattern of political campaigning. Aside from the advantage television offers in reaching large numbers of voters, it can also reduce the risk to the safety of the candidate. In light of the assassinations of President John F. Kennedy and his brother, Senator Robert F. Kennedy, the attempt on the life of George Wallace, the two attempts against President Ford, and the attack on President Reagan in which he was seriously wounded, precautions would seem sensible.

Yet candidates are under great pressure to mingle with the voters and to show themselves in person: "Rightly or wrongly, presidential candidates judge that they must be personally seen by audiences throughout the country, through such rituals as motorcades, shopping center rallies and whistle-stop campaigns."[17] After Robert Kennedy was fatally shot during the preconvention campaign of 1968, President Johnson assigned Secret Service agents to all the candidates, a practice that Congress speedily made law. Under the law, the Secret Service provides protection, unless declined, for all "major" presidential and vice presidential candidates.[18]

Political candidates also worry about timing during a campaign. Generally speaking, candidates attempt to gear their campaign to a climactic windup in the last two weeks. Often in the final weeks of a presidential campaign, the airwaves are saturated with a "media blitz" of TV commercials.

Political campaigns help to weld political parties together. For instance, campaign rallies and personal appearances by the candidate generate enthusiasm among partisan workers and volunteers. Candidates are concerned about maintaining their momentum and a certain level of excitement, not only with the voters, but for the sake of their own party organization as well.

## The President as Candidate

Although presidents have been defeated when they ran for reelection, an incumbent at least starts out with a great potential advantage over an opponent in a presidential campaign. As noted earlier, not only do the prestige and power of the office follow the president on the

© 2004 AP/Wide World Photos

President Bush waves from Air Force One after a campaign stop in Arkansas.

hustings, but all the visible trappings go along as well: Air Force One, the gleaming presidential jet, lands for an airport rally; the band plays "Hail to the Chief"; and the voters are enveloped by the aura and mystique of the presidency. Just before a president speaks, an aide hangs a portable presidential seal on the lectern.

Aside from prestige, an incumbent president already has a huge organized staff and all the advantages of White House communications and other facilities, including extensive arrangements for handling the press. And, as noted earlier, he may be able to dominate the news by taking actions as president that are carefully timed for maximum political advantage. Some of the perquisites of office may also help a vice president who is a candidate for president.

An incumbent president can use the power of his office as he campaigns. Besides channeling large federal grants to key states, he may seize on a foreign policy crisis to try to gain political advantage and display his leadership as commander in chief. On the other hand, an unexpected foreign policy crisis in the middle of an election campaign can cause political problems for the president.

Sometimes, an incumbent president may be in such a strong position that he will decide to restrict his campaigning, allow the dignity of his office to work for him, and, in effect, campaign from the White House. He may adopt the "lofty, nonpartisan pose."[19] It does not always work, however. In 1976 President Ford attempted for a time to campaign from the White House, but when Carter accused him of trying to "hide in the Rose Garden," he soon took to the campaign trail.

In 2004, President George W. Bush did not adopt a "Rose Garden" strategy. Even before he was officially re-

© Andrew Sacks

Robert F. Kennedy campaigning in Detroit, 1968

## Seven Tips for Vice Presidential Hopefuls

When presidential nominees look for running mates, it's hardly love at first sight. The vetting process that's used today would confound political matchmakers of years ago.

Now small, volunteer armies of lawyers, accountants, former law enforcement officials, and even private eyes, comb through almost every detail of a prospective vice presidential candidate's life. The advent of computerized databases that are searchable from desktops has increased the speed at which vetting teams can go about their task. . . .

There are some things vice presidential wanna-bes can do to improve their chances of being chosen.

1. Get your FBI file now. It's not uncommon for the presidential nominee to ask for a peek, but if you wait until then to request a copy, it might not arrive on time. If you're a run-of-the-mill elected official, chances are your file is less than 500 pages, small by FBI standards.
2. Get a major outside accounting firm to go over your back tax returns.
3. Get a medical checkup. If you haven't been to the doctor for a while, better go for a comprehensive physical. . . . Health questions are common.
4. Raise your visibility. Now's the time to give a few big policy speeches. Chat up your friends in the national press corps or make some new ones. Some favorable press clips can help you get on the long list, which is the first step to getting on the short list.
5. Don't treat the vetter like hired help. The vetter may be the only individual that the presidential nominee talks to who's had an in-depth look at all the contenders on the short list. Comparisons are inevitable.
6. Don't hold anything back. If there's dirt out there, do the dishing yourself. Make an honest inventory of your vulnerabilities before you meet with your vetter. This will be your opportunity to explain and put potential problems in context.
7. Don't apply pressure in public. It's OK for your allies in the interest-group community to lobby on your behalf. Indeed, it may help your cause. But make sure they do it in private.

—*National Journal,* April 29, 2000

nominated at the Republican National Convention, he was out on the campaign trail, speaking energetically to crowds in several states, often in shirtsleeves, a sartorial choice designed to give him a "just folks" appearance that would appeal to voters.

## The Issues

Political candidates in most cases develop a central theme for their campaign. Sometimes it emerges as the battle progresses, or it may be conceived well in advance. Candidates attempt to choose their terrain and stay "on message," staking out certain issues that they believe will give them the advantage over their opponents.

But to a great extent the campaign theme is shaped by the candidate's status—candidate of the "out party," incumbent president, or political heir to an incumbent. For example, in 2004, as president, George W. Bush defended the record of his administration, extolling his record on tax cuts, education, and health care. By contrast, in 2000, when Bush was the governor of Texas and a Washington outsider, he assailed the federal government as "slow to respond, slow to reform . . . irrational, running things without any standard of what is necessary."[20] Little of that sort of talk was heard from Bush in 2004—because he was now the president, in charge of the executive branch of the government.

Even a popular president cannot always transfer his appeal to a successor. As Polsby and Wildavsky noted, "One of the most difficult positions for a candidate is to try to succeed a President of his own party. . . . No matter how hard he tries to avoid it he is stuck with the

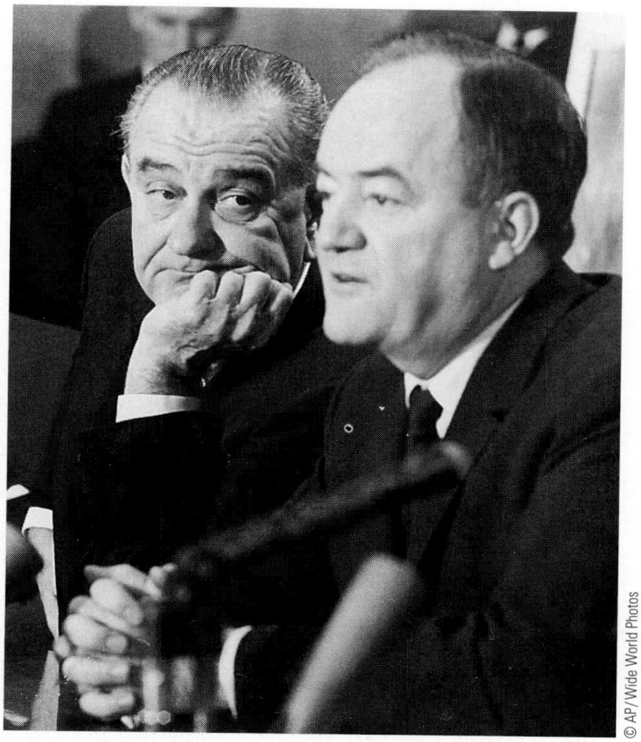



President Johnson and Vice President Hubert Humphrey

## "Ask President Bush": A Campaign Infomercial

HUDSON, WIS., Aug. 18—The audience gathered at Lakefront Park is small, intimate, the size of a crowd at a high school play. They've been instructed before he arrives not to be shy; this is their one chance to ask the president anything, and the president wants them to; after all, he calls this event "Ask President Bush."

"Mr. President," begins a young man in a baseball hat. "I just want to say I'm praying for you and God bless you."

[It's] the campaign equivalent of the infomercial, with an audience designed to look as if it's been plucked randomly off the street. . . . The campaign insists that the audience is not heavily screened and the questions are not planted.

"We have an obligation that people can come and have a level of comfort that the event won't be disrupted," says campaign spokesman Terry Holt. "A few people can ruin the experience for everyone. This will be the first or only time some of our supporters will have a chance to see the president, and we feel strongly that people should have good manners and not work to disrupt the events."

There are protesters . . . but they are several blocks away, invisible to the crowd at Lakefront Park.

There were only about 1,500 tickets issued for the event. The local paper reported that half were handed out to party leaders.

It's no mystery why Bush likes them. Each session is like a 90-minute support group dedicated to him. . . . For most of the question-and-answer sessions, the president is endlessly being thanked, for "serving our country," for "everything you did after September 11th."

Wisconsin followed the pattern of most. Bush stood on a small platform in shirtsleeves and no tie, the sun turning his face red. He ambled around the stage as he had all day, goofed around with the locals. . . .

One person . . . asked about the presence of the real enemy—Satan—which Bush soft-pedaled into something about faith-based initiatives. Luckily, for those uncomfortable moments the microphone wasn't working.

"Don't worry, I'll be the interpreter," Bush said. "And if I don't like the question I'll just change it."

—"Ask President Bush," by Hanna Rosin, *The Washington Post,* August 19, 2004, p. C1.


record made by the President of his own party."[21] And a vice president attempting to succeed the president sometimes "faces the worst of all possible worlds. . . . He cannot attack the administration in office without alienating the president and selling his own party short, and he cannot claim he has experience in the presidential office. . . . His is the most difficult strategic problem of all the candidates."[22]

There is evidence, in fact, that some incumbent presidents are a bit reluctant to expend their prestige on behalf of the heir apparent—who may not always want their help. In 1968, for example, President Johnson's attitude toward Vice President Hubert Humphrey, the Democratic nominee, seemed ambivalent at first, although in the end he publicly supported him. But Humphrey lost the election.

In much of the 2000 campaign, President Clinton kept a relatively low profile, lest the personal scandals that had enveloped him impair Vice President Al Gore's own quest for the White House. At the Democratic National Convention, Gore had pointedly drawn a line between himself and Clinton by declaring: "I stand here tonight as my own man." Gore won the popular vote but lost the election to Bush when the Supreme Court halted a recount in Florida.

## Negative Campaigning

All too often, the substantive issues in a campaign become submerged as the candidates devote more time to attacking each other than to discussing policies and programs.

Early in the 2004 campaign, the Bush strategists attacked Kerry as a "flip-flopper" for allegedly changing his positions on various issues, particularly the war in Iraq. The label stuck, even though, as Kerry partisans pointed out, Bush had also changed his position on several issues. To emphasize the Republican charge that the Democratic candidate often shifted his stance whichever way the wind was blowing, the Bush campaign ran a commercial that mocked Kerry by showing him windsurfing, with the sail first one way, and then the other.

When the anti-Kerry group calling itself "Swift Boat Veterans for Truth" ran commercials attacking the Democratic candidate's Vietnam War record, it touched off an extremely nasty dispute soon after the Republican National Convention. Kerry had emphasized his service in the Navy on the small, aluminum Swift boats, and the medals he earned, to persuade voters he was qualified to serve as commander in chief and lead the battle against international terrorism. On their side, Bush and his strategists had counted on the president's role in conducting the war on terrorism as the centerpiece of his reelection campaign.

Undermining Kerry's war record was therefore crucial to the Republican camp. The Bush campaign publicly disavowed any connection with the ads, and the president said that Kerry had "served admirably" in Vietnam. But, as noted earlier, the veterans' group attacking Kerry was bankrolled by Bush supporters in Texas. And it developed that the top outside lawyer for the Bush reelection campaign was also a lawyer for the Swift boat attack group; he resigned when his dual role was pub-

© 2004 AP/Wide World Photos

One of President Bush's commercials showed him signing the controversial Patriot Act.

licized. Although Kerry had been awarded three purple hearts, a silver star, and a bronze star in Vietnam, many of the veterans in the anti-Kerry group resented his actions when he returned from Vietnam and in 1971 led antiwar protests and testified to the Senate against the war.

The controversy was by no means the first time that a presidential campaign turned personal. Four years earlier, in 2000, a Bush commercial sought to portray Al Gore, the Democratic candidate, as someone who puffed up and misrepresented his credentials. It quoted Gore as announcing on *Larry King Live:* "I took the initiative in creating the Internet." In the commercial, a woman watches the Gore claim on her kitchen TV and cracks: "Yeah, and I invented the remote control, too. Another round of this, and I'll sell my television."[23]

Mudslinging and charges of corruption are common in campaigns. Under the unwritten rules governing the seamier side of American politics, a candidate may attempt to "get something" on an opponent. The information might not be publicized, however, if the other side possesses equally damaging information, or if it is believed that the opponent can successfully cry "smear." Because mudslinging, rumors, and scandals presumably influence some voters, their use in political campaigns persists. It is often near the end of a campaign that a candidate's supporters try to leak such stories to the news media to damage a rival.

## Bread-and-Butter Issues

Peace and pocketbook issues have tended to dominate presidential campaigns. On domestic issues, the Democrats can point to a wide range of social legislation passed during Democratic administrations. Not all of these programs have worked equally well, and one, the federal

www.georgewbush.com

A Bush ad featured John Kerry windsurfing, to suggest that his positions changed with the wind. In 2004, Republicans claimed that Kerry was a "flip-flopper" on the issues.

FIGURE 10-1

**Political Party Rated Best for Prosperity (1966–2005)**

*"Which political party—the Republican or Democratic—will do a better job of keeping the country prosperous?"*

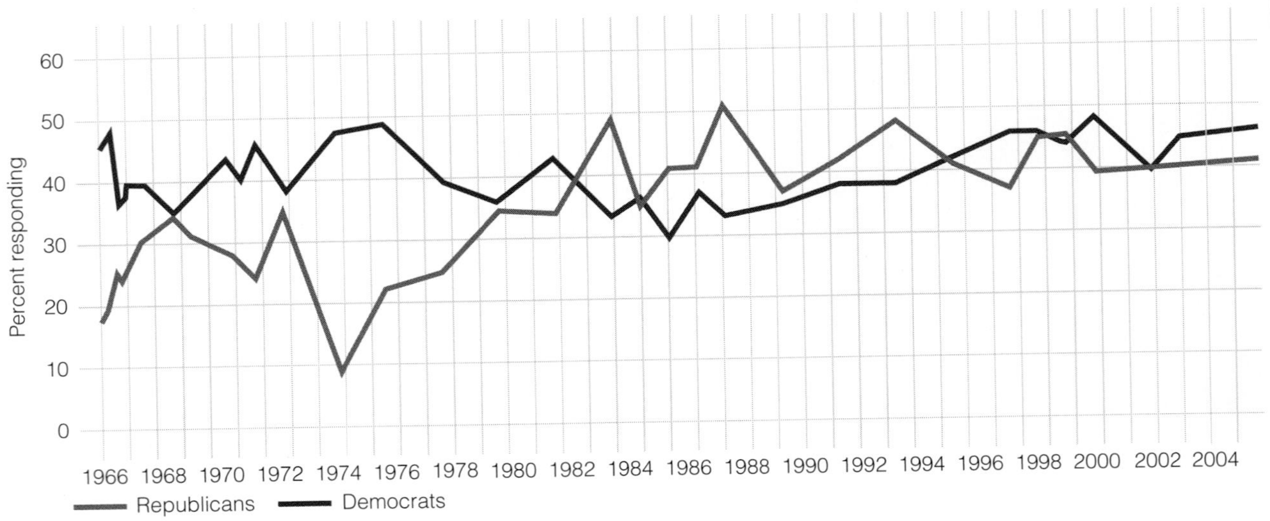


SOURCES: Gallup Opinion Index, Report no. 106 (April 1974), p. 21; Report no. 135 (October 1976), p. 5; Report no. 159 (October 1978), p. 21; Report no. 181 (September 1980), p.8; Report no. 223 (April 1984), pp. 18–19; and Gallup poll news release (September 23, 1984). Data for 1985 through 1999 provided by the Gallup Organization. Data for 2000 through 2003 from USAToday/CNN/Gallup poll, online at www.commondreams.org. Data for 2005 from the Gallup Poll News Service, September 29, 2005.

welfare program, was widely criticized and ultimately restructured with the support of a Democratic president, Bill Clinton. Nevertheless, Democratic candidates since the New Deal have been able to campaign on the party's efforts toward achieving social progress at home. And, perhaps remembering that the Great Depression began in 1929 under a Republican president, voters have, in some years, tended to associate prosperity with Democrats. (See Figure 10-1.)

Bread-and-butter issues do not always work for the Democrats, however. In 1980, for example, double-digit inflation and continued high unemployment made the economy one domestic issue that President Carter preferred not to emphasize. It proved to be, in fact, one of the weakest issues for Carter, who lost.

By 1992, with the economy troubled and unemployment high, the Democrats had regained a powerful domestic issue for the presidential campaign, an issue, perhaps more than any other, that helped the party and its candidate, Bill Clinton, to recapture the White House. In 2004, the weak economy appeared to work to Kerry's advantage as a campaign issue. But President Bush, who won, insisted to voters that economic conditions were improving and that the nation was "turning the corner."[24]

## Foreign Policy Issues

In the area of foreign affairs, the Republicans often have had an advantage. (See Figure 10-2.) Because the Democrats were in power during the First World War, the Second World War, Korea, and Vietnam, the Republicans frequently have been able to tag the Democrats, fairly or not, as the "war party." Yet in 2004 it was a Republican president, George W. Bush, who had launched the war in Iraq, a conflict that became a key campaign issue that his opponent, John Kerry, assailed as a diversion from the war on terrorism. In 1968, Richard Nixon, a Republican, was able to promise new leadership to bring an end to the war in Vietnam. Although Nixon did not succeed in ending the American combat role in Vietnam until more than two months after his reelection in 1972, his trips to Beijing and Moscow earlier that year, and the appearance of progress toward a Vietnam peace agreement during the campaign, once again provided the Republican candidate with an advantage in the area of foreign policy.

In 2004 President Bush, the Republican candidate, argued that the U.S. invasion of Iraq, despite the failure to find any weapons of mass destruction, had removed a brutal dictator and made America and the world safer. In Iraq, "freedom is on the march," Bush said repeatedly in his stump speeches. Because Kerry, as a senator, had voted to authorize the president to invade Iraq, it was difficult at first, and for many weeks, for him to exploit the Iraq war as an issue, even though American forces were still being killed there almost daily and were actively engaged in combat during the presidential campaign.

By mid-September, however, with Kerry behind in the polls, he launched an aggressive attack on Bush's Iraq war policies, calling the invasion "a profound diversion from the battle against our greatest enemy—al Qaeda."

FIGURE 10-2

**Political Party Rated Best for Peace**

*"Looking ahead for the next few years, which political party do you think would be more likely to keep the United States out of war—the Republican or the Democratic Party?"*

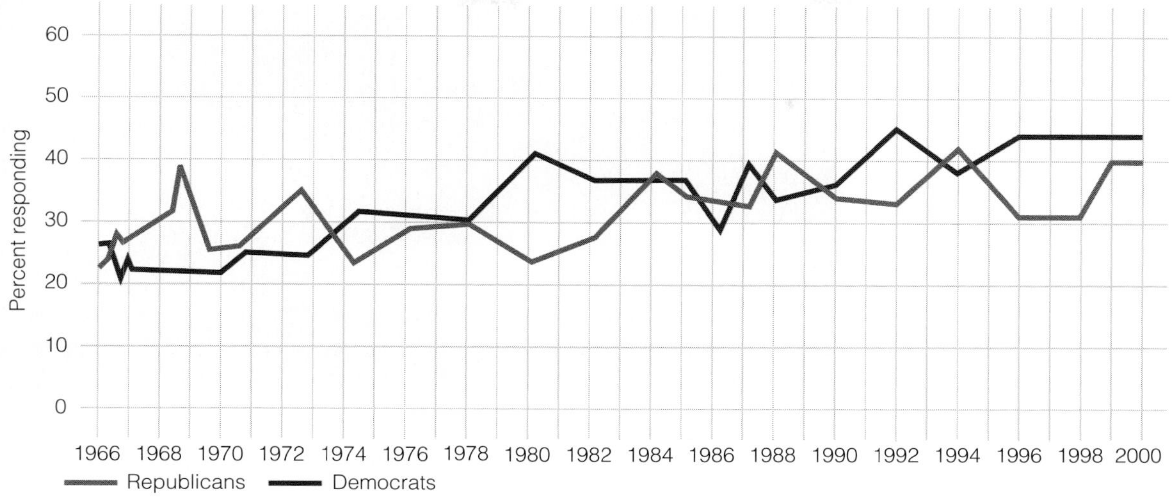


NOTE: Prior to 1992, the question was phrased, ". . . keep the United States out of World War III . . ." Question not asked after 2000.
SOURCES: Gallup Opinion Index, Report no. 106 (April 1974), p. 19; Report no. 135 (October 1976), p. 6; Report no. 159 (October 1978), p. 22; Report no. 181 (September 1980), p. 7; Report no. 223 (April 1984), pp. 18–19; and Gallup poll news release (September 23, 1984). Data for 1985–1999 provided by the Gallup Organization.

Kerry charged that the president's "misjudgment, miscalculation and mismanagement of the war in Iraq all make the war on terror harder to win. Iraq is now what it was not before the war—a haven for terrorists."[25]

Although presidents customarily present foreign policy decisions in lofty terms unrelated to their election prospects, the truth is that foreign affairs and domestic politics are closely intertwined. In making foreign policy choices, presidents often have one eye on potential voter reaction at election time. This was well illustrated by a remark the first President Bush made early in 1992 as he campaigned in the New Hampshire presidential primary: "If I'd listened to the leader of the United States Senate, George Mitchell, Saddam Hussein would be in



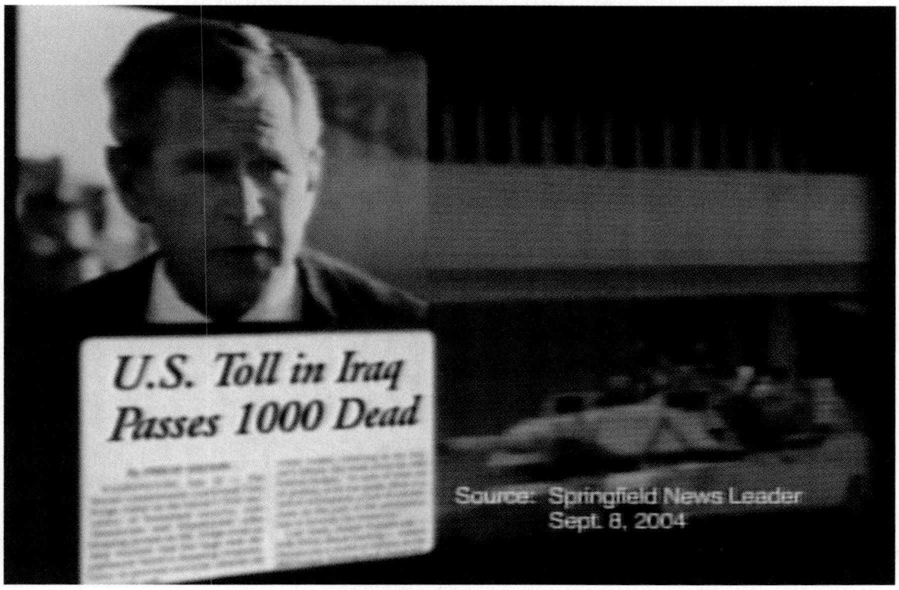


A negative ad by John Kerry's campaign criticized President Bush over casualties in Iraq.

A John Kerry commercial said he would plan to strengthen domestic programs.



Saudi Arabia and you'd be paying twenty bucks a gallon for gasoline. Now try that one on for size."[26]

## The Imponderables

A sudden foreign policy crisis, a personal scandal, a chance remark—these are among the many imponderables that may affect voter attitudes in political campaigns.

In 1884, when Grover Cleveland was the Democratic nominee, his Republican opponents chanted: "Ma, Ma, where's my Pa? Gone to the White House, ha, ha, ha." The slogan was a gleeful reference to the illegitimate child that Cleveland was accused of fathering.

During the campaign, the story broke in a Buffalo, New York, newspaper under the headline: "A Terrible Tale—A Dark Chapter in a Public Man's History." Ten years earlier, Maria Crofts Halpin, an attractive widow, had given birth to a son, whom she named Oscar Folsom Cleveland, charging Cleveland with the baby's paternity. Cleveland said he was not certain that he was the boy's father, but he had assumed full responsibility for supporting the child. When the scandal broke, he telegraphed his friends in Buffalo: "Tell the truth." Because of his open attitude, Cleveland managed to minimize the damage to his presidential campaign.*

Cleveland won the presidency, perhaps aided by another unexpected event during the campaign. A few days before the election, a Protestant minister supporting James G. Blaine, the Republican candidate, referred to the Democrats as the party of "rum, Romanism, and rebellion." The insult to Roman Catholics may have cost Blaine New York State and thereby the election.

In 1948 Thomas Dewey's campaign train, the "Victory Special," lurched backward into the crowd while the Republican nominee was orating at Beaucoup, Illinois. "Well, that's the first lunatic I've had for an engineer," snapped Dewey. The remark was widely publicized and did not sit well with the railroad unions. Overnight, "Lunatic Engineers for Truman" and other similar groups sprang up to plague the Republican candidate along the right-of-way traveled by the "Victory Special."

In 1952 Richard Nixon's place as vice presidential candidate on the Republican ticket was endangered when newspapers reported the existence of the "Nixon fund," some $18,000 contributed by a group of California businessmen to meet Nixon's political expenses as a U.S. senator. Nixon went on nationwide television and, in his famed "Checkers" speech, defended his use of the $18,000 fund, listed his personal finances, noted that his wife Pat wore a "respectable Republican cloth coat," and announced that, come what may, his family intended to

Richard M. Nixon delivering his "Checkers" speech on television, 1952



*After Cleveland's election, the Democrats celebrated their first presidential victory in 28 years by singing: "Hurrah for Maria, / Hurrah for the kid. / We voted for Grover, / And we're damned glad we did!"

## "Be Sure to Cry Scandal!"

The following is an excerpt from a publication of the Republican National Committee that advised GOP candidates on campaign techniques:

> **Researching Scandals in the Democratic Party.** With proper research and publicity, exposure of scandals can serve as a public service and as a source of votes. . . . Most scandals evolve from "tips," usually coming from newsmen, victims of the "scandal," public reports such as those of the State Auditor, or abused factions within or on the fringes of the wrongdoer's organization. . . .
>
> **Publicizing the Scandal.** A "believable" springboard from which to break the scandal must be found. A newsman, a disenchanted insider, or a local prosecutor are possible means for breaking the scandal to the public.
>
> Once the public has been informed that a scandal in fact does exist, it must be kept continually aware that its trust has been violated. . . . Question the principles of the opposition at every opportunity—at public gatherings as well as in the press. In other words, take advantage of every possible form of publicity—and be sure to cry, SCANDAL!

—Republican National Committee, *Research Techniques for Republican Campaigns*

keep a black-and-white cocker spaniel named Checkers, which had been given to his two children. Although the speech was a patently emotional appeal for which Nixon was often assailed by later critics, it turned the tide of public opinion and impressed General Eisenhower, the Republican presidential nominee. Nixon stayed on the ticket.

Checkers was not the first canine to gain fame in a presidential campaign. Running for a fourth term in 1944, Franklin D. Roosevelt ridiculed the Republicans for charging that he had left his dog behind on an Aleutian island and sent a destroyer to fetch him: "These Republican leaders have not been content with attacks on me—or my wife, or on my sons . . . they now include my little dog, Fala. . . . I don't resent attacks, and my family don't resent attacks, but Fala *does* resent them. . . . I am accustomed to hearing malicious falsehoods about myself . . . but I think I have a right to object to libelous statements about my dog."[27] (Roosevelt and his party, including Fala, returned from a trip to the Aleutian Islands in 1944 aboard a Navy destroyer. FDR was extremely fond of his Scottie; he did not leave him behind and did not send the ship to fetch his dog. Fala is buried close by Franklin and his wife, Eleanor Roosevelt, in Hyde Park, New York.)

Perhaps the most startling and disturbing surprise development of any modern presidential campaign occurred in June 1972, when five men, wearing surgical rubber gloves and carrying electronic eavesdropping equipment, were arrested inside the Washington headquarters of the Democratic National Committee in the Watergate building. One of the men, James W. McCord, Jr., a former CIA agent, turned out to be director of security for President Nixon's campaign organization. Three weeks before the election, a federal grand jury in Washington indicted the five men plus two former White House aides, E. Howard Hunt, Jr., and G. Gordon Liddy, on charges of burglary, illegal wiretapping, and bugging.

The case immediately raised a host of questions about who had sent the men on their felonious mission to the Democratic headquarters. The White House and President Nixon repeatedly denied involvement. But one of the Watergate defendants, it developed, had $89,000 in his bank account that had been delivered to the Republican campaign committee and "laundered" through Mexico to disguise its origin.

The charges of espionage and financial irregularities, however, seemed to have little impact on the voters in the 1972 election.[28] The Watergate case and the issue of political espionage began to grow into a major scandal only well after the presidential election campaign. Early in 1973, five of the defendants pleaded guilty, and two others were convicted by a federal jury. Within months, the scandal had reached the president; several of his top aides resigned and some went to prison. A year later, facing certain impeachment, Nixon resigned in disgrace, his presidency shattered less than two years after his landslide reelection.

In 1984 a joke by President Reagan at the start of the presidential campaign caused him some embarrassment. Preparing for his weekly radio broadcast, Reagan was asked for a "voice check" by technicians. The president replied: "My fellow Americans, I'm pleased to tell you today that I've signed legislation that would outlaw Rus-

## Ronald Ziegler on Watergate

White House spokesman Ronald L. Ziegler told reporters in Florida with the President that he would not comment on "a third-rate burglary attempt." In addition, Ziegler said that "certain elements may try to stretch this beyond what it is."

—*Washington Post,* June 20, 1972

sia forever. We begin bombing in five minutes." The remark was not broadcast, but it was recorded by two networks and became public, arousing a storm of controversy. The comment was denounced by the Soviet Union, criticized by Walter Mondale, the Democratic candidate, and apparently triggered a partial Soviet military alert.[29]

At the very start of the 1992 presidential election year, Gennifer Flowers, a former lounge singer, claimed in the *Star,* a supermarket tabloid, that she had engaged in a 12-year affair with Governor Bill Clinton. In an appearance with his wife, Hillary, on the CBS television program *60 Minutes,* Clinton denied Flowers's allegations but conceded marital "wrongdoing." For a time, however, the charges of infidelity threatened to derail Clinton's presidential hopes. Afterward, Clinton's supporters worried about what they termed "the bimbo factor"—fearing that one or more other supposed lovers would surface during the campaign.

Much later, under siege by the Lewinsky scandal, Clinton testified in a deposition in the Paula Jones lawsuit that he had once had a sexual encounter with Flowers, but he did not admit to a 12-year relationship.[30]

The Republicans experienced some unexpected gaffes as well in 1992, thanks to Vice President Dan Quayle. In a speech upholding "family values," Quayle caused a nationwide uproar when he attacked Murphy Brown, a popular fictional television character, for having a baby as a single, unmarried mother. Not long afterward, Quayle visited a school in Trenton, New Jersey, and coached a 12-year-old student, William Figueroa, to add an "e" to the word "potato." Political cartoonists had a field day. The schoolboy, an instant celebrity, appeared on the David Letterman show. The principal got a call from the Potato Museum in Great Falls, Virginia. "Potatoe" T-shirts sprouted on college campuses.

In 1996, Bob Dole, the Republican candidate, fell off a platform in Chico, California, when a railing gave way as he was shaking hands with the crowd. A picture of the Republican candidate lying on the ground, grimacing in pain, made some newspaper front pages. Dole got to his feet quickly and made light of the episode. But there was speculation in the press that the minor incident was somehow symbolic of his presidential campaign.

In the 2000 campaign, George W. Bush was preparing to speak at a rally in Naperville, Illinois, when he was caught by an open microphone as he pointed out a *New York Times* reporter, Adam Clymer, whom he described as a "major league [expletive]."[31] His running-mate, Dick Cheney, dutifully chimed in, "Oh, yeah. He is, big time."[32] Because Bush had promised, if elected, to restore "dignity" to the Oval Office, the remark appeared to contradict his public pledge and the image he was trying to project to the voters.

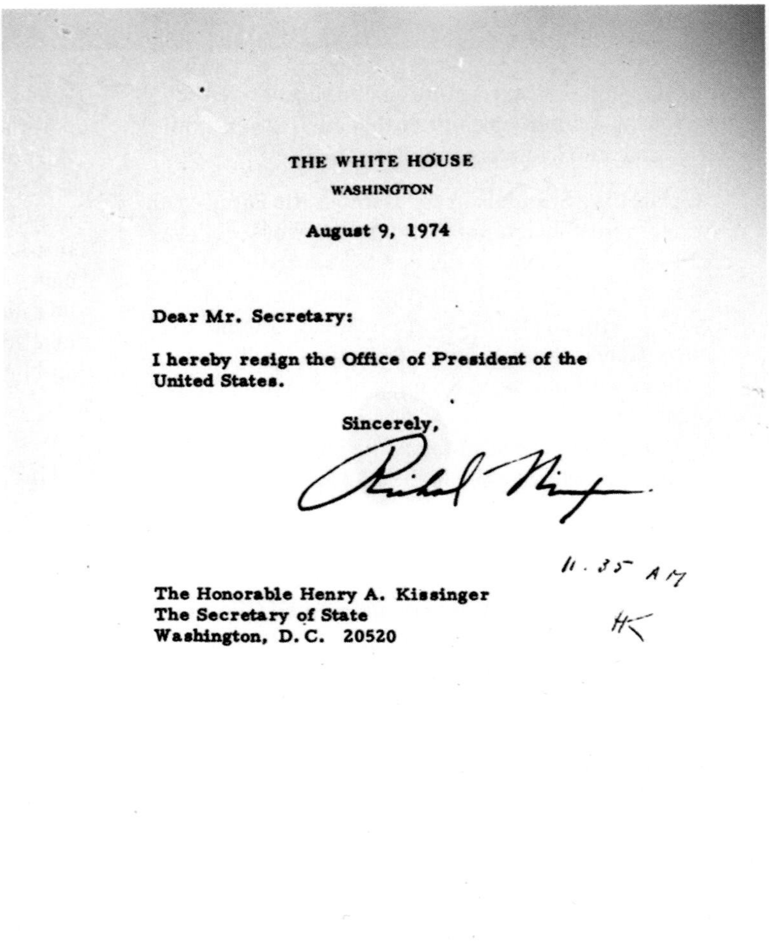
THE WHITE HOUSE

WASHINGTON

August 9, 1974

Dear Mr. Secretary:

I hereby resign the Office of President of the United States.

Sincerely,

Richard Nixon

11.35 AM

The Honorable Henry A. Kissinger
The Secretary of State
Washington, D.C. 20520

HK



"His presidency shattered": The Watergate scandal led President Nixon to resign two years later.

But Al Gore was embarrassed when he told an audience in Tallahassee, Florida, that his mother-in-law paid $108 a month for the same arthritis medicine that for his dog cost only $37.80. While it was true that Gore had both a mother-in-law and a dog, and they did take human and animal versions of the same drug, the dollar figures he cited, his campaign was forced to admit, came from a House study of drug prices.[33] Bush charged that Gore was "misleading" the voters, and the Bush camp put out a press release titled "Gore Makes Things Up."[34]

Incidents of this sort may be trivial, but they can leave their mark on a campaign. Voters may tend to remember them long after they have forgotten the details of a weighty policy address by a candidate dealing with health care or some other important issue.

World crises that erupt suddenly during a campaign are still another category of imponderables that may affect voter decisions. In general, foreign policy crises may tend to help the party in power because of voter reluc-

## Keep On Smiling: John McCain, Bob Dole's Cheshire Cat

As Bob Dole, the Republican candidate for president, prepared for his first debate with President Clinton in 1996, his advisers tried to make sure that he remembered to smile a lot, according to the following news account:

> Dole and his staff . . . were afraid that he would come across as too dour and old, and they made every effort to protect against those perceptions. In the final rehearsal, his wife, Elizabeth, sat behind the cameras and chirped, "Your smile looks great on the monitor, Bob!"—words she hoped her husband would replay in his mind as he stood at the podium at Bushnell Hall.
>
> To reinforce that notion, the Dole camp planted their smile specialist, Sen. John McCain (R-Ariz.) in a prime seat inside the hall with the sole mission of beaming so broadly that the senator might notice the crescent flash of whiteness in the audience. McCain performed the same Cheshire cat role during a crucial debate in the South Carolina primary; Dole looked out, saw his Senate pal giving it the ear-to-ear and—so the legend goes—loosened up and won the debate.

—"With 'Zingers,' Dole Tactic Is Polite Aggression," by David Maraniss, *The Washington Post,* October 7, 1996, p. A1. Copyright © 1996, The Washington Post

tance to "change horses in midstream." On the other hand, a foreign crisis that leads to a war, as in Korea or Vietnam, or that damages the prestige of the country, such as the seizure of American hostages in Iran, may, in the long run, erode the strength of the party in power and lead to retribution at the polls.

# Campaign Techniques

## Television and Politics

In September 2000, as the presidential race grew in intensity, the Republican National Committee sponsored a television commercial attacking Al Gore's plan to provide prescription drug benefits for senior citizens. Suddenly the word "RATS," in huge capital letters, flashed on the screen, so quickly that most viewers could not have seen it. But if the commercial was replayed and slowed down, there it was.

Were George W. Bush's supporters trying to characterize the Gore campaign? "It's absurd to think it was intentional," a Bush aide said, "it was an editing mistake." Other Bush advisers claimed it was part of the word "bureaucrats." The firm that produced the commercial said the word RATS was an error. Bush himself went on *Good Morning America* and denied there was "a plot to try to put subliminal messages into people's minds."[35]

The controversy might have seemed amusing, though perhaps less so to the Gore camp, but it was another reflection of the enormous importance of television in political campaigns. The acrimonious debate over the "Swift Boat Veterans for Truth" commercials in 2004 was only another example of the power of television and of political ads.

Perhaps the most famous commercial of all aired in 1964. It made a brief appearance during the presidential contest between Barry Goldwater, the conservative Republican candidate, and Lyndon Johnson, the Democratic incumbent.

The little girl in that television commercial stood in a field of daisies, plucking the petals and counting, as birds chirped in the background. Then, as the little girl reached number 10, a doomsday voice began a countdown. When the voice reached zero, there was a rumbling explosion and a huge mushroom cloud filled the screen. As it billowed upward, President Johnson's voice boomed out: "These are the stakes. To make a world in

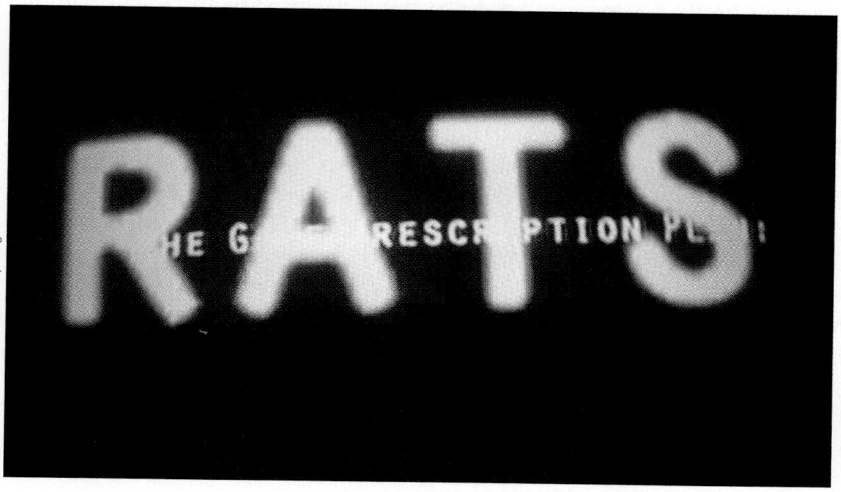




2000: George W. Bush denied there was "a plot to try to put subliminal messages into people's minds" when a campaign commercial flashed the word "RATS" quickly on screen.

"Ten, nine, eight, seven . . .

six, five, four, three . . .

two, one . . .

VOTE FOR PRESIDENT JOHNSON
ON NOVEMBER 3.

These are the stakes. To make a world in which all of God's children can live . . .

or to go into the dark. We must either love each other or we must die . . .

The stakes are too high for you to stay home."

Photos courtesy of Tony Schwartz

which all of God's children can live. Or to go into the dark. We must either love each other, or we must die." A message was then flashed on the screen reading: "Vote for President Johnson on November 3."[36]

Millions of Americans saw the famous "Daisy Girl" commercial during the 1964 campaign, even though it was shown only once before being withdrawn because of the controversy it created. To many it seemed to suggest that Barry Goldwater, the Republican candidate, might lead the nation into nuclear war. As Theodore White noted, "The film mentioned neither Goldwater nor the Republicans specifically—but the shriek of Republican indignation fastened the bomb message on them more tightly than any calculation could have expected."[37]

The marriage of television and politics took place in 1948, the first year in which a small but significant number of Americans tuned in to parts of the national nominating conventions. It was not the first year that the national conventions were televised. But very few people owned television sets in the 1940s, and fewer than 100,000 people saw broadcasts of the 1940 and 1944 conventions.

Because fewer than 200,000 homes had television sets even in 1948, the real impact of the new medium was not felt until the 1952 and 1956 Eisenhower-Stevenson campaigns. By 1956 almost 35 million homes had television sets. In 1960, of America's 53 million households, 46.6 million, or 88 percent, had sets. By this time, television was playing a central role in presidential campaigns.

**The Presidential Debates** Televised debates sometimes can have a dramatic effect on the dynamics of an election campaign. For example, on September 30, 2004, in Coral Gables, Florida, John Kerry, lagging substantially in the polls, met President George W. Bush for their first presidential debate before a vast national and worldwide television audience. Kerry charged that Bush had made a "colossal error of judgment" by invading Iraq and diverting forces from the war on terrorism and against Osama bin Laden.[38] Bush countered that Kerry had originally supported the war and was sending "mixed messages" to the world.[39]

A reported 62.5 million people watched the debate in the United States. Several times, the cameras caught Bush, lips pursed, frowning, and looking tense, while Kerry spoke. The next day, polls reported that Kerry had "won" the debate. According to a Gallup poll of registered voters, Kerry prevailed by 53 to 37 percent, a lift his campaign badly needed at that point.[40] In a two-way contest among registered voters, a *Newsweek* poll put Kerry ahead of Bush 49 to 46 percent.[41] Since Kerry had been behind Bush by 8 points in a leading poll published four days earlier, the debate, at least for that moment, appeared to have had an effect on the campaign.[42]

In the second debate in St. Louis, in a town meeting format, Bush recovered some ground but appeared strident and defensive to some observers. In the third presidential debate in Tempe, Arizona, Bush and Kerry traded sharp attacks on domestic issues.

It was in 1960 that the major-party candidates were first able to reach vast audiences in a series of televised debates. Congress in 1960 made the debates possible by abolishing a section of the Federal Communications Act that had required broadcasters to give "equal time" to all

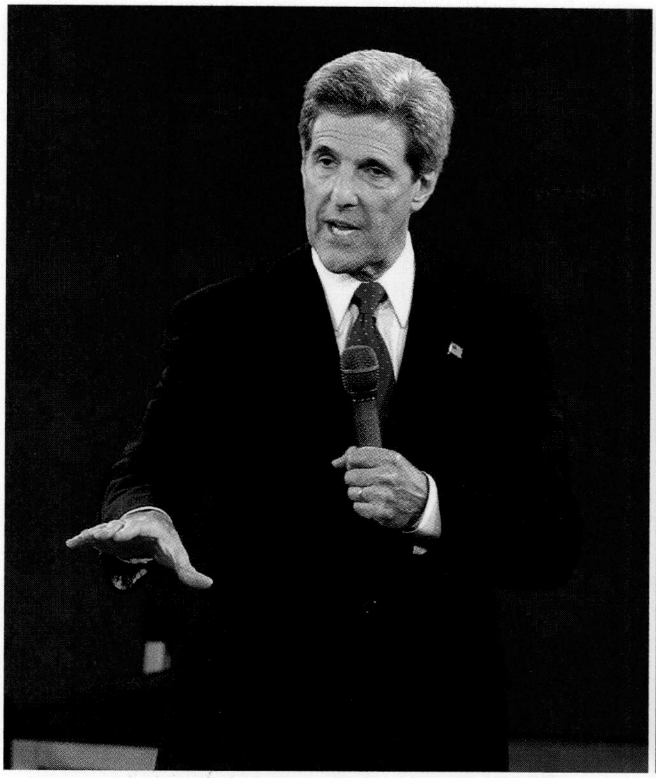

© STF/AFP/Getty Images

Senator John Kerry and President George W. Bush during their second televised debate in St. Louis, Missouri, October 8, 2004

legally qualified candidates. This cleared the way for the networks to limit the debates to major candidates. In that year there were four debates between Senator John F. Kennedy and Vice President Richard Nixon, his Republican opponent. Most observers believed that the debates helped Kennedy win the election, in part because Nixon looked pale and haggard in the first debate and wore "Lazy Shave" powder as makeup to cover the dark five-o'clock shadow on his face. By contrast, Kennedy, looking tanned and vigorous, presented a much more telegenic image to the public.

© 2004 AP/Wide World Photos

Vice President Dick Cheney, left, listens to a point made by John Edwards, his Democratic opponent, during their 2004 televised debate.

The millions of voters watching the first debate may have remembered little of what the candidates said, but they noticed that Nixon did not look as pleasing as Kennedy. As Theodore White put it, "Probably no picture in American politics tells a better story . . . than that famous shot of the camera on the vice president as he half slouched, his 'Lazy Shave' powder faintly streaked with sweat, his eyes exaggerated hollows of blackness, his jaw, jowls, and face drooping with strain."[43]

***for more about the 1960 presidential debates, see: http://www.debates.org/pages/his_1960.html***

Sixteen years went by before another televised presidential debate took place. In 1976, the debates between President Ford, the Republican incumbent, and Jimmy Carter, his Democratic challenger, were credited by some analysts with providing Carter's narrow margin of victory. Normally, an incumbent president, or the better known of two candidates, has little incentive to debate an opponent; the television exposure only serves to help his rival become better known. But Ford, behind by 33 points in the polls, sought to regain the initiative by challenging his opponent to debate, and Carter accepted.

John F. Kennedy and Richard M. Nixon in a televised debate, 1960



*for more about the 1976 presidential debates, see: http://www.debates.org/pages/his_1976.html*

Again in 1980, voters watched the candidates debate. The main debate took place between President Carter, now the incumbent, and former governor Ronald Reagan of California. Reagan hammered away at the faltering economy of 1980. Near the end of the 90-minute debate, he urged voters to ask themselves: "Are you better off than you were four years ago? Is it easier for you to go and buy things in the stores than it was four years ago?"[44] It was an effective sales pitch. Polls showed that Reagan had won the debate.

*for more about the 1980 presidential debates, see: http://www.debates.org/pages/his_1980.html*

In 1984, President Reagan debated his Democratic opponent, Walter Mondale. In 1987, before the next presidential election, a bipartisan Commission on Presidential Debates, a nongovernmental group, was established by the two major parties to schedule presidential debates in future elections.

*for more about the 1984 presidential debates, see: http://www.debates.org/pages/his_1984.html*

In 1988, the presidential candidates, Vice President Bush and Governor Michael Dukakis of Massachusetts, debated twice on television. In the vice presidential debate, Senator Dan Quayle, the Republican candidate, did not fare well against Senator Lloyd Bentsen of Texas, his Democratic opponent. When Quayle compared his experience in Congress to that of John F. Kennedy, Bentsen snapped: "Senator, I served with Jack Kennedy. I knew Jack Kennedy. Jack Kennedy was a friend of mine. Senator, you're no Jack Kennedy."[45] The retort became famous and entered the nation's political lore. A CBS poll reported Bentsen the winner of the debate by more than 2 to 1.[46]

*for more about the 1988 presidential debates, see: http://www.debates.org/pages/his_1988.html*

When Bill Clinton challenged the first President Bush to a series of televised debates in 1992, Bush at first refused and found himself on the defensive for several days. The Clinton camp had taken to dressing volunteers in chicken suits to heckle the president at campaign stops, implying he was afraid to face his Democratic opponent. The giant fowl were known as "Chicken George," and they appeared to greatly annoy the president. At an appearance in the Midwest, Bush got into an argument with one of the chickens, accusing the bird of polluting the Arkansas River.

Then Bush, who was lagging in the polls, agreed to three debates. Because Ross Perot had jumped back into the race, he was invited to take part.

The unexpected star of the first debate was Perot, whose biting, homespun comments and humor contrasted with the more ponderous arguments of the two major-party candidates. Asked how, if elected, he

## Spin Control: "Call and Praise the President's Performance"

After every televised presidential debate, members of the candidates' staffs—so-called "spin doctors"—circulate among the news media to try to persuade reporters that their candidate won, or at least did not lose. The staffers try to put a favorable "spin," or twist, on events to help their candidate. The spin doctors' marching orders are supposed to be confidential, but in 1992, by mistake some copies of the Bush-Quayle instructions for action after the October 15 debate were faxed to the news media. Here are some excerpts:

> Call your local political reporter and give the spin. Don't wait for him or her to call you—call ASAP. Remember, they are under a tight deadline due to the hour of the debate. *It is vital that you call right away and give your reaction.*
>
> If there are any talk-radio shows on the air, call and praise the president's performance. Please use the talking points. It is imperative that all surrogates are giving the same message. . . . Issue a news release declaring the president the winner.

The instructions include these "talking points":

> Tonight was a clear win, a big win for the president. Bill Clinton came in a cautious and weak third place. . . . The president forcefully stated that character is a key issue in this campaign. The person the American people choose to be president must be of unquestioned character and integrity. President Bush is known for his strength of character. . . .
>
> Tonight the president asked the key issue in this campaign. If a major domestic or international crisis breaks out, who is it you trust to solve the crisis and get the job done? The answer is George Bush.

—"Talking Points Spin Out of Control in Fax Fiasco," by Howard Kurtz, *The Washington Post,* October 17, 1992, p. A12. Copyright © 1992, The Washington Post

planned to get his program passed by Congress, Perot replied: "Now, all these fellows with thousand-dollar suits and alligator shoes running up and down the halls of Congress that make policy now—the lobbyists, the PAC guys, the foreign lobbyists, and what-have-you—they'll be over there in the Smithsonian, you know, because we're going to get rid of them, and the Congress will be listening to the people."[47]

In the second presidential debate that year Bush attacked Clinton for taking "different positions" on issues and said: "You can't turn the White House into the Waffle House." During the final two weeks of the campaign Bush narrowed the gap in the polls, but it was not enough; Clinton was elected president, and reelected in 1996, when he debated Bob Dole, the Republican candidate, on television.

***for more about the 1992 presidential debates, see: http://www.debates.org/pages/his_1992.html***

***for more about the 1996 presidential debates, see: http://www.debates.org/pages/his_1996.html***

In 2000, George W. Bush debated Al Gore three times. Because it was expected that both the popular vote and the electoral vote might be close, the presidential debates took on especial importance that year.

***for more about the 2000 presidential debates, see: http://www.debates.org/pages/his_2000.html***

In one sense, it may be unfair to the candidates and the voters for so much to depend on the impression that the presidential office-seekers make in one or more 90-minute televised debates. Candidates often misstate some facts, which many viewers at home probably do not realize. On the other hand, the televised debates give millions of voters an opportunity they would not otherwise have to watch the candidates in action, to hear and contrast their views on a wide range of domestic and foreign issues, and to make judgments about each candidate's style and character.

Studies of the effect of televised debates on elections have reached varying conclusions. To an extent, some studies suggest, viewers see what they wish to see; that is, their perception of the candidates and issues hews closely to their "original voting preference."[48] But other studies suggest that debates may have "a measurable direct influence on the outcome of the election."[49]

In 2004, there were three presidential debates and one vice-presidential debate. As in all recent presidential election years, the tradition of televised debates provided the voters a chance to see the candidates interact, and the debates may have helped the viewers to make their choice about who was best qualified to lead the nation as president of the United States.

***for more about the 2004 presidential debates, see: http://www.debates.org/pages/his_2004.html***

## Madison Avenue: The Packaging of the President

By 2004 there were more than 248 million television sets in about 102 million homes in America; 98 percent of all homes with electricity in the United States had televisions—more than had bathtubs or telephones. The ability of political candidates to reach greater numbers of voters through television was reflected in a dramatic rise in campaign spending for commercials. In 1972,

$10.8 million was spent for political broadcasts at the presidential level. By 2000, $606 million was spent on political television commercials.[50] In 2004 that figure was expected to more than double to $1.5 billion.[51]

The increasing use of television and Madison Avenue advertising techniques has raised the question of whether political candidates can be merchandised and packaged like toothpaste. To some extent the answer must be yes; many of the advertising executives who handle political accounts think in just those terms.

As a professional actor for most of his adult life, President Reagan enjoyed an added advantage on television. "Reagan," the *Washington Post* reported in 1980, ". . . calls upon his actor's training to get misty on cue, near the end of his talks. . . . His Sunday night closer was an anecdote . . . about looking into the faces of young people in Kansas City and feeling all warm and lumpy about it."[52]

In 1984, several of President Reagan's commercials portrayed happy Americans in various everyday activities—going to work, raising flags, getting married, painting a picket fence. "It's morning again in America," a syrupy-voiced announcer intoned, "and under the leadership of President Reagan, our country is prouder . . . and stronger . . . and better." The commercials were primarily designed to win votes for Reagan by making Americans feel good about themselves.

Besides praising the candidate, television ads often jab at opponents. This kind of **negative advertising**—political commercials that strongly attack a rival candidate—has become increasingly frequent in political campaigns.

In 1988, a commercial for the first President Bush became notorious. Bush's Democratic opponent was Massachusetts governor Michael Dukakis. The controversy began with an ad in which Massachusetts crime statistics flashed on the screen, and an announcer attacked Dukakis's "revolving door prison policy [that] gave weekend furloughs to first-degree murderers. . . . While out, many committed other crimes like kidnapping and rape, and many are still at large."[53] To underscore the point, Bush partisans enlisted the aid of a Maryland man who, with his fiancée, had been brutally assaulted by a Massachusetts convict, Willie Horton, a murderer out on a furlough.

Then, a conservative, pro-Bush political action committee aired television commercials featuring a photograph of Horton and linking him to Dukakis. So effective was the commercial that the name "Willie Horton" entered the political lexicon and became synonymous with negative, attack commercials. The "Willie Horton" commercial was credited with helping the first Bush win the election.

The appearance of Bush on a boat in Boston harbor, charging that the Massachusetts governor's own seaport was one of the most polluted in the nation, was another television image that stuck with the voters. Somehow, when Dukakis tried the same tactic, it didn't work. He rode in an Army tank, wearing an outsized helmet, to emphasize his commitment to a strong national defense—a campaign appearance that appeared silly and contrived to many viewers.

Television ads can, demonstrably, make the difference in the outcome of some elections:

> For example, in 1984, Senator Walter Huddleston (D.-Ky) was forty-six points ahead in the polls and appeared headed for relatively easy reelection to a third term until the campaign of his opponent was ignited and the voters' interest captured by a series of

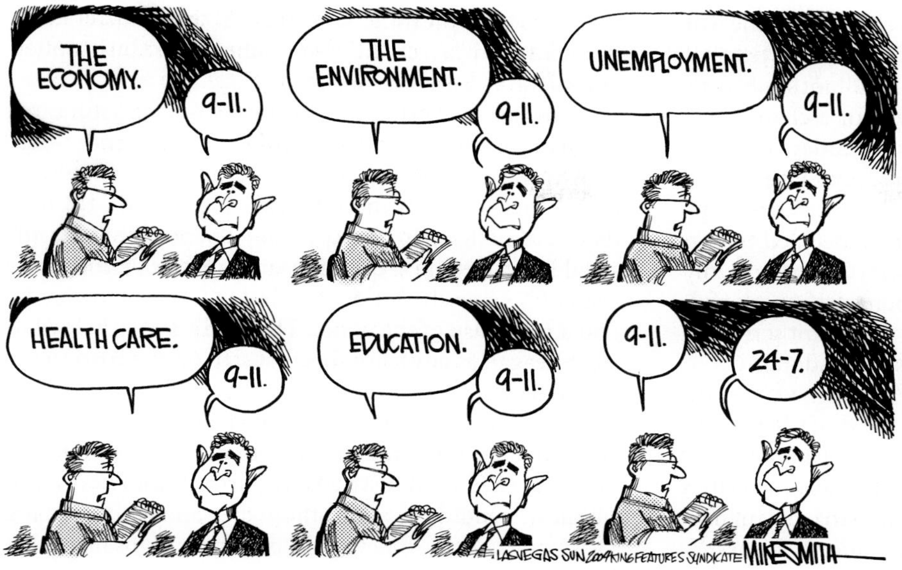


Cartoon by Mike Smith. © Reprinted by special permission of King Features Syndicate

imaginative campaign ads. These ads sought to portray the incumbent as a man who shirked his senatorial duties and obligations to his constituents by taking junkets to plush vacation spots at government expense. His challenger's television ads showed bloodhounds on the seemingly elusive senator's trail first at the Capitol, where he was nowhere to be found, and then at a posh Caribbean resort, where his trace was discovered. By the end of the campaign, Senator Huddleston had seen his comfortable lead disappear and on Election Night Kentucky had a new senator, Republican Mitch McConnell.[54]

What is the impact of television in a political campaign? Thomas E. Patterson and Robert D. McClure have argued that the "nightly network newscasts of ABC, CBS, and NBC present a distorted picture of a presidential election campaign. These newscasts pay only limited attention to major election issues. These newscasts almost entirely avoid discussion of the candidates' qualifications for the Presidency. Instead . . . [they] devote most of their election coverage to the trivia of political campaigning that make for flashy pictures. Hecklers, crowds, motorcades, balloons, rallies, and gossip—these are the regular subjects of network campaign stories."[55]

In a study of the effect of television on voters in Summit County, Ohio, Harold Mendelsohn and Garrett J. O'Keefe found that people who made up their minds late in a campaign were more likely than others to be influenced by television commercials. Similarly, they reported that "switchers," those who changed their minds during the course of a campaign, were more likely to be influenced by commercials.[56]

Although the impact of television on American politics should not be underestimated, it is easy to exaggerate the influence of Madison Avenue and political commercials. The idea that a few advertising executives in New York can manipulate the mass of voters ignores other important factors—such as party identification or the voters' personal economic circumstances—that affect how people cast their ballots.

With the increased importance of television, however, there is at least a danger that a candidate with more money, more skilled media advisers, or a better television style will enjoy a substantial advantage over a rival. Under federal election laws the two major-party presidential candidates in 2004 and other recent elections accepted public funding for the general election campaign and were held, in theory, to equal spending levels.

With access to an audience of millions of voters through television, however, a political candidate may be tempted to display an image that masks the real person, to present the issues in capsulized, simplistic form, and to become a performer rather than a leader. But the candidate who goes too far in this direction takes the risk that the voters may see through the slickness and, in effect, switch channels—by voting for the opposing candidate. And even the cleverest media advisers must work within the existing political framework; their advertising campaigns are limited by the issues that seem important to the voters, by campaign spending laws, by party loyalties, and by the strengths and weaknesses of their client, the candidate. There are, in short, limits to the ability of Madison Avenue to package and sell a candidate.

## Professional Campaign Managers

When Bill Clinton first ran for president, James Carville, a Washington political consultant, gained national recognition as a key behind-the-scenes adviser to Clinton, then governor of Arkansas and the Democratic nominee. During the campaign, a reporter asked Carville to assess his job. He replied: "Let's say you ask a politician what time it is. Some pols will tell you the time. Some will tell you how to build a clock. Bill Clinton will tell you how to build a Swiss village. The consultant's job is to say: 'Governor, just tell them it's time for a change.'"[57]

Today, and for the past several decades, political consultants and professional campaign managers have been part of almost every major campaign. When Representative John B. Anderson of Illinois decided to run for president in 1980, he hired David Garth, a highly successful professional campaign manager. A colorful, cigar-smoking New Yorker, Garth at one point scribbled a note on a sign-up sheet at Anderson headquarters in Washington. The sheet encouraged campaign workers to enter an upcoming softball game. "We don't have time for softball," Garth wrote. "We're playing hardball."[58]

Garth was quick to defend his craft against critics who argue that professional campaign managers manipulate the voters. "What is not manipulation?" he asked. "One of the great stupidities is that somehow what we do is manipulation, which it is, and that nothing else is. . . . When Roosevelt sat down to discuss his next fireside chat did they say 'You go ahead and say just what you think is right'? What I'm trying to say is, what happens behind the scenes hasn't changed in politics."[59]

At all levels of politics, candidates turn to professional campaign managers and consultants. The firms earn large fees for their varied services, which include advertising, public relations, research on issues, public opinion sampling, creating websites, organizing focus groups to test voter reaction, fund-raising, telephone solicitations, computer analysis, and speech-writing.

As Larry Sabato has pointed out, however, the importance of campaign consultants can be overstated, although they "in at least a few cases can convincingly be given credit or blame for the margin of victory or defeat." But because consultants are often treated favorably in the press, and are skilled at self-promotion, "the perception is that consultants and technology make the difference in a greater percentage of elections than they likely do."[60]

Sabato suggests that members of the press, who value consultants as key sources of information, tend to treat them "with kid gloves." And he adds: "Political consultants and the new campaign technology may be producing a whole generation of officeholders far more skilled at running for office than in the art of governing. Who can forget Robert Redford as a newly elected, media-produced U.S. senator at the end of the film *The Candidate* asking pathetically, 'Now what do I do?'"[61]

In the spring of 1965, when Ronald Reagan was thinking about running for governor of California, he approached the Spencer-Roberts political management firm to see whether it would handle his campaign. Such was the reputation of the California firm that aspirants for political office sought out Spencer-Roberts rather than vice versa. George Christopher, the former mayor of San Francisco, had also approached Spencer-Roberts. After meeting with Reagan, the political management firm "accepted" him, rather than Christopher, as a client.[62]

Spencer-Roberts managed Reagan's successful campaign against incumbent governor Edmund "Pat" Brown. Because Reagan was an actor, some voters believed that he was simply playing the part of a candidate and memorizing his speeches. Spencer-Roberts advised Reagan to hold question-and-answer periods after each of his speeches to demonstrate to the voters that he had a real grasp of the issues. The firm's advice helped to elect Reagan as governor, his first step on the road to the presidency.

From its beginnings in California in the 1930s, campaign management rapidly grew to the status of a profitable nationwide industry. Some firms handle only Republican candidates, and others specialize in managing Democrats. Almost inevitably, public relations firms that have branched out into campaign management have evolved from technicians giving advice on press releases to strategists helping candidates make major campaign policy decisions. As Stanley Kelley, Jr., accurately predicted: "It is hard to see why the same trends which have brought the public relations man into political life will not also push him upward in political decision-making. His services are valuable because effective use of the mass media is one of the roads to power in contemporary society. . . ."[63]

One political scientist, Dan Nimmo, has contended that the use of professional campaign managers raises disturbing questions about American politics. The campaign consultants, he has observed, tend to approach elections as "contests of personalities" rather than choices between political parties or principles. And, he warns, the professional image-makers "can make a candidate appear to be what he is not."[64]

## The Polls

Public opinion polls are widely used in political campaigns not only by the news media, but by the candidates themselves. Political leaders are always concerned about their standing in the polls published by the press. But the public opinion surveys used by campaigns have become much more sophisticated than a simple comparison of the relative standing of competing candidates. Politicians may order a confidential poll to be taken well before a campaign in order to gauge their potential strength and may decide whether to run on the basis of the findings.

Once candidates are committed to running in a primary or a general-election campaign, they may commission private polls to test voter sentiment. The results then assist them in identifying the issues and planning their campaign strategy. After the campaign is under way, additional private polls may be taken to measure the success of a candidate's personal appeal and handling

© Dennis Brack/Black Star/Stockphoto.com

of the issues; both the candidate's style and positions on the issues may be adjusted accordingly. If elected, officials may rely on polls to measure voter reaction to their performance in office.

Political leaders often complain about polls, but almost all candidates rely on them. After Ronald Reagan was first elected president in 1980, it was revealed that during his campaign he had employed a highly sophisticated, computerized polling system. With fresh data flowing in constantly from national-sample interviews and surveys in 20 states, Reagan's staff was able to track shifts in opinion among the electorate, and to take action based on the information. As his chief poll-taker, Richard Wirthlin, described it, "Tracking allows you to watch a campaign almost the same way you watch a movie."[65]

In 1988, Michael Dukakis, the Democratic presidential nominee, trailed in the polls during the fall campaign. The polls were having a "terrible effect," Dukakis complained in mid-October, after a major poll showed him behind by 17 points. He argued that matters had reached the point where "polls drive the process."[66]

In 1992, the first president Bush was behind Bill Clinton in the polls. Bush—modeling himself on Harry Truman—took a whistle-stop train tour through three southern states. He told the crowd gathered along the tracks: "Don't believe these crazy polls. Don't believe these nutty pollsters. Don't let these guys tell you what you think. . . . We don't need that in the United States."[67] Bush lost.

But whether polls influence voters and affect election outcomes is not entirely clear. It might also be argued that polls are merely a mirror reflecting public opinion at a given moment. And candidates who are leading in the polls also may worry that their supporters will be less inclined to bother to vote. (For further discussion of the possible effect of polls on elections, see Chapter 6.)

There is a close interrelationship among the various tools and techniques of modern politics. The images that candidates try to project on television may be tailored to advice provided by professional campaign managers, who in turn rely on polls that they have taken or commissioned. Many of these expensive, interlocking, and highly professionalized services were relatively new in the campaigns of the 1960s; today they are taken for granted.

## The News Media

After he lost the California governor's race in 1962, Richard Nixon held a famous news conference in which he declared: "You won't have Nixon to kick around any more, because, gentlemen, this is my last press conference." The press, Nixon added, should recognize "that they have a right and a responsibility, if they're against a candidate, to give him the shaft, but also recognize if they give him the shaft, put one lonely reporter on the

© 2004 AP/Wide World Photos

Democratic presidential candidate John Kerry answers questions from reporters in 2004.

campaign who will report what the candidate says now and then."[68]

Nixon was exhausted and upset when he made these remarks, but his comments reflected his feelings after the 1960 presidential campaign and the 1962 California contest that he had been treated unfairly by the press. The complaint was not a new one; in 1807 President Jefferson had lamented "the falsehoods of a licentious press."[69] Modern candidates for political office, however, can ill afford to ignore the press.

In most presidential election years, more newspapers have endorsed Republican presidential candidates than Democratic candidates in their editorials. "Democratic candidates probably have to work a little harder at cultivating good relations [with the press] in order to help counteract the editorial slant of most papers. But Republicans have to work harder to win the sympathies of reporters of liberal tendency who dominate the national press corps," one study asserted.[70]

No doubt personal bias does color reporting at times. However, it is also true that the personal politics of news reporters may not be reflected in their stories, because many news reporters attempt to adhere to professional standards of fairness in covering the candidates.

In 1992, the supposedly liberal press intensely scrutinized whether Clinton, the Democratic candidate, told the truth about his draft status while a student during the Vietnam War. Only just before the election did the press pay much attention to the issue of whether the first President Bush told the truth about his involvement in the Iran-contra scandal while he was vice president.

And as noted in Chapter 8, the tangled Whitewater story, a continuous source of embarrassment to the Clintons, was first brought to public attention in 1992 by the *New York Times,* usually regarded as the most prominent liberal paper in the country. It was not until September 2000, in the last months of Clinton's presidency, that a special prosecutor closed the Whitewater investigation, announcing that there was "insufficient" evidence to bring charges against Clinton or his wife, Hillary Rodham Clinton.

National political correspondents and columnists play an influential role in interpreting political developments and even in recruiting candidates. Speculation in the press about who may or may not become a candidate, and published stories analyzing the relative strengths and abilities of rival contenders, may affect what happens at the conventions and on Election Day.

In contrast, editorial support of political candidates by newspapers has a less demonstrable effect on the outcome of presidential campaigns. (See Table 10-2.) During the New Deal years, Roosevelt was consistently opposed by one-half to two-thirds of the nation's daily newspapers; Harry Truman in 1948 and John Kennedy in 1960 were endorsed by only 15 percent of the daily papers, but both won. So did Jimmy Carter in 1976, with endorsements from only 12 percent of the daily papers.

Despite the importance of television in politics and campaigns, daily newspapers in the United States have a circulation of about 55 million, and the impressions that voters receive in political campaigns are formed in part by what they read. As a result, candidates must include the written press in their calculations of campaign techniques and strategy, even if they rely on television for direct mass appeal to the electorate.

## Campaign Finance

When Abraham Lincoln ran for Congress in 1846, it cost him 75 cents: "I made the canvass on my own horse; my entertainment, being at the houses of friends, cost me nothing; and my only outlay was 75¢ for a barrel of cider, which some farm-hands insisted I should treat to."[71]

Clearly, times have changed. (See Figure 10-3.) The immense cost of American political campaigns can be

### The Campaign: "Some Kind of a Cross-Country Race"

Reporters and candidates live at a breakneck pace during presidential campaigns. A sense of the hectic nature of life on the campaign trail was captured by author Timothy Crouse in a conversation with reporter James Doyle of the *Washington Star:*

> Doyle was slouching in an armchair by the picture window of his bedroom, dead tired from a week on the road. . . . He took a gulp of beer and looked out the window at the sun setting on the river.
>
> "A lot of people," he said, "look at this coverage as if it were some kind of a cross-country race—you gotta get two paragraphs in when he stops at Indianapolis and two more when he stops at Newark. If you do it that way, without making any meaning out of it, it is going to come out like some crazy disjointed trip across the country.
>
> "The problem is, if you try to write every day, you get caught up in sheer exhaustion. It's as simple as that. You do it by rote, because that's all you've got the energy for. It's the lack of sleep, the keeping up with deadlines, the disorientation from all this flying around—your mind just goes blank after a while. When it comes time to write the story, all you can do is just kind of a level job of stumbling through the day's events. I don't think I know how to cover a campaign."

—Timothy Crouse, *The Boys on the Bus*

TABLE 10-2

**Political Division of Daily Newspapers in Presidential Elections, 1932–2004**

| Year | Republican | Democratic | Independent or Neutral |
|---|---|---|---|
| 1932 | 55.5% | 38.7% | 5.8% |
| 1936 | 60.4 | 34.5 | 5.1 |
| 1940 | 66.3 | 20.1 | 13.6 |
| 1944 | 60.1 | 22.0 | 17.9 |
| 1948 | 65.2 | 15.4 | 19.4 |
| 1952 | 67.3 | 14.5 | 18.2 |
| 1956 | 59.0 | 17.0 | 24.0 |
| 1960 | 54.0 | 15.0 | 31.0 |
| 1964 | 34.7 | 42.4 | 22.9 |
| 1968* | 60.8 | 14.0 | 24.0 |
| 1972 | 71.4 | 5.3 | 23.3 |
| 1976 | 62.0 | 12.0 | 26.0 |
| 1980† | 42.2 | 12.0 | 42.0 |
| 1984 | 57.7 | 9.4 | 32.7 |
| 1988 | 31.2 | 13.3 | 55.4 |
| 1992‡ | 14.9 | 18.3 | 66.8 |
| 1996§ | 18.7 | 10.9 | 69.9 |
| 2000 | 59.1 | 40.9 | NA |
| 2004 | 56.0 | 44.0 | NA |

NOTE: Figures represent percentages of total number of papers replying to questionnaires. The number responding varied from year to year.
*George Wallace had the support of 1.2 percent.
†John Anderson had the support of 3.8 percent.
‡Ross Perot had the support of 0.12 percent.
§Other, 0.5 percent.
SOURCES: Data for 1932–1960 from William B. Dickinson, Jr., "Politicians and the Press," in Richard M. Boeckel, ed., *Editorial Research Reports,* vol. 2, no. 2 (September 2, 1964), p. 659. Data for 1964–1996 from *Editor & Publisher,* October 31, 1964; November 2, 1968; November 4, 1972; October 30, 1976; November 1, 1980; November 3, 1984; November 5, 1988; November 7, 1992; and October 26, 1996; data for 2000 from George Washington University; data for 2004 from *Editor & Publisher,* October 23, 2004.

seen at a glance from the following figures, which represent total spending at all levels—federal, state, and local—in presidential years since 1972:

$425 million in 1972
$540 million in 1976
$1.2 billion in 1980
$1.8 billion in 1984
$2.7 billion in 1988
$3.2 billion in 1992
$4.2 billion in 1996
$3.8 billion in 2000
$4.3 billion in 2004[72]

Beginning with the presidential election of 1976, the nature of political spending in the United States was significantly reshaped by the Watergate scandal, Congress, and the Supreme Court. For the first time, under the Federal Election Campaign Act amendments of 1974 and 1976, both major candidates, Jimmy Carter and Gerald Ford, financed their 1976 election campaigns with federal funds. Major-party presidential candidates have since continued to use federal funds in their general-election campaigns.

In addition to the federal money provided to the major candidates and parties for the national conventions and the general election, some candidates in primary elections may receive federal money. Those who raise the $100,000 necessary to qualify to receive federal dollars are eligible to receive matching funds from the government to help pay for some of the costs of their primary election campaigns.

In 2004, however, both George W. Bush and John Kerry declined federal money during the primaries, relying instead on their own highly successful fundraising efforts—which also meant they were not subject to federal restrictions on how much they could spend. With the donations pouring in, Bush raised $270 million before the convention and Kerry raised $235 million.[73] Bush and Kerry each accepted $75 million in public funds for the general election campaign.

The most significant feature of the federal campaign spending laws enacted in the 1970s was that they utterly failed to control the size of contributions and spending in political campaigns.

The goals of these laws were simple: First, limit political contributions so that wealthy individuals, corporations, or interest groups could not exercise undue influence on the politicians to whom they give money. Second, limit the amount that candidates could spend so that all would compete on a level playing field, thereby denying an advantage to a wealthy candidate.

But loopholes in the law, court decisions, and new patterns of financing campaigns all combined to undermine the effectiveness of the election law. The problem with efforts at campaign finance reform is that laws are made by lawmakers, the very people who have the least incentive to control the money flowing into their campaigns.

As Larry J. Sabato, a political scientist who has studied campaign reform, put it bluntly: "This is all about self-preservation and survival. . . . It may be a rotten system, but it has one redeeming feature—it elected you."[74]

The presidential election of 1976 was the first in which the law sought to provide effective limits on the size of contributions to candidates. In 1972 Max Palevsky, a California millionaire, gave almost $320,000 to George McGovern, the Democratic candidate. In 1976 he could give only $1,000 to Jimmy Carter. The conclusion that might logically be drawn is that a candidate who receives a $1,000 contribution will feel less obligated to the donor than one who receives $320,000. As will be seen, however, the loopholes that developed greatly weakened the effectiveness of the law.

By the 1988 presidential campaign, so-called "soft money" and "independent expenditures" on behalf of the presidential candidates totaled as much as or more

**FIGURE 10-3**

**Major-Party Campaign Spending in Presidential Elections, 1956–2004**

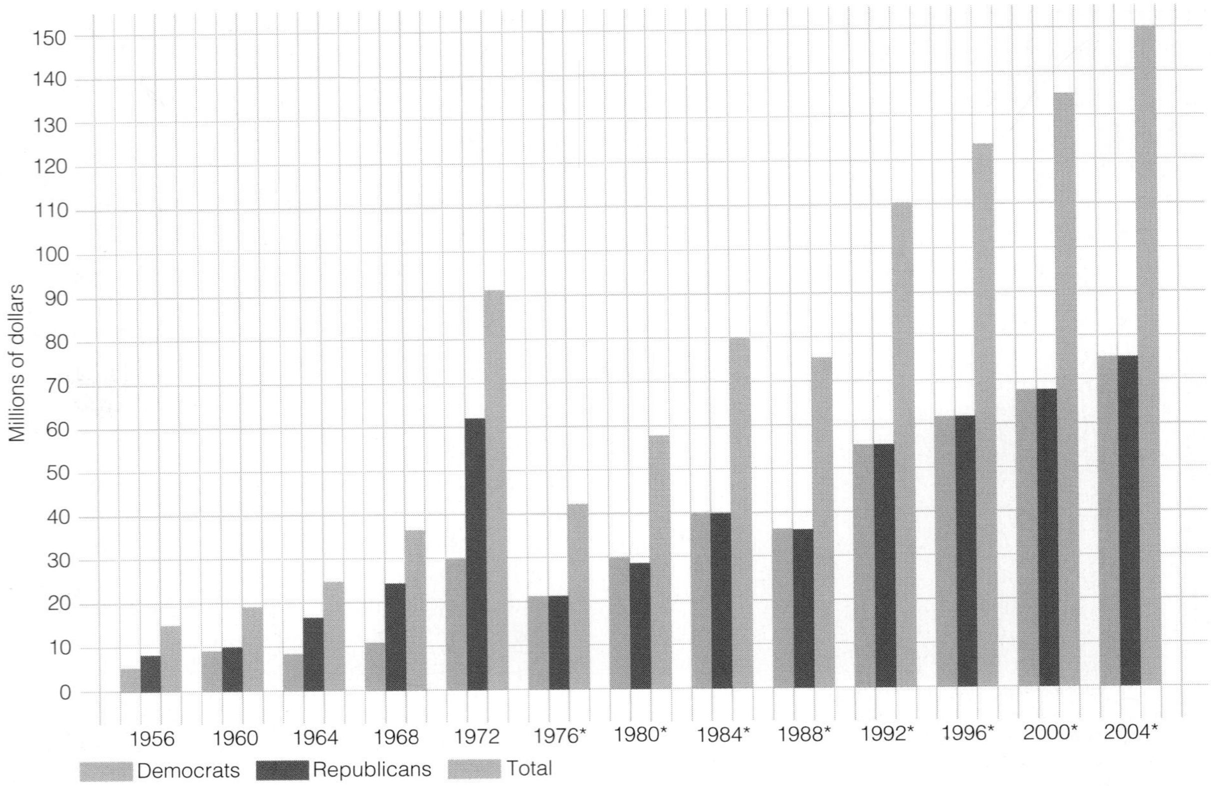


NOTE: Figures are for the postconvention campaigns.
*Both major-party presidential candidates accepted public funding in 1976, 1980, 1984, 1988, 1992, 1996, 2000, and 2004. Totals for those years reflect total federal funding for such candidates under the Federal Election Campaign Act amendments of 1974.
SOURCES: Herbert E. Alexander, *Financing Politics: Money, Elections, and Political Reform*, 3rd ed. (Washington, D.C.: CQ Press, 1984), p. 7. Data for 1984, 1988, 1992, 1996, 2000, and 2004 provided by the Federal Election Commission. In 1992, in addition to the totals that include the full spending by major-party national committees shown above, independent candidate Ross Perot spent $68.4 million to finance his presidential campaign. In 1996, Perot received $29.1 million in federal funds when he ran as a candidate of his Reform Party.

than the funds allotted under the Federal Election Campaign Act.

**Soft money,** until the law was changed in 2002, described the unregulated campaign funds from corporations, unions, and wealthy donors that were not subject to the limits of federal law because they went to party committees and not directly to candidates.

**Independent expenditures** are funds spent for or against a candidate by committees not formally connected to a candidate and without coordination with the campaign. These two types of campaign spending amounted to a huge gap in the law and undercut the post-Watergate efforts at reform. Big contributors in both parties were donating $100,000 or more, gifts to party or "independent" committees that would be illegal if made to the candidates directly.

For the presidential election of 2000, soft money expenditures by the two major parties far exceeded the spending by their presidential candidates, who had accepted federal funds subject to a cap. Critics called soft money "the loophole that ate the law," because political committees could not only accept large donations but did not have to make them public.[75] The money came from business, individuals, and labor unions. Once again, "fat cats"—big contributors—and special interests were influencing election campaigns.

In 2002, the Bipartisan Campaign Reform Act, usually known as the McCain-Feingold law for its Senate sponsors, banned contributions of soft money to national political parties. In addition the law prohibited the use of such funds to broadcast "issue ads" that mentioned a specific candidate if the ads ran within 60 days of a general election or 30 days before a primary. The law did allow limited contributions of soft money to state parties for voting and registration drives, but not for use in federal elections.

The new law also doubled the amount that individuals can give to a candidate from $1,000 to $2,000. Even before the new law went into effect after the 2002 congressional elections, however, the two major political parties had created the new 527 organizations to accept the continuing flow of soft money. And more soft money was being shifted to the state parties.

The 2002 campaign finance reform law resulted from a long effort by senators John McCain, an Arizona Republican, and Russell D. Feingold, a Wisconsin Democrat. The law was immediately challenged by a group of senators, led by Mitch McConnell, a Kentucky Republican, who argued that restrictions on campaign contributions violated the First Amendment's protection of freedom of speech.

In December 2003, however, the Supreme Court upheld the McCain-Feingold campaign finance law. The 5-4 decision rejected the argument that the law, by banning soft money and restricting television ads during political campaigns, curtailed free speech. The Court affirmed the power of Congress to regulate the flood of money in politics because, the justices said, the whole system of campaign finance was mired in "corruption, and in particular the appearance of corruption. . . . the manner in which parties have sold access to federal candidates and officeholders has given rise to the appearance of undue influence."[76]

Several years earlier another issue, that of foreign contributions, arose during the 1996 presidential campaign. The FBI investigated allegations that money from China had found its way into the Clinton campaign. And it was disclosed that almost $1 million had been given to the Democratic Party by donors linked to a wealthy Indonesian family and their conglomerate, the Lippo Group. One Indonesian couple, permanent residents of the United States at the time, gave $450,000.

Money in election campaigns is a subject cloaked by a good deal of secrecy, and a vast amount of confusion. Even before the passage of the 1974 law, Congress over the years had attempted to control the sources, amounts, and reporting of campaign expenditures. But it was not until after the Watergate scandal that the political climate was favorable for the first comprehensive attempt to regulate campaign finance. As mentioned earlier in this chapter and discussed in more detail in Chapter 13, that scandal had begun when, in 1972, burglars, employed by President Nixon's reelection campaign, broke into the Democratic Party headquarters in the Watergate office building in Washington. The burglary and cover-up, Nixon's resignation to avoid impeachment, and the widespread financial abuses in his 1972 campaign that were revealed by the Senate Watergate committee and by the press increased sentiment for public financing of elections and related reforms. The result was passage of the Federal Election Campaign Act amendments of 1974.

Despite the law, no politician or political scientist would accept the officially reported campaign spending figures as fully reflecting actual political campaign costs. Of the iceberg that is campaign finance, only a portion shows above the surface. Partly as a result, an atmosphere of public cynicism and mistrust has tended to surround the subject of money and politics. Voter attitudes on the subject are reflected in such statements as: "Money wins elections," "Politicians can be bought," or "Politics is a rich man's game."

Money is important. It did not, however, win the Democratic nomination for Averell Harriman in 1956, nor did it put Nelson Rockefeller in the White House in three attempts in the 1960s—and neither man lacked money. Since the Second World War, the Republicans have generally spent more than the Democrats on national campaigns. Therefore, if money alone had determined the result of presidential elections, the Democrats could not have won. There are, in other words, some limits to the influence of money in elections.

## Regulating Campaign Finance

For many years, a patchwork of federal legislation had also sought to limit spending and require disclosure of gifts to elected officials, but the laws had fallen far short of achieving these goals.

The Federal Election Campaign Act of 1971 required disclosure of the names of all contributors giving more than $100 to a federal campaign, and placed limits on what candidates could spend. The law also repealed certain provisions of the Hatch Act of 1940, which had sought, with little success, to limit political contributions and spending in federal elections.

As far back as 1907, Congress prohibited corporations from contributing to candidates for office in federal elections. The Taft-Hartley Act of 1947 bars gifts by labor unions or corporations to federal election campaigns. But the law did not stop unions or corporations from financing political campaigns; they simply set up separate political arms to make campaign contributions, such as the AFL-CIO Committee on Political Education (COPE), and BIPAC, the Business-Industrial Political Action Committee.

Beginning in 1973, Congress provided that taxpayers could specify a small amount of each person's federal income taxes—$3 in 2004—to go into a campaign fund to be distributed among the candidates in the next presidential election. The "checkoff law" was designed to provide public financing of presidential campaigns in order to free political parties of dependence on private contributions. Beginning in 1974, this option was included on the standard income tax forms to make it more convenient for taxpayers.

**The Federal Rules** The 1974 amendments to the Federal Election Campaign Act rewrote the laws of campaign finance. The law was modified by the Supreme Court in *Buckley* v. *Valeo,* an important ruling in January 1976 that opened the way to independent expenditures.[77] The campaign finance law of 2002 made further changes. The law as of 2004 provided as follows:

*Contribution limits.* Individuals may give up to $2,000 to federal candidates in primary elections and general elections; individuals may also give up to $95,000 over two years, distributed among candidates, party committees, or political action committees (PACs), such as those sponsored by corporations or labor unions. (These limits are indexed to increase with inflation.)

*Public financing.* Presidential—but not Senate or House—candidates may accept federal money to pay for primaries or general elections. In 2004, both major party candidates accepted funds for the general-election campaign, but neither major-party candidate accepted matching funds during the primary elections. To qualify for public funds in the preconvention period, a candidate must raise at least $5,000 in each of 20 states in contributions of up to $1,000, for an overall total of $100,000. In addition, public funds may be used to help each major political party to finance its national convention.

*Spending limits.* Presidential candidates who accept federal funds are limited to spending the amount they receive—$75 million each for Bush and Kerry in 2004.[78] Candidates who receive federal funds in the general election can accept no private contributions.

*Disclosure.* Candidates must file periodic reports with the government disclosing the names and addresses of all donors of more than $200 and listing all expenditures of more than $200.

*Federal Election Commission.* In 1975, Congress created a bipartisan, six-member Federal Election Commission to enforce the campaign finance laws and administer the public financing machinery.

The 1974 law had sought to limit campaign expenditures in all federal elections and to restrict individual spending by candidates or their families. But two years later, in *Buckley* v. *Valeo,* the Supreme Court ruled that these limits, in general, restricted freedom of expression and it struck them down—except for presidential candidates who accept public financing. The Court upheld the limits on contributions, ruling that this imposed less of a burden on free expression.

The Supreme Court's decision in *Buckley* v. *Valeo* opened the way for wealthy candidates to spend vast amounts of their own money in their campaigns. The ruling also permitted independent expenditures to be made by committees not formally connected with a candidate. This opened up one part of the enormous loophole in the law discussed earlier in this chapter.

As political writer Elizabeth Drew has noted, "The law that established public financing of Presidential campaigns was intended to remove the role of private money from Presidential contests, but great rivers of private money, much of it untraceable, still flow into them." That is because the "'independent' committees working on a Presidential candidate's behalf . . . are independent in name only."[79]

And the Supreme Court has held, 7–2, that state and national political parties may spend unlimited amounts on congressional campaigns as long as the party and the candidate are not working together.[80] Under the ruling, the parties are able to pay for commercials that specifically urge voters to vote for or against a candidate.

## How Much Does It Cost?

In many districts it costs several hundred thousand dollars to run for Congress, and some candidates for the House spend several million dollars in the hope of being sent to Washington by the voters. The $1 million threshold in a House race was crossed for the first time in 1978 by Carter Burden, a wealthy candidate in Manhattan's "silk stocking" district, who lost, and Robert L. Livingston, a Louisiana Republican, who won.[81] In 1990, there were 11 candidates for the House who spent $1 million or more.[82] By 1994, the number had increased to 48.[83] By 2004, $1 million for a House race no longer seemed all that unusual; for example, House Speaker Dennis Hastert, an Illinois Republican, spent $3.7 million on his reelection campaign even before the fall campaign got under way.[84]

To run for the U.S. Senate, candidates may spend even more staggering amounts. In 1988, the average cost of Senate campaigns was almost $4 million.[85] But the cost of Senate races keeps spiraling upward; in the 2000 elections, Jon S. Corzine, a Wall Street millionaire, spent $35.5 million to win the Democratic nomination for the U.S. Senate in New Jersey.[86] In 2004 Blair Hull, a wealthy Democratic candidate for the Senate in Illinois and a political novice, spent almost $29 million of his own money on his primary campaign, only to be defeated by Barack Obama, a young, charismatic state senator from Chicago's South Side.[87]

Gubernatorial races also often prove to be very expensive. In 1980, Jay Rockefeller, a member of one of America's wealthiest families and heir to the Standard Oil fortune, spent about $12 million in winning reelection as governor of West Virginia. Almost all of the money was his own.[88] By 2002, Tom Golisano, a businessman, spent $65 million of his personal fortune in an unsuccessful independent gubernatorial campaign in New York.[89]

The candidate who spends the most does not always win. "Money also can turn off voters," Herbert E. Alexander has noted. "Wealthy candidates can create a backlash among the electorate."[90]

Running for president is vastly more expensive than running for Congress. The cost of nominating and electing a president has increased steadily. The presidential election of 1980, including the preconvention campaigns and the national conventions, cost about $275 million. The figure rose to more than $1 billion in 2004.[91]

Although presidential candidates have been accepting public funds to finance their campaigns, as already noted, in 2004 soft money could still be contributed to

Illinois state senator Barack Obama delivers the keynote speech at the Democratic National Convention in 2004. He was elected to the U.S. Senate later that year and quickly emerged as a star within his party.

influence presidential campaigns through 527 organizations and other supposedly independent groups.

Alexander Heard, author of a number of authoritative studies of campaign finance, has concluded that money is particularly important in "the shadow land of our politics" where it is decided who will be a nominee of a political party: "Cash is far more significant in the nominating process than in determining the outcome of elections."[92]

## Where Does the Money Go?

Today, radio and television costs are by far the biggest single item in campaign spending at the presidential level and in many congressional contests. The cost of TV commercials is the chief reason that presidential candidates take time to appear at fund-raisers even in the midst of barnstorming around the country to win votes.

Candidates' political committees also spend money on other forms of publicity and advertising. They must pay for polls and data processing, printing costs, telephone bills, headquarters costs, and salaries of party workers. A great deal of money is spent on Election Day to pay poll workers, to provide transportation to get the voters to the polls—and, sometimes, illicitly, to pay voters. Alexander Heard has estimated that Election Day spending accounts for "as much as one-eighth of the total election bill in the United States."[93]

## Where Does the Money Come From?

By the 1980s, long before John Kerry and George W. Bush battled for the White House in 2004, **political action committees (PACs)** had become a powerful and controversial source of campaign money. PACs are independent organizations, or more often, political arms of corporations, unions, or interest groups. (See Chapter 7 for a detailed discussion of PACs.) PAC spending in all 1984 campaigns at the federal level totaled $113 million. By 2000 PAC spending had increased to $579 million.[94]

PACs tend to give to candidates already serving in Congress (and who therefore have a better chance of winning), not to their challengers: "PACs have tended to move away from ideology and instead have become incumbent-oriented. . . . Three out of four PAC dollars in 1988 went to incumbents of both parties."[95]

By mid-2006, the number of PACs had increased rapidly to 4,600, up from 2,279 two decades earlier.[96] The growth of PACs was due, in part, to the 1976 Supreme Court decision permitting independent expenditures in political campaigns by groups not formally connected with a candidate.[97] PACs often contribute to political campaigns because they hope a candidate will support legislation that will benefit a specific industry, union, or interest group.

The reasons why people give money to campaigns vary widely. Some contributors simply believe in a party or a candidate and wish to express their support. Others give because they do expect some tangible benefit or reward from the winning candidate. Others hope to buy access to a public official; for some who long for social recognition, an invitation to a White House dinner may be reward enough.[98]

Some of America's wealthiest families have contributed heavily to political campaigns. The bulk of the contributions from these families—whose wealth is rooted in oil, steel, autos, railroads, and other large industries—went to the Republican Party. Although the contribution limits in the 1974 act have reduced the influence of individual donors, wealthy individuals and families can still contribute substantially, if indirectly, to congressional

Hillary Rodham Clinton and a well-known supporter during her campaign for the U.S. Senate in New York in 2000

and presidential candidates, because the law permits an aggregate contribution of $95,000 over two years by each person, distributed among candidates, party committees, or PACs. And the federal law does not apply in state or local elections, where wealthy individuals can make their presence felt.

Both major parties rely on a variety of sources to raise money: PAC contributions, individual contributions from the public, $100-a-plate and $1,000-a-plate dinners, direct-mail and Internet solicitation, televised appeals, contributions from members of labor unions and corporation executives, and corporate advertising in convention programs and political booklets.

An unadvertised source of campaign funds is the underworld. In some communities, close ties exist between organized crime and politics. Elected officials may take graft to protect criminal operations, and sometimes the payoffs take the form of campaign contributions. Heard has guessed that perhaps "15 percent of political campaign expenditures at state and local levels" comes from the underworld.[99]

## Campaigns, Money, and Democracy

The reforms in election laws during the 1970s sought, however unsuccessfully, to limit contributions, to provide meaningful public disclosure of campaign gifts and spending (in place of laws that invited evasion), to broaden the base of campaign giving, and to provide public funding for part of the costs of presidential campaigns. The reforms were based on the belief that candidates should not have to depend on big contributors to whom they might become obligated and that roughly equal resources should be available to candidates for public office.

The case for this reform effort was compelling, because inadequate controls only served to reinforce voter cynicism about politics. But the growth and influence of soft money and independent expenditures mocked these reforms and led to the McCain-Feingold law in 2002.

Clearly, special interest money from PACs has achieved undue influence in the electoral process. President Carter, in his farewell address to the nation, warned that single-issue groups and special interest organizations had become "a disturbing factor in American political life."[100]

As presidential candidates have relied more on public funding, PAC money has been diverted elsewhere. Millions of dollars in special interest money that might otherwise have gone into presidential campaigns is funneled into congressional races through PACs.

The growth and power of the PACs helped to undermine the reforms of the federal election laws. Vari-

"Senator, according to this report, you're marked for defeat by the A.D.A., the National Rifle Association, the A.F.L.-C.I.O., the N.A.M., the Sierra Club, Planned Parenthood, the World Student Christian Federation, the Clamshell Alliance . . . "

## Making a Difference

### "WAKE UP, AMERICA"

She is 90 and has arthritis, emphysema, a bunion on her big left toe, and a steel brace supporting her back. However, Doris "Granny D" Haddock completed a 14-month, 3,200-mile walk across America for campaign finance reform. The passion that drove this great-grandmother was sparked after her weekly women's club discussed campaign finance reform.

"I believe very strongly that democracy is threatened by illegal money that corporations, unions and wealthy men are giving to political candidates," said Haddock, who retired in 1972 as an executive secretary at a shoe firm.

The Dublin, N.H., woman scolded lawmakers for turning "this temple of our fair republic into a bawdy house where anything and everything is done for a price."

"Along my 3,000 miles through the heart of America . . . did I meet anyone who thought that their voice as an equal citizen counts for much in the corrupt halls of Washington? No, I did not. Did I meet anyone who felt anger or pain over this? I did indeed, and I watched them shake with rage sometimes when they spoke, and I saw tears well up in their eyes," she said.

When her son Jim first heard about his mother's plan to walk across the nation, he placed her on a "Herculean" training program. She walked 10 miles a day, practiced carrying a 25-pound backpack and slept on the ground.

"If your mother is 88 years old with emphysema and arthritis, you're not just going to say, 'Have a good time,'" her son said. "I'm proud of her."

Not once has Haddock missed a meal or slept on the floor. Friends and strangers have given her shelter and motels have let her stay for free.

Haddock began her trip in Pasadena, California, on January 1, 1999, and arrived in Washington, D.C., on February 29, 2000. Three members of Congress aided Granny D as she climbed the east steps of the Capitol, saying they wanted to support her on the final leg of her trip because of her extraordinary efforts to draw attention to an issue they've championed for years.

As she arrived at the Capitol, Granny D had this to say: "Wake up, America, recognize what is happening to your country and do something about it."

—Adapted from *USA Today,* February 29, 2000; the Associated Press, March 1, 2000; and the *Los Angeles Times,* March 1, 2000

ous suggestions have been made for controlling PACs, plugging loopholes in the law, and banning the 527 organizations that sprang up like mushrooms after passage of the McCain-Feingold law. Some analysts also have suggested that public financing, available since 1976 in presidential campaigns, be extended to congressional campaigns.

Efforts to circumvent the reform laws and the fact that some candidates have unequal financial resources tend to undermine public confidence in the American political process. And campaigns are a vital part of that process, for, within limits, they give the voters a chance to decide who shall govern.

## CHAPTER HIGHLIGHTS

- For every candidate, between nomination and election there stands the campaign. In American politics, the campaign is the battleground of power.
- Campaigns are organized chaos. On the national level, large numbers of people—professionals and volunteers—are thrown together for a relatively short period of time to mount an incredibly complex effort to elect a president.
- Studies have shown that many voters, more than half in recent decades, are committed to one candidate or another in advance of the campaign. Nevertheless, a large group of voters, often one-third or more, make their decision during the campaign.
- Long before they can get into a general-election campaign, aspiring presidential candidates must, as a rule, enter the bruising arena of the primaries.
- Political candidates in most cases develop a central theme for their campaign. Sometimes, the substantive issues in a campaign become submerged as the candidates devote more time to attacking each other than to discussing policies and programs.
- Television is an essential part of a modern political campaign. Candidates normally spend much of their budgets on TV commercials. In all recent presidential elections, the major-party candidates have also debated each other on television. In 2004, the candidates appeared on talk and entertainment shows and campaigned on the Internet as well. All offered websites that featured the latest speeches, news, and pronouncements of the presidential campaign.
- Public opinion polls are widely used in political campaigns, not only by the news media, but by the candidates themselves.
- At all levels of politics, candidates have turned to professional campaign managers and consultants. The firms earn large fees for their varied services, which

include advertising, public relations, research on issues, public opinion sampling, creating websites, fund-raising, telephone solicitations, computer analysis, and speech-writing.

- In 1976 for the first time, under the Federal Election Campaign Act amendments of 1974 and 1976, both major candidates financed their election campaigns with federal funds. Major-party presidential candidates have since continued to accept federal funds in their general-election campaigns.
- The most significant feature of the federal campaign spending laws of the 1970s was that they had utterly failed to control the size of contributions and spending in political campaigns. And the growth and influence of soft money and independent expenditures mocked the reforms. But Congress in 2002 banned gifts of soft money to national political parties. The new law also prohibited the use of such funds to broadcast "issue ads" for a specific candidate within 60 days of a general election.
- After the 2002 campaign finance law was passed, groups known as 527 organizations were created to continue to accept soft money to influence elections and to exploit a loophole in the law.
- Political action committees (PACs) are a powerful and controversial source of campaign money.
- Efforts to circumvent the federal election reform laws and the fact that some candidates have unequal financial resources tend to undermine public confidence in the American political process.

## KEY TERMS

527 organizations, p. 290
negative advertising, p. 316
soft money, p. 322
independent expenditures, p. 322
political action committees (PACs), p. 325

## SUGGESTED WEBSITES

**http://www.publicintegrity.org/default.aspx**
*The Center for Public Integrity*
A nonprofit center dedicated to government accountability, ethics, and campaign finance reform. The center's research is accessible from the Internet and includes selected reports, newsletters, and databases.

**http://www.opensecrets.org**
*The Center for Responsive Politics*
A nonpartisan, nonprofit organization that tracks money in politics and its effects on public policy and elections. Contains extensive data about lobbyists, soft money contributions, PACs, presidential and congressional races, and political donors.

**http://www.commoncause.org**
*Common Cause*
A nonprofit, nonpartisan organization that promotes government accountability. Visitors to the website can research contributions to the Republican and Democratic Parties by donor name, donor location, or industry, as well as news about a wide range of government agencies and topics.

**http://www.fec.gov**
*Federal Election Commission*
The branch of the federal government that oversees federal elections. The website contains a citizens' guide to elections, including current rules for upcoming campaigns, how to support a candidate, and FEC publications.

## SUGGESTED READING

Bennett, W. Lance. *The Governing Crisis: Media, Money, and Marketing in American Elections*, 2nd edition* (St. Martin's, 1996). A trenchant critique of the conduct and content of recent presidential election campaigns. Includes several proposals for improving the quality of the national debate.

Bibby, John F. *Politics, Parties, and Elections in America*, 5th edition* (Thomson / Wadsworth, 2002). An overview of the role of the Republican and Democratic Parties in recruiting leaders, nominating candidates, and contesting elections. Argues that political parties are still a strong force in American elections even though many voters do not vote for the candidate of their party.

Drew, Elizabeth. *The Corruption of American Politics** (Carol Publishing, 1999). A critical examination of campaign finance. Drew, a long-time Washington journalist, argues that the incessant demands of fund-raising have eroded the quality of American politics and politicians over the past generation.

Jamieson, Kathleen Hall. *Dirty Politics: Deception, Distraction, and Democracy** (Oxford University Press, 1992). A careful analysis of deceptive television ads and other manipulative practices used in modern election contests. Argues that the news media focus too much attention on the polls and the candidates' campaign strategies and give too little attention to the candidates' proposals.

Magleby, David B., Anthony Corrado, and Kelly D. Patterson, eds. *Financing the 2004 Election** (The Brookings Institution, 2006). A comprehensive analysis by leading scholars of political money in the 2004 presidential, congressional, and state elections. This is the latest in a series of books, sponsored by the Citizens Research Foundation that begins with Herbert E. Alexander's volume on the 1960 election.

Maisel, Louis Sandy. *Parties and Elections in America: The Electoral Process,* 4th edition* (Rowman & Littlefield, 2004). An excellent general analysis of how election campaigns are conducted in America. The author was himself a major-party candidate for the U.S. House of Representatives.

Malbin, Michael J., ed. *Life After Reform: When the Bipartisan Campaign Reform Act Meets Politics** (Rowman & Littlefield, 2003). An examination of the evolution, content, and likely impact of the 2002 campaign finance reform law on campaigns, contributors, and especially political parties. A central focus is how the parties have adapted to the ban on soft money contributions to national political parties, and the increased use of "527" groups.

Patterson, Thomas E. *Out of Order** (Vintage Books, 1994). A detailed study of the influence of the mass media in presidential elections. The author argues that the media, and especially television, have replaced political parties as the main factor in screening and selecting potential presidential candidates.

Polsby, Nelson W., and Wildavsky, Aaron B. *Presidential Elections,* 11th edition* (Rowman & Littlefield, 2003). An excellent, concise analysis of the basic strategic considerations affecting the conduct of presidential election campaigns.

Sabato, Larry J., ed. *Midterm Madness: The Elections of 2002** (Rowman & Littlefield, 2003). A study of the 2002 midterm elections, covering national trends and case studies of individual campaigns for the U.S. Senate and governorships. The editor concludes that the popularity of President George W. Bush and campaigning by him greatly helped the Republicans to win the 2002 elections.

Schantz, Harvey L., ed. *Politics in an Era of Divided Government: Elections and Governance in the Second Clinton Administration* (Routledge, 2001). An analysis of the 1996 reelection campaign of President Clinton with chapters on the U.S. House and Senate elections, the presidential and congressional nominations, and the general election for president.

Schroeder, Alan. *Presidential Debates: Forty Years of High-Risk TV** (Columbia University Press, 2001). A thorough analysis of presidential debates from 1960 through 1996, covering the candidates' strategies and tactics and the effects which the debates may have had on specific elections.

Sorauf, Frank J. *Inside Campaign Finance: Myths and Realities* (Yale University Press, 1992). A comprehensive examination of the American system for financing election campaigns. Questions that are explored include: Who gives money for election campaigns? How much do they give? Why do people give? And, what are the consequences of the current financing system for American politics?

Thurber, James A., and Nelson, Candice J., eds. *Campaigns and Elections American Style,* 2nd edition* (Westview Press, 2004). A useful collection of essays on what it takes to enter and win elections in America today.

Troy, Gil. *See How They Ran: The Changing Role of the Presidential Candidate,* revised and expanded edition* (Harvard University Press, 1996). A survey of how presidential candidates—from George Washington to Bill Clinton—have campaigned for the office. Emphasizes campaign tactics and strategies, and how they have changed over time.

Wayne, Stephen J. *The Road to the White House 2004: The Politics of Presidential Elections** (St. Martin's, 2004). A clearly written analysis of the strategy and tactics of winning the American presidency. Includes sections on campaign finance, delegate selection, national conventions, the media, and voting.

White, Theodore H. *The Making of the President, 1960* (Atheneum, 1961); *The Making of the President, 1964* (Atheneum, 1965); *The Making of the President, 1968* (Atheneum, 1969); and *The Making of the President, 1972* (Atheneum, 1973). Colorful, detailed accounts of American presidential campaigns, set against the background of the social and cultural forces at work in American society. White, a leading political analyst, had access to many of the political figures he wrote about.

*Available in paperback edition.

# Chapter 11

# Voting Behavior and Elections

THERE COMES A MOMENT in every campaign when the bands are silent and the cheering stops. The candidate has given the last speech, made the last promise, answered the last question from reporters, smiled at the red light on the television camera for the last time. There is nothing left to do but to board the campaign plane and fly home to await the verdict of the voters.

There is a certain majesty and mystery in this moment, for until the votes are counted, no one—not the candidates, the voters, the poll-takers, the news reporters, not even the computers blinking and buzzing in the control centers of the television networks—knows what the precise outcome will be. And in the extraordinary presidential election of 2000, the suspense lasted for weeks after Election Day; nobody knew who had won.

In a democracy, the people choose who will govern, and that choice is expressed in the voting booth. Although the right to vote is basic to the American political system, it is not as common elsewhere as might be thought. Only about half of the world's countries hold regular free elections in which the people may choose among rival candidates.

Chapter 1 examined the reciprocal nature of power in a democracy: Government makes authoritative, binding decisions about who gets what in society, but derives its power from the people. People may influence government in a number of ways—by taking part in political activity, by the opinions they hold, by belonging to interest groups, by direct action. But a fundamental way that people influence government is through the ballot box; voting is a very powerful input in the political system.

For example, as the presidential election of 2000 demonstrated, one of the most potent weapons of popular control in a democracy is the ability of the electorate to remove a party from power. In that year, George W. Bush of Texas, the Republican presidential nominee, defeated Al Gore, the candidate of the Democratic Party, which at that time controlled the presidency.

In the federal system that exists in the United States, the voters choose at all levels of government. In a presidential year, for instance, the voters select many of the nation's more than 500,000 local, state, and federal elected officials, including the president and vice president, 435 members of the House, one-third of the Senate, and 11 state governors.

American voters normally may choose among two or more competing candidates for the same office. In a democracy, voting is an act of choice among alternative candidates, parties, and, depending on the election, alternative policies.

Under a democratic form of government, then, the voter is theoretically supreme. Yet, as we have seen, there is often a gap between democratic theory and practice. For example, candidates for public office—at least below the presidential level—may compete with vastly unequal financial resources. TV commercials often attempt to manipulate the voters and create "images" of candidates, rather than informing the electorate. What the voters perceive may be distorted if one side or the other engages in unethical campaign practices or "dirty tricks." Some voters may be unenthusiastic about the nominees of both major parties and may believe that their choice is between the lesser of two evils. In some years, they may choose to support a minor-party or independent candidate. Or they may easily come to feel that, for them, voting is a waste of time.

Key Question In this chapter we will explore a key question: ***What are the consequences of voting and elections in a democratic society?*** There are also a number of related questions to consider: Do enough people vote? Why do large numbers of people fail to vote? How do voters make up their minds? What do elections mean in a democracy—do voters speak in a voice that can be understood by those whom they elect? Do their votes influence government policies? In other words, do elections make a difference in terms of who gets what, when, and how?

## WHO VOTES?

The voter may have the final say in the United States—but how many people vote? To those who hold an idealized view of representative democracy, the statistics are bound to be disappointing. In some elections there are as many nonvoters as voters.

### The Voter

Almost half or more of the Americans of voting age have voted for president in each election since 1928. But in nonpresidential election years, considerably less than half have bothered to vote for members of Congress. In the 11 off-year congressional elections from 1962 to 2002, an average of only 38 percent voted for members of the House of Representatives. By contrast, in the 12 presidential elections from 1960 through 2004, an average of 55.4 percent cast their ballots for president. During these elections, voter turnout declined in every presidential year but four: 1984, 1992, 2000, and 2004. In 2004, for example, the voter turnout for president increased substantially—from 51.2 percent in 2000 to 58.3 percent four years later. (See Figure 11-1.)

Although 21st-century Americans have made great technological progress, their forebears in the horse-and-buggy era scored much higher in voter participation. A much larger proportion of voters took part in presidential elections in the 1890s than in recent years. In the election of 1896, for example, almost 80 percent of the eligible voters cast their ballots. The drop in turnout since then is often attributed to the fact that the adoption of women's suffrage in 1920 brought into the electorate a large new group unaccustomed to voting because they had previously been barred from casting ballots. But the decline in voter participation had begun well before then. After voter turnout dipped to a low point in the early 1920s, it moved to generally higher levels in 1928 and in subsequent elections. (See Figure 11-2.) Despite this trend, voting participation in the United States is substantially lower than it is in many other countries of the world, including Great Britain, Germany, France, and Canada. (See Table 11-1.) Because other nations calculate voter turnout in varying ways, however, the comparison with the United States is not precise.

**Socioeconomic Factors** It is clear that who votes varies with factors of geography, age, sex, education, ethnic background, religion, income, social class, and occupation. This does not necessarily mean that people vote or do not vote because of such social, demographic, and economic factors; it merely means that these factors often coincide with higher or lower voting participation.[1] For example, regional differences in voter participation may be associated with social and economic factors in those areas or with differences in the election laws governing registration and voting.

Middle-aged people vote more than the young or the very old. Although some college students and young people take an active part in election campaigns, poll data indicate that almost half of Americans between the ages of 18 and 24 did not register to vote in 2004.[2]

In the past, studies showed that voting and political participation increased slowly with age, peaked in the mid-forties and fifties, and declined after age 60.[3] More recently, however, a higher percentage of older citizens have voted.

During the first several decades after the women's suffrage amendment was ratified in 1920, men voted more than women. By 2000, however, about 3 percent more women voted than men.[4]

Because there are more women than men in the

## FIGURE 11-1

**Voter Participation in Presidential and House Elections, 1960–2004**

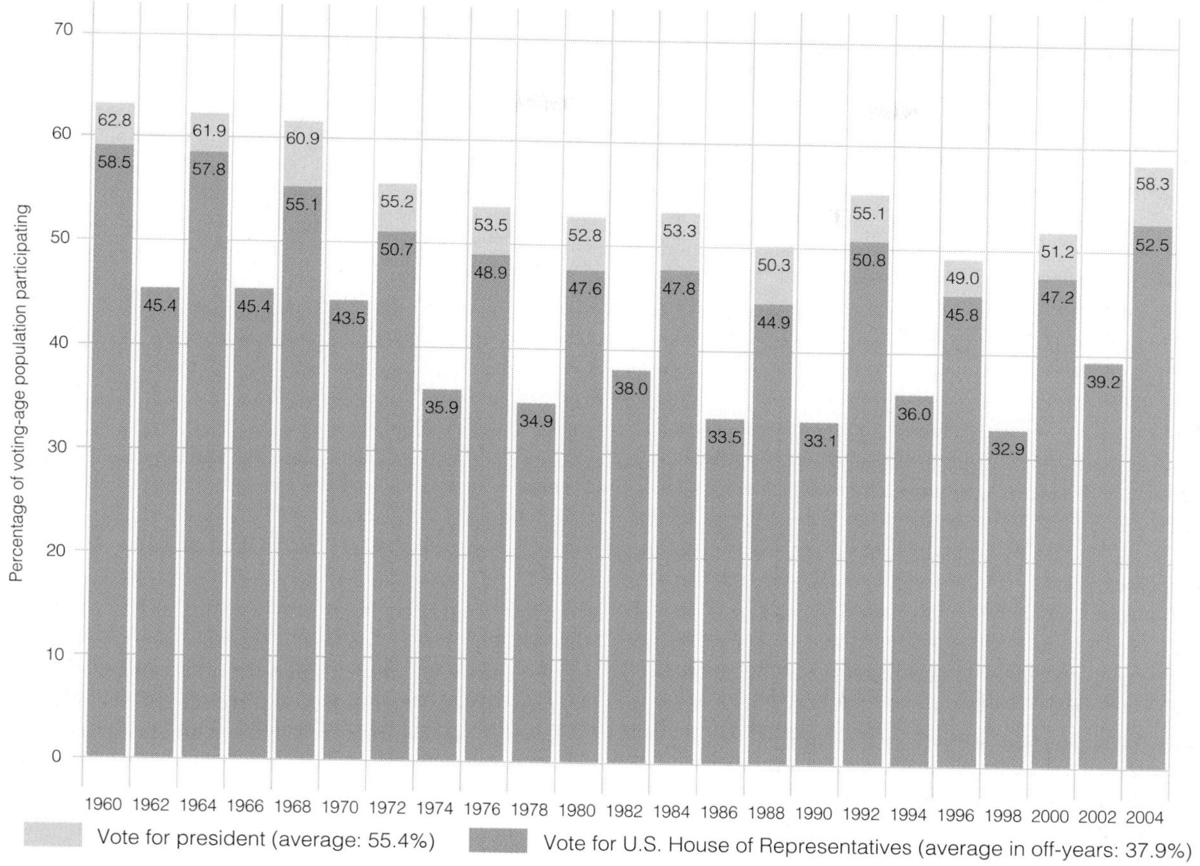


SOURCE: Data provided by U.S. Bureau of the Census, *Statistical Abstract of the United States: 2006*, p. 251; 2002 data provided by The Center for Voting and Democracy.

United States, in absolute numbers there are likely to be more women than men voters in future elections. Sandra Baxter and Marjorie Lansing concluded in a 1980 study: "A major shift has occurred in the voting balance in the last decade: more women than men have gone to the polls to vote for president."[5]

College graduates vote substantially more than people with a high school or grade school education. One survey found that 77.5 percent of college-educated Americans reported that they voted in the 2004 presidential election, whereas only 56.4 percent of those with four years of high school and 39.5 percent of those with some high school edu-

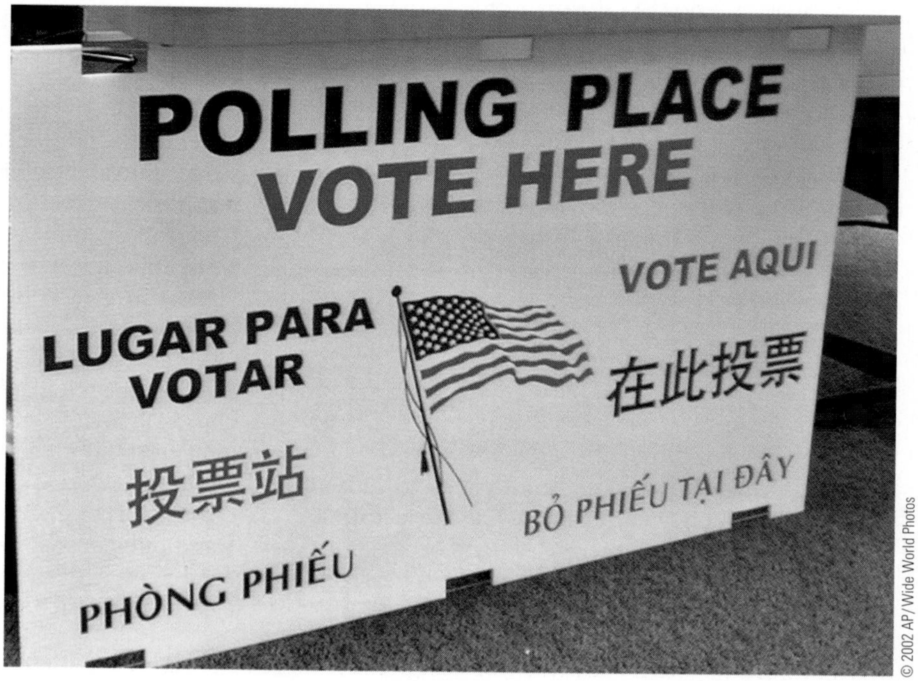

FIGURE 11-2

**Voter Participation in Presidential Elections, 1880–2004**

SOURCES: Figures for 1880 to 1916 in Robert E. Lane, *Political Life* (New York: Free Press, 1965), p. 20. Reprinted with permission of Macmillan Publishing Co., Inc., from *Political Life* by Robert E. Lane. Copyright 1959 by The Free Press. Figures for 1920 to 1948 in *Statistical Abstract of the United States: 1969,* p. 368. Data for 1952 to 1980 from *Statistical Abstract of the United States: 1984,* p. 262. Data for 1984 from *Washington Post,* January 8, 1985, p. A3. Data for 1988 from *New York Times,* November 13, 1988, p. 32. Data for 1992 provided by the Committee for the Study of the American Electorate, Washington, D.C. Data for 1996 from U.S. Bureau of the Census, *Statistical Abstract of the United States: 1999,* p. 301. Data for 2000 from U.S. Bureau of the Census, *Statistical Abstract of the United States: 2003,* p. 270. Data for 2004 from the Census Bureau.

TABLE 11-1

**Voter Participation in Other Countries**

| Nation | Election Year | Turnout (%) |
|---|---|---|
| Australia* | 2004 | 94 |
| Belgium* | 2003 | 96 |
| Canada | 2006 | 65 |
| France | 2002 | 60 |
| Germany | 2005 | 78 |
| Great Britain | 2005 | 61 |
| Greece | 2004 | 76 |
| India | 2004 | 58 |
| Ireland | 2002 | 63 |
| Netherlands | 2003 | 80 |
| New Zealand† | 2005 | 62 |
| Portugal | 2005 | 64 |
| Russia | 2004 | 64 |
| Switzerland | 2003 | 45 |

*Compulsory registration and voting.
†Compulsory registration.
NOTE: Turnout for Russia is for the country's presidential election. Data for all other countries are for elections for the national legislature.
SOURCES: International Foundation for Election Systems; International Institute for Democracy and Electoral Assistance.

cation said they voted.[6] Education seems to cause the greatest variation in voter turnout of all the factors.[7]

Income, education, social class, and occupation are closely related; the higher the level in all these categories, the more likely a person is to vote. (See Table 11-2.)

Jews vote more than Catholics, and Catholics vote more than Protestants. Churchgoers are more likely to vote than nonchurchgoers, a phenomenon perhaps associated with the willingness of the churchgoer to participate in organized activity and the inclination of some religious groups to get involved in politics. African Americans vote less often than whites—but historically black voters in the South were often prevented from voting by legal subterfuge, violence, or intimidation. As was noted in Chapter 5, the number of black registered voters in the South increased dramatically after passage of the Voting Rights Act of 1965.

**Voter Attitudes** Voter turnout does vary with demographic and social differences, but other research has identified additional factors that seem to influence participation at the polls. This research has focused on voter attitudes.

For example, a strong Democrat or a rock-ribbed Republican is more likely to get out and vote than a citizen whose party loyalties are casual. The higher the *intensity of partisan preference,* therefore, the more likely it is that the person will vote. Similarly, the *degree of interest* that people have in the campaign and their *concern over the election outcome* appear to be related to whether they vote. If people think the election is close, they are more likely to vote because they may believe that their votes will count. And if people think they can understand and influence politics, they are more likely to vote than are those who regard politics and government as distant and complicated. The greater a person's *sense of political*

Comparing Governments

## IN AUSTRALIA, NOT VOTING CAN MEAN JAIL TIME

In the United States people are free to vote or not, as they wish. But in Australia, voting is compulsory. Under the law, citizens must pay a $10 fine if they fail to vote—or go to jail if they refuse to pay up. Voter registration is compulsory for everyone over the age of 18.

Australia's law has produced turnout levels above 95 percent, compared with 51 percent in the November 2000 U.S. presidential election and England's 60 percent in June 2001. Several other countries have compulsory voting laws—with a wide range of actual enforcement.

Eight Australians were jailed after the 1998 general election for refusing to vote. Another 6,246 were summoned to court and had assets seized as a forced payment of the fine—or escaped imprisonment when they came across a sympathetic judge. More than 40,000 simply ponied up $10 and were done with it.

A retired Australian diplomat and civil servant, Bill Smithies, is preparing to go to jail. Smithies has not voted in nearly 20 years, so prison surely beckons. Opposed to Australia's compulsory voting law, Smithies, 66, is willing to spend a few days behind bars rather than pay a $10 fine for failing to vote. Smithies and others assert that the law making Australian citizens vote is wrong.

Jail time is most likely a result of not paying the fines given to nonvoters, and jail times are usually short. However, the idea of going to jail—even briefly—is enough to compel the majority to vote.

According to Special Minister of State Eric Abetz, who oversees elections, voting is a civic duty, like paying taxes, and only full participation can ensure a chosen government is legitimate.

—Adapted from the *Washington Post*, November 4, 2001

*effectiveness,* in other words, the greater the chance that he or she will vote. Americans, moreover, are indoctrinated with the importance of voting long before they are old enough to do so. Thus the voter's *sense of civic duty* also bears on whether he or she goes to the polls.[8]

### The Nonvoter

Some 35 to 45 percent or more of Americans do not vote in presidential elections. Who are they? Why don't they vote? The preceding discussion indicated that the nonvoter is more likely to be less educated, rural, nonwhite, very young or very old, a person "whose emotional investment in politics . . . is on the average much less than that of the voter."[9] Although a rough portrait of the nonvoter can be sketched in these terms, the picture does not explain why he or she does not vote.

As noted earlier, about 58.3 percent of the voting-age population—or 122.3 million people—voted in the 2004 election. However, millions of Americans of voting age did not. After the 2004 election, the Census Bureau released the following breakdown of nonvoters and the reasons they gave for not voting:

- 32.4 million were not registered
- 19.9 percent were too busy, had to work, or had problems getting child care
- 15.4 percent were sick or disabled
- 10.7 percent did not care or were not interested
- 9.9 percent did not like the candidates
- 9.0 percent were out of town

TABLE 11-2

**Voter Turnout by Group and Region, 2004**

| Voting Group | Percentage Voting |
|---|---|
| College graduate | 77.5 |
| 65–74 years and older | 73.3 |
| 45–64 years old | 68.7 |
| Midwest | 67.8 |
| 1–3 years college | 68.9 |
| Female | 65.4 |
| White | 65.4 |
| Northeast | 64.1 |
| 35–44 years old | 64 |
| West | 64 |
| Male | 62.1 |
| South | 61 |
| African American | 60 |
| High school graduate | 56.4 |
| 25–34 years old | 55.7 |
| Unemployed | 51.4 |
| Hispanic | 47.2 |
| 18–24 years old | 46.7 |
| Some high school education | 39.5 |

SOURCE: U.S. Bureau of the Census, *Voting and Registration in the Election of November 2004.*

*The American Past*

## SUSAN B. ANTHONY AND THE BATTLE FOR WOMEN'S SUFFRAGE

In 1920, the nineteenth amendment to the Constitution guaranteed women the right to vote. But the struggle for women's suffrage had begun in 1848. For many years, the leader of that battle was Susan B. Anthony. The following account tells of her attempt to influence the Republican convention of 1880 to recognize the rights of women in the party's platform. Anthony described her plans in a letter to one of her followers:

> "I want the rousingest rallying cry ever put on paper—first, to call women by the thousand to Chicago; and second, to get every one who can not go there to send a postal card to the mass convention, saying she wants the Republicans to put [an] Amendment pledge in their platform. Don't you see that if we could have a mass meeting of 2,000 or 3,000 earnest women, June 2, and then receive 10,000 postals from women all over the country, what a tremendous influence we could bring to bear on the Republican convention, June 3? We can get Farwell Hall for $40 a day, and I think would do well to engage it for the 2d and 3d, then we could make it our headquarters—sleep in it even, if we couldn't get any other places. . . ."

The mass meeting opened in Farwell Hall, Chicago, June 1, the day before the Republican convention, with delegates from twenty-six states, and continued in session three days. . . . The audience numbered 3,000 and the enthusiasm was unprecedented in all the records of this movement. . . .

The Chicago press gave very satisfactory reports of this meeting, but the *Springfield Republic* was vulgar and abusive, called the ladies "withered beldames," "cats on the back roof," and advised them to "go home and attend to their children, if they had any, and if not, to engage in that same occupation as soon as they could regularly do so."

The charge being so often made that the leaders of the suffrage movement were a lot of old maids and childless wives, Miss Anthony prepared a list showing that sixteen of the most prominent were the mothers of sixty-six children. Of the pioneers she herself was the only one who never married.

—Ida Husted Harper, *The Life and Work of Susan B. Anthony*

6.8 percent cited registration problems

2.1 percent had no transportation

17.8 percent mentioned a variety of other reasons.[10]

Even taking into account the fact that some people had good reasons for not voting, a nation with more than 100 million citizens who do not turn out in a presidential election would seem to fall somewhat short of the idealized model of popular democracy. But some political scientists believe that what might work in a simple, agrarian society does not apply in a modern, highly industrialized society like the United States today.[11] The harassed parent with five young children may well find it difficult to get to the polls on Election Day. Most people spend more time worrying about money, sex, illness, crime, the high cost of living, automobile repairs, and a host of other things than they do worrying about politics.

Al Gore and Joe Lieberman wave to supporters at a rally in 2000.

© AP/Wide World Photos

The MTV bus toured college campuses across the nation in an effort to register first-time voters.

So if we ask whether enough people vote in the United States, we must also ask: How much is enough? A turnout of 50 to 60 percent in a presidential election may not meet the classic standards of democracy, but it may be the best that can be expected in the United States today. In any event, it is the reality.

One overall pattern that emerges from all the data about the voter and the nonvoter in the United States is that those who are more advantageously situated in the social system vote more than the "have-nots," or less advantaged. If members of all social groups in the United States voted in equal proportions, candidates might have to offer programs that appealed more to the disadvantaged groups, many of whose members do not now go to the polls. In short, if everybody voted, the candidates and policies of the American political system might be somewhat different from what they are today.

## How the Voter Decides

We have an idea who votes and who does not. The next question is: Why do people vote the way they do? How people make up their minds to vote for one candidate instead of another is obviously of great interest to politicians, campaign managers, advertising executives, and pollsters. But the question also has much broader implications for all citizens and for democratic government; the kind of society in which we live depends in part on whether voters flip a coin in the voting booth or choose on a somewhat more rational basis—satisfaction or dissatisfaction with the incumbent administration, for example.

Although American voters have been extensively analyzed, we still do not know precisely why they behave the way they do. We do not know which of many factors ultimately will cause a person to stay home or to vote for one candidate or party instead of another. To say, for example, that many Catholics are Democrats does not mean a person is a Democrat because he or she is a Catholic. And, although party loyalty appears to be related to voting habits, we do not know, for example, that a Kansas farmer votes Republican *because* he identifies with the Republican Party. Psychologists know that it is extremely difficult to judge people's motives from their behavior; even asking voters to explain their actions may not produce satisfactory answers.

So there are limits to the ability of political scientists to interpret the behavior of voters. Even allowing for these limits, however, a great deal has been learned about voting habits in recent decades.

Two basic approaches have been followed in studying how the voters decide:

1. *The sociological method.* This approach focuses on the social and economic background of the voters—their income, class, ethnic group, education, and similar factors—and attempts to relate these factors to how they vote.
2. *The psychological method.* This approach attempts to go beyond socioeconomic factors and find out what is going on inside the minds of the voters, to measure their perceptions of parties, candidates, and issues. This second approach is based on the premise that how the voter responds depends less on static factors, such as social class, than on dynamic changing factors of issues and politics. In short, voting behavior may change as the issues and candidates change.

© 2003 AP/Wide World Photos

## TABLE 11-3

**Votes by Groups in Presidential Elections, 1960–2004**

| | 1964 | | 1968 | | | 1972 | | 1976* | | | 1980 | | | |
|---|---|---|---|---|---|---|---|---|---|---|---|---|---|---|
| | Dem. | Rep. | Dem. | Rep. | Wallace | Dem. | Rep. | Dem. | Rep. | McCarthy | Dem. | Rep. | Anderson | Other |
| National | 61.3% | 38.7% | 43% | 43.4% | 13.6% | 38% | 62% | 50% | 48% | 1% | 41% | 50.8% | 6.6% | 1.4% |
| Men | 60 | 40 | 41 | 43 | 16 | 37 | 63 | 53 | 45 | 1 | 38 | 53 | 7 | 2 |
| Women | 62 | 38 | 45 | 43 | 12 | 38 | 62 | 48 | 51 | † | 44 | 49 | 6 | 1 |
| White | 59 | 41 | 38 | 47 | 15 | 32 | 68 | 46 | 52 | 1 | 36 | 56 | 7 | 1 |
| Nonwhite | 94 | 6 | 85 | 12 | 3 | 87 | 13 | 85 | 15 | † | 86 | 10 | 2 | 2 |
| College education | 52 | 48 | 37 | 54 | 9 | 37 | 63 | 42 | 55 | 2 | 35 | 53 | 10 | 2 |
| High school education | 62 | 38 | 42 | 43 | 15 | 34 | 66 | 54 | 46 | † | 43 | 51 | 5 | 1 |
| Grade school education | 66 | 34 | 52 | 33 | 15 | 49 | 51 | 58 | 41 | 1 | 54 | 42 | 3 | 1 |
| Professional and business people | 54 | 46 | 34 | 56 | 10 | 31 | 69 | 42 | 56 | 1 | 33 | 55 | 10 | 2 |
| White-collar workers | 57 | 43 | 41 | 47 | 12 | 36 | 64 | 50 | 48 | 2 | ‡ | ‡‡ | ‡ | ‡ |
| Manual workers | 71 | 29 | 50 | 35 | 15 | 43 | 57 | 58 | 41 | 1 | 48 | 46 | 5 | 1 |
| Union members | 73 | 27 | 56 | 29 | 15 | 46 | 54 | 63 | 36 | 1 | 50 | 43 | 5 | 2 |
| Farmers | 53 | 47 | 29 | 51 | 20 | ‡ | ‡ | ‡ | ‡ | ‡ | 31 | 61 | 7 | 1 |
| Under 30 | 64 | 36 | 47 | 38 | 15 | 48 | 52 | 53 | 45 | 1 | 47 | 41 | 11 | 1 |
| 30–49 years | 63 | 37 | 44 | 41 | 15 | 33 | 67 | 48 | 49 | 2 | 38 | 52 | 8 | 2 |
| Over 49 | 59 | 41 | 41 | 47 | 12 | 36 | 64 | 52 | 48 | † | 41 | 54 | 4 | 1 |
| Protestants | 55 | 45 | 35 | 49 | 16 | 30 | 70 | 46 | 53 | † | 39 | 547 | 6 | 1 |
| Catholics | 76 | 24 | 59 | 33 | 8 | 48 | 52 | 57 | 42 | 1 | 46 | 4 | 6 | 1 |
| Republicans | 20 | 80 | 9 | 86 | 14 | 5 | 95 | 9 | 91 | † | 8 | 86 | 5 | 1 |
| Democrats | 87 | 13 | 74 | 12 | 14 | 67 | 33 | 82 | 18 | † | 69 | 26 | 4 | 1 |
| Independents | 56 | 44 | 31 | 44 | 25 | 31 | 69 | 38 | 57 | 4 | 29 | 55 | 14 | 2 |

*Figures for some groups do not add to 100 percent because of the vote for other minor-party candidates.
†Less than 1 percent.
‡Not available.

The difference between these two approaches is not as great as it might seem at first glance: How the voters currently perceive the issues may well be shaped by their social and economic backgrounds. The social psychologists who followed the second approach beginning in the 1950s built on the foundations laid by the political sociologists in the 1940s.

## The Sociological Factors

In the first of two classic voter studies, 600 residents of Erie County, Ohio, were interviewed during the 1940 presidential election.[12] The study found a pattern that has been repeated over and over in American national elections. Wealthier people usually voted Republican, and poorer people voted Democratic: "Different social characteristics, different votes."[13]

But the voter is a member of several groups simultaneously. Sometimes the claims of one group conflict with those of another. For example, the study concluded that rich people were more likely to vote Republican, Catholics were more likely to vote Democratic. What of wealthy Catholics? Such people are said to be "cross-pressured" because their social affiliations are pulling them in opposite directions. The study found that these voters were more likely than others to delay their decision and change their minds during a campaign. In 1948 the same research method was used in a study of how 1,000 voters in Elmira, New York, made up their minds during the Truman-Dewey campaign.[14] This more detailed study also concluded that social class influenced voting behavior.

Today, however, many of the more recent voter analyses, whether following the sociological or the psychological approach, are based on national rather than local poll data. From these various studies, it is possible to draw a picture of the American voter in terms of his or her social class and other sociological factors. (Table 11-3 provides a breakdown of how different groups have voted in presidential elections.)

| 1984 | | 1988 | | 1992 | | | 1996 | | | 2000 | | | 2004 | |
|---|---|---|---|---|---|---|---|---|---|---|---|---|---|---|
| Dem. | Rep. | Dem. | Rep. | Dem. | Rep. | Perot | Dem. | Rep. | Perot | Dem. | Rep. | Nader | Dem. | Rep. |
| 41% | 59% | 46% | 54% | 43.2% | 37.8% | 19.0% | 50.0% | 41.0% | 9.0% | 48.4% | 47.9% | 2.7% | 48.5% | 51.5% |
| 36 | 64 | 44 | 56 | 41 | 37 | 22 | 45 | 44 | 11 | 45 | 52 | 3 | 44 | 56 |
| 45 | 55 | 48 | 52 | 46 | 38 | 16 | 54 | 39 | 7 | 53 | 45 | 2 | 52 | 48 |
| 34 | 66 | 41 | 59 | 39 | 41 | 20 | 46 | 45 | 9 | 43 | 55 | 3 | 44 | 56 |
| 87 | 13 | 82 | 18 | 77 | 11 | 12 | 82 | 12 | 6 | 87 | 9 | 4 | 83 | 17 |
| 39 | 61 | 43 | 57 | 43 | 40 | 17 | 47 | 45 | 8 | 49 | 49 | 2 | 48 | 52 |
| 43 | 57 | 46 | 54 | 40 | 38 | 22 | 52 | 34 | 14 | 52 | 46 | 2 | 54 | 46 |
| 51 | 49 | 56 | 44 | 56 | 28 | 16 | 58 | 27 | 15 | 55 | 42 | 3 | 69 | 31 |
| 34 | 66 | ‡ | ‡ | ‡ | ‡ | ‡ | ‡ | ‡ | ‡ | ‡ | ‡ | ‡ | ‡ | ‡ |
| 47 | 53 | ‡ | ‡ | ‡ | ‡ | ‡ | ‡ | ‡ | ‡ | ‡ | ‡ | ‡ | ‡ | ‡ |
| 46 | 54 | ‡ | ‡ | ‡ | ‡ | ‡ | ‡ | ‡ | ‡ | ‡ | ‡ | ‡ | ‡ | ‡ |
| 52 | 48 | ‡ | ‡ | ‡ | ‡ | ‡ | ‡ | ‡ | ‡ | ‡ | ‡ | ‡ | 67 | 33 |
| ‡ | ‡ | ‡ | ‡ | ‡ | ‡ | ‡ | ‡ | ‡ | ‡ | ‡ | ‡ | ‡ | ‡ | ‡ |
| 40 | 60 | 37 | 63 | 40 | 37 | 23 | 54 | 30 | 16 | 47 | 47 | 6 | 60 | 40 |
| 40 | 60 | 45 | 55 | 42 | 37 | 21 | 49 | 41 | 10 | 45 | 47 | 6 | 43 | 57 |
| 41 | 59 | 49 | 51 | 46 | 39 | 15 | 50 | 45 | 5 | 53 | 45 | 2 | 50 | 50 |
| 39 | 61 | 36 | 64 | 41 | 41 | 18 | 44 | 50 | 6 | 42 | 55 | 3 | 38 | 62 |
| 39 | 61 | 51 | 49 | 47 | 35 | 18 | 55 | 35 | 10 | 52 | 46 | 2 | 52 | 48 |
| 4 | 96 | 7 | 93 | 7 | 77 | 16 | 10 | 85 | 5 | 7 | 92 | 1 | 5 | 95 |
| 79 | 21 | 85 | 15 | 82 | 8 | 10 | 90 | 6 | 4 | 89 | 10 | 2 | 93 | 7 |
| 33 | 67 | 43 | 57 | 39 | 30 | 31 | 48 | 33 | 19 | 44 | 49 | 7 | 52 | 48 |

SOURCE: Data provided by the Gallup poll.

**Social Class, Income, and Occupation** Upper-class and middle-class voters are more likely to vote Republican than are voters of lower economic and social status, who tend to be Democrats. The vote of union members has usually gone Democratic.

Professional and business people have been more likely to support Republicans than Democrats. For example, with the exception of 1964—when Republicans in droves deserted Goldwater for Johnson—business and professional people voted heavily Republican in the seven elections from 1960 to 1984. (See Table 11-3.) Among people in the highest income brackets, Republican candidates usually draw more votes than do Democrats. In a 1996 survey, for example, the one income group where Bob Dole had a substantial lead over Bill Clinton was among voters with an annual family income of $75,000 or more.

**Education** In 1996 Bill Clinton received 47 percent of the votes of college graduates, compared with 45 percent voting for Dole. More often, however, college graduates have tended to vote for Republicans rather than Democrats. A majority of college-educated voters were in the ranks of the GOP during the elections of Kennedy, Nixon, and Reagan, and during Vice President George Bush's 1988 race for the presidency, and his son's two presidential victories in 2000 and 2004. Although Nixon averaged 43.4 percent of the popular vote in 1968, he received 54 percent of the votes of college graduates; by contrast, only 33 percent of voters with a grade school education voted for Nixon. (See Table 11-3.) In 1996, Clinton, who received 49.2 percent of the total popular vote, was supported by 58 percent of voters with a grade school education.

**Religion and Ethnic Background** In a 1992 survey, 59.5 percent of Jews and 41.8 percent of Catholics, but only 36 percent of Protestants, said they considered themselves Democrats.[15] In 1960, Jews, Catholics, and Protestants voted 81, 78, and 38 percent, respectively, for

Kennedy. Because Kennedy was the first Roman Catholic to be elected president, the 1960 election was carefully analyzed to assess the effect of his religion on the result. The Michigan Survey Research Center concluded that Kennedy won a "bonus" from Catholics of 4.3 percent of the two-party vote (2.9 million votes) but lost 6.5 percent (4.4 million votes) from Protestant Democrats and independents. His religion cost him a net loss of 2.2 percent, or 1.5 million popular votes.[16] On the other hand, the heavy Catholic vote in big northern industrial states probably helped him win in the electoral college.[17] It cannot be demonstrated, however, that Kennedy won because he was a Catholic.

Various studies have shown that voters of Irish, Italian, Polish, East European, and Slavic descent often favor Democrats, although President Reagan made strong gains among several of these groups in 1980 and 1984. Black Americans, who generally had voted Republican until the New Deal, shifted away from the party of Lincoln to give approximately 94 percent of their votes to the Democrats in 1964. And in the next nine presidential elections from 1968 to 2000, the support among nonwhites for the Democratic presidential nominee never dropped below 77 percent. In 2004, Kerry, the Democratic presidential nominee, received 83 percent of the vote from African Americans.[18]

**Primary Groups** In addition to conventional social groups, voters are influenced by personal contacts with much smaller "primary" groups, such as families, coworkers, and friends. Sometimes these influences may change a voter's mind. However, because people of similar social background tend to associate with one another, primary groups often merely reinforce the political views that the voter already holds.

**Geography** In general, the Democrats still draw their strength from the big cities of the North and East. Voters in rural areas in the North are more likely to be Republicans. Until the 1960s, Democrats normally ran strongly in the South. But the Democrats can no longer count on the South in presidential contests. In 1972, for example, President Nixon polled 71 percent of the popular vote in the South, and for the first time since Reconstruction, the Republican presidential ticket carried all 11 states of the Old Confederacy. In 1976 the Democratic candidate, Jimmy Carter, was a former governor of the Deep South state of Georgia, and he carried every southern state except Virginia. But in 1980 Republican Ronald Reagan polled 51 percent of the popular vote in the South and won 10 southern states. And in 1984, Reagan won every state in the South by a decisive margin; he also polled 62.4 percent of the popular vote in the region.[19] This trend continued when the first President Bush, at the time vice president, won every southern state in 1988 and polled 58.7 percent of the vote in the South.

In 1992 the Democrats nominated a pair of southerners for president and vice president, and this time the presidential race in the South was much closer. The Clinton-Gore Democratic ticket received 41.5 percent of the popular vote in the region, while Bush and Quayle won 42.7 percent for the Republicans, and Ross Perot and James B. Stockdale polled 15.8 percent. Clinton carried four states in the South in 1992; the remaining seven went to Bush. Two years later, in the midterm elections of 1994, the Republican Party made big gains in southern congressional races. For the first time since Reconstruction, Republican candidates for the House of Representatives decisively outpolled their Democratic opponents in the popular vote in the South. In 2000, both major parties nominated a candidate from a southern state to head their presidential ticket; and the Republican, George W. Bush, then the governor of Texas, carried all 11 of the states in the South. President Bush also carried all 11 southern states in 2004.

The suburbs, originally Republican strongholds after the Second World War, are today more a mixture of Democrats and Republicans. Democratic strength has grown in suburbia as lower- and middle-class whites and many blacks have left the cities, but Republicans still dominate some suburban areas.

**Sex** Until 1980, in most presidential elections, whether voters were men or women did not seem to have a significant influence on how they voted.[20] In 1980, however, it was different. The election that year provided the most striking example of a difference in voting behavior between men and women since voter polls began in the 1930s. In 1980 men voted for Ronald Reagan rather than Jimmy Carter by a dramatic margin of 15 percentage points or more. By contrast, women—perhaps because they perceived Reagan as being more likely to engage in a military adventure than Carter—split their votes more evenly between the two candidates.[21] (Virtually all surveys on the subject have shown that women are substantially less likely than men to favor military action.[22])

At the beginning of 1984, some Republican electoral strategists were worried that this "gender gap" might seriously hamper President Reagan in his bid for reelection. But when Reagan won his sweeping victory in November 1984, women voters as well as men gave him a solid reelection margin. There was still a substantial difference in the voting preferences of men and women in 1984, however. Reagan won the votes of 64 percent of the men, compared with 55 percent of women. In 1996 there again was a gender gap in the vote for president. The polls indicated that Clinton and Dole ran almost even among male voters. Among women who voted, by contrast, Clinton's lead was sizable—54 percent to 39 percent. (See Table 11-3.) The 1980, 1984, and 1996 elections all suggested that men and women may vote differently—when the images and issue positions of the candidates coincide with differences in political attitudes between men and women.

In 2000 and 2004, once again there was a gender gap. In 2004, for example, the democractic nominee, John Kerry, led among women voters, 52 percent to 48 percent. Among male voters, President Bush won decisively, 56 percent to 44 percent. (See Table 11-3.)

**Age** In most national elections since 1960, younger voters were more likely to vote Democratic than Republican. Older voters seemed to find the GOP attractive. From 1960 to 1980, the Democrats consistently got a higher percentage of the vote from those under age 30 than from voters 50 and older. In 1984, however, this pattern changed. Ronald Reagan, the oldest person ever to serve as president, showed surprising strength among the nation's youngest voters. Reagan, the Republican, ran as strongly among voters under 30 (60 percent) as among the older age groups. After his election in 1992 Bill Clinton became America's third-youngest president. Clinton led George Bush by 47 percent to 31 percent among voters under 25, but his lead was only 3 percent among voters in their fifties.[23]

In the 1996 presidential election, the Dole campaign was concerned about their candidate's age—at 73, Bob Dole was the oldest major-party nominee to seek a first term in the White House. Dole's advisers worried about whether Dole's age would diminish his appeal to the voters, and especially to younger voters. And Dole did run far behind Clinton among voters under 30; Clinton received 53 percent of those votes, to 34 percent for Dole.[24] In 2004, John Kerry also won the youth vote, with support from 60 percent of voters under 30. (See Table 11-3.)

## The Psychological Factors

It would be wrong to give too much weight to sociological factors in determining how voters behave. To do so would be to ignore the very important question of people's changing attitudes toward politics. After the Second World War, a group of scholars at the University of Michigan conducted new studies of voting behavior, concentrating on the psychology of voting—on how individuals perceive and evaluate politics.

The Michigan researchers noted that social characteristics of the population change only slowly over a period of time. The percentage of Catholics or Jews in the United States does not change overnight, for example. Yet the electorate may behave very differently from one election to the next. Long-term factors such as social class did not seem adequate to explain such sudden shifts; candidates and issues, which change in the short term, provided a more likely explanation: "It seemed clear that the key to the finer dynamics of political behavior lay in the reactions of the electorate to these changes in the political scene."[25]

In measuring voter attitudes, the Michigan electoral analysts identified three powerful factors: *party identification, candidates,* and *issues.*

**Party Identification** Many Americans display persistent loyalties to the Democratic or Republican Party. Voters may form an attachment to one party or the other and often do not change. Most national elections have taken place within the framework of this basic division in the electorate. However, in 1992, many voters, dissatisfied with the candidates and platforms of the major parties, turned their loyalties to independent candidate Ross Perot.

From the late 1930s through the 1990s, substantially more people in the United States identified themselves as Democrats than as Republicans. (See Table 11-4.) In fact, in 1964, 1976, and 1980, Democrats outnumbered Republicans by more than 2 to 1. By 1984 this Democratic advantage in party identification had narrowed considerably. By 1999, 34 percent of the electorate said they were Democrats, compared with 28 percent for Republicans. And a very large group—38 percent—called themselves independents.

In 2006, party identification in the United States stood at 35 percent Democrats, 32 percent Republicans, and 33 percent independents. (See Table 11-4.)

TABLE 11-4

**Party Identification among the American Electorate, 1940–2006**

| | Percentage of Voters Identifying Themselves as: | | |
|---|---|---|---|
| Year | Democrats | Republicans | Independents |
| 1940 | 42% | 38% | 20% |
| 1950 | 45 | 33 | 22 |
| 1960 | 47 | 30 | 23 |
| 1964 | 53 | 25 | 22 |
| 1966 | 48 | 27 | 25 |
| 1968 | 46 | 27 | 27 |
| 1970 | 45 | 29 | 26 |
| 1972 | 43 | 28 | 29 |
| 1974 | 44 | 23 | 33 |
| 1976 | 46 | 22 | 32 |
| 1980 | 47 | 23 | 30 |
| 1984 | 41 | 29 | 30 |
| 1986 | 40 | 30 | 30 |
| 1988 | 43 | 29 | 28 |
| 1990 | 40 | 32 | 28 |
| 1992 | 38 | 29 | 33 |
| 1994 | 39 | 28 | 33 |
| 1996 | 35 | 30 | 35 |
| 1998 | 34 | 29 | 37 |
| 1999 | 34 | 28 | 38 |
| 2004 | 33 | 29 | 38* |
| 2006 | 35 | 32 | 33 |

*Includes "Other" and "Don't Know."

SOURCE: Data for 1940–1999 provided by the Gallup poll; data for 2004 and 2006 from The Pew Research Center for the People and the Press, July 26, 2004, and September 27, 2006, online at <http://www.people-press.org>.

Democratic presidential candidate John Kerry greets veterans after a campaign speech in Minnesota.



Although party identification remains a key factor in American politics, it may be growing somewhat less important. As far back as the 1972 presidential election, according to the University of Michigan election analysts, "issues were at least equally as important as party identification" as an explanation of the vote.[26] Moreover, as shown in Table 11-4, the number of people who identified with either of the two major parties dropped from 80 percent in 1940 to 67 percent in 2006, as the number of independents rose from 20 to 33 percent. And in most elections since the Second World War, there also has been extensive ticket-splitting by many voters. As explained in Chapter 10, a ticket-splitter is a voter who votes for candidates of more than one party in the same election. For example, a person may vote for a Republican presidential candidate and a Democratic senator or representative. In 1988 the first President Bush won by a sizable margin despite the Democratic advantage in party identification.

**The Candidates** Between 1952 and 1992 the GOP won seven of the 11 presidential elections that were held. How was this possible, given the higher percentage of those who identified at that time with the Democratic Party?

The answer is that although people may identify with a party, and frequently vote for its candidates, they do not always vote that way. Short-term factors, such as changes in candidates or issues, may cause enough voters to switch from the party they normally favor to have a decisive effect on the outcome of the election. In 1952 and 1956 Dwight Eisenhower, the Republican candidate, easily defeated Adlai Stevenson, a Democrat. Eisenhower's personal appeal, his smile, his image as an outstanding military hero of the Second World War, and—in the second election—his popularity as president all helped to offset normal party loyalties.

Clearly, the personal impression a candidate makes on the voters may have a powerful influence on the election returns. Thus, dour Calvin Coolidge looked like he had been "weaned on a pickle." Thomas E. Dewey, in the classic phrase of Alice Roosevelt Longworth, resembled "the bridegroom on a wedding cake." Richard Nixon in 1968 remained "Tricky Dick" to many strong Democratic partisans. Hubert Humphrey "talked too much." Gerald Ford struck many voters as "well-meaning but dull." Jimmy Carter was often seen as "decent but ineffective." Ronald Reagan, particularly during his highly successful 1984 reelection campaign, was a "leader who inspired confidence" for many voters. In 1988 George H. W. Bush, for a time at least, had difficulty overcoming his image as a rich "Ivy League" patrician who was ill at ease among the common folk.

In 1992 and 1996, Bill Clinton, not yet tarred by scandal, was seen favorably by many voters as "an ordinary guy" who wolfed donuts and enjoyed mingling with the people. In 1996 Bob Dole was often viewed as a solid, capable legislator, but also by some as dull, "too old," and painfully laconic. And in the 2000 campaign, some voters perceived Al Gore as "stiff" and "wooden." George W. Bush, by contrast, was seen as more at ease with rank-and-file voters, but was ridiculed on late-night television for his occasional tangled syntax and mispronounced words. And in 2004, John Kerry, the Democratic presidential nominee, encountered some of the same problems in connecting with the voters that the first President Bush had faced in 1988. Kerry had to work hard during the primaries and in the general election campaign to convince voters that he was not a New England patrician unable to understand the problems of ordinary Americans. Appearance, personality, and popularity of the candidates obviously bear some relation to the number of votes they receive.

2000—the morning after: Headlines on four editions of the *Chicago Sun-Times* on November 8, 2000, reflect the confused result of that election.

**The Issues** Two central questions should be asked about the role issues play in a political campaign: Do voters vote according to their opinions about public issues? If so, do their policy preferences later affect the direction of the government? Both points will be discussed later in this chapter. For now, it is enough to note that a voter must be aware of the existence of an issue and must have an opinion about it if he or she is to be directly motivated by it.*

If an issue is to have a direct effect on an individual's voting behavior, a voter must not only recognize the issue and have a minimum degree of feeling about it, but he or she also must come to think that one candidate or the other is closer to his or her own position. Research shows, however, that human beings are sometimes highly selective in accepting political messages. If they do not happen to be tuned in to the proper "wavelength," the messages may be received only as so much noise. Increasing the volume may only make the voter flick the "off" switch. Like mechanisms that control the body's blood pressure and temperature, this mental fuse "seems to protect the individual citizen from too strenuous an overload of incoming information."[27] In some elections, even among voters who do hold opinions on public issues, only 40 to 60 percent can perceive differences between the parties on those issues.[28]

On certain major issues, or on issues that affect them directly, the voters do seem to "tune in" and form definite party preferences. It was noted in Chapter 10 that, in some years, voters have tended to associate prosperity with Democrats. However, some voters have thought that Republicans were more likely to keep the peace.

When one group of voters is directly affected by a political issue, its members may listen carefully to the political debate. For example, in 1964 Barry Goldwater voted against the first major civil rights bill since Reconstruction. Partly because black voters seemed to know in general where Goldwater stood on civil rights, they turned out in unprecedented numbers to vote for his Democratic opponent, Lyndon Johnson.

Moreover, issues may be more important in some elections than in others. Research by Norman H. Nie, Sidney Verba, and John R. Petrocik suggests that substantial "issue voting" occurred during the elections of 1964, 1968, and 1972. Issues such as the Vietnam War, race, and several controversial social issues sharply divided the voters during those election years.[29] In 1980, however, the public's evaluation of the candidates played a very important role.[30]

In 1996, one survey found 21 percent of those polled said that the "economy/jobs" was one of the issues that mattered most in deciding how to vote. Among that sizable bloc of voters, 61 percent voted for Clinton, compared with 27 percent who supported Dole and 10 percent who voted for Perot. In addition, among the one-sixth of the voters who said that "Medicare, Social Security" was important in deciding how to vote, 67 percent voted for Clinton.[31]

## Retrospective Voting

The relative importance of candidates, issues, and party identification thus appears to vary from election year to election year. But in most elections another factor also seems to be at work: Many voters appear to make up their minds by looking back at what has happened under the country's current political leadership and making a rough judgment about their leaders' performance in office. Morris P. Fiorina and other political scientists have explored this concept of **retrospective voting.** Fiorina points out that citizens "typically have one comparatively hard bit of data: they know what life has

*Issues also may have an *indirect* effect on voters. For example, if a candidate takes a position pleasing to labor union leaders, the union leaders may work enthusiastically on a voter-registration drive among union members. That in turn may result in more votes for the candidate.

A Florida election official examines a ballot during a hand recount in the disputed 2000 presidential election.

been like during the incumbent's administration." He explains:

> They need *not* know the precise economic or foreign policies of the incumbent administration in order to see or feel the *results* of those policies. And is it not reasonable to base voting decisions on results as well as intentions? In order to ascertain whether the incumbents have performed poorly or well, citizens need only calculate the changes in their own welfare. If jobs have been lost in a recession, something is wrong. If sons have died in foreign rice paddies, something is wrong. If polluters foul food, water, or air, something is wrong. And to the extent that citizens vote on the basis of such judgments, elections do not signal the direction in which society should move so much as they convey an evaluation of where society has been. Rather than a prospective decision, the voting decision can be more of a retrospective decision.[32]

### Rational Choice

In addition to such factors as social class, income, party identification, and retrospective voting, some political scientists emphasize "rational choice"—the concept that individuals engage in political behavior, such as voting, to serve their own best interests.

For example, Fiorina has argued: "The central premise of the [rational choice] approach . . . is that behavior is purposive. Political behavior is not solely the product of psychological drives, socialization, or organizational norms. Rather individuals have goals they try to achieve, acting as rationally as their knowledge, resources, and the situation permit."[33]

## Voting Patterns

Although the act of voting represents an individual decision, the result of an election is a group decision. On Election Day as the sun moves westward across the continent's four time zones, the tides and patterns of electoral choice are already beginning to form. The polls have closed in the East as voters in California, elsewhere along the Pacific Coast, and in Hawaii are still casting their ballots.* The results from the first precincts in New England trickle in, then more, and in time, the decision takes shape and gains definition.

Sometimes the resulting picture is sharp, quickly seen, and its meaning clear; other times it is as blurred as an impressionist painting. Yet the trained eye analyzing the results of American elections can detect patterns and trends, interrelationships, currents, sectional nuances, and sometimes national meaning.

### Control

For national political parties, the prize is control of the presidency. But party success or failure is measured in terms of states won or lost. Broad voting patterns on the national level can easily be seen by comparing political maps in presidential years, such as those found inside the front and back covers of this book. Some political results are geographically dramatic—for example, Lyndon Johnson's 1964 landslide, in which the map is predominantly Democratic except for a cluster of states in the Deep South and Arizona. Ronald Reagan's strong electoral victory in 1984 also covered nearly every part of the map; the Democrats that year carried only one state, Walter Mondale's Minnesota, and the District of Columbia. By contrast, GOP bedrock strength in parts of the Midwest is illustrated by the maps of the elections of 1940, 1944, and 1948; in each case the Plains States are a Republican island in a Democratic sea.

In 2000, when the electorate was divided almost 50–50 between Al Gore, the Democrat, and George W. Bush, the Republican presidential nominee, there was a strong sectional pattern in the vote. The Democrats carried every state in the Northeast except New Hampshire and also showed strength in the midwestern states near the Great Lakes and in California, Washington, and Oregon on the West Coast. George W. Bush, by contrast, carried the southern states and the Plains States, and he also

*In the past, sometimes the major television networks projected the winner of a presidential race before the polls had closed in the West. In 1980 President Carter conceded while the polls were still open in California, Oregon, Washington, Alaska, and Hawaii.

won every state in the Rocky Mountains region except New Mexico.

## Coalitions

The broad outline of the national vote can be shown on a map, but much that is politically significant is less visible. Electoral victories are built not merely on simple geographic foundations; they also are formed by alliances of segments of the electorate and of interest groups, and by unorganized masses of voters who coalesce behind the winner. Politicians and political scientists are interested, therefore, in coalitions of voters.

Roosevelt's New Deal brought together a coalition of the South, the urban North, minority groups, and labor unions. Nixon's winning coalition in 1968 included part of the South, most of the Midwest, the West, whites, Protestants, businesspeople, and white-collar workers. Long-term trends in American politics can be traced by analyzing the makeup of winning and losing coalitions.

## Congress

In analyzing these alignments, however, congressional as well as presidential voting patterns should be considered. Although, as will be shown, the two are often linked, in most presidential elections since the New Deal days, the Democratic Party has been stronger in congressional elections than in contests for the presidency. During the period from 1932 to 1992, Republican presidential nominees were elected to seven four-year terms in the White House. Yet during that same period, the Republicans won full control of Congress for a total of only four years (1947–1948, and 1953–1954).

Then, in 1994, the Republican Party brought about a dramatic change in the balance of power in congressional elections, winning control of the House of Representatives for the first time in 40 years, and also winning a majority in the Senate. The GOP gained House seats in all major regions of the country in 1994, but its gains were particularly large in the South, the Midwest, and the West. The change in the South was especially striking. There, in 1994, for the first time since Reconstruction, more Republicans than Democrats were elected to the U.S. House of Representatives.[34] And the Republicans continued to win more southern seats than the Democrats in the next six congressional election years from 1996 through 2006.

© Archaubault/U.S. News & World Report

## Coattails

The entire House of Representatives and one-third of the Senate are elected every two years. In a presidential election year, the vote for president may affect the vote for Congress and for state and local offices, although there are signs that in recent years the effect of the presidential vote on contests for other offices may be lessening.

The relationship between the vote for president and for members of the House is illustrated in Figure 11-3. Some individual members of Congress are strong enough to withstand the tides of presidential voting, but at times a president has been able to carry into office with him a majority of his own party in the House.

The fortunes of presidential and senatorial candidates are also sometimes linked, especially in the more competitive two-party states. In the 20th century, however, four presidents were elected along with a Congress controlled by the opposition party in both the House and the Senate—Eisenhower in 1956, Nixon in 1968 and 1972, George H. W. Bush in 1988, and Clinton in 1996. (See Table 11-5.)

As Table 11-6 shows, the president's party often has lost strength in midterm congressional elections. In off-year elections since 1920, the party in power has lost an average of 28 seats in the House; in some of those election years, the party's losses were well above average, as in 1922 and 1938. Occasionally, the party in power may actually gain a few seats, as in 1934, or suffer only minor losses, as in 1962 and 1990. In 1998, the Democrats gained five seats in the House and held on to the same number of seats as before in the elections for the U.S. Senate. It was the first time since 1934 that the president's party gained seats in a midterm election.

In 2002, the president's party also did well at midterm. President George W. Bush's popularity was high, just a little over a year after the terrorist attacks on New York and Washington, D.C. In the November congressional elections, Bush's Republican Party also gained five seats in the House, and the GOP regained a majority in the Senate.

Still, the more common pattern has been for the incumbent president's party to lose ground in midterm congressional elections. Why the voters have normally reduced the strength of the party of the president they elected two years earlier has been the subject of considerable scholarly research. It is clear that substantially fewer voters turn out in off-years. (See Figure 11-1.) Angus Campbell has suggested that in presidential elections that stimulate a high degree of public interest, the normally "less involved peripheral voters" tend to turn out

FIGURE 11-3

**Presidential and House Vote, 1928–2004**

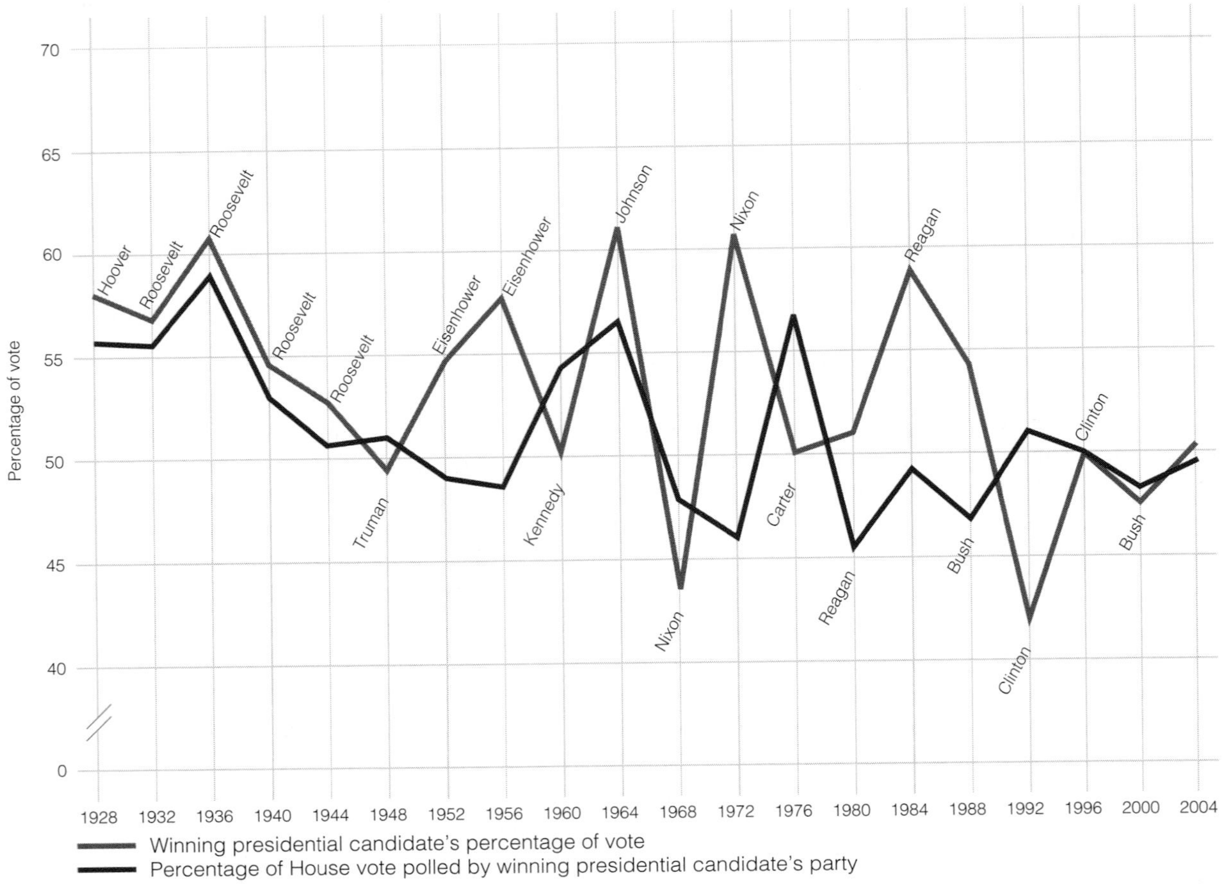


SOURCES: Congressional Quarterly, *Politics in America* (Washington, D.C.: Congressional Quarterly, May 1969), p. 41. Reprinted with permission. Data for 1972 and later from Congressional Quarterly, *Weekly Reports.* Data for 1996 House vote from *New York Times,* November 7, 1996, p. B3. Data for 2000 from U.S. Bureau of the Census, *Statistical Abstract of the United States: 2002,* p. 241.

and vote for the winner, as do many independents and people who switch from the opposing party. In the midterm elections, the peripheral voters tend to drop out, and many independents and party switchers move back to their usual positions. The result is a decline in the proportion of the vote for the president's party.[35] Barbara Hinckley, in an analysis of midterm House results from 1954 through 1966, found that the "midterm loss was concentrated" in marginal House districts where the president ran ahead of his party's winning congressional candidate in the preceding election.[36] In the ensuing off-year election, when the party's presidential nominee was not heading the ticket, these members of Congress were particularly vulnerable to defeat.

But why are the midterm losses of the president's party sometimes very large and sometimes quite small? Edward R. Tufte has suggested that such variations are related to two factors: "The vote cast in midterm congressional elections is a referendum on the performance of the president and his administration's management of the economy." The size of the midterm loss, Tufte added, "is substantially smaller if the President has a high level of approval, or if the economy is performing well, or both."[37]

Nevertheless, the kind of campaigns that individual House candidates run in local congressional districts also shape the midterm verdict. In 1982, near the bottom of a severe recession, President Reagan's approval rating was only 42 percent. Republican House candidates took great pains to demonstrate their independence from the Republican president's economic policies. In November, however, Republicans lost 26 seats in the House—the second-largest midterm loss for a president in his first term in the 20th century. But as Thomas Mann and Norman Ornstein have argued, "the losses would have been much deeper had national economic conditions alone determined the net shift in House seats."[38]

Although the "coattail" effect in presidential voting exists, it can be overstated. In most elections, many can-

## TABLE 11-5

### Major-Party Lineup: Winning Presidential Candidate and Congress, 1932–2004

| Election Year* | President and Party | | Congress | House | Senate | President's Popular Vote Percentage |
|---|---|---|---|---|---|---|
| | | | | D R | D R | |
| **1932** | Roosevelt | D | D | 313–117 | 59–36 | 57.4 |
| 1934 | Roosevelt | D | D | 322–103 | 69–25 | |
| **1936** | Roosevelt | D | D | 333–89 | 75–17 | 60.8 |
| 1938 | Roosevelt | D | D | 262–169 | 69–23 | |
| **1940** | Roosevelt | D | D | 267–162 | 66–28 | 54.7 |
| 1942 | Roosevelt | D | D | 222–209 | 57–38 | |
| **1944** | Roosevelt | D | D | 243–190 | 57–38 | 53.4 |
| 1946 | Truman | D | R | 188–246 | 45–51 | |
| **1948** | Truman | D | D | 263–171 | 54–42 | 49.6 |
| 1950 | Truman | D | D | 234–199 | 48–47 | |
| **1952** | Eisenhower | R | R | 213–221 | 47–48 | 55.1 |
| 1954 | Eisenhower | R | D | 232–203 | 48–47 | |
| **1956** | Eisenhower | R | D | 234–201 | 49–47 | 57.4 |
| 1958 | Eisenhower | R | D | 283–154 | 66–34 | |
| **1960** | Kennedy | D | D | 263–174 | 64–36 | 49.5 |
| 1962 | Kennedy | D | D | 259–176 | 68–32 | |
| **1964** | Johnson | D | D | 295–140 | 67–33 | 61.1 |
| 1966 | Johnson | D | D | 248–187 | 64–36 | |
| **1968** | Nixon | R | D | 243–192 | 58–42 | 43.4 |
| 1970 | Nixon | R | D | 255–180 | 54–44† | |
| **1972** | Nixon | R | D | 243–192 | 56–42 | 60.7 |
| 1974 | Ford | R | D | 291–144 | 60–37‡ | |
| **1976** | Carter | D | D | 292–143 | 61–38 | 50.0 |
| 1978 | Carter | D | D | 277–158 | 58–41 | |
| **1980** | Reagan | R | D/R | 243–192 | 46–53 | 50.8 |
| 1982 | Reagan | R | D/R | 269–166 | 46–54 | |
| **1984** | Reagan | R | D/R | 253–182 | 47–53 | 58.8 |
| 1986 | Reagan | R | D | 258–177 | 55–45 | |
| **1988** | Bush | R | D | 260–175 | 55–45 | 53.9 |
| 1990 | Bush | R | D | 267–167§ | 56–44 | |
| **1992** | Clinton | D | D | 259–175§ | 57–43 | 43.2 |
| 1994 | Clinton | D | R | 203–231§ | 47–53 | |
| **1996** | Clinton | D | R | 207–227§ | 45–55 | 49.2 |
| 1998 | Clinton | D | R | 211–223§ | 45–55 | |
| **2000** | Bush | R | R | 212–221** | 50–50†† | 47.9 |
| 2002 | Bush | R | R | 205–229§ | 48–51†† | |
| **2004** | Bush | R | R | 202–231** | 44–55 | 50.8 |

NOTE: Does not include independents and minor parties.

*Presidential years appear in boldface.

†Harry Byrd, Jr., of Virginia was elected as an independent and is therefore not included in this and subsequent totals until his retirement in 1982. However, he received committee assignments as a Democrat. Also in 1970, James Buckley was elected as a Conservative from New York. He generally voted Republican but is not included in this table. In 1976 he was defeated.

‡The total became Democrats 61, Republicans 37, after a disputed Senate contest in New Hampshire was won by the Democratic candidate in a special election in September 1975.

§After the 1990, 1992, 1994, 1996, and 1998, 2002, and 2004 elections, there was one independent in the House.

**In 2000, there were two others—one independent and one socialist—in the House.

††In May 2001 Senator James A. Jeffords, a Vermont Republican, switched to independent, giving Democrats control of the Senate 50–49 until January 2003.

SOURCES: Adapted from Congressional Quarterly, *Politics in America* (Washington, D.C.: Congressional Quarterly, 1979), pp. 120–121; Congressional Quarterly, *Weekly Reports; National Journal,* and the *Statistical Abstract of the United States: 2006,* p. 256.

## TABLE 11-6

### Midterm Loss in House of Representatives of Party in Control of Presidency, 1922–2002

| Size of Loss (average 28 seats) | Net Number of Seats Lost or Gained Since Previous Election | Year | Incumbent President |
|---|---|---|---|
| Massive | −75 | 1922 | Harding |
| | −71 | 1938 | Roosevelt |
| | −55 | 1946 | Truman |
| | −53 | 1994 | Clinton |
| | −49 | 1930 | Hoover |
| | −48* | 1974 | Ford |
| Above average | −47 | 1958 | Eisenhower |
| | −47 | 1966 | Johnson |
| | −45 | 1942 | Roosevelt |
| | −29 | 1950 | Truman |
| | −26 | 1982 | Reagan |
| | −18 | 1954 | Eisenhower |
| | −12† | 1970 | Nixon |
| | −12 | 1978 | Carter |
| | −10 | 1926 | Coolidge |
| Below average | −8 | 1990 | Bush |
| | −5 | 1986 | Reagan |
| | −4 | 1962 | Kennedy |
| | +5 | 1998 | Clinton |
| | +5 | 2002 | Bush |
| | +9 | 1934 | Roosevelt |

*Republicans lost five House seats in special elections in 1974; their net loss on Election Day in 1974 was 43 seats.
†Republicans lost three House seats in special elections in 1969; their net loss on Election Day in 1970 was nine seats.
SOURCE: Adapted from Congressional Quarterly, *Weekly Reports*.

didates of the party that loses nationally are able to survive. This is because voters are selective: Some do not vote for all candidates on the ballot; others pick and choose and split their tickets. At times the coattail effect may work in reverse, as when a local candidate pulls a larger vote than the national ticket.[39]

Sometimes, candidates for governor may ride into the statehouse on a sufficiently long presidential coattail. "The great tides of presidential politics," V. O. Key, Jr., observed, "tend to engulf the affairs of states and often to determine the results of state elections."[40]

One reason for the relationship between presidential and gubernatorial voting is that many voters find it convenient to vote a straight party ticket by making a single mark or pulling a single lever (in states where they are permitted to do so). Even so, ticket-splitting between candidates for president and governor is common, particularly in states where there is strong two-party rivalry.

Moreover, three-fourths of the gubernatorial races cannot be directly affected by the presidential campaign because those states have scheduled gubernatorial elections in off-years to insulate the outcomes from the tides of national presidential politics. (See Table 11-7.) In 2004, a presidential year, 11 governors were elected, but in 2006, a midterm election, 36 governors' races were scheduled. (See Table 11-8.) This separation of gubernatorial and presidential races may help candidates of the party that is out of power nationally.[41]

***for more information about the gubernatorial issues, see: http://www.nga.org***

## TABLE 11-7

### Party Control of Governorships, 1946–2004

| After Elections of* | Democrats | Republicans |
|---|---|---|
| 1946 | 23 | 25 |
| **1948** | 30 | 18 |
| 1950 | 23 | 25 |
| **1952** | 18 | 30 |
| 1954 | 27 | 21 |
| **1956** | 28 | 20 |
| 1958 | 35 | 14 |
| **1960** | 34 | 16 |
| 1962 | 34 | 16 |
| **1964** | 33 | 17 |
| 1966 | 25 | 25 |
| **1968** | 19 | 31 |
| 1970 | 29 | 21 |
| **1972** | 31 | 19 |
| 1974 | 36 | 13† |
| **1976** | 37 | 12† |
| 1978 | 32 | 18 |
| **1980** | 27 | 23 |
| 1982 | 35 | 15 |
| **1984** | 34 | 16 |
| 1986 | 26 | 24 |
| **1988** | 28 | 22 |
| 1990 | 28 | 20† |
| **1992** | 30 | 18† |
| 1994 | 19 | 30† |
| **1996** | 17 | 32† |
| 1998 | 17 | 31† |
| **2000** | 19 | 29† |
| 2002 | 22 | 28† |
| **2003** | 24 | 26 |
| 2004 | 22 | 28 |

*Presidential years appear in boldface.
†After the 1974, 1976, 1994, 1996, and 1998 elections, there was an independent governor in Maine. After the 1990 and 1992 elections, independents held the governorship in Alaska and Connecticut. The Reform Party won the governorship of Minnesota in 1998. After 2002, there were no independent governors. After 2000 there was one independent and one Reform Party governor. In 2003, California's Democratic Governor Gray Davis was recalled and replaced by Republican Arnold Schwarzenegger.
SOURCES: Congressional Quarterly, Politics in America (Washington, D.C.: Congressional Quarterly, 1969), p. 69; Congressional Quarterly, *Weekly Reports; National Journal;* and *The World Almanac and Book of Facts 2004,* p. 69. Data for 2003 and 2004 from the *Statistical Abstract of the United States: 2006,* p. 258.

**TABLE 11-8**

**How the States Elect Governors (through 2006)**

| | |
|---|---|
| **Two-Year Term** | |
| Election in even-numbered years | 2 |
| **Four-Year Term** | |
| Election in presidential years | 9 |
| Election in even-numbered years at midterm | 34 |
| Election in odd-numbered years | 5 |
| **Total, all states** | 50 |

SOURCE: Data provided by the National Governors Association.

# ELECTION 2004: A CASE STUDY

In the election of 2004 President George W. Bush, the Republican nominee, won a sharply contested but clear-cut victory over Senator John F. Kerry, his Democratic opponent. Bush carried 31 of the 50 states and won 286 electoral votes to 251 for John Kerry. Bush also became the first son of a former president in American history to win two terms in the White House. The results were as follows:

| Candidate | Popular Vote* | Electoral Vote* | Percentage |
|---|---|---|---|
| George W. Bush (R) | 62,040,610 | 286 | 50.73% |
| John F. Kerry (D) | 59,028,439 | 251 | 48.27 |
| Ralph Nader (Independent) | 463,655 | 0 | 0.38 |
| Michael Badnarik (Libertarian) | 397,265 | 0 | 0.32 |
| Others | 363,579 | 0 | 0.3 |
| Totals | 122,293,548 | 538 | 100.0 |

*Data from http://uselectionatlas.org.

## The Republicans

As the 2004 presidential campaign approached, it was almost universally assumed that President George W. Bush would, at age 58, seek reelection. But Bush and his Republican supporters realized that four broad factors could have a powerful effect on their party's prospects for victory.

First, how popular would the president and his administration be with the voters in the summer and fall of 2004? Since 1950, every American president who sought a second term whose job approval rating in the polls was significantly above 50 percent had been reelected. On the other hand, three American presidents who sought a second term with job ratings below 50 percent—Ford, Carter, and the first President Bush—had all been defeated.[42] And two other presidents with low job ratings—Harry Truman and Lyndon Johnson—had chosen not to run again.

Second, how much would George W. Bush be helped by the fact that he was president—and commander in chief—while the United States was involved in a war on terrorism? In previous elections, many American voters had been reluctant to change presidents during wartime.

Third, although the continuing military struggle in Iraq underscored the president's status as a wartime chief executive, how would the voters perceive the Iraq war in the fall of 2004? If events in Iraq appeared to be going badly for the United States, that could weaken the president.

Fourth, how would the American economy be performing by the summer and fall of 2004? If the economy were doing well during the second half of 2004, the chances of a Republican victory would be increased. But the nation had been in a recession during George W. Bush's first year in office. If the economy did not recover by the summer of 2004, the Republican effort to reelect the president would be more difficult.

President Bush greets voters in Florida in 2004.

© Matthew Cavanaugh/EPA/Landov

John Kerry, the Democratic candidate for president, and running mate John Edwards campaign in North Carolina in 2004.

As expected, George W. Bush announced in May 2003 that he would seek the Republican nomination and run for a second term. Standing on the rain-soaked south lawn of the White House, Bush said: "The American people will decide whether or not I deserve a second term. In the meantime, I am focusing my attention . . . on helping people find work. . . . I want this economy to be robust and strong . . ." He wanted to make sure, he added, that the world knew "that the war on terror continues."[43]

## The Democrats

During 2002 and much of 2003, President George W. Bush's poll ratings stood at record or near-record highs. There was much talk of a Republican presidential landslide in 2004; and in fact, to some observers, the Democratic nomination did not appear to be a prize worth having. Throughout 2002, former vice president Al Gore, the Democratic presidential nominee in 2000, led in public opinion polls when Democratic voters were asked their choice for the 2004 Democratic nomination.

Then, on December 15, 2002, Gore surprised many political analysts by announcing that he would not be a candidate in 2004. The road to the nomination was now open to what became a flock of other Democratic aspirants. Howard Dean, the former governor of Vermont and a physician, had been campaigning extensively. Dean was first formally to declare his candidacy, in June 2003. "The president," he said, "pushes forward an agenda and policies which divide us."[44] On September 2, 2003, in front of the USS *Yorktown* near Charleston, South Carolina, Kerry, the junior Democratic Senator from Massachusetts, formally declared his candidacy.

In January 2003, several other candidates declared that they would seek the Democratic nomination, including Senator John Edwards, the first-term Democratic senator from North Carolina; the Reverend Al Sharpton of New York; Representative Dick Gephardt of Missouri, the former leader of the Democrats in the House of Representatives; and Senator Joseph Lieberman of Connecticut, who had been the Democratic candidate for vice president in 2000.

Late in the summer, it began to become clear that the U.S. military involvement in Iraq had not ended with a quick victory; and Howard Dean emerged as the most visible Democratic critic of the Iraq war. The American attack on Iraq, he contended, had been both a military and a foreign policy disaster.

Suddenly, the Dean campaign began to take life. Large crowds turned out for the former Vermont governor's rallies, and the Dean organization, which made extensive and innovative use of the Internet, began to receive a flood of campaign contributions. And Dean began to move up in the polls. The Democratic party had a frontrunner.

The surge of support for Howard Dean late in 2003 was particularly frustrating for John Kerry. The Massachusetts senator had expected to win the Democratic nomination fairly easily after Gore decided he would not be a candidate. But by the fall of 2003, the Kerry campaign had faltered. In November, Kerry fired his campaign manager.

In addition, Kerry decided to shift most of his campaigning to Iowa, where the Iowa caucuses would be held on January 19. The way to come from behind and win the New Hampshire primary, several of his advisers argued, was first to score a clear-cut victory in Iowa.

For the Kerry campaign, the decision to concentrate on the Iowa caucuses turned out to be the right strategy. Kerry's campaign in Iowa received a lift with the arrival in the state of his "band of brothers," Vietnam War veterans with whom Kerry had served on Swift boats during the war. In an emotional meeting that was widely televised across the state, one of the veterans credited Kerry with having saved his life by pulling him from the river after he had fallen overboard.

During the final two weeks before the Iowa caucuses, Senator Edwards also showed a special ability to connect with Iowa voters. Kerry won with 38 percent of the vote, and Edwards got 32 percent. Dean, the former frontrunner, won only 18 percent; and Dean hurt himself further as he tried to rally his supporters by letting loose on television what came to be called the "Dean scream." (In Washington, one highly interested observer drew his own conclusions about Dean's viability as a candidate. "This guy ain't coming back," President Bush said to one of his closest political advisers.)[45]

Eight days after Iowa, John Kerry won the New Hampshire primary. In the Gallup poll taken after the New Hampshire results were in, the support for Kerry among Democrats nationwide jumped from 9 percent to 49 percent. After winning decisive victories in almost every state he contested on February 3 and on "Super Tuesday," March 2, Kerry had an insurmountable lead in the delegate count for his party's national convention. The Democrats, like the Republicans, had their nominee for 2004.

One other candidate created a stir in early 2004 by announcing that he was going to run. On February 22, Ralph Nader announced on NBC's "Meet the Press," "I have decided to run as an independent candidate for president."

Democrats were horrified that Nader had entered the race. Nader had polled 2,834,000 votes when he ran for president in 2000, and it was widely assumed that in 2004 his candidacy would cut into Kerry's voter support more than Bush's. Republican strategists, by contrast, were delighted.

## April to August 2004, and the Democratic and Republican Conventions

In the weeks after April 1, each party prepared for its national convention. Kerry was assured of the nomination, but who would he pick to run with him for vice president?

The keynote speech by Barack Obama, the Democratic Senate candidate in Illinois and an African American, electrified the crowd on the second night. Almost overnight, the speech made Obama a rising figure in the Democratic Party.

Kerry worked at length on his own acceptance speech, "writing it out in longhand."[46] He began his speech by saluting and declaring: "I'm John Kerry, and I'm reporting for duty." His appearance produced an ovation in the packed hall. Democratic partisans thought on that final night that their convention had been a great success. But the first nationwide Gallup poll after the convention ended did not show a large pro-Democratic "convention bounce." Bush was ahead of Kerry in the polls.

August did not go well for Kerry. He came under a widely publicized attack by the Swift Boat Veterans for Truth who tried to discredit his service in Vietnam and the medals he had won. They also attacked his protest against the war after he had returned from Vietnam. Kerry was woefully slow to respond to the assault the Swift boat group aired in TV commercials and repeated in a best-selling book.

Four weeks after the Democrats had met in Boston, the Republicans launched their counterattack at their national convention in New York City. Republican party strategists had picked New York for the convention to remind voters of the president's leadership in the weeks

January 19, 2004: Howard Dean, an early Democratic presidential hopeful, conceded defeat in the Iowa caucus with what became known as "The Dean Scream." Dean ended his speech with: "We're going to Washington, D.C. to take back the White House. Yeah!"

Consumer advocate Ralph Nader ran for president as an independent in 2004.

© Kevin Casey/Getty Images

that followed the September 11, 2001, attacks on the World Trade Center.

President Bush's acceptance speech was preceded by a moving video that evoked images of September 11 and Bush's visit to the firefighters at ground zero. Then the president gave an address in which he forcefully outlined some of his goals for a second term in the White House. The first Gallup poll after the Republican gathering in New York put Bush seven percentage points ahead of Kerry. Bush had won his "convention bounce." There were now just nine weeks until Election Day.

## The Fall General Election Campaign

The nationally televised presidential and vice presidential debates dominated the fall election contest.

In the first television debate, in Coral Gables, Florida, Kerry vigorously attacked Bush's decision to go to war in Iraq: "This president has made, I regret to say, a colossal error of judgment. And judgment is what we look for in the president of the United States of America. Iraq is not even the center of the focus of the war on terror. . . . He rushed the war in Iraq without a plan to win the peace." Bush disagreed, and he defended his policy in Iraq, saying, "The world is better off without Saddam Hussein. . . . We're spending reconstruction money. And our alliance is strong. That's the plan for victory. And when Iraq is free, America will be more secure." But Bush appeared uncomfortable, even angry, in the face of Kerry's verbal challenges. He frowned frequently and looked irritated as Kerry spoke. To some observers watching on television, Kerry seemed more "presidential" than the president.

Huge numbers of Americans—more than 62 million—watched the first presidential debate on September 30. Kerry was judged the winner, by 53 percent to 37 percent. (Table 11-9.) Polls taken after the remaining debates suggested that the second presidential debate in St. Louis, in a town hall format, was a tie, and that Kerry was again considered the winner in the last debate in Tempe, Arizona, on October 13. In the vice-presidential debate, some of the polls gave Cheney the edge over Edwards.

2004: Republican workers encourage young voters to register outside MTV's studio in Times Square.

© 2004 AP/Wide World Photos

**TABLE 11-9**

**Which Candidate "Won" the 2004 Television Debates—The Voters' Response***

| | | | |
|---|---|---|---|
| First Presidential Debate, September 30, 2004** | | | |
| Kerry | 53% | Neither | 1 |
| Bush | 37 | Both | 8 |
| Vice Presidential Debate, October 5, 2004** | | | |
| Edwards | 35 | Neither | n /a |
| Cheney | 43 | Both | 19 |
| Second Presidential Debate, October 8, 2004 | | | |
| Kerry | 47 | Neither | 1 |
| Bush | 45 | Both | 7 |
| Third Presidential Debate, October 13, 2004 | | | |
| Kerry | 52 | Neither | 1 |
| Bush | 39 | Both | 8 |

*After the three presidential debates, the question was phrased: "Regardless of which candidate you happen to support, who do you think did the better job in the debate—John Kerry (or) George W. Bush?" After the vice presidential debate, the question was phrased: "Who, in your opinion, won the debate?"

**Does not add up to 100 percent because some questioned had no opinion or were undecided.

SOURCE: For the presidential debates, the Gallup poll, available online at <www.usatoday.com>, released October 14, 2004. For the vice presidential debate, an ABC News poll, October 5, 2004, online at <www.pollingreport.com>.

There were now just a little over two and a half weeks until Election Day. Only about 10 states were regarded as "swing states" that might be won by either candidate. Ohio, Florida, and Pennsylvania, all with large electoral votes, were considered the most important of the battleground states. And no Republican had ever been elected president without carrying Ohio.

The four national candidates crossed and recrossed the swing states for a series of campaign rallies. Late in the campaign, the two major parties together were spending $10 million a day on television and radio ads.[47] In addition, a full two weeks before Election Day on November 2, another trend was clear. Millions of Americans were voting early in states where it was possible to do so. In 2000, 13 states offered early voting. By 2004, that number had increased to 23 states. In addition, laws governing absentee voting had become much less stringent in many states. In some states it was no longer necessary to give a reason for requesting an absentee ballot. This, too, amounted to a form of early voting and raised the total number of states where it was possible to vote early to 31. Some analysts predicted that as many as 20 million votes would be cast before November 2.[48]

Over the final weekend and on Monday, the day before Election Day, both parties mounted unprecedented efforts to turn out their vote. And on the morning of Election Day, November 2, it looked as though the weather were going to help make it easy for many people to vote. There would be rain in Ohio and parts of western Pennsylvania; but in most of the country it would be dry, and in many areas the sun was shining. Everywhere, however, the people voted; more than 122 million Americans went to the polls, the largest number of voters in U.S. history.

Democrats enjoyed some high turnout rates among their core constituency groups. But voters who leaned Republican also went to the polls in very heavy numbers, at least matching the turnout rates of the Democrats. Bush defeated Kerry by a margin of 2.5 percentage points, or by just over 3,000,000 popular votes.

Several noteworthy features of the voting patterns of 2004 were clear:

Senator John Kerry . . . and President George W. Bush during their first televised debate, September 30, 2004.

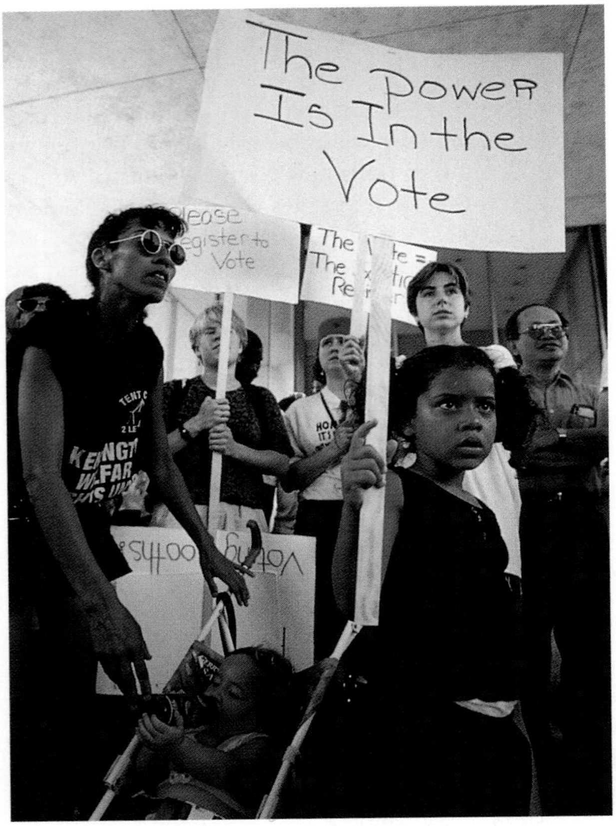


© Nicole Bengiveno

1. As noted, more than 122 million people voted. About 17 million more people voted in the presidential election of 2004 than in 2000; and the percentage of the voting age population who voted—around 58.3 percent—was about seven percentage points higher than the 51.2 percent who voted in 2000. It was the highest turnout since Richard Nixon, Hubert Humphrey, and George Wallace ran for president in 1968.
2. In some of the most closely contested swing states, the increase between 2000 and 2004 in the number of people voting was remarkable. In Pennsylvania, 856,471 more people voted in 2004 than had voted in 2000. In Ohio, the number voting was up by 922,451. And in Florida, where the state population had also been rising rapidly, the jump in the number of people who voted was 1,646,700.
3. George W. Bush's share of the total popular vote was 50.7 percent. Bush became the first presidential candidate since his father ran in 1988 to win more than half of the total popular vote.
4. Ralph Nader made a weak showing. He received just over 463,655 votes (about 0.38 percent)—an enormous drop from the 2,834,000 votes he polled in 2000.
5. The Libertarian candidate Michael Badnarik, with 397,265 votes, ran slightly behind Nader. And David Cobb, who defeated Nader for the Green Party's nomination, got slightly more than 119,859. Overall, third-party and independent candidates did poorly in 2004. As Micha Sifry, an analyst of third parties, declared: "This was not a year for third-party protest movements. The election was a referendum on George W. Bush, and most people felt that their vote had to either go for him or against him."[49]
6. There was a pronounced sectional pattern in the voting returns. Kerry ran ahead of Bush in nearly all of the Northeast, carrying every state from Maryland and the District of Columbia northward to the Canadian border. Kerry also carried the three West Coast states of Washington, Oregon, and California. Bush ran well ahead of Kerry throughout the South, sweeping all 11 states of the former Confederacy. And Bush also had a large lead in the Plains States and carried all eight Rocky Mountain States. In the Great Lakes industrial states of the Midwest, the vote totals of the two candidates were often close.
7. Kerry ran well among some traditionally Democratic groups. Among members of union households, Kerry led by 61 to 38 percent. Exit polls also showed that Kerry did very well among two groups that were heavily Democratic throughout the 1980s and 1990s. African Americans voted 88 percent for Kerry, and 74 percent of Jewish voters cast their ballots for him. (See Table 11-10.)
8. Hispanic Americans, who voted for Clinton in 1996 and Gore in 2000, were still in the Democratic column in 2004—but by a much smaller margin. Hispanic Americans gave 53 percent of their votes to Kerry and 44 percent to Bush. (See Table 11-10.) It was the highest vote that Hispanic Americans had ever given to a Republican candidate for president. The number of Hispanic Americans who voted also increased sharply.
9. President Bush won among all groups of voters who were 30 and older. The one age group where Kerry was in the lead was among voters aged 18 to 29; he carried this group 54 percent to 45 percent. In addition, the get-out-the-vote efforts aimed at the "youth vote" seemed to have some effect. Between 2000 and 2004 the number of voters who were younger than 30 increased by 4.6 million.[50]
10. In 2004 there was a continuation of the "gender gap"—the tendency of women and men to vote differently in the presidential race. Among men, Bush led Kerry 55 to 44 percent. Women favored Kerry over Bush 51 to 48 percent. But the gender gap narrowed considerably in 2004. Kerry's advantage over Bush among women in

## TABLE 11-10

### How Groups Voted in 2004

| | Kerry | Bush | Independent |
|---|---|---|---|
| All (100%) | 48% | 51% | —% |
| Men (46%) | 44 | 55 | — |
| Women (54%) | 51 | 48 | — |
| Whites (77%) | 41 | 58 | — |
| Blacks (11%) | 88 | 11 | — |
| Hispanics (8%) | 53 | 44 | 2 |
| Asian (2%) | 56 | 44 | — |
| Married (63%) | 42 | 57 | — |
| Unmarried (37%) | 58 | 40 | — |
| Didn't complete high school (4%) | 50 | 49 | — |
| High school graduate (22%) | 47 | 52 | — |
| Some college (32%) | 46 | 54 | — |
| College graduate (26%) | 46 | 54 | — |
| Postgraduate (16%) | 55 | 44 | — |
| Age: | | | |
| 18–29 (17%) | 54 | 45 | — |
| 30–44 (29%) | 46 | 53 | — |
| 45–59 (30%) | 48 | 51 | — |
| 60 and up (24%) | 46 | 54 | — |
| Family income: | | | |
| Less than $15,000 (8%) | 63 | 36 | — |
| $15,000–30,000 (15%) | 57 | 42 | — |
| $30,000–50,000 (22%) | 50 | 49 | — |
| $50,000 or higher (55%) | 43 | 56 | — |
| Protestants (54%) | 40 | 59 | — |
| Catholics (27%) | 47 | 52 | — |
| Jews (3%) | 74 | 25 | — |
| Family financial situation compared with 2000: | | | |
| Better (32%) | 19 | 80 | — |
| Worse (28%) | 79 | 20 | — |
| About the same (39%) 50 | 49 | — | |
| Democrats (37%) | 89 | 11 | — |
| Republicans (37%) | 6 | 93 | — |
| Independents (26%) | 49 | 48 | 1 |
| Liberals (21%) | 85 | 13 | 1 |
| Moderates (45%) | 54 | 45 | — |
| Conservatives (34%) | 15 | 84 | — |
| 2000 votes: | | | |
| Gore (37%) | 90 | 10 | — |
| Bush (43%) | 9 | 91 | — |
| First-time voters (11%) | 53 | 46 | — |
| Union households (24%) | 61 | 38 | — |
| Gay, lesbian, or bisexual (4%) | 77 | 23 | — |

SOURCE: Based on CNN exit polls, online at <http://www.cnn.com/election/2004>

2004 was much smaller than Gore's advantage had been in 2000.

11. Voters' evaluations of their own economic circumstances were strongly reflected in the returns. About a third (32 percent) of the voters reported that their family's financial situation was better in 2004 than it had been in 2000. Among these voters, Bush led Kerry by 80 to 19 percent. Among the 28 percent of all voters who said that their family's financial situation was worse, Kerry polled 79 percent.
12. The issue of same-sex marriages emerged as a highly visible issue on Election Day in 2004. Six months after gay and lesbian couples began legally marrying in Massachusetts, voters in 11 states approved constitutional amendments codifying marriage as an exclusively heterosexual institution. The amendments were endorsed by the voters in every state where they appeared on the ballot—including Ohio, Michigan, and Oregon.[51] They also may have raised the turnout among conservative voters, who then voted for President Bush.
13. The Republicans gained seats and retained control of the House of Representatives. In the U.S. Senate, the Republicans made a net gain of four seats. Overall, the elections of 2004 left the Republican Party in the strongest position the party had enjoyed in several decades. The GOP had solid majorities in the House and the Senate, and they controlled the presidency.

## ELECTION 2006: A CASE STUDY

From the White House to the state house, and down to the precinct level, an atmosphere of gloom hung over the Republican Party as the midterm congressional elections of 2006 approached.

Party leaders and strategists were well aware that the normal pattern has been for the party of the president to lose seats in both houses of Congress in midterm general elections. In the eighty years through 2002, the average midterm loss in the House of Representatives was 28 seats. (See Table 11-6.)

But in 2006, the Democrats needed only 15 seats to gain control of the House. To win control of the Senate, the Democrats needed to gain six seats, a considerably more difficult challenge. But even if the Democrats

succeeded only in wresting control of the House, the Republicans faced the prospect of investigations into administration policies—and scandals—by Democratic-controlled congressional committees armed with subpoena power. It was a daunting prospect for the GOP as the party prepared for the next presidential election in 2008.

The leaders of both major parties knew that two broad factors could have a major impact on the midterm election results. First was the war in Iraq, which had now dragged on for more than three years. By September, as the fall campaign got underway, the war had cost more than 2,700 lives of American military men and women, with more than 20,000 wounded, and $2 billion a week. As voters tuned in to television news or surfed the Internet, they saw the flames of suicide bomb explosions, the daily toll of sectarian violence in Baghdad and other Iraqi cities, and at home the images of grieving widows, parents, sons, and daughters as the fallen returned home for the last time to be buried in the small towns and villages of the heartland.

All of this could not help but have an enormous impact on the electorate, and the polls showed that the war in Iraq was indeed a driving force in the midterm elections.

In addition to the cost of the war in lives and treasure, there was a lingering unease among many voters that America had gone to war for the wrong reasons. The Bush administration had warned that Saddam Hussein's Iraq possessed weapons of mass destruction that threatened American national security. Yet no such weapons were found after U.S. forces successfully invaded in 2003 and captured the Iraqi despot, who was convicted and, two days before the midterm congressional elections, sentenced to be hanged.

A second broad factor that both parties agreed could be important to the election outcome was President Bush's low approval ratings in the polls. When Bush responded to the 9/11 terrorist attacks by ordering the military into Afghanistan, his approval rating soared to 90 percent in the Gallup poll. It remained high during the initial phase of the war in Iraq, hovering around 70 percent. But in May of 2005, it dropped below 50 percent and did not rise above that number through the midterm elections, sinking to a low of 31 percent in May of 2006. It was a dramatic drop in public approval and coincided with the increasingly bad news in Iraq.[52] (See Table 11-11.)

In previous midterm elections when the incumbent president's popularity was low (as measured by the public's assessment of his job performance), the president's party usually sustained substantial losses in the House and Senate. When the incumbent president's job rating was high, by contrast, his party, although perhaps losing some seats in Congress, usually did considerably better in the midterm congressional races.

With Bush's approval rating in the mid-to-upper thirties during the fall campaign, many Republican can-

"And now with a rebuttal . . ."

## TABLE 11-11

**President Bush's Job Rating, 2001–2006***

| Date of Interviews | Approve | Disapprove | No Opinion |
|---|---|---|---|
| Bush elected with 47.9% of the vote (December 2000); Bush's first inauguration (January 2001). | | | |
| February 1–4, 2001 | 57% | 25% | 18% |
| Attacks of September 11, 2001, destroy both towers of the World Trade Center and damage the Pentagon; Bush declares "War on Terror," invades Afghanistan. | | | |
| September 14–15, 2001 | 86% | 10% | 4% |
| October 21–22, 2001 | 90%** | 6% | 4% |
| Bombing campaign and search for Osama Bin Laden continue in Afghanistan (November 2001). | | | |
| November 26–27, 2001 | 87% | 8% | 5% |
| 2002 State of the Union address: Bush declares Iran, Korea, and Iraq "Axis of Evil." | | | |
| January 25–27, 2002 | 84% | 13% | 3% |
| Bush begins making the case for war with Iraq. | | | |
| November 8–10, 2002 | 68% | 27% | 5% |
| 2003 State of the Union address: Bush says there's evidence Hussein was trying to acquire uranium from Africa. | | | |
| January 31–February 2, 2003 | 61% | 35% | 4% |
| Invasion of Iraq begins (March 2003). | | | |
| March 29–30, 2003 | 71% | 26% | 3% |
| Administration and CIA admit errors in asserting that Iraq tried to acquire uranium from Africa. | | | |
| July 25–27, 2003 | 58% | 38% | 4% |
| Saddam Hussein is captured in a spider hole in Iraq (December 2003). | | | |
| December 15–16, 2003 | 63% | 34% | 3% |
| 2004 State of the Union address: Bush continues to defend war with Iraq (January 2004). | | | |
| January 29–February 1, 2004 | 49% | 48% | 3% |
| Democratic National Convention (July–August 2004)/Republican National Convention (August–September 2004) | | | |
| September 13–15, 2004 | 52% | 45% | 3% |
| October 11–14, 2004 | 48% | 49% | 3% |
| August 2005: Hurricane Katrina hits Gulf Coast leaving hundreds of thousands homeless. | | | |
| August 28–30, 2005 | 45% | 52% | 3% |
| March 2006: Third Anniversary of Iraq War | | | |
| March 13–16, 2006 | 37% | 59% | 5% |
| May 5–7, 2006 | 31% | 65% | 5% |
| September 2006: American troop death toll in Iraq passes 2,700. | | | |
| September 15–16, 2006 | 44% | 51% | 5% |

*Responses to the question: "Do you approve or disapprove of the way George W. Bush is handling his job as president?"
**Highest approval rating ever recorded for any president by Gallup.
SOURCE: Data provided by the Gallup poll.

didates found it convenient to distance themselves from the chief executive. Although Bush campaigned energetically for some candidates, others did not invite him into their states or districts, and some openly criticized the president's policies, particularly on the war in Iraq. A few Republicans even called on Secretary of Defense Donald H. Rumsfeld to resign.

Karl Rove, the president's chief political adviser, had laid out the Republicans' 2006 strategy at the start of the year. At a meeting of the Republican National Committee, Rove declared: "At the core, we are dealing with two parties that have fundamentally different views on national security." The Democrats, he added, were "wrong—deeply and profoundly and consistently wrong."[53]

Traditionally, national security issues had worked well for the Republicans. Bush's comfortable margin of victory in the presidential election of 2004, for example, was attributed in part to the belief of many voters that the president, in the wake of the attacks of 9/11, was leading a vigorous war on terrorism. But the protracted war in Iraq had turned Republican strength into weakness. In 2006, a majority of voters disapproved of the way Bush was managing the conflict in Iraq. For example, a Gallup poll in early October found that 66 percent disapproved of how he was handling the war.[54]

Political scandals, which often plague presidents in their second term, had also come home to roost for the Republicans. In 2005, Vice President Dick Cheney's chief of staff, I. Lewis "Scooter" Libby, was indicted and charged with perjury and obstruction of justice in connection with the leak to the press of the name of a CIA officer whose husband was an opponent of the administration. In 2006, lobbyist Jack Abramoff pleaded guilty to charges of fraud, tax evasion, and conspiracy to bribe public officials, and agreed to testify against members of Congress and executive branch officials whom he had paid off and entertained. Representative Bob Ney, an Ohio Republican, pleaded guilty to accepting bribes from Abramoff to help the lobbyist and his clients.

As the midterm election campaigns took place, other factors gave the Republican Party cause to worry. The federal government had reacted slowly and ineffectively to Hurricane Katrina, which struck New Orleans and the Gulf Coast in 2005, leaving more than 1,700 people dead and hundreds of thousands homeless. That, too, reflected badly on Bush, who early on had publicly praised the director of the Federal Emergency Management Agency for doing "a heckuva job" in responding to the hurricane.

Overall, the public had a low opinion of the Republican-controlled Congress. In September 2006 a Gallup poll reported that 63 percent of those questioned did not approve "of the way Congress is handling its job.[55] Since Congress was Republican-controlled, its low approval ratings could not be expected to help the fortunes of the GOP.

Despite the political environment that seemed to favor the Democratic Party in 2006, there were several factors that Republicans hoped would work to their advantage. Because the GOP controlled both houses of Congress, the power of incumbency was a plus factor for the Republicans; a senator or representative often enjoys an edge over a challenger who may have less name recognition. Beyond that, in a number of states where the GOP controlled the legislature and the governor's office, the Republicans made sure that congressional district lines were redrawn to favor their party in elections for the House of Representatives.

In addition, the Republicans enjoyed a traditional advantage in fund-raising, assisted by President Bush, who traveled to many states and helped garner millions of dollars for the party at private dinners and events often closed to the press and public.

The GOP's organizational skills at the grass roots had served it well in the 2004 presidential election, and the party hoped for a large turnout of Republican voters in the midterm contests. However, the Democrats were better organized in 2006 than they had been two years earlier, and they made a concerted effort to turn out their voters as well.

The economy might also have been expected to help the Republicans in 2006. The Dow-Jones Industrial Average broke the 12,000 mark for the first time in its 110-year history on October 18, less than three weeks before the election, and unemployment dropped to a new low. The Bush administration had orchestrated tax cuts. But wages were stagnant, the housing market had declined, and many voters expressed discontent with their personal economic condition. And with the Iraq war overshadowing many other issues, Republicans had difficulty getting voters to focus on the economy.

The GOP also struggled to promote "family values" and social issues that had aided the party in past elections. But the party's efforts to ban flag-burning or oppose gay marriage appeared to have lost some of their magic.

## The Setting

When the 2006 election year began, there were 55 Republicans, 44 Democrats, and one independent in the U.S. Senate. A total of 33 Senate seats (out of a hundred) were to be filled in the November general elections. Of these, the Democrats had 17 seats to defend and the Republicans 15. Thus, to gain control, the Democrats faced a difficult challenge—they would have to hold on to all of their seats and gain six more.

Even if the Democrats won in three states—Ohio, Pennsylvania, and Rhode Island—where they appeared to be leading their Republican rivals, they would have to win three out of four states where the contests were extremely close—Missouri, Montana, Virginia, and Tennessee—to overturn Republican control of the Senate.

The Democrats had made a major effort in 2006 to recruit strong candidates for both the House and the Senate. And Senator Barack Obama of Illinois, a rising

© AP Images/Evan Vucci

2006: President Bush campaigned in Tennessee for Bob Corker, the Republican candidate for the U.S. Senate.

star in the party who was not himself running, campaigned extensively for Democratic candidates.

In the House of Representatives, the strategic situation was markedly different. As the campaign began, the Republicans controlled the House, 229 to 201, with one independent and four vacancies. There were 435 House seats to be filled, and at least 60 were considered competitive. Of these, 53 were in districts held by the Republicans. And all ten of the most endangered seats were Republican. Democrats were therefore optimistic they could win at least the 15 seats they needed to end 12 years of Republican rule in the House.

Thirty-six of the nation's 50 governorships were to be filled in 2006, and more than 6,000 legislative seats in 46 states. When the election year began, Republicans controlled 28 governorships; 22 were held by Democrats. Many of the races for governor were close, and the Democrats hoped to win enough gubernatorial contests to control a majority of the 50 states for the first time since 1994.

## The Election Campaign

Ironically, one of the first harbingers of trouble brewing for the Republican Party in 2006 came in the Democratic Senate primary in Connecticut on August 8. Ned Lamont, a wealthy political newcomer, upset Senator Joseph I. Lieberman, who had served three terms and had been the Democratic nominee for vice president in 2000. But Lieberman was a strong backer of the Iraq war, and that proved a fatal flaw in his primary campaign. Although defeated for his party's nomination, Lieberman announced he would run as an independent, and, as expected, he defeated both Lamont and his Republican opponent in the general election in November.

Nevertheless, Lieberman's defeat in the primary was an indication of how risky it could be for a candidate to align himself with Bush in support of an unpopular war. As the fall campaign progressed, a number of Republican candidates either openly or obliquely criticized the conduct of the war or called for a change in strategy in Iraq.

There were other problems faced by the Republicans in 2006. Tom DeLay, the Texas Republican who was the powerful House majority leader, was forced to give up his post after he was indicted in Texas on charges of money laundering. He announced he would not run for reelection in 2006. Another Republican, Randy "Duke" Cunningham, a former Republican member of the House from San Diego, was sentenced to eight years in prison after admitting he took $2.4 million in bribes from two defense contractors. As already noted, Representative Bob Ney, an Ohio Republican, pleaded guilty to accepting bribes from the disgraced lobbyist Jack Abramoff.

Then, in late September, Mark Foley, a Florida Republican, abruptly resigned from the House after news reports disclosed that he had sent sexually graphic e-mails to underage House pages. The scandal tended to undermine the Republican argument that it was the party of moral values. The fallout from the Foley affair cast a shadow over House Speaker Dennis Hastert, who insisted he had not known about Foley's inappropriate e-mails.

The Democrats had an unexpected public relations problem as well. A week before the election, in a talk to a group of students in California, Senator John Kerry of Massachusetts, the Democratic presidential nominee two years earlier, stumbled badly as he tried to tell a joke aimed at Bush, with the result that many took his words as a jibe at the troops in Iraq. Kerry apologized, but Bush pounced on the mistake during a flurry of last-minute campaign appearances in Republican states to try to energize the GOP base.

Bush unleashed some of his most intense rhetoric in the fading days of the campaign. In Sugar Land, Texas, a week before the election, he again promised "victory" in Iraq and said of the Democrats, "Well, however they put it, their approach comes down to this: The terrorists win and America loses."[56]

## The Results

Election Day, November 7, dawned clear and mild in the east and across much of the rest of the country; in the Pacific Northwest, however, voters faced floods and rampaging rivers, and in southern California they faced record-breaking heat. There were reports during the day of heavy voter turnout and of some problems with electronic voting machines. President Bush voted near his ranch in Crawford, Texas, then flew back to the White House to watch the returns.

The polls had not been closed in the east for very long before the first indications of a Democratic sweep were perceptible. As the TV networks began their major election coverage at 10 p.m., the Democrats picked up five, then 12, of the 15 seats they needed to control the House. During the night it became clear that the Democrats would gain close to double the number of House seats they needed, ending 12 years of Republican rule in the House of Representatives.

In the Senate races, the picture was less clear. Early on, Democrats picked up Senate seats in Ohio, Pennsylvania, and Rhode Island. For control of the Senate, however, they needed three more seats—and the key races for those seats were extremely tight. In New York, Senator Hillary Clinton, as expected, coasted to an easy victory over her Republican opponent, strengthening her hand for a possible bid for her party's presidential nomination in 2008.

Nancy Pelosi, the California Democrat, was now in position to become the first woman, and the first Italian American, to be speaker of the House. It was well after midnight when she stepped to the microphone at a hotel ballroom in Washington to speak to the cheering, dancing, flag-waving Democrats. Many had linked arms and were kicking in a chorus line.

"You go, girl!" someone in the crowd shouted.

"Today the American people voted for change and they voted for Democrats to take our country in a new direction," Pelosi said. "And nowhere did the American people make it more clear that we need a new direction than in the war in Iraq . . . we cannot continue down this catastrophic path . . . Mr. President, we need a new direction in Iraq."

Americans awoke the morning after the election to high drama. The Democrats were within inches of capturing the Senate as well as the House. Although Republicans had prevailed in Tennessee, Democrats had won in Missouri. And Jon Tester, the Democratic candidate for the Senate in Montana, held a slim lead over Conrad Burns, the three-term Republican incumbent, whose reelection effort had been damaged by the fact that he had taken more money from lobbyist Jack Abramoff than any other Republican.

The real cliffhanger was in Virginia, where Jim Webb, the Democratic challenger, led the Republican incumbent, George Allen, by about 7,400 votes. Webb claimed victory on November 8. Unless his lead were overturned by a possible recount, the Democrats would gain the six seats they needed to control the Senate.

At 1 p.m. that same Wednesday, President Bush, admitting he had taken a "thumpin'" from the voters, held a televised news conference. He appeared in a conciliatory mood, holding out an olive branch to the Democrats and calling for bipartisan cooperation. He invited Nancy Pelosi to lunch at the White House. And he dropped a bombshell: Donald Rumsfeld, the controversial defense secretary, was out, to be replaced by Robert Gates, the former director of the CIA.

By firing Rumsfeld, who had become a lightning rod for criticism of the war in Iraq, Bush was acknowledging that voter anger over the war was a driving force in the Republican losses. More than any other issue, it had returned power to the Democrats.

Just before 1 p.m. on November 9, Conrad Burns conceded in Montana. And across the country, in Alexandria, Virginia, at 3:11 p.m., George Allen faced the television cameras. "The people of Virginia have spoken," he said, " . . . and I respect their decision."

With that, the Democrats had captured the United States Senate. They now controlled both houses of Congress for the first time in 12 years. The era of one-party rule in Washington was over.

Several noteworthy features marked the voting patterns of 2006:

1. Almost 79 million voters went to the polls. According to the Center for the Study of the American Electorate, there was a turnout of 40.4 percent of all citizens of voting age—an increase in turnout of 1.1 percent from the last midterm election in 2002. In Virginia and Montana, two states that had closely contested races for the U.S. Senate, the turnout exceeded 50 percent—52 percent in Virginia and 63.5 percent in Montana. In Montana, for the first time, voters were allowed to register on election day.
2. Democrats emerged from the 2006 midterm elections with a majority of state governors—28 Democrats to 22 Republicans—for the first time since 1994. Democrats won in major states, including Ohio, New York, Maryland, and Massachusetts, which elected its first African-American governor, Deval Patrick. Nationwide, in the 36 contests for governor in 2006, the Democrats made a net gain of six, winning 20 races, while Republicans won only 16 statehouses.
3. Republicans lost key Senate races in several different regions of the country. Six Republican incumbents failed to hold onto their seats. They lost Senate seats they had previously controlled in the South (Virginia), the Midwest (Missouri, Ohio), the west (Montana), and the Northeast (Pennsylvania, Rhode Island). The Republicans failed to pick up seats they had hoped to win in

the Northeast (Maryland, New Jersey) and in the Midwest (Minnesota).

4. The Senate that convened in January 2007 would be controlled by the Democrats 51–49. The Democratic total included two independents, Senator Joseph Lieberman of Connecticut and Senator Bernie Sanders of Vermont, who both said they would caucus with the Democrats. Harry Reid of Nevada, the Democratic minority leader, would become the majority leader in the new Democratic-controlled Senate.
5. In the battle for control of the House of Representatives, the Democrats' net gain of at least 29 House seats was a dramatic shift of power that marked the first time the Democrats had controlled the House since 1994. The results left the Democrats with a comfortable majority of 230 to 195, pending final tallies in ten districts. No independents were elected to the House. Thirty-four House candidates ran without major-party opposition.
6. The Democratic sweep was also visible in the contests for the state legislatures. Before the election, Republicans held the majority of both houses of legislatures in 21 states; Democrats controlled 17 states, and 11 were divided. After the election, Democrats controlled both houses of the legislatures in 23 states, Republicans in 15, and 10 were split. As a result, the Democrats controlled the legislatures in more states than they had since 1994. Nationwide, Democrats also gained more than 320 state legislative seats. Of the 7,382 state legislators, 3,984 were Democrats and 3,324 were Republicans; most of the rest were independents or members of third parties.
7. Voters in several states approved or rejected ballot measures. In South Dakota, a measure that would have banned almost all abortions in the state was turned down. Seven states voted to ban same-sex marriages, but in Arizona gay rights advocates helped to defeat such a measure. Eight states approved restrictions on the government's use of eminent domain to take property for private projects. Two states rejected measures to legalize possession of an ounce of marijuana, and South Dakota turned down legalizing its medical use. And six states approved increases in the minimum wage.
8. Exit polls indicated that Democrats received the support of 55 percent of women, compared with 43 percent for Republicans—the highest percentage of women who voted for Democrats since 1988. Democrats also won 18 percent of independent voters, the highest proportion in 25 years, and registered a 14 percent increase in votes by Hispanics, from 55 percent in 2004 to 69 percent in 2006.[57]

Ned Lamont celebrates his victory over Senator Joseph Lieberman in the 2006 Democratic primary in Connecticut. Lieberman then ran as an independent candidate for the U.S. Senate, and won.

9. In House races, Republicans received 70 percent of the vote of white Christian evangelicals, an important element in the party's base, a seven percentage point drop from the vote in 2004 by that group. Democrats led Republicans among Catholic voters, 55 to 44 percent, a reversal from 2004, when Republicans won a narrow majority of Catholics.[58]
10. The most important fact about the 2006 elections was that the Democrats took control of Congress, one of the three branches of the national government—the legislative branch. Speaker-elect Nancy Pelosi told President Bush, "We've made history. Now we have to make progress."

Although in the immediate aftermath of the voting, the president and Democratic leaders of the House and Senate pledged to work together in a spirit of bipartisanship, for at least two years, the government will be divided, and with it at least a strong possibility of "partisan gridlock."

As President Bush accepted the political sea change, he said he was "open to any idea or suggestion that will help us achieve our goals of defeating the terrorists and ensuring that Iraq's democratic government succeeds."

At the same time, the Democrats were firmly committed to making progress on extricating the nation from the war in Iraq, a key issue that helped them win their majority in the midterm elections. And there also remained a number of major domestic issues—from health insurance to federal funding for stem cell research—on which Democrats and Republicans had taken sharply differing positions.

How well the two parties were seen as handling the challenging and potentially divisive issues ahead would go a long way toward determining their prospects in the 2008 presidential election.

## The Electoral System

The act of choice performed by the American voter on Election Day takes place within a legal and structural framework that strongly influences the result. The electoral system in the United States is not neutral—it affects the dynamics of voting all along the way. Before voters can step into the voting booths, they must meet a number of legal requirements. The candidates whose names appear on the ballot must have qualified under state law. The form of the ballot may influence voters' decisions; if they are allowed to make a single mark or pull a single lever, for example, they are more likely to vote a straight party ticket than if they must make several marks, pull many levers, punch several holes, or push several buttons to vote that way. How their votes count in a presidential election is controlled by custom, state law, and the Constitution, for all three affect the workings of the electoral college. In short, the structure, details, and workings of the electoral system affect the people's choice.

Perhaps the most striking example of this occurred in the presidential contest of 2000. On November 7 of that year, the voters went to the polls to choose a new president and a new Congress to lead the nation in the new century. But as the dawn broke the next morning, America was stunned to learn that the contest was not over. There was no clear winner because the crucial result in Florida hung in the balance. Nationwide, Vice President Al Gore was ahead of Texas Governor George W. Bush in the popular vote by a thin margin, but Bush was slightly ahead in Florida, where the state's 25 electoral votes would determine who became the next president. Teams of lawyers descended on the Sunshine State, the Democrats demanding a hand recount in four largely Democratic counties. At first, the dispute focused on Palm Beach County, where voters who said they had meant to vote for Gore claimed they were confused by the "butterfly" layout of the ballot—with the names of the presidential candidates on both the left and right sides—and punched the wrong hole. Instead of voting for Gore, they had voted for Pat Buchanan, the conservative candidate of the Reform Party.

The major controversy between the two parties centered on a tiny piece of paper known as a "chad." As Americans soon learned, a chad was the bit of paper that normally fell out when a ballot was punched by the voter with a stylus. Sometimes, however, voters failed to punch the ballot all the way through. A tiny dangling piece of paper—a "hanging chad"—may remain and can fall back to fill the hole in the card. Voting machines read such ballots as not having cast any vote. Democrats argued that they had lost a substantial number of votes intended for Gore. They demanded the hand recount in order to identify those votes.

On December 8, Florida's highest court ordered a statewide recount of any votes that the machines had not counted. The Bush camp appealed to the U.S. Supreme Court, which halted the recount. Then in a historic decision on December 12, a bitterly divided Supreme Court ruled 5–4 for Bush, declaring that because the recount lacked uniform standards, it was unconstitutional. Finally, it was official: George W. Bush was the next president of the United States.

### Suffrage

The Constitution provides for popular election of members of the House of Representatives, a provision extended to the election of senators by the Seventeenth Amendment, ratified in 1913. In electing a president, the voters in each state actually choose electors, who meet in December of the election year and cast their ballots for a chief executive. (See the discussion about the electoral college later in this chapter.)

Voting is a basic right provided for by the Constitution. Under the Fourteenth Amendment, it is one of the privileges and immunities of national citizenship that the states may not abridge and that Congress has the power to protect by federal legislation. For example, in 1970 Congress limited state residence requirements for voting in presidential elections. The states, however, do set many requirements for voting. State laws in part govern the machinery of choice—residence and other voting requirements, registration, primaries, and the form of the ballot. And state laws regulate political parties.

Until the age of Andrew Jackson, voting was generally restricted to men who owned property and paid taxes. Since then, suffrage has gradually been broadened. Most states lifted property requirements in the early 19th century. In 1869 Wyoming became the first state to enact women's suffrage, and three other western states did so in the 1890s. In 1917 the suffragettes, who fought for women's right to vote, began marching in front of the White House; they were arrested and jailed. In 1919 Congress passed the Nineteenth Amendment, making it unconstitutional to deny any citizen the right to vote on account of sex. The amendment was ratified by the states in time for women to vote in the presidential election of 1920.

The long struggle of African Americans for the right to vote is described in Chapter 5. As we have seen, even though the Fifteenth Amendment specifically gave black citizens the right to vote, it was circumvented when the South regained political control of its state governments after Reconstruction. Poll taxes, all-white primaries, phony literacy tests, intimidation, and violence were all effective in disenfranchising blacks in the South. In 1964 the Twenty-fourth Amendment eliminated the last vestiges of the poll tax in federal elections.[59]

But blacks still faced many of the other barriers to voting; only 44 percent of voting-age black citizens in the South voted in the 1964 presidential election. The Voting Rights Act of 1965, which was extended in 1970, in 1975, and in 1982 to the year 2007, sought to throw the mantle of federal protection around these voters. It was followed by a dramatic increase in blacks voting in the South.

Suffragettes marching to the White House, 1917

Although these anachronistic character tests were suspended along with literacy tests by the 1970 amendments to the Voting Rights Act, a number of states retained on the statute books other odd barriers to voting. The laws of nine states, for example, disqualified paupers, and Louisiana law disqualified parents of illegitimate children. The laws of seven states disqualified people engaging in duels. Such oddities were not affected by the Voting Rights Act or its various extensions, but the states generally did not enforce them.

Most states bar mentally incompetent people and inmates of prisons from voting. People convicted of certain types of crimes lose the right to vote under the laws of 46 states and the District of Columbia. Some states restore the right to vote on release from prison, or after a set number of years of imprisonment, or by executive or legislative clemency.

***for more information about voting rights, see:***
***http://www.usdoj.gov:80/crt/voting/intro/intro_a.htm***

**Residence Requirements** When Congress extended the Voting Rights Act in 1970, it included a provision permitting voters in every state to vote in presidential elections after living in the state for 30 days. This uniform federal standard was designed to override state residence requirements, some of which had prevented millions of people from voting for president. The Voting Rights Act also required states to permit absentee registration and voting. Subsequently, the Supreme Court ruled that states may not require residence of more than 30 days for a person to be able to vote in federal, state, and local elections,[60] although in 1973 the Court modified this standard to permit a state residency requirement of 50 days, at least in state and local elections.[61] But neither case changed the 30-day maximum residence requirements for voting in presidential elections.

**Literacy and Character Tests** Historically, literacy tests were used to keep recent immigrants and blacks from voting. The Voting Rights Act of 1965 suspended literacy tests in the six southern states and all or part of four other states where fewer than half the voting-age population had registered or voted in the 1964 election. The law also suspended in those areas tests requiring voters to prove "good moral character."

Later amendments to the Voting Rights Act extended the ban against literacy and character tests to all states. Before passage of the law, 12 states—including California and New York—still listed literacy as a requirement for voting. Two states, Idaho and Connecticut, had "good character" tests. Under Idaho law, prostitutes, their customers and madams, bigamists, persons of Chinese or Mongolian descent, and others who "lewdly or lasciviously cohabit together"[62] were banned from voting. And Connecticut had a law on its books requiring that voters be of "good moral character."

**Age Requirements** In the late 1960s, with young Americans fighting and dying in Vietnam—but denied the right to vote—pressure to lower the voting age to 18 built up rapidly. After November 1970 eight states had lowered their legal voting age to younger than 21. In all other states, however, the minimum voting age was 21.

In 1970 Congress, by statute, lowered the voting age to 18 in all elections, but later that year the Supreme Court ruled that Congress had power to do so only in federal elections.[63] The result was confusion. In 1971 Congress passed, and the necessary three-fourths of the states ratified, a constitutional amendment lowering the voting age to 18 in all elections.

The Twenty-sixth Amendment enfranchised 10.5 million people between the ages of 18 and 21 in time to vote in the 1972 presidential election. Many political observers reasoned that the addition of so large a group of young voters could have a major impact on the political system. But the lower voting age did not result in dramatic political change, in part because younger voters traditionally have had a low rate of turnout. In fact, in the first election in which all people aged 18 through 20 could vote (1972), fewer than half (48 percent) voted.[64] In 2000, about 8 percent of the total vote for president was cast by people aged 18 through 24.[65]

**Citizenship Requirements** Only U.S. citizens can vote in U.S. elections. This was not always the case, however. In the 19th century, 22 states and territories gave aliens the right to vote; the last state to abolish alien voting was Arkansas, in 1926. As a result, the presidential election of

1928 was the first in which only U.S. citizens could cast ballots. More than 17 million U.S. residents could not vote in 2000 because they were not American citizens.[66]

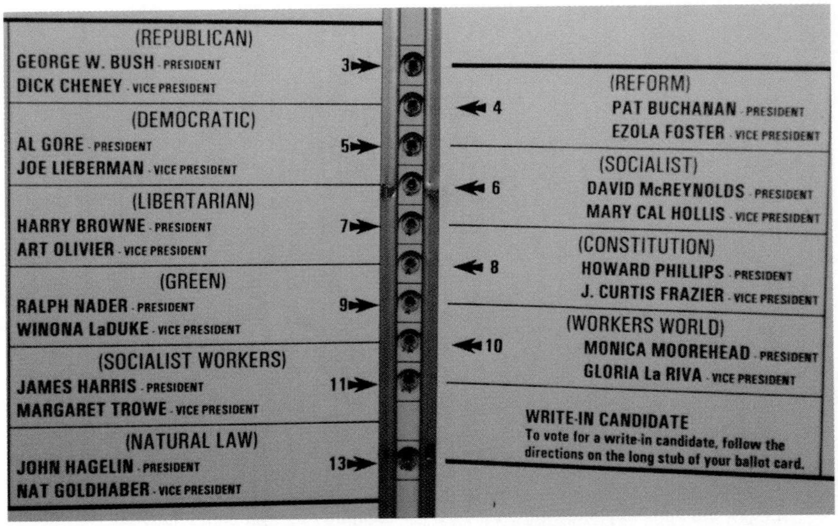




The controversial ballot in Palm Beach County, Florida, in 2000. Democrats argued that because of its design, some Gore supporters mistakenly voted for Pat Buchanan.

**Voter Indentification Requirements** For more than 50 years, the broad trend in the United States has been to reduce barriers and other requirements that might impede voting. But in recent years there has been a counter trend that could depress voter turnout. Twenty-four states—13 of them between 2003 and 2006—have passed laws requiring voters to produce voter identification cards, often containing a photo ID, when they vote. And in Congress, the House of Representatives passed a bill in September 2006 that would require would-be voters to have a government-issued photo ID to vote in federal elections in 2008. (As of October 2006, the Senate had not acted on the House bill.)

Proponents of the voter ID laws, often Republicans and conservatives, argue that the laws are necessary to prevent election fraud. Opponents of the laws, often Democrats and their political allies, argue that the new requirments are likely to reduce voting among minority, poor, elderly, and young voters—potential voters who are least likely to have the documentation, such as driver's licenses or birth certificates, that they would need to establish their identity.

## Winning Votes—Machine Style

I know every man, woman, and child in the Fifteenth District, except them that's been born this summer—and I know some of them, too. I know what they like and what they don't like, what they are strong at and what they are weak in, and I reach them by approachin' at the right side.

For instance, here's how I gather in the young men. I hear of a young feller that's proud of his voice, thinks he can sing fine. I ask him to come around to Washington Hall and join our Glee Club. He comes and sings, and he's a follower of Plunkitt for life. Another young feller gains a reputation as a baseball player in a vacant lot. I bring him into our baseball club. That fixes him. You'll find him workin' for my ticket at the polls next election day. . . . I don't trouble them with political arguments. I just study human nature and act accordin'.

—Boss Plunkitt, in William L. Riordon, *Plunkitt of Tammany Hall*

In some states, state judges have voided their states' voter ID legislation. In September 2006, for example, a Missouri circuit court judge threw out that state's law, ruling that it placed an unconstitutional burden on voters because the ID was not free.[67] As a result, in late 2006 the full impact of the movement to establish voter ID legislation was yet to be determined.

## The Nominating Process: Primaries and Conventions

Voting requirements restrict the number of people who can step into the voting booth. The nominating process restricts choice because the voter is effectively limited to those candidates nominated by parties or running as independents and placed on the ballot. (Write-in votes, where permitted, seldom elect anyone.)

State laws govern the nominating process and the selection of party leaders. Although the Constitution provides for election of members of Congress and the president, it makes no direct mention of how they shall be nominated and placed on the ballot. In the 19th century, candidates for public office were chosen by backroom caucuses of politicians or by local or state conventions. The abuses of that manner of selection led to demands for reform. By 1915 two-thirds of the states had some kind of law providing for primary elections to choose candidates for the general elections. Today, every state has provisions for primary elections to choose some candidates who run in statewide contests. Party officials also may be chosen in primaries.

Currently, most states hold direct primaries to nominate candidates for the House and Senate. In a handful of other states, nominations are by convention, by party committee, or by a combination of methods. In states using primaries, the most common form is the **closed**

© 2000 AP/Wide World Photos

**primary,** in which only registered members of a party or people declaring their affiliation with a party can vote. About 20 states use the **open primary,** in which any voter may participate and vote for one political party's slate of candidates.

In recent years, four states—Alaska, California, Louisiana, and Washington—used the **blanket primary,** a system in which any registered voters are able to vote for candidates from more than one party. A voter, for example, could vote for a Democratic nominee for the U.S. Senate and for a Republican gubernatorial nominee. In 2000, however, the U.S. Supreme Court ruled against California's blanket primary system, declaring that it violated the constitutional right to freedom of association by forcing political parties to allow nonmembers to choose a party's candidates.[68] The Court's decision struck down the blanket primary in Alaska and Washington, as well as in California, but left intact a somewhat different "nonpartisan" version of the blanket primary in Louisiana. Political party leaders have usually opposed the blanket primary, arguing that it weakens party identification and loyalty.

Political parties still hold conventions to nominate candidates for president and vice president. Delegates to these conventions are usually, but not always, selected in presidential primaries. In 2004, 33 states, the District of Columbia, and American Samoa held Democratic presidential primaries; and 28 states and Puerto Rico held Republican presidential primaries in which voters chose all or some convention delegates.[69]

Other states chose delegates to national nominating conventions by different methods, including selection by state conventions, party caucuses, and party committees. But because most of the large states held presidential primaries in 2004, about three-fourths of the delegates to the national conventions were selected in presidential primaries that year.

## Voter Registration

The old Tammany Hall slogan, "Vote Early and Vote Often," still brings nostalgic smiles to the faces of some political leaders in New York. But the use of "repeaters" to vote more than once, and of "tombstone voters" (using the names of deceased voters) and similar devices, is made much more difficult—although by no means impossible—by modern systems of voter registration.

Before voters can vote, they must register. Under state laws, when voters register, their names are entered on a list of people qualified to vote. They may, if they wish, declare their party affiliation when they register. On Election Day, the registration list may be checked for each voter who comes to the polling place to ensure that he or she is qualified to cast a ballot.

**Permanent registration,** under which the voter registers only once in his or her district, prevails in all but a few states. **Periodic registration,** under which the voter must register every year or at other stated intervals, is used in a very small number of states.

Like other forms of election machinery, registration procedures can affect the political result. For example, Idaho has used roving canvassers to remind people to register to vote, and the turnout has consistently been higher than the national average. No doubt other factors are at work in Idaho, but as a presidential commission concluded: "The average American is far

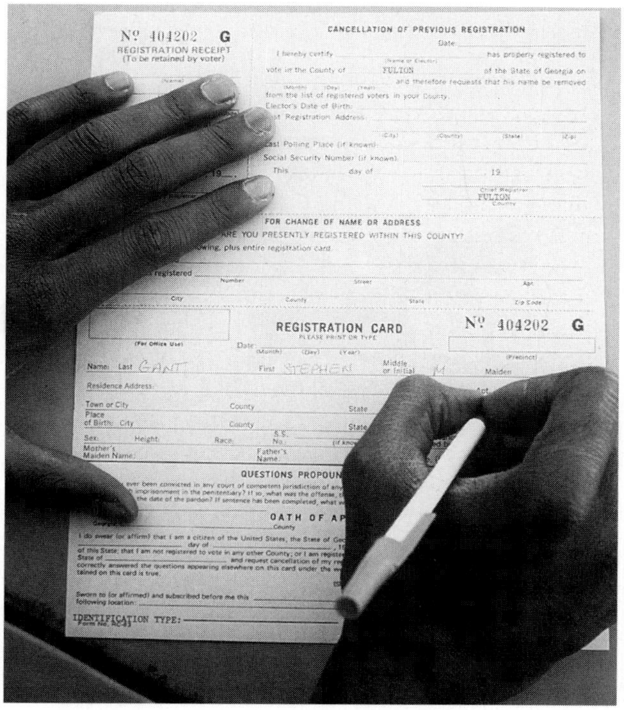


© Thomas England/Photo Researchers

## Making a Difference

# ROCK THE VOTE: EMPOWERING YOUNG AMERICANS

Only 33 percent of 18- to 21-year-olds voted in the 1988 presidential election. That low turnout continued a steady decline that began in 1971, when the Twenty-sixth Amendment lowered the voting age to 18.

That was the situation in 1991 when Patrick Lippert, a Los Angeles political activist, became executive director and later president of Rock the Vote, an organization founded in 1990 by record industry executives to counter efforts at censorship. When Lippert joined, he expanded the focus of the nonpartisan organization's goals to include the political empowerment of young Americans.

Lippert's political work began in California in the early 1980s when the Minnesota native volunteered as an activist to help organize the entertainment community around progressive causes. At the helm of Rock the Vote, he was credited with an 18 percent increase in turnout by 18- to 24-year-old voters in 1992. He was helped by music videos on MTV produced for Rock the Vote and featuring Madonna and rapper Ice-T. In her video, Madonna wraps herself in the American flag and cries out "Vote!" to the music of her hit song, "Vogue." In his video, Ice-T intones: "We're youth, we have to change things."

Lippert seemed an unlikely candidate to awaken the slumbering political conscience of twenty-something rock and rollers; he didn't own a stereo and rarely watched MTV. Yet, Lippert stirred a potent mix of celebrity and politics that sent young Americans to the polls in record numbers. His passion and sharp political sense won him a special place at the intersection of entertainment and politics. Lippert was one of the few people that both stodgy legislators and outlaw rock stars could trust.

Besides increasing young voter participation, Rock the Vote also played a key role in congressional passage of the "motor voter" bill, a law that added millions of people to the voter rolls by allowing people to register to vote when they receive or renew their driver's licenses. He was invited to the White House by President Clinton for the bill-signing ceremony. For his work, Lippert was honored with many awards, including the Congressional Arts Caucus Award.

Patrick Lippert wrote in the *Los Angeles Times* Opinion section: "For a democracy to be truly realized, all citizens eligible to vote must exercise their constitutional right. For this reason, until this happens, Rock the Vote is committed to registering America's youth on college campuses, in high schools and at record stores and concerts."

On July 13, 1993, Patrick Lippert died from complications due to AIDS. He was 35 years old. Until the end, he was devoted to his cause. In lieu of flowers, he had asked that any memorial donations be made to Rock the Vote.

—Adapted from the *Los Angeles Times, Time, Rolling Stone,* and Rock the Vote

"People of North Dakota! Or possibly South Dakota!"



more likely to vote if few barriers stand between him and registration."[70]

A basic factor affecting registration and voting in the United States is that an American who wishes to register usually must take the initiative and appear in person at the local registration office. (In Great Britain and a number of European countries, the government takes the initiative in trying to register eligible voters.) In more recent years, however, some attempts have been made to make it easier to register in the United States. In some states, potential voters may register at tables set up in stores, or with citizen registrars or party volunteers who go from door to door seeking new voters. Or voters may register online at websites such as http://www.rockthevote.com.

***for more information about voter registration, see: http://www.rockthevote.com and http://www.justvote.org***

In 1993, Congress passed and President Clinton signed a "motor voter" bill, which was designed to make it easier for people to register to vote. The law required states to allow people to register when they applied for a driver's license or when they visited public assistance agencies or military recruitment offices.[71] The law, which went into effect in January 1995, survived a Supreme Court challenge by then governor Pete Wilson of California and by public officials in six other states.

"Good God! He's giving the white-collar voters' speech to the blue collars."

## Ballots

The secret (so-called Australian) ballot was not adopted by every state in the United States until 1950. Early in American history the voter often announced his vote orally at the polling place. After the Civil War, this method was replaced by ballots printed by each political party; since the ballots were often of different colors, it was easy to tell how someone voted. Concern over voter intimidation and fraud led to pressure for secret ballots printed by public authorities. By 1900 a substantial number of states had adopted the secret ballot. This ballot has two chief forms:

1. The **party-column ballot,** or Indiana ballot, lists the candidates of each party in a row or column, beside or under the party emblem. In most cases, the voter can make one mark at the top of the column, or pull one lever, and thus vote for all the party's candidates for various offices. This ballot encourages straight-ticket voting.
2. The **office-column ballot,** or Massachusetts ballot, groups candidates according to the office for which they are running—all the presidential candidates of all the parties appear in one column or row, for example.

Research has demonstrated that the form of the ballot may influence the vote. Among independent voters, one study found that a party-column ballot increased straight-ticket voting by 60 percent.[72]

The first voting machine was used in 1892 by the city of Lockport, New York. By 1990 more than half the states used machines statewide or in most areas.

Although states have long permitted voting by mail for people who are out of town on Election Day, a growing number of states have tried additional strategies to increase voter turnout and to decrease the cost of conducting elections. Some states now allow voting by mail, even for people who may be at home on Election Day. Other states permit early voting weeks before Election Day. By 2000, some 21 states permitted either mail balloting or early voting, and a few, such as Arizona and Colorado, allowed both.[73]

In 1996, Oregon allowed all of its registered voters to vote by mail in an election for the U.S. Senate. Under this method, voters did not have to go in person to a polling place. Ballots were mailed to registered voters and had to be mailed back (or dropped off at specified locations) by three weeks later.[74] When the ballots were counted, Democratic Congressman Ron Wyden defeated his Republican opponent, Gordon Smith, and became the first U.S. senator to be elected by mail ballots.[75]

In 2000, following a statewide referendum, Oregon went to an all-mail ballot, in which every vote in statewide elections would be cast through the mail. Advocates of the new system argued that it would improve voter participation. Critics worried that it would increase election fraud.[76]

## Counting the Votes

On Election Night the results in each state are tabulated by state and local election officials and reported to the nation through the National Election Pool (NEP), a cooperative organization formed by ABC, CBS, NBC, CNN, Fox News, and the Associated Press.

The drama of Election Night is in a sense entirely artificial. As the night wears on, one candidate may appear to lead, then fall behind, and perhaps forge ahead again. Actually, once the polls close, the popular vote result is already recorded inside the ballot boxes and voting machines.

In recent years the nation has no longer had to wait until the votes actually were counted to know the results of some elections because the television networks have developed systems of projecting the vote with the aid of

computers. In 1996 the three major broadcast networks promised not to call the presidential winner until the polls had closed in enough states to guarantee the 270 electoral votes needed for victory. The *New York Times* reported, "That happened at 9 p.m. Eastern Standard Time, when the polls closed in Minnesota, New Mexico, New York, Rhode Island, and Wisconsin. Moments later, all three networks announced President Clinton's victory."[77] But in the 2000 presidential election, the vote projections led to an embarrassing disaster for the major television networks. First, the networks called Florida for Vice President Gore, only to retract that news two hours later. Early the next morning, the networks awarded Florida to Bush, then retracted that as well. As it turned out, the gap between the two candidates in Florida was razor thin.

The computerized vote-projection systems are based on exit polls and on the analysis of key precincts that are chosen at random from each state. Past election data about the sample precincts are coded and stored in the computers and compared with actual returns as they come in on Election Night. As the computer processes the data flowing in, it is able to make a statistical forecast of the probable outcome. In 1980 a number of western Democratic candidates as well as other political leaders complained sharply when the television networks declared Reagan the projected winner early in the evening, and President Carter conceded at 8:50 p.m. EST. These events, coming while the polls were still open on the West Coast, they argued, discouraged many potential voters from voting. Again in 1984, the television networks declared President Reagan the winner before the polls had closed on the West Coast.

In 1992, in order to deflect criticism, the television networks agreed that they would not project the winner in a state until the majority of the polls had closed in that state.

## Fraud

With so much at stake on Election Night, it is not surprising that from time to time there are charges of voting fraud, even in presidential elections.

In 1960, after John Kennedy's narrow popular-vote victory over Richard Nixon, some Republicans charged that there had been election frauds in Cook County, Illinois, and in Texas. If Kennedy had failed to carry these two states, Nixon would have won in the electoral college. Kennedy carried Illinois by a mere 8,858 votes, but his margin in Texas was much larger, 46,257 votes. Nixon considered, but decided not to ask for, an investigation or a recount.[78]

Proposals to allow voting via the Internet were generally not adopted in 2004 because of widespread fear that hackers could compromise the election results. Further disputes occurred that year over the touch-screen voting machines adopted in many states. An estimated 50 million people voted in 2004 using touch-screen or other types of computerized voting. Many of these voters cast their ballots on machines from Diebold Election Systems. Some experts said the machines were flawed, but the company asserted that the problems had been fixed. But the effort to apply new technology to make voting easier remained controversial.

## The Electoral College

The Constitution does not provide for the popular election of the president. Instead, it provides that each state "shall appoint, in such manner as the legislature thereof may direct," electors equal in number to the representatives and senators that the state has in Congress. Instead of voting directly for president, an American, in casting his or her ballot, votes for a slate of electors that is normally pledged to the presidential candidate of the voter's choice. Together, the electors are known as the **electoral college,** the body composed of electors from the 50 states who formally have the power to elect the president and vice president of the United States.

Many voters are unaware that they are voting for electors because their names do not even appear on the ballot in about two-thirds of the states. The slate of electors that receives the most votes meets in the state capital in December of a presidential election year and casts its ballots. Each state sends the results to Washington, where the electoral votes are officially counted in a joint session of Congress early in January. The candidate with a majority of the electoral votes is elected president. (In 2000, as in every presidential election since 1964, there

were a total of 538 members of the electoral college; 270 electoral votes were required to win the presidency.) If no one receives a majority, the House of Representatives must choose the president from among the three candidates with the largest number of electoral votes, with each state delegation in the House having one vote. Members of the electoral college also vote for vice president in a separate balloting procedure. If no candidate for vice president receives a majority of the electoral votes, the Senate must choose the vice president from one of the two candidates with the most electoral votes.*

***for more information about the electoral college, see the "Electoral College" link at:***
***http://ap.grolier.com/browse?type=pep***

Custom, not the Constitution, is the reason electors are chosen in each state by popular vote. In the first four presidential elections, state legislatures chose the electors in most cases. South Carolina was the last state to switch to popular election, in 1860. Although there is hardly any possibility that a state would discontinue the popular election of electors, legally, a state may select them any way it wishes.[79]

The framers of the Constitution had great difficulty in agreeing on the best way to elect the president. Some favored direct election by all of the voters, but others thought this would give an advantage to the more populous states. The provision for presidential electors represented a compromise between the big and little states for "only a few delegates to the Constitutional Convention felt that American democracy had matured sufficiently for the choice of the President to be entrusted directly to the People."[80]

Over the decades, the electoral college has been severely criticized as an old-fashioned device standing between the people and their choice of a president. The criticism may be summarized as follows:

1. The "winner-take-all" feature of the electoral college means that if a candidate carries a state by even one popular vote, he wins all the state's electoral votes, distorting the will of the voters because the minority votes cast within a state count for nothing. As a result, a president may be elected who has lost the total popular vote. This actually happened in the elections of John Quincy Adams in 1824, Rutherford B. Hayes in 1876, Benjamin Harrison in 1888, and George W. Bush in 2000.
2. The system, with its winner-take-all feature, gives an advantage to the populous states that have many electoral votes and to the members of minority groups that constitute powerful voting blocs within those states. At the same time,

Ralph E. Becker Collection/Smithsonian Institution

*The House chose the president twice: after the election of 1800, when it elected Jefferson, and following the election of 1824, when it elected John Quincy Adams. The Senate chose the vice president only once, when it elected Richard M. Johnson of Kentucky in 1837. In the case of a tie in the presidential balloting in the House that is not resolved by Inauguration Day, January 20, the vice president–elect becomes acting president. Since the Senate chooses the vice president in the event of an electoral vote deadlock, the Senate, in effect, would select the new president on Inauguration Day; if no president or vice president has been selected by January 20, the presidency would go to the speaker of the House, or next to the president pro tempore of the Senate, or down through all the cabinet posts under the Presidential Succession Act.

very small states are overrepresented because every state has a minimum of three electoral votes.

3. Electors are not bound by the U.S. Constitution to vote for the candidate to whom they are pledged. In 2004, in 26 states and the District of Columbia electors were bound by state law or pledges to vote for their party's candidate, although most legal scholars believed those statutes were unconstitutional; 24 states had no such laws. From 1796 through 2004, 157 electors had failed to vote for the candidate to whom they were pledged.

In 1968 major-party supporters feared that George Wallace would receive enough electoral votes to deprive Nixon or Humphrey of a majority; the third-party candidate then might be in a position to win concessions in return for his electoral votes, or force the election into the House of Representatives, where he might strike further bargains.

The closeness of the 2000 election, and the lengthy postelection dispute over Florida's 25 electoral votes, created new pressures for electoral college reform. Past debates had centered on plans to award each candidate electoral votes in proportion to his share of the popular vote within each state. In the 1960s, the idea of direct election of the president gained in popularity. It seemed closest to the principle of "one person, one vote" enunciated by the Supreme Court.

© Leslie Hugh Stone/The Image Works

## Proposals for Direct Election of the President

In September 1969 the House passed a proposed constitutional amendment to abolish the electoral college and substitute direct election of the president and vice president. Under the amendment, if no candidate received 40 percent of the popular vote, a runoff election would be held between the top two presidential candidates. The amendment did not pass, but some similar proposals were put forward after the 2000 postelection crisis.

One reason the 1969 amendment and the proposals after the 2000 election did not pass was a widespread reluctance, in and out of Congress, to change a fundamental aspect of the American political system. There were also a number of specific objections. Critics argued that it would encourage the growth of splinter parties. The result, they warned, could be the fragmentation of American politics and destruction of the two-party system.[81] And the two-party system, these critics have contended, is a vital instrument in resolving social conflict and managing the transfer of power.

Those opposed to direct election also argued that the electoral college is compatible with the federal system and that direct election would (1) increase the temptation for fraud in vote counting, leading to prolonged recounts and chaos, (2) rob minority groups of their influence in big electoral-vote states, and (3) tempt states to ease voter-qualification standards in order to fatten the voter rolls.

## One Person, One Vote

During the 1960s the Supreme Court ruled in a series of reapportionment decisions that each person's vote should be worth as much as another's. Yet the decisions were controversial because they upset the balance of political power between urban and rural areas in the United States. The result was a concerted but unsuccessful effort in Congress and the states to amend the Constitution to overturn the Supreme Court rulings.

**The State Legislatures** All votes are equal when each member of a legislative body represents the same number of people. In the United States, however, successive waves of immigration and the subsequent growth of the cities resulted in glaring inequalities in the population of urban and rural state legislative districts by the turn of the 20th century. The 1920 census showed that for the first time more Americans lived in urban than in rural areas. The rural state legislators, representing sparsely populated districts, passed state laws to maintain their advantage over the cities. By 1960, in every state the largest legislative district was at least twice as populous as the smallest district.

In Tennessee that year, the smallest district in the lower house had a population of 3,400 and the largest had 79,000. Obviously, the people in the biggest district were not as equally represented as the voters in the smallest. Because the legislature had refused to do anything about it, a group of urban residents, including a county judge named Charles W. Baker, sued Joe C. Carr, Tennessee's secretary of state. The case went to the U.S. Supreme Court, which in 1946 had refused to consider a case involving malapportionment in Illinois (*Colgrove* v. *Green*). Justice Felix Frankfurter, in that earlier opinion, ruled that the Supreme Court "ought not to enter this political thicket."[82]

But in 1962, in *Baker* v. *Carr,* the Supreme Court ruled in favor of the voters who had challenged the established order in Tennessee.[83] In 1964, in *Reynolds* v. *Sims,* the Supreme Court made it clear that the Fourteenth Amendment required that seats in both houses of a state legislature be based on population. Second, the Court ruled that although legislative districts might not be drawn with "mathematical exactness or precision," they must be based "substantially" on population.[84] The Court had laid down the principle of "one person, one vote."

The reapportionment decisions had an immediate effect on the political map of America. The legislature of Oregon had reapportioned on the basis of population in 1961; between the *Baker* v. *Carr* ruling in 1962 and 1970, the other 49 states took similar steps.

**Congressional Districts** It was not just the state legislatures that were malapportioned before the mid-1960s. Although the average congressional House district had a population of 410,000 in the 1960s, the actual population of these districts varied greatly. For example, in Georgia, one rural district had 272,000 people, but the 5th Congressional District (Atlanta and its suburbs) numbered 823,000 people. In 1964, in the case of *Wesberry* v. *Sanders,*[85] the Supreme Court ruled that this disparity in the size of Georgia's congressional districts violated the Constitution. As a result, the states were required to redraw the boundaries of their congressional districts to conform to the Court's ruling.

The Supreme Court's reapportionment decisions left open the question of how much the population of state legislative and congressional districts might vary from one another without violating the principle of "one person, one vote." In a series of decisions the Court shifted ground as it grappled with this difficult question, eventually ruling that deviations as high as 10 percent in state legislative districts were too small to merit attention by the courts.[86]

Under the Constitution and federal law, Congress determines the total size of the House of Representatives, which grew from 65 members in 1790 to 435 in 1912. Congress has kept the House membership at 435 since then, although it could change that semipermanent figure.[87] After each 10-year census, federal law requires that the number of representatives for each state be reapportioned on the basis of population. If a state gains or loses members of Congress, the state legislature redistricts by drawing new boundary lines for its House districts. (In some instances federal courts have drawn the new lines.) In 1972, for example, California gained a total of five seats as a result of the 1970 census, making its House delegation the largest in the nation. Previously, New York's was the largest. Again, after the 1980, 1990, and 2000 censuses, California, Florida, and Texas gained seats, and New York, Pennsylvania, Ohio, and Illinois lost seats. The average population of House districts had risen to about 690,000 by 2006.

As a result of the reapportionment revolution of the 1960s, rural areas had been expected to lose power to the cities. But because of the population exodus from the cities, the suburbs have proved to be the areas that gained the most from reapportionment of state legislatures and congressional districts. As far back as 1965 an official of the National Municipal League noted that almost half of the big cities in the United States had less population than their suburbs: "No center city contains the necessary 50 percent of the people to dominate the state. . . . The U.S. is an urban nation, but it is not a big-city nation. The suburbs own the future."[88]

Because the suburbs have grown much faster than the nation as a whole, in the 1970s, for the first time, there were more members of the House of Representatives from the suburbs than from the cities. And since then, this trend has continued. (See Table 11-15.) As the political battle shifts to the suburbs, Gerald M. Pomper has predicted: "Suburban power will influence the way both politics and government are conducted."[89]

After the 1990 census, state legislatures created a number of congressional districts in which the majority of the population was black or Hispanic. The lines of

**TABLE 11-12**

**Suburban, Central City, and Rural Congressional Districts in the United States House of Representatives, 1962–1992**

| | 1962 | 1966 | 1974 | 1986 | 1992 |
|---|---|---|---|---|---|
| Metropolitan districts | 254 | 264 | 305 | 347 | 351 |
| Central city | 106 | 110 | 109 | 98 | 86 |
| Suburban | 92 | 98 | 132 | 167 | 196 |
| Mixed metropolitan | 56 | 56 | 64 | 82 | 69 |
| Rural districts | 181 | 171 | 130 | 88 | 84 |
| Total | 435 | 435 | 435 | 435 | 435 |

SOURCES: Data for 1962–1974 provided by Richard Lehne, "Suburban Foundations of the New Congress," *Annals of the American Academy of Political and Social Science,* November 1975, p. 143; and analysis extended for 1986 and 1992 by Harvey L. Schantz, State University of New York, Plattsburgh.

these new districts, subject to approval by the Justice Department, were drawn to conform with judicial interpretations of the Voting Rights Act requiring that minority voters have the maximum opportunity to elect minority members to Congress. Thirteen new African Americans and six new Hispanic Americans were elected to the House in these newly created districts in 1992. Also elected that year was Carol Moseley-Braun of Illinois, who became the first African American woman and the first African American Democrat to serve in the Senate. In all, there were 38 African American and 17 Hispanic American members at the start of the 103rd Congress in January 1993. By January 2005, there were 43 African Americans and 29 Hispanic Americans in Congress.[90]

As noted in Chapter 5, the Supreme Court in 1993 and 1995 ruled that congressional districts that had been specifically drawn to contain a majority of black voters were open to challenge on the grounds that they were unconstitutional. On June 13, 1996, in two 5–4 decisions, the Court went a step further, as it invalidated two districts in Texas and one in North Carolina with black majorities, and another district with a majority of Hispanic voters in Houston, Texas.[91] (See Figure 11-4.)

All of the affected districts were oddly shaped rather than compact—the 12th Congressional District in North Carolina, for example, followed a narrow, winding course along 160 miles of Interstate Highway 85, in the central part of the state. The two decisions of the Court totaled 189 pages, and Justice Sandra Day O'Connor's opinion in the Texas case included a detailed analysis of the challenged districts. "Significant deviations from traditional districting principles, such as the bizarre shape and noncompactness demonstrated by the districts here, cause constitutional harm insofar as they convey the message that political identity is, or should be, predominantly racial," Justice O'Connor declared.[92]

The two decisions suggested that the high court was likely to examine on a case-by-case basis districts in which minority-group voters predominated. The decisions also suggested that additional congressional districts, as well as districts drawn to increase minority representation in state and local legislative bodies, would be scrutinized by the court.[93]

After the Supreme Court's decisions and the redrawing of the congressional districts' boundary lines, one question remained: Would the black candidates who had won in the gerrymandered districts be able to retain their seats now that they had to run in districts where white voters were in the majority? The answer, to the surprise of many observers, was yes. In 1996, all five of the black members of Congress running in redrawn districts were reelected. All of the redrawn districts were in southern states; and all five of the districts had white majorities. For some observers, the victories of these black congressional candidates were evidence of changing racial attitudes in the South; for others, they were proof of the power of incumbency.[94]

Although the Supreme Court has struck down districts gerrymandered along racial lines, in 2004 it ruled that districts redrawn two years earlier by the Republican-controlled legislature in Pennsylvania were constitutional. By a vote of 5–4 it rejected a complaint by Democrats that the oddly shaped districts—one was only 300 yards wide in some places—deprived voters of equal protection of the laws. Justice Anthony M. Kennedy said that correcting district boundaries for partisan purposes would involve the courts in "unprecedented intervention in the American political process."[95]

In June 2006, the Supreme Court also approved most parts of a fiercely disputed 2003 congressional redistricting plan in Texas. Normally, congressional redistricting has taken place in the year immediately follow-

**FIGURE 11-4**

**Irregular House Districts**

*The Supreme Court ruled in 1996 that four congressional districts, one in North Carolina and three in Texas, were unconstitutional.*

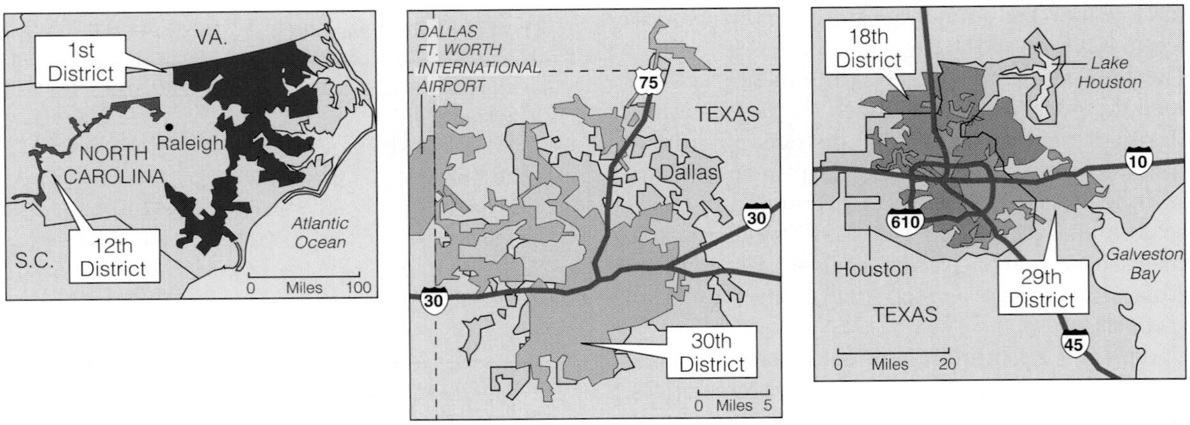

ing a 10-year census. But the Republican party first won full control of the Texas state legislature in 2002; and the next year, the Republican legislators overturned a congressional redistricting plan that had been put in place by a federal court in 2001. The Republican plan created new districts that led to the election of six additional Republican members of the House of Representatives from Texas in 2004.

The Court's 2006 decision appeared to open the door to redistricting efforts at any time during a decade—not just in the year immediately after a 10-year census. But the Court did rule that the state's largest district created in 2003, covering much of West and South Texas, violated the voting rights of Hispanics.[96] The boundaries of that district were subsequently redrawn.

## Elections and Democratic Government

Who won the election? In the United States, with its federal system, the question must be asked on all levels—national (the president, Congress), state (the governor and state legislatures), and local (county and city governments). Since candidates of both major parties win these offices, the outcome of American elections is mixed. Which party won or lost is not always as simple as it might appear. In 1984, for example, Reagan, a Republican, won by a landslide in the presidential election and

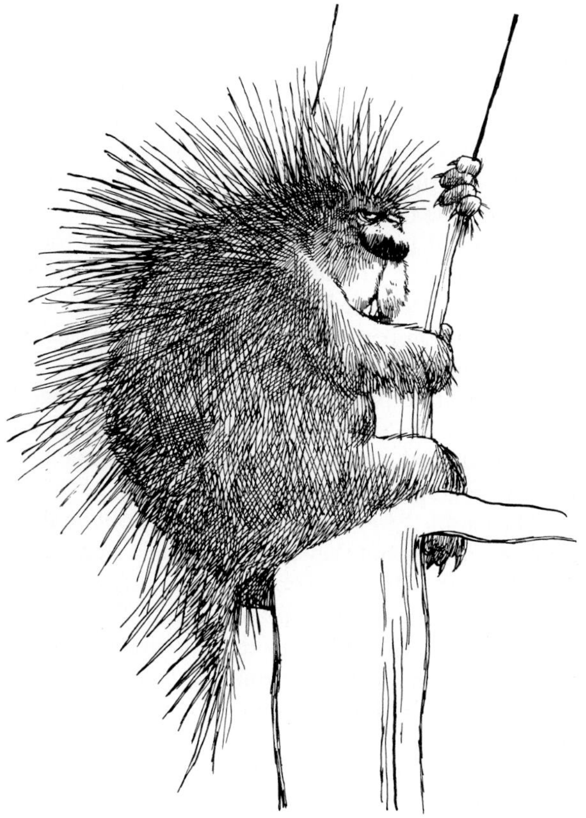

Drawing by Jeff MacNelly from *A Political Bestiary* by Eugene J. McCarthy and James J. Kilpatrick, McGraw-Hill, Inc. Reprinted by permission.

"The Untouchable Incumbent. Incumbents . . . evolved in the manner of the porcupine. They grew longer and longer quills."

the GOP won a majority in the Senate. But the Democrats retained control of the House of Representatives and a majority of the nation's statehouses and state legislatures. Yet there are differences in elections; the voice of the voter speaks more clearly in some years than in others.

### Types of Elections

V. O. Key, Jr., has suggested three broad types of presidential elections.[97] A *landslide for the out-party* "expresses clearly a lack of confidence in those who have been in charge of affairs." Some observers felt that the defeat of President George Bush in 1992 was fundamentally an election of this type. In other election years, however, the voters may approve an incumbent administration in a vote of confidence that amounts to a *reaffirmation of support.* Moreover, both in elections that oust the party in power and in those that produce a reaffirmation of support, people appear to be engaged in retrospective voting—looking back and making a judgment on the way things have gone and the kind of government they have had during their political leaders' time in office.

A third type of election, a *realignment,* may return the party that controls the presidency to power, but with the support of a new coalition of voters. (There also may be a major realignment when the president's party loses control of the White House.) When the realignment within the electorate is "both sharp and durable," Key suggests that a "critical" election has taken place, one that results in "profound readjustments" in political power.[98]

Angus Campbell and his associates have classified presidential elections in somewhat similar fashion: They relate the election returns to the basic pattern of party identification. They speak of **maintaining elections,** which reflect the standing party identification of the voters; of **deviating elections,** in which the majority party (according to party identification) is defeated in a temporary reversal; and of **realigning elections,** which may lead to a basic shift in the party identification of the electorate.[99]

### The Meaning of Elections

Much of the discussion in this chapter has focused on the wide variety of reasons, sociological and psychological, that may cause different voters to vote for the same political candidate. Regardless of these individual reasons, the overall election verdicts have broad meaning for the political system as a whole.

First of all, elections decide which individuals shall govern. Who wins can make a difference—in the political philosophy and caliber of those appointed to the Supreme Court by the president and approved by Congress, to take but one example.

Second, elections can have important consequences for the broad direction of public policy. Naturally, many specific questions are not settled by elections, but 1936 was rather clearly a broad approval of the New Deal, just

© AP/Wide World Photos

as 1964 was a repudiation of conservative Republicanism in that year. The series of four Democratic presidential victories from 1936 to 1948 ("maintaining elections" in Angus Campbell's terminology, "reaffirmations of support" in Key's classification) served to ensure that most of the policy innovations of the New Deal would become established public programs.

The voice of the people is not always so clear. The meaning of a particular election, the "mandate" of the people to the president on specific issues, may be subject to varying interpretations. As we have noted, many different people vote for the same candidate for different reasons; this candidate, once elected, may make decisions that cause some of the voters to feel misled. For example, in 1964 Americans voted for a president who seemed to promise, among other things, to avoid a war in Asia, but did not.* In the presidential election of 1968 some voters retaliated by voting Republican.

It is also true that issues may be warped and facts concealed from the public in campaign debate, so that people may cast their votes on the basis of inadequate information. For example, during the 1972 campaign, President Nixon, his press secretary, and spokespeople for the president's election committee all repeatedly denied responsibility for the burglary and bugging of the Democrats' Watergate headquarters. In the summer of 1973 Senate hearings disclosed in great detail the involvement of high government officials in the incident and in subsequent attempts to cover it up. And in the 1976 presidential election, Watergate, which had occurred during a Republican administration, worked to Gerald Ford's disadvantage.[100] Ford, the Republican incumbent, lost to Carter, the Democratic challenger.

To summarize, elections leave elected officials with a great deal of flexibility in governing. Yet elections also often set broad guidelines within which decision makers must stay—or risk reprisal by the voters.

## Continuity and Change

It is true that most American elections have tended to be fundamentally centrist, or middle-of-the-road in character. Parties and candidates have competed for the center ground in American politics because that is where the parties believed the biggest bloc of voters were.[101] For this reason candidates do not as a rule endorse radical programs of social change. Yet the New Deal marked a considerable departure in government's approach to America's problems. Since 1932 government has intervened in the social and economic order to an unprecedented extent. Even President Reagan's conservative approach and extensive budget cuts did not fundamentally alter the major social role played by the federal government. Its role as economic regulator has been approved by many voters in elections for five decades. At the same time, on many public issues, the coming to power of the Reagan administration did change the terms of the debate over social policy in America. Moreover, the Republican Party's capture of both the House and the Senate in 1994 was followed by a serious challenge within Congress to a number of long-established domestic programs and enactment of a law that ended the largest federally run welfare program. And President George W. Bush's election in 2000 also was followed by more conservative domestic policy initiatives. Elections do at times set broad parameters for change.

"The people," Key has observed, "may not be able to govern themselves but they can, through an electoral uprising, throw the old crowd out and demand a new order, without necessarily being capable of specifying exactly what it shall be. An election of this type may amount, if not to revolution, to its functional equivalent."[102]

Besides establishing a framework for change, elections also provide continuity and a sense of political community, for they are links in a chain that bind one generation of voters to the next. Every four years the voters come together in an act of decision that is influenced by the past and present, but designed to shape the future.

*At the start of the 1964 campaign there were 16,000 American troops in Vietnam as "advisers." Three months after his election in 1964, President Johnson ordered the bombing of North Vietnam. By June 1965, U.S. troops were admittedly fighting, not advising. By 1968 more than 500,000 American troops were in Vietnam. The last U.S. forces were pulled out by President Nixon in March 1973.

## CHAPTER HIGHLIGHTS

- In a democracy, the people choose who will govern, and that choice is expressed in the voting booth. The right to vote is basic to the American political system.
- In the federal system that exists in the United States, the voters choose at all levels of government.
- One overall pattern that emerges from all the data about the voter and the nonvoter in the United States is that those who are more advantageously situated in the social system vote more than the "have-nots," or less advantaged.
- Although American voters have been extensively analyzed, we still do not know precisely why they behave the way they do. We do not know which of many factors ultimately causes a person to stay home on Election Day or to vote for one candidate or party instead of another.
- Although party identification remains a key factor in American politics, it may be growing somewhat less important.
- In most elections since the Second World War, many voters have split their tickets when they vote.
- For national political parties, the prize is control of the presidency. But party success or failure is measured in terms of states won or lost. Broad voting patterns on the national level can easily be seen by comparing political maps in presidential years, such as those found inside the front and back covers of this book.
- The entire House of Representatives and one-third of the Senate are elected every two years. In a presidential election year, the vote for president may affect the vote for Congress and also can have an effect on state and local offices, although there are signs that in recent years the effect of the presidential vote on contests for other offices may be lessening.
- Voting requirements restrict the number of people who can step into the voting booth. The nominating process restricts choice because the voter is effectively limited to those candidates nominated by parties or running as independents and placed on the ballot.
- State laws govern the nominating process and the selection of party leaders. Although the Constitution provides for election of members of Congress and the president, it makes no direct mention of how they shall be nominated and placed on the ballot.
- In states using primaries, the most common form is the closed primary. About 20 states use the open primary.
- Permanent registration prevails in all but a few states. Periodic registration is used in a very small number of states.
- The secret (so-called Australian) ballot was not adopted by every state in the United States until 1950. Concern over voter intimidation and fraud led to pressure for secret ballots printed by public authorities. This ballot has two chief forms: the party-column ballot, or Indiana ballot, and the office-column ballot, or Massachusetts ballot.
- The Constitution does not provide for the popular election of the president. Instead, it provides that each state "shall appoint, in such manner as the legislature thereof may direct," electors equal in number to the representatives and senators that each state has in Congress. The electors form the electoral college.
- Instead of voting directly for president, an American, in casting his or her ballot, votes for a slate of electors that is normally pledged to the presidential candidate of the voters' choice.
- In the early 1960s, the Supreme Court made it clear that the Fourteenth Amendment required that seats in both houses of a state legislature and congressional districts be based on population. The Court had laid down the principle of "one person, one vote."
- Most American elections have tended to be fundamentally centrist, or middle-of-the-road in character. Parties and candidates have competed for the center ground in American politics because that is where the parties have believed the biggest bloc of voters were. But elections do at times set broad parameters for change.

## KEY TERMS

retrospective voting, p. 343
closed primary, p. 364
open primary, p. 364
blanket primary, p. 364
permanent registration, p. 365
periodic registration, p. 365
party-column ballot, p. 366
office-column ballot, p. 366
electoral college, p. 368
maintaining elections, p. 373
deviating elections, p. 373
realigning elections, p. 373

## SUGGESTED WEBSITES

**http://www.gallup.com**
*The Gallup Organization*
Since 1935, the Gallup Organization has conducted surveys to measure public opinion on various issues. Its polls cover five subject areas: Politics and Elections, Business, Social Issues and Policy, Managing, and Lifestyle.

**http://www.pollingreport.com**
*The Polling Report*
An independent and nonpartisan website that features public opinion polls from a variety of sources arranged by topic. The national survey data are updated whenever new polls are released.

**http://www.rockthevote.org**
*Rock the Vote*
A nonpartisan organization dedicated to educating young Americans about the importance of voting and the issues facing them as voters. Includes links to register to vote and education about important issues.

**http://www.vanishingvoter.org**
*Vanishing Voter Project*
A project of the Harvard University Kennedy School of Government, includes weekly polls of the electorate and a voter involvement index.

## SUGGESTED READING

Abramson, Paul R., Aldrich, John H., and Rhode, David W. *Change and Continuity in the 2000 and 2002 Elections** (CQ Press, 2003). A comprehensive study of recent voting behavior and historical trends in presidential and congressional elections. Includes sociological and psychological influences on voter choice, the nomination process, campaign strategies, voter turnout, and election outcomes.

Berelson, Bernard R., Lazarsfeld, Paul F., and McPhee, William N. *Voting: A Study of Opinion Formation in a Presidential Campaign** (University of Chicago Press, 1986). An influential study of how voters decide for whom they will vote. Based on interviews with about 1,000 residents of Elmira, New York, during the Truman-Dewey presidential contest of 1948.

Campbell, Angus, Converse, Philip E., Miller, Warren E., and Stokes, Donald E. *The American Voter* (University of Chicago Press, 1986). (Originally published in 1960 and an abridged paperback in 1964.) A landmark study of voting behavior, based on interviews with national samples of the American electorate.

Conway, M. Margaret. *Political Participation in the United States,* 3rd revised edition* (CQ Press, 2000). A comprehensive analysis of patterns of political participation. The author examines who gets involved in politics, for what reasons, and with what effects.

Fiorina, Morris P. *Retrospective Voting in American National Elections** (Yale University Press, 1981). An important analysis of voting behavior. Emphasizes that many voters make a rough judgment about the performance of the incumbent administration, and then cast their votes accordingly.

Flanigan, William H., and Zingale, Nancy. *Political Behavior of the American Electorate,* 11th edition* (CQ Press, 2005). A concise analysis and summary of research on how and why Americans vote.

Jacobson, Gary C. *The Politics of Congressional Elections,* 6th edition* (Longman, 2003). A comprehensive, general analysis of congressional elections. Focuses on the candidates, their campaigns, the voters, and the relationship between national politics and congressional elections.

Judis, John B., and Teixeira, Ruy. *The Emerging Democratic Majority, with a New Afterword** (Scribner, 2004). The author, two democratic-leaning writers, use census data, public opinion polls, and election returns to argue that long-term demographic trends favor the Democratic party. The book, written before President Bush won the 2004 election, contends that women, minorities, professionals, and working-class voters will over time help form a new Democratic majority.

Key, V. O., Jr. *The Responsible Electorate** (The Belknap Press of Harvard University Press, 1966). An examination of American voting behavior in presidential elections, based primarily on analyses of Gallup poll data from 1936 to 1960. Key argues that the voters' views on issues and government policy are quite closely related to how they vote in such elections.

Key, V. O., Jr. *Southern Politics in State and Nation,* 2nd edition* (University of Tennessee Press, 1984). (Originally published in 1949.) A landmark study of the politics of the South. Analyzes why the Democratic Party dominated that region for nearly three generations after the Civil War, and what the political consequences were.

Lazarsfeld, Paul F., Berelson, Bernard, and Gaudet, Hazel. *The People's Choice: How the Voter Makes Up His Mind in a Presidential Campaign,* 3rd edition (Columbia University Press, 1968). (Originally published in 1944.) A classic in the study of voting behavior, based on a series of interviews with potential voters in Erie County, Ohio, during the Roosevelt-Willkie presidential contest of 1940. The book stresses the relationship between the voters' socioeconomic status and how they voted.

Mayhew, David R. *Electoral Realignments: A Critique of an American Genre** (Yale University Press, 2002; softcover, 2004). The author examines 15 major propositions of realignment theory and then tests them. He argues there is little support for these propositions, concludes that realignment theory should be discarded, and suggests that other factors, such as the impact of war or race on elections, shape the voters' choice.

Nelson, Michael, ed. *The Elections of 2004** (CQ Press, 2005). Informative analysis of the 2000 elections. Includes a chapter on the postelection battle for control of the presidency.

Nie, Norman H., Verba, Sidney, and Petrocik, John R. *The Changing American Voter,* enlarged edition (Harvard University Press, 1979). An important sequel to the classic 1960 study, *The American Voter,* based primarily on public opinion polls from 1956 to 1973. The authors conclude that, compared with the 1950s, issues were more visible and had a greater effect on voting in the elections from 1964 through 1972.

Peirce, Neal R., and Longley, Lawrence D. *The Electoral College Primer 2000** (Yale University Press, 2000). A detailed study of the history of the electoral college and its effects in past presidential elections. Presents the case for abolishing the electoral college and electing presidents directly by popular vote.

Scammon, Richard M., and Wattenberg, Ben J. *The Real Majority* (Coward-McCann, 1970). A lively analysis of political attitudes and voting patterns. Argues that the majority of American voters are "unyoung, unpoor, and unblack," and contends that candidates who take moderate positions on issues—close to the "political center"—are more likely to be elected than candidates who take more extreme positions.

Schantz, Harvey L., ed. *American Presidential Elections: Process, Policy, and Political Change** (State University of New York Press, 1996). A comparative analysis of the 52 U.S. presidential elections held between 1788 and 1992. Emphasizes the basic patterns of presidential elections, and traces the impact of various types of presidential elections on public policy and American society.

Sundquist, James L. *Dynamics of the Party System: Alignment and Realignment of Political Parties in the United States,* revised edition* (The Brookings Institution, 1983). A comprehensive historical analysis of the relative electoral strength of America's political parties over a 150-year period.

Wattenberg, Martin P. *Where Have All the Voters Gone?** (Harvard University Press, 2002). A study of the decline of voter turnout between 1960 and 2000. Covers both presidential and midterm elections and compares U.S. turnout with turnout levels in other democratic countries. Argues that lower turnout benefited the Republicans in the presidential election of 2000, and especially in the midterm election of 1994.

*Available in paperback edition.

# Chapter 12

# The Congress

ON OCTOBER 10, 2002, the U.S. House of Representatives, by a vote of 296 to 133, authorized the president to use "the armed forces of the United States" in a war against Iraq. At 1:15 a.m. the next morning, the Senate also voted, 77 to 23, to authorize the use of military force against "the continuing threat" posed by the government of Saddam Hussein.[1] The congressional resolution also asserted that Iraq might use weapons of mass destruction in a "surprise attack" against the United States, or give such weapons to terrorists who would use them to attack America.

When American forces invaded Iraq in the spring of 2003, however, no nuclear, chemical, or biological weapons were found. By 2006, with the war going badly and U.S. casualties mounting, many of the same members of Congress who had voted to authorize military action against Iraq had become critics of the conduct of the war.

But back in 2002, with President George W. Bush warning that American national security was in danger, relatively few members of Congress—only 156 out of 535—risked voting against the resolution. Four members who were leading contenders for the Democratic presidential nomination in 2004—Senators John Kerry of Massachusetts, John Edwards of North Carolina, and Joseph Lieberman of Connecticut, and Representative Dick Gephardt of Missouri—all supported the congressional authorization to invade Iraq.

Before long, however, out on the primary campaign trail, the Democratic presidential aspirants were questioned about their votes on the Iraq resolution. In particular, Senator Kerry, who first came to national attention as a young veteran opposed to the war in Vietnam, had considerable difficulty in explaining his early support for the war in Iraq. His awkward efforts to defend his vote may have contributed to his defeat by Bush in the 2004 presidential election.

The legislative process forces members of Congress to take public positions on a host of controversial issues every year. Members know they may have to defend their votes in the next election.

Congress formulates the basic laws of the land. As one of the three separate branches of the government, it is an institution essential to the operation of the American political system. At times, it may resolve conflict between dueling political interests. And it provides an important window on American politics.

Key Question Against this background, in this chapter we will explore a key question: ***Can Congress meet the needs of the American people in the 21st century?***

There are other important questions to consider. Is Congress an outmoded institution, hobbled by powerful special interests and partisanship? Because senators and representatives are normally concerned about getting re-elected—and because campaigns are increasingly costly—are members too easily influenced by campaign contributions from business or labor? Are too many members of Congress insensitive to ethical standards? Can Congress legislate in those times when there is "divided government," with one party in control of the White House and the opposition party in control of Congress? How well does Congress represent the voters, and should its members lead or follow public opinion? What is the role of Congress in the American political system as a whole? How well does it perform that role?

### THE INTERNET AGE: LOBBYING BY BLACKBERRY

Early in 2004 the Senate defeated a bill that would have protected gun manufacturers by giving them immunity from lawsuits. A powerful interest group, the National Rifle Association, favored the bill but turned against it when an amendment was passed to extend a ban on assault weapons. Through the miracle of modern electronics, the NRA was able to communicate directly with senators on the floor of the Senate to kill the bill:

> WASHINGTON—Wayne LaPierre, executive vice president of the NRA . . . sent e-mail messages to senators urging them to reject it. Some Senate Democrats who supported immunity were spotted reading the e-mail message on their BlackBerry pagers; within minutes, a copy of the message—in which Mr. LaPierre said his group would use the vote "in our future evaluations and endorsement of candidates"—was circulating in the Democrats' cloakroom.
>
> "I'm a bit numb," said Senator Dianne Feinstein, Democrat of California, the lead sponsor of the assault weapons ban, after the final vote. Of the rifle association, she said: "They had the power to turn around at least 60 votes in the Senate. That's amazing to me . . . "

—Adapted from the *New York Times,* March 3, 2004

## CONGRESS: CONFLICT AND CONTROVERSY

Congress is like a big tent. And as in a circus, all sorts of balancing acts, distractions, and acrobatics are going on simultaneously under the Big Top. This should not be surprising. Most of the conflicts and pressures in the political system as a whole are reflected in the institution of Congress.

© Owen Franken/Corbis

## Senator Rudman: "This Isn't Much Fun"

In March 1992, Warren B. Rudman, a Republican senator from New Hampshire, announced that he would not seek a third term. Rudman later described why he left Congress:

> The Republican Party I grew up with was starting to vanish: the party of Eisenhower, Taft, Dirksen and Baker, men who believed in a strong defense and less government, and who didn't think you could solve every problem by passing a law. If someone had told me in the 1960s that one day I would serve in a Republican Party that opposed abortion rights—which the Supreme Court had endorsed—advocated prayer in the schools, and talked about government-inspired "family values," I would have thought he was crazy.
>
> To me the essence of conservatism is just the opposite: Government should not intrude in anything as personal as the decision to have a child, it should not be championing prayer or religion, and family values should come from families and religious institutions, not from politically inspired, Washington-based moralists. . . .
>
> I thought the essence of good government was reconciling divergent views with compromises that served the country's interests. But that's not how movement conservatives or far-left liberals operate. The spirit of civility and compromise was drying up. By the 1990s, many nights I would go home and shake my head and think, We're not getting a hell of a lot done here. And then I would think, This isn't much fun. . . .
>
> I kept my decision a secret from everyone except my family and a few close friends. . . . On December 28, 1992, while most of my staff was on vacation, I went to my Senate office for the last time, to pack up all my photographs and personal belongings and have them shipped back to New Hampshire. . . . I turned to Marion Phelan, my longtime aide, and said, "I never carved my name in the Daniel Webster desk," and we headed for the Senate floor.
>
> Each senator has a desk, the old-fashioned kind with tops that lift up like those that once were used in schoolrooms. By tradition each senator carves his name inside his desk, and the senior New Hampshire senator has the special privilege of carving his name in Daniel Webster's desk because, although Webster represented Massachusetts, he was a New Hampshireman.
>
> The Senate wasn't in session, so Marion could go onto the floor with me. We took a chisel and other tools I'd need to do the job right. Several of the Capitol Police came over to watch as I lifted the top of the desk and started to work. When I finished carving my name in the desk, I shook hands with everyone and made my exit.

—Warren B. Rudman,
the *Washington Post Magazine,* April 21, 1996

At its best, Congress can enact far-reaching and vital legislation that affects people's lives for the better—as, for example, when it passes laws and appropriations dealing with health care, education, and cancer or AIDS research. It doesn't always act in this fashion, however. Individual lawmakers often succeed in pushing through **pork-barrel legislation,** bills that benefit their home districts, or powerful corporate contributors, with sometimes wasteful or unnecessary public works or other projects.

Congress is a much-criticized institution, often attacked for failure to act, obstructionist rules, low ethical standards, and a variety of other imperfections. As an institution, it is seldom held in high esteem by the voters.

To take one example, for more than 20 years, until the enactment of Medicare in 1965, Congress declined to pass health care legislation for the elderly. Yet the need for such help was clear enough: In March 1965, a few months before passage of Medicare, the median income of Americans aged 65 and older was $1,355 a year (an amount equal to $7,909 in 2003).[2] Obviously, on such incomes most older Americans were unable to afford adequate health care in the face of rising medical costs.

What is more, the public supported such legislation; a Gallup poll in 1962 showed 69 percent in favor of Medicare.[3] By 1940 every West European country had some form of government health insurance. Yet the United States, the richest country in the world, had failed to act. A powerful interest group, the American Medical Association, fought Medicare as "socialized medicine," and for two decades Congress would not be moved.

But is all of the criticism leveled at Congress entirely fair? Many political scientists who have studied the operation of Congress have concluded that Congress does a fairly good job on the whole. Those who defend Congress argue that it is a generally representative assembly that broadly mirrors the desires of the people. If it fails to act "fast enough" to meet social needs, perhaps it is because the people do not want it to act any faster. And one may ask: How fast is fast enough? Congress to an extent, at least, reflects the diversity of American society. And often when Congress is divided on an issue and fails to act, it is because the country is divided on that issue.

## The Varied Roles of Congress

Congress is the national legislature. It plays a central and crucial role in the political system by making laws, the general rules that govern American society. Congress is

The American Past

## VIOLENCE IN THE SENATE

The Kansas-Nebraska Act of 1854, which opened up the territories to slavery if their residents voted for it, prompted heated—and ultimately violent—debates in Congress between pro- and antislavery legislators:

> Charles Sumner, a scholar and a radical lawyer, senator from Massachusetts as the result of a political deal, had begun to rival William H. Seward as the spokesman of antislavery sentiment. His handsome features and oratorical talent caused him to be compared with [Senator John C.] Calhoun; but he had none of Calhoun's restraint. He was one of those fortunately rare and rarely fortunate persons who are not only thick-skinned themselves but assume that everyone else is. In a turgid oration on 19 May 1856, "The Crime against Kansas," he exhausted the vocabulary of vituperation. The elderly and moderate Senator Butler of South Carolina he described as a Don Quixote whose Dulcinea was "the harlot slavery," and Stephen A. Douglas as Sancho Panza, "the squire of slavery, ready to do its humiliating offices." The tone of this speech was so nasty that it would probably have ended Sumner's political career, had not "Southern chivalry" demanded physical chastisement. Three days after its delivery a South Carolina congressman [Preston Brooks], a distant cousin of Senator Butler, passed up the opportunity to attack Sumner on the steps of the Capitol . . . then, with a stout stick, beat him senseless when sitting helplessly at his desk in the Senate chamber. The assailant was praised by the Southern press and presented by admirers with suitably inscribed sticks. Sumner, badly injured, returned to his seat only at intervals for the next three years; but he was now a hero and martyr in the North.
>
> —Samuel Eliot Morison, *The Oxford History of the American People*

called upon to deal with all of the major issues confronting the nation—the economy, the tax structure, protection of the environment, and many other problems. No less than the president, Congress, by legislating, decides national policy.

Most of the controversy over congressional performance focuses on lawmaking. But Congress plays other important roles. It has several nonlegislative functions: it proposes amendments to the Constitution; it may declare war; it can impeach and try the president or other civil officers of the United States, including judges; it may rule on presidential disability; it regulates the conduct of its members; and it has power to decide whether a prospective member has been properly elected or should be seated. The House may choose the president in the event of electoral deadlock. The Senate approves or rejects treaties and presidential appointments, and, through the unwritten custom of **senatorial courtesy,** individual senators who belong to the same political party as the president exercise an informal veto power over presidential appointments in their states.

In addition, Congress oversees and supervises the operations of the executive branch and the independent regulatory agencies. For example, when bureaucrats are closely questioned at appropriations hearings, Congress is exercising its supervisory powers, or, as its members like to call it, "legislative oversight"—the power of Congress to examine and supervise the operations of the executive branch.*

The power of the purse, which the Constitution grants to Congress, carries with it the power to monitor how well the money is spent. For this purpose Congress conducts investigations and holds hearings. These are ostensibly tied to a legislative purpose, but often they serve a broader function of focusing public attention on specific social problems.

For example, in February 2002, the House and Senate intelligence committees began a joint investigation

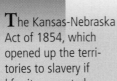

© George Tames/New York Times

*The term "legislative oversight" can be a bit confusing since "oversight" often means a mistake, or omission, as in to "overlook" something. But Congress uses it in the sense of overseeing or supervising.

*Making a Difference*

## FOR CAROLYN MCCARTHY, "THE ROAD IS ALWAYS LONG"

It all started for Carolyn McCarthy on December 7, 1993, when a deranged gunman opened fire with a 9-mm pistol on a Long Island Rail Road commuter train and killed six people, including her husband Dennis, and wounded 19 others, including her son Kevin.

The Long Island Rail Road massacre transformed Carolyn McCarthy into an advocate of gun control. Before it thrust her into the media spotlight, McCarthy was a Republican whose idea of political involvement was volunteering to pick up litter at the local beach. But when her congressman, Dan Frisa, voted in 1996 to repeal an assault weapons ban, she became incensed. When local party officials squelched her inquiries about mounting a primary challenge to Frisa, she gave up her GOP registration and launched a Democratic campaign to unseat him.

She raised more than $1 million and outspent Frisa. Frisa seemed at a loss for an effective response to McCarthy, and in the final days of the campaign, Frisa did a disappearing act, shunning appearances and interviews. McCarthy rolled to victory by 17 percentage points, taking 57 percent of the vote. She has been reelected ever since.

Drawing on more than 30 years' experience as a licensed practical nurse, McCarthy has worked on health-related bills. And as one who struggled with learning disabilities as a child, she has spoken for more federal aid for school districts to cope with the costs of educating learning-disabled children.

But make no mistake: Gun control legislation is her raison d'être on Capitol Hill. More than three-fifths of her substantive floor speeches so far in the 106th Congress have been on gun control matters or on issues arising from the Long Island shooting.

She often becomes teary-eyed when discussing gun control, a reminder to all how deeply personal the issue remains. She told the *New York Daily News* that her Long Island colleague, Republican Peter T. King, had urged her to try not to take politics so personally, but she finds that impossible.

Colleagues in the House say she has evolved from being a symbol to being an effective legislator as well. "She has the passion, the moral authority and the know-how to get things through," says Rep. Rosa DeLauro, Democrat of Connecticut.

© AP/Wide World Photos

Even opponents find her difficult to counter.

"I think Carolyn McCarthy is a very sincere, dedicated advocate for gun control unlike a number of other advocates," says the National Rifle Association's chief lobbyist, Jim Baker.

"The road is always long but I have faith," she says.

—Adapted from the Associated Press; and *Congressional Quarterly 50: 50 Ways to Do the Job of Congress*

into whether the nation's intelligence agencies had failed to provide adequate warning of the terrorist attacks of September 11, 2001.[4] A year later, the committees released a report critical of the FBI and CIA performance before 9/11.[5]

Perhaps even more important than congressional power to conduct investigations and hearings is the role of Congress in "legitimizing" the outputs of the political system. People are more likely to accept the policy decisions of a political system if major decisions are made by representative institutions. Congress, therefore, at times plays a key role in the resolution of conflict in American society. As in the case of all political institutions, Congress is subject to external pressures by organized interest groups, unorganized public opinion, the press, and individual constituents. Not every problem can be solved by passing a law. But in responding to social needs with legislation, Congress can at least help to ease the friction points.

In thus managing conflict (or making conflict manageable), Congress helps to integrate various groups and interests within the community by acting, to some extent, as a referee. However, as was noted in Chapter 7, not all groups in a pluralistic society have equal power. And highly organized, well-financed, business and single-issue lobbies may exercise an influence out of proportion to their number of supporters. Disadvantaged groups—the poor and African Americans, for example—may find it more difficult to influence Congress than does the oil industry. Consequently, in resolving conflict, Congress may still leave many groups unsatisfied.

Yet Congress does provide one of several points of access to the political system for many individuals and groups. The inputs, in the form of demands and supports by segments of the community, are transformed by Congress through the legislative process into policy outputs and binding decisions for all of society.

But Congress is more than just a legislature. It is also

"Perhaps the witness would care to reconsider his answer to the last question?"



a representative assembly of 535 men and women, and who they are is worth examining in some detail, for it may affect what they do.

## THE LEGISLATORS

### Portrait of a Lawmaker

When the 109th Congress convened in January 2005, the average age of members of the House of Representatives was 55 and the average of senators was 60.[6] In part, members of Congress are older than the average American because of constitutional restrictions: A member of the House must be at least 25 (and a citizen for seven years) and a senator must be at least 30 (and a citizen for nine years). In part, of course, it is explained by the fact that senators and representatives usually do not achieve their office without considerable prior experience in politics or other fields.

More than half the nation's population are women, but in the 109th Congress only 15.7 percent, or 70 representatives and 14 senators, were women.[7] (See Table 12-1.) Two of these senators chaired standing committees: Susan Collins headed Homeland Security and Governmental Affairs and Olympia Snowe chaired Small Business and Entrepreneurship. Women held seats on the four most exclusive standing committees: Appropriations (Dianne Feinstein, Kay Bailey Hutchison, Mary Landrieu, Barbara Mikulski, and Patty Murray); Armed Services (Hillary Rodham Clinton, Susan Collins, and Elizabeth Dole); Finance (Blanche Lincoln and Olympia Snowe); and Foreign Relations (Barbara Boxer and Lisa Murkowski).[8]

The 109th Congress had 42 African Americans and 29 Hispanic members, 26 in the House of Representatives and three in the Senate. There were six Asian or Native Hawaiian/Pacific Islanders in the House and two in the Senate. Congress had one Native American, serving in the House of Representatives.[9]

In many other respects, the socioeconomic makeup of Congress is not representative of the general population. For example, 218 out of 535 members, or about 41 percent of the 109th Congress, were lawyers. In the population as a whole, lawyers compose only about 0.7 percent of the labor force. Other major occupational groups of members of Congress were: business, 193; education, 98; agriculture, 33; journalism, 17; medical profession,

**TABLE 12-1**

**Women in the U.S. Senate, 109th Congress, 2004–2006**

| Name | Party | State | First Elected |
|---|---|---|---|
| Barbara Boxer | D | California | 1992 |
| Maria Cantwell | D | Washington | 2000 |
| Hillary Rodham Clinton | D | New York | 2000 |
| Susan Collins | R | Maine | 1996 |
| Elizabeth Dole | R | North Carolina | 2002 |
| Dianne Feinstein | D | California | 1992 |
| Kay Bailey Hutchison | R | Texas | 1993 (special) |
| Mary Landrieu | D | Louisiana | 1996 |
| Blanche Lincoln | D | Arkansas | 1998 |
| Barbara Mikulski | D | Maryland | 1986 |
| Lisa Murkowski | R | Alaska | 2002 (appointed) |
| Patty Murray | D | Washington | 1992 |
| Olympia Snowe | R | Maine | 1994 |
| Debbie Stabenow | D | Michigan | 2000 |

© Hyungwon Kang/Reuters/Corbis

Relatives of victims of the 9/11 terrorist attacks testify to a joint congressional investigating committee.

20; and law enforcement, 9.[10] As Roger Davidson has suggested, representatives "are recruited almost wholly from the same relatively high-status occupations."[11]

Although America is a highly urbanized society, Congress historically has been predominantly Main Street and rural. However, this is much less true today, since many members represent city and suburban districts.[12] Congress is also mostly Protestant; although a majority listed their religion as Protestants of various denominations, there were also 153 Roman Catholics and 37 Jewish members.[13] If one were to draw a portrait of a typical member of Congress, that person might turn out to be about 56, male, white, Protestant, and a lawyer.

How significant is it that in many ways Congress is not literally a cross section of America? Obviously, Congress does not have to be an exact model of the population in order to represent its constituents. Nor is it entirely surprising that lawyers are overrepresented in a body that makes laws. Yet it is not hard to see how some blacks, other minorities, women, blue-collar workers, the poor, and members of underrepresented socioeconomic groups in general may feel left out of a system that produces a predominantly white, male, Protestant, and upper-middle-class national legislature.

## The Life of a Legislator

"It is true that we just don't have much time to legislate around here."[14] The complaint was voiced by a Republican congressman who participated in a series of roundtable discussions about life on Capitol Hill. It could easily have come from almost any one of the 100 senators or 435 members of the House. There are so many demands on members of Congress that lawmakers soon discover they cannot possibly do all that is expected of them. One House member attempted some years ago to list all the aspects of his job. Only a sample is quoted here: "A Congressman has become an expanded messenger boy, an employment agency . . . wardheeler . . . kisser of babies, recoverer of lost luggage . . . contributor to good causes—cornerstone layer . . . bridge dedicator, ship christener."[15]

Although members of Congress differ in how they choose to allocate their time, it is constituents who elect legislators, so most of those elected spend a fair portion of their day trying to take care of the problems of their constituents. Many lawmakers bounce back and forth between Washington and their districts like Ping-Pong balls.

As of 2006, members of the House and Senate received salaries of $165,200 a year, plus funds to hire a staff and certain other allowances for office supplies, telephone calls, and travel. Although the basic salary and benefits are considerable, members of Congress also have substantial expenses—many maintain residences in both Washington and their hometowns, for example.

The mail and e-mail pour in from constituents and must, somehow, be answered. Because the volume of mail is so great, many lawmakers use computers to churn out personalized form letters. Thanks to the franking privilege, members of Congress are entitled to send mail to constituents without charge by putting their frank, or mark, on the envelope. A 1973 law restricts use of the frank to official business and forbids its use to solicit votes or money, or for mass mailings 60 days before an election. Even so, the privilege is widely abused by members who are simply puffing their accomplishments. Controversy over the franking privilege led to reforms in the 1990s, including rules to limit the amount of mail that members can send out to their constituents.

Computers enable senators and representatives to target specialized groups with their mailings. In addition, almost all members of Congress have e-mail addresses, and their own Web page as well. All of this technology has increased the advantages that incumbents enjoy over their challengers, who do not have free mailing privileges.

Not all of the incoming mail is friendly, of course. But few senators and representatives dare to reply to abusive letters as Congressman John Steven McGroarty of California once did. He wrote to a constituent: "One of the countless drawbacks of being in Congress is that I am compelled to receive impertinent letters from a jackass like you in which you say I promised to have the Sierra Madre mountains reforested and I have been in Congress two months and haven't done it. Will you please take two running jumps and go to hell."[16]

On a typical day, a member of Congress may spend an hour reading mail, making calls, dictating memos, then rush off to a 10 a.m. committee meeting, eat lunch (if there is time), dash to the floor for a vote, and then return to a committee hearing. Perhaps late in the afternoon the member manages to get back to the office, where a group of constituents is waiting. A powerful interest group (a labor union or business association, for example) has invited the member to one or more cocktail receptions, and he or she must dutifully put in an appearance, have a drink, and chew on a rubbery shrimp before getting home for dinner—that is, on the nights not spent at a dinner in some dreary hotel banquet hall. And some nights members must remain on Capitol Hill if debates or votes are scheduled. Members spend many weekends in their home state or district, flying there to march in the Veterans Day parade or listen to constituents' woes. All of this can be difficult for the family of a representative or senator.

One congressional survey asked a sample of representatives and senators how they allocated their time. More than two-thirds responded that they spent a "great deal" of their time meeting with constituents in their home districts. Just under half said they spent a "great deal" of time attending committee meetings. A smaller proportion of members said they spent a "great deal" of time speaking with lobbyists and government officials about legislative issues, studying legislation, working with informal groups of colleagues, and attending floor debate or watching it on television.[17]

Although members of Congress do spend much of their time handling problems of constituents, 77 percent of House members questioned in one study listed legislative work as their most time-consuming job; only 16 percent listed "Errand Boy; lawyer for constituents."[18]

"We're like automatons," one senator said. "We spend our time walking in tunnels to go to the floor to vote."[19]

Members of Congress must choose among alternative roles open to them—whether, for example, to concentrate on working for the interests of their districts, on seeking to become party leaders, on running for higher office, on specializing in a committee, or on seizing an issue that may bring them national recognition.

## The Image of the Legislator

Congress and its individual members enjoy a rather mixed public image. In recent years, voters have had a generally negative view of Congress, although this was

**TABLE 12-2**

**Public Attitudes toward Congress, 1965–2006**

| | Approve | Disapprove | Don't Know |
|---|---|---|---|
| 1965 | 64% | 26% | 10% |
| 1967 | 38 | 55 | 7 |
| 1968 | 46 | 46 | 8 |
| 1969 | 34 | 54 | 12 |
| 1970 | 34 | 54 | 12 |
| 1971 | 26 | 63 | 11 |
| 1974 | 38 | 54 | 8 |
| 1978 | 34 | 63 | 3 |
| 1982 | 29 | 54 | 17 |
| 1987 | 42 | 49 | 9 |
| 1990 | 24 | 68 | 8 |
| 1991 | 32 | 53 | 15 |
| 1992 | 19 | 78 | 3 |
| 1993 | 24 | 65 | 11 |
| 1994 | 23 | 70 | 7 |
| 1995 | 38 | 53 | 9 |
| 1996 | 39 | 49 | 12 |
| 1997 | 39 | 52 | 9 |
| 1998 | 42 | 52 | 6 |
| 1999 | 37 | 56 | 7 |
| 2000 | 51 | 42 | 7 |
| 2001 | 72* | 19 | 9 |
| 2002 | 50 | 40 | 10 |
| 2003 | 43 | 50 | 7 |
| 2004 | 42 | 51 | 7 |
| 2005† | 37 | 53 | 10 |
| 2006‡ | 27 | 67 | 7 |

*The spike in public approval occurred in the months after the terrorist attacks of September 11, 2001.

†Data from March 2004, 2005.

‡Data from May 2006.

SOURCES: Louis Harris; the *Washington Post;* and the Gallup poll.

A legislator's work is never done, as seen in this series of photographs of Representative Loretta Sanchez, Democrat of California.

A member of Congress must meet with constituents . . .

communicate with voters . . .

attend committee meetings . . .

and campaign for reelection . . .

By kind permission from the Office of Loretta Sanchez

not always the case. Voter attitudes toward Congress fluctuate markedly. For example, in 1965, after Congress passed landmark Great Society legislation, 64 percent of the public approved of its performance. By 2004, however, only 42 percent approved of the performance of Congress.

Low public confidence in Congress was reflected in demands to limit the terms of senators and representatives. In 1992, voters in 14 states approved term limits for members of both houses of Congress. However, in 1995 the U.S. Supreme Court ruled that the states could not pass laws limiting the terms of members of Congress.[20] As a result of that decision, only an amendment to the Constitution could impose congressional term limits.

There is a paradox in public attitudes toward the legislative branch: Public opinion of Congress as a whole may be negative, but individual lawmakers are often popular and frequently reelected. Since the Second World War, through 2002, some 93 percent of House members and 80 percent of senators who sought reelection were victorious.[21] As Richard F. Fenno, Jr., has asked: "How come we love our Congressmen so much more than our Congress?"[22]

## Representation: The Legislators and Their Constituents

Should members of Congress lead or follow the opinions of their constituents? The question poses the classic dilemma of legislators, mixing as it does the problems of the proper nature of representation in a democracy with practical considerations of the lawmaker's self-interest and desire for reelection.

One answer was provided by Edmund Burke, the 18th-century British statesman, in his famous speech to the voters of Bristol, who had just sent him to Parliament. As Burke defined the relationship of a representative to his constituents: "Their wishes ought to have great weight with him; their opinion high respect. . . . But his unbiased opinion, his mature judgment, his enlightened conscience, he ought not to sacrifice to you. . . . Your rep-

"And if I'm elected I promise to go with the flow."



resentative owes you, not his industry only, but his judgment."[23] Parliament, Burke contended, was an assembly of one nation, and local interests must bow to the general, national interest.

The Burkean concept of the legislator as **trustee** for the people, the belief that legislators should act according to their conscience, clashes with the concept of the representative as **instructed delegate,** the idea that legislators should automatically mirror the will of the majority of their constituents. (Burke encountered political difficulties with his own constituents; those who cite his independence as a role model for legislators seldom note that six years after his speech, he withdrew as the member from Bristol.)

On the other hand, members of Congress who attempted faithfully to follow opinion in their districts would soon discover that it was very difficult to measure opinion accurately. They would face the practical problem of how to go about it. And they would find that on some issues many voters had no strong opinions.

Despite these hurdles, members do try, of course, to gauge the thinking back home. They rely on conversations with friends, party leaders, and journalists in their states or districts; the mail, particularly personal letters; local newspapers; and political polls published in their states. Some lawmakers have turned to professional polling organizations for help. Others have mailed questionnaires to the voters. But such mail "polls" may be taken not so much to gauge constituency thinking as to promote legislators by flattering their constituents with a questionnaire.[24]

Even when opinions can be discerned and measured, the members are aware that a constituency is made up of competing interests and is actually several constituen-

## The Art of Pork-Barrel Politics

In an angry election year, when the worst name a politician can be called is "incumbent," Rep. Steny H. Hoyer (D-Md.) has found something good about that awful condition. In fact, Hoyer has come up with millions of good things.

There's the $10 million Hoyer wedged into the federal budget for a new aircraft testing facility at Patuxent River Naval Air Station. There's the $5 million for research on airplane ejection seats at Indian Head Naval Surface Warfare Center. And there's the $2 million for a new day-care center there.

Those projects have three things in common. They are in southern Maryland, three largely rural counties that the state legislature placed in Hoyer's district earlier this year. They are included in the House's defense appropriations bill at least in part because of Hoyer's lobbying. And they offer solid proof that, even at a time when voters seem eager to throw the bums out, being one of the bums ain't all bad.

Hoyer, the House's fourth-ranking Democrat and a senior member of the Appropriations Committee, is dramatically demonstrating to his new constituents the art of pork-barrel politics. He unabashedly declares that one man's pork is another man's national priority.

"'Pork' is an epithet that applies to projects that are not in one's district," Hoyer says. "It's politics. I'm trying to represent my area as effectively as I can. And I plead guilty to representing my area very effectively."

—*Washington Post,* July 5, 1992

cies. Often they can please one group only at the expense of offending another.

A large proportion of House and Senate members, therefore, reject the role solely of trustee or solely of instructed delegate. Instead, they try to combine the two by exercising their own judgment and representing constituency views. As Roger Davidson has suggested, "Many congressmen observe that their problem is one of balancing the one role against the other."[25] In interviews with 87 members of the House of Representatives, Davidson found that almost half, by far the largest group of respondents, sought to blend the trustee and delegate conceptions.[26]

Davidson and his colleague Walter J. Oleszek have emphasized the dual nature of Congress. On one hand, they note, Congress is an institution that makes laws and public policy. But, equally important, it is also a representative body of 535 men and women who must constantly relate to their home districts and constituents in order to be reelected. Thus, "there are two Congresses."[27]

Sometimes a member of Congress faces the dilemma of local versus national interest. Constituents may feel foreign aid is a waste of money, but the legislator may decide it is in the best interests of the United States and vote accordingly. Often, however, local interests are put first—that is where the voters are. And some members of Congress feel that their first obligation is to the constituency that elected them.

Political scientists have studied the process of how legislators make up their minds on an issue. David R. Mayhew has suggested that the "electoral connection," the relationship between members of Congress and their constituents, profoundly influences congressional behavior. "United States congressmen are interested in getting reelected," Mayhew emphasizes, and that basic fact, he adds, influences the kinds of activities members of Congress find it "electorally useful to engage in."[28] And Richard F. Fenno, Jr., has suggested that the reelection prospects of members of Congress depend greatly on their "home style"—the way they present themselves to constituents back in the district.[29]

Aage R. Clausen has concluded that members of Congress generally vote according to their known policy positions and display substantial stability and continuity in their voting patterns.[30] Donald R. Matthews and James A. Stimson have reported that when members of Congress must cast a vote on a complex issue about which their knowledge is limited, they search "for cues provided by trusted colleagues" who may possess more information about the legislation in question.[31]

To an extent the dilemma faced by the members of Congress may be artificial. One major study of constituent influence discovered that average voters know little about their representative's activities—a finding that contrasted with the view of most members of Congress, who regard their voting record as important to their reelection.[32] Approximately half the voters surveyed in one House election year said they had heard nothing about either the incumbent or the opposing candidate.[33]

## The House

Although Congress is one branch of the federal government, the House and Senate are distinct institutions, each with its own rules and traditions and each jealous of its own powers and prerogatives. (See Table 12-3.)

One basic difference, of course, was established by the Constitution, which provided two-year terms for members of the House and staggered six-year terms for senators. The result is that all members of the House, but only one-third of the Senate, must face the voters every other year.

TABLE 12-3

**Major Differences between the House and Senate**

| House | Senate |
|---|---|
| Larger (435 members) | Smaller (100 members) |
| Shorter term of office (2 years) | Longer term of office (6 years) |
| Less flexible rules | More flexible rules |
| Narrower constituency | Broader, more varied constituency |
| Policy specialists | Policy generalists |
| Power less evenly distributed | Power more evenly distributed |
| Less prestige | More prestige |
| More expeditious in floor debate | Less expeditious in floor debate |
| Less reliance on staff | More reliance on staff |
| Less press and media coverage | More press and media coverage |
| More partisan | Less partisan |

SOURCE: Adapted from Walter J. Oleszek, *Congressional Procedures and the Policy Process*, 4th ed. (Washington, D.C.: CQ Press, 1996), p. 26.

© Dennis Brack/Black Star/Stockphoto.com

Because the House has 435 members compared with 100 in the Senate, the House is a more formal institution with stricter rules and procedures. For example, the Senate permits unlimited debate most of the time, but representatives in the House may be limited to speaking for five minutes or less during debate.

And because there are so many representatives, they generally enjoy less prestige than senators. At Washington dinner parties where protocol is observed, House members sit below the salt, ranking three places down the table from their Senate colleagues. (House members are outranked not only by senators, but also by governors and former vice presidents.[34]) In the television age, some senators, especially those who are presidential aspirants, have become celebrities, instantly recognizable to the spectators in the galleries. By contrast, visitors in the House galleries find it difficult to pick out their own representative, let alone any other.

One survey reported that less than half of Americans—just 47 percent—could name their representative in Congress.[35] While the figure is somewhat low, it does not give the whole picture. Although many voters cannot *remember* the name of their own representative, a much higher percentage can *recognize* the name from those on a list. In a selected group of congressional districts, "virtually all voters recognized the name of the incumbent when they heard it," and "most had a positive or negative response."[36]

Despite its size, the House has achieved a stability of tenure and a role never envisioned by the Founding Fathers. The men who framed the Constitution distrusted unchecked popular rule and provided an indirectly elected Senate to restrain the more egalitarian House of Representatives (the Seventeenth Amendment in 1913 provided for the direct election of the Senate). As Gouverneur Morris put it: "The second branch [the Senate] ought to be a check on the first [the House]. . . . The first branch, originating from the people, will ever be subject to precipitancy, changeability, and excess. . . .The second branch ought to be composed of men of great and established property—an aristocracy. . . . Such an aristocratic body will keep down the turbulency of democracy."[37]

*for more information about the U.S. House of Representatives, see: http://www.house.gov*

Ironically, the House and Senate have on some issues exchanged places in terms of these expectations of the framers. One reason is that House seats are safer. A commonly cited standard for a "safe" congressional district is one in which the winner receives 55 percent of the vote or more. Less than that is considered "marginal." And House elections have shown a pattern of what David Mayhew has called "vanishing marginals."[38] That is, the percentage of congressional districts that are unsafe and marginal is relatively low.

Morris P. Fiorina has suggested one possible explanation for these "vanishing marginals." He contends that "the Washington System" (discussed in Chapter 14) may be responsible. Under it, members of Congress create new bureaucracies in the executive branch and then gain credit by helping constituents deal with the complex rules issued by the new agencies. Representatives from marginal districts, Fiorina contends, have increasingly found it possible to base their reelection on such casework for constituents and on "procuring the pork."[39]

Senate seats are less safe; often, a third of those running are elected with less than 55 percent of the vote. Since Senate races often tend to be close, there is a greater possibility of dramatic shifts in party strength in the Senate. Because members of the House are more likely to come from safe districts than their colleagues in the Senate, the House has sometimes been less responsive than the Senate to pressures for change in the status quo. Senators have statewide constituencies that are frequently dominated by urban areas with powerful labor and minority-group vote blocs; as a result, the Senate at times has proved to be the more "liberal" branch of Congress.[40] When the Republicans captured both houses of Congress in 1994, for example, the House, with its 73 freshman Republicans, was decidedly the more strongly conservative branch.

Despite the relative safety of House seats, there has been a dramatic turnover in the membership of the House in recent years. For example, a majority of the members of the Congress that convened in January 2003 were relative newcomers who had been elected in one of the previous five elections.[41] Some members, tired of constituent pressures and election campaigns every two years, have quit. Others, of course, have been defeated.

## Power in the House: The Leadership

The **speaker,** who leads the majority party in the House, is the presiding officer and the most powerful member. The position of speaker is provided for in the Constitution ("The House of Representatives shall chuse their Speaker and other Officers").

The speaker has a number of official powers: to preside over the House, to recognize or ignore members who wish to speak, to appoint the chair and the party's members of the Rules Committee, to appoint members of special or select committees that conduct special investigations, to refer bills to one or more committees, and to exercise other procedural controls.

Much of the speaker's real power, however, stems from the combination of these formal duties with that of political leader of the majority party in the House. Technically, the speaker is elected by the House, with each party offering a candidate. In practice, the speaker is chosen at the start of each Congress by a caucus, or meeting, of the majority party. Because in the past, at least, the formal voting in the House has been strictly along party lines, the majority party's candidate for speaker has automatically won.

Historically, the speaker exercised great power until 1910, when the rules were revised to strip much of the speaker's formal power. But a speaker with a strong personality and great legislative skill can still exert broad influence in the House, as Newt Gingrich did briefly, after the Republicans won control of the House in 1994, and as Sam Rayburn of Texas demonstrated when he held that post for 17 of the 21 years between 1940 and 1961. Over bourbon and branch water in a small room in the Capitol, Rayburn and his intimates would plan strategy for the House and swap political stories in an informal institution known as the "Board of Education."[42] Today, the speaker remains a key figure, exercising more formal powers than at any time since 1910.

For 10 years, until he retired in 1987, Thomas P. "Tip" O'Neill, Jr., of Massachusetts reigned as speaker, and he made a considerable impact on both Congress and the nation. As a member of the House, he had succeeded John F. Kennedy. He became majority leader in 1972 and speaker in 1977. O'Neill, a huge barrel-chested man with a thatch of shaggy white hair and a booming, easy laugh, proved to be a colorful speaker. He looked exactly like what he was—an old-time Irish politician from Boston. But he was more than that. Early in his career as a House leader, he was called upon to take actions of historic importance for the nation. As majority leader, O'Neill played a key role in the decision to hold the impeachment hearings that became an important factor in Richard M. Nixon's decision to resign as president in 1974.

O'Neill's successor was Representative Jim Wright, a Texas Democrat from Fort Worth. He was able to guide a good deal of legislation through Congress but was pugnacious, often quick-tempered, and controversial. Wright resigned in 1989 after the House Ethics Committee charged him with violating House rules over a dubious book contract that earned him $55,000. The House then chose Representative Thomas S. Foley, a liberal Democrat from Spokane, Washington, as the new speaker.

Then, after the election of 1994, Newt Gingrich of Georgia became the Republican speaker of the House. Gray-haired, stocky, and combative, Gingrich exercised great power as speaker and became almost as familiar to the public as the president, Bill Clinton. It was Gingrich who had brought the ethics charges against Jim Wright.

Ironically, Gingrich himself became a subject of controversy over his own book deal, for which he had agreed to accept a $4.5 million advance from the publisher. Because of criticism that he was exploiting his position as speaker, Gingrich backed down and instead accepted normal royalties on the book's sales. Gingrich was also criticized for his actions as head of GOPAC, the political action committee he had headed that was a powerful force when the Republicans won both houses of Congress in 1994 for the first time in 40 years. Gingrich was investigated by the House Ethics Committee and was reprimanded and fined.

In 1999 Republican J. Dennis Hastert of Illinois became the 51st speaker of the House. A former high school wrestling coach, Hastert was promoted to speaker only because of the sudden resignations and retirements of Gingrich and his expected successor, Bob Livingston,

© Ron Sachs/Corbis

J. Dennis Hastert was the longest-serving speaker of the House, from 1999 until the Democrats won control of the body in November 2006.

of Louisiana. As speaker, Hastert ably consolidated his power among House Republicans.

Hastert also campaigned hard for his fellow Republicans, raising "more money for House candidates than any previous Speaker."[43] Hastert, whom some had dubbed the "accidental speaker," had become an effective leader.

The speaker has two chief assistants, the majority leader and the majority whip, both elected by the party caucus. The majority leader is the party's floor leader and a key strategist. Together with the speaker and the members of the House Rules Committee, the majority leader schedules debate and negotiates with committee chairs and party members on procedural matters. The majority **whip,** along with a number of deputy whips, is responsible for rounding up party members for important votes and counting noses. (The term "whip" comes from "whipper-in," the person assigned in English fox hunts to keep the hounds from straying.) Tom DeLay, the majority whip for eight years, was so effective in that job that he earned the nickname "The Hammer." He later became the House majority leader but resigned that post, and then retired from Congress, after being indicted in Texas in 2005 on charges of money laundering.

The minority party also elects a minority leader, a minority whip, and deputy whips. In January 2003 Nancy Pelosi, a liberal from San Francisco, became the Democratic minority leader—the first woman to lead a major party on Capitol Hill. Democrats chose Steny Hoyer of Maryland to be their new whip. Pelosi's leadership position meant that she often appeared on television to speak for her party.

## The Rules Committee

The House Committee on Rules exercises considerable control over what bills are brought to the floor. Most major legislation cannot be debated without a special rule from the Rules Committee that limits the time for floor debate and the extent to which a bill may be amended. The whole House must adopt each special rule before it goes into effect.[44]

In 1961 President Kennedy and Speaker Sam Rayburn barely won a fight to enlarge the House Rules Committee and thus curb the power of its conservative chairman. Democrats at that time controlled the House, but a coalition of southern Democrats and Republicans frequently succeeded in blocking passage of liberal legislation. In the 1961 change, the committee's size was increased, and the new members were chosen for their support of the administration's position on controversial bills.[45] By the 1970s, the Rules Committee was no longer a bottleneck to legislation. The most important change made during the early 1970s empowered the speaker of the House to nominate all majority-party members of the Rules Committee. Since then, as a result, the committee has operated as an arm of the leadership of the political party in control of the House, with nine of its 13 members drawn from the majority party.

## The Legislative Labyrinth: The House in Action

The basic power structure of the House, then, consists of the speaker, the floor leaders and whips of the two major parties, the Rules Committee, and the chairs of the 19 standing committees. How these individuals and committees interact powerfully affects the fate of legislation. But the business of making laws is also governed by a complicated, even Byzantine, set of rules and procedures. Although most citizens are not familiar with them, these procedures can affect policy outcomes. Whether a bill is steered through the legislative labyrinth or gets lost along the way often depends on how the rules and procedures are applied.

About 5 percent of all bills and joint resolutions introduced in Congress become public law. In the 107th Congress (2001–2003), for example, 7,439 public bills and joint resolutions were introduced but only 377 became public laws.[46]

After a House member introduces a bill, the speaker

refers it to a committee. Often, the choice is limited by the jurisdictions of the standing committees, but when jurisdictions overlap or when new kinds of legislation are introduced, the speaker may have considerable discretion in deciding where to assign a bill.

Only about 16 percent of bills get out of committee in the House. The committee chair may assign the measure to one of the 88 subcommittees of the standing committees. If the bill is reported out of committee, it is placed on one of four calendars, or lists of business eligible for House floor consideration. The various House calendars and the kinds of bills referred to them are shown in Table 12-4.

On three days a week any bill may be debated under a procedure called "suspension of the rules." More than half of the bills passed by the House are enacted under this procedure; only 40 minutes of debate is permitted, with no floor amendments, and a two-thirds vote is required for passage. Some uncontroversial bills in the House are passed by unanimous consent.

A quorum consisting of a majority of the House, 218 members, is required for general debate. When the House is considering legislation that deals with taxes and spending, however, it sits as a **Committee of the Whole,** a device that allows the House to conduct its business with fewer restrictions on debate and a quorum of only 100 members.

In both the House and the Committee of the Whole, there are various ways of voting. If 25 representatives in the Committee of the Whole (or 44 in the House) demand a **recorded vote,** members vote electronically and the position of each is noted and published in the *Congressional Record.* Sometimes the House uses a voice vote, in which members shout "aye" or "no" and the chair decides the result.

When an electronic vote is taken, members insert a plastic identification card in one of 44 voting stations on the floor and press one of three buttons. If the member votes "yes," a green light appears on a display board over the speaker's head; for "no," a red light appears, and for "present," an amber light. The use of electronic voting has greatly reduced the time needed for recorded votes; under the old system, the clerk called the roll and each member present had to answer by name. The changes in voting procedure in the Committee of the Whole and the inauguration of electronic voting in the House itself have greatly increased the number of on-the-record votes by representatives.

Supporters or opponents of a bill sometimes request recorded votes as a delaying tactic to gain time to round up their forces. Often, however, such votes are demanded to place members on the spot; in a recorded vote each representative's position must become a matter of public record. Some interest groups regularly rate the records of members on the basis of their recorded votes. Constituents may not pay much attention to how representatives vote, but opponents in an election campaign may use legislators' recorded votes on key issues against them.

When debate is concluded in the Committee of the Whole, the House may vote on final passage. On rare occasions, the House may vote instead to send the bill back to its committee of origin (thereby killing it permanently), or it may send the bill back to the committee with instructions to make further changes in the bill (thereby delaying it temporarily).

TABLE 12-4

**Regulating Legislative Traffic: The House Calendars**

|  |  |
|---|---|
| **Union** | Bills that directly or indirectly appropriate money or raise revenue are placed on the Union Calendar. |
| **House** | Bills that do not appropriate money or raise revenue go on the House Calendar. Most bills go either to the Union Calendar or House Calendar. |
| **Private** | Bills that affect specific individuals and deal with private matters, such as claims against the government, immigration, or land titles, are placed on the Private Calendar and are called on the first and, with the speaker's approval, third Tuesdays of each month. |
| **Discharge** | Motions to force a bill out of committee are placed on the Discharge Calendar if they receive the necessary 218 signatures from House members. The procedure is rarely successful. |

## Televising Congress

In March 1979, amid much controversy, the House began live television and radio broadcasts of floor debate. The Senate permitted televising of its deliberations starting in 1986. The broadcasts from both chambers are carried gavel-to-gavel over the nonprofit C-SPAN network by nearly 7,900 cable television systems in all 50 states, with a potential audience of 86 million households as of 2004.* In addition, local stations and the major networks sometimes carry excerpts.

*for more information about the C-SPAN network, see:*
*http://www.cspan.org*

When the television coverage began, there were dire predictions that publicity-seeking members would en-

*Data provided by C-SPAN, online at <http://www.cspan.org/about/company/>. C-SPAN carries proceedings of the House and presidential campaigns. A second cable network, C-SPAN2, televises Senate proceedings and current events and issues. C-SPAN3 during the day televises public affairs events from Washington and elsewhere; at night and on weekends it carries programs about American history.

gage in ham acting and long-winded oratory. Although some members did play to the cameras, a majority of House members reported they were satisfied with the results. Nevertheless, the opportunity to posture for audiences at home has lengthened House sessions. "There are an awful lot of added speeches that we wouldn't have without television," Speaker O'Neill once complained.[47]

Not all members of the public have been impressed by watching Congress on television. "The results of government in action are disgusting enough without having to have it aired," a woman in Winston-Salem, North Carolina, wrote to the House. But a man in Chelsea, Massachusetts, wrote: "This has given me much more knowledge of the manner in which the laws of this great nation are devised, debated, amended and finally resolved."[48]

Many viewers do not know, however, that television in the House operates under restrictions. The cameras are operated by employees of the House, not by the cable networks. And under the rules set by the speaker, the cameras are not permitted to pan around the floor and show members yawning, sleeping, or fidgeting. Most of the time, during regular floor debate, the cameras must focus on the person speaking. However, occasionally the reaction of a member to the debate is shown. The cameras also show members when they file into the chamber and vote.

The Senate, after resisting television for many years, finally voted in 1986 to permit the deliberations on the Senate floor to be televised. Since the 1950s, Senate committee meetings, particularly important investigations that attracted widespread public interest, have often been televised.

© Paul Conklin/PhotoEdit

## THE SENATE

The Senate may not be "the most exclusive club in the world" or a "rich man's club," although it has been called both. But it certainly has both the atmosphere and appearance of a club. Its membership is relatively small; its quarters are ornate and gilded; its ways are slow. In 2003, there were 40 millionaires in the Senate.[49] And with good reason; the growing costs of Senate campaigns, and legal limits on contributions by individuals, mean that rich candidates and incumbents may spend millions of dollars of their personal fortunes to finance their own campaigns. Senator Jon Corzine of New Jersey spent a record $63.2 million, including a record $60.2 million of his own money, in his successful 2000 Senate campaign.[50]

***for more information about the U.S. Senate, see: http://www.senate.gov***

But the folkways and customs of the Senate have changed markedly since the late 1950s when William S. White, then Senate correspondent of the *New York Times,* wrote of the "Inner Club" run by southerners.[51] Around the same period, Donald Matthews, a political scientist, described the Senate's "unwritten rules of the game, its norms of conduct." The freshman senator, Matthews wrote, was expected to serve a silent apprenticeship, to be one of the Senate "work horses" rather than one of the "show horses," to develop a legislative specialty, pay homage to the institution, and observe its folkways.[52] At the time, these included the elaborate courtesy with which senators, even bitter enemies, customarily addressed each other on the floor.

A decade later Nelson W. Polsby argued that "the role of the Senate in the political system has changed over the last 20 years," decreasing the importance of Senate norms. He contended that television, with its ability to publicize individual senators, had made the Senate "an incubator of presidential hopefuls" and eroded the significance of its rules of behavior.[53] And Ralph K. Huitt observed that the Senate has always had a place for "mavericks" and "independents."[54]

Today, newcomers to the Senate often speak up and speak out, sometimes gaining national recognition very rapidly. Many of the old ways have faded. As political scientist Barbara Sinclair has noted, senators now seek "broad involvement across multiple issues and arenas."[55] She adds: "In the contemporary Senate, freshmen are not expected to remain on the sidelines, nor even to be restrained in their participation in committee or on the

© Randy Duchaine/Corbis

floor."[56] Thus, a "new Senate style" has emerged, replacing the old behavior.[57] Although courtesy is still observed in floor debate, "it seems to be breached more often than it used to be."[58] It is not unknown for senators to yell at each other on the Senate floor; the sedate solons of yesteryear might not recognize the old club today.

When a Democratic senator, Patrick Leahy of Vermont, questioned lucrative no-bid contracts awarded in Iraq to Vice President Dick Cheney's former company, Halliburton, the vice president famously used an obscene four-letter word in an acrimonious exchange with Leahy on the Senate floor. As *USA Today* reported the incident, the vice president suggested that the senior senator from Vermont "do something to himself that is not anatomically possible."[59]

Political scientists Robert L. Peabody, Norman J. Ornstein, and David W. Rohde have also analyzed the decline of folkways and norms in the Senate. The emergence of the Senate as "a major breeding ground for presidential candidates," they suggest, has affected the behavior of "a wider circle of senators." For example, when Senator John F. Kennedy set his sights on the presidency, he spoke out on a variety of subjects "beyond the jurisdictions of his original committee assignments." Kennedy was contributing to the decline of the silent apprenticeship as a Senate norm. Soon, other senators with presidential ambitions began to speak out, adding to "the breakdown of apprenticeship."[60]

In 2004, five of the nine candidates for the Democratic presidential nomination were senators or a former senator. Two years later, some ten senators, including the Republican Senate Majority Leader, Bill Frist, were hoping to move into the White House in 2008. As more senators run for president, or hope to be picked for vice president, they can be expected to ignore the norm of "legislative work," the authors of the study of Senate folkways argued. And the tradition that senators should specialize in certain subjects has been weakened by the need for presidential contenders to be generalists, with a wide knowledge of public policy questions.[61] For example, when Senator John Kerry of Massachusetts clinched the Democratic presidential nomination early in 2004, he spoke out on a wide range of issues, from taxes and job losses to foreign policy.

Another reason that senators today are more vocal even as newcomers is that they have become much more vulnerable to electoral challenges. In a sense, they must begin working for reelection from day one. To the public, "senators are right out front as visible targets for the expression of voter dissatisfaction."[62]

## Power in the Senate: The Leadership

Just as the speaker is elected by the House, the Senate elects a president pro tempore, who occasionally presides in the absence of the vice president. Although the office is provided for in the Constitution, it has little formal power. Usually, this position is filled by the senior member of the majority party. In 2006, the president pro tempore, a Republican, was Senator Ted Stevens of Alaska, a senator for 36 years, since 1968.

The closest parallel to the speaker is the Senate majority leader, who is the most powerful elected leader of the Senate—although, as in most political offices, a great deal of the power wielded by the majority leader depends on the person and political circumstances. Lyndon Johnson, the Democratic Senate leader from 1953 to 1960, was widely regarded as an extraordinarily skillful and powerful floor leader.[63] Johnson's power to persuade was formidable. A big man, he towered over most other senators as, on occasion, he subjected them to "The Treatment"—a prolonged exercise in face-to-face persuasion that combined elements of a police "third degree" with Johnson's flair for dramatic acting.[64]

© Mark Wilson/Getty Images

Female senators of the 108th Congress; seated: Olympia Snowe (R-ME) , Mary Landrieu (D-LA, in blue), Blanche Lincoln (D-AR), Barbara Boxer (D-CA), Susan Collins (R-ME), Dianne Feinstein (D-CA), Maria Cantwell (D-WA); standing: Hillary Rodham Clinton (D-NY), Elizabeth Dole (R-NC), Kay Bailey Hutchison (R-TX), Barbara Mikulski (D-MD), Lisa Murkowski (R-AK), Debbie Stabenow (D-MI), Patty Murray (D-WA).

In contrast, Johnson's successor as majority leader was the soft-spoken Mike Mansfield of Montana. When Mansfield was accused of not providing sufficient leadership for the Senate, he declared: "I am neither a circus ringmaster, the master of ceremonies of a Senate nightclub, a tamer of Senate lions, or a wheeler and dealer."[65] When Mansfield retired from the Senate in 1977, Robert C. Byrd of West Virginia was elected the majority leader. In June 2006 Byrd, at 88, became the longest-serving member in the history of the Senate.

© George Tames/New York Times

Senator Lyndon B. Johnson giving Senator Theodore F. Green "The Treatment"—a forceful exercise in face-to-face persuasion.

Byrd, who rose from rural poverty in the hills of West Virginia, played country music on his fiddle for the voters and even released a record album. Extremely hardworking, Byrd, when he served as majority leader, concentrated more on making the Senate work than on influencing legislation ideologically.[66] By 2003, Byrd, no longer the Senate leader, had achieved the status of an elder statesman. His was a lonely, often eloquent voice cautioning against the rush to war in Iraq.

Senator George J. Mitchell of Maine succeeded Byrd in 1988. He grew up in Waterville, Maine, in modest circumstances; his father was a janitor at Colby College and his mother was a Lebanese immigrant. As majority leader, Mitchell projected an image of calm and confidence.

Before Bob Dole of Kansas left the Senate in 1996 to campaign for the presidency, he served as the Republican majority leader. He was defeated that year by President Clinton, who was reelected to a second term.

When George W. Bush, a Republican, was inaugurated in 2001, he could look forward to working with a Republican Congress. His party controlled the House, and although the Senate was divided 50–50, Republicans effectively were in control, because in case of a deadlock, Vice President Dick Cheney, a Republican, would cast the tie-breaking vote.

But after only four months, in a dramatic move, Senator James M. Jeffords of Vermont, a moderate, left the Republican Party and became an independent. That gave control of the Senate to the Democrats by a razor-thin margin, 50–49. Overnight, the Senate minority leader, Thomas A. Daschle of South Dakota, became majority leader. Although he operated in a low-key style, he became much more visible on television as a party spokesman. The sudden shift in the Senate gave Democrats the chairs of all the committees and subcommittees and control of the legislative agenda. Trent Lott of Mississippi, who had been the majority leader until Jeffords' move, became the Senate minority leader.

© Joe Raedle/Getty Images

Senate Democratic leader Harry Reid of Nevada

After the Republicans captured the Senate in the 2002 midterm elections, Lott was again poised to become majority leader when Congress reconvened in January. However, Republican senators forced Lott to withdraw and resign as party leader in December after he praised Senator Strom Thurmond and his 1948 presidential bid in which the South Carolina senator, then a Democrat, had advocated racial segregation.[67] Republican senators, by conference call, chose Senator William H. Frist of Tennessee to be the new majority leader.[68] A legislator for only eight years, Frist's claim to party leadership rested on his success as chairman of the National Republican Senatorial Committee. The White House also strongly endorsed Frist, a surgeon turned politician, to be the leader of Senate Republicans.

As party leader, Frist sought input from many Republican senators, especially committee chairs, with whom he held weekly meetings.[69] During his first year as majority leader, Frist's biggest legislative victory was passage in November 2003 of the Medicare bill that provided a prescription drug benefit for the first time.

## The Senate in Action

Unlike the House, with its complex procedures, calendars, and tight restrictions on debate, the Senate is more informal and less bound by rules. In part this is because the Senate is smaller than the House.

Senate bills appear on only one legislative calendar, and they are usually called up by unanimous consent. Since a single senator may object to this procedure, the majority leader, in conducting floor business, consults with the minority leader across the aisle on most major matters to avoid objections. A separate, second Senate calendar is used to schedule debate on treaties and nominations.

The Senate does not have electronic voting as the House does; instead, the clerk calls the roll, reading out the name of each senator. The yes or no vote of each member is checked off by the clerk on a printed form and the tally is announced.

## The Filibuster

Most of the time, the Senate allows unlimited debate. Because of this, a single senator, or a group of senators, may stage a **filibuster** to talk a bill to death and prevent it from coming to a vote. (The word "filibuster" originally meant a privateer or pirate, and its origin in American politics is not certain.[70]) Usually, the filibuster is used to defeat a bill by tying up the Senate so long that the measure will never come to a vote. But a number of factors, including a 1975 rule change making it easier to cut off debate, have combined to diminish the importance of the filibuster as a weapon to block legislation.

The traditional filibuster, of the kind staged by the actor James Stewart in the classic 1939 movie *Mr. Smith Goes to Washington,* is rarely seen now. Rather, the mere threat of a filibuster, or "extended debate," may be enough to bring about compromise on a bill. Or senators may invoke various points of order and other procedural rules to tie up the Senate without actually making a long speech.

Senators more often can delay or even kill floor action on legislation or other Senate matters simply by asking their party leaders not to schedule them—an informal tactic known as a **hold.** This maneuver can effectively stall action on bills or a nomination for an ambassador or other administration official whose appointment requires senate confirmation.

To conduct an old-style filibuster, all that senators must do is remain on their feet and keep talking. For the first three hours, their comments must relate to the subject of the debate, but after that, they may, if they wish, read the telephone book. The record for such marathon performances by a single senator was set by Senator Strom Thurmond, who spoke against the Civil Rights Act of 1957 for 24 hours and 18 minutes.

A group filibuster may go on for many days or even months. When one senator tires, he or she merely "yields" to a fresher colleague, who takes over. To counter these tactics, the Senate may meet round-the-clock in the hope of wearing down the filibusterers. But the senators conducting the filibuster may retaliate by suggesting the absence of a quorum (51 senators). Such a demand voiced at, say, 4 a.m. is inconvenient for other senators. So, senators attempting to break the filibuster set up cots in the halls and straggle in to answer the roll; then they try to go back to sleep.

Today, however, more often than not, the Senate permits "gentleman's filibusters" that run from 9 a.m. to 5 p.m. and allow senators to get home in time for dinner.

"Listen, pal! I didn't spend seven million bucks to get here so I could yield the floor to you."



This was not always the case. Donald A. Ritchie, the associate historian of the Senate, recalled the days when senators such as Huey Long, the Louisiana Democrat, would take the floor for marathon filibusters. "He used to read recipes for gumbo and for pot liquor and greens, the Bible and Shakespeare," Ritchie said.[71]

Under Rule XXII of the Senate, a filibuster may be ended if three-fifths of the entire Senate (60 members) vote for **cloture.** (To cut off debate on changes in Senate rules, a vote of two-thirds of the senators present is still required.) Cloture is difficult to impose. From 1919 through May 2006, it was voted only 253 times in 684 attempts.[72] Under the rules, even when cloture is invoked to cut off debate, senators may continue to talk for 30 hours.

In 2005 Bill Frist, the Senate Republican leader, threatened to change the rules to prevent Democrats from using filibusters to block Senate confirmation of judges nominated by President George W. Bush. The rule change, the so-called "nuclear option," was averted by a compromise fashioned by a bipartisan group of senators.

One of the most dramatic—some thought comic—episodes surrounding a filibuster took place early in 1988, when Senate Republicans tried to defeat a Democratic bill that would have limited the cost of Senate campaigns. Senator Robert C. Byrd invoked a rule to compel the attendance of senators in the chamber. He ordered the sergeant-at-arms to arrest any senators who could be found and bring them to the floor. The sergeant-at-arms and a posse of Capitol police began scouring the buildings: "They spotted Sen. Steven D. Symms (R-Idaho), but he fled before they could apprehend him."[73] Then the police "forced their way into the office of Sen. Bob Packwood (R-Ore.), arrested him and carried him feet-first into the Senate chamber in a flamboyant climax to a bitter all-night filibuster."[74] Angry Republicans accused the Democrats of turning the Senate into a "banana republic." The Democrats failed in their effort to invoke cloture to end the filibuster, and the bill, having been successfully blocked by the Republicans, did not pass.

## The Party Machinery

Senate and House Republicans and Democrats are organized along party lines for both political and legislative purposes. As noted earlier, in the House and Senate, the leader of each party is assisted by a whip, and several deputy whips, to round up members for key votes.

In addition, the party conference (or caucus, in the case of House Democrats) consists of all the members of that party in each branch of Congress. The party conferences elect leaders, who assume the title of majority or minority leader, depending on which party controls the House and Senate.

## Circus in the Senate

In 2003, Republicans staged a filibuster to try to outmaneuver Democrats who threatened to use the same tactic to block four of President George W. Bush's nominees for federal judgeships. The resulting chaos was less than dignified:

> WASHINGTON—The great Senate 30-hour anti-filibuster filibuster started at 6 o'clock Wednesday evening . . . and the much-touted dignity of the Senate reigned supreme until . . . about 6:10, when Tom Harkin (D-Iowa) held up a sign that revealed his plans for the night: "I'll Be Home Watching *The Bachelor*. . . ."
>
> This "reverse filibuster" was different. It was . . . designed by the majority (the Republicans) to pressure the minority (the Democrats) to give up its threat to filibuster against four of President Bush's nominees for judgeships. . . .
>
> "This is a travesty," said Minority Whip Harry Reid (D-Nev.). Reid . . . responded by launching a time-wasting filibuster of his own last Monday, talking for more than eight hours—a speech that included goulash recipes, advice on how to keep rabbits out of a garden, and a dramatic reading of six chapters of "Searchlight: The Camp That Didn't Fail," his 1998 book about his Nevada home town. . . .
>
> Downstairs . . . the Democrats are holding a pep rally for supporters, some of whom wear T-shirts that read: "We Confirmed 98% of Bush's Judges And All We Got Was This Lousy T-Shirt." . . . There's also a box billed as a "Care Package for Courageous Senators." Its contents include coffee, candy bars, a copy of the Constitution and Pepto-Bismol tablets that are said to counteract the nausea induced by Republican rhetoric.
>
> Outside, the sun is fighting through heavy gray clouds, illuminating the magnificent dome of the Capitol. Police in heavy coats are standing guard. . . . "I could see if it was something important like the budget or Iraq," the cop says, "but who cares about judicial appointments? This marathon has been going on for more than 13 hours now. There's still nearly 17 hours to go.
>
> "They should get a life," the cop says.
>
> —*Washington Post,* November 14, 2003

In addition, the policy committees of each party provide a forum for discussion of party positions on legislative issues. In both the House and Senate, members actively compete for assignment to choice committees. In the House, the Republicans and Democrats each have a Steering Committee that makes committee assignments. In the Senate, this task is performed by the Republican Committee on Committees and for the Democrats by the Steering and Coordination Committee.

Finally, the major parties in both houses have congressional campaign committees that funnel contributions and other assistance to their party's candidates for Congress. All four of these campaign committees "have a common overriding goal of maximizing the number of seats their parties hold in Congress."[75]

## The Committee System

Committees and subcommittees are where Congress does most of its work. Policies are shaped, interest groups heard, and legislation hammered out.

Long before Woodrow Wilson became president, he described what he called "government by the chairmen of the Standing Committees of Congress." Wilson saw congressional committees as "little legislatures," and added that the House sat "not for serious discussion, but to sanction the conclusions of its Committees" as rapidly as possible. "Congress in its committee-rooms," Wilson concluded, "is Congress at work."[76]

The growth of the modern presidency has modified the Wilsonian view of the power of Congress and its

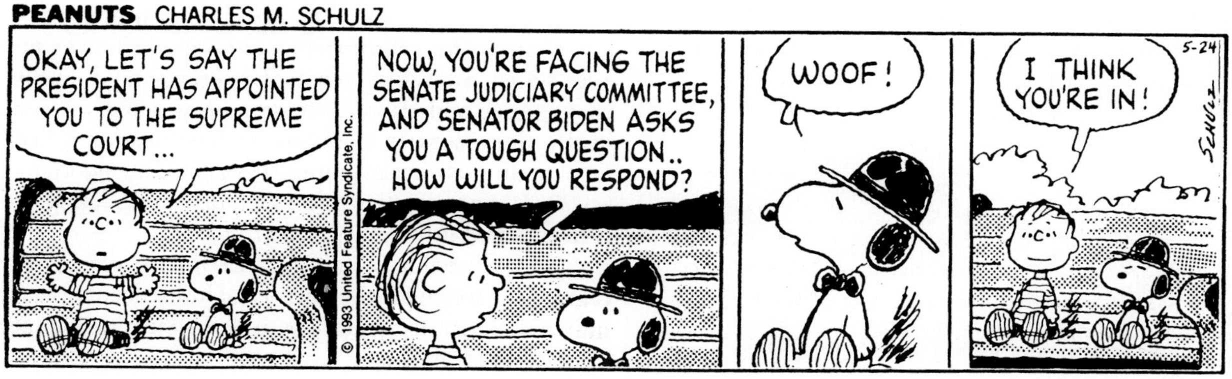

committees. Moreover, since the 1980s, party leaders have often worked around recalcitrant standing committees, bypassing them or adjusting legislation after committee consideration.[77] The committees are, nevertheless, vital centers of congressional activity.

The **standing committees** of Congress are the permanent committees that consider bills and conduct hearings and investigations. In the 109th Congress there were 17 standing committees of the Senate and 20 standing committees of the House. (The 37 standing committees of Congress are listed in Table 12-5.)

The standing committees constitute the heart of the committee system. At times, Congress also creates **special committees** or **select committees** to conduct special investigations. In addition, there are **joint committees** of the House and Senate dealing with such subjects as the economy and taxes. **Conference committees** are a fourth type of committee. These committees are temporary and their purpose is to reconcile House-Senate differences on legislation that has passed through both chambers.

Members of the House and Senate are assigned to committees in a three-step process. First a committee on committees or steering committee matches committee requests and vacancies. Then, the party conference or caucus must ratify these committee lineups. And finally, the new Congress must approve the list of committee assignments. By tradition, each party is usually allotted seats on committees roughly in proportion to its strength in each house of Congress.

Various factors are taken into account in making committee assignments, including party loyalty, geographical balance, the interests of the legislators' districts, and whether the assignment will help their reelection. Certain committees are more prestigious than others. In the House, members compete for places on Appropriations, Rules, and Ways and Means. In the Senate, particularly desirable committees include Appropriations, Finance, Foreign Relations, and Armed Services.

**TABLE 12-5**

**Standing Committees of the 109th Congress**

| Senate Committees | House Committees |
|---|---|
| Agriculture, Nutrition and Forestry | Agriculture |
| Appropriations | Appropriations |
| Armed Services | Armed Services |
| Banking, Housing and Urban Affairs | Budget |
| Budget | Education and the Workforce |
| Commerce, Science, and Transportation | Energy and Commerce |
| Energy and Natural Resources | Financial Services |
| Environment and Public Works | Government Reform |
| Finance | Homeland Security |
| Foreign Relations | House Administration |
| Health, Education, Labor, and Pensions | International Relations |
| Homeland Security and Government Affairs | Judiciary |
| Indian Affairs | Resources |
| Judiciary | Rules |
| Rules and Administration | Science |
| Small Business and Entrepreneurship | Small Business |
| Veterans' Affairs | Standards of Official Conduct |
| | Transportation and Infrastructure |
| | Veterans' Affairs |
| | Ways and Means |

SOURCE: *Congressional Directory*, 109th Congress (2004–2006) (Washington, D.C.: Government Printing Office, 2006), www.gpoaccess.gov/congress/index.html

## Committee Chairs

The party that controls the House or Senate selects the chairs and the party's members of the standing committees for that body. Most committee chairs still achieve their power and position by the **seniority system.** Until modified and reformed in the 1970s, that system automatically resulted in the selection as committee chair of the member of the majority party in Congress who had the longest continuous service on a particular committee. The seniority system (sometimes assailed as "the senility system") was criticized for rewarding age, rather than merit, and for concentrating too much power in the hands of a few old, often conservative, committee chairs who were accountable to no one. Today, in both the Senate and the House, members can no longer count on length of service to guarantee them committee chairs. Instead, in the House, party members vote by secret ballot to select committee chairs and ranking minority members. In the Senate, both parties also provide for the election of committee chairs and ranking minority members.

Republican members of Senate committees select their chairs when Republicans control the Senate, or ranking members when they do not, subject to approval by the party conference. Senate Democrats vote as a group for committee chairs or ranking members. Until the reforms of the seniority system were adopted, no aspect of Congress had been criticized more often. The system has not been entirely abandoned, however, since older members usually are selected as committee chairs. Members of committees are rarely assigned to committees solely on the basis of seniority, although they are ranked by seniority once they are on a committee.

Despite the reforms, the seniority principle had been set aside only rarely in the House. However, Speakers Gingrich and Hastert occasionally violated seniority in selecting chairs. In 1995, House Republicans replaced 13 of their most senior committee chairs. Then in January 2003, Hastert again ignored seniority in selecting two committee chairs.[78]

Not only seniority but the ability of a member to raise campaign money for the party may influence the selection of a committee chair. Seniority is generally stronger in the Senate, although Senate and House Republicans adopted a party rule limiting chairs to six years of service.

The chief argument against seniority has been that it bestows power not necessarily on the most qualified or most party-loyal, but on the longest-lived. Yet seniority allows a committee chair to build up expertise in policy and to become more skilled in the legislative process.

Committee chairs still wield considerable influence. They schedule meetings, decide which bills will be taken up, and usually control the hiring and firing of the majority committee staff. In some cases a committee chair can pigeonhole a bill simply by refusing to hold hearings. But today, chairs must also pay attention to the views of the majority party and its leaders. In recent years, there has been a trend toward greater democracy within some of the committees. Some committees have adopted rules giving rank-and-file members a greater voice in committee operations and providing for regularly scheduled meetings.

## The Subcommittees

The 37 chairs of the standing committees of the House and Senate possess substantial power. Yet here, too, Congress has changed. As Anthony King observed, "by the late 1970s, committee chairmen, although still very influential people, had lost much of their former power. They felt bound to defer to the other members of the committee; much of the committees' work had been devolved onto subcommittees, often chaired by junior, even freshman, congressmen, and senators."[79]

As a result of these changes, Congress had become somewhat decentralized. "The most striking feature of congressional organization is decentralization," Samuel C. Patterson observed, and "congressional government by subcommittee" increased in the 1970s.[80] The pendulum began to swing back toward greater centralization in the 1980s, however. When the Republicans won control of Congress in 1994, they reduced the number of subcommittees and curtailed the authority of subcommittee chairs. As a result, the heads of the standing committees once again exercised considerable power. Congress became a more centralized body.

The subcommittee explosion and subsequent contraction can be clearly traced by studying the subcommittee totals in the House over the past several decades. In 1951 there were only 69 subcommittees in the House; by 1992 the total had reached 135—an increase since 1951 of 96 percent. By 2000, the number of House subcommittees had dropped to 87, and the total of Senate subcommittees had also declined, to 69, for a total in both branches of 156. In 2006 there were 93 subcommittees in the House and 67 in the Senate, for a total of 160. Thus, the number and power of the subcommittees has varied with the times.

## The Committees at Work

Committees perform the valuable functions of division of labor and specialization in Congress. No member of the House or Senate could hope to know the details of all 7,439 bills introduced, for example, in the 107th Congress.* For that reason, senators and representatives tend to rely on the expert knowledge that members of committees may acquire. If a committee has approved a bill, other members generally assume that the committee has considered the legislation carefully, applied its expertise, and made the right decision. That is why Congress, for the most part, approves the decisions of its committees.

As a result of the committee system, members of Congress specialize in various fields. Sometimes they become more knowledgeable in their areas than the bureaucrats in the executive branch. Finally, many scholars argue that a legislative body should have some forum where members of competing parties can resolve their differences. Committees serve this purpose; they are natural arenas for political bargaining and legislative compromise.

Not all committees are alike. Richard F. Fenno, Jr., has identified a number of factors that may affect a committee's degree of independence, influence in Congress, and success in managing legislation. Fenno found five key variables in committee behavior: *Member goals* reflect the benefits desired by each committee member; for instance, those serving on the Senate Armed Services Committee may be primarily interested in improving their own chances of reelection by getting new military bases for their districts. *Environmental constraints* are the outside influences that affect a committee—primarily the other members of the House, the executive branch, client groups, and the two major political parties. *Strategic premises* are the basic rules of the game for a committee—the Appropriations Committees often try to reduce presidential budget requests, for example, and thus appear more responsible with taxpayers' money. *Decision-making processes* are the internal rules for each committee. Finally, *decisions of committees* vary; the Appropriations Committees, for example, generally do cut the president's budget, but the Armed Services Committee tends to respond to the president's wishes.[81]

## Congressional Investigations

Although committees basically process legislation, they perform other tasks, such as educating the public on important issues through hearings and investigations. In 1973 the Senate Select Committee on Presidential Campaign Activities began its far-reaching inquiries into the Watergate affair. Those hearings revealed that President Nixon had tape-recorded his White House conversations, a disclosure that precipitated the legal confrontation between the president and the courts over access to the tapes.

More than anything that had gone before, the Watergate hearings revealed the inside workings of the executive branch at that time. The hearings demonstrated the

*It should be noted that many of the bills introduced were either private bills for the benefit of individuals or duplicates of other bills. In contrast to a private bill, a public law applies to whole classes of citizens.

© 2004 AP/Wide World Photos

Senior U.S. military officers in Iraq testified as the Senate Armed Services Committee investigated abuse of Iraqi prisoners.

tremendous power of a congressional investigation, particularly a televised Senate investigation, to focus the nation's attention on its political process. In 1974, the hearings were followed by the House Judiciary Committee's impeachment investigation and Nixon's resignation.

Again in 1987, the televised hearings on the Iran-contra scandal were viewed by millions of Americans and revealed a great deal of information about the secret foreign policies of the Reagan administration. For 250 hours, the committee and a House panel had taken testimony from witnesses who unfolded a tale of how President Reagan's administration had secretly sold arms to Iran to try to free American hostages in the Middle East, then siphoned off the profits to the contra rebels in Nicaragua. Somehow, even more millions of dollars had also ended up in the Swiss bank accounts of the private individuals involved.

© Alex Webb/Magnum Photos

Marine Lt. Col. Oliver L. North, who ran the secret operation from the White House, briefly captured the imagination of the American public; he wore his uniform when he testified, and many viewers saw him as a hero. But he admitted to the congressional committees that he had misled Congress and shredded key documents. Rear Adm. John M. Poindexter, the president's national security adviser, also said he had destroyed evidence to save the president embarrassment.

Congressional investigations also have been used to publicize risks to consumers. For example, in 2000 a House committee investigated when it became apparent that some car tires manufactured by Firestone were defective, resulting in tread separation and causing fatal accidents, most involving Ford Explorers. The committee hauled in Firestone and Ford executives to testify, as well as the federal officials responsible for auto safety. Congressional investigations have also looked into the problems of American policy during the war in Vietnam, the tragedy of hunger in the midst of plenty, the violation of individual rights by government intelligence agencies, and intelligence failures before the 9/11 terrorist attacks and the 2003 war in Iraq.

During the early 1950s, Senator Joseph R. McCarthy achieved formidable personal political power by using the Senate's investigatory function to conduct "witch hunts" in search of alleged Communists in government. McCarthy succeeded in creating an atmosphere of fear in which the rights of witnesses were frequently violated. In the 1990s, with the end of the Cold War, documents became available indicating that several Soviet agents had indeed worked inside the government in Washington, in some cases acting as spies and passing secrets to Moscow, but that hardly justified McCarthy's abuses of power.

A series of Supreme Court decisions, starting in 1957, has attempted to give some protection to witnesses

## Iran-Contra: "Disdain for the Law"

The common ingredients of the Iran and Contra policies were secrecy, deception, and disdain for the law. . . . [Marine Lt. Col. Oliver L.] North admitted that he and other officials lied repeatedly to Congress and to the American people about the Contra covert action and Iran arms sales, and that he altered and destroyed official documents. . . .

Secrecy became an obsession. Congress was never informed of the Iran or the Contra covert actions, notwithstanding the requirement in the law that Congress be notified of all covert actions in a "timely fashion." . . .

The President's N.S.C. staff secretly diverted millions of dollars in profits from the Iran arms sales to the Contras, but the President said he did not know about it and [Vice Adm. John M.] Poindexter claimed he did not tell him.

The Chairman of the Joint Chiefs of Staff was not informed of the Iran arms sales, nor was he ever consulted regarding the impact of such sales on the Iran-Iraq war or on U.S. military readiness.

The Secretary of State was not informed of the millions of dollars in Contra contributions solicited by the N.S.C. staff from foreign governments with which the State Department deals each day. Congress was told almost nothing—and what it was told was false.

—Report of the Congressional Committees Investigating the Iran-Contra Affair, 1987

before committees. For example, the Supreme Court has ruled that Congress has no power to "expose for the sake of exposure" and that questions asked by a congressional investigating committee must be relevant to its legislative purpose.[82] On the other hand, the Supreme Court has ruled that witnesses cannot refuse under the First Amendment to answer questions about their political beliefs if the questions are pertinent to the committee's legislative purpose.[83] Of course, witnesses before a committee can invoke the Fifth Amendment on the grounds that their answers might tend to incriminate them. But many people infer that witnesses who invoke this constitutional privilege are guilty of something, and the witnesses may lose their jobs or suffer other social penalties as a result.

### Congressional Staffs

Congress has become a bureaucracy. In recent years, the number of people on the congressional payroll has increased enormously. In addition to staff members on their office payrolls, senators and representatives have large committee and subcommittee staffs to serve them. Office staffs are likely to concentrate on legislative and constituent services, whereas on the committees, staff members draft and analyze bills, coordinate with officials in the executive branch, and prepare for hearings. In 1957 congressional staffs totaled 4,489 workers; by 2000 the figure had increased to approximately 24,000.[84]

In 2005, each member of the House was allowed to spend up to $806,258 on staff, including up to 18

Louisiana Governor Kathleen Blanco testifies to a House committee hearing in 2005 on Hurricane Katrina.

fulltime workers. Senators were allowed up to $472,677 for legislative staff and between $1.9 and $3.2 million for clerical and administrative staff, the exact amount based on state population.[85]

Typically, members of the House have a chief of staff who manages the office and may be a top political adviser to the representative. A legislative director and a few legislative assistants focus on policy details. A press secretary sees to it that the member is well covered in the hometown press. Many House offices also have college interns to help answer mail from constituents. Personal staffs are much larger in the Senate. In addition to their offices on Capitol Hill, senators and representatives maintain offices in their home districts and states.

Although congressional staff members have been criticized for having too much influence, one study concluded that members of the staff "do much of the congressional work and . . . in many instances, this work could not be done without staff."[86] The staffs have grown because of "a greater congressional workload" and the desire of senators and representatives to have "the assistance of skilled experts."[87]

Staff members on some key committees wield power almost comparable to that of White House staff members. Along with the explosion in congressional staff has been a corresponding increase in cost. Between 1970 and 2005 the cost of running the legislative branch rose from $361 million to $3.8 billion.[88]

In addition to their staffs, members of Congress have several legislative support agencies that help them do their jobs. The Congressional Research Service of the Library of Congress provides quick answers and long-range studies on a wide range of issues and has computerized databases available to members and their staffs. The Government Accountability Office (GAO) serves as an important watchdog into waste or fraud in the bureaucracy and conducts investigations at the request of congressional committees. The Congressional Budget Office provides Congress with an independent analysis of the president's budget and economic assumptions.

***for more information about the Government Accountability Office, see: http://www.goa.gov***

## Congressional Reforms

Congress has reformed and modernized its procedures in recent decades and has opened up most of its committee meetings. The seniority system, as noted, has been reformed and modified.

Congress, especially the Senate, is sometimes assailed for rules and procedures designed to block rather than facilitate the passage of legislation. And Congress does not always get its work done on time. Frequently, for example, it has failed to act on the federal budget in time for the government to meet its payroll. When this happens, Congress has usually resorted to "continuing resolutions" to fund the departments and keep federal workers on the job. When it does not act to do so, the government has to temporarily shut down. These problems, though, may reflect policy and partisan differences rather than procedural pitfalls. In a national emergency, Congress is able to legislate quickly.

Furthermore, Richard Fenno concluded that the House enjoys stability as a result of "internal processes which have served to keep the institution from tearing itself apart while engaged in the business of decision making." For example, it is generally assumed that members will not "pursue internal conflicts to the point where the effectiveness of the House is impaired."[89]

In short, the House operates under a set of rules that may be necessary for system maintenance—that is, to keep a diverse, unwieldy institution functioning. From this basic premise has flowed the defense of such congressional procedures as the committee system and the tradition of elaborate courtesy that senators normally, although certainly not always, display in addressing one another on the floor.

A case may even be made for some of the other procedures of Congress that are often condemned. Much of the earlier criticism of Congress originated with liberals and activists who were impatient for the national legislature to get on with the business of meeting social needs. Some analysts argue that congressional procedures may protect the country in a crisis against hasty or misguided action that could result from bowing to popular emotion.

In the field of foreign affairs, Congress has often been criticized for yielding too much power to the president. Under the Kennedy, Johnson, and Nixon administrations, the United States engaged in a major, divisive military conflict in Vietnam, although Congress never declared war. The War Powers Resolution, passed in 1973, was an important attempt by Congress to reassert its authority. In the three decades since the resolution was passed, however, the law has not effectively restricted the president's military power. In the Persian Gulf in 1991, for example, the first President Bush embarked on a major war against Iraq without a declaration of war by Congress. Again in 2003, America went to war in Iraq without a formal congressional declaration. However, in both instances, the full House and Senate authorized the president to use force.

As congressional investigations in the mid-1970s revealed, Congress—and the executive branch—failed to exercise proper control over the activities of the federal intelligence agencies. Although intelligence committees were established in the House and Senate in the wake of those investigations, they have performed their task of overseeing the intelligence agencies with mixed results.

But if Congress sometimes fails to monitor executive agencies, to an extent that is perhaps underemphasized, Congress innovates and initiates, sometimes on matters of great importance. And since the passage of the

Congressional Budget and Impoundment Control Act of 1974, Congress has taken a greater role in the entire budget process—the way in which the government decides how its money is spent.

## Congress and the Budget

In preparing the government's annual budget, Congress acts in two stages. First, it passes **authorizations,** laws that recommend maximum levels of funding for federal programs. Then it enacts **appropriations bills,** separate legislation that allows the money to be spent. Annual spending for the government is divided into 13 separate appropriations laws. Each one covers a functional category or categories of governmental spending. For example, each year the Congress and president must agree on a defense appropriations bill. Appropriations bills must be passed in time for the start of a new fiscal year on October 1.

Before Congress passed the Congressional Budget and Impoundment Control Act of 1974, it was hard for members to keep track of the dollar total of the appropriations bills it passed. Lawmakers proved unable to control federal spending. Conflict over the budget on the one hand and soaring costs on the other were the twin factors that helped to bring about passage of the 1974 act.[90] The law required Congress to adopt budget resolutions each year setting target figures for total spending.

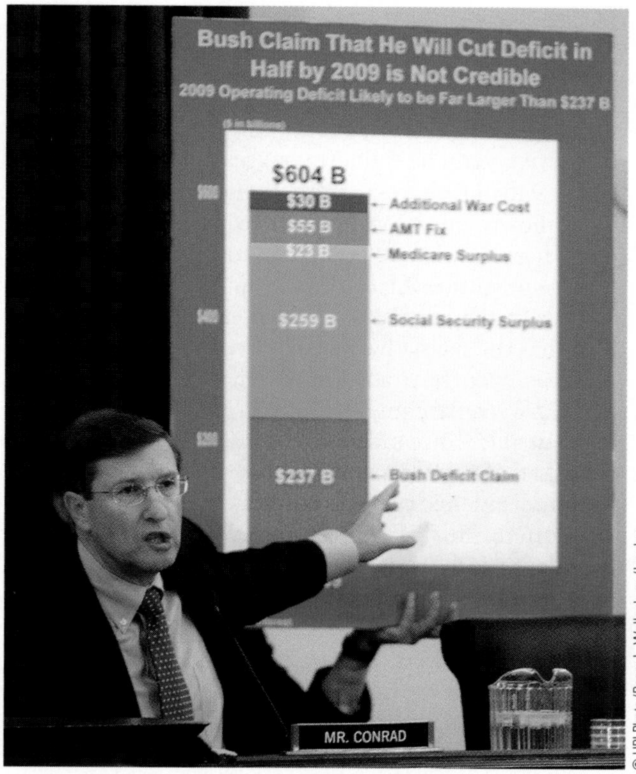


© UPI Photo/Roger L. Wollenberg/Landov

Kent Conrad, Democrat of North Dakota, questions President Bush's budget estimates.

The act also created a House Budget Committee, a Senate Budget Committee, and a Congressional Budget Office to provide the experts and the data the members needed. Moreover, the law established a timetable for Congress and its committees to act on spending bills. This schedule was an attempt to give Congress time to evaluate the president's budget and to choose among competing programs.

Later legislation revised the timetable for the budget process. The Budget Enforcement Act of 1990 set caps on appropriations for domestic, international, and defense programs. Under the law the president's budget request is due the first Monday in February of each year. Congress is required to adopt a budget resolution by April 15. On October 1 the federal fiscal year begins, running until the following September 30. On more than one occasion, however, Congress has failed to meet the October 1 deadline and has been forced to enact stopgap measures to keep the government operating. Deadlock in the battle of the budget resulted in two government shutdowns in the mid-1990s.

These budgetary reforms have shifted more power to Congress in dealing with the federal budget. The laws gave Congress new tools to manage the federal budget. And the creation of the Congressional Budget Office meant that Congress no longer had to rely on the executive branch for fiscal facts and figures.

## A Bill Is Passed

All of the institutions, people, and procedures we have discussed in this chapter—the formal organization of Congress, the party leadership, the floor maneuvering, the committee system, staff work—bear some relation to whether a bill will make its way into law. To do so, it must cross hurdles every step of the way.

The formal route that a bill must follow is shown in Figure 12-1. Any member may introduce a bill. (Some legislation is introduced as a "joint resolution," which becomes law in the same manner as a bill.*) The member who introduces a bill is called the sponsor, and other members who sign on to the bill are called cosponsors. After a bill is introduced in either the House or the Senate, or both, it is referred to a standing committee, which may hold hearings or assign the bill to a subcommittee. Hearings are almost always open to the public. They may be closed by an open vote of the committee, but this normally occurs only when national security or classified information is being discussed. Detailed changes to bills are made in the mark-up sessions. After receiving the subcommittee's recommendations, the full committee

*There are two other kinds of congressional resolutions. A "simple" resolution is passed by one branch of Congress and relates to matters entirely within the jurisdiction of that house. A "concurrent" resolution must be passed by both houses. Neither a simple nor a concurrent resolution goes to the president for his signature and neither has the force of law.

FIGURE 12-1

**How a Bill Becomes Law**

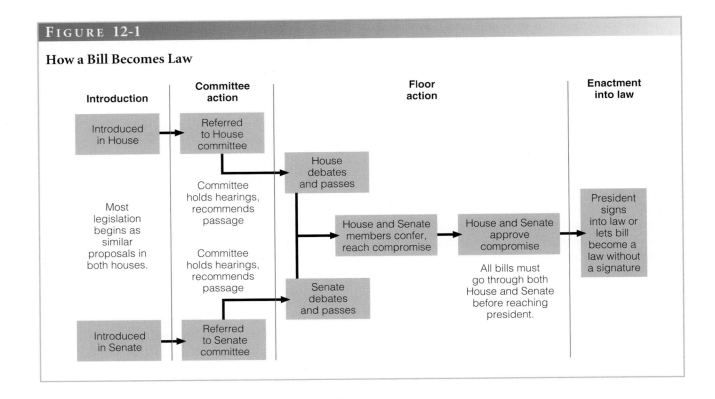

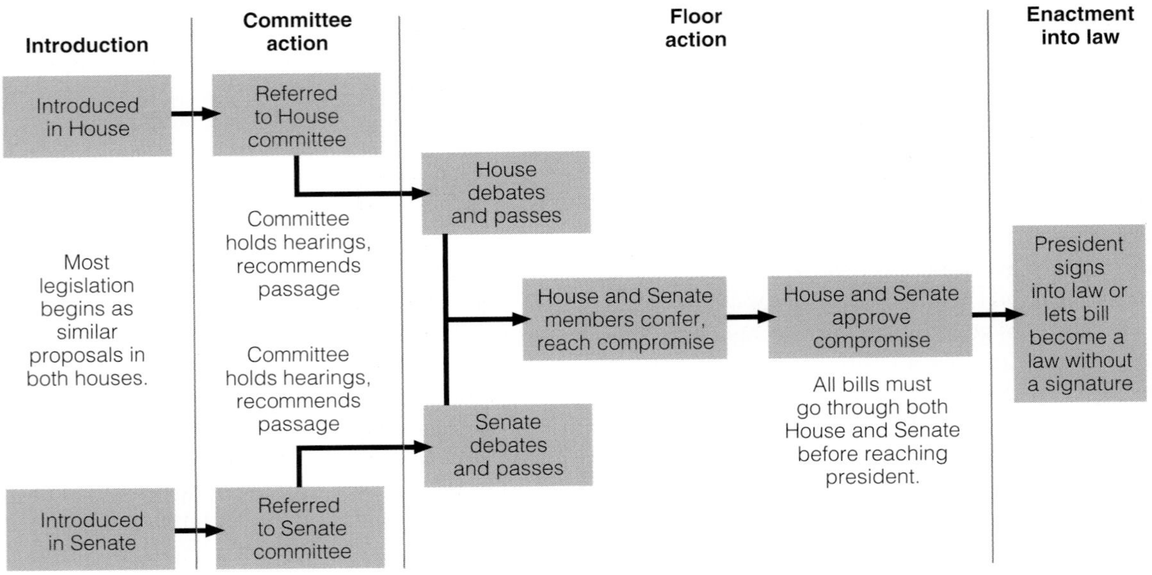


meets to decide what action to take on the bill. It may do nothing, or it may rewrite the bill completely, or it may report out the original bill to the House or Senate, with or without amendments. A written report, often with minority views, accompanies the bill from committee. The bill is placed on one of the House calendars or the Senate calendar to await floor action.

If a bill is passed by one house, it is sent to the other chamber, which may pass the bill as is, send it to committee, or ignore it and continue to press its own version of the legislation. If there are major differences in the final bill passed by each house, one house may ask for a conference. The presiding officer of each house names a conference committee composed of members of the standing committees or subcommittees that have considered the bill.

A great deal of what Congress does happens behind closed doors in the conference committees. The selection of members to serve on the conference committee may influence whether any legislation emerges or the nature of the legislation that is reported out. The conferees try to iron out disagreements and reconcile the two versions. Usually, they reach some form of agreement and report back to their respective houses. But agreement is not always reached, or it may be reached only after important changes in the legislation are made. Each house then approves or rejects the conference report. If both houses approve, the final version is signed by the speaker and the president pro tempore of the Senate and is sent to the president, who may sign the bill into law, let it become law without his signature, or veto or pocket veto the bill, as described in Chapter 13. If Congress overrides a presidential veto by a two-thirds vote in both houses, the bill becomes law without the president's signature.

## Legislative Vetoes

In recent decades, Congress enacted many laws containing a legislative veto over acts of the executive branch. A **legislative veto,** as the term suggests, is a provision of law in which Congress asserts the power to override or strike down an action by the executive branch. Presidents have consistently opposed such provisions as being unconstitutional, and in 1983 the Supreme Court agreed. In the landmark *Chadha* case, the Court ruled 7–2 that the legislative veto violated the constitutional requirement of separation of powers among the branches of the government.[91]

But the Court's decision, although historic, left a great deal of uncertainty in its wake. One of the most important legislative vetoes is contained in the War Powers Resolution, which Congress passed in 1973 to limit the president's authority to commit troops to combat overseas. Many constitutional scholars thought it unlikely that any president would directly challenge Congress over the war powers law.

And despite the Court's decision, Congress continued to pass laws containing legislative veto provisions. Both Congress and the president, however, have found it convenient to compromise rather than fight over the issue.

Even after Congress enacts a law, it can continue to influence the executive branch in ways other than legislative vetoes. It controls spending authority, it oversees the executive branch agencies, it can enact new legislation to strengthen or modify earlier laws, and it can conduct congressional investigations.

## Congressional Ethics

Congress at times has been tarnished by scandal and by the questionable ethics and activities of some of its members. Some members of Congress travel abroad on "junkets" for dubious legislative purposes. Some have relatives on their office payroll. In the past many accepted speaking fees from lobbyists. Some have taken outright bribes.

In 2005 the Securities and Exchange Commission investigated allegations that Bill Frist, the Senate majority leader, had engaged in insider stock trading. Frist denied any wrongdoing.

In 2006 Randy "Duke" Cunningham, a former member of the House from San Diego, was sentenced to eight years in prison after admitting he took $2.4 million in bribes from two defense contractors. Cunningham, a decorated fighter pilot ace in Vietnam, used his position on key House committees to steer millions of dollars in defense work to the two contractors.

The scandal surrounding the activities of lobbyist Jack Abramoff, discussed in Chapter 7, led to federal investigations of members of Congress linked to him. Tom DeLay, the powerful House majority leader, who had close ties to Abramoff, was forced to give up his leadership post after he was indicted in a separate case in Texas on charges of money laundering. DeLay did not run for reelection in 2006.

"You've been around here longer than I have. What are 'congressional ethics'?"

That same year it was disclosed that the FBI had raided the house in Washington of Representative William J. Jefferson, a Louisiana Democrat, and found $90,000 in cash in his freezer. The FBI said it had videotaped Jefferson receiving the cash and accused him of taking hundreds of thousands of dollars in bribes from a Kentucky businessman who sought his help in obtaining government contracts. The FBI also searched Jefferson's House office at night and removed documents, an action that drew protests from both Republicans and Democrats, who argued that the raid violated the constitutional separation of powers between the executive and legislative branches. The House ethics committee launched investigations of both Jefferson and Bob Ney, an Ohio Republican involved with Abramoff. Ney agreed to plead guilty to accepting bribes from Abramoff. Then it was disclosed that Representative Mark Foley, a Florida Republican, had sent sexually explicit e-mails to teenage House pages. Foley resigned and Republican House leaders faced a barrage of criticism for not having acted sooner when they first learned of inappropriate contacts by the congressman with the young pages.

This pattern of corruption or lax ethical standards was not new. In 1991, the American public was outraged at disclosures that members of the House of Representatives had written 8,331 bad checks on the private bank maintained for members. But unlike checks written by ordinary citizens who overdraw their accounts, those written by the representatives did not bounce—the bank honored them. Some legislators had written hundreds of bad checks totaling hundreds of thousands of dollars. The check writing did not go unpunished by the electorate, however. In 1992 representatives who had written 100 or more bad checks were much more likely to lose reelection.

In 2002 the House expelled Representative James A. Traficant, Jr., Democrat of Ohio, because of his convictions on 10 counts of bribery, racketeering, and tax evasion.[92] Traficant was subsequently sentenced to eight years in prison.

The one congressman to support Traficant was Gary A. Condit, Democrat of California, who had already lost his 2002 primary. Although it is rare for an incumbent to lose a primary, the voters turned against Condit because of his reported affair with Chandra Levy, a young intern who had worked in Condit's office and who was found murdered in a Washington park.

A Senate career also came to an end in 2002 because of allegations of wrongdoing. Late in the campaign, Senator Robert Torricelli, Democrat of New Jersey, withdrew from his reelection campaign after the Senate determined that he had accepted "several gifts from businessman David Chang, a former campaign contributor."[93]

Despite these cases, scandal of various kinds and dishonesty among members of Congress are the exception and not the rule. The majority of senators and representatives are hardworking and honest. In the wake of various scandals, however, both the House and Senate established ethics committees, and in 1968 both houses adopted weak codes of conduct for their members. In 1977 the House and Senate strengthened their ethics codes, requiring financial disclosure by members and limiting outside earned income. Beginning in 1991, members of the House and Senate could no longer accept fees for speeches or articles, and in 1995 Congress set limits on the value of gifts that members of both houses may receive.

"I'm sorry, sir, Congressman Clayborne isn't in at the moment. He's doing two to five for mail fraud."

## Congress and the American Political System

Congress is a major battleground of American democracy. But in attempting to manage the external demands placed on it, Congress often finds itself caught in the crosscurrents of a restless and rapidly changing society.

In today's political system, two of the most important crosscurrents are the revitalization of parties and the rise of partisanship.[94] In Congress, these trends are reflected in the increased policy differences between Republicans and Democrats and the greater cohesion of each party on recorded votes.[95] In the contemporary Congress, a substantial majority of all Republicans are conservative and most Democrats are liberal. "In other words," according to Davidson and Oleszek, "the two parties are more cohesive internally and further apart externally than they were in the recent past."[96] These changes have promoted a breakdown of courtesy between members of the two parties in the House and Senate.

Another important political trend has been the frequency of divided government. One study noted that "in the eight presidential administrations" between January 1969 and January 2001, "there has been divided partisan control of the Congress and president for 26 of 32 years."[97] Most often, this has involved a Republican president with a Democratic Congress; "in 1995, though, Bill Clinton became the first Democratic president since Harry Truman in 1947–1948 to share control of the government with a Republican Congress."[98] The election of 2002 once again brought about unified Republican control of the Congress and presidency.

Still another political trend has been the close balance in voting strength between the two major parties, as exemplified by the slim margin of victory in the presidential election of 2000. In Congress, this has been reflected in "narrow party margins in both chambers."[99] This has been especially true in the Senate, where only a seat or two separated the parties in 2004.

There are times when Congress seems to be stalemated by partisanship. But Congress may simply be reflecting the partisan divisions in the electorate. In other words, Congress is perhaps slow to act because the consensus in the country that Congress needs to act and to innovate is absent or slow to develop. A powerful argument can be made that Congress does act when the people demand it, their voice is clear, and the need unmistakable. E. E. Schattschneider has described American government as a political system "in which the struggle for democracy is still going on."[100] Viewed in this context, Congress is neither ideal nor obsolete, but rather an enduring arena for political conflict and a crucible for democratic change.

## CHAPTER HIGHLIGHTS

- Congress is the national legislature. It plays a central and crucial role in the political system by making laws, the general rules that govern American society.
- In part, members of Congress are older than the average American because of constitutional restrictions: A member of the House must be at least 25 (and a citizen for seven years) and a senator must be at least 30 (and a citizen for nine years).
- Although Congress is one branch of the federal government, the House and Senate are distinct institutions, each with its own rules and traditions and each jealous of its own powers and prerogatives.
- One basic difference between the House and Senate was established by the Constitution, which provided two-year terms for members of the House and staggered six-year terms for senators.
- In the House, the speaker is the presiding officer and the most powerful member. The position of speaker is provided for in the Constitution. The basic power structure of the House consists of the speaker, the floor leaders and whips of the two major parties, the Rules Committee, and the chairs of the standing committees.
- In March 1979, amid much controversy, the House began live television and radio broadcasts of floor debate. The Senate permitted televising of its deliberations starting in 1986. The broadcasts from both chambers are carried gavel-to-gavel over the nonprofit C-SPAN network by nearly 7,900 cable television systems in all 50 states, with a potential audience of 86 million households as of 2004.
- The Senate majority leader is the most powerful elected leader of the Senate. Most of the time, the Senate allows unlimited debate. Because of this, a single senator, or a group of senators, may stage a filibuster to talk a bill to death, although the device is now rarely used.
- Senators more often can delay or even kill floor action on legislation or other Senate matters simply by asking their party leaders not to schedule them—an informal tactic known as a hold.
- Under Rule XXII of the Senate, a filibuster may be ended if three-fifths of the entire Senate (60 members) vote for cloture.
- Although committees of Congress basically process legislation, they perform other tasks, such as educating the public on important issues through hearings and investigations.
- The party that controls the House or Senate selects the committee chairs and their party's members of the standing committees for that body. Most committee chairs still achieve their power and position by seniority.
- In preparing the government's annual budget, Congress acts in two stages. First, it passes authorizations, laws that recommend maximum levels of funding for federal programs. Then it enacts appropriations bills, separate legislation that allows the money to be spent.
- In the wake of various scandals, both the House and Senate established ethics committees, and in 1968 both houses adopted weak codes of conduct for their members. In 1977 the House and Senate strengthened their ethics codes, requiring financial disclosure by members and limiting outside earned income. Beginning in 1991, members of the House and Senate could no longer accept fees for speeches or articles, and in 1995 Congress set limits on the value of gifts that members of both houses may receive.
- A powerful argument can be made that Congress does act when the people demand it, their voice is clear, and the need unmistakable.

## KEY TERMS

pork-barrel legislation, p. 381
senatorial courtesy, p. 382
trustee, p. 388
instructed delegate, p. 388
speaker, p. 391
whip, p. 392
Committee of the Whole, p. 393
recorded vote, p. 393
filibuster, p. 397
hold, p. 397
cloture, p. 398
standing committees, p. 400
special committees, p. 400
select committees, p. 400
joint committees, p. 400
conference committees, p. 400
seniority system, p. 400
authorizations, p. 405
appropriations bills, p. 405
legislative veto, p. 406

## SUGGESTED WEBSITES

**http://www.cspan.org**
*C-SPAN*
The website companion to the C-SPAN cable television channels includes video and audio clips of Congress, interviews and debates, sorted by subject, and allows visitors to watch or listen to C-SPAN live on the website. Additional information about current events and special topics in American history are available.

**http://www.senate.gov** **http://www.house.gov**
*The Senate* *The House of Representatives*
The official websites of the U.S. Senate and House of Representatives include a list of members of Congress and ways to contact them via e-mail, their websites, office phone numbers, and mailing addresses. Also includes home pages for House and Senate committees.

**http://thomas.loc.gov**
*Thomas—Legislative Information on the Internet*
A comprehensive official guide to the current status in Congress of a bill, resolution, or amendment. Includes

bills and issues that various congressional committees and subcommittees are considering. The site also includes links to the websites of members of Congress.

## SUGGESTED READING

Baker, Ross K. *House and Senate,* 3rd edition* (Norton, 2001). A study of Congress that emphasizes the difference between the House and Senate. Based largely on interviews with legislators, lobbyists, and journalists who have worked on both sides of Capitol Hill. The author rejects the argument that the two chambers are becoming more alike.

Barone, Michael, and Cohen, Richard E. *The Almanac of American Politics 2004,** published biennially (*National Journal,* 2003). A comprehensive guide to political leaders at the local, state, and national levels. Includes political profiles of the governors, members of Congress, their constituencies, their voting records on major issues, and ratings by various interest groups.

Binder, Sarah A. *Stalemate: Causes and Consequences of Legislative Gridlock** (The Brookings Institution, 2003). A study for the years 1947 to 2000 of legislative gridlock, defined as the percent of major issues that are not enacted into law by each two-year Congress. The authors found that slightly more than half of all such items were not enacted and that gridlock was more frequent during periods of divided party government than when one party controlled both Congress and the presidency.

Congressional Quarterly, *Weekly Report* and annual *Almanac* (Congressional Quarterly, Inc.). A detailed and very useful report on American politics, with emphasis on Congress and current legislation. Published weekly, with an annual almanac that contains much of the material from the weekly reports.

Davidson, Roger H., and Oleszek, Walter J. *Congress and Its Members,* 9th edition* (CQ Press, 2004). An outstanding general introduction to Congress and to the men and women who are elected to serve. Includes the changes instituted by the Republicans after their party won control of Congress in 1994.

Dodd, Lawrence C., and Oppenheimer, Bruce I. *Congress Reconsidered,* 8th edition* (CQ Press, 2005). A collection of essays analyzing the evolving institutions and folkways of Congress, and the effects of the "Republican revolution" of 1994.

Fenno, Richard F., Jr. *Home Style** (Longman, 2002) (Originally published in 1978.) A thoughtful analysis of a very important aspect of the political behavior of House members—their relationships with the constituents in their home districts.

Fiorina, Morris P. *Congress: Keystone of the Washington Establishment** (Yale University Press, 1989). A lively and interesting discussion of how Congress creates new bureaucracies in Washington and then gains credit at home by helping voters to deal with those agencies. The author argues that House seats are safer as a result.

Herrnson, Paul S. *Congressional Elections: Campaigning at Home and in Washington,* 4th edition* (CQ Press, 2004). A detailed study, based on hundreds of interviews, of what it takes to run a successful congressional campaign.

King, David C. *Turf Wars: How Congressional Committees Claim Jurisdiction** (University of Chicago Press, 1997). An expert examination of the struggle for power among committees in Congress. King shows how members of Congress may gain political advantage by having legislative authority over certain policy areas, and describes the tug-of-war among members of Congress for slots on desirable committees.

Loomis, Burdett A., and Schiller, Wendy. *The Contemporary Congress,* 4th edition* (Thomson / Wadsworth, 2004). A useful overview of policymaking in the modern Congress.

Mayhew, David R. *Congress: The Electoral Connection,* second edition* (Yale University Press, 2004). A stimulating analysis of congressional behavior. Argues that the basic motivation of members of Congress is to win reelection and traces the effects this has on a member's legislative behavior and the way Congress makes policy.

Oleszek, Walter J. *Congressional Procedures and the Policy Process,* 6th edition* (CQ Press, 2003). An extremely valuable, clearly written examination of the rules and procedures in the Senate and the House of Representatives. Describes the congressional legislative process in detail, from the introduction of a bill to final presidential action.

Ornstein, Norman J., Mann, Thomas E., and Malbin, Michael J. *Vital Statistics on Congress 2003–2004** (AEI Press, 2004). A comprehensive summary of today's Congress—its membership, political orientation, and performance. Includes numerous historical tables and figures illustrating congressional elections, committees, voting patterns, budget, and campaign finance.

Polsby, Nelson W. *How Congress Evolves: Social Bases of Institutional Change* (Oxford University Press, 2004). A colorful history of the U.S. House of Representatives from 1937 to the mid-1990s. Emphasizes the increased acceptance by Congress of liberal democratic initiatives during these years. In 1995, the author says, the Republicans took control of a Congress that was more amenable to party government than it had been from 1937 to the 1970s.

Sinclair, Barbara. *The Transformation of the U.S. Senate** (Johns Hopkins University Press, 1989). A perceptive analysis of how and why Senate norms have been transformed in recent decades. Argues that senatorial folkways have changed because senators are now rewarded for broad involvement in multiple issues and policy arenas.

Smith, Steven S., and Deering, Christopher J. *Committees in Congress,* 3rd edition* (*Congressional Quarterly,* 1997). A detailed analysis of the dynamics of congressional committees. Argues that during the 1980s and 1990s, for a variety of reasons, committees of Congress have become less powerful and less autonomous.

Sundquist, James L. *The Decline and Resurgence of Congress** (The Brookings Institution, 1981). A study that focuses on the efforts made by Congress in the early 1970s to recapture some of the powers it had lost to the presidency. Discusses the expansion of congressional staff, procedural changes, the strengthening of legislative oversight, and reforms in the congressional budget process.

Wilson, Woodrow. *Congressional Government: A Study in American Politics** (Transaction Publishers, 2002). (Originally published in 1885.) A classic study of congressional government in the late 19th century by a scholar who later became president of the United States. Stresses the separation of powers in the American political system, the importance of congressional committees and committee chairs, and what Wilson viewed as the dominance of congressional power over that of the president in that era.

*Available in paperback edition.

# Chapter 13

# THE PRESIDENT

"THE EXECUTIVE POWER shall be vested in a President of the United States of America." These 15 words in Article II of the Constitution established the presidency, but they hardly reflect either the magnitude of that power in the 21st century or its limitations.

When Harry S Truman suddenly became president during the Second World War upon the death of Franklin D. Roosevelt, he described how he felt to a group of reporters. "I don't know whether you fellows ever had a load of hay fall on you," he said, "but when they told me yesterday what had happened, I felt like the moon, the stars and all the planets had fallen on me. Boys, if you ever pray, pray for me now."[1]

Even as Truman, who was Roosevelt's vice president, moved into the White House, he grasped the pitfalls and dangers that lay ahead in the highest office in the land. To the reporters, he invoked the heavens because he knew he had moved into a crucible where, as the nation's leader, he would surely be blamed for whatever might go wrong.

As Truman and other chief executives have learned, public approval of a president often resembles a roller coaster, with highs and lows that vary with his performance and external events. For example, President George W. Bush enjoyed extraordinary public support after the 9/11 terrorist attacks and during the war in Afghanistan that followed. But that level of public approval later eroded sharply halfway into his second term.

By the time Bush ran for reelection in 2004, his approval ratings in the polls had dropped dramatically. That spring and summer, the war in Iraq was not going well; American forces, private contractors, and Iraqi citizens

Photo by Bruce White, copyright White House Historical Association (3075)

AP Images/Susan Walsh

President George W. Bush and Secretary of State Condoleezza Rice at the United Nations in 2005

were being killed almost every day. The weapons of mass destruction that Bush had warned Iraq possessed—and which he gave as the principal reason to go to war—had not been found more than a year after he had proclaimed an end to major combat. Despite these problems, Bush was reelected.

By 2006, however, Bush's approval rating had dropped even further. In May 2006, only 31 percent of respondents approved of the way Bush was "handling his job as president."[2] (See Figure 13-1.) The poor approval rating followed a series of setbacks for the administration, including the government's failed response to Hurricane Katrina, which devastated New Orleans and parts of the Gulf Coast, and the mounting U.S. casualties from the continuing war in Iraq. There were almost daily attacks by insurgents against American forces and Iraqis. Sectarian violence, horrific suicide bombings, and attacks by Shiites and Sunnis against each other raised fears that Iraq might be on the brink of civil war. Bush's continuing decline in the polls during April 2006 also coincided with a steep rise in gasoline prices that left many voters angry.

Even as Bush's public approval declined, however, he continued to assert broader presidential powers than those claimed by many modern presidents. After 9/11, Bush, with strong support from Vice President Cheney, had invoked the war on terrorism to proclaim a wide range of expanded presidential powers. He promulgated a policy of pre-emptive war if necessary to strike an enemy before the United States was attacked.

He declared the right to imprison "enemy combatants," even American citizens, indefinitely. He secretly ordered the National Security Agency to eavesdrop on persons in the United States who telephoned or e-mailed suspected terrorists overseas. His order bypassed the Foreign Intelligence Surveillance Act, a 1978 law that required approval of domestic wiretaps by a secret federal court. He claimed, in part, that his constitutional powers as commander in chief gave him the right to engage in such warrantless surveillance of Americans. His justice department argued that the Geneva Conventions, international treaties designed to protect prisoners of war, did not apply in the fight against terrorism or prevent the use of harsh interrogation methods to extract information from suspects.

Bush's predecessor, Bill Clinton, had spent eight years in the White House on the same kind of roller-coaster ride. Clinton was the first Democratic president

FIGURE 13-1

**President George W. Bush's Popularity during Times of Crisis**

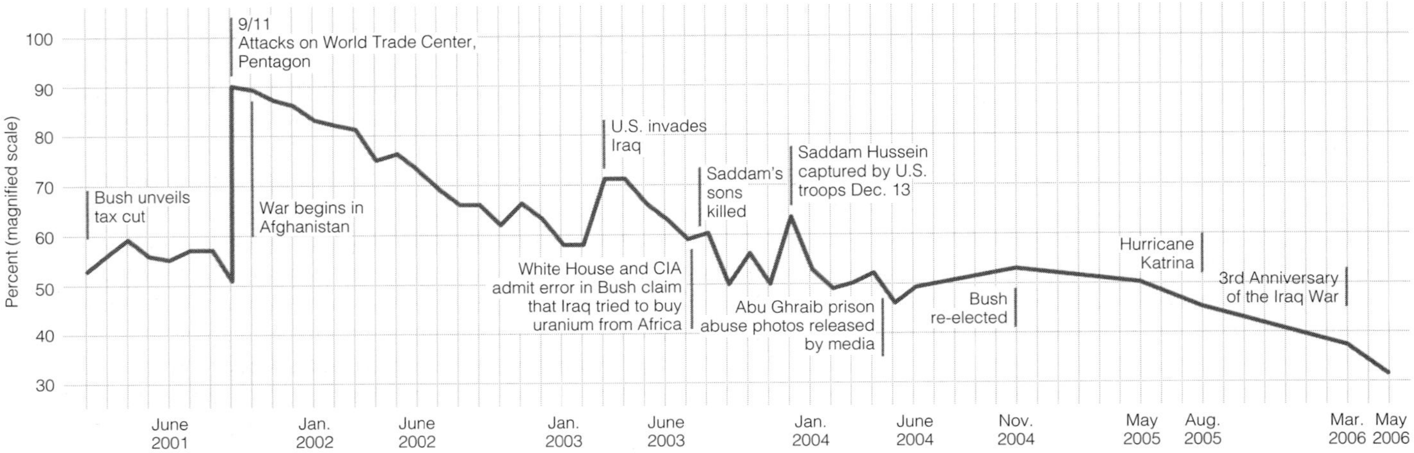


SOURCE: Data provided by the Gallup poll. Respondents were asked: "Do you approve or disapprove of the way George W. Bush is handling his job as president?"

## A President Views His Power

**P**ower? The only power I've got is nuclear—and I can't use that.

—Lyndon Johnson, quoted in Hugh Sidey, *A Very Personal Presidency*

to be elected for two terms since Franklin D. Roosevelt. He was only the second president ever to be impeached, but like the first, Andrew Johnson, he was not convicted or removed from office.

Clinton was brilliantly articulate, a former Rhodes scholar at Oxford University, and a resourceful political leader. Yet, in sworn testimony and in public statements, he misled the nation about his sexual liaison with a young White House intern, Monica Lewinsky, a scandal that seriously tarnished his legacy. Although millions of voters disapproved of his personal behavior and felt it had brought disgrace to his high office, his approval ratings in the polls remained extraordinarily high. For the nation had enjoyed unprecedented prosperity and a booming economy during his years in office, and the enormous budget deficits to which the voters had become accustomed turned into a huge surplus. Americans seemed willing, perhaps for the first time, to make a distinction between a president's personal life and his public performance.

It was as though in his own person, Clinton embodied the peaks and valleys, the contradictions and contrasts, and the paradox of the presidency itself. At the very least, he reminded the American public that the president is also a human being, subject to all the failings, foibles, and weaknesses of the human spirit.*

# The Paradox of the Presidency

The American presidency is a place of paradox. It is an office of enormous contrasts, of great power—and great limits. Over the past several decades, a number of factors and events have altered the public's perception of the presidency.

Although once viewed as extraordinarily powerful, the presidency at times has seemed an institution of uncertain power. Although a president can wield enormous military might, even in that arena, he may not achieve every objective. In 2003, although President George W. Bush was able to launch a major attack on Iraq, he could not enlist the support of some European allies. Although he proclaimed "victory" in Iraq, three years after the U.S. invasion, the war continued.

President Kennedy was assassinated in 1963, and his four immediate successors left office under adverse circumstances: President Johnson, harshly criticized over the war in Vietnam, chose not to run again; President Nixon was forced to resign because of the Watergate scandal; Presidents Ford and Carter were defeated. Less than three months after his first inauguration, President Reagan was wounded in an assassination attempt. In 1992 the first President Bush failed in his bid for reelection. In 1998, as the Lewinsky scandal intensified, Congress impeached President Clinton.

Of the 11 presidents who have served since the Second World War, only five—Dwight Eisenhower, Richard Nixon, Ronald Reagan, Bill Clinton, and George W. Bush—were elected twice, and Nixon, who resigned to avoid impeachment, failed to complete his second term.

Reagan was a popular chief executive, whose death in 2004 was widely mourned. But his public approval had declined midway into his second term. His image was diminished by the disclosure that he had approved a secret foreign policy, allowing the sale of arms to Iran, and that—without the knowledge of the American people—millions of dollars in profits had been diverted to the contra rebels in Central America who were seeking to overthrow the government of Nicaragua. It was revealed that secret operations, many of them illegal, were being run out of the White House by Marine Lt. Col. Oliver L. North and concealed from Congress and the public.

Why has presidential power sometimes appeared so fragile? Perhaps one reason is that many of the problems presidents face have become more difficult to manage. The first President Bush's problems in managing the economy were compounded by his most famous campaign promise; as a candidate for president in 1988, he had proclaimed to the Republican National Convention, "Read my lips, no new taxes." The delegates cheered wildly. But two years later, with the government running at a deficit, he broke that celebrated pledge, agreed to raise taxes by $165 billion over five years, and thereby lost the trust of many voters.

The presidency was perceived by many scholars as having been weakened by the Vietnam War in the 1960s and the Watergate scandal in the 1970s. Both of those traumatic events diminished public trust in the institution of the presidency, and—some analysts believed—diminished the actual power of that office as well.

In the wake of presidential scandals and public skepticism, some observers have asked whether any chief executive, however able, can manage the nation's problems. Yet only a few decades ago, many commentators had been concerned with a different issue. They worried about the expansion of presidential power and the emer-

* Franklin D. Roosevelt had an extramarital relationship with a close female friend, and another admired president, John F. Kennedy, had several mistresses. The difference was that their affairs did not become general public knowledge until long after their presidencies; Clinton's became headline news while he still occupied the White House.

## The American Past

### DINING WITH THE PRESIDENT: HOT DOGS FIT FOR A KING

Andrew Jackson was the People's President, and it seemed fitting that on the day of his inauguration in 1829 the doors of the White House should be opened to the common man. At the reception, food and drink vanished as soon as they were served; glassware, china, and furniture were shattered by the boisterous mob. The new President, astonished and trapped, was finally rescued by friends who locked arms, formed a flying wedge, and led Jackson out. Since then, Presidents have understandably preferred to entertain only invited guests. Their problem has been to do so in a way that is dignified and elegant yet does not appear excessively lavish. Jefferson, who believed in democratic informality, was criticized for wearing "yarn stockings and slippers down at the heels" while receiving the British ambassador; Martin Van Buren, on the other hand, was denied reelection in 1840 partly because the sumptuous banquets he gave offended many voters. For modern Presidents the solution has been to provide the proper formality and pomp at state dinners at the White House, and to demonstrate their informality by inviting dignitaries to their own homes. Thus F.D.R. served hot dogs to the king of England at Hyde Park, and Lyndon Johnson entertained the chancellor of Germany at a barbecue on his ranch.

—Marcus Cunliffe and the editors of *American Heritage, The American Heritage History of the Presidency*

gence of what the historian Arthur M. Schlesinger, Jr., termed "the imperial Presidency."[3] Particularly in the area of foreign and military policy, Schlesinger and others contended, the presidency had exceeded constitutional bounds and usurped congressional war powers.

The growth of the power of the presidency, many of these historians noted, was accompanied by excessive reverence for the person of the president, a phenomenon that one scholar called "the Sun King complex."[4] Another scholar, Thomas E. Cronin, criticized the "textbook Presidency," the creation, he argued, of political scientists, journalists, and others who endow the chief executive with a "halo." Cronin perceived a "cult of the Presidency," in which the occupant of the White House becomes "benevolent, omnipotent, omniscient."[5]

During the period of tension between the United States and the Soviet Union in the decades after World War II, danger from abroad had fueled presidential power. With the fall of the Soviet system in 1991, Schlesinger wrote, "the imperial Presidency collapsed."[6] In 2004, however, Schlesinger said he feared that the continual wars conducted by the administration of George W. Bush were bringing about a resurgent imperial presidency.[7]

Any discussion of the modern presidency is inevitably colored by Watergate, the scandal that led to Richard Nixon's resignation. To some extent, that scandal may have resulted from political and institutional factors—among them the growth of presidential power, increasing government secrecy, a lack of government credibility, a burgeoning national security bureaucracy, and the use of intelligence agencies and techniques in domestic politics.

President Clinton was impeached, charged with lying about his affair with Monica Lewinsky. For most of his presidency he was dogged by the Whitewater affair—his participation with his wife Hillary in a real estate development and their ties to a failed savings and loan association in Arkansas.

Long before Bill Clinton's problems, Congress, in the wake of Vietnam and Watergate, moved in the early 1970s to try to reassert its power within the political system. It enacted the **War Powers Resolution,** a law passed in 1973 in an effort—largely unsuccessful—to limit a president's use of combat forces abroad. Congress also created a new structure to deal with the federal budget, an action designed to permit the lawmakers to share power with the president over the budget process.

The opposing perceptions of the presidency—either as an office grown too powerful, or in some areas too weak—leave unresolved the question of how the presidency can be controlled without so reducing its powers that the president cannot manage national problems and lead the nation. "The American democracy," Schlesinger has suggested, "must discover a middle ground between making the President a czar and making him a puppet."[8]

Key Question

In this chapter we will explore a key question: ***In the light of the nation's experience over recent decades, has the presidency grown too powerful, or too weak?*** Other questions to consider flow from this central issue. For example, are there enough checks on presidential power? Should a president be able to send American forces into combat, as several chief executives have, without a formal declaration of war by Congress? Does a president have enough control over the bureaucracy and policy formation, and enough influence with Congress, to solve the nation's problems? Can any president govern? Are the public's expectations of presidential performance so high that any president is doomed to failure from the start? Is the press so determined to find scandal in high places that every president will be tarred and feathered by the news media?

## The American Presidency

The day before he took the oath of office as 35th president of the United States, John F. Kennedy called on President Eisenhower at the White House. "There are no easy matters that will ever come to you as President," Eisenhower told the younger man. "If they are easy, they will be settled at a lower level."[9]

The president is not merely the symbolic and actual leader of more than 300 million Americans, sworn to "preserve, protect and defend" the Constitution, but also a world leader, whose decisions may affect the future of the more than 6 billion inhabitants of the globe. Yet the presidency is an office of both power and limits—that is the paradox of the modern presidency, discussed earlier. The core of the dilemma is that the technology of the nuclear age and the growth of government in a modern industrial society have combined to concentrate great power in the hands of a chief executive in some policy areas, while restricting his options in others. For example, the president's power to use military force without a declaration of war by Congress was demonstrated during the 1960s in Southeast Asia, in the Persian Gulf in 1991, and in Iraq in 2003. Yet, the Constitution provides that only Congress can declare war.

When in 1973, over President Nixon's veto, Congress enacted a law designed to recapture its war powers, that effort did not effectively limit presidential power. President Reagan, the first President Bush, and President Clinton all sent military forces into combat with no congressional declaration of war. President George W. Bush invaded Afghanistan in 2001 and Iraq in 2003. True, Congress passed resolutions authorizing the use of force in both cases, but it did not declare war. In none of these instances did the War Powers Resolution restrict presidential power.

But these actions all took place abroad. The president's sheer military power, which he exercises as commander in chief, remains formidable. Presidential power at home, in contrast, may be more limited. A president may not be able to get a tax bill through Congress or strengthen the Social Security system.

George Tames/The New York Times

"There are no easy matters that will ever come to you as president. . . ." President Kennedy (left) is visited by former President Eisenhower at Camp David, Maryland.

### A President Looks to the Future

It is not by any means the sole task of the Presidency to think about the present. One of the chief obligations of the Presidency is to think about the future. We have been, in our one hundred and fifty years of constitutional existence, a wasteful nation, a nation that has wasted its natural resources and, very often, wasted its human resources.

One reason why a President of the United States ought to travel throughout the country and become familiar with every State is that he has a great obligation to think about the days when he will no longer be President, to think about the next generation and the generation after that.

—Franklin D. Roosevelt, in Arthur Bernon Tourtellot, *The Presidents on the Presidency*

### "God, What a Job!"

I can't make a damn thing out of this tax problem. I listen to one side and they seem right, and then God! I talk to the other side and they seem just as right, and there I am where I started. I know somewhere there is a book that would give me the truth, but hell, I couldn't read the book. . . . God, what a job!

—Warren G. Harding, in Richard F. Fenno, Jr., *The President's Cabinet*

## The Institution, the Person

The presidency is both an institution and a person. The institution is the office created by the Constitution, custom, cumulative federal law since 1789, and the gradual growth of formal and informal tools of presidential power. The person is a human being, powerful yet vulnerable, compassionate or vain, ordinary or extraordinary. To the institution, the president brings the imprint of his personality and style. Under the Twenty-second Amendment, the incumbent must normally change at least once every eight years.[10] The presidency is, then, both highly institutionalized and highly personal.

George Washington assumed the office feeling not unlike "a culprit who is going to the place of his execution." William Howard Taft thought it "the loneliest place in the world." Harry Truman declared that "being a President is like riding a tiger. A man has to keep on riding or be swallowed." Warren Harding thought the White House "a prison." Lyndon Johnson spoke of "the awesome power, and the immense fragility of executive authority." Jimmy Carter called it "the most difficult job, maybe, on earth." Ronald Reagan complained that "you live in a fishbowl." The first president Bush observed, "You have to have a fairly thick skin."

Bill Clinton, however, musing about the presidency in his final months in office, insisted he enjoyed the job, despite his troubles. "Some people who have been in this position," he said, ". . . talk about what a terrible burden it is, and how the White House is the crown jewel of the federal penal system, and how they can't wait to get out of there. . . . Frankly, most of those guys didn't have a tougher time than I've had there—and I don't know what in the heck they're talking about."[11]

© Bettmann/Corbis
The presidency is both an institution and a person.

The strands of power have come together in the person and the institution of the modern presidency. When the president speaks to the nation, millions listen. His words are instantly transmitted around the globe by satellite and high-speed communications. When he pulls his beagle's ears, as Lyndon Johnson did, the bark of dog lovers is heard around the world. If he cancels a subscription to a newspaper, as John Kennedy did, a thousand thunderous editorials denounce him. When he says he does not like broccoli, as the first President Bush revealed, crates of the vegetable are shipped to the White House by indignant growers. Is his kitten ill? His chef disloyal? Does he carry his own garment bag aboard the plane? Does he dye his hair? Does he eat too much fast food? Does his wife consult astrologers? Does she have imaginary conversations with celebrated figures from the past? Did he fall off his mountain bike? No detail in the life of a modern president (and these are real examples) escapes the eyes of the media, which provide such information to a public apparently hungry for more.

Public disclosure of intimate details of a president's life is not limited to the press, revelations of scandal, or the literary endeavors of White House cooks, seamstresses, and bottle-washers. His own distinguished, high-level staff assistants may be secret diarists, scribbling away at night for the sake of posterity and the best-seller lists. Indeed, presidents themselves write books, not only for money but to give their own version of events and, they hope, to secure their place in history. Truman, Eisenhower, Johnson, Nixon, Ford, Carter, Reagan, the first President Bush, and Clinton all published memoirs after they left the White House.

The intense public interest in the person and office of the president is a reflection of how the job of chief executive has become magnified. The immense pressures on the human being who occupies the office of president have intensified because the institution of the presidency has evolved and grown with the nation.

# The Expanding Presidency

## "We Never Once Thought of a King"

The framers of the Constitution who met at Philadelphia toiled in the greatest secrecy. No television cameras invaded their privacy in 1787. Yet even in that preelectronic age, the framers felt it necessary to issue a press release (their only one) to counteract rumors that were circulating around the country. The statement was leaked to the *Pennsylvania Herald* in August: "Tho' we cannot, affirmatively, tell you what we are doing; we can, negatively, tell you what we are not doing—we never once thought of a king."[12] (Alexander Hamilton, however, did propose a virtual monarchy in the form of a lifetime chief executive, but his plan won no support.)

The colonists who made the American Revolution were, perhaps understandably, prejudiced against kings. At the same time, the difficulties encountered under the Articles of Confederation had exposed the shortcomings of legislative government and demonstrated the need for a strong executive. But how strong?

James Wilson and Gouverneur Morris championed a single powerful chief executive, and James Madison eventually adopted that view. Many of the framers considered legislatures to be dangerously radical; the blessings of liberty could best be enjoyed, they felt, if popular government was checked by a strong executive branch that could protect wealth, private property, and business. Support for a powerful single president was by no means unanimous, however; some of the framers had specifically proposed a plural executive, and some wanted the president to be chosen by Congress. The framers, as Thomas E. Cronin has observed, knew that the American presidency is always a "potentially dangerous institution. . . . The framers wanted a more authoritative and decisive national government, yet they were keenly aware that the American people were not about to accept too much centralized power vested in a single person."[13]

Out of the debates at Philadelphia emerged the basic structure of the presidency as we know it today: a single president who headed one of three separate branches of government and was elected independently for a four-year term. The great authority the framers gave to the president was limited by the separation of powers among the three branches of government, by the checks and balances engraved in the Constitution, by the federal system, and, in time, by other informal controls generally unforeseen in 1787—the rise of political parties and mass media, for example.

## The Growth of the American Presidency

"I prefer to supervise the whole operations of the government myself . . . and this makes my duties very great," President James Polk wrote in his diary in 1848.[14]

So great had those duties become in the 21st century that by fiscal 2007 the president proposed an estimated federal budget of $2.7 trillion and presided over a bureaucracy of 2.7 million civilians and 1.4 million members of the armed forces. He would not have dreamed of attempting to "supervise the whole operations of the government" by himself.

Great crises and great presidents have contributed to the growth of the presidency since 1789. George Washington, Andrew Jackson, Abraham Lincoln, Theodore Roosevelt, Woodrow Wilson, and Franklin Roosevelt all placed their personal stamp on the presidency. When a president strengthens and reshapes the institution, the change may endure even after he leaves. The modern presidency, for example, is rooted in the style of Franklin D. Roosevelt.

© AP/Wide World Photos

Franklin D. Roosevelt influenced the modern presidency more than any other chief executive.

Although presidents and events have played a decisive role in the development of the presidency, several broad historical factors have combined to create a powerful chief executive today.

**The Nuclear Age and the End of the Cold War** For more than four decades after the end of the Second World War, the United States and the Soviet Union lived under the terrible shadow of nuclear war. Each possessed nuclear missiles that could destroy the other country in half an hour or less; given the time factor, the president, rather than Congress, of necessity became the one who had to decide whether to use such hideous, and ultimately irrational, weapons. (As Clinton Rossiter noted, the next wartime president "may well be our last."[15])

In 1991, the collapse of the Soviet Union and the breakup of the communist central government into 15 separate nations marked the formal end to the **Cold War** (1945–1991), the period after the Second World War marked by rivalry and tension between the two nuclear superpowers, the United States and the communist government of the Soviet Union. Although both sides had moved to cut strategic weapons drastically, the United States and Russia in 2005 still possessed long-range missiles with powerful nuclear warheads. At least six other countries were nuclear powers, and a number of Third World nations were attempting to develop nuclear arms. Despite the disintegration of the Soviet Union, the world

## Lyndon Johnson Leaves the White House

Of course I miss it. . . . President Nixon said to me, "How did you feel when you weren't President any more?" And I said, "I don't know whether you'll understand this now or not, but you certainly will later. I sat there on that platform and waited for you to stand up and raise your right hand and take the oath of office, and I think the most pleasant words . . . that ever came into my ears were 'So help me God' that you repeated after that oath. Because at that time I no longer had the fear that I was the man that could make the mistake of involving the world in war, that I was no longer the man that would have to carry the terrifying responsibility of protecting the lives of this country and maybe the entire world, unleashing the horrors of some of our great power if I felt that that was required. But that now I could ride back down that avenue, being concerned about what happened, being alarmed about what might happen, but just really knowing that I wasn't going to be the cause of it." . . . The real horror was to be sleeping soundly about three-thirty or four or five o'clock in the morning and have the telephone ring and the operator say, "Sorry to wake you, Mr. President." . . . There's just a second between the time the operator got me on the line until she could get . . . Mr. Bundy in the Situation Room, or maybe . . . Secretary McNamara. . . . And we went through the horrors of hell that thirty seconds or minute or two minutes. Had we hit a Russian ship? Had an accident occurred? We have another *Pueblo?* Someone made a mistake—were we at war? Well, those experiences are gone.

—Lyndon B. Johnson, excerpts from a CBS television news special, "LBJ: Why I Chose Not to Run," December 27, 1969

was still a volatile place, and the president continued to control the "nuclear button."

In sum, the constitutional power of Congress to declare war was eroded in the last half of the 20th century by the power of the president to use nuclear weapons, to commit U.S. forces to meet sudden crises, and to fight so-called limited wars. Even in a changed world, the president remains the dominant figure in responding to crisis with military force.

**Foreign Affairs** The president, under the Constitution, has the prime responsibility for conducting the foreign affairs of the United States. From its isolationism before the Second World War, the United States emerged in the postwar period as one of two major world powers. During the Eisenhower administration, when John Foster Dulles exercised a powerful influence as secretary of state, the United States adhered to the principle of collective security to "contain" communism and entered into a series of military alliances with other nations for this purpose.

The wisdom of the role of the United States as a "world policeman" was seriously questioned in the 1960s and 1970s, when the United States became bogged down in the Vietnam War. By 1980, following the seizure of hostages in the American embassy in Iran and Soviet intervention in Afghanistan, some of the post-Vietnam emphasis on détente and disarmament had given way to a renewed concern over national security and military strength. And in that year, and again in 1984, the voters in the presidential election chose Ronald Reagan, who increased defense spending and emphasized military preparedness. In 1991, after Saddam Hussein's military invaded Kuwait, the first President Bush sent troops to force Iraq to withdraw. His son, President George W. Bush, announced a strategy of preemptive war, allowing the United States to strike first when it deemed such action necessary because of "imminent danger."[16] Because the United States remains one of the most powerful nations, the president is inevitably a world leader as well as a national leader.

**Domestic Affairs** The great increase in presidential power in the 20th century took place in the domestic field as much as in foreign affairs. Franklin Roosevelt's New Deal, as Edward S. Corwin pointed out, brought "social acceptance of the idea that government should be active and reformist, rather than simply protective of the established order of things."[17]

This concept of a large, activist government as the engine of social progress was dramatically challenged by House Speaker Newt Gingrich and other leaders of the Republican-controlled Congress elected in 1994. They supported an agenda to reduce government's role in the lives of Americans, to cut the rate of growth of social programs, and to turn more power back to the states. With the political winds blowing strongly against the traditional Democratic, New Deal philosophy, even President Clinton could announce in 1996: "The era of big government is over."[18] But after the Democrats made surprising gains in the House of Representatives in the 1998 off-year elections, Gingrich quit as speaker and left Congress.

The years after the New Deal brought a tremendous growth of government as manager. As a result, the president today directs a huge bureaucracy. Although political leaders may continue to argue over the nature and extent of Washington's role, modern government is expected to deal with social problems, from substandard schools to health care, and the president is at the center of the debate. Nor have Republican presidents necessar-

© 2002 AP/Wide World Photos

Bush chose Mt. Rushmore and the chiseled faces of famous predecessors as the backdrop for a speech about homeland security.

ily been successful in turning back the tide of big government, try as they might. President Nixon cut back and dismantled some federal programs, but the federal budget increased substantially during his presidency. Ronald Reagan, too, attacked the bureaucracy in his 1980 campaign, but its size increased during his eight years in office.

**The Mass Media** Television and the other news media have helped to magnify the person and the institution of the presidency. (The relationship between the president and the press is discussed later in this chapter.) All the major television and radio networks, newspapers, magazines, and wire services have correspondents assigned full-time to covering the president. These "White House regulars" accompany the chief executive wherever he travels, sending out a steady flow of news about his activities.

When a president wants to talk to the people, the networks (whose stations are licensed by the federal government) often make available free prime time. Presidential news conferences are frequently televised live. People identify with a president they see so often on television; his style and personality help to shape the times and the national mood.

Modern presidents, to a greater extent than the public is aware, often tailor their daily activities to television, scheduling upbeat events in time to appear in a "sound bite" on the evening news. Conversely, bad news that the White House wants to play down may be announced late on a Friday, on the theory that people, involved in their weekend activities, pay less attention to the news on a Saturday. Presidents and their media affairs experts attempt to orchestrate and dominate the news to the advantage of the presidency.

A president's media advisers—George W. Bush recruited a team of former television network producers—carefully plan the settings and backdrop for his appearances, with an eye to how they will appear on TV. If he gives a speech in a blue-collar neighborhood, there are likely to be workers in hard hats sharing the stage. If he visits an elementary school, he will be surrounded by happy children. And a president's image-makers are always alert to a "photo-op" that will make him appear presidential, or warm and fuzzy, as the occasion demands.

At the same time, the press may weaken a president when it reports news that reflects unfavorably on his actions and policy decisions, or his personal conduct. In that sense, the news media is a two-edged sword.

## The Impossible Burden: The Many Roles of the Chief Executive

During George W. Bush's first week in office in January 2001, he delivered his inaugural address at the Capitol; danced at more than a half dozen balls that night with his wife and daughters; had coffee with his parents on his first morning in the White House; gave a tour of his new home to supporters; greeted more than 2,200 people who attended the traditional open house; redecorated the Oval Office; sent cabinet nominations to the Senate; reinstated a policy banning the use of taxpayer money for abortions; swore in several cabinet officials and appointees; sent major education legislation to Congress; lunched with freshman House members; invited the prime minister of Canada to the White House; and signed an order to help keep power flowing to California, which was having an energy crisis.

The president of the United States is one individual but fills many separate roles: chief of state, chief executive, commander in chief, chief diplomat, chief legislator, chief of party, and popular leader. All but the last two are required of him by the Constitution. In addition, as one scholar of the presidency suggested, the president is expected to be the voice of the people, protector of the peace, manager of prosperity, and world leader.[19]

A modern president is presumed to be all these things and more. He is looked to as a sort of role model for the nation. Sometimes it almost seems that a president is expected to combine the talents of a matador, a shortstop, a ballet dancer, a police chief, a parent, a public relations expert, an expert economist, a political wizard, and a military genius. But of course, no human being can live up to such expectations.

Moreover, it would be simplistic and misleading to think of the president as rapidly "changing hats" as he goes about filling these various roles. Many of the presidential roles blend and overlap; some may collide. Being a vigorous party leader, for example, will often conflict with playing the role of chief of state, of being president of all the people. For a president's roles, as Cronin has noted, "are not compartmentalized, unrelated functions, but rather a dynamic, seamless assortment of tasks and responsibilities."[20]

For purposes of analysis, however, it is possible to separate out the principal roles of the president. When we do so, we see that the "awesome burden" has identifiable parts.

### Chief of State

The president of the United States is the ceremonial and symbolic *head of state.* In another role, he is also *head of government,* the official who presides over the machinery of the executive branch.

In many countries, the two jobs are distinct: a figurehead king, queen, or president is head of state, but the premier or prime minister is head of government and exercises the real power. It is because the two functions are combined in the person of the American president that he finds himself declaring National Codfish Week or toasting the grand duchess of Luxembourg at a state dinner on the same day that he makes a vital foreign policy decision or vetoes a major bill sent to him by Congress.

The distinction between head of state and head of government may seem trivial—of interest only to protocol officers and society columnists—but it is not. Much of the mystique and aura of power that have surrounded the institution of the presidency are due to the fact that the president is more than a prime minister; he is a symbol of nationhood as well as a custodian of the

"Okay, bring in the new guy. . . ."

As the train bearing the body of Franklin D. Roosevelt left Warm Springs, a tearful Chief Petty Officer Graham Jackson played "Going Home."

people's power. In Theodore Roosevelt's famous phrase, he is both "a king and a prime minister." [21]

*for more information about Theodore Roosevelt, see:*
***http://lcweb2.loc.gov/ammem/trfhtml/trhome.html***

As noted earlier in this chapter, some critics of presidential power have argued that presidents lose their perspective and their ability to make sound judgments because they are treated too much like monarchs and are isolated from the problems faced by ordinary citizens. In part, this may happen because a president is surrounded by the trappings of power—large staffs, private aircraft, and the Secret Service.

Because the chief executive is such a symbolic and familiar figure, when a president dies in office people often react as though they have suffered a great personal loss. Even the radio announcers wept in 1945 as they told of Franklin Roosevelt's death. After President Kennedy's assassination in 1963, the nation went through a period of mourning; 250,000 people braved cold weather to line up to pass his bier in the Capitol rotunda; 100 million people watched the funeral on television. Social scientists studying the impact of the assassination on children and adults found definite physical and psychological effects.[22] Similarly, when former President Reagan died in 2004, people waited for hours in California and in Washington to view his flag-draped casket.

## Chief Executive

The president runs the executive branch of the government. When President George W. Bush took office in 2001, he headed a federal establishment with an estimated total payroll of $133 billion. No executive in private industry has responsibilities that match the president's. The president receives a salary of $400,000 a year plus $50,000 in nontaxable expenses and up to $100,000 in travel expenses, also tax-free, as well as handsome retirement benefits, including a lifetime pension of $171,900 a year.[23]

There are few legal qualifications for the office. The Constitution requires only that the president be a "natural-born" citizen, at least 35 years old, and 14 years a resident of the United States.[24]

Obviously, there would be more than enough work in the president's in-basket to keep him busy if he did nothing else but administer the government. And, in fact, presidents do find themselves bogged down under a mountain of paper. Most presidents work at night to try to keep up; the sight of Franklin Roosevelt, a polio victim, being wheeled to his office at night, preceded by wire baskets full of paperwork, was a familiar one to White House aides during the New Deal era. President Eisenhower tried to solve the paperwork problem by ordering his staff to prepare memos no more than one page long. Lyndon Johnson took a swim and nap each afternoon, then began a second working day at 4 p.m., often summoning weary aides for conferences at the end of *their* working day.

*for more information about Franklin Roosevelt, see:*
***http://www.fdrlibrary.marist.edu***

Because administering the government is only one of seven major presidential roles, the president cannot spend all of his time running the executive branch. The White House staff, other agencies in the Executive Office of the President, and the cabinet all help to run the government. The president tries to confine himself to *presidential* decisions, such as resolving major conflicts within the bureaucracy, or among his own advisers, and initiating and approving major programs and policies.

Beneath the president in the executive branch are the 15 cabinet departments (as of January 2005) and about 50 major independent agencies, boards, and commissions. (See Figure 14-3 in the next chapter.) These agencies are of two main types: executive agencies and independent regulatory agencies. The **executive agencies** are independent agencies of government under the president within the executive branch, but not part of a cabinet department. They report to the president in the same manner as departments, even though they are not within any cabinet department. They are, therefore, independent of the departments, but not of the president. The **independent regulatory agencies** exercise quasi-judicial and quasi-legislative

© UPI/Bettmann/Corbis

November 1963: President John F. Kennedy lies in state in the Capitol rotunda.

powers and are administratively independent of both the president and Congress (although politically independent of neither). The members of the major regulatory agencies are appointed by the president from both major parties to staggered, fixed terms but do not report to him.

The neat organizational charts do not show the overlapping and intricate real-life relationships among the three branches of government. Nor do they give any hint of the difficulties a president faces in controlling his own executive branch and in making the bureaucracy carry out his decisions.

President Truman understood the problems that Eisenhower would have as an Army general elected president: "He'll sit here," Truman would remark (tapping his desk for emphasis), "and he'll say, 'Do this! Do that!' *And nothing will happen.* Poor Ike—it won't be a bit like the army. He'll find it very frustrating."[25]

© Bettmann/Corbis

President Johnson working late as he prepared an address on the war in Vietnam

*for more information about President Harry S Truman, see: http://www.trumanlibrary.org*

Despite their vast constitutional and extraconstitutional powers, presidents are sometimes as much a victim of bureaucratic inertia as anyone else. "I sit here all day," Truman said, "trying to persuade people to do the things they ought to have sense enough to do without my persuading them. . . . That's all the powers of the President amount to."[26]

Richard Neustadt agreed with Truman that "Presidential power is the power to persuade."[27] In persuading people, however, the president can draw upon formidable resources, not the least of which is his power to appoint and remove officials. Under the Constitution, the president, "with the advice and consent of the Senate," appoints ambassadors, Supreme Court justices, other federal judges, the heads of regulatory agencies, and other senior officials.

The Constitution does not specifically give the president the power to remove government officials, but the Supreme Court has ruled that Congress cannot interfere with the president's right to fire officials whom he has appointed with Senate approval.[28] In this instance, and in many others, decisions of the Supreme Court have increased the growth of presidential power.

During Franklin Roosevelt's administration, on the other hand, the Court held that the president did not have the right to remove officials serving in administratively independent "quasi-legislative or quasi-judicial agencies."[29] Even though commissioners of regulatory agencies are thus theoretically immune from removal by presidential power, in practice they may not be. When scandal touched the chairman of the Federal Communications Commission in 1960, the incident embarrassed President Eisenhower; within a week the official resigned.

To the task of bureaucrat in chief, therefore, the president brings powers of persuasion that go beyond his formal, constitutional, and legal authority. By the nature of his job, he is the final decision maker in the executive branch. As the sign on Harry Truman's desk said: "The buck stops here."

The president also has the power to grant "reprieves and pardons for offenses against the United States," a power that seemed relatively unimportant in modern times until President Ford granted a pardon to his predecessor, Richard Nixon (who had appointed Ford vice president). Ford noted that in the Watergate affair, the former president had "become liable to possible indictment and trial for offenses against the United States." Ford said that such a trial would divide the country, and he pardoned Nixon for all crimes that he "has committed or may have committed" as president. Ford later testified under oath that, prior to taking office, he had not entered into any arrangement with Nixon to grant the pardon. Last-minute pardons of several individuals by President Clinton as he was leaving office also proved controversial.

## Commander in Chief

When President Kennedy died at Parkland Hospital in Dallas on November 22, 1963, an Army warrant officer named Ira D. Gearhart, armed but dressed in civilian clothes, picked up a locked briefcase known as the "football," or "black box," and walked down a hospital corridor to a small room where Vice President Lyndon Johnson was being guarded by Secret Service agents. The officer who carries the "football" must be near whoever is the president, to guard "a national security portfolio of cryptographic orders the president would send his military chiefs to authorize the launching of nuclear missiles.

The orders can be dispatched by telephone, teletype, or microwave radio."[30] Although the Cold War is over, the "football" still exists; when George W. Bush visited Pope John Paul II in the Vatican in 2004, a Marine major held the football nearby.

In effect, the warrant officer has custody of the "nuclear button," which is not a button but a set of coded orders. That such a person and such machinery exist is a reminder of the fact that, regardless of his other duties, the president is at all times commander in chief of the armed forces of the United States.

Although a president normally delegates most of this authority to his generals and admirals, he is not required to do so. During the Whiskey Rebellion of 1794, President Washington personally led his troops into Pennsylvania. During the Civil War, Lincoln often visited the Army of the Potomac to instruct his generals. Franklin Roosevelt and Prime Minister Winston Churchill conferred on the major strategic decisions of the Second World War. Truman made the decisions to drop the atomic bomb on Japan in 1945 and to intervene in Korea in 1950. In 1961, Kennedy authorized the Bay of Pigs invasion of Cuba by Cuban exiles armed and trained by the Central Intelligence Agency. He blockaded Cuba in 1962 to persuade the Soviet Union to withdraw its missiles from that island. Johnson personally approved bombing targets in Vietnam. Nixon made the decision to send U.S. troops into Cambodia in 1970, to bomb North Vietnam, and to bomb Cambodia in 1973. Reagan made the decision to send troops to invade Grenada in 1983 and to bomb Libya in 1986. The first President Bush dispatched 27,000 troops to invade Panama in 1989 and sent more than half a million men and women to the Persian Gulf in 1990. Clinton sent armed forces into Haiti and Bosnia, bombed Iraq, and authorized American warplanes to lead NATO's bombing campaign against Yugoslavia. George W. Bush sent the American military into Afghanistan in 2001 and dispatched 130,000 troops to invade Iraq in 2003.

Lieutenant Commander Vivian Crea, United States Coast Guard, first woman to serve as military aide to the president, carries the "football."



*for more information about Abraham Lincoln, see:*
***http://lcweb2.loc.gov/ammem/alhtml***

**Civilian supremacy,** the principle of civilian control of the military, is based on the clear constitutional power of the president as supreme commander of the armed forces. In many other countries, particularly in the Third World, military commanders often topple civilian leaders and seize power for themselves.

In the United States, the principle of civilian supremacy was put to a severe test during the Korean War when General Douglas MacArthur repeatedly defied President Truman's orders. The hero of the Pacific theater during the Second World War, MacArthur enjoyed personal prestige to rival the president's and had a substantial political following of his own. Truman finally dismissed MacArthur in April 1951. In the most dramatic conflict in modern times between the military and the president, the president prevailed.

The Constitution declares that "Congress shall have Power . . . to declare War," but Congress has not done so since December 1941, when it declared war against Japan, following the Japanese attack on Pearl Harbor, and later against Germany.* In the intervening years presidents have made the decision to go to war, although four times—in Vietnam, the Persian Gulf, Afghanistan, and Iraq—they had congressional approval. By 1970, Congress was trying to regain some of its control over the war power. Congress repealed the Tonkin Gulf Resolution, which it had passed in 1964 to support President Johnson's Vietnam policy, and it restricted President Nixon's future use of U.S. troops in Cambodia. Sentiment continued to grow in Congress to curb the president's power to wage undeclared war.

Then, in 1973, Congress passed legislation to attempt to limit presidential war-making power. President Nixon vetoed the measure as an unconstitutional restraint on his power as commander in chief. Congress overrode the president's veto, however, and the War

* Congress has declared war five times: in the War of 1812, the U.S.-Mexican War, the Spanish-American War, the First World War, and the Second World War. It did not declare war in Korea, Vietnam, the Persian Gulf, Afghanistan, or Iraq. However, it authorized military action in Vietnam with the Tonkin Gulf Resolution of 1964, in the Persian Gulf in 1991, in Afghanistan in 2001 under a broad grant of authority to pursue terrorists, and in Iraq in 2002 with joint resolutions.

© MPI/Getty Images

President Harry S Truman and General Douglas MacArthur met on Wake Island in 1950 before Truman fired MacArthur for insubordination.

Powers Resolution became law. The measure provided that the president must report to Congress within 48 hours after sending armed forces into combat abroad, and that their use would have to end in 60 days unless Congress authorized a longer period. Within the authorized period, Congress could order an immediate withdrawal of U.S. forces.

By 2006, however, under six presidents, however, the War Powers Resolution had not effectively restricted presidential military power. Presidents Ford, Carter, Reagan, the first President Bush, Clinton, and George W. Bush all took military actions that they did not report to Congress under the War Powers Resolution. In some instances, they did report the actions to Congress but either stated or implied that they had authority as president to deploy American forces.

In September 1983, after President Reagan sent marines to Lebanon, Congress invoked the War Powers Resolution for the first time since its passage 10 years earlier. It enacted legislation declaring that the law applied to the conflict in Lebanon and authorizing continued deployment of the marines there for 18 months. President Reagan signed the bill but said this did not mean he accepted the principle that the War Powers Resolution applied in Lebanon.

Other presidents followed this pattern; they informed Congress of military actions but maintained they did so, in effect, as a courtesy, not as a legal requirement.

The War Powers Resolution, or at least that portion giving Congress authority to order a withdrawal of American forces, is a form of legislative veto, a device ruled unconstitutional by the Supreme Court in 1983.[31] As discussed in Chapter 12, however, the ruling in another case did not directly affect the War Powers Resolution.

The **military-industrial complex**—the term often used to describe the ties between the military establishment and the defense-aerospace industry—is another limit on the president's power as commander in chief. For example, a president may find it difficult to cancel production of a fighter plane, a bomber, an aircraft carrier, or some other weapons system that enjoys the strong support of the Joint Chiefs of Staff, Congress, and private industry.

Politics may also narrow a president's options. President Reagan proposed a space-based missile defense program, popularly known as "Star Wars," to protect against Soviet ICBMs. The project cost $60 billion and produced nothing. President Clinton felt it necessary to support a more modest, land-based missile shield against smaller countries. Aside from the fact that defense contractors had a huge stake in building the system, Clinton had to weigh the political costs of killing the program. To do so would open the Democrats to Republican charges that they were "soft on defense." In the end, Clinton postponed a decision and left it to his successor, George W. Bush, who continued to fund the program.

Despite these limits, presidents have claimed and exercised formidable war powers during emergencies. In the 10 weeks after the fall of Fort Sumter, South Carolina, in April 1861, Lincoln called out the militia, spent $2 million without authorization by Congress, blockaded Southern ports, and suspended the writ of habeas corpus in certain areas. Lincoln declared: "I felt that measures otherwise unconstitutional might become lawful by becoming indispensable to the preservation of the Constitution through the preservation of the nation. Right or wrong, I assumed this ground and now avow it."[32]

During the Second World War, Franklin Roosevelt exercised extraordinary powers over food rationing and the economy, only partly with congressional authorization. And in 1942, with the consent of Congress, he permitted the forced removal of 112,000 people of Japanese descent—most of them native-born citizens of the United States—from their homes in California and other western states to internment camps called "relocation centers."

During the Korean War, Truman seized the steel mills in the face of a strike threat, but the Supreme Court ruled he had no constitutional right to do so, even as commander in chief.[33] President Johnson expanded American forces in Vietnam after Congress passed the Tonkin Gulf Resolution, empowering the president to take "all necessary measures" in Southeast Asia. The president contended, however, that he did not need congressional approval to fight the war in Vietnam.

***for more information about Lyndon Johnson, see: http://www.lbjlib.utexas.edu***

1942: Japanese Americans lining up in California before being sent to internment camps



## Chief Diplomat

"I make American foreign policy," President Truman declared in 1948. By and large, presidents do make foreign policy; that is, they direct the relations of the United States with the other nations of the world. The Constitution does not specifically confer this power on the president, but it does so indirectly. It authorizes him to receive foreign ambassadors, to appoint ambassadors, and to make treaties with the consent of two-thirds of the Senate. Because it requires that the president share some foreign policy powers with Congress, the Constitution has been characterized as "an invitation to struggle for the privilege of directing American foreign policy."[34]

In this struggle the president usually enjoys the advantage. Because the State Department, the Pentagon, and the CIA report to him as part of the executive branch, the president—or so it is often assumed—has more information about foreign affairs available to him than do members of Congress. But senators and representatives also have sources of information—official briefings, background memoranda from the Library of Congress, data from the Congressional Budget Office, unofficial "leaks" from within the bureaucracy, and friends in the press and the universities. A president, therefore, does not have a monopoly on information. Much of the information he does receive is conflicting, because it represents different viewpoints within the bureaucracy; even with the best intelligence reports, a president may make decisions that prove to be misguided. Nevertheless, the information that flows in daily is a substantial source of power for the president.

Those who lack the information that the president has, or is presumed to have, including senators and representatives, find it difficult to challenge the president's actions. This was true in 2002 when President George W. Bush claimed Iraq had weapons of mass destruction to justify his invasion of that country, and Congress repeated the president's allegation in authorizing the war. More than three years later, no such weapons had been found. Often, at least in the short run, a foreign policy crisis may increase the public's support of the president's actions. (See Figure 13-1.) Over time, however, public opinion can change and Congress can chip away at a president's power in foreign affairs.

The president has sole power to negotiate and sign treaties. That power was reaffirmed by the Supreme Court in 1936.[35] The Senate may block a treaty by refusing to approve it, but it seldom does so. In 1920, however, it did refuse to ratify the Treaty of Versailles and its provision for U.S. membership in the League of Nations. Sometimes a president does not submit a treaty to the Senate because he knows it will not be approved, or he may modify the treaty to meet Senate opposition.

**Executive agreements** are international agreements between the president and foreign heads of state that, unlike treaties, do not require Senate approval. Today, these are employed by the president in the conduct of foreign affairs more often than treaties. Some executive agreements are made by the president with the prior approval of Congress. For example, in the Trade Act of 1974, Congress restored the president's power to negotiate tariff agreements with other countries. And sometimes, to gain political support, a president will submit an executive agreement to Congress after it is signed, although he is not legally required to do so.

Because a president can sign an executive agreement with another nation without the constitutional necessity of going to the Senate, the use of this device has increased

© Kevin Lamarque/Reuters/Corbis

President Bush and Secretary of Defense Donald H. Rumsfeld confer during a NATO summit meeting in 2002. Bush replaced the controversial defense secretary one day after the Democratic congressional victories in 2006.

enormously. This has been particularly true since the Second World War, as the U.S. role in international affairs has expanded. Today, in a single year, a president may sign several hundred executive agreements.

The president also has sole power to recognize or not recognize foreign governments. The United States did not recognize the Soviet Union until November 1933, some 16 years after the Russian Revolution. Since Woodrow Wilson's day, presidents have used diplomatic recognition as an instrument of foreign policy. President

© Bettmann/Corbis

Presidents do make foreign policy: British Prime Minister Winston Churchill, President Truman, and Soviet Premier Stalin at Potsdam, 1945.

Nixon's historic journey to Beijing early in 1972 marked the start of diplomatic contacts between the United States and the People's Republic of China. President Carter recognized China in 1979, and the two countries opened full diplomatic relations.

*for more information about the first President George Bush, see: http://bushlibrary.tamu.edu*

In acting as chief diplomat, the president, as commander in chief, can back up his diplomacy with military power. Both the arrows and the olive branch depicted in the presidential seal are available to him, a good example of how presidential roles overlap.

## Chief Legislator

"He shall from time to time give to the Congress Information of the State of the Union, and recommend to their Consideration such Measures as he shall judge necessary and expedient." With this statement in Article II, "the Constitution puts the President right square into the legislative business," as President Eisenhower once observed.

Today, presidents often use their televised State of the Union address, usually delivered to a joint session of Congress in January, as a public platform to unveil their annual legislative program. The details of proposed legislation are then filled in through a series of special presidential messages sent to Capitol Hill in the months that follow.

This was not always the case. Active presidential participation in the legislative process is a 20th-century phenomenon, and the practice of presidents sending a comprehensive legislative package to Congress developed only after the Second World War during the Truman administration.[36]

The success of the president's role as chief legislator depends on the cooperation of Congress. A president faced with a Congress controlled by the opposition party or a coalition of opponents may find his role as chief legislator frustrating. President Kennedy, a Democrat whose legislative program was blocked by a coalition of Republicans and southern Democrats, observed ruefully: "It is very easy to defeat a bill in the Congress. It is much more difficult to pass one. . . . They are two separate offices and two separate powers, the Congress and the Presidency. There is bound to be conflict."[37]

That conflict reached extraordinary levels during the budget battle of 1995–1996, when the government shut down twice because the Republican Congress and

© Corbis

1972: President Nixon inspects the Chinese military.

the Democratic chief executive were unable to agree on spending programs to achieve a balanced budget.

As one scholar, Charles O. Jones, has concluded, the president is often less influential in the legislative process than the public thinks: "Few, if any, major policy proposals are likely to pass both houses unchanged. Presidents rarely expect that to happen, and if they do, they are inevitably disappointed."[38]

The conflict between the president and Congress at times revolves around the doctrine of **executive privilege,** the claim by presidents of an inherent right to withhold information from Congress and the judiciary. This doctrine is nowhere explicitly stated in the Constitution but rests on the separation of powers of the three branches of government. Although presidents may invoke executive privilege, Congress in turn has argued that its legislative powers include the right to investigate the executive branch and to obtain all necessary information from the president and his administration. Usually conflicts over executive privilege arise when a congressional committee demands documents from, or testimony by, presidential assistants.

As the Watergate scandal unfolded during the Nixon administration, the president was accused by his former counsel of participating in an illegal plot to cover up the break-in and bugging at the Democratic Party headquarters in the Watergate office building in Washington. Nixon's tapes of his own White House conversations became the crucial evidence, although an 18½-minute segment of a key tape had apparently been erased. Eventually, the Watergate special prosecutor demanded the tapes for use in the trial of several high-ranking officials accused of covering up the break-in and the issue went to the U.S. Supreme Court. In ruling 8–0 that Nixon must surrender his tapes, the Court for the first time recognized the doctrine of executive privilege, but it also declared that the right of the president to keep some matters confidential must yield to the need for evidence in a criminal trial.[39]

Every president has staff assistants in charge of legislative liaison. Their job is to pressure Congress to pass the president's program. The senators or representatives who want the administration to approve a new federal building, or dam, or public works project in their state or district may discover that the price is their vote on a bill that the president wants passed. There are other, more subtle pressures. A senator who opposes a president's foreign policies may no longer be invited to White House social functions. Often, on an important measure, the president himself takes charge of the "arm twisting"—telephoning members of Congress in their offices or inviting them to the White House for a chat about the merits of his program.

On the other hand, political scientist George C. Edwards, III, has argued, "while legislative skills may at times gain support for presidential policies, this is not typical." Examining the various resources available to a president, Edwards concluded that a chief executive "has relatively little influence to wield over Congress."[40]

As chief legislator, however, the president is not limited entirely to the art of persuasion. He has an important constitutional weapon in the **veto,** the constitutional power of the president to disapprove a bill and return it with his objections to the branch of Congress in which it originated. By a vote of two-thirds of each house, Congress may pass the bill over the president's veto. If he approves a bill, he may sign it—often in front of news photographers and with much fanfare and handing out of pens.

If the president does not either sign or veto a bill within 10 working days after he receives it, the measure becomes law without his signature. If Congress adjourns during the 10-day period after the president receives a bill, he can exercise his **pocket veto,** the power of a pres-

© Stephen Jaffe/AFP/Getty Images

2003: President Bush signs the bill modifying the nation's Medicare system.

ident to kill a bill by taking no action when Congress has adjourned.

But the Constitution is unclear on whether a president can pocket-veto a bill when Congress is in recess. During the 1970s, Senator Edward M. Kennedy successfully challenged in court three pocket vetoes by Presidents Nixon and Ford. The court rulings suggested that a president may not pocket-veto legislation when Congress is in recess but only when it adjourns for good at the end of the second session of a Congress.

Except for joint resolutions, which are the same as bills, resolutions of Congress do not require presidential action because they are expressions of sentiment, not law.

Because Congress normally finds it difficult to override a presidential veto, merely the threat of a veto is often enough to force Congress to tailor a bill to conform to administration wishes. Only about 4 percent of presidential vetoes have been overridden by Congress. (See Table 13-1.)

**TABLE 13-1**

**Presidential Vetoes, 1789–2006**

| | Regular Vetoes | Pocket Vetoes | Total Vetoes | Vetoes Overridden |
|---|---|---|---|---|
| Washington | 2 | — | 2 | — |
| Madison | 5 | 2 | 7 | — |
| Monroe | 1 | — | 1 | — |
| Jackson | 5 | 7 | 12 | — |
| Van Buren | — | 1 | 1 | — |
| Tyler | 6 | 4 | 10 | 1 |
| Polk | 2 | 1 | 3 | — |
| Pierce | 9 | — | 9 | 5 |
| Buchanan | 4 | 3 | 7 | — |
| Lincoln | 2 | 5 | 7 | — |
| A. Johnson | 21 | 8 | 29 | 15 |
| Grant | 45 | 48 | 93 | 4 |
| Hayes | 12 | 1 | 13 | 1 |
| Arthur | 4 | 8 | 12 | 1 |
| Cleveland | 304 | 110 | 414 | 2 |
| B. Harrison | 19 | 25 | 44 | 1 |
| Cleveland | 42 | 128 | 170 | 5 |
| McKinley | 6 | 36 | 42 | — |
| T. Roosevelt | 42 | 40 | 82 | 1 |
| Taft | 30 | 9 | 39 | 1 |
| Wilson | 33 | 11 | 44 | 6 |
| Harding | 5 | 1 | 6 | — |
| Coolidge | 20 | 30 | 50 | 4 |
| Hoover | 21 | 16 | 37 | 3 |
| F. Roosevelt | 372 | 263 | 635 | 9 |
| Truman | 180 | 70 | 250 | 12 |
| Eisenhower | 73 | 108 | 181 | 2 |
| Kennedy | 12 | 9 | 21 | — |
| L. Johnson | 16 | 14 | 30 | — |
| Nixon | 26 | 17 | 43 | 7 |
| Ford | 48 | 18 | 66 | 12 |
| Carter | 13 | 18 | 31 | 2 |
| Reagan | 39 | 39 | 78 | 9 |
| G. H. W. Bush | 29 | 15 | 44 | 1 |
| Clinton | 36 | 1 | 37 | 2 |
| G. W. Bush* | 1 | — | — | — |
| Total | 1,485 | 1,066 | 2,550 | 106 |

*President George W. Bush vetoed a bill for the first time on July 19, 2006. The legislation would have expanded federal funds for embryonic stem cell research.
SOURCES: U.S. House of Representatives, Office of the Clerk, "Presidential Vetoes"; CRS Report for Congress, *Congressional Overrides of Presidential Vetoes,* April 7, 2004, pp. 3–5.

President Clinton briefly enjoyed a **line-item veto,** the power of the president—struck down by the Supreme Court in 1998—to veto specific parts of appropriations bills. Most state governors have this power. In 1996 Congress passed and President Clinton signed a law to give the president such power for the first time, for a period of eight years. Clinton used that power to veto parts of 11 bills.[41] In 1998, however, the Supreme Court, in a 6–3 decision, ruled the line-item veto unconstitutional.[42]

In the words of Justice John Paul Stevens, who wrote the Supreme Court's opinion, "The Line-Item Veto Act authorizes the president himself to effect the repeal of laws, for his own policy reasons, without observing the procedures set out in Article I" of the Constitution.[43] The Court thus held that Congress cannot, simply by passing a law, modify a power granted by the Constitution; to do so would require a constitutional amendment.

Several presidents have asked Congress to enact a constitutional amendment to give the president a line-item veto. One reason is that Congress often passes **riders,** provisions tacked on to a piece of legislation that are not relevant to the bill. The president may find the rider objectionable, but must swallow the legislation whole or veto the entire bill—he cannot veto the rider alone.

As chief legislator, the president may call Congress back into session. He also may adjourn Congress if the House and the Senate should disagree about when to adjourn, although no president has exercised this constitutional power. The Supreme Court has held that Congress may not delegate legislative authority to the president, but Congress has in some cases passed legislation setting broad guidelines within which the president may act. For example, under such laws the president may be authorized to reduce tariffs. And since 1939 Congress has periodically passed a series of Reorganization Acts that permit the president to restructure federal agencies under plans that he must submit to Congress. Unless Congress disapproves the plans within 60 days, they go into effect.

The president's real ability to persuade Congress often rests on his personal popularity rather than on his formal or informal powers. The veto, "arm twisting," threats to withhold funds for a public works project, and social ostracism of a representative or senator are, over the long run, less important than the ability of a president to enlist public support for his programs and the extent of his prestige with both Congress and the electorate.

## Chief of Party

"No President, it seems to me, can escape politics," John Kennedy said in 1960 when he sought the presidency. "He has not only been chosen by the Nation—he has been chosen by his party."[44]

Not every president has filled the role of party chief with the same enthusiasm that Kennedy brought to it. President Eisenhower, a career Army officer for most of his life, displayed a reluctance to engage in the rough-and-tumble of politics. As he told a press conference in 1955: "In the general derogatory sense . . . I do not like politics . . . the word 'politics' as you use it, I think the

© AP/Wide World Photos

President Clinton vetoes a budget bill in 1997.

answer to that one, would be, no. I have no great liking for that."[45]

For many months in 1980, President Carter declined to campaign actively for reelection, claiming that the hostage crisis in Iran took precedence over his political duties and made it necessary for him to remain in the White House. "I am not going to resume business as usual as a partisan campaigner out on the campaign trail until our hostages are back here, free and at home," Carter declared.[46] Carter thus attempted to adopt a presidential "above politics" stance. But two and a half months later, when Carter announced that the country's foreign and domestic problems "are manageable enough now for me to leave the White House," his statement brought hoots of disbelief from his critics.[47] He lost the election to Ronald Reagan.

***for more information about Jimmy Carter, see:***
***http://www.jimmycarterlibrary.org***

Whether or not a president enjoys his partisan role, he is the chief of his party. The machinery of the national committee reports to him; he can install his choice as national chairperson; he can usually demand his party's renomination and can stage-manage the convention that acclaims him. Since success as chief legislator depends to a considerable degree on the political makeup of Congress, the president may find it advantageous to campaign for congressional candidates in off-year elections.

Nor does the president always prevail with members of his party in Congress. The nature of the American political system is such that a basic weakness is built into the president's role as party leader: His own leaders in Congress may not bow to his political wisdom or policy wishes in every case. A president may be hobbled in achieving his domestic policy goals, and even his foreign policy objectives, by the fact that he cannot always count on the support of his own party's members in Congress. By contrast, a British prime minister can generally depend on the disciplined support of the members of the majority party in Parliament.

When a president makes decisions, he is, in the broadest sense, engaging in politics. A successful president must lead and gauge public opinion, must be sensitive to change, and must have a sure sense of the limits of the possible. All of these are political skills. As chief of party, the president is also the nation's number one professional politician. And, as Richard Neustadt suggested, "The Presidency is no place for amateurs."[48]

## Popular Leader

The president also plays a vital role as the popular leader of the nation, the one person who speaks—in theory at least—for all of America. The president, aside from all of his more formal, constitutional, and political roles, is also expected to act as the national leader. In times of crisis, the people tend to look to the president for reassurance. For example, when the president addresses the nation on television from the Oval Office to explain why he is sending U.S. forces to some remote corner of the globe, as has often happened, he is technically acting as commander in chief, but in a larger sense he is acting as national leader, the powerful figure to whom the voters turn, perhaps as much for psychological support as for factual explanations.

To this role of popular leader, the president normally brings an ideology and a philosophy. Franklin D. Roosevelt was identified with the social-welfare programs of the New Deal, Lyndon Johnson with their echo in the Great Society of the 1960s. Ronald Reagan, by contrast, was identified with limited government. To an extent, his successor, the first President Bush, shared that view, often contending that individuals could accomplish more than government programs. Clinton portrayed himself as a New Democrat, somewhat more conservative than his party's New Deal tradition. President George W. Bush, like his father and Ronald Reagan, also advocated limited government and a greater role for the private sector. Bush described himself as a "compassionate conservative," as someone willing to help citizens in need but insisting on accountability and results.

As national leader, the president does more, of course, than expound a philosophy. The policies of his administration, the legislative agenda he sends to Congress, and the actions of his bureaucrats often reflect his point of view. He may hope, although he may often be disappointed, that the justices he appoints to the Supreme Court will also march to his tune. In fact, Supreme Court decisions sometimes cause troubles for a president. The 1954 *Brown* decision, requiring desegregation of public schools, resulted in turmoil for Presidents Eisenhower and Kennedy. The *Roe* v. *Wade* decision legalizing abortion in 1973 crystallized an emotional issue that still divides the nation more than three decades later.

Today, presidential rhetoric—a chief executive's skills as an orator and persuader—powerfully affects his ability to govern. Indeed, "rhetorical leadership," in the view of presidential scholar Jeffrey K. Tulis, "is the essence of the modern presidency."[49] He adds: "Since the presidencies of Theodore Roosevelt and Woodrow Wilson, popular or mass rhetoric has become a principal tool of presidential governance. Presidents regularly 'go over the heads' of Congress to the people at large in support of legislation and other initiatives. . . . The doctrine that a president ought to be a popular leader has become an unquestioned premise of our political culture."[50] Presidents now are expected to inspire the public, Tulis notes: "And for many, this presidential 'function' is not one duty among many, but rather the heart of the presidency—its essential task."[51] President Reagan's "stunning string of partisan successes," including budget cuts and a military buildup, were due in no

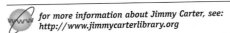

Making a Difference

## THE UNFINISHED PRESIDENCY

What to do on the miserable January morning when you wake up and find you are no longer the most powerful man in the world?

Theodore Roosevelt mounted a grand, year-long safari to East Africa—where, nearsighted as Mr. Magoo, he fired off an astonishing amount of ammunition at every species in God's creation, to be stuffed for the American Museum of Natural History. Lyndon Johnson returned to his Texas ranch to drink and smoke and grow his hair long like a hippie and wait to die. Richard Nixon did brooding penance beside the Pacific, then went back East to reinvent himself as an elder statesman.

Perhaps a president's life after the White House is the real manifestation of his character. Consider the interesting case of Jimmy Carter. Buried, after one term, in the Ronald Reagan landslide of 1980, widely scorned as the micromanager of malaise, held hostage by the Ayatollah, Carter in his post–White House incarnation performed a cunning reversal. An engineer by training, he did not so much reinvent himself as reconstruct, in another dimension, the job from which the American people had fired him.

When Carter left the White House in 1981 at the relatively young age of 56, logic dictated that he continue to be politically active, although he promised he would never try to regain the presidency. The question was how he wanted to spend the rest of his life. He knew he wanted to do a lot more than build a museum-library in tribute to himself and give a lot of after-dinner speeches. What Carter really wanted was to find some way to continue the unfinished business of his presidency. In *Keeping Faith,* the memoir Carter wrote at home in Plains, Georgia, during his first 18 months out of office, he set forth the goals of "alleviating tension in the troubled areas of the world, promoting human rights, enhancing environmental quality. . . . These were hazy ideas at best, but they gave us something to anticipate which could be exciting and challenging during the years ahead." These "hazy ideas" evolved into a grand design: the Carter Center in Atlanta, which has become his lasting institutional legacy to peace, democracy, health, and human rights.

Since leaving office Carter had been involved in mediating an impressive list of foreign disputes, civil wars, and political transitions. For his work, he was awarded the Nobel Peace Prize in 2002.

Some observers have suggested that Carter used the White House as a stepping-stone to the status of elder statesman. It is more accurate to say that instead of abandoning his agenda when he lost badly to Ronald Reagan in 1980, he chose to continue working toward programs and policies he believed in, in office or out of it. That he has tried to complete his unfinished agenda with such vigor and such success is a testament to his stubborn will and tenacious refusal ever to throw in the towel. Jimmy Carter may be many things, but a quitter is not among them.

—Adapted from *Time* magazine and *The Unfinished Presidency: Jimmy Carter's Journey beyond the White House*

small measure to his skills as a popular leader, a "great communicator."[52]

But the president's role as popular leader is not without its perils. Modern presidents, Theodore J. Lowi has argued, are doomed to failure. Because of the "exalted rhetoric and high expectations surrounding the presidency," even a degree of success is considered a failure by the mass public, Lowi contends.[53] The presidency is thus a no-win situation, in Lowi's view, because for a successful presidential candidate, victory in November is the beginning of the end: "His political career is finished before he can fully enjoy the prize."[54]

In this view, as soon as a president wins, he loses. This paradox is a direct result of the enormous attention focused on modern presidents in the American political system. As Lowi puts it: "Since the president has become the embodiment of government, it seems perfectly normal for millions upon millions of Americans to concentrate their hopes and fears directly and personally upon him. It is no wonder that [the] United States has developed such a tremendous stake in the 'personal president' and his personal capacity to govern."[55]

The president, it must be emphasized again, fills all of these various presidential roles at once. The powers and duties of the office are not divisible. The roles conflict and overlap; in performing one role, the president may incur political costs that make it more difficult for him to perform another. In short, the presidency is a balancing act.

In addition to these basic roles, Americans expect the president to take on many other roles. In the event of a major civil disturbance, he is expected to act as a police officer and restore domestic tranquility. As the manager of the economy, he is expected to prevent recession, ensure prosperity, and hold down the cost of butter and eggs. He is expected to set an example in his personal life—which is why accusations of marital infidelity became a campaign issue when Bill Clinton ran for president in 1992, and why his later sexual affair with a young intern cast a long shadow over his legacy.

A president is expected to be a teacher, to educate the people about great public issues. In some mysterious way, the president is expected to speak for all the people and to give voice to their deepest aspirations and ideals.

"The Presidency," Franklin Roosevelt said, "is not merely an administrative office. That is the least of it. It is preeminently a place of moral leadership."[56]

© 2004 AP/Wide World Photos

## The Tools of Presidential Power

In the exercise of power, the president of the United States has available a formidable array of tools, money, and people. In ever widening circles, this last category includes the White House staff (secretaries and advisers), the Executive Office of the President (a conglomerate of presidential substaffs), the vice president, the cabinet, the 15 cabinet departments, the many other agencies of the executive branch, and the more than 4 million employees of the federal bureaucracy and the military.

He has almost unlimited personal resources as well. When President Johnson had reviewed the marines in California on one occasion and was walking back to a helicopter, he was stopped by an officer who pointed to another helicopter and said, "That's your helicopter over there, sir." Johnson replied, "Son, they are all my helicopters."[57]

When the president travels, he has at his disposal not only helicopters, but a fleet of jets; aboard Air Force One, he can communicate with his aides or with the military anywhere in the world. If he flies to Kansas City to deliver a speech, a special Pentagon communications unit that travels with the president links him to the White House.

In addition to the formal machinery of government at the president's command, he has other, informal resources—his reputation, personality and style, ability to arouse public opinion, political party, and informal advisers and friends.

As one leading presidential scholar, Thomas Cronin, has warned, however, listing the president's cabinet and all the other panels, staffs, and informal advisers that serve him might create the impression that a president "must have just about all the inside information and good advice anyone could want." As Cronin points out, one might even erroneously conclude that a president "can both set and shape the directions of public policy and can see to it that these policies work as intended."[58] Yet, that is often not the case. As we have already seen, there are limitations on presidential power at almost

© Martin H. Simon/Corbis

President Bush appointed Joshua Bolten as his chief of staff in 2006.

**TABLE 13-2**

**The President's Cabinet**

| The Executive Departments, in Order of Formation* | |
|---|---|
| State | 1789 |
| Treasury | 1789 |
| Interior | 1849 |
| Justice† | 1870 |
| Agriculture‡ | 1889 |
| Commerce§ | 1913 |
| Labor§ | 1913 |
| Defense¶ | 1947 |
| Housing and Urban Development | 1965 |
| Transportation | 1966 |
| Energy | 1977 |
| Education | 1979 |
| Health and Human Services# | 1979 |
| Veterans Affairs | 1989 |
| Homeland Security | 2002 |

*As of 2006. The office of postmaster general, created in 1789, received cabinet rank in 1829 and was made a cabinet department in 1872. In 1970 Congress abolished the Post Office as a cabinet department and replaced it with the U.S. Postal Service, an independent federal agency.
†The office of attorney general, created in 1789, became the Department of Justice in 1870.
‡Created in 1862 and elevated to a cabinet department in 1889.
§The Department of Commerce and Labor, created in 1903, was divided into two departments in 1913.
¶The Department of War (the Army), created in 1789, and the Department of the Navy, created in 1798, were consolidated with the Air Force into the Department of Defense in 1947.
#Created as the Department of Health, Education, and Welfare in 1953, it was divided into two cabinet departments in 1979.

every turn. Indeed, one of the measures of a president's power is how well he can use the tools at his command.

## The Cabinet

The president, the vice president, the heads of the major executive departments of the government, and certain other senior officials who may hold "cabinet rank" constitute the **cabinet.** (See Table 13-2.) But the cabinet is an informal institution. The Constitution speaks of "the principal Officer in each of the executive Departments" and of "Heads of Departments." The Twenty-fifth Amendment, ratified in 1967, allows for the possibility of the department heads acting as a group in case of presidential disability. But the cabinet as an organized body is nowhere specifically provided for by law or in the Constitution.

When George W. Bush took office in 2001, he assembled a diverse cabinet, naming two African Americans, two Asian Americans, four women, and one Cuban American. He appointed retired general Colin Powell as secretary of state and Donald H. Rumsfeld as secretary of defense. However, Powell clashed with Rumsfeld over the Iraq war and other issues and resigned days after Bush was re-elected in 2004. Rumsfeld came under increasing criticism as the war dragged on. When in 2006 several retired generals attacked Rumsfeld over the conduct of the war in Iraq, he was strongly defended by the president. Bush's choice of John Ashcroft for attorney general also proved controversial; opponents asserted that Ashcroft had violated constitutional rights in detaining and prosecuting terrorist suspects. Ashcroft resigned in 2004, and Bush named Alberto Gonzales, the White House counsel, to replace him.

But shuffling cabinet posts may not deflect criticism from the White House. When Tom Ridge, the first secretary of the newly created Department of Homeland Security, resigned, Bush appointed Michael Chertoff, an assistant attorney general and former federal judge, to the post. In August 2005, six months after Chertoff was sworn in, the United States suffered one of the worst natural disasters in its history. Hurricane Katrina destroyed much of New Orleans and other parts of the Gulf Coast, leaving more than 1,300 people dead and stranding thousands of others without food, water, or shelter. Chertoff was among those blamed in the aftermath for the federal government's failure to prepare for and respond swiftly to the disaster.

The president, Richard F. Fenno points out, "is not required by law to form a Cabinet or to keep one," and the cabinet has become "institutionalized by usage alone."[59] Perhaps because the cabinet is entirely a creature of custom, it is a relatively weak institution. The weakness of the cabinet under a strong president is often illustrated by the story of how Lincoln counted the votes when the entire cabinet was opposed to him: "Seven nays, one aye—the ayes have it."

In any case, a cabinet member may not be competent to discuss problems of a general nature, for "beyond his immediate bailiwick, he may not be capable of adding anything to the group conference."[60] For this reason, President Kennedy thought that cabinet meetings were "a waste of time."[61]

Modern presidents have made varied use of the cabinet. Lyndon Johnson met regularly with his cabinet, but the conduct of the war in Vietnam was normally discussed not in the cabinet, but at regular Tuesday luncheon meetings of the president and selected officials.

During the 1980 campaign, Ronald Reagan promised, if elected, to institute a "cabinet government," in which the president and the members of his cabinet arrived at decisions together. But in practice, it was the president and a small group of White House staff aides who usually made the real decisions. "Cabinet government is an illusion," one administration official acknowledged.[62] As one account put it, "Full Cabinet meetings, scornfully referred to as 'dog-and-pony shows' by one Cabinet member and as 'pep rallies' by another, were largely informational. The busier Cabinet members and White House staff members alike tended to regard them

Secretary of Defense Donald H. Rumsfeld briefs reporters in the Pentagon.



as a waste of time. 'I can't think of a single major decision that has been made at the full Cabinet meeting,' said one secretary."[63]

*for more information about Ronald Reagan, see: http://www.ronaldreagan.com*

Several members of President Clinton's cabinet caused him political problems, among them Housing and Urban Development Secretary Henry Cisneros, who was investigated for payments to his mistress, pleaded guilty to lying to the FBI, and was later pardoned by Clinton.

On the other hand, cabinet members can sometimes serve as useful "lightning rods" to divert blame from a president.[64] In April 1993, for example, 85 people died during the federal siege of the Branch Davidian religious sect at Waco, Texas. Attorney General Janet Reno, who had ordered the FBI to attack the compound, took full responsibility afterward. As a result, in the immediate aftermath of Waco, President Clinton escaped some of the public outrage over the government's handling of the matter. Later, Reno's repeated refusal to appoint an independent counsel to investigate financial abuses by the Clinton-Gore ticket during the 1996 election campaign subjected her to repeated Republican attacks. Again, Clinton let Reno take most of the criticism. In 2004, when the prisoner abuse scandal in Iraq became public, it was Donald H. Rumsfeld, the secretary of defense, who took much of the political heat, rather than President Bush.

Although the cabinet is often considered to be a device to assist the president, it also limits his power to some extent. "The members of the Cabinet," Vice President (under Calvin Coolidge) Charles G. Dawes said, "are a President's natural enemies."[65] In part, this is because cabinet members after a time tend to adopt the parochial view of their own departments. They may become narrow advocates of the programs and needs of their bureaucracies, competing with other cabinet members for bigger budgets and presidential favor. As Fenno has noted, a cabinet member's "formal responsibilities extend both upward toward the President and downward toward his own department."[66]

## The White House Staff

When President Clinton moved into the White House in January 1993, his staff at first was young, inexperienced, and still operating in the informal, chaotic fashion of the political campaign organization that had elected him.

After appointing a boyhood friend, an Arkansas businessman with no Washington experience, as chief of staff, Clinton eventually was obliged to replace him with Leon E. Panetta, a former congressman from northern California, wise in the ways of Washington. Panetta imposed order and discipline on the White House staff and emerged as a key player in the Clinton administration.

Presidents do not always choose wisely in making this key appointment. Soon after the 1988 election, the first George Bush appointed John H. Sununu chief of staff at the White House. As governor of New Hampshire, Sununu had helped Bush win the presidential primary in that state, a crucial victory in Bush's drive for the nomination. Now he was being rewarded. But Sununu's abrasive manner grated on his colleagues and members of Congress, and his high-living style caught the attention of the press. Stories appeared about Sununu using official limousines and military aircraft on personal trips, including ski trips and a visit to his dentist; soon commentators on the television networks were

## Ronald Reagan on the Iran-Contra Scandal

As the Iran-contra scandal began to unfold in 1986, President Reagan offered shifting interpretations of what had occurred:

**November 13, 1986:**
"We did not—repeat—we did not trade weapons or anything else for hostages."

**November 19, 1986:**
"I don't think a mistake was made."

**November 24, 1986:**
"I'm not going to lie about that. I didn't make a mistake."

**December 6, 1986:**
"It's obvious that the execution of these policies was flawed, and mistakes were made."

**March 4, 1987:**
"I told the American people I did not trade arms for hostages. My heart and my best intentions still tell me that's true. But the facts and the evidence tell me it is not. . . . What began as a strategic opening to Iran deteriorated in its implementation into trading arms for hostages."

—*Washington Post,* March 4, 1987, and September 6, 1987

talking about "Air Sununu." When the criticism became too intense to withstand, Sununu resigned.

Modern presidents depend on large staffs. And great power is often wielded by those who surround the president, some of whom rise from relative obscurity to great influence. Wilson had his Colonel House, Franklin Roosevelt his Harry Hopkins. Eisenhower relied heavily on Sherman Adams, who—much to Eisenhower's distress—was forced to resign for accepting a vicuña coat and other gifts from Bernard Goldfine, a Boston textile manufacturer for whom Adams had interceded with federal regulatory agencies.

President Johnson had his Bill Moyers, later a successful television personality, and Nixon his H. R. (Bob) Haldeman and John D. Ehrlichman—both of whom went to prison for their actions in the Watergate scandal. In 2006, when Republicans worried that the administration of George W. Bush was faltering, there was pressure for a White House staff shakeup; Bush's chief of staff, Andrew Card, departed and was replaced by Joshua Bolten, the administration's budget director. All modern presidents have come to rely on their advisers, and in every case, some aides have emerged as more influential than others.

The power of the president's assistants, however, flows from their position as extensions of the president. Seldom possessing any political prestige or constituency of their own, they depend entirely on staying in the president's good graces for their survival. Their power is derivative, though nonetheless real—it is not uncommon in the White House to see a cabinet member waiting to confer with a member of the president's staff.

President Coolidge and his cabinet pose for photographers in 1924.

In recent administrations, the president's assistant for national security affairs has often taken a central role in foreign policy formation and crisis management. With access to the president and the White House Situation Room, the downstairs office into which all military, intelligence, and diplomatic information flows, the national security adviser may emerge as a powerful rival to the secretary of state. Henry A. Kissinger, for example, took the post in the Nixon administration and quickly emerged as the most powerful White House adviser in the field of foreign affairs, overshadowing Secretary of State William P. Rogers. Eventually, Kissinger himself was named secretary of state by Nixon.[67]

The members of the president's staff fill a variety of functions that are essential to presidential decision making. Some act as gatekeepers and guardians of the president's time. Others deal almost exclusively with Congress. Still others serve as links with the executive departments and agencies, channeling problems and conflicts among the departments to the president. Some advise the president on political questions, patronage, and appointments. Others may write his speeches. The press secretary issues presidential announcements on matters large and small and fences with correspondents at press briefings.

Presidents use their staffs differently. Eisenhower had a tight, formal system, with Sherman Adams, his chief of staff, screening all problems and deciding what the president should see. Kennedy favored a less structured arrangement, regarding his staff as "a wheel and a series of spokes" with himself in the center.[68] In his first term, George W. Bush ran a usually disciplined staff modeled on corporate America; his advisers prided themselves on running a White House in which information was, at least much of the time, tightly controlled. But in his second term, as noted, Bush felt obliged to shake up his staff.

In 2005 the White House staff had 402 employees and a payroll of $25.7 million a year.[69] Inevitably, a chief executive's vision, to a degree, is filtered through the eyes of his assistants. An Eisenhower or a Nixon, with a rigid staff system, may become isolated in the White House. A Lyndon Johnson, with an overpowering, demanding personality, may surround himself with deferential aides. In short, the president's staff may not let him hear enough, or it may tell him only what he wants to hear.

## The Executive Office of the President

The White House staff is only a small part of the huge presidential establishment that has burgeoned since Franklin D. Roosevelt's day. Under the umbrella of the Executive Office of the President, more than half a dozen key agencies serve the president directly, with a combined payroll in 2003 of $15.8 million and a total staff of 1,693.[70] (See Figure 13-2.) Many of these employees have offices in the Executive Office Building just west of the White House.

Roosevelt established the Executive Office of the President in 1939 by executive order after a committee of scholars had reported to him: "The President needs help." Since that time, the office has grown substantially.

FIGURE 13-2

**Executive Office of the President, 2006**

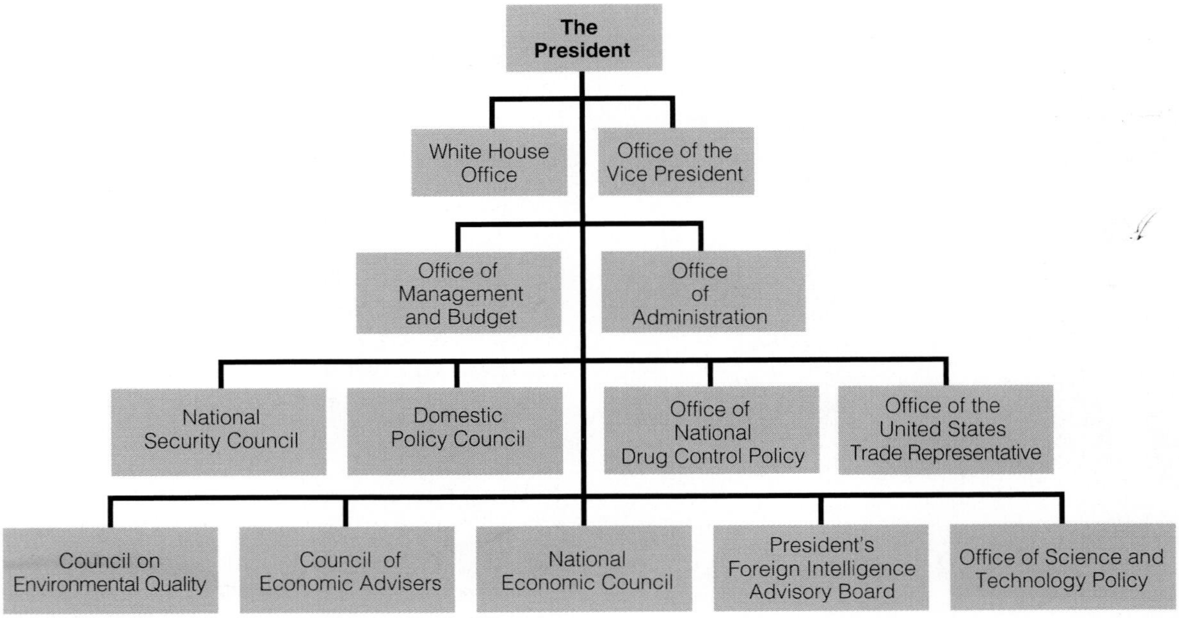

As the Executive Office of the President existed in 2004, its major components included the following:

**National Security Council** When the United States emerged as a major power after the Second World War, no central machinery existed to assist the president in conducting foreign and military affairs. The **National Security Council (NSC)** is a White House office created under the National Security Act of 1947 to advise the president and help coordinate American military and foreign policy. By statute, its four members are the president, the vice president, and the secretaries of state and defense. The president's assistant for national security directs the NSC staff.

President George W. Bush's first national security adviser, Condoleezza Rice, enjoyed a close relationship with the president. She came under fire in 2004, however, when she relied on the concept of executive privilege in refusing at first to testify in public to a presidential commission investigating events that led to the 9/11 terrorist attacks. Eventually, Bush allowed her to appear. When Bush appointed Rice as Secretary of State in 2004, her deputy, Stephen J. Hadley, succeeded her as the national security adviser.

Like the cabinet, the NSC has been put to vastly different uses by different presidents. Eisenhower used the NSC extensively, and during his administration a substructure of boards and committees mushroomed beneath it. During the Cuban Missile Crisis in 1962, Kennedy established an informal body known as the Executive Committee of the National Security Council (ExCom). Much larger than the statutory membership of the NSC, it consisted of some 16 top officials and advisers in the foreign policy, military, and intelligence fields whom the president felt it appropriate to consult.

President Bush and then National Security Adviser Condoleezza Rice depart the White House to board the Marine One helicopter. Bush named Rice secretary of state when Colin Powell resigned after the 2004 election.

Under Reagan, the NSC played a central role in the events that became known as the Iran-contra scandal. A major covert operation—the arms sales to Iran and diversion of money to the contra rebels in Nicaragua—was run out of the White House by the National Security Council staff, an operational role that Congress had not intended for the NSC.

In 1990, retired Admiral John M. Poindexter, who had been Reagan's national security adviser, was convicted of felonies in the Iran-contra affair and sentenced to six months in prison, a conviction later overturned by a federal appeals court. Poindexter had admitted to Congress, however, that he had destroyed a secret and highly classified presidential finding about trading arms for hostages in Iran because he thought the document might be "politically embarrassing" to Reagan. The entire episode illustrated that the president's national security adviser may wield great power, not only in foreign affairs, but in domestic politics as well.

**Domestic Policy Council** All recent presidents have had a staff to assist them in formulating domestic policy. Creation of a formal staff for this purpose began under Lyndon Johnson in the 1960s. Although the name of the unit has changed several times, later presidents continued to rely on a domestic policy staff. The Domestic Policy Council was created by an executive order in 1993. Under George W. Bush, the council specialized in such fields as education, health, welfare, justice, federalism, transportation, environment, labor, and veterans affairs.

**Office of Management and Budget** The Office of Management and Budget (OMB) was created in 1970. The office was designed to tighten presidential control over the federal bureaucracy and improve its performance.

The OMB has two overlapping functions: preparing the federal budget and serving as a management tool for the chief executive. The director of the office advises the president on the allocation of federal funds and attempts to resolve the competing claims of the departments and agencies for a larger share of the federal budget. The task of preparing and administering the annual budget gives OMB enormous power within the government.

**National Economic Council** The National Economic Council, a relatively new body modeled on the National Security Council, was created by President Clinton in 1993 to coordinate all economic policy decisions at the presidential level. It deals with the budget, international trade, and other economic issues and programs.

**Council of Economic Advisers** Since the Great Depression of the 1930s, the president has been expected to manage the nation's efforts to achieve prosperity. Because few presidents are economic experts, presidents since 1946 have relied on a Council of Economic Advisers to assist them in the formation of national economic policy.

The three members, one of whom is designated as the chair by the president, are subject to Senate confirmation. The council is expected to give impartial professional advice, but because its members are also part of the president's administration, they perform a difficult task.

**Office of the United States Trade Representative** The United States trade representative, who carries the rank of ambassador, represents the president in often difficult and complex international trade and tariff negotiations. The role of the trade representative has become increasingly influential in recent years because of the growing importance of trade issues. For example, the trade representative has sought to persuade Japan to accept more American products, including automobiles.

**The Vice President** "I am Vice President," said John Adams. "In this I am nothing, but I may be everything."[71] The remark remains apt today. Under the Constitution, the vice president's only formal duties are to preside over the Senate, to vote in that body in case of a tie, and (under the Twenty-fifth Amendment) to help decide whether the president is disabled, and, if so, to serve as acting president. If the president dies, resigns, or is removed from office, however, the vice president becomes president. As of 2004, this had occurred nine times as the result of the death or resignation of a president. In four of those cases, the president had been assassinated.

Often in the past, the candidate for vice president has been chosen by the presidential nominee to "balance the ticket," to add geographic or some other strength to the campaign. In 2004, for example, John Kerry chose Senator John Edwards of North Carolina as his running mate. Democrats felt that Edwards's smiling, sunny personality, relative youth, and working-class roots would benefit the ticket, and that his geographic base might help the party in some southern states.

But sometimes the choice of a vice presidential candidate creates problems. In 1988, George Bush, the Republican presidential nominee, selected Senator Dan Quayle of Indiana as his running mate in an effort to appeal to younger voters and conservatives. But Bush's choice was controversial from the start. As vice president, Quayle was regarded by many voters, and widely in the media, as a lightweight. He soon became the butt of jokes by stand-up comics on late-night television. During the 1992 campaign, Quayle took on an aggressive role as Bush's point man, but he soon became embroiled in controversy by attacking Murphy Brown, a fictitious character in a popular television situation comedy, for her decision to become a single parent. Quayle's difficulties reached their peak later that spring when he encouraged an elementary school boy to spell *potato* with an unnecessary "e" at the end.

In 1968 Richard Nixon, the Republican presidential nominee, chose Spiro Agnew of Maryland, a relatively obscure governor, in an effort to strengthen the ticket's appeal in southern and border states. Agnew quickly emerged as a controversial political figure. He attacked Vietnam War protest leaders and assailed network news commentators who had been critical of the president. In the midst of the Watergate crisis, however, at a time when Nixon was battling for his own political survival, a federal prosecutor in Baltimore gathered evidence that Agnew had asked for and accepted more than $100,000 in cash payments from highway engineering firms that were awarded state contracts while Agnew was governor of Maryland, and that one payoff was even made to Agnew in the office of the vice president. Agnew resigned, pleaded no-contest to income tax evasion, received a $10,000 fine, and was placed on probation for three years.

Under George W. Bush, Vice President Dick Cheney has played an influential and sometimes controversial role in the administration. Cheney has been considered more powerful in the post than previous vice presidents.

Before the start of the Iraq war in 2003, Cheney was one of the most vocal advocates of invading that country. In 2002, for example, Cheney told a veterans' group that "there is no doubt that Saddam Hussein now has weapons of mass destruction."[72] When U.S. forces invaded in 2003, no such weapons were found. Cheney insisted that Saddam Hussein, Iraq's dictator, had ties to al Qaeda even after the 9/11 commission concluded there was no "collaborative relationship" between Iraq and the terrorist group.

In 2005, a federal grand jury investigating the leak of the name of a CIA officer, Valerie Plame, indicted Cheney's long-time chief of staff, I. Lewis "Scooter" Libby, on charges of perjury, obstruction of justice, and making false statements. Libby resigned.

Then, early in 2006, while hunting quail in Texas, Cheney accidentally shot and wounded a 78-year-old companion, attorney Harry Whittington. The vice president was criticized for waiting until the next day before making the incident public. Some analysts saw the vice president as a continuing liability to President Bush. Cheney, however, appeared completely unfazed by his critics.

In the 20th century seven vice presidents succeeded to the presidency through the death or resignation of an incumbent president, or by election.* As a result, during that century a former vice president served as president almost 40 percent of the time. These statistics would sug-

*The vice presidents who succeeded to the presidency in the 20th century were Theodore Roosevelt, Calvin Coolidge, Harry S Truman, Lyndon B. Johnson, Gerald R. Ford, Richard M. Nixon, and the first President George Bush. Nixon became president in 1969, eight years after serving as vice president.

## Some Vice Presidents View Their Office

**John Adams**
My country has in its wisdom contrived for me the most insignificant office that ever the invention of man contrived or his imagination conceived.

**Thomas Jefferson**
The second office of this Government is honorable and easy, the first is but a splendid misery.

**John Nance Garner**
The vice presidency isn't worth a pitcher of warm spit.

**Harry Truman**
Look at all the Vice Presidents in history. Where are they? They were about as useful as a cow's fifth teat.

**Thomas R. Marshall**
Like a man in a cataleptic state [the vice president] cannot speak; he cannot move; he suffers no pain; and yet he is perfectly conscious of everything that is going on about him.

**Spiro Agnew**
Now I know what a turkey feels like before Thanksgiving.

**Walter Mondale**
They know who Amy [Carter] is, but they don't know me.

**George H. W. Bush**
If I fall out of favor at the White House, I might end up attending a lot of funerals in funny little countries.

**Dan Quayle**
The president gets the plums, and I get what's left.

**Al Gore**
If you close your left eye and turn your head . . . the great seal of the Vice President reads—"President of the United States."

**Dick Cheney**
My image might be better . . . if I spent more time as a public figure trying to improve my image, but that's not why I'm here.

—Adams, Jefferson, Garner, Truman, and Marshall quoted in Donald Young, *American Roulette;* Spiro Agnew quoted in the *Los Angeles Times West Magazine,* June 22, 1969; Walter Mondale quoted in the *Los Angeles Times,* January 13, 1978; George Bush quoted in the *Chicago Tribune,* August 18, 1981; Dan Quayle quoted in the *Washington Post,* August 17, 1992; and Al Gore appearing on the *Late Show with David Letterman,* September 6, 1993; Cheney quote from *Vanity Fair,* June 2006.

gest that vice presidents be carefully selected on merit rather than solely for political considerations.

**Presidential Commissions** From time to time, presidents appoint ad hoc "blue ribbon" commissions of prominent citizens to study special problems. Such panels can help a president by dealing with a crisis, by providing influential support for his programs, or by deflecting political pressure. But they also may cause him headaches by criticizing his administration, by proposing remedies he does not favor, or in other ways.

For example, in 1986 President Reagan named a special review board headed by former Senator John Tower, a Texas Republican, to investigate the Iran-contra affair.

Vice President Dan Quayle tries to teach William Figueroa, 12, to spell.

© Larry Downing/Reuters/Corbis

The panel strongly criticized the president personally as well as his administration, and some of its language was harsh. It concluded that top officials had lied to each other and to the public, and had possibly broken the law.[73]

Similarly, in 1976 President Ford named the Rockefeller Commission to study published reports of spying within the United States by the CIA. But the commission also gathered information about CIA plots to assassinate foreign leaders, causing Ford political embarrassment.

In 2002, Congress created the National Commission on Terrorist Attacks upon the United States, known as the 9/11 commission, to investigate the attacks on New York and Washington. President Bush appointed the chairman, and congressional leaders named the other members. The commission, in its final report in 2004, was sharply critical of the Bush administration and the intelligence agencies.

After President Kennedy's assassination, the nation was torn by doubt and speculation over the facts of his death. President Johnson convinced Chief Justice Earl Warren to head an investigating commission. The Warren Commission concluded that Lee Harvey Oswald shot the president and had "acted alone." At first this conclusion seemed to reassure much of the public that no conspiracy existed, but later the Warren Commission's conclusions were widely attacked by many critics who refused to accept the shooting as the act of one person.

## The Informal Tools of Power

Many factors affect a president's ability to achieve his objectives. The president is the chief actor on the Washington stage. He is carefully watched by bureaucrats, members of Congress, party leaders, and the press. The decisions he makes affect his professional reputation among these groups. In turn, his effectiveness as president depends on this professional reputation.[74]

THE TIMES-PICAYUNE ©2004
MOM! BILLY USED VICE-PRESIDENTIAL LANGUAGE!

© 2004 Steve Kelley. *The Times Picayune.* Reprinted by permission.

In the exercise of presidential power, the president has available to him not only the formal tools of the office, but a broad range of informal techniques. All presidents rely on these in varying degrees.

Television is a powerful, informal tool of presidential power. With the development of electronic mass media, presidents can make direct appeals to the people. Franklin Roosevelt began the practice with his famous

### Harry Truman: This Great White Jail . . .

President Harry S Truman kept a diary that was discovered only decades later. Here is part of the entry for January 6, 1947:

> Arose at 5:45 A.M.[,] read the papers and at 7:10 walked to the station to meet the family. Took 35 minutes. It was a good walk. Sure is fine to have them back. This great white jail is a hell of a place in which to be alone. While I work from early morning until late at night, it is a ghostly place. The floors pop and crack all night long. Anyone with imagination can see old Jim Buchanan walking up and down worrying about conditions not of his making. Then there's Van Buren, who inherited a terrible mess from his predecessor as did poor old James Madison. Of course Andrew Johnson was the worst mistreated of any of them. But they all walk up and down the halls of this place and moan about what they should have done and didn't . . . It's a hell of a place.

—*Washington Post,* July 11, 2003

"fireside chats" over radio. Today, the president may schedule a live televised speech or press conference to publicize his policies. He may call a White House conference to dramatize a major issue.

Many presidents since Andrew Jackson have had a "kitchen cabinet" of informal advisers who hold no official position on the White House staff. Theodore Roosevelt had his "tennis cabinet," Warren Harding his "poker cabinet," and Herbert Hoover, who liked exercise, his "medicine ball cabinet." Lyndon Johnson often called on friends such as Washington attorneys Abe Fortas, James H. Rowe, Jr., and Clark Clifford for advice. Ronald Reagan, too, had a "kitchen cabinet" of old friends who were for the most part California businessmen.

Long before Bill and Hillary Clinton moved into the White House, it was apparent that a president's spouse may, in some cases at least, be an important influence on both politics and policy. Both Eleanor Roosevelt and Lady Bird Johnson, for example, each in their own way had an impact on their husbands, Franklin Roosevelt and Lyndon Johnson. Hillary Rodham Clinton, a bright, successful lawyer, became a controversial figure in the Clinton White House. Breaking with precedent, President Clinton placed the First Lady in charge of his early efforts to reform the nation's health care system. That effort failed.

Thereafter, Hillary Clinton sought to adopt a lower profile and to become involved in issues, such as children's and women's rights and the arts and historic preservation, that were closer to the traditional concerns of previous presidential spouses. That strategy ran into difficulty when Mrs. Clinton was blamed for the dismissals of several employees of the White House travel office and when she became embroiled in the congressional investigation of the Whitewater affair. In January 1996, she was subpoenaed to answer questions about Whitewater before a federal grand jury—an embarrassment to the president, who was running for reelection that year.

Despite those problems, Hillary Clinton emerged as a powerful figure in the White House and an important, although unofficial, presidential adviser. She defended the president amid the sex scandal that threatened for a time to destroy his presidency, and in 2000 she ran as the Democratic candidate for the U.S. Senate in New York. She won the election by a large margin, creating speculation that she might seek the Democratic presidential nomination in 2008.

A president can take advantage of many of the perquisites of power. He may flatter key members of Congress by telephoning them for advice on key issues or inviting them to ride with him on Air Force One. He bargains with congressional leaders who frequently call on him at the White House, an informal arrangement that pays presidential homage to the importance of the leaders and incidentally allows them to make statements for the television cameras as they emerge from the Executive Mansion.

## The President Versus the Press

Every President, when he first enters the White House promises an "open Administration." He swears he likes reporters, will cooperate with them, will treat them as first-class citizens. The charade goes on for a few weeks or months, or even a couple of years. All the while, the President is struggling to suppress an overwhelming conviction that the press is trying to undermine his Administration, if not the Republic. He is fighting a maddening urge to control, bully, vilify, prosecute, or litigate against every freethinking reporter and editor in sight. Then, sooner or later, he blows. Teddy Roosevelt sued newspapers. Franklin Roosevelt expressed his displeasure over a certain article by presenting its author with an Iron Cross. Lyndon Johnson . . . but there is no sense singling out a few. Every president from Washington on came to recognize the press as a natural enemy, and eventually tried to manipulate it and muzzle it.

—Timothy Crouse, *The Boys on the Bus*

**The President and the Press** A president's ability to gain almost constant access to the news media, especially television, is a vital instrument of presidential power in the electronic age. A president relies on a press secretary to speak for him in day-to-day dealings with the news media.

When President George W. Bush's poll numbers plunged in the spring of 2006, he named a new chief of staff but also replaced his beleaguered press secretary, Scott McClellan, with Fox TV commentator Tony Snow. McClellan appeared to have had little leeway in answering reporters' questions, which often led to friction between the White House and the press corps.

President Clinton ran through three assistants to handle press relations before he imported Michael McCurry from the State Department. Under McCurry, a gentle man with a straightforward manner, Clinton's press relations reached a more stable level. McCurry often leavened his news briefings with humor, even though it was his lot to deal with the press during the Lewinsky scandal and the impeachment trial. He once told reporters, for example, "I'm double-parked in the no comment zone."[75] In his final press briefing he summed up his turbulent time in the White House: "I have been the chum in the feeding frenzy."[76]

Some press secretaries have more power than others. Several years earlier, Larry Speakes, a former public relations executive, left the White House after serving as press spokesman to President Reagan. Speakes wrote a book in which he disclosed that as press secretary, he had made up quotes and attributed them to President Reagan.[77] The disclosure caused a storm, forcing Speakes to resign his job on Wall Street.

The controversy focused attention on the crucial role of the White House press secretary. A president relies on a press secretary to speak for him in day-to-day dealings with the news media. Often, the press secretary acts as a buffer, standing between the president and the press and public, fielding questions that the president might prefer not to answer.

In recent years, most presidential press secretaries have held daily briefings for the White House press corps. The press secretary becomes a familiar personality to the public—but not always to the president's advantage. When the Watergate affair surfaced, President Nixon's press spokesman, Ronald L. Ziegler, repeatedly denied White House involvement and dismissed the break-in at Democratic headquarters as a "third-rate burglary attempt." After the truth began to emerge in April 1973, Ziegler announced that all previous White House denials were "inoperative," an explanation that did little to restore confidence in the administration's veracity—or Ziegler's. The White House had lied to the people, and the president found confidence in his administration shattered. After Nixon left the White House, he told television interviewer David Frost: "I want to say right here and now, I said things that were not true."[78]

The White House Office of Communications was created during the Nixon administration, in part to enable the White House to bypass the Washington press corps and reach the local news media directly. The office has often played a significant role in attempts at news management.[79] Administrations normally believe it to be in their self-interest to suppress embarrassing information. Mistakes, errors in judgment, or poorly conceived or badly executed policies are seldom brought to light unless discovered by the press or congressional investigators. Even then, White House spokespersons try to minimize unfavorable events. In describing military or intelligence operations, in particular, the government sometimes tends to conceal or distort. If the truth later becomes known, public confidence may be undermined.

Most presidents grant private interviews with a few television anchors, syndicated columnists, and influential Washington correspondents. They hope in that way to gain support for their views in the press and among readers. But the presidential press conference is a more direct device used by the chief executive to reach the public. (See Table 13-3.) Wilson began the practice by inviting reporters into his office. Harding, Coolidge, and Hoover accepted only written questions, and their press conferences were generally dull. Roosevelt held regular news conferences, canceled the requirement for written questions, and played the press like a virtuoso. Truman moved the press conference from his office to the Executive Office Building, establishing a more formal atmosphere.

Wilson established the policy that reporters could not quote the president directly without permission, but Eisenhower changed this, allowing his news conferences to be filmed and released to television after editing. Ken-

### The President and the Press: "A Symbiotic Relationship"

A president and his top aides enjoy almost unchecked powers of communication to define and defend their policies and to attack their adversaries. They can shape the agenda of public discussion, commanding the airwaves and headlines with the slightest hint of crisis. They can bury their mistakes by sealing their files on the pretext of national security. The Washington press, in turn, feels so dependent on government information and so dutiful in disseminating official propaganda that it grows desperate to prove its mettle by also exposing error, hyperbole, hypocrisy, and abuses of power. Thus are government and press condemned to a symbiotic relationship, a precarious balance of collaborations and antagonisms.

—Max Frankel, *The Times of My Life and My Life with* The Times

© Luke Frazza/AFP/Getty Images

2004: President Bush briefs reporters before boarding Air Force One.

**TABLE 13-3**

**Presidential Press Conferences**

| President | Number | Years in Office* | Average per Year† |
|---|---|---|---|
| Roosevelt | 998 | 12 | 83 |
| Truman | 322 | 8 | 40 |
| Eisenhower | 193 | 8 | 24 |
| Kennedy | 64 | 3 | 21 |
| Johnson | 135 | 5 | 27 |
| Nixon | 37 | 5.5 | 7 |
| Ford | 39 | 2.5 | 16 |
| Carter | 59 | 4 | 15 |
| Reagan | 46 | 8 | 5.8 |
| G. H. W. Bush | 142 | 4 | 36 |
| Clinton | 192 | 8 | 24 |
| G. W. Bush | 26 | 5.5† | 4.7 |

*Figures rounded.
†As of June 2006.

nedy instituted "live," unedited TV press conferences in the modern auditorium of the State Department, and he dazzled the press with his skill in fielding questions. Johnson had some full-dress press conferences, but he often preferred to answer questions from reporters while loping rapidly around the White House South Lawn. Nixon reverted to formal, televised press conferences, but he held very few. To an extent that exceeded any modern predecessors, the Nixon-Agnew administration considered the press a political target. Ford's amiable personality helped him maintain fairly good relations with the press. Carter also had reasonably good relations with the press during much of his presidency, although political cartoonists had a field day, invariably caricaturing him with "blubber lips." President George W. Bush did not appear comfortable in the press conference format, and in the four years after he took office in January 2001 he held fewer news conferences than any modern chief executive.

President Reagan enjoyed the traditional "honeymoon" from intense press criticism normally afforded to any new chief executive. But as Fred I. Greenstein has noted, it does not take the press very long to begin criticizing a president: "Media coverage of the President-elect and the first few months of an administration tends to emphasize the endearing personal touches—Ford's preparation of his own English muffins, Carter's fireside chat in informal garb. No wonder both of these Presidents enjoyed high poll ratings during their initial months in office. But the trend can only go downward. . . . After idealizing Presidents, the media quickly search out their warts."[80]

And, in time, Reagan's relations with the press became somewhat less amicable. Reporters wrote stories pointing out that Reagan sometimes misstated facts and statistics. Other accounts suggested that Reagan napped, relaxed, or vacationed a good deal, leaving work to his aides, who hesitated to awaken him if a crisis developed in the middle of the night.

In his book, Larry Speakes gave support to this image of Reagan. The president, he wrote, read few newspapers and preferred to "read the comics first."[81] Preparing Reagan for a news conference, the former press secretary added, was like "reinventing the wheel."[82] Despite some unfavorable news accounts during Reagan's first term, criticism of his policies or the errors of his subordinates did not seem to stick to him personally, so much so that Reagan's stewardship was frequently referred to in the press as "the Teflon presidency."[83]

In Chapter 10, we discussed the advantages that a president normally enjoys as a political candidate, including the ability to dominate the news. But a president

## "You Could Get a Million Dollars"

On March 21, 1973, President Nixon, White House counsel John Dean, III, and H. R. Haldeman, Nixon's chief of staff, met in the Oval Office to discuss payoffs to buy the silence of the Watergate burglars. Their conversation, recorded by the president's secret taping system, became a crucial part of the evidence in the House Judiciary Committee's impeachment investigation of President Nixon. Following are excerpts from the March 21 conversation:

**NIXON:** How much money do you need?

**DEAN:** I would say these people are going to cost a million dollars over the next two years.

**NIXON:** We could get that. . . . You could get a million dollars. You could get it in cash. I know where it could be gotten. It is not easy, but it could be done. But the question is who the hell would handle it? Any ideas on that?

**HALDEMAN:** . . . We thought [Former Attorney General John] Mitchell ought to be able to know how to find somebody who would know how to do all that sort of thing, because none of us know how to.

**DEAN:** That's right. You have to wash the money. You can get $100,000 out of a bank, and it all comes in serialized bills.

**NIXON:** I understand.

**DEAN:** And that means you have to go to Vegas with it or a bookmaker in New York City. I have learned all these things after the fact. I will be in great shape for the next time around.

**HALDEMAN:** (Expletive deleted).

—From the White House transcripts, released April 30, 1974

can wield that power day in and day out, even when no political campaign is under way. On the afternoon of March 16, 1988, the Iran-contra independent counsel, Lawrence E. Walsh, announced the indictments of President Reagan's former national security adviser, retired Admiral John M. Poindexter; Marine Lt. Col. Oliver L. North, the former NSC aide; and two other key participants in the Iran-contra scandal. A few hours later, the president announced he was sending 3,200 troops to Honduras on a "training exercise." The president's action was undoubtedly designed to place pressure on the left-wing government of Nicaragua. But some Reagan critics voiced suspicions that the dispatch of the troops was an obvious attempt to divert attention from, and overshadow, the unwelcome news of the indictments of the president's men.

## The Watergate Scandal: A President Resigns

It had begun shortly after 1 a.m. on the morning of June 17, 1972, when Frank Wills, a 24-year-old, $80-a-week security guard at the Watergate office building, had pulled a piece of masking tape from the edge of a garage-level door. The tape presumably had been placed there to keep the door from latching shut. He left, but returned in a few minutes. To his astonishment, he found the door had been taped again—apparently by a persistent but foolish burglar. He called the police.

When Wills pulled the tape off the door of the Watergate, it was as though one tiny strand of thread had unraveled a whole skein of corruption and criminal activity planned and condoned in what—until then—had seemed the least likely of places, the White House.

At first, however, the press treated the break-in as little more than a routine crime story. Five men had been arrested inside the headquarters of the Democratic National Committee in the Watergate office building, part of a high-rise complex along the Potomac River. But one of the men turned out to be James W. McCord, Jr., director of security for the Committee for the Reelection of the President (CREEP). Later, two other suspects were arrested, E. Howard Hunt, Jr., and G. Gordon Liddy, both former White House aides. Liddy, like McCord, was an official of CREEP. Several of the burglars had worked for the CIA.

It soon developed that the break-in had been ordered by high officials of the administration and of President Nixon's 1972 election campaign, and financed by money contributed to the campaign. Two young reporters from the *Washington Post,* Bob Woodward and Carl Bernstein, pursued the story.

As the scandal unfolded, it was disclosed that the burglars had bugged the Democratic headquarters and that telephone conversations of Democratic Party officials had been broadcast by a concealed transmitter to a motel across the street.

In the White House, Nixon's advisers took steps to cover up the links between the burglars and the president's campaign. Nixon was overwhelmingly reelected in November. Watergate seemed to have been "contained."

In January 1973, however, five of the defendants pleaded guilty and two others who chose to stand trial were convicted by a federal jury. In March, McCord, facing a long prison term from U.S. District Judge John J. Sirica, suggested that White House and other officials had advance knowledge of the Watergate bugging. President Nixon denied prior knowledge of the Watergate

© J P Laffont/Corbis Sygma

Senator Sam J. Ervin, Jr. presides over Senate Watergate hearings in 1973.

bugging or the subsequent cover-up by his staff. He accepted the resignations of his two principal aides, H. R. Haldeman and John Ehrlichman, and of his attorney general, Richard Kleindienst, and authorized the new attorney general to appoint a special prosecutor to investigate the Watergate case. But the storm did not abate.

Nixon admitted that he had established a special investigative unit, known as "the Plumbers," to find the source of national security news leaks. The Plumbers had been headed by Howard Hunt and G. Gordon Liddy.

In the weeks that followed McCord's disclosure, the daily headlines brought one startling disclosure after another: In 1970 Nixon had approved a plan for burglary and electronic surveillance of people suspected of endangering national security, although he was warned, in writing, that burglary was "clearly illegal"; Nixon had ordered the secret wiretapping of 17 people, including a number of his own assistants and several journalists; the president's personal attorney raised and secretly distributed funds totaling $220,000 to the Watergate burglars and their attorneys; the acting director of the Federal Bureau of Investigation had destroyed vital Watergate evidence; the attorney general of the United States, John Mitchell, was present during a discussion of proposals for bugging the Democratic Party's Watergate headquarters and for kidnapping American citizens and taking them to Mexico; and the president's assistants compiled an "enemies list" and requested tax audits of political opponents.

In May 1973 a Senate select committee under chairman Sam J. Ervin, Jr., a North Carolina Democrat, began holding televised hearings into Watergate and the 1972 campaign. The hearings revealed that Nixon had concealed microphones in his offices at the White House to record conversations on tape, in most cases without the knowledge of the people being recorded. The tapes became key evidence in the scandal.

Within a few months, all seven of the Watergate burglars had been given jail sentences by Judge Sirica. In October Nixon dismissed the Watergate special prosecutor, in what became known as "the Saturday night massacre," but he was forced by the tremendous public outcry to appoint another. The House of Representatives began an impeachment investigation. Nixon agreed to surrender some of the tapes of his conversations about Watergate.

Then came the climactic events of the summer of 1974. The Supreme Court ordered Nixon to surrender more tapes to the new Watergate special prosecutor, and the House Judiciary Committee voted to impeach the president. The committee approved three articles of impeachment and sent them to the full House. In addition, one of the newly released tapes showed that Nixon had lied when he denied he had participated in the cover-up of the Watergate burglary. On June 23, 1972, the tapes revealed, Nixon had ordered the CIA to try to confine the FBI investigation of the break-in, and he now admitted he knew that he would gain political advantage from that order.

Nixon's support in Congress within his own Republican Party crumbled. He did not have enough votes in Congress to avoid impeachment and removal from office.

Richard Nixon resigned on August 9, 1974, the first president in the nation's history to do so. A month later, he accepted a pardon from his successor, President Ford, and thus could not be prosecuted for acts committed while president. Many of Nixon's high advisers were less fortunate. In 1975 John Ehrlichman, H. R. Haldeman, and John Mitchell were convicted of covering up the Watergate break-in. All three went to prison.

A total of 19 people were convicted or pleaded guilty in connection with Watergate-related crimes, including 10 Nixon aides and three CREEP officials. All 19 served prison sentences.

## Presidential Impeachment, Disability, and Succession

Despite the enormous power of the president, under the Constitution he may be impeached by Congress and, if convicted of "Treason, Bribery or other high Crimes and Misdemeanors," removed from office.* Only the House can bring impeachment proceedings against a president, by majority vote. The president is then tried by the Senate with the chief justice presiding. A two-thirds vote of

*Not only the president, but also the vice president and other federal officials and federal judges—as the Constitution puts it, all "civil officers of the United States"—are subject to impeachment. From 1789 through 2004, a total of 16 federal officials were impeached and tried by the Senate. Seven were convicted and removed from office, seven were acquitted, and in two cases the charges were dismissed. Members of Congress are subject to discipline and expulsion by their respective houses, but it is not clear whether they are "civil officers" subject to impeachment. At least some scholars believe that members of Congress are not exempt from removal by impeachment. See, for example, Raoul Berger, *Impeachment: The Constitutional Problems* (Cambridge, Mass.: Harvard University Press, 1973), pp. 214–223.

President Nixon bids a tearful farewell to the White House staff after announcing his resignation.



the Senate is required to convict a president and remove him from office, a fate that Andrew Johnson escaped by one vote in 1868.

The unsuccessful attempt to remove Johnson from office grew out of the turmoil following the Civil War. The president hoped to carry out Lincoln's conciliatory Reconstruction policies toward the South after the war. This placed him in direct conflict with the Radical Republicans in Congress, who favored much harsher policies. When Johnson dismissed his secretary of war, the House charged he had violated the Tenure of Office Act and brought impeachment proceedings. The trial and balloting in the Senate went on for more than two months.

Historically, Congress has hesitated to impeach and remove a president, for several reasons. First, there has been an understandable reluctance to act against the highest official in the land, who—unless he succeeds to his office—is elected by all the people. Second, there has been a fear that impeachment, as a political remedy, might become a partisan weapon to remove a president whenever he displeases a Congress controlled by the opposition political party or by political opponents in his own party.

Third, the language of the Constitution dealing with impeachment, scattered in four places, leaves many unanswered questions. For example, can officials be indicted before they are impeached, or in place of impeachment? Many legal scholars believe the answer is yes, for judges and officials up to and including the vice president. But they also contend that a president must first be impeached and removed before prosecution. Otherwise the country might find itself in the untenable position of having its national leader behind bars while still holding office. Yet another difficult problem is whether the "high crimes and misdemeanors" required as grounds for an impeachment conviction must literally be crimes in the legal sense—the breaking of specific laws—or whether that constitutional language encompasses serious abuses of the office of the president that might fall short of actual, indictable crimes. During the controversy leading up to the impeachment of President Clinton, his lawyers and other supporters argued that the actions he had committed did not rise to the level of an impeachable offense.

## The Nixon Impeachment Proceedings and Resignation

Before 1973 it seemed most unlikely that any modern president could be impeached, but the Watergate scandal and the Clinton scandal changed all that. A resolution to impeach President Nixon was introduced in the House on July 31, 1973, by Robert F. Drinan, a Massachusetts Democrat who was also a Roman Catholic priest. Some of those who might otherwise have favored such a course were dismayed at the prospect of the succession of Vice President Agnew to the presidency in the event of Nixon's removal from office. But Agnew resigned the following October on the day he was convicted of criminal charges, and that same month the House Judiciary Committee began an inquiry into the possible impeachment of Nixon. It was the first time since 1868 that Congress had taken steps to consider whether a president of the United States should be impeached.

The formal proceedings of the committee, under chairman Peter W. Rodino, Jr., began in February 1974. The committee staff amassed 38 volumes of evidence dealing with the Watergate break-in, Nixon's wiretapping of 17 aides and news reporters, the White House enemies list, and other abuses. The committee members, earphones clamped to their heads, listened for hours to the White House tapes. They also heard presentations by the president's attorney, James D. St. Clair, and by the committee's special counsel, John Doar. They heard witnesses in closed session, and then on July 24 began six historic days of public deliberation. The sessions were televised and watched by millions of Americans.

The Judiciary Committee voted three articles of impeachment. Article I accused Nixon of obstruction of justice by "using the powers of his high office" to "delay, impede, and obstruct" the investigation of the break-in at Democratic headquarters. The article specifically charged that Nixon had made false public statements "for the purpose of deceiving the people of the United States" into believing that the president's campaign organization had not been involved. Article II accused the president of violating the constitutional rights of citizens by misusing the FBI, the CIA, the Internal Revenue Service, and other agencies, and by establishing a secret investigative unit, the Plumbers, in the White House itself. Article III charged that Nixon had defied the committee by failing to produce subpoenaed tapes and documents.

On July 24, 1974, the Supreme Court ruled 8–0 that Nixon had to yield 64 tapes of his White House conversations to the Watergate special prosecutor. His support in Congress collapsed when the tapes were released soon afterward and showed that Nixon had participated in the Watergate cover-up. As these climactic events unfolded, the full House had no opportunity to vote on the articles of impeachment, nor was there a Senate trial, as occurred in the case of Andrew Johnson. On August 9, 1974, just 10 days after the last of the articles had been approved by the Judiciary Committee, Nixon resigned.

## The Clinton Scandal and Impeachment

Bill Clinton was only the second president to be impeached. Like the first, Andrew Johnson, he was not convicted and removed from office.

Clinton's troubles began with an Arkansas land deal in which he and his wife had invested in 1978 with the owners of a local savings and loan association that later failed. The deal envisioned a real estate development called Whitewater on 230 acres in the Ozark Mountains in northern Arkansas, at the juncture of Crooked Creek and the White River. The plan was to sell the lots for vacation homes. The Whitewater venture was unsuccessful, and it led to charges of fraud and allegations that Clinton, as governor, had helped the bank's owners obtain federally insured loans, which Clinton denied.

The clamor over Whitewater had become so loud by early in 1994 that Clinton's attorney general, Janet Reno, appointed a special prosecutor to investigate. Five months later, a new problem surfaced for the president when Paula Jones, a clerk in the Arkansas state government, filed a lawsuit claiming that Clinton, while governor, solicited oral sex from her in a hotel room in Little Rock. In August, Kenneth W. Starr, who had been solicitor general in the first President Bush's administration, took over as independent counsel investigating the president.

In 1995, Monica S. Lewinsky, a dark-haired, 21-year-old intern from Beverly Hills, California, began working for the White House; by November Clinton was in a sexual relationship with her that had begun when Lewinsky showed the president her thong underwear. The following year, Clinton broke off but later resumed

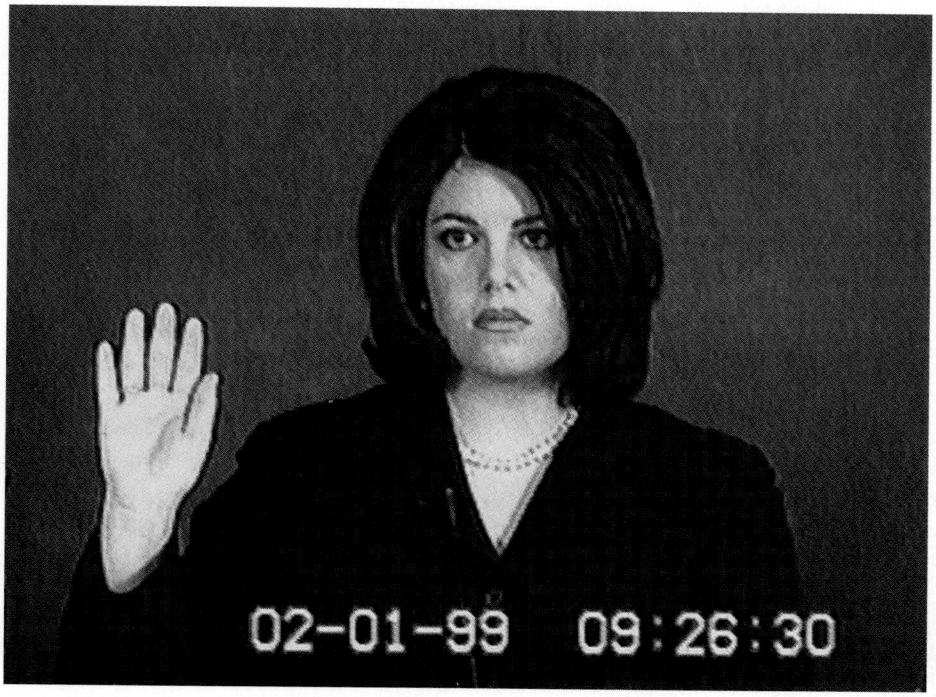




Monica Lewinsky is sworn in for the Senate impeachment trial of President Clinton.

his affair, but that spring Lewinsky was transferred to a job in the Pentagon after the president's aides realized she seemed to be spending too much time in the West Wing of the White House. At the Pentagon, Lewinsky became friendly with Linda Tripp, another ex–White House employee.

In 1997, Tripp began secretly taping her conversations with Lewinsky, in which the young intern confided details of her affair with the president. In December, Lewinsky was subpoenaed to give a deposition in the Paula Jones case. Coached by the president, she signed a false affidavit saying she had no "sexual relationship" with Clinton. In the meantime, the president's friend, Vernon Jordan, a powerful Washington attorney, was arranging a job interview for Lewinsky in New York.

In January 1998, in a famous finger-wagging denial in front of the TV cameras, Clinton said, "I did not have sexual relations with that woman, Miss Lewinsky." Earlier that same month, the president also testified in the Jones lawsuit.

What he did not know was that Linda Tripp had secretly tipped off Paula Jones's attorneys, and Kenneth Starr, about Clinton's affair with Lewinsky. During his testimony, Clinton was presumably caught off guard when it became apparent that Jones's lawyers possessed detailed information about his affair with Lewinsky and began questioning him about the intern. At the deposition, he denied under oath that he had had "sexual relations," as defined by Jones's lawyers, with Lewinsky.

A week earlier, Tripp had turned over to Starr 20 hours of tape recordings of Lewinsky's conversations with her, and the next day at Starr's request, she wore a hidden microphone while having lunch with Lewinsky at a hotel in Arlington, Virginia.

Kenneth Starr opened a grand jury inquiry into the Lewinsky matter. Under a grant of immunity, Lewinsky admitted the affair to the grand jury. In August 1998, Clinton testified before the grand jury in the White House, now admitting an "improper relationship" with the young intern, and insisting that "sexual relations," as defined by Jones's lawyers, meant intercourse only, not oral sex. Afterwards, in a brief nationally televised speech, Clinton conceded, "I did have a relationship with Miss Lewinsky that was not appropriate."

In September 1998, Starr delivered to Congress a lengthy, 445-page report. The document recited in minute and explicit detail the president's 10 sexual encounters with Lewinsky in rooms next to the Oval Office. The report accused the president of perjury, obstruction of justice, witness tampering, and other acts that Starr claimed constituted grounds for impeachment. It said nothing about Whitewater, the original purpose of the investigation.

That same month, Henry J. Hyde, the House Judiciary Committee chairman, proposed a resolution for the impeachment of the president, and in October, the House voted 258–176 to begin impeachment proceedings. The following month, Clinton agreed to settle the Paula Jones lawsuit with a payment of $850,000.

In December, the Judiciary Committee approved four articles of impeachment. The articles charged that Clinton had committed perjury to the federal grand jury, and in his testimony in the Jones case; had obstructed justice by influencing Lewinsky and Clinton's personal secretary to conceal evidence and testify falsely; and had abused the powers of his office by lying to Congress in his answers to questions sent to him by the committee.

On December 19, the full House voted for two of the articles, alleging that Clinton "willfully provided perjurious, false and misleading testimony to the grand jury" and "prevented, obstructed, and impeded the administration of justice." The House rejected the other two articles of impeachment. The vote came at the end of an extraordinary week in which the United States and Britain bombed Iraq, and the House speaker-designate, Bob Livingston, a Louisiana Republican, withdrew his candidacy after admitting past adulterous affairs of his own.

*for more information about William Jefferson Clinton, see:*
*http://www.clintonlibrary.gov*

The trial of President Clinton in the Senate began on January 9, 1999, with Chief Justice William H. Rehnquist presiding in a black robe oddly festooned with gold stripes. Thirteen House "managers," Republican representatives acting as prosecutors, presented the case against Clinton, who was defended by the White House counsel, Charles F. C. Ruff. No witnesses were called, but the Senators viewed videotaped depositions from Lewinsky, Vernon Jordan, and a White House aide, Sidney Blumenthal.

From the start, public opinion polls showed a solid majority of Americans were opposed to the removal of the president from office. The senators and the public knew that there was little chance Clinton would be convicted. To a considerable extent, therefore, the senators were going through the motions, acting out a story with a predictable ending. Knowing the likely outcome, the senators wanted to get the trial over with as soon as possible. The numbers were in the president's favor; even if all 55 Senate Republicans voted to convict, 12 Democrats would have to cross party lines to vote against the president to achieve the two-thirds majority needed to remove him from office.

On February 12, 1999, the Senate found the president not guilty. Article I, alleging perjury to the grand jury, failed, with 45 senators voting in favor, and 55 against. Article II, alleging obstruction of justice, failed by a vote of 50 for and 50 against.

The first impeachment trial of a president of the United States in 131 years was over.

## Disability and Succession

Twice in American history, presidents were incapacitated for long periods. Garfield lived for 80 days after

## November 22, 1963: Lyndon Johnson Learns He Is President

We arrived at Love Field in Dallas, as I remember, just shortly after 11:30 a.m. . . . The President and Mrs. Kennedy walked along the fence, shaking hands with people in the crowd that had assembled. . . .

Mrs. Johnson, Senator Ralph Yarborough, and I then entered the car which had been provided for us in the motorcade. . . . We were the second car behind the President's automobile. . . .

After we had proceeded a short way down Elm Street, I heard a sharp report. . . .

I was startled by the sharp report or explosion, but I had no time to speculate as to its origin because Agent Youngblood . . . shouted to all of us in the back seat to get down. . . . He vaulted over the back seat and sat on me. I was bent over under the weight of Agent Youngblood's body. . . .

When we arrived at the hospital, Agent Youngblood told me to get out of the car, go into the building, not to stop, and to stay close to him and the other agents. . . .

In the hospital room to which Mrs. Johnson and I were taken, the shades were drawn—I think by Agent Youngblood. . . .

It was Ken O'Donnell who, at about 1:20 p.m., told us that the President had died. I think his precise words were "He's gone." . . .

I found it hard to believe that this had happened. The whole thing seemed unreal—unbelievable. A few hours earlier, I had breakfast with John Kennedy; he was alive, strong, vigorous. I could not believe now that he was dead. I was shocked and sickened.

—Statement of President Lyndon B. Johnson to the Warren Commission, July 10, 1964

he was shot in 1881. Wilson never fully recovered from the stroke that he suffered in September 1919, yet he remained in office until March 1921. To a considerable extent, his wife, Edith Wilson, was president. President Eisenhower suffered three serious illnesses, including a heart attack in 1955 that incapacitated him for four days and curtailed his workload for 16 weeks. Sherman Adams, the White House chief of staff, and Press Secretary James Hagerty ran the executive branch machinery during this period.

Eisenhower's heart attack raised anew the question of presidential disability. The Constitution was exceedingly vague on the subject. It spoke of presidential "inability" and "disability," but it left it up to Congress to define those terms and to decide when and how the vice president would take over when a president was unable to exercise his powers and duties. If a president became physically or mentally ill, or disappeared, or was captured in a military operation, or was under anesthesia in a hospital, what was the vice president's proper role? Did he become president or merely assume the "powers and duties" of the office? And for how long? Eisenhower and Nixon sought to cover these contingencies with an unofficial written agreement, a practice followed by Kennedy and Johnson, and Johnson and Humphrey.

But suppose a president were unable or unwilling to declare that he was disabled? Who would then decide whether he was disabled or when he might resume his duties? Could a scheming vice president, with the help of psychiatrists, somehow have a perhaps temporarily unstable president permanently removed from office?

The Twenty-fifth Amendment, ratified in 1967, sought to settle these questions. It provides that the vice president becomes acting president if the president informs Congress in writing that he is unable to perform his duties. Or, the vice president may become acting president if the vice president and a majority of the cabinet, or of some "other body" created by Congress, decide that the president is disabled. The president can reclaim his office at any time unless the vice president and a majority of the cabinet or other body contend that he has not recovered. Congress would then decide the issue. But it would take a two-thirds vote of both houses within three weeks to support the vice president; anything less and the president would resume office.

Until the Twenty-fifth Amendment was ratified, there was no constitutional provision for replacing a vice president when that office became vacant.* So the amendment also provided that the president shall nominate a vice president, subject to the approval of a majority of both houses of Congress, whenever that office becomes vacant. The provision reduces the possibility of presidential succession by the House speaker or the Senate president pro tempore, or by cabinet members, unless the president and vice president die simultaneously, or unless a president dies, resigns, or is impeached while the vice presidency is vacant and before Congress has acted to approve a new vice president.[84] (See Table 13-4.)

The Twenty-fifth Amendment was used for the first time in October 1973 when President Nixon nominated Gerald Ford to succeed Agnew. Congress approved his choice, 92–3 in the Senate and 387–35 in the House. Until Ford was sworn in that December, the office of vice president was vacant for 57 days. During that period, if Nixon had ceased to be president, his successor would have been House Speaker Carl Albert.

* As of 2004, the nation had been without a vice president 18 times for a total of 37 years.

**TABLE 13-4**

**The Order of Succession in the Event a President Is No Longer Able to Serve**

1. The Vice President
2. The Speaker of the House
3. The President Pro Tempore of the Senate
4. The Secretary of State
5. The Secretary of Treasury
6. The Secretary of Defense
7. The Attorney General
8. The Secretary of Interior
9. The Secretary of Agriculture
10. The Secretary of Commerce
11. The Secretary of Labor
12. The Secretary of Health and Human Services
13. The Secretary of Housing and Urban Development
14. The Secretary of Transportation
15. The Secretary of Energy
16. The Secretary of Education
17. The Secretary of Veterans Affairs
18. The Secretary of Homeland Security

SOURCES: Presidential Succession Act of 1947, as amended; Twenty-fifth Amendment to the U.S. Constitution.

The Twenty-fifth Amendment was used for the second time to fill a vice presidential vacancy after Nixon resigned and Ford succeeded him as president. In August 1974 Ford nominated former New York governor Nelson A. Rockefeller to be vice president. After lengthy hearings and approval by the House and Senate, Rockefeller took the oath of office in December.[85]

## THE SPLENDID MISERY: PERSONALITY AND STYLE IN THE WHITE HOUSE

Thomas Jefferson described the presidency as "a splendid misery." Others, like Franklin Roosevelt and John Kennedy, brought great vigor and vitality to the job; they seemed to enjoy being president. The personality, style, and concept of the office that each president brings with him to the White House affect the nature of his presidency. William Howard Taft expressed the classic restrictive view of the presidency: "The President can exercise no power which cannot be fairly and reasonably traced to some specific grant of power."[86] Theodore Roosevelt adhered to the "stewardship" theory. He saw the chief executive as "a steward of the people" and believed that "it was not only his right but his duty to do anything that the needs of the Nation demanded unless such action was forbidden by the Constitution or by the laws."[87]

Dallas, November 22, 1963: President Lyndon Johnson takes the oath of office.

Abraham Lincoln and Franklin Roosevelt went even further, contending that in great emergencies the president could exercise almost unlimited power to preserve the nation. (See Figure 13-3.)

Louis W. Koenig has classified presidents as "literalist" (Madison, Buchanan, Taft, and, to a degree, Eisenhower) or "effective" (Washington, Jackson, Lincoln, Wilson, and the Roosevelts), adding that many chief executives fall somewhere in the middle. A literalist president, as defined by Koenig, closely obeys the letter of the Constitution; an effective president, who generally flourishes in times of crisis and change, interprets his constitutional powers as broadly as possible.[88]

A president's personality and approach to the office may leave a more lasting impression than his substantive accomplishments or failures. We think of Teddy Roosevelt shouting "Bully!"; Wilson, austere and idealistic, in the end shattered by events; Franklin Roosevelt in a wheelchair, cigarette holder tilted at a jaunty angle, conquering paralysis with élan. We think of Eisenhower's golf, Kennedy's glamour, Johnson's cowpuncher image, Nixon's isolation, the first President Bush at the helm of his speedboat as it churned across the waters at Kennebunkport, Maine, Clinton's living on the edge, and George W. Bush jogging or clearing brush at his Texas ranch.

**FIGURE 13-3**

**Presidential Greatness**

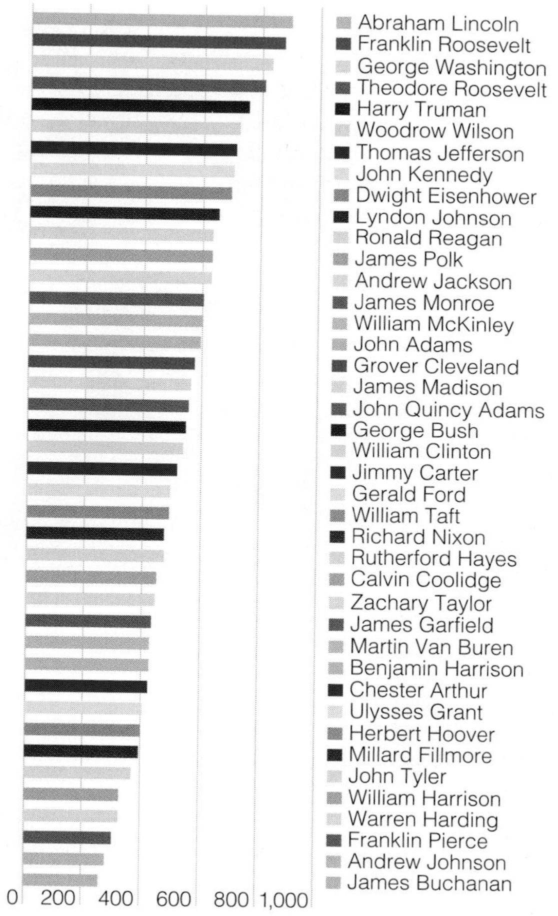


NOTE: Points earned from ratings by 58 historians based on the following categories: Public Persuasion, Crisis Leadership, Economic Management, Moral Authority, International Relations, Administrative Skills, Relations with Congress, Vision/Setting Agenda, Pursued Equal Justice for All, and Performance within Context of Times.

SOURCE: C-Span survey, February 21, 2000.

James David Barber attempted to systematize the study of presidential behavior by analyzing how childhood and other experiences may have molded a president's character and style. Barber proposed four broad character types into which presidents may be grouped, and he suggested that from such an analysis it might ultimately be possible to theorize about future presidential behavior.[89] Barber contended, for instance, that Eisenhower reluctantly ran for president because he was "a sucker for duty" as a result of his background, that Johnson ruled through "manipulative maneuvering," and that Nixon "isolated himself."[90]

In an accurate prediction of Watergate and Nixon's downfall, Barber warned in 1972 that Nixon's character "could lead the President on to disaster. . . . The danger is that crisis will be transformed into tragedy. . . . The loss of power to forces beyond his control would constitute a severe threat. That would be a time to go down, if go down one must, in flames."[91]

Some observers contend that because of the many variables affecting human behavior, presidents may not act in ways that psychological analysis of their lives might suggest.[92] But because of the work of Barber and others, this approach has gained increasing attention.

## The American Presidency: Triumph and Tragedy

Running for president in 1980, Ronald Reagan said he wanted to "bring our government back under control and make it acceptable to the people."[93] He would, he declared, eliminate "extravagance and fat in government."[94] Twenty years earlier, John F. Kennedy, seeking the presidency in 1960, viewed it as "the vital center of action in our whole scheme of government." The problems of America, he said, "demand a vigorous proponent of the national interest—not a passive broker for conflicting private interests," a president who will "place himself in the very thick of the fight."[95]

Whether a president takes an activist approach, like Kennedy, or a more conservative approach, like Reagan, the voters tend to look to the White House for solutions to major problems. Yet the president may not be able to

Lyndon Johnson issues orders to a doubtful steer on his Texas ranch.

© AP/Wide World Photos

John F. Kennedy viewed the presidency as a "vital center of action."

© John Atherton/UPI/Bettmann/Corbis

Theodore Roosevelt strikes a typically exuberant pose.

Brown Brothers

William Howard Taft, who weighed 332 pounds, displays a graceful follow-through.

Brown Brothers

solve the worst national problems that confront him. He may be hobbled by divided government if Congress is controlled by the opposition party. He cannot single-handedly end environmental pollution, nor control economic problems such as inflation, budget deficits, and unemployment. Nor can he easily use the nation's nuclear power in foreign policy crises—to prevent the seizure of American hostages, for example, or to fight international terrorism. Koenig has suggested the concept of "the imagined presidency," which is "vested in our minds with more power than the presidency really has."[96] The difference between the real and the imagined presidency, he contends, may lead to public frustration over presidential performance.

Although the great power of the presidency tends to overshadow its limitations, we have seen how, in many spheres, that power is circumscribed. As chief executive, the president faces an often intractable bureaucracy. As chief legislator, under the constitutional separation of powers, he faces an independent and often hostile Congress. As military and foreign policy leader, his powers are enormous, but he must, at least to some extent, consider the public's reaction and sentiment in Congress and the bureaucracy. He may also consider the response of other nations as well. The Twenty-second Amendment limits the president to two terms and thereby weakens his power in the second term (since everyone knows he will not be president again). Federal law may restrict his options. The Supreme Court may strike down his programs. The press may expose corruption in the

© AP/Wide World Photos

President Clinton reviewing U.S. troops in Bosnia

### The President Is Not Above the Law

After the Watergate scandal, a Senate intelligence committee under Senator Frank Church, Democrat of Idaho, investigated abuses by the FBI, CIA, and other federal intelligence and police agencies. Former President Nixon, responding to written questions from the committee, attempted to argue that a President was in some way above the law: "It is quite obvious," he said, "that there are certain inherently governmental actions which if undertaken by the sovereign in protection of the interest of the nation's security are lawful but which if undertaken by private persons are not." The committee emphatically rejected this concept of the President as "sovereign," and noted in its final report: "There is no inherent constitutional authority for the President or any intelligence agency to violate the law."

—Excerpt from the final report of the Senate Select Committee on Intelligence, Book IV, 1976

bureaucracy or in the White House itself. Public opinion may turn against him. The necessities of politics may force him to weigh his actions in terms of their effect on his party. Finally, he may be impeached and removed from office.

Whether the presidency is too powerful, or not powerful enough, depends, then, to some extent not only on how a president uses his power but also on what he hopes to accomplish. Presidents have different goals. Many Democratic presidents have tried to press forward with energetic programs of social reform, but other presidents have tried to cut back on such programs.

The answer to the question of whether presidents have too much power depends ultimately on what voters expect of the office and of the American political system. In the domestic arena, those who regard the presidency as an essential instrument for meeting the social challenges and problems of the nation today do not necessarily tend to regard that office as too powerful. Others, alarmed at the size of the federal bureaucracy and opposed to social-welfare programs, take a different view. They argue that the federal government intrudes too much into the lives of citizens.

In any event, presidential power fluctuates, depending in part on the situation in which it is being exercised. Franklin Roosevelt was able to wield extensive economic power during the early years of the New Deal because the nation was in the throes of an acute depression. By 1938

## "A Small, Select Club"

It's a small, select club, a peerage, the few men alive at any one time who have served as president. What unites them, ultimately, overwhelms partisan differences or even the bitter memories of past political battles. Only they know what it's like to be president—to order troops into battle; to hate the press; to sacrifice privacy in return for power; to face the nation from the West Front of the Capitol and swear to defend the Constitution against all foes, foreign and domestic, so help you, God; to sit alone in the Oval Office late at night and contemplate the imperfect choices that are the stuff of history.

—George Stephanopoulos, *All Too Human: A Political Education*

© AP/Wide World Photos

Five former United States presidents: George H. W. Bush, Ronald Reagan, Jimmy Carter, Gerald Ford, and Richard Nixon

he was encountering substantial domestic opposition. When the Second World War came along, he was able once more to exercise great powers; people expected it.

The power a president exercises depends not only on the times and the circumstances but also on the policy area involved. Until the relatively ineffective War Powers Resolution of 1973, for several decades there had been few serious attempts to curb the president's power to commit military forces abroad. In the field of domestic legislation, however, presidential powers may not be strong enough. For example, Reagan could not persuade Congress to shift responsibility for the welfare program from the federal government to the states, although later Clinton succeeded in doing so. Clinton's major effort to revamp the nation's health care system fizzled in 1994. As of 2006, George W. Bush has been unable to modify the Social Security system.

The president (along with the vice president) is the only official of the U.S. government elected by all the people. The presidency, therefore, would seem to be the branch of government best situated to view and act on national problems in the interest of a national constituency. In a diverse democracy of conflicting interests and competing groups, the president is the one official who represents all the people and who can symbolize their aspirations. He is the custodian of the future. Despite the limits on his powers, he can be the greatest force for national unity—or disunity. He can recognize the demands of minorities for social justice, or he can repress or ignore their rights. He can protect constitutional liberties or turn loose federal police power to wiretap, eavesdrop, and burglarize. He can lead the nation into war or preserve the peace. Such is his power that he leaves his indelible mark on the times, with the result that the triumph or tragedy of each presidency is, in some measure at least, also our own.

## CHAPTER HIGHLIGHTS

- The American presidency is an office of enormous contrasts, of great power and great limits.
- The presidency is both an institution and a person. The institution is the office created by the Constitution, custom, federal laws since 1789, and the gradual growth of various tools of presidential power. The person is a human being who brings a particular personality and style to the White House. The presidency, then, is both highly institutionalized and highly personal.
- Under the Twenty-second Amendment, in normal circumstances the incumbent must change at least once every eight years.
- There are few legal qualifications for the office; the Constitution requires only that the president be a "natural-born" citizen, at least 35 years old, and 14 years a resident of the United States.
- The president is one individual but fills many separate roles: chief of state, chief executive, commander in chief, chief diplomat, chief legislator, chief of party, and popular leader. All but the last two are required of him by the Constitution. Many of the presidential roles blend and overlap.
- The president of the United States is the ceremonial and symbolic head of state. In another role, he is also head of government, the official who presides over the machinery of the executive branch.
- The president runs the executive branch of government with the aid of a White House staff, various other agencies in the Executive Office of the President, and the cabinet.
- The president is commander in chief of the armed forces of the United States. The Constitution declares that "Congress shall have Power . . . to declare War," but Congress has not done so since 1941. In the intervening years the president has made the decision to go to war. The War Powers Resolution, a law Congress passed in 1973, was an effort to set a time limit on the use of combat forces abroad by a president. The resolution has not effectively restricted presidential military power, however.
- Civilian supremacy, the principle of civilian control of the military, is based on the clear constitutional power of the president as supreme commander of the armed forces.
- Presidents make foreign policy; they direct the relations of the United States with other nations of the world. The Constitution does not specifically confer this power on the president, but it does so indirectly. The president has sole power to make treaties with the consent of two-thirds of the Senate. The president also can sign executive agreements with other nations that do not require Senate approval.
- Beneath the president in the executive branch are the 15 cabinet departments (as of January 2007) and about 50 major independent agencies, boards, and commissions. These agencies are of two main types: executive agencies and independent regulatory agencies.
- The conflict between the president and Congress at times revolves around the doctrine of executive privilege, the claim by presidents of an inherent right to withhold information from Congress and the judiciary. This doctrine is nowhere explicitly stated in the Constitution but rests on the separation of powers of the three branches of government.
- As chief legislator, the president has an important weapon in the veto, the constitutional power of the president to disapprove a bill and return it with his objections to the branch of Congress in which it originated.
- Because of the Watergate scandal, Richard Nixon resigned on August 9, 1974, the first president in the nation's history to do so.
- Only the House can bring impeachment proceedings against a president, by majority vote. The president is then tried by the Senate with the chief justice of the United States presiding. A two-thirds vote of the Senate is required to convict a president and remove him from office.
- Andrew Johnson was the first president to be impeached, in 1868. At his Senate trial, he escaped being removed from office by one vote. In 1998, Bill Clinton became the second president to be impeached. Like Andrew Johnson, he was not convicted and removed from office.
- If the president dies, resigns, or is removed from office, the vice president becomes president. The Twenty-fifth Amendment sets forth the procedures under which the vice president becomes acting president if the president is unable to perform his duties.

## KEY TERMS

War Powers Resolution, p. 416
Cold War, p. 419
executive agencies, p. 423
independent regulatory agencies, p. 423
civilian supremacy, p. 426
military-industrial complex, p. 427
executive agreements, p. 428
executive privilege, p. 431
veto, p. 431
pocket veto, p. 432
line-item veto, p. 433
riders, p. 433
cabinet, p. 437
National Security Council (NSC), p. 440

## SUGGESTED WEBSITES

**http://www.thepresidency.org**
*The Center for the Study of the Presidency*
A nonpartisan, nonprofit organization dedicated to the study of the presidency. The Reference Center provides

access to the center's publication, *Presidential Studies Quarterly,* and to special reports produced by the center.

**http://www.whitehouse.gov**
*The White House*
The official website of the White House offers presidential speeches, press conferences, interviews, and other documents. Provides links to the personal home pages of the president, the First Lady, and the vice president. Also contains links to the websites of departments that make up the cabinet, independent agencies that report to the president, and special presidential commissions.

## SUGGESTED READING


Barber, James David. *The Presidential Character: Predicting Performance in the White House,* 4th edition* (Prentice-Hall, 1992). An important analysis of why presidents act as they do. Based on research on presidents from Taft to the first Bush, Barber's study explores the relationships between each president's personality type and his performance in office.

Burns, James MacGregor. *Roosevelt: The Lion and the Fox** (Harcourt Brace Jovanovich, 1963). (Originally published in 1956.) A political biography of Franklin D. Roosevelt, one of the foremost practitioners of the art of presidential leadership. Focuses primarily on Roosevelt's first two terms in office.

Campbell, Colin, and Rockman, Bert A., eds. *The George W. Bush Presidency: Appraisals and Prospects** (CQ Press, 2004). A collection of essays on the George W. Bush administration through the end of 2003. Focuses on foreign policy and the Iraq war, presidential leadership, relations with Congress, judicial appointments, and opinion polls.

Cohen, Jeffrey, and Nice, David. *The Presidency** (McGraw-Hill, 2003). A comprehensive study of the presidency stressing the conflict between the limited constitutional foundations of the office and public expectations for strong presidential leadership.

Corwin, Edward S. *The President: Office and Powers,* 5th revised edition* (New York University Press, 1984). A classic analysis of the American presidency. Stresses the historical development and the legal powers of the office.

Cronin, Thomas E., and Genovese, Michael A. *The Paradoxes of the American Presidency,* 2nd edition* (Oxford University Press, 2004). A wide-ranging survey of the history and power of the presidency. Includes a chapter on the role of the vice president.

Donald, David Herbert. *Lincoln** (Simon & Schuster, 1995). An absorbing, revealing, and superbly written biography of one of the greatest American presidents. The book emphasizes Lincoln's remarkable skills as a political leader.

Fenno, Richard F., Jr. *The President's Cabinet: An Analysis in the Period from Wilson to Eisenhower* (Harvard University Press, 1959). A thoughtful study of the development of the cabinet and its role as a distinct political institution. Examines the dual role of cabinet members as presidential advisers and department heads and the place of the cabinet in the larger political system.

Genovese, Michael A. *The Power of the American Presidency, 1789–2000** (Oxford University Press, 2001). A highly readable study of American presidents. Provides a biography and portrait or photo of each president.

Greenstein, Fred I. *The Presidential Difference: Leadership Style from Roosevelt to Clinton* (Free Press, 2000). An informative examination of the differing approaches to presidential leadership, by a leading presidential scholar.

Jones, Charles O. *The Presidency in a Separated System** (The Brookings Institution, 1994). A thoughtful analysis of factors that may limit and check "presidential leadership" in a system in which power is divided among separate branches of government. It argues that—over time—the role, the resources, and the relative power of the president vary greatly in such a system.

Koenig, Louis W. *The Chief Executive,* 6th edition (Harcourt Brace Jovanovich, 1996). An excellent, readable, and comprehensive study of the many facets of the presidency.

Light, Paul C. *The President's Agenda: Domestic Policy Choice from Kennedy to Clinton,* 3rd revised edition (Johns Hopkins University Press, 1999). An analysis of how specific policy proposals get on the agenda as part of the president's domestic program.

Lowi, Theodore J. *The Personal President: Power Invested, Promise Unfulfilled** (Cornell University Press, 1985). An analysis of the modern presidency that concludes that the president has become the personal embodiment of government in the United States. Argues that the high expectations surrounding today's presidents doom them to failure.

Milkis, Sidney M., and Nelson, Michael. *The American Presidency: Origins and Development, 1776–2002* (CQ Press, 2003). An excellent history of the presidency.

McCulloch, David. *Truman** (Touchstone, 1993). A warm, engaging biography of the plain-speaking president.

Nelson, Michael, ed. *The Presidency and the Political System,* 7th edition* (CQ Press, 2002). A collection of interesting essays on some central aspects of the presidential office. Includes useful analyses of both the legal and political sources of presidential powers.

*National Journal* (Government Research Corporation). An excellent weekly report on American politics and government. Provides comprehensive detailed stories about current policy issues in many areas, and analyzes how Congress, the executive branch, and various interest groups interact.

Neustadt, Richard E. *Presidential Power: The Politics of Leadership from Roosevelt to Reagan** (Free Press, 1990). (Originally published in 1960.) A knowledgeable exploration of the problems faced by a modern president in seeking to exercise his power. The first edition of this book was influential in the Kennedy Administration, in which its author served for a time as a special consultant.

Pfiffner, James P. *The Modern Presidency,* 4th edition* (Wadsworth Thomson, 2005). An analysis of the development of the presidency since Franklin Roosevelt. The author stresses the organizational aspects of the presidency, especially the working styles of each president's chief of staff.

Rozell, Mark J. *Executive Privilege: Presidential Power, Secrecy, and Accountability,* 2nd edition, revised* (University Press of Kansas, 2002). An examination of the use of executive privilege by presidents since Nixon. The author argues that there is a constitutional basis for executive privilege, but that presidents should use the power judiciously and the two other branches of government should provide a check on excessive use of this power by presidents.

Schlesinger, Arthur M., Jr. *A Thousand Days* (Houghton Mifflin, 1965). A well-written, detailed account of the Kennedy years by a scholar and former presidential aide. Although Schlesinger was not at the center of power in the Kennedy White House, he had the advantage of viewing events with the eye of a trained historian.

Skowronek, Stephen. *The Politics Presidents Make: Leadership from John Adams to Bill Clinton* (Belknap Press of Harvard University Press, 1997). A study, rich in historical detail, of the varying leadership strategies that American presidents have pursued. Emphasizes the differences in the impact that presidents have had on the politics of their time.

Tulis, Jeffrey K. *The Rhetorical Presidency** (Princeton University Press, 1987). An important analysis suggesting that a president's skills as an orator and communicator, and as a popular leader, are directly related to his success. The development of the "rhetorical presidency," the author argues, has fundamentally transformed American politics in the 20th century.

Walch, Timothy, ed. *At the President's Side: The Vice Presidency in the Twentieth Century* (University of Missouri Press, 1997). A useful collection of essays on an often neglected political office.

Wise, David. *The Politics of Lying: Government Deception, Secrecy, and Power* (Random House, 1973). An analysis, with detailed examples from several presidential administrations, of how government deception and official secrecy led to an erosion of confidence in the government during the late 1960s and early 1970s. Explores the relationship between the government and the press.

*Available in paperback edition.

CAUTION
Airport
Security
Checkpoint

# Chapter 14

# The Bureaucracy

ON MARCH 1, 2003, 22 agencies previously scattered around the federal government moved into the headquarters in Washington of the newly created Department of Homeland Security. A few months earlier, Tom Ridge, former governor of Pennsylvania, had been sworn in as the first secretary of the new cabinet department; in 2005 he was succeeded by a federal judge, Michael Chertoff.

The department was created as a direct result of the terrorist attacks on September 11, 2001, that killed almost 3,000 people, destroyed the twin towers of the World Trade Center in New York City, and seriously damaged the Pentagon in Washington.

The Homeland Security Act of 2002, which created the new department, bluntly stated its mission:

> There is established a Department of Homeland Security, as an executive department of the United States within the meaning of title 5, United States Code.
>
> The primary mission of the department is to (a) prevent terrorist attacks within the United States; (b) reduce the vulnerability of the United States to terrorism; and (c) minimize the damage, and assist in the recovery, from terrorist attacks that do occur within the United States.

Like many previous cabinet departments, DHS was established by Congress to meet a specific need, in this case the threat that terrorism posed to America's national security. In short, a bureaucracy was created to deal with a new and frightening problem facing the nation.

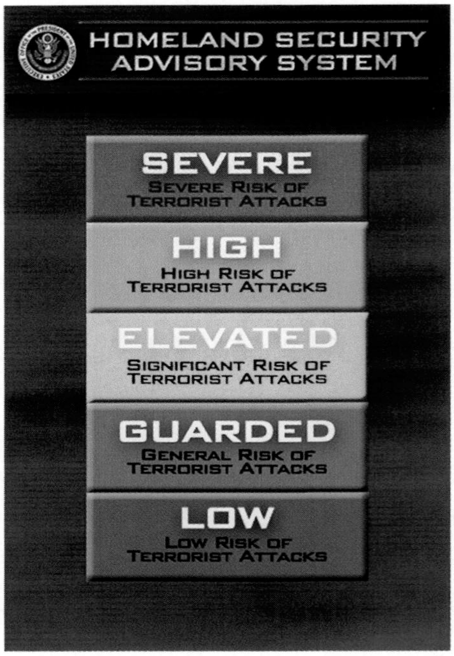


The color-coded terrorism alert system was assailed by some critics as too broad to be useful.

© 2002 AP/Wide World Photos

DHS was more than a typical new department because the law establishing the department moved nearly two dozen existing agencies out of previous departments and placed them under the new homeland security umbrella.

The department, with a proposed budget of $42.7 billion in 2007 and 180,000 employees, was the third largest in the government; only the Department of Defense and the Department of Veterans Affairs had more employees.

DHS has five major directorates: Border and Transportation Security, which includes the Customs Service and part of the Immigration and Naturalization Service, and several other agencies; Emergency Preparedness and Response, including the Federal Emergency Management Agency (FEMA), which is responsible for responding to disasters; Science and Technology; Information Analysis and Infrastructure Protection; and Management. Many other agencies were transferred to the new department, including the Coast Guard and the Secret Service.

***For more information about the Department of Homeland Security see: http://www.dhs.gov***

The terrorist attacks, in other words, led to the creation of a giant new bureaucratic structure. Only three years before the creation of the new cabinet department, in Bush's first campaign for the White House, he had adopted the classic stance of the outsider campaigning against the government in Washington. At the time, in 2000, he was the governor of Texas.

In a speech in Philadelphia, he attacked the federal bureaucracy as being too large and inefficient. "The federal government," Bush said, is "responsible for the safety of our nation's food supply. The way things work now, there's one agency that inspects cheese pizza. There's another that inspects pepperoni pizza. There is one agency that inspects food grown outside the United States. Another that inspects food grown here inside the United States. Apparently, the revolutionary idea that maybe these functions could be combined hasn't dawned on anyone yet. . . . Americans hear examples like this and conclude, quite reasonably, that government is out of touch, that it is too big and it spends too much."[1]

Once in power, however, and in response to the 9/11 terrorist attacks, Bush presided over the creation of DHS, a large new bureaucracy into which many agencies were reshuffled. To meet a huge new challenge, he had created a huge new bureaucracy. As often happens, "bureaucracy" looks very different from outside Washington than it does to political leaders inside the capital.

Challengers seeking the presidency tend to portray themselves as outsiders ready to do battle against the bureaucratic fortress in Washington. But when outsiders are elected, they immediately, by definition, become insiders, responsible for the very bureaucracy they attacked so readily on the campaign trail.

Sometimes the importance of "the bureaucrats in Washington" is brought home dramatically by unexpected events—a budget crisis, a flood in the Midwest, or the 1995 bombing of the federal building in Oklahoma City. Then the public may form a more favorable view of the men and women who run the federal government.

Conversely, when the government fails to respond rapidly and effectively to a natural disaster—as happened in 2005, when Hurricane Katrina devastated New Orleans and parts of the Gulf Coast—the public reaction may be swift. The storm, with fierce winds and horrendous floods, left more than 1,700 people dead and tens of thousands driven from their homes. In the aftermath, public outrage was directed not only at President George W. Bush, but also at Michael Chertoff, whose Homeland Security Department was responsible for FEMA, the Federal Emergency Management Agency, which responded slowly to the disaster. Michael Brown, FEMA's director, soon resigned in disgrace.

When the people are deprived of government services they tend to take for granted, they may also form a different view of "bureaucrats." For example, twice in late 1995 and continuing into early 1996 the federal government shut down for days and weeks because President Clinton and leaders of the Republican-controlled Congress were locked in a battle over the budget. Hundreds of thousands of federal workers were thrown off the job temporarily.

Visitors to the nation's capital and to popular national parks such as Yellowstone were turned away. The Park Service was shut down. Washington's museums and monuments were closed to tourists, as were the Statue of Liberty and Ellis Island in New York. Americans planning to travel abroad could not get passports because the State Department office that issues them was closed.

© Mario Tama/Getty Images

New Orleans, August 2005: Victims of Hurricane Katrina are rescued from a school rooftop.

Business executives and citizens who needed to deal with government agencies, such as the Commerce Department, were frustrated, for there was no one to call. Many voters voiced their disgust with both sides in the squabble in Washington. The shutdown caused great inconvenience to many people. But it also brought home the fact that perhaps the "bureaucrats in Washington"—so often the target of political brickbats—were necessary, after all.

As past presidential election campaigns have illustrated, bureaucracy—and bureaucrats—are often handy political targets to blame for society's ills. By one dictionary definition, "bureaucrat" is a neutral word—it simply means "an administrator"—but its connotations are far from complimentary. "Bureaucrat" and "bureaucracy" are words that, to some people, conjure up an image of self-important but inefficient petty officials wallowing in red tape. It has been wryly suggested, and is widely believed, that once established, bureaucracies tend to mushroom under "Parkinson's Law": "Work expands so as to fill the time available for its completion."[2] The political theorist Hannah Arendt has described bureaucracy as "rule by Nobody," that is, "an intricate system of bureaus in which no men, neither one nor the best, neither the few nor the many, can be held responsible."[3]

There are checks on bureaucratic power, however, including the news media and congressional scrutiny. And government at every level—federal, state, and local—could not function without people to run it. Many government programs are highly complex and require experts and professional people to administer them. **Public administration** is the term preferred by most political scientists to describe the bureaucratic process—the business of making government work—and bureaucrats are public administrators. The same bureaucrats who are blamed for red tape have also accomplished some remarkable tasks: The National Aeronautics and Space Administration (NASA) put men on the moon, and the Tennessee Valley Authority (TVA) brought about the greening of a large area of America.

Today, Americans may turn to the federal government to solve or alleviate problems of the economy, of the cities, of mass transportation, of poverty, pollution, education, public health, and energy. In all of these fields, public administrators—bureaucrats—make important decisions and bear great responsibilities. So, of course, do bureaucrats working for state and local governments.

The millions of people who receive Social Security checks every month would not be getting them unless

NASA

the Social Security Administration were part of the federal bureaucracy. The same "faceless bureaucrats" who are attacked in political campaigns process the Social Security checks. There is waste and red tape and inefficiency in the federal government, but, as in any large organization outside government, there are also thousands of honest, competent people.

Americans tend to be against "Big Government" in the abstract, but they also demand all kinds of government services. The "bureaucracy in Washington" did not grow overnight, but developed gradually, largely in response to public needs. Most government departments and agencies have been created as a result of pressure from some segment of the population. And the same citizens who complain about "the bureaucracy" may protest the loudest if Washington proposes to close a defense installation that provides jobs in their local community.

Criticism of bureaucracy is not limited to attacks on the government in Washington. The student in a large university may feel like a statistic, crushed by an impersonal bureaucracy. So may an employee of a big corporation. Computer technology and the tendency to assign numbers to individuals (credit cards, bank accounts, Social Security) have made many people feel that they are mere cogs in a vast bureaucratic machine. Voice mail, e-mail, and answering machines have replaced human beings. Once, callers to companies, banks, or other institutions could talk to other people; today, more often than not, they must push buttons, leave messages—and hope for a reply as they listen to the familiar refrain: "Your call may be monitored for quality assurance. Please listen carefully as our menu options have changed. . . . Your call is important to us, please continue to hold."

But the fattest bureaucratic target of all is the federal government. Some of the sentiment directed against the federal bureaucracy can be traced to the social-welfare programs of the New Deal, which vastly expanded the role of government in the lives of individual citizens. For three decades much of the criticism of the bureaucracy came from Republicans and conservatives opposed to the welfare state and the concentration of power in Washington. Yet, during eight years of Republican rule under President Eisenhower, the federal government increased in size. In the late 1960s Democratic liberals began to voice similar criticisms. Ideological disenchantment with the federal bureaucracy had come full circle; conservatives and liberals joined in an antibureaucratic alliance of sorts.

The antigovernment sentiment reached a peak in the aftermath of the 1994 congressional elections, when Republicans captured both houses of Congress for the first time in 40 years and Newt Gingrich was elected speaker of the House. With Gingrich as the point man, the Republicans set out to dismantle or slow down major social programs, cut back the regulation of business, and greatly reduce the size and reach of the federal government. As noted in Chapter 13, even President Clinton—adopting some of his opponents' rhetoric—announced in his January 1996 State of the Union message: "The era of big government is over."[4]

Some critics, such as Peter F. Drucker, have gone so far as to conclude that "modern government has become ungovernable." Drucker contends that because of bureaucratic inertia and "administrative incompetence," government is unable to perform the tasks assigned to it. He adds: "There is no government today that can still claim control of its bureaucracy and of its various agencies. Government agencies are all becoming autonomous, ends in themselves, and directed by their own

Officials of the Federal Emergency Management Agency (FEMA) meet with flood victims in Cuero, Texas.

## Bureaucracy: How to Break an Ashtray

The federal government is often criticized for having too many or unnecessary regulations, as the following news story reflects:

> At the General Services Administration, the current "federal specification" for a glass or metal ashtray runs nine pages, including two pages of drawings. . . . [T]he ashtray rules . . . govern "breakage, type I glass." To test for potential defects, paragraph 4.5.2 states:
>
> > The test shall be made by placing the specimen on its base upon a solid support (1¾-inch, 44.5 mm, maple plank), placing a steel center punch (point ground to a 60-degree included angle) in contact with the center of the inside surface of the bottom and striking with a hammer in successive blows of increasing severity until breakage occurs.
> >
> > The specimen should break into a small number of irregular shaped pieces not greater in number than 35, and it must not dice. Any piece ¼ inch (6.4 mm) or more on any three of its adjacent edges (excluding the thickness dimension) shall be included in the number counted. Smaller fragments shall not be counted (see 3.4.1).
>
> Time will be needed to determine whether the . . . ashtray example assumes the legendary status accorded the 1985 discovery that the military was paying $640 each for toilet seats.
>
> —*Washington Post,* August 17, 1993

Courtesy of Alan Singer/CBS

1993: Then vice president Al Gore, dramatizing burdensome federal regulations, shows David Letterman how to break an ashtray.

desire for power, their own rationale, their own narrow vision rather than by national policy."[5]

Even if such criticisms are overstated, they raise important, valid questions about the role of bureaucracy in modern society. But as long as people demand more and more services from their government—Social Security, health care, aid to education, housing, and the like—some form of bureaucracy is inevitable.

The classic concept of the bureaucracy was developed by the pioneering German sociologist Max Weber, who saw it as a secretive, strict hierarchy, with authority flowing from the top down within a fixed framework of rigid rules and regulations. In Weber's view, the bureaucracy draws its power from its expertise. Political rulers are in no position to argue with the technical knowledge of the trained bureaucrat: "The absolute monarch is powerless opposite the superior knowledge of the bureaucratic expert."[6] Even the Russian czar of old,

## Buttering Up the Farmers: The Federal Popcorn Board

WASHINGTON—Since taking control of Congress, Republicans have repeatedly vowed to shrink the Government and its role in the nation's economy. But some matters are just too important to be left alone.

Popcorn, for example. The Senate this month passed a far-reaching farm bill that would scale back Federal subsidies for farmers. A little-noticed provision would establish a Federal Popcorn Board. . . .

The Popcorn Board got strong support from the chairman of the Senate Agriculture Committee, Richard G. Lugar of Indiana (a state that grows lots of popcorn), and from the Popcorn Institute, a trade association.

Andy Fisher, a spokesman for Mr. Lugar, a Republican Presidential candidate, said the board would operate "at no cost to the taxpayer" because it could levy assessments on popcorn processors. But the board could issue regulations, and violators would be subject to civil fines up to $1,000.

—*New York Times,* February 25, 1996

Weber noted, could seldom act against the wishes of his bureaucracy.

Government in the United States today, of course, does not in every respect fit Weber's classic view of bureaucracy. Court decisions, probing by the press, the Freedom of Information Act, and congressional investigations place pressure on the bureaucracy to operate in public view. Bureaucrats may prefer to operate in secrecy, but they also know they risk embarrassing public disclosure if they cover up incompetence, lavish spending, or corruption. And the expertise of the bureaucracy, while still a formidable source of power, has been balanced in part by the fact that both the president and Congress are able to access other sources of expert opinion in framing national policies. For example, the Executive Office of the President has advisers in every important policy area. Similarly, Congress has the Congressional Budget Office, the Government Accountability Office, and professional committee and office staffs to provide it and its members with expert advice.

In the 19th century, elected officials in the United States customarily rewarded their supporters with government jobs. Selection of bureaucrats on the basis of merit rather than politics was the goal of the civil service reform movement of the late 19th century.

One result was that during the first third of the 20th century, classic theories of public administration emerged that were rooted in the civil service reform movement. As Dwight Waldo noted, early theorists in the field of public administration concluded that "politics and administration are distinct" and that "politics in any 'bad' sense ought not to intrude upon administration."[7] Today, however, political scientists recognize that politics and bureaucracy are inseparable, and that bureaucratic decision making involves political as well as policy choices.

Since bureaucrats have great discretion in the deci-

## Donald Duck Goes to Washington

WASHINGTON—The General Accounting Office disclosed Thursday that it put Donald Duck's name on the payroll of the Department of Housing and Urban Development, and gave him a salary of $99,999 a year—without being challenged.

The department's computer, which is supposed to head off such shenanigans, not only failed to detect the "hiring" of the cartoon character, it raised no objections to a salary more than twice the legal limit, $47,500, for civil service pay.

It was not revealed what, if any, task the loquacious duck was supposed to perform at HUD, where 16,000 employees are charged with "providing for sound development of the nation's communities and metropolitan areas."

Officials of the GAO, Congress' watchdog over federal spending, disclosed the incident in testimony before the subcommittee on compensation and employee benefits of the House Post Office and Civil Service Committee.

—*Los Angeles Times,* October 27, 1978

"99,999 bucks! I've been working here in Washington for 30 years, and I only make 72,000!"

"I'm sorry, dear, but you knew I was a bureaucrat when you married me."

sions they make, a central problem is how to make bureaucracy accountable to popular control—in short, how to reconcile bureaucracy and democracy.[8]

Because civil servants are not elected and are free of direct control by the voters, the bureaucracy is semipermanent in character and, at times, an independent center of power. Moreover, a government agency may yield to pressure from an interest group or from some narrow segment of society rather than respond to broader public interests.

There is another danger. The executive branch may abuse its power and seek to misuse the bureaucracy—particularly police and intelligence agencies—against its political opponents. So, at the same time that it is responsive, bureaucracy, particularly in its law enforcement and regulatory functions, must also, in some degree, be independent. If it is too responsive, it may yield to improper political pressures.

The bureaucracy also must be effective if government is to solve the social problems that face it. A job-training program that fails to help many displaced workers but creates jobs for bureaucrats, or a clean air program that issues regulations but fails to eliminate smog, adds to the taxpayers' burden without alleviating social ills.

Today, many students of public administration contend that bureaucracy should be designed to serve people and to be sensitive to human needs and social inequality. They argue that the first goal of bureaucracy should not be efficiency and economy, but influencing and carrying out public policies "which more generally improve the quality of life for all."[9]

Key Question

In this chapter we will explore a key question: ***Can a large bureaucracy be efficient and effective and meet social needs in a democratic system? Or by its very nature, does bureaucracy tend to become inefficient and unresponsive to people's needs?*** There are a number of other complex questions to consider in assessing the role of public administration in a democracy: Can government really be "too big" if people demand increased services? Should the federal bureaucracy be broken up and decentralized, and power shifted to the states?

Closely tied to these questions is the important issue of whether the bureaucracy has been captured by industry or other interest groups, whether government regulators are tools of the regulated. In other words, to whom is the bureaucracy responsive? Does the bureaucracy make public policy solely by its own decisions? Can the president or Congress control it? In a democracy this is a serious question, for democratic institutions should be responsive to the people. How effective are the checks on bureaucratic power?

## Bureaucracy and the Policy Process

In theory, bureaucrats are simply public servants who administer policy decisions made by the accountable officials of the government—the president, his principal appointees, and Congress. In fact, government administrators by their actions—or inaction—often make policy. That is, they play an important role in choosing among alternative goals and selecting the programs to achieve those goals. As Francis E. Rourke has noted, "Bureaucrats themselves have now become a central factor in the policy process: in the initiation of proposals, the weighing of alternatives, and the resolution of conflict."[10]

Moreover, there is no single bureaucracy in America, and the term is not limited to the federal govern-

Drawing by Jeff MacNelly from *A Political Bestiary* by Eugene J. McCarthy and James J. Kilpatrick, McGraw-Hill Book Company, 1979.

"Among the most familiar creatures of the political seas is the Bloated Bureaucracy . . . it cannot be hurried; it swims at its own pace."

ment: Bureaucrats administer programs at every level, down to the smallest units of state and local government. Public administration in the United States is fragmented by the system of federalism. And at each level of government there are hundreds of bureaus and divisions.

Bureaucrats have great discretionary powers; what they decide to do, or not to do, constitutes a policy output of the political system. Bureaucrats have discretion when the power they exercise leaves them "free to make a choice among possible courses of action or inaction."[11]

Bureaucrats also help to shape policy through the advice they give to elected officials. The elected officials have the final say on decisions, but their choices may be limited by the options the bureaucrats present to them. As a practical matter, elected officials are confined to choosing policies and programs that the bureaucracies are capable of carrying out.

## Bureaucracy and Client Groups

The American bureaucracy is deeply involved in politics as well as policy. As in the case of the president and members of Congress, government agencies also have **constituencies**—interest groups, or client groups, either directly regulated by the bureaucracy or vitally affected by its decisions.

Sometimes, through close political and personal association between a government agency and its client group, the regulating agency becomes a captive of the industry it is supposed to regulate. "In its most developed form," Rourke observes, "the relationship between an interest group and an administrative agency is so close that it is difficult to know where the group leaves off and the agency begins."[12] One reason for this close relationship is that a bureaucracy is often able to increase its political strength by building a constituency. As Rourke notes: "The groups an agency provides tangible benefits to are the most natural basis of . . . political support, and it is with these interest groups that agencies ordinarily establish the firmest alliances. Such groups have often been responsible for the establishment of the agency in the first place. Thereafter, the agency and the group are bound together by deeply rooted ties that may be economic, political, or social in character."[13]

Viewed in this light, the behavior of the bureaucracy becomes somewhat predictable. Thus, the Agriculture Department is a natural representative for farmers; the Commerce Department is friendly toward business; and the Pentagon is allied with defense contractors. These close relationships illustrate how some government agencies have mobilized the support of client groups.

Client groups do not always dominate, however. Although a government bureau may be influenced by its clients, it may at the same time be sensitive to, and responsive to, pressures from the public, Congress, and other actors in the political system. For example, often bureaucrats are particularly sensitive to the wishes of the congressional committees that monitor their activities and control their appropriations. At the same time, many senior bureaucrats complain that they are subject to so many pressures and controls that they are unable to do the work that the law requires their agency to perform.

The bureaucracy acts and reacts in a political way. It responds to a variety of pressures because it is at once accountable to several groups—its clients, the public at large, the press, Congress, and the president. Public administrators, in short, play a major role in the American political system, and their decisions are of crucial importance to government and society as a whole.

## Bureaucracy and Congress

In addition to client groups, another source of bureaucratic power stems from the political support that an agency may enjoy in Congress, particularly among influential committee chairs. For a long time, the military services were able to count on the friendly support of powerful chairmen of the House and Senate Armed Services Committees. Similarly, the FBI and the CIA long enjoyed the protection of a small group of influential representatives and senators.

But not always. In the mid-1970s Congress investigated and exposed illegal or questionable operations by both the FBI and the CIA. In the mid-1990s, both agencies were severely criticized in Congress. The CIA was

© CNN via Getty Images

FBI agent Robert Hanssen is arrested for espionage in 2001.

taken to task over the disclosure that Aldrich H. Ames, a CIA officer, had betrayed the agency's secrets to Moscow, costing the lives of 10 Soviets serving as CIA agents and causing the imprisonment of several others.[14] The FBI was criticized after the arrest in 2001 of Robert P. Hanssen, a special agent who spied for Moscow over more than two decades.[15] Both intelligence agencies were blamed for the failure to uncover and warn of the terrorist plot that led to the 9/11 attacks on the World Trade Center and the Pentagon. And in the aftermath of the invasion of Iraq in 2003, the CIA was severely faulted for wrongly estimating that stockpiles of weapons of mass destruction would be found in that country.

Agencies that do not have cordial relations with important members of the legislative branch may find their power diminished. The Department of Energy (DOE) was battered by congressional critics in the year 2000 after a series of security lapses at the Los Alamos National Laboratory in New Mexico, including the disappearance for a time of computer hard drives containing secrets of the nation's nuclear weapons program. The government prosecuted one scientist at the laboratory, Wen Ho Lee, whom it suspected of revealing secret data about nuclear weapons to China. But the government lacked evidence that Lee had ever done so. He was charged instead with 59 counts of removing and downloading nuclear secrets onto computer tapes. Lee pleaded guilty in 2000 to only one charge of mishandling classified information. He said he threw the tapes he had made into a dumpster at the lab, but the FBI was unable to retrieve them to verify his account. The judge apologized to Lee and strongly denounced the government for its harsh treatment of the mild-mannered scientist, who had been shackled and kept in solitary confinement for nine months.

Other agencies have fared better than DOE. The U.S. Army Corps of Engineers is a classic example of a federal agency that won virtually independent status by mobilizing political support in the legislative branch. Its river-and-harbor, navigation, and flood-control projects brought important benefits to local communities—and to members of Congress in those districts.[16]

Government agencies exert considerable effort to maintain cordial relations with Capitol Hill. That task has become more complex in recent years because congressional reforms have resulted in the creation of many new subcommittees, and the agencies must deal with them. The cabinet departments employ hundreds of people to engage in liaison with Congress. Liaison offi-

© Joe Raedle/Newsmakers/Getty Images

Wen Ho Lee celebrates his release from prison in 2000.

cers watch over legislation concerning their agencies; they also field requests that members of Congress make on behalf of constituents who have business pending before their agency.

Political scientist Morris P. Fiorina has formulated an intriguing theory about the symbiotic relationship between Congress and the bureaucracy. He suggested that "the Washington System" follows a cycle: First, members of Congress earn credit from their constituents by establishing federal programs. Second, the legislation is drafted in very general terms, so that some government agency must create rules and regulations—which means "the trampling of numerous toes. At the next stage, aggrieved and/or hopeful constituents petition their members of Congress to intervene in the complex (or at least obscure) decision processes of the bureaucracy. The cycle closes when the congressman lends a sympathetic ear, piously denounces the evils of bureaucracy, intervenes in the latter's decisions, and rides a grateful electorate to ever more impressive electoral showings. Congressmen take credit coming and going. They are the alpha and the omega."[17]

Few members of Congress have ever served in the bureaucracy, a factor that adds to the tensions between legislators and bureaucrats. By contrast, in Britain, with its parliamentary system, many members of Parliament have been, or hope to be, cabinet ministers or junior ministers. As a result, the gulf between lawmakers and bureaucrats in Britain is much narrower.

Of course, in the relationship between Congress and the bureaucracy, the bureaucracy is not without powerful resources. Members of Congress, for example, are particularly sensitive to any plans by the Defense Department to close military bases in their districts. And when some members of Congress talked about reducing the subsidies for rail lines, Amtrak countered by revealing plans for reduced operations. As Fiorina pointed out, "Just coincidentally, lines to be eliminated seemed to run through the districts of critical members of the Appropriations and Commerce committees."[18]

## Bureaucracy, Triangles, and Subgovernments

The bureaucracy, interest groups, and congressional committees interact. In some areas, such as agriculture and defense, the relationship among the three actors is so close that it is sometimes referred to as a **triangle,** an **iron triangle,** or a **subgovernment.** (See Figure 14-1.) Although the terms may vary, they refer essentially to the same phenomenon: a powerful alliance of mutual benefit among an agency or unit of the government, an interest group, and a committee or subcommittee of Congress.

As Robert L. Lineberry has suggested, in such a situation, policymaking is a result of "close cooperation and interaction among these triads of power." Lineberry adds: "When a group becomes strong enough, it gets a part of the government, its own piece of the action. The measure of an interest group's strength is how many 'shares' of the government it controls. 'Little' interests, such as the fisheries or tobacco growers, may have only an agency or two within a cabinet department and only a subcommittee of Congress. 'Big' interests, such as business and labor, have whole cabinet departments."[19]

**FIGURE 14-1**

**The Veterans Affairs "Triangle"**

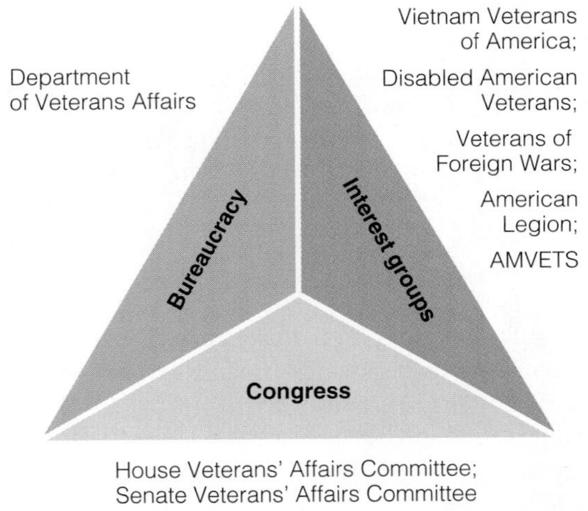


There are numerous examples of triangles or subgovernments. In many cases the movement of people among the three corners of the triangle is also an important element; a Pentagon general may, after a required waiting period, end up as a lobbyist for a missile manufacturer, or a staff member of the House Armed Services Committee may go to work for a defense contractor. Typically, in such triangles, many of the participants know one another and play "musical chairs," changing jobs within the triangle.

The existence of such triangles or subgovernments raises questions about the nature of the pluralist system. Instead of competing with one another, some analysts argue, interest groups merely capture a segment of the bureaucracy and call it their own.[20]

For most government agencies today, however, Francis Rourke has argued, the "highly exclusionary" closed system of iron triangles "is long gone."[21] In Rourke's view, this is the result of greater openness in the bureaucracy enforced by Congress, the increase in the number of competing interest groups trying to influence agency policies, and the increased power of the news media.[22] Moreover, client groups today, Rourke has observed, are "less supportive and considerably less deferential toward their administrative patrons than was once the case."[23]

## Issue Networks: The Policy Activists

While the concept of iron triangles and subgovernments is helpful, it may not tell the whole story. Political scientist Hugh Heclo has suggested that **issue networks,** a loose grouping of people and organizations who seek to influence policy formation, play an important role in the shaping of public policy. As Heclo has defined it, "An issue network is a shared-knowledge group having to do with some aspect . . . of public policy."[24] As the term implies, issue networks are made up of "policy activists, those who care deeply about a set of issues and are determined to shape the fabric of public policy accordingly."[25]

In Heclo's model, an issue network is rather fluid, a loose grouping of people and organizations who seek to influence policy formation. Thus, an issue network is not as easily identifiable or as neatly categorized as an iron triangle or subgovernment: "Looking for the closed triangles of control, we tend to miss the fairly open networks of people that increasingly impinge upon government."[26]

These loose networks of policy activists not only help to shape the programs that the government adopts, Heclo contends, but increasingly they influence the appointment of the bureaucrats who administer those programs. Presidents today may be somewhat less likely than in the past to appoint party politicians to fill cabinet and subcabinet posts. Instead, they tend to choose executives whose reputations have been established by word of mouth in the various issue networks that swirl and merge around the policy process in Washington.

# The Politics of Bureaucracy

A new cabinet secretary in Washington often discovers that a title does not assure actual authority over his or her department. "I was like a sea captain who finds himself on the deck of a ship that he has never seen before," wrote one. "I did not know the mechanism of my ship; I did not know my officers—even by sight—and I had no acquaintance with the crew."[27]

As the cabinet member had quickly realized, the bureaucracy has its own sources of power that enable it to resist political authority. Cabinet secretaries come and go; the civil service remains. The expert technician in charge of a bureau within a department may have carved out considerable independence over the years and may resent the efforts of a political appointee to take control of the bureau.

This was precisely the problem Bill Richardson faced when President Clinton appointed him secretary of energy in 1998. In attempting to improve security at Los Alamos and the other DOE weapons laboratories, Richardson discovered that the scientists at the labs resisted rules and regulations designed to protect secrets. Scientists by nature and training are used to a free exchange of ideas, a culture that ran counter to the secretary's efforts to tighten security. The problems at Los Alamos and the other national laboratories sank Richardson's hopes of running for vice president on the Democratic ticket in 2000; he was elected governor of New Mexico two years later.

In Francis Rourke's study of the politics of bureaucracy, he developed three central themes: the bureaucracy exercises an *impact on policy;* it does so by *mobilizing political support* and *applying its expertise.*[28] As Rourke points out, the growth of the civil service and the removal of much of the appointment power from politics does not mean that politics has been removed from the bureaucracy. Quite the contrary: Federal departments and bureaus are extremely sensitive to the winds of politics. A request or inquiry from a member of Congress usually brings speedy action by a government agency—the officials in that agency know where appropriations come from.

Furthermore, in mobilizing support, the bureaucracy practices politics, often in expert fashion. The bureaucracy draws support from three areas—the public, Congress, and the executive branch.[29]

## Bureaucracy and Public Opinion

A government agency that enjoys wide public support has an advantage over agencies that do not. The president and Congress are both sensitive to public opinion, and a popular, prestigious agency may receive more appropriations and achieve greater independence than others. In the mid-1970s it was disclosed that the FBI under J. Edgar Hoover had committed burglaries to search for evidence or to gather intelligence, and in other ways had violated the constitutional rights of Americans.[30] But for more than four decades, the FBI had managed to build such a favorable image with the general public that, until Hoover's death in 1972, both the bureau and its chief enjoyed a status of virtual independence. No president of the United States dared to fire J. Edgar Hoover.*

During the 1960s the National Aeronautics and Space Administration (NASA) and its Apollo astronauts captured the public imagination. To enable it to place men on the moon in 1969, NASA received massive appropriations at a time when some Americans were demanding a reordering of national priorities to meet social needs on earth.

In order to improve their image and enlist public support for their programs, many federal agencies employ substantial numbers of public relations people and information officials. These information specialists issue news releases and answer questions from members of the press and the general public. One CBS News study, which the network dubbed its "Flack Census," estimated that the executive branch employed 10,858 people in

*Hoover's confidential files, in which he squirreled away potentially embarrassing information about political leaders, were another significant source of his extraordinary power.

Astronauts Neil A. Armstrong and Edward "Buzz" Aldrin walk on the moon, July 20, 1969.

© AP/Wide World Photos

public relations activities.[31] In one year, the Department of Defense alone listed 1,066 civilian and military public relations officials worldwide at a cost of $44.3 million.[32] And the actual cost and number of people performing public relations activities in the federal government are probably much higher than the "official" figures.

## Bureaucracy and the President

The image of the department head as a sea captain aboard a strange ship with an unknown crew may be applied as well to a president seeking control over the bureaucracy. President Kennedy was particularly exasperated by vacillation and delay in the foreign policy bureaucracy. "The State Department is a bowl of jelly," he once declared. "It's got all those people over there who are constantly smiling. I think we need to smile less and be tougher."[33]

Other presidents have voiced similar complaints. Franklin Roosevelt complained that it was "almost impossible" to get results from the Treasury Department. Then he added:

> But the Treasury is not to be compared with the State Department. You should go through the experience of trying to get any changes in the thinking, policy, and action of the career diplomats. . . . But the Treasury and the State Department put together are nothing compared with the Na-a-vy. The admirals are really something to cope with—and I should know. To change anything in the Na-a-vy is like punching a feather bed. You punch it with your right and you punch it with your left until you are finally exhausted, and then you find the damn bed just as it was before you started punching.[34]

Often, presidents try to gain tighter control of the bureaucracy by reorganizing its structure. After the Second World War, efforts toward administrative reform led in 1947 to creation of the first of two Hoover Commissions. Formally designated the Commission on Organization of the Executive Branch of the Government, the study panel was headed by former President Herbert Hoover. It first reported in 1949, and of its nearly 300 recommendations for streamlining, simplifying, and centralizing authority in the federal government, about half were adopted.[35]

Since 1918 Congress has from time to time given presidents the right to restructure the executive branch. Presidents have made extensive use of this power under a series of reorganization acts passed since 1939; this power was increased by the Reorganization Act of 1949 and granted to later presidents for varying lengths of time.

The creation in 1970 of the Office of Management and Budget (OMB) was designed to shift to the president and his budget officials tighter control over management of the federal bureaucracy. Since 1921 presidents have been required to submit to Congress an annual budget for the federal government. OMB is a unit of the Executive Office of the President. (See Chapter 13.)

The budget process, which OMB manages, can be a major tool of presidential control over the executive branch. The federal government runs on a fiscal year that starts October 1 and ends the following September 30. Each spring, agencies and departments begin planning their requests for the fiscal year starting 17 months later. Matching these requests against economic forecasts and revenue estimates from his advisers, the president establishes budget guidelines; within this framework individual agency requests are studied by OMB and presented to the president for decision. Unless there is a political deadlock between the president and Congress, as has

Culver Pictures, Inc.

Franklin Delano Roosevelt: "But the Treasury and the State Department . . . are nothing compared with the Na-a-vy."

sometimes occurred, the budget then goes to Capitol Hill in January.

The infighting and competition among government agencies for a slice of the budget pie give the president, through OMB, an important lever for bureaucratic control. Indeed, as Aaron Wildavsky observed, "the budget lies at the heart of the political process."[36] Moreover, the bureaucrat "whose requests are continually turned down in Congress finds that he tends to be rejected and in his own department as well. . . . [OMB] finds itself treating agencies it dislikes much better than those it may like better but who cannot help themselves nearly as much in Congress."[37]

## Bureaucracy and Policymaking

In theory, presidents make policy and bureaucrats carry it out. In fact, officials often play a major role in policy formation. In large part, this is because presidents rely on bureaucratic expertise in making their policy decisions. Frederick C. Mosher has noted the tendency of professionals with "specialized knowledge, science, and rationality" to dominate many areas of the bureaucracy.[38] On the other hand, that kind of expertise is a less reliable source of bureaucratic power today. As Francis Rourke has observed, "the private sector now abounds with think tanks, consulting firms, and watchdog groups that are widely regarded as more reliable sources of information and advice than the government itself."[39]

Other factors have combined to reduce the influence of bureaucrats in setting policy agendas. For example, the "divided government" that has characterized the American political system during some administrations has reduced the influence of the bureaucracy. During the Reagan years, for example, Republicans controlled the White House and competed with the Democrats, who controlled the House of Representatives and, for two years, the Senate. In these circumstances, the White House sought to centralize executive power in the president's hands, while Congress tried to "micromanage" the bureaucrats. The result in each case was less power and discretion for the administrators.[40]

But presidents who rely too much on such expertise may get into trouble. For example, in April 1980, President Carter ordered a military force to attempt to rescue the American hostages being held in the U.S. embassy in Iran. Although the secretary of defense, Harold Brown, and the Joint Chiefs of Staff had apparently assured the president the mission would have a reasonable chance of success, Operation Eagle Claw failed. It also cost the lives of eight American servicemen, who died when a helicopter and a transport plane crashed into each other on the ground in a remote desert staging area. Of course, Carter was not only relying on his military experts. He undoubtedly felt that a successful rescue mission would be of enormous political benefit to him in an election year.

Other administrations have suffered similar setbacks. In 1961 President Kennedy approved a CIA plan to invade Cuba and topple Premier Fidel Castro. After the invasion of the Bay of Pigs proved a disaster, Kennedy publicly took responsibility for the mess, although privately he complained: "All my life I've known better than to depend on the experts. How could I have been so stupid, to let them go ahead?"[41] Of the Joint Chiefs of

Iran rescue mission, 1980: the advisers . . .

. . . the result



Staff, who had approved the CIA plan, Kennedy bitterly told a visitor: "They don't know any more about it than anyone else."[42]

Just as federal officials can promote policies that get the nation into trouble, they also can be instrumental in changing those policies. In 1968, during the war in Vietnam, several high-level Pentagon officials privately urged Clark M. Clifford, the secretary of defense, to try to bring about a reversal of President Johnson's Vietnam policy. As Clifford studied administration policy in Vietnam—and a request by the military for 206,000 more troops—he gradually became convinced of the folly of further escalation. Although his warm friendship with the president "grew suddenly formal and cool," Clifford and an advisory group of prestigious civilians were apparently instrumental in persuading the president to reverse his policies.[43]

## A Profile of the American Bureaucracy

### Who Are the Administrators?

In 1792 the federal government had 780 employees. Today there are 2,677,999 civilian employees of the federal government.[44] A study of this total reveals some surprising facts. In the first place, "the bureaucracy in Washington" is not in Washington—at least most of it is not.

One recent statistical breakdown, for example, showed that only 327,270 government employees—about 12 percent of the federal total—worked in the metropolitan Washington area. The rest were scattered throughout the 50 states and overseas. California alone had 244,863 federal workers, and 73,702 federal employees worked overseas.[45]

In addition to workers on the federal payroll, however, several million people work indirectly for the federal government. These employees work for defense contractors, as outside consultants, or in other programs funded by the government. Some of this outside consulting work has been criticized as wasteful or as a way of expanding the bureaucracy without seeming to do so.

In 2006 one-quarter (25.2 percent) of the civilian

### The Paper Chase

The sheer volume of paper generated by the federal bureaucracy has long been the target of criticism. In one year, according to the government's own figures, it took Americans 913 million hours to fill out 4,900 different kinds of government forms. Congress, responding to public complaints about the amount of paperwork demanded by the government, established the Commission on Federal Paperwork. The task of the commission was to reduce the flood of official paper.

The commission acquired a staff of some three dozen people and issued 36 reports and 770 recommendations before it went out of business in 1977. Its major recommendation was that a new cabinet-level Department of Administration be created to manage federal paperwork.

Congress was less than enthusiastic over the idea of creating yet another bureaucracy to manage the bureaucracy. Representative Peter H. Kostmayer, a Pennsylvania Democrat, declared: "We can encourage each department to tighten up its operations without hiring thousands of more bureaucrats who, as we know, have an unsurpassed ability to produce paperwork." Congress did not establish the new department.

—Adapted from Congressional Quarterly, *Weekly Report,* December 10, 1977; and *New York Times,* December 1, 1979 employees of the federal government worked for the Department of Defense. The 675,111 civilian workers in the Pentagon and other military installations, added to the 758,035 employees of the Postal Service and the 235,654 in the Department of Veterans Affairs, composed almost two-thirds (62.3%) of the entire federal bureaucracy. In contrast, the State Department employed only 33,945 people.[46]

The federal civilian bureaucracy of 2,677,999 people is unquestionably large compared with private industry; Wal-Mart, the biggest corporation in America, and in the world, had more than 1.8 million employees in 2003. Yet federal civilian workers comprise only 13 percent of total government employment—federal, state, and local—in the United States. More than five times as many people work for state and local governments as for the federal government.

According to one Census Bureau analysis, local governments had 11,379,390 employees, 39 percent of them teachers, and state governments employed about 5,072,130 people.[47]

A comparison of federal, state, and local bureaucracies is shown in Figure 14-2. A rough portrait can be drawn of the "average" man or woman in the federal service: He or she is 46.8 years old, has worked for the government for 16.6 years, and earns an annual salary of $61,714.[48] The president receives $400,000 a year, the vice president $212,100, and members of the cabinet $183,500. The great majority of federal workers are members of the career civil service, with their salaries in most cases fixed on a General Schedule that ranges from

© Justin Sullivan/Getty Images

The Postal Service has the most civilian employees.

FIGURE 14-2

**Government Employment—Federal, State, and Local**

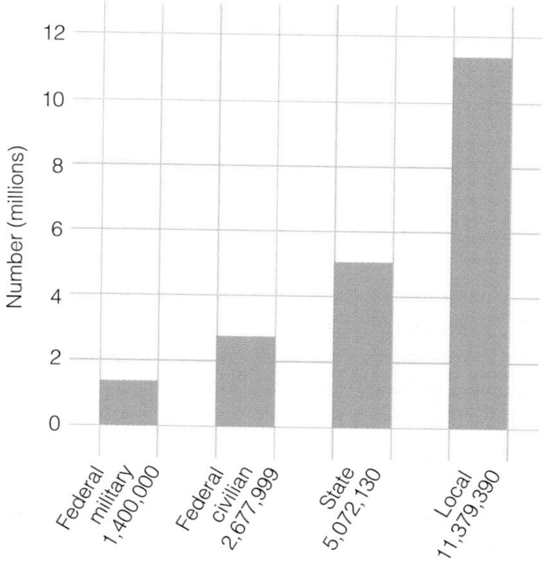


SOURCES: Data for military, U.S. Department of Defense, 2002; for civilian workforce, for local and state governments, U.S. Bureau of the Census, 2005. Federal military includes active, reserve, and National Guard.

a starting salary of $16,352 for clerks (GS-1) to $118,957 for a relative handful of top civil servants (GS-15).[49] However, members of the Senior Executive Service (SES), a group of high-level administrators and managers at the top of the government bureaucracy, can earn salaries ranging up to $165,200.[50]

What kinds of workers make up the bureaucracy? Although almost half a million fit the conventional image of bureaucrats—general administrative and clerical employees—the government also employs 20,452 electronic engineers; 65,932 computer specialists; 46,692 nurses; 24,010 air traffic controllers; and 37,409 criminal investigators. Among federal white-collar workers, 786,118 (49.1 percent) are women.[51]

## The Structure of the Bureaucracy

As noted in Chapter 13, the federal bureaucracy consists of three basic types of agencies: the cabinet departments, the executive agencies, and the independent regulatory agencies. Figure 14-3 shows the major executive branch agencies as of the year 2004, but approximately 100 smaller independent units of government existed, some even too small to warrant a line in the *United States Government Manual.*

As Richard E. Neustadt once emphasized, the executive branch is not a monolith: "Like our governmental structure as a whole, the executive establishment consists of separated institutions sharing powers. The president heads one of these; cabinet officers, agency administrators, and military commanders head others."[52]

A president attempts to control the bureaucracy through his White House staff and other units of the Executive Office of the President—particularly the Office of Management and Budget—and through his department heads. Because of the sheer size of the federal government, however, no president can really hope to supervise all the activities of the administrators. And the effort to control the bureaucracy has led to the growth of the White House staff—creating a new bureaucracy at the presidential level. Thus, attempts to control bureaucracy may create new layers of bureaucracy.

**The Cabinet Departments** The 15 **cabinet departments** are major components of the federal bureaucracy. Some idea of the structure of the executive branch and the problem of presidential control can be grasped by studying the organizational chart of a cabinet department. At first glance, it might appear to be a tightly organized agency, with lines of authority flowing upward to the secretary, who in turn reports to the president. In fact, the chart masks entrenched bureaus and key civil servants, some of whom enjoy close outside ties with interest groups and congressional committees—relationships that give them power independent of the cabinet secretary and the president. The sheer size of most departments would seem to defy presidential control. To take one example, the Department of Transportation, formed in 1966, had more than 53,000 employees in 2006. As shown in Figure 14-4, the department was headed by a secretary, a deputy secretary, and an under-secretary for policy, and five assistant secretaries.

In addition, several major agencies—with sometimes competitive client groups—were loosely grouped under the Department of Transportation, including the Federal Aviation Administration (FAA), the Federal Railroad Administration, the Federal Highway Administration, and the Maritime Administration. Although the organizational chart does not show it, the Department of Transportation, like the other cabinet departments, is dispersed geographically. The air traffic controllers of the FAA operate airport towers across the United States; the Federal Highway Administration has field offices in several cities.

President George W. Bush meets with his cabinet.

The creation of the cabinet departments parallels the growth of the American nation. Only three departments—State, War, and Treasury—were created in 1789. But new areas of concern have required the establishment of executive departments to meet new problems. This fact is reflected in the names of some of the departments created in past decades—Housing and Urban Development in 1965, Transportation in 1966, Energy in 1977, Education in 1979, Health and Human Services, also in 1979, and the Department of Homeland Security in 2003.[53]

**The Executive Agencies** The **executive agencies** are units of government under the president, within the executive branch, that are not part of a cabinet department. They do, however, report to the president in the same manner as departments and therefore are not independent of the president. Their heads are appointed by the president and may be dismissed by him. The executive agencies include several powerful units of the bureaucracy, such as NASA, the CIA, and the Environmental Protection Agency, to name a few.

Grouped with the executive agencies but somewhat different in status are **government corporations,** agencies that were at one time semiautonomous, but through legislation since 1945 have been placed under presidential control. In 1970 Congress abolished the Post Office as a cabinet department and established the U.S. Postal Service as an independent, government-owned corporation. The hope, at least, was to increase efficiency, remove postal employees from politics, and give the new service power to raise rates to meet expenses.

But new forms of organization do not automatically solve bureaucratic problems. Although the Postal Service made efforts to streamline its operations, many citizens have complained that under the new system postal rates have increased but the mail often remains slow in reaching its destination. As one result, several private delivery services, such as Federal Express and UPS (United Parcel Service), compete actively with the government. To try to keep up with its competitors in the private sector, the Postal Service has offered some innovations; beginning in 2004, for example, customers could go online or telephone and have packages picked up the next day, avoiding a trip to (and sometimes long lines at) the post office. And online shopping has improved Postal Service revenues because many shippers mail packages to their customers.

Some other examples of government corporations are the Federal Deposit Insurance Corporation (FDIC), which protects bank deposits, and the Tennessee Valley Authority (TVA), which has built dams and provided hydroelectric power and other economic benefits to an area covering seven states.

**The Independent Regulatory Agencies** The **independent regulatory agencies** exercise quasi-judicial and quasi-legislative powers and are administratively independent of the president, Congress, and the courts. These agencies thus occupy a special status in the bureaucracy. In fact, however, as has been made abundantly clear over the years, the regulatory agencies and commissions are sometimes susceptible to pressures from the White House, Congress, and the industries they regulate.

The regulatory agencies decide such questions as who will receive a license to operate a television station or build a natural gas pipeline to serve a large city. These licenses and franchises are worth millions of dollars, and the competition for them is fierce. As a result, the regulatory agencies are the target of intense pressures, including, at times, approaches by skillful and well-paid

## FIGURE 14-3

### Executive Branch of Government

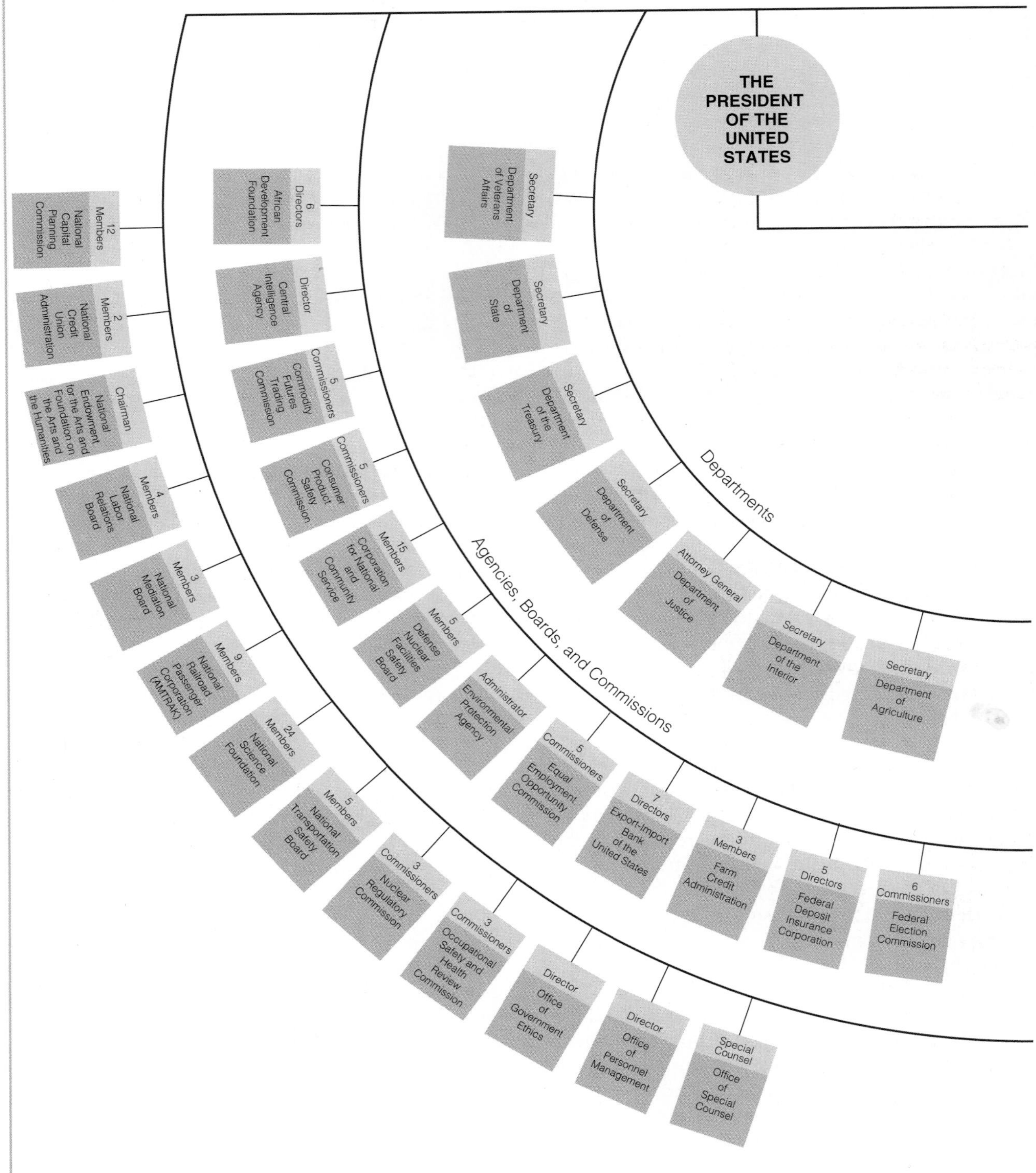


SOURCE: Adapted from National Archives and Records Administration, online at <http://www.gpoaccess.gov/gmanual/browse.html>.

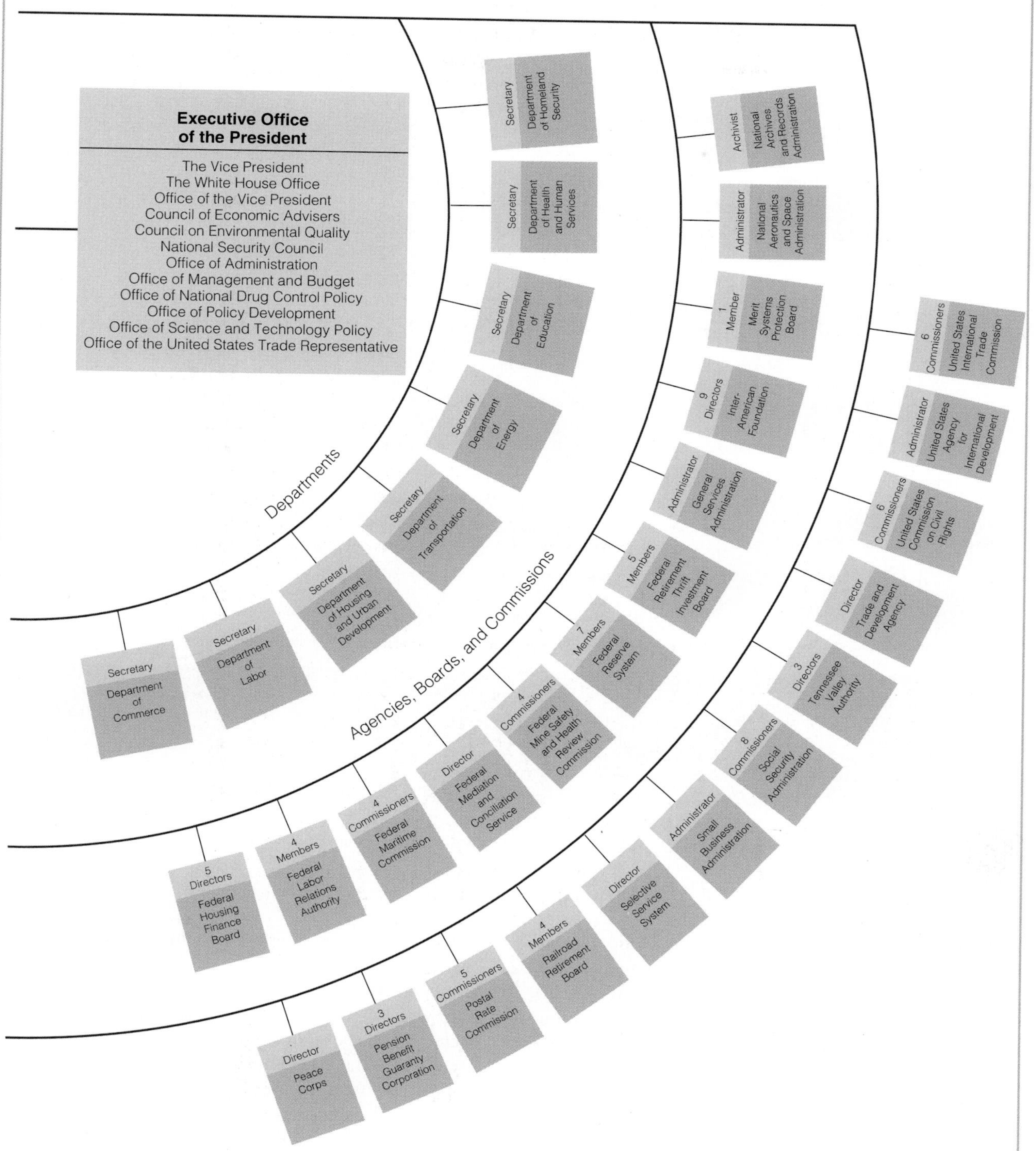

Executive Office of the President
The Vice President
The White House Office
Office of the Vice President
Council of Economic Advisers
Council on Environmental Quality
National Security Council
Office of Administration
Office of Management and Budget
Office of National Drug Control Policy
Office of Policy Development
Office of Science and Technology Policy
Office of the United States Trade Representative
Departments
Secretary Department of Homeland Security
Secretary Department of Health and Human Services
Secretary Department of Education
Secretary Department of Energy
Secretary Department of Transportation
Secretary Department of Housing and Urban Development
Secretary Department of Labor
Secretary Department of Commerce
Agencies, Boards, and Commissions
Archivist National Archives and Records Administration
Administrator National Aeronautics and Space Administration
1 Member Merit Systems Protection Board
9 Directors Inter-American Foundation
Administrator General Services Administration
5 Members Federal Retirement Thrift Investment Board
7 Members Federal Reserve System
4 Commissioners Federal Mine Safety and Health Review Commission
Director Federal Mediation and Conciliation Service
4 Commissioners Federal Maritime Commission
4 Members Federal Labor Relations Authority
5 Directors Federal Housing Finance Board
6 Commissioners United States International Trade Commission
Administrator United States Agency for International Development
6 Commissioners United States Commission on Civil Rights
Director Trade and Development Agency
3 Directors Tennessee Valley Authority
8 Commissioners Social Security Administration
Administrator Small Business Administration
Director Selective Service System
4 Members Railroad Retirement Board
5 Commissioners Postal Rate Commission
3 Directors Pension Benefit Guaranty Corporation
Director Peace Corps

FIGURE 14-4

**Department of Transportation**

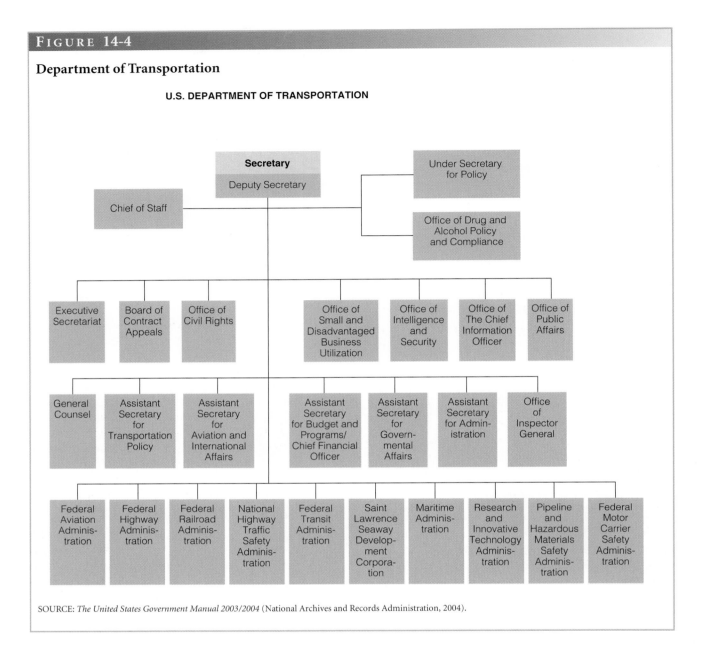

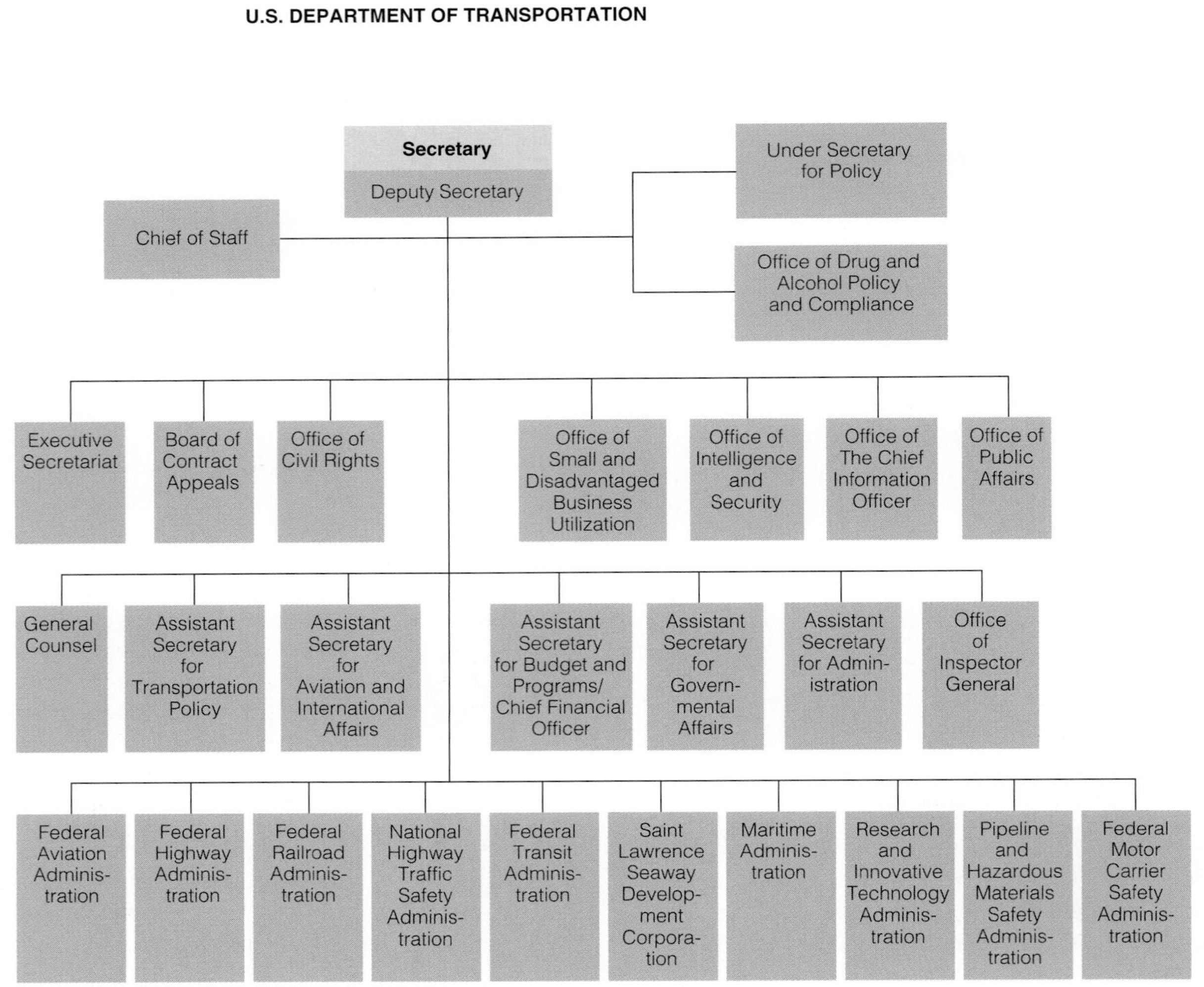


SOURCE: *The United States Government Manual 2003/2004* (National Archives and Records Administration, 2004).

Washington lawyers who go in the "back door" to argue their clients' cases in private meetings with agency officials. The Government-in-the-Sunshine Act (1976), which opened up most agency meetings to the public and also prohibited secret contacts, was designed to discourage such ex parte (one-sided) backdoor meetings. However, the Supreme Court later appeared to allow the agencies more latitude in their contacts with regulated industries.[54]

The regulatory agencies were created because of the need for rule making and regulation in highly complex, technical areas involving the interests of the public. In awarding licenses, they also exercise a quasi-judicial function. Despite the separation of powers provided for in the Constitution, regulatory agencies combine aspects of all three branches of government—legislative, executive, and judicial.

Commission members are appointed by the president with the consent of the Senate, but unlike cabinet members, they do not report to the president. Although members of the regulatory commissions cannot, by law, all be drawn from the same political party, the president designates the chairperson. Through his appointive powers a president may in time gain political control of the commissions.

A House inquiry into regulatory agencies some years ago demonstrated during a dramatic series of hearings that the agencies had, in many cases, become servants of industry instead of regulating in the interest of the larger public. The hearings, and subsequent disclo-

## Hold the Pepperoni: Bureaucracy Defines Pizza

There is no easy way to describe why Pizza Hut is locked in combat with the Agriculture Department. . . . Pizza Hut wants to be able to sell pepperoni pizzas to school lunch programs around the country. The Agriculture Department says the company can do that only if it puts no more than 20 slices of pepperoni on each one. . . .

What is a pizza? According to Agriculture Department reckoning, the cheese on a standard pizza makes it a dairy product unless the meat on top comes to more than 2 percent of its total weight. That translates to 20 slices of pepperoni per large pizza.

Pizza Hut can, in other words, legally sell pepperoni pizza to local schools. It just can't sell pizza with a lot of pepperoni on it, which is what it would like to do.

—*Washington Post,* October 11, 1991

sures, revealed a pattern of fraternization by commissioners and regulated industries.

Some regulatory agency members have accepted free transportation, lecture fees, hotel rooms, and gifts from businesses subject to their authority.[55] Others have left the government for well-paying jobs in the regulated industry. Many have seemed more concerned with protecting pipeline companies, airlines, railroads, and television networks than with making sure the industries are serving the public satisfactorily. On the other hand, at times, the regulatory agencies have been defenders of the public interest; for example, the Securities and Exchange Commission has protected investors from stock frauds, and the Federal Trade Commission has tried to curtail false television advertising.

The major regulatory agencies, in order of their creation, are:

1. *The Federal Trade Commission* (1914): five members, seven-year terms; regulates industry; responsible for preventing unfair competition, price fixing, deceptive advertising, mislabeling of textile and fur products, false packaging, and similar abuses.
2. *The Federal Communications Commission* (1934): five members, five-year terms; licenses and regulates all television and radio stations in the United States; regulates frequencies used by police, aviation, taxicabs, citizens' band and "ham" operators, and others; fixes rates for telephone and telegraph companies in interstate commerce.
3. *The Securities and Exchange Commission* (1934): five members, five-year terms; created to protect the public from investing in securities on the basis of false or misleading claims; requires companies offering securities for sale to file an accurate registration statement and prospectus; registers brokers; regulates stock exchanges.
4. *The Federal Energy Regulatory Commission* (1978): five members, five-year terms; although within the Department of Energy, is an independent regulatory commission; regulates and has jurisdiction over natural gas companies, electric utilities, and interstate oil pipelines.

Many other government agencies have regulatory functions in whole or in part. For example, the Federal Maritime Commission regulates shipping; the National Labor Relations Board (NLRB) prohibits unfair labor

"All those in favor of establishing government regulatory agencies say 'Aye.' "

practices; and the Board of Governors of the Federal Reserve System regulates the money supply, interest rates, and the banking industry. Many units of the regular cabinet departments also have regulatory functions. Examples include the Food and Drug Administration (FDA) in the Department of Health and Human Services; the Occupational Safety and Health Administration (OSHA) in the Labor Department; and the Antitrust Division of the Justice Department.

## Deregulation: The Pattern Changes

The government regulation of industry, which blossomed during the New Deal administration of Franklin D. Roosevelt, had, by the 1970s, become a target of criticism by many Republicans and Democrats alike. For example, President Carter, a Democrat, called for deregulation of airlines, banking, trucking, railroads, and telecommunications.

Even before Carter took office in 1977, Congress had begun exploring deregulation of the airline and other industries. The rising tide of sentiment in Congress reflected complaints by business of excessive and costly government regulation, red tape, delay, and paperwork. In 1978 Congress enacted the Airline Deregulation Act, which in 1985 ended federal control over airline routes and fares.

In 1980 Congress deregulated the trucking industry and substantially deregulated the railroads. In 1995, the oldest regulatory agency, the Interstate Commerce Commission (ICC), which had regulated the railroads, was abolished and its powers assigned to the Department of Transportation.

In the rush to deregulate, some observers felt, the government may have gone too far. The airline industry is a case in point. After airlines were deregulated in 1978, they could, with some exceptions, fly anywhere they pleased on domestic routes. As a result, major carriers dropped all service to 132 cities.[56] A number of smaller communities suffered severely because of these changes. New carriers sprang up to compete with the giants, and price wars broke out on transcontinental and other routes. The public sometimes benefited through lower air fares, and some airlines had a sharp increase in business at first. But after an initial surge of profits, the industry, beginning in 1981, operated at a loss for three years in a row. Eventually, Braniff, Pan Am, and Eastern airlines all went out of business. Thousands of airline workers lost their jobs.

Today, flight delays and cancellations have become common, with some hapless passengers stranded overnight in airport terminals or trapped for hours on planes sitting on runways, waiting to take off. Travelers in economy class were often jammed into seats that provided little legroom because the airlines tried to squeeze as many people as possible into each plane. Many passengers complained of being treated like cattle. In the airline industry, at least, deregulation had proved a mixed blessing.

The airlines were hard hit as well by the sharp drop in passenger travel in the aftermath of the 9/11 attacks, in which terrorists used commercial airliners to destroy the World Trade Center and damage the Pentagon. United Airlines, the second-largest airline after American Airlines, filed for bankruptcy in December 2002. Even after economy measures and concessions by labor unions, United lost $2.8 billion in 2003.[57] The stringent security protections felt necessary after 9/11, combined with cost cutting by the airlines, often made air travel an unpleasant experience for millions of travelers.

## The Growth of Social Regulation

Although considerable deregulation of transportation, communications, and financial institutions has taken place in recent decades, social regulation by the federal

© AP/Wide World Photos

"Flight delays and cancellations have become common."

government increased during the 1970s and 1980s. The term **social regulation** refers to laws, rules, and government programs designed to protect individual rights and specific groups, as well as to benefit society as a whole in such areas as health, worker safety, consumer protection, and the environment. For example, social regulation includes laws and rules to protect the employment rights of blacks, other minorities, and women; legislation to preserve the natural environment and to protect the public from air or water pollution; and laws and rules to guard the health and safety of employees in the workplace.

Although the authority of the federal government has been narrowed in such fields as transportation and communications, during the 1970s and 1980s the power of the Environmental Protection Agency (EPA), the Equal Employment Opportunity Commission (EEOC), and the Occupational Safety and Health Administration (OSHA) was strengthened.

But the Republican capture of Congress in 1994 coincided with a backlash against what some voters and political leaders perceived as excessive government regulation in these very areas. The Republican Congress in 1995 attempted to reduce or remove altogether a broad range of regulations designed to protect the environment. Although Congress did not achieve all of these goals, it was able to weaken the Clean Water Act and the Endangered Species Act, and it cut back funding for the EPA.

Those opposed to government rules designed to protect the environment argued that they placed burdensome requirements on businesses. Environmental groups, by contrast, contended that only the federal government could crack down on corporate polluters.

Inevitably, the relatively recent growth of federal intervention in such fields as safety and the environment was accompanied by a political struggle over the proper scope of these kinds of regulations. And underlying that conflict over specific policy issues was the larger gulf between liberals and conservatives over the role of government itself.

As Michael D. Reagan has observed, "Traditional economic regulation and the alphabet soup of New Deal regulatory commissions" were designed to control "abuses of private economic power. . . . There was . . . almost no concept of what we now call social regulation: programs designed to achieve positive social benefits in such areas as protection of health, safety, and individual rights."[58]

And public attitudes toward government regulation can vary dramatically with circumstances. In 2000, Firestone recalled 6.5 million defective tires after more than 148 deaths and more than 500 injuries were caused in accidents, most involving Ford Explorers; in many of these accidents, the tire treads had separated, causing drivers to lose control.[59] In the wake of the recall and resulting controversy, there were demands by the public, by members of Congress, and by the Department of Transportation for more stringent laws to deal with tire safety defects.[60] Before the year was out, Congress enacted legislation increasing the penalties for concealing defects and requiring U.S. manufacturers to report to American regulators when they recall tires overseas.[61]

## Those at the Top

When the newly elected president of the United States took office in January 2005, he was viewed as the leader, not only of the nation, but also of his "administration." But what, exactly, does that mean? Although no formal definition of the term exists, in general a president's administration consists of the president, the heads of the 15 cabinet departments, 425 subcabinet officials and agency heads, 183 ambassadors, and 2,800 aides, assistants, and confidential secretaries. In all, an incoming president makes approximately 4,000 key appointments, for the most part exempt from civil service competitive exams. Of this total, perhaps 1,200 are important policy advisory posts.

Most of the 2,677,999 federal civilian workers are civil servants, not "the president's men" or women. They are not appointed by him to the key policy jobs in the bureaucracy.

In presidential election years, the House Govern-

© AP/Wide World Photos

A Firestone tire from a sport utility vehicle involved in a two-car accident in Arizona

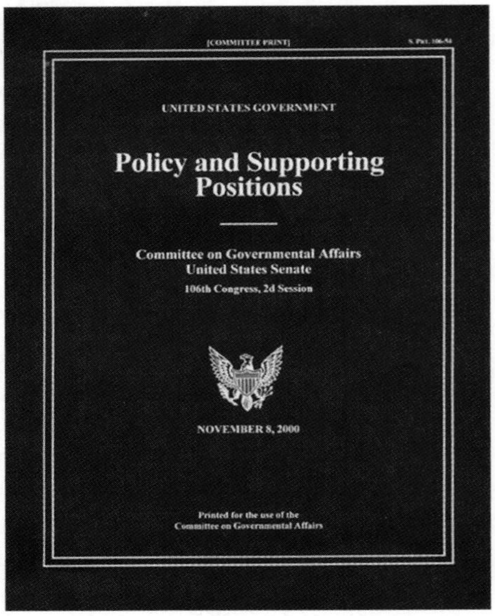


"The plum book"

© Bettmann/Corbis

Andrew Jackson was credited with introducing the "spoils system" in American politics.

ment Reform and Oversight Committee or the Senate Governmental Affairs Committee has obligingly published something known affectionately in Washington as "the plum book" (as in "political plum"), a listing of the non–civil service jobs that the incoming president may fill.[62] For White House aides who screen patronage appointees for the new administration, the plum book is an indispensable reference guide. Job-seekers in George W. Bush's administration who studied the new edition published after the 2000 presidential election found more than 7,000 positions listed in the 334-page book.

## The Civil Service

Today, the majority of government jobs are filled through the competitive civil service system. Yet presidents have always rewarded their political supporters and friends with government jobs. (In many cases, of course, presidents appoint people recommended by powerful senators or House members.) Although George Washington declared that he appointed officials on the basis of "fitness of character," he favored members of his own party, the Federalists. Jefferson dismissed hundreds of Federalists when he became president, replacing them with members of his own party.

**The Spoils System** After Andrew Jackson was elected in 1828, he dismissed more than a third of the 612 presidentially appointed officeholders and 10 to 20 percent of the 10,000 lesser government officials. Although Jackson thereby continued a practice started by Jefferson, he is generally credited with introducing to the national government the **spoils system,** the practice, known more often today as **political patronage,** under which victorious politicians reward their followers with jobs. (Jackson preferred to call it "rotation in office.")

In 1832 Senator William Learned Marcy of New York, defending a Jackson ambassadorial appointment, declared: "To the victor belong the spoils." The phrase became a classic statement of the right of victorious politicians to reward their followers with jobs. Political workers expected such rewards; when Lincoln became president, office-seekers prowled the White House stairways and hallways.

**The Road to Reform** Inefficiency and corruption in the federal government led to the first efforts at reform in the 1850s. After the Civil War the reform movement gathered momentum. Although President Grant's administration was riddled by corruption, it was Grant who persuaded Congress in 1871 to set up the first Civil Service Commission. But the reform efforts had faltered by 1875, partly because Congress declined to appropriate new funds for the commission.

In 1880 the Republican Party was divided into two factions, for and against civil service reform. James A. Garfield, the Republican presidential candidate, ran on a reform platform. To appease the "Stalwarts," or antireform faction, Chester A. Arthur was chosen for vice president.

After Garfield's election, Charles J. Guiteau, an eccentric evangelist and lawyer, decided he deserved the post of ambassador to Austria or at least the job of Paris

© Bettmann/Corbis

Chester A. Arthur

consul. In 1881 it was easy to get into the White House, and Guiteau actually had an unsuccessful interview with President Garfield. Brooding over his failure to join the diplomatic service, Guiteau purchased a revolver. On July 2, he approached Garfield at the railroad station in Washington and shot him in the back, crying, "I am a Stalwart and now Arthur is President!" Garfield died 80 days later, and his assassin was hanged.

To the dismay of his political cronies, Chester Arthur—who as collector of the Port of New York had been a major dispenser of political patronage—now became a champion of civil service reform. In the wake of public indignation over the assassination, Congress passed the Civil Service Reform Act of 1883 (the Pendleton Act). It established a bipartisan Civil Service Commission under which about 10 percent of federal employees were chosen through competitive examinations.

The basic purpose of the 1883 act was to transfer the power of appointment from politicians to a bipartisan commission that would select federal employees on merit. In recent decades Congress has placed more and more government workers under the protective umbrella of civil service. Today, most of the federal bureaucracy is appointed under the merit system. During the Carter administration, Congress enacted the Civil Service Reform Act of 1978, which replaced the Civil Service Commission with the Office of Personnel Management (OPM) and two other agencies.

To a degree, the removal of civil service appointments from politics has done the president a favor. No matter whom a president selects for a government post, he may antagonize others. William Howard Taft complained that every time he made an appointment he created "nine enemies and one ingrate."[63]

In 2003 1.3 million government jobs were exempt from the competitive civil service system. But many of these were in agencies such as the Postal Service, the Foreign Service of the Department of State, and the FBI, which have their own merit systems.

**Recruiting the Bureaucrats** People interested in working for the federal government can get in touch directly with the agency where they seek employment. Most agencies of the federal government have their own websites that explain how they can be contacted, either online directly, or through USAJOBS, the government's official employment website, or by telephone. The government also holds nationwide recruitment fairs that list what jobs are available.

Applicants can apply directly to the agency that has the job openings and either fill out a federal job form (optional), or submit their résumés directly to the agency or through the USAjobs website. Sometimes, although rarely, an examination for a position is required.

WWW ***For more information about the Office of Personnel Management, see: http://www.opm.gov; and the OPM's job and information site at http://usajobs.opm.gov***

These procedures are followed for competitive civil service jobs. The government also has "excepted" or exempt jobs, which are often political appointments not subject to the usual civil service rules. However, as noted, some agencies, such as the FBI and the State Department's Foreign Service, have "excepted" jobs only because they have their own employment systems.

When a federal agency wants to fill a vacancy, the Office of Personnel Management may refer to it a list of names of qualified, eligible applicants. Or the agency may fill the job from among eligible candidates who already have civil service status and can be promoted or transferred from within the government.

Under a system of "veteran preference," many military veterans who served during certain years or in specific campaigns receive special consideration. For example, preferences go to veterans of the Vietnam War, the 1991 Persian Gulf War, the war in Afghanistan, the war in Iraq that began in 2003, and deployments in Somalia or Bosnia. Disabled veterans and certain members of their families also are given preference.

Before being accepted for government employment, applicants are told that an investigation will be made of their reputation, character, and loyalty to the United States. OPM conducts most of these investigations, but if the job is in the national security area, in which the applicant has access to classified material, the FBI may conduct the background check. New government employees must swear or affirm that they will support and defend the Constitution. Employees must also swear that they will not participate in a strike against the government or any agency of the government. Within that framework, they are free to join one of the numerous unions and

The American Past

## CIVIL SERVICE: "THE ROOT OF ALL EVIL"

George Washington (Boss) Plunkitt, a 19th-century political boss in Tammany Hall, New York City's Democratic machine, had a low opinion of civil service:

> I know that the civil service humbug is stuck into the constitution . . . but, as Tim Campbell said: "What's the constitution among friends?" . . .
>
> The people's voice is smothered by the cursed civil service law; it is the root of all evil in our government. . . . Let me tell of one case. After the battle of San Juan Hill [in the Spanish-American War of 1898], the Americans found a dead man with a light complexion, red hair and blue eyes. They could see he wasn't a Spaniard, although he had on a Spanish uniform. . . . A private of the Seventy-first Regiment saw him and yelled, "Good Lord, that's Flaherty." That man grew up in my district, and he was once the most patriotic American boy on the West Side. He couldn't see a flag without yellin' himself hoarse.
>
> Now, how did he come to be lying dead with a Spanish uniform on? . . . Well, in the municipal campaign of 1897, that young man, chockful of patriotism, worked day and night for the Tammany ticket. Tammany won, and the young man determined to devote his life to the service of the city. He picked out a place that would suit him, and sent in his application to the head of department. He got a reply that he must take a civil service examination to get the place. . . . He read the questions about the mummies, the bird on the iron, and all the other fool questions—and he left that office an enemy of the country that he had loved so well. The mummies and the bird blasted his patriotism. He went to Cuba, enlisted in the Spanish army at the breakin' out of the war, and died fightin' his country. . . .
>
> If that young man had not run up against the civil examination, but had been allowed to serve his country as he wished, he would be in a good office today, drawin' a good salary.
>
> —Boss Plunkitt, in William L. Riordon, *Plunkitt of Tammany Hall*

employee organizations that represent federal workers. Unions of government workers at the federal, state, and local levels have in recent years advocated a national law to give full collective-bargaining rights to their members. But in a number of cases, the courts have ruled against the position favored by the unions.

Government workers receive annual vacations that increase from two to four weeks with length of service, sick leave, and fringe benefits. Under the merit system, they almost certainly will be promoted if they remain in the career service.

Federal employees may express political opinions, contribute to political parties, vote, badger their representatives in Congress, wear a campaign button, display a bumper sticker on their cars, and attend political rallies. But they are limited by law from certain other forms of political participation. The **Hatch Act** is a federal law Congress passed in 1939 to restrict political activities by federal workers. Under the law, federal employees are protected from political pressure to make campaign contributions or to work in political campaigns. Until 1993, the law barred federal workers from taking an active part in party politics or campaigns. In that year, Congress amended the Hatch Act to make it less restrictive by allowing federal workers to take an active part in political activities while off duty.*

But federal employees may not run for public office as the candidate of a political party. Many federal workers have considered the law a violation of their rights of free speech. In 1973, however, the Supreme Court upheld the constitutionality of the Hatch Act; the Court noted that Congress had passed the law because of the danger that a political party might use federal workers in campaigns and that promotions and job security might depend on party loyalty.[64]

There is no mandatory retirement age for federal employees, but they can voluntarily retire with a pension on reaching the age range of 55 to 62, depending on length of service. Retired government workers drawing a pension receive from 7 percent to 80 percent of their salaries for the rest of their lives, depending on length of service and their job. On average, federal employees retire after 26 years at age 58.

Federal workers hired after 1983 must usually join the Federal Employees' Retirement System (FERS), a pension program that combines Social Security, an annuity, and a savings plan. For most of the bureaucracy below the level of political appointees, a government career has offered a relatively high degree of security. It is true that federal employees may be fired for cause (such as misconduct or inefficiency) or if they are adjudged a security risk. Or employees may be given little to do, or dull work, or be transferred to the bureaucratic equivalent of Siberia if they offend a superior. But, by and large, they are protected from arbitrary dismissal. Firing most career federal workers is difficult because it still entails a

*Some federal employees, such as those at the FBI, the CIA, and the Justice Department, are not permitted to take an active part in political activities even while off duty.

complex and lengthy series of hearings and appeals. On the other hand, Congress may end a government program or cut the appropriation, resulting in a "reduction in force" in the bureaucracy. Workers who are thus "riffed" may be transferred to another job in their agency or to some other government unit, or they may be fired.

## The Carter Reforms

The shape of the federal bureaucracy changes with the times. In 1978, for example, President Carter proposed major changes in the civil service system, changes designed to reward merit and penalize incompetence. Before the year was out, Congress had passed, and the president had signed, the Civil Service Reform Act of 1978.

This law, the first major overhaul of the government civil service system in almost a century, established three new agencies: the Office of Personnel Management, to act as the president's personnel arm, handling recruitment, examinations, pay policy, job classification, and retirement; the Merit Systems Protection Board, to hear appeals and conduct investigations, including inquiries into complaints by **whistle-blowers,** government employees who publicly expose evidence of official waste or corruption that they have learned about in the course of their duties; and the Federal Labor Relations Authority, to oversee labor-management relations and arbitrate labor disputes between federal agencies and employee unions.

Under the law, federal officials were given somewhat more flexibility in firing employees for incompetence, although not nearly as much as Carter had requested. The appeals process still gave employees substantial job protection. For the first time, a system of merit pay increases, rather than entirely automatic raises, was established at the upper-middle levels of the bureaucracy.

**The Senior Executive Service** Perhaps the most important feature of the reform act was the establishment of the **Senior Executive Service (SES),** a corps of about 7,700 high-level administrators and managers at the top of the government bureaucracy. Those senior executives who chose to join the SES knew they would have less job tenure and could be transferred more easily within an agency or to another agency. At the same time, they became eligible for substantial cash bonuses for merit. Well over 90 percent of eligible government executives joined the SES.

The idea behind the creation of the SES was to establish a nucleus of top executives in the government in a way that would balance career risk-taking against rewards for high performance, and at the same time would emphasize mobility, managerial discretion in assignments, and accountability.[65]

The senior executives receive substantially higher pay than other officials who are not in the SES. In enacting the reform law, Congress sought to apply the carrot-and-stick incentives of private industry to the massive federal bureaucracy. To an extent, at least, the experiment succeeded.

## Bureaucracy and Society

During President Carter's administration Congress, at his request, established the Department of Energy. It also created the Department of Education and the Department of Health and Human Services, largely by splitting the old Department of Health, Education, and Welfare. And the Carter Administration reorganized some other parts of the bureaucracy, including agencies dealing with civil rights, civil defense, and international communications. A decade later, Congress established the Department of Veterans Affairs, and then in 2003, in response to the terrorist threat to America, the huge Department of Homeland Security was created.

Ronald Reagan promised during the 1980 campaign to abolish the Department of Energy and the Department of Education if elected. But as president, he found it easier said than done. Twenty-seven years later, the two cabinet departments still existed.

Reagan had campaigned against the bureaucracy, however, and as president he moved to try to control the bureaucracy and to reduce its power. When the nation's

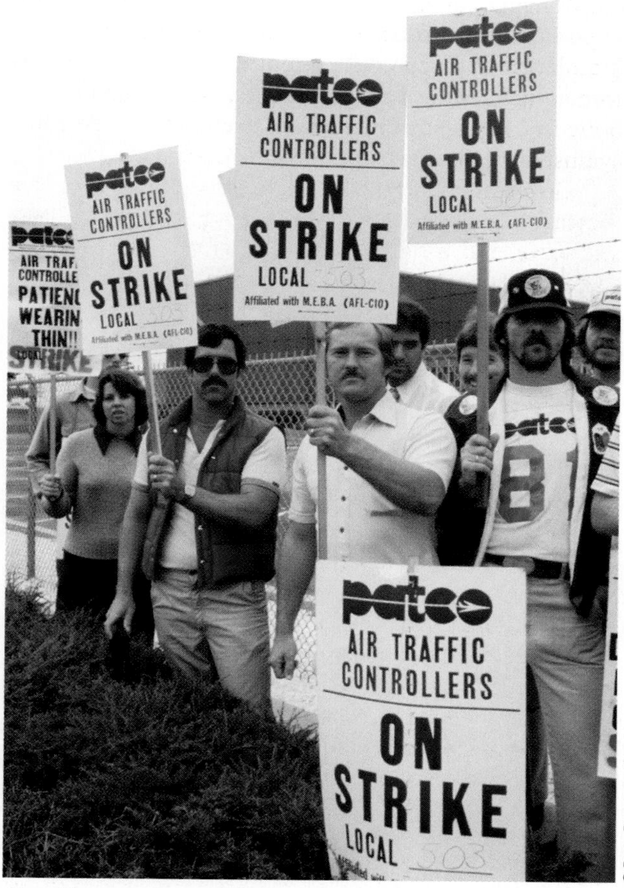




Air traffic controllers picketing in 1981

air traffic controllers went on strike in August 1981, Reagan fired 12,000 of them. The strikers were members of the Professional Air Traffic Controllers Organization (PATCO), ironically one of the few unions to have endorsed Reagan in the 1980 presidential campaign. Supervisory personnel of the Federal Aviation Administration and military air controllers watched the radar screens, and many flights were curtailed. In time, the strike was broken. Reagan emphasized that the walkout was illegal because the strikers had defied a court order to return to their jobs, but his tough stance was a message to the bureaucracy as a whole.

## Rational Decision Making

One of the criticisms of bureaucracy is that its decision making tends to be "incremental"—that is, what was decided yesterday limits the scope of choice today. New policies, instead of replacing old ones, tend to be "added on" to existing programs because government officials are usually wary of sweeping change or policy innovations.

Peter Drucker has suggested: "Certain things are inherently difficult for government. Being by design a protective institution, it is not good at innovation. It cannot really abandon anything. The moment government undertakes anything it becomes entrenched and permanent."[66]

Because of the obstacles to innovation, bureaucracy may overlook problems that do not fit into established forms. A former surgeon general of the United States, Dr. William H. Stewart, once told a Senate subcommittee on poverty that the federal government did not know the extent of hunger and malnutrition in America. "We just don't know," he said. "It hasn't been anybody's job."

On the other hand, bureaucracy is sometimes able to perceive and attack the problems of society. For ex-

### The Clock-Watchers

The request from an Upper West Side restaurant to erect a large clock on a Broadway sidewalk had proceeded smoothly through the city's complicated approval process.

Only one defect marred the project's otherwise orderly flow through the city bureaucracy: The black, 19-foot-high clock has been standing in front of the Ancora Restaurant at Broadway and 85th Street off and on for more than a year. When city officials discovered that last month, they issued an ultimatum to the restaurant's owners. If you want permission to erect the clock, you must first remove it.

But discussions produced a less severe solution. The restaurant's owners agreed to donate to a community cause the $5,000 it would have cost to tear down and then reinstall the clock. In addition, they agreed to remove the restaurant's name from above the clock.

"You would think 18 months would be enough to finish the normal planning process," [Douglas] Griebel [one of the partners in the restaurant] said. "I'm not putting up Trump Tower, after all."

—Adapted from the *New York Times*, August 5, 1986

© Vic DeLucia/The New York Times

## Regulating the Size of Holes in Swiss Cheese

In August of the year 2000, *NBC Nightly News* revealed that federal bureaucrats were actually proposing to measure and regulate something that—well—isn't there.

**BOB FAW reporting:** Imagine Uncle Sam, spending billions to defend us, making sure the air we breathe and the water we drink are safe, is also busily engaged in regulating—are you ready for this—the size of the holes in Swiss cheese. . . . The United States Department of Agriculture has now proposed, in 15 dense pages of regulation, that the holes in Swiss cheese—the industry calls them "eyes"—be made smaller, from the size of a nickel now—11⁄16 of an inch—to about the size of a dime—3⁄8 of an inch.

For cheesemakers, it is really a matter of economics. If the holes are bigger, there is more trim, more waste, and less profit.

**UNIDENTIFIED WOMAN:** It could be a pinhole, I don't care. As long as the taste is there.

**FAW:** There is, however, some dismay that your government is cracking down on those holes in your Swiss cheese.

**JOHN FRYDENLUND (Citizens Against Government Waste):** They really are doing something that is completely pointless, irrelevant, and—and unnecessary.

**FAW:** His taxpayer watchdog group asks, "Doesn't Uncle Sam have better things to do?" The USDA, which spends $40 million a year setting prices for milk and standards for cheese, says taxpayers don't foot the bill for those regulatory changes—that the industry does. And that when it comes to the size of holes, the USDA is only doing what cheesemakers want. That, say critics, is part of the problem.

**RUTH REICHL (*Gourmet Magazine*):** I mean, that's—it's emblematic of how we think about food. It's not about flavor, it's not about its deliciousness. It's about, you know, "Oh, my God! The holes may be too big!"

—Adapted from *NBC Nightly News,* in cooperation with the *Washington Post,* August 8, 2000

ample, earlier than many private employers, the federal government was active in helping minorities, women, and the disadvantaged through affirmative action hiring policies and programs. Although these programs came under sharp political attack in the mid-1990s, for the most part they remained in place.

Often, when government is confronted with a new task, a new agency is established to handle it. For example, during the Kennedy administration, the Peace Corps was made independent of the State Department, and during the Johnson administration, the poverty program was created as a separate agency. The tendency to start new agencies for new programs to some extent reflects resistance to change on the part of existing old-line agencies.

Beginning in the 1960s during the Kennedy administration, the federal government tried to apply newer techniques of management technology to policy problems. The goal of the "rationalists," as advocates of the new techniques were sometimes called, was to arrive at decisions on the basis of systematic analysis, rather than on the basis of guesswork or custom.

Efforts to apply the tools and techniques of rational decision making and computer analysis to reform the management of the executive branch have been both praised and criticized. The system works best for areas in which goals can be "quantified"—expressed in dollar amounts. Thus, within limits, the Pentagon can use this technique to measure the relative merits and cost of weapons systems and military hardware. But in areas such as health care, education, and foreign policy, cor-

## True Grits: A President Versus the Bureaucracy

President Clinton said good riddance to 16,000 pages of federal regulations yesterday and took special satisfaction in saying goodbye to a rule on how to test the consistency of southern grits. . . .

Of the 39 pounds of pages of regulations being eliminated, Clinton said one of the best examples of unnecessary rules was one governing how to test a southern dish, corn grits, for proper consistency. He proceeded to read the lengthy passage.

"Grits, corn grits, hominy grits, is the food prepared by so grinding and sifting clean white corn with removal of corn bran and germ that on a moisture-free basis its crude fiber content is not more than 1.2 percent and its fat content is not more than 2.25 percent," he said.

The crowd roared as he read on, then he cited as a "real sacrifice" a 2,700-word regulation on french fries.

—*Washington Post,* June 13, 1995

## *Making a Difference*

## WHISTLE-BLOWING: "UNDERSTAND THE RISKS"

The kingpin of Washington whistle-blowers may be Casey Ruud. Ruud put himself in the public hot seat in 1986 after his inspection audits at the Hanford nuclear reservation contended the plutonium production plants in southeast Washington were unsafe and needed to be shut down.

His reports initially were ignored, then minimized by Hanford authorities. However, Ruud's conclusions were later deemed accurate, and led to his congressional testimony and an end to bomb making at Hanford.

Still, Ruud was laid off from Hanford in 1988 and shunned at another weapons site before resigning. He fought in court, claiming unlawful retaliation for whistle-blowing, and eventually got a job back at Hanford with the state Department of Ecology, where he now works.

Along the way, Ruud has been lauded by former Energy Secretary Hazel O'Leary as a model whistle-blower and received a $10,000 Cavallo Foundation award in 1996 for moral courage in government.

Last month, a judge ruled the Westinghouse Corp. owes Ruud "front pay" for the rest of his working life—the difference between his state salary and the money he would have been making if he hadn't been canned at Hanford a decade ago.

Meanwhile, Ruud . . . still blows the whistle. During the past two years, he and Hanford scientist John Broeder proved that radioactive fluids leaking from massive storage tanks have spread much further than Hanford authorities conceded.

Ruud says his recent efforts to expose that problem further alienated him at Hanford. "I am absolutely resented in every way by my superiors," he says.

Ruud estimates that he has counseled more than 200 Hanford employees on whistle-blowing. "The majority of the people who come to me only come to me because they are desperate," he says. His advice? He tells them to make sure their spouses and relatives understand the risks. And he discourages them from thinking like victims.

"That's the key. The public doesn't want to deal with victims."

—*Seattle Times,* January 3, 1999

rect choices cannot so easily be arrived at by measuring benefits against costs. The long-range benefits to American society from an improved educational system, for example, cannot be evaluated wholly by a computer.

## Checks on Bureaucratic Power

Bureaucracy is big and powerful. There are, however, some visible checks on that power. First, government agencies must share power with other elites in the political system, not only competing agencies in the executive branch, but also Congress, the courts, and groups and leaders outside the government. When government agencies mobilize political support among private industry or other client groups, they give up some of their independence and power in the process.

Congress exercises checks on bureaucratic power in several ways—through congressional oversight of departments and agencies of the executive branch, for instance, and through committee hearings and investigations. In addition, congressional staff members may intervene with government agencies to help citizens who feel the bureaucracy is unresponsive to their problems.

The courts and the legal system also play a role in controlling bureaucracy. Court rulings may narrow or overturn regulations issued by federal agencies. The courts may reject claims of executive privilege and require the production of documents that the bureaucracy would rather keep secret.

Or the courts may punish bureaucrats who break the law. Ten officials of the Nixon administration were convicted and jailed in the Watergate scandal. Several high-level officials of the Reagan administration and other individuals were charged with crimes as a result of the Iran-contra scandal; some were convicted. All told, more than 100 officials of the Reagan administration were accused of illegal or unethical conduct, forced to resign, indicted, or convicted.[67] The unusual number of aides involved in improprieties of one sort or another gave the Democrats a "sleaze factor" issue that they sought to exploit during the 1988 presidential campaign. Despite that effort, the Democrats lost. During the 2000 presidential contest, the Republicans were able to remind voters of the various scandals of the Clinton administration.

In addition to sharing power with other parts of government and with interest groups, officials are held in check by the press. Fear of adverse publicity is a powerful factor in decision making in Washington, as well as in state and local governments. Moreover, some government employees have become whistle-blowers, publicly exposing evidence of waste or corruption that they discover in the course of their duties.

**Whistle-Blowers** Whistle-blowing can sometimes turn out to be a significant factor within the bureaucracy. During the Nixon administration, A. Ernest Fitzgerald, a Pentagon official, exposed a $2 billion cost overrun in the C-5A aircraft program. After this, Fitzgerald was forced out of his job; he was not reinstated for five years.

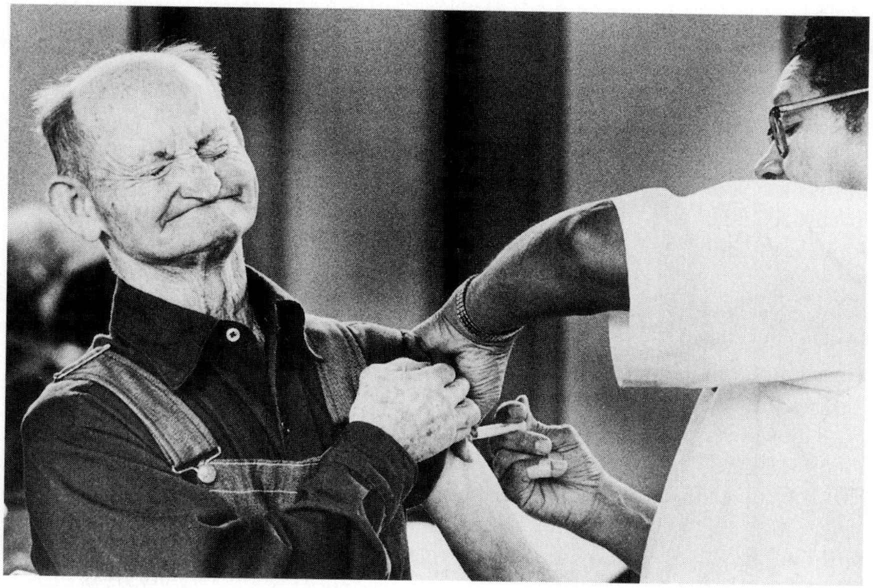
© Bettmann/Corbis

Fifty million Americans were given swine flu vaccine, despite the risks.

Later it was revealed that President Nixon had personally ordered Fitzgerald fired.

Whistle-blowers often pay a high price for their actions. Others, less well known, also have been fired. Consider, for example, the case of Dr. J. Anthony Morris, a government virologist. In 1976 a soldier at Fort Dix, New Jersey, died of swine flu. Fearing a nationwide epidemic, federal authorities began a massive inoculation program. Alone within the government, Morris opposed the program; he had been questioning the value of flu shots for several years. He vigorously protested that there was no evidence the swine flu would cause an epidemic like the flu epidemic that had occurred in 1918 and killed millions of people worldwide. And, he warned, the vaccine was dangerous. At age 58, Morris was fired from his research job by the head of the Food and Drug Administration, who found him guilty of "insubordination and inefficiency."[68]

Inoculations started in October 1976, were suspended for a time, and then cut off entirely in February 1977. Fifty million Americans were given swine flu vaccine, but the program was halted after several people became seriously ill with Guillain-Barré syndrome, a rare and serious paralytic disease.[69] By January 1988, some 4,178 claims totaling $3.2 billion had been filed against the government. The lawsuits also claimed that at least 360 deaths and more than 1,600 cases of Guillain-Barré disease had resulted from the flu shots.[70]

There have been many similar stories. When John Kartak, an Army recruiter in Minneapolis, discovered his office had forged high school diplomas and concealed criminal records to meet recruiting quotas, he called the Army whistle-blower hotline. The Army responded by ordering two psychological evaluations of Kartak, whose superior said he had been filing a lot of complaints lately and was "highly unstable." But Kartak was vindicated when the Army eventually determined his charges were true and found 58 people in the office guilty of engaging in illegal acts.[71] Less fortunate was Joseph Setepani of the Food and Drug Administration, who protested the use of carcinogens and mutagens in food supplies. Setepani was "reassigned to long-term research in a trailer on an experimental farm."[72]

In 1989 Congress strengthened the Whistleblower Protection Act, and the first President Bush signed it into

© 2004 AP/Wide World Photos

Government whistle-blower Richard Foster testifies to Congress about Medicare costs.

## The Case for Bureaucracy: It's Like Your Old Car

Despite endless rantings to the contrary, American bureaucracy does work—in fact, it works quite well. It is something like your ten-year-old car, an immensely complex mechanism made up of tens of thousands of parts, which is by no means perfect or totally reliable. But it starts more than it stalls, and completes the majority of the trips you take. . . .

It is the same with government agencies, especially big ones. They are imperfect, vastly complex, and usually reliable, and they come to our attention only when they break down. One of the most visible, and certainly one of the largest and most complex, is the U.S. Postal Service, which collects and delivers 650 million items to 130 million addresses six times a week, with 93 percent of them arriving on time. Rarely is any piece lost. Still, we take this service for granted—and without knowing a thing about the immense administrative, processing, and transportation systems needed to make it work. We complain when one letter is a few days late, allowing that one late letter, not the thousand of on-time deliveries we have received, to shape our image of the whole. . . .

In popular culture, bureaucracy's image is that of a huge, impersonal organization. Yet when one investigates the actual number of employees working in government offices, the common pattern is not massiveness but small-to-modest size. Another false image . . . is that bureaucracy inevitably expands in size and, over time, deteriorates in quality. Both allegations are refuted by evidence. . . .

It is often argued that bureaucracy is too powerful to be safely compatible with democracy. A number of surveys and field studies . . . have concluded, however, that bureaucrats respond with remarkable loyalty to policy guidance from elected officials . . . foot dragging, leaks, and sabotage are relatively rare.

—Charles T. Goodsell, *The Case for Bureaucracy: A Public Administration Polemic*

law. Although whistle-blowers may still pay a high price—despite the law they risk retaliation from their superiors—the possibility of exposure from within the bureaucracy sometimes acts to curb potential abuses.

In 2004, Richard S. Foster, the government's chief expert on Medicare costs, disclosed to the press and to Congress that he had estimated that the true cost of the prescription drug benefit added to the program a few months earlier would be $500 billion to $600 billion over 10 years, not $400 billion as the administration had claimed. Foster said his superior had warned him that he would be fired if he revealed the true figure to Congress. Foster later told a House committee about the effort to muzzle him. Despite the risk to his career, he had blown the whistle.

**Other Checks on Bureaucracy** In addition, there are certain "inner checks" on the bureaucracy. To some extent, bureaucrats may be inhibited from abusing their power by the social and political system in which they operate. Like other citizens, bureaucrats have been politically socialized, and in many cases they may tend to

A Louisiana Department of Wildlife and Fisheries officer rescues a three-month-old victim of Hurricane Katrina.

adhere to standards of fair play and respect for individual rights. But relying on individual conscience is rather uncertain, and the search continues for institutionalized methods of control. The device of the ombudsman, for example, has proved popular in Sweden and in some other countries. The ombudsman is an official complaint-taker who tries to help citizens wronged by the actions of government agencies. In broader terms, public opinion and the political culture may also serve as a check on bureaucratic power. Because the public tends to be suspicious of bureaucracy, bureaucrats may act more cautiously than they would otherwise.

Despite these checks, the problems posed by bureaucracy remain. Yet as long as government has responsibility for allocating things of value, for deciding who gets what in American society, there will be bureaucrats to help make and carry out those decisions. The size of the bureaucracy at any particular time, then, depends on the demands made on the political system by the voters.

Bureaucrats are convenient political targets, vulnerable to attack, and their shortcomings will no doubt continue to be criticized. Nevertheless, the government could not function without bureaucrats. At the same time, the problem of controlling bureaucracy and making it serve the people is a continuing challenge to the American system.

## CHAPTER HIGHLIGHTS

- Bureaucracy and bureaucrats are often handy political targets to blame for society's ills. Yet, government at every level—federal, state, and local—could not function without people to run it. Many government programs are highly complex and require experts and professionals to administer them.
- "Public administration" is the term preferred by most political scientists to describe the bureaucratic process—the business of making government work—and bureaucrats are public administrators.
- Americans tend to be against "Big Government" in the abstract, but they also demand all kinds of government services. The "bureaucracy in Washington" did not grow overnight, but developed gradually, largely in response to public needs. Most government departments and agencies have been created as a result of pressure from some segment of the population.
- Because civil servants are not elected and are free of direct control by the voters, the bureaucracy is semipermanent in character and, at times, an independent center of power. A central problem is how to make bureaucracy accountable to popular control—in short, how to reconcile bureaucracy and democracy.
- In theory, bureaucrats are simply public servants who administer policy decisions made by the accountable officials of the government—the president, his principal appointees, and Congress. In fact, government administrators by their actions—or inaction—often make policy.
- There is no single bureaucracy in America, and the term is not limited to the federal government. Bureaucrats administer programs at every level, down to the smallest units of state and local government. Public administration in the United States is fragmented by the system of federalism.
- The American bureaucracy is deeply involved in politics as well as policy. As in the case of the president and members of Congress, government agencies also have constituencies—interest groups, or client groups, either directly regulated by the bureaucracy or vitally affected by its decisions.
- The bureaucracy, interest groups, and congressional committees interact. In some areas the relationship among the three actors is so close that it is sometimes referred to as a triangle, an iron triangle, or a subgovernment.
- Issue networks, a loose grouping of people and organizations who seek to influence policy formation, play an important role in the shaping of public policy.
- The great majority of federal workers are members of the career civil service.
- The 15 cabinet departments are major components of the federal bureaucracy.
- The executive agencies are units of government under the president, within the executive branch, that are not part of a cabinet department.
- The independent regulatory agencies exercise quasi-judicial and quasi-legislative powers and are administratively independent of the president, Congress, and the courts.
- Andrew Jackson is generally credited with introducing to the national government the spoils system, the practice, known more often today as political patronage, under which victorious politicians reward their followers with jobs.
- Whistle-blowers are government employees who publicly expose evidence of official waste or corruption that they have learned about in the course of their duties.

## KEY TERMS

public administration, p. 465
constituencies, p. 470
triangle, p. 472
iron triangle, p. 472
subgovernment, p. 472
issue networks, p. 473
cabinet departments, p. 478
executive agencies, p. 479
government corporations, p. 479
independent regulatory agencies, p. 479
social regulation, p. 485
spoils system, p. 486
political patronage, p. 486
Hatch Act, p. 488
whistle-blowers, p. 489
Senior Executive Service (SES), p. 489

## SUGGESTED WEBSITES

**http://www.whistleblower.org**
*Government Accountability Project*
A nonpartisan, nonprofit organization that promotes government and corporate accountability and assists whistle-blowers. The organization offers advice and referrals for whistle-blowers. GAP also does its own research on government programs and offices. The reports of its investigations are available on the website.

**http://www.opm.gov**
*Office of Personnel Management*
The federal government's human resources agency; contains general information for current and prospective federal employees and statistics about federal government workers.

**http://www.pogo.org**
*Project on Government Oversight*
A nonpartisan, nonprofit organization that investigates, exposes, and tries to remedy abuses of power within the government. The site includes POGO Alerts, which are brief reports about the project's investigations, and legal resources for those who are considering becoming a whistle-blower.

**http://www.usajobs.opm.gov**
*USAJobs*
The federal government's official site for jobs and employment information. Current job openings, online applications for jobs, and information about working for the government are available.

## SUGGESTED READING


Heclo, Hugh. *A Government of Strangers** (The Brookings Institution, 1977). An important analysis of the relations between political leaders and the bureaucracy. Heclo identifies weaknesses in the nation's political leaders and the bureaucracy as well as weaknesses in the nation's political structure and suggests reforms to bring about more effective executive leadership.

Johnson, Roberta Ann. *Whistleblowing: When It Works—and Why** (Lynne Rienner Publishers, 2003). A series of interesting case studies of government whistleblowers. Explores their motivation, impact on policy, and the effects that whistleblowers' actions have on their careers and their employing agency.

Kerwin, Cornelius M. *Rulemaking: How Government Agencies Write Law and Make Policy,* 3rd edition* (CQ Press, 2003). An analysis of the important role of rulemaking by government agencies. Examines the process of rulemaking, and the ways by which rule makers can be held accountable to executive agencies and the other branches of the government. The author believes there should be more public participation in this process.

Meier, Kenneth J. *Politics and the Bureaucracy: Policymaking in the Fourth Branch of Government,* 4th edition* (Wadsworth, 1999). A broad overview of the federal bureaucracy and its growing role in the policymaking process.

Mosher, Frederick C. *Democracy and the Public Service,* 2nd edition (Oxford University Press, 1982). An excellent and readable discussion of various trends in the public service, including professionalization, unionization, and the merit system. Discusses their implications for democratic government.

Osborne, David, and Plastrik, Peter. *Banishing Bureaucracy: The Five Strategies for Reinventing Government** (Addison-Wesley Longman, 2000). An influential set of prescriptions, drawing on numerous case studies, for making government more efficient through the reform of public management.

Rourke, Francis E. *Bureaucracy, Politics, and Public Policy,* 3rd edition* (Little, Brown, 1984). A concise general introduction to the role of the bureaucracy in the making of public policy. Among other topics, the book analyzes the sources of power of government bureaucracies, and new approaches to policymaking in bureaucratic agencies.

Salamon, Lester M. *Partners in Public Service* (Johns Hopkins University Press, 1995). A thorough account of the emergence of nonprofit organizations as major instruments for the delivery of public services.

Seidman, Harold, and Gilmour, Robert S. *Politics, Position, and Power: From the Positive to the Regulatory State,* 5th edition (Oxford University Press, 1997). An enlightening discussion of the operations of government agencies and the political realities affecting proposals for their reorganization.

Simon, Herbert A. *Administrative Behavior: A Study of Decision-Making Processes in Administrative Organizations,* 4th edition* (Free Press, 1997). A classic theoretical and empirical analysis of decision making in government bureaucracies. This book, first published in 1947, has influenced modern scholarly work on bureaucratic organizations.

Skowronek, Stephen. *Building a New American State: The Expansion of National Administrative Capacities, 1877–1920** (Cambridge University Press, 1982). A valuable study of the factors that led to the emergence and development of bureaucratic institutions as an integral part of the national government of the United States.

Skrzycki, Cindy. *The Regulators: Anonymous Power Brokers in American Politics** (Rowman & Littlefield, 2003). A Washington journalist offers a portrait of the federal bureaucracy at work. The book covers important issues, such as auto safety, as well as issues of less general concern, to illustrate the broad reach of federal regulations.

White, Leonard D. *The Federalists* (Macmillan, 1948); *The Jeffersonians, 1801–1829* (Macmillan, 1951); *The Jacksonians, 1829–1861* (Macmillan, 1954); and *The Republican Era, 1869–1901* (Macmillan, 1958). A notable study, in four volumes, of the historical development of the American public service from 1789 to the turn of the 20th century.

Wildavsky, Aaron, and Caiden, Naomi. *The New Politics of the Budgetary Process,* 5th edition* (Longman, 2003). A revealing analysis of the nature of the federal budgetary process and its relationship to the making of public policy. Discusses and summarizes the important changes in the 1990 budget reconciliation act.

Wilson, James Q. *Bureaucracy: What Government Agencies Do and Why They Do It,* 2nd edition* (Basic Books, 1991). A comprehensive survey of why government agencies in the United States behave in the ways they do. Stresses the important differences that can be found among various agencies.

Wood, B. Dan, and Waterman, Richard W. *Bureaucratic Dynamics: The Role of Bureaucracy in a Democracy** (Westview Press, 1994). Argues that executive bureaucracies, contrary to the belief of many of their critics, do respond to election results and alter the policies of their agencies accordingly.

*Available in paperback edition.

# Chapter 15

# JUSTICE

IN THE HIGH-CEILINGED marble chamber of the Supreme Court late in June 2006, the marshal of the Court rapped his gavel on a wooden block and cried: "The honorable, the chief justice and the associate justices of the Supreme Court of the United States. Oyez, oyez, oyez. All persons having business before the honorable, the Supreme Court of the United States, are admonished to draw near."

As the marshal spoke, Chief Justice John G. Roberts and the associate justices, wearing their black robes, filed in through the red velvet curtains behind the bench. It was the last day of the Court's term before the summer adjournment, and decisions were announced in a number of important cases.

In a powerful rebuke to the administration of President George W. Bush, the high court held 5–3 that the military tribunals created to try terror suspects held at Guantanamo Bay, Cuba, violated both military law and the Geneva Convention on the treatment of prisoners of war.[1] The Court ruled in the case of Salim Ahmed Hamdan, a former driver for Osama bin Laden. The important decision in *Hamdan* v. *Rumsfeld* meant that the 450 prisoners held at Guantanamo could not be brought before the military tribunals. The Supreme Court's decision came at a time when the prison at Guantanamo had come under increased criticism from other nations. In response to the Court's ruling, the Bush administration agreed to apply the Geneva Convention to all terrorist suspects in U.S. custody, including those at Guantanamo and al Qaeda detainees held by the Central Intelligence Agency.

Collection, The Supreme Court Historical Society, photograph by Steve Petteway, Supreme Court

Yaser Esam Hamdi, a U.S. citizen, after he was captured fighting for the Taliban in Afghanistan

One day before the Court's decision, the justices upheld a controversial Republican redistricting plan in Texas.[2] By redrawing congressional district lines in 2003, the party had increased Republican control of the House of Representatives. The decision meant that states could redraw district lines at any time, not necessarily only after the annual 10-year census, as had been traditional.

At the start of the week, the justices struck down Vermont's law limiting campaign contributions and spending.[3] The 6–3 decision left intact the Court's landmark 1976 ruling in *Buckley* v. *Valeo,* which upheld limits on political contributions but not on spending, except for presidential candidates who accept public funding.

It was a different Court that handed down these decisions in June 2006. President George W. Bush had nominated Roberts to be chief justice in September 2005, and he was easily approved by the Senate. He replaced Chief Justice William Rehnquist, who died earlier that month.

Originally, the president had nominated Roberts to replace Associate Justice Sandra Day O'Connor, who unexpectedly announced her retirement in 2005 after almost 25 years on the high court. That created an important vacancy on the Court, because O'Connor was known as the "swing vote" whose opinions often decided key Supreme Court cases. Most notably, her vote had decided the politically volatile case that determined Bush's election in 2000 over Vice President Al Gore.

Then, in September 2005, Chief Justice Rehnquist died, creating another vacancy on the high court. Bush announced that he would switch Roberts's nomination from associate justice to chief justice. To replace O'Connor, Bush nominated his White House counsel, Harriet E. Miers. Almost from the start, the Miers nomination was in trouble. Democrats and Republicans alike were skeptical of her qualifications. Miers had never been a judge, and she had written a number of highly flattering letters to Bush that used phrases such as "Cool!" and "You're the best!"

In an October press conference, Bush expressed his support for Miers by saying she was "plenty bright," words that seemed to fall somewhat short of an ecstatic endorsement. As discontent with Miers mounted in Congress, she withdrew her nomination.

Bush quickly nominated another candidate for O'Connor's seat. He chose Samuel A. Alito, Jr., 55, a judge of the federal appeals court in Philadelphia. Alito, a Yale law school graduate, was considered a conservative jurist. As a lawyer in private practice, he had argued 12 cases in front of the Supreme Court, losing only two. Many Democrats opposed Alito, comparing him to Justice Anthony Scalia, one of the Court's most conservative members.

Under intense questioning during five days of Senate hearings, Alito declined to discuss his views on several key issues that might reach the Supreme Court. Some liberal senators threatened to filibuster Alito's nomination, but their efforts failed. In January 2006 Alito was confirmed, 58–42, the second closest confirmation vote for a Supreme Court nominee in 100 years. He was quickly sworn in less than two hours later so that he could sit with the other justices that night during the president's annual State of the Union address.

Until O'Connor retired, and for several years before that, many of the Court's key decisions were decided by a vote of 5–4. The narrow margin in the Supreme Court meant that a change of even one justice in the makeup of the high court could alter the ideological trend of its decisions. With the passage of time, as justices grow older, vacancies occur. As a result, presidential elections may determine the makeup of the Court. In this case, a year after the 2004 presidential election, Bush had the opportunity to appoint both a new chief justice and a new associate justice. With the addition of Chief Justice Roberts, regarded at the time as moderately conservative, together with Alito, the Supreme Court was expected by many observers to move in a generally more conservative direction.

Ronald Reagan, elected in 1980 as a conservative Republican, was able, over two terms, to place his imprint

### William O. Douglas on the Supreme Court

The Court is and always will be a storm center of controversial issues. For to it come most of the troublesome, contentious problems of each age, problems that mirror the tensions, fears and aggressiveness of the people. It will be denounced by some group, whatever it does.

—William O. Douglas, *The Court Years: 1939–1975*

© Michael Newman/PhotoEdit

on the Court. During his first term, he filled only one vacancy, in 1981, choosing Sandra Day O'Connor, 51, a state appeals court judge in Arizona, to become the first woman to serve on the Supreme Court.

But in Reagan's second term, two more vacancies occurred. First, in 1986, Chief Justice Warren E. Burger retired. That allowed Reagan to promote Justice Rehnquist, then 61, to chief justice and to appoint Antonin Scalia, 50, like Rehnquist a conservative, and the first Italian American to serve on the Supreme Court. The following year, Justice Lewis F. Powell, Jr., retired, and Reagan named Anthony M. Kennedy, 52, a federal appeals court judge in San Francisco, to the Court. Kennedy was confirmed by the Senate in 1988, ending a bitter seven-month battle over the vacant seat.

Reagan's successor, the first President Bush, had additional opportunities to attempt to shape the Court's conservative majority. When Justice William J. Brennan, Jr., one of the two remaining liberals on the Court, retired in July 1990, Bush nominated David H. Souter, 51, a little-known federal appeals court judge from New Hampshire. A year later, Justice Thurgood Marshall, a giant of the civil rights movement before he was named to the high court by President Lyndon Johnson, stepped down at the age of 82, citing his advanced years and health problems. Bush named Clarence Thomas, a conservative federal appeals court judge, to succeed him.

Thomas, a 43-year-old African American born in rural Georgia and raised in poverty, was on his way to Senate confirmation when Anita Hill, an Oklahoma law professor, accused him of sexual harassment. Hill's charges, aired on television for days by the Senate Judiciary Committee, erupted into a major political controversy and an extraordinary drama. Hill said that when she worked with Thomas at two government agencies, he had repeatedly asked her for dates and engaged in explicit sexual conversations with her about pornographic movies and his own sexual abilities.

Thomas categorically denied Hill's charges and accused the committee of a "high-tech lynching for uppity blacks."[4] The committee, unable to resolve the conflicting stories, approved the Thomas nomination, and he was narrowly confirmed by the full Senate, 52–48.

In 1993, President Clinton nominated Ruth Bader Ginsburg, a judge of the federal Court of Appeals in Washington, D.C., to the Supreme Court. Justice Ginsburg, 60, whose first job out of law school was as a legal secretary, was known as a strong advocate for women's rights. She joined Sandra Day O'Connor as the second woman to serve on the high court. Ginsburg was considered a moderate.

The following year, Clinton named Stephen G. Breyer, the chief judge of the federal Court of Appeals in Boston, to the Supreme Court. Breyer, 55 years old, was also known as a moderate and a pragmatist.

The Supreme Court and the lower federal courts comprise one of the three independent, constitutionally coequal branches of the federal government. But the Supreme Court is only one part of the fragmented, decentralized system of justice in America, a system that encompasses a network of federal courts, state and local courts and prosecutors, the U.S. Department of Justice, state and local police, the Federal Bureau of Investigation, prisons and jails, probation and parole officers, and parole boards.

*Key Question* Against this background, we will explore a two-part key question: ***What is the role of the Supreme Court in the American political system, and how well does the criminal justice system work?***

Many related questions to consider also arise. Since the Constitution created three separate branches of the federal government, can the Supreme Court, as head of the judicial branch, overrule the other two branches—the president and Congress? Because its members are appointed and not accountable to the voters, should the Supreme Court "legislate" and make social policy? Should the Supreme Court adhere closely to what it perceives as the "original intent" of the framers, or should it interpret the Constitution broadly and infer new constitutional principles to meet changing conditions?

The Supreme Court stands at the pinnacle of the judicial system. But is the system of criminal justice stacked against African Americans and other minorities? Do the rich have a better chance under the system than the poor? Should America continue to have capital punishment? What steps can be taken to protect the public against corrupt officials at the highest level of the government? Who can investigate impartially, if a president, other White House officials, or cabinet members are potential targets of a criminal investigation?

## The System of Justice

### Crime, Terrorism, Politics, and the Public

In the wake of the September 11, 2001, terrorist attacks on America, Congress passed the controversial USA Patriot Act, expanding the federal government's authority to act against suspected terrorists. President George W.

Attorney General Alberto Gonzales

Bush created military tribunals to try non-U.S. citizens who were suspected terrorists, and he asserted the right to label some persons, including American citizens, as "enemy combatants" and hold them indefinitely without the right to have an attorney. In 2004, however, the Supreme Court ruled that all detainees have the right to a hearing and could not be held indefinitely.[5]

Critics focused much of their attention on the attorney general, then John Ashcroft, whom they accused of being too willing to disregard constitutional rights in his zeal to pursue those he labeled terrorists or their supporters. Opponents of Bush, Ashcroft, and the Patriot Act argued that civil liberties and freedoms could be lost under the guise of protecting these same liberties and freedoms. After Bush's reelection in 2004, Ashcroft resigned. To replace him Bush named Alberto Gonzales, the White House counsel. In 2006 the Patriot Act was renewed and most of its major provisions, which would otherwise have expired, were made permanent. Some modest privacy safeguards were added to the law; for example, libraries would no longer be required to turn over the names of borrowers without a warrant signed by a judge.

The actions by Congress and the Executive Branch in the aftermath of 9/11 in some ways echoed the atmosphere at the height of the Cold War, when the perceived enemy was the Soviet Union and international communism rather than terrorism. In those years, the FBI conducted illegal break-ins at the offices of left-wing groups, fomented trouble among militants, drew up lists of supposed subversives to be rounded up in the event of war, and opened files on entertainers and other prominent figures. And during the Second World War, after Japan attacked Pearl Harbor, President Roosevelt approved the forced removal of Japanese Americans to detention camps in Arizona, California, and four other Western states.

In all of these instances, the government, faced with what it believed to be threats, either foreign or domestic, has reacted in ways that violated individual rights. It has done so knowing that, in times of apparent danger, public opinion tends to support strong government actions even at the expense of constitutional protections.

During a period of political activism, as in the 1960s and early 1970s—the era of protests against the Vietnam War—the police and the courts became the cutting edge and the enforcement arm of the "Establishment" in the eyes of dissident groups. To most Americans, however, the police and courts represent "law and order."

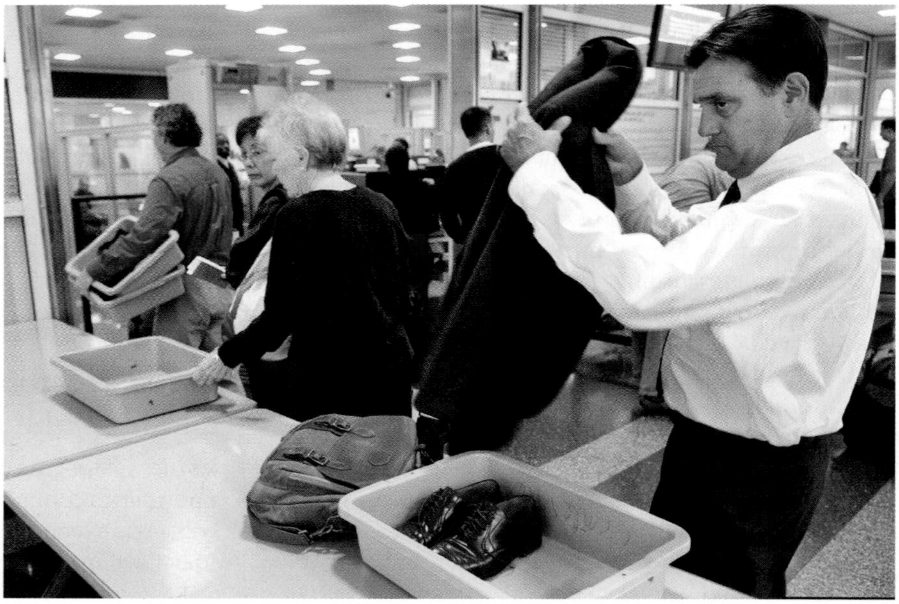


Passengers face increased security screening at the nation's airports.

Comparing Governments

## CRIME AND PUNISHMENT AROUND THE WORLD

Differing historical and cultural traditions have produced strikingly divergent approaches to crime and punishment around the world. For example, the death penalty, which is widely accepted in the United States, has been rejected by most countries, and its use has been condemned by the European Parliament as inhumane. According to Amnesty International, 108 nations have abolished the death penalty, and 87 still retain it. (About 60 percent of all executions in the world each year are conducted in China.)

Differences in the system of justice go well beyond the use of capital punishment. Singapore imposes caning for vandalism and other offenses, such as illegal immigration. Jaywalking, littering, spitting, and the importation and sale of chewing gum carry stiff penalties as well. In the Netherlands, by contrast, the use of marijuana is permitted, and prostitution is legal.

In Saudi Arabia, the Mutawwa (religious police) enforce strict Islamic law. Public music and dancing are prohibited, as are "immodest" dress, pornography, and public interaction between a male and female who are not close relatives. Non-Muslim public religious services are forbidden, as are the display of Bibles, crucifixes, and other non-Islamic religious artifacts. Possession of alcohol may result in a jail sentence, fine, or public flogging, and drug trafficking carries a mandatory death sentence. Those convicted of homosexuality are subject to imprisonment, lashing, or death. Stealing is punished—in accord with Islamic law—by the cutting off of a hand.

A Pakistani soccer team learned firsthand about the differences among countries in the summer of 2000, on a sports trip to Afghanistan. When the athletes showed up for their match wearing soccer shorts, they were arrested for violating the ruling Taliban's strict Islamic dress code, which requires men to wear long shirts and trousers and women to be covered from head to toe. The visiting Pakistanis had their heads shaved, and were expelled from the country.

—Adapted from Amnesty International, U.S. State Department, and the *New York Times,* July 18, 2000

In a society plagued by crime and violence, and more recently by fear of terrorist attacks, most citizens look to government, to law enforcement authorities, to keep them safe on the streets and in their homes. Others seek more direct means to protect themselves; they buy guns and keep them in their homes or carry them.

Today, crime and terrorism and their prevention influence American life in a variety of ways. Airline passengers must pass through metal detectors, are often required to remove their shoes so that screeners can search for explosives or knives, and submit their baggage to be X-rayed in order to prevent hijackers from taking weapons aboard a plane, or terrorists from planting a bomb. Closed-circuit television guards stores and the lobbies of apartment and office buildings. Many private homes, especially in affluent areas, have burglar alarms. Many drivers have remote-controlled key fobs to open or lock their car doors. Armed, uniformed guards are commonplace in shopping malls and office buildings. Gas station cashiers and tellers in some banks sit behind protective glass windows, talking to customers through microphones. These practices, many almost unheard of even two decades ago, grew so gradually that we now tend to accept them as a normal part of the landscape. Today, they are symbols of how crime and fear of terrorism affect the quality of life.

In recent years, the nature of justice in America, the crime rate, and the actions of the police have sometimes themselves become political issues.

During the 1960s, when the Supreme Court was headed by Chief Justice Earl Warren, the Court handed down a series of decisions favoring the rights of criminal defendants. The resulting backlash from conservatives played a major part in making crime a political issue.

The political system has also been troubled in recent decades by wrongdoing and criminal investigations at the highest level—the presidency. In 1973 the extraordinary developments in the Watergate scandal led to the appointment of a special prosecutor, operating outside regular Justice Department channels, to handle the case. The appointment symbolized public skepticism over whether the normal machinery of justice could be relied on in a case involving the highest officials of the government. The special prosecutor demanded tape recordings that President Richard Nixon had secretly made of his White House conversations. Instead of complying, the president fired the prosecutor. The strong public reaction forced Nixon to name another special prosecutor. For months, Nixon and his attorneys resisted the courts; the president yielded his tapes only after the Supreme Court ruled 8–0 that he was required to produce them, and then only in the face of the growing sentiment in the House of Representatives for his impeachment.[6]

In time, Attorney General John Mitchell and several high officials of the White House went to prison. The president himself was named by a federal grand jury as an unindicted coconspirator in the cover-up of the Watergate burglary and eventually resigned and received a presidential pardon. It was clear that the president and his aides had tried to block the investigation of a crime. The Watergate controversy intensified the doubts sometimes raised about the system of justice in America.

In 1986 and afterward, the Iran-contra scandal cast a shadow over the final years of the Reagan presidency and led to the indictment and trial of senior presidential aides and other participants.

Beginning in 1994, President Clinton and his wife, Hillary Rodham Clinton, were scrutinized by an independent counsel investigating the Whitewater affair, a probe that shifted to Clinton's sexual relationship with White House intern Monica Lewinsky and led to his impeachment, trial by the Senate, and acquittal. Not until September 2000 did the independent counsel close the Whitewater investigation, concluding that there was "insufficient" evidence to charge the Clintons with any crime.

In 2005, I. Lewis "Scooter" Libby, the chief of staff for Vice President Dick Cheney, was indicted and charged with perjury and obstruction of justice by a special counsel investigating the leak to the press of the name of Valerie Plame, a CIA officer married to former ambassador Joseph Wilson, a critic of the Bush administration.

The emergence of crime and "law and order" as political issues was accompanied by a series of spectacular events: the shoot-out between federal agents and a group of white supremacists at Ruby Ridge, Idaho, in 1992; the deadly siege of a religious sect near Waco, Texas, in 1993; the first attack on the World Trade Center that year; the bombing of the federal building in Oklahoma City in 1995; the bombing in Atlanta during the 1996 summer Olympic games; and the 9/11 terrorist attacks on targets in New York and Washington in 2001.

The political scandals, shoot-outs, bombings, and terrorist attacks were an indication of the pressures on the system of justice in America. It is a system, of course, that rests on a foundation of law.

## The Law

In a political sense, law is the body of rules made by government for society, interpreted by the courts, and backed by the power of the state. While this is a simple, dictionary-type definition, there are conflicting theories of law and little agreement on precisely how it should be defined.

If law were limited to what can be established and enforced by the state, then Louis XIV would have been correct in saying, "It is legal because I wish it." The founders of the American nation were influenced by another tradition, rooted in the philosophy of John Locke and in the principle of **natural rights,** the belief that all people possess certain basic rights that may not be abridged by government. Under this theory, human beings, living in a state of nature, possessed certain fundamental rights that they brought with them into organized society. The tradition of natural rights was used by the American revolutionaries of 1776 to justify their revolt against England. In modern times, the principle was embraced by Dr. Martin Luther King, Jr., and by others who practiced "civil disobedience" against laws they believed to be unjust, unconstitutional, or immoral.

Still another approach to law is sociological. In this view, law is seen as the gradual growth of rules and customs that reconcile conflict among people in societies; it is as much a product of culture, religion, and morality as of politics. There is always a problem of incorporating majority morality into criminal law; if eventually enough people decide to break a law, it becomes difficult to enforce. One example was Prohibition, which was widely ignored and finally repealed.

Much American law is based on English **common law,** the cumulative body of judicial decisions, custom, and precedent, rather than law created by statute. In 12th-century medieval England, judges began to dispense law, and their decisions came to be called common law, or judge-made law, as opposed to written law passed by legislatures. In deciding cases, judges have often relied on the principle of ***stare decisis,*** the Latin phrase meaning "stand by past decisions." In other words, judges generally attempt to find a precedent for a decision in an earlier case involving similar principles. Most law that governs the actions of Americans is **statutory law,** law enacted by Congress, or by state legislatures or local legislative bodies; but many statutes embody principles of English common law.

Laws do not always ensure fairness. If a man discovers that his apple trees are gradually being cut down by a neighbor, he can sue for damages, but by the time the case is decided the trees may all be felled. Instead, he may seek help through **equity,** a legal principle of fair dealing,

Dr. Martin Luther King, Jr., in jail in Birmingham, Alabama, 1967

## The American Past

## "SEPARATE BUT EQUAL HAS NO PLACE"

In 1954 the U.S. Supreme Court, in an historic decision, *Brown* v. *Board of Education of Topeka, Kansas,* voted unanimously to end racial segregation in the nation's public schools. The Court's opinion was written by Chief Justice Earl Warren:

> In approaching this problem, we cannot turn the clock back to 1868 when the [Fourteenth] Amendment was adopted, or even to 1896 when *Plessy* v. *Ferguson* was written. We must consider public education in the light of its full development and its present place in American life throughout the Nation. . . .
>
> Today, education is perhaps the most important function of state and local governments. . . . It is the very foundation of good citizenship. Today it is a principal instrument in awakening the child to cultural values, in preparing him for later professional training, and in helping him to adjust normally to his environment. In these days, it is doubtful that any child may reasonably be expected to succeed in life if he is denied the opportunity of an education. . . . We come then to the question presented: Does segregation of children in public schools solely on the basis of race, even though the physical facilities and other "tangible" factors may be equal, deprive the children of the minority group of equal educational opportunities? We believe that it does. . . .
>
> We conclude that in the field of public education the doctrine of "separate but equal" has no place. Separate educational facilities are inherently unequal. . . . The plaintiffs and others similarly situated . . . are, by reason of the segregation complained of, deprived of the equal protection of the laws guaranteed by the Fourteenth Amendment.
>
> —*Brown* v. *Board of Education of Topeka, Kansas,* 347 U.S. 483 (1954)

which may provide preventive measures and legal remedies that are unavailable under existing common law and statutory law. The man, for example, might ask a court for an immediate injunction to prevent any further tree chopping.

Cases considered by federal and state courts are either civil or criminal. **Civil cases** concern relations between individuals or organizations, such as a divorce action, or a suit for damages arising from an automobile accident or for violation of a business contract. The government is often party to a civil action—when the Justice Department files a civil antitrust suit against a corporation, for example. It is in the lower courts that ordinary citizens are most likely to experience the system of justice, whether paying a speeding or a parking ticket, defending against some other misdemeanor, suing a neighbor, or filing for divorce. The majority of citizens, in other words, are not defendants in serious criminal cases. **Criminal cases** concern crimes committed against the public order. Most crimes are defined by local, state, and federal statutes, which set forth a range of penalties as well.

A growing body of cases in federal courts concerns questions of **administrative law,** the rules and regulations made and applied by federal regulatory agencies and commissions. Corporations and individuals can go into federal court to challenge the rulings of these agencies. Supreme Court Justice Robert Jackson once observed that people are governed either by the will of one person, or group of people—or by law. He added, "Law, as the expression of the ultimate will and wisdom of a people, has so far proven the safest guardian of liberty yet devised."[7]

## THE SUPREME COURT

The Supreme Court is a political institution that makes both policy and law. Although insulated by tradition and judicial tenure from the turmoil of everyday politics, the Supreme Court lies at the heart of the ongoing struggle in the American political system. "We are very quiet there," said Justice Oliver Wendell Holmes, Jr., "but it is the quiet of a storm centre."[8]

*for more information about the Supreme Court, see:*
*http://www.supremecourtus.gov*

In giving the Constitution contemporary meaning, the Supreme Court inevitably makes political and policy choices. "To consider the Supreme Court of the United States strictly as a legal institution," Robert A. Dahl has suggested, "is to underestimate its significance in the American political system. For it is also a political institution, an institution, that is to say, for arriving at decisions on controversial questions of national policy."[9]

### The Supreme Court: Politics, Policy, and Public Opinion

A basic reason for the political controversy surrounding the Supreme Court is that its precise role in the American political system was left ambiguous by the framers of the Constitution. The Supreme Court is at the apex of the judicial branch, one of the three independent, constitutionally coequal branches of the federal government. But does it have the constitutional right to resolve conflicts among the three branches?

The Court may be seen, on the one hand, as one of

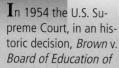

three "coordinate" branches of the federal government, or it may be viewed as the final arbiter of constitutional questions. As Robert G. McCloskey noted, "The fact that the Constitution is supreme does not settle the question of who decides what the Constitution means."[10]

This was dramatically illustrated during the 1974 court battle over the Nixon tapes. When the Watergate special prosecutor subpoenaed tape recordings of the president's conversations for use in the criminal trial of Nixon's former subordinates, the president invoked executive privilege and refused to comply. Nixon claimed that because the Constitution established three independent branches of government, the Supreme Court could not compel the president to release the tapes. The Court held otherwise; it recognized the existence of executive privilege, but ruled that the president could not hold back evidence needed for the criminal trial of his subordinates.[11] Nixon yielded to the Supreme Court and surrendered the tapes.

## Judicial Review

Since the era of Chief Justice John Marshall (1801–1835), the Supreme Court has exercised the right of **judicial review,** the power to declare acts of Congress or actions by the executive branch—or laws and actions at any level of local, state, and federal government—unconstitutional. Lower federal courts and state courts may exercise the same power, but the Supreme Court normally has the last word in deciding constitutional questions. "We are under a Constitution," Charles Evans Hughes declared, "but the Constitution is what the judges say it is."[12]

Yet why, it is often asked, should nine justices who are appointed for life and not elected by the people have the power in a democratic system to strike down the laws and decisions of popularly elected legislatures and leaders? The question is asked most often by people who disapprove of what the Supreme Court is doing at a particular time. Those who approve of the philosophy of a given Court seldom complain that it is overstepping its power.

And judicial review is in effect a coin with two sides. Although the Supreme Court may exercise judicial review and strike down a law as unconstitutional, it may also affirm that a law or executive act is constitutional. To date, only a little more than 150 acts have been declared unconstitutional; thousands more have been sustained by the Court.

One view of the Supreme Court holds that because the justices are not popularly elected, the Court should move cautiously and avoid "legislating" social change. Popular democracy and the principle of majority rule are more consistent, in this view, with legislative supremacy.

An opposite view holds that the Court is the cornerstone of a system of checks and balances and restraints on majority rule provided by the Constitution. In this view, the Supreme Court often may be the only place in the political system where minorities are protected from the majority.

The debate over the role of the Supreme Court in the American system is sharpened by the fact that the Constitution is written in broad and sometimes ambiguous language. As a result, the Supreme Court has interpreted the meaning of the Constitution very differently at different times. Justice Felix Frankfurter once observed:

> The meaning of "due process" and the content of terms like "liberty" are not revealed by the Constitution. It is the justices who make the meaning. They read into the neutral language of the Constitution their own economic and social views. . . . Let us face the fact that five Justices of the Supreme Court are the molders of policy rather than the impersonal vehicles of revealed truth.[13]

"The way I see it, the Constitution cuts both ways. The First Amendment gives you the right to say what you want, but the Second Amendment gives me the right to shoot you for it."

The Supreme Court must, however, operate within the bounds of public opinion, and, in the long run, within the political mainstream of the times. The Court possesses no armies, and it must finally rely on the executive branch to enforce many of its rulings. It was this truth that supposedly led President Andrew Jackson to declare of his chief justice, "John Marshall has made his decision—*now let him enforce it.*"[14] The Court cannot completely ignore the reactions to its decisions in Congress and in the nation because, as a political institution, its power ultimately rests on public opinion.

**The Road to Judicial Review** The Constitution gives the Supreme Court power to consider "all Cases . . . arising under this Constitution." The principle of judicial review traces back to English common law, although the Constitution nowhere explicitly gives this power to the Court. The question of the framers' intent is still debated, but in 1788 Alexander Hamilton argued in *The Federalist* that the judicial branch did in fact have the right to judge whether laws passed by Congress were constitutional.[15] James Madison made the same point during the debate in Congress over the Bill of Rights. Later, so did James Wilson, another influential framer of the Constitution. And, according to political scientist Henry J. Abraham, "a vast majority" of the delegates to the Constitutional Convention favored the idea of judicial review.[16] The principle of judicial review was largely taken for granted in the debates of the convention and in the state conventions that ratified the Constitution.

During the colonial period, the British Privy Council in London exercised judicial review over laws passed by the colonial legislatures. And during the first decade of the nation's existence, the Supreme Court, in a few cases, ruled on whether federal laws were constitutional. It invalidated one federal statute, for example, and at least twice struck down minor state laws.[17]

The power of judicial review, however—although it had already been exercised—was not firmly enunciated and established by the Supreme Court until 1803 in the case of ***Marbury* v. *Madison*,** which declared a portion of an act of Congress unconstitutional.[18]

When Jefferson became president in 1801 he was angered to find that his Federalist predecessor, John Adams, had appointed a number of federal judges just before leaving office, among them one William Marbury as a justice of the peace in the District of Columbia. When Jefferson discovered that Marbury's commission had not actually been delivered to him, he ordered Secretary of State James Madison to hold it up. Under a provision of the Judiciary Act of 1789, Marbury sued in the Supreme Court for a writ of mandamus compelling the delivery of his commission. The Supreme Court under Chief Justice John Marshall dismissed the case, saying it lacked jurisdiction to issue such a writ. The Court held that the section of the Judiciary Act under which Marbury had sued was unconstitutional, since the Constitution did not empower the Court to issue a writ of mandamus, as the act provided. The ruling thus avoided an open political confrontation with the executive branch over Marbury's commission but at the same time established the power of the Court to void acts of Congress. "The Constitution is superior to any ordinary act of the legislature," Marshall wrote, and "a law repugnant to the Constitution is void."[19]

Although the Court's power of judicial review was thus established, the question of how the Court should

Courtesy of Chicago Historical Society/Declan Haun. ICHi-35488

apply its great power has remained a subject of controversy to the present day. The debate has centered on whether the Court should practice judicial activism or judicial restraint. **Judicial activism** is the philosophy that Supreme Court justices and other judges should boldly apply the Constitution to social and political questions. **Judicial restraint** is the philosophy that the Supreme Court should avoid constitutional questions when possible and uphold acts of Congress unless they clearly violate a specific section of the Constitution.

As one scholar has posed the central questions: "Should the Court play an active, creative role in shaping our destiny, equally with the executive and legislative branches? Or should it be characterized by self-restraint, deferring to the legislative branch whenever there is room for policy judgment and leaving new departures to the initiative of others?"[20]

The philosophy of judicial activism was embraced on many issues by a majority of the members of the Warren Court, which vigorously applied the Constitution to social and political questions. For example, in protecting the rights of criminal defendants and in its reapportionment decisions, the Court moved into controversial areas that earlier Supreme Court justices had avoided.

The philosophy of judicial restraint is associated with Justices Felix Frankfurter, Louis D. Brandeis, and Oliver Wendell Holmes, Jr. Frankfurter, for example, held that the Court should avoid deciding "political questions" that could involve it in conflicts with other branches of the federal government.

## The Changing Role of the Supreme Court

Although John Marshall had set forth the right of judicial review in 1803, the Supreme Court did not declare another act of Congress unconstitutional until the *Dred Scott* decision in 1857. Under Marshall's successor, Roger B. Taney (1836–1864), the Court protected states' rights and stressed the power of the states over that of the federal government.

After the Civil War, the Court refused to apply the Fourteenth Amendment to protect the rights of black Americans, even though Congress had passed the amendment for this specific purpose (see Chapter 5). Instead, the Court used the amendment's due process clause to protect business from state regulation. The Fourteenth Amendment provides that no state shall "deprive any person of life, liberty, or property, without due process of law." The Court accepted the argument that a corporation was a "person" within the meaning of the amendment. In a series of cases, it used the Fourteenth and Fifth Amendments to protect industry, banking, and public utilities from social regulation. In the 1890s the Supreme Court struck down the federal income tax[21] and emasculated the federal antitrust laws. In general, the Court during this era served as a powerful guardian of the "robber barons"—the businessmen who amassed great fortunes in the late 19th century—as well as a champion of **laissez-faire** capitalism, a philosophy that government should interfere as little as possible in economic affairs.

The Court continued to expound a conservative philosophy under Chief Justice William Howard Taft in the 1920s. The election of Franklin D. Roosevelt in 1932 was followed by vast social change in America, but a majority of the Supreme Court was not in sympathy with the programs of the New Deal. Between 1933 and 1937 the Court struck down one after another of Roosevelt's programs. In 1936 the average age of members of the Court was 71, and the justices were dubbed the "nine old men."[22]

Reelected by a landslide that year, Roosevelt risked his prestige in 1937 when he proposed his famous "court-packing" plan to expand the number of justices. The size of the Supreme Court is set by Congress and over the years has varied from five justices to 10; the number has been set at nine since 1869. Roosevelt's objective was to put on the Court younger justices who would be more sympathetic to the New Deal. His plan to bring the Supreme Court out of what he termed "the horse and buggy age" provided that whenever a justice refused to retire at age 70, the president could appoint an additional justice. Under the plan, the Court could have been expanded to a maximum of 15 members.

The debate raged in and out of Congress all that spring, but in less than six months the proposal was dead. Although Roosevelt's plan failed, by the time the Court recessed that summer it had already begun to shift to a more liberal position and to uphold New Deal programs. As a result, 1937 is regarded as a watershed year in the history of the Supreme Court. From that date on, the Court for many years often emerged as the protector not of big business but of the individual.

## The Warren Court

During Earl Warren's 16 years as chief justice (1953–1969), the Supreme Court had a profound impact on politics and government in America. The Warren Court was an extraordinarily activist, innovative tribunal that wrought far-reaching change in the meaning of the Constitution.

Among its major decisions, the Warren Court outlawed official racial segregation in public schools, set strict national standards to protect the rights of criminal defendants, required the equal apportionment of state legislatures and the House of Representatives, and ruled that prayers and Bible reading in the public schools were unconstitutional. And it handed down other dramatic decisions that won it both high praise and sharp criticism—and engulfed it in great controversy.

Riding the crest of the tidal wave of social change that swept through America in the 1950s and 1960s, the Court became a natural target of those who felt it was moving too fast and too far. The political reaction to its bold decisions was symbolized by automobile bumper stickers and roadside billboards that read "Impeach Earl War-

© Fred Ward/Black Star/Stockphoto.com

Chief Justice Earl Warren

ren." Before he retired as chief justice in 1969, Warren was asked to name the most important decisions of the Warren Court.[23] He singled out those dealing with reapportionment, school desegregation, and the right to counsel, in that order.[24] Each of these cases symbolized one of three broad fields in which the Warren Court brought about far-reaching changes in America: the political process itself, civil rights, and the rights of the accused.

In its reapportionment decisions, the Warren Court required that each citizen's vote count as much as another's. The decision in *Brown* v. *Board of Education* has not eliminated racial segregation in American schools or American society. But by striking down the officially enforced dual school system in the South, the Court implied that "all racial discrimination sponsored, supported, or encouraged by government is unconstitutional."[25] Thus the decision foreshadowed a social upheaval. The civil rights movement, the civil rights legislation of the 1960s, and the controversy over the busing of public school children all followed.

The *Brown* decision remains a judicial milestone; by its action at a time when much of white America was complacent and satisfied with the existing social order, the Supreme Court provided moral as well as political leadership—it reminded the nation that the Constitution applies to all Americans.

The third broad area of decision by the Warren Court—the protection of the rights of criminal defendants—was discussed in Chapter 4. In a series of controversial decisions, including *Miranda, Gideon,* and *Mapp,* the Court, bit by bit, threw the mantle of the Bill of Rights around people accused of crimes. In so doing, the Court collided directly with the electorate's rising fear of crime; it was condemned for "coddling criminals" and "handcuffing the police." Under the Burger Court the pendulum swung back substantially, in favor of the police and prosecutors.

The Warren Court moved aggressively in several other areas as well—banning prayers in the public schools, curbing the anti-Communist legislation of the 1950s, and easing the laws dealing with obscenity. All this activity provided ample ammunition to the Warren Court's conservative critics. Moreover, as many of the Court's critics frequently pointed out, it decided many important cases by a one-vote margin.

The Burger Court and the Rehnquist Court moved more cautiously in the 1970s and thereafter and narrowed the sweep of some of the Warren Court's decisions, particularly in the areas of criminal justice and pornography. The Supreme Court might do so even more dramatically in the future. Yet one leading scholar predicted that

> the doctrines of equality, freedom, and respect for human dignity laid down in the numerous decisions of the Warren Court cannot be warped back to their original dimensions. . . . Generations hence it may well appear that what is supposedly the most conservative of American political institutions, the Supreme Court, was the institution that did the most to help the nation adjust to the needs and demands of a free society.[26]

## The Burger Court

In 1969, Chief Justice Warren retired, and Nixon named Warren E. Burger to succeed him. In Chief Justice Burger, Nixon made it clear, he believed he had found a "strict constructionist" who would fit his political and philosophical requirement that the Supreme Court interpret the Constitution but not make law. Over the next three years, Nixon appointed three more justices to the Court, and in 1975 President Gerald Ford chose one justice. Thus by 1976 a majority of the nine-member Court had been appointed since Earl Warren's retirement.

The more conservative trend represented a sea change from the Warren Court era. For example, the Burger Court handed down a number of decisions more favorable to police than to defendants. It narrowed the reach of the Fourth Amendment's protections against unreasonable search and seizure, making it easier for state and local prosecutors to use illegally seized evidence to convict defendants. (See Chapter 4.) And the Burger Court restored the death penalty.

After appointing Burger, Nixon sought to change the political balance on the Court further by nominating a conservative as an associate justice. Twice, the Senate rejected Nixon's nominees. Finally, Nixon nominated Harry A. Blackmun, a Minnesota Republican and federal appeals court judge. Blackmun, a moderate, was confirmed. Over time, Blackmun often voted with the Court's liberal bloc; he was the chief architect of the Court's 1973 decision in *Roe* v. *Wade,* legalizing abortion.

In some policy areas such as desegregation and privacy, the Burger Court gave little comfort to conservatives and even broadened the decisions of the Warren Court. For example, the Burger Court legalized abortion; declined to stop the publication of the Pentagon

Chief Justice William H. Rehnquist presided over the Senate impeachment trial and acquittal of President Clinton. He wore a special robe he designed with gold stripes, modeled after a costume he admired in a Gilbert and Sullivan operetta.



Papers, the secret history of the Vietnam war; extended the right to counsel to poor defendants even in misdemeanor cases; outlawed wiretapping of domestic groups without a court warrant; limited the power of local communities to ban pornography; and ruled that even the president must yield evidence to the courts. In the field of civil rights, the Burger Court banned racial discrimination in private schools and upheld affirmative action in education, jobs, and in federal contracts. And it held that all-male groups can be compelled to admit women—a ruling that the Rehnquist Court extended to include private clubs.[27] Even as the Supreme Court shifted to the right, many of its decisions still protected individual liberties and minority groups.

In 1981, President Reagan named the first woman to serve on the Supreme Court, Judge Sandra Day O'Connor of the Arizona Court of Appeals. With the O'Connor appointment, the associate justices of the Supreme Court found it necessary to drop the traditional title of "Mr. Justice." From then on, their title became "Justice."

## The Rehnquist Court

After Warren Burger retired in 1986, President Reagan elevated William Rehnquist to chief justice and appointed Antonin Scalia, another conservative, to the Supreme Court. The appointment of Anthony Kennedy in 1987, and President Bush's appointments of Justices David Souter in 1990 and Clarence Thomas in 1991, meant that for a time, eight of the nine members of the Court had been appointed by Republican presidents. In the space of a relatively few years, the members and political philosophy of one of the three branches of the federal government had changed measurably.

By 1988 the Rehnquist Court shifted in a more conservative direction, giving public school officials the right to censor school newspapers and plays, for example.[28] The Court in several decisions made it more difficult for workers to sue employers for discrimination.[29] And it ruled 6–2 that police may, without a warrant, search through trash that people leave outside their home to be collected.[30]

The Court's decisions alarmed liberals and led to speculation that a conservative majority had finally emerged. But, as is often the case, the decisions varied; the Court in 1990 struck down the federal law that sought to ban flag-burning.[31] And in 1991, it invalidated New York's "Son of Sam" law, which had barred criminals from earning money from books about their crimes; the Court said the state law violated the First Amendment's provisions of free press and free speech.[32]

As these opinions demonstrated, the decisions of the Supreme Court are often unpredictable, and the Court's direction not always easily categorized. Although by 2004 the Court's conservative bloc was often a dominant force, it did not always prevail.

In 2004, for example, the Rehnquist Court ruled that persons held as "enemy combatants," both U.S. citizens and nearly 600 foreigners imprisoned at Guantanamo Bay, Cuba, had the right to challenge the government in court. The prisoners held at the U.S. naval base at Guantanamo had been captured during the war in Afghanistan. The court ruled 6–3 that they could not be denied the right to contest their detention.[33] That decision opened the way for the Court's subsequent landmark ruling in 2006 that the military tribunals created to try the prisoners at Guantanamo violated U.S. law and the Geneva Convention.

The justices in 2004 also held, 8–1, that Yaser Hamdi, an American citizen captured in Afghanistan, could not be held indefinitely without a hearing. President Bush had asserted the right to detain for any length

**TABLE 15-1**

**The Supreme Court, 2006**

| Justices | Appointed by | Date |
|---|---|---|
| John G. Roberts* | George W. Bush | 2005 |
| John Paul Stevens | Ford | 1975 |
| Antonin Scalia | Reagan | 1986 |
| Anthony M. Kennedy | Reagan | 1988 |
| David H. Souter | Bush | 1990 |
| Clarence Thomas | Bush | 1991 |
| Ruth Bader Ginsburg | Clinton | 1993 |
| Stephen G. Breyer | Clinton | 1994 |
| Samuel A. Alito Jr. | George W. Bush | 2005 |

*Chief justice of the United States.

of time persons labeled "enemy combatants" by the government. Although the Court upheld the president's power to detain enemy combatants, it ruled they are entitled to a hearing. Justice Sandra Day O'Connor, writing for the Court, declared that "a state of war is not a blank check for the president."[34] She also wrote: "It is during our most challenging and uncertain moments that our Nation's commitment to due process is most severely tested; and it is in those times that we must preserve our commitment at home to the principles for which we fight abroad."[35] Soon after the Court's decision, Yaser Hamdi, in an agreement reached by the government with his lawyers, was released and sent to Saudi Arabia, where his family lives.

In a companion 5–4 decision, the Court declined on procedural grounds to hear the case of another American citizen, Jose Padilla, arrested for allegedly planning to detonate a radioactive bomb in the United States. It ordered Padilla to refile his appeal in South Carolina, where he was held in a military brig.[36]

In striking down the president's claimed right to combat terrorism by holding detainees without due process, the Court reached back to the Magna Carta in 1215 and its promise that "no free man should be imprisoned . . . save by the judgment of his peers or by the law of the land." The justices also cited English common law and a long string of Supreme Court precedents, among them cases from the Civil War and the Second World War.

And Justice John Paul Stevens, in a dissent urging that the Court decide the Jose Padilla case, declared: "At stake in this case is nothing less than the essence of a free society. . . . If this nation is to remain true to the ideals symbolized by its flag, it must not wield the tools of tyrants even to resist an assault by the forces of tyranny."[37]

In 2004 the Court also reaffirmed its historic 1966 Miranda decision protecting the rights of criminal suspects. It ruled that police could not try to trick people into confessing a crime by interrogating them without telling them of their right to a lawyer and their right to remain silent, and then questioning them a second time after properly informing them of those rights.[38]

That same year, however, the Supreme Court ruled 5–4 that people do not have a constitutional right to refuse to give their names to police.[39] The case arose in 2000 when Larry Hiibel, a Nevada cattle rancher, was arrested after refusing to identify himself in an encounter with a deputy sheriff on a rural road. And the high court ruled unanimously that patients cannot sue health maintenance organizations (HMOs) for damages in state courts if they are refused care recommended by doctors.[40] The decision had the effect of ruling out large, unlimited medical malpractice suits against HMOs.

And in 2005 the Supreme Court ruled 6–3 that Congress could prohibit the use of marijuana for medical purposes, even in the states that allowed it.[41] Advocates of using marijuana for medical reasons planned further legal challenges to the federal drug law, however, so the case did not settle the issue.

That same year, in a controversial decision, the Court ruled 5–4 that the city of New London, Connecticut, could take private property for a project that included research centers and a hotel.[42] The city claimed the plan would create jobs and increase tax revenues. Under the principle of eminent domain, the government, as provided in the Fifth Amendment, can take property for "public use" with "just compensation" to the owners. Normally, the federal government and states and cities do so for projects such as highways; the Court, by expanding that power to include economic development, aroused widespread opposition—citizens do not want their homes bulldozed to make way for a shopping mall. In the wake of this decision, in one year 31 states passed laws restricting the use of eminent domain for commercial projects.

These decisions struck a balance between conservative and liberal values. The decisions that detainees are entitled to a hearing tended to please liberals, while the portion of the opinions supporting the president's right to imprison "enemy combatants," and the Nevada case supporting police power, were more likely to satisfy conservatives. On the whole, however, although the Rehnquist Court was unpredictable, it tended to be a somewhat conservative body ideologically, and one that favored judicial caution in many of its decisions.

## The Roberts Court

When John G. Roberts took his place on the Supreme Court in 2005, at age 50, he was the youngest chief justice in 204 years. A federal appeals court judge in Washington, D.C., a high school wrestler and co-captain of his football team, Roberts was a Harvard graduate and a former law clerk for Chief Justice Rehnquist. He had argued in front of the Supreme Court 39 times, winning 25 of those cases.

His appointment, along with that of Justice Samuel A. Alito, Jr., was widely viewed as an effort by President George W. Bush to move the Court in a more conservative direction. How Roberts would shape the

© Bettmann/Corbis

Nixon leaves the White House in 1974 on the morning he resigned.

Supreme Court, and his own positions on important issues, would take time to become clear.

In one of the first cases handed down after Roberts was sworn in, the justices voted 6–3 that former Attorney General John Ashcroft had acted without legal authority in 2001 when he tried to block Oregon's law permitting physician-assisted suicide.[43] Ashcroft had declared that the federal Controlled Substances Act gave him power to stop Oregon doctors from writing prescriptions for the purpose of suicide. Chief Justice Roberts joined in a strong dissent written by Justice Antonin Scalia, who argued that Ashcroft had acted reasonably in declaring that writing prescriptions to assist in suicide was not a legitimate medical purpose.

In March 2006, the Court held 5–3 that police violated the Fourth Amendment when they searched a home at the invitation of a wife to look for evidence of her husband's use of cocaine, although her husband was present and objected to the search.[44] In writing his first dissent, Chief Justice Roberts argued that a man's home "is not his castle if he happens to be . . . asleep or otherwise engaged when the constable arrives at the gate. Then it is his co-owner's castle."[45]

## The President and the Court

Historically, presidents have picked Supreme Court justices for their politics more than for their judicial talents. By nominating justices whose political views appear compatible with their own, they try to gain political control of the Supreme Court. (Table 15-1 lists the current justices and the presidents who appointed them.)

When Franklin Roosevelt unsuccessfully attempted to pack the Supreme Court, he was aiming not so much at the age of its members as at their political views. As Justice Hugo Black put it, "Presidents have always appointed people who believed a great deal in the same things that the President who appoints them believes in."[46]

This practice is not necessarily bad if it does not lead to the appointment of mediocre judges. In fact, it is one important way in which the Supreme Court is at least indirectly responsive to the electorate. Along with the power of public opinion and the power of the Senate to confirm or reject the president's nominee, the presidential appointment power to some degree links the Court to the voters and the rest of the political system.

Approximately 90 percent of all Supreme Court justices in American history have belonged to the appointing president's political party; some have been selected from the president's inner circle of political advisers.

The requirement that a majority of the Senate approve a Supreme Court nominee restricts the president's ability to shape the Court completely to his political liking. Up to 2005, the Senate had refused to approve 28, or almost 20 percent, of the 141 Supreme Court nominations sent to it.

Nor do justices always act as presidents expect. Supreme Court justices have a way of becoming surprisingly independent once they are on the bench; more than one president has been disappointed to find that he misjudged his appointee. As governor of California, Earl Warren helped to elect President Dwight Eisenhower. There was nothing in Warren's background as a moderate Republican to make the president think his chief justice would preside over a social upheaval. Later, Eisenhower reportedly called the Warren appointment "the biggest damn-fool mistake I ever made."[47] And President Nixon was bitterly disappointed when Chief Justice Burger, joined by two other Nixon appointees, voted with the rest of the Court to require the president to yield his crucial tape recordings, a decision that set the stage for Nixon's resignation.[48]

At times, presidential nominations of Supreme Court justices touch off memorable political battles. Such was the case in 1991, when President Bush nominated Clarence Thomas, and in 1987, when President

The interior of the Supreme Court

Reagan nominated Robert Bork. A coalition of liberal and moderate forces sought to block the nomination of Bork, a former Yale University law professor who had opposed the Supreme Court's landmark 1973 ruling permitting abortions and who had taken other outspoken conservative positions. Opponents charged that Bork would attempt to undo rulings favoring women's rights, civil rights, privacy, and other individual rights. After televised Senate hearings and acrimonious debate, the Senate rejected Bork, by a vote of 58–42.

President Reagan then nominated another conservative, Douglas H. Ginsburg, to the Court vacancy. But his nomination went up in a puff of smoke when it was disclosed that he had used marijuana both as a student and as a professor at Harvard Law School. For an administration pledged to a war against drugs, it was too much; within two days Ginsburg asked the president to withdraw his nomination.

## Congress and the Court

As Supreme Court Justice Robert Jackson once suggested, conflict among the branches of the federal government is always latent, "ready to break out again whenever the provocation becomes sufficient."[49] The Supreme Court, in deciding cases, must worry not only about public opinion, but about how Congress may react. Walter F. Murphy has suggested that the Court's conflicts with Congress ebb and flow in a three-step pattern: First, the Court makes decisions on important aspects of public policy. Second, the Court receives severe criticism coupled with threats of remedial or retaliatory action by Congress. The third step, according to Murphy, has generally been "judicial retreat."[50]

Robert A. Dahl has concluded that the dominant policy views of the Court "are never for long out of line" with the dominant views of the legislative majority.[51] Or, as "Mr. Dooley," a character created by humorist Finley Peter Dunne put it, "the Supreme Court follows the election returns."

Under the Constitution, Congress can control the Supreme Court's **jurisdiction,** the kinds of cases that a court has the authority to decide. For instance, after the Civil War, Congress blocked the Court from reviewing Reconstruction laws.

In the 1980s, conservatives in Congress led by Senator Jesse Helms, a North Carolina Republican, introduced "court-stripping" bills designed to restrict the Supreme Court's jurisdiction and remove its power over cases dealing with abortion and school prayer. These attempts were defeated and did not become law.

Congress (in conjunction with the states) also possesses the power to overturn Supreme Court decisions by amending the Constitution. The Sixteenth

© Lester Lefkowitz/Corbis

The Supreme Court

Amendment, establishing the federal income tax, passed by Congress in 1909 and ratified in 1913, was adopted as a direct result of a Supreme Court decision; in 1895 the Court had ruled unconstitutional an attempt by Congress to levy a national income tax.[52] And the Twenty-sixth Amendment, giving people aged 18 and older the right to vote in all elections, was passed by Congress in 1971 and ratified that year because the Supreme Court had ruled that Congress could lower the voting age only in federal, not in state and local, elections.[53]

Finally, Congress may attempt to overturn specific Supreme Court rulings by legislation. For example, in 1988, Congress reinstated civil rights protections that had been narrowed by the Supreme Court's 1984 decision in the *Grove City* case.[54] Congress did so by passing the Civil Rights Restoration Act that increased civil rights for women, minorities, the elderly, and the disabled. The new law stated that federal antidiscrimination laws apply to an entire institution even if it accepts federal aid for only one program. The legislation had the effect of protecting expanded athletic programs for women in colleges that receive federal money. The law directly overturned the Supreme Court decision in *Grove City.*

## The Supreme Court in Action

Unlike Congress and the presidency, institutions that are the subject of continual scrutiny by the press, the Supreme Court has usually operated in secrecy. One result is that the public has had only limited knowledge about the high court. In one poll, for example, 59 percent of respondents could name the Three Stooges,* but only 17 percent could name three of the court's nine justices.

Until relatively recently, the internal workings and deliberations of the Supreme Court went largely unreported. That picture began to change, however, with a series of disclosures in books, and papers of the justices themselves.

In 1993, the papers of the late Justice Thurgood Marshall were made public by the Library of Congress. They contained a treasure trove of detail about the inner workings of the Court, the backstage dealings among the justices, and their very human concerns.

The justices refer to each other by first names or even nicknames in Marshall's papers. Scalia was called "Nino," and Anthony M. Kennedy was "Tony." Rehnquist was known as "Chief" or "CJ." When, in anticipation that women would be appointed to their ranks, the justices in 1980 dropped the "Mr." from their formal titles, at least two justices, Blackmun and Powell, objected. They preferred to wait until a woman was actually named. If the change was adopted, Blackmun pointed out, the Court would have "to remove and replace the brass plates that are on the backs of the chairs at the bench" and on the doors of their chambers. In a "Dear Chief" letter to Rehnquist, Blackmun strongly implied that he was not about to let anyone strip the brass plate off *his* chair.[55]

In 2004, a huge cache of Blackmun's own papers were released by the Library of Congress, providing an extraordinary view of the clashes, personalities, and private views of the justices on a series of major decisions, including abortion, capital punishment, and school prayer. (See box, "Inside the Supreme Court: The Blackmun Papers.")

Even earlier, in 1979, much of the Court's traditional secrecy had been stripped away with the publication of *The Brethren,* a book by two investigative reporters about the operations of the Supreme Court.[56] The book disclosed internal memoranda of the justices and reported in great detail on the private weekly conferences during which justices discuss pending cases. The book revealed a degree of conflict and intense competition among the justices that had not been reported before in such great detail.[57] As already noted, the Supreme Court is a political institution. As the book related, the justices engage in trade-offs and deals and form shifting alliances, much as do political participants in the executive and legislative branches.

*The Brethren* was particularly harsh on Chief Justice Warren Burger, whom it portrayed as a jurist of distinguished bearing, but a man of personal pomposity and

*The Three Stooges, a slapstick comedy team popular in films of the 1930s through the 1950s, were, for more than a decade, Larry, Moe, and Curly. An earlier Stooge, Shemp, dropped out of the team for a time and upon his death was replaced, in succession, by two actors named Joe. The 1995 poll of 1,200 people by Luntz Research of Arlington, Virginia, did not require respondents to provide the last names of the comedians or the first names of the Supreme Court justices. Nor were the respondents required to name Joe or Shemp.

## Inside the Supreme Court: The Blackmun Papers

Justice Harry A. Blackmun's 24-year tenure on the Supreme Court produced more than 1,500 boxes of drafts, letters, and transcripts. Five years after his death on March 4, 1999, the papers were released, as Blackmun wished. The Blackmun papers provide a detailed behind-the-scenes account of historic decisions by the Court, most importantly *Roe* v. *Wade,* the 1973 ruling that legalized abortion.

When the case reached the Court, Blackmun reviewed the Court's previous decisions recognizing a constitutional right to privacy. In one note to himself he indicated he might seek to extend the privacy principle to the issue of abortion. The right to privacy, he wrote, "is broad enough to encompass the decision whether to terminate a pregnancy. . . . But, despite the arguments, the right is not absolute. There is a point at which another interest is involved—life or the potential of life. . . . I avoid any determination as to when life begins. Therefore, a balancing of interests."

Blackmun's note added: "1. A majority of state statutes go down the drain. 2. It will be an unsettled period for a while." He added: "It is not a happy assignment—will be excoriated."

He was right about that. After the Court's 7–2 ruling, which Blackmun wrote, he received thousands of angry letters. There were so many that the Library of Congress, which houses the papers, kept only a small sample.

Blackmun's reaction is recorded in another document. "I never thought that I would be standing against the combined might of the Roman Catholic Church and the Mormon Church and 1600 Pennsylvania Avenue and other forces, with all their respected political power," he wrote. "It showed me once again that the federal bench is no place to win a popularity contest. . . . I suspect I've been called every possible epithetical name, Hitler, butcher of Dachau, Pontius Pilate, Herod, murderer, madman."

After 1973, as the membership of the Court gradually changed, Justice Blackmun worked to preserve *Roe* v. *Wade.* When Justices Sandra Day O'Connor, Anthony Kennedy, and David Souter arrived, he worried that they might vote to abolish the right to abortion. But in 1992, in another case, the Supreme Court upheld *Roe.* The outcome hung in the balance until, at the last moment, Justice Kennedy told Blackmun he would vote for the right of women to have an abortion. Harry Blackmun had triumphed, by a vote of 5–4.

shallow intellect. It quoted Justice William J. Brennan, Jr., as calling Burger a "dummy," and quoted Justice Lewis F. Powell, Jr., as saying of Burger's draft in a busing case: "If an associate in my law firm had done this . . . I'd fire him."[58]

**How Cases Reach the Court** Most cases never get to the Supreme Court. Those that do usually reach the Court in one of two ways. The Court has **original jurisdiction,** the right under the Constitution to hear certain kinds of cases directly, such as cases involving foreign diplomats, or cases in which one of the 50 states is a party. But the Court rarely exercises original jurisdiction. Rather, the overwhelming majority of cases presented to the Court come in the form of petitions for a **writ of certiorari.** The Court can choose which of the cases it wants to hear by denying or granting certiorari, a Latin term meaning "made more certain." The votes of four justices are needed to grant "cert." Between 90 and 95 percent of all such applications are denied.[59]

Cases may reach the Supreme Court for review from either state or federal courts. The cases come from a state court of last resort (usually a state supreme court), or from federal courts of appeals, U.S. district courts, or special-purpose federal courts.

Of the more than 10 million cases tried annually in American courts, only some 7,000 are taken to the Supreme Court. Of this total, the Court customarily hears argument on fewer than 100. The rest of the cases on the Court's docket are denied, affirmed, or reversed by written "memorandum orders." In choosing whether even to consider a case, the Supreme Court makes law (because, usually, the Supreme Court's refusal to take a case means that a lower court decision stands).

**Court Tradition** The Court normally sits from October through June. The Court building on Capitol Hill is a majestic structure of white marble, completed in 1935 and modeled after the Greek Temple of Diana at Ephesus, one of the seven wonders of the ancient world. The great bronze doors weigh six and a half tons each; the courtroom seats 300 and has a ceiling 44 feet high. Tradition is observed; the federal government's lawyers appearing for oral argument still wear morning clothes—a formal cutaway coat with tails and striped pants. Most private attorneys simply wear dark suits. The rather grandiose setting of the building and the formal atmosphere are designed to preserve the dignity of the nation's highest tribunal, but they also provide some comfort to its critics, particularly political cartoonists, who find it easy to lampoon the Court's elaborate Grecian setting.

Lawyers arguing before the Court usually have one-half hour to make their case. Five minutes before their time expires a white light comes on; when a red light flashes on they must stop. But the justices often use up some of the precious time by interrupting to question the attorneys, a procedure that can be totally unnerving for lawyers making their initial appearance before the Supreme Court.

## The Chief Justices of the United States

John Jay (1789–1795)
John Rutledge (1795)
Oliver Ellsworth (1796–1800)
John Marshall (1801–1835)
Roger B. Taney (1836–1864)
Salmon P. Chase (1864–1873)
Morrison R. Waite (1874–1888)
Melville W. Fuller (1888–1910)
Edward D. White (1910–1921)
William Howard Taft (1921–1930)
Charles Evans Hughes (1930–1941)
Harlan F. Stone (1941–1946)
Fred M. Vinson (1946–1953)
Earl Warren (1953–1969)
Warren E. Burger (1969–1986)
William H. Rehnquist (1986–2005)
John G. Roberts (2005– )

Justice William O. Douglas

On Fridays when the Court is sitting, the justices meet in conference to discuss and vote on pending cases and petitions for certiorari. The justices, by a tradition established in 1888, shake hands as they file into the oak-paneled conference room. The meetings are secret and presided over by the chief justice. Beneath a portrait of Chief Justice John Marshall, which hangs over the marble fireplace, the members of the Court gather around a conference table. Behind each justice is a cart on which law clerks have placed all the legal documents the justices may need to expound their positions on the various cases. During these discussions, no one other than the nine justices is allowed in the conference room, not even a clerk. The chief justice and the other justices take notes during their deliberations.

**The Chief Justice** Although theoretically equal to the other eight justices, "the Chief" has four important advantages: prestige, the power to influence the Court's selection of cases, the power to chair the conference, and the power to assign the writing of opinions by the justices. The chief justice, therefore, may play a very important role as "Court unifier."[60] Or the chief justice may be a source of disunity.

Leadership styles among chief justices differ. Charles Evans Hughes, chief justice during the 1930s, was popular among the justices on the Court even though he ran the conference with a firm hand. His successor, Harlan Fiske Stone, was much less reserved and delighted in joining the debate. "'Jackson,' he would say, 'that's damned nonsense.' 'Douglas, you know better than that.'"[61]

The chief justice, if in the majority, decides who will write the Court's opinion; otherwise, the ranking justice among the majority assigns the writing of the opinion. According to *The Brethren,* Chief Justice Burger often maneuvered in conference to assign opinions (and thus perhaps influence their content) even when he was not in the majority on a case. In one such instance, the authors reported, Justice William O. Douglas threatened to make public a 1972 memo in which he complained that Burger should not have assigned a group of major abortion cases to Justice Harry A. Blackmun:

> When . . . the minority seeks to control the assignment, there is a destructive force at work in the Court. When a Chief Justice tries to bend the Court to his will by manipulating assignments, the integrity of the institution is imperiled.
>
> . . . Perhaps the purpose of the Chief Justice, a member of the minority in the Abortion Cases, in assigning the opinions was to try to keep control of the merits. If that was the aim, he was unsuccessful.[62]

Douglas eventually withdrew his threat to publish the explosive memo. But clearly, the interaction among the justices on the Court is a political process, in which votes are sometimes traded and positions compromised.

Shortly after Justice Lewis F. Powell, Jr., retired in 1987, he granted an interview in which he talked frankly about this process. "Whenever you're assigned to write a 5-to-4 decision, you know that you cannot afford to lose a vote," he said. "And sometimes you end up on the short end of a case when you started out with five votes, and that makes you more than a little unhappy."[63] He added: "You receive memos from other Justices, saying 'Dear Lewis, I'm inclined to join your opinion but it would help me if you changed so and so.' And sometimes a Justice will suggest language."[64]

The justices, Powell added, call uninteresting cases "dogs." "A dog is a case that you wish the Chief Justice had assigned to some other justice," he said—a deadly dull case, "a tax case, for example."[65]

**Dissenting Opinions** Once an opinion is assigned, justices are free to write dissenting opinions if they disagree with the majority, or concurring opinions if they reach the same conclusion as the majority, often for different reasons. Important bargaining takes place backstage among the justices as the opinions are written and circulated informally, and justices may trade their votes to influence the shape of an opinion. Some legal experts believe that dissents, because they publicly reveal disunity, weaken the prestige of the Court—the large number of 5–4 decisions by the Warren Court, for example, provided fuel for its enemies. But many of the most eloquent arguments of the Supreme Court have been voiced in dissents by justices including the first John Marshall Harlan (of Kentucky), as well as Holmes, Brandeis, Stone, Black, and Douglas. Today's dissent may become tomorrow's majority opinion when the Court, as it has frequently done, overrules past decisions to meet new problems.

When it is in session, the Court usually hands down its opinions in the first part of each week. The justices read or summarize their opinions in the courtroom, sometimes adding informal comments. The words that echo through the marble chamber, often with enormous consequences for society, become the law of the land and renew the meaning of constitutional government.

## The American Court System

Because the United States encompasses both a federal government and 50 state governments, it has a dual court system. As one scholar noted, "In effect, this means that there exist, side by side, two major court systems—one could even say fifty-one—which are wholly distinct."[66]

At the top of the system is the U.S. Supreme Court. But as we have seen, relatively few cases get there. The average citizen has neither the time nor the money to fight a case all the way to the highest tribunal. In any event, the Court considers only cases involving a substantial federal question or constitutional issue, and normally after all remedies in the state courts have been exhausted.

### The Federal Courts

The bulk of the cases that come before the judicial branch of the federal government are handled in the "inferior" courts created by Congress under the Constitution. Immediately below the Supreme Court are the U.S. courts of appeals, also known as circuit courts. The nation is divided geographically into 13 judicial circuits, each with a court of appeals. Every state and territory falls within the jurisdiction of one of these circuit courts. Each court of appeals has from six to 28 judges, but usually three judges hear a case. The circuit courts hear appeals from lower federal courts and review the decisions of federal regulatory agencies. Each year about 61,000 cases reach the circuit courts.

*for more information about the federal courts, see: http://www.uscourts.gov*

Below the circuit courts are the federal district courts. In 2004 there were 89 district courts in the 50 states, plus one each for the District of Columbia, Puerto Rico, the Virgin Islands, Guam, and the Northern Mariana Islands, making a total of 94. Each district has from two to 28 judges, making a total of 679 district judgeships.[67]

More than half of the federal judicial districts coincide with state lines, but some populous states, such as California, Texas, and New York, are divided into multiple districts. The federal district courts are trial courts; they handle cases involving disputes between citizens of different states, and violations of federal law—for example, of civil rights, patent and copyright, bankruptcy, immigration, counterfeiting, antitrust, and postal laws.

### Special Federal Courts

Congress has created special-purpose courts to deal with certain kinds of cases. These include the U.S. Court of Federal Claims, which has jurisdiction over such cases as claims for compensation for property taken by the government, claims for income tax refunds, or claims by government workers for back pay; the U.S. Court of Appeals for the Federal Circuit, which hears copyright, trademark, and patent cases; the U.S. Tax Court, which hears a variety of tax cases; and the U.S. Court of Appeals for the Armed Forces, often termed the "GI Supreme Court." This court, whose three judges are civilians, is the final appellate tribunal in court-martial convictions. It was established by Congress in 1950, along with a Uniform Code of Military Justice. The code represented the first major overhaul of the system of military justice since the early 19th century.

The Vietnam War focused new attention on the process of military justice. The most controversial case growing out of that war was the murder conviction of 1st Lt. William L. Calley, Jr. In 1968 American soldiers swept through the South Vietnamese hamlet of My Lai and killed somewhere between 100 and more than 300 men, women, and children, all civilians. The tragedy was covered up for more than a year, until journalist Seymour M. Hersh publicized the story, for which he won a Pulitzer Prize. The government brought charges in connection with the massacre and its cover-up against 25 officers and enlisted men, including the general who commanded the division at the time of the murders. But only Lieutenant Calley, who led his platoon through My Lai, was convicted. In 1971 an Army court found Calley guilty of the premeditated murder of at least 22 South Vietnamese civilians at My Lai. He was sentenced to life imprisonment, but the Army later reduced the sentence to 10 years. Calley was paroled by the Army after he had served one-third of his sentence.

Military courts drew attention again after 9/11 when the government asserted the right to try some suspects before military tribunals, and again when several U.S. soldiers were charged with abusing prisoners in Iraq.

The cases stemming from the wars in Iraq and Vietnam dramatized the fact that many Americans—about

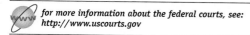

© Bettmann/Corbis

Lt. William Calley, Jr.

1.4 million in 2006 in the armed forces, active reserve, and national guard when called up—were subject to military courts and therefore were at least temporarily outside the civilian system of justice as it has evolved under the Constitution. Moreover, there is always the danger that military trials will be swayed by command influence—that is, that the decisions of prosecutors, and officers who serve on military juries, may be affected by the views of their commanding officers.

In recent years, the Court of Appeals for the Armed Forces itself has moved to broaden the legal rights of servicemen and servicewomen. For example, it held that the Supreme Court's *Miranda* decision, ruling out involuntary confessions, must also apply in military cases.[68]

Although defendants charged under military law have a right to counsel, they do not have a right to trial by a jury of 12 people. And except in cases that carry the death penalty, juries in military courts do not have to be unanimous to convict.

In 1987 the Supreme Court ruled that military personnel suspected of a crime of any type may be tried in military courts, whether or not the crime was committed at a military installation.[69] As a result, military defendants may be tried in either civilian or military courts for crimes unrelated to the service.

More than a decade earlier, in 1974, the Supreme Court upheld the controversial Article 134, the "general article" of the Uniform Code of Military Justice, which permitted the military to impose criminal penalties for any offense that imperiled "good order and discipline" in the armed forces.[70] The rules of evidence used in federal criminal trials also apply to military courts-martial.

## The State Court System

State and local courts, not the federal courts, handle most cases in the United States. The quality and structure of the state court systems vary tremendously, but most states have several layers of courts:

1. *Magistrates' courts* are courts in which justices of the peace, or magistrates, handle **misdemeanors,** minor criminal offenses such as speeding, and perform civil marriages. Most "JPs" do not have law degrees, but what they may lack in legal training they make up for in their well-known zeal for convictions, which average 80 percent in criminal cases.[71]
2. *Municipal courts* are known variously as police courts, city courts, traffic courts, and night courts. These courts, generally one step up from the magistrates' courts, usually hear civil and lesser criminal cases.
3. *County courts,* also called superior courts, try **felonies,** serious crimes, such as murder, arson, or rape. These courts also try major civil cases. At this level, jury trials are held in some cases.
4. *Special jurisdiction courts* are sometimes created at the county level to handle domestic relations, juveniles, probate of wills and estates, and other specialized tasks.
5. *Intermediate courts of appeals,* or appellate divisions, exist in some states to hear appeals from the county and municipal courts.
6. *Courts of appeals,* often called state supreme courts, are the final judicial tribunals in the states.

## The Judges

**Federal Court Judges** All federal court judges are appointed by the president, subject to Senate approval. Historically, federal judges have been selected under a Senate patronage system that has often drawn criticism. The system changed briefly under President Jimmy Carter, but traditionally it has worked this way: Senators present the president with the names of three candidates for federal judgeships; from these, the president selects one; the Justice Department and the FBI check the background of the person selected; the American Bar Association files a report; and the name is submitted to the Senate for confirmation.

During the 1976 presidential campaign, however, Carter promised to appoint all federal judges "strictly on the basis of merit without any consideration of political aspect or influence." As president, Carter issued two executive orders, one creating merit commissions to recommend circuit court judges, and another encouraging the creation of such commissions in the states to recommend candidates for federal district courts.

Commissions were established in about half the states. Despite the loose, partly voluntary nature of the merit system, Carter's orders had an impact; more women and members of minority groups were appointed to the federal bench. President Reagan canceled both Carter orders and returned to the Senate patronage system. Fewer women and minority judges were named by Reagan and his successor, the first President Bush, although their numbers increased during the Clinton years.

**State and Local Judges** A majority of the 30,552 state judges in the United States are elected, as are many local judges.[72] Some, most, or all judges are elected in 30 states. In other states, judges are appointed. Sixteen states and the District of Columbia employ the merit system for the selection of judges, patterned after the "Missouri plan."[73] The basic elements of that plan, which went into effect in Missouri in 1940, are as follows:

1. Nomination of the judges by a nonpartisan commission made up of lawyers, a judge, and citizens.
2. Appointment by the governor.
3. Approval by the voters after an initial term on the bench.

Despite the efforts to bring about judicial reform, in most cases "it is the politicians who select the judges. The voters only ratify their choices."[74] Political parties sometimes do not run competing candidates for the judiciary; rather, political leaders of both major parties get together and carve up the available judgeships. The nominees then run with the endorsement of both parties. In the process, political hacks are sometimes elevated to the bench.

But a presidential commission has warned: "The quality of the judiciary in large measure determines the quality of justice."[75] Bad judges do more than administer bad law; in the process they erode public respect for the entire system of criminal justice and the political system of which it is a vital part.

## Criminal Justice in America

A presidential commission has observed that "the poor—like the rich—can go to court. Whether they find satisfaction there is another matter. . . . Too frequently courts . . . serve the poor less well than their creditors. . . . The poor are discouraged from initiating civil actions against their exploiters. Litigation is expensive; so are experienced lawyers."[76]

The commission that issued this critical report included a mixture of liberals, moderates, and conservatives. The report went on to criticize the nation's criminal justice system in words that were often harsh. In fact, the commission said, there is no real system of criminal justice:

> There is, instead, a reasonably well-defined criminal process . . . through which each accused offender may pass: from the hands of the police, to the jurisdiction of the courts, behind the walls of a prison, then back onto the street. . . . Criminal courts themselves are often poorly managed and . . . seriously backlogged. . . . Prisons . . . are . . . schools in crime. . . . The typical prison experience is degrading . . . and the outlook of most ex-convicts is bleak.[77]

### The Criminal Justice Treadmill

- Half of all major crimes are never reported to police.
- Of those that are, fewer than 25 percent are solved by arrests.
- Half of these arrests result in dismissal of charges.
- Ninety percent of the rest are resolved by a plea of guilty.
- The fraction of cases that do go to trial represent fewer than 1 percent of all crimes committed.
- About 25 percent of those convicted are sent to prison; the rest are released on probation.
- Nearly everyone who goes to prison is eventually released.
- Between half and two-thirds of those released are arrested and convicted again; they become repeat criminals known as recidivists.

—Adapted from *To Establish Justice, to Insure Domestic Tranquility,* Final Report of the National Commission on the Causes and Prevention of Violence

© AP/Wide World Photos

A robbery occurs in America every 1.2 minutes. A bank video surveillance camera showed a young woman believed responsible for six Boston area bank holdups.

Most criticism of the administration of justice in the United States is directed not at the principles of the system—the presumption that a defendant is innocent until proven guilty and the protections of the Bill of Rights—but at the failure of the system to work the way it is supposed to work.

Americans, Edward L. Barrett, Jr., has noted, tend to think that the procedure of the criminal courts protects the dignity of the individual against the power of the government:

> Such is the general image we have of the administration of criminal justice. But if one enters the courthouse in any sizable city and walks from courtroom to courtroom, what does he see? One judge, in a single morning, is accepting pleas of guilty from and sentencing a hundred or more persons charged with drunkenness. Another judge is adjusting traffic cases with an average time of no more than a minute per case. A third is disposing of a hundred or more other misdemeanor offenses in a morning. . . . Suddenly it becomes clear that for most defendants in the criminal process, there is scant regard for them as individuals. They are numbers on dockets, faceless ones to be processed and sent on their way. The gap between the theory and the reality is enormous.[78]

## A Profile of Crime in America

In 2003 an estimated 11.7 million violent and property crimes were reported to law enforcement agencies in the United States, of which 1,367,009, or 12 percent, fell into the category of crimes that people fear the most: murder, forcible rape, robbery, and aggravated assault. (See Table 15-2.)

In the United States in 2003, a total of 16,137 people were murdered, an increase of 0.4 percent in four years. More than 2.1 million burglaries were reported, 65.7 percent of these in homes. More than 1.2 million cars were stolen. Put another way, on the average a violent crime was committed every 23 seconds, a murder every 33 minutes, a rape every 5.6 minutes, a robbery every 1.2 minutes, a burglary every 14.7 seconds, and a car stolen every 26 seconds.[79] (See Figure 15-1.)

These figures, compiled annually by the FBI from reports received by law enforcement agencies, indicate a decrease in recent years in the rate of violent and major crime. Various factors have been cited to explain the apparent lower crime rates, including a strong economy in the 1990s, the decline of the crack cocaine epidemic that had gripped the inner cities in the mid-1980s, tougher police tactics, and new gun laws.

However, there is no broad agreement among

**TABLE 15-2**

**Crime in the United States, 2003**

| Crime Offenses | Estimated Number of Crimes | Rate per 100,000 Inhabitants |
|---|---|---|
| Total | 11,695,264 | 3,982.6 |
| Violent | 1,367,009 | 465.5 |
| Property | 10,328,255 | 3,517.1 |
| Murder | 16,137 | 5.5 |
| Forcible rape | 94,635 | 32.2 |
| Robbery | 401,326 | 136.7 |
| Aggravated assault | 854,911 | 291.1 |
| Burglary | 2,143,456 | 729.9 |
| Larceny-theft | 6,947,685 | 2,356.9 |
| Auto theft | 1,237,114 | 421.3 |
| Arson | 63,215 | 48.8 |

SOURCE: Adapted from *Crime in the United States 2004,* Uniform Crime Reports, Federal Bureau of Investigation, tables 1, 2.30, and 2.31.

**FIGURE 15-1**

**Crime Clocks, 2003**

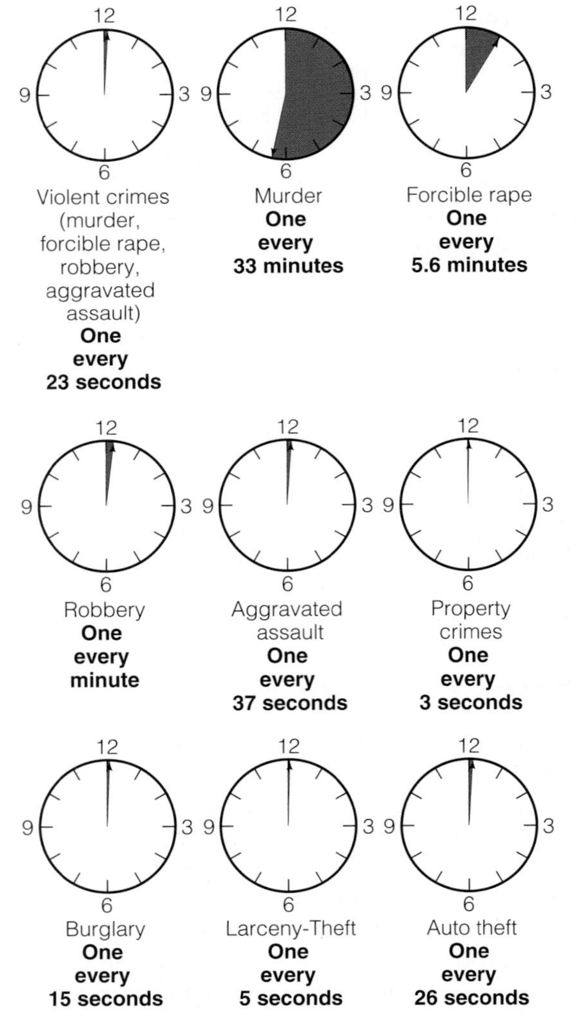


SOURCE: Adapted from *Crime in the United States 2004,* Uniform Crime Reports, Federal Bureau of Investigation, p. 7.

experts even that crime has really declined, let alone a consensus on the possible causes of any decrease. For example, one study found that despite a short-term drop in crime from a peak in the early 1990s, there had been an increase of 40 percent over 30 years in the overall level of violence in major cities, as well as a sharp increase in the fear of crime.[80] And a preliminary FBI report for 2005 indicated that violent crime had increased that year for the first time in four years.[81]

Moreover, the annual crime statistics may not reflect the full magnitude of lawbreaking in the United States. A presidential commission has estimated that the actual amount of crime committed is "several times" greater than the amount of crime reported to the authorities.[82] People fail to report crime for a variety of reasons, including a reluctance to "get involved," doubt that police can do anything about it, or fear of reprisal by the criminal.[83]

There are some popular misconceptions about crime. As the president's commission noted, "the risks of personal harm are spread very unevenly," because they are much higher for residents of the inner city than for most other Americans.[84] Author Richard Harris reported, for example, that for a black resident of Chicago's inner city, "the chance of being physically assaulted, on the basis of reported crimes, was one in seventy-seven, whereas for the white resident of a nearby suburb the chance was one in ten thousand."[85] But even people who live in relatively "safe" areas have either been victims of crime or know someone who has been a crime victim.

Crime by youths accounts for a substantial share of all crime. In 2003, for example, 27.5 percent of the arrests for violent and property crimes were of persons under age 18.[86] Drug addiction is another source of crime. Estimates vary greatly as to how much crime is committed by drug addicts in order to get money to support their habit. Some estimates have attributed as much as three-quarters of all serious crime in New York City and Washington, D.C., to drug addicts.[87]

Because the population is increasing, when crime statistics drop, the actual number of such crimes remained disturbingly high. Even if the crime rate stayed level, there would be more crime because of population growth.

One approach in the effort to reduce crime is gun control, legislation designed to restrict criminals from acquiring handguns or assault weapons. It is an approach strongly opposed by many gun owners and their powerful lobby, the National Rifle Association. In 1993, President Clinton signed the Brady Bill, which requires the buyer of a handgun to wait five days while authorities check to see whether the purchaser has a criminal record or a history of drug addiction or mental problems.

The law was named after James Brady, the White House press secretary severely injured when he was shot in the head during an assassination attempt against President Reagan in 1981. During six years after the law went into effect, almost 700,000 of 30 million applications from would-be gun buyers were rejected by the FBI or state and local agencies.[88] In 1998, under the Brady law, the Justice Department began a program of instant background checks of potential gun buyers; in the first year of operation, 160,000 of 8.7 million people who attempted to buy guns were turned down.[89] The screening turned up some startling statistics; for example, in 2004, 8.3 percent of the applicants rejected were actual fugitives from justice.[90]

The Brady law continued to draw criticism from opponents of gun control, and one study reported that

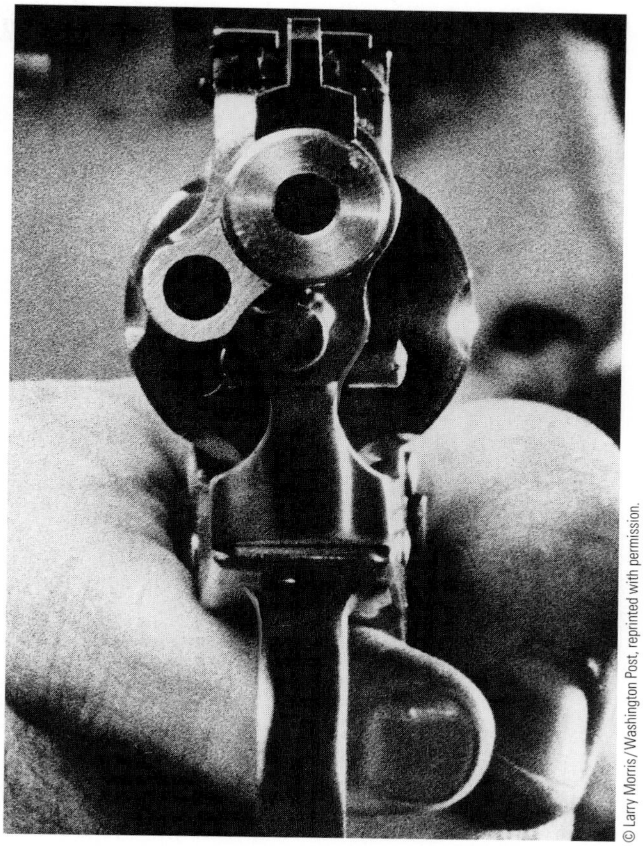

© Larry Morris/Washington Post, reprinted with permission.

TABLE 15-3

**Death and Guns: A Look around the World**

*The high rate of deaths from guns in the United States is not reflected in many other countries, as these numbers show. The statistics are for gun deaths in one year.*

| Gun Deaths | Country | Population |
|---|---|---|
| 2 | New Zealand | 3,547,983 |
| 15 | Japan | 125,449,703 |
| 30 | Great Britain | 58,489,975 |
| 106 | Canada | 28,820,671 |
| 213 | Germany | 83,536,115 |
| 9,390 | United States | 265,562,845 |

SOURCE: Center to Prevent Handgun Violence. Data for 1996.

## The Million Mom March: "It Would Have Been Her Seventh Birthday"

WASHINGTON, May 14—With a rallying cry of "enough is enough," hundreds of thousands of mothers and other gun control advocates marched on the nation's capital and in several cities around the country today, demanding "sensible gun laws," mourning the loss of children to gun violence and vowing to transform the politics of gun control.

Under a clear spring sky, the Million Mom March crowded the grassy expanse of the National Mall, cheering one speaker after another who assailed the National Rifle Association and its power over Congress. Many of the demonstrators wept at the stories of mothers who had lost their children, listening transfixed to the families shattered by shootings from Columbine High School, in Littleton, Colorado, where 15 died last year to the Michigan elementary school where a 6-year-old girl was killed by a classmate on Feb. 29.

"I come to you today, two days after what would have been her seventh birthday," said Veronica McQueen, the Michigan girl's mother. "I am a mom with a terrible tragedy, and I hope it never, ever happens again."

It was a Mother's Day of high emotion and powerful imagery, both here and in more than 60 other demonstrations scheduled around the country this weekend. Many in the crowd on the Mall today wore T-shirts with the photographs of family members killed by guns. Judi Ellis of Toledo, Ohio, carried a placard that declared, "I march today to save a child tomorrow," with a picture of her son, who was killed in 1995, before he left for college. "You're not supposed to bury your son," she said.

—From Robin Toner, "Mothers Rally to Assail Gun Violence," *The New York Times,* May 15, 2000. © 2000 The New York Times Company. Reprinted by permission.

the background checks had not reduced homicide rates.[91] However, other analyses showed that the law had reduced interstate gun trafficking, and a California study reported that state laws requiring background checks had reduced crimes committed with guns by 25 to 30 percent.[92]

In 1994, as part of a crime bill enacted into law and signed by President Clinton, the manufacture or sale of 19 types of new semiautomatic assault-style weapons was prohibited; the law did not apply to assault weapons people already owned. Law enforcement authorities said such weapons were used primarily to commit crimes. As many as 78 percent of the public supported the measure.[93] But the ban expired in 2004.

In recent years there have been a number of school shootings, including the carnage at Columbine High School in Littleton, Colorado, in the spring of 1999. Then in February 2000, a 6-year-old boy took a handgun to school and shot and killed Kayla Rolland, his first-grade classmate in Flint, Michigan.

In response to these tragedies, thousands of people gathered on the mall in Washington, D.C., in May of 2000 in a "Million Mom March" for gun control and an end to violence.

Despite the shocking school shootings, repeated workplace killings by disgruntled or mentally disturbed current or former employees, and the mass protest in Washington, Congress by 2004 had not passed more stringent gun control legislation.

Kayla Rolland, 6, the first-grade Michigan student shot and killed at school by a 6-year-old classmate

## The Prisons

The Department of Justice reported in 2002 that a record 2,186,230 people were in federal and state prisons and local jails in the United States. Of the total, 184,484 were inmates of federal prisons.[94] The majority of prisoners are in the state prison systems, where uprisings, often violent, and the seizure of hostages have become familiar occurrences in recent years.

Prison overcrowding is recognized as a serious problem in America, which has the highest incarceration

Attica, 1971

rate in the world. Many states have passed laws providing for early release of prisoners when overcrowding reaches certain levels. In a number of states, prisoners sleep on floors, or two and three prisoners are jammed into cells built for one. Overpopulation is a major factor in the outbreaks of riots and cases of hostage-taking in the prisons.

Yet the U.S. Supreme Court has ruled 8–1 that prison overcrowding is not forbidden by the Constitution. In a 1981 decision, the Burger Court held that "harsh" prison conditions are the price of crime, "part of the penalty that criminal offenders pay for their offenses against society." Although prison conditions may not be "grossly disproportionate to the severity of the crime . . . persons convicted of serious crimes cannot be free of discomfort."[95] The case challenged the housing of two men in cells of 63 square feet in an Ohio prison. In 1984 the Court held that the Constitution protected prisoners far less than other citizens.[96]

In 1992, the Supreme Court ruled that federal courts are no longer obliged to hear appeals by state prison inmates.[97] In the same year, however, the Court decided an important case strengthening prisoners' rights when it ruled that beatings or other excessive use of force by guards may violate the Constitution even when there is no serious injury to the prisoner.[98]

The nation's prisons, instead of rehabilitating offenders, may contribute to the crime rate by simply serving in many instances as "human warehouses" for the custody of convicts. Close to half of felons released from prison commit new crimes. In many cases little is done to prepare prisoners for their return to the outside world. More than half of all state prisons have no vocational training programs. A presidential study commission concluded that "for a great many offenders . . . corrections does not correct."[99] Moreover, state parole systems are badly overburdened. As a result, the decision on when to release prisoners is often arbitrary and unfair, creating further bitterness among those who must remain behind bars. Inmates sentenced to federal prisons for crimes committed after October 1987 are not eligible for parole.

As noted earlier, tensions in America's prisons sometimes run so high that they explode into prison riots, in which guards or other hostages are seized and inmates demand better conditions. One of the most dramatic and tragic outbreaks occurred in 1971 at Attica, a maximum-security state prison in New York. The dismal conditions at Attica were typical of many state prison systems: old and overcrowded buildings, with guards who were often poorly trained and sometimes brutal. Racial tensions ran high at Attica, as at other prisons where many inmates are African American and most of the guards white.

For four days, convicts took control of the courtyard of a cell block and held hostages. Governor Nelson Rockefeller ordered 200 state troopers to storm the prison. Thirty-two inmates and 11 hostages died. Almost all of them had been killed in the hail of troopers' bullets. A special New York State commission that investigated the bloodshed at Attica concluded that the conditions that sparked the revolt were, in a sense, universal: "Attica is every prison; and every prison is Attica."[100]

## The Police

Police in the United States walk a tightrope; often underpaid, with inadequate personnel and resources, they are expected to fight crime, enforce the law, keep the peace, and provide a wide variety of social and community services.

Police must spend much of their time performing community services—from directing traffic to rescuing stray cats. These duties greatly reduce the amount of time police can spend fighting crime. And police face violence in their work. From 1970 to 2006 a total of 6,904 police officers in the United States were killed in the line of duty.[101]

© 2003 Steve Kelley/*The Times Picayune*. Reprinted with permission.

Many Americans strongly support and defend the police. Even when police employed violence against young antiwar demonstrators at the 1968 Democratic National Convention in Chicago, 56 percent of the public approved of the way the police had acted.[102] Later, a staff study of a presidential commission adjudged the events at Chicago "a police riot."[103] But in times of turmoil and fear of violence, many Americans appear to regard "law and order" as a requirement that takes precedence over all other considerations, including the constitutional right of peaceful dissent.[104]

On the other hand, when a state jury acquitted four white Los Angeles police officers in the beating of black motorist Rodney King, 77 percent of respondents thought that the jury verdict was "not justified."[105] In this instance, the beating had been videotaped by a citizen and shown repeatedly on television. The acquittal touched off the devastating riots in Los Angeles in April 1992. In 1993, two of the police officers, Stacey C. Koon and Laurence Powell, were convicted in federal court of violating King's civil rights, and sent to prison. The two other officers were acquitted of the federal charges. Because so many Americans had viewed the brutal beating on TV, the episode, the trials, and the riots focused new attention on the controversial question of how far police may go in enforcing the law before they themselves become lawbreakers.

And police do break the law. In New York, in 2000, three officers were convicted and given substantial prison terms in the brutalization of a Haitian immigrant, Abner Louima, in the bathroom of a police station in Brooklyn. A year earlier, four New York City plainclothes officers

Wally Skalij/Daily Breeze/Zuma Press

fired 41 shots at Amadou Diallo, an immigrant from Guinea, who had been standing, unarmed, outside his house in the Bronx. Diallo's death—he had been hit by 19 bullets—led to widespread protests in the city, but the four officers were acquitted of all charges.

In Philadelphia, several police officers pleaded guilty to charges ranging from creating false evidence to implicate innocent people, to selling drugs, lying under oath, and beating up victims, mostly poor blacks. In a typical case, James Morris, a restaurant owner, was convicted of drug trafficking and sentenced to three years in prison on completely false evidence given by a police officer, who claimed he witnessed a drug buy that never took place. As a result of the Philadelphia police scandal, 300 criminal convictions were overturned or cases dismissed and the city paid $11 million in damages.[106]

In Los Angeles a similar police scandal erupted. It was disclosed that some L.A.P.D. officers had planted guns, drugs, or other evidence on suspects they arrested. More than 100 cases may have been tainted in this manner, many in a gang-infested inner-city neighborhood. Police planted a gun on one unarmed man, Javier Francisco Ovando, after he was shot by officers, leaving him paralyzed for life. He was sentenced in 1997 to 23 years in prison but freed by a judge two years later when the truth emerged.[107]

As "the cop on the beat" dealing with everyday social conflict and crime, police exercise great discretionary powers.[108] Should a fight be broken up, a speeding car stopped, a street-corner crowd dispersed? The police officer must decide. To a great extent, law enforcement policy is made by the police.

Police do not capture most lawbreakers, however. There is a huge gap between the number of crimes reported and the number of criminals arrested. Crime can be viewed as a series of concentric circles, in which the smallest, innermost circle represents people actually convicted and sent to prison. (See Figure 15-2.)

## The Department of Justice

Although criminal justice and law enforcement are primarily the responsibility of state and local authorities, the federal government wields substantial power in this field. The Department of Justice in recent years has emerged as a major policy-making agency in relation to a broad range of political, legal, and social issues. The department is headed by the attorney general, who is both a cabinet officer and the president's chief legal adviser.

***for more information about the Department of Justice, see: http://www.usdoj.gov***

One of the Justice Department's basic responsibilities is to conduct criminal prosecutions in the federal courts. This means that the attorney general has tremendous power to make political as well as legal decisions about who will be prosecuted and who will not.

Sometimes the attorney general can deflect public criticism from the president. Under George W. Bush, At-

FIGURE 15-2

**Crime and Law Enforcement**

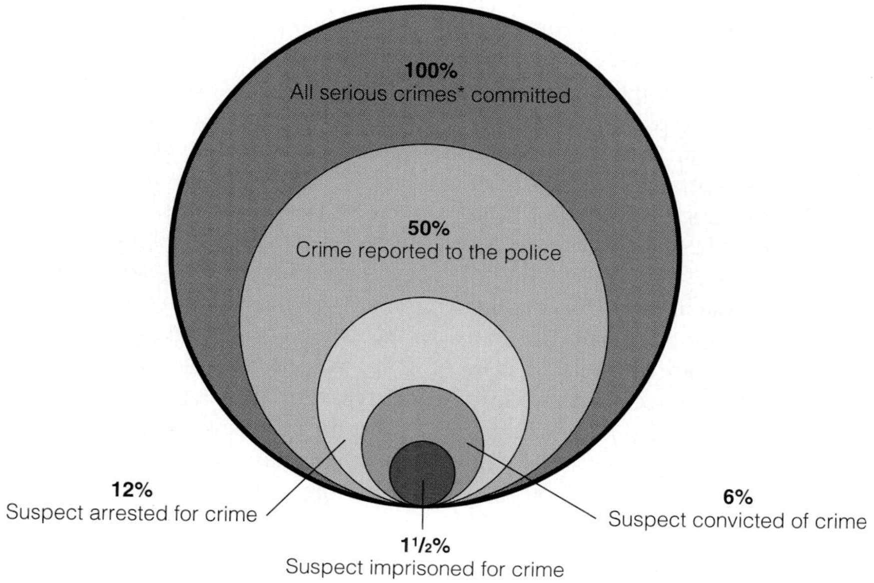


*Homicide, forcible rape, robbery, aggravated assault, burglary, larceny over $50, auto theft. Based on estimates.

SOURCE: *To Establish Justice, to Insure Domestic Tranquility,* Final Report of the National Commission on the Causes and Prevention of Violence (Washington, D.C.: U.S. Government Printing Office, December 1969), p. xviii.

© AP/Wide World Photos

Los Angeles, March 2000: A police scandal led to this protest by demonstrators.

torney General John Ashcroft became a lightning rod for criticism of the administration. Ashcroft's critics claimed that in combating terrorism, he was overzealous and disregarded individual rights.

During the Clinton administration, after 85 people died in 1993 in the FBI siege of a religious sect's compound near Waco, Texas, Attorney General Janet Reno took responsibility. As a result, much of the criticism of the attack was focused on Reno and the FBI rather than on Clinton and the White House. As attorney general, Reno was the target of a constant drumbeat of Republican criticism, much of it centered on her refusal to name an independent counsel to investigate charges of fundraising abuses by the Democrats in the 1996 presidential campaign.

During the Watergate scandal in the 1970s, a special prosecutor, Harvard law professor Archibald Cox, was named to pursue the Watergate case and related cases. When Cox sought presidential tape recordings to learn whether Nixon himself had participated in covering up the burglary of Democratic headquarters and in obstructing justice, Nixon dismissed him. Attorney General Elliot L. Richardson then resigned, along with the deputy attorney general. There were immediate demands for the appointment of a new special prosecutor. Responding to these pressures, Nixon named Texas attorney Leon Jaworski to the post. The appointment, dismissal, and replacement of the special Watergate prosecutor was a dramatic illustration of the politically sensitive nature of the Justice Department.

In the wake of Watergate, Congress in 1978 passed the Ethics in Government Act, providing for appointment of an independent counsel, not subject to control by the president, the attorney general, or Congress, in cases involving possible crimes by high officials. The law proved controversial, in part because of independent counsel Kenneth Starr's relentless pursuit of President Clinton in what had begun as the Whitewater investigation. Congress allowed the law to expire in 1999, except for investigations already in progress.

The attorney general can, however, appoint a "special counsel" to investigate officials in the executive branch and Congress. For example, Patrick J. Fitzgerald, the U.S. attorney in Chicago, was appointed in 2003 as a special counsel to investigate the leak to the press of the name of Valerie Plame, a CIA officer. But a special counsel is subject to oversight by the attorney general.

An attorney general might publicly disclaim any suggestion that the decisions of that office are political. But the attorney general is a cabinet officer responsible to the president. As a result, both the attorney general and the Justice Department play a significant political role.

The attorney general's political viewpoint is normally an important factor weighed by the president in selecting an individual for that post. In exercising discretion about whom to prosecute, an attorney general may also reflect personal ideology and outlook. Should an antitrust suit be brought against a major American corporation, such as Microsoft? Should the department increase its efforts to combat organized crime? The attorney general may decide.

When it was revealed that some U.S. soldiers had tortured prisoners in Iraq, various inquiries were begun into whether higher-ups in the government had approved such abuses. A controversial 2002 Justice Department memo surfaced that appeared to be an attempt to define and justify torture to obtain information from suspected terrorists. Even if a government interrogator "knows that severe pain will result from his actions," the memo said, "if causing such harm is not his objective, he lacks the specific requisite intent" to be guilty of torture.[109] The White House later asserted that the memo did not reflect the policy of the Bush administration.

The Justice Department prosecutes persons accused of federal crimes through its U.S. attorneys in each of the federal judicial districts. Although U.S. attorneys are appointed by the president, subject to Senate approval, they serve under the attorney general. Under the supervision of the department's criminal division, the U.S. attorney in each district initiates investigations and decides whether to prosecute or to seek a grand jury indictment in criminal cases.

Separate divisions of the Justice Department deal with criminal, civil, antitrust, tax, civil rights, and environmental and natural resources cases. A special unit in the criminal division handles cases involving organized crime. The Justice Department also includes the Drug Enforcement Administration, and the Bureau of Prisons, which is in charge of federal prisons and youth centers.

## The FBI

Best known of all the arms of the Justice Department is the Federal Bureau of Investigation. After the terrorist attacks of September 11, 2001, the FBI shifted its main focus from general criminal cases to trying to prevent another terrorist attack on the United States.

Congress, as a result of the FBI's changed mission, provided more money to the bureau. In fiscal 2006, the FBI had a budget of $5.7 billion and employed more than 30,400 people (about 30 percent of all the Justice Department's employees). Of the total, 12,515 were FBI special agents; most of the rest were support personnel.[110]

The FBI is the investigative arm of the Justice Department, and its jurisdiction is limited to suspected violations of federal law. It has 56 field offices, about 400 smaller offices called resident agencies, a training base in Quantico, Virginia, and 45 representatives in foreign countries, known as "Legal Attachés," or Legats, for liaison with foreign police and intelligence services.[111] In the FBI's files are 226 million fingerprint cards, representing approximately 79 million individuals.[112] In 1999 the FBI switched to a much faster Integrated Automated Fingerprint Identification System that digitally records fingerprints.

*for more information about the FBI, see:*
***http://www.fbi.gov***

Senate and House investigations of the FBI during the 1970s, in the wake of the Watergate scandal, revealed that for years—while the FBI enjoyed a highly favorable public image—the bureau had systematically engaged in illegal activities that violated the constitutional rights of American citizens. FBI agents, for example, engaged in hundreds of burglaries of individuals and groups to plant microphones or to photograph documents. From 1956 to 1971, the bureau, through its counterintelligence program (COINTELPRO), harassed American citizens and disrupted their organizations through a wide variety of clandestine techniques, some of which broke up marriages or endangered lives.

Moreover, it was disclosed that since the administration of Franklin D. Roosevelt, the FBI had gathered intelligence on domestic groups and individuals with only the shakiest legal authority to do so. It had files on entertainers such as John Lennon, Elvis Presley, and Lucille Ball; on movie stars, including Marilyn Monroe; and on a wide range of other people, from Eleanor Roosevelt, Pablo Picasso, and Albert Einstein to Al Capone and Walt Disney—even on justices of the U.S. Supreme Court.[113] For years the bureau compiled various indexes or lists of people it considered politically unreliable who were to be rounded up in an emergency. And as the congressional investigations also disclosed, the FBI opened first-class mail in violation of the law.[114] All of these disclosures of FBI abuses surfaced several years after the death of the bureau's longtime chief, J. Edgar Hoover, but many of the illegal practices had taken place under his leadership.

For 48 years, until his death in 1972 at the age of 77, Hoover was director of the FBI. Under eight presidents, Hoover and the FBI acquired an unprecedented degree of power and independence. One major source of Hoover's

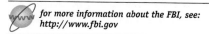

J. Edgar Hoover

power was the secret dossiers and files of the FBI. A member of Congress who had a drinking problem, or who had accepted a campaign contribution from someone rumored to have connections with organized crime, or who was having an extramarital affair, might have good reason to fear the contents of the FBI's file on him or her.

Even presidents respected Hoover's power, and under his reign the FBI, although an arm of the Justice Department, became largely independent of the attorney general. With a masterful gift for publicity, Hoover invented the "Ten Most Wanted" list and helped to project the image of the "G-man" as square-jawed, clean-cut, and infallible. Through movies, a television series, and guided tours of its headquarters for the millions of tourists who visit Washington each year, the FBI became the most publicized agency of the federal government. During Hoover's years, it was able to obtain almost anything it wanted from Congress, including a new $126 million headquarters building, still named for Hoover, that opened in 1975.

Even before Hoover's death, the FBI had become controversial. The majority of Americans traditionally thought of it in favorable terms, as an agency adept at catching bank robbers and spies. But other Americans worried about the concentration of power in the hands of the FBI, and they feared that its wiretaps and dossiers might be used for political ends, or to enhance the power of the director. Because Hoover's political views were generally conservative, liberals feared that the FBI was more concerned about pursuing domestic radicals than organized crime.

In addition, events during the Vietnam War focused widespread public attention on the American system of justice and raised important questions about its operations, adequacy, and fairness. For example, in prosecuting antiwar protesters, the government sometimes relied on informers who encouraged or committed the same acts for which their associates were later tried. During the same period, federal grand juries were used to gather intelligence against the peace movement and to suppress political dissent. And as mentioned earlier, through COINTELPRO, its domestic counterintelligence program, the FBI secretly harassed American citizens and in some cases even endangered lives.

The FBI's reputation suffered after President Nixon named an old political associate, L. Patrick Gray, as acting director to succeed Hoover. Gray—at Nixon's request, relayed through the Central Intelligence Agency—initially slowed down and restricted the FBI investigation of the Watergate burglary. And Gray admitted that he had burned key files in the Watergate case.

In 1976 Congress enacted a law that limits the director of the FBI to one 10-year term of office. President Carter named a federal judge, William Webster of Missouri, as head of the FBI in 1978. The FBI's image improved substantially under Webster, who remained director until 1987, when President Reagan named him to head the CIA. President Clinton appointed Louis J. Freeh, a federal judge in New York and a former prosecutor, as FBI director. President George W. Bush named Robert S. Mueller, III, a former Justice Department official, as director.

The FBI's entanglement in the Watergate case had raised a question exactly opposite of that posed by Hoover's independence. Patrick Gray's actions had illustrated the danger of an FBI chief who was too responsive to political control. In the early 1980s, some critics questioned whether the FBI had improperly entrapped members of Congress in its "Abscam" investigation, in which seven lawmakers were indicted and convicted for taking bribes from agents posing as wealthy Arabs. Clearly the role and power of a secretive police agency raises disturbing problems in a democracy.

At the same time, in the aftermath of the 9/11 attacks the FBI was expected to take the lead in protecting the nation from terrorism. In 2002, a joint congressional committee investigating the attacks criticized both the FBI and the CIA for failing to predict or prevent the attacks on the World Trade Center and the Pentagon. Some of the criticism centered on an unheeded warning by an FBI agent in Phoenix that potential terrorists might be training in flight schools in the United States—as the 9/11 hijackers had done. The memo was sent to FBI headquarters, but no action was taken, despite the warning.

In addition, the FBI drew criticism for its handling of the case of Zacarias Moussaoui, a man suspected of close links to the nineteen 9/11 hijackers. Coleen Rowley, an agent in the Minneapolis office of the FBI, complained that efforts to obtain permission to search the

© Chris Kleponis/Bloomberg News/Landov

FBI director Robert S. Mueller III testifies to the 9/11 commission in 2004.

suspect's laptop computer were rejected by officials at FBI headquarters in Washington. Moussaoui pleaded guilty in 2005 to conspiracy to engage in terrorism; when a jury a year later rejected the death penalty for him, he was sentenced to life imprisonment.

Less than a month after the 9/11 attacks, letters containing deadly anthrax spores were mailed to media offices and two U.S. senators, Patrick J. Leahy, Democrat of Vermont, and Tom Daschle, Democrat of South Dakota, causing the death of five people, including two postal workers, and infecting 22 others.

The FBI had the responsibility of trying to identify and arrest the anonymous mailer of the anthrax letters. It was not immediately clear whether the murders-by-mail were the work of homegrown or foreign terrorists, but the authorities believed that the letters were most likely mailed by a scientist or laboratory worker, perhaps someone who had been employed in a government lab that conducted research on biological weapons. The FBI questioned and gave polygraph tests to dozens of scientists who had access to anthrax in their laboratories, and searched the homes of some of them, focusing on one man in particular, in an effort to find the person or people responsible. Five years later, the case had not been solved.

## The Criminal Courts

Americans who have never had a brush with the law may tend to think of the system of criminal justice in terms of "due process of law," trial by jury, and the right to counsel—in short, the adversary system of justice, in which the power of the state is balanced by the defendant's constitutional rights and by the presumption, not specifically written in the Constitution, but deeply rooted in Anglo-Saxon law, that a person is innocent until proven guilty beyond a reasonable doubt.[115]

**Plea Bargaining** These protections may prevail when a case goes to trial. But in fact, the great majority of cases never go to trial. According to one report, "Most defendants who are convicted—as many as 90 percent in some jurisdictions—are not tried. They plead guilty, often as the result of negotiations about the charge or the sentence."[116] In other words, the machinery of the adversary system of justice exists—but it may not be used. Most guilty pleas are the result of backstage discussions between the prosecutor and defense counsel. The practice is commonly known as plea bargaining, or, less elegantly, as "copping a plea."

The practice sometimes serves everyone's needs but the defendant's. The government is saved the time and expense of a public prosecution; the defense attorney can collect a fee and move on to the next client; the judge can keep the business of the court moving along. But the guilt or innocence of the accused person is not proved.

Usually, the plea bargaining process works this way: A defendant agrees to plead guilty to a less serious charge than might be proved at a trial, and often to cooperate as a witness for the prosecution; in return the prosecutor agrees to reduce the charges or recommend leniency. Often, the accused person will get a lighter sentence this way than if the case went to trial and resulted in a conviction. There is no guarantee, however, that the judge will act as the prosecutor has promised. And, an innocent person may be persuaded to plead guilty to a crime he or she did not commit.

In 1970 the Supreme Court upheld the practice of plea bargaining.[117] The Court ruled that a guilty plea, entered voluntarily and intelligently with the advice of counsel, was constitutional.

Sometimes an accused person will simply plead guilty without plea bargaining, perhaps in the hope of receiving a lighter sentence. If the accused pleads not guilty, a trial date is set.

**Court Delay** American courts do not have enough judges to handle the volume of cases that come before them. In a single year the courts may dispose of more than 3 million cases.[118] The high caseload, the lack of judges, and poor administration of the courts all result in major delays in the criminal process. The courts are badly backlogged; in many large cities the average delay between arrest and trial is close to a year. In Great Britain the period from arrest to final appeal frequently takes four months, but the same process in many states in America averages 10 to 18 months.

**Bail Reform** During the long wait for their trials, accused people may be free on bail or detained. Bail is a system designed to ensure that defendants will appear in court when their cases are called; typically, arrested persons go before a judge or magistrate who fixes an amount of money to be "posted" with the court as security in exchange for the defendant's freedom. If defendants do not have the money, a bondsman may post bail for them, but the defendants must pay the bondsman a premium, usually 10 percent. If the accused cannot raise bail either way, they may have to remain in jail until their case comes up. If they go free on bail but fail to appear for their trial, the bail is forfeited.

The rights of the individual and the community conflict during the pretrial period. The accused person may have a job and a family to support, and he or she needs to be free in order to prepare a defense. On the other hand, the community demands that the accused appear for trial; that, after all, is the rationale of the bail system.

Such a system obviously discriminates against the poor, who may not be able to buy their way out of jail. "Millions of men and women are, through the American bail system, held each year in 'ransom' in American jails, committed to prison cells often for prolonged periods before trial," Ronald Goldfarb has written. "Because they are poor or friendless, they may spend days, weeks, or months in confinement, often to be acquitted of wrongdoing in the end."[119]

In 2001, five people died and 22 people contracted anthrax from letters sent to political leaders and members of the news media.

Until the Bail Reform Act of 1966, federal judges had often deliberately set a high bail for defendants they considered dangerous, in the hope that the bail could not be paid; the practice was an illegal but widespread system of pretrial detention. Under the 1966 act this subterfuge was no longer possible. Federal judges were required to release defendants before trial except in capital cases—in which death was the possible punishment—and unless there were good reasons to believe that the defendant would flee if released. A federal judge might still set bail, but defendants could no longer be held because they did not have the money. The reform legislation does not apply to state or local courts, however, where the amount of bail remains up to the judge. And in those courts, many defendants are still imprisoned because they lack bail money.

**The Trial** Under the Fifth Amendment, a person charged with a serious federal crime must first be accused in an **indictment,** a finding by a grand jury that there is enough evidence against an individual to warrant a criminal trial. The Supreme Court has not applied this requirement to the states, where defendants are more often brought to trial on a **criminal information,** a formal accusation by a prosecutor, made under oath before a court, charging a person with a crime. The grand jury, so named because it is larger than the trial jury, does not determine guilt or innocence. It does seek to establish whether there is enough evidence to justify a criminal trial.

Within the states, although procedures vary in different jurisdictions, in general, arrested people are brought before a magistrate for a preliminary hearing at which they are either held or released on bail. They may be assigned counsel if they cannot afford a private attorney. The district attorney or prosecutor next may seek a grand jury indictment or may present an information to a judge. In two-thirds of the states, however, most grand juries have been eliminated in recent years. Many people are reluctant to serve, sometimes for months, on a grand jury. And, because of police corruption in some localities and skepticism by the public about police testimony, prosecutors can no longer depend on grand juries to issue indictments. For that reason, district attorneys often prefer to go before a judge to present an information.

Once formally accused, either by an indictment or information, defendants are brought into court for **arraignment,** the proceeding before a judge in which the formal charges of an indictment or information are read to an accused person, who may plead guilty or not guilty. (In some cases they may plead "no-contest" and put themselves at the mercy of the court.) At every critical stage, a criminal suspect is entitled to have the advice of a lawyer, and defendants too poor to hire one must be offered or assigned counsel in all criminal cases where conviction might mean imprisonment.

Jury trials are required in federal courts in all criminal cases and in all common-law civil suits where the sum involved is larger than $20. Under a 1968 Supreme Court decision, states must also provide jury trials in "serious" criminal cases,[120] which the Supreme Court defined in 1970 as all cases in which the penalty for conviction could exceed six months' imprisonment.[121] In a federal court, if a defendant wishes to waive the right to a jury trial and have the judge try the case, it is usually possible, but many states do not permit this practice.

Federal juries must render a unanimous verdict in all criminal and civil cases, but more than two-thirds of the states permit a less-than-unanimous verdict (usually by three-fourths of the jurors) in civil cases. In 1972 the Supreme Court ruled that unanimous jury verdicts were not required even in state criminal cases.[122]

In a number of states, juries may consist of fewer than the traditional number of 12 people; the Supreme Court in 1970 upheld the constitutionality of such juries.[123] Federal criminal juries contain 12 members. But most federal civil cases may be tried with juries of six people.[124]

Although courtroom procedures vary on the federal, state, and local levels, in general the pattern is the same. First, the jury is chosen, with the prosecution and the defense each having the right to challenge and replace prospective jurors. Then the prosecution presents its case, and the defense cross-examines the witnesses for the prosecution. After that, the defense presents its own witnesses, who are cross-examined in turn by the prosecutor. A defendant does not have to take the stand to testify on his or her own behalf. A trial may be over in a few hours or drag on for months. Finally, the judge delivers a charge to the jury, explaining the law and emphasizing that the defendant's guilt must be proved beyond a reasonable doubt. The jury deliberates, and then renders its verdict.

After the trial, of course, comes sentencing if the defendant is convicted. In federal courts, judges have relatively little discretion because since 1987 they have been required to mete out prison terms under guidelines resulting from the Sentencing Reform Act of 1984. The law created a commission that wrote guidelines for sentencing people convicted of federal crimes. The purpose of the law was to ensure uniform sentencing so that defendants in different parts of the country convicted of the same type of crime received similar sentences. The guidelines take into account both the seriousness of the crime and the prior convictions of the person to be sentenced. But some critics argue that the law has reduced the power of judges to take into account special circumstances that might apply in some cases. As noted, the law also eliminated parole in the federal prison system for crimes committed after October 1987.

Congress, in addition, has set mandatory minimum penalties for certain federal crimes. One of the most controversial, enacted in 1988, imposed a five-year mandatory sentence for anyone convicted of possession of 5 grams of crack cocaine with intent to distribute. But a person must be convicted of possessing 100 times that amount of powdered cocaine with intent to distribute to receive the same sentence. In the mid-1980s, crack cocaine, an inexpensive drug, was widely used, often by African Americans, in the inner city. Powdered cocaine, by contrast, was often the drug of choice for many affluent white-collar users. The disparity meant that many low-income blacks were crowded into federal prisons for crack possession, compared with a much lower proportion of whites convicted on cocaine charges.

In California and almost half the states, public reaction to increased crime resulted in passage of "three strikes and you're out" laws. In California, for example, anyone convicted of a third felony was required to serve a minimum of 25 years in prison. In 1996, however, the California Supreme Court ruled that judges could ignore the law and give felons lighter sentences. Several other states have adopted some version of these "three strikes" laws. And the crime bill passed by Congress in 1994 contained a "three strikes" provision mandating life in prison for a third violent federal offense.[125] Critics contend that the laws have little impact because most states already provide long prison terms for habitual offenders. Others argue that the laws may eventually result in a prison population of older offenders who are no longer a likely threat to society. Crime, however, is a popular political issue, and many political leaders, particularly in election campaigns, try to outdo one another in portraying themselves as public servants who will "get tough" on crime.

Critics of both state and federal mandatory minimum sentencing laws contend that they are unjust, deprive judges of necessary discretion, and have resulted in a greatly increased prison population of nonviolent criminals, many serving time for drug offenses. A 2004 study by an American Bar Association commission urged that both state and federal mandatory sentencing laws be repealed.

## Capital Punishment

In January 2000 the then Republican governor of Illinois, George Ryan, halted all executions in the state because of a "shameful record of convicting innocent people and putting them on death row."

It was the first time the governor of a state had declared a halt to executions. Although Ryan supported the death penalty in principle, he noted that 13 men had been sentenced to death in Illinois since 1977 for crimes

"Of course everybody is looking at you accusingly. You are, after all, the accused."

"We find the defendant not guilty but not all that innocent, either."



they did not commit, but were later found innocent and set free by the courts. "I cannot support a system, which in its administration, has proven so fraught with error," he said, "and has come so close to the ultimate nightmare, the state's taking of innocent life."[126] Ironically, Ryan himself was later found guilty of accepting payoffs for state contracts and sentenced to six and a half years in prison.[127]

Governor Ryan's action reflected increasing concern by many Americans that the death penalty in some cases may have resulted in the execution of people who were not guilty of the crimes for which they were convicted. In addition, there was growing concern over racial disparity in sentencing; many opponents of capital punishment argued that a disproportionate number of African Americans were awaiting execution, compared with the nation's total black population. For example, 42 percent of death row inmates were black, although African Americans constitute only 13 percent of the U.S. population.[128]

By 2006, more than 3,370 convicts were on death row in the United States, the largest number in any country in the world.[129] Poll data indicated that 74 percent of the public supported capital punishment. (See Table 15-4.)

The death penalty even became embroiled in the 2000 presidential election because George W. Bush, the Republican nominee, was the governor of Texas, the state that led the nation in executions. "As far as I'm concerned," Bush declared in June 2000, "there has not been one innocent person executed since I've been governor."[130] He made this statement, a standard reply to critics, shortly before the controversial execution in Texas of Gary Graham, who was convicted on the testimony of one woman who said she had glimpsed his face for a few seconds in a parking lot. During the campaign, both Bush and his Democratic opponent, Al Gore, supported the death penalty.

For a brief period of four years, between 1972 and 1976, the U.S. Supreme Court had suspended the death penalty. In 1972, in a 5–4 decision, it had ruled out executions under any law then in effect, holding that capital punishment, as then administered, was unconstitutional.[131] At that time, 38 states, the federal government, and the District of Columbia had laws authorizing the death penalty for various crimes, although no one had been executed in the United States since 1967.

In the years following the 1972 decision, 38 states and the federal government passed new laws providing for capital punishment and designed to satisfy the standards set forth by the Supreme Court. Most of the state laws prescribed death sentences for such crimes as mass murder; killing a police officer, firefighter, or prison guard; and murder while committing rape, kidnapping, arson, or hijacking. Federal law provided the death penalty for crimes including air hijacking resulting in death, and for murder linked to drug trafficking.

On July 2, 1976, the Court ruled 7–2 that the death penalty was constitutional.[132] Specifically, the majority held that capital punishment, if administered under ad-

**TABLE 15-4**

**Public Support for the Death Penalty, 1960–2004**

| Year | Favor | Opposed |
|---|---|---|
| 1960 | 53% | 36% |
| 1971 | 49 | 40 |
| 1978 | 62 | 27 |
| 1981 | 66 | 25 |
| 1985 | 75 | 17 |
| 1988 | 79 | 16 |
| 1991 | 76 | 18 |
| 1995 | 77 | 13 |
| 2000 | 66 | 28 |
| 2001 | 68 | 26 |
| 2002 | 70 | 25 |
| 2003 | 64 | 32 |
| 2004 | 71 | 26 |
| 2005 | 74 | 23 |

SOURCE: *National Journal,* "The Hotline," May 19, 2005.

*Making a Difference*

## JOURNALISM 101: FREEING PRISONERS ON DEATH ROW

David Protess, a journalism professor at Northwestern University, examines death row cases, assigning them to his students, and teaching them to pore over documents, reenact crimes, and interview witnesses.

In 1996, Protess and three students helped prove the innocence of four men who had spent 18 years in prison for a double murder in Ford Heights, Illinois.

Last month, an investigation by Protess and six students led to the release of Anthony Porter, 43, who had spent 16 years on death row for the murder of a Chicago couple.

Protess's pursuit of cases, his enthusiastic style, and the skills he teaches have earned him admirers among students, journalists, and professors. Still, he gets questions about his passion in these cases.

"Do I bring a passion to my work?" he asked. "Yeah, I do. Some believe that the higher calling of journalism is that after you find the truth, you can in fact right the wrong."

He added: "In some cases, the truth was the guy was guilty, and those students got an A."

Protess now gets three to four requests a day from inmates and lawyers around the country.

He looks for cases with no incriminating physical evidence like blood or semen, no credible witness, no reliable confession, and other "viable suspects." He emphasizes that his investigations are collaborative efforts.

David Protess wants his students to learn investigative skills, but he also wants to solve cases.

—Adapted from Pamela J. Belluck, "Death Row Lessons," *The New York Times,* March 6, 1999. Copyright © 1999 The New York Times Co. Reprinted with permission. Please see full-text article at the back of the book.

equate guidelines, did not violate the Eighth Amendment's prohibition against "cruel and unusual punishments." The Supreme Court ruled that judges and juries could impose the death sentence as long as they had sufficient information to determine whether the sentence was appropriate in each case. The Court upheld state laws providing for capital punishment in Georgia, Florida, and Texas, but it struck down two other state statutes requiring automatic death sentences for murder.[133]

"We now hold that the punishment of death does not invariably violate the Constitution," the Supreme Court declared. And it noted that the framers of the Constitution accepted capital punishment: "At the time the Eighth Amendment was ratified, capital punishment was a common sanction in every state. Indeed, the first Congress of the United States enacted legislation providing death as the penalty for specified crimes."

In upholding the new capital punishment laws in 1976, the Court concluded: "It is an extreme sanction, suitable to the most extreme of crimes." Approximately half of the 611 inmates then on death row faced possible execution as a result of the Court's decision; they were imprisoned either in the three states whose laws were upheld or in states with similar statutes. In 1977 Gary Gilmore, a killer who had demanded to die, was shot by a Utah firing squad in the first execution in America in a decade. And on November 2, 1984, Margie Velma Barfield, age 51, became the first woman to be executed in the United States in 22 years. As the executions continued, the Supreme Court set a minimum age for capital punishment; in 1988, it declared unconstitutional the death penalty for juveniles who are under age 16 when they commit murder.[134]

## Life and Death in Angola Prison

Howard has just served us four plates of the best chocolate chip cookies I've ever eaten when Warden Burl Cain tells us that Howard killed a man and is going to die an old man in prison for it. It's as blunt as that, but it exposes the intimate, relevant detail of Howard's life. "I don't know how Howard killed somebody, and I don't care," says Cain about his favorite prisoner. "I care about how he is now." Even though Louisiana offers no hope for parole, Cain says he believes Howard is rehabilitated and should be freed if he can meet the family of the man he killed and receive its forgiveness. Howard nods in agreement, because justice is as simple and brutal as that, even if he is going to die here in Angola prison.

There are 88 men on death row, and Burl Cain has killed more people than most of them. He has set five down by lethal injection, and he has held each of their hands as they died. The table has five straps on the gurney—two leg manacles, two wristbands and one chest belt.

At 18,000 acres, it's the largest prison in the United States, with the lowest-paid guards, few of whom have graduated from high school. It's a place that *Collier's* magazine once called "the worst prison in America," where in 1951, in an effort to protest the brutal conditions, 31 prisoners sliced their Achilles tendons so they wouldn't be sent to work.

At the prison museum Cain . . . points his thick fingers at the pictures of men he has executed. "They're special people to me."

There are 88 more men waiting to be made special. Everyone spends all day on his bed, silent, reading the Bible or playing chess against a neighbor he can't see except for the hand that reaches through the bars into the hall to move pieces.

These men, like most prisoners, don't get many visitors. So Cain says his main job is to give the 5,018 hopeless men on this former slave-breeding farm hope, even though 86 percent of them will stay here for "life and one dark day." The dark day is the one after they die, when their body gets embalmed and waits to go home and get buried, although the truth is that when they die, no one comes, and they get buried right here on the Farm. Cain thinks he can summon hope through a four-year Bible college, or the amateur rodeo the prisoners put on every year, or having them pick cotton by hand in the fields that were once a real plantation, and still really are, for 4 cents an hour.

A few months ago, though, some prisoners lost it, lost the hope, and one of them took a guard hostage. Burl Cain couldn't talk the hope back into him, and they had a shootout. "He got one of ours, and we got one of theirs," he says. "It all worked out in the end." And wrong as that sounds, in Angola that's how it is.

—Adapted from Joel Stein, "The Lessons of Cain," *Time,* July 10, 2000

Among the states with laws providing for the death penalty, lethal injection is the most common method, employed by 37 states, then electrocution, the gas chamber, hanging, and the firing squad. Since the federal government began keeping statistics on executions in 1930, some 3,891 people had been executed by civil authority in the United States before the Supreme Court's ruling in 1972. After the death penalty was restored in 1976, there were an additional 915 executions by mid-2004, some 332 in Texas alone, bringing the total since 1930 to 4,806.[135]

At the time the U.S. Supreme Court faced the constitutional issue in 1972, at least 37 nations worldwide had abolished imposition of the death penalty in peacetime. In western Europe, for example, only France and Spain retained capital punishment. Increasingly in the United States as well, the death penalty has come under attack, and intense legal battles have been fought to save some of the condemned prisoners. In Texas, James D. Autry was scheduled to die in 1983: "Already strapped to the execution table, with the intravenous needles stuck in place and only 24 minutes before the poison was to flow at midnight, Autry was rescued by a stay order from Associate Justice Byron R. White."[136] The reprieve was only temporary, however; Autry was executed on March 14, 1984.

Proponents of capital punishment argue that it is appropriate punishment by society for terrible, brutal crimes, including serial murders. They argue as well that capital punishment brings a measure of justice to the families of the victims of homicides. Moreover, the proponents contend, the death penalty may deter other murders. They also note that people convicted of murder may in time be released from prison and may kill again.

A number of studies, however, have concluded that capital punishment is not necessarily an effective deterrent—there have been more than 350,000 slayings in the United States since the death penalty was restored—and opponents also argue that there is always the possibility that innocent people will be executed if justice miscarries. One study of hundreds of capital cases between 1900 and 1985 concluded that in 350 of these cases an innocent person had been convicted, and that 23 of these prisoners were executed.[137] Since 1972, the study found, 24 innocent people had been sentenced to death; one was executed but the others were eventually released from prison.[138]

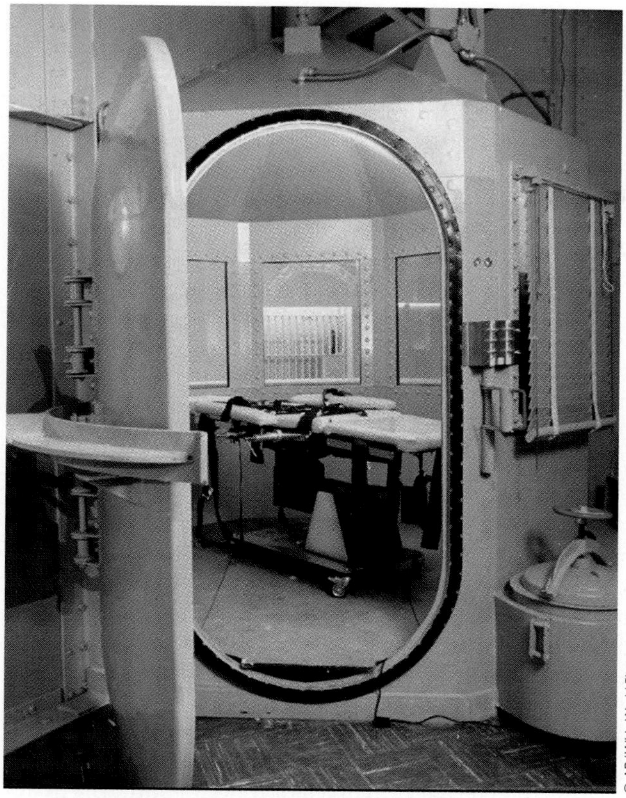

© AP/Wide World Photos

The death chamber at San Quentin prison, California

© Ezio Petersen/Corbis

John Gotti

In 1996, Congress passed an antiterrorism law that included a provision designed to make it much more difficult for prisoners on death row to file successive appeals in federal courts to delay their executions. The Supreme Court upheld the law but ruled that prisoners awaiting execution could still appeal directly to the Supreme Court in extraordinary circumstances.

In 2002, the Supreme Court, in a landmark decision, ruled 6–3 that the Constitution does not allow the execution of mentally retarded offenders.[139] Daryl R. Atkins, who was on death row in Virginia after his conviction for robbery and murder, had an IQ of 59. In 2005 the Supreme Court ruled 5–4 that the Constitution bars execution for juveniles under the age of 18.[140]

## Organized Crime

In April 1992, John Gotti, the head of the Gambino crime family based in New York City, was convicted in federal court on murder and racketeering charges. Gotti was found guilty of arranging the slaying of Paul Castellano, his predecessor as crime boss of the Gambinos, who was gunned down on the streets of Manhattan seven years earlier. He was sentenced to life in prison without parole. He died in a prison hospital in 2002.

With his $1,000 double-breasted suits, his smile, and his mobster's swagger, Gotti had become a sort of media celebrity, a real-life "godfather." Previously acquitted in three other trials, Gotti had seemed so immune to prosecution that he had earned the sobriquet "the Teflon don." But this time, his underboss, Salvatore ("Sammy the Bull") Gravano testified against his chief. Gotti's conviction symbolized both the government's increased success in fighting organized crime and the gradual deterioration of crime families in many cities across the country. In Los Angeles, New Jersey, New England, New Orleans, Detroit, and St. Louis, the conviction of top crime bosses had weakened but not destroyed the mob.

One important tool the federal government employed in fighting the mob was the 1970 Racketeer Influenced and Corrupt Organizations Act (RICO). In addition, the FBI had used electronic surveillance to penetrate the crime families, and it relied on the federal witness-protection program to provide safety and new identities for mobsters willing to testify.

Many years before the conviction of John Gotti, a flurry of federal indictments, along with tape recordings of "bugged" conversations made public by the FBI, suggested that mobsters virtually dominated the government of Newark, New Jersey. Much of the power in Newark, at least according to these documents, was wielded not by the elected mayor, Hugh Addonizio, but by the local crime chieftain, Anthony ("Tony Boy") Boiardo, heir to a crime empire built by his father, Ruggiero ("Richie the Boot") Boiardo.[141]

The FBI transcripts included this conversation between Angelo ("Gyp") De Carlo, identified as "Ray," and an associate named "Joe":

> Joe: You know . . . it's going to take three weeks but we'll own this Hughie [Addonizio]. This guy here, I'll guarantee we'll own him. I'll use that term—in three or four weeks. . . .
> Ray: Hughie [Addonizio] helped us along. He give us the city.[142]

There is still argument over whether organized crime in America should be called the Mafia, but there is little doubt that it has existed on a major scale. (Some Italian American groups have objected to the term "Mafia" on the grounds that it reflects unfairly on the majority of law-abiding Italian Americans.) Organized crime controls illegal gambling, loan sharking, narcotics, and other unlawful activities. It also owns legitimate businesses and infiltrates labor unions. In some instances it corrupts public officials by paying them to permit the mob to operate.

A presidential commission estimated that the mob operated in 80 percent of all cities of more than a million residents.[143] According to the commission, each mob "family" is organized to resemble the structure of the Mafia that has operated for more than a century in Sicily: a "boss" at the top; an underboss; a counselor; several lieutenants; beneath them, the "soldiers" or "button men"; an "enforcer" whose job is "the maiming and killing of recalcitrant members"; and a "corrupter" who buys off public officials. "The highest ruling body of the twenty-four families is the 'commission,'" a combination supreme court and board of directors composed of nine to 12 of the most powerful bosses.[144]

"All available data indicate that organized crime flourishes only where it has corrupted local officials," the presidential commission emphasized.[145] Donald R. Cressey, an expert on organized crime, reports that in one instance a congressman resigned when ordered to do so by a crime boss. In this district, the crime syndicate "also 'owns' both judges and the officials who assign criminal cases to judges. About 90 percent of the organized crime defendants appear before the same few judges."[146]

The Justice Department's Organized Crime and Racketeering Section is the government unit in charge of attempts to curb the power of the crime syndicate. In recent years the department and the FBI have had considerable success in infiltrating and prosecuting organized crime, particularly in New York City. Despite the diminishing power of the mob there and in many cities, and the conviction of hundreds of organized crime figures, the problem has not been eradicated.

Organized crime could not thrive if some segments of the public did not demand the services it provides, including illegal drugs. Corruption of the political system is the most disturbing threat posed by the mob. "The extraordinary thing about organized crime," the presidential commission concluded, "is that America has tolerated it for so long."[147]

## Justice and the American Political System

Although the Supreme Court and the Constitution may seem remote from the lives of most citizens, the decisions of the Court—the ultimate outputs of the system of justice—have direct, immediate relevance for the individuals involved and much broader meaning for the political system as a whole. As Chief Justice Earl Warren noted in his last words from the bench, "The Court develops the eternal principles of our Constitution in accordance with the problems of the day."[148]

Although each specific case decided by the Supreme Court may affect only one person directly, the Court's rulings often affect society as a whole. For example, the decision of the Court in favor of the heirs of Rose Cipollone, who had smoked cigarettes for 42 years, meant that the families of people who died of lung cancer after smoking could sue the tobacco companies on grounds that the industry knew the hazards of smoking but had conspired

### Sandbox Justice

BOSTON—For generations, maybe forever, parents have been telling their children to settle their differences with words, not fists. But usually those words didn't include phrases like "subpoena," "restraining order," or "temporary injunction."

That was before the sandbox case, pitting a 3-year-old girl, and her mother, against a 3-year-old boy, and his mother. In a possible index of the soaring litigiousness of American society, a literal sandbox squabble has turned into a full-blown legal case between statutory grown-ups, their lawyers and the state Supreme Court. . . .

The daughter of Anne Pevnev was playing with the son of Margareth Inge. The two families are neighbors, and both 3-year-olds go to the same preschool. Neither has a criminal record. . . .

Said Pevnev in her official complaint about the incident: "My daughter came to me and told me that a boy was kicking her. . . . I ran up and shouted at him to stop kicking her in the head. . . . The mother took exceptional offense at this and started screaming at me and yelling at the top of her lungs at both myself and my daughter." . . .

Judge Charles Spurlock issued a temporary restraining order to keep Jonathan away from Stacey, then summoned the parties to court. . . . After learning in court that the parties were still in diapers, he modified his order somewhat.

Attorney Howard Speicher, who represents the 3-year-old boy, said the entire affair has gotten out of hand. . . . "This is something that really never should have left the playground. . . . It's an incident that happens in every sandbox in the country, and somehow people manage to deal with it every day."

—From "Stacey Versus Jonathan: Once in the Sandbox, Now in Court," by Christopher B. Daily. *The Washington Post,* March 9, 1996. 

to cover up the risks.[149] The rulings in 2004 in the case of Yaser Hamdi and the 600 Guantanamo detainees meant that even when the American democracy is under pressure, the Constitution may protect individual rights.

The decisions of the Supreme Court have great political significance as well. In the field of civil rights, for example, the Warren Court was well ahead of the executive branch or Congress. Because its power rests on public opinion, the Court cannot get too far ahead of the country, but it can, in the words of Archibald Cox, attempt to respond to the "dominant needs of the time."[150] And it can also serve as the conscience of the nation and a guardian of minorities, the poor, and the forgotten.[151]

There are serious inequalities and flaws in the American system of justice, as we have seen—backlogged criminal courts and a bail system that often penalizes poor defendants; plea bargaining in the place of trial by jury; some judges and officials who are puppets of organized crime; prisons that are overcrowded and do not rehabilitate. Some of these problems can, of course, be solved by specific reforms—bringing defendants to trial more rapidly by appointing more judges, strengthening law enforcement, improving facilities for handling juvenile offenders, and so forth. At the same time, as one report concluded: "The most significant action that can be taken against crime is action designed to eliminate slums and ghettos, to improve education, to provide jobs. . . . We will not have dealt effectively with crime until we have alleviated the conditions that stimulate it."[152]

Ultimately, as Justice Robert Jackson observed, the third branch of government, the judiciary, maintains "the great system of balances upon which our free government is based"—the balances among the various parts of the federal system, between authority and liberty, and between the rule of the majority and the rights of the individual.[153] Chief Justice Earl Warren confessed on the day he retired that performing this task is extremely difficult "because we have no constituency. . . . We serve only the public interest as we see it, guided only by the Constitution and our own conscience."[154]

The resolution of conflict in American society through law, rather than through force, depends on public confidence in the courts and in the process of justice. And confidence in the system of justice requires that the words "Equal Justice Under Law," carved in marble over the entrance to the Supreme Court, be translated into reality at every level of the system.

## CHAPTER HIGHLIGHTS

- The Supreme Court and the lower federal courts comprise one of the three independent, constitutionally coequal branches of the federal government.
- The Supreme Court is only one part of the fragmented, decentralized system of justice in America, a system that encompasses a network of federal courts, state and local courts and prosecutors, the U.S. Department of Justice, state and local police, the Federal Bureau of Investigation, prisons and jails, probation and parole officers, and parole boards.
- Law is the body of rules made by government for society, interpreted by the courts, and backed by the power of the state.
- Much American law is based on English common law, the cumulative body of judicial decisions, custom, and precedent, rather than law created by statute.
- Most law that governs the actions of Americans is statutory law, law enacted by Congress, or by state legislatures or local legislative bodies; but many statutes embody principles of English common law.
- Civil cases concern relations between individuals or organizations, such as a divorce action, or a suit for damages arising from an automobile accident, or for violation of a business contract.
- Criminal cases concern crimes committed against the public order.
- The Supreme Court has exercised the right of judicial review, the power to declare acts of Congress or actions by the executive branch—or laws and actions at any level of local, state, and federal government—as unconstitutional.
- Judicial activism is the philosophy that Supreme Court justices and other judges should boldly apply the Constitution to social and political questions.
- Judicial restraint is the philosophy that the Supreme Court should avoid constitutional questions when possible and uphold acts of Congress unless they clearly violate a specific section of the Constitution.
- Congress (in conjunction with the states) also possesses the power to overturn Supreme Court decisions by amending the Constitution. And Congress may attempt to overturn specific Supreme Court rulings by legislation.
- The Supreme Court has original jurisdiction, the right under the Constitution to hear certain kinds of cases directly, such as cases involving foreign diplomats, or cases in which one of the 50 states is a party. But the overwhelming majority of cases presented to the Court come in the form of petitions for a writ of certiorari.
- Under the Fifth Amendment of the Constitution, a person charged with a serious federal crime must first be accused in an indictment, a finding by a grand jury that there is enough evidence against an individual to warrant a criminal trial. In state courts, defendants are more often brought to trial on a criminal information,

a formal accusation by a prosecutor, made under oath before a court, charging a person with a crime.

- Although the Supreme Court and the Constitution may seem remote from the lives of most citizens, the decisions of the Court—the ultimate outputs of the system of justice—have direct, immediate relevance for the individuals involved and much broader meaning for the political system as a whole.

## KEY TERMS

natural rights, p. 504
common law, p. 504
*stare decisis,* p. 504
statutory law, p. 504
equity, p. 504
civil cases, p. 504
criminal cases, p. 505
administrative law, p. 505
judicial review, p. 506
*Marbury* v. *Madison,* p. 507
judicial activism, p. 508
judicial restraint, p. 508
laissez-faire, p. 508
jurisdiction, p. 513
original jurisdiction, p. 515
writ of certiorari, p. 515
misdemeanors, p. 518
felonies, p. 518
indictment, p. 530
criminal information, p. 530
arraignment, p. 530

## SUGGESTED WEBSITES

**http://supct.law.cornell.edu/supct/**
*Cornell Law School—Legal Information Institute*
Contains material about cases presented to the U.S. Supreme Court, and the full text of many decisions, including concurring and dissenting opinions.

**http://www.deathpenaltyinfo.org**
*Death Penalty Information Center*
The center is a nonprofit organization that examines the death penalty. Contains state-by-state analysis, including the number of executions, and issues related to the death penalty.

**http://www.fbi.gov**
*Federal Bureau of Investigation*
The official website of the FBI offers crime reports, history of the FBI, and information about job opportunities.

**http://www.uscourts.gov**
*Federal Judiciary Homepage*
The website for federal courts, not including the Supreme Court.

**http://www.findlaw.com**
*FindLaw*
Focuses on law and government and provides access to a comprehensive and fast-growing online library of legal resources and court cases for anyone with an interest in the law.

**http://www.oyez.org/oyez/frontpage**
*The Oyez Project*
Offers synopses and texts of U.S. Supreme Court decisions. Some arguments and decisions are available in Real Audio. Also has a "tour" of the Supreme Court and biographies of current and past justices.

**http://www.sentencingproject.org**
*The Sentencing Project*
The Sentencing Project is a nonprofit organization focusing on the problems in the U.S. prison system. Offers fact sheets and policy reports about the penal system.

**http://www.supremecourtus.gov**
*The Supreme Court*
The official website of the Supreme Court offers the text of recent opinions, biographies of the current and past justices, and the history of the Court.

## SUGGESTED READING

Abraham, Henry J. *The Judicial Process,* 7th edition* (Oxford University Press, 1998). A useful general introduction to the American judicial process. Explains the operations of local, state, and federal courts and the legal system, and compares the U.S. judicial system with that of other countries.

Baum, Lawrence. *The Supreme Court,* 8th edition (CQ Press, 2003). A general overview of the Supreme Court, its personalities, the way it conducts its business, and the Court's impact upon American politics and society.

Canon, Bradley, and Johnson, Charles. *Judicial Policies,* 2nd edition* (CQ Press, 1999). An insightful study of the practical consequences of Supreme Court decisions. Examines the range of people and organizations responsible for interpreting and applying the Supreme Court's rulings—including bureaucrats, local groups, Congress, and the media. The authors also suggest that implementation of the Court's decisions can be influenced as much by politics as by legal doctrine.

Cooper, Phillip. *Battles on the Bench: Conflict on the Supreme Court** (University of Kansas Press, 1999). A revealing examination of conflict and competition among the Supreme Court justices.

Ewick, Patricia, and Silbey, Susan. *The Common Place of Law: Stories from Everyday Life** (University of Chicago Press, 1998). A thoughtful analysis, drawing upon more than 400 interviews, of the varying ways in which citizens perceive the law. The authors explore why some people are willing to use legal institutions for dispute resolution, while others view the law with suspicion and distrust.

Friedman, Lawrence M. *American Law: An Introduction,* 2nd edition* (W.W. Norton, 1998). An excellent survey of the American legal system by a respected authority.

Howard, J. Woodford, Jr. *Courts of Appeals in the Federal Judicial System* (Princeton University Press, 1981). An innovative study of three U.S. courts of appeals. Analyzes the political values, role perceptions, and judicial opinions of the judges and examines the flow of litigation to and from the courts of appeals.

Maltz, Earl M., ed. *Rehnquist Justice: Understanding the Court Dynamic** (University Press of Kansas, 2003). A valuable study of the nine justices of the Supreme Court as of 2003. Each chapter covers the judicial philosophy and career of a member of the court.

McCloskey, Robert G., and Levinson, Sanford. *The American Supreme Court,* 4th edition* (University of Chicago Press, 2005). A lucid and penetrating analysis of the role of the Supreme Court in the American system of government.

Neubauer, David W., and Meinhold, Stephen S. *Judicial Process: Law, Courts, and Politics in the United States,* 3rd edition* (Wadsworth / Thomson, 2003). A comprehensive overview of the American judicial system.

O'Brien, David. *Storm Center: The Supreme Court in American Politics,* 6th edition (W.W. Norton, 2002). A lively introduction to the Supreme Court. The author, a noted legal scholar, examines the place of the Court in American society and politics, and concludes that it has become increasingly politicized in recent years.

Pacelle, Richard L., Jr. *The Role of the Supreme Court in American Politics: The Least Dangerous Branch?** (Westview Press, 2002). A study of Supreme Court policymaking focusing on the case for judicial activism versus the case for judicial restraint. The author argues that the Court should actively protect civil rights and civil liberties but should exercise judicial restraint on economic issues.

Perry, H. W. *Deciding to Decide: Agenda Setting in the U.S. Supreme Court** (Harvard University Press, 1994). A scholarly and award-winning book exploring the internal dynamics of the Supreme Court. Analyzes how the justices select the cases they consider.

Ryden, David K., ed. *The U.S. Supreme Court and the Electoral Process,* 2nd edition* (Georgetown University Press, 2002). A detailed study of the Supreme Court's considerable and growing influence on electoral politics. The book focuses on the Court's treatment of political parties and redistricting issues, and its impact on the outcome of the 2000 presidential election.

Segal, Jeffrey A., and Spaeth, Harold J. *The Supreme Court and the Attitudinal Model Revisited** (Cambridge University Press, 2002). An important analysis of the Supreme Court that emphasizes the role of the justices' policy preferences, or attitudes, in decision making. Topics covered include filling vacancies on the Court, case selection, the assignment of opinions, and how cases are decided.

Walker, Samuel. *Police in America,* 5th edition* (McGraw-Hill, 2004). A readable introduction to police and policing practices in the United States.

Wilson, James Q., ed. *Crime and Public Policy* (University of Oregon Press, 2002). (Originally published in 1983.) A collection of 13 articles examining crime control policies in America. Proposes a number of initiatives that might be used in the effort to combat crime.

Wise, David. *The American Police State* (Random House, 1976). Details and summarizes the abuse of power and violation of constitutional rights of individuals by the federal intelligence agencies, including the FBI, CIA, and others. Includes the major findings of the Senate and House select committees on intelligence, and additional case studies.

*Available in paperback edition.

U.S. NAVY

# Chapter 16

# Foreign Policy and National Security

IN THE SUMMER OF 2006, there seemed to be no end to the violence and bloodshed in the Middle East. In Iraq, where U.S. forces had invaded more than three years earlier, the daily toll of death and destruction claimed large numbers of civilians as well as American troops.

On a typical day in August, 44 Iraqis were killed and 57 wounded when a roadside bomb killed a busload of Iraqi soldiers and a suicide bomber drove a car toward a Baghdad bank where Iraqi troops were collecting their pay. The next day a dozen people were killed, many of them children, when a bomb exploded at a soccer field. That same day 15 bodies were found in Baghdad, many showing signs of torture. A day later, a dozen people were killed and 29 wounded when a bomb strapped to a motorcycle exploded in a busy market street.

The United Nations announced that in June, an average of more than 100 civilians were killed each day in Iraq. In Washington, two of the senior U.S. generals in Iraq testified to the Senate Armed Services Committee that Iraq might be moving toward civil war.

Amid the mounting sectarian violence in Iraq, the daily car bombings, mass kidnappings, and brutal murders, Congressional Democrats called on President Bush to begin a withdrawal of American troops by the end of the year. "Mr. President, simply staying the course in Iraq is not working," the Democrats argued.[1] The letter to the president, signed by the party's leaders in both the Senate and the House, signaled that the Democrats were united in their decision to make the war a central issue in the midterm elections. In turn, Karl Rove, Bush's wiley political strategist, sought to put the Democrats on the defensive by accusing them of a "cut and run" strategy in Iraq. Bush argued that the United States could not leave Iraq until that country was stable and able to maintain security.

The carnage in Iraq, the decision of the Democratic strategists to make the war a dominant theme of the fall congressional campaign, and the charge by Bush's chief political adviser that the Democrats favored a policy of "cut and run" were an illustration of the fact that in today's world, foreign policy and issues of national security and defense, often no less than domestic concerns, may influence voters and determine election outcomes.

© Adress Latif/Reuters/Corbis

2004: U.S. Marines honor fallen comrades in Iraq.

Public opinion polls that summer showed widespread voter discontent with Bush and with the progress of the war in Iraq. The percent of people who thought the U.S. war in Iraq was "a mistake" rose above 50 percent for the first time, in June 2004; although the poll numbers fluctuated after that, in January of 2006, 51 percent thought the war a mistake, a number that rose in the months that followed to 56 percent in July.[2]

As if the trouble in Iraq were not enough, in that same month of July the Middle East exploded in new violence. The militant Lebanese group Hezbollah, in a surprise cross-border raid, killed eight Israeli soldiers and captured two. Israel responded with fierce air attacks on Hezbollah positions in southern Lebanon and the southern suburbs of Beirut. Hundreds of civilians, including many children, were killed. Hezbollah in turn lobbed a steady rain of Katyusha rockets into Israel, killing civilians in Haifa and other areas. Israel sent thousands of troops into Lebanon to try to secure a buffer zone.

The Bush administration was slow at first to call for a ceasefire, arguing that any halt to the fighting should be "sustainable" and enduring. Many other nations perceived the administration's policy as simply buying time for Israel to try to destroy Hezbollah. In August, under pressure from the United States and several other nations, the UN brokered a ceasefire.

Two years earlier, in 2004, Bush sought a second term in the White House in what was the first presidential contest to take place since the attacks of 9/11. The president made those attacks and the "war on terrorism" the centerpiece of his reelection campaign. Bush won, defeating his Democratic opponent, John Kerry, by more than 3 million popular votes.

It was on September 20, 2001, nine days after the attack on the World Trade Center in New York and the Pentagon in Washington, that President Bush stood before a joint session of Congress and pledged a global war against terrorism.

He demanded that the Taliban rulers of Afghanistan hand over Osama bin Laden, the terrorist responsible for the attack on America. Beyond that, he warned that any nation that harbors terrorists would be regarded as an enemy. "Americans should not expect one battle, but a lengthy campaign, unlike any other we have seen," he said.[3]

Less than a month later, the United States began bombing Taliban targets in Afghanistan, and later in October American troops began ground assaults in that country. In the fighting, the United States supported the forces of the Northern Alliance, a loose grouping of tribal leaders opposed to the ruling Taliban. By mid-November, Kabul, the capital, fell. By January 2002, the war was over. But bin Laden was nowhere to be seen, and many of his men had escaped over the border into Pakistan.

Even so, the success of the short-lived war in Afghanistan was not only a foreign policy victory for President Bush, it was also a political triumph. The president's approval rating soared to 90 percent in the immediate aftermath of the 9/11 attacks.[4] It was months before opposition Democrats dared to question his policies.

Only later was it revealed that on August 6, a month before the 9/11 terrorist attacks, Bush had received an intelligence briefing warning that bin Laden was planning to bring his terrorist fight to America, and might even hijack airliners. The Presidential Daily Brief was titled "Bin Ladin Determined to Strike in the U.S."[5] The disclosure that the president had received the briefing touched off a political controversy, because it raised the question of whether the administration could have done more to avoid the attack. A joint committee of Congress and then a special 9/11 commission investigated why the nation's intelligence agencies—the Central Intelligence Agency (CIA) and the Federal Bureau of Investigation (FBI) in particular—had failed to detect the hijackers, several of whom had received flight training in the United States.

Opponents of the administration criticized the way in which Attorney General John Ashcroft and the Justice

A hearing of the 9/11 commission that investigated the 2001 terrorist attacks on America

Department had rounded up more than 1,200 people, most of them foreign nationals, in the aftermath of the attack, detaining them for months on immigration and other charges and refusing to release their names. Critics maintained that in the effort to combat terrorism, the government was infringing on civil liberties and constitutional rights.

President Bush, however, buoyed by the administration's success in Afghanistan, said in June 2002 that the United States might launch a preemptive strike against another country if it believed America was in danger of being attacked. "If we wait for threats to fully materialize, we will have waited too long," he said in an address to graduates of the United States Military Academy at West Point.[6]

In September 2002, Bush formally announced a new strategy of preemptive war, under which the United States, when faced with "imminent danger," would, "if necessary, act preemptively."[7] He was, clearly, setting the stage for the invasion of Iraq. Some members of Congress, however, argued that an unprovoked attack on another country would run counter to America's traditions and its foreign policy.

The administration, undeterred, called for "regime change" in Iraq as a necessary move in the fight against terrorism, although there was scant evidence that Saddam Hussein, that country's brutal dictator, was in league with Osama bin Laden or al Qaeda.

The CIA gave support to the administration by estimating that Iraq possessed weapons of mass destruction—both biological and chemical weapons—and might have nuclear weapons by the end of the decade or sooner with outside help.

Bush warned that Iraq might give biological or chemical weapons to terrorists. Both the president and Condoleezza Rice, his national security adviser, also warned of a "mushroom cloud" that might visit nuclear devastation on America.[8]

In October 2002 Congress adopted a joint resolution authorizing the use of force in Iraq. After the Persian Gulf War of 1991, the United Nations (UN) had required Saddam to destroy any weapons of mass destruction and allow UN inspectors in the country to verify compliance. Iraq expelled the inspectors in 1998 and defied continuing UN resolutions designed to enforce the weapons ban. In November 2002, the UN adopted a new resolution demanding that Saddam disarm.

In his State of the Union address in January 2003, Bush made it clear that the United States would use force in Iraq even without further UN action. A week later, Secretary of State Colin Powell addressed the UN. With intercepted voice recordings, satellite photographs, and CIA reports, he made what seemed at the time to be a powerful case for invading Iraq, which he said possessed weapons of mass destruction.[9] More than a year later it was disclosed that much of the CIA information on which Powell had relied for his UN speech was bogus. Reports from several Iraq sources cited by Powell, including one "eyewitness" who claimed to have seen actual production of biological weapons at a mobile laboratory, turned out to be fabricated. Powell resigned in 2004. Later, he expressed deep regret for his UN speech, calling it a lasting

## Exporting Democracy to the Middle East: The Risks

If the American hawks have their way—that is, if we move to consolidate our position in the Arab world and to transform its society—then the U.S. "moment" in the Middle East could be a fairly long one, with all manner of unintended consequences. To be sure, history never repeats itself exactly, but it often deals hard blows to those who ignore it entirely. It would therefore be best to approach these ideas with caution, if not outright skepticism, to have some humility about whether a Western-led crusade for democratization is a wise policy, and to insist that Congress play its proper role in asking hard questions and setting reasonable limits on the republic's future foreign policy in this troubled region. . . .

With all that is crying out for attention—from our inner cities to the slaughters in central Africa—can we really afford this missionary zeal to remake the Middle East in our own image? We could end up merely creating for ourselves even more crumbling frontiers of insecurity.

—From "The Perils of Empire," by Paul Kennedy, *Washington Post,* April 20, 2003, p. B1. © 2003 The Washington Post Writers Group.

"blot" on his record. He said he had been misled by unnamed intelligence officials "who knew at the time that some of these sources were not good and shouldn't be relied upon, and they didn't speak up."[10]

In March 2003, the United States invaded Iraq with about 130,000 troops. The British sent 8,400 troops and Australia provided 2,000.[11] No other country provided troops until the initial combat operations had subsided the following month; several nations then sent troops for peacekeeping, humanitarian, and other occupation duties. France and Germany opposed the war and sent no troops. Forty-three nations expressed various levels of support for the invasion and formed what Washington called an international "coalition," but the brunt of the fighting was conducted by the American military. Within less than three weeks, the battle seemed over. Baghdad, the capital, fell and a giant statue of Saddam Hussein was toppled, a symbol of the dictator's defeat. Months later, U.S. forces pulled him from a hole where he had been hiding.

But the weapons of mass destruction that Bush had cited as the rationale for war were nowhere to be found. And the National Commission on Terrorist Attacks upon the United States concluded in its final report that Iraq and Osama bin Laden had no "collaborative operational relationship." Nor was there evidence, the 9/11 commission said, "that Iraq cooperated with al Qaeda in developing or carrying out any attacks against the United States," including the attacks on September 11, 2001.[12]

The military action against Iraq, the opposition of some major U.S. allies, the argument over what the government had known before September 11, the failure of the intelligence agencies to provide advance warning of the 9/11 attacks, and the CIA's erroneous estimate that Iraq possessed weapons of mass destruction—all were subjects of intense political debate. The controversy over these questions once again underscored the fact that foreign policy and national security are closely related to, and interwoven with, domestic politics. In the 2004 campaign, for example, the question of which candidate was best suited to defend America against terrorists was a central issue.

Presidents may be reluctant to admit that their foreign policy decisions are influenced by domestic political considerations. They usually prefer to describe their actions in terms of national security and global complexities. But they are always well aware of the impact of foreign policy on politics at home. Often, they consider how a particular defense or foreign policy may affect their chances for reelection.

In an uncertain era of nuclear proliferation, terrorism, regional conflicts, assassinations, famine, and genocide, American foreign policy often plays an important

© Bill Strode / Woodfin Camp & Associates

Vietnam: The costs were high.

role when the voters, every four years, choose their president. Who has more experience in foreign affairs? Which candidate will be most likely to protect the nation from further terrorist attacks? To keep America out of war? To maintain its military strength? Whose policies seem best in trouble spots such as the Middle East?

Events in other countries often affect public opinion in the United States. Domestic issues, bread-and-butter concerns, may mean more to American voters than foreign policy, but that is not always the case. President Lyndon Johnson, for example, chose not even to run in 1968, because the Vietnam War—and therefore Johnson—had become unpopular.

Key Question In this chapter we will explore a key question: ***What is foreign policy, and how is it formulated in a democratic political system such as the United States?*** Many related questions also arise. Who makes foreign policy? What role should the president play? The Congress? And how, in a democratic society, can people make their views felt and influence foreign policy? What should America's objectives be in its relations with the rest of the world? Should it attempt to be the world's police force, intervening in conflicts around the globe? When should the United States intervene? Do circumstances ever justify a preemptive attack on another country? How much of the nation's resources should go into military spending? What dangers are posed to American institutions by a multibillion-dollar defense budget? What are the responsibilities of richer nations toward less developed nations?

# The United States and World Affairs

## American Foreign Policy

**Foreign policy** is the sum of the goals, decisions, and actions that govern a nation's relations with the rest of the world. But the world changes, and so does foreign policy. A president may adopt one policy only to discard it later; a new president may reverse the policies of his predecessor. Alliances shift; the Soviet Union, America's ally against Nazi Germany in the Second World War, became its principal adversary in the Cold War that began soon afterward and lasted more than four decades. Japan, which had been America's wartime enemy, became its peacetime ally, as did West Germany.

So "foreign policy" is a changing and elusive concept. Roger Hilsman, a former assistant secretary of state, has suggested that the problem of foreign policy is not so much one of relating decisions to a single set of goals as it is "precisely one of choosing goals" in the midst of onrushing events and crises, and reconciling the views of advocates of competing policies. "The making of foreign policy," he concluded, "is a political process."[13]

The preservation of national security is a fundamental consideration in the formulation of foreign policy. **National security** is a broad concept that may be defined in many ways, but the term is generally used to refer to the basic protection and defense of the nation. But "national security" is so broad and vague a term that it can be used to justify almost any action that a nation or a president takes. President Nixon, for example, invoked it to attempt to justify a wide range of abuses of power that eventually led to his near-impeachment and resignation.

After the Second World War, there were two broad approaches to the question of national security and American foreign policy. One view emphasized threats to U.S. security posed by the power of Communist or unfriendly nations. Another regarded U.S. security as dependent on some form of world order "compatible with our values and interests."[14] This second view holds that there can be no real security for the United States without world peace and security for all people.

Yet national security proved a relative term in the thermonuclear age. During the Cuban Missile Crisis of 1962, President Kennedy's advisers knew that their decisions, if wrong, "could mean the destruction of the human race."[15] So any description of national security and

President Kennedy, standing, right, leaning forward, meets with advisers, including his brother, Attorney General Robert F. Kennedy, standing at left, during the Cuban Missile Crisis, October 1962.

*The American Past*

## TRUMAN FIRES GENERAL MACARTHUR

On April 11, 1951, in the midst of the Korean War, President Harry S Truman fired General of the Army Douglas MacArthur for insubordination. MacArthur had consistently defied the president's orders. Truman describes what led to his decision in his memoirs:

> On March 24 General MacArthur released a statement that was . . . entirely at cross-purposes with the one I was to have delivered. . . . This was a most extraordinary statement for a military commander of the United Nations to issue on his own responsibility. It was an act totally disregarding all directives to abstain from any declarations on foreign policy. It was in open defiance of my orders as President and as Commander in Chief. This was a challenge to the authority of the President under the Constitution. It also flouted the policy of the United Nations.
>
> By this act MacArthur left me no choice—I could no longer tolerate his insubordination. In effect, what MacArthur was doing was to threaten the enemy with an ultimatum—intimating that the full preponderance of Allied power might be brought to bear against Red China. . . .
>
> If there is one basic element in our Constitution, it is civilian control of the military. Policies are to be made by the elected political officials, not by generals or admirals. . . .
>
> That is why our Constitution embodies the principle of civilian control of the military. This was the principle that General MacArthur threatened. I do not believe that he purposefully decided to challenge civilian control of the military, but the result of his behavior was that this fundamental principle of free government was in danger.
>
> It was my duty to act. . . . I felt compelled to have Joseph Short, my press secretary, call a special news conference for 1 a.m., April 11. . . . The reporters were handed a series of papers, the first being my announcement of General MacArthur's relief. . . .
>
> —*Memoirs by Harry S. Truman: Years of Trial and Hope 1946–1952*

foreign policy must take into account the changed nature of the world since the beginning of the atomic age.

In Korea and Vietnam, the United States fought a protracted war against Communist power in Asia. Faced with often hostile, armed Communist nations, the United States sought to maintain a high level of military strength. American policymakers argued that this costly arms burden was necessary to protect the national security, American liberties at home, and the freedom of other nations. Only the shield of American power, they contended, prevented Communist expansion to a degree that would threaten American security.

Critics of this view maintained that the United States often used its vast power to support military governments in Asia, Latin America, and elsewhere in the world, including dictators who violated human rights and civil liberties, and tortured or killed political opponents. For example, the United States supported the government of El Salvador despite the operations of right-wing "death squads" that murdered thousands of people with the apparent approval of high-ranking Salvadoran military and civilian officials. In Guatemala, the army, supported by millions of dollars from Washington, murdered an estimated 100,000 people in four decades of guerrilla warfare. A presidential panel concluded in 1996 that the CIA had recruited and paid as sources of information Guatemalan military officers who engaged in assassinations, torture, kidnappings, murder, and widespread violations of human rights.[16]

A major foreign policy issue often debated, but unresolved, is: when should the United States intervene militarily abroad? One view maintains that it should do so only when its vital interests are clearly at stake and it can act with the broad support of the American public and the nation's allies. Another view was adopted by the administration of George W. Bush, which, as noted, promulgated a strategy of preemptive war when the nation believed it faced "imminent danger." Others argue that humanitarian values may also sometimes require armed intervention. In Africa in 1998, for example, at least 500,000 Tutsis were massacred by Rwanda's Hutu majority. The UN was unable to halt the genocide, and the United States stood by and did nothing.

The creation of a "national security state" at times has threatened liberties at home. During the Watergate scandal, President Nixon argued that the wiretapping of his own aides and of journalists, the formation of a special White House investigative unit known as "the Plumbers" to plug news leaks, and a plan to open first-class mail and burglarize the homes or offices of suspected people were all justified by "national security."

As the **Cold War**—the period of intense rivalry between the United States and the Soviet Union after

### NATIONAL SECURITY: A PRESIDENT'S VIEW

Together we shall save our planet, or together we shall perish in its flames.

—John F. Kennedy, Address to the General Assembly of the United Nations, September 25, 1961 the Second World War—faded into history, new global issues came to the fore, centering on challenges that transcended national boundaries. Increasingly, political leaders and economists spoke of **globalization,** a world economy characterized by the free movement of goods, capital, labor, and information across national borders. It was a process that opponents argued benefited giant multinational corporations and other industries but harmed the environment, American labor unions, and poor workers in less developed countries.

Globalization has focused attention on another foreign policy issue—the powerful multinational corporations, many of them based in the United States, whose activities cut across national borders. Critics argue that these giant corporations are primarily concerned with profits, ignoring the social or environmental effects of their activities. They ask: "By what right do a self-selected group of druggists, biscuit makers, and computer designers become the architects of the new world?"[17]

**Nuclear proliferation**—the spread of nuclear weapons to more nations—threatens the world. The nuclear peril; the danger to the global environment; overpopulation; famine; disease, including the AIDS epidemic; a rising tide of nationalism; and ethnic and religious conflicts—all are issues broader than the old rivalry of competing political systems. They are also issues that in many cases involve the future of humanity and the survival of the planet.

As more countries attempted to acquire nuclear weapons, and with the spread of terrorism, it was possible that the world might actually become more unstable than it was during the Cold War years when the superpowers faced off against each other.

All of these issues and conflicts provide a challenge to the policymakers seeking to manage America's foreign policy.

## The Historical Setting

A nation's foreign policy is rooted in its politics and in its past. In discussing the history of American foreign policy, we can identify some recurring strands and major themes that are relevant today.

One fundamental characteristic of America's early foreign policy was **isolationism,** a policy of avoiding foreign involvement. President George Washington declared that it was the nation's policy "to steer clear of permanent alliance," and Thomas Jefferson said that America wanted peace with all nations, "entangling alliances with none."

During the 19th century, the diplomats of Europe maneuvered to preserve the "balance of power" in the Old World; America, protected by the broad Atlantic, could afford to remain relatively aloof from the problems of Europe. The **Monroe Doctrine,** a declaration by President James Monroe in 1823, warned European powers to keep out of the Western Hemisphere and pledged that the United States would not intervene in the internal affairs of Europe.

"If we don't comply, they're threatening us with liberation."



American isolation, of course, was only relative. The United States fought a war with Great Britain in 1812; it annexed Texas, which led to a war with Mexico in 1846; and it took possession of Puerto Rico, Guam, and the Philippines under the treaty ending the Spanish-American War in 1898. (The Philippines gained independence in 1946.) However, the United States did not become a major colonial power, with vast overseas territories, on a scale comparable with Great Britain or some of the nations of Europe.

By the end of the 19th century, an opposite strand of American foreign policy was visible—**interventionism,** or military involvement by the United States in various parts of the world. In the early 20th century, the United States practiced "gunboat diplomacy," intervening militarily in Mexico, the Caribbean, and Latin America. The First World War brought major U.S. military involvement in Europe for the first time. After the war, however, the United States declined to join with other countries in the League of Nations. President Woodrow Wilson's dream of world order was shattered, and America retreated "back to normalcy" and isolationism.

But during the Second World War, the United States and its allies defeated Nazi Germany and Japan, and America emerged from that conflict a great world power. The United States moved from isolationism to **internationalism,** the policy that America must take an active leadership role in world affairs.

A world weary of war and destruction centered its hopes for peace on the United Nations, created in 1945. It quickly became clear, however, that the future of the postwar world would be shaped not in the UN but in the relations between the two superpowers, the United States and the Soviet Union.

## The Era of the Cold War

In a speech at Westminster College in Fulton, Missouri, in March 1946, Britain's great wartime prime minister, Winston Churchill, declared that from the Baltic to the Adriatic seas, "an iron curtain has descended across the continent."[18] In retrospect, it became clear that the Cold War had begun.

During this period, the United States adopted a policy of **containment** of the power of the Soviet Union. George F. Kennan, a senior American diplomat and later ambassador to Moscow, was the architect of that approach. He advocated that U.S. policy toward the Soviet Union be one of "firm and vigilant containment of Russian expansive tendencies."[19]

Under the Truman Doctrine, Washington began a program of military aid to Greece, which was fighting Communist guerrillas, and Turkey, which was under pressure to cede military bases to the Soviet Union. As enunciated by President Harry S Truman, the doctrine declared that American security and world peace depended on U.S. protection for the "free peoples of the world."[20]

In the summer of 1947, the United States launched the **Marshall Plan** (named for its creator, Secretary of State George C. Marshall) and poured more than $13 billion in four years into Western Europe to speed its postwar economic and social recovery. The Soviet Union and other East European nations declined to join the Marshall Plan.

In 1949 the United States and many of the nations of Western Europe formed the North Atlantic Treaty Organization (NATO), whose members were pledged to defend each other against attack. NATO was the first and most important of a series of postwar collective security pacts signed by the United States. These arrangements were greatly expanded during the Eisenhower administration. In 1997, Russia agreed to the expansion of NATO, and the Czech Republic, Poland, and Hungary became members in 1999. In 2006 the United States was pledged under security pacts to defend 53 nations. (See Figure 16-1.)

In the Pacific a new war broke out only five years after the end of the Second World War. During the Korean War (1950–1953), the United States became involved for the first time in a land war in Asia. After North Korea invaded South Korea in June of 1950, U.S. forces were sent to Korea in a conflict that eventually cost the lives of 33,667 Americans killed in combat.

New forces, sometimes obscured by the rhetoric of the Cold War, were loose in the world. The United States, the sole nuclear power at the end of the Second World War, lost that advantage when the Soviet Union developed atomic weapons in 1949. About the same time, however, world Communist unity began to come apart. As early as 1948, Yugoslavia's President Tito had broken with the Soviet Union. In 1956 Soviet tanks crushed a revolt against Communist rule in Hungary.

By 1961 Russia and its former ally, Communist China, were open and bitter adversaries. In 1968 Soviet and Warsaw Pact troops invaded Czechoslovakia in order to put down a movement toward democratic reforms in that country.

During the same postwar period, a rising tide of nationalism brought independence to various nations in Africa, Asia, and the Middle East and stirred political currents in Latin America. **Nationalism** can be defined in different ways. In its best sense it is a love of country and a desire for independence. But it can also mean an excessive form of patriotism that unscrupulous political

U.S. Army Photo

President Truman and Secretary of State George C. Marshall

FIGURE 16-1

**U.S. Security Pacts**

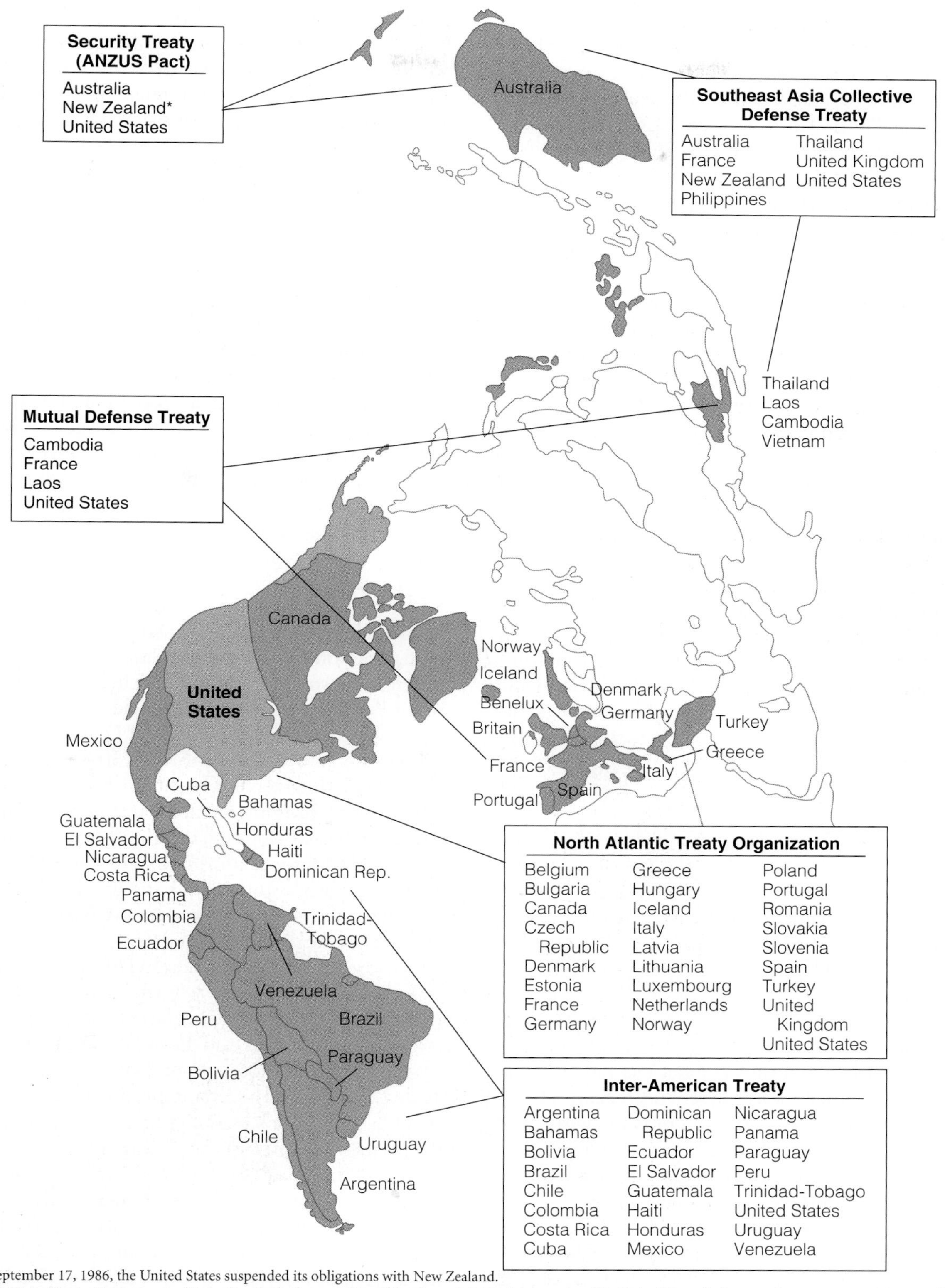


*As of September 17, 1986, the United States suspended its obligations with New Zealand.

SOURCE: United States Department of State, Treaties In Force: A List of Treaties and Other Agreements of the United States in Force on January 1, 2003. Data as of 2006.

leaders may exploit to whip up one group against another, leading to civil war and bloody "ethnic cleansing," such as occurred in the former Yugoslavia under the Serbian dictator Slobodan Milosevic.

In 1947 India and Pakistan gained their independence from Britain. The 1960s saw a second wave of nationalism, this time in Africa. As European powers withdrew from what remained of their 19th-century colonial empires, the Third World became a Cold War battleground, as the United States and the Soviet Union competed for power in Africa, and in the Middle East. In many of these areas of the globe, poverty, hunger, disease, illiteracy, and political instability were combined in a volatile mixture.

Not all relationships that cut across national boundaries are controlled by governments. Modern scholars have also focused on **transnational relations,** which may be defined as "contacts, coalitions, and interactions across state boundaries that are not controlled by the central foreign-policy organs of governments."[21] Transnationalism, for example, includes such global activities as trade, personal contacts, communications between private groups, and business relationships. Today, that concept is more often described as part of the process of globalization, in which multilateral trade and lending institutions are deeply involved.

Foreign policy analysts often speak of interdependence, or mutual dependence among nations. Sometimes this mutual dependence is cooperative, as when several nations agree to combat an environmental problem. Or it can be involuntary, as was the case of the United States and the Soviet Union, whose strategic interdependence derived "from the mutual threat of nuclear destruction."[22]

## Vietnam and Its Aftermath

In Vietnam, the United States gradually moved into the power vacuum created when the French withdrew from Indochina following their defeat in 1954 by Ho Chi Minh, the Vietnamese nationalist leader. Presidents Eisenhower and Kennedy supported the government of South Vietnam, and Kennedy sent 16,000 troops there as "advisers."

But it was President Johnson who, in 1965, committed the United States to a full-scale war against Communist North Vietnam and the National Liberation Front, or Vietcong. Eventually, Johnson sent more than 500,000 combat troops to Vietnam. The war proved divisive and increasingly unpopular at home. In August 1968, for the first time, more than half of Americans thought the war in Vietnam was a mistake, a figure that remained above 50 percent thereafter.[23]

Richard Nixon's promise to end the war helped to bring about his election in November 1968. Yet it took Nixon four years to redeem his pledge. By the time the peace agreement was signed in Paris in January 1973, more than 47,000 Americans had died in combat in eight years, and more than 303,000 U.S. troops had been wounded. Perhaps a million Vietnamese soldiers, North and South, were killed. In addition at least 415,000 civilians died in South Vietnam. The United States dropped more than 7 million tons of bombs in Southeast Asia in eight years. The war cost more than $140 billion.

The Vietnam War illustrated the limits of American world power, and in its wake much of the crusading zeal that had marked the nation's foreign policy gave way to a more cautious, pragmatic approach. For a time, one of the legacies of Vietnam was a reluctance on the part of many Americans and their political leaders to undertake another foreign venture that might embroil the United States in a war.

For almost a decade and beyond, the Vietnam issue divided the nation and cast a shadow over the quality of American life. The lengthy war caused many Americans to become disillusioned with the workings of the political system itself. For that reason alone, the cost of the Vietnam War may continue to be felt for many years to come. As recently as 2004, details of John Kerry's service in Vietnam, and questions about George W. Bush's attendance record at National Guard bases in the United States during the war, emerged as issues in the presidential campaign.

## From Détente to the End of the Cold War

Even before the United States had disengaged from Vietnam, a period of **détente,** or relaxation of tensions, between the two superpowers had begun in May 1972, when President Richard Nixon held a summit meeting in Moscow with Soviet party chief Leonid Brezhnev. In Moscow, Nixon signed the SALT (Strategic Arms Limitation Talks) agreement placing a measure of control over nuclear weapons, and a separate **Antiballistic Missile (ABM) Treaty** limiting the number of defensive missiles each country could build. The meeting followed Nixon's historic trip to China, the first by an American president. Secretary of State Henry A. Kissinger was the architect of the new policy of détente.

President Jimmy Carter, elected in 1976, achieved an important foreign policy breakthrough in the Middle East. In 1979 Carter brought about the signing of a peace treaty between Israel and Egypt after a generation of hostility between those two nations. The signing of the agreement followed a summit meeting between the leaders of Egypt and Israel six months earlier at Camp David, the presidential retreat near Washington.

The same year that the Camp David peace accords were signed the United States under President Carter entered into full diplomatic relations with the People's Republic of China and ended diplomatic relations with the Republic of China (Taiwan). But the pro-democracy movement that swept through Eastern Europe and ended with the collapse of the Soviet Union in 1991 had much more difficulty taking root in China, whose leaders continued to practice police-state repression against

© Don Wright

"Thanks a lot"

© AP/Wide World Photos

January 1973: The Vietnam peace accords are signed in Paris.

those who challenged the Communist leadership. In May and June of 1989, hundreds of thousands of Chinese students and other citizens demonstrated for democracy in Beijing's Tiananmen Square. The students erected a replica of the Statue of Liberty. The army opened fire on the demonstrators, and tanks crushed some of them. Thousands were killed or injured, and there were mass arrests in the wake of the demonstrations. For the moment, at least, democracy had been crushed in China.

A decade earlier, in 1979, Soviet troops invaded Afghanistan and established a pro-Soviet government there. Through the CIA, the United States provided money and arms to support the Afghan rebels fighting the Soviet forces. By early in 1989, the rebels had won and the Soviets left Afghanistan. The various rebel factions then fought each other; the Taliban, a fundamentalist Islamic movement, prevailed and imposed its harsh rule over most of the country. In the 1990s, the Taliban allowed Osama bin Laden to establish terrorist

© AP/Wide World Photos

Beijing's Tiananmen Square, 1989: A lone protester defies the tanks.

training camps in Afghanistan. As noted, in response to the 9/11 attacks, U.S. forces invaded Afghanistan and toppled the Taliban government.

In November 1979, Iranian militants forced their way into the U.S. embassy in Teheran and seized more than 60 Americans as hostages. The militants demanded that the deposed shah of Iran, then in New York, be returned to Iran by the United States. Their demands were backed by the Ayatollah Khomeini, leader of Iran's Islamic revolution.

In April 1980 President Carter approved a military rescue mission to Iran that turned into a disaster in the desert, leaving eight American servicemen dead and the hostages still imprisoned. Carter lost the election that year to Ronald Reagan. Finally, on Inauguration Day 1981, only moments after Reagan had taken the oath of office, all 52 remaining hostages were flown out of Iran, ending their 444 days in captivity.

President Reagan had promised to strengthen the nation's diplomacy and its military power. True to his

© UPI/Bettmann/Corbis

American hostages are seized at the United States embassy in Teheran in November 1979.

© Steve Liss/Time Life Pictures/Getty Images

word, Reagan presided over a major buildup of military strength.

Early in his presidency, Reagan denounced the Soviet Union as an "evil empire."[24] But later in the Reagan years, after initial tensions, relations with the Soviet Union improved substantially. In 1987 Reagan and Soviet leader Mikhail Gorbachev signed the first treaty in history reducing the size of their nations' nuclear arsenals.

During the 1980s, the United States pursued policies in Central America aimed at defeating forces in Nicaragua and El Salvador that were supported, President Reagan charged, by the Soviet Union and Cuba. In Nicaragua, Reagan supported a covert CIA-backed war against that country's leftist Sandinista rulers.

Under Reagan, the National Security Council (NSC), operating from within the White House, conducted a secret foreign policy. U.S. arms were sold to Iran to try to persuade the Iranian government to pressure groups holding hostages seized in Lebanon to free them. Millions of dollars in profits from those arms sales were then diverted to support the contra rebels in Nicaragua, at a time when Congress had banned such aid. Even larger sums ended up in the Swiss bank accounts of the private individuals who ran the secret operations for Marine Lt. Col. Oliver L. North, a staff member of the NSC.

The Iran-contra scandal eventually created a dilemma for Reagan's vice president, George H. W. Bush, who was elected president in 1988. When he ran for reelection in 1992, his role in the scandal became a major campaign issue. As vice president, Bush had emphasized his importance as a key official within the Reagan White House. Yet he professed to have only marginal knowledge of the Iran-contra affair, claiming he was "out of the loop," a position that seemed contradictory and opened him to attack by his Democratic opponent, Bill Clinton.

Only a year earlier, in 1991, the first President Bush had faced a crisis in the Middle East. The United States and its West European allies depended on the oil fields of the Persian Gulf region to fuel their economies. In 1990, Iraq's Saddam Hussein invaded oil-rich Kuwait, threatening Saudi Arabia, an even bigger oil supplier. Bush deployed American forces to the area as part of a coalition of allied nations. In the Persian Gulf War in 1991, U.S. military forces drove Iraq out of Kuwait.[25]

## The Cold War Ends

For more than 40 years, the United States and the Soviet Union had been locked in a seemingly insoluble era of conflict, somewhere between peace and war. With both sides possessing unimaginably destructive nuclear missiles and bombs, the possibility of Armageddon was never far in the background. Indeed, during the Cuban Missile Crisis of 1962, the world went to the brink of nuclear war.

But in the fall of 1989, the tide of history once more swept across Eastern Europe. In one country after another, democratic forces were able to break the grip of the Communist dictatorships, closely allied with Moscow, that had come to power in the aftermath of the Second World War. In Hungary, Poland, East Germany, Czechoslovakia, and Bulgaria, governments fell, often after mass

Taking down the Berlin Wall, November 1989

Christopher J. Wise

demonstrations by angry citizens. In Romania, the revolt was bloody as security forces fired into the crowds, and dictator Nicolae Ceausescu and his wife, who attempted to flee by helicopter, were caught and shot.

In November, East Germany opened its borders to the West, and on television the world watched the memorable scene of crowds dancing in celebration atop the Berlin Wall, the symbol of a divided Germany. Soon afterward, the wall itself came down, and chunks of its stones became souvenirs of a vanished and unlamented era. A year later, in October 1990, East and West Germany were united.

Still, the mighty Soviet Union stood, seemingly impervious to change. But Mikhail Gorbachev, who had come to power in 1985, had unleashed *glasnost,* or change, and *perestroika,* the restructuring of Soviet society, which had become much more open in just a few years. The new policies had some unexpected results. On May Day of 1990, something extraordinary happened in Red Square—the crowds jeered President Gorbachev and the other Kremlin leaders who were atop Lenin's tomb. As the loudspeakers blared out martial music, demonstrators marched across the cobblestones carrying banners that said "Down with the Politburo! Resign!" and calling for freedom for Lithuania.

In August 1991, a cabal of hardliners led by Vladimir A. Kryuchkov, the chairman of the KGB, the Soviet secret police and spy agency, briefly held Gorbachev prisoner at his dacha on the Black Sea. As demonstrators in Moscow rallied in support of Gorbachev, Boris Yeltsin, the president of Russia, climbed onto a tank and defied the coup plotters. The tide turned, the plotters were arrested, and a weakened Gorbachev returned briefly to power. But within four months, the republics of the Soviet Union declared their independence of central control, Gorbachev resigned, and Yeltsin, as president of Russia, emerged as the most important leader in the former Soviet empire, which had broken up into 15 independent states.

At 7:32 p.m. on December 25, 1991, the red flag of the Soviet Union with hammer-and-sickle fluttered in the wind for the last time as it was slowly lowered over the Kremlin in Moscow, marking the formal end to the Soviet Union. The breakup of the Communist empire had seemed inconceivable only a few years earlier.

The superpower conflict that had most threatened the survival of humanity was history. On February 1, 1992, President Bush and President Yeltsin of Russia met at Camp David, Maryland, and formally declared what was already apparent to the world: The Cold War was over.

## The Post–Cold War World

The end of the Cold War did not mean an end to conflict around the globe. Ethnic and religious strife—in the Balkans, Africa, Asia, and the Middle East—demonstrated that the world was still not a peaceful place.

There was progress in some areas, however. In South Africa, for example, where blacks had been repressed for decades by a policy of apartheid, or forced separation of the races, the transition to democracy took place rapidly despite sporadic violence. In 1990, the white government lifted its ban on the African National Congress, and the congress's leader, Nelson Mandela, was freed after more than 27 years in prison. Apartheid laws were ended and a new constitution was written. In 1994, Mandela was elected president.

And in 1993, a breakthrough—which at the time

appeared to hold at least a promise of peace—occurred in the Middle East. Israel and the Palestinians reached a peace agreement, ending their 48-year state of war. The accords were signed at the White House in September, and in a ceremony on the south lawn, Prime Minister Yitzhak Rabin of Israel and Palestinian leader Yasir Arafat reached across President Clinton in an historic handshake. Under this and related agreements, the Palestinians were supposed to gradually gain self-rule in Gaza and the West Bank of the Jordan. Israel and a Palestinian state, it was hoped, would coexist peacefully.

But peace in the Middle East proved an illusion. In November 1995, Rabin was assassinated, and his successor, Benjamin Netanyahu, had campaigned in favor of a much tougher policy toward Arafat and the Arab countries. He was defeated in 1999 in a landslide by Ehud Barak, the Labor Party candidate.

In September 2000, Ariel Sharon, a hard-line former Israeli general, visited the Temple Mount, Islam's holiest shrine in Jerusalem, leading to rock-throwing and then violent clashes between Palestinians and Israeli forces. Barak resigned and in 2001 Sharon, the leader of the Likud Party, was elected prime minister. But the clashes continued and tensions in the area remained high. The violence followed a familiar pattern. Young Palestinian suicide bombers blew up civilians in Israel and the Israeli military retaliated with strikes on the West Bank and in the Gaza Strip. The Israeli military assassinated leaders of the Palestinian militant group Hamas, touching off a new round of suicide bombings and military actions. Early in 2006 Hamas won a large majority in the Palestinian parliament and named a prime minister, leading to further tensions with Israel, which refused to deal with what it regarded as a terrorist group.

Meanwhile, in 1999, Boris Yeltsin resigned as Russia's president. He was succeeded by Vladimir Putin, a former KGB officer who had served in East Germany. Like his predecessor, Putin became bogged down by the war in Chechnya, a southern region that had rebelled against Russian rule. Chechen separatists set off bombs in Moscow, and in 2004 caused two airliners to crash and seized a school in Beslan, in southern Russia, in a siege

President Nelson Mandela of South Africa

In September 1993, Israeli prime minister Yitzhak Rabin, left, and Palestinian leader Yasir Arafat shook hands on a peace agreement.

## Comparing Governments

# PRESIDENTIAL ELECTIONS, RUSSIAN STYLE

MOSCOW, March 14—President Vladimir V. Putin cruised to a second term on Sunday in an election that had never been in doubt and that consolidated his centralized control of power in Russia.

Mr. Putin, 51, had already taken command of Parliament in an election in December and marginalized his opponents by limiting press access and harassing their campaigns. . . . With nearly 90 percent of the ballots counted, Mr. Putin had received more than 70 percent of the vote. A candidate representing the Communist Party, Nikolai M. Kharitonov, was projected to win about 15 percent . . . four other challengers did not rise above single digits. . . .

Rights groups and some political commentators said this election signaled the end of Russia's post-Soviet experiment with democracy. Political opposition has been effectively eliminated. . . .

Some people stayed away from the polls, however, either because of apathy or as a protest against what they said was overbearing government manipulation. "What's the point?" said Mikhail I. Krendeshev, 29, a manager in a private company. "The system has deprived us of any choice. My refusal to vote is not even a protest. It's just deep disillusionment in the way our country is heading and disillusionment after the collapse of the democratic forces."

Four years ago, Mr. Putin won the presidency as the anointed successor of Boris N. Yeltsin at a time of disarray and a weakened Kremlin.

Since then Mr. Putin [a former official of the KGB, the Soviet spy agency] has asserted his control by limiting press freedoms, neutralizing political opposition and demonstrating his readiness to exercise power by arresting the nation's richest man, the oil baron Mikhail B. Khodorkovsky. . . .

One 43-year-old marketing executive angrily said he would not vote, saying: "I don't want to be part of this farce. For 70 years these people have been oppressed by the K.G.B. and they vote again for the K.G.B."

—From "As Expected, Putin Easily Wins Another Term," by Seth Mydans, *New York Times,* March 15, 2004, p. A3. 

that led to the death of more than 300 children and adults. In the aftermath, Putin, who had already cracked down on the press and wealthy business opponents, consolidated even more political power in his hands.

During the 1990s the long war in the former Yugoslavia posed a challenge to the Clinton administration's foreign policy. After intense fighting among Serbs, Muslims, and Croats, peace accords were signed in 1995, and Clinton dispatched American troops to Bosnia as part of a NATO peacekeeping force.

But in 1999, Serbia invaded Kosovo, a province in southern Yugoslavia, forcing an estimated 700,000 ethnic Albanians to flee and creating an enormous refugee crisis. Acting through NATO, U.S. warplanes bombed Yugoslavia for more than two months. Slobodan Milosevic, then Yugoslavia's president, finally allowed international peacekeeping forces, including American troops, to enter Kosovo. The residents of Kosovo, mostly Muslims, returned to what was left of their homes.

Terrorism continued to afflict the post–Cold War world, with bombings not only in the United States and Russia, but in Spain, Indonesia, Saudi Arabia, and other countries. The bombings; the murder or kidnapping of diplomats, business people, educators, or others; the kidnapping and beheading of hostages; aircraft hijackings; and other forms of terror were becoming increasingly familiar. These violent actions have been carried out by various political groups, many with links to al Qaeda, for a variety of reasons. By 2004, some 29,021 people had been killed in 15,613 terrorist incidents since 1968.[26]

United Nations peacekeepers patrol the Lebanese-Israeli border.

On August 7, 1998, almost simultaneous terrorist bombings of the U.S. embassies in Kenya and Tanzania killed at least 213 people, including 12 Americans, and injured 5,000. The attacks were the work of Osama bin Laden, who was committed to a *jihad,* a so-called holy

## False Alarm: "A U.S. Missile Attack!"

It was just past midnight as Stanislav Petrov settled into the commander's chair inside the secret bunker at Serpukhov-15, the installation where the Soviet Union monitored its early-warning satellites over the United States.

Then the alarms went off. On the panel in front of him was a red pulsating button. One word flashed: "Start."

It was September 26, 1983, and Petrov was playing a principal role in one of the most harrowing incidents of the nuclear age: a false alarm signaling a U.S. missile attack.

The episode resonates today because Russia's early-warning system has fewer than half the satellites it did back then, raising the specter of more such dangerous incidents.

As Petrov described it, one of the Soviet satellites sent a signal to the bunker that a nuclear missile attack was under way. The warning system's computer concluded that a missile had been launched from a base in the United States.

The responsibility fell to Petrov, then a 44-year-old lieutenant colonel, to make a decision: Was it for real?

Petrov was situated at a critical point in the chain of command. He reported to superiors at warning system headquarters; they reported to the general staff, which would consult with Soviet leader Yuri Andropov on the possibility of launching a retaliatory attack.

Petrov's role was to evaluate the incoming data. At first, the satellite reported that one missile had been launched—then another, and another. Soon, the system was "roaring," he recalled—five Minuteman intercontinental ballistic missiles had been launched, it reported.

Less than five minutes after the alert began, however, Petrov decided the launch reports must be false. He recalled making the tense decision under enormous stress—electronic maps and consoles were flashing as he held a phone in one hand and juggled an intercom in the other, trying to take in all the information at once. Another officer at the early-warning facility was shouting into the phone to him to remain calm and do his job.

Petrov's decision was based partly on a guess. He had been told many times that a nuclear attack would be massive—an onslaught designed to overwhelm Soviet defenses at a single stroke. But the monitors showed only five missiles. "When people start a war, they don't start it with only five missiles," he remembered thinking at the time. "You can do little damage with just five missiles." Another factor, he said, was that Soviet ground-based radar installations showed no evidence of an attack.

Thus, Petrov decided—and advised the others—that the satellite alert was a false alarm, a call that may have averted a nuclear holocaust. But he was relentlessly interrogated afterward and was never rewarded for his decision. According to Petrov and other sources, the false alarm was eventually traced to the satellite, which picked up the sun's reflection off the tops of clouds and mistook it for a missile launch. The computer program that was supposed to filter out such information was rewritten. Today Petrov is a long-forgotten pensioner living in a town outside Moscow.

—Adapted from the *Washington Post,* February 10, 1999

Heavily armed guards patrol the Washington D.C. Metro during a security alert in 2004.

war, against the United States. Two years later, on October 12, 2000, 17 U.S. sailors were killed in a terrorist attack on the USS *Cole,* a Navy destroyer in Yemen. That attack was also carried out by al Qaeda and bin Laden and foreshadowed the 9/11 2001 attacks on New York and Washington.

Not only terrorism, but also international drug trafficking had an increasing effect on foreign policy. In 1988 the federal government indicted General Manuel Antonio Noriega, the military dictator of Panama, for drug dealing. In 1989, the first President Bush sent troops into Panama. They toppled Noriega, who was arrested, brought back to Miami, placed on trial, convicted of drug trafficking, and sentenced to 40 years in prison.

The drug overlords had gained extraordinary power in some countries, such as Colombia, a major cocaine producer. Even though several leaders of the Colombian cartels had been captured or killed, these actions and the best efforts of American authorities had done relatively little to stem the flow of illegal drugs into the United States.

By 2005, Americans had become increasingly aware that the United States, while still a superpower—indeed, the only surviving superpower—was but one nation in an increasingly interdependent, multipolar world, that is, a world in which there are many competing centers of power. The American who watches television on a Sony, uses a Toshiba laptop computer, and drives a Volkswagen could hardly fail to understand the reality of globalization. Nor was it possible to separate military and diplomatic policies from domestic economic policies. Economic factors affected the strength of the dollar abroad, the cost of imported goods and foreign travel by Americans, and the balance of trade.

Despite the collapse of the Soviet Union, the threat of nuclear war remained, even if substantially diminished. The United States, Britain, France, Russia, and China still retained nuclear weapons, and North Korea claimed it had them. Several Third World nations, including Iran, were attempting to acquire such weapons. In May 1998 both India and Pakistan, two countries often in conflict, conducted underground tests of nuclear weapons. The threat of nuclear proliferation continued. Even small wars carry the potential of growing out of control into nuclear war. Although political candidates and leaders debate about America's military strength and the best way to ensure "national security," it is also possible to ask whether nations and people can ever really achieve security in the nuclear age.

## How Foreign Policy Is Made

### The President and Foreign Policy

In the field of foreign affairs, as President Kennedy once remarked, "the President bears the burden of the responsibility. . . . The advisers may move on to new advice."[27]

As noted in Chapter 13, the president is both chief diplomat and commander in chief. The two roles overlap; national security, foreign policy, and domestic programs are closely related because the president must decide how much money to allocate for each area within the overall framework of his annual budget.

A large defense budget means less money for meeting priorities at home, and the level of defense expenditures affects the economy. As a Senate subcommittee on national security put it: "The boundary between foreign and domestic policy has almost been erased."[28]

The president has the responsibility of deciding whether to use nuclear weapons. The collapse of the Soviet system has diminished, but not eliminated, that terrible responsibility. During the Cold War, Richard Neustadt could write that the president "lives daily with the knowledge that at any time he, personally, may have to

### JFK: A Strategy of Peace

In June 1963, at the height of the Cold War, President John F. Kennedy delivered a dramatic appeal for world peace in a speech at American University in Washington:

> What kind of peace do I mean? What kind of peace do we seek? Not a Pax Americana enforced on the world by American weapons of war. . . . I am talking about genuine peace, the kind of peace that makes life on earth worth living, the kind that enables men and nations to grow and to hope and to build a better life for their children—not merely peace for Americans but peace for all men and women—not merely peace in our time but peace for all time. . . . Total war makes no sense . . . in an age when the deadly poisons produced by a nuclear exchange would be carried by wind and water and soil and seed to the far corners of the globe and to generations yet unborn. . . .
>
> First: Let us examine our attitude toward peace itself. Too many of us think it is impossible. . . .
>
> We need not accept that view. Our problems are manmade—therefore, they can be solved by man. . . . No problem of human destiny is beyond human beings. . . . And if we cannot end now our differences, at least we can help make the world safe for diversity. For, in the final analysis, our . . . common link is that we all inhabit this small planet. We all breathe the same air. We all cherish our children's future. And we are all mortal.

—John F. Kennedy, Commencement Address at American University in Washington, June 10, 1963

"Can I nuke something for you?"

make a human judgment . . . which puts half the world in jeopardy."[29] Although fear of nuclear war eased with the end of the Cold War, as noted, several nations still possess the bomb, and others are trying to acquire nuclear weapons. As a result, the president's finger remains on the nuclear "button." The vast power of the president in the realm of foreign policy carries with it great risks—risks that a president will exercise his judgment unwisely or that he will act without public or congressional support.

In conducting foreign policy, the president must often choose among conflicting advice as he makes decisions. "The State Department wants to solve everything with words, and the generals, with guns," President Johnson was quoted as saying.[30] A president's background, experience, and beliefs may strongly influence his attitude toward foreign affairs. President Nixon, for example, had long been identified with international affairs as vice president; as president he put great emphasis on foreign policy and negotiations. In time, however, a domestic event—Watergate—beclouded his diplomatic initiatives and ended his presidency.

President Reagan's strong anti-Communist philosophy colored his early rhetoric against the Soviet Union, but his views appeared to have softened substantially by the time of his fourth summit meeting with Mikhail Gorbachev in the spring of 1988. Reagan also took a strong stance against dealing with terrorists. Yet he secretly sold arms to Iran to try to persuade terrorists who had seized American hostages to release them. The Iran-contra disclosures in the latter years of his presidency lessened public confidence in his leadership.

Presidents have different leadership styles in dealing with foreign policy. Like both Reagan and Nixon, the first President Bush appeared more confident dealing with foreign rather than domestic issues. President Clinton, by contrast, was slow at first to exercise leadership in foreign affairs. By the end of his two terms in office, however, his efforts to secure peace in the Middle East and Northern Ireland, and his intervention in Bosnia and Kosovo, had enhanced his image as a world leader. President George W. Bush moved aggressively in foreign affairs, launching two wars and making the battle against terrorism the centerpiece of his 2004 reelection campaign.

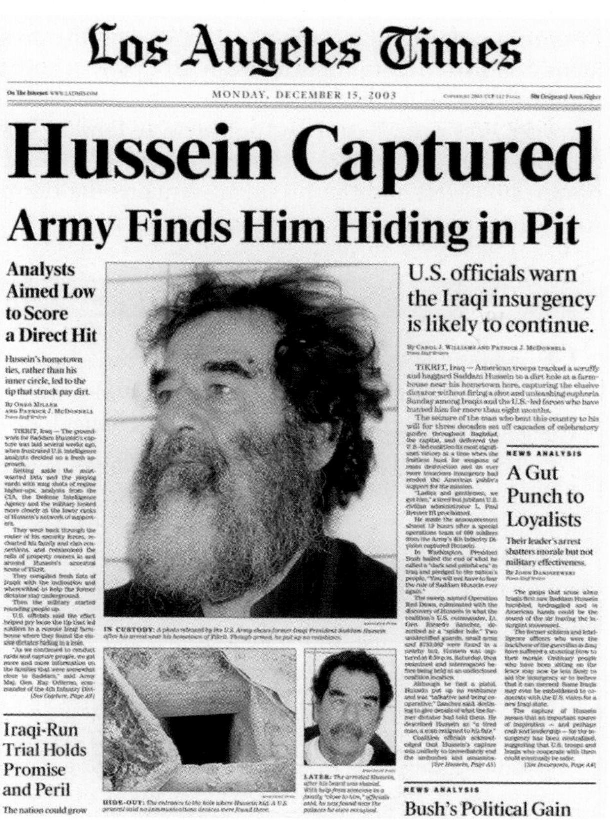
Los Angeles Times

MONDAY, DECEMBER 15, 2003

# Hussein Captured

## Army Finds Him Hiding in Pit

**Analysts Aimed Low to Score a Direct Hit**

Hussein's hometown ties, rather than his inner circle, led to the tip that struck pay dirt.

**U.S. officials warn the Iraqi insurgency is likely to continue.**

NEWS ANALYSIS

**A Gut Punch to Loyalists**

Their leader's arrest shatters morale but not military effectiveness.

IN CUSTODY: A photo released by the U.S. Army shows former Iraqi President Saddam Hussein after his arrest near his hometown of Tikrit. Though armed, he put up no resistance.

**Iraqi-Run Trial Holds Promise and Peril**

The nation could grow

HIDE-OUT: The entrance to the hole where Hussein hid. A U.S. general said no communications devices were found there.

LATER: The arrested Hussein, after his beard was shaved. With help from someone in a family "close to him," officials said, he was found near the palaces he once occupied.

NEWS ANALYSIS

**Bush's Political Gain**

## Congress and Foreign Policy

Under the Constitution, power to conduct foreign and military affairs is divided between Congress and the president. While the Constitution gave the president power to appoint ambassadors and command the armed forces, Congress was given power to declare war, raise and support armies, and appropriate money for defense; and the Senate was granted power to approve or disapprove treaties and ambassadorial nominations made by the president.

But the Constitution does not spell out the boundaries of the power that each branch shall exercise. The result has been intermittent conflict between the president and Congress over foreign policy. Although the Constitution gives Congress the power to declare war, Congress never did so in Vietnam, the Persian Gulf War, Afghanistan, or Iraq. In all of these instances a president made the decision to go to war.

In the struggle between Congress and the president, at various times in history one branch has dominated. After the Second World War, however, Congress lost to the president much of its war power and control over foreign policy. In the late 1960s and early 1970s, as a result of the increasing unpopularity of the war in Vietnam, a movement began in Congress to try to restore some of the war power to the legislative branch. (These efforts are traced in Chapter 12.)

It was not until 1973 that Congress made any significant effort to place restrictions on presidential power to wage war. In 1973, Congress passed the **War Powers Resolution,** designed to limit to 60 or 90 days the president's ability to commit American troops to combat without congressional authorization. The bill became law over President Nixon's veto. The War Powers Resolution failed to restrict presidential use of military power, however, and the president remains the dominant partner in the conduct of foreign policy.

Meanwhile, Congress made efforts to gain greater control over secret intelligence operations. Beginning in 1974, Congress required that before a covert operation can take place the president must issue a "finding" that the proposed operation is important to the national security. Congress also specified that the CIA report covert operations to the House and Senate intelligence committees and give them prior notice of most secret operations.

Between 1950 and 2006, 10 American presidents committed U.S. troops to foreign soil (in Korea, Lebanon, the Dominican Republic, Vietnam, Cambodia, Iran, Grenada, Honduras, Panama, the Persian Gulf, Somalia, Haiti, Rwanda, Bosnia, Kosovo, Afghanistan, and Iraq) without any declaration of war by Congress. In several instances, however, Congress had passed resolutions broadly supporting presidential action in various geographic areas. For example, Congress passed resolutions authorizing the use of force against those responsible for the 9/11 terrorist attacks and supporting the use of force in Iraq.

Because presidents have substantial control over the channels of information about military actions, they may be able to shape how Congress responds. For example, Congress passed the Tonkin Gulf Resolution after President Johnson announced on nationwide television on August 4, 1964, that two U.S. destroyers, the *Maddox* and the *Turner Joy,* had been attacked in the Gulf of Tonkin off Vietnam. Secretary of Defense Robert S. McNamara declared that the two ships had been under "continuous torpedo attack." Up to this point 163 Americans had died in Vietnam, and 16,000 troops were there as "advisers." After passage of the Tonkin Gulf Resolution, President Johnson—beginning early in 1965—vastly expanded the war.

It developed, however, that reports of the attack in the Tonkin Gulf had been considerably exaggerated. For example, the captain of the *Maddox,* Commander Herbert L. Ogier, later said he thought that two torpedoes

### "This Chamber Reeks of Blood"

On September 1, 1970, the U.S. Senate rejected an amendment sponsored by Senators George McGovern, Democrat of South Dakota, and Mark O. Hatfield, Republican of Oregon, to withdraw U.S. troops from Vietnam. Just before the vote, Senator McGovern arose on the Senate floor to plead for an end to a war that Congress had never declared:

> Every senator in this chamber is partly responsible for sending 50,000 young Americans to an early grave. This chamber reeks of blood. Every senator here is partly responsible for the human wreckage at Walter Reed and Bethesda Naval and all across our land—young boys without legs, or arms, or genitals, or faces, or hopes. There aren't very many of these blasted and broken boys who think this war is a glorious venture. Don't talk to them about bugging out, or national honor, or courage. It doesn't take courage at all for a congressman, or a senator, or a President to wrap himself in the flag and say we're staying in Vietnam. Because it isn't our blood that is being shed. But we are responsible for those young men and their lives and their hopes. And if we don't end this foolish, damnable war, those young men will someday curse us for our pitiful willingness to let the Executive carry the burden the Constitution puts on us.

—Quoted in Robert Sam Anson, *McGovern: A Biography*

Early each morning, officials meet at the CIA to prepare the president's daily intelligence briefing on world developments.

were fired but that subsequent reports of torpedoes were actually sonar readings caused by the destroyer's own propellers.[31] Indeed, as the task force commander warned Washington: "Freak weather effects and an over-eager sonarman may have accounted for many reports."[32] At a Senate hearing four years later, Senator Albert Gore, Democrat of Tennessee (whose son and namesake was elected vice president in 1992 and 1996 and ran for president in 2000), told Secretary McNamara to his face: "I feel that I have been misled, and that the American people have been misled."[33]

As the Tonkin Gulf episode illustrates, one major reason Congress has lost to the president so much of its power over foreign affairs is that diplomatic, military, and intelligence information flows directly to the president. As a result, Congress and the public have tended to assume that the president "has the facts" and is acting on the basis of expert advice. Second, foreign policy decisions are often made in crisis situations, in "an atmosphere of real or contrived urgency."[34]

This, too, puts pressure on Congress to defer to presumed presidential wisdom. More recently, however, there has been an increasing realization that the extensive flow of information to the president does not guarantee that his foreign policy decisions will necessarily prove correct or wise.

## The Machinery

Today the president of the United States has powerful tools available for the conduct of foreign policy, including a personal staff and that of the National Security Council, the State Department, the Pentagon, the CIA, and other agencies.

The existence of this machinery does not mean, however, that the United States can always influence, let alone control, the course of international events. American policymakers may not be able to affect the price of Middle East oil, stop the seizure of American diplomats by Islamic revolutionaries, or prevent terrorist attacks on U.S. installations or military forces.

Until 1947 no formal centralized machinery existed to aid the president in his foreign policy tasks. In that year, Congress attempted to give the president the tools to match his responsibilities.

**The National Security Council** The National Security Act of 1947 created the National Security Council, a White House panel designed to help coordinate American military and foreign policy. The NSC, in the language of the statute, advises the president on "the integration of domestic, foreign, and military policies relating to the national security." In one sense the act, amended and expanded in 1949, was an effort to institutionalize the power that had been wielded over military-diplomatic affairs by President Roosevelt during the Second World War. It was also an effort to provide continuity from one administration to the next in the conduct of national security affairs. The NSC, however, has been used very differently by a succession of presidents.

***for more information about the National Security Council, see: http://www.whitehouse.gov/nsc/***

Eisenhower, who had spent most of his career in the military, relied upon it frequently. During both the Kennedy and Johnson administrations, the NSC was occasionally used for "window dressing" during a crisis to give the appearance of somber decisions being made by the president with his highest national security advisers. Real decisions were sometimes reached in less formal meetings. During the Cuban Missile Crisis of 1962, however, Kennedy expanded the NSC, creating an executive committee, or Ex Comm, that met almost continuously to deal with the threat of Soviet nuclear missiles that had been sent to Cuba.

President Nixon directed that the NSC "be reestablished as the principal forum for presidential consideration of foreign-policy issues."[35] Various interagency groups and committees began to flourish once again under Nixon and his adviser for national security, Henry Kissinger. During the Reagan administration, it was a member of the NSC staff, Marine Lt. Col. Oliver North, who, with help from the CIA, coordinated the secret operations that burgeoned into the Iran-contra scandal. The president's national security adviser, Vice Adm. John M. Poindexter, worked closely with North in carrying out and concealing the Iran arms sales and the diversion of profits to the contras in Nicaragua.

After an investigation by an independent counsel, North, Poindexter, and others were indicted for conspiring to defraud the government and then covering up their actions. North was convicted in 1989 of falsifying and destroying documents, but his conviction was overturned by a federal appeals court, which questioned whether his testimony to congressional investigators had been unfairly used against him. The independent counsel then dropped all charges. But in North's testimony to Congress he had admitted shredding documents sought by investigators.

Poindexter was convicted of deceiving Congress and lying to Congress, but the appeals court also overturned his conviction on similar grounds. At the congressional hearings into the scandal, however, Admiral Poindexter, calmly puffing on his pipe, admitted that he had destroyed a presidential "finding," a statement permitting the covert arms-for-hostages sales. He also asserted that he had never informed Reagan of the diversion of millions of dollars to the contras. Thus, under Reagan, the NSC and the post of national security adviser fell, for a time, into disrepute.

President George W. Bush named Condoleezza Rice, a former NSC staff member and academic, as his national security adviser, and she served as an influential member of the White House staff. She was criticized, however, for her testimony to the 9/11 commission in which she had difficulty explaining why the Bush administration had not paid more attention before the 9/11 attacks to warnings of the threat of terrorism. Rice enjoyed strong support from Bush, who named her secretary of state after Colin Powell resigned in 2004.

**The State Department** George F. Kennan once described the American State Department in a less turbulent era: "The Department of State . . . in the 1920s when I entered it, was a quaint old place, with its law-office atmosphere, its cool dark corridors, its swinging doors, its brass cuspidors, its black leather rocking chairs, and the grandfather's clock in the Secretary of State's office."[36]

Today the State Department, with an annual budget of more than $13 billion, is huge; it occupies a large, antiseptically modern building that houses about a third of its 33,945 employees. Department couriers hand-carry diplomatic documents 10 million miles a year in travels between Washington and the 177 U.S. embassies abroad. High-speed coded communications link the secretary of state to American embassies overseas, handling more than 300,000 words daily. In the Operations Center on the seventh floor, behind a locked door that is opened by a buzzer, the secretary can monitor a developing crisis. A device flashes incoming cables on a screen; the center can reach any U.S. post abroad in two minutes.

***for more information about the State Department, see: http://www.state.gov***

Despite all this, the State Department's level of efficiency has been the target of periodic criticism. As the United States became a world power, the size of the department increased vastly; bureaus and assistant secretaries proliferated. The department's snail-like replies to President Kennedy's requests were a constant source of frustration in the White House, where McGeorge Bundy was the national security adviser. By one account Kennedy would say, "Damn it, Bundy and I get more done in one day in the White House than they do in six months at the State Department. . . . They never have any ideas over there . . . never come up with anything new."[37]

The role of the secretary of state varies greatly according to the secretary's personal relationship with the president. In theory the principal foreign policy adviser and the ranking officer of the cabinet, the secretary in practice may be overshadowed by the president's national security assistant or the secretary of defense.

The department has six geographic bureaus covering the world. Within the geographic bureaus are more than 226 country desks. In addition, there are functional bureaus dealing with subjects such as economic and business affairs, arms control, nuclear nonproliferation, intelligence and research, educational and cultural affairs, consular affairs, international narcotics and law enforcement, refugees, and international organizations (the bureau that manages U.S. policy at the United Nations).[38]

The U.S. Foreign Service consists of the professional diplomats who represent the United States overseas and staff key policy posts in the State Department in Washington. Most Foreign Service officers—the nation's professional diplomats—are stationed abroad as ambassadors, ministers, and political and consular officials. Posts are normally rotated, and members of the Foreign Service periodically return to Washington between tours of duty overseas. In 2004, the Foreign Service numbered 9,608 men and women, of whom 3,038 were Foreign Service officers.[39]

Overseas, the ambassador is the president's personal representative to the chief of state and government to which he or she is accredited. Appointed by the president and subject to Senate confirmation, the ambassador is formally in charge of the entire U.S. mission in a foreign capital. The mission may include representatives of the Agency for International Development (AID), as well as the military service attachés, military assistance advisers, and officers of the CIA, all of whom make up the so-called "country team." Often it is a team in name only, however, with each element reporting back to its own headquarters in Washington and some officials working at cross-purposes to the ambassador. "To a degree," a Senate subcommittee concluded, "the primacy of the ambassador is a polite fiction."[40]

In addition to problems of coordination with other agencies of government, the State Department also faces competition from those agencies. In the past it has competed for the president's attention, not only with the White House national security adviser but with other agencies involved in foreign policy—the Office of International Security Affairs in the Defense Department, for example, and the CIA. To some extent the State Department must also compete with outside sources of advice in foreign policy—defense research firms, universities, presidential task forces, "think tanks"—private organizations interested in foreign or defense policy—and former government officials who may be called in and consulted by the president.

**Information and Arms Control** In 1999, the U.S. Information Agency (USIA) and the Arms Control and Disarmament Agency (ACDA), formerly independent entities, were merged into the State Department, along with the 7,000 employees of the two agencies. The goal of the information program remained unchanged: to present America's image to people overseas in the best possible light and to try to gain support for U.S. policies.

The arms control component of the State Department prepares and manages U.S. participation in international arms control and disarmament negotiations. It also conducts research on techniques of arms control. In the past, as an independent agency, ACDA played an active role in negotiations between the United States and the Soviet Union to reduce the number of nuclear arms in the two countries.

The State Department must share the foreign policy field with dozens of other agencies of the federal government involved in various aspects of foreign affairs. These include not only the Department of Defense and the CIA, but the departments of Agriculture, Labor, Commerce, Justice, Treasury, and Transportation, all which have some foreign responsibilities.

**Intelligence and Foreign Policy: The Central Intelligence Agency (CIA)** The U.S. government today has 16 intelligence agencies that employ nearly 100,000 people at a total cost of $44 billion a year.[41] The best known of these spy agencies is the CIA. Until 2004, when Congress restructured the intelligence machinery, the director of the CIA was responsible for coordinating the work of all of the intelligence agencies. Under the 2004 law, that job was given to the new director of national intelligence, John Negroponte.

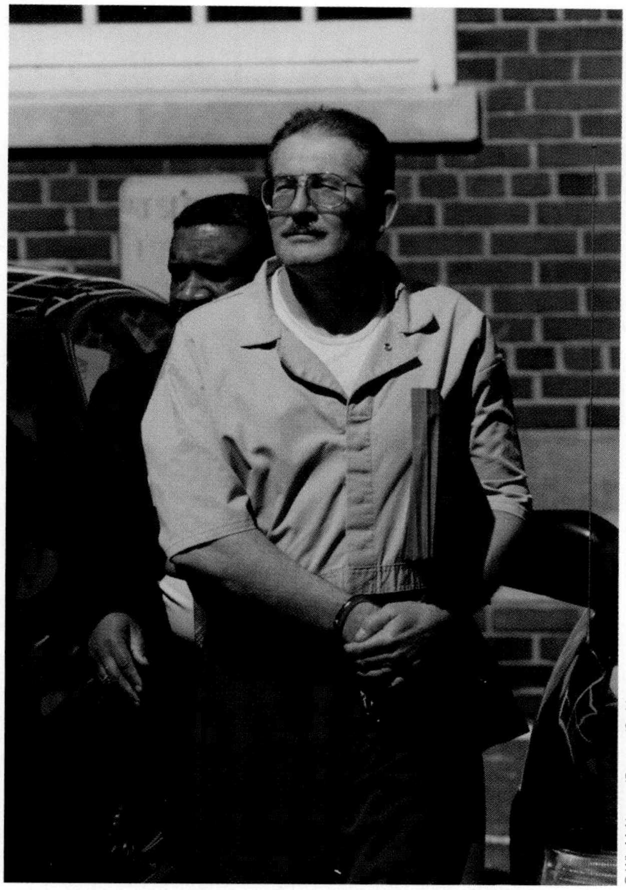



CIA officer Aldrich Ames, the highest-paid KGB spy in history

Over the years, the CIA has often been plagued by problems. In February 1994, FBI agents arrested Aldrich H. Ames, an officer of the CIA, and his wife, Rosario, touching off a spy scandal that shook public and congressional confidence in the agency. Ames had acted as a Soviet mole for nine years, betraying to the KGB the names of Soviet intelligence officers and other Russians who were secretly working for the CIA. Ten were executed and many others imprisoned. Ames was paid or promised a total of $4.6 million by the Russians, making him the highest-paid spy in history. He was convicted and sentenced to life in prison with no possibility of parole. His wife received a prison sentence of five years. Investigations by the CIA and the Senate and House intelligence committees criticized the intelligence agency for its failure to detect the spy inside its own ranks.[42]

All major powers, and many smaller countries, have intelligence services. In the United States, the CIA gathers information from human spies, satellites, and open sources, and the agency's analysts prepare reports for the president to assist him in making foreign policy decisions. But the CIA has also engaged in covert operations—secret political action in other countries, usually conducted with presidential approval—that have sometimes caused the United States embarrassment.

The Central Intelligence Agency, Langley, Virginia

*for more information about the CIA, see: http://www.cia.gov*

During the mid-1970s Senate and House investigating committees disclosed a series of startling actions by the CIA: The agency had hired two underworld figures, Sam Giancana and Johnny Rosselli (both of whom were later murdered), to assassinate Cuban Premier Fidel Castro with poison. During four presidential administrations, the CIA had also plotted the assassination of, or coups against, seven other foreign leaders.[43] The congressional committees also disclosed abuses by the FBI, the National Security Agency (NSA), and other branches of the intelligence community.

The congressional inquiries were launched after Seymour M. Hersh, then an investigative reporter for the *New York Times,* disclosed that for several years, beginning in the late 1960s, the CIA had, in violation of its charter, spied on American citizens at home and infiltrated antiwar and other dissident groups.[44] These charges were later documented in a report of a presidential commission headed by Vice President Nelson A. Rockefeller, which found that some of the CIA's actions were "plainly unlawful."[45]

The Rockefeller report and the congressional committees disclosed that the CIA had photographed and followed American citizens; engaged in break-ins, wiretapping, and bugging of Americans; and for 20 years had opened, read, and photographed first-class mail in violation of federal law. The agency had also experimented with mind-altering drugs and administered them to Americans who were not aware of what was happening; one subject, an army civilian researcher, died by committing suicide—according to the government's official account—several days after the CIA had laced his after-dinner drink with LSD. He was not told about the drug until 20 minutes after it had been administered.

Activities of this sort were not mentioned in the law passed by Congress in 1947 establishing the CIA. The law said that the agency was to advise the National Security Council and to acquire and analyze political, military, and economic knowledge about other countries on which the president could base his decisions about foreign affairs.

The 1947 law makes no specific reference to covert operations abroad, although the statute does permit the CIA to perform such "other functions and duties" as the National Security Council may direct. Presidents have authorized covert operations under this language in the law. But as the Senate Intelligence Committee concluded: "Authority for covert action cannot be found in

© Roger Ressmeyer/Corbis

the National Security Act."[46] Yet the committee reported that the CIA had carried out 900 major covert operations between 1961 and 1975. In 1984, the CIA was reported to be conducting 50 covert operations around the globe.[47] And the Senate panel found that the CIA's widespread domestic spying, to which it gave the code name Operation CHAOS, violated the provisions of the 1947 act designed to prohibit the agency from acting as a domestic police force.

Before the Japanese attack on Pearl Harbor in 1941, the United States had no central intelligence-gathering agency. After Pearl Harbor, President Roosevelt created the Office of Strategic Services (OSS) to gather intelligence, conduct secret political warfare, and carry out sabotage operations behind enemy lines during the Second World War. The CIA was the direct descendant of the wartime OSS.

The 1947 act that first established the intelligence machinery provided that the Director of Central Intelligence (DCI) wear one hat as head of the CIA and principal intelligence adviser to the president. But the director simultaneously was responsible for coordinating the work of the other government intelligence agencies, including the National Security Agency (NSA), the code-making and code-breaking arm of the Pentagon; the National Reconnaissance Office (NRO), which manages spy satellites; the Defense Intelligence Agency (DIA), the military rival to the CIA; the FBI; and the State Department's Bureau of Intelligence and Research (INR). Together, these agencies spend an estimated $40 billion a year.[48] But 80 percent of the total was controlled by the secretary of defense, funds outside the authority of the CIA director. As noted, in 2004 Congress established a new position, the director of national intelligence, to coordinate the work of intelligence agencies.

The CIA has two principal divisions. An Intelligence Directorate engages in overt collection, research, and analysis of foreign intelligence. Most of the criticism of the CIA has been directed at its Operations Directorate, renamed the National Clandestine Service, which engages in the secret collection of intelligence (espionage) and in secret political action (covert operations). On occasion this directorate has helped to overthrow governments—in Iran in 1953 and Guatemala in 1954, for example. It was this clandestine arm of the CIA that plotted the assassination of such leaders as Cuba's Fidel Castro and Patrice Lumumba in the Congo (now Zaire), launched the invasion of Cuba at the Bay of Pigs in 1961, and supported a secret army of 30,000 people in Laos.

Although, unlike the FBI, the CIA has no police

## CIA: Don't Talk about Assassinations

The difficulty with this kind of thing, as you gentlemen are all painfully aware, is that nobody wants to embarrass a President of the United States by discussing the assassination of foreign leaders in his presence. This is something that has got to be dealt with in some other fashion. Even though you use euphemisms you've still got a problem. . . . I think any of us would have found it very difficult to discuss assassinations with a President of the U.S. I just think we all had the feeling that we're hired to keep those things out of the Oval Office.

—Richard M. Helms, former CIA director, testifying to the Senate Intelligence Committee, June 13, 1975

power within the United States, in 1967 it was disclosed that the CIA was subsidizing the National Student Association and dozens of foundations and private groups within the country. President Johnson ordered that most of the secret funding be ended.

In 1972 the CIA again became enmeshed in domestic activities. Most of the burglars caught in the Watergate break-in had CIA backgrounds, and one was on the intelligence agency's payroll at the time of the break-in. A year earlier, at the request of the White House, the CIA had secretly assisted E. Howard Hunt, Jr., a former CIA operative and White House "plumber," and one of the men eventually convicted in the Watergate burglary. And President Nixon tried to use the CIA to block the FBI from probing the burglary of Democratic headquarters. For several days, Richard M. Helms, then the CIA director, went along with Nixon's effort to limit the investigation.

The CIA's size and budget are secret, but it has been unofficially estimated that the agency spends about $4.5 billion a year and employs some 17,000 people.[49] The CIA has its headquarters in a secluded, wooded area of Langley, Virginia, across the Potomac River from Washington.

Until the 1960s, the American public knew little about the activities of the intelligence agencies. During the 1950s, the CIA, under its director, Allen W. Dulles, toiled largely out of the limelight. The loss of a U-2, a CIA spy plane, on a flight over the Soviet Union in 1960 and the disaster at the Bay of Pigs in 1961 thrust the CIA into the headlines and focused attention on its activities. By 1964 critics charged that the CIA stood at the center of what had become "an invisible government."[50] Former assistant secretary of state Roger Hilsman wrote: "The root fear was that the CIA represented . . . a state within a state, and certainly the basis for fear was there."[51]

On the other hand, because the CIA is a secret agency and usually does not make any public comment, it is sometimes blamed for things it does not do. Defenders of the CIA argue that it operates under sufficient control and does not carry out any covert operations abroad "without appropriate approval at a high political level in our government outside the CIA."[52] This approval usually comes from an interagency board that has responsibility for authorizing covert operations. However, in the mid-1970s the Senate Intelligence Committee (known at the time as the Church Committee for its chairman, Senator Frank Church, an Idaho Democrat) reported that the interagency board seldom met. And former CIA director Richard Helms conceded in testimony to the committee that the board has acted as a "circuit breaker" to insulate the president from responsibility for covert CIA operations.[53] Nor has the interagency board always been advised of CIA covert operations.

The CIA's defenders have argued that despite the agency's mistakes, it is an essential arm of the government. Allen Dulles wrote, for example, that an intelligence service "is the best insurance we can take out against surprise." As for covert CIA operations inside other countries, Dulles contended that the United States could not limit its activities "to those cases where we are invited in."[54]

In the wake of the various investigations of the CIA and the FBI in the 1970s, Congress finally moved to strengthen its control over the intelligence establishment. The Senate and the House each created a permanent Select Committee on Intelligence with authority over the CIA and the other intelligence agencies. Congress declined to enact detailed reform bills to control the intelligence agencies, but it did pass a law requiring the president to notify the intelligence committees in advance of covert operations in most circumstances.

When President Reagan appointed William J. Casey, a millionaire New York lawyer, as director of the CIA in 1981, the choice proved controversial, in part because Casey had managed Reagan's 1980 presidential campaign. There was concern over whether a political figure in charge of the intelligence agency would provide objective analyses.

Casey died in May 1987, before he could be fully questioned by Congress about his role in the Iran-contra scandal. After several other directors had served as head of the intelligence agency, President Clinton named the CIA's deputy director, George J. Tenet, as CIA chief in 1997.

During Tenet's tenure, however, the CIA, and the FBI as well, failed to penetrate and foil the al Qaeda terrorists who carried out the 9/11 attacks on the U.S. And the CIA estimated that Iraq had weapons of mass destruction, which President George W. Bush cited as the reason to invade that country. No such weapons were found, and Tenet resigned in June 2004.

As his successor, Bush named Porter J. Goss, a Florida Republican who chaired the House Intelligence Committee. Goss brought several committee staff members with him to the CIA, and clashes between the staff

© Luke Frazza/AFP/Getty Images

CIA director George Tenet, along with other high officials, testified to the 9/11 commission.

and career spies led to the departure from the agency of several senior officials.

With the appointment of the new director of national intelligence, the CIA lost some of its power. For example, the DNI, rather than the CIA director, was responsible for briefing the president each morning. In 2006 Bush abruptly forced Goss out as CIA chief, naming Air Force general Michael V. Hayden, former head of the National Security Agency, as his successor.

**National Security Agency (NSA)** The budget of the National Security Agency (NSA) is also secret, but it was reported several years ago that the code agency had a budget of $3.7 billion, with 38,000 employees—more workers than the CIA or any of the other intelligence agencies.[55]

The ability of the NSA to intercept all forms of communication, including telephone conversations and e-mail, raised privacy concerns both at home and abroad. The issue created sharp controversy when it was disclosed that a presidential order issued by George W. Bush in 2002 instructed the NSA, without warrants, to monitor international telephone calls and e-mails of hundreds of thousands of people in the United States, including Americans, in an attempt to track down terrorists. The program was first revealed to the public by the *New York Times* in December 2005. Critics argued that the surveillance violated both the Fourth Amendment of the Constitution and the 1978 Foreign Intelligence Surveillance Act (FISA), which created a secret court to approve warrants to wiretap spies or terrorists.

The Bush administration insisted that the eavesdropping was necessary in the fight against terror. The president argued that his power to order the warrantless surveillance was based on his constitutional role as commander in chief and a resolution passed by Congress after 9/11, which authorized the executive branch to "use all necessary and appropriate force" to combat international terrorism.

Testifying to Congress, Attorney General Alberto R. Gonzales suggested that President Bush might even have the power to tap purely domestic conversations between two Americans within the United States without a warrant, if the conversation related to terrorists.[56] Under the 1978 FISA law, however, the NSA is prohibited from intercepting strictly domestic conversations or communications in the United States without a court order.

In May 2006, *USA Today* revealed that soon after the 9/11 attacks, the NSA began secretly collecting the phone call records of millions of Americans with the help of three major telephone companies.[57] According to the newspaper, the NSA did not listen in on conversations but analyzed the records to try to detect terrorist activity.

While the ability of the NSA to eavesdrop, and the debate over the extent of its legal and constitutional powers, has raised privacy concerns, at the same time the agency has been criticized in Congress for failing to keep up with new technology. For example, data encryption, widely available commercially, the use of fiber-optic cables, and the overwhelming number of e-mails crisscrossing the globe have made it more difficult for the NSA to do its job.

**National Reconnaissance Office** The National Reconnaissance Office (NRO) builds and operates the nation's spy satellites, which circle the globe capturing images of potential targets in other countries and electronic signals. With some 3,000 employees and an estimated annual budget of around $6.2 billion, the NRO spends far more than any of the government's other intelligence agencies. Its budget is twice as big as that of the CIA. It has some 15 satellites in orbit photographing the world and eavesdropping on telephone conversations, diplomatic traffic, and other electronic signals. The satellites bear code names like CRYSTAL, LACROSSE, TRUMPET, and CLASSIC WIZARD.

The images beamed back digitally to NRO ground stations by its satellites are extraordinarily detailed. The agency's cameras reputedly can pick out an object the size of a license plate from hundreds of miles in outer space. The intelligence captured by the NRO's spies in the sky has played a key role in virtually every major foreign policy event of the last several decades.

**Director of National Intelligence (DNI)** The failure of the intelligence agencies to prevent the attacks of 9/11, together with the CIA's mistaken estimate that Iraq had weapons of mass destruction—which helped to trigger the U.S. invasion of that country in 2003—led to insistent demands for reform. It was these twin failures, and the recommendations of the 9/11 commission, that persuaded Congress to change the structure of the intelligence agencies.

The 9/11 commission recommended that an "intelligence czar" with authority over intelligence agency budgets be placed over the CIA director and the other intelligence agency heads to try to bring about better coordination among the 16 government units that deal with intelligence.

In 2004 Congress passed a law creating the position of Director of National Intelligence (DNI) for this purpose. Early in 2005 President Bush appointed a career diplomat, John Negroponte, to the post. At the same time, Congress established the National Counterterrorism Center to centralize efforts to combat terrorist attacks. The creation of the center had also been recommended by the 9/11 commission.

Some analysts saw a danger that centralizing too much power in the hands of the DNI, an intelligence "czar," might threaten liberties at home. However necessary it may be to protect American security, the existence of a clandestine intelligence and espionage establishment creates special problems in a free society. The operations of the CIA and the other U.S. intelligence agencies pose the continuing dilemma of how secret intelligence machinery, even if necessary to protect the nation, can be made compatible with democratic government.[56]

**Other Instruments: The Agency for International Development, the Peace Corps, and the Voice of America** The State Department must compete in the foreign policy field with the president's NSC staff, the CIA, and the Pentagon. Several other agencies and units of the federal government also are involved in foreign policy.

One of the agencies with foreign policy responsibilities both in Washington and in the field is the Agency for International Development (AID). As its initials imply, AID is responsible for carrying out programs of financial and technical assistance to less economically developed nations.

From 1946 through 2004, the United States has spent more than $1.6 trillion on foreign aid, contributions to international organizations, and military assistance.[58] For fiscal 2005, for example, the president's budget request for foreign aid totaled $21.3 billion and included economic assistance for about 150 countries in Latin America, Asia, Africa, the Middle East, Eastern Europe, and the former republics of the Soviet Union. In recent years, the United States has placed greater emphasis on channeling aid through multilateral financial institutions, and it has increased its participation in the International Bank for Reconstruction and Development (the World Bank), which makes loans to and promotes foreign investments in underdeveloped nations.

AID is politically unpopular because many Ameri-

Two Afghan women carry cans of cooking oil provided by the U.S. Agency for International Development.

## Making a Difference

# INSPIRING HOPE: MIDDLE EAST TEENAGERS WORKING FOR PEACE IN MAINE

OTISFIELD, MAINE—This pine-scented camp on the shore of Pleasant Lake, Maine, may hold hope for the tormented Holy Land. It is the site of "Seeds of Peace," a program that brings together Arab and Israeli teenagers for a month of fun and serious discussions.

The camp is part of a private program launched in 1993 by John Wallach, former foreign editor of the Hearst newspapers, to bring together children from troubled lands. Wallach says that he was tired of "being a fly on the wall of history" and wanted to "inspire hope."

Aside from swimming and other summer camp activities, the heart of "Seeds of Peace" is a daily, 90-minute discussion known in camp shorthand as "coexistence." Many of the sessions center on fear. Israeli teenagers tell of being afraid that someone—anyone—standing next to them might be a suicide bomber. They talk a lot about the Holocaust, which many of their co-campers know little about because it is not taught in most Arab schools.

Sara Jabari, a 15-year-old Palestinian, said her father, a gas station owner in Hebron, was warned by Hamas, the extremist Palestinian group responsible for the suicide bombings, not to send her to the peace camp. He ignored the warning "because he believes in peace, and I believe in peace," Jabari said.

Jabari said she was wary of the Israeli campers at first. "I thought all Israelis were like the [Israeli] settlers, and the settlers are always killing our people." Then she met Dana Naor. "She is my friend. She is so nice and I know [among] the Israelis, there is good and there is bad from them. And from the Palestinians, there is good and there is bad too. I really had a new idea of the Israelis from Dana."

"Seeds of Peace" takes no government money, and Wallach said he raises the necessary funds each year from individuals and corporations.

"The whole point of it is to let people recognize that the differences are wide, that they are deep, but that it's up to them to find a way to resolve it," said Wallach. "This may seem like a simple thing, but you have to understand that many of these boys and girls have never heard the other side."

Wallach says it is nearly impossible to do the same with adults because, in his words, "They have too much baggage." That is why Wallach founded this program centered on young people who would return to their homelands as "ambassadors of peace."

This program has so impressed agencies in other countries that Wallach has been asked to create similar pilot programs for Greek and Turkish Cypriot youths and one for youngsters from Serbia, Croatia, and Bosnia.

The teens leave camp full of hope. Then they return home. There most will face criticism from those, including friends, who say they have been brainwashed.

They will keep in touch with their newfound friends via e-mail and will try to visit each other. For some, that will mean traveling in secret.

Adi Fassler, an Israeli, says now she knows why building peace is so difficult. She believes if adults and government leaders went through the same camp experience, they would learn to accept each other.

—Adapted from the *Washington Post,* August 22, 1997; *USA Today,* August 4, 1998; the *Boston Globe,* August 15, 1999; and online at <http://www.seedsofpeace.org>

cans regard it as a "give-away" program with little visible benefit to taxpayers. But the aid program can be defended both on humanitarian grounds and, more narrowly, on political grounds. As the richest nation in the world, the United States has felt a moral obligation to try to alleviate poverty, disease, and malnutrition in other nations. At the same time, supporters of the aid program contend, peace and stability are unlikely to be achieved for the United States or the world as a whole as long as such conditions exist in the poorer nations.

Despite some popular misconceptions, most foreign aid is not given to other countries in the form of cash. Most AID dollars are spent in the United States to buy commodities and to hire technical experts for projects overseas. AID provides technical assistance by sending abroad specialists in such fields as health, economic growth, the environment, and democratic forms of government. Through development loans, repayable in U.S. dollars, AID offers other countries long-term, low-interest financing for such projects as highways, dams, schools, and hospitals. In addition, the United States donates and sells agricultural commodities at low cost to other countries.

Many poorer countries, however, have been burdened by debt as a result of loans by industrial nations and multilateral organizations.

The Peace Corps was created under President Kennedy in 1961 to provide a trained corps of highly motivated American volunteers, many of them young, to help people in developing nations. In 2006, some 7,810 Peace Corps volunteers were in training or serving abroad in countries as teachers, agricultural aides, doctors, and in many other capacities. In 1990, after democratic governments emerged in Eastern Europe, the Peace Corps sent volunteers for the first time to many of those countries, including Czechoslovakia, Hungary, Poland, Russia, and Ukraine.

Peace Corps volunteers, who must be U.S. citizens

and at least 18 years old, serve abroad for two years and receive a monthly allowance for food, clothing, housing, and other living expenses. Upon completing a "tour," Peace Corps volunteers receive an additional $225 for each month served. By 2006, some 182,000 volunteers had served in the Peace Corps.

The Voice of America became an independent government agency in 1999. As the government's official radio, it beams news broadcasts, music, and feature programs in 52 languages to some 100 million listeners around the globe. Although its purpose is to promote American democracy abroad, its staff attempts to report the news objectively in order to maintain credibility with its foreign audience. A bipartisan Broadcasting Board of Governors, an independent agency of the executive branch, oversees the agency.

## The United Nations

The **United Nations (UN)** was founded in San Francisco in 1945 to fulfill the dream of a community of nations, a world body that could take collective action to keep the peace and work for the betterment of humanity. The opening words of the UN charter declared: "We the peoples of the United Nations determined to save succeeding generations from the scourge of war, which twice in our lifetime has brought untold sorrow to mankind."

*for more information about the United Nations, see:*
*http://www.un.org*

During the Cold War years, however, the UN was generally unable to keep the peace on issues that divided the major world powers. Decisions affecting world peace were made in Washington, Moscow, Beijing, and other capitals, but less often at UN headquarters in New York City. In part, this was predictable given the structure of the UN and the nature of international relations.

The UN Security Council, with 15 members, cannot act over the veto of any of the five permanent members—as of 2006, the United States, Russia, Britain, France, and China. Other countries, including Germany and Japan, have been pressing to become permanent members of the Security Council. Because the former Soviet Union frequently exercised a veto in the Security Council, UN members sought a way to circumvent the council. In November 1950, the UN General Assembly decided that it could act to meet threats to peace when the Security Council failed to do so because the permanent members lacked unanimity. There is no veto power in the General Assembly, to which all member nations belong. Although the General Assembly has thus increased somewhat in importance, it, too, has proved unable to cope with many major conflicts.

The UN has acted with varying success in several world crises: in Korea in 1950, Suez in 1956, the Congo in 1961, and Cyprus in 1964. In the Arab-Israeli War of October 1973, the UN played a significant role in reducing tensions and avoiding a military confrontation between the United States and the Soviet Union. But the UN was not able to end war in Vietnam, and it had scant success in the Middle East during the Arab-Israeli Six-Day War in 1967. The UN failed in its attempt to end Israel's invasion of Lebanon in 1982.

On the other hand, the UN played a role in bringing about the Soviet withdrawal from Afghanistan and in halting the long war between Iran and Iraq in the 1980s. And it provided the umbrella for the coalition of nations, led by the United States, that forced Iraq to withdraw from Kuwait in 1991. The following year UN teams, at great risk and with casualties, brought relief supplies by air and land to beleaguered Sarajevo in the civil war that followed the breakup of Communist Yugoslavia, but was unable to end the siege of that city.

In 2006, 69,838 UN military personnel were deployed around the world as peacekeepers. (See Table 16-1.)

The United States provides almost one-quarter of the UN's $3.6 billion annual budget, plus several hundred million dollars more each year as its share of the UN's peacekeeping costs. However, the United States lost much of its influence in the UN during the 1960s as the UN shifted from a pro-Western to a neutralist stand. As many of the former colonial territories of Africa and Asia gained independence, they joined the UN, and the United States could no longer count on winning its political battles in that body.

© Cris Bouroncle/AFP/Getty Images

2004: U.S. soldiers fighting insurgents in Iraq

**TABLE 16-1**

**United Nations Peacekeeping Forces, 2006**

*Member states of the United Nations provide troops and officers for UN peacekeeping forces that are periodically sent to crisis areas around the world. In 2006, there were almost 67,000 UN military personnel in the field. Among the larger peacekeeping forces were the following:*

| UN Force (year created) | Location | Troops |
|---|---|---|
| UN Mission in Liberia | Liberia | 14,576 |
| UN Peacekeeping Force in Cyprus (1964) | Cyprus | 866 |
| UN Operations in Cote d'Ivoire | Cote d'Ivoire | 6,705 |
| UN Mission in the Sudan | Sudan | 8,895 |
| UN Disengagement Observer Force (1974) | Golan Heights (Syria-Israel border) | 1,046 |
| UN Interim Force in Lebanon (1978) | Southern Lebanon | 5,490* |
| UN Mission in Sierra Leone (1999) | Freetown, Sierra Leone | 17,500 |
| UN Transitional Administration in East Timor (1999) | Dili, East Timor | 5,000 |
| UN Organization Mission in the Democratic Republic of the Congo (1999) | Democratic Republic of the Congo and the subregion, including Namibia, Rwanda, Uganda, Zambia, and Zimbabwe | 15,854 |
| UN Mission in Ethiopia and Eritrea (2000) | Ethiopia and Eritrea | 3,156 |

SOURCE: Data provided by the United Nations, "Current Peacekeeping Operations," online at <www.un.org/Depts/dpko/dpko/cu_mission/body.htm>.

With the loss of American leadership in the UN, criticism of the world body increased in the United States, particularly during the 1980s among conservatives associated with the Reagan administration. At the same time, public support for the UN diminished. Some segments of the public view the world organization as a threat to American sovereignty. Some militia groups even imagined that "black United Nations helicopters" were coming to invade America.[59]

In 1984, discontented with anti-American and anti-Western sentiments in the United Nations Educational, Scientific, and Cultural Organization (UNESCO), the United States withdrew from the body. In 2003, however, the United States rejoined UNESCO.

In 2002, President George W. Bush tried to persuade the UN to approve his use of force against Iraq, but when he failed to do so, he made it clear that the United States would invade without the UN's approval. Bush sent U.S. troops into Iraq in 2003.

By 2006 the UN had expanded from its original 50 to 192 members, with a staff of 61,000 around the world.[60] The UN is administered by a secretariat, staffed by the member nations, and headed by a secretary-general, who in 2006 was Kofi Annan of Ghana. The UN General Assembly elected Ban Ki-moon, the foreign minister of South Korea, as his successor, beginning in 2007. The United States is represented in the UN by an ambassador who heads a U.S. mission in New York. Corruption in the UN's oil-for-food program, which was designed to allow medical supplies and food into Iraq in return for limited oil exports, provided ammunition for the UN's critics. One highly controversial critic, John Bolton, a State Department official and conservative Republican partisan, was appointed by Bush as U.S. ambassador to the world body in 2005, although Bolton had openly criticized the UN on a number of occasions. Bolton argued, for example, that the UN should not be allowed to interfere with military action by the United States when Washington considered it necessary. Bush exercised his constitutional power to make a temporary appointment when the Senate is not in session and named Bolton to the UN job during the congressional recess. Bush acted after the Senate had refused to confirm the nominee, in part because of testimony that Bolton had berated, demeaned, and intimidated his subordinates.

Although the UN has had limited success as a peacekeeping agency, it has served several other constructive purposes. It provides a forum for discussion, a place where new and small nations can be heard. It sometimes helps to defuse world crises by allowing nations to talk instead of fight. And its economic, social, and health agencies have made significant contributions in improving the lives of millions of people all over the world. The UN has also had some success in dealing with such international environmental issues as the peaceful use of outer space and seabeds, pollution of the oceans, and overpopulation. Finally, the UN, for all its limitations, still remains a symbol of hope, the tangible embodiment of humanity's fragile dream of peace.

## The Politics of Foreign Policymaking

Over a period of time, widespread or intense domestic reaction to foreign policy may have an impact on government. During the late 1960s, there was domestic protest against the war in Vietnam by students, professors, and many other citizens. Some Americans reacted against the protesters, but others were undoubtedly favorably influenced by the peace movement. Eventually, a majority of Americans felt the war was a mistake, and a climate developed in which President Johnson felt it prudent not to run for reelection. The growing opposition to the war provided the political backdrop for President Nixon's decision in 1969 to begin the withdrawal of American troops and for the lengthy peace negotiations, conducted initially in secret, that finally brought an end to U.S. participation in the war in 1973.

**The Role of the Public** Despite public awareness of highly publicized issues like the war in Vietnam or in Iraq, some political scientists have argued that on most foreign policy issues, the public is both uninterested and uninformed. Gabriel A. Almond observed that "Americans tend to exhaust their emotional and intellectual energies in private pursuits." While members of the public may develop well-defined views on domestic questions that affect them directly, he argued, on questions of foreign policy they tend to react in changeable, "formless and plastic moods." Almond suggested that relatively small leadership groups play the major role in the making of most specific foreign policy decisions, and that the public's role is largely confined to the expression of mass attitudes that provide a framework within which officials may work.[61]

James N. Rosenau has also differentiated between public response to domestic issues and foreign policy issues, but he emphasizes that when a foreign policy question becomes so big that it involves "a society's resources and relationships," it quickly turns into a domestic political issue—and he cites the war in Vietnam as an example.[62] The same was true for the divisive war in Iraq that began with the U.S. invasion in 2003.

Nevertheless, a president has wide latitude in conducting foreign policy. Kenneth N. Waltz has suggested that as a rule, "The first effect of an international crisis is to increase the president's popular standing." But, Waltz points out, a president sometimes risks political unpopularity in a foreign policy crisis no matter what he does.[63] And a president who responds too readily to public opinion may be pushed into dangerous choices if public sentiment is running high for quick or simple solutions. Just as the public may demand peace, at other times it may demand retaliation that risks war.

Domestic influence on foreign policy is not limited to mass public opinion as reflected in polls, e-mails, letters, or protest demonstrations. Congress, individual legislators or committee chairs, interest groups, private organizations concerned with foreign policy, opinion leaders, the press, TV commentators, and proximity to an election all may have some effect on policy outcomes.

Some foreign policy questions are of special importance to particular groups. A president who is interested in carrying New York, California, and Illinois, for example, in his reelection campaign may frame U.S. policy toward Israel with some thought to the likely reaction among the many Jewish voters in those states. On Polish patriotic days, members of Congress from heavily Polish areas such as Buffalo or Chicago stand in the House and Senate and carefully pay homage to the contribution of Polish heroes to the nation's heritage.

**Presidential Credibility** A president's conduct of foreign policy depends in large measure on whether he is able to carry the public along with him on big decisions. Without public trust in his leadership, he may fail.

© Mian Khursheed/Reuters/Corbis

## After 9/11: A Strategy for Preventive War

In 2002, following the terrorist attacks of 9/11, President George W. Bush outlined a new national security strategy for America, a controversial policy allowing for preemptive, or, as it is also called, preventive war to foil terrorists. The strategy formed the basis for the U.S. invasion of Iraq in 2003. Some of the highlights:

- "We must be prepared to stop rogue states and their terrorist clients before they are able to threaten or use weapons of mass destruction against the United States and our allies and friends. . . . We cannot let our enemies strike first."
- "For centuries, international law recognized that nations need not suffer an attack before they can lawfully take action to defend themselves against forces that present an imminent danger of attack. . . . We must adapt the concept of imminent threat to the capabilities and objectives of today's adversaries."
- "The greater the threat, the greater is the risk of inaction—and the more compelling the case for taking anticipatory action to defend ourselves. . . . To forestall or prevent such hostile acts by our adversaries, the United States will, if necessary, act preemptively."

—President George W. Bush, "The National Security Strategy of the United States of America," September 17, 2002

## Preventive War: A Failed Doctrine

So far, the preventive war doctrine has had one real test: the invasion of Iraq. Mr. Bush terrified millions of Americans into believing that forcibly changing the regime in Baghdad was the only way to keep Iraq's supposed stockpiles of unconventional weapons out of the hands of Al Qaeda. Then it turned out that there were no stockpiles and no operational links between Saddam Hussein's regime and Al Qaeda's anti-American terrorism. Meanwhile, America's long-standing defensive alliances were weakened and the bulk of America's ground combat troops tied down in Iraq for what now appears to be many years to come. If that is making this country safer, it is hard to see how. The real lesson is that America dangerously erodes its military and diplomatic defenses when it charges off unwisely after hypothetical enemies.

Before the Iraq fiasco, American leaders rightly viewed war as a last resort, appropriate only when the nation's vital interests were actively threatened and reasonable diplomatic efforts had been exhausted.

—From "Preventive War: A Failed Doctrine," *New York Times* editorial, September 12, 2004, p. A12. 

President Reagan's approval rating plummeted after the disclosure in 1986 that—despite his stated public policy of never dealing with terrorists—he had secretly sold arms to Iran to try to extricate American hostages seized by terrorists in Lebanon.

Other presidents have encountered credibility problems. Since the Second World War, the government has on more than one occasion told official lies designed to protect secret intelligence operations. Under President Eisenhower, for example, the administration claimed at first that the CIA's U-2 spy plane shot down 1,200 miles inside the Soviet Union was a "weather research" aircraft that had strayed off course. Under President Kennedy, the government initially denied, but later admitted, that it was responsible for the CIA-backed invasion of Cuba at the Bay of Pigs.

President Johnson suffered from a "credibility gap" that seriously hampered his presidency. The Tonkin Gulf episode, discussed earlier in this chapter, was one example of an event during his presidency that took on a far different coloration after the fact. During the Watergate scandal, President Nixon claimed he had concealed certain information for "national security" reasons, but he later admitted political motivation as well; "national security" had been used as a pretext to cover up a crime.[64] Misleading official statements about foreign policy and national security, in short, have contributed to an erosion of public confidence in government honesty.

**Political Parties, Campaigns, and Foreign Policy** The two-party system tends to push both major parties toward the center on foreign policy issues. Kenneth Waltz explains that "failure to do so will give a third party the chance to wedge itself in between its two larger competitors. . . . The policy positions of two competing parties begin to approach one another, and the candidates even begin to look and talk very much alike."[65]

Nevertheless, foreign policy questions often become campaign issues. In 2004, for example, George W. Bush repeatedly sought to persuade the voters that he was the best candidate to keep America safe from international terrorists. Senator Kerry argued that Bush had mismanaged the conduct of the war in Iraq and then "failed to tell you the truth" about how badly it was going.[66]

Advocates of bipartisanship in foreign policy contend that both major political parties should broadly support the president, that it is in the nation's interest to appear united to the rest of the world, and that foreign policy issues should not be sharply debated in political campaigns. If that was ever the case, it certainly does not reflect today's realities. As a concept, bipartisanship now seems rather quaint. Most candidates today maintain that foreign policy issues must be discussed in political campaigns precisely because those issues are so important.

Bipartisanship flourished particularly in the period shortly after the Second World War. It was symbolized by the phrase "Politics stops at the water's edge," a concept popularized in 1950 by Senator Arthur H. Vandenberg, a Michigan Republican who served as chairman of the Senate Foreign Relations Committee under a Democratic president, Harry Truman.

© Reuters/Landov

The Pentagon

**The Economics of Foreign Policymaking** In a world in which the American economy is so directly affected by trade, foreign policy cannot be concerned with political and military power alone. As the nation moved further into the 21st century, foreign policy increasingly involved major economic questions, such as trade restrictions, import quotas, the balance of trade, and interest rates. The impact of economic policy and globalization on foreign affairs is discussed in Chapter 17.

## The Defense Establishment

In late September 2004, in a remote base at Fort Greely, Alaska, the United States began deploying a controversial antimissile system designed to protect America from a nuclear attack. An outgrowth of a program first envisioned by Ronald Reagan and dubbed "Star Wars," the system deployed in 2004 cost billions of dollars to develop.

In theory, a "kill vehicle" launched from Alaska would intercept an incoming ballistic missile in space and collide with it at 15,000 miles an hour, destroying it; the impact alone was designed to accomplish this, since the kill vehicle carried no warhead. The system was not planned to counter an all-out attack, but, at best, to ward off a small number of missiles that might be launched by so-called "rogue" nations.

Two years earlier President George W. Bush had ordered the system deployed. The Pentagon maintained that the interceptors had worked in five out of eight tests. But critics said that the system had not been adequately tested. They noted that in the tests, the team knew the exact time, place, and trajectory of the target missile—conditions unlikely to prevail in the event of a real attack. Even the Pentagon's chief weapons evaluator estimated that the system could hit its targets only 20 percent of the time.

Some saw the deployment as a political missile timed for the 2004 presidential election. President Bush praised the system in his campaign. For example, in a campaign speech in Pennsylvania—a hotly contested battleground state—Bush talked about the ABM system and suggested that its opponents, including John Kerry, the Democratic presidential candidate, were jeopardizing America's safety: "We say to those tyrants who believe they can blackmail American and the free world, 'You fire, we're going to shoot it down.'"[67]

Since the Second World War the United States has spent more than $3 trillion on national defense; in fiscal 2007 the Defense Department's budget request was $439.3 billion.[68] Because of expanding technology, however, some weapons systems become obsolete even as they are deployed. And during the years when the Soviet Union stood as a rival superpower, a strong argument could be made that, because of the threat of nuclear war, as spending for armaments increased, national security actually diminished.

Aside from this paradox, the existence of a multibillion-dollar military machine has created numerous problems for American society. Within the military-industrial complex, whole industries depend on government defense contracts; aerospace industry lobbyists attempt to guard their clients' interests in Washington; and some universities compete for classified military research contracts. A society that devotes some 18 percent of the national budget to defense-related spending cannot allocate as much as it otherwise might to eliminate poverty or improve health, schools, and the natural environment. The "cost" of a defense economy cannot be measured simply in terms of the size of the annual Pentagon budget.

Since the Second World War, America's nuclear weapons have remained in their underground silos and beneath the sea in submarines. With the end of the Cold War, their use seems less likely. But since the Second World War, the United States has fought a series of "limited" or conventional wars in Korea, Vietnam, the Persian Gulf, Afghanistan, and Iraq. Despite its vast weaponry, military personnel, and technology, the

United States learned in Vietnam that superior size and resources were of little advantage against an elusive and politically dedicated enemy skilled in guerrilla warfare. In Iraq, after the U.S. invasion in 2003, insurgents using roadside bombs, rocket-propelled grenades, and suicide car bombs caused mounting casualties among U.S. troops and Iraqi civilians.

The military was finding it difficult to use its superior firepower against hostile guerrilla forces in an urban environment. The practical limits of American power apply as well to the most terrible weapons in its arsenal. The United States could not employ nuclear weapons against a smaller nation without being morally condemned by most of the rest of the world as well as by millions of citizens at home. The use of such weapons has been considered, however. During the Korean War, for example, President Eisenhower discussed with his advisers the possible use of nuclear arms.[69] But the use of tactical or strategic nuclear weapons in a conventional "limited war" may carry with it the threat of escalation into a larger war. To an extent, therefore, the "usable power" of the United States has been limited.

Furthermore, domestic opposition to U.S. involvement in Southeast Asia, the Middle East, Central America, and the Persian Gulf has demonstrated the potential political risks and limitations for American leaders pursuing military solutions to foreign policy problems.

Foreign policy and defense policy are intimately linked. Ideally, as Burton M. Sapin noted: "Foreign policy establishes the broad outlines within which the defense establishment must do its work."[70] A modern president must contend with the problems of controlling a huge, powerful military establishment with its friends and protectors in Congress and its clients in private industry. The president must see that the generals serve his foreign policy goals, rather than the other way around.

## The Department of Defense

The principle of civilian control over the American military establishment is deeply rooted in the Constitution and the nation's tradition. The president is commander in chief of all the armed forces, and the secretary of defense, by law, must be a civilian. Yet the effectiveness of civilian control of the military has sometimes been open to question.

Across the Potomac River from Washington, in Arlington, Virginia, lies the Pentagon. Completed in 1943 at a cost of $83 million, the Pentagon houses some 24,000 civilian and military employees. In its concourse is a shopping center large enough for most suburban cities. The Pentagon has its own bank, post office, barbershop, department stores, florist—even an optometrist and medical and dental clinics.

The secretary of defense is the Western world's biggest employer, in charge of 675,111 civilians and 1,100,000 members of the armed forces as of 2006. Indirectly, the Pentagon is also the biggest private employer in America; in 2003, for example, the Defense Department's contracts were running at a level of $208 billion a year.[71]

The National Security Act of 1947, as amended in 1949, unified the armed forces under the control of a single secretary of defense. The Army, Navy, and Air Force continue to exist as separate entities within the Defense Department, each with its own secretary. The secretaries of the armed services do not control their military operations, however; that is the responsibility of the president, acting through the secretary of defense and the Joint Chiefs of Staff.

The Pentagon has its own "little State Department," the Office of International Security Affairs (ISA), which serves both as the Defense Department's link with the State Department and as a competing source of foreign policy formulation.

The Pentagon also has its own intelligence organization, the Defense Intelligence Agency (DIA), created in 1961, as well as the supersecret National Security Agency (NSA), discussed earlier in this chapter, which intercepts the coded messages of other nations and conducts electronic espionage. The military services have their own intelligence units as well.

In the months before the 2003 invasion of Iraq, Pentagon conservatives established a small office, the Policy and Counterintelligence Evaluation Group, that acted as a sort of rival to the CIA, collecting intelligence that tried to show a link between Iraq's leader, Saddam Hussein, and al Qaeda terrorists to help justify the war. The Pentagon's efforts were later discredited; the CIA and the 9/11 commission found no evidence that Iraq and Osama bin Laden were working together.

## The Joint Chiefs of Staff

The members of the **Joint Chiefs of Staff** are the chair, the chiefs of staff of the three armed services, and, when Marine Corps matters are under consideration, the commandant of the Marines. By law the chair, whose powers were greatly strengthened by the Defense Reorganization Act of 1986, advises the president and the secretary of defense.

The chair and other members of the Joint Chiefs are appointed by the president. Sometimes the president may skip over senior officers to appoint a more dynamic, younger service chief. The chair of the Joint Chiefs outranks the other members. Together, the Joint Chiefs are responsible for the day-to-day conduct of military operations as well as long-range strategic planning. They are assisted by a Joint Staff of 1,200 officers and civilians from the three services. Although the president relies on the chair of the Joint Chiefs for military advice, he may choose to disregard the chair's views. The president has the responsibility to weigh military risks against the nation's total foreign policy objectives.

Robert Kennedy related that during the Cuban Missile Crisis in 1962, one member of the Joint Chiefs advocated the use of nuclear weapons: "I thought, as I listened, of the many times that I had heard the military take positions which, if wrong, had the advantage that no one would be around at the end to know."[72]

But not every military officer is a "hawk." A series of leading military figures in recent decades—generals like George Marshall, Omar Bradley, Matthew Ridgway, James Gavin, Maxwell Taylor, and Colin Powell—clearly demonstrated that they could view foreign policy in its broadest context, not merely in narrow, military terms. Another career military man, President Eisenhower, resisted the advice of some of his military advisers and refused, for example, to intervene in Southeast Asia in 1954. And some high-ranking military officers and ex-officers criticized the wars in Vietnam and Iraq.

## Selective Service

Although in peacetime the United States has usually relied on a volunteer army, the government has registered or drafted men for military service during times of international tension or war. During the Second World War, the Korean War, and the Vietnam War, for example, men were conscripted for military duty.

Early in 1980, in response to events in Iran and Afghanistan, President Carter asked Congress to resume draft registration. Congress approved the legislation, and registration at 34,000 post offices began that summer. The Selective Service System did not issue draft cards or classify those who registered. There could not be an actual draft unless Congress approved a call-up. Although Carter had asked for authority to register both men and women, Congress refused to approve draft registration for women. In 1981, the Supreme Court ruled that a draft of men only was constitutional.[73] Draft registration of men continued under Presidents Reagan, Bush, Clinton, and George W. Bush. Male U.S. citizens age 18 through 25 and most noncitizens in that age bracket are required to register for the draft and may do so by various means, including registration at post offices, many high schools, by mail, and online.

## Strategic Arms: The Balance of Terror

The United States and Russia, as noted, in 2004 still possessed intercontinental nuclear missiles, as did China and several other nations, including India, Pakistan, and Israel. North Korea claimed it already possessed nuclear bombs, and Iran appeared to be actively pursuing a nuclear weapons program. The al Qaeda terrorist organization had also attempted to acquire nuclear arms.

The proliferation of these powerful weapons meant that the world still lived in the shadow of the bomb. The reality is that the U.S. military still spends about $27 billion a year to keep about 7,800 active nuclear weapons ready for use.[74] The single nuclear bomb the United States dropped on Hiroshima in 1945 killed about 75,000 people and, with the bomb dropped on Nagasaki three days later, led to the Japanese surrender that ended the Second World War. And today's nuclear bombs are many times more powerful than those dropped on Japan.

In the decades after the 1950s, the world lived with the knowledge that it was less than 30 minutes away from nuclear disaster. (Figure 16-2 illustrates the potential destruction of two major U.S. cities.)

FIGURE 16-2

**Potential Destruction from Nuclear Weapons**

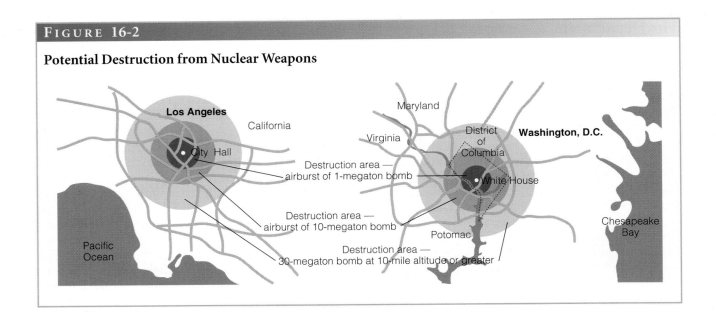

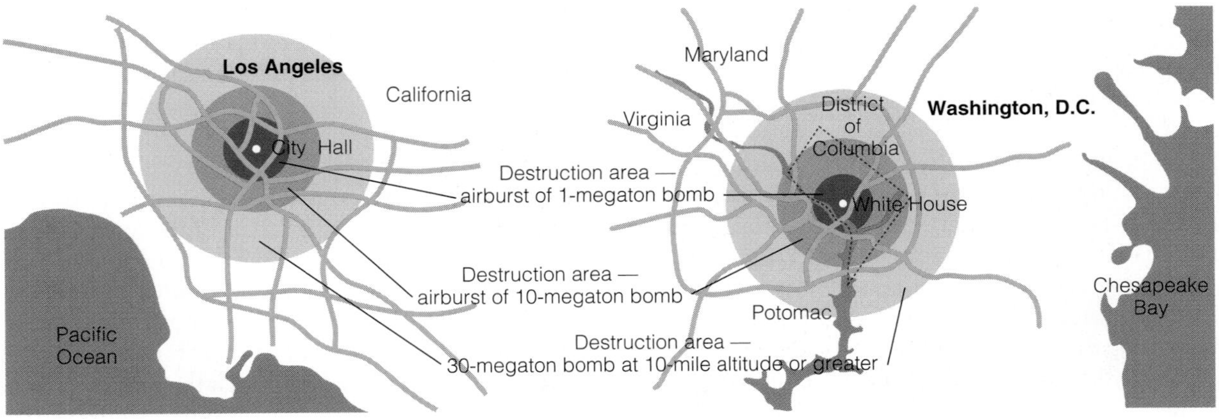

## How to Waste $5.7 Billion: A Case Study

The history of the U.S. development of its first antiballistic missile (ABM) system illustrates how costly weapons systems may waste taxpayer dollars and become outmoded by the time the systems are ready to be deployed.

By 1967 the Soviet Union had deployed an ABM system around Moscow. The Johnson administration opposed deployment of an ABM system by the United States, arguing that Soviet countermeasures would leave both countries with no net increase in security.

But the Joint Chiefs of Staff and powerful members of Congress favored the ABM system. So the United States in 1969 embarked on a multibillion dollar program to build the Safeguard ABM system.

On October 1, 1975, the enormous complex of radars, missiles, and computers, located in the wheat fields near Grand Forks, North Dakota, was completed, at a cost of $5.7 billion. The Pentagon announced that Safeguard was fully operational. By an irony of history, however, the next day the House of Representatives voted to dismantle the project. The Senate concurred and the missile facilities were shut down.

The reason: Even before its completion, the ABM had become obsolete when the Soviets developed MIRV—multiple independently targetable warheads that could overwhelm the antimissile defense system. This was precisely the argument that critics of the ABM system had used during a Senate debate over the system in 1968.

The American nuclear monopoly was broken when the Soviet Union exploded an atomic bomb in 1949. In 1957 the Soviet Union launched the first Sputnik, or earth satellite. The military implications were clear: If Russia possessed the technology to boost a satellite into outer space, it had long-range missiles that could be targeted on American cities. In October 1964 Communist China exploded its first nuclear bomb, and the "nuclear club" then had five members—the United States, the Soviet Union, Britain, France, and China. India became the sixth member when it exploded a nuclear device in May 1974. Both India and Pakistan held underground tests of nuclear weapons in 1998. Israel has nuclear weapons. South Africa has said it built six nuclear bombs and then destroyed them.

After the Second World War, the United States adopted a policy of **strategic deterrence.** The theory of deterrence, developed in the Pentagon with the assistance of defense "think tanks" such as the Rand Corporation, involved deploying enough nuclear weapons so that an enemy would not, in theory, attack the United States, for fear of being attacked in retaliation.

But how, if it relied on nuclear arms alone, could the United States respond to nonnuclear military challenges? President Kennedy believed it was necessary for the United States to supplement its nuclear power by expanding its capacity to fight "conventional" wars. During the 1960s, the policy of massive nuclear retaliation changed to one of "limited" or "flexible" response, and the Pentagon trained its Special Forces (the Green Berets) in guerrilla warfare and "counterinsurgency." In Vietnam, at least, the new theory and techniques did not prove to be very successful.

Some defense intellectuals shocked many people by their attempts at rational analysis of an essentially irra-

"General Hoskins, I don't care if you are in charge of our star-wars defense. You must wear a regulation uniform."

tional process—thermonuclear war. For example, Herman Kahn wrote in 1961 that a nuclear war "would not preclude normal and happy lives for the majority of survivors and their descendants."[75] The picture of nuclear survivors living joyful lives amid the charred, radioactive debris did not convince everyone. Other analysts, such as Ralph E. Lapp, argued that the nation's arsenal of weapons had grown into "a monstrous stockpile which could not only kill, but overkill, any possible enemy."[76]

The strategy of deterrence had a language all its own. Military theorists spoke of "first-strike capability" and "second-strike capability," "stable deterrent," or "counterforce." By the late 1960s the jargon included ominous new acronyms: MIRV (multiple independently targetable reentry vehicle), MAD (mutual assured destruction), and ABM (antiballistic missile). Whatever parity had been achieved in the "balance of terror" was threatened by new technology—the simultaneous development of the ABM as a defense against ballistic missiles, and the MIRV, designed to overwhelm an ABM system by firing from one missile a cluster of real and dummy warheads to confuse radar defenses. The spiraling arms race, in short, threatened to spin out of control.

As a result, both superpowers signed a series of disarmament agreements. The 1972 SALT agreements limited ABM deployment by the United States and the Soviet Union and included a five-year freeze on production and testing of offensive nuclear weapons. Both sides, however, continued to possess immense destructive power despite the agreement and later accords.

American strategic deterrence has long rested on a "triad" of nuclear weapons—land-based missiles, submarines armed with nuclear missiles, and bombers. But the theories of how these deadly weapons should be used have changed over the years. In 1983, President Reagan announced the Strategic Defense Initiative (SDI), or "Star Wars" program, designed to develop and test components for tracking and shooting down Soviet nuclear missiles in space. SDI assumed the development of such advanced technology as lasers or particle beams that could intercept incoming missiles. The Reagan strategy thus meant a shift from the traditional doctrine of "massive retaliation" to a defensive posture.

Critics of the program said it would be overwhelmed by countermeasures, would cost vast sums of money, and, most of all, might encourage an enemy to attack first, before such a defensive net could be deployed. With the end of the Cold War, the program was scaled down. Proponents argued that it was still necessary because more nations were acquiring nuclear weapons and ballistic missiles, increasing the chance of accidental or intentional use. The original Star Wars program was never built, but as noted, President George W. Bush began the deployment of a version of the system in 2004.

In 2001, the Bush administration announced it was pulling out of the 1972 ABM Treaty that limited the deployment of ABMs by the United States and the Soviet Union. President Bush said the withdrawal was necessary so that America could build an ABM system to defend itself. Russia strongly objected to the U.S. decision.

Even as the arms race spiraled, scientists raised new questions about whether a nation that launched a nuclear attack, even a "successful" attack, might destroy itself and the planet. Some experts questioned whether any nuclear strategy could provide true security for any nation. In 1984, for example, the chief of staff of the U.S. Air Force, General Charles A. Gabriel, declared, "I don't think anyone in his right mind would argue that nuclear war is winnable."[77]

## Arms Control and Disarmament

For years, leaders of both the United States and the Soviet Union realized that the arms race and the strategy of deterrence, however "logical," could lead to disaster. One obvious but elusive alternative was arms control and disarmament, the subject of intermittent negotiations between Moscow and Washington since the Second World War.

In 1963 the United States, the Soviet Union, and Great Britain reached agreement on a limited nuclear test-ban treaty. The treaty, banning tests in the air, under water, and in outer space—but not underground—was ratified by the U.S. Senate and signed by more than a hundred nations, but two nuclear powers—France and China—refused to do so.

Despite progress between Washington and Moscow, nuclear proliferation continued. Even as the superpowers were cutting back, other nations were attempting to acquire nuclear weapons and join the "nuclear club." As this has happened, some analysts believe, global stability may be threatened even more than it had been during the Cold War era.

In 1968 the UN General Assembly voted approval of a draft treaty banning the spread of nuclear weapons to states not already possessing them. The United States, the Soviet Union, and 60 other nations signed the Nonproliferation Treaty, and the Senate ratified it in 1969. But Israel, India, Japan, France, and China did not sign. The treaty was extended indefinitely in 1995.

In 1972, as noted, the United States and the Soviet Union signed the SALT agreement to limit strategic arms; and the separate ABM Treaty, which as modified, limited each side to one ABM site. In 1979, another agreement, known as SALT II, was reached with the Soviets, although it was never ratified by the U.S. Senate.

In the summer of 1982, a new round of arms control talks began in Geneva. SALT was renamed START (Strategic Arms Reduction Talks) by the Reagan administration. Finally in 1987, the United States and the Soviet Union agreed to dismantle all of their intermediate- and shorter-range missiles, and Soviet leader Mikhail Gorbachev journeyed to Washington to sign the treaty. The agreement, the Intermediate-range Nuclear Forces (INF) treaty, was historic because it marked the first time that the two countries had agreed to reduce their nuclear arsenals. And in 1991, both sides signed the START I agreement to reduce strategic, long-range missiles as well.

In January 1993, the first President Bush and President Boris Yeltsin of Russia met in Moscow and signed a far-reaching treaty to destroy three-quarters of their nuclear warheads over 10 years. The treaty, known as START II, also called for the elimination of all land-based intercontinental ballistic missiles with multiple warheads. The Senate ratified the pact in 1996.

That same year, the United States, Russia, and most of the nations of the world signed the Comprehensive Test Ban Treaty (CTBT), banning all underground nuclear weapons tests and explosions, just as testing in the atmosphere was already banned. But it was rejected by the Republican-controlled Senate in 1999 after the Republicans made it clear they would not approve the treaty unless the White House moved forward with a missile defense system. President George W. Bush's administration opposed the treaty, and as of 2004 the CTBT had not been ratified by the Senate.

In 2002 Bush and President Putin of Russia signed yet another agreement committing both nations to reducing their nuclear arsenals to a maximum of 2,200 warheads over 10 years. The treaty was ratified by the Senate in 2003.[78]

Despite these agreements, the world still faced the threat of nuclear, chemical, and biological warfare. In 1969 President Nixon announced that the United States was renouncing germ warfare and would no longer stockpile biological weapons. But he said the United States would continue to engage in "defensive research" in biological weapons. At that time the United States did not renounce chemical warfare, including the production of deadly nerve gases like sarin or VX—a tiny drop of which can kill instantly.

In 1970, however, President Nixon submitted to the Senate the Geneva Protocol outlawing chemical and biological warfare among nations. The United States had signed the treaty in 1925, but the Senate never ratified it until 1974. In 1972 the United States, the Soviet Union, and some 70 other nations signed an international agreement to outlaw biological weapons. This treaty, too, was ratified by the Senate in 1974. Thus, today, the United States is formally pledged not to use chemical or biological weapons.

But the treaties did not prohibit the production or stockpiling of chemical weapons. In 1992 the Chemical Weapons Convention banned the production, sale, and use of nerve gas and other chemical weapons. By 1995, a total of 159 nations, including the United States and Russia, had signed the treaty. It was ratified by the Senate in 1997 and went into effect that same year.

## The Military-Industrial Complex

In his final speech to the nation, President Eisenhower warned against what he called "unwarranted influence" by the "**military-industrial complex.**"[79] The term has often been used since that time to describe the economic and political ties between the military establishment and the defense-aerospace industry. Eisenhower thus focused attention on the consequences for America of a vast military establishment linked to a huge arms industry. In the years after Eisenhower's 1961 warning, the concept of the military-industrial complex

### Eisenhower's Warning: The Military-Industrial Complex

This conjunction of an immense military establishment and a large arms industry is new in the American experience. The total influence—economic, political, even spiritual—is felt in every city, every statehouse, every office of the federal government. We recognize the imperative need for this development. Yet we must not fail to comprehend its grave implications. Our toil, resources, and livelihood are all involved; so is the very structure of our society.

In the councils of government, we must guard against the acquisition of unwarranted influence, whether sought or unsought, by the military-industrial complex.

The potential for the disastrous rise of misplaced power exists and will persist.

We must never let the weight of this combination endanger our liberties or democratic processes. We should take nothing for granted. Only an alert and knowledgeable citizenry can compel the proper meshing of the huge industrial and military machinery of defense with our peaceful methods and goals, so that security and liberty may prosper together.

—Dwight D. Eisenhower, Farewell Radio and Television Address to the American People, January 17, 1961

**TABLE 16-2**

**The Top 10 Defense Contractors**

| Rank | Company | Amount of Defense Contracts (in billions) |
|---|---|---|
| 1 | Lockheed Martin | $19.4 |
| 2 | Boeing Company | 18.3 |
| 3 | Northrop Grumman | 13.5 |
| 4 | General Dynamics | 10.6 |
| 5 | Raytheon Company | 9.1 |
| 6 | Halliburton | 5.8 |
| 7 | BEA Systems PLC | 5.6 |
| 8 | United Technologies | 5.0 |
| 9 | L-3 Communications Holdings | 4.7 |
| 10 | Computer Science | 2.8 |

SOURCE: Figures are rounded. Data from The Statistical Information Analysis Division, "Top Ten Companies Receiving The Largest Dollar Volume of Prime Contract Awards—Fiscal Year 2005," online at <http://siadapp.dior.whs.mil/procurement/historical_reports/statistics/p01/fy2005/top100.htm>.

was expanded to encompass universities conducting defense research, scientists, laboratories, aerospace industry contractors, and research firms.

Entire communities in some areas are dependent on defense industries or military installations. In fiscal 2006 the Lockheed Martin Corporation received $19.4 billion in defense contracts from the government, heading the list of the 100 largest defense contractors in the United States.[80] The top 10 defense contractors in America are shown in Table 16-2.

Defense spending fattens the congressional "pork barrel." Powerful individual legislators can, and do, obtain multimillion-dollar contracts for their states and districts. Another example of the interrelationships within the military-industrial complex is the fact that retired military officers are frequently hired by aerospace industry contractors.

The effect of the military-industrial complex is pervasive and difficult to measure. But with many billions of dollars at stake, the scramble for contracts, the pressure on Congress and the Pentagon, and the political and economic rewards involved have given some Americans a substantial interest in an economy geared to defense production.

A military-industrial complex spawned to protect American security has created numerous problems for American society. America faced, and still faces, the problem of how to balance its military needs against social needs at home. Billions of dollars that might, in part at least, have been used for education, housing, transportation, and similar programs were siphoned off into arms. Even when the United States lost its main adversary, with the disintegration of the Soviet Union, the vast defense and aerospace industries continued to flourish.

Professor Paul Kennedy has also argued: "If . . . too large a proportion of the state's resources is diverted from wealth creation and allocated instead to military purposes, then that is likely to lead to a weakening of national power over the longer term."[81]

Huge military expenditures are often the result of intense political battles and pressures. The debate over the controversial B-1 and B-2 bombers provided an example of the enormous economic stakes in a new weapons system. For years the Air Force, backed by the aerospace industry and influential members of Congress, had pushed for production of the supersonic missile-firing B-1 bomber. Killed by President Carter, it took wing again under President Reagan, who announced plans to produce 100 of the supersonic aircraft at a cost of billions. The bomber was the most expensive weapons system in the federal budget.

The first B-1 rolled off the production line in October 1986. But accidents and serious flaws in its performance raised questions about whether the costly plane really worked. As author Nick Kotz wrote in 1988: "By now the B-1 is more than a bomber. It has become a cause."[82] Whether a weapons system gets built may depend as much on political factors as on military necessity, Kotz argued. The result may be "billions wasted on weapons and military facilities we don't need," and an arms program "totally out of control."[83] A total of 97 B-1 bombers was built, but the aircraft was never used in the 1991 war in the Persian Gulf; the Air Force depended on older, more reliable aircraft.

Next, Congress funded the B-2, the stealth bomber, which was designed to evade enemy radar, and production began on 21 of the planes, which cost $2 billion each, at a total cost of $44.7 billion. The aircraft experienced a series of technical problems during years of flight tests, including faulty radar; and the General Accounting Office reported in 1997 that the plane's skin was so sensitive it had to be sheltered from heat and rain. The B-2 was finally used in combat for the first time in 1999 during the NATO bombing of Yugoslavia. One of the planes mistakenly bombed the Chinese embassy in Belgrade because the CIA had relied upon inaccurate maps.

One result of the military-industrial complex is that the United States has become arms merchant to the world. In 2003 alone, for example, American contractors sold more than $14.5 billion in weapons to other nations, making the United States by far the world's biggest arms merchant.[84] The total was larger than arms sales by all European countries combined. In addition, the United States ships war matériel, ranging from rifles to jet fighter planes, to other nations under a military assistance program.

The military-industrial complex also has had so-

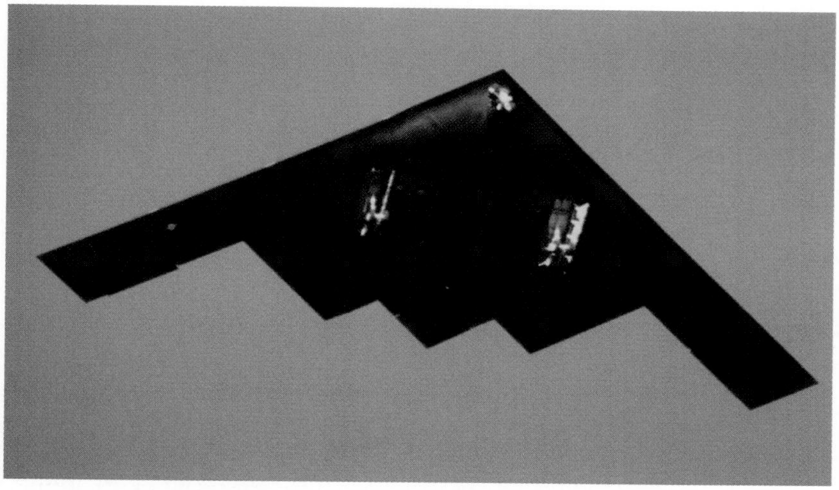


A B-2 stealth bomber

cial and political effects. Demographically, it has been partly responsible for increased population in states such as California, Texas, and Florida, with large defense or aerospace industries. This, in turn, has increased the political power of those states. Influential committee chairs in Congress have channeled huge defense expenditures to their states, bringing economic benefits to those states and political benefits to the legislators. Conversely, in the early 1990s, cutbacks in defense spending caused by the end of the Cold War led to increased unemployment among defense workers in these states.

Finally, the huge amounts of money flowing into defense contracts can lead to fraud and bribery in the Pentagon's procurement of military weapons. In 1988, for example, it was disclosed that billions of dollars in contracts had been awarded to companies improperly and that some Pentagon officials had been bribed.

## America's World Role in the 21st Century

By 2006, as we have seen, foreign policy issues had arisen in many new forms. International terrorism remained a central concern. Other issues tended, perhaps even more than in the past, to involve economics—world trade, import restrictions, oil reserves and prices—and other subjects, such as the international environment and the ocean bed, hunger, overpopulation, nuclear proliferation, genocide, and disease, including the AIDS epidemic.

In the environmental area alone, the United States and other countries faced the daunting challenges of dealing with global warming, acid rain, depletion of the ozone layer, and oil spills; controlling pesticides; preserving the rain forests that help to provide oxygen; and ensuring biodiversity—that is, maintaining the diversity

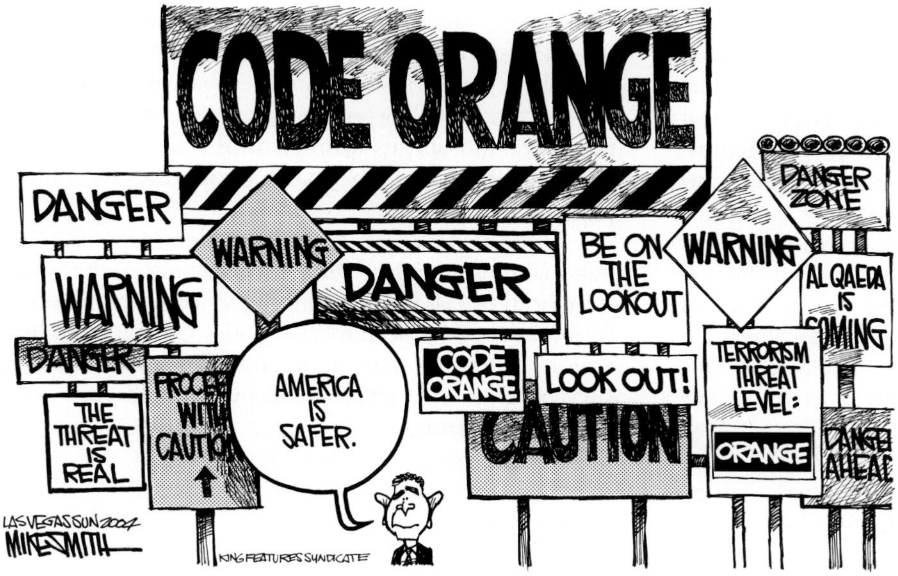

© Rina Castelnuovo/The New York Times

of animals and plants in a world that human beings share with other species.

These global problems suggest a new definition of the term "national security." As one study concluded, "the new concept of security in terms of common global threats, including threats to the environment, now presents an alternative to the traditional definition."[84]

Yet the old tensions among nations continued to exist, even if their shape had changed. The United States emerged from the Second World War as a major power, and it could not wish away its power and global responsibility. At the same time, it faced the challenge of redefining its foreign policy goals and reordering its priorities in a world where tensions had been reduced by the end of superpower rivalry, but international terrorism had increased.

In the 20th century, many changes had taken place in the relations among nations. In the 1970s, American forces had returned from Vietnam, and an American president had opened the door to the People's Republic of China. In the 1980s, the United States and the Soviet Union had moved part of the way down the road to limiting nuclear armaments. In the 1990s, both sides, now with Russia as the new player on the world stage, pledged drastic cuts in their nuclear arsenals. Democracy had come to Eastern Europe and South Africa. But the collapse of communism had created new ethnic strife, for example, among nationalities in the former Soviet republics and in the former Yugoslavia. The Middle East remained volatile, with continuing strife between Israel and the Palestinians.

In the immediate aftermath of the Vietnam War, the conviction grew among many Americans that the nation should exercise great caution in intervening in armed conflicts beyond its borders. There was concern over the danger of U.S. involvement in "another Vietnam." In the wake of the 9/11 attacks, however, the United States under President George W. Bush sent American forces into Afghanistan and embarked on a policy of preemptive war, leading to the invasion of Iraq. In the 21st century, the danger of terrorism had eclipsed many other foreign policy issues. But policymakers grappled as well with the threat of nuclear weapons in North Korea and Iran, and whether and how to confront those challenges.

At the same time, domestic issues increased the pressures on policymakers in Washington to weigh the legitimate concerns of American national security against needs at home. And it was increasingly clear that in addition to military power alone, a strong domestic economy—and with it, an increased ability to compete in world markets—would be a key measure of the nation's strength and its position in the world. It was no longer really possible to separate economic and foreign policies.

America in the new century remained a major international power. U.S. relations with the rest of the world were both broad-ranging and highly complex. And the formation of American foreign policy continued to be a major challenge to the nation's political leadership. The survival of the planet might depend on the decisions made in America.

## CHAPTER HIGHLIGHTS

- Foreign policy is the sum of the goals, decisions, and actions that govern a nation's relations with the rest of the world.
- National security is a broad concept that may be defined in many ways, but the term is generally used to refer to the basic protection and defense of the nation.
- One fundamental historical characteristic of American foreign policy was that of isolationism, a policy of avoiding foreign involvement.
- An opposite strand of American foreign policy is interventionism, or military involvement by the United States in various parts of the world.
- After the Second World War, the United States moved from its former position of isolationism to one of internationalism, the policy that America must take an active leadership role in world affairs.
- In 1973, Congress passed the War Powers Resolution, designed to limit to 60 or 90 days the president's ability to commit American troops to combat without congressional authorization. The law proved ineffective, however.
- Today the president of the United States has powerful tools available for the conduct of foreign policy, including a personal staff and that of the National Security Council, the State Department, the Pentagon, the Director of National Intelligence, the CIA, and other agencies.
- The role of the secretary of state varies greatly according to the secretary's personal relationship with the president. In theory the principal foreign policy adviser and the ranking officer of the cabinet, the secretary in practice may be overshadowed by the president's national security assistant or the secretary of defense.
- The Peace Corps was created under President Kennedy in 1961 to provide a trained corps of highly motivated American volunteers, many of them young, to help people in developing nations.
- The United Nations was founded in San Francisco in 1945 to fulfill the dream of a community of nations, a world body that could take collective action to keep the peace and work for the betterment of humanity.
- The principle of civilian control over the American military establishment is deeply rooted in the Constitution and the nation's tradition. The president is commander in chief of all the armed forces, and the secretary of defense, by law, must be a civilian.
- Members of the Joint Chiefs of Staff are the chair, the chiefs of staff of the three armed services, and, when Marine Corps matters are under consideration, the commandant of the Marines. By law the chair, whose powers were greatly strengthened by the Defense Reorganization Act of 1986, advises the president and the secretary of defense.
- The term "military-industrial complex" has often been used to describe the economic and political ties between the military establishment and the defense-aerospace industry.

## KEY TERMS

foreign policy, p. 545
national security, p. 545
Cold War, p. 546
globalization, p. 547
nuclear proliferation, p. 547
isolationism, p. 547
Monroe Doctrine, p. 547
interventionism, p. 547
internationalism, p. 547
containment, p. 548
Marshall Plan, p. 548
nationalism, p. 550
transnational relations, p. 550
détente, p. 550
Antiballistic Missile (ABM) Treaty, p. 550
War Powers Resolution, p. 560
National Security Council (NSC), p. 561
United Nations (UN), p. 570
Joint Chiefs of Staff, p. 575
strategic deterrence, p. 577
military-industrial complex, p. 579

## SUGGESTED WEBSITES

**http://www.cia.gov**
*Central Intelligence Agency*
The CIA's website describes the agency's work and provides information about world affairs in two CIA publications, *The World Factbook,* and *Factbook on Intelligence.* Information is also available about careers in the CIA.

**http://www.defenselink.mil**
*DefenseLink—The official website of the U.S. Department of Defense*
DefenseLink offers links to the branches of the armed forces, news about the military, a virtual tour of the Pentagon, job listings for civilians, and the *Defense Almanac,* a comprehensive book containing information and statistics about the Department of Defense.

**http://www.peacecorps.org**
*The Peace Corps*
The website offers information on joining the Peace Corps, stories about individual volunteers, and facts and news about the Peace Corps.

**http://www4.sss.gov/Default.htm**
*The Selective Service System*
The Selective Service System provides information about registering for the draft, factual information about the draft procedure during a crisis, history and changes to the draft, and news about current legislation affecting the draft.

**http://www.state.gov**
*State Department*
The official website of the U.S. Department of State. Offers advice for those traveling or living abroad, including travel warnings about countries considered dangerous for U.S. citizens to visit; information about careers with the State Department; and "Background Notes," a detailed description of the geography, government, and politics of foreign countries.

**http://www.voanews.com**
*Voice of America*
The Voice of America is the U.S. government's official radio station. The website includes short-wave frequencies for the Voice of America, schedules of its programs, and a link that enables visitors to listen to its broadcasts over the Internet.

## SUGGESTED READING


Allison, Graham, and Treverton, Gregory F., eds. *Rethinking America's Security: Beyond Cold War to New World Order** (Norton, 1992). A valuable collection of essays on foreign policy after the end of the Cold War. The editors and some of the authors argue that responding to the nation's social problems is the first priority in preserving America's national security.

Almond, Gabriel A. *The American People and Foreign Policy*, 2nd edition (Temecula Textbook publishers, 2003). (Originally published in 1950.) An influential study of public opinion and how it relates to the formation and conduct of American policy.

Bush, George Herbert Walker, and Scowcroft, Brent. *A World Transformed** (Knopf, 1998). An account of the end of the Cold War by the former president and his national security adviser. They argue for continued internationalism, and against isolationism, in the post–Cold War era.

Cohen, Eliot. *Supreme Command: Soldiers, Statesman, and Leadership in Wartime** (Random House, 2003). An analysis of relations between national civilian political leaders and generals during wartime. Focuses on Lincoln and three leaders of foreign democracies, as well as U.S. leadership during the Vietnam War, and the Persian Gulf War of 1990–1991.

Daalder, Ivo H., and Lindsay, James M. *America Unbound: The Bush Revolution in Foreign Policy** (Brookings Institution, 2003). An analysis of the Bush doctrine of preemption and how President George W. Bush was willing to exercise military power unilaterally. Traces the intellectual origins and history of Bush's foreign policy, and the personalities of the policymakers who shaped it. The authors are generally critical of Bush's diplomatic style and foreign policy.

Halberstam, David. *The Best and the Brightest** (Random House, 2001). A detailed account of the men and the policies that led the United States into the costly war in Vietnam. Written in a highly readable, anecdotal style by a leading journalist who was one of the first to challenge the optimistic official reports on the progress of the war.

Hendrickson, Ryan C. *The Clinton Wars: The Constitution, Congress, and War Powers** (Vanderbilt University Press, 2002) An examination based on six case studies of the roles played by Congress and the president in deciding to use force during the Clinton presidency. The author concludes that the president exceeded his constitutional powers and that Congress has not fulfilled its obligations under the War Powers Resolution.

Huntington, Samuel P. *The Third Wave: Democratization in the Late Twentieth Century** (University of Oklahoma Press, 1993). A study of countries seeking to achieve a democratic form of government after the breakup of the Soviet Union and the demise of formerly Communist regimes in Eastern Europe. The author argues that a variety of factors may affect the success or failure of transitions to democracy.

Johnson, Loch K. *Secret Agencies: U.S. Intelligence in a Hostile World** (Yale University Press, 1998). A valuable and wide-ranging examination of the activities of the U.S. intelligence community.

Kennedy, Paul. *The Rise and Fall of the Great Powers: Economic Change and Military Conflict from 1500 to 2000** (Random House, 1987). An analysis of the shifts in global power over the past five centuries and how historical patterns are reflected in modern times. The author argues that nations actually lose power by "overextending" militarily and not allocating enough resources to the creation of wealth.

Kennedy, Robert F. *Thirteen Days** (Norton, 1999). (Originally published in 1969.) A short, fascinating account of the Cuban Missile Crisis of 1962 as it appeared to a key participant in the crucial decisions made by the Kennedy administration. Reflects the great tension during the world's first nuclear confrontation.

Kissinger, Henry A. *Diplomacy** (Diane Publishing, 1998). A sweeping history of relations between nations by a prominent figure in 20th-century diplomacy. Kissinger, who was President Nixon's secretary of state, recounts his own experiences in foreign affairs.

Maynes, Charles William, and Williamson, Richard S., eds. *U.S. Foreign Policy and the United Nations System* (Norton, 1996). A useful collection of essays on the role the United Nations can play in managing global problems and advancing U.S. foreign policy interests. The contributors discuss proposals for reforming the UN, as well as a number of major foreign policy issues.

Nye, Joseph S., Jr. *Soft Power: The Means to Success in World Politics** (Public Affairs, 2004). "Soft power" is the ability of a nation to achieve its foreign policy goals by attracting other countries and peoples to its side because of the appeal of its culture and policies. The author explores this vital component of a nation's power in world affairs and urges U.S. leaders to emphasize soft power in the conduct of foreign policy.

Ohmae, Kenichi. *The End of the Nation State* (Diane Publishing, 1998). A provocative study on the transformation of the global economy. The author argues that nation-states have lost their key role in the management of economies, and are being supplanted by private corporations and by regional economic units.

Porter, Gareth, and Brown, Janet Welsh. *Global Environmental Politics,* 3rd edition (Westview Press, 2000). A brief but useful exploration of global environmental issues, such as acid rain and depletion of the ozone layer, that transcend national boundaries. The authors argue that threats to the global environment are replacing traditional definitions of national security.

Richelson, Jeffrey T. *The U.S. Intelligence Community,* 4th edition* (Westview Press, 1999). A detailed look at the American intelligence community, including its organization, operations, and structure. The author also examines the challenges that the intelligence community faces in the 21st century.

Woodward, Susan L. *Balkan Tragedy: Chaos and Dissolution after the Cold War* (The Brookings Institution, 1996). A detailed examination of the forces that led to political disintegration and war in the former Yugoslavia. Argues that differences among the Western powers prolonged the conflict and led to crises and frustration in the United Nations and in NATO.

*Available in paperback edition.

# Chapter 17

# Government and the Economy

AS PRESIDENT GEORGE W. BUSH and Senator John Kerry battled for control of the White House in the 2004 presidential election campaign, the state of the economy emerged as a major issue.

Bush, the Republican candidate, pointed to steady if moderate job growth and other signs of recovery from a long period of uncertain economic conditions. Kerry, the Democrat, argued that 1.8 million jobs had been lost during the years since Bush took office in 2001 and that many of the new jobs were low-paying.

The president, whose approval ratings had soared after his resolute response to the terrorist attacks in September 2001, could no longer count on his image as a leader in the war on terrorism to carry him through to victory in November. For the war in Iraq had not gone well. More than a year after the U.S. invasion of that country, the weapons of mass destruction that Bush cited as the chief reason for the war had not been found, and Iraq's prewar link to al Qaeda terrorists seemed equally elusive.

By June, opinion polls indicated that more than half the public considered the war in Iraq to have been a mistake, disapproved of Bush's handling of the situation, and believed America was less safe from terrorist attack as a result of the war.[1] Perhaps even more significant, as the election year began, a third of the public considered the economy the "most important" issue in deciding whom to vote for; only 18 percent cited the war in Iraq.[2]

As the national conventions of the two major parties approached, Kerry and Bush both campaigned in Ohio, a key battleground state that had been severely affected by job losses. Early in July, the government reported that job growth had slowed in June; although 112,000 jobs had been added, the number was less than half of what had been predicted. As might be expected, Bush and Kerry each put their own spin on the numbers.

NASDAQ
NASDAQ COMPOSITE
1184.93
-36.16 -2.96%
1,457,633,902
© Peter Foley/Bloomberg News/Landov

The focus on jobs underscored a basic fact of life in American politics: The president of the United States is expected to manage the economy, and voters are keenly aware of whether they are out of work, or employed and able to put bread on the table for themselves and their families.

There is a certain amount of irony in this, because the ability of any president to influence the economy, control inflation, and maintain prosperity is somewhat limited. The tools at his command are imperfect, and economists disagree on the best way to keep the economic ship of state on an even keel.

Moreover, economic cycles may trip up investors and Wall Street experts as well as political leaders. On March 29, 1999, the Dow Jones Industrial Average of 30 leading stocks rose above the 10,000 mark for the first time in history. On Wall Street, brokers and traders celebrated and uncorked the champagne.

Three years later, by the early fall of 2002, the champagne had gone flat. The Dow had fallen to below 7,500, and the NASDAQ index, which tracks high-technology stocks, had plunged as well. Millions of investors had lost an estimated $8.4 trillion in stock market value. Many small, first-time investors worried about their futures.

Corporate fraud, the collapse of Enron—the giant energy trading company—and the indictment of top executives of major firms, including Enron's former chairman, Kenneth L. Lay, and its former CEO, Jeffrey K. Skilling—both convicted in 2006—had shaken the faith of many ordinary citizens in the nation's business establishment. (Lay's conviction was vacated after he died before sentencing.)

*for more information about the Dow Jones Industrial Average, see: http://www.djindexes.com/jsp/industrialAverages.jsp?sideMenu=true.html#*

Along with Enron, the problems of WorldCom, a major telecommunications company, symbolized the corporate and accounting scandals. The firm, the nation's second-largest long-distance telephone company, had concealed more than $7 billion in expenses in order to show a profit on its books. The Securities and Exchange Commission charged WorldCom with defrauding its investors; the company filed for bankruptcy; and its founder, Bernard J. Ebbers, was indicted on criminal fraud charges, convicted, and sentenced to 25 years in prison. Other leading business executives were charged, including Martha Stewart, the domestic lifestyle icon, who was convicted in 2004 with her former broker of lying to federal investigators about a stock sale. She served five months in jail.

The boom of the 1990s had started to fade well before then. A panel of economic experts declared that an economic recession had officially begun in March 2001. By the spring of 2002, Alan Greenspan, then the chairman of the Federal Reserve Board, expressed optimism that the nation was recovering from the recession. Nevertheless, unemployment remained high, and the market continued its downward trend for many months. As the market declined, investors withdrew billions from mutual funds. The Dow did not climb back above 10,000 again until December 2003.

The market slide at the start of the decade directly affected Americans who had counted on their 401(k) and other pension plans to support them during their retirement years. Many workers were remaining on the job longer than they had expected; others who had

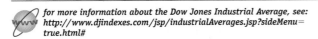

MIKE PETERS
SAME OLD STORY...
I STARTED RUNNING AROUND WITH THE WRONG CROWD AND EVENTUALLY I BECAME A CEO.
grimmy.com
Cartoon by Mike Peters © 2002. Reprinted with special permission of King Features Syndicate.

The floor of the New York Stock Exchange

already retired were forced to return to work to make ends meet.

The sharp fluctuations in the stock market, and the huge losses, hit people on Main Street as well as in the skyscraper canyons of downtown Manhattan. In 2000, before the market declined, more than half of Americans had invested in stocks, a substantial increase from one-third only a decade earlier.[3] Millions of ordinary Americans, from auto mechanics to bank presidents, had bought stocks, bonds, or mutual funds. About 80 million Americans were shareholders, as individuals or through their company or union pension funds.

Much of the earlier growth in the stock market had been driven by high-technology stocks such as Microsoft, the computer giant, and Intel, the chip maker, both among the components of the Dow. But many of the high-tech stocks on the NASDAQ exchange did poorly in 2000, as a large number of so-called dot-com companies fell by the wayside. Many, even some of the most glamorous, had failed to turn a profit. It began to dawn on people that they had invested their savings in companies that had not made any money. Much of the initial excitement over the Internet firms faded.

www *for more information about the NASDAQ, see: http://www.nasdaq.com*

In 2004, as in previous elections, the nation's economy had a measurable impact on the political system. Not only the presidential contest but also many congressional races were, to a great extent, debates over economic conditions, and about which party and which candidate might bring prosperity.

The economic downturn at the start of the decade also dramatically affected the federal budget. In 2001, President Bush proposed and signed into law a $1.35 trillion tax cut that provided rebate checks of $300 for single people and $600 for couples filing joint returns. The legislation reduced the federal estate tax and provided for its repeal in 2010. The theory behind the huge tax cut was that the rebates would jump-start the economy by giving people more money to spend, and the tax breaks for businesses would encourage companies to expand.

But the tax cuts, combined with the faltering economy, turned the federal government's budget surpluses into deficits. A **budget surplus** is the amount of money available when the government's income is greater than what it spends in a fiscal year. On the other hand, a **deficit** occurs when the government's income is less than its outlays. For decades, the government had incurred multibillion-dollar annual deficits. But by the late 1990s, during the Clinton administration, there were substantial budget surpluses each year.

President George W. Bush inherited a budget surplus of $236 billion, which soon turned into large deficits. By 2006, the budget deficit for the next fiscal year was projected to be $423 billion, although later that year the White House forecast a reduced deficit of $248 billion. Critics asked how the government could fight a war in Iraq that cost billions and still find money to meet needs at home, such as education and health care.

*Key Question* In this chapter, we will explore a key question: ***How well does government manage the economy?*** Several related questions also may be asked. For

"Well, if the economic boom benefits everyone, what good is it?!"



example: What are the politics of economic policy? To what extent should the government be involved in economic policy? What tools are available to the government in attempting to manage the economy, to maintain full employment, and to control inflation?

# Managing the Economy

## The Political Context of Economic Policy

The political battle between George W. Bush and John Kerry over the economy in the 2004 presidential election campaign echoed a similar theme in earlier years. During the 2000 presidential campaign, for example, Bush, the successful Republican candidate, offered the voters a tax cut that Congress later approved. "If you pay taxes, you ought to get tax relief," he said. "I believe the people who pay the bills ought to get some money back. . . . I trust you with your own money."[4] Al Gore, his Democratic opponent, advocated more limited, targeted tax cuts to help the middle class, leaving more money available for social programs.

It was no accident that during Bill Clinton's successful campaign for the presidency in 1992, the sign on the wall of his headquarters in Little Rock, Arkansas, said: "It's the economy, stupid!" The sign was there to remind campaign workers that the biggest issue on the minds of the voters that year was the economy. When Clinton took office in 1993, the deficit was $290 billion; five years later, in 1998, he was able to announce a surplus of $70 billion, the first surplus in 29 years. By 2000, as his presidency was ending, the surplus, as noted, had grown to $236 billion.[5]

Voters may be concerned about foreign policy, education, abortion, guns, and a host of other issues, but often they think first about how well off they are, the so-called "bread-and-butter" or "pocketbook" issues. They are interested in whether they can afford to buy a home, or fix a leaky roof, or pay for quality health care—including health insurance and prescription drugs—or, even more basically, whether they can feed and clothe their children.

Sometimes, a major foreign policy issue such as the Vietnam War or Iraq will preoccupy the public. But often, the voters' personal financial situation may be of primary concern. Hence the sign on the wall in Little Rock.

Although America is a nation that prides itself on its system of free enterprise, most voters, whether conserva-

## The American Past

### THE CRASH OF 1929

In October 1929, the stock market crashed, touching off the Great Depression of the 1930s. Economist John Kenneth Galbraith describes what did—and did not—happen:

> Dr. Julius Klein, Assistant Secretary of Commerce, friend of President Hoover, and the senior apostle of the official economic view, took to the radio to remind the country that President Hoover had said that the "fundamental business of the country" was sound. . . .
>
> Most important, perhaps, from Pocantico Hills came the first public statement by John D. Rockefeller in several decades. So far as the record shows, it was spontaneous. However, someone in Wall Street—perhaps someone who knew that another appeal to President Hoover to say something specifically encouraging about stocks would be useless—may have realized that a statement from Rockefeller would, if anything, be better. The statement ran: "Believing that fundamental conditions of the country are sound . . . my son and I have for some days been purchasing sound common stocks."
>
> The statement was widely applauded, although [entertainer] Eddie Cantor . . . said later, "Sure, who else had any money left?" . . .
>
> In the week or so following Black Thursday, the London penny press told delightedly of the scenes in downtown New York. Speculators were hurling themselves from windows; pedestrians picked their way delicately between the bodies of fallen financiers. . . . In the United States the suicide wave that followed the stock market crash is also a part of the legend of 1929. In fact, there was none.
>
> Since the market crash took place late in the year, there could have been a substantial increase in suicides in late October. . . . However . . . the number of suicides in October and November was comparatively low. . . . During the summer months, when the market was doing beautifully, the number of suicides was substantially higher.
>
> —John Kenneth Galbraith, *The Great Crash, 1929*

tive or liberal, look to the government in Washington to provide remedies to the country's economic problems. Those problems vary with the times, but whether they concern health care, prescription drugs, inflation, unemployment, interest rates, or foreign competition, the president and his advisers are expected to provide solutions. Today most people look to the federal government to exercise a major responsibility for the health, stability, and growth of the national economy.

Since political leaders are normally interested in winning reelection, they realize it is in their self-interest, as well as in the interest of millions of Americans, to try to promote a strong, healthy economy. How to accomplish that goal, of course, is the subject of wide disagreement among politicians, political parties, and economists.

## The Historical Context

The federal government took a major role in economic affairs with the coming of Franklin D. Roosevelt's New Deal. When Roosevelt was inaugurated in 1933, at the height of the Great Depression, 13 million people—25 percent of the labor force—were unemployed.

The New Deal marked a dramatic shift from what had gone before. Although the government had invested in canals and railroad development in the 19th century, in the 1930s the government for the first time committed itself not simply to repairing problems in the economy, but to assuming a key role in the nation's economic system. It did so in a variety of ways, including regulation of business; economic support for the unemployed, the poor, and the retired; and using the government's taxing and spending powers to try to control the business cycle—the level of unemployment and inflation.

Despite these measures, unemployment remained high until the rapid recovery of the economy during the Second World War. In the postwar world, with the nation still concerned about avoiding another economic depression, national growth with full employment and low inflation became a major goal.

The Employment Act of 1946 spelled out in law the responsibility of the federal government for the economy and its obligation "to promote maximum employment, production, and purchasing power." The law directed the president to submit an annual economic report to Congress; it created a three-member Council of Economic Advisers to assist the president; and it established a Joint Economic Committee, made up of members of the House and Senate, to study the president's report and the economy.

Most U.S. economists believe that a stock market crash and a depression as severe as that which began in 1929 are unlikely to happen again because there are more built-in economic stabilizers today. Even so, the sudden dip in the stock market in October 1987, and the sharp decline in the Dow in 2001 and 2002, caused great

## A Modern-Day Hero: "I Feel That I Am a Symbol"

LAWRENCE, MASS.—Six months after a fire nearly destroyed his textile company, Malden Mills Industries, Aaron M. Feuerstein has set himself up as a hero of corporate responsibility, insisting that his loyalty to his workers should be the model for all chief executives. But in playing the role of model chief executive—lionized in the media for promising to re-employ all his workers once he rebuilt and for paying most of them in the interim—he is risking his company and his reputation.

© 2002 AP/Wide World Photos

Loyal to his workers: Aaron M. Feuerstein, owner of Malden Mills Industries

And therein, his wife worries, lies the potential for a modern-day tragedy.

There were certainly safer alternatives. He could have closed and walked away with tens of millions of dollars in fire insurance, giving up to rivals his company's flagship product, Polartec, a synthetic fabric much in demand for sporty outerwear. Or he could have reduced the risk by being far more parsimonious in his payments to his workers and less ambitious in rebuilding.

Mr. Feuerstein will have none of that. He is rebuilding in the grand style, installing huge quantities of the best machinery and restoring the fine details of 19th-century factory buildings—spending in two years what he normally invests in a decade. By relying on insurance to pay the entire bill and on the efficiency and inventiveness of loyal workers to make the investment pay off, he is gambling the solvency of his company. . . .

"I feel that I am a symbol of the movement against downsizing and layoffs that will ultimately produce an answer. People see me as a turning of the tide."

—Adapted from Louis Uchitelle, "The Risks of Keeping a Promise," *The New York Times*, July 4, 1996. © 1996 The New York Times Co. Please see full-text article at the back of the book.

alarm on Wall Street, in Washington, and in the country, and had repercussions in markets around the world.

### Theories of Economic Policy

The United States operates predominantly under an economic system of free enterprise, or **capitalism.** Under capitalism, there is private ownership of the means of production. In such a system, in its purest form, there is little room for government; people own private property, either directly or as shareholders; and as consumers they participate in a free marketplace that responds to the laws of supply and demand. In practice, however, the United States has a mixed, or modified, free enterprise

© 2002 AP/Wide World Photos

Monday, October 19, 1987: The Dow Jones Industrial average plunged more than 500 points for the biggest one-day percentage loss in history.

© Doug Armand/Stone/Getty Images

The U.S. financial center in New York City

system in which both private industry and government play important roles.

The individual's economic freedom is sharply limited by federal, state, and local economic policies. To begin with, the higher the federal, state, and local taxes a person pays, the less money he or she will have to spend on consumer goods. If government fails to prevent a recession, the person may be out of work. If government fails to prevent inflation, the dollar buys less and retired people living on pensions and savings may find their fixed incomes inadequate.

There is, obviously, an interaction between government policies and the economy. What the government does influences economic conditions; in turn, the state of the economy affects government actions and policies.

In general, Democrats have favored a larger role for government in regulating the welfare of society and the individual, and Republicans generally have favored less government intervention. But the basic responsibility of government for economic policy is now well established.

That said, there are still great differences among political leaders and economists about how to exercise that responsibility. There is conflict, as well, not only about the proper extent of government action, but also about the underlying economic theory. Economists have different views about how to prevent cycles of recession and unemployment, about growth and productivity, and about government taxing and spending. They may belong to one "school" or another that has different perspectives on economic policy. There is, in short, a good deal of crystal-ball gazing involved, for no one economist or school has all the answers. If they did, there would never be periods of recession, high unemployment, layoffs, downsizing, or hardship.

Because there is so much difference among economists about economic theory, politicians can choose the economic advice—and advisers—that suits their own brands of politics. As a result, a change in the presidency often means a change in economic policy; the occupant of the White House does not normally appoint economic advisers who are in sharp disagreement with him.

**Laissez-Faire Economics** In French, **laissez-faire** means to "leave alone."[6] It describes a theory that an economic system works best when free of government interference. Although the principles were first developed in France, laissez-faire is associated with Adam Smith, the Scottish economist and founder of the classical school of economics, and his book *Wealth of Nations*, published in 1776.

There are echoes of laissez-faire philosophy in modern politics—for example, when House Republicans in 1995 sought to roll back government regulation of the workplace and the environment. They believed that government had become too intrusive and burdensome to business.

**Keynesian Economics** John Maynard Keynes, later Baron Keynes of Tilton, died in 1946, but he was perhaps the most influential economist of the 20th century. Keynes's views were just the opposite of laissez-faire. He advocated government intervention in the marketplace. The English economist argued that when people did not consume and invest enough to maintain national income at full employment levels, government must step in and regulate the economy, primarily through **fiscal policy**—by cutting taxes or increasing spending in the public sector, or both. In Keynes's view, during an economic downturn if the government spent more than it took in from taxes and other revenues, the deficit that resulted was not bad, it was good. Thus, Keynes argued

John Maynard Keynes

that deficit spending by the government was necessary to combat a recession.

Keynesian economics provided the underpinning of economic policy for President Franklin Roosevelt's New Deal administration in the 1930s and 1940s. Since that time, many government economists have been influenced by the thinking of Keynes.

Today, however, the political framework has changed. In the mid-1990s, a Democratic president, Bill Clinton, and the leaders of a Republican-controlled Congress agreed publicly on the need to balance the budget. Their arguments were over how to do so and how soon.

Keynesian economists and their modern successors place major emphasis on fiscal policy to guide the economy, although they also recognize the role of **monetary policy,** the control of the supply of money and the supply of credit through the actions of the Federal Reserve Board.

**Supply-Side Economics** In 1981, when President Reagan took office, the United States was experiencing severe inflation. Reagan and his advisers advocated economic policies that were a sharp departure from the past.

They called for a program of federal tax and spending cuts to try to assure growth without inflation and to end recessions. The theory was that inflation could be controlled by increasing the supply of goods. The concept was called **supply-side economics,** an economic philosophy that advocates both tax and budget cuts to increase incentives to produce in order to expand the total supply of the nation's goods and services.

The money moving into the economy because of tax reductions, it was hoped, would be used by industry to build new factories and machinery to provide jobs and growth. The benefits would thus flow to the public, in theory. Supply-side economists attacked the Keynesian model of the economy for Keynes's view that inflation is the result of too much demand—too many dollars chasing after too few goods. The supply-siders argued that inflation is caused by a lack of supply—not enough goods on the market. Thus, their solution is to cut taxes to encourage greater production.

Congress went along with Reagan's program, enacting extensive tax and spending cuts. Journalists dubbed the program "Reaganomics." The Reagan cutbacks had an immediate impact on millions of Americans: Government social services were cut or their projected rate of increase reduced.

At first, economic conditions worsened. Unemployment reached 10.7 percent at one point in 1982, the highest figure since the Second World War, and 12 million people were jobless. The government's budget deficits soared to unprecedented multibillion-dollar levels, in part because the Reagan administration increased defense spending.

Taken together, the Reagan budget and tax cuts reduced the income of the poor and increased the income of the rich.[7] The percentage and number of poor people increased substantially under Reagan.[8] But by mid-1984, the economy was booming, and Reagan was overwhelmingly reelected.

**Monetarism** Some economists argue that the money supply—the quantity of money in circulation—is the key to government regulation of the economy. Monetarists contend that the government should confine its role in economic affairs to ensuring that the money supply expands fast enough to accommodate economic growth. These theories are identified with the "Chicago school" of economists, led by Milton Friedman of the University of Chicago. Friedman argued that interest rates, which are one aspect of monetary policy, and fiscal policy—taxes and spending—have little effect or importance. He also argued that the money supply should be increased at a constant rate. Friedman received the Nobel Prize in 1976. His views won increasing, but by no means universal, acceptance in the United States and abroad.

In sum, in the more than six decades since the New Deal, the government has advocated and carried out sharply differing economic theories. But during this period, complex fiscal and monetary policies—even direct economic controls—have not always avoided the twin evils of recession and inflation.

## The Machinery

In making economic policy, the president has a number of tools and advisers available to him—the Council of Economic Advisers, the National Economic Council, the Office of Management and Budget, the secretary of the treasury, the Department of Labor, and the economists and experts who staff these government agencies. He can invoke his power to delay major strikes under the Taft-Hartley Act. Various presidents have had power to negotiate and alter U.S. tariffs.

*for more information about the National Economic Council and the Council of Economic Advisers, see:*
*http://www.whitehouse.gov/nec/ and*
*http://www.whitehouse.gov/cea/*

Through his appointment power, the president can influence the makeup of the Federal Reserve Board. And, of course, the president is free to consult outside economists and experts in the private sector, including the universities. The president can also impose economic controls or voluntary guidelines on prices and wages. He may call upon all of these resources in shaping the fiscal and monetary policies of the federal government. Yet, despite the boom times of the 1990s, presidents in recent decades often have not been successful in controlling inflation, recession, or high unemployment. In part, this may be due to world economic conditions—factors that are beyond any president's control. But it also may stem from the nature of the American economic system, in which there are limits on the government's ability to manage the economy.

## The Tools of Economic Policy

Usually, the federal government has attempted to influence the total shape of the economy through two sets of tools: *fiscal policy* and *monetary policy.* The fiscal tools of the government, as noted, are primarily spending and taxation. The monetary tools are control of the supply of money and control of the supply of credit through the Federal Reserve System.

## Fiscal Policy

**The Budget** The federal budget reflects an allocation of resources by the national government. It spells out the programs and purposes for which the government will spend money and it estimates the source of federal revenues. (See Figure 17-1.) But the budget is also an important tool of fiscal policy. During a time of inflation, the president may cut spending and ask for higher taxes to cool down the economy. In a recession he may propose a bigger budget, more public works spending, and lower taxes. Or, as Reagan did in 1981, a president may call for both lower taxes and less domestic spending. By planning a budget surplus or deficit, the federal government attempts to pump money into or out of the economy, to stimulate it or slow it down.

The president must share with Congress his fiscal control over the economy. Only Congress can vote to spend federal funds. It does so in a three-step process. First, it passes **budget resolutions** to set overall spending targets. Second, it passes **authorizations** to spend federal money. Third, it passes **appropriations bills** to pay for the spending it has authorized. The budget process is described in more detail in Chapter 14.

Under this system, legislative committees deal with the substance of programs and, by authorizing funds, set forth their views of what ought to be spent. Within that framework, the appropriations committees decide what actually may be spent.

The idea behind this system is that appropriations committees have an overview of expenditures by Congress—something that legislative or "program" committees do not have—and are therefore in a better position to allocate funds. Because an authorization without an appropriation is meaningless, the system places great power in the hands of the House and Senate appropriations committees and subcommittees. Congress may increase or cut the president's appropriations requests.

Once money is appropriated, Congress has its own

### Cutting the Federal Budget: Farewell to the Tea Board

The government's tea party is over.

President Clinton, without fanfare, signed legislation Tuesday abolishing the federal Board of Tea Experts. . . .

The tempest over the teapots has steamed along since the early 1970s, when the Nixon administration tried to dump the board. Clinton brought the issue back to a boil in 1993 as part of his budget review of federal advisory panels, and a Congress intent on downsizing the government finally passed legislation last month.

Congressional opponents of the board argued the government did not need tea tasters on its payroll, but hanging up the kettles probably won't make a dent in the deficit. . . .

The 99-year-old law created the tea board, mandating it meet for two days every year to set minimum quality standards for whole-leaf tea imported into the United States. In most years, the board selected one tea from each tea category—the black, oolong and green—to serve as the standard. . . . Some tea experts suggested Washington's willingness to throw the tea tasters overboard has more to do with political posturing than with saving money.

"It's the silliest cost-cutting measure that I can think of," said John Frederick Walter, author of "Coffee and Tea" and a contributing editor at *Food & Wine* magazine.

"Somehow this image of people sitting around a table with their pinkies raised galled a lot of people who don't understand it serves a valid function," Walter said.

—From "Clinton Signature Leaves the FDA Holding the Bag: Board of Tea Experts Liquidated Along with 1897 Importation Act," by Stephen Barr. *The Washington Post,* April 11, 1996.

## FIGURE 17-1

**The Federal Government Dollar**

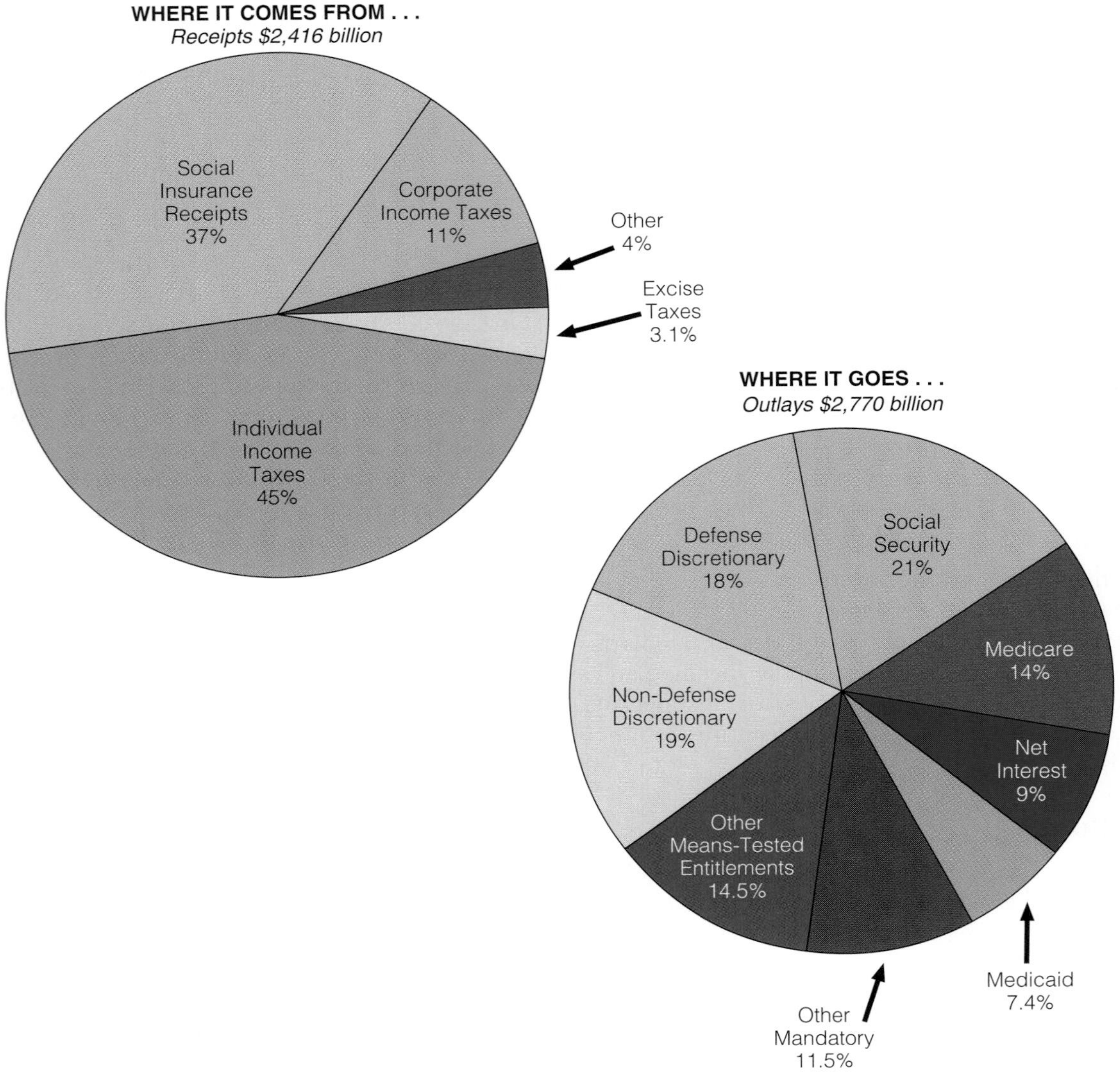


NOTE: Fiscal year 2007, estimated.
SOURCE: *Budget of the United States Government, Fiscal Year 2007* (Washington, D.C.: U.S. Government Printing Office, 2006), tables S-11 and S-8, percentages add to more than 100 because of rounding.

accountant—the comptroller general of the United States, who heads the Government Accountability Office (GAO)—to check up on how it is spent.

In the 1980s and early 1990s, the deficit became a hot political issue. When the Republicans were out of power in the 1960s, they assailed the "deficit spending" of the Democrats, whom they labeled the party of "tax and spend." But when two Republicans, Ronald Reagan and his successor, the first President Bush, served as president from 1981 until 1993, the annual deficit more than tripled.

Mounting deficits led both major political parties to call for a balanced budget. But the battle over just how to balance the budget led to the struggle between President Clinton and the Republican Congress and caused the two government shutdowns in 1995 and 1996.

Congress passed a series of laws in an attempt to come to grips with the budget process and the federal deficit. Budget, tax, and spending policies were uncoordinated, and sometimes seemed to be moving in different directions; Congress sought to impose a structure and coherence on the budget process. The Congressional Budget and Impoundment Act of 1974 established the budget committees in the House and Senate and created a framework for Congress to use in dealing with the president's budget. The Gramm-Rudman Acts of 1985

FIGURE 17-2

**Federal Budget Deficit and Surplus, 1940–2010**

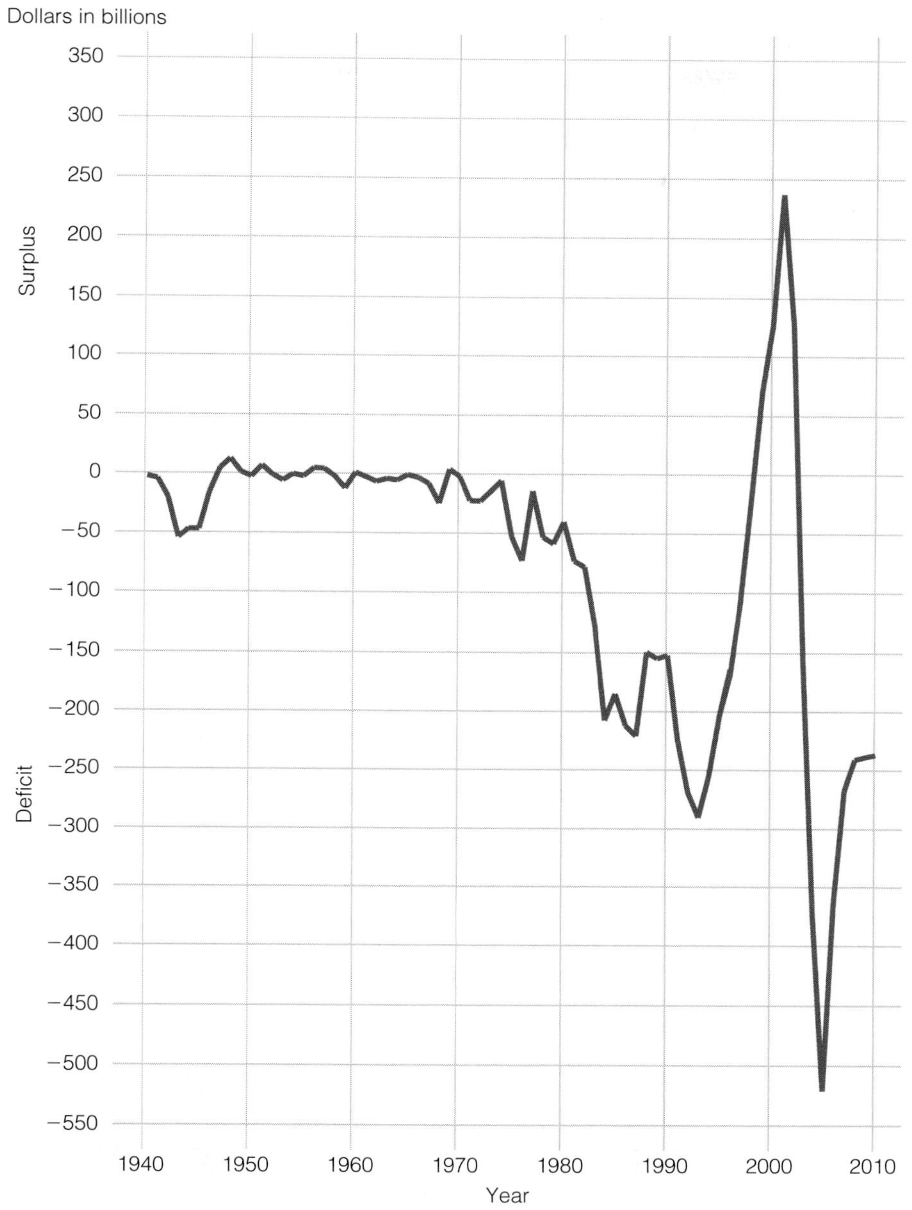


NOTE: Data after 2004 are projections.
SOURCE: *Budget of the United States Government, Fiscal Year 2005* (Washington, D.C.: U.S. Government Printing Office, 2004), p. 21, table 1.1.

and 1987 were congressional attempts to control spending and eliminate the deficit.

The complicated Budget Enforcement Act of 1990 set limits on appropriations for domestic, international, and defense programs. It put mandatory spending programs such as Medicare on a "pay-as-you-go" basis. Under the act, as discussed in Chapter 12, the president submits his budget request on the first Monday of each February. Congress is required to adopt a budget resolution by April 15, and the fiscal year begins on October 1.

These laws did not make much of a dent in the annual federal deficit, which had soared to $290 billion by 1992. By fiscal 1996, however, when both the Democratic president and the Republican-controlled Congress publicly agreed on the goal of balancing the budget within six years, the deficit had dropped dramatically. (See Figure 17-2.)

The deficit was not only an economic problem; it had also become a major political issue. The government closings in 1995 and early 1996 were the result of an impasse over the federal budget and over how to balance the budget by 2002. But the goal of a balanced budget was reached earlier than expected. As already noted, President Clinton was able to announce a $70 billion surplus in 1998, a surplus of $123 billion in 1999, and a surplus of $236 billion in 2000. Within two years, however, after the election of President George W. Bush, the surplus had vanished, to be replaced by massive deficits.

Why does a balanced budget or a budget surplus matter? The government finances a budget deficit by issuing and selling bonds and other securities to the public. But a budget deficit means the government has to borrow more and pay more interest than it would otherwise. Some economists believe that eliminating deficits helped to keep interest rates down during the Clinton years, which in turn stimulated the stock market. Other economists believe that the deficit has relatively little impact on interest rates. Finally, a surplus makes large amounts of money available for social programs to improve American society, or for tax cuts, or both.

**Borrowing** Just as individuals do, governments may spend more than their income. When that happens, governments—like individuals—borrow to make up the difference. The United States, for example, borrows money by selling federal securities. It issues interest-bearing Treasury bills, long-term Treasury bonds, and other notes, which are purchased by institutions, corporations, individuals, and foreign governments.

When the government runs at a deficit for many years, the amount of money it owes piles up. The **national debt** is exactly what it sounds like—the total amount of money that the United States owes to its creditors. The national debt stood at $16.2 billion in 1930. By 2004, the national debt stood at more than $7.6 trillion.[9]

In 1917 Congress passed a statutory debt limit, or ceiling, on government borrowing, which limits the amount of debt the nation may incur—but the limit has been revised upward many times. Borrowing costs money; in fiscal 2005 the government expected to spend $180.5 billion, or some 7.5 percent of the federal budget, on interest payments.

**Taxes** "The Congress shall have Power to lay and collect Taxes." And Congress, as every taxpayer knows, exercises this constitutional authority. Under the budget for fiscal 2005 the federal government planned to spend $2.4 trillion, most of it raised from taxes. Of every dollar the government expected to take in during fiscal 2005, 42 cents came from individual income taxes, 39 cents from social-insurance taxes, 11 cents from corporate income taxes, 3.5 cents from excise taxes (taxes on certain goods such as gasoline and cigarettes), and another 4 cents from other revenue sources.[10]

Estimated tax receipts for 2005 appear in Table 17-1. As these figures show, individual income taxes are the federal government's largest single source of revenue. The federal income tax is graduated on the theory that people with higher incomes should be taxed at a higher rate. But taxpayers at all levels grumble about the tax squeeze; not many enjoy paying their taxes or consider them low.

Until the 20th century, the Constitution required the federal government to collect income taxes in proportion to state population. The Sixteenth Amendment, ratified in 1913, permitted the government to levy a general income tax. Since that time, however, various interest groups have lobbied Congress and won special tax advantages. Until 1975 the major oil producers had a

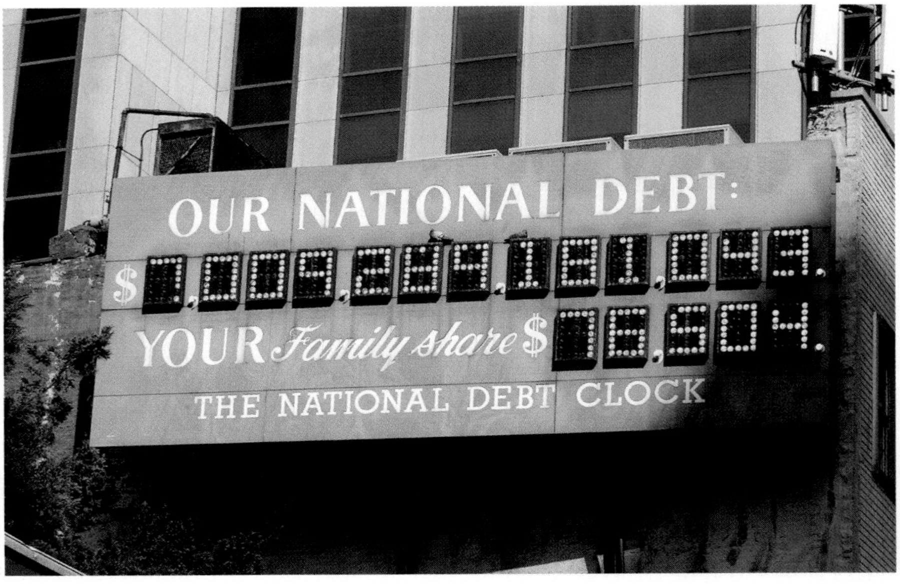




New York, February 19, 2004: The National Debt clock in New York City

**TABLE 17-1**

**The Federal Budget: Where the Money Comes From**

| Source | 2007 estimate (in billions) | Percent |
|---|---|---|
| Individual income taxes | $1,096.4 | 45% |
| Social-insurance taxes and contributions | 884.1 | 37% |
| Corporation income taxes | 260.6 | 11% |
| Excise taxes | 74.6 | 3% |
| All other receipts | 100.2 | 4% |
| Total budget receipts | $2,415.9* | 100% |

SOURCE: Adapted from *Budget of the United States Government, Fiscal Year 2007* (Washington, D.C.: U.S. Government Printing Office, 2006), Federal Receipts, table S-8.

"depletion allowance," which reduced their taxes. Business executives and many other people still enjoy certain "expense account" deductions. There are also other loopholes in the tax law. Rich people can afford to hire high-priced tax attorneys to find them. People in high-income brackets may set up foundations, take business losses that enable them to avoid high taxes, or invest in tax-free municipal bonds or various types of "tax shelters"—businesses or other activities that receive special tax breaks, such as real estate, oil and gas equipment leasing, and cattle breeding.

By the end of the 1960s, growing public awareness of inequalities in the federal tax laws led to talk of "a taxpayers' revolt." Congress responded by passing several tax reform laws over two decades.

The 1986 tax reform measure, passed during the Reagan administration, was the most extensive revision in the nation's tax laws in 40 years. The Tax Reform Act of 1986 cut individual and corporate tax rates. The measure for a time ended the preferential treatment for capital gains, and ended or modified a wide variety of taxpayer deductions.

The politics of taxation results in intense pressures on Congress from interest groups when changes in the structure of the tax laws are under consideration. And Congress and the president often fight political battles over how tax policy should be used as a fiscal tool to slow down or stimulate the economy. The use of fiscal policy to control the economy depends, in theory, on delicate timing; but Congress tends to move very slowly in passing tax legislation.

And, as noted earlier, tax and spending policies are often at the center of the nation's political debate. The size and nature of proposed tax cuts was a central issue in the 2000 presidential race. After George W. Bush was elected, he proposed and Congress passed the largest tax cut in 20 years, reducing personal income tax rates over a period of five years.

Again in 2004, taxes were a subject of political debate in the presidential campaign. President Bush argued that his administration's tax cuts had spurred the economy by providing individuals and businesses with more money, since they had to pay less taxes to the government. John Kerry vowed to repeal the cuts that benefited taxpayers making more than $200,000 a year and spend the resulting revenues on domestic programs, such as reducing the cost of college tuition and health care.

The Internal Revenue Service (IRS), the agency responsible for collecting federal taxes, is not the most popular agency in Washington. Most citizens regard tax forms as far too complicated. Political leaders do not hesitate to tap into this frustration with both the tax code and the IRS.

In 1997, Senate hearings revealed that the IRS had harassed taxpayers for money they did not owe, or had paid or tried to pay. The agency suspended a number of midlevel employees after it was disclosed that field agents had been rated on the number of seizures, levies, and liens they imposed on taxpayers.

Although Americans complain about high taxes, compared with other democratic countries the United States stands near the bottom of the ladder in terms of how much it taxes its citizens. As a percentage of the **gross domestic product (GDP),**[11] the yearly value of goods and services produced within a country, the United States, at 32.2 percent, ranks much lower than Sweden, with a tax burden of 59.3 percent, Denmark at 57.1 percent, or France at 50.9 percent.[12] (See Figure 17-3.)

## Monetary Policy

Government also attempts to regulate the economy by monetary policy—controlling the supply of money and the cost and availability of credit. It does this through the operations of the Federal Reserve System. "The Fed," as the system is often called, was established in 1913. Before that time, the United States had no way to expand and contract the money supply according to the needs of the economy. To provide such an elastic system, Congress created the Federal Reserve.

For many years, the chairman of the Federal Reserve, Alan Greenspan, was as one of the nation's best-known and most powerful figures. Greenspan was first appointed chairman in 1987 by President Reagan, and he was reappointed by the first President Bush, twice by President Clinton, and again by President George W. Bush.

Greenspan became so influential that his words and actions could affect the economy at home and abroad. In December 1996, when Greenspan remarked that the stock market might be exhibiting "irrational exuberance" and used the word "bubble" in the same speech, the Dow plunged and markets shook in Japan and Germany.

In 2005, when Greenspan, 79, was approaching the end of his term after almost 19 years as chairman,

## FIGURE 17-3

**Tax Burdens of Selected Countries**

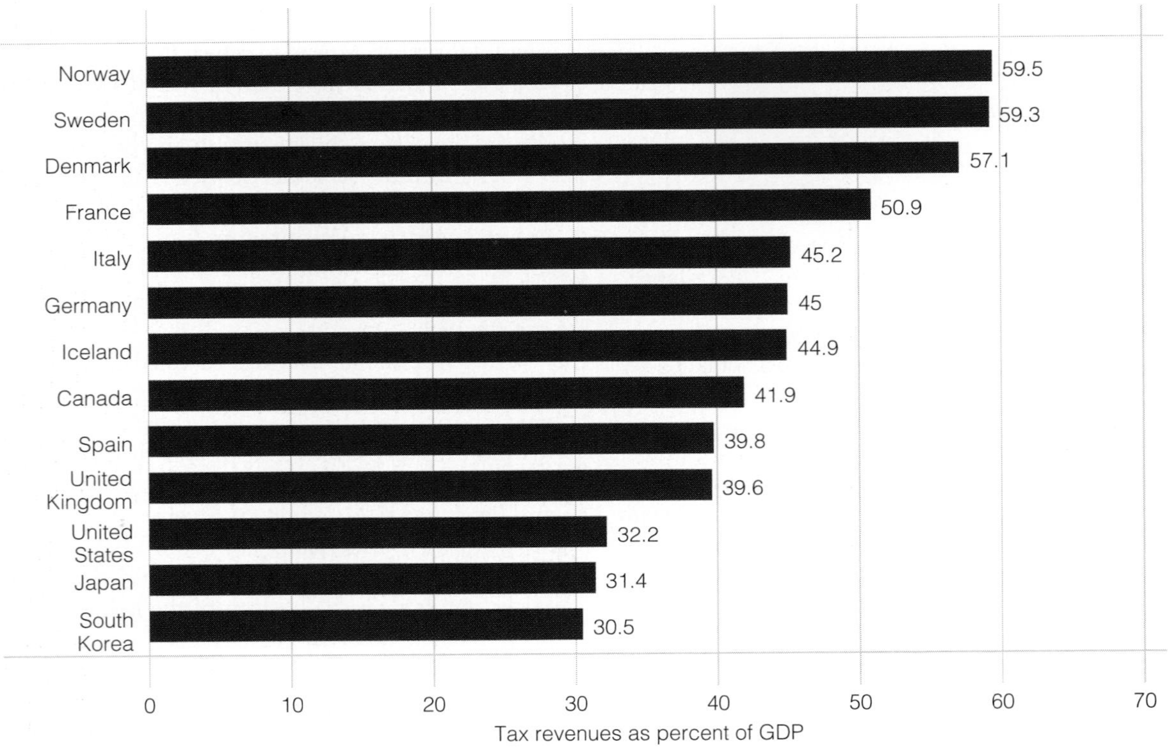


NOTE: Data for 2002.
SOURCE: Adapted from *Statistical Abstract of the United States: 2003*, p. 856.

Federal Reserve Chairman Ben S. Bernanke

Bush named the senior White House economic adviser, Ben S. Bernanke, as the new chairman of the Fed. Bernanke, 51, was a former economics professor at Princeton University.

Wall Street listens carefully to the Fed chairman because it is within the chairman's and the board's power to raise interest rates to stem inflation. A big increase in interest rates can have an adverse effect on the stock market because investors then fear that corporations in which they hold shares will not be able to borrow as much at higher rates in order to expand their factories, production, and profits.

Higher interest rates affect more than the stock market. For example, higher rates mean college loans cost more. Mortgage loans cost more as well, and that may influence young couples to put off buying a home, which in turn affects the construction industry and many other parts of the economy.

For almost four years after 2000, however, the Fed gradually lowered interest rates to stimulate the economy. That attracted more new home buyers and led to a flood of refinancing at lower rates by existing homeown-

## Why Not Just Print Money?

Since the federal government prints all the money in circulation in the United States, when it faces a budget deficit why not just print more money?

The answer is, it could, but it doesn't. The Federal Reserve Board, created by Congress in 1913, decides how much money to print, largely based on the public's demand for currency. For example, a shopper in a supermarket may pay for groceries with a credit card or a bank debit card, but many people prefer to pay in cash, so there have to be enough bills and coins to go around. So the demand for currency determines the supply, not the size of the deficit.

Another important reason that the government does not simply print money when it runs short is that to do so would create inflation. Why? Because printing more money does not increase the amount of goods produced by a society. Putting a lot more money in circulation would drive up prices, reducing the value of money, and creating inflation.

The Federal Reserve Board tells the U.S. Treasury Department how much money to print. If you look closely at a dollar bill, or a larger denomination, it says "Federal Reserve Note" along the top. Paper money is printed by the Bureau of Printing and Engraving, and coins are produced by the U.S. Mint, both divisions of the Treasury Department.

© Rob Crandall / The Image Works

The Bureau of Printing and Engraving prints about 37 million bills each day, but 95 percent of the new currency printed each year is simply to replace old, worn-out bills. The average life span of a $1 bill is about 18 months. A $20 bill lasts about two years, and a $100 bill—they don't circulate as much—may be around for eight and a half years. Coins are much hardier; the average life of a coin is 25 years.

—Information provided
by the Federal Reserve Board,
U.S. Department of the Treasury

ers. Then in 2004, the Fed began increasing interest rates in an effort to prevent inflation.

The Fed is headed by a Board of Governors. Although the board's seven members are appointed by the president with the approval of the Senate, they serve overlapping 14-year terms and are largely independent of both Congress and the White House. The Fed's chair, appointed by the president for a term of four years, can, and sometimes does, oppose the policies of the administration. During the Reagan administration, for example, there was frequent tension between the president and the chairman of the Fed.

The Federal Reserve is the central banking system of the United States; it operates through 12 Federal Reserve Banks and 25 branches across the nation. All national banks and about 12 percent of state banks are members of the system.

When individuals or corporations need money, they normally borrow from a bank. When banks need money, they may borrow from the Federal Reserve System. The Federal Reserve is, therefore, a banker's bank. When it lends to the banks, it can, in effect, create money.

Through its control of the flow of money and credit within the United States, the Fed attempts to pump more money into the economy when a recession threatens. In a time of rising prices and excessive spending, the Fed normally tries to tighten the supply of money and credit so that people will have less to spend.

When the Fed raises interest rates, in other words, it does so in the hope of slowing down the economy. To take one example, millions of Americans have credit cards, and the interest they pay every month is a major source of income for the nation's banks. If the Fed raises interest rates, then the rate charged by credit card companies goes up, and consumers—or so the Fed hopes—may spend less money in order to save on finance charges. When the Fed cuts interest rates, as it did repeatedly beginning early in 2001, it hopes to stimulate the economy.

As one chairman remarked, the Fed tries "to lean against the prevailing economic winds." It does so chiefly in four ways:

1. *Open market operations.* Banks lend money to people in relation to the amount of reserves the banks have on deposit with the Federal Reserve. When the Fed sells government bonds on the open market, they are purchased by individuals

and commercial banks. When people take money out of the bank to buy bonds, or when the banks pay for the securities, the banks have fewer dollars on hand. The effect is to reduce bank reserves and tighten credit; banks then have less money to lend to people. Or, the Federal Reserve can buy government securities and expand credit. When the Fed buys government securities, banks have more cash to lend, and interest rates go down, which should encourage people to borrow money.

2. *The discount rate.* The Fed can raise or lower the discount rate that it charges member banks for loans. This affects interest rates in the economy generally. If the rate is lowered, banks borrow more from the Fed and have more money to lend to their customers.
3. *Reserve requirements.* The Fed can raise or lower the size of the reserves that member banks must keep in the Federal Reserve banks against their deposits and thus tighten or expand credit. For example, if the Fed wants to speed up the growth of the economy, it can lower the reserve requirement, which gives the banks access to more of their money to lend to customers.
4. *Margin requirements.* The Fed can raise or lower the margin requirements for investors buying securities. The margin requirement defines how much money someone can borrow to purchase stocks.

The Fed's actions can influence the federal funds rate, which banks charge each other for the overnight sale of federal funds. A lower federal funds rate encourages banks to lend more money; a higher rate makes it more difficult for people and businesses to borrow money.

As discussed earlier, economists and politicians disagree over the best way to maintain price stability, full employment, and economic growth. Some measures are politically safer to take than others; for example, it is easier for government to spend money on public works to combat recession than it is to impose wage-price controls to fight inflation.

Whatever steps an administration takes carry great political risks if they fail. Normally both the president and Congress try to steer a safe course between the twin reefs of recession and inflation.

At times, although rarely, when fiscal policy and monetary policy prove unable to control inflation, the government has imposed direct economic controls—on wages and prices, for example. Most presidents have been reluctant to take such a drastic step, although President Richard Nixon did so in 1971, instituting a sweeping three-phase program that began with a 90-day freeze on wages, prices, and rents; later a Cost of Living Council supervised the program of controls, which lasted three years. There was precedent for Nixon's actions; economic controls were imposed during the First World War, the Second World War, and the Korean War. There was also some peacetime precedent, since for a time controls were kept on prices and rents during the Truman administration.

## International Trade Policy

When members of the World Trade Organization (WTO) met in Seattle in December 1999, they were not prepared for what happened. Thousands of protesters surrounded the convention hall, blocked delegates from leaving their hotels, and braved the tear gas, pepper spray, and rubber pellets of the city's police, who moved about in armored personnel carriers.

***for more information about the World Trade Organization, see: http://www.wto.org***

Seattle, Washington, 1999: Protesters demonstrate against the World Trade Organization.

## The Seattle Protests: Tear Gas and Ponytails

SEATTLE, Dec. 2—If there is any clear message coming through the clouds of tear gas and the broken glass in Seattle this week, it is that the terms of debate about free trade have changed in the United States.

It is no longer a debate about trade at all, but rather a debate about globalization, a process that many now understand affects not only traditional economic factors such as jobs and incomes but also the food people eat, the air they breathe, the quality of medical care, and the social and cultural milieu in which they live.

The demonstrators in Seattle this week were a thoroughly mixed bunch, from anarchistic hooligans at one extreme to pacifist nuns at the other. Some were aging hippies, their gray hair now pulled back in ponytails. Others were kids with nose rings cruising the streets on skateboards. Both were outnumbered by the thousands of union workers in baseball caps and nylon jackets. And not surprisingly, there was a large contingent of Washington wonks on hand from policy shops on Capitol Hill.

By and large, these are the people who have never bought into the New Economy, either because it has left them behind or because they never embraced its values. They are folks who don't check each day to see how their 401(k) is doing or hang out with people who have become millionaires after their companies went public. Their perspective on globalization is less economic than it is cultural and political.

What they all seem to agree on is that giant corporations have gone too far in gaining control over their lives and defining the values of their culture, and that the WTO has become a handmaiden to those corporate interests.

—Adapted from the *Washington Post,* December 3, 1999

© AP/Wide World Photos

As a few delegates managed to gather to meet in the hall, the demonstrators outside chanted: "Whose world? Our world! Whose streets? Our streets!"[13]

Downtown Seattle was in turmoil, the area was placed under curfew, and the governor called in the National Guard to try to keep order. More than 600 people were arrested. The majority of the protesters were peaceful, but a small group, most wearing masks, smashed store windows. The United Nations secretary general, Kofi Annan, was unable to deliver his speech to the delegates.[14]

The WTO was created in 1995 and had 135 nations as members by the time of the Seattle protests. Its task was to act as a global referee to resolve international trade disputes. The organization, with headquarters in Geneva, Switzerland, was also given the authority to reduce international tariffs by 38 percent.

But the WTO acted largely in secret and soon emerged as a symbol of **globalization,** a term that refers to a world economy characterized by the free movement of goods, capital, labor, and information across national borders. The WTO became the target of a diverse group of environmentalists, human rights activists, labor unions, and others.

The trade talks collapsed as a result of the protests, and the failure shattered President Clinton's hopes of beginning a new round of trade negotiations, one of the major foreign policy goals of his second administration.

In 2000, the Seattle protests had a more peaceful echo in Washington, D.C., as protesters tried to shut down the spring meetings of the World Bank and the International Monetary Fund (IMF). This time, police were ready, and although the capital was disrupted the protesters were allowed to march and chant, and the demonstrations ended with voluntary arrests. In the spring of 2004 a smaller and more subdued group of protesters again targeted the World Bank and the IMF.

But, as in Seattle, the message of the protesters was

clear—that the policies of the two lending institutions had harmed the environment, and actually led to cuts in spending for health and education in poor countries. Critics charged that the IMF imposed rigid economic conditions on less developed, Third World countries in exchange for its loans and ignored humanitarian concerns.

The protests and demands for reform of international organizations such as the WTO and the IMF underscored the fact that globalization and international trade policies—once the province of bankers, economists, and specialists meeting in quiet anonymity—have become volatile political issues both at home and abroad.

But trade and tariff policies have often been caught up in domestic politics throughout U.S. history. In the United States, a **tariff** is a federal tax on imports. A high tariff discourages other nations from sending goods to U.S. markets and is therefore "protective" of American manufacturers. When American corporations are hurt by foreign competition, it often creates pressures to protect industries at home by setting high tariffs. That makes the price of foreign products higher and may encourage people to buy domestically manufactured products instead.

But a tariff wall can work two ways. Other countries can and do retaliate by setting up trade barriers of their own; they raise their tariffs on imports from the United States. As a result, most presidents favor free trade.

Pressure from American industry seeking foreign markets for its products, and from consumers wanting lower prices for imported goods, has resulted in a gradual reduction of U.S. tariff barriers since the 1930s.

In 1947 the United States and 22 other nations signed the General Agreement on Tariffs and Trade (GATT)—the predecessor of the WTO—which provided a formal framework for international tariff reductions. More trade barriers fell during the 1960s.

During the same period, however, industry in Japan and the creation of the European Community in western Europe threatened the competitive advantage previously enjoyed at home by American business.

Protectionist sentiment succeeded in placing many restrictions on tariff reductions—for example, by imposing quotas on certain categories of imports. In 1988 Congress passed and the president signed a trade bill that provided protection for industries seriously injured by imports.

In 1992, the United States, Mexico, and Canada completed negotiations on an agreement to create a free-trade area for the three countries. President Bush submitted the North American Free Trade Agreement (NAFTA) to Congress. But in an election year, many members of Congress were cautious about the pact, fearing that some U.S. companies would move their plants to Mexico, where labor is cheaper. Ross Perot, an independent candidate for president that year, repeatedly voiced this argument. Although business generally supported the agreement, it was bitterly opposed by organized labor, which feared job losses. Opponents of NAFTA also worried that the pact would lead to expanded competition from Mexico, since products manufactured there could now enter the United States more freely. Despite strong opposition by organized labor and by many Democrats, President Clinton supported the pact, Congress approved it in 1993, and it went into effect on January 1, 1994.

NAFTA bolstered Mexico's economy. By NAFTA's 10-year anniversary in 2004, trade between the United States and Mexico, which totaled $81.5 billion before the agreement, had almost tripled to $232 billion. Mexico became the second-largest buyer of U.S. goods and services. Although opponents of NAFTA said it had cost 200,000 U.S. jobs, some economists estimated that the total expansion of the American economy had created 18 million jobs, far more than went south of the border.[15] The benefits of NAFTA were still a subject of considerable debate, however, and the trade agreement had not stemmed the flow of undocumented immigrants across the Mexican border into the United States.

In 1994 Congress approved a new international trade agreement that created the WTO, which officially came into being on January 1, 1995. But well before the protests in Seattle, various groups were opposed to the WTO; in the United States, some unions feared loss of jobs; and textile manufacturers and other businesses worried about foreign competition.

American steel manufacturers have complained about low-priced imports.

For example, a coalition of labor unions, environmentalists, religious groups, and veterans opposed China's entry into the WTO. The unions feared that American industry would move high-paying jobs to China, where the same work could be done at much lower wages; others objected to rewarding a Communist government that threatened its neighbors and harshly repressed all dissent. But business organizations, eager to open China's vast market to American industry, lobbied hard for eliminating trade restrictions against China. In 2000, Congress approved normal trade relations with Beijing.

Then in 2002, Congress enacted legislation granting President George W. Bush "fast track" authority to negotiate trade agreements with other countries, pacts that Congress could approve or reject but not change. Most Democrats voted against the bill, warning that it might cost jobs for American workers. Previous presidents, beginning with Gerald Ford, had been granted such authority, but it had expired in 1994 under President Clinton.

International economics has a direct effect on the relations among nations and on the economy at home. Across the industrial heartland of America, many workers lost their jobs to foreign competition in the 1980s and 1990s. During those years, layoffs, plant closings, and unemployment became all too familiar in what some called "the rust belt." (See Figure 17-4.)

That happened in part because the United States had become less competitive with the rest of the world. Not only are the wages of its workers higher, thanks to strong unions, but the salaries and benefits of its executives

**FIGURE 17-4**

**Annual Rate of Unemployment in the United States, 1982–2006**

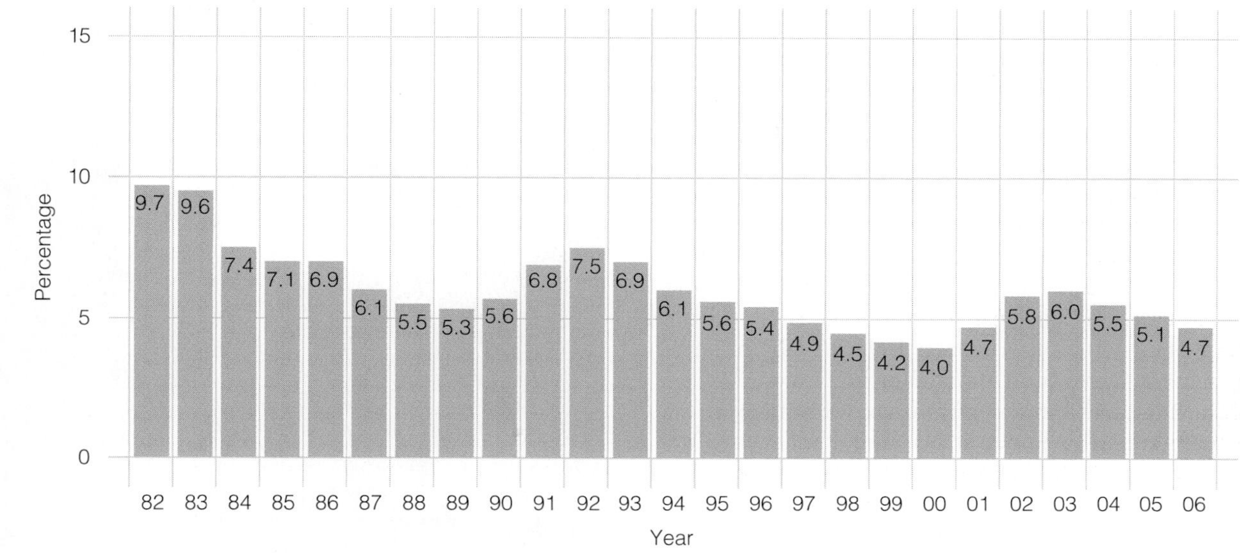


*Data as of August 2006.
SOURCE: U.S. Bureau of Labor Statistics.

© William Campbell/Corbis Sygma

Workers at an American-owned electric plant in Juarez, Mexico. NAFTA raised fears that American jobs would move south of the border.

have skyrocketed. Many CEOs of major U.S. corporations earn salaries and stock options in the millions of dollars a year.

Trade policy remains a politically volatile issue. Many American companies have moved their manufacturing operations overseas to China, other parts of Asia, or Latin America to take advantage of cheap labor in less developed countries. Today, as often as not, telephone operators in India or the Philippines may answer when a consumer in the United States calls an American company for technical support or customer service. The people calling with questions may not realize they are talking to someone a world away. These cost-cutting moves may result in higher profits for corporations but the loss of American jobs to workers overseas who earn much lower pay. Look closely at the running shoes you buy and chances are the label will say "Made in Taiwan" or "Made in China."

In Japan, South Korea, Taiwan, and other countries, industry, often heavily subsidized by government, has been turning out products that are sometimes better and often cheaper than those produced in California, Ohio, or Pennsylvania. And Americans are buying those products. Europe, dependent on America for foreign assistance after the destruction of the Second World War, has also emerged as a powerful economic rival.

In 1958, the European Economic Community, known as the Common Market, was established to integrate the nations of western Europe by the gradual removal of trade and tariff barriers. This led in 1967 to the formation of the European Community (EC), which Great Britain joined in 1973. In 1994, the EC became known as the European Union (EU).

The 25-nation European Union has eliminated most tariffs among its member states. On January 1, 2002 most members of the EU, but not Britain, Denmark, or Sweden, began using a common currency, the euro.

The American auto industry can be studied as an example of how the nation has had to adjust to globalization. For many years after the Second World War, Detroit did not have to worry about significant competition from foreign auto manufacturers. General Motors, Ford, and Chrysler could compete at home for the domestic auto market.

Gradually, however, German Volkswagens and then Japanese small cars began appearing on U.S. highways. In 2002, more than 6 million American-made passenger cars were sold in the United States, but another 2.3 million foreign cars were imported, including almost 1 million from Japan and 564,910 from Germany. In other words, nearly 28 percent of cars sold in the United States that year were foreign.[16]

To the extent that Americans buy cars made in Japan, for example, some American auto workers lose jobs, which in turn creates protectionist pressures on the American government to erect trade barriers against imports. By the mid-1990s, however, the American auto industry was increasing domestic sales and expanding its markets overseas, including in Japan.

At the same time, when large numbers of foreign cars are sold in the United States, the flow of dollars to Japan and other nations adversely affects the U.S. **balance of trade,** the relationship between the total cost of foreign goods imported to this country and sales of U.S. products overseas. In 2003, for example, the United States spent $496.5 billion more to buy foreign goods than it earned from sales abroad, an increase of $75 billion over the previous year.[17]

The deficit in the balance of trade with China in 2003 was $123 billion, or about 25 percent of the total trade imbalance. The deficit in the balance of trade with Japan decreased somewhat that year, from $70 billion in 2002 to $65 billion in 2003. Japan accounted for about 13 percent of the total U.S. trade deficit.[18]

Foreign policy and economic policy also are con-

© Rob Nelson/Black Star/Stockphoto.com

cerned with the **balance of payments,** the net balance or relationship between total income and total expenditures by the nation in its dealings with the rest of the world, including trade, loans, and investments.

So complex is the trade picture, however, that even citizens who want to "buy American" to support the economy at home may find themselves frustrated. Globalization has meant that some Japanese car manufacturers have opened plants in the United States, employing American workers. Is a Japanese auto made in Kentucky a "foreign" car?

Because some foreign manufacturers enjoy help from their governments, Congress has legislated against "dumping," a term that means selling goods in the United States at prices below their cost of production, usually because of subsidies by a foreign government to its own industries. Brazil, for example, subsidizes its steel industry, and American steelmakers complained that this gives Brazilian steel an unfair advantage over the U.S. steel industry.

In recent decades, there has been a shift from manufacturing to service industries. Here, chefs are trained at a culinary institute in New England.

In 1988, Representative Richard A. Gephardt, Democrat of Missouri, sponsored what became known as the "Gephardt amendment" to a trade bill then pending in Congress. The amendment would have opened the way to retaliation by Washington against countries that had a trade surplus with the United States. Congress rejected the amendment but passed a major trade bill to stiffen the U.S. response to unfair trading practices by other countries. It was signed into law by President Reagan.

Economic policy affects U.S. foreign policy in various ways. Even interest rates in the United States have an impact overseas. For more than two decades, for example, Third World nations sought some relief from re-

## Making a Difference

## HOW TWO GRADUATE STUDENTS CREATED GOOGLE

For Google's founders, Sergey Brin and Larry Page, it is as if the dot-com glory days never ended. . . . Google has maintained a casual corporate culture with on-site massage therapists, free health-conscious meals and games of roller hockey in the parking lot.

Mr. Brin, 30, and Mr. Page, 31 . . . met in 1995 when Mr. Page was at a weekend for new graduate students at Stanford University. . . . Mr. Brin was one of a group of students assigned to show Mr. Page around the campus.

In 1996, the two men, working out of Mr. Page's dormitory room, began collaborating on the development of a new Internet search technology. They called their program BackRub. . . . The two spent until mid-1998 working on BackRub, and then set out to sell licenses to the technology. Their immediate goal was to move out of the dorms and pay off the credit card debt they had amassed trying to expand their network.

Andy Bechtolsheim, a co-founder of Sun Microsystems . . . gave them $100,000 at the first meeting. . . . Mr. Bechtolsheim made the check out to Google Inc., essentially forcing the two men to set up a corporation, if only to cash the check.

Ultimately, Mr. Brin and Mr. Page raised $1 million . . . enough to set up shop in a rented house and garage in Menlo Park, Calif. Within a year, the company moved to a suite of offices above a bicycle store. . . . Soon after, America Online and Yahoo also invested in the new business.

Today, Google has nearly 2,000 employees and operates out of a 500,000-square-foot headquarters in Mountain View, Calif. . . . known as the GooglePlex.

Google filed with the Securities and Exchange commission. . . . Mr. Brin and Mr. Page . . . will become billionaires with the company's initial public offering.

Despite the company's meteoric growth the last few years, Mr. Brin and Mr. Page made clear in their letter on the registration statement that they intended to maintain Google's unconventional culture and way of doing business by "applying the values it has developed as a private company to its future as a public company."

"With our products, Google connects people and information all around the world for free," the letter said, adding that "by releasing services for free, we hope to help bridge the digital divide."

—From Laurie J. Flynn, "The Google IPO," *The New York Times,* April 29, 2004. © 2004 The New York Times Company. Reprinted by permission.

payment of loans to American banks. Interest rates in America, which at times have been high, have made it difficult for the poorer nations to repay their debts. As discussed in Chapter 16, growing concern by many prominent figures, including Pope John Paul II, over the plight of poor countries burdened by debt led Congress in 2000 to agree to provide $435 million for the U.S. share of a $90 billion global debt relief program.

Other factors that have little to do with foreign competition have markedly reshaped the American economy. In recent decades, for example, there has been a shift from manufacturing into high-tech and service industries in the United States. Inevitably, this has led to dislocation and loss of jobs by many blue-collar workers.

## THE AMERICAN ECONOMY IN THE 21ST CENTURY

By the presidential election campaign of 2004, economic indicators, the various guideposts that the government uses to measure the health of the economy, were better in some areas, but weaker in others. The economic recovery was fitful. By the midterm congressional elections of 2006, unemployment was low but wages were flat, and home sales were no longer booming as they had been for several years. Gas prices were very high that spring and summer, topping an average of more than $3 a gallon before dropping in September, and interest rates on mortgages and on credit card debt

A ticker on the New York Stock Exchange

© AP/Wide World Photos

had increased, leaving many middle-class households feeling economically squeezed.

Many Americans felt uncertain about the future. Large numbers of small investors, having put their savings into mutual funds and stocks, lost money at the start of the decade. So-called baby boomers, men and women in their 50s, were concerned that they could not depend on Social Security benefits when they retired. They worried that the program might disappear or that the amount of the payments would be greatly reduced. Some corporate profits were up, but corporate chief executive officers still earned enormous salaries. (See Table 17-2.) And more business executives were indicted and convicted for various fraudulent practices.

In the wake of the high-profile cases of corporate fraud, particularly the collapse of the telecommunications giant WorldCom, Congress in 2002 passed the Sarbanes-Oxley Act, a law designed to foster greater transparency in the activities of corporations and their accountants. The law imposed new criminal penalties for top corporate officers and required stricter auditing and oversight of the accounting industry.

Economic policies have important and far-reaching social and political consequences. Americans continue to expect the government to maintain prosperity, and to protect their economic security, both now and in the future, in a rapidly changing world.

Nevertheless, there is little agreement over what precise steps the government should take to meet the goals of full employment, low inflation, and economic stability. There is a contradiction in all this, for Americans philosophically want as little government interference as possible in their lives. At the same time, they expect their political leaders to preserve a healthy, growing economy for the nation and its citizens. Whether a president or a political party remains in power may depend on how well that challenge is met.

"Five percent of my income is from lemonade, and the rest is from charity."



TABLE 17-2

**Top 10 Chief Executive Officer Salaries**

| CEO | Company | Pay (in millions)* |
|---|---|---|
| Reuben Mark | Colgate-Palmolive | $141.1 |
| Steven P. Jobs | Apple Computer | 74.8 |
| George David | United Technologies | 70.5 |
| Henry R. Silverman | Cendant | 54.4 |
| Sanford I. Weill | Citigroup | 54.1 |
| Richard S. Fuld, Jr. | Lehman Brothers | 52.9 |
| Lew Frankfort | Coach | 45.8 |
| Lawrence J. Ellison | Oracle | 40.6 |
| Howard Solomon | Forest Laboratories | 36.1 |
| Richard M. Kovacevich | Wells Fargo | 35.9 |

*Includes 2003 salary, bonuses, and long-term compensation.
SOURCE: *Business Week,* April 19, 2004.

## CHAPTER HIGHLIGHTS

- The United States operates predominantly under an economic system of free enterprise, or capitalism. Under capitalism, there is private ownership of the means of production.
- In practice, however, the United States has a mixed, or modified, free enterprise system in which both private industry and government play important roles.
- Keynesian economists and their modern successors place major emphasis on fiscal policy to guide the economy, although they recognize the role of monetary policy—the control of the supply of money and the supply of credit through the actions of the Federal Reserve Board.
- Supply-side economics is an economic philosophy that advocates both tax and budget cuts to increase incentives to produce, in order to expand the total supply of the nation's goods and services. The Reagan administration adopted this policy in the 1980s.
- The federal government, which for decades had incurred multibillion-dollar deficits, was, by the late 1990s, producing substantial budget surpluses. A budget surplus is the amount of money available when the government's income is greater than what it spends in a fiscal year. By 2002, however, the surplus had vanished and was replaced by large deficits.
- A budget deficit occurs when the government's income in a fiscal year is less than its outlays.
- When the government runs at a deficit for many years, the amount of money it owes piles up. The national debt is the total amount of money that the United States owes to its creditors.
- Government also attempts to regulate the economy by monetary policy—controlling the supply of money and the cost and availability of credit. It does this through the operations of the Federal Reserve System.
- When individuals or corporations need money, they normally borrow from a bank. When banks need money, they may borrow from the Federal Reserve System. The Fed is, therefore, a banker's bank. When it lends to the banks, it can, in effect, create money.
- In the United States, a tariff is a federal tax on imports. A high tariff discourages other nations from sending goods to U.S. markets and is therefore "protective" of American manufacturers.
- The balance of trade is the relationship between the total cost of foreign goods imported to this country and sales of U.S. products overseas.
- Foreign policy and economic policy also are concerned with the balance of payments, the net balance or relationship between total income and total expenditures by the nation in its dealings with the rest of the world.
- In the 21st century, globalization has become the target of a diverse group of environmentalists, human rights activists, labor unions, and others.

## KEY TERMS

budget surplus, p. 589
deficit, p. 589
capitalism, p. 592
laissez-faire, p. 593
fiscal policy, p. 593
monetary policy, p. 594
supply-side economics, p. 594
budget resolutions, p. 595
authorizations, p. 595
appropriations bills, p. 595
national debt, p. 598
gross domestic product (GDP), p. 599
globalization, p. 603
tariff, p. 604
balance of trade, p. 606
balance of payments, p. 607

## SUGGESTED WEBSITES

**http://www.federalreserve.gov**
*Board of Governors of the Federal Reserve System*
Contains background information on the work of the Federal Reserve Board and biographies of current members. The *Beige Book*, an informal review conducted by the Federal Reserve Banks that summarizes current economic conditions in their districts, and the *Monetary Policy Report* to Congress are both available online.

**http://www.whitehouse.gov/cea/**
*Council of Economic Advisers*
Contains the council's current economic report to the president and other economic data.

**http://www.gao.gov**
*Government Accountability Office*
The website of the GAO, the investigative arm of Congress, provides daily reports about the GAO's latest findings. The GAO site also includes FraudNET, a section that encourages and allows people to report fraud, waste, abuse, or mismanagement of federal government funds.

**http://www.whitehouse.gov/omb/**
*Office of Management and Budget*
The OMB's website offers the current federal budget, along with previous recent budgets.

## SUGGESTED READING


Collins, Robert M. *The Politics of Economic Growth in Postwar America** (Oxford University Press, 2002). A history of the U.S. economy since World War II, focusing on economic growth, one of the three major goals of the Employment Act of 1946. Organized by presidential administrations, the book covers periods of economic growth and contraction, along with economic policies and politics.

Destler, I. M., and Balint, Peter. *The New Politics of U.S. Trade Policy** (Institute for International Econom-

ics, 1999). A concise examination of the politics of foreign trade in an increasingly global economy.
*Economic Report of the President* (U.S. Government Printing Office, 2006). The annual assessment of the state of the nation's economy written by the president's Council for Economic Advisors. The Report, called for by the Employment Act of 1946 and the Full Employment and Balanced Growth Act of 1978, contains a wealth of economic data.
Galbraith, John Kenneth. *The Affluent Society,* 40th anniversary edition* (Mariner Books, 1988); and *The New Industrial State*, 4th edition* (Houghton Mifflin, 1985). Two well-known works by an influential American economist. In both, Galbraith examines the economic structure of the United States.
Heilbroner, Robert, and Milberg, William. *The Crisis of Vision in Modern Economic Thought** (Cambridge University Press, 1996). A thorough historical analysis of the events that shaped the various schools of economic thought. Examines the divisions among economists in the post-Keynesian era.
Kotlikoff, Laurence J., and Burns, Scott. *The Coming Generational Storm: What You Need to Know About America's Economic Future* (MIT Press, 2004). An analysis of demographic trends that suggests that the U.S. government and economy will be in serious trouble when baby boomers retire and draw upon Medicare and Social Security. The authors suggest options for government policymakers and strategies for individuals seeking to ensure their own economic security.
Krugman, Paul. *The Age of Diminished Expectations** (MIT Press, 1997). A lively examination of major economic issues. Krugman argues that although for a time American voters were content to let economic policy drift, as the Baby Boom generation moves into retirement this will no longer be possible.
Morris, Irwin. *Congress, the President, and the Federal Reserve: The Politics of American Monetary Policy-Making** (University of Michigan Press, reprint edition, 2002). A comprehensive overview of the politics of monetary policy in the United States.
Phillips, Kevin P. *The Politics of Rich and Poor: Wealth and the American Electorate in the Reagan Aftermath* (Random House, 1990). An analysis of the economic policies of the Reagan administration and the consequences of those policies for American society. The author argues that the Reagan policies widened the income gap between the wealthy and those with low incomes.
Rivlin, Alice M. *Reviving the American Dream: The Economy, the States, and the Federal Government** (The Brookings Institution, 1992). A thoughtful and perceptive account of the state of the American economy. The author later became a key economic adviser to President Clinton.
Sampson, Anthony. *Company Man: The Rise and Fall of Corporate Life* (Times Books/Random House, 1995). A lively account by a well-known British author detailing the history of corporations in the United States and England.
Schick, Allen. *The Federal Budget: Politics, Policy and Process** (The Brookings Institution, 2000). A revealing analysis, including detailed case studies and an array of statistical data, of how the federal budget is formulated.
Smith, Hedrick. *Rethinking America** (Avon Books, 1996). An examination of the modern American economy by a distinguished journalist. Smith proposes reforms to cope with a changed world order.
Stein, Herbert. *The Illustrated Guide to the American Economy,* 3rd revised edition* (American Enterprise Institute for Public Policy Research, 1999). A concise overview, with numerous charts and graphs, of the state of the American economy.
Stein, Herbert. *Presidential Economics: The Making of Economic Policy from Roosevelt to Clinton,* 3rd revised edition* (American Enterprise Institute for Public Policy Research, 1994). A stimulating analysis of how economists participate in making federal economic policy. The author served as chief economic adviser to President Nixon.

*Available in paperback edition.

EXIT 533
Welfare

# Chapter 18

# PROMOTING THE GENERAL WELFARE

MILLIONS OF OLDER AMERICANS count on their monthly Social Security checks to help make ends meet. But many workers worry that the money to fund the program may not be there when the Baby Boom generation—people in their 40s and 50s—retire. During the presidential campaign of 2004, the candidates of both major parties, President George W. Bush and Senator John Kerry, talked about the public's growing concern over the fate of Social Security.

The managers of the Social Security program had warned that by 2018 payroll taxes would no longer be enough to cover Social Security payments to retirees, and by 2042, unless changes were made to the system, Social Security would be broke and able to pay, from current payroll taxes, only about 70 percent of promised benefits.[1] One survey had found that more young people believed in UFOs than believed Social Security would be solvent when they reached retirement age.[2]

The candidates of the two major parties proposed two very different approaches to rescuing the Social Security system. Their disagreement reflected long-standing philosophical differences between the Democratic and Republican Parties.

George W. Bush, the Republican candidate, proposed a sweeping overhaul of Social Security. Bush called for partially privatizing the program. Under his plan, Social Security taxes would be reduced, and younger workers could invest the amount they saved in taxes in the stock market, creating "personal retirement accounts." In his second term as president, however, Bush failed to persuade Congress to divert part of Social Security payroll taxes to such private accounts. He ran into strong opposition by Democrats, many Republicans, and AARP, the powerful lobby for older Americans.

John Kerry, the Democratic nominee in 2004, insisted that the structure of the Social Security program should remain basically unchanged. His plan called for a bipartisan approach to maintaining the system.

Critics of Bush's plan claimed that his reforms would undermine the basic principle of the Social Security system, which was created as a "pay-as-you-go" public safety net, in which the contributions of people currently working are used to pay the benefits of those who have retired. They saw Bush's proposal as the first step in transforming Social Security from a social-welfare program into a private pension system.

Opponents also expressed concern that in a wobbly stock market, many would lose money, as large numbers of Americans did from 2000 to 2002, and in the Great Depression of the 1930s. If millions of Americans lost money in stocks, would they pressure the government to bail them out with tax money? How would the government make sure that individuals invested their retirement account funds prudently, and would that mean an expanded role for Washington in regulating the stock market? Or would the government manage the personal savings accounts that Bush envisioned? Many such questions about the future of Social Security remained unanswered during the presidential campaign.

Kerry's plan to shore up Social Security also drew criticism. Opponents argued that it would not resolve the basic problem facing the system, which was the growing imbalance between revenues and promised benefits to increasing numbers of retirees.

Well before the 2004 presidential campaign, the large social programs begun by President Franklin D. Roosevelt during the New Deal and expanded by John F. Kennedy and Lyndon B. Johnson had come under increasing scrutiny. One observer, Anthony King, pointed to what he called "the decline of the ideas of the New Deal as the principal organizing themes of American political life. The central idea of the New Deal was a simple one: that the federal government could, and should, solve the country's economic and social problems."[3]

By contrast, in the 1980s, during the administrations of Ronald Reagan and the first President Bush, the White House sought to restrict the government to a more limited role; where possible, social programs were eliminated or cut back. Conservatives argued that government programs had not worked and that the federal bureaucracy, and the rules and regulations spawned by these programs, had proved burdensome to individuals. To the Reagan conservatives, government was not the solution; it was the problem.

Kerry, in contrast to George W. Bush, advocated the view that government should intervene more often to manage the economy and to provide social programs

© J. L. Atlan/Corbis Sygma

A soup kitchen in the nation's capital

*The American Past*

## FDR ON SOCIAL SECURITY: "A LAW THAT WILL TAKE CARE OF HUMAN NEEDS"

On August 14, 1935, President Franklin D. Roosevelt signed the Social Security Act into law with a ringing statement:

> Today a hope of many years' standing is in large part fulfilled. The civilization of the past hundred years, with its startling industrial changes, has tended more and more to make life insecure. Young people have come to wonder what would be their lot when they came to old age. The man with a job has wondered how long the job would last.
>
> This social security measure gives at least some protection to thirty millions of our citizens who will reap direct benefits through unemployment compensation, through old-age pensions and through increased services for the protection of children and the prevention of ill health.
>
> We can never insure one hundred percent of the population against one hundred percent of the hazards and vicissitudes of life, but we have tried to frame a law which will give some measure of protection to the average citizen and to his family against the loss of a job and against poverty-ridden old age. . . .
>
> If the Senate and the House of Representatives in this long and arduous session had done nothing more than pass this Bill, the session would be regarded as historic for all time.
>
> —*The Public Papers and Addresses of Franklin D. Roosevelt*

for people. However, like the previous Democratic president, Bill Clinton, he sought to avoid the "liberal" label and to move closer to the political center than had Democrats in the past.

Although the presidential candidates in 2004 battled over such diverse subjects as Iraq, terrorism, education, tax cuts, health care, and the environment, many of the domestic issues reflected a philosophical divide over the proper role of government.

But the heated rhetoric of a presidential campaign does not always match reality. Although views about the role of government vary greatly, no modern president would propose to shut down a program like Social Security, on which millions of retirees depend. The responsibility of the national government to make social policy was recognized at the beginning of the American nation, for the Constitution was established, among other purposes, to "promote the general welfare."

To take one example of the need for federal intervention, it would be difficult, if not impossible, for individuals, or even groups of people, to compel American industry to reduce pollution of the environment. But government, supported by public opinion and public demands, possesses the power to accomplish that task.

To "promote the general welfare," the federal government fills several major roles. It is regulator, promoter, manager, and protector. It performs these roles in a wide variety of ways and with a degree of zeal that varies with the political climate and the administration in power. It regulates business and labor. But it also promotes business and labor. It assists farmers. It runs such agencies as the Food and Drug Administration and the Tennessee Valley Authority. It tries to manage the economy through fiscal and monetary policies. It acts, to some extent—and with varying success—as protector in consumer affairs, health, education, welfare, science, and the environment, and in attempting to alleviate poverty and hunger.

The government does not necessarily perform all of its roles well. By 2005 there were still 37 million people struggling below the poverty level, and large numbers of homeless people were living on the streets of the nation's cities in rain, snow, heat, and cold. Although economic conditions had improved somewhat, two-income households had become the norm, as families—often uncertain about their economic future—struggled to make ends meet. As a result, many Americans took a rather dim view of the ability of the government to manage the economy.

As noted throughout this book, there are many areas in which government and society have failed to live up to American expectations. So in discussing government in operation, a careful distinction must be made between the various roles of the government and its actual performance.

A government like that of the United States, which exercises responsibility for the welfare of its citizens in such areas as social security, housing, and education, is sometimes described as a welfare state. The term is often used as one of criticism. But the role of the federal government in making social policy has been well established, particularly since the days of the New Deal. As one study suggested, "social welfare programs substantially improve the well-being of most beneficiaries and . . . retrenchment does have serious repercussions. . . . There is no reason to abandon the aim of providing a minimal level of support for all who remain in need."[4]

Despite the cutbacks in government social programs under President Reagan, and the sharply differing philosophy of his administration from Democratic administrations in the past, Washington did not ignore its domestic role during the administrations of President Reagan and the first and second President Bush. Programs such as Social Security, Medicare, and Medicaid continued to aid millions of Americans.

Today, regardless of who occupies the White House, the terms of the argument usually concern the proper extent of government intervention in domestic problems, as well as how government should respond to national needs. Government services require government spending, and the size of government programs is directly related to the level of taxes. The level of government taxing and spending for welfare and social programs is a volatile political issue, directly affecting election outcomes.

Key Question In this chapter we will explore a key question: ***How and to what extent should the federal government "promote the general welfare"?*** There are many other questions to consider. How efficiently does government regulate corporate power on behalf of the consumer? And how well has it performed in the field of social welfare; in eliminating poverty and hunger; in coping with rising medical costs, including the high price of prescription drugs; in providing health insurance for everyone; in meeting educational needs; and in protecting the environment?

## Government as Regulator and Promoter

### Government and Business

The Constitution, as Justice Oliver Wendell Holmes, Jr., once wrote, "is not intended to embody a particular economic theory."[5] But the Supreme Court, which interprets the meaning of the Constitution, has often embodied the particular economic theory of its time. For half a century, from the late 1880s until 1937, during Franklin Roosevelt's New Deal, the Court generally interpreted the Constitution in such a way as to prevent government from regulating industry. It adopted the prevailing **laissez-faire** philosophy, which held that government should intervene as little as possible in economic affairs.

During the late 19th century, economic power was concentrated in the "trusts" and in the hands of the "robber barons." But a rising tide of populism created public demands that led to the passage of state and federal laws regulating industry. Nevertheless, the Supreme Court, as was noted in Chapter 15, interpreted the Fourteenth Amendment to protect business from social regulation by the states and by Congress.

Justice Holmes made the comment quoted above in his famous dissent in the *Lochner* case. In that 1905 decision the majority of the Supreme Court struck down a New York State law that had limited bakery employment to "sixty hours in any one week" and "ten hours in any one day." Today it might seem incredible that the Supreme Court would permit a bakery owner to work his employees more than 60 hours a week. But in 1905 the Supreme Court refused to approve the use of the power of the state to regulate private property—in this case a bakery.

The Great Depression and the New Deal brought about a reversal of Supreme Court thinking. Since 1937 the Court has upheld laws policing business; the right of government to regulate wages, hours, and working conditions of employees is now firmly established.

Industries often protest government rules, however. Some of the regulations of the Occupational Safety and Health Administration (OSHA) have been so detailed and stringent that they brought a storm of protests from business and industry. And corporate power often counterbalances government power. As one scholar has suggested, the scope and effectiveness of the federal government's efforts "have been sharply limited by business's success in weakening the content and constraining the enforcement of the legislation."[6]

But business, even as it objects to government regulation, asks for government protection: "A powerful campaign has been mounted [by industry] to contain government; reduce its size—or rate of growth—especially as regards social welfare functions; and diminish its regulatory encroachments. . . . On the other hand, business clamors for government protection, [and] decisive efforts to control inflation. . . . This is a whipsaw treatment of government."[7]

**Regulating Business: Antitrust Policy** In 1890 Congress passed the Sherman Antitrust Act, which was designed to encourage competition in business and prevent the growth of monopolies. The Supreme Court severely limited the scope of the act, however, by ruling that it was up to the states to control industrial monopolies. Then in 1914 Congress passed the Clayton Act, which sought to put teeth into the federal antitrust law by defining illegal business practices, by providing the remedy of court injunctions, and by giving the Federal Trade Commission power to issue cease-and-desist orders. The same measure exempted labor unions from antitrust actions.

Subsequent legislation has strengthened the antitrust laws, and both the Federal Trade Commission and the antitrust division of the Justice Department have blocked many large corporate mergers. But the degree of enforcement of the antitrust laws varies with the attitudes of the administration in power in Washington.

Nevertheless, there have been a number of landmark cases in which the government has changed the shape of major industries. In a famous case in 1957, the Supreme Court, under the Clayton Act, forced du Pont to divest itself of 23 percent of the stock of General Motors.[8] In 1982, American Telephone and Telegraph Company, AT&T, was broken up into "Baby Bells." At the time, AT&T was the largest corporation in the world.

In 1998, the Justice Department filed an antitrust suit against the powerful Microsoft Corporation (headed by billionaire Bill Gates). The government charged that the computer software giant was using its monopoly in personal computer operating systems to gain competitive advantage in other software fields, such as Internet browsers.

In 2000, after a fiercely contested legal battle, a federal judge found Microsoft guilty of violating antitrust law, ruling that it had used the predominance of its Windows operating system to stifle competition, and to pressure computer makers into using Microsoft's Web browser.[9] The judge ordered that Microsoft be broken up into two companies, one for computer operating systems and one for software applications. But a year later, a federal appeals court in Washington, D.C., overruled the lower court and held that Microsoft would not have to be split in two, although it said that the Seattle-based computer giant had repeatedly abused its software monopoly. The government appealed, but the Supreme Court declined to hear the case. Microsoft had won.[10]

Although government regulation has had some success at blocking **monopoly,** the control of a market by a single company, it has not been able to prevent **oligopoly,** the concentration of economic power in the hands of a relatively few large companies. Economist John Kenneth Galbraith has noted that "in the characteristic market of the industrial system, there are only a handful of sellers."[11] Even as the government was pursuing the breakup of Microsoft, for example, oil giants Exxon and Mobil merged in 1999, creating the world's second-biggest oil company. And in 2000, the Federal Communications Commission (FCC) approved media giant Viacom's $30 billion acquisition of CBS, a merger that gave Viacom control of 35 percent of the American broadcasting market.[12] In 2004, General Electric, which already owned NBC, merged with Vivendi Universal, the owners of Universal Pictures and theme parks. The 10 largest corporations in the United States are shown in Table 18-1.

TABLE 18-1

**The 10 Largest Corporations in the United States, 2004**

| Rank (by sales volume) | Company | Profits (in billions) | Assets (in billions) |
|---|---|---|---|
| 1 | Wal-Mart Stores | $263.009 | $104.812 |
| 2 | Exxon Mobil | 222.883 | 174.278 |
| 3 | General Motors | 195.324 | 448.508 |
| 4 | Ford Motor | 164.505 | 312.564 |
| 5 | General Electric | 134.187 | 647.483 |
| 6 | Chevron Texaco | 112.937 | 81.470 |
| 7 | Philip Morris | 99.468 | 82.455 |
| 8 | Citigroup | 94.713 | 1,264.032 |
| 9 | American International Group | 81.501 | 104.457 |
| 10 | Hewlett-Packard | 73.061 | 677.000 |

SOURCE: Data provided by *Fortune,* July 2004.

Thus, despite government regulation, some American corporations have increased in both size and diversity. Nothing illustrates the trend better than the rise in recent years of **conglomerates:** large multi-interest, and often multinational, corporations that may, under one corporate roof, manufacture products ranging from missiles to baby bottles. Because conglomerates are formed by mergers of companies in unrelated fields, they have long been considered exempt from most antitrust regulation.

The ordinary consumer cannot keep up with the complexities of corporate ownership in what Galbraith has called "the new industrial state." Indeed, large corporations have become more powerful than many nations. Of the 100 largest economic units in the world, only 49 were countries; 51 were multinational corporations.[13] As ownership of industry becomes more and

The nation's two biggest oil companies merged in 1998.

more impersonal and remote, it is increasingly difficult for the private citizen to fix responsibility for corporate actions.

Whether government can be expected to intervene to regulate corporate power on behalf of consumers and individuals is not always clear. Government regulation, no matter how desirable and necessary, is a source of potential and actual tension in a mostly free enterprise capitalist economy such as that of the United States. Many of the conflicts of American politics concern the degree to which government should intervene in the private sector.

Some political theorists have contended that political liberty exists only where there is a free market system and private enterprise, with a minimum of government intervention. In the view of Charles E. Lindblom, for example, much of the personal liberty that people have sought "is freedom to engage in trade . . . freedom also to move about, to keep one's earnings and assets."[14]

On the other hand, E. E. Schattschneider has suggested that "the struggle for power is largely a confrontation of two major power systems, government and business." The function of democracy, he argues, has been "to provide the public with a second power system, an alternative power system, which can be used to counterbalance the economic power."[15]

As discussed in Chapter 17, the nation was jolted in 2001 and later years by corporate fraud inside huge companies such as Enron, the energy trader, and WorldCom, a communications giant. In the wake of the scandals, criminal prosecutions sent dozens of executives to prison. In 2003, a Corporate Fraud Task Force established by the government to prosecute such cases reported that it had obtained more than 500 convictions, a total that included more than 25 former chief operating officers (CEOs).[16]

But the issue of corporate responsibility extends beyond individual wrongdoers in the executive suites of major companies to the larger question of the responsibility of corporations toward society as a whole. The consumer movement, public concern over pollution by industry, and similar pressures led some corporations to take steps to improve their public image in the area of corporate responsibility.

Ralph Nader's crusade for auto safety in the 1960s brought federal legislation and prodded the automobile industry to produce safer cars and to recall those with suspected defects. Increasing awareness of the issue of corporate responsibility led in the 1960s and 1970s to the emergence of public interest law firms composed of young law school graduates. Instead of joining traditional, old-line law firms representing large corporations, the graduates offered their skills to protect consumers, minorities, and the poor. Today, these public interest firms are much fewer in number, although some conventional law firms perform a limited amount of public interest work. A number of private organizations, such as environmental and consumer groups, also have staff attorneys who practice public interest law in representing their organizations.

**The Regulatory Agencies** Although the Justice Department has responsibility for fostering competition through the antitrust laws, much of the day-to-day contact between government and industry is carried on through federal regulatory agencies, including the major commissions discussed in Chapter 14. Thus the Securities and Exchange Commission (SEC) has responsibility for regulating the stock market; the Federal Communications Commission (FCC), the broadcast industry; the Federal Energy Regulatory Commission (FERC), power companies and pipelines; and the Federal Trade Commission (FTC), industry as a whole. Other federal agencies, such as the Food and Drug Administration, the Environmental Protection Agency, the Federal Maritime Commission, and the Consumer Product Safety Commission, have also played an important role in regulating business.

As also noted in Chapter 14, many of the commissions have, to varying degrees, become captives of their client industries, and deregulation has reduced the authority of some of these agencies. Nor has regulation always been successful. A case in point is the railroad industry, which long asserted that its passenger operations lost money while its freight operations made money. The great increase in air and highway travel in the past few decades was a major factor in reducing railroad revenues. Poor management by some railroads was certainly another factor.

But some would argue that the government was also partly responsible for the deterioration of the railroads. Federal regulators permitted passenger service to decline to a point approaching extinction. Americans visiting Japan or Europe found better rail service in cleaner, more modern trains than in many parts of their own country. On the other hand, the railroads have complained that government regulation forced the railways to continue service on unwanted passenger routes and in other ways made it difficult for them to compete with the airlines.

In 1970 Congress passed legislation to establish a federally subsidized national rail network of passenger trains. The law created a government-sponsored corporation to run many of the nation's intercity passenger trains (but not commuter lines). The National Railroad Passenger Corporation, better known as Amtrak, lost money. But the corporation expanded its Metroliner service between Washington, New York, and New Haven, providing comfortable high-speed train service at frequent intervals. Because the Metroliner was well run and competitive with the airlines in the heavily traveled northeast corridor, it initially made a profit, even though Amtrak as a whole did not. By 2000, Amtrak had only 0.3 percent of the nation's total passenger traffic.[17]

© AP/Wide World Photos
Amtrak's high-speed Acela began service between Washington, New York, and Boston in 2000.

In that year, in an effort to compete with low-fare air flights in the Northeast, it began operating a new generation of high-speed trains, the Acela, along the busy corridor between Boston and Washington, D.C.

Amtrak in 2004 asked Congress for an average of $1.7 billion a year through 2009, warning that without substantial subsidies Amtrak faces bankruptcy. President George W. Bush and many members of Congress objected to continuing subsidies for Amtrak, which since its creation has received more than $24 billion in government assistance.

As noted in Chapter 14, deregulation of the nation's airlines also added to that industry's woes. By 2006, several major airlines were bankrupt or in deep trouble, facing higher labor costs, rising fuel prices, and stiff competition from a number of no-frills carriers that offered cheaper fares.

**Aiding Business** Related to the concept of government as regulator is that of government as promoter. Government promotes commerce by providing services and direct and indirect subsidies to producers and farmers. Many business firms and farmers benefit from government aid. Appropriations for highways are indirect subsidies to truckers, bus lines, and automobile manufacturers and users. The federal government pays the airlines and the railroads to carry the mail; it helps support the merchant marine through subsidies to shipbuilders and ship operators; and it finances airport construction.

In the "alphabet soup" of government agencies in Washington, there are several service agencies for industry—the Department of Commerce and the Small Business Administration (SBA), for example—as well as the Department of Agriculture, which serves farmers.

At times the government has even extended direct aid to large corporations in financial trouble. In 1979, for example, Congress authorized a massive $3.5 billion aid package for the ailing Chrysler Corporation, the nation's third-largest automobile manufacturer. Chrysler had underestimated the increased consumer demand for small cars that use less gasoline and started building them too late; as a result it was losing more than $1 billion a year. Congress acted because of growing concern over the impact on the economy if a major auto manufacturer went under. By 1983, Chrysler showed a profit, and in 1998, it merged with the German automaker Daimler-Benz.

In addition to subsidies and services, the federal government assists industry through its trade and tariff policies, as discussed in Chapter 17.

**Aiding Agriculture** In 1996, Congress passed and President Clinton signed a major new law to assist farmers and replace the program adopted during Franklin D. Roosevelt's New Deal that paid farmers not to plant certain crops.

The new law ended the Depression-era subsidies that were paid to farmers when prices for farm products dropped below certain levels. Instead, the law guaranteed farmers fixed annual payments, regardless of the prices of farm products. No longer did Washington have power to tell farmers what crops to plant, or to leave some land unplanted. Farmers themselves could decide what to plant. The legislation also phased out dairy price supports over four years.

The new farm law marked a victory for the Republican Congress elected in 1994, since it moved farming away from many government controls and toward a free market approach. At the same time, it provided an estimated $56 billion to farmers over seven years.[18] A farm bill signed into law in 2002 continued the fixed payments but reinstituted payments to farmers when prices of farm products dropped below certain levels.

Because the nation's 3 million farmers sometimes produce more than they can sell profitably and are often hostage to drought, or floods, or extreme cold, there were still enormous problems in agriculture. The government's programs over many decades to aid farmers reflect not only the political power of the farm belt, but also recognition by Washington of the responsibility of the federal government to promote and assist a vital segment of the nation's economic life.

## Government and Labor

As in the case of business, labor is both regulated and helped by the federal government. Today organized labor wields great economic and political power in the United States. This was not always the case; the history of the labor movement in America is one of long struggle, intermittent violence, and only gradual recognition.

The industrialization of the 19th century brought American laborers job opportunities in factories but scant bargaining power with employers. As a result they worked long hours at low wages and under hazardous working conditions. In 1881 Samuel Gompers, a London-born cigarmaker, founded what became the American Federation of Labor (AFL). The AFL fought for "bread-and-butter" improvements—the eight-hour day, higher pay, fringe benefits, and restrictions on child labor. It was largely a federation of craft unions—groups of skilled workers organized by trades: construction, printing, mining, clothing manufacturing, and others.

The Great Depression, which threw millions of people out of work, and the liberal policies of the New Deal created a favorable climate for the labor movement. In the mid-1930s a group of labor leaders within the AFL began to organize industrial unions in the mass-production industries, thus bringing unskilled workers into a labor movement dominated until then by craft unions. Led by John L. Lewis, head of the United Mine Workers, the dissidents formed a new labor organization that became known in 1938 as the Congress of Industrial Organizations (CIO). The CIO rapidly won recognition from the automotive, steel, rubber, and other industries. In 1955 the AFL merged with the CIO. In 2004 there were 15.8 million union members in the United States, of which more than 13 million belonged to unions in the AFL-CIO.[19]

As early as 1926, the Railway Labor Act stated labor's right to organize and established the National Mediation Board to assist in settling rail strikes. The Norris-LaGuardia Act of 1932 sharply restricted the power of the courts to issue injunctions in labor disputes. Up to that time employers were frequently able to break strikes by obtaining court injunctions against the unions.

The National Labor Relations Act of 1935 was labor's great milestone. Sponsored by Senator Robert F. Wagner, Democrat of New York, it established labor's right to collective bargaining and barred employers from setting up "company unions" (unions controlled by the employer) or discriminating against any worker for union activity or membership. The act also established the National Labor Relations Board (NLRB), an independent regulatory agency that supervises union elections and determines unfair labor practices.

The Fair Labor Standards Act of 1938 established a minimum wage for American workers, a maximum 40-hour workweek, and time-and-a-half for overtime. It also outlawed child labor. Over the years, the minimum-wage law has been amended by Congress and its coverage expanded. In 2004, the federal minimum wage was $5.15 an hour, although some states had higher or lower minimum wages. More than 7.4 million workers earned the federal minimum wage.

The power labor gained during the New Deal inevitably brought a political reaction. The National Labor Relations Act had placed restrictions on employers but none on unions. In 1947 Congress passed the Taft-Hartley Act, which sought to shift some of labor's newly won power back to management. The act prohibited the **closed shop,** under which only union members may be hired, but it did permit the **union shop,** under which any person may be hired provided he or she joins the union within a specified time. Under Section 14B of the Taft-Hartley Act, 21 states (10 in the South) passed state **right to work laws** to outlaw the union shop. The act also defined and prohibited unfair labor practices by unions; expanded the membership of the NLRB, an agency that employers had considered too favorable to labor; barred labor unions from making political contributions; and outlawed strikes by government employees. Finally, the law provided that in strikes creating a national emergency, the president can seek a court injunction against a union during an 80-day "cooling off period."

*for more information about the National Labor Relations Board, see: http://www.nlrb.gov*

Big labor unions continued to prosper, despite the restrictions of the Taft-Hartley Act. And the legislation had one result that its Republican sponsors had not intended: Because passage of the law demonstrated to labor that legislation aimed at unions could win support in Congress, it had the effect of increasing the political activity of labor unions. Often that labor support went to Democrats.

In the late 1950s a Senate committee held a series

## Surviving on the Minimum Wage: The Working Poor in America

Many Americans may assume that because Congress sets a minimum wage, even people in low-paying jobs are assured of enough money to get by. After all, the Fair Labor Standards Act of 1938 promised to provide for everyone "minimum standards of living necessary for health, efficiency and well-being of workers."

The reality is different. Shop clerks, parking attendants, fast-food workers, and many other minimum wage earners actually earn less than the federal government's official definition of poverty.

The federal poverty threshold in 2005 for a family of three—for example, a single mother with two young children—was $15,735, before taxes. A head of a household working full-time year round for the federal minimum wage of $5.15 an hour would earn $10,712 before taxes, well below the poverty line.

Moreover, states set their own minimum wage standards, sometimes below the federal minimum. Kansas has the lowest, $2.65, and Washington state has the highest, $7.16. The higher minimum wage, federal or state, applies to businesses with sales of $500,000 or more. But many smaller businesses are exempt from paying the minimum wage to their workers. And all employers can pay less than the federal minimum wage to students, and to people younger than 20. An employee subject to a state minimum wage could make as little as $5,512 a year.

More than 7.4 million workers, 6 percent of the workforce, earn a minimum wage. Of these, 61 percent are women.

The average American family earns an income of almost $50,000 with annual expenditures before taxes averaging $40,000 for basics such as food, housing, transportation, and other expenses. Comparable standards of living are not enjoyed by the millions of people working for minimum wage.

The average American spends more than $1,100 on housing per month. Minimum wage workers can spend only $123 to $333 per month. The average American spends about $646 a month, or $21 a day, on transportation; the working poor can spend only $2.37 to $6.40 a day on transportation, which may not be enough for them to get to work and back each day. Taking care of the basics leaves little or no funds for personal insurance, bill payments, health care, clothing, or entertainment of any kind. Child care—in many families the second largest expense after housing—can cost up to half of the total income of people earning minimum wage.

The reality is that the minimum wage falls short of securing an adequate standard of living for millions of workers and their families.

A minimum wage worker in Iowa

of hearings to investigate labor racketeering. Two successive Teamsters Union presidents, Dave Beck and James R. Hoffa, eventually went to jail after the disclosures, and the AFL-CIO expelled the Teamsters. (Hoffa was later murdered.) The televised hearings brought national recognition to the Senate committee's chief counsel, Robert F. Kennedy. It also led to demands for reform legislation.

The Labor Reform Act of 1959 (Landrum-Griffin Act) grew out of the hearings. The act (1) required unions to file elaborate financial reports, constitutions, and bylaws with the secretary of labor; (2) granted union members the right to elect officers by secret ballot; (3) barred ex-convicts from holding union office; and (4) tightened Taft-Hartley provisions against secondary boycotts, organizational picketing, and other labor practices that employers felt gave unions an unfair advantage.

Despite provisions for injunctions that sometimes avert or delay major strikes, the public is often unprotected against walkouts that may inconvenience millions of people—airline, rail, and garbage strikes, for example. Compulsory arbitration to settle major labor disputes has not won wide acceptance, and the problem of disruptive strikes in an industrial society remains.

Because unions have concentrated on bread-and-butter gains through collective bargaining, organized labor has made great economic progress in the United States. The extent of labor's political power is less clear. Unlike many industrial nations, the United States has never had a major, enduring "labor party." Rather than run its own candidates for political office, labor has usually worked through the two-party system. Since the New Deal era, labor has usually supported the national Democratic Party, but it carefully watches the records of

Senator John Kerry was endorsed by labor unions in the 2004 presidential race.

members of Congress in both parties and supports those whom it considers friendly to labor.

Although labor support is vital to many political candidates, the concept of a deliverable "labor vote" is dubious, because union members are also Republicans and Democrats as well as members of other groups. In the 2004 presidential campaign John Kerry enjoyed the support of organized labor, as has almost every modern Democratic presidential candidate.

As the nation has shifted away from manufacturing industries, shrinking labor's traditional blue-collar base, union membership in the United States has declined steadily. In the 1950s, 35 percent of the nation's nonagricultural workers were union members, but by 2003, that figure had fallen to 12.9 percent. Although unions have conducted aggressive membership drives, the numbers continued downward; union membership dropped by 370,000 in 2003, in part as a result of layoffs of workers.[20]

The Department of Labor, which achieved cabinet status in 1913, administers and enforces laws relating to the welfare of wage earners in the United States. Its responsibilities include providing job-training programs, administering the wages and hours law, and enforcing the safety and health standards for workers set by various federal laws.

## Government as Protector

In 2003, President George W. Bush signed a controversial bill revamping the Medicare program and providing drug benefits for senior citizens for the first time.

In his reelection campaign the following year, Bush cited the law as an example of his administration's accomplishments. His opponent, John Kerry, the Democratic candidate, emphasized that 45 million Americans were still without health insurance.

When Democrat Bill Clinton won the presidency in 1992, he appointed his wife, Hillary Rodham Clinton, to head a task force to draw up a plan to provide health insurance coverage for all Americans. The task force labored in secret and produced a plan so complicated that it was doomed to failure. Its defeat in 1994 contributed to the Republican capture of Congress that year.

Nevertheless, the goal of providing good, affordable health care to all Americans, including those too poor to pay for it, continued to be a key political issue.

Despite differing approaches to the issue by political leaders, the fact that neither presidential candidate in 2004 could explicitly reject any government role in providing health coverage for seniors or for the needy was an indication of how much public opinion had shifted in recent decades. Helping people to obtain health care in an era of astronomical medical costs remained one of the most important tasks of government as protector of the public. Individuals do not have the power to reduce health costs or require insurance coverage for everyone. They look to the government to accomplish those objectives.

When Social Security was enacted in 1935, President Franklin D. Roosevelt's opponents criticized the expansion of government and voiced fears of "creeping socialism." Times change. The government now spends hundreds of billions of dollars each year on social programs, ranging from school lunches to health care for the elderly. And while many Americans might criticize specific programs, by and large most Americans expect the government to act as protector of the general welfare. Proposing to abolish or modify established social programs that enjoy broad public support carries a high political risk.

In the rest of this chapter, we will explore some of the important aspects of government as protector. It

"I'll stop downloading illegal music files as soon as you stop importing your prescription drugs from Canada."

should be kept in mind, of course, that the government does not always successfully fulfill its role as protector of the public.

Despite screening by the Food and Drug Administration, dangerous prescription drugs have been sold to the public. Some 800 innocent people, without their knowledge, were deliberately exposed to radiation in government medical experiments conducted between the 1940s and the 1960s. In addition, thousands of people were exposed to radiation leaking from hundreds of underground nuclear tests conducted in Nevada without any notice to the public. Hazardous nuclear waste escaped into the atmosphere and into the ground for years from the government's plutonium plant in Rocky Flats, Colorado, until the plant was finally shut down for safety violations in 1988. Congress has passed laws to clean up the air we breathe, but the executive branch has sometimes enforced those laws in ways that favor the polluters, not the public. As always, in studying the operations of government we should remember that there is often a gap between the goal and the reality.

## Government and the Consumer

Today, most Americans would agree that government has a responsibility to protect ordinary consumers from the perils of the marketplace. Three decades ago few citizens were aware of consumer issues. That the picture changed dramatically was, to a considerable extent, the work of a single crusader for consumer protection: attorney Ralph Nader.

In his book *Unsafe at Any Speed,* published in 1965, Nader charged that the automobile industry bore partial responsibility for many highway accidents and deaths by making cars that emphasized style over safety. Nader was then investigated by private detectives hired by attorneys for the General Motors Corporation (GM). A Senate subcommittee disclosed that the private detectives had

### Unsafe to Attack General Motors

In 1965, Ralph Nader, then a 31-year-old Connecticut attorney, criticized the safety of American automobiles, particularly the General Motors Corvair, in his book *Unsafe at Any Speed.* General Motors, through an attorney in Washington, hired a "private eye" to investigate Nader. Senate investigators found that the New York detective agency, Vincent Gillen Associates, Inc., had issued the following instructions to its operatives:

> [Nader] apparently is a freelance writer and attorney. Recently he published a book *Unsafe at Any Speed,* highly critical of the automotive industry's interest in safety. Since then our clients' client apparently made some cursory inquiries into Nader to ascertain his expertise, his interest, his background, his backers, etc. They have found out relatively little about him, and that little is detailed below. Our job is to check his life and current activities to determine "what makes him tick," such as his real interest in safety, his supporters, if any, his politics, his marital status, his friends, his women, boys, etc., drinking, dope, jobs—in fact all facets of his life. This may entail surveillance which will be undertaken only upon the OK of Vince Gillen as transmitted by him to the personnel of Vincent Gillen Associates, Inc.

—Hearings before the Subcommittee on Executive Reorganization, Committee on Government Operations, U.S. Senate, *Federal Role in Traffic Safety,* March 22, 1966

"Granted the public has a *right* to know what's in a hot dog, but does the public really *want* to know what's in a hot dog?"



put Nader under surveillance and had even checked into his sex life. As a result of the Senate investigation, James M. Roche, the president of GM, found it prudent to apologize publicly to Nader at a committee hearing.[21]

The congressional investigation of GM's flagrant action against a private citizen made Nader a national figure overnight. In the years that followed, he played a vital role in the passage of five major federal consumer laws (listed later in this section). GM removed the Corvair from production after Nader charged that the car was hazardous to drive under certain conditions. Today, major auto companies routinely recall cars from consumers to correct safety defects. Ralph Nader's crusades found a response among the public, the press, Congress, and the executive branch. In the 2000 election, Nader ran for president on the Green Party ticket; four years later he ran in some states as an independent and on the Reform Party ticket.

The basic demand of the consumer movement is that government step in to protect buyers from hazardous products, shoddy merchandise, mislabeling, fraudulent sales techniques, consumer credit abuses, and other deceptive or dangerous practices. "Consumerism" holds that when business will not police itself, government must act.

The person who must return a TV set to the repair shop three times before it is fixed properly; the child playing with a flammable toy; the inner-city resident talked into buying an overpriced bedroom suite for "only $899"; the family injured in an auto crash because of defective tires—all are victims of consumer abuses. Many products that Americans buy seem to have "built-in" obsolescence—that is, they are designed to wear out after a certain amount of time.

Consumer frauds victimize the most those who can afford it the least. Various studies have shown that "the poor pay more." Residents of the inner city often buy low-quality merchandise at high prices. Why? One reason is that neighborhood merchants extend "easy" credit terms to poor people who may not be able to buy on credit in major department stores. And, as David Caplovitz noted in his study of poverty areas in Manhattan, "neighborhood merchants . . . compensate for extending credit to poor risks by high markups." The result is that poor families often end up paying higher prices for appliances such as television sets and washing machines than do more affluent families.[22] To deal with customers who cannot keep up the payments, the merchant can use the weapons of repossession and salary garnishment, backed by the power of the law.

During the 1960s and 1970s, legislation was passed to deal with consumer problems, and limited machinery to deal with those problems was established within the executive branch. Presidents Kennedy, Johnson, Nixon, Ford, Carter, Reagan, the first President Bush, and Clinton all appointed staff assistants for consumer affairs. Several federal agencies are involved in consumer matters, but the primary responsibility is in the hands of the Federal Trade Commission.

The principal consumer laws include the following:

1. *Auto safety* (1966). One law requires manufacturers to meet federal standards for automobile and tire safety, and another requires each state to establish federally approved highway safety programs or lose 10 percent of federal highway construction funds.
2. *Truth-in-packaging* (1966). To help shoppers make price comparisons, a law was passed requiring manufacturers to label their products more clearly. But it does not require standard package sizes, which would aid shoppers in threading their way through the supermarket jungle of "jumbo," "family," and "large economy" sizes.
3. *Meat and poultry inspection* (1967 and 1968). Two laws were designed to tighten consumer protection against poor-quality meat and poultry. Before this legislation, these products were subject to federal inspection when shipped between states, but products consumed within a state were subject only to state inspection. Seven states had no meat inspection at all.
4. *Truth-in-lending* (1968). This legislation requires merchants and lenders to provide full, honest, and understandable information about credit terms. For example, a customer who agrees to pay "only 3 percent per month" must be told that the annual interest rate is actually 36 percent.
5. *Product safety* (1972). The law establishes the independent five-member Consumer Product Safety Commission. The commission has broad power to act against hazardous products that in 2002 caused an estimated 14.2 million injuries to consumers.

In almost every case, industry has lobbied against consumer bills and has often weakened the final ver-

## Accelerating Problems of the Consumer

The gas gauge was nearing "empty" so the University of Arizona co-ed pulled off the freeway into the nearest service station. All went routinely enough until suddenly she noticed white smoke billowing out from under the open hood. The attendant, standing over it with a properly concerned expression, informed her that the car needed "a new accelerator in its generator" and that if she tried to drive out of the station without having it fixed, the car would be ruined.

One tank of gas and $119 later the student was back on the freeway, heading for the university campus. To confirm her growing suspicion, she took the car to her regular mechanic for a recheck. His verdict: Potassium powder had been used to simulate smoke, and she had been "conned" (a generator does not have an accelerator).

The case is not as exceptional as one might think. Despite stepped-up efforts by law-enforcement agencies and more widespread and vehement complaining on the part of car owners, deceptive auto-repair practices persist as a major consumer problem.

—*Christian Science Monitor*

sions. There is some danger, therefore, that the passage of consumer legislation may create the appearance of government regulation without the reality. Consumer advocates now are increasingly focusing their attention on how consumer laws are put into effect and on their real impact once enacted. At the same time, the power of the consumer movement had diminished as Congress and the electorate became preoccupied with other issues.

## The General Welfare

In 2006, almost 49 million Americans—retired or disabled workers and their dependents—received about $450 billion in Social Security payments. Another 2.3 million families received public assistance (welfare) payments totaling about $17 billion, of which the federal government paid about half (with state and local governments paying the rest).

But the federal government no longer administers the welfare program. In 1996 President Clinton, who was seeking reelection, signed a bill that completely restructured the nation's welfare plan.

The new law, passed by the Republican-controlled Congress, dismantled the program established 60 years earlier during President Roosevelt's New Deal administration. The federal government no longer guarantees payments to poor families with children. Instead, the law provides that each state receives federal money to design and run its own welfare programs.

People who receive assistance under the new welfare law are required to find work within two years, and lifetime benefits are limited to five years, although states are free to set even stricter limits. The law preserved the Medicaid program of health care for people with low incomes but placed restrictions on the Food Stamp program.

Although some liberal Democrats and advocates for children sharply criticized the president's decision to sign the bill into law, the measure redeemed Clinton's pledge in the 1992 campaign to "end welfare as we know it."[23] The law was strongly backed by Republicans and conservatives. It marked a fundamental change in social policy after six decades.

By 2004, $33.2 billion a year in federal benefits went to 6.9 million persons under the Supplemental Security Income (SSI) program of aid to needy aged, blind, and disabled people. SSI is part of the Social Security system. In addition, it was estimated that a monthly average of 8.2 million jobless workers would collect $39.1 billion in unemployment insurance.[24]

Yet before 1935 these programs did not exist. The hardships of old age, ill health, poverty, unemployment, blindness, or disability were problems for individuals, their families, private charity, states, and local communities.

The Great Depression of the 1930s changed all that. Millions lost their jobs, and a blight of hunger and poverty descended on the land. "Brother, Can You Spare a

Photo by Dorothea Lange. Culver Pictures, Inc.

## Comparing Governments

### SWEDEN'S WELFARE STATE—AND HIGH TAXES

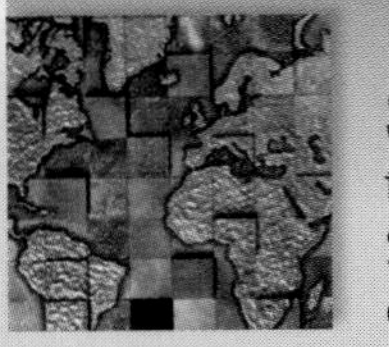

Swedes pay high taxes—very high taxes. So high that a family earning $100,000 might only take home $50,000 or possibly even less. Under Sweden's social democracy, the highest income tax bracket is about 55 percent compared with 38.6 percent in the United States. Sweden's retail prices also add a 25 percent tax.

Sweden is a welfare state where high taxes provide guaranteed free or low-cost health care, education, and many other services. Welfare and social insurance provide security for anyone who gets sick or injured and is unable to work. Education for the most part is free and open to everyone. Sweden's broad range of social-welfare benefits includes child allowances, housing allowances, unlimited paid sick leave, and 12 months of leave shared by both parents during the first eight years of a child's life. The gap between wealthy and poor is one of the smallest in the world. Everyone older than 65 is guaranteed a pension.

By contrast, welfare in the United States is limited to some people whose incomes are too low to support themselves and their families. Under a 1996 law the government no longer guarantees payments to poor families with children. Instead, each state is given money to design and run its own welfare program. Recipients are required to find work. Social Security in the United States mainly covers older people who have accrued benefits during their careers from the taxes they paid into the system.

Residents of Sweden never worry about losing health coverage while unemployed or how to pay for a college education. Americans have lower taxes but pay high prices for college tuition and health care. Sweden's high taxes provide security and a lifetime of services and benefits. But a fifth of Sweden's labor force is on sick leave or enjoying early retirement; as a result some Swedes worry that too many people are taking advantage of the system.

---

Dime?" was a popular song of 1932. America realized that individuals needed help from the national government to provide income to meet basic needs during hard times. In the midst of the Depression, Franklin D. Roosevelt proposed, and Congress passed, the landmark Social Security Act of 1935. Although to some Americans it seemed a revolutionary step at the time, the United States was the last major industrial nation in the world to adopt a general system of social security.

There are two kinds of social-welfare programs, both designed to guarantee personal economic security to individuals. One is called *social insurance.* The Social Security program is, in effect, a compulsory national insurance program, in theory self-financed by taxes on employers and employees. The other kind of program, *public assistance,* had no pay-as-you-go features; until the 1996 welfare law changed the system and ended the federal guarantee, it simply distributed public funds to poor families. (Recipients were usually said to be "on welfare.") The distinction is important, because each approach has significant political consequences.

Social insurance is widely accepted because it is "earned." People assume that they have a "right" to retirement income after a lifetime of work. But "welfare" programs have not enjoyed the same acceptance by the public. Many Americans who have received welfare payments, and many others who have not, believe that society has a responsibility to care for those who are less fortunate. Some Americans, however, as Gilbert Y. Steiner has pointed out, hold a different view:

> [They] resent supporting those who can't make their own way. . . . The idea of "toughening up" is forever popular. Toughening up, it is argued, will drive the cheaters out, the slackers to work, the unwed mothers into chastity; and it will save money. It is this clash between the ideas of public aid as a right and public aid as a matter of sufferance, to be granted with suspicion, with strings, and with restraints, that is reflected in public policy debates and political action.[25]

By the mid-1990s, politicians of both parties, relying on polling data and other information, realized that many voters, rightly or wrongly, had concluded that welfare was a program of "handouts" of their tax money to loafers and "welfare queens." Both Republicans and Democrats agreed that welfare needed to be modified. And it was. By shifting responsibility for welfare programs to the states, however, the law meant that states and localities would be under new financial pressures to provide for poor families.

**Social Security** The Social Security Act of 1935 and its later amendments provide for both social insurance and public assistance programs. The insurance aspects fall into four categories: old-age and survivors insurance, disability insurance, Medicare, and unemployment insurance.

***for more information about Social Security, see: http://www.ssa.gov***

When people talk about receiving **Social Security,** they generally mean the monthly cash payments received by retired, older people through a compulsory national insurance program financed by taxes on employers and

SOMEDAY SON, NONE OF THIS WILL BE YOURS..

SOCIAL SECURITY

© Mike Peters. Reprinted by special permission of King Features Syndicate.

employees. A man or woman who reaches the age of 62 may draw partial Social Security payments if he or she has worked enough years to qualify (10 years in 2004). Men and women who have worked long enough to qualify may receive Social Security at the full, higher rate beginning at age 65, a figure that will gradually rise to age 67 by 2027. In other words, people born in 1960 and later must reach age 67 in order to receive full benefits.

Social Security payments depend on a person's average earnings over a period of years. In October 2006 the average monthly benefit for a retired worker was $1,002. (Examples of Social Security payments are shown in Table 18-2.)

As originally passed, Social Security payments provided only retirement benefits. In 1939 the program was expanded to provide payments to dependents and survivors of workers covered by the system. And in 1956 it was expanded to include disabled workers.

Over the years, Congress has extended Social Security coverage to virtually all types of workers. The system is financed by a Social Security tax levied equally on employers and employees. Self-employed people also must pay a Social Security tax. In 2006, employers and employees each paid 7.65 percent of an employee's income for Social Security and Medicare taxes (up to a ceiling of $94,200 for Social Security in 2006); self-employed people paid 15.3 percent.[26]

Inflation hits hardest those who live on fixed incomes, such as retired workers who depend on Social Security payments. Because of this, Congress has linked the benefits to the cost of living; increases in the amounts paid out under the program are now as a rule automatic.

Social Security is the largest of the various federal **entitlement programs,** which are programs mandated by law and not subject to annual review by Congress or the president. By fiscal 2004, these entitlement programs accounted for almost half of the total federal budget.

Well before that year, the Social Security program was in crisis. The expansion of the Social Security system, the looming retirement of the Baby Boom generation, and inflation have created enormous financial strains. To put it simply, Social Security was getting closer to the time when it would run out of money. Social Security taxes go into trust funds so that the program can be self-sustaining. But payments to recipients are in danger of outpacing the growth of the system's reserves.

Part of the problem is demographic: Compared with the year the program started, there were, proportionately, fewer people of working age to pay taxes and more people of retirement age to draw benefits, and this trend was expected to continue. In 30 years, there are likely to be twice as many older Americans as there are today. Because people are living longer, further changes probably will have to be made in the system; for example, Congress might decide to reduce benefits for wealthier individuals.

Certainly some measures will have to be taken if Social Security is to survive. As noted earlier, government officials estimate that the program, without changes, will remain solvent only until 2042, when the reserves will run out because benefit payments will exceed income from taxes. After that year, benefits for all retirees could be cut by 27 percent, and will be reduced every year thereafter. Social Security would still collect taxes but would have to spend all of what it collects to pay the benefits.[27]

**Medicare**   In 1965 Congress created **Medicare,** a federal program of health insurance to provide hospital and medical services to people 65 years old and older through the Social Security system. Medicare helps to pay hospital bills, and for those who choose to pay an extra amount ($88.50 a month in 2006) to enroll in Part B, it also pays a portion of doctors' bills. Starting in 2007 people with higher incomes will pay substantially higher premiums for this additional coverage. In general, Medicare pays 80 percent of doctors' bills for those who pay the extra premium, but less for some hospital outpatient services. In 2006 an estimated 42 million people were eligible for Medicare, most of whom had also enrolled in the voluntary insurance program for doctors' bills. Those who could afford it purchased "medigap" policies from private insurance companies to make up the difference between the 80 percent the government pays and the full amount of the doctors' bills.

## TABLE 18-2

### Examples of Average Monthly Cash Payments under Social Security

| | |
|---|---|
| Retired worker, all ages | $1,002 |
| Retired couple | $1,648 |
| Disabled worker | $ 939 |
| Disabled worker with spouse and child | $1,571 |
| Widow(er) | $ 967 |
| Young widow(er) with two children | $2,074 |

SOURCE: Data provided by the Social Security Administration, as of October 2006.

© John Davis/Pictor International/ImageState

But Medicare, like Social Security, was in danger of running out of money. Officials estimated that the trust fund that pays for hospital bills would run out of cash by 2023 unless changes were made in the program. Medicare cost $294 billion in fiscal 2005, and will undoubtedly cost more in the future, even if it is merged one day into a general program of national health insurance.

In 1988, Congress passed a controversial new law to pay for more of the costs of catastrophic illness for those eligible for Medicare. The new law would have meant an extra tax for many older Americans, as much as $1,600 a year in the case of the wealthiest 5 percent. Highly vocal opposition led by this affluent minority killed the measure in little more than a year; Congress repealed the law in 1989 before it could go into effect.

As of 2006 about 47 million Americans had no health insurance. Some proposals to create a national health insurance system would keep Medicare; others would absorb Medicare into a general plan covering everyone. But universal health insurance, an enormously costly program, would require political support that in 2006, at least, it lacked.

Following the 1994 defeat of President Clinton's plan to provide health insurance for all Americans, politicians of both political parties largely avoided the issue of universal health coverage. One issue that did receive increasing attention, however, was the problem of rising prescription drug costs. This was partly a result of the political power of seniors: Although only 12.3 percent of Americans were older than 65, they comprised one-fifth of all voters in the 2000 elections.

Paying for drugs was a serious problem for many older Americans, for whom the cost of prescriptions may cut heavily into their retirement income. Because Medicare did not cover the cost of prescription drugs, many lower-income seniors and other Americans were forced to go without needed medications, or to choose between buying drugs or food.[28]

In 2003, Congress passed and President George W. Bush signed a law that provided prescription drug benefits under Medicare. More than 31 million people had enrolled in Medicare Part D, the drug benefit, when it went fully into effect in 2006. Proponents of the measure said it was an important reform that would help millions of seniors. Critics argued that out-of-pocket costs would be too high for many people and that few Medicare recipients would end up saving money. (For a detailed discussion of the 2003 Medicare law see the box titled "The Medicare Debate: Pros and Cons.") The law did not provide for the importation of prescription drugs from Canada, which many people favored because of the lower prices available there.

**Unemployment Insurance** The Social Security benefits discussed above are paid directly by the federal government. But the Social Security Act of 1935 also virtually forced the states to set up unemployment insurance programs to pay benefits to people who are out of work. The program is financed by federal and state taxes on employers. Every state has an unemployment insurance program, but the size of benefits and the amount of time they are granted vary greatly. Most, but by no means all, workers are covered.

By 2004, the majority of states paid unemployment benefits of 26 weeks (up to 30 weeks in a few states). But a weekly payment in 2004 of $262.18—the national average—was scarcely enough to support a jobless worker with a family.

**Welfare: Politics and Programs** The Social Security Act of 1935 created three public assistance or "welfare" programs: old-age assistance; aid to the blind; and the largest program, known later as Aid to Families with Dependent Children (AFDC). The AFDC program was eliminated by the 1996 welfare reform law. It was replaced by Temporary Assistance for Needy Families

## The Medicare Debate: Pros and Cons

In 2003 Congress overhauled the Medicare program to provide drug benefits for seniors for the first time. President George W. Bush supported and signed the highly contested law, known as the Medicare Prescription Drug, Improvement and Modernization Act of 2003. The law has affected millions of baby boomers and seniors. Opponents and supporters of the law debated its pros and cons:

**Pros**

- Prescription Drug Benefit began in January 2006 for people covered by Medicare, with an average $24-per-month premium in 2007.
- Varying plans are offered; some plans pay for and cover more drugs than others.
- Each plan has a list of drugs it covers; seniors may appeal to get a drug addded to their coverage list.
- After a deductible, Medicare covers 75 percent of drug costs up to $2,250.
- After a gap in coverage from $2,250 to $5,100, termed the "donut hole" gap, Medicare covers 95 percent of drug costs. This is called the *catastrophic benefit.*
- Under the catastrophic benefit seniors pay $2 for generic drugs and $5 for brand-name drugs or 5 percent of the prescription drug cost, whichever is greater.
- Low-income seniors are eligible for extra coverage with no premiums, no coverage gap, and no copayment after their total drug costs exceed $3,600.
- The plan focuses on preventive medicine.
- Consumers are eligible for health savings accounts that will allow money to be saved tax free and used to pay for medical expenses.

**Cons**

- The drug benefit program is run by private companies.
- The premium increases each year.
- There is a $250 deductible.
- After the deductible, seniors pay 25 percent of drug costs.
- With the "donut hole" coverage gap, after total drug costs reach $2,250 seniors pay an additional $2,850 in out-of-pocket drug costs before Medicare will continue coverage.
- Each drug plan will only cover a specific list of drugs.
- Changes will increase the federal budget deficit and cost taxpayers $400 billion over the next 10 years.
- In 2010 private insurers can compete with Medicare on a test basis.
- Drug companies and private health insurers may profit from the increased number of prescriptions filled.

—Adapted from Department of Health and Human Services, *Medicare & You 2006.*

(TANF), which set limits on cash benefits of five years, and allowed states to set their own shorter limits. TANF also required recipients to work after being on assistance for a maximum of two years, and gave bonuses to states that reduced the number of out-of-wedlock births.

In 1950 a fourth program was added—aid to the permanently and totally disabled. Then in 1974 the Supplemental Security Income (SSI) program was established to provide uniform federal benefits to needy aged, blind, and disabled people. SSI supplemented Social Security payments to these recipients.

As the system operated for many decades, the federal government provided most of the money for welfare in the form of grants to the states. In some states, local governments also assumed part of the cost. State and local welfare agencies administered the programs.

The welfare system came under attack on several grounds. First, its advocates argued, the program did not cover all the poor. Moreover, because the states control the programs, benefits varied sharply. Southern states paid lower welfare benefits than did the big industrial states of the North.

The program also drew criticism that it "creates a class of dependent persons and then sustains them in their dependency."[29] It was frequently attacked as well on the grounds that it degrades the people it is attempting to help. Welfare agencies regularly investigate those receiving payments, and poor people often regard welfare workers as unwelcome detectives. Behind all this is the public suspicion that many welfare recipients are "loafers" and "chiselers." The 1996 welfare reform law, as noted earlier, provides that each state receives federal money to design and run its own welfare programs.

What has been the result of the changes in the wel-

## Welfare Reform: Does It Work When the Jobs Are Few?

GREENVILLE, MISS.—While President Clinton has flatly declared "the debate is over—we now know that welfare reform works," the hard-luck counties of the Mississippi Delta show the difficulties that can emerge when tough laws collide with a weak economy.

The welfare rolls have fallen sharply across this 200-mile stretch of cotton fields and catfish farms, as they have in most of the country. But with unemployment rates hovering at 10 percent or more, many of those leaving the rolls are failing to find jobs.

Across the Delta, mothers dropped from the welfare rolls are now turning to relatives, boyfriends or other Federal programs—most notably disability payments—or traveling long distances in search of work. Maggie Miller lost her benefits and moved in with her sister, raising the number of children in the two-bedroom house to 15. Patricia Watson worked a day at a distant catfish-processing plant but quit after returning home to discover that her baby-sitter could not find her 6-year-old daughter. . . .

It was scenarios like these, in places like this, that critics of last year's landmark law feared. The landmark measure ended a 61-year-old guarantee of Federal aid and transferred money and authority to the states. While some states might make good use of their autonomy, the critics said, others would prove unwilling or unable to construct safety nets of their own. Mindful of this state's last-place rankings on socioeconomic scales, they summarized their fears with a frequent refrain: "What about Mississippi?"

—From "What about Mississippi," by Jason DeParle, *New York Times,* October 16, 1997. Copyright © 1997, by The New York Times Co. Reprinted with permission.

© AP/Wide World Photos

A farm worker in the Mississippi Delta picks peas under the broiling sun for $2.50 a box.

fare system? By one account, "hundreds of thousands of Americans have moved from welfare to work, many of them substantially raising their incomes."[30] However, several studies by state governments and urban-policy researchers conclude that "a significant number of those who have left the welfare rolls have no jobs, and are sinking deeper into poverty."[31]

A study by the Urban Institute, a private policy organization, found that among unemployed former welfare recipients, 48 percent reduced or skipped meals for lack of food; 63 percent often or sometimes run out of food with no money to buy more; and 46 percent have been unable to pay the rent, utility bills, or a mortgage.[32]

## The Politics of Poverty

"This administration," President Lyndon B. Johnson declared in his first State of the Union address, "today here and now declares unconditional war on poverty in America."[33]

When President Johnson spoke these words in January 1964, many Americans might have wondered what he was talking about. Through the picture window of split-level suburbia, the poor could not be seen. Yet they were there, millions of people living in poverty in the mountains of Appalachia and in the inner cities. When the black urban neighborhoods exploded in flames during the second half of the decade, the poor became more visible.

The federal antipoverty program resulted in part from the publication in 1962 of Michael Harrington's *The Other America,* a book that forcefully described the extent of poverty in the United States and had a substantial impact among segments of the public and within the federal government. The poor, he noted, were "across the tracks," out of view of more comfortable Americans.[34] The poor lived, in Ben H. Bagdikian's words, "in the midst of plenty," occupying "a world inside our society in which the American dream is dying." Yet poor people "are not made so differently from their fellow Americans."[35]

Who are the poor? The federal government answers the question in terms of how many people have incomes below a certain "poverty" level. But to some extent poverty is a relative term; people may feel poor if they have a good deal less than most other people have. And with affluence no farther away than the commercials shown on television, the poor in American society are constantly reminded of their poverty.

In statistical terms the Census Bureau estimated that in 2005 there were almost 37 million poor people in the United States. The government defined poverty in that

© Rob Crandall

year as an income of less than $19,971 for a family of four.[36] The profile of the poor included these facts:

1. About 12.6 percent of the nation's population was poor.
2. There were almost three times as many poor white people as poor African Americans—25.3 million as compared with 9 million. But a higher percentage of African Americans was poor—almost one in every four African Americans as opposed to about one in every 10 whites.[37]

In response to President Johnson's "war on poverty," Congress in 1964 passed legislation creating the Office of Economic Opportunity (OEO). Community-action programs became a highly controversial aspect of the antipoverty agenda. They were designed to give federal grants to a wide range of programs organized and administered by local public or private groups, "with maximum feasible participation" of the poor. While successful in some areas, the community-action programs led in some other cases to what one critic, Daniel P. Moynihan, termed a "maximum feasible misunderstanding."[38]

Supporters of the antipoverty program argued that through community action the poor could be organized politically to express their grievances to the "power structure." But in some cases the strategy led to widely publicized confrontations between the poor and established political leaders. Big-city mayors and other critics charged that the federal government was funding community-action groups to march on City Hall and challenge the entrenched power of local political organizations. Conflict over the program was inevitable. President Johnson, by promising, in effect, to end poverty in the United States, had created public expectations that exceeded the ability of the program to achieve its goal.

President Nixon did not support the poverty program and dissolved OEO. Then in 1994, Congress, with President Clinton's support, created AmeriCorps, a kind of domestic Peace Corps. In exchange for one or two years of community service, those enrolled in 2004 received up to $4,725 a year to help finance their college education or vocational training, or to pay back student loans. AmeriCorps members tutored schoolchildren, assisted disabled people, helped to restore national parks, and participated in recycling, poverty programs, and other activities to benefit communities.

## The Politics of Hunger

As the Republican Party held its national convention in Philadelphia in the summer of 2000, the *Philadelphia Inquirer* ran an editorial titled "In Gilded Times, Some Children Languish." In the midst of economic abundance, the editorial declared, millions of American children remained mired in poverty. "Leave no child behind. The failure to honor that phrase is bipartisan. It's always painfully clear at election time that children don't vote."[39]

Children living in poverty often go to bed hungry. And the statistics of hunger in America are indeed startling. According to one study, nearly 35 million Americans went hungry or lived in households with inadequate food supplies in 2002. Thirteen million were children. The antihunger organization Second Harvest reported that 23.3 million Americans had received food from food banks in 2001. Requests for emergency food assis-

*Myth vs. Reality*

## AMERICA: THE AFFLUENT SOCIETY?

The United States is the richest country in the world, an affluent society where the less fortunate are taken care of by a government "safety net." But the typical American family is well off and lives in a comfortable house in the suburbs, perhaps with a white picket fence. That, at least, is the idealistic image of America that many voters hold. The facts are rather different:

- The per capita income of Americans is $37,610, ranking fifth among nations.
- 35.9 million people live in poverty, according to the official definition by the federal government.
- 3 million are homeless, according to the National Law Center on Homelessness and Poverty.
- 4.9 million live in substandard housing.
- 45 million have no health insurance.
- 2.2 million are confined in federal and state prisons.
- 8.8 million are unemployed.
- The murder rates in Washington, D.C., and many other U.S. cities are the highest in the world compared with those of cities of the same size in other countries.
- Women and many minorities face discrimination in employment and housing, and in other ways.

—U.S. Department of Labor, Bureau of Labor Statistics; U.S. Bureau of the Census; National Law Center on Homelessness and Poverty; Department of Justice; U.S. Conference of Mayors; the World Bank; the World Health Organization

tance had risen 9 percent since 1997, and nearly two-thirds of the requests were coming from families with children.[40]

Part of the problem had to do with low wages. Having jobs did not necessarily mean that people escaped poverty. And to some extent the problem of hunger in America was related to what appeared to be a growing population of homeless people. Estimates of the size of that population varied. As far back as 1983, in one government estimate the number was put at 2 million.[41] By 2000, a study by the Urban Institute concluded that the number of people who were homeless at least once in the course of the previous year had risen to 3.5 million. Of those, 1.2 million were children.[42] In an affluent society, these figures are shocking. Despite government and private programs, hunger and homelessness have not been eliminated.

Many low-income Americans benefit from an extensive federal Food Stamp program. In 1961 President Kennedy, by executive order, initiated the Food Stamp program to increase the buying power of low-income families. Congress established the system by law in 1964. Most recipients of food stamps have incomes well below the national poverty level.

From its modest beginnings, the Food Stamp program rapidly spiraled into one of the federal government's largest social welfare programs. However, legislation passed as part of the 1996 welfare reform plan cut billions from the program and barred most adults without children from receiving food stamps for more than three months.

By 2002, $20.7 billion a year was budgeted for food stamps. An average of 17.2 million people received food stamps at any given time that year. Monthly benefits averaged $141 for each recipient.[43] In addition to food stamps, the federal government distributed surplus food crops to the poor through local welfare agencies, and it financed a school lunch program and a special milk program for children.

## Health

In fiscal 2005 the federal government planned to spend $604 billion, or 25 percent of the national budget, for health services.[44] The funds were allocated for research, training and education, hospital construction, Medicare and Medicaid, and prevention of disease.

The Medicare program, established in 1965 and discussed earlier in the chapter, provided hospital and medical services to older people through the Social Security system. **Medicaid,** also established in 1965, is a public assistance program created to help pay hospital, doctor, and medical bills for people with low incomes. It is financed through general federal, state, and local taxes. Washington pays 50 to 83 percent of the cost of state programs established under Medicaid.[45] By 2004, Medicaid served 42.4 million people at a cost of $252.6 billion in federal and state funds.[46]

Some states have received permission from the federal government to design their own programs of medical aid to the poor. In Tennessee, and in other states that established their own programs, patients were funneled into "managed care" programs that cut costs by limiting the specialists, drugs, and treatments allowed. By 2004, however, because of rising medical costs, Tennessee's model plan was in serious financial trouble.[47]

But some states cut back on the program. In a three-year period in the late 1990s, 1 million low-income parents were dropped from the Medicaid roles of 15 states. In Georgia and Texas, the number of parents receiving

## Doctors on Duty: "What Is More Basic?"

MUNSTER, IND.—Seventy-year-old Myra Rosenbloom will not be ignored. Her questions are relentless, her energy unflagging. "What is more basic than a doctor in a hospital?" she asks. "What is more basic?"

Rosenbloom has asked that question of nearly everyone she has met since her husband, Jack, a patient at a Lake County, Ind., hospital, died two years ago unattended by a physician. Angered by what she saw as lack of proper care, Rosenbloom began investigating hospital regulations in Indiana.

To her surprise, she discovered that Indiana had no law requiring a doctor to be on duty in a hospital; state regulations required only that a doctor be contacted "within a reasonable amount of time" after a patient arrived. . . . Rosenbloom, with the help of researcher William Rutherford, has investigated medical statutes in 20 states. Not one has a law requiring a doctor to be in a hospital, even in emergency rooms.

"I tell people they're better off checking into a Holiday Inn if they are sick," Rosenbloom said. "At least they know what they are getting. Because without doctors all we are doing is running medical motels."

A grandmother who is only five feet tall, Myra Rosenbloom does not look like a public avenger. Yet she got an entire state legislature to pay attention by spending six days and nights on a bench inside the Indiana statehouse during the dead of winter. Her sleep-in marked the end of a two-year battle against one of the state's most powerful lobbies, the Indiana Hospital Association. . . .

"Myra Rosenbloom turned the Indiana General Assembly upside down last session," said State Rep. Charlie Brown (D). "She stole my heart in terms of stick-to-itiveness." . . .

In the end a compromise was struck, requiring hospitals to have a doctor on duty at all times but accepting emergency room doctors as meeting the requirement. . . .

"It's not good enough," [Rosenbloom] said of the hard-fought win. She said she won't stop until all 50 states have laws in place that assure her sort of tragedy will not recur.

—From "Widow Makes Hospitals Change Their Ways," by Megan Garvey, *Washington Post*, September 9, 1994, p. A3. Copyright © 1994, The Washington Post Writers Group.

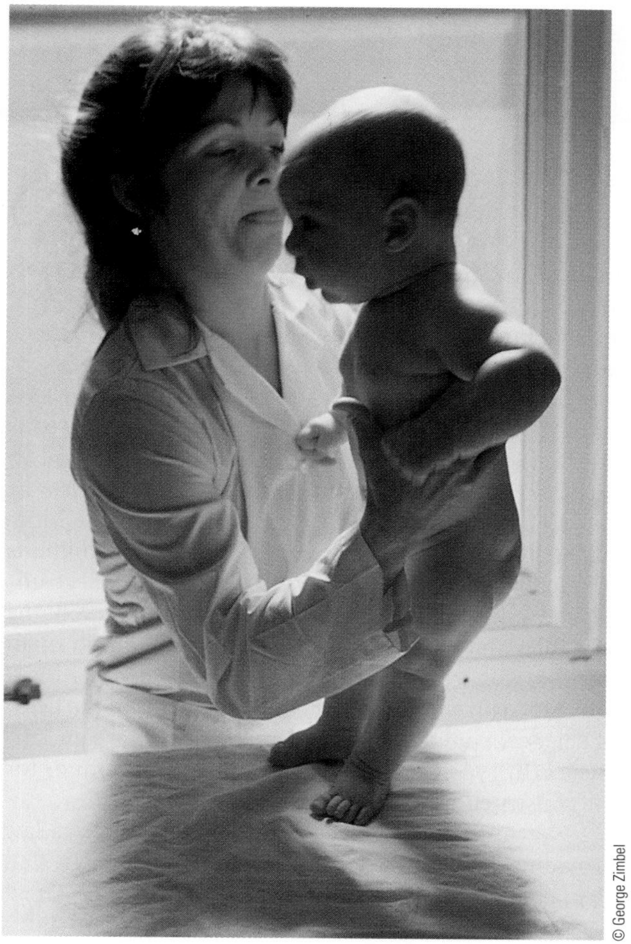
© George Zimbel

Medicaid benefits was cut in half. And parents in 32 states who worked for the minimum wage earned too much to qualify for Medicaid.[48]

Federal programs have assisted the aged and the needy but have not helped the majority of Americans to obtain adequate health care at a reasonable cost. The price of hospital rooms, physicians' care, and other health services has increased at an alarming rate. Major illness can quickly wipe out the financial resources of the average American family, and private insurance plans often fail to cover the cost of prolonged hospitalization or medical treatment, or long-term care for infirm older people.

Although about 47 million Americans had no health insurance in 2006, there was little prospect that Congress, without a major change in the political climate, would enact a universal health care plan. Debate on the issue centered on the question of who would pay for such a vast, multibillion-dollar program—to cover the cost of an estimated 26.5 million operations and more than 3 billion prescriptions a year.

## Education

Many Americans agree that the nation's educational system faces formidable challenges. Parents, students, and other citizens are concerned that the nation's public schools are not doing a good enough job of educating children in a world where the United States faces increasing economic competition with other countries.

*Comparing Governments*

## HEALTH CARE IN CANADA AND THE UNITED STATES

Although the United States and Canada are neighbors, they are, on many cultural and policy issues, far apart. One of the public policies on which they differ the most markedly is health care. In the United States, medical care is, like any other industry, profit-driven. In recent years, medicine has been increasingly dominated by for-profit health maintenance organizations (HMOs), corporations whose interest in health care is matched by their concern for the bottom line.

In Canada, where most industries are private and for-profit, health care is treated differently. Since the creation of a national health system in 1971, the Canadian government has used tax funds to pay for universal medical coverage, and sets the costs of medical services through negotiations with health care providers. Every citizen is guaranteed access to needed medical treatment.

Both systems have their advocates and their critics. The American health care system boasts many of the finest doctors and hospitals in the world, and the most advanced medical technology. As in other industries, the profit motive has been a spur to innovation. For those who are able to afford it, the best of American health care is the best available anywhere, and patients travel from all over the world to have complicated medical procedures performed by American doctors in American facilities. But for many Americans, access to basic medical care is unavailable. In 2006, there were about 47 million Americans who lacked health insurance.

Critics of the Canadian system point to delays in receiving specialized treatments, reduced availability of the most advanced technologies, and the rationing of certain expensive procedures, such as organ transplantation. They also warn that government involvement leads to greater inefficiency and bureaucratic red tape. They argue that the American health care system provides excellent care for a majority of those who need it.

It should. Per capita health care spending in the United States is nearly twice that of any other country. In 1997, Americans spent an average of $4,090 per person for health care, compared with $2,090 in Canada. But, according to a 2000 study by the Commonwealth Fund, 25 percent of Americans reported that they have difficulty getting health care when it is needed, compared with 21 percent of Canadians.

In 2000, the World Health Organization evaluated the health care systems of 191 nations. Canada was ranked 30th in the world. The American system was ranked 37th, positioned between Costa Rica and Slovenia.

—The Commonwealth Fund, "Multinational Comparisons of Health Care Expenditures, Coverage, and Outcomes," October 1998, online at <http://www.cmwf.org>; and "Despite Big Spending, U.S. Ranks 37th in Study of Global Health Care," *Los Angeles Times,* June 21, 2000

Economic difficulties in the early 1990s compounded the problem, forcing many states—even large states like California—to make deep cuts in their education budgets. Across the nation, teachers were often underpaid, their status not equal to that of other important professions. Political candidates vied with one another in offering solutions to the challenge.

When George W. Bush ran for president in 2000, he promised he would insist on strict performance standards for the nation's public schools. With his backing, Congress in 2002 passed the No Child Left Behind Act, designed to ensure that all students were proficient in reading and math within a decade and a half.

The law immediately proved controversial. It required the states to give reading and math tests to students in the third to eighth grades and provided some federal funds for tutoring students in schools designated as "failing." Many states, however, contended that the law's stringent requirements for standardized tests would place unfair financial burdens on the states and would label schools as failing even if only a small group of students performed poorly. Critics charged that the No Child Left Behind law was drastically underfunded, and its title ironic and misleading.

As the debate over the law illustrated, education remained a volatile political issue. In 2004, more than 69.7 million students were enrolled in the nation's schools and colleges. Of the total, 15.9 million were in colleges, 15.7 million in high schools, and 38.1 million in elementary schools and kindergartens.[49]

In fiscal 2005 the federal government budgeted a total of $63.9 billion for various kinds of direct aid to education. (See Table 18-3.) This aid was channeled in two ways: to educational institutions and to individuals.

As far back as 1862, Congress had passed the Morrill Act to establish "land-grant" colleges. And millions of veterans of the Second World War went to college under the federally financed GI Bill of Rights. In 1958, the year after the Soviet Union launched its Sputnik earth satellite, Congress enacted the National Defense Education Act to provide loans for college students in the fields of science, engineering, mathematics, and foreign languages. In 1963 Congress began appropriating funds for the construction of college classrooms.

Not until 1965, however, did Congress pass a law providing for general federal aid to education. In that year, the high-water mark of President Johnson's "Great Society," it enacted the Elementary and Secondary Edu-

## TABLE 18-3

**Federal Outlays for Education, 1968–2005 (in billions of dollars)**

| | 1968 | 1976 | 1979 | 1985 | 1989 | 1993 | 1998 | 2001 | 2005 |
|---|---|---|---|---|---|---|---|---|---|
| Elementary and secondary education | 3.2 | 4.7 | 5.9 | 6.2 | 9.8 | 12.6 | 14.9 | 17.2 | 37.8 |
| Higher education | 4.4 | 2.6 | 4.5 | 7.2 | 9.6 | 14.1 | 15.9 | 17.9 | 23.1 |
| Adult and other education | 1.2 | 0.8 | 2.0 | 2.1 | 1.4 | 1.2 | 1.5 | 1.8 | 3.1 |
| Total | $8.8 | $8.1 | $12.4 | $15.5 | $20.8 | $27.9 | $32.3 | $36.9 | $63.9 |

SOURCE: Adapted from *Budget of the United States Government,* for fiscal years 1968–2005, table 3.2.

cation Act and the Higher Education Act. Until 1965 the church-state controversy had blocked passage of a general aid to education bill. (See the discussion of the establishment clause in Chapter 4.) The Elementary and Secondary Education Act bypassed that dispute by providing aid to children in both public and private (including religious-affiliated) schools on the basis of economic need. The bulk of the money was concentrated in urban and rural areas with a high percentage of children from poor families. Under the law, the federal government also provided general purpose grants, plus money for textbooks, library books, special programs for handicapped children, and teacher training.

The Higher Education Act of 1965 for the first time provided federal money for undergraduates. These were later named Pell grants for their sponsor, Senator Claiborne Pell, Democrat of Rhode Island. The law also provided federally insured loans for college students, federal subsidies to pay the interest on student loans from private lenders, and a work-study program to help the colleges pay the wages of students with part-time jobs obtained through the schools.

The same law channeled money to colleges to buy library books and created a program of fellowships for graduate students. It also established a Teacher Corps in which future teachers who received federal aid while studying agreed, after graduating, to teach in schools in inner cities and poor rural areas.

For fiscal year 2005, the government budgeted more

© Bob Daemmrich

"Continuing problems in the nation's public schools . . .": An overcrowded first-grade classroom in Texas than $60 billion to assist 10 million college undergraduate and graduate students.

But federal spending has failed to avert continuing problems in the nation's public schools. The quality of education in many big-city public school systems has deteriorated. As large numbers of middle-class residents have moved to the suburbs, big cities have found their tax dollars dwindling; one result is that schools are often poorest where their services are needed most—in low-income, inner-city communities.

In 1979 Congress created a new Department of Education at the cabinet level. The department was given responsibility for the entire federal educational effort, and absorbed the education branches of the old Department of Health, Education, and Welfare, as well as units concerned with education in several other government departments.

Ronald Reagan, the California Republican who was elected president in 1980, opposed the new department, and during the campaign he called for its abolition. However, as president, Reagan in 1981 appointed a secretary of education to his cabinet, and the department survived his presidency. Later efforts by Republicans in Congress to abolish the Department of Education failed.*

The Supreme Court, as discussed in Chapter 4, has upheld the use of public money for school vouchers to send children to religious and other private schools. The decision approved the voucher program in Cleveland. Critics worried that vouchers would drain needed funds from the public school system; some opponents argued that vouchers used to send children to religious schools violated the constitutional separation of church and state.

In 2004 Washington, D.C., began the nation's first federally funded school voucher program. More than 1,000 students from low-income families that participated in the $12.5 million experimental program received as much as $7,500 to pay tuition and fees at private schools.[50]

## Science

In an age of science and technology some people have come to feel that, more and more, decisions affecting their lives are being made not by elected political leaders, but by "faceless technocrats in long, white coats."[51]

Should American astronauts try to land on Mars? Should a new weapons system, such as a scaled-down version of the Strategic Defense Initiative, or "Star Wars," be developed? What should government medical researchers be doing about AIDS? Should they be allowed to use federal funds to expand stem cell research, which might lead to cures for some diseases? For the answers to such questions, the president may turn to scientists. Government today has become far too complicated for political leaders to know all the scientific data they need to make policy decisions.

*A cabinet department can be abolished only by Congress, and not solely by a president.

The federal government spends billions of dollars every year on scientific research and development. In fiscal 2005, more than $124 billion was budgeted for this purpose. Of the total, more than $67 billion went to military programs. The National Aeronautics and Space Administration (NASA) accounted for $7.9 billion.[52]

Most of the government's basic research is conducted at colleges and universities. That in turn has raised questions about the relationship of science and government. For instance, what is the proper role of science within the political system? Some critics regard science as "something very close to an establishment . . . a set of institutions supported by tax funds, but largely on faith, and without direct responsibility to political control."[53] Another question is whether universities can accept government funds for research without restricting or losing their academic independence.

The president has a science adviser within the White House. The adviser heads the Office of Science and Technology Policy, which has broad responsibility for advising the president on scientific affairs. In addition, the National Science Foundation, a government agency established in 1950, supports basic and applied research.

In the years after 1957 the federal science effort in large part was geared to responding to Soviet space accomplishments, particularly the launching of Sputnik, the world's first earth satellite. American scientists were called on to solve scientific, military, and technological problems, and America soon surpassed the Soviet Union in outer space. In 1969 the Apollo 11 astronauts landed on the moon. In 1976 America's Viking robot spacecraft landed on Mars and transmitted photographs back to earth. And in 1980, Voyager 1 photographed the rings of Saturn, almost a billion miles away in outer space. In January 2004 NASA landed two rovers, Spirit and Opportunity, on the surface of Mars. The rovers touched down on opposite sides of the red planet that is 302.6 million miles away, and beamed back images in an effort to discover whether life once existed on Mars.

But there have been disasters as well, notably the explosion that sent the space shuttle *Challenger* plunging into the ocean shortly after launch in 1986, killing all seven people aboard; and the disaster that struck the space shuttle *Columbia* in 2003 when it broke up during reentry, killing all seven crew members.

The government has also funded a variety of scientific research projects. In 2000, scientists announced that the first stage of the Human Genome Project had been completed. The project was begun in 1990, with the goal of mapping the approximately 100,000 genes in the human genetic code. It would provide insights into genetic diseases and lay the groundwork for treatments based on genetic engineering.

Meanwhile, the growing ability to manipulate the genetic characteristics of plants and animals—including cloning—was raising concerns over possible unforeseen consequences. Consumer groups in the United States

"All the News That's Fit to Print"

The New York Times

EARLY EDITION

Sunday: Breezy, high 45. Sunday night, cloudy, low 34. Monday, cloudy, late shower possible, high 43. Weather map is on Page 38.

VOL. CLII . . . . No. 52,382 — NEW YORK, SUNDAY, FEBRUARY 2, 2003 — THREE DOLLARS

# SHUTTLE BREAKS UP, 7 DEAD

## COLUMBIA, WITH SIX AMERICANS AND ISRAELI, IS LOST OVER TEXAS AT START OF ITS DESCENT

### New Blow To a Nation

*War, Hard Times And Yet More Loss*

By TODD S. PURDUM

### 'Roger,' and Then Silence

By DAVID E. SANGER

WASHINGTON, Feb. 1 — The space shuttle Columbia broke up this morning on re-entry into the earth's atmosphere, killing all seven astronauts aboard and sending fiery debris over Texas in the second loss of a space shuttle in 17 years.

There was no immediate explanation of what caused the disintegration of the oldest shuttle in NASA's fleet. The disaster occurred roughly 40 miles above Earth as the shuttle slipped into the netherworld between outer space and the upper atmosphere, slowing to 12,500 miles an hour toward its destination, the Kennedy Space Center in Florida.

The Columbia crew appeared, from space, on television on Jan. 20. From left were David M. Brown, Ilan Ramon, Rick D. Husband, Kalpana Chawla, William C. McCool, Michael P. Anderson and Laurel Salton Clark. Yesterday, a firefighter inspected debris believed to be from the shuttle near Palestine, Tex.

Continued on Page 25

Continued on Page 34

### Mass of Data but No Clear Image As NASA Begins Hunt for Cause

By WILLIAM J. BROAD

Continued on Page 34

### A Diverse Crew, Four on Their First Space Mission

Profiles, Page 27.

IN OTHER NEWS

Plans for Iraq Air Assault

Powell Surprises Europe

Bush's Ambitious Budget

NEWS SUMMARY



protested against "Frankenfoods," and European nations threatened to prohibit the importation of bioengineered produce.

## Protecting the Environment

During the 1992 presidential campaign, the first President Bush, seeking votes in the timber country of the Pacific Northwest, took aim at the spotted owl in a speech in Colville, Washington. "It is time," Bush declared, "to make people more important than owls."[54]

Bush was well aware that preserving the old-growth forests that are the habitat of the spotted owl, an endangered species, had cost thousands of jobs in Oregon and Washington. Calling the owl "that little furry, feathery guy,"[55] Bush said he would not sign an extension of the Endangered Species Act unless it were changed to balance economic costs against wildlife protection. Although he had promised four years earlier to serve as the "environmental president," Bush calculated in 1992 that owls don't vote. But in appealing to the economic self-interest of workers in the Northwest, he risked the wrath of pro-environment voters, also an important constituency in the western states, and particularly in California.

The owl is about 2 feet tall and weighs 22 ounces, its chocolate-colored plumage marked with white spots. There are perhaps 2,000 pairs left. Officials of the Bush administration had estimated that saving the bird could cost 32,000 jobs in the Pacific Northwest.[56]

To try to resolve the controversy, the administration proposed that logging be allowed only on some acres of federal land in Oregon, action that would still cost thousands of timber jobs. Two years later, President Clinton established reserves for the spotted owl where very limited amounts of logging could take place.

Despite the fact that protecting the owl cost jobs in Oregon, the state's economy thrived in the 1990s. Over a five-year period, the state gained about 5,000 more jobs in high-technology industries than it lost in the mills.

As recently as the 1960s, words and phrases like "pollution," "the environment," and "energy crisis" were unfamiliar. Within a few years, however, Americans were acutely aware of the danger to the environment posed by technology. At the same time, they wanted to enjoy the benefits of that technology. Americans wanted clean air and water—but they were also aware that cars that met clean-air standards would cost more money. They were concerned about oil spills polluting their beaches—but they wanted plenty of gasoline for their automobiles at the lowest possible price. There was a conflict, in other words, between the environment and energy.

In the winter of 1973–1974 the nation found itself facing a major energy crisis. The president appointed an "energy czar" to allocate oil supplies; motorists waited in long lines to buy gas; speed limits were lowered; the federal government ordered cutbacks in deliveries of heat-

### The Polluted Land

Those of us who were born after 1900, or even after 1920, inherited a land that was generally pleasant, livable, and lovely to look at. To be sure, there were slums and tenements and soft coal soot, and quite a lot of mud mixed with the horse manure, but the quality of life, as measured in clean air, clean water, and verdant hills, was something to remember with wonder—and with dismay.

For the generations of this century have squandered that inheritance. Never was so great a trust so grossly violated. We turned our valleys into dust bowls and our rivers into sewers, killed the lakes, fouled the air, choked the cities. With the brute efficiency of systematic vandals, we combined stupidity and greed. Now we measure the quality of our life by the tons of litter we leave behind. The hallmark of our society is stamped on 10 million roadside bottles: No deposit, no return.

—James J. Kilpatrick, *Washington Star,* January 8, 1970

"I don't see why all the fuss over dioxin. . . . Shoot, it didn't even kill the chickens. . . ."



ing oil to homes and offices; and airlines laid off thousands of pilots, flight attendants, and other employees as a shortage of jet fuel forced the cancellation of many flights. Other industries that depended on oil were adversely affected as well. The immediate shortages were the result of a cutoff of oil shipments by the Arab states after the Arab-Israeli War in October 1973.

By the time of the energy crisis, Americans had begun to understand that humanity in the technological age was slowly destroying nature and the earth itself—and endangering its own survival. Scientists warned that economic growth combined with overpopulation might end in disaster for the world. In the United States, cities had become enveloped in smog, rivers clogged with human and industrial waste, seabirds and shorelines ravaged by oil spills and litter. Alarmed and concerned, many Americans became aware of the science of ecology, which deals with the relationship between living organisms and their environment.

The upsurge of interest in the quality of the natural environment was soon reflected in the political environment. Political leaders of both major parties scrambled to stake out a position. Public pressure for a cleanup led rapidly to major legislation. First, the Clean Air Act amendments of 1970 set federal air quality standards to control automobile and industrial pollution. Legislation to clean up the nation's waterways followed two years later. A new government unit, the Environmental Protection Agency (EPA), began operating in 1970.

***for more information about the Environmental Protection Agency, see: http://www.epa.gov***

Pollution is a result of industrialization and increased energy consumption, combined with population growth. In 1804, after 100,000 years of human history, the earth's population reached 1 billion. By 2004, just 200 years later, as a result of advances in life expectancy made during the industrial revolution, there were 6.4 billion people living on the planet.[57] Scientists worried that the rapidly expanding "population bomb" was putting unsustainable demands upon the air, water, and natural resources. The National Academy of Sciences and 57 other scientific organizations issued a warning that humankind was "approaching a crisis point" in population growth.[58]

As with most major national problems, progress toward restoring the environment requires cooperation by individuals, corporations, and institutions—but it also requires government action in the form of legislation and enforcement. When the Reagan administration came to power in 1981, environmentalists feared that protection of the environment would be given a lower priority than searching for new energy sources or reducing government regulation of industry.

As secretary of the interior Reagan appointed

*Making a Difference*

## SAVING THE REDWOODS: TWO YEARS IN A TREE

SACRAMENTO, CALIF.—When Julia Hill decided to leave Arkansas and travel the world, her reasons were simple enough. She was a mixed-up 23-year-old who had been dragged around America as a child by her father, a "preacher man," and then had been involved in a near-fatal car crash. Her plan was to follow the old hippie trail through the Far East in search of spiritual enlightenment.

In the end, Miss Hill only got as far as the Pacific Coast of Northern California. Without really planning to, she drifted into the ranks of environmental "guerrillas" determined to save the last remaining sequoias, or giant redwoods, the world's tallest and oldest trees, from commercial logging. She joined the cause, climbed into a tree—and stayed there.

For 738 days, her feet did not touch the ground. She lived on a plywood platform the size of a double bed, perched 180 feet high in the branches of one of the oldest trees of all, a "grandmother" that she named Luna, a 600-year-old redwood. Her supporters brought food and supplies to her every two days, hauled up by rope. She vowed that she would stay there until she won a promise that her tree would be saved.

Julia came down from Luna in December 1999, after she had reached an agreement with the Pacific Lumber Company. The company agreed to spare Luna along with other trees in 2.9 acres near Stafford, California. Julia also gets to visit with the 200-foot-tall Luna regularly with company permission. Also as part of the agreement, Hill and her supporters will pay the lumber company $50,000 for lost logging revenue. The company, in turn, will donate $50,000 to Humboldt State University for forestry studies. She had also picked up a "green" nom de guerre, and become Julia "Butterfly" Hill, all-time champion of the tree-hugging world and an international celebrity.

Now 25, she has—inevitably—secured a book deal and a huge advance payment for her story. Although she swears that everything was unplanned, she has unwittingly achieved the dream of her generation: instant fame and fortune. However, as part of the agreement, HarperCollins, the publisher for her book, *The Legacy of Luna,* agreed to print it on special paper—30 percent recycled and 70 percent pulped from wood produced by a forestry group in Canada that employs American Indian loggers and specializes in preserving natural biodiversity.

"I was not about to use a forest just to make this book," she says.

—Adapted from *USA Today,* December 20, 1999; and the *Washington Times,* February 4, 2000

James G. Watt, a conservative lawyer from Wyoming who had fought for business against environmentalists. Watt was eventually forced to resign from the cabinet because of indiscreet remarks he made about minorities and the disabled. Several months earlier, the EPA became entangled in scandal over the government's handling of toxic wastes. After many years of concern over toxic waste dumps, especially the contamination of Love Canal near Buffalo, New York, Congress in 1980 had created a $1.6 billion "superfund" to clean up such sites. The dangers of hazardous industrial waste were underscored again in 1983 when residents of the entire town of Times Beach, Missouri, had to be moved because of deadly dioxin contamination.

The dollar cost of a cleaner environment and counterpressures for development of energy sources created many conflicts. Nevertheless, the environmental movement became firmly rooted in only a few years, with some visible results. In 1971, for example, Congress canceled plans to build an American supersonic jet transport (SST) in part because of the danger that the plane's exhaust would deplete the ozone layer in the stratosphere. The ozone layer filters out ultraviolet sunlight, and some studies concluded that because damage to the ozone layer would expose more people to ultraviolet radiation, the SST exhaust might lead to an increase in skin cancer in human beings.

Americans became much more aware of the need to preserve the environment, and some tried to do something about it in their daily lives. For example, many people voluntarily separated their trash for recycling, and in a number of cities the law began requiring it.

With the competing pressures in American society, environmentalists will inevitably lose many battles. Energy needs will often prevail over environmental concerns. Nevertheless, the political power of the environmental supporters is tangible. Millions of people belong to an estimated 2,000 to 3,000 environmental organizations across the country. Public interest in the environment has been followed by legislation and expansion of the government's role as environmental regulator. Clean air, clean water, land use, and other similar issues are significant factors in political campaigns.

However, critics complained about the effects of environmental laws. Many businesses and industries chafed under antipollution regulations. When the Republicans won both houses of Congress in 1994, they were determined at first to roll back many environmental laws.

Congress suspended the law protecting endangered species for more than a year. In the spring of 1996, the Endangered Species Act went back into effect when Congress and President Clinton reached an agreement on spending. The federal government then complied with a court order and granted protection under the act to the California red-legged frog.[59]

By the late 1990s, some Republicans worried that a backlash had developed among voters against policies that weakened environmental laws. As a result, the Republicans began to pull back from their efforts to overturn or weaken environmental legislation.

**The Environmental Protection Agency** The environment is a major arena of conflict, with competing interest groups clashing over policy. The EPA was established in 1970 as an independent unit of the executive branch. The creation of the EPA pulled together under one roof various regulatory powers that had been scattered through a dozen bureaus and agencies. The EPA's administrator is often called on to make hard and controversial decisions—whether to grant the auto industry more time to manufacture cars with cleaner engines, for example.

In past years Congress has passed major legislation dealing with the environment. The laws have dealt with clean air, clean water, and endangered species.

**Air Pollution** The Clean Air Act amendments of 1970 set strict federal air quality standards governing major forms of pollution by industry, including automobile emissions. The law provides heavy fines for violators. Under the 1970 act, auto manufacturers were required by 1975 to reduce by 90 percent the levels of carbon monoxide, hydrocarbons, and nitrogen oxides in engine exhaust. When the big auto companies in Detroit claimed they needed more time to comply, Congress and the administrator of the EPA granted extensions. The act also required cities to meet national clean-air standards by 1982. These deadlines were also moved forward after many cities failed to meet the initial target dates.

In 1990, Congress passed major revisions to the Clean Air Act. The law was designed gradually to phase out the use of chlorofluorocarbons and the chemicals used in aerosol sprays that deplete the ozone layer, and to reduce automobile emissions. It also set new rules to reduce urban smog, to curb the chemicals that produce acid rain, and to regulate toxic pollutants.

By the mid-1990s alarm over the depletion of the ozone layer had subsided somewhat. In Montreal, Canada, in 1987, 23 nations had signed an agreement to phase out the use of ozone-destroying chemicals. In the years following this pact, researchers concluded from test results that the amount of these chemicals in the atmosphere had declined. Although some scientists predicted that beginning in 2000 the ozone layer would begin to improve and eventually recover, NASA satellites reported that the hole in the ozone layer had reached a record size, larger than North America, in 2003. By 2004, however, the hole appeared to have shrunk by 20 percent.[60]

Air pollution is a global, not merely a national, problem. For example, acid rain is an increasing concern that has caused friction between the United States and Canada, which has complained that sulfur dioxide and nitrogen oxides from U.S. factories cause acid rain that destroys lakes, forests, and fish and other wildlife in Canada. Acid rain knows no geographic boundaries, and similar damage has been caused by this form of pollution in the United States. In 1988 the United States joined with 23 other nations in signing a treaty aimed at controlling acid rain.

There was widespread agreement among scientists that gases—such as carbon dioxide—that are emitted in the burning of fossil fuels were producing a "greenhouse effect," trapping heat in the atmosphere. In 2000, an international panel of scientists warned that global warming would raise the temperature of the Earth's surface by 2 to 9 degrees in the next 100 years.[61] By comparison, the world has warmed an estimated 5 to 9 degrees since the peak of the last ice age.[62] The rising temperature is expected to have major consequences for the global environment, including melting the polar icecaps, raising the sea level, causing coastal flooding and erosion, reducing soil moisture, and causing deforestation.[63]

In 1992, at the first Earth Summit, the United States joined with 106 other countries in signing the Climate Change Treaty, which established nonbinding targets for reducing emissions. In Japan in 1997, 160 nations drafted the Kyoto Protocol, an international agreement that set specific targets to reduce emissions of six greenhouse gases that cause global warming. The target for the United States was a 7 percent reduction from 1990 levels by the year 2012. The United States during the Clinton administration signed the treaty, although the Senate did not ratify it. But in 2001, President George W. Bush abandoned the Kyoto Protocol on the grounds that many heavily populated developing nations such as India and China would not be bound by its terms. Bush also argued that the cost of reducing emissions would cause serious damage to the U.S. economy. Many nations criticized the United States, which produces about one-fifth of the world's greenhouse gases, for rejecting the Kyoto Protocol.

**Water Pollution** On March 24, 1989, the 987-foot supertanker Exxon *Valdez* ran aground on a reef 25 miles south of Valdez, Alaska, spilling nearly 11 million gallons of crude oil into Prince William Sound. It was the largest oil spill from a tanker in U.S. history, and it had a devastating effect on fish, birds, and other wildlife, and on the beaches of Alaska. The spill also caused great hardship among those who lived in the area, especially the Alaska Natives and others who fished the sea or depended on its bounty for their livelihood. Exxon spent $2.5 billion to clean up the spill. Two years later, the company paid $1.1 billion as part of a plea bargain in which federal criminal and state charges were dropped. In 1994, a federal jury ordered Exxon to pay $5 billion in punitive damages to 14,000 commercial fishers, Alaska Natives, businesses, and landowners who had sued the oil giant over the oil spill.

The Exxon *Valdez* episode was only the most dra-

matic example of a larger problem that had begun to cause concern some two decades earlier. By the start of the 1970s, all across America, rivers, lakes, and streams were getting dirtier. Cities and towns were dumping their waste into rivers. Industrial plants pumped chemical wastes and toxic compounds into once-clear waters. The result: fouled drinking water, polluted beaches unfit for swimming, dead fish, and algae-clogged streams.

Congress responded by passing the Water Pollution Control Act of 1972, which had as its goal the complete elimination of discharges of pollutants into the nation's waterways by 1985. The law allotted $18 billion to the

April 1989: cleaning up the Exxon Valdez oil spill

Rina Castelnuovo/The New York Times

states to build the waste treatment plants they needed to clean up the water. Within five years pollution began to diminish in at least some of the nation's waterways. According to one federal report, of 12 major rivers studied, five—including the Colorado and the Ohio—showed significant reductions in bacterial counts.[64]

Oil spills from drilling rigs or tankers like the Exxon *Valdez* are also a major form of pollution that has fouled the nation's beaches and endangered wildlife. There have been several other major oil spills, such as those off Santa Barbara, California, in 1969; near Nantucket, Massachusetts, in 1976; and in the Gulf of Mexico in 1979. In the summer of 1988 many East Coast beaches were closed because of a new type of pollution—syringes, blood bags, and other forms of medical waste dumped by hospitals and laboratories.

**Environmental Impact and Endangered Species** The National Environmental Policy Act of 1969 required the government to assess the impact on the environment of all new projects involving the federal government. The provision is important because it has since been adopted by many states and communities; in addition, it has provided the basis for environmental lawsuits. The 1969 act also established a three-member Council on Environmental Quality to advise the president, and required the president to submit an annual "state of the environment" report to Congress.

The Endangered Species Act was passed by Congress in 1973 to protect wildlife and plants that might otherwise vanish forever from the earth. The law helped to save the American bald eagle, the national symbol, and more than 700 other species.[65] But long before the northern spotted owl became a presidential campaign issue, the law proved controversial.

The battle over the tiny snail darter, a rare fish in the Little Tennessee River, is a case in point. In 1973 David Etnier, a University of Tennessee zoologist, discovered the 3-inch fish in an area where the Tennessee Valley Authority (TVA) planned to build the Tellico Dam. The fish was placed on a list under the Endangered Species Act, entitling it to protection from actions of the government. Opponents of the dam took their case to the U.S. Supreme Court and won a ruling in 1978 requiring the TVA to halt the project.[66] A special board created by Congress studied the problem and also sided with the fish. But in 1979 Congress voted to finish construction of the dam and also voted to allow exemptions to the Endangered Species Act in the future. Reluctantly, President Carter signed the bill. The snail darter had lost.

But the story had a happy ending after all. In 1976, some 710 snail darters had been transplanted to a tributary of the Little Tennessee, 10 miles downstream from the dam, and the species thrived there. In 1980, 14 baby snail darters were unexpectedly discovered 80 miles below the dam in the South Chickamauga Creek. And in July 1984, the tiny fish was removed from the endangered species list.

**Energy Policy** A few minutes after 4 p.m. on August 14, 2003, New York City and parts of eight states in the Northeast and Midwest suddenly suffered a massive power blackout. In New York City, the power failure on a stiflingly hot day cut off lights, air conditioning, and computers and brought subways to a halt. It forced the evacuation of office buildings, trapped people in elevators, and stranded thousands of commuters. Planes were grounded as the city's three major airports shut down.

Some states and part of Ontario, Canada, were without power for as long as four days. The estimated cost of the blackout ranged as high as $10 billion.

The blackout had begun when generators of FirstEnergy Corporation, one of the nation's largest utilities, tripped in central Ohio when electric transmission lines came in contact with trees. The failure touched off a cascading series of power outages that spread rapidly eastward. The huge blackout underscored the fact that the nation's power grid was antiquated, fragile, and unable to keep up with demand.

"We are a major superpower with a third-world electrical grid," said Bill Richardson, New Mexico's governor and a former secretary of energy. The nation's power grid, he said, "needs serious modernization."[67]

Nuclear power is one alternative energy source. Even before the 1990s, however, the nuclear power industry in America was in serious trouble. Five plants, including Seabrook in New Hampshire and another in Midland, Michigan, had shut down in one two-month

## Breathing Coal Dust: The Government Bows to Industry

WASHINGTON—In 1997, as a top executive of a Utah mining company, David Lauriski proposed a measure that could allow some operators to let coal-dust levels rise substantially in mines. The plan went nowhere in the government.

Last year, it found enthusiastic backing from one government official—Mr. Lauriski himself. Now head of the Mine Safety and Health Administration, he revived the proposal despite objections by union officials and health experts that it could put miners at greater risk of black-lung disease.

The reintroduction of the coal dust measure came after the federal agency had abandoned a series of Clinton-era safety proposals favored by coal miners while embracing others favored by mine owners.

The agency's effort to rewrite coal regulations is part of a broader push by the Bush administration to help an industry that had been out of favor in Washington. As a candidate four years ago, Mr. Bush promised to expand energy supplies, in part by reviving coal's fortunes, particularly in Appalachia, where coal regions will also help decide how swing states like West Virginia, Pennsylvania and Ohio vote this year.

The president has also made good on a 2000 campaign pledge to ease environmental restrictions that industry officials said were threatening jobs in coal country. That promise led many West Virginia miners, who traditionally voted Democratic, to join coal operators in supporting Mr. Bush. It helped him win the state's five electoral votes, ultimately the margin of victory. . . .

In all, the mine safety agency has rescinded more than a half-dozen proposals intended to make coal miners' jobs safer, including steps to limit miners' exposure to toxic chemicals. . . .

Mr. Lauriski said the coal dust measure would improve miners' health by encouraging the use of equipment to limit how much dust miners breathe.

—From "Rewriting Coal Policy: Friends in the White House," by Christopher Drew, Richard A. Oppel, Jr., and Claire Hoffman, *New York Times,* August 9, 2004, p. A1. Copyright © 2004 by The New York Times Co. Reprinted with permission.

period because of excessive cost or safety reasons. Orders for about 100 other reactors had been canceled, representing a loss of billions of dollars, and there had been no orders for new nuclear plants since 1978.

A combination of skyrocketing costs and public opposition because of accidents, such as that in 1979 at the Three Mile Island nuclear power plant in Pennsylvania, had turned many of the nuclear construction projects into financial disasters. The problems besetting the nuclear power industry meant higher prices for consumers, but beyond that, disappointment for those who hoped that nuclear power would solve the nation's future energy needs.

Groups such as the Clamshell Alliance and other foes of nuclear power did not win every round, however: In 1984, after massive and prolonged protests, the Nuclear Regulatory Commission gave the Diablo Canyon nuclear plant near San Luis Obispo, California, permission to open. All told, there were 102 nuclear plants in operation in the United States in 2004, producing 20 percent of the nation's electricity. Nuclear plants have become the most important source of electric power after coal.

But the public continued to fear the release of deadly radiation in the event of an accident or a terrorist attack on a nuclear power plant. The Nuclear Regulatory Commission conceded in 1982 that 100,000 people could be killed in a worst-case accident at the Salem plant in New Jersey, assuming a total meltdown of the nuclear core and adverse weather conditions.[68]

Concerns about nuclear power did not pose the only problems for the nation's energy policy. In the summer of 2006, gasoline prices rose for a while to more than $3 a gallon; even Americans who normally paid little attention to foreign policy were aware that their ability to take the family out for a Sunday drive or to work in a job requiring a long commute by car might depend on what happened 6,000 miles away in the Persian Gulf. America's dependence on foreign oil from the Middle East was never more apparent than in 1991 when the United States went to war against Iraq's Saddam Hussein, who had seized Kuwait and was then in a position to threaten Saudi Arabia and its vast oilfields.

For the ordinary citizen, energy shortages were difficult to understand. Some argued that there had been no shortage at all in the 1970s—that gas lines and the crisis were artificial, created by the actions of "Big Oil." Many Americans were reluctant to adjust their affluent

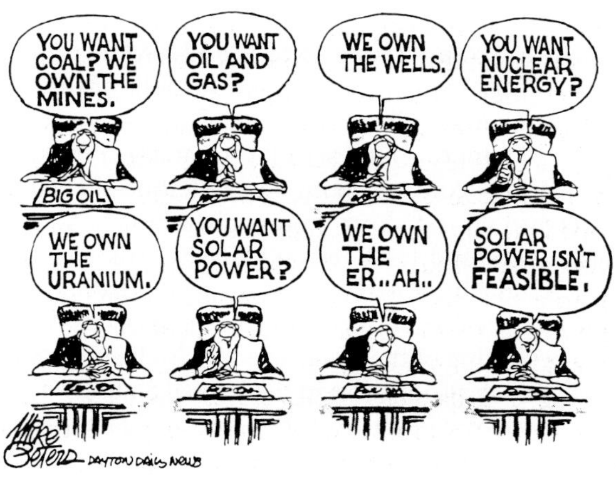

lifestyles to energy needs—to commute to work in car pools or turn down their thermostats in winter.

Some of the basic facts were not all that complicated, however. The United States has abundant petroleum deposits in Texas, Louisiana, Oklahoma, California, and Alaska and offshore in the oceans and the Gulf of Mexico. Before the Second World War, domestic fields supplied about 95 percent of the oil used in this country. By 2004, however, the United States was using more than 20 million barrels of oil a day, and domestic sources were providing only 50 percent of the total. The other 50 percent was imported, about half of that amount from the nations included in the Organization of the Petroleum Exporting Countries (OPEC) in the Middle East. Although the United States had only 4.6 percent of the world's population, it was consuming almost 24 percent of the world's energy.[69]

The dependence on foreign oil created problems at home. Rising fuel prices contributed to inflation. In October 2004, crude oil prices topped $50 a barrel for the first time, and gasoline prices at the pump began rising. By the summer of 2006, oil was selling for a time at more than $70 a barrel. The billions of dollars paid annually to import oil accounted for a substantial share of U.S. trade and balance-of-payments deficits. In Iraq, oil pipelines were bombed and sabotaged by insurgents opposed to the U.S. occupation. Energy problems were directly linked to the nation's foreign policy, as the war in the Persian Gulf in 1991 and the war in Iraq illustrated. The wars were a dramatic reminder that events in the Middle East could quickly endanger the flow of oil to the rest of the world. And escalating oil prices attested to the influence of OPEC on the American economy.

Over the years, the federal government and Congress attempted to deal with the energy problem. In 1977 President Carter asked for and got a new cabinet-level Department of Energy. The creation by Congress of the new department underscored the importance of the energy issue and its continuing impact on the political system and the lives of individual Americans.

***for more information about the Department of Energy, see: http://www.doe.gov***

## Three Mile Island: The Worst Fear

Pennsylvania Gov. Richard L. Thornburgh, in unusually forceful testimony, told the Nuclear Regulatory Commission yesterday that the health and safety of people living around the crippled Three Mile Island nuclear reactor will be at risk if the NRC allows a twin reactor on the island to resume operation.

The statement from Thornburgh, a Republican who was in office when the nation's worst commercial nuclear power accident occurred more than five years ago, intensified one of the most emotional nuclear-power debates—whether the NRC should restore the license of the undamaged reactor on Three Mile Island.

"I was there when the worst fear of modern man almost came to pass in central Pennsylvania," Thornburgh said. . . . "I saw anger and confusion on the faces of good and innocent people who realized, for the first time, that there was something out there powerful and strange and not entirely under control."

—From "Restarting the TMI Reactor," by Dale Russakoff, *Washington Post,* August 16, 1984, p. A2. Copyright © 1984, The Washington Post Writers Group.

**Nuclear Power: Three Mile Island** March 28, 1979, was a routine night in the control room of the nuclear power plant on Three Mile Island in the Susquehanna River, 11 miles southeast of Harrisburg, Pennsylvania. Inside the control room, a horseshoe-shaped panel stretched 40 feet along three walls. It was lined with dials, gauges, and 1,200 red and green warning lights.

Suddenly, at 4 a.m., a Klaxon sounded. A voice on the loudspeaker intoned: "Turbine trip in Unit 2." It was the beginning of the worst accident in the history of nuclear power production in the United States.

A valve had failed in the nuclear reactor's cooling system, and the nuclear core of the reactor was rapidly overheating, raising the possibility of a meltdown. If that happened, the nuclear core would burn through steel and concrete walls and would release lethal levels of radioactivity into the atmosphere. What opponents of nuclear power had always warned against—a nuclear disaster in a populated urban area—seemed close at hand.

The governor of Pennsylvania closed nearby schools and advised pregnant women and preschool children within 5 miles of the site to leave and people within 10 miles to stay indoors. An evacuation of up to 300,000 people was planned but not ordered. Many residents left on their own.

It took technicians and government experts seven days to bring the danger under control. Although the feared meltdown did not take place, some radiation was released. There were no reported injuries to the public, but the incident sowed fear and confusion among residents of the area and alerted millions of Americans to the dangers of nuclear power. A presidential commission studied the accident and recommended that new nuclear plants be built in areas remote from population centers.

Despite the dangers dramatized by the accident at Three Mile Island, advocates of nuclear power argued that nuclear plants were an important element in the nation's energy supply. Opponents maintained that the disaster averted at Three Mile Island would surely come, sooner or later.

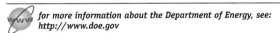

In 1986, it did. The meltdown of a reactor in a Soviet nuclear plant at Chernobyl, near Kiev, released high levels of radiation into the air. At least 23 people were killed, hundreds were hospitalized, and 40,000 were evacuated from the area. European nations banned the import of food from eastern Europe for fear of contamination. It was the worst nuclear power disaster in history.

By the end of the 20th century, the nuclear power industry was facing another challenge: a growing problem in disposing of its nuclear waste. With insufficient disposal facilities for the hazardous waste produced by nuclear power plants, by 2002 there were 45,000 tons of spent nuclear fuel—which remains radioactive for 10,000 years—stored in temporary containers on the grounds of the nation's nuclear plants.[70]

## Can Government Meet the Challenge?

This discussion of government in operation has examined a number of crucial areas in which government—and therefore American society—has attempted to solve urgent social and economic problems. The results have been mixed.

In some policy areas, the government has had only limited success. Economic stability has been endangered by soaring budget deficits, even as Congress and the president struggled to control them. Government has been slow to develop new and alternative sources of energy to meet the nation's future needs. In many cases, regulatory agencies have served corporate interests and have failed to protect the public. In America's free enterprise economy, it has not always been clear whether government has the will or the power to regulate industry on behalf of consumers.

In the field of social welfare, the federal government has promised much and delivered less. President Johnson declared his "war on poverty" in 1964, but more than three decades later more then 35 million Americans were still poor. The public assistance program helped millions of people, but it had also been widely criticized. As a result, the 1996 federal law reshaping the welfare program shifted much of the burden to the states.

Despite government programs, in the early 21st century there remained a wide gap between rich and poor in the United States, and the number of people living in poverty continued to increase steadily. Indeed, Benjamin I. Page, a political scientist, concluded that government welfare programs do little to redistribute wealth and have been largely offset by other government policies that favor the rich: "After all government actions are taken into account . . . after New Deals and Fair Deals and Wars on Poverty, the incomes of Americans remain very unequal. The welfare state may help establish a minimum level of existence for its citizens, but . . . it does not produce a substantial degree of equality."[71]

On the other hand, Congress has continued to fund a wide variety of programs to assist the people it represents. Environmental legislation and the creation of new federal agencies dealing with the environment are an example of government responding to public demands and societal needs. And the Social Security program provides benefits to nearly 49 million Americans.

Achieving desirable social and economic ends requires money, however, and not all Americans want to or can afford to pay the price in higher taxes. How to deal with the complex social and economic problems confronting America is by no means clear. Not every problem may have an answer. But effective programs at any level of government—whether national, state, or local—may mean hard choices, high taxes, and other sacrifices. Better public schools, for example, require money for more teachers and classrooms, as well as higher standards. In the area of social policy, the real question facing Americans today is whether they are willing to pay the costs of "promoting the general welfare" and attempting to build a better society.

## CHAPTER HIGHLIGHTS

- To "promote the general welfare," the federal government fills several major roles. It is regulator, promoter, manager, and protector.
- For half a century, from the late 1880s until 1937, the Supreme Court generally interpreted the Constitution in such a way as to prevent government from regulating industry. It adopted the prevailing laissez-faire philosophy, which held that government should intervene as little as possible in economic affairs.
- Although government regulation has had some success at blocking monopoly, the control of a market by a single company, it has not been able to prevent oligopoly, the concentration of economic power in the hands of a relatively few large companies.
- As in the case of business, labor is both regulated and helped by the federal government. Today organized labor wields great economic and political power in the United States.
- The power gained by labor during the New Deal inevitably brought a political reaction. The National Labor Relations Act had placed restrictions on employers but none on unions. In 1947 Congress passed the Taft-Hartley Act. The act prohibited the closed shop, but it did permit the union shop. Under Section 14B of the Taft-Hartley Act, 21 states passed state right to work laws to outlaw the union shop.
- The Social Security Act of 1935 and its later amendments provide for both social insurance and

public assistance programs. The insurance aspects fall into four categories: old-age and survivors insurance, disability insurance, Medicare, and unemployment insurance.

- When people talk about receiving Social Security, they generally mean the monthly cash payments received by retired, older people through a compulsory national insurance program financed by taxes on employers and employees.
- Social Security is the largest of the various federal entitlement programs, which are programs mandated by law and not subject to annual review by Congress or the president.
- In 1965 Congress created Medicare, a federal program of health insurance to provide hospital and medical services to people aged 65 and older through the Social Security system. A prescription drug benefit was added to the program and went fully into effect in 2006.
- Medicaid, also established in 1965, is a public assistance program created to help pay hospital, doctor, and medical bills for people with low incomes. It is financed through general federal, state, and local taxes.
- Public concern over environmental pollution in the 1970s led to the passage of laws to try to bring about clean air and water.
- The Environmental Protection Agency (EPA) was established in 1970 as an independent unit of the executive branch. The creation of the EPA pulled together under one roof various regulatory powers that had been scattered through a dozen bureaus and agencies.

## KEY TERMS

laissez-faire, p. 616
monopoly, p. 617
oligopoly, p. 617
conglomerates, p. 617
closed shop, p. 620
union shop, p. 620
right to work laws, p. 620
Social Security, p. 626
entitlement programs, p. 627
Medicare, p. 627
Medicaid, p. 632

## SUGGESTED WEBSITES

**http://www.census.gov/**
*The Census Bureau*
The official website of the U.S. Census Bureau provides access to current national- and state-level demographic data.

**http://www.movingideas.org/**
*Electronic Policy Network*
The website of the Electronic Policy Network is a useful source of information on a broad range of public policy issues.

**http://www.lcweb.loc.gov/global/executive/fed.html**
*Official U.S. Executive Branch Websites*
A service of the Library of Congress, this site provides a comprehensive listing of the websites of federal executive branch departments and agencies, with links to each.

**http://www.secondharvest.org/**
*Second Harvest*
Second Harvest is the largest hunger-relief organization in the United States. Their website provides access to news stories about hunger and related issues, as well as links and other information to assist individuals who want to become involved in efforts to alleviate hunger.

**http://www.ssa.gov/**
*Social Security Administration*
The official website of the Social Security Administration contains useful information related to Social Security, including the most recent trustees' reports.

**http://www.urban.org/**
*The Urban Institute*
The Urban Institute is a policy research organization concerned with social and economic issues.

## SUGGESTED READING

Benedick, Richard Elliot. *Ozone Diplomacy: New Directions in Safeguarding the Planet** (Harvard University Press, 1998). A revealing account, written by a leading U.S. negotiator, of the delicate politics of an important global environmental treaty.

Browning, Robert X. *Politics and Social Welfare Policy in the United States** (University of Tennessee Press, 1986). A detailed analysis of the development of the federal government's social-welfare programs since the 1940s. Emphasizes the effects that various economic and political factors have had on the growth of these programs.

Bryner, Gary C. *Politics and Public Morality: The Great American Welfare Reform Debate** (Norton, 1998). A useful examination of the politics of welfare reform in the 1990s.

Derthick, Martha. *Policymaking for Social Security** (The Brookings Institution, 1979). A comprehensive study of policymaking for Social Security. Examines the basic policies that have shaped the program, the small group of people who influence decisions, and the future of the Social Security system.

Dubos, René. *Reason Awake: Science for Man* (Columbia University Press, 1970). A collection of essays by a distinguished microbiologist focusing on the threat to people and the environment caused by the technological and population explosions. Analyzes a range of problems—from nuclear weapons

to urban sprawl—that have resulted from a constantly expanding technology.
Dye, Thomas R. *Understanding Public Policy,* 11th edition* (Prentice Hall, 2004). A comprehensive analysis of public policy and how it is made.
Goldberg, Gertrude S., and Collins Sheila D. *Washington's New Poor Law: Welfare Reform and the Roads Not Taken, 1935 to the Present** (Apex Press, 2001) An analysis of welfare programs throughout American history, stressing that Americans' attitudes toward welfare recipients are ambivalent. The book covers the years 1935 to 2001, and concentrates on the welfare reform law of 1996.
Gore, Albert. *Earth in the Balance,* 2nd revision (Rodale Press, 2006). A passionate polemic about mankind's effects on the environment by the Democratic nominee for president in 2000. Gore makes several specific recommendations for policy reforms, including the gradual elimination of the internal-combustion engine.
Hacker, Jacob S. *The Divided Welfare State: The Battle Over Public and Private Social Benefits in the United States** (Cambridge University Press, 2002) In the United States, welfare policy is composed of government programs and, unlike the situation in other liberal democracies, policies that encourage private systems of support. The authors discuss the development of pensions and health insurance in both the private and public sectors.
Harrington, Michael. *The Other America** (Scribner reprint edition, 1997). (Originally published in 1962.) One of the most widely read introductory surveys of the nature and extent of poverty in the United States in the early 1960s.
Johnson, Haynes, and Broder, David S. *The System: The American Way of Politics at the Breaking Point** (Little, Brown, 1997). A revealing analysis of the failed effort to enact major new health care legislation in the 1993–1994 congressional session. The authors, each a Pulitzer Prize–winning political reporter, conducted extensive interviews with both supporters and opponents of President Clinton's health care proposals.
Light, Paul C. *Government's Greatest Achievements: From Civil Rights to Homeland Defense** (Brookings Institution, 2002). A survey of historians and political scientists that cites successes in the government's efforts to promote the general welfare: reducing disease, ensuring safe food and drinking water, increasing access to health care for older Americans, and improving water and air quality.
Nader, Ralph, Green, Mark, and Seligman, Joel. *Taming the Giant Corporation* (Norton, 1977). A critical analysis of the political, economic, and social consequences of large corporations. Argues that big corporations should be chartered by the federal government and made to reveal far more information about their activities to the public.
Page, Benjamin I. *Who Gets What from Government** (University of California Press, 1983). An analysis of the redistributive effect of government economic and social programs. Concludes that significant inequality persists in the United States and that recent governmental policies have been making it worse.
Price, Don K. *The Scientific Estate* (Belknap Press of Harvard University Press, 1965). A thoughtful and perceptive analysis of science and scientists, and their relation to public policymaking in the United States.
Rosenbaum, Walter A. *Environmental Politics and Policy** (Congressional Quarterly, 2004). A useful overview of the forces that work to shape American environmental policy.
Schlesinger, Arthur M., Jr. *The Coming of the New Deal** (Houghton Mifflin, 1959). A revealing and highly readable historical account of the inauguration of Franklin Roosevelt's New Deal, which established the basis for much of the nation's current economic welfare legislation. Part of Schlesinger's multivolume historical study of Roosevelt and New Deal politics.
Sundquist, James L. *Politics and Policy: The Eisenhower, Kennedy, and Johnson Years* (The Brookings Institution, 1968). An informative and valuable study of the battles in Congress and in the country to pass what became the new domestic social-welfare programs of the Johnson Administration.
Waldman, Steven. *The Bill,* revised edition* (Penguin 1996). A revealing analysis of how President Clinton's proposal to create a national service corps moved through Congress and—after some modifications—became law.
Wilson, William Julius. *When Work Disappears: The World of the New Urban Poor** (Vintage Books, 1997). An insightful examination of the decline in the number of manufacturing jobs in American cities, and how this decline has helped to shape urban culture. The author calls for a government program of jobs creation to restore economic vitality, and hope, to inner cities.

*Available in paperback edition.

# *Chapter 19*

# State and Local Government

IN THE WASHINGTON SUBURB of Suitland, Maryland, 5 miles southeast of the Capitol dome and far from familiar paths trod by tourists, a complex of federal buildings houses a group of men and women whose business is to count people and, in part, to peer into the future.

The building is the headquarters of the U.S. Bureau of the Census, a division of the Commerce Department. On October 17, 2006, the bureau's demographers reported that the population of the United States had passed a historic milestone—300 million people. Using computers, and by calculating birth and death rates and other factors, the Census Bureau is also able to make population projections for the future. It cannot do so with precision, because there is a wide margin for error in such tabulations. Nevertheless, the Census Bureau is able to guess that the population of the United States may increase by 2020 to 336 million.[1]

Although this projection is only an estimate, an increase of 36 million people in 14 years would be like adding the populations of Australia, Denmark, Ireland, and Sweden to that of the United States. And by 2050, the population of the United States may reach 420 million, according to Census Bureau estimates.[2] In other words, there is a possibility that the 2006 population of 300 million will increase by about 120 million in 44 years. The world population is expected to reach more than 9 billion by 2050.[3]

***for more information about the U.S. Census Bureau, see:***
***http://www.census.gov***

America today, although relatively prosperous compared with many other countries, is nevertheless burdened with multifold, interlocking

© Jeff Greenberg/Photo Researchers, Inc.

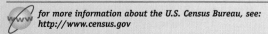

problems—environmental pollution, inadequate public schools, limited energy resources, racial discrimination, crime, drug abuse, poverty, and homelessness. If, as seems possible, the population increases substantially in five decades, will the American political system and American society be able to cope with these problems? To take a random example—and assuming there is enough gasoline or alternative sources of fuel to go around—would anyone care to visualize what it might be like driving along the San Bernardino Freeway during the morning rush hour in 2050? It is bad enough now, as Los Angeles commuters can attest.

Not only the size of the population but also its geographic distribution affect the nature of a society. In the United States, more than 70 percent of the people are crowded into just over 10 percent of the land area. More than half of the population of the United States lives in just nine states.*

Since 1920 the population of the United States has been more urban than rural. In 2000, when the population stood at 281.4 million, 226 million Americans, or 80 percent, lived in metropolitan areas. Of this total, 81 million lived in central cities and about 139 million lived outside the cities, mostly in the suburbs. About 52 million lived in rural or other nonmetropolitan areas.[4] (See Figure 19-1.)

In 2004 almost 163 million people, or more than half of the population of the United States, lived in metropolitan areas of at least 1 million.[5] As America has become urbanized, many of the nation's difficult problems have developed in their most acute form in urban areas—in the central "core" cities and the surrounding suburbs. Obviously, the decisions and actions of state, city, and other local governments have a direct impact on the quality of American life.

In turn, the national economy affects states and communities. By 2004, three years of slow job growth, spiraling health costs, and reduced tax revenues had helped to create a budget crunch in the states. With income from taxes down, the states were forced to cut their budgets and reduce services.

When the economy faltered, states were the first to be affected because they depend heavily on income from sales taxes, the first type of tax to reflect a downturn in economic activity. A decade earlier, reduced revenues because of a lagging economy meant that one state after another had been forced to raise taxes and cut services drastically. Schools, libraries, health facilities, and other basic needs suffered as a result.

One of the most dramatic examples occurred in California in 1992. For 64 days, Governor Pete Wilson and state legislators were unable to agree on a budget, and the mighty state of California had to issue IOUs of uncertain worth to pay its own employees. The fiscal package finally approved meant increased fees for students at community colleges and universities, reduced hours for many public facilities, and the closing of trauma centers in hospitals in many counties.

After the 9/11 attacks in New York and Washington, D.C., job losses and a waning economy hit the states'

FIGURE 19-1

**Where the People Are, 2002**

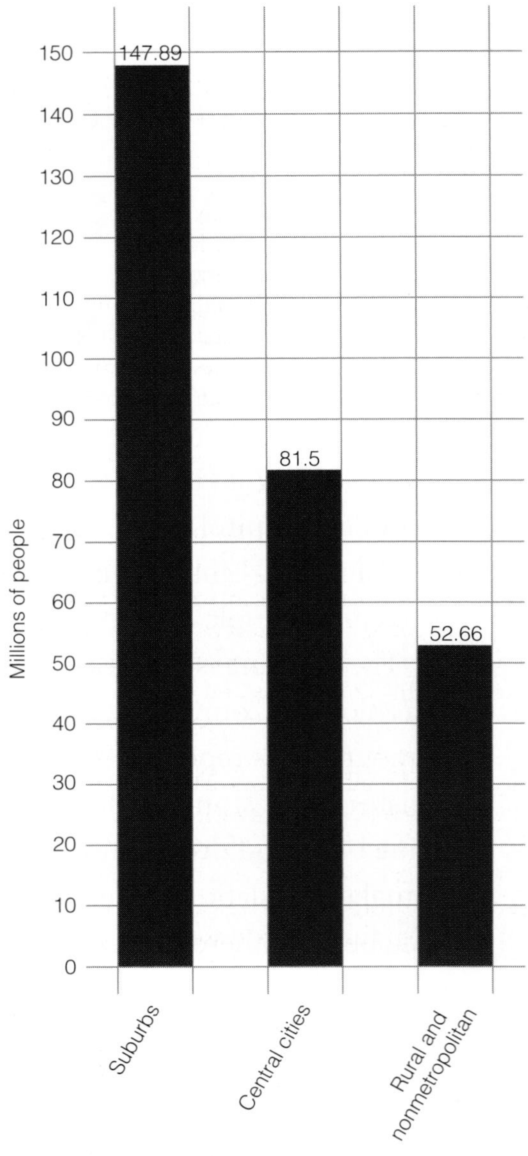


SOURCE: Data provided by U.S. Bureau of the Census, "Population by Metropolitan-Nonmetropolitan Residence, Sex, and Race and Hispanic Origin: March 2002," table 21.1.

*California, Texas, New York, Florida, Illinois, Pennsylvania, Ohio, Michigan, and New Jersey. Together, these large states, ranked here in order of population in 2003, comprised 51.2 percent of the population. See U.S. Bureau of the Census, *Statistical Abstract of the United States: 2003*, p. 24.

## Killington, Vermont, Votes to Move Out of Town

Two things go up in Killington, Vermont—ski lifts, and taxes. Since a Supreme Court ruling in 1997 transformed the state's tax system into a pool of funds that are divided among the state's towns, much of Killington's taxes now go to needier areas of the state. Killington, a popular ski resort with a median income almost $7,000 higher than the rest of the state, has been contributing more than $20 million in property and sales taxes to Vermont and only getting back about 10 percent in aid.

In 2004, almost a third of Killington's 1,095 residents met at an elementary school and voted to move the small ski resort town 25 miles east to the state of New Hampshire, where there are no income or sales taxes. Research predicted they would be taxed less, and would get more back in aid. Some came to the annual town meeting with new bumper stickers that read "Killington, New Hampshire."

The vote, which many deemed as only a symbolic show of frustration, is likely to be squashed by the state's legislators, but Killington town officials planned to draft a petition to gain approval from New Hampshire, before presenting the plan to Vermont officials.

Ironically, Killington was originally chartered by New Hampshire in 1761, three decades before Vermont became a state.

—*Washington Post,* March 3, 2004, p. A12; U.S. Census Bureau; Fox News, "Killington, Vt., Voters Choose to Secede"; *New York Times,* March 3, 2004, p. A7

budgets hard. States suffered decreased income and sales tax revenues and an increase in unemployment insurance claims. Most states were forced to cut programs and services and some increased fees, college tuitions, and cigarette taxes. Governors declared it the worst state budget problem since the Second World War.

Unlike the federal government, states must balance their budgets by adjusting spending and taxing. And the states were under added pressure to increase emergency services for homeland security while footing the bill until they received funding from Washington.

In late 2003 the economy showed some signs of improvement and only 10 states reported budget shortfalls.[6] Some even reported increased revenue for the first time since 2001. But in 2004 a number of states continued to struggle to balance their budgets.

By late 2005, however, a majority of states found themselves enjoying billions of dollars of unexpected tax receipts. The economic turnaround was the result of a general improvement in the economy and more careful budgeting by state officials. The windfall allowed some states to cut property taxes and others to restore money for schools, roads, and other transportation needs.[7]

Part of the problem that states had faced during leaner times was that Congress has shifted programs to the states, as it did in 1996 when it ended the largest federal welfare program and turned over responsibility for public assistance to the states. Washington still gave

block grants for welfare to the states, but the restrictions in the welfare law meant that state and local governments would end up paying a much larger portion of welfare costs.

Because the law restructuring the welfare system initially prohibited most aid—including welfare, food stamps, and Medicaid—to undocumented immigrants and legal immigrants who are not citizens, the law greatly affected California, home to about 40 percent of the nation's estimated 1.5 million legal immigrants. Officials predicted that the state's counties might have to pay $10.7 billion in medical and social services for noncitizens over a six-year period.[8] One California welfare executive declared: "The counties have virtually no ability to raise general tax revenues, but they'll still have to care for these people. It's a disaster in the making."[9] In 1998, Congress restored welfare and Medicaid benefits for the nation's legal immigrants, but California and other states with a high percentage of undocumented immigrants were still faced with providing basic services for low-income residents.

Much of this book has focused on the national government and national politics, but at last count there were, in addition to the government in Washington, 87,576 units of state and local government in the United States.[10] The performance of these governments is often criticized for failure to keep pace with the complex problems they face—transportation, housing, schools, drugs, crime, pollution, and welfare services to name some of the major ones. This inability to keep pace is not always the fault of the state or community; many of the problems that exist have been compounded by urbanization and patterns of population migration in recent decades. These factors have interacted to place a serious strain on the federal system.

Since the Second World War, for a variety of reasons, large numbers of low-income African Americans and whites have migrated from rural areas to big cities. At the same time, many middle-class families and business firms have moved out to the suburbs, taking the city tax base with them. The newcomers to the inner city have required costly government services—schools, welfare, police and fire protection, for example—but have not had sufficient taxable incomes and property to finance these services.

By the early 1970s the flow of African American migrants to the cities had declined sharply.[11] And by that time African Americans were also migrating to the suburbs. But many African Americans in the suburbs continued to live in highly segregated neighborhoods. Moreover, the percentage of African Americans living in the central cities was more than twice that of whites.[12]

For the most part, cities rely on the property tax to finance the bulk of municipal services. Suburban governments now collect the taxes on the property of families and industries that have left the cities—and suburban residents have little desire to "bail out" City Hall. Big-city mayors look to Washington and the statehouses for relief. But, the mayors maintain, what limited federal funds are available have been siphoned off in part by the states for use in the suburbs and in rural areas.

Key Question

In this chapter we will explore a key question: ***How well are the state and local governments meeting their responsibilities?*** There are many other questions to consider. For example, in the federal system in the United States (discussed in Chapter 3), how should responsibilities be divided among the federal, state, and local governments? How are state and local governments organized? What are the major problems of the cities and the suburbs? Given the politics and existing structure of state and local governments, can they hope to solve problems that are larger than their geographic boundaries and financial resources? What are the implications of these problems for America's future?

## The States

America is a nation of states. The political institutions of the 13 colonies foreshadowed the shape of the federal system created under the Constitution. The states, in short, were here before the American nation. They grew in number as the frontier was pushed westward to the Pacific. They are not mere administrative or geographic units established for the convenience of the central government. Rather, the states are key political institutions rooted in the nation's historical development, sharing power under the federal system with the national government in Washington. But the federal system was constructed when the United States was a small, rural nation. In today's predominantly urban America—a nation of congested cities, inner-city neighborhoods devastated by poverty and drugs, and sprawling suburbs—are the states any longer relevant? Can they meet the new demands placed on them by urbanization?

Moreover, states vary greatly in size and character. California has the fifth-largest economy in the world, and a huge influx of immigrants, both legal and undocumented, from south of the border. It is very different in many ways from a state such as Vermont or Delaware. Some states have several metropolitan areas; others have none.

Many critics of state government feel that the states are not doing as much as they should, particularly in the crucial area of urban problems. However, the states have been making an effort to meet their responsibilities. For example, in recent decades state and local spending has increased at an even faster rate than federal spending.

In addition, in recent years the staffs of the bureaucracies that run the state governments, and the staffs of the state legislatures, have become more professional; that is, they tend to be better educated, better trained, and to have a longer-term commitment to their gov-

The American Past

## MUNICIPAL CORRUPTION: BOSS TWEED LOOTS NEW YORK

For more than a decade after 1857, William Marcy Tweed ruled politics in New York City and state, enriching himself by at least $30 million through padded construction contracts and other skullduggery. This account captures the flavor of Tweed and an era:

> On the night of October 27, 1870, it was raining hard and steadily. . . . Very early in the evening thousands of loyal Democrats had assembled outside their district political clubs. All these storm-defying citizens were wearing red shirts. This was a compliment to William Marcy Tweed, State Senator, Grand Sachem of Tammany and boss of the city. Tweed had begun his political career, twenty-two years earlier, by helping to organize the celebrated "Big Six" brigade of volunteer firemen whose engine, at his suggestion, was adorned with the emblem of a ferocious tiger. It was the emblem of Tammany Hall, to which, under the driving rain, fifty thousand red-shirted citizens carrying flaring torches were marching in the largest political parade that New York had ever witnessed. . . .
>
> For two years, in nearly every issue of *Harper's Weekly,* the great cartoonist Thomas Nast had been attacking Tweed as head of a ring that was systematically looting the city. . . . While the great torchlight parade was in progress, Tweed faced an enthusiastic audience in Tammany Hall. He was forty-seven years old, tall, heavily bearded, growing bald, a man of enormous bulk. His eyes glittered as coldly as the huge diamond adorning his shirt front, but his ruddy face wore a jovial expression.
>
> Tweed received a frenzied ovation when he arose to speak, and his brief address was constantly interrupted by outbursts of cheers and applause. . . .
>
> But a scandal of this magnitude could not be ignored. Eventually, Tweed was prosecuted. At Tweed's first trial, the jury disagreed. At a second, he was convicted. Tweed was confined in the debtors' prison, where he was accorded all the privileges to which so distinguished a citizen was entitled. That was how, on a visit to his home accompanied by a warden and a keeper, he managed to make his escape. After remaining in hiding near New York, he made his way to Florida in disguise, thence to Cuba, finally to Spain. On landing in Vigo, Tweed was recognized; a cartoon by Thomas Nast revealed his identity. The Spanish authorities delivered him to an American warship sent to bring him back to the United States. . . . Tweed died in jail in the Spring of 1878.
>
> —Adapted from Lloyd Morris, *Incredible New York*

ernment jobs than in the past. The states and localities do not, of course, spend as much as the federal government, but their level of spending for domestic programs often actually exceeds that of the federal government.

Yet states are often under pressure to increase or create new taxes. One reason for this is that state and local governments rely heavily on consumer and property taxes, which do not reflect the general growth of the economy as rapidly as the federal income tax does. The federal government collects more than half of all taxes; the states and communities divide the remainder.

A little less than half of state revenues comes from taxes, about 15 percent from federal aid, and the rest from a variety of sources.[13] The general sales tax is the largest single category of state income, amounting to about 20 percent of all state revenues.[14] One rapidly growing revenue source for the states is the sales tax and gross receipts tax on the $45 billion-a-year gambling industry.[15]

But higher state taxes have met with resistance. For example, in the 1970s there was a significant tax revolt in some states, most notably in California. In 1978 California voters approved by 2 to 1 a constitutional amendment that appeared on the ballot as Proposition 13. It limited real estate taxes in the state to 1 percent of previous property values and was approved by the electorate despite warnings that it would result in severe cuts in government services. In Washington, and across the na-

tion, political leaders read the election returns as a general "taxpayers' revolt" and a demand for lower taxes.

At first, the impact of Proposition 13 was cushioned by a $5 billion state surplus that had accumulated in California. Two years later, in 1980, a new proposition, which would have cut the state's income tax in half, was offered to the voters. By that time, however, the atmosphere in California had changed. People had begun to feel the pinch in government services brought about by the passage of Proposition 13. This time, the new tax-cutting initiative was defeated by a margin of 5 to 3.

In 2006 seven states still had no personal income tax, and many other states taxed incomes at relatively low rates.* States are cautious about raising taxes in part because they must compete with one another. They "must be wary of increasing taxes or redistributing income in a way that will enable neighboring states to attract away industry." [16]

The federal government provides some financial help. In fiscal 2007, federal aid to the states and local governments was estimated at $459 billion, or almost 17 percent of the federal budget.

What do the states do? They have major responsibilities in the fields of education, welfare, transportation, the administration of justice, the prisons, housing, public health, and the environment. (See Figure 19-2.) States share with local governments the responsibility for delivery of these and many other vital public services. And this responsibility is the source of many of the difficulties that states, and local governments, face.

To provide these services, state and local governments employ more people than does the federal government—with all of the accompanying problems of labor negotiations, strikes, and control of bureaucracy. Even though states are spending more money on public services, they have not always been successful in attacking the urban problems they face. There is a wide variation in the performance and effectiveness of the 50 states, just as there are substantial differences in state politics and state political institutions.

As noted in Chapter 3, however, many states have adopted innovative programs in education and other areas that the federal government has later copied. Particularly during the 1980s, when Washington cut back on social programs, the states experimented with their own programs.

Wisconsin introduced the first welfare plan linking payments to school attendance, and Wisconsin and other states experimented with new welfare programs in the 1990s; Illinois introduced self-management of public housing projects; Vermont proposed a system of universal access to health care; and Minnesota, the state of Washington, and Alaska established programs to target parents who evade child support by changing jobs frequently. Arkansas made its schools accountable for students' performance as measured by test scores.

More recently, in 2006 Massachusetts became the first state in the nation to adopt a law that required all residents to purchase health insurance or face fines and other legal penalties. At the same time, the state made available low-cost health insurance policies, subsidized by the state, to uninsured residents.[17] And nearly half the states had taken the lead in raising the minimum wage above the federal level.[18]

Beyond providing services, states have a major impact on people's lives. It is the states, not the federal government, that regulate marriage, divorce, child custody, driver's licenses, auto inspection, transfer of property, wills and estates, and many other matters. And it is the states, as well as the federal government, that determine the penalty for possession of marijuana, or whether capital punishment shall be applied for certain crimes. The federal courts may eventually review state cases that involve constitutional questions, but initially at least, in cases that do not involve federal laws, the states decide.

## The State Constitutions

State constitutions spell out the basic structure of each state government. Every state constitution provides for an executive, legislative, and judicial branch. Although each includes a bill of rights, some state constitutions are more liberal than others. For example, the constitutions of the newest states, Alaska and Hawaii, have strong civil rights provisions.

State constitutions tend to be lists of what the state cannot do; they limit the power of the governor and of the legislature—to levy taxes and borrow money, for example. As a result, state constitutions are often

*States with no income tax in 2006 were Alaska, Florida, Nevada, South Dakota, Texas, Washington, and Wyoming. New Hampshire and Tennessee taxed only dividends and interest.

FIGURE 19-2

**Major Expenditures of State and Local Governments (in billions of dollars)**

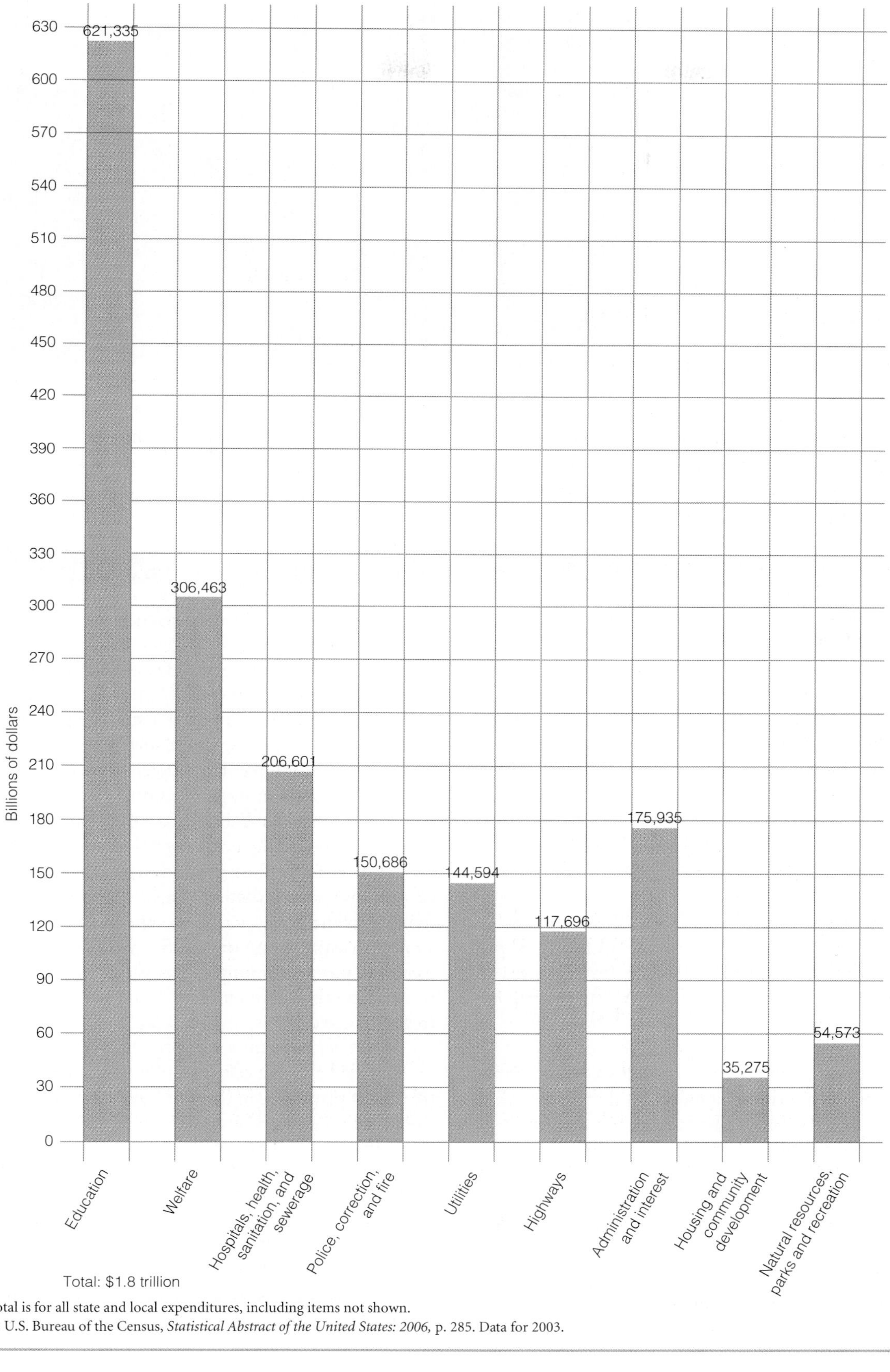


NOTE: Total is for all state and local expenditures, including items not shown.

SOURCE: U.S. Bureau of the Census, *Statistical Abstract of the United States: 2006,* p. 285. Data for 2003.

Boston 2004: Gay rights supporters protest outside the statehouse against a proposition to amend the Massachusetts constitution to ban gay marriages.



condemned as restrictive, negative documents that impede the ability of states to meet modern problems.

In the late 1960s and early 1970s, many states streamlined their constitutions. But modernizing state constitutions does not in itself improve governmental performance unless the political climate in those states also changes. In many areas of the nation, there is political resistance to major, costly undertakings by governments to solve urban problems.

The state constitutions, as Duane Lockard pointed

## Initiatives: "Democracy in Its Purest Form" or "Democracy Run Amok"?

SCAPPOOSE, ORE., Oct. 24—Forgive Carolyn Knowles for feeling a bit "overwhelmed," as she put it, when Volume I of the Oregon voters' guide—all 376 pages of it, encompassing 26 ballot measures and 607 arguments for or against them—showed up in her mailbox a few days ago.

Make federal income taxes fully deductible on Oregon returns? Limit total state spending to 15 percent of taxpayers' personal income? Prohibit public school instruction "encouraging, promoting or sanctioning" homosexual or bisexual behaviors? Ban the use of all "body-gripping animal traps"?

"It's like a full-time job trying to figure all these out," said Ms. Knowles, who already has a full-time job as a cashier in a nearby casino. "It's totally confusing. Sometimes I'm not even sure if a yes vote really means yes or no. Unless you're a real intellectual, you can get mighty bogged down."

It may be democracy in its purest form, as proponents of Oregon's initiative process like to say, or democracy run amok, as critics contend. But no one disputes that voters here face a staggering number of policy decisions, or that the official voters' guide hardly helps cut through the fog for voters who mark their ballots at home in a state where almost all votes are mailed in.

"For most voters, it resembles something written in Greek as poorly translated from the original Urdu," said William M. Lunch, a political science professor at Oregon State University.

Some 102 years after South Dakota became the first state to allow citizens to vote directly on their laws, Oregon is sticking to its tradition of using the process more than any other state. Not since North Dakota did so in 1932 has a state put so many citizen-sponsored initiatives before its people in a single election. . . .

Oregon's crowded ballot this year also illustrates two broader themes in the initiative process around the nation: its ever-expanding use and the growing number of questions about whether it is such a wise method of making public policy. Critics say the initiative process is subject to exploitation, especially by those who have the wealth to pay professional signature gatherers to get a measure on the ballot and finance an advertising blitz to get it passed.

"Whatever happened to representative government?" said Darryl Sykes, an operator in the local wastewater treatment plant here in this Portland suburb. "A lot of the stuff in the voters' guide is not written in layman's terms that the average guy can understand. I thought we elected people to figure this stuff out."

—From "The 2000 Campaign," by Sam Howe Verhovek, *New York Times,* October 25, 2000. Copyright © 2000 by The New York Times Co. Reprinted with permission.

© R. Derek Smith/The Image Bank/Getty Images

Salt Lake City, Utah

out, "have been amended more than 3,000 times and in some instances it is necessary to read the constitution backwards like a Chinese newspaper, in order to see what the last word is on an original provision." [19] Lockard also found a number of oddities; the California constitution, for example, limited the power of the legislature to regulate the length of wrestling matches, and the Georgia constitution provided a $250,000 reward for the first person to strike oil within the borders of the Peach State.[20]

Alabama's constitution, the longest at 340,000 words, has been amended 746 times.[21] The most common means of amending state constitutions is by a majority or two-thirds vote of the legislature and approval by a majority of the voters at the next election. In addition, all states permit constitutional conventions to amend their constitutions, with the changes subject to approval by the voters. In a few states, the legislature may appoint a commission to recommend constitutional changes, again subject to voter approval.[22]

Most states now either permit their constitutions to be amended, or laws enacted, by **initiative.**[23] Under this method, proposed constitutional amendments or legislation can be placed on the ballot if enough signatures are obtained on a petition. California's Proposition 13 was an example of a constitutional amendment approved by the voters in this fashion.

About half the states—mostly in the West and Midwest—permit voters to enact laws by initiative. For example, voters in these states have chosen to enact or repeal taxes, and have approved or rejected initiatives dealing with issues such as abortion, gay rights, and state lotteries and banning trucks with triple trailers, requiring employers to provide health insurance, and outlawing the hunting of nursing mother bears.[24]

In 2004, people in 34 states could vote on a total of 162 ballot measures. In California, voters faced 16 propositions, the most of any state.[25] Because many voters found it confusing to have to deal with so many choices, a backlash had developed in several states against the use of the initiative. Other voters liked the idea of direct control over laws or state constitutional amendments. Many state legislators, however, felt that the use of the initiative poached on their lawmaking authority. In the two years after 1998, seven states took steps to make it more difficult to get initiatives on the ballot.[26]

In addition to the initiative, every state has provisions for a **referendum,** a method that allows voters, in effect, to "veto" a bill passed by the legislature or to accept or reject a proposal, such as a bond issue, made by a government agency.

Seventeen states also allow the **recall,** a procedure that in certain circumstances permits voters to remove elected state officials from office before their terms have expired.[27] In many local units of government, citizens also may vote for the recall of local public officials.

In 2003, for the second time in the nation's history, a state governor was recalled.[28] Gray Davis, the Democratic governor of California, plagued by an energy and budget crisis, was recalled after opponents collected more than 1.3 million signatures. Arnold Schwarzenegger, the actor married to television personality Maria Shriver, announced on the *Tonight Show* that he would seek the California governor's seat. Schwarzenegger, a Republican, was on the ballot along with 130 other candidates, including former actors, porn stars, and actual politicians. He won with 48.5 percent of the votes in a highly Democratic state, gaining a major prize for the Republican Party.

## States of Confusion: "It's Not Funny"

SOUTHWICK, MASS., Jan. 24—Up here in the Notch, a tidy pocket of land where Connecticut borders Massachusetts on three sides, strange things happen to ordinary people.

Take Rocco Cianfarani, 64, a supermarket manager who thought he had built his wood-frame house squarely in Southwick. Because of modern-day confusion spawned by a 359-year-old surveying blunder that created the Notch, Mr. Cianfarani is now the owner of a Connecticut address, a Connecticut phone number and Connecticut tax bills he wants nothing to do with. And when he calls the police, Connecticut officers may or may not drive up his Massachusetts driveway.

"It's not funny," he said.

Norma Yourous, 82, is another Notch resident. . . . Unlike Mr. Cianfarani, Ms. Yourous officially lives in Southwick. But since she can walk to Granby, Conn., without leaving her backyard, she also pays Connecticut property taxes, which are higher than those in Massachusetts.

"That's just how it's always been," she said.

Then there are Janice and Thomas Carr, whose camper caught fire and was quickly devoured by the Notch 10 years ago. Because the Carrs technically live in Granby, Granby firefighters responded to their 911 call. But when they saw that the flaming camper was parked in a Massachusetts patch of the Carrs' property, the firefighters rolled up their hoses and urged the Carrs to call a fire department from that state.

Result: "The damn thing burned down," Mrs. Carr said.

—From "The Driveway? In Another State," by Paul Zielbauer, *New York Times,* January 26, 2001, p. B1. 

## The Governors

At first glance, it might appear as though the 50 states are federal governments in miniature. Each has the familiar three branches with checks and balances. The governors are usually prestigious figures, at least within their states; like the president, they head an executive branch. And, like the president, they have armed forces under their command in the form of the state police and the National Guard. Appearances are deceptive, however, for the position of governor in some states is generally much less powerful than may be imagined.

To begin with, the actions of a governor, and of other state officials, and the laws passed by state legislatures cannot conflict with federal law and are subject to judicial review by the U.S. Supreme Court. During the 1950s and 1960s, at Little Rock, Arkansas, and elsewhere in the South, federal power prevailed over that of state governors in confrontations over public school and university desegregation.

Beyond this, the position of governor has been weakened by historical and political factors. During the colonial period, the royal governors clashed with the elected legislatures. The state constitutions written at the time of the American Revolution reflected the prevailing distrust of executive power; in most states, the legislature chose the governor. During the 19th century, popular election of governors spread through the states, but the power of the governors remained relatively weak. Not until the 20th century were state governments reorganized and executive power increased in some states. But even today, the office of governor is weak in a number of states.

At the same time, political scientists have noted marked improvements in the abilities and stature of American governors in recent decades. Larry Sabato has suggested that the political hacks of the past have faded away: "The good-time Charlies are gone." In their place, Sabato observes, there has arisen "a new breed of governor," more highly skilled, better trained, and better able to lead their states in the modern age.[29]

© 2004 AP/Wide World Photos

California governor Arnold Schwarzenegger endorsed a proposition that would restrict state control over local tax revenues.

Variations in the power of state governors were shown in a study published by a federal commission. In only 10 states was the governor said to be "very strong."[30] Another study, by Thad L. Beyle, a political scientist, ranked the states on a scale according to the formal powers of the governors—including tenure, appointment, budget, veto powers, and party control—and concluded that nine governors had the most institutional power; 21 states ranked next, followed by a group of 17 states. Three states ranked at the low end of the scale.[31]

As Beyle also noted, the governors of the biggest states, such as California, New York, and Texas, "are important and powerful in political circles. They have greater influence in national political conventions and larger congressional delegations. They are often elevated to potential presidential candidacy just because they are the governors of these states. The national press covers them closely. . . . In short, these governors have national power because of the states they head."[32] This tendency was demonstrated once again in 2000 when the governor of Texas, George W. Bush, was nominated and elected as the Republican candidate for president.

In recent years, a number of states have taken steps to strengthen the power of the governor. In 30 states, the governor has power to reorganize the executive branch and create agencies by executive order, subject to veto by the legislature.[33] Several governors have been given broader power to appoint department heads and other state officials.[34]

In most states, the governor shares executive power with at least one other popularly elected official. Typically, the officials elected by the voters along with the governor may include the lieutenant governor, attorney general, secretary of state, treasurer, auditor, and superintendent of education. The governor's difficulties are increased if one or more of these elected executive branch officials belong to the opposing political party. The power of governors to appoint important officials (in states where they are not elected independently) varies from state to state; in some cases their choices are subject to approval by the state senate.

All states grant their governors the power to veto state legislation. Governors in 43 states could also exercise a **line-item veto,** the power to reject single parts of appropriations bills.[35]

As of 2004, 35 states limited the term of office of the governor, restricting the governor in almost every case to two four-year terms. (In one state, Virginia, the governor cannot serve more than one successive four-year term.) Twelve states had four-year terms with unlimited succession; only two states, New Hampshire and Vermont, had two-year terms with unlimited succession.[36]

In general, a governor's power and ability to develop long-range policies are greater if the term in office is four years and he or she is permitted to seek reelection. Otherwise, to some extent, the governor becomes a "lame duck" as soon as the inauguration takes place.

Pennsylvania Democrat Ed Rendell won a four-year term as governor in 2002 with the support of organized labor.

The degree of the governor's control over the state budget is another index of power. In all but a few states, the governor prepares an executive budget and submits it to the legislature. Even though this usually serves to increase the governor's strength, much still depends on the skill a governor shows in managing the state bureaucracy and on other fiscal and political practices within the state.

Nevertheless, the fact that the governor develops the state's budget and presents it to the legislature is a major source of gubernatorial power. State legislatures may revise or change the details, but it is the governor who sets the agenda.

Because federal grants provide a substantial share of state revenues, the power of governors also varies with the degree of control they have over state participation in federal programs. Even so, the power of governors to use federal grants is limited by the administrative "strings" attached to money flowing from Washington; states receiving grants must comply with federal laws—such requirements as affirmative action, for example—and with various federal reporting and record-keeping rules.

## The Legislatures

When the American nation began, state legislatures were powerful and prestigious political institutions. Today, they are sometimes described in unflattering terms.

## Making a Difference

### BRYANT HALL: WHEN HE SPEAKS THE LEGISLATORS LISTEN

On the agenda today in the Maryland General Assembly in Annapolis, there is a bill to limit the number of passengers a teenage driver can carry in a car, and Bryant Hall is there to fight it.

Bryant Hall is 15. He doesn't vote. He doesn't even drive. But he understands the workings of government better than most adults. . . . He represents a mammoth constituency: all the state's teenagers. So when Bryant speaks, leaders listen.

Bryant is a sophomore at Southern High School in rural Anne Arundel County. He plays varsity football and is a shot putter. He lives in a tiny house in Galesville, a bay town south of Annapolis, with his mother and their snaggletooth old poodle named Cody. He buses tables Sunday evenings and is learning how to drive.

He is also state legislative affairs coordinator for the Maryland Association of Student Councils, which represents 250,000 kids, and vice president of the Chesapeake Region Association of Student Councils, which represents 35,000, and for this his opinion matters in Annapolis. . . . He plans to get a poli-sci degree, and become a "politician or something." He's immensely charismatic and popular and not obnoxious at all—"he's what everyone hopes their politician to be," says Anne Arundel student council adviser Sue Barnes Hannahs.

If you ask them all, his advisers are divided between those who say he'll be president one day and those who say he might be "too nice a guy" for that.

He is nice and he is not a geek. Bryant may fall asleep to C-SPAN radio, but he gets dressed to MTV. He got the *Sports Illustrated* swimsuit calendar for Christmas, and he was homecoming prince this year.

The headline March 15, 2000, reads "Passengers Increase Teen Drivers' Risk," and it makes Bryant feel a little guilty about opposing the bill. But not too guilty. And it apparently doesn't make the legislators feel too guilty either, because a week later they convert the bill from one that would limit the number of passengers into one that just requires them to wear seat belts.

"I guess this means my lobbying effort on this part was a success!!!!!!!!!!!" he e-mails when he reads about the conversion of the passenger bill to a seat belt requirement. "I am ecstatic right now. I guess the power of the student voice shouldn't be doubted!"

Later, Bryant contemplates the situation, and decides that what really matters is the end result and he shouldn't bother trying to figure out how much of the success was attributed to "the student voice"—attributable to him.

"Then," he says, "I would be like a politician."

—Adapted from the *Washington Post*, April 6, 2000

During the 19th century, in the era of Jacksonian democracy and again after the Civil War, voters in many states wrote into the state constitutions various restrictions on legislative power—limiting state expenditures and borrowing power, for example. Many of these curbs are still in effect.

Public respect for state legislators and legislatures also has been eroded by occasional disclosures of bribes and corruption among the lawmakers. One result has been a suspicion that some state legislators manage to use their position for private gain. Closely tied to this assumption is the belief that lobbyists and special interest groups can perhaps work their will at the statehouse more easily than in Washington. An industry, utility, or labor union that exercises great power within a state capital may sometimes achieve its legislative aims more easily at the state level than in Congress, where its power may be diffused and it must compete with many other interest groups.

Finally, until the Supreme Court's reapportionment decisions of the 1960s, overrepresentation of rural areas in the state legislatures diminished legislative prestige in urban areas. City dwellers grumbled about state legislatures controlled by "appleknockers" and "farmers" who primarily served rural interests.

One of the most important and politically powerful jobs of the state legislators is to redraw the district lines for the U.S. House of Representatives, normally every 10 years after the census. This task often leads to fierce political infighting, because the party in power in the legislature can draw the lines to favor its own members of Congress. Because of population shifts, some states lose representatives after a census and others gain.

In 2000, both major parties spent millions of dollars on polls, television commercials, and consultants to try to sway a handful of state legislative races that might decide control of the U.S. House for the next 10 years. As described by Tom Hofeller, redistricting director for the Republican National Committee, "It's the hidden national election of 2000."[37]

In most states, the two branches of the legislature redraw the congressional district lines, but the governor has veto power. If one party controls both houses of the legislature and the governorship, then it can tailor districts to help its candidates. For example, a conservative Republican House member might benefit from a newly shaped district that excluded minority voters in an inner-city neighborhood. Conversely, a liberal Democrat might prefer a district that included exactly those areas. The stakes, therefore, are high after a decennial census year.

As discussed in Chapter 15, in 2006 the U.S. Supreme Court upheld a controversial Republican redistricting plan in Texas. The Republican-controlled state legislature had redrawn congressional district lines in

2003, which had the result of increasing the party's control of the U.S. House of Representatives. The decision meant that states could redraw district lines at any time, not only in the year after the 10-year census, as had been customary.

Although state legislatures are often criticized, there have been some signs of improvement. By the 1980s, a number of state legislatures had begun modernizing both their procedures and facilities—for example, strengthening their committee systems, installing computers, and initiating other reforms. As noted, this has been accompanied by a trend toward greater professionalism in the staffing of state legislatures.

Every state has a two-house **bicameral legislature** except Nebraska, which has a one-house **unicameral legislature.** The 7,570 state lawmakers serve in legislatures that range in size from 49 in Nebraska to 424 in New Hampshire. Typically, the upper house has about 40 members and the lower house about 100 members. Most state senators serve four-year terms, although in 12 states senators serve two-year terms; most state representatives in the lower house serve for two years. In 41 states the legislature meets annually. In most of the other states, the legislatures meet regularly only every two years, normally in January.[38] (See Table 19-1.)

For the majority of state legislators, public service is only a part-time job. In more than two-thirds of the states the length of regular legislative sessions is constitutionally limited, sometimes to 60 days. Even then, the legislators may spend only a few days in the capital each week, often ending the session with a great flurry of last-minute legislation. Sometimes the clock is literally stopped to permit the passage of bills within the time limit.

In 2004, California legislators were paid $99,000 a year, the highest state legislative salaries in the nation. Although seven states—California, Illinois, Massachusetts, Michigan, New York, Ohio, and Pennsylvania—paid legislators $50,000 or more annually, eight states paid only a per diem rate.[39]

Who are the legislators? State lawmakers tend to come from a higher-than-average social and economic background. As Samuel C. Patterson has noted:

> The largest occupational group among state legislators is that of lawyers. . . . Few white- and blue-collar workers serve in the legislatures, even in the industrial states with large labor union memberships. . . . In the last decade women have been winning legislative seats in increasing numbers, but the percentages are not very large.[40]

However, this occupational profile is changing. In part because the federal government has given more responsibilities to the states, legislatures tend to meet more often for longer periods. As a result, people with careers who need to work cannot always afford to serve in the legislature. In some states, the number of lawmakers who are lawyers has declined, their place taken by retired people.

Democratic state senator Angela Monson, of Oklahoma City, was elected president of the National Conference of State Legislators.

By 2004, the number of state legislators who were women had increased from 10 percent in 1980 to 22.4 percent.[41] Of the 7,382 state legislators, 1,655 were women. In the state senates there were 410 women, or 20.8 percent of 2,069 state senate seats; and women held 1,245, or 23 percent, of the 5,411 house seats. Washington State, with 36.7 percent women in the legislature, led the nation, followed by Colorado, Maryland, and Vermont.[42]

Perhaps the most important aspect of state legislatures today is their changing nature as a result of the "reapportionment revolution" discussed in Chapter 11. In *Baker* v. *Carr* in 1962, the Supreme Court held that the voters of Tennessee did have the right to challenge unequal representation in the state's legislature.[43] And in *Reynolds* v. *Sims* in 1964, it ruled that apportionment of both houses of state legislatures must be based closely on population and the principle of "equal representation for equal numbers of people."[44]

The Court's decisions did not, despite popular expectations, shift the base of state political power from rural areas to the central cities. Instead, the main beneficiary has proved to be the suburbs. And suburban legislators have often proved to be just as conservative on many social-welfare and urban issues as lawmakers from a state's rural areas.

As a result of voter discontent with politicians, by the year 2000 a total of 18 states had amended their constitutions to limit the terms of elected officials and legislators; 11 states had already done so, and the other seven would have limits in effect by 2007.[45] California, Oklahoma, and Colorado led the way, adopting term limits in 1990. The movement to limit terms of office has had the most success in states that have the initiative; limiting the number of years that a legislator may serve has been very popular with voters. The legislators, of course, do not like term limits, since it means they must give up their

**TABLE 19-1**

**The State Legislatures, 2004**

| | Senate Members | Length of Term | House Members | Length of Term | Years Sessions Are Held | Salary* |
|---|---|---|---|---|---|---|
| Alabama | 35 | 4† | 105 | 4 | annual | $ 10(d) |
| Alaska | 20 | 4† | 40 | 2 | annual | 24,012 |
| Arizona | 30 | 2† | 60 | 2 | annual | 24,000 |
| Arkansas | 35 | 4† | 100 | 2 | odd | 12,796 |
| California | 40 | 4† | 80 | 2 | annual | 99,000 |
| Colorado | 35 | 4† | 65 | 2 | annual | 30,000 |
| Connecticut | 36 | 2† | 151 | 2 | annual | 28,000 |
| Delaware | 21 | 4† | 41 | 2 | annual | 33,400 |
| Florida | 40 | 4† | 120 | 2 | annual | 27,900 |
| Georgia | 56 | 2† | 180 | 2 | annual | 16,200 |
| Hawaii | 25 | 4† | 51 | 2 | annual | 32,000 |
| Idaho | 35 | 2† | 70 | 2 | annual | 15,646 |
| Illinois | 59 | 4*† | 118 | 2 | annual | 55,788 |
| Indiana | 50 | 4† | 100 | 2 | annual | 11,600 |
| Iowa | 50 | 4† | 100 | 2 | annual | 20,758 |
| Kansas | 40 | 4† | 125 | 2 | annual | 78.75(d) |
| Kentucky | 38 | 4† | 100 | 2 | annual | 163.56(d) |
| Louisiana | 39 | 4† | 105 | 4 | annual | 16,800 |
| Maine | 35 | 2† | 151 | 2 | even | 10,815 |
| Maryland | 47 | 4† | 141 | 4 | annual | 31,509 |
| Massachusetts | 40 | 2† | 160 | 2 | biennial | 50,123 |
| Michigan | 38 | 4† | 110 | 2 | annual | 77,400 |
| Minnesota | 67 | 4† | 134 | 2 | biennial | 31,140 |
| Mississippi | 52 | 4† | 122 | 4 | annual | 10,000 |
| Missouri | 34 | 4† | 163 | 2 | annual | 31,561 |
| Montana | 50 | 4† | 100 | 2 | odd | 71.832(l) |
| Nebraska | 49 | 4† | ‡ | ‡ | annual | 12,000 |
| Nevada | 21 | 4† | 42 | 2 | odd | 130(d) |
| New Hampshire | 24 | 2† | 400 | 2 | annual | 200 |

seats. Advocates argue that it keeps lawmakers from becoming entrenched and too powerful and has opened the way for more women and minorities to serve.

In more than a dozen states, voters approved limits on the terms of members of the U.S. Congress, restricting senators to two terms and representatives to two or three terms. In 1995, however, the U.S. Supreme Court ruled that the states could not pass laws limiting the terms of members of Congress.[46] That meant that only an amendment to the U.S. Constitution could impose congressional term limits.

## The Judges

Most Americans never see the inside of the U.S. Supreme Court, or even of a federal district court. But many have been to state and local courts—for example, traffic court to pay a fine, or divorce court—where most criminal and civil cases are handled. The quality of justice in America, therefore, depends to a great extent on the

| | Senate Members | Length of Term | House Members | Length of Term | Years Sessions Are Held | Salary* |
|---|---|---|---|---|---|---|
| New Jersey | 40 | 4 | 80 | 2 | annual | $49,000 |
| New Mexico | 42 | 4 | 70 | 2 | annual | 145(d) |
| New York | 62 | 2 | 150 | 2 | annual | 79,500 |
| North Carolina | 50 | 2 | 120 | 2 | biennial | 13,951 |
| North Dakota | 47 | 4 | 94 | 4 | odd | 125 |
| Ohio | 33 | 4 | 99 | 2 | annual | 51,674 |
| Oklahoma | 48 | 4 | 101 | 2 | annual | 38,400 |
| Oregon | 30 | 4 | 60 | 2 | odd | 15,396 |
| Pennsylvania | 50 | 4 | 203 | 2 | annual | 61,889 |
| Rhode Island | 38 | 2 | 75 | 2 | annual | 11,236 |
| South Carolina | 46 | 4 | 124 | 2 | biennial | 10,400 |
| South Dakota | 35 | 2 | 70 | 2 | annual | 12,000 |
| Tennessee | 33 | 4 | 99 | 2 | annual | 16,500 |
| Texas | 31 | 4 | 150 | 2 | odd | 7,200 |
| Utah | 29 | 4 | 75 | 2 | annual | 120(d) |
| Vermont | 30 | 2 | 150 | 2 | annual | 536(w) |
| Virginia | 40 | 4 | 100 | 2 | annual | 18,000 (Senate)<br>17,640 (House) |
| Washington | 49 | 4 | 98 | 2 | annual | 32,064 |
| West Virginia | 34 | 4 | 100 | 2 | annual | 15,000 |
| Wisconsin | 33 | 4 | 99 | 2 | annual | 44,333 |
| Wyoming | 30 | 4 | 60 | 2 | annual | 125(d) |

*Salaries as of 2002. Amounts are annual unless otherwise noted as (d) per day, (l) per legislative day, (w) per week, (m) per month, (o) odd year, or (e) even year.
†Terms vary from two to four years.
‡Unicameral legislature.
SOURCE: *The Book of the States, 2004 Edition,* vol. 33 (Lexington, Ky.: Council of State Governments), pp. 78–80, 82, 83–84, 94–95.

quality of justice in the states and communities. These courts, rather than federal courts, are most visible to the average citizen.

Just as the Supreme Court may strike down federal, state, or local laws that conflict with the U.S. Constitution, state courts often strike down state laws that conflict with their state constitutions. But the decisions of state and local courts must conform to the U.S. Constitution as interpreted by the Supreme Court.

State and local judgeships can be important political prizes. Young lawyers who "go into politics" may serve in the legislature or in a state or municipal administration. But often their hope is to be appointed a judge, as their safe, prestigious, and ultimate political reward. The power to appoint legislators as judges is used by many governors to enhance their ability to get bills through the legislature and reward their political allies.

The majority of state judges are elected, however, and the costs and intensity of many of these campaigns have increased. Election contests for judgeships in many states have begun to resemble other political campaigns, sometimes raising troublesome questions about the source of campaign contributions. For example, judges can accept contributions from law firms whose partners or associates may later appear before them in court.

The structure of the state and local judiciary and the problems of the nation's criminal justice system are discussed in detail in Chapter 15.

## Politics and Parties

In Chapter 9 we examined the structure of state political party organizations, their relation to national parties, the geographic cleavage that exists between "upstate" and "downstate" urban-rural areas in many states, and the decline of big-city political machines. In Chapter 11 we mentioned the various national influences on state politics and the increasing effort of states to isolate themselves from the tides of presidential politics by scheduling elections for governor in the off-years. In the American federal system, state politics and state political parties cannot be separated from any discussion of politics and government at the national level.

In the eight presidential elections from 1976 through 2004, four former or incumbent governors were elected president: Jimmy Carter of Georgia in 1976,

**FIGURE 19-3**

**Party Competition in the States**

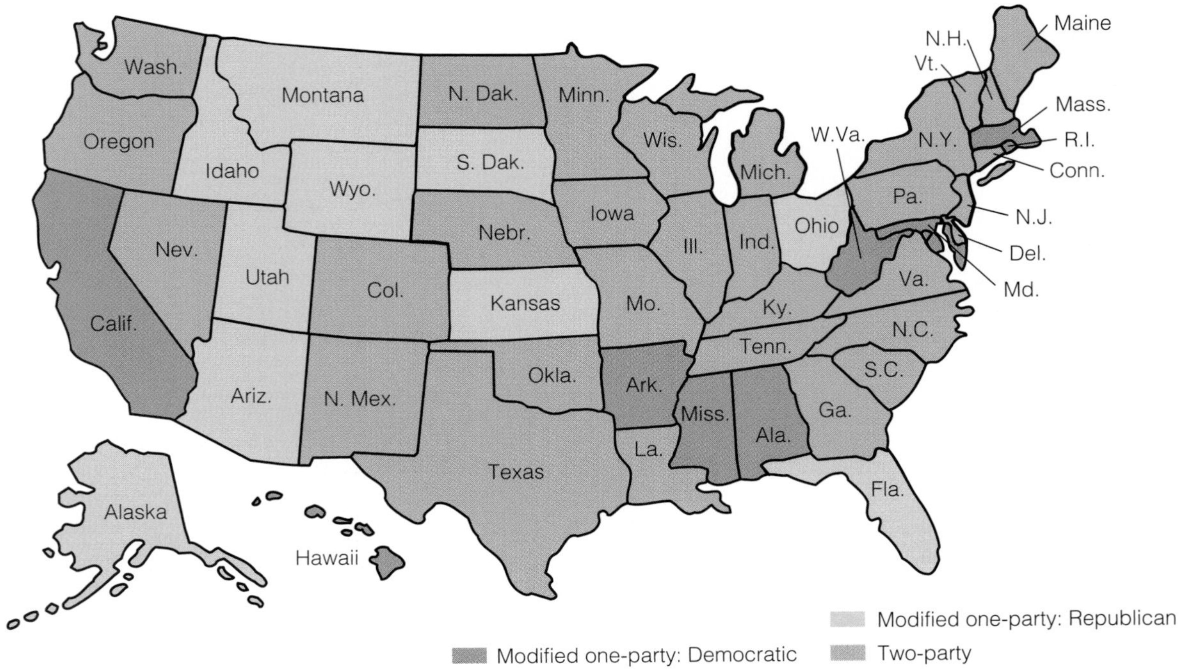


SOURCE: Adapted from data from John F. Bibby and Thomas M. Holbrook, "Parties and Elections," in Virginia Gray and Russell Hansen, eds., *Politics in the American States: A Comparative Analysis,* 8th ed., p. 88. Data for states from 1999 through 2003.

Ronald Reagan of California in 1980 and 1984, Bill Clinton of Arkansas in 1992 and 1996, and George W. Bush in 2000 and 2004. Thirteen other presidents also had served as governors.

The states are the building blocks of the national political parties. But among the states, the pattern of party competition differs widely. For example, for many years in the one-party states of the Deep South, competition was largely within the Democratic Party. The real battles were fought for the Democratic nomination; the winner of the nomination was virtually assured of victory over a Republican opponent in the general election.

The emergence of Alabama Governor George Wallace's third party in the 1960s, combined with major Republican inroads in the "Solid South," changed the face of southern politics. In 1968 Richard Nixon, the Republican presidential candidate, carried five southern states, and in 1972 he won the entire South. Four years later a southerner, Jimmy Carter, headed the Democratic ticket and carried all but one southern state. But in 1980 the Republican candidate, Ronald Reagan, accomplished exactly the reverse, carrying the entire South except for Carter's home state of Georgia. And in 1984, Reagan carried every southern state, as the first President Bush did in 1988. In 1992, however, the Democratic ticket was headed by Bill Clinton, a southern governor, and Al Gore, a southern senator, and the Democrats captured four of the 11 states of the former Confederacy. In 1996, Clinton again carried four southern states, and in 2000 and 2004, George W. Bush carried all 11 southern states.

Some states have vigorous two-party competition. Other states have modified one-party competition—one party is on average stronger than the other. But in both situations, control of the statehouse and the legislature can swing back and forth. One study measuring party competition for state offices characterized nine states as modified one-party Democratic, 31 as two-party, and 10 as modified one-party Republican.[47] (See Figure 19-3.) The pattern changes over time, but most states have competitive two-party systems.

Within the states, political parties show considerable ideological variation. A Democrat from rural Florida may be much closer to a Republican in ideological hue than to a Wisconsin Democrat. The Republican Party in Mississippi bears little resemblance to the Republican Party in Massachusetts.

The rise of the direct primary for state political nominations (discussed in Chapter 11) has weakened control of state political machines by party leaders. The primary has at least partially shifted control over nominations to the voters, in those states where they care to exercise that power.

© Ryan Beyer/Stone/Getty Images

Downtown Minneapolis

## Local Governments

A cartoon in the *New Yorker* showed a woman sitting at a table on her apartment terrace, calling to her husband, "Hurry, dear, your soup is getting dirty." For most city dwellers, air pollution is no joke. And a city's laws and regulations affect the battle for cleaner air. Whether a person lives in a skyscraper, a tenement, or a small town, the quality of local government is likely to have an immediate impact on that person's life. In this sense, local government is "closer" to the citizen, even though the federal government may have a greater effect on one's life in the long run.

New York City is a case in point. Residents have lived through financial crises and strikes by sanitation workers, transit workers, and teachers. One way or another, these inconveniences involved the city government. If New Yorkers watched noxious trash piling up on the sidewalks, if they had to walk several miles to work because of a labor dispute, or if they could not send their children to school, they had ample reason to be aware of the impact of local government on their lives.

Although the connection is not always well understood, local governments are in actuality legal creatures of the states. The state constitutions vest power in the state governments; local governments merely exercise the power that the state gives to them.

### Cities

Cities are municipal corporations chartered by the states. The charters define the municipal powers. About half the states have widely varying provisions for local home rule. As the term implies, **home rule** empowers municipalities to modify their charters and run their affairs without approval by the legislature, subject to the constitution and laws of the state. While home rule may give municipalities more freedom in choosing their form of government, in most states their freedom is not much greater than that of other localities in such fields as education, police power, and other substantive areas. Home rule, in other words, may not help cities solve problems. At a time when so many urban problems cut across the boundaries of local government units, many urban specialists believe there is a need for greater interdependence and cooperation among local governments, not greater autonomy and independence.

There are three basic forms of city government: the mayor-council plan, the council-manager plan, and the commission plan.

**The Mayor-Council Plan** Under the **mayor-council plan,** power is divided between a mayor and an elected city council. Today, most of the nation's cities of half a million people or more employ a strong mayor-council form of government in which the mayor has substantial formal power over the executive agencies and in dealings with the council. In some cities, however, a weak mayor-council form is still in use. In these cases, the mayor is merely a figurehead and must share administrative power with the council and other elected officials. Some cities employ a mixture of the two systems. Almost half the cities of 2,500 or more people use the mayor-council plan.[48]

**The Council-Manager Plan** The council-manager form of government was first adopted before the First World War by the communities of Staunton, Virginia, and Sumter, South Carolina. Under the **council-manager plan,** a council, usually elected on a nonpartisan ticket, hires a professional city manager, who runs the city government and has power to hire and fire city officials. The council in turn has power to fire the city manager (although the city council is not supposed to interfere in the day-to-day administration of city affairs).

City managers often bring professional skills to the business of running a city and may frequently receive high salaries. Although city managers are nominally "nonpolitical," they may be dismissed as a result of a political battle within the community. More than half of all cities with populations of 2,500 or more have city managers.[49] The plan is employed all across the nation but is particularly popular in California and other western states. It is also used widely in Virginia and Ohio. In cities with a population of more than 10,000, this plan is the form of government used the most.[50]

**The Commission Plan** When a hurricane and high waves smashed Galveston, Texas, in 1900, more than 5,000 people were killed and property damage was estimated to be in the millions. During the emergency, while the city government was paralyzed, the Texas state legislature appointed a commission of five local businessmen to run Galveston.

The plan caught on and for a time, at least, was extremely popular in American cities. Under the **commission plan,** a board of city commissioners, usually five, is popularly elected (on a nonpartisan ballot, in a majority of cities that use the system). The commissioners make policy as a city council, but they also run the city departments as administrators. One commissioner is usually designated mayor but often has no extra power.

In time, the commission plan proved disappointing to reformers. Responsibility was diffused under the system, and commissioners frequently lacked the skills needed to administer city departments. More than 140 cities of 2,500 or more people, but only 2 percent of such municipalities, still use the commission plan.[51] But in 1960 it was abandoned by Galveston, which turned to the council-manager plan.

### Counties

In rural areas the county is the most important geographic unit of local government. There are 3,034 counties in the United States.[52] Their size and power vary, but typically the elected officials include the sheriff, county prosecutor, coroner, clerk, and treasurer. These officials share governing power with elected county boards, most frequently called a "board of commissioners" or a "board of supervisors." Some large counties elect a county executive to act as chief administrator, and others appoint an administrator, much like city managers. The county courthouse is usually the local center of political power, the gathering place of those local officials, political leaders, and hangers-on referred to in some counties as "the courthouse gang." But county governments are changing. Of the total, about two-thirds were run by commissioners, and most of the rest by professional county administrators or elected county executives. County governments exist in every state except Connecticut and Rhode Island. In Alaska they are called boroughs and in Louisiana, parishes.

### Towns and Townships

The New England **town meeting** has long stood as a symbol of direct participatory democracy. These meetings are still held in many New England towns: The townspeople come together for an annual meeting in the spring, at which they elect a board of selectmen and settle local policy questions. More than 300 local governments still hold town meetings. But today, urbanization and a vastly increased population have sapped the town meeting of much of its former strength.

In New England and New York, the "town" includes the village and the surrounding countryside. In the Middle Atlantic states and the Midwest, counties are often subdivided into townships. By order of Congress, many Midwest townships were laid out early in the nation's history in 6-by-6-mile checkerboard fashion. For this reason, many townships today are 36 square miles in area. Rural townships are declining in importance and number. But in a number of urban areas, townships perform the function of cities. Twenty states have townships.

### Special Districts

Special districts are established within states to deal with problems that cut across the boundary lines of local units of government or to spread the tax burden over a geographic area larger than that of the preexisting local units. They are created for such purposes as fire protection, sewage, water, schools, transportation, and parks. The number of special districts has been growing at a rapid rate.

The existence of so many kinds and layers of local government results in fragmentation and overlapping, contributing to the inability of local governments to respond effectively to their problems. For example, the existence in so many states of a separate system of government control for schools often makes it difficult for local governments to coordinate education with other programs. Special districts often mean that problems will be dealt with by experts and specialists. But such districts may also mean that local governments give up control over those programs. And the tax revenues raised by special districts cannot be used by other units of government to meet other needs.

## Cities and Suburbs: The Metropolitan Dilemma

For more than three decades, the suburbs, by Census Bureau estimates, have formed the largest segment of the American population. It was one day in 1970—no one knows the exact date—that the number of people living in suburbia exceeded the population living in the central cities or rural areas.[53] There were no ceremonies to mark the occasion, no presidential ribbon cutting, no television coverage. But the date was a milestone, nevertheless.

One political result can be measured in the increase in suburban representation in Congress and in state legislatures. Another result has been to sharpen the conflict between the suburbs and the cities on issues where their interests differ. Even before the suburbs outgrew the cities in population, the urban-suburban rift was clearly visible. In state after state, suburban legislators, sometimes in alliance with rural forces, defeated legislation to aid central cities.

At the turn of the 20th century, George Washington Plunkitt, the Tammany district leader, complained that rural legislators had imposed an unfair tax burden on New York City:

> This city is ruled entirely by the hayseed legislators at Albany. . . . In England . . . they make a pretense of givin' the Irish some self-government. In this state, the Republican government makes no pretense at all. It says right out in the open: "New York City is a nice big fat Goose. Come along with your carvin' knives and have a slice." They don't pretend to ask the Goose's consent.[54]

Today, the white suburban resident has largely replaced the "hayseeds" of yesteryear as the adversary of the city dweller. If Boss Plunkitt were around today, he probably would be complaining about the "commuters" in New York City's suburban Nassau and Westchester counties.

The picture of conflict between cities and suburbs might be even bleaker but for two emerging factors. First, the pattern of metropolitan growth has created an interdependence among all governments in the area, especially in such fields as air pollution, mass transit, and land use, where no single government's boundaries conform to the size of the problem. Suburbs and cities can, and have, cooperated on problems in which their mutual benefit is at stake. Second, many of the problems of the cities—crime, overcrowding, welfare rolls, traffic, housing—exist in the suburbs as well. Suburban residents have discovered that, to some extent, they "took the city with them."

As a result, more and more suburbs and cities may come to realize that, on certain issues at least, they are in the same boat. This happened in Georgia; urban and suburban legislators, formerly political enemies, joined in an "Urban Caucus"—in part because the area around Atlanta, including Cobb County, began experiencing many of the same problems afflicting the core city. With the population shift to suburbia, the "urban crisis" in America has become the "urban-suburban crisis," or, more accurately, a "metropolitan crisis."

## The Problems of the Cities

In Greece more than 2,000 years ago planners dreamed of a new city-state called Megalopolis. *Polis* was the Greek word for "city-state" (from which "politics" is derived), and *mega* comes from the word for "large," so Megalopolis meant a very large city. In 1961 Jean Gottmann used the word to describe "the unique cluster of metropolitan areas of the northeastern seaboard of the United States."[55]

Stretching 600 miles through 11 states and the District of Columbia, in a band ranging from 30 to 100 miles wide, this region in 2000 contained more than 54 million people and includes the cities of Boston, New York, Philadelphia, Baltimore, and Washington.[56] Driving through the area seems almost like traveling in one continuous community. Some urban experts foresee the time when the United States will have three megalopolises, "Boswash" (the corridor from Boston to Washington), "Chipitts" (a strip from Chicago to Pittsburgh), and "San-San" (San Francisco to San Diego).

But is this how people were meant to live? Since the beginning of civilization, people have clustered together in cities, which have served as magnets of communication, commerce, and culture. But critics of the mega-

© George Hall/Woodfin Camp & Associates

The Inner Harbor, Baltimore, Maryland

lopolis have deplored the effect of the modern city on the quality of life. Lewis Mumford has asked, "Will the whole planet turn into a vast urban hive?" Mumford argued that the modern metropolis has grown in "a continuous shapeless mass" and that its residents are subject to constant frustration and harassment in their daily lives while becoming increasingly removed from nature.[57]

On the other hand, Edward C. Banfield has argued that most city dwellers "live more comfortably and conveniently than ever before." In Banfield's view, many urban problems—congestion, for example—are overstated: "People come to the city . . . precisely because it is congested. If it were not congested, it would not be worth coming to." In defending the city, Banfield adds: "To a large extent, then, our urban problems are just like the mechanical rabbit at the racetrack, which is set to keep just ahead of the dogs no matter how fast they may run. Our performance is better and better but because we set our standards and expectations to keep ahead of performance, the problems are never any nearer to solution."[58]

Despite Banfield's defense of urban life, a more general view is that the nation's cities are in difficulty and that problems such as poverty, crime, drugs, racial inequalities, housing, transportation, and the quality of public education are not being solved fast enough in what is often perceived as the world's richest society.*

Part of the problem is that cities are no longer performing the same role they did in the past. In the 19th and early 20th centuries, America's cities were great socializing engines, taking unskilled immigrants from Europe and, in a generation or two, turning many of them into middle-class or even affluent Americans. Some of this is still happening; the Cubans who migrated to Miami and the Mexicans and other Hispanics who settled in Texas, California, and other areas have become a political force, and in the past two decades Asian immigrants have contributed significantly to the urban mix.

But to an extent, the socializing process has stopped. Many of the migrants to the cities in recent decades have been African Americans who historically, especially among those with lower incomes, have not been integrated into American society in the same way as the Irish, Italians, Jews, Poles, and other groups; African Americans have faced greater and more persistent discrimination.

Who will pay for the cost of providing schools, housing, and other social services for residents of the inner city? That remains the core of the dilemma: The cities say they cannot do it, and many residents of the suburbs either have little desire to do so or feel they cannot afford higher taxes. City mayors complain that the federal government has simply not allocated enough money to bridge the gap. And many taxpayers—82 percent in one survey—either do not want an increase in services that would require higher taxes, or they favor a decrease in taxes and services.[59]

Despite the popular image of poor whites and African Americans pouring into the cities to go on welfare, one study of urban migration indicates that people move to the cities for jobs, not social services, and that, compared with the nonwhite population already living in the cities, the average nonwhite who moves to the city has a higher occupational and educational background.[60] But the newcomers face job and housing discrimination; they are not in the same position as whites moving to a pleasant suburban neighborhood. As one observer put it, "The Welcome Wagon rarely calls in the ghetto."[61] (See Figure 19-4.)

One approach to revitalizing the inner cities is the creation of **enterprise zones,** areas in which businesses are encouraged to locate because of tax breaks and other incentives. The first President Bush supported this concept, but in 1992 he vetoed a bill to create 50 such zones, saying the measure would have raised taxes. By then, however, 36 states and the District of Columbia had already established more than 1,000 enterprise zones. Many local governments in these areas combined tax benefits to businesses in the zones with increased police and fire protection and street improvements.[62] By 2004, more than 40 states had enterprise zone programs, including some in rural areas.

Urban problems are complex and often have resulted in physical deterioration of the cities. Some cities have attempted to reverse the trend by building attractive new commercial or residential complexes in the downtown area. Baltimore's impressive Inner Harbor complex of markets, restaurants, and museums, which opened in 1980, is one example, and similar projects have been developed in Boston and Philadelphia. But some critics have argued that expensive downtown centers, catering mainly to business executives, visitors, and the affluent, may only serve to mask the continuing and serious social and economic problems of the cities.

The challenges faced by America's cities were dramatically illustrated in New York City three decades ago. On a bleak day in October 1975, the city stood literally only two hours away from financial default. The proud eastern metropolis, which considers itself America's cultural and business leader, the city that is the home of Wall Street and the great television networks, stood on the brink of insolvency. It was unable to meet its fiscal obligations to its bondholders.

At that perilous moment, Albert Shanker, the leader of the city's teachers' union, came forward and saved New York from default by investing $150 million from union pension funds in the bonds of the Municipal Assistance Corporation, known colloquially as "Big Mac."

There was widespread fear at the time that if New York went under, other cities facing similar financial problems might find it impossible to sell their bonds

*It isn't; as of 2005, the United States ranked seventh among the world's nations in per capita income, behind Luxembourg, Norway, Switzerland, Bermuda, Denmark, and Iceland.

FIGURE 19-4

**Distribution of White, African American, and Hispanic Population, 2000**

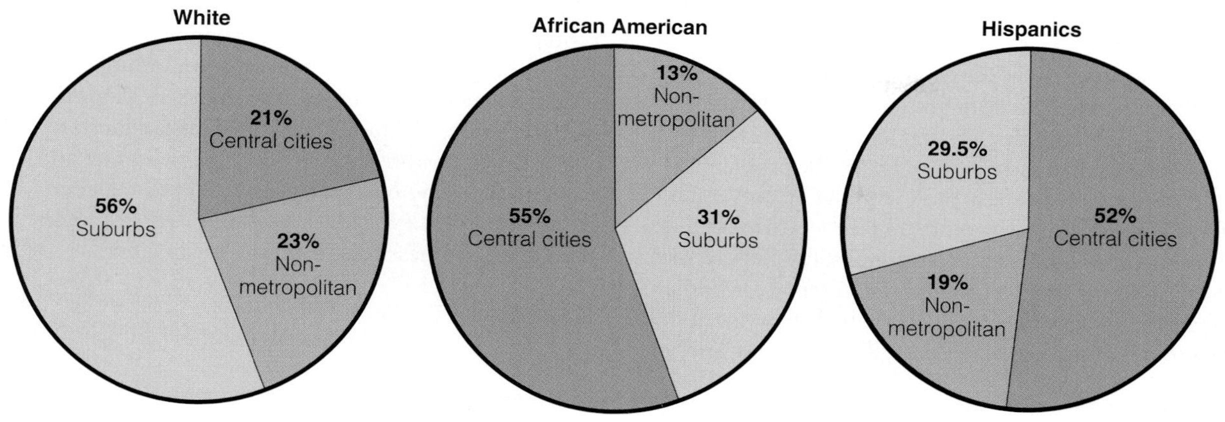


SOURCE: Adapted from U.S. Bureau of the Census, 2000 Census of Population, "Population by Metropolitan-Nonmetropolitan Residence, Sex, and Race and Hispanic Origin."

to investors, which in turn could have serious effects on the national economy. The crisis New York City faced had historical roots. For many years, the city, which has a liberal political tradition, spent billions for social services and welfare programs. At the same time, its expenditures were rising much faster than its revenues.[63]

But mounting city deficits—despite heavy borrowing—had shaken the municipal bond market. Put simply, the city found that no one wanted its bonds. New York State moved to help the city and also established an emergency financial control board to monitor city spending. That meant that the governor and a state-dominated board, rather than the city's mayor, were then in control of the city's finances.[64]

In the 1976 election year, President Ford, sensing a profitable political issue, campaigned for a time against New York City. "I am prepared to veto any bill that has as its purpose a federal bailout of New York City to prevent a default," he said.[65] By November the hostility toward New York had given way to fear; bankers, economists, and politicians worried that the snowballing effect of default by the city might cause a more general financial crisis. Ford reversed course and proposed a $2.3 billion package of aid to New York City, which Congress approved. The immediate crisis was over.

In Donald H. Haider's view, the city's troubles stemmed from "an insufficient tax base to carry out the range of services and redistributive programs to which it gradually had become wedded."[66] By 1987, however, New York City had paid off all of its loans and was considered one of the most stable economic regions in the country. But the crisis a decade earlier, the precarious

© Gail Mooney/Corbis

The South Street Seaport in lower Manhattan

## The Myth of Money

There is a wistful myth that if only we had enough money to spend—the figure is usually put at a hundred billion dollars—we could wipe out all our slums in ten years, reverse decay in the great, dull, gray belts that were yesterday's and day-before-yesterday's suburbs, anchor the wandering middle class and its wandering tax money, and perhaps even solve the traffic problem.

But look what we have built with the first several billions: Low-income projects that become worse centers of delinquency, vandalism, and general social hopelessness than the slums they were supposed to replace. Middle-income housing projects which are truly marvels of dullness and regimentation, sealed against any buoyancy or vitality of city life. Luxury housing projects that mitigate their inanity, or try to, with a vapid vulgarity. Cultural centers that are unable to support a good bookstore. Civic centers that are avoided by everyone but bums, who have fewer choices of loitering place than others. Commercial centers that are lackluster imitations of standardized suburban chainstore shopping. Promenades that go from no place to nowhere and have no promenaders. Expressways that eviscerate great cities. That is not the rebuilding of cities. This is the sacking of cities.

—Jane Jacobs, *The Death and Life of Great American Cities*

situation that had been faced by the nation's largest city and its more than 7 million residents, had served as a dramatic reminder of the serious nature of the problems confronting America's cities.

## Housing, HUD, and Community Development

Officials of the federal government and others who have studied urban problems differ widely on how to break the circle of poverty in the inner city. Where should government begin in attempting to eliminate poverty? With housing? Schools? Jobs? All of those things at once? Nobody really knows the answer.

The difficulties of making progress in attacking the overall problem can be illustrated by a close look at just one aspect of urban needs: housing. Substandard housing exists in rural as well as urban areas. Nevertheless, deteriorating inner-city neighborhoods were and are a highly visible, urgent social problem.

How well has government coped with that problem? In the Housing Act of 1949, Congress proclaimed the goal of "a decent home and a suitable living environment for every American family." That goal, the law states, shall be met "as soon as feasible." Yet, more than four decades later, 4.9 million dwellings were still listed as physically inadequate in the United States.[67]

The government has spent billions on housing, yet the federal effort has nowhere near kept pace with the need for better housing. And many public housing projects tend to be institutional-looking sterile places plagued by crime, drugs, and vandalism. In St. Louis, the government razed the Pruitt-Igoe housing project, which had been built with federal support, because vandals and the high crime rate had led to the abandonment of most of the apartments.

In many cities—most notably in St. Louis and the South Bronx in New York—whole neighborhoods have become wastelands of rubble-strewn streets, boarded-up and abandoned buildings, vacant lots, and stripped automobiles. Across the nation, tens of thousands of deteriorated housing units have been abandoned.

Sometimes federal programs appear to have conflicting goals. More than 800 communities and practically every large city in America participated in the federal urban renewal program that began in 1949. Under the program, the federal government defrayed two-thirds to three-fourths of the cost. In many cases, however, urban renewal merely added to inner-city tensions by forcing poor people from their homes to make way for middle- or upper-income housing and commercial centers. Fannie Lou Hamer, an outspoken African American civil rights leader in Mississippi, made this observation on the subject of urban renewal: "We're already living nowhere, and now they're going to move us out of that."[68]

Two examples of urban renewal in New York City are the South Street Seaport, a nautical shopping area on the East River in lower Manhattan, and Harlem, where growth and development includes trendy coffee shops, clothing stores, and large movie theatres. Urban renewal often creates an environment of less crime and higher property values, making things better for current property owners, but worse for renters.

The responsibility of the federal government for housing was given recognition at the cabinet level in 1965 when Congress established the Department of Housing and Urban Development (HUD). The same year, Congress passed a comprehensive housing bill, including for the first time a program of rent supplements for low-income families.

***for more information about HUD, see: http://www.hud.gov***

President Nixon curtailed or ended a number of federal housing programs, arguing that federally aided public housing had often failed. "All across America, the federal government has become the biggest slumlord in history," Nixon said.[69]

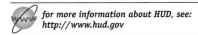

### Twin Cities: An Urban Makeover

ST. LOUIS PARK, MINN.—On a frigid afternoon, the Starbucks at the center of town lures people from nearby offices and homes like an open hearth—a common scene in downtown America.

Until recently, though, this Minneapolis suburb of 44,000 had no downtown. That made it difficult to attract the prized young professionals and others who can reinvigorate a city's tax base—but who demand urban centers near public transportation where they can live, work and play.

So St. Louis Park decided to create a downtown. But the city needed money to buy land, demolish old bars and build streets and sewer lines. City officials turned to the powerful Metropolitan Council, a 17-member body that controls many aspects of daily life in the Twin Cities' seven core counties.

The council gave St. Louis Park $3 million for the first phase of a new "downtown" along Excelsior Boulevard. The district now includes apartments, offices, an amphitheater and a park. Even with temperatures in the teens and a dusting of snow on the ground, it seems to pulse with vitality.

"I was just driving by and saw this and decided this was where I wanted to live," says Michelle Hecker, 27, sipping a steaming coffee. "It has everything I want right here."

Now the "Met Council" is being touted as a national model for a country whose local government structures have failed to keep pace with the demographic reality of how Americans live.

—From "Metro-sized Solutions to Urban Problems," by Larry Copeland, *USA Today,* February 9, 2004, p. 13A. Copyright © 2004 USA Today.

As an alternative to public housing, the Nixon administration started a program of rent subsidies in private housing for very low-income families. The program, known as Section 8, provides vouchers that people can present to participating landlords. Families that qualify pay about 30 percent of their income in rent, and the federal government makes up the rest. In 2004, Section 8 was the nation's major public housing program, providing help to 3 million people with low incomes.

Some middle-class voters have opposed spending tax money for housing for the poor. Yet middle-income and more affluent homeowners receive what amounts to a federal housing subsidy because they can deduct the interest they pay on their mortgage loans in figuring their federal income taxes. Low- and middle-income homeowners benefit as well from the fact that the Federal Housing Administration (FHA) insures the mortgages of many homes.

Federal housing policy is closely related to civil rights issues. In 1977 the Supreme Court held that suburban communities could not be compelled to change their zoning to permit low- and middle-income housing unless the "intent" of the zoning was to keep out African Americans or other minorities.[70]

As a result, suburbs had considerable power to exclude public housing. "For large numbers of suburbanites," Michael N. Danielson has observed, "subsidized housing is a threat, the incarnation of everything in urban society they have sought to insulate themselves from in politically autonomous communities."[71] Danielson suggests that racial prejudice is an important factor in such suburban resistance to housing projects, but he argues that many suburbanites are also concerned about the socioeconomic impact in their communities of low-income families; they fear lower property values, increased crime, and higher taxes for social services.[72]

In the 1980s, a goal of President Reagan's administration was to end construction of low-cost public housing. Although Congress funded some public housing during the eight Reagan years, total outlays for new public housing dropped by 80 percent.[73]

In fiscal 2007 the federal government budgeted $33.6 billion for housing programs, including funds designed to allow people with low incomes to buy their own homes, and block grants to help state and local governments to assist low-income families. About 4.8 million households were receiving assistance from HUD to pay the rent. But the number of people living in substandard housing was much greater than the number receiving help from the federal government.

Taken as a whole, the federal housing program illustrates the difficulties confronting the nation in meeting the urban crisis. Although housing has been recognized as a cabinet-level problem, the provision of decent housing for all Americans remains a goal rather than a reality.

## Urban Transportation

The reporter in the traffic helicopter seldom broadcasts good news; getting in and out of the nation's cities during morning and evening rush hours, or getting to work within the city limits, is often an ordeal. Americans spend a substantial part of their lives commuting to and from their jobs; and time spent in a crowded subway, as Lewis Mumford has suggested, takes its toll: "Emerson said that life was a matter of having good days, but it is a matter of having good minutes too. Who shall say what compensations are not necessary to the metropolitan worker to make up for the strain and depression of the twenty, forty, sixty, or more minutes he spends each night and morning passing through these metropolitan man-sewers?"[74]

Metropolitan transportation in the United States has been dominated by the automobile and the highway. Commuter railroads and other forms of mass transit were permitted to decline during the 1950s and 1960s. Federal policy has to some extent influenced the dominance of highways over rails. The federal government pays 90 percent of the cost of the huge interstate highway

## LIFE AND DEATH IN A HOUSING PROJECT

Herman Everett bounded down the stairs, his grandmother's voice filling the graffiti-smeared hallway behind him. "Be safe," she called. "Be safe."

In Mr. Everett's neighborhood these days, people don't usually say, "See you later" or "Have a nice day." They say, "Be safe."

Mr. Everett's neighborhood is the Martin Luther King Jr. Towers, a sprawling public housing project that rises from the faded Harlem checkerboard of tenements lived-in, tenements abandoned and lots now vacant but for the weeds and the rats. . . .

A few days after Thanksgiving, as they walked through King Towers to a store out on Lenox Avenue, the 19-year-old Mr. Everett and two boyhood friends were attacked by an armed mugger who was after Mr. Everett's black shearling coat—the current dangerous-to-wear status symbol on the city's fast and hard streets.

Only Mr. Everett escaped unharmed. One of his friends, 18-year-old Desmond Lawrence, was wounded in the shoulder. The other, Bernard Richardson, a quiet young man of 20 with a wisp of a goatee, was shot in the back and killed. . . .

Just after 1 a.m., the three friends left the apartment and began walking across the project. . . . A young man, not much past his teens, stepped away from a group on the street and said, "Give me your shearlings."

The three friends ignored him and kept on walking. . . . "I looked back, and that's when I saw the gun," Mr. Lawrence recalled. "Then I heard the shot. Then I fell to the ground. It was like a numbness in my arm. It was like my chest was on fire. Then I heard two or three more shots. I thought he was trying to kill me real bad."

The next shot hit Mr. Richardson in the back. . . . And when it was over, the killer walked back into the project, leaving the coats.

—From "Life in the Towers," by Don Terry, *New York Times,* February 4, 1991, p. A1. 

program, a massive incentive for states and cities to build roads rather than transit lines. The federal funds come from highway user taxes on trucks and buses, tires, and gasoline; the program, passed by Congress in 1956, was designed to link the nation's cities with 41,000 miles of superhighways, almost all of them four-lane.

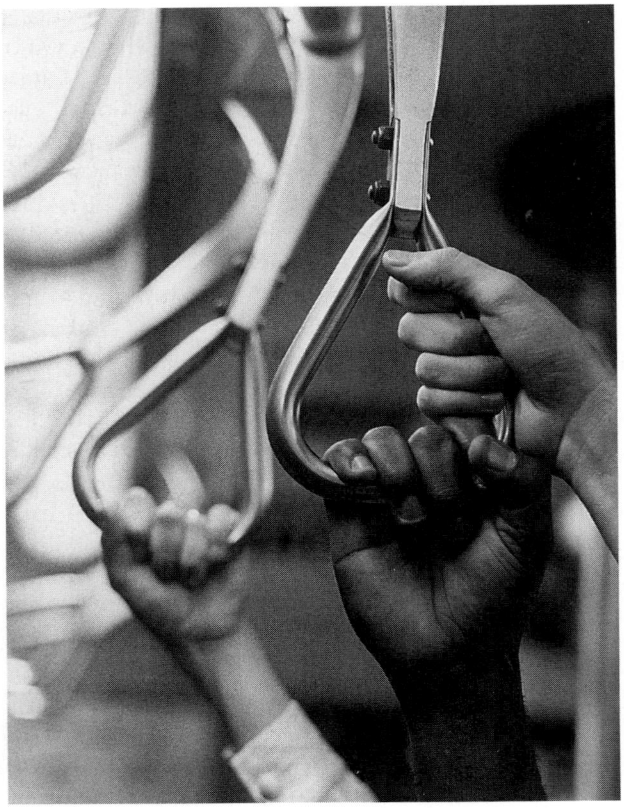
Neal Boeniz/The New York Times

Powerful interest groups have major stakes in highway politics. But the nation has been slow to develop an overall transportation policy, one that would balance highways and rapid transit, and ease congestion in metropolitan centers. The nation's dependence on the automobile became painfully obvious when Americans were confronted in 1973 and 1979 with a shortage of oil and gasoline, and more recently, when crude oil prices soared to a record $54 a barrel in the fall of 2004. At the pump, regular-grade gasoline was more than $2 a gallon that fall along most of the East Coast, and even higher in California.

The Urban Mass Transportation Act of 1970 authorized a 10-year, $12 billion program to enable cities to build or improve rapid rail, subway, and bus commuter lines. Congress in 1973 for the first time approved the use of millions of dollars in the Highway Trust Fund for urban transit needs. In the years since then, Congress has provided more billions for urban mass transit and highways, including bridge repairs and highway construction, financed in part from an increase in the tax on gasoline.

San Francisco's gleaming BART subway system, the Metro subway in Washington, D.C., and Atlanta's MARTA and Dallas's DART are examples of both the benefits and limitations of mass transit. BART has provided modern transportation for many residents of the San Francisco Bay area, but it has not—as its sponsors hoped—substantially reduced traffic jams on the highways or the bridges over the bay. The commuters who now use BART instead of cars to get to work appear to have been replaced by other drivers. In 2004 the first part of a planned $8 billion rail system opened in Houston; it was scheduled to be completed by 2019.[75]

© Robert W. Ginn/PhotoEdit

Metro, Washington, D.C.

*for more information about San Francisco's BART, Washington's Metro, Atlanta's MARTA, and Dallas's DART, see: http://www.bart.gov; http://www.wmata.com; http://www.itsmarta.com; and http://www.dart.org*

The first segment of Washington's Metro opened in 1976 and provided fast, clean, comfortable, and esthetically pleasing downtown transportation for the nation's capital. In 2001, the 103-mile system that was originally planned had been completed. Metro's construction costs had soared to $10 billion, but the system had proved an enormous benefit to the area's commuters and visitors to the nation's capital. And additional lines were under consideration, including one to Dulles Airport in Virginia.

Urban rapid transit systems are often affected by local politics. In Dallas, for example, the two branches of the first section of DART served mostly black and Hispanic neighborhoods south of the downtown area. Political leaders from these neighborhoods had successfully fought earlier plans to build the first part of the system in white areas north of downtown. Lines to serve the communities to the north and west were to open later.

As attractive as these urban rail systems are, they are unsuitable for many cities, which cannot afford them. Because commuters travel to widely scattered destinations, rail lines do not take most people where they want to go, so the automobile still offers the most convenient form of transportation. As a result, urban rail links are often difficult to justify in economic terms. And, many cities that have rail systems have been forced to hike fares in recent years when states could no longer maintain their share of the cost.

Problems interlock. The dominance of the automobile and the highway is directly related both to the energy crisis and to the problem of pollution, since automobiles produce at least 60 percent of total air pollution in the United States (electric power plants and industry account for most of the rest).

## Poverty

Poverty remains a pervasive problem in American cities, overshadowing or underlying almost all other problems. According to the Census Bureau, in 2002 about 78 percent of all people with low incomes lived in metropolitan areas.[76] About half of poor whites lived in the central cities, but for African Americans the total was more than 76 percent.[77]

This does not mean that urban and racial problems are synonymous. However, often the African American, Mexican American, or Puerto Rican child in the inner city is caught up in a cycle of poverty from which there is no easy exit. Education may be one key to eliminating poverty, but inner-city schools often occupy the oldest buildings and have the least experienced teachers, since many teachers with seniority shun assignments to those schools. African Americans and other minorities face discrimination in employment and housing as well. Unlike such physical problems as transportation or air pollution, racial bias involves social attitudes that work against certain minority groups. Many of the problems of the nation's cities, therefore, are bound up with the larger problem of ensuring full equality for all Americans.

## Urban Politics: Governing the Cities

The term **power structure** was popularized in the 1950s by Floyd Hunter, a sociologist who studied community leadership in Atlanta, Georgia.[78] Hunter concluded that a group of about 40 people, mostly top business leaders, determined policy in Atlanta and used the machinery of government to attain their own goals.

But in a study of New Haven, Connecticut, Robert A. Dahl concluded that the city was not run by a single power elite of economic or social notables, and that policy decisions were made by changing coalitions of leaders drawn from different segments of the community.[79] As noted in Chapter 6, scholars have provided diverse answers to the question of "Who governs?" Some scholars argue that power elites make public policy, but other political scientists see American society as pluralistic, with many—although not all—groups sharing in the decision making.

Edward C. Banfield and James Q. Wilson have contended that, regardless of how decisions are made in various American cities, all cities have one thing in common: "Persons not elected to office play very considerable parts in the making of many important decisions."[80] Banfield and Wilson have suggested the term "influentials" for powerful citizens who hold no official position.

When most people think of city government, however, they usually think of decisions being made by officials elected to political office by the voters. As on the national and state levels, parties, politics, and the ballot box play a central role in the decisions made at the city level that affect people's lives. But cities are not nations. Paul E. Peterson has argued that cities "cannot make war or peace; they cannot issue passports or forbid outsiders from entering their territory" and as a result are limited in the policies they can adopt.[81]

Moreover, cities are limited in size and geographical jurisdiction and they must compete with each other for new industry. As a result, Peterson maintains, cities tend to favor policies that "enhance the economic position of a community in its competition with others."[82] They do not favor policies that benefit the poor but cost money and create economic risks for the cities. If cities attempt to redistribute income—to raise taxes to finance large-scale social programs—they face the danger that businesses and employees will leave. Given these constraints, Peterson concludes, the cities are, for the most part, unable to redistribute income effectively to help the disadvantaged.[83]

Population trends, as well as economic factors, affect city government. One result of the migration of many whites to the suburbs has been that more cities with a large African American electorate have chosen African American officials. In 2002, many large cities, including Detroit, New Orleans, Atlanta, Memphis, Denver, and Washington, D.C., had black mayors. In several of these cities the African American population exceeded the white population. In all, more than 500 American cities had African American mayors.[84]

Historically, the big-city political machine, which traded jobs and social services for the votes of immigrants, has characterized urban politics. But with the changing nature of American society, urban political machines have declined. The power of Tammany Hall was broken in New York City in the early 1960s by a Democratic reform movement. In Chicago the reign of Chicago's powerful political leader Mayor Richard J. Daley, often described as the last of the big-city bosses, ended with his death in 1976.

### Honest Graft: Boss Plunkitt's Philosophy

Nobody thinks of drawin' the distinction between honest graft and dishonest graft. There's all the difference in the world between the two. . . . My party's in power in the city, and it's goin' to undertake a lot of public improvements. Well, I'm tipped off, say, that they're going to lay out a new park at a certain place.

I see my opportunity and I take it. I go to that place and I buy up all the land I can in the neighborhood. Then the board of this or that makes its plan public, and there is a rush to get my land, which nobody cared particular for before.

Ain't it perfectly honest to charge a good price and make a profit on my investment and foresight? Of course, it is. Well, that's honest graft.

—Boss Plunkitt, quoted in William L. Riordon, *Plunkitt of Tammany Hall*

As the tightly structured, old-style political machines have faded away, mayors of large cities have found it more difficult to govern. Their power has become diffused. One reason for this is the growth of "functional fiefdoms," specialized government agencies that operate specific programs, such as urban renewal or highway construction.[85] As these agencies have increased in number, they have often made independent decisions, bypassing mayors and city councils.

Just as public administrators exercise great power in the federal government, on the local level bureaucracies influence and limit the power of a big-city mayor, as do other factors. One study of urban politics noted that the mayor of New York must share power with party leaders, appointed and elected public officials, the bureaucracy, nongovernmental associations, the media, and officials and agencies of governments outside New York City. Since no one group dominates, decisions are actually the result of "mutual accommodation."[86] In short, the business of governing a metropolis usually means that mayors are constantly striving to build and maintain workable coalitions of interest groups; their power is limited and they are handy targets when things go wrong.

Another study of how mayors govern found at least five distinct mayoral styles and concluded that no one approach was necessarily the "best." And the study noted that mayors, because of the difficulties and frustrations of their jobs, may not ever achieve any higher political office.[87]

## The Face of the Suburbs

As far back as the 1990 census, the figures confirmed the existence of a trend that urban specialists had begun to

Rafael Maldonado/Santa Barbara News-Press. Reprinted with permission from the Santa Barbara News-Press.

suspect several years earlier—some suburbs closest to central cities were actually losing population.

"This is a national phenomenon," Dr. George Sternlieb of Rutgers University said. "It is a pattern that is occurring within every large metropolitan area." Blue- and white-collar workers, he said, are "leapfrogging" farther out into "exurbia" to find housing they can afford.[88]

The changing population pattern in the suburbs was in marked contrast to the massive migration to the closer-in suburbs after the Second World War. One of the phenomena of that migration was the construction of whole new communities by a single builder. In 1958 Herbert J. Gans, a young sociologist, moved with his family into one such instant suburb, Levittown, New Jersey. His purpose was to study the community as a participant and observer. In recording the quality of social life in this suburb of Philadelphia, Gans quoted one woman describing her next-door neighbor: "We see eye to eye on things, about raising kids, doing things together with your husband, living the same way; we have practically the same identical background."[89]

Although most suburbs are not modeled on Levittown, the quote summarizes both sides of the argument about suburbia. In an impersonal society, where people toil on assembly lines or in beehive offices of large corporations, many Americans long for a sense of identity and belonging. In part, people have moved to the suburbs in "a search for community." In more recent years, some upscale, gated communities have reflected a search for security—a place where suburban residents may feel they are safe from crime and unwanted visitors.

To some extent, the migration to the suburbs may be seen as a turning back to the grass-roots, a yearning for the small-town America celebrated by writers like Booth Tarkington and Mark Twain. On the other hand, the suburbs have been assailed as centers of conformity and homogeneity, in which community pressures tend to produce narrow social and political attitudes among suburbanites and massive unconcern for urban and national problems.

Why do people move to the suburbs in the first place? According to Peter H. Rossi, they are both "pushed" and "pulled."[90] The "push" reasons are often emphasized: crime in the cities, bad schools, deteriorating housing. But the "pull" reasons are also highly important: the desire for more space and to "own our own home" and the attraction of suburban schools, for example. The automobile and FHA mortgage guarantees, allowing lower- and middle-income families to purchase their own homes, have been powerful factors as well.

The move to suburbia has brought change to the center of America's cities. A number of cities have revitalized their downtown districts. In many metropolitan areas, however, not only people, but also jobs and industry, have moved to the suburbs. Suburban residents no longer need to go to the city to shop; the department stores have moved to suburban shopping malls to be near them. Or people can shop on the Internet. There is still a need for downtown business areas, but often less as centers of retail trade than as places for the conduct of businesses that require face-to-face contact—banking, finance, and communications, for example. More recently, in some cities, such as Washington, D.C., downtown areas have been revitalized and new retail stores built. Even so, the suburbs remain the major shopping centers for most people in metropolitan areas.

Not all suburbs are alike. Some of the older, more

David Wise

affluent suburbs have been able to preserve their residential character. But the newer suburbs have mammoth retail shopping malls, office buildings, industrial parks, and other hallmarks of cities. As Louis H. Masotti has noted, suburbia is "becoming increasingly less suburban and more urban."[91]

In the popular image, however, life in the suburbs tends to be centered around home and family. And the stereotype of the suburban father happily barbecuing steaks on his outdoor grill or fussing with his lawn sometimes reflects the reality. But what about his less fortunate fellow citizens back in the city? Gans suggests that the Levittowners "deceive themselves into thinking that the community, or rather the home, is the single most influential unit in their lives. . . . The real problem is that the Levittowners have not yet become aware of how much they are a part of the national society and economy."[92]

Today, the suburbs face many of the same problems that cities face. The suburbanites who take pride in their shrubs, homes, and communities are also part of a larger American community with many unpleasant problems that cannot be wished away. Particularly the older suburbs, closest to the central cities, are experiencing difficulties, including rising welfare costs, crime, and physical deterioration. The quality of life in the nation as a whole is to a great extent reflected in the suburbs. For example, it might surprise most Americans to know that the majority of welfare recipients live in suburbs, small towns, and rural areas—not in the inner cities.[93]

Although social problems such as inferior education, poor housing, crime, and inadequate health care are often acute in the cities, "they are not unknown to the suburbs and are increasingly being found there. . . . More and more suburban communities have city-like characteristics and all the problems associated with those characteristics."[94] There is, in short, no place to hide from the problems American society faces as a whole.

## The Politics of Suburbia

The fact that more Americans live in what could be termed "the suburbs" might be expected to have a major impact on the political system. A closely related question is whether people who live in the suburbs really hold different political views from residents of other areas, or whether the suburbs are merely experiencing the first stages of urbanization—growing into cities, as it were.

### How One Woman Moved a Pipeline

CLINTON CORNERS, N.Y., May 28—In the tradition of ordinary people who wage crusades against big business, Anne Marie Mueser may set a new standard of stubbornness. To fight a pipeline, she put aside just about everything for 10 years, including, she says, cleaning her rickety farmhouse and painting her dilapidated barn.

Her target was a company that built one of the largest utility projects in the Northeast in years, the Iroquois Pipeline, which brings Canadian natural gas through New York State and Connecticut to Long Island.

She was vindicated on May 23, when the Iroquois Pipeline Operating Company, its former president and three other former executives pleaded guilty to violating Federal environmental laws by failing to install required erosion-control devices. The company agreed to pay $22 million in fines in what prosecutors said was the biggest environmental settlement since the Exxon *Valdez* case.

The battle she started in 1987 and, for some reason, refused to give up, is one of those David-and-Goliath yarns that include dozens of boxes of evidence, angry farmers and suggestions about which actors to cast in the movie. The most dramatic scene would undoubtedly be the one in which just about everyone acknowledges that she is largely responsible for the humiliation of a big company. . . . She quickly defeated a plan to put [the pipeline] through her . . . property here. . . .

In a baggy T-shirt, with long gray hair, she chortled about the buttoned-down types she had tied in knots. "It was kind of interesting," she said, "being in a room full of $300-an-hour-plus suits and beating them at their own game."

—From "She Pushed and Pipeline Moved," by William Glaberson, *New York Times,* June 4, 1996, p. B1. Copyright © 1996 The New York Times Co. Reprinted with permission.

One way to measure the political impact of the population shift to suburbia is to study the reflection of that growth in Congress. Richard Lehne noted that in 1974, following the redistricting in Congress after the 1970 census, the 132 representatives from suburban areas for the first time comprised the largest single group in Congress. In other words, there were more legislators from the suburbs than from the cities or from rural areas. That trend has continued.

"The election of large and increasing numbers of suburban representatives to Congress means that, today and in the future, Congress must come to grips with the policy positions and reform preferences of suburbanites," Lehne suggested. Analyzing ratings of representatives by interest groups, Lehne concluded that central-city legislators take liberal policy positions, rural representatives favor conservative policies, and men and women who represent suburban constituents "strike a moderate balance between the other two groups."[95]

But Lehne also discovered that members of Congress from older, established suburbs tend to take more liberal positions on most issues than representatives from the newer suburbs. These findings, Lehne concluded, support those who contend that the process of urbanization has extended to the suburbs. The members of Congress from older suburbs tended to vote much like their city cousins.[96]

Another study of suburban political power, by Thomas P. Murphy and John Rehfuss, found great diversity among the suburbs and their representatives in Congress. "Despite the increase in the number of [members] representing suburban districts," the authors said, "a strong suburban bloc has not emerged." One reason they cite is that "different types of suburbs have different needs." The study concluded: "'Suburban power' remains a paper tiger, but it has the potential to exert great influence."[97]

# Exploding Metropolis and America's Future

## Metropolitan Solutions

Two overriding conclusions may be drawn from a number of studies of state and local problems:

1. Many of the problems are larger than the boundaries of the governmental units that are attempting to deal with them. Smog, for example, respects no city lines, and the issue of commuter transportation in a metropolitan area may involve as many as two dozen local communities.
2. The solutions frequently cost more than the governmental units have available or are willing to spend. A suburban area cannot possibly afford, for example, to build a mass-transit line to carry its residents to downtown offices, nor can the central cities raise the tax revenues to provide adequate social services for those inner-city residents who need them most.

If metropolitan problems are larger than the boundary lines of local governments, why not create larger political units to solve these problems? The approach might seem logical, but there are many obstacles to metropolitan government. Not the least of these is the reluctance of suburban areas to give up their political independence and to pay for services for residents of the central cities. And African American residents of the cities, having finally achieved greater political power—and with African American mayors elected in several major cities—are equally reluctant to lose that hard-won power to a metropolitan government.

Some efforts at "metro" solutions are being made, however, including the creation of special districts to handle specific functions, interstate compacts, areawide planning agencies, consolidated school and library systems, and various informal intergovernmental arrangements. Annexation of outlying areas by the central city and the consolidation of cities and surrounding counties have all been tried; in many cases, they have been found wanting. Another approach has been the plan adopted in Los Angeles, under which the county has assumed responsibility for many areawide functions, but local communities have retained their political autonomy.

Some urban experts have advocated metropolitan federalism as the best solution. Toronto, Canada, and its suburbs have operated under this system since 1953. Mass transit, planning, highways, and many other functions are run by a council made up of elected officials from the central city and surrounding suburbs.

In Florida, Miami and Dade County narrowly opted for "Metro" government in 1957. Under the plan, Miami and 27 suburban cities retain control of local functions but have ceded to "Metro" many areawide functions such as fire and police protection and

© Michael Sulik/The Image Works

Seattle, Washington

transportation. Political control is vested in an elected board of commissioners, which appoints a county manager.

Varying degrees of areawide consolidation have been established in Nashville, Tennessee; Jacksonville, Florida; Baton Rouge, Louisiana; Indianapolis, Indiana; Columbus and Athens, Georgia; Lexington, Kentucky; and Butte, Montana. By 1996 there had been 27 consolidations.[98] In 2003 in the nation's first such metropolitan consolidation in 25 years, Louisville, Kentucky, merged with surrounding Jefferson County to create Louisville Metro. As a result, Louisville climbed from the 67th largest city to the 16th.[99]

Despite steps toward consolidation and metropolitan government in many areas of the country, some scholars have strongly disputed the "reformist" belief that a single metropolitan government, by eliminating overlapping jurisdictions, will promote greater efficiency. For example, one study concluded that because individuals have different preferences in government services, "a system of government composed of many different units will be more responsive to the interests of citizens than a single government for any one urban region."[100]

As urban growth continues, however, old concepts of metropolitan areas may change. The cities of the industrial Northeast, for example, may indeed come closer to the concept of "Boswash." One scholar suggested that tomorrow's metropolis may look less like a fried egg, with a clearly defined center and outer ring, and more like "a thin layer of scrambled eggs over much of the platter."[101]

## Intergovernmental Relations

Although this chapter has focused on state and local problems, any real solution to metropolitan ills depends in large measure on the relationship among federal, state, and local governments.

Although the states were doing relatively well financially in 2000, state and local governments often do not have enough revenues to meet the social demands of both urban and rural areas. In the wake of the 9/11 attacks, many localities complained that they did not have the money to provide increased security to their citizens. The confusing, overlapping programs of federal grants have been widely criticized. At the same time, state and local revenues have frequently lagged behind national economic growth. The federal system, insofar as intergovernmental fiscal relations are concerned, has become rather creaky at the joints.

## The American Challenge

The problems discussed in this chapter involve the question of what kind of nation America wants to be. How people live in their local communities reflects the quality of American life.

Do Americans have a sense of national community? Will comfortable or affluent Americans be willing to have their taxes used to provide better schools and other social services for those with lower incomes? There is no constitutional requirement that an affluent majority take such steps on behalf of a less affluent minority. But the future of the nation's democratic institutions may be affected by the answer. John Gardner, a former cabinet member, once suggested:

> If Americans continue on their present path their epitaph might well be that they were a potentially great people—a marvelously dynamic people—who forgot their obligations to one another, who forgot how much they owed one another.[102]

A further question is whether political institutions created when America was a rural nation can respond to, and cope with, the demands and problems of a highly urbanized, changing society. American democracy is under pressure; its institutions are being tested. Yet, the problems of American society—education, affordable health care, environmental pollution, racial discrimination, periodic economic ills, crime, drugs, poverty, homelessness, political corruption, energy resources, and all the rest—are not necessarily beyond solution if Americans, acting through the political process, insist on change. To a great extent, the America of tomorrow can be what the American people make it.

More than 140 years ago, the English philosopher John Stuart Mill voiced much the same thought in his essay *On Liberty:* "The worth of a State, in the long run, is the worth of the individuals composing it."

## CHAPTER HIGHLIGHTS

- America is a nation of states. The political institutions of the 13 colonies foreshadowed the shape of the federal system created under the Constitution. The states, in short, were here before the American nation.
- The states have major responsibilities in the fields of education, welfare, transportation, the administration of justice, the prisons, housing, public health, and the environment.
- State constitutions spell out the basic structure of each state government. Every state constitution provides for an executive, legislative, and judicial branch. Although each includes a bill of rights, some state constitutions are more liberal than others.
- The most common means of amending state constitutions is by a majority or two-thirds vote of the legislature and approval by a majority of the voters at the next election.
- All states permit constitutional conventions to amend their constitutions, with the changes subject to approval by the voters.
- Most states now either permit their constitutions to be amended, or laws enacted, by initiative.
- Every state has provisions for the referendum, a method that allows voters, in effect, to "veto" a bill passed by the legislature or to accept or reject a proposal, such as a bond issue, made by a government agency.
- Seventeen states also allow the recall, a procedure that in certain circumstances permits voters to remove elected state officials from office before their terms have expired.
- About half the states have widely varying provisions for local home rule. As the term implies, home rule empowers municipalities to modify their charters and run their affairs without approval by the legislature, subject to the constitution and laws of the state.
- One of the most important and politically powerful jobs of the state legislatures is to redraw the district lines for the U.S. House of Representatives normally every 10 years after the national census. This task often leads to fierce political infighting, because the party in power in the legislature can draw the lines to favor their own members of Congress.
- Under the mayor-council form of government, power is divided between a mayor and an elected city council.
- The council-manager form of government has a council, usually elected on a nonpartisan ticket, that hires a professional city manager who runs the city government and has power to hire and fire city officials. The council in turn has power to fire the city manager (although the city council is not supposed to interfere in the day-to-day administration of city affairs).
- The commission plan has a board of city commissioners, usually five, that is popularly elected. The commissioners make policy as a city council, but they also run the city departments as administrators.
- One approach to revitalizing the inner cities is the creation of enterprise zones, areas in which businesses are encouraged to locate because of tax breaks and other incentives.

## KEY TERMS

initiative, p. 657
referendum, p. 657
recall, p. 657
line-item veto, p. 659
bicameral legislature, p. 661
unicameral legislature, p. 661
home rule, p. 665
mayor-council plan, p. 665
council-manager plan, p. 665
commission plan, p. 666
town meeting, p. 666
enterprise zones, p. 668
power structure, p. 673

## SUGGESTED WEBSITES

**http://www.iandrinstitute.org**
*Initiative and Referendum Institute*
A nonprofit, nonpartisan organization that focuses on the different types of initiatives and referendums at the local, state, and international levels.

**http://www.ncsl.org**
*National Conference of State Legislatures*
Offers information about state lawmakers, state legislatures, federal-state relations, issues by topic, elections, campaigns, and redistricting.

**http://www.stateline.org**
*Stateline*
Contains the latest news about the states, in-depth information about each state, and background on important issues.

## SUGGESTED READING


Banfield, Edward C., and Wilson, James Q. *City Politics* (Harvard University Press, 1963). A comprehensive examination of politics in American cities.

Beyle, Thad L., and Muchmore, Lynn, eds. *Being Governor: The View from the Office* (Duke University Press, 1983). A valuable and revealing collection of articles on the way governors view their office and responsibilities. Based on surveys of governors, former governors, and their staffs.

*Book of the States, 2005* (Council of State Governments, 2005). A useful, up-to-date compilation of statistics summarizing social, economic, and political indicators for each of the American states.

Cox, George H., and Rosenfeld, Raymond A. *State and Local Government: Public Life in America** (Wadsworth / Thomson, 2001) A useful survey of political institutions and issues in the states and localities. The authors stress the impact of government on people and encourage students to become active citizens.

Dye, Thomas R., and MacManus, Susan A. *Politics in the States and Communities,* 12th edition (Prentice Hall, 2006) A comprehensive overview of politics at the state and local levels. Offers interesting comparisons of the 50 states on many dimensions of government, politics, and public policy; highlights important trends in the larger metropolitan areas.

Gottmann, Jean. *Megalopolis Revisited* (University of Maryland Press, 1987). An update of a pioneering study of the geographical, economic, social, and cultural characteristics of America's northeastern urban corridor.

Gray, Virginia, Hanson, Russell, and Jacob, Herbert, eds. *Politics in the American States: A Comparative Analysis,* 8th edition* (CQ Press, 2003). A useful collection of essays on various aspects of the political systems in the states, written by a number of leading authorities in the field.

Harrigan, John J., and Vogel, Ronald K. *Political Change in the Metropolis,* 8th edition (Longman, 2006). A detailed assessment of political change in urban America. The authors focus on the decline of the old-style political machine and on the growth of specialized government agencies that often bypass the power of elected officials.

Jewell, Malcolm E., and Morehouse, Sarah M. *Political Parties and Elections in American States,* 4th edition* (CQ Press, 2001). A thorough analysis of state party systems, covering such topics as party competition and organization, the nomination process, general elections and voting behavior, and parties in the legislature. Emphasizes the relationships between national and state parties, and the variations that are found among state party organizations.

Kaufman, Karen M. *The Urban Voter: Group Conflict and Mayoral Voting Behavior in American Cities** (University of Michigan Press, 2004). A study of the electorate in Los Angeles and New York City. Find that in times of racial tension, moderate white Democrats will cross over and provide crucial voting support for white Republican candidates.

Keefe, William J., and Ogul Morris S. *The American Legislative Process: Congress and the States,* 10th edition (Prentice Hall, 2001). A comprehensive description and analysis of legislatures and their environment. Highlights similarities and differences between the U.S. Congress and the state legislatures.

Pelissero, John P., ed. *Cities, Politics, and Policy: A Comparative Analysis** (CQ Press, 2003). An ambitious anthology, organized around the concept of a political system, that covers the basic elements of U.S. urban politics. Includes an examination of decision-making institutions and policy outputs and outcomes.

Peterson, Paul E. *City Limits** (University of Chicago Press, 1997). An important analysis of city government and politics. Argues that a city will tend to favor policies that strengthen its own economic position in its competition with other cities, counties, and states.

Rosenthal, Alan. *The Third House: Lobbyists and Lobbying in the States,* 2nd edition* (CQ Press, 2000). A revealing account, including a number of readable case studies, of the varied policy goals of those lobbying state legislators, and the techniques they employ.

Sabato, Larry. *Goodbye to Good-Time Charlie: The American Governorship Transformed,* 2nd edition (CQ Press, 1983). A lively study of modern American governors. Concludes that the political hacks who sometimes served as governors in the past have departed, their place taken by a new breed of better-prepared, better-trained governors.

Van Horn, Carl. *State of the States,* 4th edition* (CQ Press, 2005). A survey of developments and trends in the American states.

Weber, Ronald E., and Brace, Paul, eds. *American State and Local Politics: Directions for the Twenty-First Century** (Chatham House, 1999). A useful overview of the politics of state and local policymaking.

Wilson, James Q. *Thinking about Crime,* revised edition (Random House, 1985). A discussion of the problems of crime and law enforcement faced by many urban and suburban areas. Includes an analysis of the ways local communities attempt to deal with crime and offers some suggestions for improving public policies in this area.


*Available in paperback edition.

# *Appendix*

# The Declaration of Independence

**In Congress, July 4, 1776.**
**A DECLARATION**
**By the Representatives of the**
**United States of America,**
**In General Congress Assembled.**

When in the Course of human Events, it becomes necessary for one People to dissolve the Political Bands which have connected them with another, and to assume among the Powers of the Earth, the separate and equal Station to which the Laws of Nature and of Nature's God entitle them, a decent Respect to the Opinions of Mankind requires that they should declare the causes which impel them to the Separation.

We hold these Truths to be self-evident, that all Men are created equal, that they are endowed by their Creator with certain unalienable Rights, that among these are Life, Liberty, and the Pursuit of Happiness—That to secure these Rights, Governments are instituted among Men, deriving their just Powers from the Consent of the Governed, that whenever any Form of Government becomes destructive of these Ends, it is the Right of the People to alter or to abolish it, and to institute new Government, laying its Foundation on such Principles, and organizing its Powers in such Form, as to them shall seem most likely to effect their Safety and Happiness. Prudence, indeed, will dictate that Governments long established should not be changed for light and transient Causes; and accordingly all Experience hath shewn, that Mankind are more disposed to suffer, while Evils are sufferable, than to right themselves by abolishing the Forms to which they are accustomed. But when a long Train of Abuses and Usurpations, pursuing invariably the same Object, evinces a Design to reduce them under absolute Despotism, it is their Right, it is their Duty, to throw off such Government, and to provide new Guards for their future Security. Such has been the patient Sufferance of these Colonies; and such is now the Necessity which constrains them to alter their former Systems of Government. The History of the present king of Great-Britain is a History of repeated Injuries and Usurpations, all having in direct Object the Establishment of an absolute Tyranny over these States. To prove this, let Facts be submitted to a candid World.

He has refused his Assent to Laws, the most wholesome and necessary for the public good.

He has forbidden his Governors to pass Laws of immediate and pressing Importance, unless suspended in their Operation till his Assent should be obtained; and when so suspended, he has utterly neglected to attend to them.

He has refused to pass other Laws for the Accommodation of large Districts of People, unless those People would relinquish the Right of Representation in the Legislature, a Right inestimable to them, and formidable to Tyrants only.

He has called together Legislative Bodies at Places unusual, uncomfortable, and distant from the Depository of their public Records, for the sole Purpose of fatiguing them into Compliance with his Measures.

He has dissolved Representative Houses repeatedly, for opposing with manly Firmness his Invasions on the Rights of the People.

He has refused for a long Time, after such Dissolutions, to cause others to be elected; whereby the Legislative Powers, incapable of Annihilation, have returned to the People at large for their exercise; the State remaining in the mean time exposed to all the Dangers of Invasion from without, and Convulsions within.

He has endeavoured to prevent the Population of these States; for that Purpose obstructing the Laws for Naturalization of Foreigners; refusing to pass others to encourage their Migrations hither, and raising the Conditions of new Appropriations of Lands.

He has obstructed the Administration of Justice, by refusing his Assent to Laws for establishing Judiciary Powers.

He has made Judges dependent on his Will alone, for the Tenure of their Offices, and the Amount and Payment of their Salaries.

He has erected a Multitude of new Offices, and sent hither Swarms of Officers to harrass our People, and eat out their Substance.

He has kept among us, in Times of Peace, Standing Armies, without the consent of our Legislatures.

He has affected to render the Military independent of and superior to the Civil Power.

He has combined with others to subject us to a Jurisdiction foreign to our Constitution, and unacknowledged by our Laws; giving his Assent to their Acts of pretended Legislation:

For quartering large Bodies of Armed Troops among us:

For protecting them, by a mock Trial, from Punishment for any Murders which they should commit on the Inhabitants of these States:

For cutting off our Trade with all Parts of the World:

For imposing Taxes on us without our Consent:

For depriving us, in many Cases, of the Benefits of Trial by Jury:

For transporting us beyond Seas to be tried for pretended Offences:

For abolishing the free System of English Laws in a neighbouring Province, establishing therein an arbitrary Government, and enlarging its Boundaries, so as to render it at once an Example and fit Instrument for introducing the same absolute Rule into these Colonies:

For taking away our Charters, abolishing our most valuable Laws, and altering fundamentally the Forms of our Governments:

For suspending our own Legislatures, and declaring themselves invested with Power to legislate for us in all Cases whatsoever.

He has abdicated Government here, by declaring us out of his Protection and waging War against us.

He has plundered our Seas, ravaged our Coasts, burnt our Towns, and destroyed the Lives of our People.

He is, at this Time, transporting large Armies of foreign Mercenaries to compleat the Works of Death, Desolation, and Tyranny, already begun with circumstances of Cruelty and Perfidy, scarcely paralleled in the most barbarous Ages, and totally unworthy the Head of a civilized Nation.

He has constrained our fellow Citizens taken Captive on the high Seas to bear Arms against their Country, to become the Executioners of their Friends and Brethren, or to fall themselves by their Hands.

He has excited domestic Insurrections amongst us, and has endeavoured to bring on the Inhabitants of our Frontiers, the merciless Indian Savages, whose known Rule of Warfare, is an undistinguished Destruction, of all Ages, Sexes and Conditions.

In every stage of these Oppressions we have Petitioned for Redress in the most humble Terms: Our repeated Petitions have been answered only by repeated Injury. A Prince, whose Character is thus marked by every act which may define a Tyrant, is unfit to be the Ruler of a free People.

Nor have we been wanting in Attentions to our British Brethren. We have warned them from Time to Time of Attempts by their Legislature to extend an unwarrantable Jurisdiction over us. We have reminded them of the Circumstances of our Emigration and Settlement here. We have appealed to their native Justice and Magnanimity, and we have conjured them by the Ties of our common Kindred to disavow these Usurpations, which, would inevitably interrupt our Connections and Correspondence. They too have been deaf to the Voice of Justice and of Consanguinity. We must, therefore, acquiesce in the Necessity, which denounces our Separation, and hold them, as we hold the rest of Mankind, Enemies in War, in Peace, Friends.

We, therefore, the Representatives of the UNITED STATES OF AMERICA, in GENERAL CONGRESS, Assembled, appealing to the Supreme Judge of the World for the Rectitude of our Intentions, do, in the Name, and by Authority of the good People of these Colonies, solemnly Publish and Declare, That these United Colonies, are, and of Right ought to be, FREE AND INDEPENDENT STATES; that they are absolved from all Allegiance to the British Crown, and that all political Connection between them and the State of Great-Britain, is and ought to be totally dissolved; and that as FREE AND INDEPENDENT STATES, they have full Power to levy War, conclude Peace, contract Alliances, establish Commerce, and to do all other Acts and Things which INDEPENDENT STATES may of right do. And for the support of this Declaration, with a firm Reliance on the Protection of divine Providence, we mutually pledge to each other our Lives, our Fortunes, and our sacred Honor.

*Signed by* ORDER *and in* BEHALF *of the* CONGRESS,
JOHN HANCOCK, PRESIDENT.

ATTEST.
CHARLES THOMSON, SECRETARY.
PHILADELPHIA: PRINTED BY JOHN DUNLAP.

## Table A-1

### Signers of the Declaration of Independence

According to the Authenticated List Printed by Order of Congress of January 18, 1777*

*John Hancock.*

New-Hampshire.
*Josiah Bartlett,*
*Wm. Whipple,*
*Matthew Thornton.*†

Massachusetts-Bay.
*Saml. Adams,*
*John Adams,*
*Robt. Treat Paine,*
*Elbridge Gerry.*

Rhode-Island and Providence, &c.
*Step. Hopkins,*
*William Ellery.*

Connecticut.
*Roger Sherman,*
*Saml. Huntington,*
*Wm. Williams,*
*Oliver Wolcott.*

New-York.
*Wm. Floyd,*
*Phil. Livingston,*
*Frans. Lewis,*
*Lewis Morris.*

New-Jersey.
*Richd. Stockton,*
*Jno. Witherspoon,*
*Fras. Hopkinson,*
*John Hart,*
*Abra. Clark.*

Pennsylvania.
*Robt. Morris,*
*Benjamin Rush,*
*Benja. Franklin,*
*John Morton,*
*Geo. Clymer,*
*Jas. Smith,*
*Geo. Taylor,*
*James Wilson,*
*Geo. Ross.*

Delaware.
*Caesar Rodney,*
*Geo. Read,*
*(Tho. M:Kean.)*‡

Maryland.
*Samuel Chase,*
*Wm. Paca,*
*Thos. Stone,*
*Charles Carroll, of Carrollton.*

Virginia.
*George Wythe,*
*Richard Henry Lee,*
*Ths. Jefferson,*
*Benja. Harrison,*
*Thos. Nelson, Jr.*
*Francis Lightfoot Lee,*
*Carter Braxton.*

North-Carolina.
*Wm. Hooper,*
*Joseph Hewes,*
*John Penn.*

South-Carolina.
*Edward Rutledge,*
*Thos. Heyward, junr*
*Thomas Lynch, junr*
*Arthur Middleton.*

Georgia.
*Button Gwinnett,*
*Lyman Hall,*
*Geo. Walton.*

*Spelling and abbreviation of names conform to original printed list.

†Matthew Thornton's name was signed on the engrossed copy following the Connecticut members, but was transferred in the printed copy to its proper place with the other New Hampshire members.

‡Thomas McKean's name was not included in the list of signers printed by order of Congress on January 18, 1777, as he did not sign the engrossed copy until some time thereafter, probably in 1781.

# The Constitution of the United States of America*

**We the people of the United States, in Order to form a more perfect Union, establish Justice, insure domestic Tranquility, provide for the common defence, promote the general Welfare, and secure the Blessings of Liberty to ourselves and our Posterity, do ordain and establish this Constitution for the United States of America.**

## Article I

***Section 1.*** All legislative Powers herein granted shall be vested in a Congress of the United States, which shall consist of a Senate and House of Representatives.

***Section 2.*** The House of Representatives shall be composed of Members chosen every second Year by the people of the several States, and the Electors in each State shall have the Qualifications requisite for Electors of the most numerous Branch of the State Legislature.

No Person shall be a Representative who shall not have attained to the Age of twenty-five Years, and been seven Years a Citizen of the United States, and who shall not, when elected, be an Inhabitant of that state in which he shall be chosen.

[Representatives and direct Taxes shall be apportioned among the several States which may be included within this Union, according to their respective Numbers, which shall be determined by adding to the whole Number of free persons, including those bound to Service for a Term of Years, and excluding Indians not taxed, three fifths of all other Persons.][1] The actual Enumeration shall be made within three Years after the first Meeting of the Congress of the United States, and within every subsequent Term of ten Years, in such Manner as they shall by Law direct. The Number of Representatives shall not exceed one for every thirty Thousand, but each State shall have at Least one Representative; and until such enumeration shall be made, the State of New Hampshire shall be entitled to chuse three, Massachusetts eight, Rhode-Island and Providence Plantations one, Connecticut five, New-York six, New Jersey four, Pennsylvania eight, Delaware one, Maryland six, Virginia ten, North Carolina five, South Carolina five, and Georgia three.

When vacancies happen in the Representation from any State, the Executive Authority thereof shall issue Writs of Election to fill such Vacancies.

The House of Representatives shall chuse their Speaker and other Officers; and shall have the sole Power of Impeachment.

***Section 3.*** The Senate of the United States shall be composed of two Senators from each State, [chosen by the Legislature thereof,][2] for six Years; and each Senator shall have one Vote.

Immediately after they shall be assembled in Consequence of the first Election, they shall be divided as equally as may be into three Classes. The Seats of the Senators of the first Class shall be vacated at the Expiration of the second Year, of the second Class at the Expiration of the fourth Year, and of the third Class at the Expiration of the sixth Year, so that one-third may be chosen every second year; [and if Vacancies happen by Resignation, or otherwise, during the Recess of the Legislature of any State, the Executive thereof may make temporary Appointments until the next Meeting of the Legislature, which shall then fill such Vacancies].[3]

No Person shall be a Senator who shall not have attained to the Age of thirty Years, and been nine Years a Citizen of the United States, and who shall not, when elected, be an Inhabitant of that State in which he shall be chosen.

The Vice-President of the United States shall be President of the Senate, but shall have no vote, unless they be equally divided.

The Senate shall chuse their other Officers, and also a President pro tempore, in the absence of the Vice-President, or when he shall exercise the Office of the President of the United States.

The Senate shall have the sole Power to try all Impeachments. When sitting for that purpose, they shall be on Oath or Affirmation. When the President of the United States is tried, the Chief Justice shall preside: And no person shall be convicted without the Concurrence of two thirds of the Members present.

Judgment in Cases of Impeachment shall not extend further than to removal from Office, and disqualification to hold and enjoy any Office of honor, Trust, or profit under the United States: but the Party convicted shall nevertheless be liable and subject to Indictment, Trial, Judgment, and punishment, according to Law.

***Section 4.*** The Times, Places and Manner of holding Elections for Senators and Representatives, shall be prescribed in each state by the Legislature thereof; but the Congress may at any time by Law make or alter such Regulations, except as to the Places of Chusing Senators.

The Congress shall assemble at least once in every Year, and such Meeting shall [be on the first Monday in December,][4] unless they shall by Law appoint a different Day.

***Section 5.*** Each House shall be the Judge of the Elections, Returns and Qualifications of its own Members, and a Majority of each shall constitute a Quorum to do Business; but a smaller number may adjourn from day to day, and may be authorized, to compel the Attendance of absent Members, in such Manner, and under such Penalties, as each House may provide.

Each House may determine the Rules of its Proceedings, punish its Members for disorderly Behavior, and, with the Concurrence of two thirds, expel a Member.

Each House shall keep a Journal of its Proceedings, and from time to time publish the same, excepting such Parts as may in their Judgment require Secrecy; and the Yeas and Nays of the Members of either House on any question shall, at the Desire of one fifth of those present, be entered on the journal.

Neither House, during the Session of Congress, shall, without the Consent of the other, adjourn for more than three days, nor to any other Place than that in which the two Houses shall be sitting.

*The Constitution and all amendments are shown in their original form. Parts that have been amended or superseded are bracketed and explained in the footnotes.

***Section 6.*** The Senators and Representatives shall receive a Compensation for their Services, to be ascertained by Law, and paid out of the Treasury of the United States. They shall in all Cases, except Treason, Felony, and Breach of the Peace, be privileged from Arrest during their Attendance at the Session of their respective Houses, and in going to and returning from the same; and for any Speech or Debate in either House, they shall not be questioned in any other place.

No Senator or Representative shall, during the Time for which he was elected, be appointed to any civil Office under the Authority of the United States, which shall have been created, or the Emoluments whereof shall have been increased, during such time; and no person holding any Office under the United States shall be a Member of either House during his continuance in Office.

***Section 7.*** All Bills for raising Revenue shall originate in the House of Representatives; but the Senate may propose or concur with Amendments as on other bills.

Every Bill which shall have passed the House of Representatives and the Senate, shall, before it become a Law, be presented to the President of the United States; If he approve he shall sign it, but if not he shall return it, with his Objections, to that House in which it shall have originated, who shall enter the Objections at large on their Journal, and proceed to reconsider it. If after such Reconsideration two thirds of that House shall agree to pass the bill, it shall be sent, together with the objections, to the other House, by which it shall likewise be reconsidered, and if approved by two thirds of that House, it shall become a Law. But in all such Cases the Votes of both Houses shall be determined by Yeas and Nays, and the Names of the Persons voting for and against the Bill shall be entered on the Journal of each House respectively. If any Bill shall not be returned by the President within ten Days (Sundays excepted) after it shall have been presented to him, the Same shall be a Law, in like Manner as if he had signed it, unless the Congress by their Adjournment prevent its Return, in which Case it shall not be a Law.

Every Order, Resolution, or Vote to which the Concurrence of the Senate and House of Representatives may be necessary (except on a question of Adjournment) shall be presented to the President of the United States; and before the Same shall take Effect, shall be approved by him, or being disapproved by him, shall be repassed by two thirds of the Senate and House of Representatives, according to the Rules and Limitations prescribed in the Case of a Bill.

***Section 8.*** The Congress shall have Power to lay and collect Taxes, Duties, Imposts and Excises, to pay the Debts and provide for the common Defence and general Welfare of the United States; but all Duties, Imposts and Excises shall be uniform throughout the United States;

To borrow money on the credit of the United States; To regulate Commerce with foreign Nations, and among the several States, and with the Indian Tribes;

To establish an uniform Rule of Naturalization, and uniform Laws on the subject of Bankruptcies throughout the United States;

To coin Money, regulate the Value thereof, and of foreign Coin, and fix the Standard of Weights and Measures;

To provide for the Punishment of counterfeiting the Securities and current Coin of the United States;

To establish Post Offices and Post Roads;

To promote the Progress of Science and useful Arts, by securing for limited times to Authors and Inventors the exclusive Right to their respective Writings and Discoveries;

To constitute Tribunals inferior to the Supreme Court;

To define and punish Piracies and Felonies committed on the high Seas, and Offenses against the Law of Nations;

To declare War, grant Letters of Marque and Reprisal, and make Rules concerning Captures on Land and Water;

To raise and support Armies, but no Appropriation of Money to that Use shall be for a longer Term than two Years;

To provide and maintain a Navy;

To make Rules for the Government and Regulation of the land and naval forces;

To provide for calling forth the Militia to execute the Laws of the Union, suppress Insurrections and repel Invasions;

To provide for organizing, arming, and disciplining the Militia, and for governing such part of them as may be employed in the Service of the United States, reserving to the States respectively, the Appointment of the Officers, and the Authority of training the Militia according to the discipline prescribed by Congress;

To exercise exclusive Legislation in all Cases whatsoever, over such District (not exceeding ten Miles square) as may, by Cession of particular States, and the acceptance of Congress, become the Seat of the Government of the United States, and to exercise like Authority over all places purchased by the Consent of the Legislature of the State in which the Same shall be, for the Erection of Forts, Magazines, Arsenals, dock-Yards, and other needful Buildings;—And

To make all Laws which shall be necessary and proper for carrying into Execution the foregoing Powers, and all other Powers vested by this Constitution in the Government of the United States, or in any Department or Officer thereof.

***Section 9.*** The Migration or Importation of such Persons as any of the States now existing shall think proper to admit shall not be prohibited by the Congress prior to the Year one thousand eight hundred and eight, but a tax or duty may be imposed on such Importation, not exceeding ten dollars for each person.

The privilege of the Writ of Habeas Corpus shall not be suspended, unless when in Cases of Rebellion or Invasion the public Safety may require it.

No Bill of Attainder or ex post facto Law shall be passed.

[No capitation, or other direct, Tax shall be laid unless in proportion to the Census or Enumeration herein before directed to be taken.][5]

No Tax or Duty shall be laid on Articles exported from any State.

No Preference shall be given by any Regulation of Revenue to the ports of one State over those of another: nor shall Vessels bound to, or from, one State, be obliged to enter, clear, or pay Duties in another.

No Money shall be drawn from the Treasury, but in Consequence of Appropriations made by Law; and a regular Statement and Account of the Receipts and Expenditures of all public Money shall be published from time to time.

No Title of Nobility shall be granted by the United States: And no Person holding any Office of profit or Trust under them, shall, without the Consent of the Congress, accept of any present, Emolument, Office, or Title, of any kind whatever, from any King, Prince, or foreign State.

***Section 10.*** No State shall enter into any Treaty, Alliance, or Confederation; grant Letters of Marque and Reprisal; coin Money; emit Bills of Credit; make any Thing but gold and silver Coin a Tender in payment of Debts; pass any Bill of Attainder, ex post facto Law, or Law impairing the Obligation of Contracts, or grant any Title of Nobility.

No State shall, without the Consent of the Congress, lay any Imposts or Duties on Imports or Exports, except what may be absolutely necessary for executing its inspection Laws: and the net Produce of all Duties and Imposts, laid by any State on Imports or Exports, shall be for the Use of the Treasury of the United States; and all such Laws shall be Subject to the Revision and Control of the Congress.

No State shall, without the Consent of Congress, lay any duty of Tonnage, keep Troops, or Ships of War in time of peace, enter into any Agreement or Compact with another State, or with a foreign power, or engage in War, unless actually invaded, or in such imminent Danger as will not admit of delay.

### Article II

***Section 1.*** The executive Power shall be vested in a President of the United States of America. He shall hold his Office during the Term of four years, and, together with the Vice-President, chosen for the same Term, be elected, as follows:

Each State shall appoint, in such Manner as the Legislature thereof may direct, a Number of Electors, equal to the whole Number of Senators and Representatives to which the State may be entitled in the Congress: but no Senator or Representative, or person holding an Office of Trust or profit under the United States, shall be appointed an Elector.

[The Electors shall meet in their respective States, and vote by Ballot for two persons, of whom one at least shall not be an Inhabitant of the same State with themselves. And they shall make a List of all the Persons voted for, and of the Number of Votes for each; which List they shall sign and certify, and transmit sealed to the Seat of the Government of the United States, directed to the President of the Senate. The President of the Senate shall, in the Presence of the Senate and House of Representatives, open all the Certificates, and the Votes shall then be counted. The person having the greatest Number of Votes shall be the President, if such Number be a Majority of the whole Number of Electors appointed; and if there be more than one who have such Majority, and have an equal Number of Votes, then the House of Representatives shall immediately chuse by Ballot one of them for president; and if no person have a Majority, then from the five highest on the List the said House shall in like Manner chuse the President. But in chusing the President, the Votes shall be taken by States, the Representation from each State having one Vote; a quorum for this Purpose shall consist of a Member or Members from two-thirds of the States, and a Majority of all the States shall be necessary to a Choice. In every Case, after the Choice of the President, the Person having the greatest Number of Votes of the Electors shall be the Vice-President. But if there should remain two or more who have equal votes, the Senate shall chuse from them by Ballot the Vice-President.][6]

The Congress may determine the Time of chusing the Electors, and the Day on which they shall give their Votes; which Day shall be the same throughout the United States.

No person except a natural-born Citizen, or a Citizen of the United States, at the time of the Adoption of this Constitution, shall be eligible to the Office of President; neither shall any person be eligible to that Office who shall not have attained to the Age of thirty-five years, and been fourteen Years a Resident within the United States.

[In Case of the Removal of the President from Office, or of his Death, Resignation, or Inability to discharge the powers and Duties of the said Office, the same shall devolve on the Vice-President, and the Congress may by Law provide for the Case of Removal, Death, Resignation, or Inability, both of the President and Vice-President, declaring what Officer shall then act as President, and such Officer shall act accordingly, until the disability be removed, or a President shall be elected.][7]

The President shall, at stated Times, receive for his Services a Compensation, which shall neither be increased nor diminished during the period for which he shall have been elected, and he shall not receive within that Period any other Emolument from the United States, or any of them.

Before he enter on the execution of his Office, he shall take the following Oath or Affirmation:—"I do solemnly swear (or affirm) that I will faithfully execute the Office of President of the United States, and will, to the best of my Ability, preserve, protect, and defend the Constitution of the United States."

***Section 2.*** The president shall be Commander in Chief of the Army and Navy of the United States, and of the Militia of the several States, when called into the actual Service of the United States; he may require the Opinion, in writing, of the principal Officer in each of the executive Departments, upon any subject relating to the Duties of their respective Offices, and he shall have Power to Grant Reprieves and Pardons for Offenses against the United States, except in Cases of Impeachment.

He shall have Power, by and with the Advice and Consent of the Senate, to make Treaties, provided two thirds of the Senators present concur; and he shall nominate, and by and with the Advice and Consent of the Senate, shall appoint Ambassadors, other public Ministers and Consuls, Judges of the supreme Court, and all other Officers of the United States, whose Appointments are not herein otherwise provided for, and which shall be established by Law: but the Congress may by Law vest the Appointment of such inferior Officers, as they think proper, in the President alone, in the Courts of Law, or in the Heads of Departments.

The President shall have Power to fill up all Vacancies that may happen during the Recess of the Senate, by granting Commissions which shall expire at the End of their next Session.

***Section 3.*** He shall from time to time give to the Congress Information of the State of the Union, and recommend to their Consideration such Measures as he shall judge necessary and expedient; he may, on extraordinary occasions, convene both Houses, or either of them, and in Case of Disagreement between them, with respect to the Time of Adjournment, he may adjourn them to such Time as he shall think proper; he shall receive Ambassadors and other public Ministers; he shall take Care that the Laws be faithfully executed, and shall Commission all the Officers of the United States.

***Section 4.*** The President, Vice-President and all civil Officers of the United States, shall be removed from Office on Impeachment for, and Conviction of, Treason, Bribery, or other high Crimes and Misdemeanors.

### Article III

***Section 1.*** The judicial power of the United States, shall be vested in one supreme Court, and in such inferior Courts as the Congress may from time to time ordain and establish. The Judges, both of the supreme and inferior Courts, shall hold their Offices during good Behaviour, and shall, at stated Times, receive for their Services, a Compensation, which shall not be diminished during their Continuance in Office.

***Section 2.*** The judicial Power shall extend to all Cases, in Law and Equity, arising under this Constitution, the Laws of the

United States, and treaties made, or which shall be made, under their Authority;—to all Cases affecting ambassadors, other public ministers and consuls;—to all cases of admiralty and maritime Jurisdiction;—to Controversies to which the United States shall be a Party;—to Controversies between two or more States;—[between a State and Citizens of Another State;][8]—between Citizens of different States,—between Citizens of the same State claiming Lands under Grants of different States, and between a State, or the Citizens thereof, and foreign States, Citizens or Subjects.

In all Cases affecting Ambassadors, other public Ministers and Consuls, and those in which a State shall be Party, the supreme Court shall have original Jurisdiction. In all the other Cases before mentioned, the supreme Court shall have appellate Jurisdiction, both as to Law and Fact, with such Exceptions, and under such Regulations as the Congress shall make.

The trial of all Crimes, except in Cases of Impeachment, shall be by Jury; and such Trial shall be held in the State where the said Crimes shall have been committed; but when not committed within any State, the Trial shall be at such Place or Places as the Congress may by Law have directed.

***Section 3.*** Treason against the United States, shall consist only in levying War against them, or in adhering to their Enemies, giving them Aid and Comfort. No person shall be convicted of Treason unless on the Testimony of two Witnesses to the same overt Act, or on Confession in open Court.

The Congress shall have power to declare the Punishment of Treason, but no Attainder of Treason shall work Corruption of Blood, or Forfeiture except during the Life of the Person attainted.

### Article IV

***Section 1.*** Full Faith and Credit shall be given in each State to the public Acts, Records, and judicial Proceedings of every other State. And the Congress may by general Laws prescribe the Manner in which such Acts, Records and Proceedings shall be proved, and the Effect thereof.

***Section 2.*** The Citizens of each State shall be entitled to all Privileges and Immunities of Citizens in the several States.

A Person charged in any State with Treason, Felony, or other Crime, who shall flee from Justice, and be found in another State, shall on demand of the executive Authority of the State from which he fled, be delivered up, to be removed to the State having Jurisdiction of the crime.

[No person held to Service or Labour in one State, under the Laws thereof, escaping into another, shall, in Consequence of any Law or Regulation therein, be discharged from such Service or Labour, but shall be delivered up on Claim of the party to whom such Service or Labour may be due.][9]

***Section 3.*** New States may be admitted by the Congress into this Union; but no new State shall be formed or erected within the Jurisdiction of any other State; nor any State be formed by the Junction of two or more States, or parts of States, without the Consent of the Legislatures of the States concerned as well as of the Congress.

The Congress shall have power to dispose of and make all needful Rules and Regulations respecting the Territory or other property belonging to the United States; and nothing in this Constitution shall be so construed as to prejudice any Claims of the United States, or of any particular State.

***Section 4.*** The United States shall guarantee to every State in this Union a Republican Form of Government, and shall protect each of them against Invasion; and on Application of the Legislature, or of the Executive (when the Legislature cannot be convened) against domestic Violence.

### Article V

The Congress, whenever two-thirds of both Houses shall deem it necessary, shall propose Amendments to this Constitution, or, on the Application of the Legislatures of two-thirds of the several States, shall call a Convention for proposing Amendments, which, in either Case, shall be valid to all Intents and Purposes, as part of this Constitution, when ratified by the Legislatures of three-fourths of the several States, or by Conventions in three-fourths thereof, as the one or the other Mode of Ratification may be proposed by the Congress; provided that no Amendment which may be made prior to the Year One thousand eight hundred and eight shall in any Manner affect the first and fourth Clauses in the Ninth Section of the first Article; and that no State, without its Consent, shall be deprived of its equal Suffrage in the Senate.

### Article VI

All Debts contracted and Engagements entered into, before the Adoption of this Constitution, shall be as valid against the United States under this Constitution, as under the Confederation.

This Constitution, and the Laws of the United States which shall be made in Pursuance thereof; and all Treaties made, or which shall be made, under the Authority of the United States, shall be the supreme Law of the Land; and the Judges in every State shall be bound thereby, any Thing in the Constitution or Laws of any State to the Contrary notwithstanding.

The Senators and Representatives before mentioned, and the Members of the several State Legislatures, and all executive and judicial Officers, both of the United States and of the several States, shall be bound by Oath or Affirmation to support this Constitution; but no religious Test shall ever be required as a qualification to any Office or public Trust under the United States.

### Article VII

The Ratification of the Conventions of nine States shall be sufficient for the Establishment of this Constitution between the States so ratifying the same.

Done in Convention by the Unanimous Consent of the States present the Seventeenth Day of September in the Year of our Lord one thousand seven hundred and Eighty seven, and of the Independence of the United States of America the Twelfth. In Witness thereof We have hereunto subscribed our Names.

*Articles in Addition to, and Amendment of, the Constitution of the United States of America, Proposed by Congress, and Ratified by the Legislatures of the Several States, Pursuant to the fifth Article of the Original Constitution.*

### Amendment I[10]

Congress shall make no law respecting an establishment of religion, or prohibiting the free exercise thereof; or abridging the freedom of speech, or of the press; or the right of the people peaceably to assemble, and to petition the Government for a redress of grievances.

### Amendment II

A well regulated Militia, being necessary to the security of a free State, the right of the people to keep and bear Arms shall not be infringed.

**Amendment III**

No Soldier shall, in time of peace, be quartered in any house, without the consent of the Owner, nor in time of war, but in a manner to be prescribed by law.

**Amendment IV**

The right of the people to be secure in their persons, houses, papers, and effects, against unreasonable searches and seizures, shall not be violated, and no Warrants shall issue, but upon probable cause, supported by Oath or affirmation, and particularly describing the place to be searched, and the persons or things to be seized.

**Amendment V**

No person shall be held to answer for a capital, or otherwise infamous crime, unless on a presentment or indictment of a Grand Jury, except in cases arising in the land or naval forces, or in the Militia, when in actual service in time of War or public danger; nor shall any person be subject for the same offence to be twice put in jeopardy of life or limb; nor shall be compelled in any criminal case to be a witness against himself, nor be deprived of life, liberty, or property, without due process of law; nor shall private property be taken for public use without just compensation.

**Amendment VI**

In all criminal prosecutions, the accused shall enjoy the right to a speedy and public trial, by an impartial jury of the State and district wherein the crime shall have been committed, which district shall have been previously ascertained by law, and to be informed of the nature and cause of the accusation; to be confronted with the witnesses against him; to have compulsory process for obtaining witnesses in his favor, and to have the Assistance of Counsel for his defence.

**Amendment VII**

In suits at common law, where the value in controversy shall exceed twenty dollars, the right of trial by jury shall be preserved, and no fact tried by a jury, shall be otherwise reexamined in any Court of the United States, than according to the rules of the common law.

**Amendment VIII**

Excessive bail shall not be required, nor excessive fines imposed, nor cruel and unusual punishments inflicted.

**Amendment IX**

The enumeration in the Constitution, of certain rights, shall not be construed to deny or disparage others retained by the people.

**Amendment X**

The powers not delegated to the United States by the Constitution, nor prohibited by it to the States, are reserved to the States respectively, or to the people.

**Amendment XI (1795)**[11]

The Judicial power of the United States shall not be construed to extend to any suit in law or equity, commenced or prosecuted against one of the United States by Citizens of another State, or by Citizens or Subjects of any Foreign State.

**Amendment XII (1804)**

The Electors shall meet in their respective States and vote by ballot for President and Vice-President, one of whom, at least, shall not be an inhabitant of the same State with themselves; they shall name in their ballots the person voted for as President, and in distinct ballots the person voted for as Vice-President, and they shall make distinct lists of all persons voted for as President, and of all persons voted for as Vice-President, and of the number of votes for each, which lists they shall sign and certify, and transmit sealed to the seat of the government of the United States, directed to the President of the Senate;—The President of the Senate shall, in the presence of the Senate and House of Representatives, open all the certificates and the votes shall then be counted;—The person having the greatest number of votes for President, shall be the President, if such number be a majority of the whole number of Electors appointed; and if no person have such majority, then from the persons having the highest numbers not exceeding three on the list of those voted for as President, the House of Representatives shall choose immediately, by ballot, the President. But in choosing the President, the votes shall be taken by states, the representation from each state having one vote; a quorum for this purpose shall consist of a member or members from two-thirds of the states, and a majority of all the states shall be necessary to a choice. [And if the House of Representatives shall not choose a President whenever the right of choice shall devolve upon them, before the fourth day of March next following, then the Vice-President shall act as President, as in the case of the death or other constitutional disability of the President.][12]—The person having the greatest number of votes as Vice-President, shall be the Vice-President, if such number be a majority of the whole number of Electors appointed, and if no person have a majority, then from the two highest numbers on the list, the Senate shall choose the Vice-President; a quorum for the purpose shall consist of two-thirds of the whole number of Senators, and a majority of the whole number shall be necessary to a choice. But no person constitutionally ineligible to the Office of President shall be eligible to that of Vice-President of the United States.

**Amendment XIII (1865)**

***Section 1.*** Neither slavery nor involuntary servitude, except as a punishment for crime whereof the party shall have been duly convicted, shall exist within the United States, or any place subject to their jurisdiction.

***Section 2.*** Congress shall have power to enforce this article by appropriate legislation.

**Amendment XIV (1868)**

***Section 1.*** All persons born or naturalized in the United States, and subject to the jurisdiction thereof, are citizens of the United States and of the State wherein they reside. No State shall make or enforce any law which shall abridge the privileges or immunities of citizens of the United States; nor shall any State deprive any person of life, liberty, or property, without due process of law; nor deny to any person within its jurisdiction the equal protection of the laws.

***Section 2.*** Representatives shall be apportioned among the several States according to their respective numbers, counting the whole number of persons in each State, excluding Indians not taxed. But when the right to vote at any election for the choice of electors for President and Vice-President of the United States, Representatives in Congress, the Executive and Judicial Officers of a State, or the members of the Legislature thereof, is denied to any of the male inhabitants of such State, being twenty-one years of age, and citizens of the United States, or in any way abridged, except for participation in rebellion, or other crime, the basis of representation therein shall be reduced in the proportion which the number of such male citizens shall bear to the whole number of male citizens twenty-one years of age in such State.

***Section 3.*** No person shall be a senator or Representative in Congress, or elector of President and Vice-President, or hold any Office, civil or military, under the United States, or under any State, who, having previously taken an oath, as a member of Congress, or as an Officer of the United States, or as a member of any State legislature, or as an executive or judicial Officer of any State, to support the Constitution of the United States, shall have engaged in insurrection or rebellion against the same, or given aid or comfort to the enemies thereof. But Congress may by a vote of two-thirds of each House, remove such disability.

***Section 4.*** The validity of the public debt of the United States, authorized by law, including debts incurred for payment of pensions and bounties for services in suppressing insurrection or rebellion, shall not be questioned. But neither the United States nor any State shall assume or pay any debt or obligation incurred in aid of insurrection or rebellion against the United States, or any claim for the loss or emancipation of any slave; but all such debts, obligations, and claims shall be held illegal and void.

***Section 5.*** The Congress shall have the power to enforce, by appropriate legislation, the provisions of this article.

**Amendment XV (1870)**

***Section 1.*** The right of citizens of the United States to vote shall not be denied or abridged by the United States or by any State on account of race, color, or previous condition of servitude—

***Section 2.*** The Congress shall have power to enforce this article by appropriate legislation.

**Amendment XVI (1913)**

The Congress shall have power to lay and collect taxes on incomes, from whatever source derived, without apportionment among the several States, and without regard to any census or enumeration.

**Amendment XVII (1913)**

The Senate of the United States shall be composed of two Senators from each State, elected by the people thereof, for six years; and each Senator shall have one vote. The electors in each State shall have the qualifications requisite for electors of the most numerous branch of the State legislatures.

When vacancies happen in the representation of any State in the Senate, the executive authority of such State shall issue writs of election to fill such vacancies: *Provided,* That the legislature of any State may empower the executive thereof to make temporary appointments until the people fill the vacancies by election as the legislature may direct.

This amendment shall not be so construed as to affect the election or term of any Senator chosen before it becomes valid as part of the Constitution.

**Amendment XVIII (1919)**[13]

***Section 1.*** After one year from the ratification of this article the manufacture, sale, or transportation of intoxicating liquors within, the importation thereof into, or the exportation thereof from the United States and all territory subject to the jurisdiction thereof for beverage purposes is hereby prohibited.

***Section 2.*** The Congress and the several States shall have concurrent power to enforce this article by appropriate legislation.

***Section 3.*** This article shall be inoperative unless it shall have been ratified as an amendment to the Constitution by the legislatures of the several States, as provided in the Constitution, within seven years from the date of the submission hereof to the States by the Congress.

**Amendment XIX (1920)**

The right of citizens of the United States to vote shall not be denied or abridged by the United States or by any State on account of sex.

Congress shall have power to enforce this article by appropriate legislation.

**Amendment XX (1933)**

***Section 1.*** The terms of the President and Vice-President shall end at noon on the 20th day of January, and the terms of Senators and Representatives at noon on the 3d day of January, of the years in which such terms would have ended if this article had not been ratified; and the terms of their successors shall then begin.

***Section 2.*** The Congress shall assemble at least once in every year, and such meeting shall begin at noon on the 3d day of January, unless they shall by law appoint a different day.

***Section 3.*** If, at the time fixed for the beginning of the term of the President, the President elect shall have died, the Vice-President elect shall become President. If a President shall not have been chosen before the time fixed for the beginning of his term, or if the President elect shall have failed to qualify, then the Vice-President elect shall act as President until a President shall have qualified; and the Congress may by law provide for the case wherein neither a President elect nor a Vice-President elect shall have qualified, declaring who shall then act as President, or the manner in which one who is to act shall be selected, and such person shall act accordingly until a President or Vice-President shall have qualified.

***Section 4.*** The Congress may by law provide for the case of the death of any of the persons from whom the House of Representatives may choose a President whenever the right of choice shall have devolved upon them, and for the case of the death of any of the persons from whom the Senate may choose a Vice-President whenever the right of choice shall have devolved upon them.

***Section 5.*** Sections 1 and 2 shall take effect on the 15th day of October following the ratification of this article.

***Section 6.*** This article shall be inoperative unless it shall have been ratified as an amendment to the Constitution by the legislatures of three-fourths of the several States within seven years from the date of its submission.

**Amendment XXI (1933)**

***Section 1.*** The eighteenth article of amendment to the Constitution of the United States is hereby repealed.

***Section 2.*** The transportation or importation into any State, Territory, or possession of the United States for delivery or use therein of intoxicating liquors, in violation of the laws thereof, is hereby prohibited.

*Section 3.* This article shall be inoperative unless it shall have been ratified as an amendment of the Constitution by conventions in the several States, as provided by the Constitution, within seven years from the date of the submission hereof to the States by the Congress.

**Amendment XXII (1951)**

No person shall be elected to the Office of the President more than twice, and no person who has held the Office of President, or acted as President, for more than two years of a term to which some other person was elected President shall be elected to the Office of the President more than once.

But this Article shall not apply to any person holding the Office of President when this Article was proposed by the Congress, and shall not prevent any person who may be holding the Office of President, or acting as President, during the term within which this Article becomes operative from holding the Office of President or acting as President during the remainder of such term.

**Amendment XXIII (1961)**

*Section 1.* The District constituting the seat of Government of the United States shall appoint in such manner as the Congress may direct:

A number of electors of President and Vice-President equal to the whole number of Senators and Representatives in Congress to which the District would be entitled if it were a State, but in no event more than the least populous State; they shall be in addition to those appointed by the States, but they shall be considered, for the purposes of the election of President and Vice-President, to be electors appointed by a State; and they shall meet in the District and perform such duties as provided by the twelfth article of amendment.

*Section 2.* The Congress shall have power to enforce this article by appropriate legislation.

**Amendment XXIV (1964)**

*Section 1.* The right of citizens of the United States to vote in any primary or other election for President or Vice-President, for electors for President or Vice-President, or for Senator or Representative in Congress, shall not be denied or abridged by the United States or any State by reason of failure to pay any poll tax or other tax.

*Section 2.* The Congress shall have power to enforce this article by appropriate legislation.

**Amendment XXV (1967)**

*Section 1.* In case of the removal of the President from Office or of his death or resignation, the Vice-President shall become President.

*Section 2.* Whenever there is a vacancy in the Office of the Vice-President, the President shall nominate a Vice-President who shall take Office upon confirmation by a majority vote of both Houses of Congress.

*Section 3.* Whenever the President transmits to the President pro tempore of the Senate and the Speaker of the House of Representatives his written declaration that he is unable to discharge the powers and duties of his Office, and until he transmits to them a written declaration to the contrary, such powers and duties shall be discharged by the Vice-President as Acting President.

*Section 4.* Whenever the Vice-President and a majority of either the principal Officers of the executive department or of such other body as Congress may by law provide, transmit to the President pro tempore of the Senate and the Speaker of the House of Representatives their written declaration that the President is unable to discharge the powers and duties of his Office, the Vice-President shall immediately assume the powers and duties of the Office as Acting President.

Thereafter, when the President transmits to the President pro tempore of the Senate and the Speaker of the House of Representatives his written declaration that no inability exists, he shall resume the powers and duties of his Office unless the Vice-President and a majority of either the principal Officers of the executive department or of such other body as Congress may by law provide, transmit within four days to the President pro tempore of the Senate and the Speaker of the House of Representatives their written declaration that the President is unable to discharge the powers and duties of his Office. Thereupon Congress shall decide the issue, assembling within forty-eight hours for that purpose if not in session. If the Congress, within twenty-one days after receipt of the latter written declaration, or, if Congress is not in session, within twenty-one days after Congress is required to assemble, determines by two-thirds vote of both Houses that the President is unable to discharge the powers and duties of his Office, the Vice-President shall continue to discharge the same as Acting President; otherwise, the President shall resume the powers and duties of his Office.

**Amendment XXVI (1971)**

*Section 1.* The right of citizens of the United States, who are eighteen years of age or older, to vote shall not be denied or abridged by the United States or by any State on account of age.

*Section 2.* The Congress shall have power to enforce this article by appropriate legislation.

**Amendment XXVII (1992)**

No law varying the compensation for the services of the Senators and Representatives shall take effect, until an election of Representatives shall have intervened.

## Presidents of the United States

| Year | President | Party | Votes Received | Electoral Vote | Percentage of Popular Vote |
|---|---|---|---|---|---|
| 1789 | George Washington | no designation | Unknown | 69 | Unknown |
| 1792 | George Washington | no designation | Unknown | 132 | Unknown |
| 1796 | John Adams | Federalist | Unknown | 71 | Unknown |
| 1800 | Thomas Jefferson | Democratic-Republican | Unknown | 73 | Unknown |
| 1804 | Thomas Jefferson | Democratic-Republican | Unknown | 162 | Unknown |
| 1808 | James Madison | Democratic-Republican | Unknown | 122 | Unknown |
| 1812 | James Madison | Democratic-Republican | Unknown | 128 | Unknown |
| 1816 | James Monroe | Democratic-Republican | Unknown | 183 | Unknown |
| 1820 | James Monroe | Democratic-Republican | Unknown | 231 | Unknown |
| 1824 | John Quincy Adams | Democratic-Republican | 108,740 | 84 | 30.5 |
| 1828 | Andrew Jackson | Democratic | 647,286 | 178 | 56.0 |
| 1832 | Andrew Jackson | Democratic | 687,502 | 219 | 55.0 |
| 1836 | Martin Van Buren | Democratic | 765,483 | 170 | 50.9 |
| 1840 | William H. Harrison | Whig | 1,274,624 | 234 | 53.1 |
| 1841 | John Tyler* | Whig | | | |
| 1844 | James K. Polk | Democratic | 1,338,464 | 170 | 49.6 |
| 1848 | Zachary Taylor | Whig | 1,360,967 | 163 | 47.4 |
| 1850 | Millard Fillmore* | Whig | | | |
| 1852 | Franklin Pierce | Democratic | 1,601,117 | 254 | 50.9 |
| 1856 | James Buchanan | Democratic | 1,832,955 | 174 | 45.3 |
| 1860 | Abraham Lincoln | Republican | 1,865,593 | 180 | 39.8 |
| 1864 | Abraham Lincoln | Republican | 2,206,938 | 212 | 55.0 |
| 1865 | Andrew Johnson* | Democratic | | | |
| 1868 | Ulysses S. Grant | Republican | 3,013,421 | 214 | 52.7 |
| 1872 | Ulysses S. Grant | Republican | 3,596,745 | 286 | 55.6 |
| 1876 | Rutherford B. Hayes | Republican | 4,036,572 | 185 | 48.0 |
| 1880 | James A. Garfield | Republican | 4,453,295 | 214 | 48.5 |
| 1881 | Chester A. Arthur* | Republican | | | |
| 1884 | Grover Cleveland | Democratic | 4,879,507 | 219 | 48.5 |
| 1888 | Benjamin Harrison | Republican | 5,447,129 | 233 | 47.9 |
| 1892 | Grover Cleveland | Democratic | 5,555,426 | 277 | 46.1 |
| 1896 | William McKinley | Republican | 7,102,246 | 271 | 51.1 |
| 1900 | William McKinley | Republican | 7,218,491 | 292 | 51.7 |
| 1901 | Theodore Roosevelt* | Republican | | | |
| 1904 | Theodore Roosevelt | Republican | 7,628,461 | 336 | 57.4 |
| 1908 | William H. Taft | Republican | 7,675,320 | 321 | 51.6 |
| 1912 | Woodrow Wilson | Democratic | 6,296,547 | 435 | 41.9 |
| 1916 | Woodrow Wilson | Democratic | 9,127,695 | 277 | 49.4 |
| 1920 | Warren G. Harding | Republican | 16,143,407 | 404 | 60.4 |
| 1923 | Calvin Coolidge* | Republican | | | |
| 1924 | Calvin Coolidge | Republican | 15,718,211 | 382 | 54.0 |
| 1928 | Herbert C. Hoover | Republican | 21,391,993 | 444 | 58.2 |
| 1932 | Franklin D. Roosevelt | Democratic | 22,809,638 | 472 | 57.4 |
| 1936 | Franklin D. Roosevelt | Democratic | 27,752,869 | 523 | 60.8 |
| 1940 | Franklin D. Roosevelt | Democratic | 27,307,819 | 449 | 54.8 |
| 1944 | Franklin D. Roosevelt | Democratic | 25,606,585 | 432 | 53.5 |
| 1945 | Harry S Truman* | Democratic | | | |
| 1948 | Harry S Truman | Democratic | 24,105,812 | 303 | 49.5 |
| 1952 | Dwight D. Eisenhower | Republican | 33,936,234 | 442 | 55.1 |

*(continued)*

## Table A-2

**Presidents of the United States *(continued)***

| Year | President | Party | Votes Received | Electoral Vote | Percentage of Popular Vote |
|---|---|---|---|---|---|
| 1956 | Dwight D. Eisenhower | Republican | 35,590,472 | 457 | 57.6 |
| 1960 | John F. Kennedy | Democratic | 34,227,096 | 303 | 49.9 |
| 1963 | Lyndon B. Johnson* | Democratic | | | |
| 1964 | Lyndon B. Johnson | Democratic | 43,126,506 | 486 | 61.1 |
| 1968 | Richard M. Nixon | Republican | 31,785,480 | 301 | 43.4 |
| 1972 | Richard M. Nixon | Republican | 47,169,905 | 520 | 60.7 |
| 1974 | Gerald R. Ford† | Republican | | | |
| 1976 | Jimmy Carter | Democratic | 40,827,394 | 297 | 50.0 |
| 1980 | Ronald Reagan | Republican | 43,899,248 | 489 | 50.8 |
| 1984 | Ronald Reagan | Republican | 54,450,603 | 525 | 58.8 |
| 1988 | George H. W. Bush | Republican | 47,946,422 | 426 | 53.9 |
| 1992 | Bill Clinton | Democratic | 43,728,375 | 370 | 43.2 |
| 1996 | Bill Clinton | Democratic | 45,628,667 | 379 | 49.2 |
| 2000 | George W. Bush | Republican | 50,456,169 | 271 | 47.9 |
| 2004 | George W. Bush | Republican | 62,553,154 | 286 | 50.8 |

*Succeeded to presidency upon death of the incumbent.
†Succeeded to presidency upon resignation of the incumbent.

# SELECTIONS FROM THE FEDERALIST PAPERS

***The Federalist* No. 10**
James Madison
November 23, 1787

TO THE PEOPLE OF THE STATE OF NEW YORK

Among the numerous advantages promised by a well-constructed Union, none deserves to be more accurately developed than its tendency to break and control the violence of faction. The friend of popular governments never finds himself so much alarmed for their character and fate, as when he contemplates their propensity to this dangerous vice. He will not fail, therefore, to set a due value on any plan which, without violating the principles to which he is attached, provides a proper cure for it. The instability, injustice, and confusion introduced into the public councils, have, in truth, been the mortal diseases under which popular governments have everywhere perished; as they continue to be the favorite and fruitful topics from which the adversaries to liberty derive their most specious declamations. The valuable improvements made by the American constitutions on the popular models, both ancient and modern, cannot certainly be too much admired; but it would be an unwarrantable partiality, to contend that they have as effectually obviated the danger on this side, as was wished and expected. Complaints are everywhere heard from our most considerate and virtuous citizens, equally the friends of public and private faith, and of public and personal liberty, that our governments are too unstable, that the public good is disregarded in the conflicts of rival parties, and that measures are too often decided, not according to the rules of justice and the rights of the minor party, but by the superior force of an interested and overbearing majority. However anxiously we may wish that these complaints had no foundation, the evidence of known facts will not permit us to deny that they are in some degree true. It will be found, indeed, on a candid review of our situation, that some of the distresses under which we labor have been erroneously charged on the operation of our governments; but it will be found, at the same time, that other causes will not alone account for many of our heaviest misfortunes; and, particularly, for that prevailing and increasing distrust of public engagements, and alarm for private rights, which are echoed from one end of the continent to the other. These must be chiefly, if not wholly, effects of the unsteadiness and injustice with which a factious spirit has tainted our public administrations.

By a faction, I understand a number of citizens, whether amounting to a majority or a minority of the whole, who are united and actuated by some common impulse of passion, or of interest, adversed to the rights of other citizens, or to the permanent and aggregate interests of the community.

There are two methods of curing the mischiefs of faction: the one, by removing its causes; the other, by controlling its effects.

There are again two methods of removing the causes of faction: the one, by destroying the liberty which is essential to its existence; the other, by giving to every citizen the same opinions, the same passions, and the same interests.

It could never be more truly said than of the first remedy, that it was worse than the disease. Liberty is to faction what air is to fire, an aliment without which it instantly expires. But it could not be less folly to abolish liberty, which is essential to political life, because it nourishes faction, than it would be to wish the annihilation of air, which is essential to animal life, because it imparts to fire its destructive agency.

The second expedient is as impracticable as the first would be unwise. As long as the reason of man continues fallible, and he is at liberty to exercise it, different opinions will be formed. As long as the connection subsists between his reason and his self-love, his opinions and his passions will have a reciprocal influence on each other; and the former will be objects to which the latter will attach themselves. The diversity in the faculties of men, from which the rights of property originate, is not less an insuperable obstacle to a uniformity of interests. The protection of these faculties is the first object of government. From the protection of different and unequal faculties of acquiring property, the possession of different degrees and kinds of property immediately results; and from the influence of these on the sentiments and views of the respective proprietors, ensues a division of the society into different interests and parties.

The latent causes of faction are thus sown in the nature of man; and we see them everywhere brought into different degrees of activity, according to the different circumstances of civil society. A zeal for different opinions concerning religion, concerning government, and many other points, as well of speculation as of practice; an attachment to different leaders ambitiously contending for pre-eminence and power; or to persons of other descriptions whose fortunes have been interesting to the human passions, have, in turn, divided mankind into parties, inflamed them with mutual animosity, and rendered them much more disposed to vex and oppress each other than to co-operate for their common good. So strong is this propensity of mankind to fall into mutual animosities, that where no substantial occasion presents itself, the most frivolous and fanciful distinctions have been sufficient to kindle their unfriendly passions and excite their most violent conflicts. But the most common and durable source of factions has been the various and unequal distribution of property. Those who hold and those who are without property have ever formed distinct interests in society. Those who are creditors, and those who are debtors, fall under a like discrimination. A landed interest, a manufacturing interest, a mercantile interest, a moneyed interest, with many lesser interests, grow up of necessity in civilized nations, and divide them into different classes, actuated by different sentiments and views. The regulation of these various and interfering interests forms the principal task of modern legislation, and involves the spirit of party and faction in the necessary and ordinary operations of the government.

No man is allowed to be a judge in his own cause, because his interest would certainly bias his judgment, and, not improbably, corrupt his integrity. With equal, nay with greater reason, a body of men are unfit to be both judges and parties at the same time; yet what are many of the most important acts of legislation, but so many judicial determinations, not indeed concerning the rights of single persons, but concerning the rights of large bodies of citizens? And what are the different classes of legislators but advocates and parties to the causes which they determine? Is a law proposed concerning private debts? It is a question to which the creditors are parties on one side and the debtors on the other. Justice ought to hold the balance between them. Yet the parties are, and must be, themselves the judges; and the most numerous party, or, in other words, the most powerful faction must be expected to prevail. Shall domestic manufactures be encouraged, and in what degree, by restrictions on foreign manufactures? are questions which would be differently decided by the landed and the manufacturing classes, and probably by neither with a sole regard to justice and the public good. The apportionment of taxes on the various descriptions of property is an act which seems to require the most exact impartiality; yet there is, perhaps, no legislative act in which greater opportunity and temptation are given to a predominant party to trample on the rules of justice. Every shilling with which they overburden the inferior number, is a shilling saved to their own pockets.

It is in vain to say that enlightened statesmen will be able to adjust these clashing interests, and render them all subservient to the public good. Enlightened statesmen will not always be at the helm. Nor, in many cases, can such an adjustment be made at all without taking into view indirect and remote considerations, which will rarely prevail over the immediate interest which one party may find in disregarding the rights of another or the good of the whole.

The inference to which we are brought is, that the *causes* of faction cannot be removed, and that relief is only to be sought in the means of controlling its *effects*.

If a faction consists of less than a majority, relief is supplied by the republican principle, which enables the majority to defeat its sinister views by regular vote. It may clog the administration, it may convulse the society; but it will be unable to execute and mask its violence under the forms of the Constitution. When a majority is included in a faction, the form of popular government, on the other hand, enables it to sacrifice to its ruling passion or interest both the public good and the rights of other citizens. To secure the public good and private rights against the danger of such a faction, and at the same time to preserve the spirit and the form of popular government, is then the great object to which our inquiries are directed. Let me add that it is the great desideratum by which this form of government can be rescued from the opprobrium under which it has so long labored, and be recommended to the esteem and adoption of mankind.

By what means is this object attainable? Evidently by one of two only. Either the existence of the same passion or interest in a majority at the same time must be prevented, or the majority, having such coexistent passion or interest, must be rendered, by their number and local situation, unable to concert and carry into effect schemes of oppression. If the impulse and the opportunity be suffered to coincide, we well know that neither moral nor religious motives can be relied on as an adequate control. They are not found to be such on the injustice and violence of individuals, and lose their efficacy in proportion to the number combined together, that is, in proportion as their efficacy becomes needful.

From this view of the subject it may be concluded that a pure democracy, by which I mean a society consisting of a small number of citizens, who assemble and administer the government in person, can admit of no cure for the mischiefs of faction. A common passion or interest will, in almost every case, be felt by a majority of the whole; a communication and concert result from the form of government itself; and there is nothing to check the inducements to sacrifice the weaker party or an obnoxious individual. Hence it is that such democracies have ever been spectacles of turbulence and contention; have ever been found incompatible with personal security or the rights of property; and have in general been as short in their lives as they have been violent in their deaths. Theoretic politicians, who have patronized this species of government, have erroneously supposed that by reducing mankind to a perfect equality in their political rights, they would, at the same time, be perfectly equalized and assimilated in their possessions, their opinions, and their passions.

A republic, by which I mean a government in which the scheme of representation takes place, opens a different prospect, and promises the cure for which we are seeking. Let us examine the points in which it varies from pure democracy, and we shall comprehend both the nature of the cure and the efficacy which it must derive from the Union.

The two great points of difference between a democracy and a republic are: first, the delegation of the government, in the latter, to a small number of citizens elected by the rest; secondly, the greater number of citizens, and greater sphere of country, over which the latter may be extended.

The effect of the first difference is, on the one hand, to refine and enlarge the public views, by passing them through the medium of a chosen body of citizens, whose wisdom may best discern the true interest of their country, and whose patriotism and love of justice will be least likely to sacrifice it to temporary or partial considerations. Under such a regulation, it may well happen that the public voice, pronounced by the representatives of the people, will be more consonant to the public good than if pronounced by the people themselves, convened for the purpose. On the other hand, the effect may be inverted. Men of factious tempers, of local prejudices, or of sinister designs, may, by intrigue, by corruption, or by other means, first obtain the suffrages, and then betray the interests, of the people. The question resulting is, whether small or extensive republics are more favorable to the election of proper guardians of the public weal; and it is clearly decided in favor of the latter by two obvious considerations:

In the first place, it is to be remarked that, however small the republic may be, the representatives must be raised to a certain number, in order to guard against the cabals of a few; and that, however large it may be, they must be limited to a certain number, in order to guard against the confusion of a multitude. Hence, the number of representatives in the two cases not being in proportion to that of the two constituents, and being proportionally greater in the small republic, it follows that, if the proportion of fit characters be not less in the large than in the small republic, the former will present a greater option, and consequently a greater probability of a fit choice.

In the next place, as each representative will be chosen by a greater number of citizens in the large than in the small republic, it will be more difficult for unworthy candidates to practice with success the vicious arts by which elections are too often carried; and the suffrages of the people being more free, will be more likely to centre in men who possess the most attractive merit and the most diffusive and established characters.

It must be confessed that in this, as in most other cases, there is a mean, on both sides of which inconveniences will be found to lie. By enlarging too much the number of electors, you render the representatives too little acquainted with all their local circumstances and lesser interests; as by reducing it too much, you render him unduly attached to these, and too little fit to comprehend and pursue great and national objects. The federal Constitution forms a happy combination in this respect; the great and aggregate interests being referred to the national, the local and particular to the State legislatures.

The other point of difference is, the greater number of citizens and extent of territory which may be brought within the compass of republican than of democratic government; and it is this circumstance principally which renders factious combinations less to be dreaded in the former than in the latter. The smaller the society, the fewer probably will be the distinct parties and interests composing it; the fewer the distinct parties and interests, the more frequently will a majority be found of the same party; and the smaller the number of individuals composing a majority, and the smaller the compass within which they are placed, the more easily will they concert and execute their plans of oppression. Extend the sphere, and you take in a greater variety of parties and interests; you make it less probable that a majority of the whole will have a common motive to invade the rights of other citizens; or if such a common motive exists, it will be more difficult for all who feel it to discover their own strength, and to act in unison with each other. Besides other impediments, it may be remarked that, where there is a consciousness of unjust or dishonorable purposes, communication is always checked by distrust in proportion to the number whose concurrence is necessary.

Hence, it clearly appears, that the same advantage which a republic has over a democracy, in controlling the effects of faction, is enjoyed by a large over a small republic,—is enjoyed by the Union over the States composing it. Does the advantage consist in the substitution of representatives whose enlightened views and virtuous sentiments render them superior to local prejudices and schemes of injustice? It will not be denied that the representation of the Union will be most likely to possess these requisite endowments. Does it consist in the greater security afforded by a greater variety of parties, against the event of any one party being able to outnumber and oppress the rest? In an equal degree does the increased variety of parties comprised within the Union, increase this security. Does it, in fine, consist in the greater obstacles opposed to the concert and accomplishment of the secret wishes of an unjust and interested majority? Here, again, the extent of the Union gives it the most palpable advantage.

The influence of factious leaders may kindle a flame within their particular States, but will be unable to spread a general conflagration through the other States. A religious sect may degenerate into a political faction in a part of the Confederacy; but the variety of sects dispersed over the entire face of it must secure the national councils against any danger from that source. A rage for paper money, for an abolition of debts, for an equal division of property, or for any other improper or wicked project, will be less apt to pervade the whole body of the Union than a particular member of it; in the same proportion as such a malady is more likely to taint a particular county or district, than an entire State.

In the extent and proper structure of the Union, therefore, we behold a republican remedy for the diseases most incident to republican government. And according to the degree of pleasure and pride we feel in being republicans, ought to be our zeal in cherishing the spirit and supporting the character of Federalists.

PUBLIUS

## *The Federalist* No. 51

James Madison
February 8, 1788

TO THE PEOPLE OF THE STATE OF NEW YORK

To what expedient, then, shall we finally resort, for maintaining in practice the necessary partition of power among the several departments, as laid down in the Constitution? The only answer that can be given is, that as all these exterior provisions are found to be inadequate, the defect must be supplied, by so contriving the interior structure of the government as that its several constituent parts may, by their mutual relations, be the means of keeping each other in their proper places. Without presuming to undertake a full development of this important idea, I will hazard a few general observations, which may perhaps place it in a clearer light, and enable us to form a more correct judgment of the principles and structure of the government planned by the convention.

In order to lay a due foundation for that separate and distinct exercise of the different powers of government, which to a certain extent is admitted on all hands to be essential to the preservation of liberty, it is evident that each department should have a will of its own; and consequently should be so constituted that the members of each should have as little agency as possible in the appointment of the members of the others. Were this principle rigorously adhered to, it would require that all the appointments for the supreme executive, legislative, and judiciary magistracies should be drawn from the same fountain of authority, the people, through channels having no communication whatever with one another. Perhaps such a plan of constructing the several departments would be less difficult in practice than it may in contemplation appear. Some difficulties, however, and some additional expense would attend the execution of it. Some deviations, therefore, from the principle must be admitted. In the constitution of the judiciary department in particular, it might be inexpedient to insist rigorously on the principle: first, because peculiar qualifications being essential in the members, the primary consideration ought to be to select that mode of choice which best secures these qualifications; secondly, because the permanent tenure by which the appointments are held in that department, must soon destroy all sense of dependence on the authority conferring them.

It is equally evident, that the members of each department should be as little dependent as possible on those of the others, for the emoluments annexed to their offices. Were the executive magistrate, or the judges, not independent of the legislature in this particular, their independence in every other would be merely nominal.

But the great security against a gradual concentration of the several powers in the same department, consists in giving to those who administer each department the necessary constitutional means and personal motives to resist encroachments of the others. The provision for defense must in this, as in all other cases, be made commensurate to the danger of attack. Ambition must be made to counteract ambition. The interest of the man must be connected with the constitutional rights of the place. It may be a reflection on human nature, that such devices should be necessary to control the abuses of government. But what is government itself, but the greatest of all reflections on human nature? If men were angels, no government would be necessary. If angels were to govern men, neither external nor internal controls on government would be necessary. In framing a government which is to be administered by men over men, the great difficulty lies in this: you must first enable the government to control the governed; and in the next place oblige it to control itself. A dependence on the people is, no doubt, the primary control on the government; but experience has taught mankind the necessity of auxiliary precautions.

This policy of supplying, by opposite and rival interests, the defect of better motives, might be traced through the whole system of human affairs, private as well as public. We see it particularly displayed in all the subordinate distributions of power, where the constant aim is to divide and arrange the several offices in such a manner as that each may be a check on the other—that the private interest of every individual may be a sentinel over the public rights. These inventions of prudence cannot be less requisite in the distribution of the supreme powers of the State.

But it is not possible to give to each department an equal power of self-defense. In republican government, the legislative authority necessarily predominates. The remedy for this inconveniency is to divide the legislature into different branches; and to render them, by different modes of election and different principles of action, as little connected with each other as the nature of their common functions and their common dependence on the society will admit. It may even be necessary to guard against dangerous encroachments by still further precautions. As the weight of the legislative authority requires that it should be thus divided, the weakness of the executive may require, on the other hand, that it should be fortified. An absolute negative on the legislature appears, at first view, to be the natural defense with which the executive magistrate should be armed. But perhaps it would be neither altogether safe nor alone sufficient. On ordinary occasions it might not be exerted with the requisite firmness, and on extraordinary occasions it might be perfidiously abused. May not this defect of an absolute negative be supplied by some qualified connection between this weaker department and the weaker branch of the stronger department, by which the latter may be led to support the constitutional rights of the former, without being too much detached from the rights of its own department?

If the principles on which these observations are founded be just, as I persuade myself they are, and they be applied as a criterion to the several State constitutions, and to the federal Constitution it will be found that if the latter does not perfectly correspond with them, the former are infinitely less able to bear such a test.

There are, moreover, two considerations particularly applicable to the federal system of America, which place that system in a very interesting point of view.

*First.* In a single republic, all the power surrendered by the people is submitted to the administration of a single government; and the usurpations are guarded against by a division of the government into distinct and separate departments. In the compound republic of America, the power surrendered by the people is first divided between two distinct governments, and then the portion allotted to each subdivided among distinct and separate departments. Hence a double security arises to the rights of the people. The different governments will control each other, at the same time that each will be controlled by itself.

*Second.* It is of great importance in a republic not only to guard the society against the oppression of its rulers, but to guard one part of the society against the injustice of the other part. Different interests necessarily exist in different classes of citizens. If a majority be united by a common interest, the rights of the minority will be insecure. There are but two methods of providing against this evil: the one by creating a will in the community independent of the majority that is, of the society itself; the other, by comprehending in the society so many separate descriptions of citizens as will render an unjust combination of a majority of the whole very improbable, if not impracticable. The first method prevails in all governments possessing an hereditary or self-appointed authority. This, at best, is but a precarious security; because a power independent of the society may as well espouse the unjust views of the major as the rightful interests of the minor party, and may possibly be turned against both parties. The second method will be exemplified in the federal republic of the United States. Whilst all authority in it will be derived from and dependent on the society, the society itself will be broken into so many parts, interests, and classes of citizens, that the rights of individuals, or of the minority, will be in little danger from interested combinations of the majority. In a free government the security for civil rights must be the same as that for religious rights. It consists in the one case in the multiplicity of interests, and in the other in the multiplicity of sects. The degree of security in both cases will depend on the number of interests and sects; and this may be presumed to depend on the extent of country and number of people comprehended under the same government. This view of the subject must particularly recommend a proper federal system to all the sincere and considerate friends of republican government, since it shows that in exact proportion as the territory of the Union may be formed into more circumscribed Confederacies, or States oppressive combinations of a majority will be facilitated: the best security, under the republican forms, for the rights of every class of citizens, will be diminished; and consequently the stability and independence of some member of the government, the only other security, must be proportionately increased. Justice is the end of government. It is the end of civil society. It ever has been and ever will be pursued until it be obtained, or until liberty be lost in the pursuit. In a society under the forms of which the stronger faction can readily unite and oppress the weaker, anarchy may as truly be said to reign as in a state of nature, where the weaker individual is not secured against the violence of the stronger; and as, in the latter state, even the stronger individuals are prompted, by the uncertainty of their condition, to submit to a government which may protect the weak as well as themselves; so, in the former state, will the more powerful factions or parties be gradually induced, by a like motive, to wish for a government which will protect all parties, the weaker as well as the more powerful. It can be little doubted that if the State of Rhode Island was separated from the Confederacy and left to itself, the insecurity of rights under the popular form of government within such narrow limits would be displayed by such reiterated oppressions of factious majorities that some power altogether independent of the people would soon be called for by the voice of the very factions whose misrule had proved the necessity of it. In the extended republic of the United States, and among the great variety of interests, parties, and sects which it embraces, a coalition of a majority of the whole society could seldom take place on any other principles than those of justice and the general good; whilst there being thus less danger to a minor from the will of a major party, there must be less pretext, also, to provide for the security of the former, by introducing into the government a will not dependent on the latter, or, in other words, a will independent of the society itself. It is no less certain than it is important, notwithstanding the contrary opinions which have been entertained, that the larger the society, provided it lie within a practical sphere, the more duly capable it will be of self-government. And happily for the *republican cause,* the practicable sphere may be carried to a very great extent, by a judicious modification and mixture of the *federal principle.*

PUBLIUS

# Endnotes

## Chapter 1

[1] President George W. Bush's address to the nation on Katrina, September 15, 2005, online at <www.whitehouse.gov>.

[2] Gallup Poll, September 7-10, 2006, online at <www.pollingreport.com>.

[3] "President's Remarks at the United Nations General Assembly," September 12, 2002, online at <http://www.whitehouse.gov>.

[4] From "The National Security Strategy of the United States of America," September 17, 2002, online at <http://www.whitehouse.gov/nsc/nss.pdf>.

[5] *New York Times,* April 29, 2004, p. A1, reporting results of a *New York Times*/CBS News poll showing 47 percent of respondents thought the United States "had done the right thing" in invading Iraq.

[6] Code of Federal Regulations, Title 49, Volume 5, Standard 104 (2001).

[7] The National Center for Education Statistics, *Digest of Education Statistics,* 2002, Table 322; and *Statistical Abstract of the United States: 2003,* p. 187.

[8] In 2001, Congress voted to end the estate tax in 2010 for one year but to reinstate it the following year.

[9] V. O. Key, Jr., *Politics, Parties, and Pressure Groups,* 5th ed. (New York: Crowell, 1964), p. 3.

[10] David Easton, *The Political System: An Inquiry into the State of Political Science* (New York: Knopf, 1953), pp. 136–137.

[11] Key, *Politics, Parties, and Pressure Groups,* p. 2.

[12] *Observer* (London), November 29, 1964, p. 2.

[13] Key, *Politics, Parties, and Pressure Groups,* p. 2.

[14] "Remarks of Senator John F. Kennedy, Street Rally, Waterbury, Connecticut, November 6, 1960," in *The Speeches of Senator John F. Kennedy, Presidential Campaign of 1960* (Washington, D.C.: U.S. Government Printing Office, 1961), p. 912.

[15] David Easton, "An Approach to the Analysis of Political Systems," *World Politics,* vol. 9 (April 1957), pp. 383–384. Our discussion of the concept of a political system relies chiefly on Easton's work, although it should not be read as a literal summary of his approach. For example, the analogy to a stereo system is the authors' own, and Easton's analysis of a political system is both much more detailed and broader in scope than the outline presented here.

[16] Robert L. Lineberry, *American Public Policy: What Government Does and What Difference It Makes* (New York: Harper & Row, 1977), p. 3.

[17] Ibid., p. 69.

[18] Ibid., p. 71.

[19] U.S. Bureau of the Census, *Profile of General Demographic Characteristics: 2000,* table DP-1, online at <http://www.census.gov/Press-Release/www/2001/tables/dp_us_2000.PDF>; for 2010 and 2050 estimates, U.S. Bureau of the Census, "U.S. Interim Projections by Age, Sex, Race, and Hispanic Origin," March 18, 2004, online at <http://www.census.gov/ipc/www/usinterimproj/>. Figures rounded.

[20] Ben J. Wattenberg, in collaboration with Richard M. Scammon, *This U.S.A.* (New York: Doubleday, 1965), p. 18. Population projections have been lowered since this study was published.

[21] Data from U.S. Bureau of the Census, "Ancestry: 2000," online at <http://www.census.gov>.

[22] The Census Bureau does not ask the religion of Americans in the decennial census, which is taken every 10 years that end in zero, but religious groups estimate their own membership. These are rounded figures for 2000 from The Encyclopedia Britannica Library, *Year in Review 2002,* table: "Religious Adherents in the United States of America, AD 1900–2000."

[23] See Wattenberg and Scammon, *This U.S.A.,* pp. 45–46.

[24] U.S. Bureau of the Census, *Population Projections Program, Projections of the Resident Population by Race, Hispanic Origin, and Nativity: Middle Series, 2050 to 2070,* series NP-T5-G, January 13, 2000.

[25] U.S. Bureau of the Census, *Census 2000, Urban and Rural,* PCT-2, online at <http://www.census.gov>.

[26] John Kenneth Galbraith, *The New Industrial State* (Boston: Houghton Mifflin, 1967), pp. 7–9, 392–393.

[27] See Rachel Carson, *Silent Spring* (Boston: Houghton Mifflin, 1962).

[28] John F. Kennedy, "Remarks at Amherst College," October 26, 1963, in *Public Papers of the Presidents of the United States, John F. Kennedy, 1963* (Washington, D.C.: U.S. Government Printing Office, 1964), p. 816.

[29] *Parliamentary Debates, House of Commons, Fifth Series,* vol. 444 (London: His Majesty's Stationery Office, 1947), pp. 206–207.

## Chapter 2

[1] Daniel J. Boorstin, *The Americans: The National Experience* (New York: Random House, 1965), pp. 325ff.

[2] Ralph Ketcham, *Framed for Posterity: The Enduring Philosophy of the Constitution* (Lawrence: University Press of Kansas, 1993), p. 11.

[3] *Grutter* v. *Bollinger,* 123 S. Ct. 617 (2003); *Gratz* v. *Bollinger,* 123 S. Ct. 602 (2003).

[4] *Brown* v. *Board of Education of Topeka et al.,* 347 U.S. 483 (1954).

[5] *Roe* v. *Wade,* 410 U.S. 113 (1973); *Doe* v. *Bolton,* 410 U.S. 179 (1973).

[6] Carl L. Becker, *The Declaration of Independence* (New York: Vintage Books, 1942), p. 5.

[7] David Hawke, *A Transaction of Free Men* (New York: Scribner's, 1964), p. 209.

[8] Ibid.

[9] Peter Laslett, ed., *Locke's Two Treatises of Government* (Cambridge: Cambridge University Press, 1960), p. 348.

[10] Samuel Eliot Morison, "The Mayflower Compact," in Daniel J. Boorstin, ed., *An American Primer* (Chicago: University of Chicago Press, 1966), p. 19.

[11] Clinton Rossiter, *Seedtime of the Republic* (New York: Harcourt Brace Jovanovich, 1953), p. 35.

[12] Ibid., p. 87.

[13] Ibid., p. 88.

[14] Nat Hentoff, *The First Freedom: The Tumultuous History of Free Speech in America* (New York: Delacorte Press, 1980), pp. 160–161.

[15] The newspaper was published in Boston on September 25, 1690.

[16] In Charles Francis Adams, ed., *The Works of John Adams,* vol. 10 (Boston: Little, Brown, 1856), p. 282.

[17] Gordon S. Wood, *The Radicalism of the American Revolution* (New York: Knopf, 1992), p. 6.

[18] Alpheus T. Mason, "America's Political Heritage: Revolution and Free Government—A Bicentennial Tribute," in M. Judd Harmon, ed., *Essays on the Constitution of the United States* (Port Washington, N.Y.: Kennikat Press, 1978), p. 17.

[19] Merrill Jensen, *The New Nation* (New York: Knopf, 1950), pp. 347, 348.

[20] William H. Riker, *Federalism: Origin, Operation, Significance* (Boston: Little, Brown, 1964), pp. 18, 20.

[21] Letter to James Duane, in Clinton Rossiter, *1787: The Grand Convention* (New York: Macmillan, 1966), p. 53.

[22] Catherine Drinker Bowen, *Miracle at Philadelphia* (Boston: Little, Brown, 1966).

[23] Charles Warren, *The Making of the Constitution* (New York: Barnes & Noble, 1967), pp. 55–60.

[24] Bowen, *Miracle at Philadelphia,* p. 23.

[25] John P. Roche, "The Founding Fathers: A Reform Caucus in Action," *American Political Science Review,* vol. 55, no. 4 (December 1961), p. 803.

[26] Fred Barbash, *The Founding: A Dramatic Account of the Writing of the Constitution* (New York: Linden Press/Simon & Schuster, 1987), p. 58.

[27] Ibid., p. 69.

[28] Bowen, *Miracle at Philadelphia,* p. 186.

[29] James MacGregor Burns, *The Vineyard of Liberty: The American Experiment* (New York: Knopf, 1982), p. 40.

[30] Barbash, *The Founding,* p. 149.

[31] In Carl Van Doren, *The Great Rehearsal* (New York: Viking Press, 1948), p. 153.

[32] Warren, *The Making of the Constitution,* pp. 687–688.

[33] In Van Doren, *The Great Rehearsal,* p. 174.

[34] Baron de Montesquieu, *The Spirit of the Laws,* vol. 1 (New York: Hafner, 1949), p. 151.

[35] Edward S. Corwin, Harold W. Chase, and Craig R. Ducat, *The Constitution and What It Means Today* (Princeton: Princeton University Press, 1978), p. 5.

[36] Alpheus T. Mason, *The Supreme Court: Palladium of Freedom* (Ann Arbor: University of Michigan Press, 1962), p. 8.

[37] Archibald Cox, *The Court and the Constitution* (Boston: Houghton Mifflin, 1987), p. 42.

[38] *Marbury* v. *Madison,* 1 Cranch 137 (1803). Judicial review is discussed in Chapter 15.

[39] Richard F. Fenno, Jr., *The President's Cabinet* (Cambridge: Harvard University Press, 1959), pp. 19–20.

[40] Charles A. Beard, *An Economic Interpretation of the Constitution of the United States* (New York: Macmillan, 1935), p. 188. Originally published in 1913.

[41] Forrest McDonald, *We the People* (Chicago: University of Chicago Press, 1958), pp. vii, 350, 415.

[42] Robert E. Brown, *Charles Beard and the Constitution* (Princeton: Princeton University Press, 1956), p. 198.

[43] Charles Francis Adams, ed., *The Works of John Adams,* vol. 6 (Boston: Little, Brown, 1851), p. 484.

[44] Ketcham, *Framed for Posterity: The Enduring Philosophy of the Constitution,* p. 27.

[45] James Madison, "*The Federalist,* No. 40," in Edward Mead Earle, ed., *The Federalist* (New York: Random House, Modern Library), p. 257.

[46] Alexander Hamilton, "*The Federalist,* No. 84," in Earle, ed., *The Federalist,* p. 561.

[47] Seymour Martin Lipset, *The First New Nation* (New York: Basic Books, 1963), p. 2.

[48] Ibid., p. 16.

[49] *McCulloch* v. *Maryland,* 4 Wheaton 316 (1819).

[50] Alexander Hamilton, "*The Federalist,* No. 68," in Earle, ed., *The Federalist,* pp. 441–442.

[51] The year after each amendment refers to the year of ratification.

[52] *Chisholm* v. *Georgia,* 2 Dallas 419 (1793). However, citizens can sue states in state courts if they are deprived of their rights under the Constitution or federal laws, and states can appeal such cases to the federal courts. *Scheuer* v. *Rhodes,* 416 U.S. 232 (1974); *Maine* v. *Thiboutot,* 448 U.S. 1 (1980).

[53] See George Stimpson, *A Book About American Politics* (New York: Harper & Row, 1952), pp. 527–528.

[54] *Clinton* v. *City of New York,* 524 U.S. 417 (1998).

[55] "Letter to Samuel Kercheval, 1816," in Saul K. Padover, ed., *The Complete Jefferson* (New York: Duell, Sloan & Pearce, 1943), p. 291.

## Chapter 3

[1] Data as of June 2006 from Insurance Institute for Highway Safety, Highway Loss Data Institute, "Maximum Posted Speed Limits for Passenger Vehicles," online at <http://www.iihs.org/laws/state_laws/speed_limit_laws.html>.

[2] *Washington Post,* November 19, 1995, p. A16; and *New York Times,* November 19, 1995, p. A24.

[3] William H. Riker, *Federalism: Origin, Operation, Significance* (Boston: Little, Brown, 1964), p. 1.

[4] The former Soviet Union was a federal system. When it broke up in 1991, it was replaced by the Commonwealth of Independent States, a very loose grouping of 11 of the 15 former Soviet republics. Although the future of the Commonwealth was uncertain, it, too, could be roughly characterized as a federal system.

[5] Riker, *Federalism: Origin, Operation, Significance,* pp. 152–153.

[6] U.S. Department of Commerce, Bureau of Economic Analysis, "State Personal Income: 2005," online at <http://www.bea.doc.gov/bea/rels.htm>.

[7] Morton Grodzins, *The American System* (Chicago: Rand McNally, 1966), pp. 3–4.

[8] U.S. Bureau of the Census, *Statistical Abstract of the United States: 2006,* p. 272.

[9] Morton Grodzins, "Centralization and Decentralization in the American Federal System," in Robert A. Goldwin, ed., *A Nation of States* (Chicago: Rand McNally, 1963), pp. 1–4.

[10] Grodzins, *The American System;* Daniel J. Elazar, *American Federalism: A View from the States* (New York: Crowell, 1966); Daniel J. Elazar, *The American Partnership* (Chicago: University of Chicago Press, 1962).

[11] Michael D. Reagan, *The New Federalism* (New York: Oxford University Press, 1972), pp. 4, 145.

[12] Donald F. Kettl, *The Regulation of American Federalism* (Baltimore: Johns Hopkins University Press, 1987), p. 174.

[13] James L. Sundquist with David W. Davis, *Making Federalism Work* (Washington, D.C.: The Brookings Institution, 1969), p. 12.

[14] "Letter to George Washington, April 16, 1787," in Saul K. Padover, ed., *The Complete Madison* (New York: Harper & Brothers, 1953), p. 184.

[15] Riker, *Federalism: Origin, Operation, Significance,* pp. 4–5.

[16] *McCulloch* v. *Maryland,* 4 Wheaton 316 (1819).

[17] *United States* v. *Curtiss-Wright Export Corp.,* 299 U.S. 304 (1936).

[18] *McCulloch* v. *Maryland* (1819).

[19] Alfred H. Kelly and Winfred A. Harbison, *The American Constitution* (New York: Norton, 1955), p. 176.

[20] In Walter Berns, "The Meaning of the Tenth Amendment," in Goldwin, ed., *A Nation of States,* p. 138. For a spirited defense of the opposite view, see "The Case for 'States' Rights'" by James J. Kilpatrick in the same volume.

[21] *Collector* v. *Day,* 11 Wallace 113 (1871). This decision was overruled by the Supreme Court in 1939 in *Graves* v. *O'Keefe,* 306 U.S. 466 (1939).

[22] *Schechter Poultry Corporation* v. *United States,* 295 U.S. 495 (1935).

[23] *Steward Machine Co.* v. *Davis,* 301 U.S. 548 (1937); *National Labor Relations Board* v. *Jones & Laughlin Steel Corp.,* 301 U.S. 1 (1937).

[24] *United States* v. *Darby,* 312 U.S. 100 (1941).

[25] *The National League of Cities* v. *Usery,* 426 U.S. 833 (1976).

[26] *Equal Employment Opportunity Commission* v. *Wyoming,* 460 U.S. 226 (1983).

[27] *Garcia* v. *San Antonio Metropolitan Transit Authority,* 469 U.S. 528 (1985).

[28] *United States* v. *Lopez,* 514 U.S. 549 (1995).

[29] *Seminole Tribe of Florida* v. *Florida,* 517 U.S. 44 (1996).

[30] *Printz* v. *United States* and *Mack* v. *United States,* both 521 U.S. 898 (1997).

[31] *Alden* v. *Maine,* 527 U.S. 706 (1999).

[32] *Kimel* v. *Florida Board,* 528 U.S. 62 (2000).

[33] *United States* v. *Morrison,* 529 U.S. 598 (2000).

[34] *Federal Maritime Commission* v. *South Carolina Ports Authority,* 535 U.S. 743 (2002).

[35] Elazar, *American Federalism: A View from the States,* p. 164.

[36] *Williams* v. *North Carolina,* 317 U.S. 287 (1942), 325 U.S. 226 (1945).

[37] *Haddock* v. *Haddock,* 201 U.S. 562 (1906).

[38] Edward S. Corwin et al., eds., *The Constitution of the United States of America, Analysis and Interpretation* (Washington, D.C.: U.S. Government Printing Office, 1964), p. 750.

[39] *Powell* v. *Alabama,* 287 U.S. 45 (1932).

[40] *Norris* v. *Alabama,* 294 U.S. 587 (1935).

[41] *New York Times,* August 8, 1965, section 4, p. 2.

[42] *New York Times,* February 16, 1988, p. D19.

[43] *National Journal,* December 8, 1990, p. 2,957.

[44] *Budget of the United States Government, Fiscal Year 2005,* Department of Defense (Washington, D.C: U.S. Government Printing Office, 2004), and online at <http://www.gpoaccess.gov/usbudget/fy05/>, p. 1.

[45] As the system of senatorial courtesy has operated in recent years, some presidents have notified both home-state senators of potential nominees, even when one or more senators do not belong to the president's party. However, in practice, only an objection by a member of the president's party is likely to affect a nomination.

[46] V. O. Key, Jr., *Southern Politics in State and Nation* (New York: Knopf, 1949), p. 307.

[47] Richard E. Dawson and James A. Robinson, "Inter-Party Competition, Economic Variables and Welfare Policies in the American States," *Journal of Politics,* vol. 25 (1963), pp. 265–289; Thomas R. Dye, *Politics, Economics, and the Public: Policy Outcomes in the American States* (Chicago: Rand McNally, 1966), p. 293; Thomas R. Dye, *Understanding Public Policy,* 2nd ed. (Englewood Cliffs, N.J.: Prentice Hall, 1975), p. 304.

[48] Brian R. Fry and Richard F. Winters, "The Politics of Redistribution," *American Political Science Review,* vol. 64 (June 1970), pp. 508–522.

[49] Virginia H. Gray, "The Determinants of Public Policy: A Reappraisal," in Thomas R. Dye and Virginia Gray, eds., *The Determinants of Public Policy* (Lexington, Mass.: D. C. Heath, 1980), p. 217.

[50] *Analytical Perspectives, Budget of the United States Government, Fiscal Year 2007* (Washington, D.C.: U.S. Government Printing Office, 2006), p. 108.

[51] Advisory Commission on Intergovernmental Relations, *Fiscal Balance in the American Federal System,* vol. 1 (Washington, D.C.: U.S. Government Printing Office, 1967), p. 137.

[52] Advisory Commission on Intergovernmental Relations, *Summary and Concluding Observations: The Intergovernmental Grant System* (Washington, D.C.: U.S. Government Printing Office, 1978), p. 3.

[53] *Budget of the United States Government, Fiscal Year 2005,* p. 32. Of every dollar the federal government collected in fiscal 2005, approximately 54.2 cents came from the federal income tax. The total includes both individual income taxes (42.9 percent) and corporate income taxes (11.3 percent).

[54] David R. Beam, "Washington's Regulation of States and Localities: Origins and Issues," *Intergovernmental Perspective,* published by the Advisory Commission on Intergovernmental Relations, vol. 7, no. 3 (Summer 1981), p. 10. For a discussion of some of the complex issues related to regulatory federalism, see Mel Dubnick and Alan Gitelson, "Nationalizing State Policies," in *The Nationalization of State Government,* Jerome J. Hanus, ed. (Lexington, Mass.: D. C. Heath, 1981), pp. 39–74.

[55] Nelson A. Rockefeller, *The Future of Federalism* (Cambridge: Harvard University Press, 1962), p. 15.

[56] *New York Times,* December 31, 1998, p. A11.

## Chapter 4

[1] *Reno* v. *American Civil Liberties Union,* 521 U.S. 844 (1997).

[2] *New York Times,* June 27, 1997, p. A20.

[3] John Stuart Mill, *On Liberty* (New York: Appleton-Century-Crofts, 1947), p. 52.

[4] As noted in Chapter 2, some scholars regard only the first eight or nine amendments as the Bill of Rights.

[5] Earl Warren, "The Law and the Future," *Fortune,* November 1955, p. 107.

[6] Alpheus T. Mason, *The Supreme Court: Palladium of Freedom* (Ann Arbor: University of Michigan Press, 1962), p. 58.

[7] *Palko* v. *Connecticut,* 302 U.S. 319 (1937).

[8] *Feiner* v. *New York,* 340 U.S. 315 (1951).

[9] *Schenck* v. *United States,* 249 U.S. 47 (1919).

[10] *United States* v. *O'Brien,* 391 U.S. 367 (1968).

[11] *Texas* v. *Johnson,* 491 U.S. 397 (1989).

[12] *United States* v. *Eichman* and *United States* v. *Haggerty,* both 496 U.S. 310 (1990).

[13] *Smith* v. *Goguen,* 415 U.S. 566 (1974).

[14] *Rankin* v. *McPherson,* 483 U.S. 378 (1987).

[15] *Simon & Schuster* v. *New York State Crime Victims Board,* 502 U.S. 105 (1991).

[16] *Hill* v. *City of Houston,* 483 U.S. 1001 (1987).

[17] *Ward* v. *Rock Against Racism,* 491 U.S. 781 (1989).

[18] *Virginia* v. *Black,* 123 S. Ct. 1536 (2004).

[19] *R. A. V.* v. *St. Paul,* 505 U.S. 377 (1992).

[20] *Washington Post,* September 12, 1992, p. A1.

[21] Ibid.

[22] *Board of Regents of the University of Wisconsin* v. *Southworth,* 529 U.S. 217 (2000).

[23] *New York Times,* November 10, 1999, p. A20; and online at <http://www.nytimes.com/library/politics/scotus/articles/111099student-fees-edu.html>.

[24] *Tinker* v. *Des Moines School District et al.,* 393 U.S. 503 (1969).

[25] *Bethel School District No. 403* v. *Fraser,* 478 U.S. 675 (1986).

[26] *Hazelwood School District* v. *Kuhlmeier,* 484 U.S. 260 (1988).

[27] Ibid.

[28] *Board of Education, Island Trees Union Free School District* v. *Pico,* 457 U.S. 853 (1982).

[29] *Washington Post,* May 10, 1982, p. A2.

[30] Hugo L. Black, "The Bill of Rights," *New York University Law Review,* vol. 35 (April 1960), p. 867.

[31] *United States* v. *Carolene Products Co.,* 304 U.S. 144 (1938).

[32] *Roth* v. *United States* and *Alberts* v. *California,* both 354 U.S. 476 (1957).

[33] D. H. Lawrence, "Pornography and Obscenity," in Diana Trilling, ed., *The Portable D. H. Lawrence* (New York: Viking Press, 1947), p. 646.

[34] *Jacobellis* v. *Ohio,* 378 U.S. 184 (1964).

[35] *Miller* v. *California,* 413 U.S. 15 (1973).

[36] Ibid.

[37] *Pope* v. *Illinois,* 481 U.S. 497 (1987).

[38] *Jenkins* v. *Georgia,* 418 U.S. 153 (1974).

[39] *Barnes* v. *Glen Theatre,* 501 U.S. 560 (1991).

[40] *City of Erie* v. *Pap's A.M.,* 529 U.S. 277 (2000).

[41] *Sable Communications of California, Inc.* v. *Federal Communications Commission,* 492 U.S. 115 (1989).

[42] *Hamling* v. *United States,* 418 U.S. 87 (1974).

[43] *New York* v. *Ferber,* 458 U.S. 747 (1982).

[44] *Ashcroft* v. *Free Speech Coalition,* 535 U.S. 234 (2002).

[45] *United States* v. *American Library Association, et al.,* 123 S. Ct. 2297 (2003).

[46] *Ashcroft* v. *ACLU,* No. 03-218 (2004).

[47] *New York Times,* June 30, 2004, p. A19.

[48] *National Endowment for the Arts* v. *Finley,* 524 U.S. 569 (1998).

[49] *Olmstead* v. *United States,* 277 U.S. 438 (1928).

[50] *Griswold* v. *Connecticut,* 381 U.S. 479 (1965).

[51] *Roe* v. *Wade,* 410 U.S. 113 (1973).

[52] *Stanley* v. *Georgia,* 394 U.S. 557 (1969).

[53] *Cantrell* v. *Forest City Publishing Co.,* 419 U.S. 245 (1974).

[54] *Cox Broadcasting Corp.* v. *Cohn,* 420 U.S. 469 (1975).

[55] Under the law, the right of access to school records transfers from parents to students who turn 18 or attend college. But parents who declare their children as dependents still have the right to access student records.

[56] *De Jonge* v. *Oregon,* 299 U.S. 353 (1937).

[57] *Davis* v. *Massachusetts,* 167 U.S. 43 (1897).

[58] *Hague* v. *C. I. O.,* 307 U.S. 496 (1939).

[59] *Collin* v. *Smith,* 439 U.S. 916 (1978); see also *National Socialist Party* v. *Village of Skokie,* 432 U.S. 43 (1977).

[60] *Hurley* v. *Irish-American Gay, Lesbian, and Bisexual Group of Boston,* 515 U.S. 557 (1995).

[61] *United States* v. *Grace,* 461 U.S. 171 (1983).

[62] *United States* v. *Newdow,* No. 02-1574 (2004).

[63] Jefferson used the now-famous phrase in a letter to a group of Baptists in Danbury, Connecticut. See Saul K. Padover, ed., *The Complete Jefferson* (New York: Duell, Sloan & Pearce, 1943), pp. 518–519.

[64] *United States* v. *Seeger,* 380 U.S. 163 (1965).

[65] *Welsh* v. *United States,* 398 U.S. 333 (1970).

[66] Ibid.

[67] *Gillette* v. *United States,* 401 U.S. 437 (1971), and *Negre* v. *Larsen,* 394 U.S. 968 (1969).

[68] *Minersville School District* v. *Gobitis,* 310 U.S. 586 (1940).

[69] The Jehovah's Witnesses won their fight in *West Virginia Board of Education* v. *Barnette,* 319 U.S. 624 (1943). (Walter Barnett's name was misspelled in court records.)

[70] William Cohen, Murray Schwartz, and DeAnne Sobul, *The Bill of Rights: A Source Book* (New York: Benziger Brothers, 1968), pp. 267–268.

[71] *Oregon* v. *Smith,* 494 U.S. 872 (1990).

[72] *Gonzales* v. *O Centro Espirita Beneficente Uniao do Vegetal,* No. 04-1084 (2006).

[73] *Reynolds* v. *United States,* 98 U.S. 145 (1878); *Davis* v. *Beason,* 133 U.S. 333 (1890).

[74] *Church of the Lukumi Babalu Aye Inc.* v. *City of Hialeah,* 508 U.S. 520 (1993).

[75] *Bob Jones University* v. *United States* and *Goldsboro Christian Schools, Inc.* v. *United States,* both 461 U.S. 574 (1983).

[76] *Everson* v. *Board of Education,* 330 U.S. 1 (1947).

[77] *Lynch* v. *Donnelly,* 465 U.S. 471 (1984).

[78] *Engel* v. *Vitale,* 370 U.S. 421 (1962).

[79] "Almighty God, we acknowledge our dependence upon Thee, and we beg Thy blessings upon us, our parents, our teachers, and our country."

[80] *Engel* v. *Vitale* (1962).

[81] *McCreary County* v. *ACLU of Kentucky,* No. 03-1693 (2005).

[82] *Van Orden* v. *Perry,* No. 03-1500 (2005).

[83] *Abington School District* v. *Schempp* and *Murray* v. *Curlett,* both 374 U.S. 203 (1963).

[84] National Center for Education Statistics, U.S. Department of Education, <http://nces.ed.gov>.

[85] *Everson* v. *Board of Education* (1947).

[86] *Lemon* v. *Kurtzman, Earley* v. *DiCenso,* and *Robinson* v. *DiCenso,* all 403 U.S. 602 (1971). In *Lemon,* the Court set forth a three-pronged test to determine if a given practice was constitutional or if it violated the separation of church and state:

whether it had a secular purpose, whether it had the principal effect of advancing or inhibiting religion, and whether it complied with the "excessive government entanglement" standard the Court had cited in *Walz* v. *Tax Commission of the City of New York,* 397 U.S. 664 (1970).

[87] *Mitchell* v. *Helms,* 530 U.S. 793 (2000).

[88] *Board of Education of Westside Community Schools* v. *Mergens,* 496 U.S. 226 (1990).

[89] *Lee* v. *Weisman,* 505 U.S. 577 (1992).

[90] *Santa Fe Independent School District* v. *Doe,* 120 S. Ct. 2266 (2000).

[91] *Zelman* v. *Simmons-Harris,* 536 U.S. 639 (2002).

[92] *Tilton* v. *Richardson,* 403 U.S. 672 (1971).

[93] *Rosenberger* v. *Rector and Visitors of University of Virginia,* 515 U.S. 819 (1995).

[94] *Dennis* v. *United States,* 341 U.S. 494 (1951).

[95] *Yates* v. *United States,* 354 U.S. 298 (1957); *Scales* v. *United States,* 367 U.S. 203 (1961); *Noto* v. *United States,* 367 U.S. 290 (1961); *Elfbrandt* v. *Russell,* 384 U.S. 11 (1966).

[96] *Albertson* v. *Subversive Activities Control Board,* 382 U.S. 70 (1965).

[97] *McNabb* v. *United States,* 318 U.S. 332 (1943).

[98] *Wilson* v. *Layne,* 526 U.S. 603 (1999), and *Hanlon* v. *Berger,* 526 U.S. 808 (1999).

[99] *Wilson* v. *Layne* (1999).

[100] *Hanlon* v. *Berger* (1999).

[101] *Payton* v. *New York,* 445 U.S. 573 (1980).

[102] Ibid.

[103] *Hudson* v. *Michigan,* No. 04-1360 (2006).

[104] *Wilson* v. *Arkansas,* 514 U.S. 927 (1995).

[105] *United States* v. *Banks,* 124 S. Ct. 521 (2003).

[106] Ibid.

[107] *Chimel* v. *California,* 395 U.S. 752 (1969).

[108] *New York Times,* July 1, 1973, section 4, p. 6.

[109] *New York Times,* September 26, 1975, p. 1.

[110] *New Jersey* v. *T. L. O.,* 469 U.S. 325 (1985).

[111] *Vernonia School District* v. *Acton,* 515 U.S. 646 (1995), and *Board of Education* v. *Earls,* 536 U.S. 822 (2002).

[112] *Carroll* v. *United States,* 267 U.S. 132 (1925); *Texas* v. *White,* 423 U.S. 67 (1976); *United States* v. *Ross,* 456 U.S. 305 (1982).

[113] *United States* v. *Ross* (1982).

[114] *Wyoming* v. *Houghton,* 526 U.S. 295 (1999).

[115] *Pennsylvania* v. *Mimms,* 434 U.S. 106 (1977).

[116] *New York* v. *Belton,* 453 U.S. 454 (1981).

[117] *Michigan* v. *Sitz,* 496 U.S. 444 (1990).

[118] *Knowles* v. *Iowa,* 525 U.S. 113 (1998).

[119] *Atwater* v. *City of Lago Vista,* 532 U.S. 318 (2001).

[120] *Terry* v. *Ohio,* 392 U.S. 1 (1968).

[121] *Illinois* v. *Wardlow,* 528 U.S. 119 (2000).

[122] *United States* v. *Watson,* 423 U.S. 411 (1976).

[123] *Mapp* v. *Ohio,* 367 U.S. 643 (1961).

[124] *Weeks* v. *United States,* 232 U.S. 383 (1914).

[125] *United States* v. *Calandra,* 414 U.S. 338 (1974).

[126] *United States* v. *Peltier,* 422 U.S. 531 (1975).

[127] *Nix* v. *Williams,* 464 U.S. 417 (1984).

[128] *United States* v. *Leon,* 468 U.S. 897 (1984).

[129] *Massachusetts* v. *Sheppard,* 468 U.S. 981 (1984).

[130] *Maryland* v. *Garrison,* 480 U.S. 79 (1987).

[131] *Zurcher* v. *Stanford Daily,* 436 U.S. 547 (1978).

[132] *Olmstead* v. *United States* (1928).

[133] *Nardone* v. *United States,* 302 U.S. 379 (1937); *Benanti* v. *United States,* 355 U.S. 96 (1957).

[134] *Katz* v. *United States,* 389 U.S. 347 (1967). *Katz* overruled the *Olmstead* decision. In a related case, *Berger* v. *New York,* 388 U.S. 41 (1967), the Supreme Court invalidated a New York State law that permitted police to engage in electronic surveillance with a court warrant; the Court held that the state law was too broad in setting standards for electronic eavesdropping.

[135] *Tyler* v. *Berodt,* 493 U.S. 1022 (1990).

[136] *United States* v. *United States District Court for the Eastern District of Michigan,* 407 U.S. 297 (1972). In this case, sometimes also known as the *Keith* case, the Supreme Court did not address itself to the question of whether the president had power to order electronic surveillance against foreign intelligence activities or agents.

[137] Data provided by Steven Aftergood, the Federation of American Scientists, and the Department of Justice website, online at <http://www.usdoj.gov/04foia/readingrooms/oipr_records.htm>.

[138] *Dalia* v. *United States,* 441 U.S. 238 (1979).

[139] *Rumsfeld* v. *Padilla,* 124 S. Ct. 2711 (2004); *Hamdi* v. *Rumsfeld,* 124 S. Ct. 2686 (2004).

[140] *Rasul* v. *Bush,* No. 03-334 (2004).

[141] *Hamdan* v. *Rumsfeld,* No. 05-184 (2006)

[142] *Mallory* v. *United States,* 354 U.S. 449 (1957).

[143] *Escobedo* v. *Illinois,* 378 U.S. 478 (1964).

[144] *United States* v. *Henry,* 447 U.S. 264 (1980); *Illinois* v. *Perkins,* 496 U.S. 292 (1990).

[145] *Miranda* v. *Arizona,* 384 U.S. 436 (1966).

[146] *Harris* v. *New York,* 401 U.S. 222 (1971). The defendant claimed at his trial that he had sold baking soda, not heroin, to an undercover narcotics agent. The prosecution then read a statement the defendant had made, without police warnings, just after his arrest, admitting the sale and making no mention of baking soda.

[147] *Lego* v. *Twomey,* 404 U.S. 477 (1972); *Dutton* v. *Evans,* 400 U.S. 74 (1970); *Kastigar* v. *United States,* 406 U.S. 441 (1972); *Michigan* v. *Tucker,* 417 U.S. 433 (1974); *Oregon* v. *Hass,* 420 U.S. 714 (1975); *Rhode Island* v. *Innis,* 446 U.S. 291 (1980); and *New York* v. *Quarles,* 467 U.S. 649 (1984).

[148] *Michigan* v. *Mosley,* 423 U.S. 96 (1975).

[149] *Washington Post,* August 26, 1985, p. A6.

[150] *New York Times,* May 31, 1987, section 4, p. 1.

[151] *Dickerson* v. *United States,* 530 U.S. 428 (2000).

[152] *Gideon* v. *Wainwright,* 372 U.S. 335 (1963).

[153] *Betts* v. *Brady,* 316 U.S. 455 (1942).

[154] *Argersinger* v. *Hamlin,* 407 U.S. 25 (1972).

[155] Chief Justice John Marshall, in *Barron* v. *Baltimore,* 32 U.S. 243 (1833).

[156] *Gitlow* v. *New York,* 268 U.S. 652 (1925).

[157] *Fiske* v. *Kansas,* 274 U.S. 380 (1927).

[158] *Near* v. *Minnesota,* 283 U.S. 697 (1931).

[159] *Powell* v. *Alabama,* 287 U.S. 45 (1932).

[160] *Hamilton* v. *Regents of the University of California,* 293 U.S. 245 (1934).

[161] *De Jonge* v. *Oregon* (1937).

[162] *Palko* v. *Connecticut* (1937).

[163] *Robinson* v. *California,* 370 U.S. 660 (1962); *Furman* v. *Georgia,* 408 U.S. 238 (1972).

[164] *Malloy* v. *Hogan,* 378 U.S. 1 (1964).

[165] *Gideon* v. *Wainwright* (1963); *Argersinger* v. *Hamlin* (1972).

[166] *Klopfer* v. *North Carolina,* 386 U.S. 213 (1967).

[167] *Pointer* v. *Texas,* 380 U.S. 400 (1965).

[168] *Washington* v. *Texas,* 388 U.S. 14 (1967).

[169] *Duncan* v. *Louisiana,* 391 U.S. 145 (1968).

[170] *Benton* v. *Maryland,* 395 U.S. 784 (1969).

[171] *West Virginia Board of Education* v. *Barnette* (1943).

[172] In Mason, *The Supreme Court: Palladium of Freedom,* p. 171n.

[173] *Trop* v. *Dulles,* 356 U.S. 86 (1958).

[174] *Kennedy* v. *Mendoza-Martinez,* 372 U.S. 144 (1963).

[175] *Schneider* v. *Rusk,* 377 U.S. 163 (1964).

[176] *Afroyim* v. *Rusk,* 387 U.S. 253 (1967).

[177] Data from the Center for Immigration Studies, estimate for 2003, online at <http://www.cis.org/topics/illegalimmigration.html>.

[178] Data for fiscal year 2005 from the U.S. Immigration and Naturalization Service, *Yearbook of Immigration Studies,* online at <http://uscis.gov/graphics/shared/aboutus/statistics/index.htm>.

[179] *Graham* v. *Richardson,* 403 U.S. 365 (1971); *In re Griffiths,* 413 U.S. 717 (1973); *Foley* v. *Connelie,* 435 U.S. 291 (1978); *Ambach* v. *Norwick,* 441 U.S. 68 (1979).

[180] *Plyler* v. *Doe,* 457 U.S. 202 (1982).

[181] *The San Antonio Independent School District* v. *Rodriguez,* 411 U.S. 1 (1973).

[182] *New York Times,* October 4, 1989, p. B9.

[183] Data provided by the Education Trust Organization, "State Funding Gaps," press release, October 10, 2003.

[184] Data from the National Conference of State Legislatures, Education Finance Database, online at <http://www.ncsl.org/programs/educ/NCEF.htm>.

## Chapter 5

[1] The Centers for Disease Control and Prevention, *National Vital Statistics Report,* vol. 52, no. 2, table A, September 15, 2003, p. 2.

[2] The Centers for Disease Control and Prevention, *National Vital Statistics Reports,* vol. 52, no. 9, table 1, November 7, 2003, p. 30.

[3] The Sentencing Project, Briefing Sheets, online at <http://www.sentencingproject.org>.

[4] Ibid., data for 2003.

[5] Data from Bureau of Labor Statistics, U.S. Department of Labor, *Unemployment Rates by Age, Sex, Race, and Hispanic or Latino Ethnicity for 2006,* table D-16.

[6] U.S. Bureau of the Census, Current Population Survey, *Money Income in the United States: 2002,* series P60-221, 2002, table 1, p. 9.

[7] William Julius Wilson, *The Truly Disadvantaged: The Inner City, the Underclass and Public Policy* (Chicago: University of Chicago Press, 1987).

[8] U.S. Bureau of the Census, National Population Estimates-Characteristics, *Annual Estimates of Population by Sex, Race and Hispanic or Latino Origin,* table 3, April 1, 2000 to July 1, 2005.

[9] U.S. Bureau of the Census, *Selected Characteristics of the Total and Native Population,* 2004 American Community Survey.

[10] U.S. Bureau of the Census, National Population Estimates-Characteristics, *Annual Resident Population Estimates of the United States by Race and Hispanic or Latino Origin,* table 4, April 1, 2000 to July 1, 2002.

[11] U.S. Bureau of the Census, Current Population Survey, *Money Income in the United States: 2002,* series P60-221, 2002, Figure 3, p. 10.

[12] U.S. Bureau of the Census, Population Projections Program, *Projections of the Resident Population by Race, Hispanic Origin and Nativity: Middle Series, 2050 to 2070,* NP-T5-G, p. 2, January 13, 2000. See <http://www.census.gov/population/projections/nation/summary/np-t5-g.pdf>.

[13] The term "Indians" reflected the widespread belief in the time of Columbus that the peoples who lived in North America before the Europeans arrived inhabited the outer edge of the Indies, or what is now known as Asia. The term "Native Americans" initially applied to American Indians and Alaska Natives. Over time, however, the term has been expanded in some usage to include all native peoples of the United States and its territories, including native Hawaiians, Chamorros, and American Samoans. Source: Bureau of Indian Affairs, U.S. Department of the Interior.

[14] Data from U.S. Bureau of the Census, National Population Estimates, *Annual Resident Population Estimates of the United States by Race and Hispanic or Latino Origin: July 1, 2002,* table NA-EST2002-ASRO-04.

[15] U.S. Bureau of the Census, "American Indian/Alaska Native Heritage Month: November 2002," p. 3, online at <http://www.census.gov/Press-Release/www/2002/cb02ff17.html>.

[16] The federal budget for fiscal 2004 included a total of $11 billion for programs to assist American Indians. Data provided by the White House, March 2003.

[17] U.S. Bureau of the Census, "American Indian/Alaska Native Heritage Month," p. 5.

[18] U.S. Bureau of the Census, "Poverty Rate Rises, Household Income Declines, Census Bureau Reports," series CB02-124, p. 2, 2002, online at <http://www.census.gov/Press-Release/www/2002/cb02-124.html>.

[19] Indian Health Service, U.S. Department of Health and Human Services, *Regional Differences in Indian Health,* p. 64, chart 4.19.

[20] U.S. Department of Health and Human Services, Office of the Surgeon General, *Mental Health: A Report of the Surgeon General 1999,* chapter 4, "Current Status," p. 2.

[21] Dee Brown, *Bury My Heart at Wounded Knee* (New York: Holt, Rinehart and Winston, 1970).

[22] U.S. Bureau of the Census, *Poverty in the United States, 2002,* series P60-222, p. 1.

[23] U.S. Bureau of the Census, *The Hispanic Population in the United States: March 2002,* series P20-545, p. 4.

[24] *National Directory of Latino Elected Officials* (Washington, D.C.: National Association of Latino Elected Officials Educational Fund, 2003).

[25] *Washington Post,* March 29, 1978, p. A6.

[26] *New York Times,* April 21, 1978, p. 14.

[27] Federation for American Immigration Reform, online at <http://www.fairus.org>.

[28] *DeCanas* v. *Bica,* 424 U.S. 351 (1976).

[29] *Plyler* v. *Doe,* 457 U.S. 202 (1982).

[30] U.S. Bureau of the Census, *General Demographic Characteristics: 2004.*

[31] Data from U.S. Bureau of the Census, National Population Estimates, *Annual Resident Population Estimates of the United States by Race and Hispanic or Latino Origin: July 1, 2002,* table NA-EST2002-ASRO-04.

[32] U.S. Bureau of the Census, *The Asian Population 2000,* February 2002, table I, p. 4.

[33] *New York Times,* January 3, 2004, p. A1.

[34] Center for American Women and Politics, Eagleton Institute of Politics, Fact Sheet, "Women in the U.S. Congress," Rutgers University, 2003, online at <http://www.cawp.rutgers.edu>.

[35] Of the total of 15 dead, four were killed by enemy action—including three women who died when an Iraqi Scud missile hit their barracks—and 11 died in accidents or of natural causes.

[36] U.S. Department of Defense, *Active Duty Military Personnel by Rank/Grade,* September 30, 2005 (women); and Department of Defense, *Active Duty Military Personnel by Rank/Grade,* September 30, 2005.

[37] Data provided by the Center for American Women and Politics, Eagleton Institute of Politics, Rutgers University, online at <http://www.cawp.rutgers.edu>. Total for female mayors is for cities of more than 30,000 population as of June 2003.

[38] *Washington Post,* "Fortune 500 Gains Female CEO in New PepsiCo Chief," August 15, 2006, p. D1.

[39] U.S. Bureau of the Census, *Income, Poverty, and Health Insurance Coverage in the United States: 2004,* p. 7.

[40] Department of Labor, Bureau of Labor Statistics, *Employment Status of the Civilian Population by Sex and Age,* June 2006, table A-1; and U.S. Bureau of the Census, Current Employment Statistics, *Women and Men in the United States,* series P20-544, March 2002.

[41] U.S. Department of Education, National Center for Education Statistics, *First Professional Degrees Conferred by Degree-Granting Institutions.* Of the 2003 total, 6,813 women were graduates of medical schools, and 19,151 earned law degrees.

[42] U.S. Bureau of the Census, Current Employment Statistics, *Men and Women in the United States,* p. 3; Bureau of Labor Statistics, U.S. Department of Labor, *Employment Situation,* table A-1, January 18, 2000, p. 1.

[43] Carol A. Whitehurst, *Women in America: The Oppressed Majority* (Santa Monica: Goodyear Publishing, 1977), p. 69.

[44] *Rostker* v. *Goldberg,* 453 U.S. 57 (1981).

[45] Because the Supreme Court ruled in *Grove City* v. *Bell,* 465 U.S. 555 (1984), that the 1972 law applied only to specific departments or programs that received federal money, not to educational institutions as a whole, Congress in 1988, over President Reagan's veto, passed a law to undo the Supreme Court decision. As a result, federal antidiscrimination laws apply to an entire institution if any department or program receives federal funds.

[46] Joyce Gelb and Marian Lief Palley, *Women and Public Policies* (Princeton: Princeton University Press, 1982), p. 4.

[47] Center for American Women and Politics, Eagleton Institute of Politics, Rutgers University, "Women Office Holders: Historical," 2005.

[48] *New York Times,* October 11, 1991, p. A1.

[49] *Harris* v. *Forklift Systems, Inc.,* 510 U.S. 17 (1993).

[50] Ibid.

[51] The Gallup Organization, *Poll Releases,* "Many Women Cite Spousal Abuse, Job Performance Affected," October 25, 1997, pp. 1–2, online at <http://www.gallup.com/content/login.aspx?ci=4321>.

[52] *Akron* v. *Akron Center for Reproductive Health, Inc.,* 462 U.S. 416 (1983).

[53] *Thornburgh* v. *American College of Obstetricians and Gynecologists,* 476 U.S. 747 (1986).

[54] *Hartigan* v. *Zbaraz,* 484 U.S. 171 (1987).

[55] *Webster* v. *Reproductive Health Services,* 492 U.S. 990 (1989).

[56] *Washington Post,* July 4, 1989, p. A1.

[57] *Hodgson* v. *Minnesota,* 497 U.S. 417 (1990), and *Ohio* v. *Akron Center for Reproductive Health,* 497 U.S. 502 (1990).

[58] *Planned Parenthood of Southeastern Pennsylvania* v. *Casey,* 505 U.S. 833 (1992).

[59] Ibid.

[60] Ibid.

[61] The Centers for Disease Control and Prevention, *National Vital Statistics Report,* vol. 52, no. 7, October 31, 2003, p.1.

[62] *Stenberg* v. *Carhart,* 530 U.S. 914 (2000).

[63] *New York Times,* November 19, 2003, p. A1.

[64] *Washington Post,* November 19, 2003, p. A8, citing poll by the Pew Research Center and the Pew Forum.

[65] *New York Times,* November 19, 2003, p. A19.

[66] *Washington Post,* December 21, 1999, p. A1.

[67] *New York Times,* December 21, 1999, p. A1.

[68] *Washington Post,* October 7, 1994, p. A1.

[69] U.S. Bureau of the Census, *Married Couple and Unmarried Partner Households: 2000 series CENSR-5,* February 2003, pp. 1–3.

[70] Gallup poll, Gallup Poll News Service, May 31, 2006.

[71] The Gallup Organization, Gallup Poll News Service, May 20, 2005.

[72] Lambda Legal, "Summary of States, Cities, and Counties Which Prohibit Discrimination Based on Sexual Orientation," January 6, 2003, online at <http://www.lambdalegal.org/cgi-bin/iowa/documents/record?record=217>.

[73] *Bowers* v. *Hardwick,* 478 U.S. 186 (1986).

[74] *Lawrence* v. *Texas,* 123 S. Ct. 2472 (2003).

[75] *Boy Scouts of America* v. *Dale,* 530 U.S. 640 (2000).

[76] Ibid.

[77] Data as of 2004 from the U.S. Centers for Disease Control and Prevention, *Basic Statistics.*

[78] U.S. Centers for Disease Control and Prevention, *HIV Infection and AIDS: An Overview,* March 2005.

[79] *Washington Post,* June 9, 2000, p. A1.

[80] U.S. Bureau of the Census, Facts for Features, *Americans with Disabilities Act: July 26,* released July 19, 2006.

[81] *Washington Post,* May 2, 1992, p. A15.

[82] *Los Angeles Times,* October 4, 1995, p. A1. Data from an ABC News poll released the week before the October 3 verdict.

[83] James Baldwin, *The Fire Next Time* (New York: Dial Press, 1963), p. 40.

[84] Ralph Ellison, *Invisible Man* (New York: Random House, 1952), p. 3.

[85] Gunnar Myrdal, *An American Dilemma: The Negro Problem and Modern Democracy* (New York: Harper & Row, 1962).

[86] Ibid., p. lxxi.

[87] Charles E. Silberman, *Crisis in Black and White* (New York: Random House, 1964), p. 10.

[88] William Julius Wilson, *The Declining Significance of Race: Blacks and Changing American Institutions* (Chicago: University of Chicago Press, 1978), p. 22.

[89] Lucius J. Barker and Jesse J. McCorry, Jr., *Black Americans and the Political System,* 2nd ed. (Boston: Little, Brown, 1980), p. 342.

[90] Silberman, *Crisis in Black and White,* pp. 43–44.

[91] Myrdal, *An American Dilemma,* p. 33.

[92] John Hope Franklin, *From Slavery to Freedom* (New York: Knopf, 1967), p. 128. Some historians contend that Attucks was part black and part Natick Indian, a tribe in eastern Massachusetts.

[93] *Dred Scott* v. *Sandford,* 19 Howard 393 (1857).

[94] *Plessy* v. *Ferguson,* 163 U.S. 537 (1896).

[95] *Brown* v. *Board of Education of Topeka, Kansas,* 347 U.S. 483 (1954).

[96] In Robert H. Jackson, *The Supreme Court in the American System of Government* (Cambridge: Harvard University Press, 1955), p. 11.

[97] *Brown* v. *Board of Education of Topeka, Kansas,* 349 U.S. 294 (1955). John Marshall Harlan, grandson of the justice who dissented in *Plessy* v. *Ferguson,* was by this time a member of the Supreme Court and participated in the second *Brown* decision.

[98] *Alexander* v. *Holmes County Board of Education,* 396 U.S. 19 (1969).

[99] *Swann* v. *Charlotte-Mecklenburg County Board of Education,* 402 U.S. 1 (1971).

[100] Diane Ravitch, "Busing: The Solution That Has Failed to Solve," *New York Times,* December 21, 1975, section 4, p. 3.

[101] *Keyes* v. *School District No. 1,* 413 U.S. 189 (1973).

[102] *Washington Post,* July 18, 2001, p. A3. The Harvard University study reported on enrollments in 1998–1999.

[103] The Supreme Court had barred segregation on interstate transportation in a series of decisions: on buses in *Morgan* v. *Commonwealth of Virginia,* 328 U.S. 373 (1946); on trains in *Henderson* v. *United States,* 339 U.S. 816 (1950), which held that an interstate railroad could not segregate a dining car; and in other cases.

[104] *The Negro in American History, Vol. I: Black Americans 1928–1968,* with an introduction by Saunders Redding (Chicago: Encyclopedia Britannica Educational Corp., 1969), pp. 175–176.

[105] Southern Regional Council data in 1965 *Congressional Quarterly Almanac,* p. 537.

[106] United States Commission on Civil Rights, *Political Participation,* May 1968, pp. 171, 222.

[107] U.S. Bureau of the Census, Current Population Reports, *Voting and Registration in the Election of November 1988,* series P20-440, October 1989, p. 17; and "Voting and Registration: November 1988," Internet release date, October 17, 1997.

[108] U.S. Bureau of the Census, Current Population Reports, Population Characteristics, *Voting and Registration in the Election of November 1996,* series P20-504, July 1998, table 4, p. 23.

[109] U.S. Bureau of the Census, Current Population Reports, Population Characteristics, *Voting and Registration in the Election of November 2000,* series P20-542, February 2002, table A, p. 5; and U.S. Bureau of the Census, Current Population Reports, *Reported Voting and Registration, by Race, Hispanic Origin, Sex, and Age, for the United States: November 2004.*

[110] *Shaw* v. *Reno,* 509 U.S. 630 (1993).

[111] *Miller* v. *Johnson,* 515 U.S. 900 (1995).

[112] See *Shaw* v. *Hunt,* 517 U.S. 899 (1996), which invalidated the same North Carolina district that the Supreme Court had reviewed in 1993, when the case was called *Shaw* v. *Reno;* and *Bush* v. *Vera,* 517 U.S. 952 (1996).

[113] *Report of the National Advisory Commission on Civil Disorders* (New York: Bantam Books, 1968), pp. 1, 10.

[114] Stokely Carmichael and Charles V. Hamilton, *Black Power* (New York: Random House, 1967), p. 44.

[115] *New York Times,* May 23, 1970, p. 12.

[116] *Regents of the University of California* v. *Allan Bakke,* 438 U.S. 265 (1978).

[117] *United Steelworkers of America* v. *Weber,* 443 U.S. 193 (1979).

[118] *Fullilove* v. *Klutznick,* 448 U.S. 448 (1980).

[119] *Johnson* v. *Transportation Agency, Santa Clara County,* 480 U.S. 616 (1987).

[120] *Adarand Constructors* v. *Pena,* 515 U.S. 200 (1995).

[121] *Grutter* v. *Bollinger,* 123 S. Ct. 617 (2003); *Gratz* v. *Bollinger,* 123 S. Ct. 602 (2003).

[122] Total of black elected officials provided by the Joint Center for Political and Economic Studies. Data on black mayors from the National Conference of Black Mayors, online at <www.ncbm.org>.

[123] Arthur M. Schlesinger, Jr., *The Disuniting of America: Reflections on a Multicultural Society* (New York: Norton, 1992), p. 15.

[124] "Radio and Television Report to the American People on Civil Rights," June 11, 1963, *Public Papers of the Presidents of the United States,* John F. Kennedy 1963 (Washington, D.C.: U.S. Government Printing Office, 1964), p. 469.

## Chapter 6

[1] A poll taken during the Senate trial reflected Clinton's problem; it found that only 24 percent of those questioned believed Clinton to be "honest and trustworthy." Gallup poll, "Clinton Personal Characteristics," January 15–17, 1999.

[2] Gallup poll, "Presidential Impeachment Crisis," January 22–24, 1999.

[3] CNN/*USA Today*/Gallup poll, reported in the *New York Times,* September 24, 2001, p. B6.

[4] CNN/*USA Today*/Gallup poll, reported in *USA Today,* September 12, 2003, p. 6A.

[5] The Gallup Organization, "George W. Bush's Job Approval Rating—Recent Trend," January 29–February 1, 2004, online at <http://www.gallup.com>.

[6] *USA Today*/Gallup Poll, May 5–7, 2006, online at <http://www.pollingreport.com/bushjob1.htm>.

[7] James Bryce, *The American Commonwealth,* vol. 1 (New York: Putnam, Capricorn Books, 1959), p. 296.

[8] V. O. Key, Jr., *Public Opinion and American Democracy* (New York: Knopf, 1961), p. 10.

[9] Ibid., p. 14.

[10] Floyd H. Allport, "Toward a Science of Public Opinion," *Public Opinion Quarterly,* vol. 1 (January 1937), p. 23.

[11] W. Lance Bennett, *Public Opinion in American Politics* (New York: Harcourt Brace Jovanovich, 1980), pp. 12–13.

[12] Allport, "Toward a Science of Public Opinion," p. 15.

[13] Walter Lippmann, *Public Opinion* (New York: Free Press, 1965), pp. 18–19. (Originally published in 1922.)

[14] Robert E. Lane, *Political Life* (New York: Free Press, 1959), p. 204.

[15] Fred I. Greenstein, *Children and Politics* (New Haven: Yale University Press, 1965), p. 1.

[16] Ibid., pp. 71–73.

[17] Key, *Public Opinion and American Democracy,* pp. 301, 305.

[18] Bennett, *Public Opinion in American Politics,* pp. 165–166, citing Theodore M. Newcomb's study in Theodore M. Newcomb, *Personality and Social Change* (New York: Dryden Press, 1943).

[19] M. Kent Jennings and Richard G. Niemi, *The Political Character of Adolescence* (Princeton: Princeton University Press, 1974), p. 319.

[20] Ibid., p. 328.

[21] Gallup poll, April–May 1999.

[22] *The Gallup Poll Monthly,* April 1993, p. 43. Respondents were asked, "Do you think abortions should be legal under any circumstances, legal only under certain circumstances, or illegal in all circumstances?"

[23] Lloyd A. Free and Hadley Cantril, *The Political Beliefs of Americans* (New Brunswick: Rutgers University Press, 1967), p. 216. See also extensive data of the Survey Research Center (University of Michigan, 1956), quoted in Key, *Public Opinion and American Democracy,* Chapter 6.

[24] Samuel A. Stouffer, *Communism, Conformity, and Civil Liberties* (Gloucester, Mass.: Peter Smith, 1963).

[25] Poll conducted by Princeton Survey Research Associates for the Henry J. Kaiser Family Foundation, February–September 2000. Respondents were asked, "Do you think high schools should or should not provide students with condoms if they ask for them?"

[26] Greenstein, *Children and Politics,* pp. 155–156.

[27] CNN exit poll, 2004.

[28] Free and Cantril, *The Political Beliefs of Americans,* p. 148.

[29] Stanley Milgram, "Group Pressure and Action against a Person," *Journal of Abnormal and Social Psychology,* vol. 69 (1964), pp. 137–143. In a somewhat similar experiment, Solomon Asch, a psychologist at Swarthmore College, placed subjects among groups of college students whose members, unknown to the subjects, deliberately responded incorrectly when they were asked to match up black lines of varying lengths on white cards. Influenced by the group's false judgments, the subjects gave incorrect answers 37 percent of the time. S. E. Asch, *Psychology Monograph,* vol. 70, no. 416 (1956).

[30] Mark Twain, *The Autobiography of Mark Twain,* ed. Charles Neider (New York: Harper & Row, 1959), p. 386.

[31] Elisabeth Noelle-Neumann, "The Spiral of Silence: A Theory of Public Opinion," *Journal of Communication,* vol. 24 (Spring 1974), p. 43.

[32] Ibid., p. 45.

[33] Angus Campbell, Philip E. Converse, Warren E. Miller, and Donald E. Stokes, Survey Research Center, University of Michigan, *The American Voter* (New York: Wiley, 1960).

[34] The Gallup Organization, Gallup Poll Tuesday Briefing, "Who Supports Marijuana Legalization?," November 1, 2005.

[35] The Gallup Organization, *Poll Releases,* "More Americans Approve of House Vote to Impeach Clinton Now than a Year Ago", December 19–20, 1998, p. 1, online at <http://www.gallup.com/content/?ci=3397>. Forty percent of independents favored the impeachment decision.

[36] Gallup poll, "Party Identification of the American Electorate, 1940–2004." Data from January 2004 reported voters identifying themselves as Democrats, 34 percent; Republicans, 32 percent; and Independents, 34 percent.

[37] Key, *Public Opinion and American Democracy,* p. 11.

[38] Robert E. Lane and David O. Sears, *Public Opinion* (Englewood Cliffs, N.J.: Prentice Hall, 1964), p. 106.

[39] Harry S. Truman, *Memoirs by Harry S. Truman: Years of Trial and Hope,* vol. 2 (Garden City, N.Y.: Doubleday, 1956), p. 177.

[40] "New Hampshire Confounded Most Pollsters," *Washington Post,* February 8, 1988, p. A1.

[41] *Dallas Morning News,* February 1, 2000, p. 1A.

[42] Elizabeth Drew, *Showdown: The Struggle between the Gingrich Congress and the Clinton White House* (New York: Simon & Schuster, 1996), p. 103.

[43] Herbert F. Weisberg and Bruce D. Bowen, *An Introduction to Survey Research and Data Analysis* (San Francisco: Freeman, 1977), p. 24.

[44] For a discussion of the pitfalls and problems of public opinion polling, see Michael Wheeler, *Lies, Damn Lies, and Statistics: The Manipulation of Public Opinion in America* (New York: Liveright, 1976).

[45] Online at <http://www.pollingreport.com/iraq.htm>.

[46] CNN/*USA Today*/Gallup poll, November 1–3, 2000, online at <http://www.pollingreport.com>.

[47] "Polling's Dirty Little Secret: No Response," *New York Times,* November 21, 1999, section 4, p. 1.

[48] Bernard Hennessy, *Essentials of Public Opinion* (North Scituate, Mass.: Duxbury Press, 1975), pp. 70-71.

[49] Elisabeth Noelle-Neumann, "Turbulences in the Climate of Opinion: Methodological Applications of the Spiral of Silence Theory," *Public Opinion Quarterly,* vol. 41, no. 2 (Summer 1977), p. 144.

[50] *New York Times,* February 23, 2000, p. A16.

[51] NEP is run by Joe Lenski, executive vice president of Edison Media Research, and Warren Mitofsky of Mitofsky International.

[52] Free and Cantril, *The Political Beliefs of Americans,* p. 13.

[53] Ibid., p. 30.

[54] See Bennett, *Public Opinion in American Politics,* pp. 141–150.

[55] Norman H. Nie, Sidney Verba, and John R. Petrocik, *The Changing American Voter,* enlarged ed. (Cambridge: Harvard University Press, 1979), p. 348.

[56] Ibid., p. 156.

[57] U.S. Bureau of the Census, *Voting and Registration in the Election of November 2004,* series P20-556, p. 2.

[58] U.S. Bureau of the Census, *Statistical Abstract of the United States,* 2003, p. 270, and Center for Voting and Democracy, "2002 Voting-Age and Voting-Eligible Population Estimates and Voter Turnout," November 8, 2002, online at <http://www.fairvote.org/turnout/>.

[59] E. E. Schattschneider, *The Semisovereign People* (New York: Holt, Rinehart and Winston, 1960), p. 99. By 2000 the number of nonvoters totaled about 100.4 million.

[60] Free and Cantril, *The Political Beliefs of Americans,* p. 61.

[61] *Restoring America's Legacy: The Challenge of Historical Literacy in the 21st Century,* September 2002, online at <http://www.goacta.org/publications/reports.html>. The survey questioned students at 55 colleges and universities.

[62] *Washington Times,* September 16, 1997, p. A3. Survey taken by the National Constitution Center.

[63] *Washington Post,* the Kaiser Family Foundation, and Harvard University survey, *Washington Post,* January 29, 1996, p. A1.

[64] Gallup poll conducted for the National Endowment for the Humanities, Boulder (Colo.) *Daily Camera,* October 9, 1989, p. 1.

[65] Schattschneider, *The Semisovereign People,* p. 132.

[66] See David Wise, *The Politics of Lying: Government Deception, Secrecy, and Power* (New York: Random House, 1973).

[67] Richard G. Niemi and Herbert F. Weisberg, *Controversies in American Voting Behavior* (San Francisco: Freeman, 1976), p. 168. See also Bennett, *Public Opinion in American Politics,* pp. 27–30, 43–48, 90–91.

[68] "Assassination," in *To Establish Justice, to Insure Domestic Tranquility: Final Report of the National Commission on the Causes and Prevention of Violence* (Washington, D.C.: U.S. Government Printing Office, 1969), p. 120.

[69] Ross Perot interview with Dan Rather, *CBS Evening News,* June 3, 1991.

[70] Dan Nimmo, *Political Communication and Public Opinion in America* (Santa Monica: Goodyear Publishing, 1978), p. 98.

[71] Walter Lippmann, *Essays in the Public Philosophy* (Boston: Little, Brown, 1955), p. 14.

[72] Schattschneider, *The Semisovereign People,* p. 136.

[73] Key, *Public Opinion and American Democracy,* p. 7.

## Chapter 7

[1] C. Wright Mills, *The Power Elite* (New York: Oxford University Press, 1959), pp. 8, 13.

[2] See, for example, Peter Bachrach, *The Theory of Democratic Elitism* (Boston: Little, Brown, 1966); G. William Domhoff, *Who Rules America?* (Englewood Cliffs, N.J.: Prentice Hall, 1967); and Domhoff, *The Higher Circles* (New York: Vintage Books, 1970).

[3] Richard H. Rovere, *The American Establishment* (New York: Harcourt Brace Jovanovich, 1962), p. 6.

[4] Robert A. Dahl, *Who Governs?* (New Haven: Yale University Press, 1961), p. 86.

[5] See Peter Bachrach and Morton S. Baratz, "Two Faces of Power," *American Political Science Review,* vol. 56, no. 4 (December 1962), pp. 947–952.

[6] David B. Truman, *The Governmental Process* (New York: Knopf, 1951), p. 37.

[7] James Madison, "*The Federalist,* No. 10," in Edward Mead Earle, ed., *The Federalist* (New York: Random House, Modern Library), p. 56.

[8] Quoted in William Safire, *Safire's New Political Dictionary: The Definitive Guide to the New Language of Politics* (New York: Random House, 1993), p. 841.

[9] Ibid., p. 612.

[10] Alexis de Tocqueville, *Democracy in America,* vol. 1, ed. Phillips Bradley (New York: Vintage Books, 1945), p. 198.

[11] Robert H. Salisbury, *Governing America: Public Choice and Political Action* (New York: Appleton-Century-Crofts, 1973), p. 90.

[12] Ibid.

[13] Robert E. Lane, *Political Life* (New York: Free Press, 1959), p. 75.

[14] *New York Times,* May 27, 1982, p. 1. Data on contributions from CongressWatch.

[15] Ibid. Mikulski was elected to the Senate in 1986.

[16] David Bollier, *Citizen Action and Other Big Ideas: A History of Ralph Nader and the Modern Consumer Movement* (Washington, D.C.: Center for Study of Responsive Law, 1991), p. 14.

[17] Lester W. Milbrath, *The Washington Lobbyists* (Chicago: Rand McNally, 1963), pp. 212–213.

[18] Quoted in Safire, *Safire's New Political Dictionary,* p. 418.

[19] "Show Me the Money," *The Washingtonian,* January 1998.

[20] *Time,* March 3, 1986.

[21] *National Journal,* March 25, 2005, p. 32.

[22] Report of a study by Public Citizen, a Ralph Nader group, quoted in the *Washington Post,* December 20, 1997, p. A2. Nader's group was opposed to the tobacco settlement.

[23] Report of a study by Common Cause of tobacco company political contributions, quoted in the *Washington Post,* December 20, 1997, p. A2.

[24] Connally was indicted by the federal government but acquitted in 1975 on charges that he had accepted a total of $10,000 from AMPI in return for urging Nixon to raise milk price supports.

[25] For more detailed accounts of the milk producers' lobbying, see Carol S. Greenwald, *Group Power* (New York: Praeger, 1977), pp. 3–8; and U.S. Senate, 93rd Cong., 2nd sess., *The Final Report of the Select Committee on Presidential Campaign Activities,* pp. 579–929.

[26] *New York Times,* September 29, 1998, p. A22.

[27] Data for 1999 from The Center for Responsive Politics, online at <http://www.opensecrets.org/2000elect/select/AllCands.htm>.

[28] V. O. Key, Jr., *Politics, Parties, and Pressure Groups,* 5th ed. (New York: Crowell, 1964), p. 130.

[29] The AAA mounted its successful campaign in 1968, but the automobile association's victory was only temporary. In 1975 a bill became law permitting larger trucks on the roads.

[30] Data from MoveOn.org website, May 10, 2006, online at <http://MoveOn.org>.

[31] NRA membership and staff size as of 2004; approximately $200 million budget for fiscal 2004. Data provided by the National Rifle Association. Total for NRA contributions to congressional candidates provided by the Federal Election Commission.

[32] Donald Devine, *The Attentive Public* (Chicago: Rand McNally, 1969), p. 119. Data from 1964.

[33] *National Journal,* March 4, 1995, p. 552; and *Washington Post,* July 6, 1995, p. C2.

[34] Joseph C. Goulden, *The Superlawyers: The Small and Powerful World of the Great Washington Law Firms* (New York: Weybright & Talley, 1972), p. 6.

[35] Ibid., p. 70.

[36] In the early 1990s, Clifford's reputation was tarnished by his involvement in a scandal surrounding the Arab-owned Bank of Commerce and Credit International (BCCI). He was indicted on federal and New York State charges of alleged fraud and bribery for his role. But the federal charges were dropped and the state decided not to prosecute because of his ill health. See the *Washington Post,* April 8, 1993, p. A1; and December 1, 1993, p. A1. Clark Clifford died in 1998 at the age of 91.

[37] *USA Today,* March 20, 2000, p. 24A; and the *New York Times,* March 14, 2000, p. 19.

[38] NRA Fact Sheet, March 20, 2000, online at <http://www.nraila.org>.

[39] *Buckley* v. *Valeo,* 424 U.S. 1 (1976). The federal campaign spending laws and the effect of Supreme Court decisions are discussed in detail in Chapter 10.

[40] Data provided by the Federal Election Commission.

[41] *First National Bank of Boston* v. *Bellotti,* 435 U.S. 765 (1978).

[42] *Consolidated Edison* v. *Public Service Commission,* 447 U.S. 530 (1980).

[43] Institute of Politics, John F. Kennedy School of Government, Harvard University, "An Analysis of the Impact of the Federal Election Campaign Act, 1972–78," prepared for the Committee on House Administration, U.S. House of Representatives (Washington, D.C.: U.S. Government Printing Office, 1979), p. 4.

[44] Center for Responsive Politics, *Top Committee-Related Industries Giving to Committee Members, 2003–2004 election cycle,* online at <http://www.opensecrets.org>.

[45] Fred Wertheimer, "Of Mountains: The PAC Movement in American Politics" (paper written for the Conference on Parties, Interest Groups, and Campaign Finance Laws, Washington, D.C., September 1979), pp. 5–8.

[46] Federal Election Commission, "PAC Activity Increases in the 2004 Elections," April 13, 2005, online at <http://www.fec.gov>.

[47] Federal Election Commission, "PAC Financial Activity 2003–2004," online at <http://www.fec.gov>. The number of PACs is constantly changing; during congressional elections, for example, the figure may be even higher.

[48] *United States* v. *Harris,* 347 U.S. 612 (1954).

[49] *National Journal,* March 25, 2006, p. 19.

[50] *Washington Post,* July 17, 1991, p. A21.

[51] Milbrath, *The Washington Lobbyists,* p. 358.

[52] Theodore J. Lowi, *The End of Liberalism: Ideology, Policy, and the Crisis of Public Authority,* 2nd ed. (New York: Norton, 1979).

[53] Ibid., p. xvi.

[54] E. E. Schattschneider, *The Semisovereign People* (New York: Holt, Rinehart and Winston, 1960), p. 35.

[55] Mancur Olson, Jr., *The Logic of Collective Action: Public Goods and the Theory of Groups,* rev. ed. (Cambridge: Harvard University Press, 1971), p. 2.

## Chapter 8

[1] CBS News poll conducted May 20–23, 2004, online at <http://pollingreport.com>. A *Newsweek* poll conducted by Princeton Survey Research Associates a week earlier, May 13–14, 2004, reported President Bush's approval rating only slightly higher, at 42 percent; "Newsweek Poll: Bad Days for Bush," online at <http://www.msnbc.msn.com/id/4986882/site/newsweek/>.

[2] *New York Times Co.* v. *United States,* 403 U.S. 713 (1971).

[3] W. A. Swanberg, *Citizen Hearst: A Biography of William Randolph Hearst* (New York: Scribner's, 1961), pp. 107–108.

[4] U.S. Internet usage data from Nielsen//NetRatings, March 18, 2004, online at <http://www.nielsen-netratings.com>; and world data from Global Reach, Global Internet Statistics, online at <http://www.global-reach.biz/globstats>.

[5] Data provided by the Newspaper Association of America, online at <http://www.naa.org>.

[6] Data from the Federal Communications Commission, online at <http://www.fcc.gov>.

[7] Magazine circulation figures from the Audit Bureau of Circulations, 2003, online at <http://abcas3.accessabc.com/ecirc/index.html>.

[8] Data provided by the National Cable and Telecommunications Association, "2003 Year-End Industry Overview," online at <http://www.ncta.com>.

[9] U.S. Bureau of the Census, *Statistical Abstract of the United States 2003,* table 1274, online at <http://www.census.gov/prod/www/statistical-abstract-3.html>.

[10] *Washington Post,* May 8, 2004, p. C1.

[11] *USA Today,* January 25, 2004, "How Ad Meter Works," online at <http://www.usatoday.com/money/advertising/2004-01-25-ad-meter-explainer_x.htm>.

[12] It was Newton Minow, President Kennedy's chairman of the Federal Communications Commission, who called television a "vast wasteland" in a speech to broadcasters in 1961. See Arthur M. Schlesinger, Jr., *A Thousand Days* (Boston: Houghton Mifflin, 1965), p. 736.

[13] *New York Times,* August 20, 2006, p. 1.

[14] *Washington Post,* March 5, 1998, p. A1.

[15] *National Broadcasting Co.* v. *United States,* 319 U.S. 190 (1943).

[16] See Norman Dorsen, Paul Bender, and Burt Neuborne, *Political and Civil Rights in the United States,* 4th ed., vol. 1 (Boston: Little, Brown, 1976), pp. 774–777.

[17] *Turner Broadcasting Corp.* v. *Federal Communications Commission,* 512 U.S. 622 (1994).

[18] David Wise, *The Politics of Lying: Government Deception, Secrecy, and Power* (New York: Random House, 1973), p. 273.

[19] *Red Lion Broadcasting Co., Inc.* v. *Federal Communications Commission,* 395 U.S. 367 (1969).

[20] *Rosenbloom* v. *Metromedia,* 403 U.S. 29 (1971).

[21] *Federal Communications Commission* v. *Pacifica Foundation,* 438 U.S. 726 (1978).

[22] *Washington Post,* June 9, 2004, p. A1, and June 10, 2004, p. C4.

[23] *Near* v. *Minnesota,* 283 U.S. 697 (1931).

[24] Ibid.

[25] *New York Times Co.* v. *United States,* 403 U.S. 713 (1971).

[26] Ibid.

[27] *Cable News Network, Inc.* v. *Noriega,* 498 U.S. 976 (1990).

[28] *Miami Herald Publishing Co.* v. *Tornillo,* 418 U.S. 241 (1974).

[29] *New York Times,* March 30, 1996, p. 24. Justice Souter made this comment in testimony before a House Appropriations subcommittee two days earlier. In 1996, federal appeals courts were given the option of televising appellate arguments.

[30] *Sheppard* v. *Maxwell,* 384 U.S. 333 (1966).

[31] *Richmond Newspapers, Inc.* v. *Virginia,* 448 U.S. 555 (1980).

[32] *United States* v. *Caldwell, Branzburg* v. *Hayes, In the Matter of Paul Pappas,* all 408 U.S. 665 (1972).

[33] Earl Caldwell did not go to jail because the term of the federal grand jury seeking his testimony had expired by the time the Supreme Court ruled.

[34] Robert H. Phelps and E. Douglas Hamilton, *Libel* (New York: Macmillan, 1966), p. 62.

[35] In the Supreme Court's decision, the word "malice" is not used in its commonly understood meaning of "ill will."

[36] *New York Times Co.* v. *Sullivan,* 376 U.S. 254 (1964).

[37] *Curtis Publishing Co.* v. *Butts,* 388 U.S. 130 and *Associated Press* v. *Walker,* 388 U.S. 28 (1967); *Rosenbloom* v. *Metromedia,* 403 U.S. 29 (1971).

[38] *Time* v. *Firestone,* 424 U.S. 448 (1976).

[39] *Wolston* v. *Reader's Digest,* 443 U.S. 157 (1979).

[40] *Hustler Magazine, Inc.* v. *Falwell,* 485 U.S. 46 (1988).

[41] *Milkovich* v. *Lorain Journal Co.,* 497 U.S. 1 (1990).

[42] *Food Lion, Inc.* v. *Capital Cities/ABC, Inc.,* 194 F.3d 505 (4th Cir. 1999), online at <http://www.medill.northwestern.edu/faculty/doppelt/foodlion.html>.

[43] Joseph C. Wilson, "What I Didn't Find in Africa," *New York Times,* July 6, 2003, sec. 4, p. 9.

[44] Robert D. Novak, "Mission to Niger," *Washington Post,* July 14, 2003, p. A21.

[45] Matthew Cooper, Massimo Calabresi, and John F. Dickerson, "A War on Wilson," *Time,* July 17, 2003, online at <www.time.com>.

[46] Matthew Cooper, "What I Told the Grand Jury," *Time,* July 25, 2005, pp. 38–40.

[47] Judith Miller, "My Four Hours Testifying in the Federal Grand Jury Room," *New York Times,* October 16, 2005, p. 31.

[48] *New York Times,* October 29, 2005, p. A1.

[49] Ibid.

[50] Robert D. Novak, "My Leak Case Testimony," *Washington Post,* July 12, 2006, p. A15.

[51] *New York Times,* September 9, 2006, p. A22; August 29, 2006, p. A12; and *Newsweek,* September 4, 2006, pp. 40–41.

[52] *New York Times,* November 10, 2005, p. A20.

[53] *Brill's Content,* July–August 1998, p. 132.

[54] Thomas B. Ross, then chief of the *Chicago Sun-Times* Washington bureau, quoted in Wise, *The Politics of Lying,* pp. 287, 394.

[55] Ibid., pp. 105–106.

[56] John D. O'Connor, "I'm the Guy They Called Deep Throat," *Vanity Fair,* July 2005, p. 86.

[57] *Gallup Report,* January 1982, no. 196, p. 31.

[58] *The People, the Press & Their Leaders,* 1995 (Washington, D.C.: The Times Mirror Center for the People and the Press, 1995), p. 9.

[59] Ibid.

[60] U.S. Congress, House of Representatives, Committee on Government Operations, Administration of the Freedom of Information Act, 92nd Cong., 2nd sess., *Twenty-first Report* (Washington, D.C.: U.S. Government Printing Office, 1972), p. 8.

[61] *Snepp* v. *United States,* 444 U.S. 507 (1980).

[62] *New York Times,* May 26, 2004, p. A10.

[63] Ibid.

[64] *Washington Post,* August 12, 2004, p. A1.

[65] *New York Times,* November 14, 1969, p. 1.

[66] Harris Interactive poll, February 13–19, 2002, "Following the Leaders," online at the Roper Center for Public Opinion Research, at <http://www.ropercenter.uconn.edu>.

[67] Roper Starch Worldwide/History Channel, January 27–30, 2000, "The Press and the President," online at the Roper Center for Public Opinion Research at <http://www.ropercenter.uconn.edu>.

[68] *Public Perspective,* July/August 2002, p. 21, online at the Roper Center for Public Opinion Research at <http://www.ropercenter.uconn.edu/pubper/pdf/pp13_4b.pdf>.

[69] *The State of the News Media 2004,* "Overview: Public Attitudes," online at <http://www.journalism.org>.

[70] Harris poll, "Confidence in Leaders of Major Institutions Declines Modestly Since Last Year," p. 2, table 1, February 9–16, 2004, online at <http://www.harrisinteractive.com/harris_poll/index.asp?PID=447>.

[71] *The State of the News Media 2004.*

[72] Gallup poll, February 19, 1999.

[73] The Pew Research Center for the People and the Press, "Survey of Journalists," March 10–April 20, 2004, p. 62, Q27, online at <http://people-press.org/reports/display.php3?ReportID=214>.

[74] *The People, the Press & Their Leaders,* pp. 36–37.

[75] *New York Times,* November 18, 1992, p. A20. The survey, by the Freedom Forum, a nonpartisan organization that studies media issues, was based on a telephone poll of 1,400 reporters nationwide.

[76] Wise, *The Politics of Lying,* p. 367.

[77] W. Lance Bennett and David L. Paletz, *Taken by Storm: The Media, Public Opinion, and U.S. Foreign Policy in the Gulf War* (Chicago: University of Chicago Press, 1994), pp. 282–283.

## Chapter 9

[1] *New York Times,* July 30, 2004, p. A1.

[2] Ibid.

[3] *New York Times,* September 3, 2004, p. A1.

[4] *Newsweek* poll, September 3, 2004, online at <http://www.pollingreport.com>.

[5] Pew Center for the People and the Press, July 26, 2004, online at <http://www.people-press.org>.

[6] Frank J. Sorauf, *Political Parties in the American System* (Boston: Little, Brown, 1964), p. 1.

[7] Ibid.

[8] V. O. Key, Jr., *Politics, Parties, and Pressure Groups,* 5th ed. (New York: Crowell, 1964), p. 9.

[9] Key, *Politics, Parties, and Pressure Groups,* p. 167.

[10] Wilfred E. Binkley, *American Political Parties* (New York: Knopf, 1963), p. 19.

[11] Four Whig presidents occupied the White House. Only two were elected, however—William Henry Harrison in 1840 and Zachary Taylor in 1848. Both died in office and were succeeded by their vice presidents, John Tyler and Millard Fillmore.

[12] Clinton Rossiter, *Parties and Politics in America* (Ithaca, N.Y.: Cornell University Press, 1960), pp. 73–74.

[13] Rossiter, *Parties and Politics in America,* p. 7.

[14] Allan P. Sindler, *Political Parties in the United States* (New York: St. Martin's, 1966), p. 15.

[15] Herbert McCloskey, Paul J. Hoffmann, and Rosemary O'Hara, "Issue Conflict and Consensus among Party Leaders and Followers," *American Political Science Review,* vol. 54, no. 2 (June 1960), pp. 415–426. The study was based on interviews with delegates who attended the 1956 Democratic and Republican national conventions.

[16] *New York Times,* August 29, 2004, section 15, p. 1.

[17] *Gallup Opinion Index,* Report no. 131, June 1976, p. 11; *Gallup Opinion Index,* Report no. 180, August 1980, p. 31; *Gallup Report,* no. 255, December 1986, pp. 27–28; and The Gallup Organization, *Poll Releases,* April 1999, online at <http://www.gallup.com/poll/content/login.aspx?ci=3934>.

[18] Everett Carll Ladd, Jr., "The 1994 Congressional Elections: The Realignment Continues," in *Political Science Quarterly,* vol. 10, no. 1 (Spring 1995), p. 19.

[19] Everett Carll Ladd, Jr., with Charles D. Hadley, *Transformations of the American Party System: Political Coalitions from the New Deal to the 1970s,* 2nd ed. (New York: Norton, 1978), p. 329.

[20] Martin P. Wattenberg, *The Decline of American Political Parties, 1952–1980* (Cambridge, Mass.: Harvard University Press, 1984), p. xv.

[21] Austin Ranney, "The Political Parties: Reform and Decline," in Anthony King, ed., *The New American Political System* (Washington, D.C.: American Enterprise Institute for Public Policy Research, 1979), p. 245.

[22] Ladd with Hadley, *Transformations of the American Party System,* pp. 329–333.

[23] Frank J. Sorauf, *Party Politics in America,* 5th ed. (Boston: Little, Brown, 1984), p. 420.

[24] Ladd with Hadley, *Transformations of the American Party System,* pp. 258, 268.

[25] Sorauf, *Party Politics in America,* p. 148.

[26] Everett Carll Ladd, Jr., "The 1992 Vote for President Clinton: Another Brittle Mandate?" in *Political Science Quarterly,* vol. 108, no. 1 (Spring 1993), p. 5.

[27] Ibid.

[28] Ibid.

[29] Data from the Gallup poll.

[30] Jo Freeman, "The Political Culture of the Democratic and Republican Parties," *Political Science Quarterly,* vol. 101, no. 3 (Fall 1986), p. 337.

[31] Quoted in Andrew Hacker, "Is the Party Over?" *New York Times Book Review,* November 26, 1978, p. 12.

[32] Rossiter, *Parties and Politics in America,* p. 117.

[33] Theodore H. White, *The Making of the President, 1968* (New York: Atheneum, 1969), p. 33.

[34] The Center for Responsive Politics, "Soft Money Contributions," 2000 cycle, online at <http://www.opensecrets.org>.

[35] Rossiter, *Parties and Politics in America,* p. 131.

[36] Jerome L. Himmelstein, "The New Right," in Robert C. Liebman and Robert Wuthnow, eds., *The New Christian Right: Mobilization and Legitimation* (New York: Aldine, 1983), p. 16.

[37] The anti-Catholic, anti-Irish Native American Party was so secretive that its members pretended ignorance of party affairs; as a result editor Horace Greeley dubbed it the Know-Nothing Party.

[38] Key, *Politics, Parties, and Pressure Groups,* p. 255.

[39] Rossiter, *Parties and Politics in America,* pp. 5–6.

[40] Key, *Politics, Parties, and Pressure Groups,* p. 316.

[41] Robert J. Huckshorn, *Party Leadership in the States* (Boston: University of Massachusetts Press, 1976), pp. 69–95.

[42] David R. Mayhew, *Placing Parties in American Politics* (Princeton: Princeton University Press, 1986), pp. 17–77, 78.

[43] Sorauf, *Political Parties in the American System,* p. 53.

[44] David Halberstam, "Daley of Chicago," in William J. Crotty, Donald M. Freeman, and Douglas S. Gatlin, *Political Parties and Political Behavior* (Boston: Allyn and Bacon, 1971), p. 286. Reprinted from *Harper's,* August 1968.

[45] Raymond E. Wolfinger, "Why Political Machines Have Not Withered Away and Other Revisionist Thoughts," *The Journal of Politics,* vol. 34 (1972), p. 384.

[46] Ibid., pp. 384–386.

[47] For general discussions of political participation, see Chapters 6 and 11.

[48] Nelson W. Polsby and Aaron B. Wildavsky, *Presidential Elections,* 9th ed. (Chatham, N.J.: Chatham House, 1996), pp. 165, 285.

[49] Michael Kelly, "Glasshouse Conventions: How the Parties Built Their Pretty Facades—and Why They're So Fragile," *New Yorker,* September 9, 1996, p. 39.

[50] Ibid., p. 40.

[51] Nelson W. Polsby, *Consequences of Party Reform* (New York: Oxford University Press, 1983), p. 77.

[52] In 1956, in an unusual move, Adlai Stevenson, the nominee of the Democratic National Convention, threw open the choice of a vice presidential candidate to the delegates. In the floor balloting, Senator Estes Kefauver of Tennessee narrowly defeated Senator John F. Kennedy of Massachusetts to become Stevenson's running mate.

[53] *USA Today,* August 14, 2000, p. 8A.

[54] *New York Times*/CBS News poll, *New York Times,* July 25, 2004, section 15, p. 1.

[55] Key, *Politics, Parties, and Pressure Groups,* p. 398. Polk was the first "dark horse" to be nominated for president by a national political convention.

[56] Michael G. Hagen, "Press Treatment of Front-Runners," in William G. Mayer, ed., *In Pursuit of the White House: How We Choose Our Presidential Nominees* (Chatham, N.J.: Chatham House, 1996), p. 191.

[57] United States Election Project, "2004 Presidential Primary Turnout Rates," online at <http://elections.gmu.edu / Voter_Turnout_2004_Primaries.htm>.

[58] Austin Ranney, "Turnout and Representation in Presidential Primary Elections," *American Political Science Review,* vol. 66 (March 1972), p. 27.

[59] For a discussion of the pros and cons of a national presidential primary, see Judith H. Parris, *The Convention Problem* (Washington, D.C.: The Brookings Institution, 1972), pp. 172–177.

[60] Austin Ranney, *The Federalization of Presidential Primaries* (Washington, D.C.: American Enterprise Institute for Public Policy Research, 1978), pp. 33–38.

[61] Polsby, *Consequences of Party Reform,* p. 182.

[62] Rossiter, *Parties and Politics in America,* p. 34.

[63] Quoted in George Seldes, ed., *The Great Quotations* (New York: Pocket Books, 1967), p. 734.

[64] James Bryce, *The American Commonwealth* (New York: Capricorn Books, 1959), vol. 1, p. 151.

[65] Gerald M. Pomper, with Susan S. Lederman, *Elections in America: Control and Influence in Democratic Politics,* 2nd ed. (New York: Longman, 1980), p. 152.

[66] Ibid., pp. 161, 164. See also Paul T. David, "Party Platforms as National Plans," *Public Administration Review,* vol. 31, no. 3 (May-June 1971), pp. 303–315.

[67] Max Lerner, *America as a Civilization,* vol. 1 (New York: Simon & Schuster, 1967), pp. 389–390.

[68] See, for example, Report of the Committee on Political Parties of the American Political Science Association, *Toward a More Responsible Two-Party System* (New York: Holt, Rinehart and Winston, 1950).

## Chapter 10

[1] *New York Times,* August 20, 2004, p. A17.

[2] *New York Times,* September 22, 2000, p. A1.

[3] David B. Magleby, ed., *Financing the 2000 Elections* (Washington, D.C.: The Brookings Institution, 2002), chapter 2; Candice J. Nelson, *Spending in the 2000 Elections,* table 2-1, p. 24.

[4] 2004 estimate from Herbert E. Alexander, Distinguished Professor Emeritus, University of Southern California.

[5] Henry Adams, *Democracy: An American Novel* (New York: Modern Library Classics, 2003). Originally published anonymously in 1880.

[6] Nelson W. Polsby and Aaron B. Wildavsky, *Presidential Elections,* 9th ed. (Chatham, N.J.: Chatham House, 1996), p. 181.

[7] William H. Flanigan and Nancy H. Zingale, *Political Behavior of the American Electorate,* 8th ed. (Washington, D.C.: CQ Press, 1994), pp. 162–163.

[8] Dan Nimmo and Robert L. Savage, *Candidates and Their Images: Concepts, Methods, and Findings* (Pacific Palisades, Calif.: Goodyear Publishing, 1976), p. 208.

[9] Ibid., pp. 136–137.

[10] Ibid., p. 143.

[11] Dan Nimmo, *Political Communication and Public Opinion in America* (Santa Monica, Calif.: Goodyear Publishing, 1978), pp. 361–372. See also David L. Swanson, "Political Communication: A Revisionist View Emerges," *The Quarterly Journal of Speech,* vol. 64 (1978), pp. 211–222.

[12] Norman H. Nie, Sidney Verba, and John R. Petrocik, *The Changing American Voter,* enlarged edition, A Twentieth Century Fund Study (Cambridge, Mass.: Harvard University Press, 1979), p. 319.

[13] Walter DeVries and Lance Tarrance, Jr., *The Ticket-Splitter: A New Force in American Politics* (Grand Rapids, Mich.: Eerdmans, 1972), p. 37.

[14] Ibid., p. 111.

[15] In Iowa, convention delegates are selected in small face-to-face groups called caucuses, rather than in a primary election.

[16] Theodore H. White, *The Making of the President, 1968* (New York: Atheneum, 1969), pp. 326–333.

[17] "Assassination," in *To Establish Justice, To Insure Domestic Tranquility: Final Report of the National Commission on the Causes and Prevention of Violence* (Washington, D.C.: U.S. Government Printing Office, 1969), p. 132.

[18] The law states that the secretary of the treasury, after consultation with an advisory committee that includes leaders of Congress, decides who qualifies as a candidate under this definition. The law does not specifically provide protection for preconvention candidates, but the precedent was set in 1968 when the Secret Service guarded a total of 12 candidates.

[19] V. O. Key, Jr., *Politics, Parties, and Pressure Groups,* 5th ed. (New York: Crowell, 1964), p. 471.

[20] Governor George W. Bush, "Getting Results from Government," Philadelphia, June 9, 2000, online at <http://www.georgewbush.com>.

[21] Nelson W. Polsby and Aaron B. Wildavsky, *Presidential Elections,* 2nd ed. (New York: Scribner's, 1968), p. 129.

[22] Polsby and Wildavsky, *Presidential Elections,* 9th ed., p. 99.

[23] *New York Times,* September 16, 2000, p. A10.

[24] Bush used the phrase in a speech in Grand Rapids, Michigan, on July 30, 2004, online at <http://www.georgewbush.com>.

[25] *New York Times,* September 25, 2004, p. A1.

[26] The first President Bush, quoted on *NBC Nightly News,* January 15, 1992.

[27] From the text of Roosevelt's remarks to the International Brotherhood of Teamsters, Washington, D.C., September 23, 1944, as transcribed by the White House stenographer from his shorthand notes and provided to the authors by the Franklin D. Roosevelt Library.

[28] A Gallup poll published in October showed that 52 percent of the voters had heard of the Watergate scandal, but only about a third were able to recite the key facts of the situation. Eight out of 10 people who knew about the incident said it was not a strong reason for voting for Nixon's Democratic opponent, Senator George McGovern. Source: Gallup poll, *Washington Post,* October 8, 1972, p. A5.

[29] *Washington Post,* August 14, 1984, p. A6; and October 12, 1984, p. A10.

[30] *Washington Post,* March 6, 1998, p. A18.

[31] *Washington Post,* September 5, 2000, p. A4.

[32] Ibid.

[33] *USA Today,* September 20, 2000, p. 13A.

[34] *Washington Post,* September 24, 2000, p. A14.

[35] "Decision 2000," September 12, 2000, online at <http://www.msnbc.com/news>.

[36] PBS, *The American Experience,* "Vietnam: A Television History," p. 10, online at <http://www.pbs.org/wgbh/amex/vietnam/104ts.html>.

[37] Theodore H. White, *The Making of the President, 1964* (New York: Atheneum, 1965), p. 322.

[38] The Commission on Presidential Debates, debate transcript, September 30, 2004, "The First Bush-Kerry Presidential Debate," p. 4, online at <http://www.debates.org/>.

[39] Ibid., p. 30.

[40] The Gallup poll, October 1, 2004, "Kerry Wins Debate," online at <http://www.gallup.com/poll/content/login.aspx?ci=13237>.

[41] *Newsweek* poll, October 2, 2004, online at <http://www.pollingreport.com/wh2004.htm>.

[42] CNN/*USA Today*/Gallup poll, September 26, 2004, reporting Bush ahead of Kerry 52 to 44 percent in a two-way race, online at <http://www.pollingreport.com/wh2004.htm>.

[43] Theodore H. White, *The Making of the President, 1960* (New York: Atheneum, 1961), p. 289.

[44] *New York Times,* October 30, 1980, p. B19.

[45] *Washington Post,* October 6, 1988, p. A1.

[46] *Washington Post,* October 7, 1988, p. A14.

[47] *Washington Post,* October 12, 1992, p. A18.

[48] Sidney Kraus and Dennis Davis, *The Effects of Mass Communication on Political Behavior* (University Park: The Pennsylvania State University Press, 1976), p. 59.

[49] Ibid.

[50] Data for 2000 provided by the Television Bureau of Advertising, online at <http://www.tvb.org/nav/build_frameset.asp?url=/rcentral/index.asp>.

[51] CNN Money, "A Vote for Local T.V.", July 13, 2004, online at <http://www.cnnmoney.com>.

[52] *Washington Post,* October 21, 1980, p. B4.

[53] Reported in the *Washington Post,* October 5, 1988, p. 1.

[54] John F. Bibby, *Politics, Parties, and Elections in America,* 3rd ed. (Chicago, Ill.: Nelson-Hall, 1996), p. 233.

[55] Thomas E. Patterson and Robert D. McClure, *The Unseeing Eye: The Myth of Television Power in National Politics* (New York: Putnam, 1976), pp. 22–23.

[56] Harold Mendelsohn and Garrett J. O'Keefe, *The People Choose a President: Influences on Voter Decision Making* (New York: Praeger, 1976), p. 171.

[57] *New York Times,* July 16, 1992, p. A11.

[58] *New York Times,* September 19, 1980, p. B1.

[59] Ibid.

[60] Larry J. Sabato, *The Rise of Political Consultants: New Ways of Winning Elections* (New York: Basic Books, 1981), p. 15.

[61] Ibid., pp. 310–311, 337.

[62] James M. Perry, *The New Politics* (New York: Potter, 1968), pp. 25–26.

[63] Stanley Kelley, Jr., *Professional Public Relations and Political Power* (Baltimore, Md.: Johns Hopkins Press, 1956), p. 212.

[64] Dan Nimmo, *The Political Persuaders* (Englewood Cliffs, N.J.: Prentice Hall, 1970), pp. 197–198.

[65] *Time,* September 15, 1980.

[66] *Washington Post,* October 18, 1988, p. 1.

[67] Statement by the first president Bush while campaigning in South Carolina, October 20, 1992, broadcast by NBC News on the *Today* show, October 21, 1992.

[68] Earl Mazo and Stephen Hess, *Nixon: A Political Portrait* (New York: Harper & Row, 1968), p. 282.

[69] University of Virginia, Thomas Jefferson Digital Archive, "Thomas Jefferson on Politics & Government," online at <http://etext.virginia.edu/jefferson/quotations/jeff1600.htm>.

[70] Polsby and Wildavsky, *Presidential Elections,* 9th ed., p. 201.

[71] Quoted in Carl Sandburg, *Abraham Lincoln: The Prairie Years,* vol. 1 (New York: Harcourt Brace, 1926), p. 344.

[72] Herbert E. Alexander and Monica Bauer, *Financing the 1988 Election* (Boulder, Colo.: Westview Press, 1991), p. 4; Herbert E. Alexander and Anthony Corrado, *Financing the 1992 Election* (Armonk, N.Y.: Sharpe, 1995), p. 3; and John C. Green, ed., *Financing the 1996 Election* (Armonk, N.Y.: Sharpe, 1999), p. 13; 2004 data from David B. Magleby, Anthony Corrado, and Kelly D. Patterson, eds., *Financing the 2004 Election* (Washington, D.C.: The Brookings Institution Press, 2006), table 3-1, p. 71.

[73] Federal Election Commission press release, "2004 Presidential Campaign Financial Activity Summarized," February 3, 2005, <online at www.fec.gov/press>.

[74] *Washington Post,* July 8, 1996, p. A1.

[75] *Washington Post,* July 27, 1988, p. A4.

[76] *Washington Post,* December 11, 2003, p. A1.

[77] *Buckley* v. *Valeo,* 424 U.S. 1 (1976).

[78] The 1976 amendments to the Federal Election Campaign Act contained an escalator clause keyed to the cost-of-living index, allowing the amount of public funds received by candidates to increase with inflation.

[79] Elizabeth Drew, *Politics and Money: The New Road to Corruption* (New York: Macmillan, 1983), pp. 1–2.

[80] *Colorado Republican Federal Campaign Committee* v. *Federal Election Commission,* 518 U.S. 604 (1996).

[81] *New York Times,* January 18, 1979, p. 19.

[82] Larry Makinson, *The Price of Admission: Campaign Spending in the 1990 Election* (Washington, D.C.: Center for Responsive Politics, 1991), p. 35.

[83] Data for 1994 from the Federal Election Commission.

[84] Data from Center for Responsive Politics, online at <http://www.opensecrets.org>.

[85] Alexander and Bauer, *Financing the 1988 Election,* p. 53.

[86] Data from Center for Responsive Politics, online at <http://www.opensecrets.org/2000elect/storysofar/topraces.asp>.

[87] Center for Responsive Politics, "Blair Hull, Illinois Senate Race," online at <http://www.opensecrets.org/politicians/alsorun.asp?CID=N00025738&cycle=2004>.

[88] *Washington Post,* November 30, 1980, p. A1.

[89] Drug Reform Coordination Network, online at <http://stopthedrugwar.org/chronicle/262/newyork.shtml>.

[90] Herbert E. Alexander, *Financing Politics: Money, Elections, and Political Reform,* 4th ed. (Washington, D.C.: CQ Press, 1992), pp. 5–6.

[91] Federal Election Commission press release, "2004 Presidential Campaign Financial Activity Summarized," February 3, 2005, online at <www.fec.gov/press>.

[92] Alexander Heard, *The Costs of Democracy* (Chapel Hill: University of North Carolina Press, 1960), pp. 14, 35.

[93] Ibid., p. 394.

[94] Data provided by the Federal Election Commission. Figures rounded. Total expenditures by PACs for the 1980s were much higher but included their staff salaries and other overhead. 2000 numbers: Federal Election Commission, "PAC Activity Increases in 2000 Election Cycle," online at <http://www.fec.gov>.

[95] Alexander and Bauer, *Financing the 1988 Election,* pp. 68–69.

[96] Federal Election Commission press release, "PAC Financial Activity Increases," August 30, 2006, online at <http://www.fec.gov/press>.

[97] *Buckley* v. *Valeo* (1976).

[98] For a discussion of the complex motives for campaign giving, see Heard, *The Costs of Democracy,* chapter 4.

[99] Ibid., p. 163.

[100] *New York Times,* January 15, 1981, p. B10.

## Chapter 11

[1] See Lester W. Milbrath and M. L. Goel, *Political Participation,* 2nd ed. (Chicago: Rand McNally, 1977), for detailed citations of studies of political participation.

[2] U.S. Bureau of the Census, *Statistical Abstract of the United States: 2006,* p. 263.

[3] Milbrath and Goel, *Political Participation,* p. 114; and Raymond E. Wolfinger and Steven J. Rosenstone, *Who Votes?* (New Haven: Yale University Press, 1980), pp. 37–38. However, Wolfinger and Rosenstone add that "the decline in turnout among people over sixty . . . is explained not by their greater age but by differences in education, marital status, and sex" (p. 47).

[4] Data provided by U.S. Bureau of the Census, *Voting and Registration in the Election of November 2000,* series P20-542.

[5] Sandra Baxter and Marjorie Lansing, *Women and Politics: The Invisible Majority* (Ann Arbor: University of Michigan Press, 1980), p. 1.

[6] Data provided by U.S. Bureau of the Census, *Voting and Registration in the Election of November 2004.*

[7] For a discussion of the "very strong relationship between rates of voting and years of education," see Wolfinger and Rosenstone, *Who Votes?* pp. 17–20, 34–36.

[8] Angus Campbell, Philip E. Converse, Warren E. Miller, and Donald E. Stokes, *The American Voter* (New York: Wiley, 1960), pp. 96–101. Our discussion of voter attitudes is based in part on Chapter 5 of this landmark study of voting conducted at the Survey Research Center, University of Michigan.

[9] Ibid., p. 111.

[10] U.S. Census Bureau, *Voting and Registration in the Election of November 2004,* March 2006, table f, p. 15.

[11] Milbrath and Goel, *Political Participation,* p. 143.

[12] Paul F. Lazarsfeld, Bernard Berelson, and Hazel Gaudet, *The People's Choice* (New York: Columbia University Press, 1968). (Originally published in 1944.)

[13] Ibid., p. 21.

[14] Bernard R. Berelson, Paul F. Lazarsfeld, and William N. McPhee, *Voting* (Chicago: University of Chicago Press, 1966). (Originally published in 1954.)

[15] Gallup poll, July 1992.

[16] Angus Campbell, Philip E. Converse, Warren E. Miller, and Donald E. Stokes, "Stability and Change in 1960: A Reinstating Election," *American Political Science Review,* vol. 55, no. 2 (June 1961), pp. 269–280. Actual votes were obtained by applying percentages to the 1960 total two-party vote.

[17] See Ithiel de Sola Pool, Robert P. Abelson, and Samuel L. Popkin, *Candidates, Issues, and Strategies* (Cambridge: MIT Press, 1964), pp. 68, 117–118.

[18] Data provided by the Gallup poll.

[19] Congressional Quarterly, *Weekly Report,* February 10, 1973, p. 308; Congressional Quarterly, *Weekly Report,* November 6, 1976, p. 3118; *New York Times,* January 6, 1981, p. A14; and *New York Times,* December 22, 1984, p. 10. Vote totals are for the 11 states of the Old Confederacy: Alabama, Arkansas, Florida, Georgia, Louisiana, Mississippi, North Carolina, South Carolina, Tennessee, Texas, and Virginia.

[20] For a comparison of voting between men and women in the Eisenhower era, see Campbell, Converse, Miller, and Stokes, *The American Voter,* p. 493.

[21] The Gallup poll data in Table 11-3 indicated that Reagan ran 15 percentage points ahead of Carter among men. The ABC News exit poll, based on interviews of 9,341 voters leaving voting precincts on Election Day, reported that Reagan's margin over Carter was 19 percentage points among men. Both the Gallup poll and the ABC News exit poll found that among women who were interviewed, Reagan ran 5 percentage points ahead of Carter.

[22] Baxter and Lansing, *Women and Politics: The Invisible Majority,* p. 57.

[23] Voter Research and Surveys exit polls for 1992, in *National Journal,* November 7, 1992, p. 2543.

[24] Voter News Service exit polls for 1996, *National Journal,* November 9, 1996, p. 2407.

[25] Campbell, Converse, Miller, and Stokes, *The American Voter,* p. 17.

[26] Arthur H. Miller, Warren E. Miller, Alden S. Raine, and Thad A. Brown, "A Majority Party in Disarray: Policy Polarization in the 1972 Election," *American Political Science Review,* vol. 70, no. 3 (September 1976), p. 770.

[27] Campbell, Converse, Miller, and Stokes, *The American Voter,* pp. 171–172.

[28] Ibid., p. 180.

[29] Norman H. Nie, Sidney Verba, and John R. Petrocik, *The Changing American Voter,* enlarged edition (Cambridge: Harvard University Press, 1979), pp. 96–109, 156–173.

[30] See Gregory B. Markus, "Political Attitudes during an Election Year: A Report on the 1980 NES Panel Study," *American Political Science Review,* vol. 76, no. 3 (September 1982), pp. 538–560, especially p. 560.

[31] Voter News Service exit polls for 1996, *National Journal,* November 9, 1996, p. 2408.

[32] Morris P. Fiorina, *Retrospective Voting in American National Elections* (New Haven: Yale University Press, 1981), pp. 5–6.

[33] *New York Times,* February 26, 2000, p. A15.

[34] In the 11 states of the former Confederacy, the Republicans won 64 U.S. House seats in November 1994. The Democrats won 61 seats. See Milton C. Cummings, Jr., "Political Change since the New Deal: The 1992 Presidential Election in Historical Perspective," in Harvey L. Schantz, ed., *American Presidential Elections: Process, Policy, and Political Change* (Albany: State University of New York Press, 1996), pp. 56–57, 59.

[35] Angus Campbell, "Surge and Decline: A Study of Electoral Change," in Angus Campbell, Philip E. Converse, Warren E. Miller, and Donald E. Stokes, *Elections and the Political Order* (New York: Wiley, 1966), pp. 44–45, 59, 61–62.

[36] Barbara Hinckley, "Interpreting House Midterm Elections: Toward a Measurement of the In-Party's 'Expected' Loss of Seats," *American Political Science Review,* vol. 61, no. 3 (September 1967), p. 699.

[37] Edward R. Tufte, "Determinants of the Outcomes of Midterm Congressional Elections," *American Political Science Review,* vol. 69, no. 3 (September 1975), p. 824.

[38] Thomas Mann and Norman Ornstein, "Election '82: The Voters Send a Message," *Public Opinion,* December/January 1983, p. 8.

[39] For an additional discussion of the coattail phenomenon, see Warren E. Miller, "Presidential Coattails: A Study in Political Myth and Methodology," *Public Opinion Quarterly,* vol. 19, no. 1 (Spring 1955), pp. 353–368.

[40] V. O. Key, Jr., *Politics, Parties, and Pressure Groups,* 5th ed. (New York: Crowell, 1964), p. 304.

[41] In 1942 only 10 states with four-year gubernatorial terms scheduled their election for governor midway through the president's term. By 1962 the number of such states stood at 20; for 1990 it was 34, a total that remained through 2002. Adapted from Congressional Quarterly, *Politics in America* (Washington, D.C.: Congressional Quarterly, May 1969), pp. 148–155; and Congressional Quarterly, *Weekly Reports*.

[42] See Milton C. Cummings, Jr., "The Presidential Campaign and Vote in 1996: Job Ratings of Presidents—and Success or Failure at the Polls," in Harvey L. Schantz, ed., *Politics in an Era of Divided Government: Elections and Governance in the Second Clinton Administration* (New York: Routledge, 2001), pp. 63–84.

[43] CNN, *Live from the Headlines,* May 16, 2003.

[44] *New York Times,* June 24, 2003, p. A22.

[45] *Newsweek,* November 15, 2004, p. 58.

[46] Ibid., p. 81.

[47] *Newsweek,* November 15, 2004.

[48] *New York Times,* October 29, 2004, pp. A16, A1.

[49] *Washington Post,* November 5, 2004, p. A7.

[50] *Washington Post,* November 9, 2004, pp. C1 and C9.

[51] Stateline, online at <http://www.stateline.org>.

[52] The Gallup Poll and *USA Today*/Gallup Poll tracked Bush's approval rating each month. Respondents were asked, "Do you approve or disapprove of the way George W. Bush is handling his job as president?" online at <www.pollingreport.com>.

[53] *Washington Post,* January 21, 2006, p. A1.

[54] *USA Today*/Gallup Poll October 6–8, 2006, online at <www.pollingreport.com>.

[55] Gallup Poll, September 7–10, 2006, online at <www.pollingreport.com>.

[56] Remarks by the president at the Texas Victory 2006 Rally, Sugarland Regional Airport, Sugarland, Texas, October 30, 2006, online at <www.whitehouse.gov>.

[57] *Washington Post,* November 9, 2006, p. A37; and *USA Today,* November 10, 2006, p. 6A.

[58] *Washington Post,* November 11, 2006, p. A1.

[59] Only five southern states still imposed a poll tax as a requirement for voting in federal elections when the Twenty-fourth Amendment went into effect on January 23, 1964. Under the Voting Rights Act of 1965, the U.S. attorney general filed lawsuits against four of the 27 states still imposing poll taxes in state and local elections. In 1966 the U.S. Supreme Court ruled in *Harper* v. *Virginia State Board of Elections* (383 U.S. 633) that any state poll tax violated the Fourteenth Amendment. The decision outlawed the use of poll taxes at any level of election.

[60] *Dunn* v. *Blumstein,* 405 U.S. 330 (1972).

[61] *Marston* v. *Mandt,* 410 U.S. 679 (1973); and *Burns* v. *Fortson,* 410 U.S. 686 (1973).

[62] Elizabeth Yadlosky, *Election Laws of the Fifty States and the District of Columbia,* Legislative Reference Service of the Library of Congress, June 5, 1968, p. 305.

[63] *Oregon* v. *Mitchell,* 400 U.S. 112 (1970).

[64] U.S. Bureau of the Census, *Current Population Reports, Population Characteristics,* series P-20, no. 244, December 1972, p. 3.

[65] U.S. Bureau of the Census, *Voting and Registration in the Election of November 2000,* series P20-542, p. 6, table b.

[66] Department of Homeland Security, *Estimates of the Legal Permanent Resident Population and Population Eligible to Naturalize in 2004,* February 2006.

[67] *USA Today,* October 6, 2006, p. 23A.

[68] *Washington Post,* June 27, 2000, p. A1.

[69] Democratic National Committee, formerly online at <http://www.democrats.org/whitehouse/primary.html>; The Green Papers, "2004 Presidential Primaries, Caucuses, and Conventions" chronology, online at <http://www.thegreenpapers.com>.

[70] *Report of the President's Commission on Registration and Voting Participation* (Washington, D.C.: U.S. Government Printing Office, 1963), p. 32.

[71] *Washington Post,* May 12, 1993, p. A1.

[72] Campbell, Converse, Miller, and Stokes, *The American Voter,* p. 285.

[73] "Same Day Voter Registration Was the One Reform That Improved Turnout in the 2000 Election," *The Political Standard,* November/December 2001.

[74] Congressional Quarterly, *Weekly Report,* February 3, 1996, p. 310.

[75] Ibid.

[76] *Washington Post,* November 29, 1998, p. A6.

[77] *New York Times,* November 6, 1996, p. B7.

[78] Richard M. Nixon, *Six Crises* (New York: Doubleday, 1962), p. 413.

[79] In fact, in 1969 Maine changed its system of choosing presidential electors; under a state law passed that year, two electors are chosen at large and two are chosen from Maine's two congressional districts. Nebraska adopted a similar system. Other states elect their presidential electors on a statewide basis.

[80] Neal R. Peirce, *The People's President* (New York: Simon & Schuster, 1968), p. 41.

[81] See, for example, Irving Kristol and Paul Weaver, "A Bad Idea Whose Time Has Come," *New York Times Magazine,* November 23, 1969.

[82] *Colgrove* v. *Green,* 328 U.S. 549 (1946).

[83] *Baker* v. *Carr,* 369 U.S. 186 (1962).

[84] *Reynolds* v. *Sims,* 377 U.S. 533 (1964).

[85] *Wesberry* v. *Sanders,* 376 U.S. 1 (1964).

[86] *Kirkpatrick* v. *Preisler,* 394 U.S. 526 (1969); *Mahon* v. *Howell, City of Virginia Beach* v. *Howell,* and *Weinberg* v. *Prichard,* all 410 U.S. 315 (1973); *Gaffney* v. *Cummings,* 412 U.S. 735 (1973); and *White* v. *Regester,* 412 U.S. 755 (1973).

[87] The membership of the House increased only briefly, to 436 in early 1959 and to 437 from late 1959 through 1962, as a result of the admission to statehood of Alaska and Hawaii.

[88] William J. D. Boyd, in Congressional Quarterly, *Weekly Report,* November 21, 1969, p. 2342.

[89] Gerald M. Pomper, "Census '70: Power to the Suburbs," *Washington Monthly,* May 1970, p. 23.

[90] Congressional Research Service, *Membership of the 109th Congress: A Profile,* June 13, 2006. U.S. Department of State, *Record Number of Hispanics Elected to U.S. House of Representatives,* November 12, 2002.

[91] *New York Times,* June 14, 1996, p. A1.

[92] Ibid.

[93] Ibid.

[94] *Washington Post,* November 23, 1996, p. A1.

[95] *Vieth* v. *Jubelirer,* 124 S. Ct. 1769 (2004).

[96] *New York Times,* June 29, 2006, p. A22.

[97] Key, *Politics, Parties, and Pressure Groups,* pp. 520–536.

[98] V. O. Key, Jr., "A Theory of Critical Elections," *Journal of Politics,* vol. 17 (February 1955), pp. 3–18.

[99] Campbell, Converse, Miller, and Stokes, *The American Voter,* pp. 531–538.

[100] On Election Day 1976, CBS News interviewed 14,836 people as they left the polls. Those who voted for Jimmy Carter were given a list of 10 possible issues and asked to check as many as three that "led you to vote for Jimmy Carter." By far the largest group—49 percent—checked "Restoring trust in government." One in five checked "Watergate and the pardon." See *National Journal,* November 6, 1976, p. 1588.

[101] For a detailed statement of the view that elections are won and lost "in the center," see Richard M. Scammon and Ben J. Wattenberg, *The Real Majority* (New York: Coward-McCann, 1971).

[102] Key, *Politics, Parties, and Pressure Groups,* pp. 522–523.

## Chapter 12

[1] *CQ Weekly,* October 12, 2002, p. 2689, Senate vote 237; and pp. 2692–2693, House vote 455. In both chambers, an independent voted against the resolution.

[2] U.S. Bureau of the Census, *Statistical Abstract of the United States: 1969,* p. 279.

[3] Peter A. Corning, *The Evolution of Medicare,* U.S. Department of Health, Education, and Welfare (Washington, D.C.: U.S. Government Printing Office, 1969), p. 93.

[4] Chuck McCutcheon, "Former CIA Official to Head Hill Intelligence Probe of Sept. 11," *CQ Weekly,* February 16, 2002, pp. 485–487.

[5] Helen Fessenden, "Robust Intelligence Oversight Stalls at White House Door," *CQ Weekly,* July 26, 2003, pp. 1917–1921.

[6] CRS Report for Congress, "Membership of the 109th Congress: A Profile." January 18th, 2006.

[7] Ibid.

[8] *Congressional Directory, 109th Congress (2005–2006)* (Washington, D.C.: Government Printing Office, 2006), pp. 335–373.

[9] CRS Report for Congress, "Membership of the 109th Congress: A Profile." January 18th, 2006.

[10] *Congressional Quarterly Today,* November 4, 2004, p. 62.

[11] Roger H. Davidson, *The Role of the Congressman* (New York: Pegasus, 1969), p. 69.

[12] Leroy N. Rieselbach, *Congressional Politics: The Evolving Legislative System,* 2nd ed. (Boulder, Colo.: Westview Press, 1995), pp. 65, 68.

[13] *Congressional Quarterly,* "Guide to the New Congress."

[14] Charles L. Clapp, *The Congressman: His Work as He Sees It* (Washington, D.C.: The Brookings Institution, 1963), p. 61.

[15] Luther Patrick, "What Is a Congressman?" *Congressional Record,* May 13, 1963, p. A2978.

[16] In John F. Kennedy, *Profiles in Courage* (New York: Harper & Row, 1956), p. 30.

[17] Roger H. Davidson and Walter J. Oleszek, *Congress and Its Members,* 6th ed. (Washington, D.C.: CQ Press, 1998), p. 130, citing survey by Joint Committee on the Organization of Congress.

[18] Davidson, *The Role of the Congressman,* pp. 98–99.

[19] Davidson and Oleszek, *Congress and Its Members,* 9th ed., p. 129.

[20] *U.S. Term Limits, Inc.* v. *Thornton,* 514 U.S. 779 (1995).

[21] Davidson and Oleszek, *Congress and Its Members,* 9th ed., p. 448.

[22] Richard F. Fenno, Jr., "If, As Ralph Nader Says, Congress Is 'The Broken Branch,' How Come We Love Our Congressmen So Much?" in *Congress in Change,* Norman J. Ornstein, ed. (New York: Praeger, 1975), pp. 277–287.

[23] Edmund Burke, *The Works of the Right Honourable Edmund Burke,* vol. 2 (London: Oxford University Press, 1930), pp. 164–165.

[24] V. O. Key, Jr., *Public Opinion and American Democracy* (New York: Knopf, 1961), pp. 492–493.

[25] Davidson, *The Role of the Congressman,* p. 119.

[26] Ibid., pp. 117–119.

[27] Davidson and Oleszek, *Congress and Its Members,* 9th ed., p. 4.

[28] David R. Mayhew, *Congress: The Electoral Connection* (New Haven: Yale University Press, 1974), pp. 13, 49.

[29] Richard F. Fenno, Jr., *Home Style: House Members in Their Districts* (Boston: Little, Brown, 1978).

[30] Aage R. Clausen, *How Congressmen Decide: A Policy Focus* (New York: St. Martin's, 1973), pp. 9, 53.

[31] Donald R. Matthews and James A. Stimson, *Yeas and Nays: Normal Decision-Making in the U.S. House of Representatives* (New York: Wiley, 1975), p. 45.

[32] Warren E. Miller and Donald E. Stokes, "Constituency Influence in Congress," *American Political Science Review,* vol. 57 (March 1963), pp. 53–54.

[33] Ibid.

[34] Virginia F. Depew, ed., *The Social List of Washington, D.C., and Social Precedence in Washington* (Kensington, Md.: Jean Shaw Murray, 1980).

[35] *Atlanta Constitution,* September 24, 2000, p. 6A. The survey was sponsored by National Public Radio, the Kaiser Family Foundation, and the Kennedy School of Government, Harvard University.

[36] Thomas E. Mann, *Unsafe at Any Margin: Interpreting Congressional Elections* (Washington, D.C.: American Enterprise Institute for Public Policy Research, 1978), p. 30.

[37] In Robert A. Dahl, *Pluralist Democracy in the United States: Conflict and Consent* (Chicago: Rand McNally, 1967), p. 35.

[38] David R. Mayhew, "Congressional Elections: The Case of the Vanishing Marginals," *Polity,* vol. 6 (Spring 1974), pp. 295–317.

[39] Morris P. Fiorina, *Congress: Keystone of the Washington Establishment* (New Haven: Yale University Press, 1977), p. 50.

[40] Lewis A. Froman, Jr., *Congressmen and Their Constituencies* (Chicago: Rand McNally, 1963), pp. 69–84.

[41] Davidson and Oleszek, *Congress and Its Members,* 9th ed., p. 115.

[42] Neil MacNeil, *Forge of Democracy: The House of Representatives* (New York: David McKay, 1964), pp. 82–83.

[43] Gebe Martinez, "The Seasoned Speaker: Still Hastert, but Harder," *CQ Weekly,* September 14, 2002, pp. 2358–2363, quotation, p. 2362.

[44] For a detailed study of the complex rules and procedures of the House and Senate, see Walter J. Oleszek, *Congressional Procedures and the Policy Process,* 6th ed. (Washington, D.C.: CQ Press, 2003); and text of the Legislative Reorganization Act of 1970.

[45] Milton C. Cummings, Jr., and Robert L. Peabody, "The Decision to Enlarge the Committee on Rules: An Analysis of the 1961 Vote," in Robert L. Peabody and Nelson W. Polsby, eds., *New Perspectives on the House of Representatives* (Chicago: Rand McNally, 1963), p. 193.

[46] Davidson and Oleszek, *Congress and Its Members,* 9th ed., p. 236.

[47] *Congressional Quarterly,* Weekly Report, March 15, 1980, p. 735.

[48] Boris Weintraub, "TV in Congress—Measuring the Impact," *Washington Star,* March 19, 1980, p. C5.

[49] "Millionaires Populate U.S. Senate," CNN, January 13, 2003, online at <http://www.cnn.com>.

[50] Paul S. Herrnson, *Congressional Elections: Campaigning at Home and in Washington,* 4th ed. (Washington, D.C.: CQ Press, 2004), p. 160.

[51] William S. White, *Citadel* (New York: Harper & Row, 1957), pp. 2, 82–84.

[52] Donald R. Matthews, *U.S. Senators and Their World* (Chapel Hill: University of North Carolina Press, 1960), pp. 92–117.

[53] Nelson W. Polsby, "Goodbye to the Inner Club," *Washington Monthly,* August 1969, pp. 30–34.

[54] Ralph K. Huitt, "The Outsider in the Senate: An Alternative Role," in Ralph K. Huitt and Robert L. Peabody, eds., *Congress: Two Decades of Analysis* (New York: Harper & Row, 1969), pp. 159–178.

[55] Barbara Sinclair, *The Transformation of the U.S. Senate* (Baltimore: Johns Hopkins University Press, 1989), p. 79.

[56] Ibid., p. 94.

[57] Ibid., p. 101.

[58] Ibid., p. 99.

[59] *USA Today,* August 4, 2004, p. 1D.

[60] Robert L. Peabody, Norman J. Ornstein, and David W. Rohde, "The United States Senate as Presidential Incubator: Many Are Called But Few Are Chosen," *Political Science Quarterly,* vol. 91, no. 2 (Summer 1976), pp. 252–253.

[61] Ibid., pp. 253–256.

[62] Charles O. Jones, "The New, New Senate," in Ellis Sandoz and Cecil V. Crabb, Jr., eds., *A Tide of Discontent: The 1980 Elections and Their Meaning* (Washington, D.C.: Congressional Quarterly, 1981), p. 100.

[63] Johnson was Senate minority leader from 1953 to 1955.

[64] Rowland Evans and Robert Novak, *Lyndon B. Johnson: The Exercise of Power* (New York: New American Library, 1966), p. 104.

[65] *Congressional Record,* November 27, 1963, p. 22862.

[66] Mark Green, with Michael Calabrese et al., and Ralph Nader Congress Watch, *Who Runs Congress?* 3rd ed. (New York: Bantam Books, 1979), pp. 100–101.

[67] Gebe Martinez, "Issue Kept Gaining Momentum," *CQ Weekly,* January 4, 2003, pp. 24–27.

[68] John Cochran and David Nather, "Fast-Moving Events Challenge Frist's Debut at Senate Helm," *CQ Weekly,* January 4, 2003, pp. 16–17, 21–22.

[69] John Cochran, "Management by Objective: How Frist Deals in 51–49 Senate," *CQ Weekly,* August 30, 2003, pp. 2062–2063, 2066–2069, quotation, p. 2068.

[70] See William Safire, *Safire's New Political Dictionary* (New York: Random House, 1993), p. 245.

[71] *New York Times,* February 25, 1988, p. A26.

[72] Data provided by Senate Historical Office.

[73] *Washington Post,* February 25, 1988, p. A4.

[74] Ibid., p. A1.

[75] Herrnson, *Congressional Elections,* p. 94.

[76] Woodrow Wilson, *Congressional Government* (New York: World, Meridian Books, 1956), pp. 69, 82–83. (Originally published in 1885.)

[77] Barbara Sinclair, *Unorthodox Lawmaking: New Legislative Processes in the U.S. Congress* (Washington, D.C.: CQ Press, 1997), pp. 14–20, 34–38, 84–88.

[78] Derek Willis, "Republicans Mix It Up When Assigning House Chairmen for the 108th," *CQ Weekly,* January 11, 2003, pp. 89, 91–92.

[79] Anthony King, "Introduction," in Anthony King, ed., *The New American Political System,* 2nd edition (Lanham, Md.: Rowman & Littlefield, 1990), p. 2.

[80] Samuel C. Patterson, "The Semi-Sovereign Congress," in King, ed., *The New American Political System,* p. 160.

[81] Richard F. Fenno, Jr., *Congressmen in Committees* (Boston: Rowman & Littlefield, 1973). The names of many of the Senate and House committees cited in Fenno's work have changed; the committee names as of 2004 have been substituted by the authors.

[82] *Watkins* v. *United States,* 354 U.S. 178 (1957).

[83] *Barenblatt* v. *United States,* 360 U.S. 109 (1959).

[84] Data from C-SPAN, online at <http://www.cspan.org/questions/weekly35.htm>.

[85] Data provided by Walter J. Oleszek.

[86] Harrison W. Fox, Jr., and Susan Webb Hammond, *Congressional Staffs* (New York: Free Press, 1977), p. 2.

[87] Ibid., p. 27.

[88] Data provided by Walter J. Oleszek.

[89] Richard F. Fenno, Jr., "The Internal Distribution of Influence: The House," in David B. Truman, ed., *The Congress and America's Future,* prepared for the American Assembly, Columbia University (Englewood Cliffs, N.J.: Prentice Hall, 1965), p. 70.

[90] Allen Schick, *Congress and Money: Budgeting, Spending and Taxing* (Washington, D.C.: The Urban Institute, 1980), p. 42.

[91] *Immigration and Naturalization Service* v. *Chadha,* 462 U.S. 919 (1983).

[92] Gebe Martinez, "Traficant's Ouster Decided But Not Relished by His Peers," *CQ Weekly,* July 27, 2002, pp. 2036–2037.

[93] Elizabeth A. Palmer and Jonathan Allen, "Torricelli's Ethics Admonishment Quickly Becomes Campaign Issue," *CQ Weekly,* August 3, 2002, pp. 2104–2105.

[94] Gerald M. Pomper, "Alive! The Political Parties after the 1980–1992 Presidential Elections," in Harvey L. Schantz, ed., *American Presidential Elections: Process, Policy, and Political Change* (Albany: State University of New York Press, 1996), pp. 135–156.

[95] Ibid., pp. 146–149.

[96] Davidson and Oleszek, *Congress and Its Members,* 9th ed., p. 276.

[97] Harvey L. Schantz, ed., *Politics in an Era of Divided Government: Elections and Governance in the Second Clinton Administration* (New York: Routledge, 2001), p. xvii.

[98] Ibid.

[99] Roger H. Davidson and Colton C. Campbell, "The Irony of the 105th Congress and Its Legacy," in Schantz, ed., *Politics in an Era of Divided Government,* pp. 155–180, quotation, p. 164.

[100] E. E. Schattschneider, *The Semisovereign People* (New York: Holt, Rinehart and Winston, 1960), p. 102.

## Chapter 13

[1] Harry S Truman, statement to the press, April 13, 1945, quoted in Robert J. Donovan, *Conflict and Crisis: The Presidency of Harry S Truman, 1945–1948* (New York: Norton, 1977), p. 17.

[2] *USA Today*/Gallup Poll, May 5–7, 2006, online at <http://www.pollingreport.com/bushjob1.htm>.

[3] Arthur M. Schlesinger, Jr., *The Imperial Presidency* (Boston: Houghton Mifflin, 1973).

[4] Louis W. Koenig, *The Chief Executive,* 4th ed. (New York: Harcourt Brace Jovanovich, 1981), p. 11.

[5] Thomas E. Cronin, *The State of the Presidency,* 2nd ed. (Boston: Little, Brown, 1980), pp. 76, 90.

[6] Arthur Schlesinger, Jr., "So Much for The Imperial Presidency," *New York Times,* September 3, 1998, p. A23.

[7] Arthur M. Schlesinger, Jr., *War and the American Presidency* (New York: Norton, 2004).

[8] Schlesinger, *The Imperial Presidency,* p. x.

[9] From a television and radio interview: "After Two Years—A Conversation with the President," December 17, 1962, in *Public Papers of the Presidents of the United States, John F. Kennedy, 1962* (Washington, D.C.: U.S. Government Printing Office, 1963), p. 890.

[10] Under the Twenty-second Amendment, a vice president who succeeded to the presidency for less than two years could run, and if elected, serve as president for two more full terms. Thus, the same person could conceivably be president for almost 10 years.

[11] White House press release (Remarks by the president, Democratic National Committee dinner, New York City), April 24, 2000.

[12] Carl Van Doren, *The Great Rehearsal* (New York: Viking Press, 1948), p. 145.

[13] Thomas E. Cronin, in Thomas E. Cronin, ed., *Inventing the American Presidency* (Lawrence: University Press of Kansas, 1989), p. ix.

[14] In Richard F. Fenno, Jr., *The President's Cabinet* (Cambridge: Harvard University Press, 1959), p. 217.

[15] Clinton Rossiter, *The American Presidency,* rev. ed. (New York: Harcourt Brace Jovanovich, 1960), p. 225.

[16] See "The National Security Strategy of the United States of America," September 17, 2002, online at <http://www.whitehouse.gov/nsc/nss.html>.

[17] Edward S. Corwin, *The President, Office and Powers 1787–1957* (New York: New York University Press, 1957), p. 311.

[18] *New York Times,* January 24, 1996, p. 1.

[19] Rossiter, *The American Presidency,* pp. 16–41.

[20] Cronin, *The State of the Presidency,* p. 156.

[21] Letter to Lady Delamere, March 7, 1911, in Roosevelt, Theodore, 1858–1919, Correspondence and Compositions, Theodore Roosevelt Collection, Houghton Library, Harvard College Library.

[22] For example, among adults, one study found that "the assassination generally

evoked feelings similar to those felt at the death of a close friend or relative." Of a sample of the adult population, 43 percent said they did not feel like eating, 29 percent smoked more than usual, 53 percent cried, 48 percent had trouble sleeping, and 68 percent felt nervous and tense. Source: Paul B. Sheatsley and Jacob J. Feldman, "A National Survey on Public Reactions and Behavior," in Bradley S. Greenberg and Edwin B. Parker, eds., *The Kennedy Assassination and the American Public* (Stanford: Stanford University Press, 1965), pp. 158, 168.

[23] U.S. Code, Title 3, Chapter 2, Section 102, 103; and Congressional Research Service Report for Congress, "Former Presidents: Federal Pension and Retirement Benefits," pp. 1–2, November 13, 2003, online at <http://www.senate.gov/reference/resources/pdf/98-249.pdf>.

[24] A citizen born abroad of American parents might well be regarded as "natural-born." The question arose in 1968 because George Romney, a Republican hopeful, had been born in Mexico. The requirement of 14 years' residence apparently does not mean that a president must have lived in the United States for 14 successive years immediately before the election, because Herbert Hoover had not.

[25] In Richard E. Neustadt, *Presidential Power* (New York: Wiley, 1980), p. 9.

[26] Ibid., p. 9.

[27] Ibid., p. 10.

[27] *Myers* v. *United States,* 272 U.S. 52 (1926).

[29] *Humphrey's Executor* v. *United States,* 295 U.S. 602 (1935).

[30] Bob Horton, Associated Press staff writer, "The Job of Guarding the President's Code Box," *Washington Star,* November 21, 1965. See also William Manchester, *The Death of a President* (New York: Harper & Row, 1967), pp. 62, 321.

[31] *Immigration and Naturalization Service* v. *Chadha,* 462 U.S. 919 (1983).

[32] In Arthur Bernon Tourtellot, *The Presidents on the Presidency* (Garden City, N.Y.: Doubleday, 1964), p. 311.

[33] *Youngstown Sheet and Tube Co.* v. *Sawyer,* 343 U.S. 579 (1952).

[34] Corwin, *The President, Office and Powers 1787–1957,* p. 171.

[35] *United States* v. *Curtiss-Wright Export Corp.,* 299 U.S. 304 (1936).

[36] Richard E. Neustadt, "Presidency and Legislation: Planning the President's Program," *American Political Science Review,* vol. 49 (December 1955), p. 981.

[37] "After Two Years—A Conversation with the President," p. 894.

[38] Charles O. Jones, *The Presidency in a Separated System* (Washington, D.C.: The Brookings Institution, 1994), p. 182.

[39] *United States* v. *Nixon,* 418 U.S. 683 (1974).

[40] George C. Edwards, III, *Presidential Influence in Congress* (San Francisco: Freeman, 1980), pp. 10, 205.

[41] *New York Times,* June 26, 1998, p. A1; *Washington Post,* October 7, 1997, p. A1; and October 18, 1997, p. A4.

[42] *Clinton* v. *City of New York,* 524 U.S. 417 (1998).

[43] *New York Times,* June 26, 1998, p. A1.

[44] *Congressional Record,* January 18, 1960, pp. 710–712.

[45] Neustadt, *Presidential Power,* p. 166.

[46] *Weekly Compilation of Presidential Documents,* February 13, 1980, p. 310.

[47] See Dom Bonafede, "Who's He Trying to Kid?" *National Journal,* May 10, 1980, p. 781.

[48] Neustadt, *Presidential Power,* p. 180.

[49] Jeffrey K. Tulis, *The Rhetorical Presidency* (Princeton, N.J.: Princeton University Press, 1987) p. 4.

[50] Ibid.

[51] Ibid.

[52] Ibid.

[53] Theodore J. Lowi, *The Personal President: Power Invested, Promise Unfulfilled* (Ithaca, N.Y.: Cornell University Press, 1985), p. 11.

[54] Ibid., p. 10.

[55] Ibid., p. 96.

[56] Rossiter, *The American Presidency,* p. 148.

[57] Hugh Sidey, *A Very Personal Presidency* (New York: Atheneum, 1968), p. 98.

[58] Cronin, *The State of the Presidency,* p. 80.

[59] Fenno, *The President's Cabinet,* p. 19.

[60] Ibid., p. 137.

[61] "Conversation between President Kennedy and NBC Correspondent Ray Scherer," broadcast over NBC television network, April 11, 1961 (stenographic transcript), p. 17.

[62] *Washington Post,* July 18, 1982, p. 1.

[63] *Washington Post,* July 19, 1982, pp. 1, A8.

[64] See Richard J. Ellis, *Presidential Lightning Rods: The Politics of Blame Avoidance* (Lawrence: University Press of Kansas, 1994). As Ellis points out, some presidential advisers may attract blame toward a president, serving as a liability rather than a lightning rod.

[65] Neustadt, *Presidential Power,* p. 39.

[66] Fenno, *The President's Cabinet,* p. 218.

[67] In a break with tradition Nixon also permitted Kissinger to keep his title as assistant to the president for national security.

[68] "Conversation between President Kennedy and NBC Correspondent Ray Scherer," p. 3.

[69] *Washington Post,* White House Briefing, "2005 White House Office Staff List—By Salary," online at <http://www.washingtonpost.com>.

[70] Office of Personnel Management, "Federal Civilian Personnel Summary, 2005," online at <http://www.opm.gov/feddata/html.2005/november/table1.asp>.

[71] Donald Young, *American Roulette: The History and Dilemma of the Vice Presidency* (New York: Holt, Rinehart and Winston, 1965), p. 10.

[72] Remarks of the Vice President to the Veterans of Foreign Wars 103rd National Convention, August 26th, 2002, online at <www.whitehouse.gov>.

[73] *Report of the President's Special Review Board* (Washington, D.C.: U.S. Government Printing Office, February 26, 1987).

[74] Neustadt, *Presidential Power,* chapter 4.

[74] Michael McCurry, remarks to reporters at the White House, January 30, 1998, quoted in *Newsday,* February 1, 1998, p. A42.

[76] *Washington Times,* October 2, 1998, p. A2.

[77] Larry Speakes, *Speaking Out* (New York: Macmillan, 1988).

[78] *New York Times,* May 5, 1977, p. 33.

[79] See John Anthony Maltese, *Spin Control: The White House Office of Communications and the Management of Presidential News* (Chapel Hill: University of North Carolina Press, 1992).

[80] Fred I. Greenstein, "Change and Continuity in the Modern Presidency," in Anthony King, ed., *The New American Political System* (Washington, D.C.: American Enterprise Institute for Public Policy Research, 1978), pp. 74–75.

[81] Speakes, *Speaking Out,* p. 111.

[82] Ibid., p. 113.

[83] The phrase was coined by Representative Patricia Schroeder, a Colorado Democrat, in a speech to the House in August 1983, in which she said that Reagan was "perfecting the Teflon-coated presidency. He sees to it that nothing sticks to him." *Washington Post,* April 15, 1984, p. 1.

[84] Below the level of vice president, the order in which other officials might succeed to the presidency is spelled out in the Presidential Succession Act of 1947. The order of succession begins with the House speaker, followed by the president pro tempore of the Senate, and then members of the cabinet, starting with the secretary of state.

[85] Because of the extraordinary circumstances of a president and a vice president resigning during the same term, the United States had four vice presidents in a period of less than four years from 1973 to 1977: Spiro T. Agnew, Gerald R. Ford, Nelson A. Rockefeller, and Walter F. Mondale.

[86] Tourtellot, *The Presidents on the Presidency,* p. 426.

[87] Ibid., pp. 55–56.

[88] Koenig, *The Chief Executive,* pp. 16–19.

[89] James David Barber, *The Presidential Character: Predicting Performance in the White House,* 2nd ed. (Englewood Cliffs, N.J.: Prentice Hall, 1977). The four types that Barber identified are active-positive, active-negative, passive-positive, and passive-negative.

[90] Ibid., pp. 94, 159, 423–424, 441.

[91] Ibid., pp. 441–442.

[92] It is interesting to note in this connection that before President Kennedy met with Soviet Premier Khrushchev in Vienna in 1961, he had access to an assessment of Khrushchev's character prepared for the CIA by a panel of psychiatrists and psychologists. See Bryant Wedge, "Khrushchev at a Distance—A Study of Public Personality," *Trans-Action,* October 1968.

[93] *Congressional Quarterly,* Weekly Report, July 19, 1980, p. 2064.

[94] *Congressional Quarterly,* Weekly Report, November 1, 1980, p. 3282.

[95] *Congressional Record,* January 18, 1960, p. 711.

[96] Louis W. Koenig, *The Chief Executive,* 6th ed. (Belmont, Calif.: Wadsworth Publishing, 1995), p. 17.

## Chapter 14

[1] Governor George W. Bush, "Getting Results from Government," Philadelphia, June 9, 2000, online at <http://www.georgewbush.com>.

[2] C. Northcote Parkinson, *Parkinson's Law* (Boston: Houghton Mifflin, 1957), p. 2.

[3] Hannah Arendt, *Crises of the Republic* (New York: Harcourt Brace Jovanovich, 1972), p. 137.

[4] *New York Times,* January 24, 1996, p. 1.

[5] Peter F. Drucker, *The Age of Discontinuity* (New York: Harper & Row, 1969), p. 220.

[6] In H. H. Gerth and C. Wright Mills, *From Max Weber: Essays in Sociology* (New York: Oxford University Press, 1953), p. 234.

[7] Dwight Waldo, "Public Administration," *Journal of Politics,* vol. 30, no. 2 (May 1968), p. 448.

[8] Wallace Sayre, "Premises of Public Administration: Past and Emerging," *Public Administration Review,* vol. 18, no. 2 (Spring 1958), p. 105.

[9] H. George Frederickson, "Toward a New Public Administration," in Frank Marini, ed., *Toward a New Public Administration: The Minnowbrook Perspective* (Scranton, Pa.: Chandler, 1971), p. 314.

[10] Francis E. Rourke, ed., *Bureaucratic Power in National Politics* (Boston: Little, Brown, 1978), p. vii.

[11] Kenneth Culp Davis, *Discretionary Justice* (Baton Rouge: Louisiana State University Press, 1969), p. 4.

[12] Francis E. Rourke, *Bureaucracy, Politics, and Public Policy,* 2nd ed. (Boston: Little, Brown, 1976), p. 46.

[13] Ibid.

[14] David Wise, *Nightmover: How Aldrich Ames Sold the CIA to the KGB for $4.6 Million* (New York: HarperCollins, 1995).

[15] David Wise, *Spy: The Inside Story of How the FBI's Robert Hanssen Betrayed America* (New York: Random House, 2002).

[16] See Arthur Maass, *Muddy Waters* (Cambridge: Harvard University Press, 1951); and "Congress and Water Resources," in Rourke, ed., *Bureaucratic Power in National Politics.*

[17] Morris P. Fiorina, *Congress: Keystone of the Washington Establishment* (New Haven: Yale University Press, 1977), pp. 48–49. After the Republicans gained control of Congress in 1994, however, Congress sought to eliminate federal programs rather than create new ones. The cycle described by Fiorina seemed more applicable to the decades when the Democrats controlled Congress and enacted many new programs.

[18] Ibid., p. 78.

[19] Robert L. Lineberry, *American Public Policy: What Government Does and What Difference It Makes* (New York: Harper & Row, 1977), p. 55.

[20] See Theodore J. Lowi, *The End of Liberalism: Ideology, Policy, and the Crisis of Public Authority* (New York: Norton, 1969), Chapter 3.

[21] Francis E. Rourke, "American Bureaucracy in a Changing Political Setting," *Journal of Public Administration Research and Theory,* vol. 1, no. 2 (April 1991), p. 119.

[22] Ibid.

[23] Ibid., p. 112.

[24] Hugh Heclo, "Issue Networks and the Executive Establishment," in Anthony King, ed., *The New American Political System* (Washington, D.C.: American Enterprise Institute for Public Policy Research, 1978), p. 103.

[25] Ibid.

[26] Ibid., p. 88.

[27] In Richard F. Fenno, Jr., *The President's Cabinet* (Cambridge: Harvard University Press, 1959), p. 225. The cabinet secretary who voiced this nautical complaint was William Gibbs McAdoo, Wilson's secretary of the treasury.

[28] Rourke, *Bureaucracy, Politics, and Public Policy,* Chapter 3.

[29] Ibid.

[30] Frank J. Donner, *The Age of Surveillance: The Aims and Methods of America's Political Intelligence System* (New York: Knopf, 1980).

[31] CBS News survey, on *CBS Evening News,* September 7, 1993.

[32] Data provided by Department of Defense for 1987.

[33] Arthur M. Schlesinger, Jr., *A Thousand Days* (Boston: Houghton Mifflin, 1965), p. 406.

[34] Roosevelt quoted in Richard E. Neustadt, *Presidential Power* (New York: Wiley, 1960), p. 42.

[35] Commission on Organization of the Executive Branch of the Government, *Reports to Congress and Task Force Reports* (Washington, D.C.: U.S. Government Printing Office, 1949). The second Hoover Commission was established in 1953 and reported in 1955. Because it urged the government to eliminate many activities that competed with private enterprise, its proposals were more politically controversial. The second Hoover Commission report had little effect. See Commission on Organization of the Executive Branch of the Government, *Reports to Congress and Task Force Reports* (Washington, D.C.: U.S. Government Printing Office, 1955).

[36] Aaron Wildavsky, *The Politics of the Budgetary Process* (Boston: Little, Brown, 1964), p. 5.

[37] Ibid., pp. 41–42.

[38] Frederick C. Mosher, *Democracy and the Public Service* (New York: Oxford University Press, 1968), pp. 21, 109.

[39] Rourke, "American Bureaucracy in a Changing Political Setting," *Journal of Public Administration Research and Theory,* p. 120.

[40] Ibid., pp. 113–114.

[41] Theodore C. Sorensen, *Kennedy* (New York: Harper & Row, 1965), p. 309.

[42] David Wise and Thomas B. Ross, *The Invisible Government* (New York: Random House, 1964), p. 185.

[43] Townsend Hoopes, *The Limits of Intervention* (New York: David McKay, 1969), p. 181, Chapters 8–10.

[44] U.S. Office of Personnel Management, *Federal Civilian Workforce Statistics, Employment and Trends as of January, 2006,* table 2, and online at <http://http://www.opm.gov/feddata/html/2006/january>.

[45] Ibid., Table 1.

[46] Ibid., Table 2.

[47] U.S. Bureau of the Census, "State Government Employment Data, March 2002," online at <http://www.census.gov/govs/apes/02stus.txt>; and "2002 Public Employment Data: Local Governments," <http://www.census.gov/govs/apes/02locus.txt>.

[48] U.S. Office of Personnel Management, *Fact Book, Federal Civilian Workforce Statistics,* 2005 ed., pp. 10, 14.

[49] U.S. Office of Personnel Management, 2004 Salary Tables, online at <http://www.opm.gov>.

[50] U.S. Office of Personnel Management, Salary Table 2006-ES, "Rates of Basic Pay for Members of the Senior Executive Service (SES)," online at <http://www.opm.gov>.

[51] Data provided by U.S. Office of Personnel Management, as of 2002.

[52] Neustadt, *Presidential Power,* p. 39.

[53] The Department of Education and the Department of Health and Human Services replaced the old Department of Health, Education, and Welfare, which had been created in 1953.

[54] *Vermont Yankee Nuclear Power Corporation* v. *Natural Resources Defense Council, Inc.,* 435 U.S. 519 (1978).

[55] Bernard Schwartz, *The Professor and the Commissions* (New York: Knopf, 1959), p. 48.

[56] *National Journal,* March 6, 1982, p. 405.

[57] *New York Times,* March 18, 2004, p. C1.

[58] Michael D. Reagan, *Regulation: The Politics of Policy* (Boston: Little, Brown, 1987), p. v.

[59] *Washington Post,* December 19, 2000, p. E1.

[60] *Washington Post,* September 20, 2000, p. E1.

[61] *New York Times,* November 7, 2000, section C, p. 4.

[62] U.S. Congress, Senate Committee on Governmental Affairs, *United States Government Policy and Supporting Positions,* 106th Cong., 2nd sess. (Washington, D.C.: U.S. Government Printing Office, 2000).

[63] In Louis W. Koenig, *The Chief Executive,* 4th ed. (New York: Harcourt Brace Jovanovich, 1981), p. 132.

[64] *Civil Service Commission* v. *National Association of Letter Carriers, AFL-CIO,* 413 U.S. 548 (1973).

[65] James P. McGrath, *Civil Service Reform Act: Implementation* (Washington, D.C.: Library of Congress, Congressional Research Service, 1980), p. 9.

[66] Drucker, *The Age of Discontinuity,* p. 226.

[67] *Washington Post,* February 9, 1988, p. E7.

[68] Helen Dudar, "The Price of Blowing the Whistle," *New York Times Magazine,* October 30, 1977, pp. 48–49.

[69] See Richard E. Neustadt and Harvey V. Fineberg, M.D., *The Swine Flu Affair* (Washington, D.C.: U.S. Department of Health, Education, and Welfare, 1978).

[70] Data provided by Torts Division, Department of Justice; and *New York Times,* June 10, 1979, p. 1.

[71] *Washington Post,* August 25, 1989, p. A19.

[72] Ibid.

## Chapter 15

[1] *Hamdan* v. *Rumsfeld,* No. 05-184 (2006).

[2] *League of United Latin American Citizens* v. *Perry,* No. 05-204 (2006).

[3] *Randall* v. *Sorrell,* No. 04-1528 (2006).

[4] *Chicago Tribune,* October 13, 1991, p. A1.

[5] *Rasul* v. *Bush,* 542 U.S. 466 (2004), and *Hamdi* v. *Rumsfeld,* 542 U.S. 507 (2004).

[6] *United States* v. *Nixon,* 418 U.S. 683 (1974).

[7] Robert H. Jackson, *The Supreme Court in the American System of Government* (Cambridge, Mass.: Harvard University Press, 1955), p. 27.

[8] Speech at a dinner of the Harvard Law School Association of New York, February 15, 1913, in Oliver Wendell Holmes and Harold Joseph Laski, *Collected Legal Papers* (New York: Harcourt, Brace and Co., 1920), pp. 291–292.

[9] Robert A. Dahl, "Decision-Making in a Democracy: The Role of the Supreme Court as a National Policy-Maker," in Raymond E. Wolfinger, ed., *Readings in American Political Behavior* (Englewood Cliffs, N.J.: Prentice Hall, 1966), p. 166.

[10] Robert G. McCloskey, *The American Supreme Court* (Chicago: University of Chicago Press, 1960), p. 8.

[11] *United States* v. *Nixon* (1974).

[12] Alpheus T. Mason, *The Supreme Court: Palladium of Freedom* (Ann Arbor: University of Michigan Press, 1962), p. 143. Hughes, later chief justice of the United States, made this comment in 1907 as governor of New York.

[13] Felix Frankfurter, "The Supreme Court and the Public," *Forum,* vol. 83 (June 1930), pp. 332–334.

[14] Quoted in Robert H. Jackson, *The Supreme Court in the American System of Government,* p. 11.

[15] Edward Mead Earle, ed., *The Federalist, No. 78* (New York: Modern Library), p. 506.

[16] Henry J. Abraham, *The Judicial Process,* 4th ed. (New York: Oxford University Press, 1980), p. 322.

[17] Ibid., pp. 324–336.

[18] *Marbury* v. *Madison,* 1 Cranch 137 (1803).

[19] Ibid.

[20] Archibald Cox, *The Warren Court* (Cambridge, Mass.: Harvard University Press, 1968), p. 2.

[21] The Sixteenth Amendment to the Constitution, ratified in 1913, allowed Congress to restore the federal income tax, which it did that year.

[22] A phrase popularized by columnists Drew Pearson and Robert S. Allen. See William Safire, *Safire's New Political Dictionary* (New York: Random House, 1993), pp. 499–500.

[23] *1968 Congressional Quarterly Almanac,* p. 539.

[24] *Baker* v. *Carr,* 369 U.S. 186 (1962); *Brown* v. *Board of Education of Topeka, Kansas,* 347 U.S. 483 (1954); and *Gideon* v. *Wainwright,* 372 U.S. 335 (1963), respectively.

[25] Robert L. Carter, "The Warren Court and Desegregation," *Michigan Law Review,* vol. 67, no. 2 (December 1968), p. 246.

[26] William M. Beaney, "The Warren Court and the Political Process," *Michigan Law Review,* vol. 67, no. 2 (December 1968), p. 352.

[27] *Roberts* v. *U.S. Jaycees,* 468 U.S. 609 (1984); *New York State Club Association* v. *New York City,* 487 U.S. 1 (1988).

[28] *Hazelwood School District* v. *Kuhlmeier,* 484 U.S. 260 (1988).

[29] Among the cases were *Patterson* v. *McLean Credit Union,* 491 U.S. 164 (1988), and *Wards Cove Packing Co., Inc.* v. *Atonio,* 490 U.S. 642 (1988). The series of decisions was overturned by the civil rights bill passed by Congress in 1991.

[30] *California* v. *Greenwood,* 486 U.S. 35 (1988).

[31] *United States* v. *Eichman* and *United States* v. *Haggerty,* both 496 U.S. 310 (1990).

[32] *Simon & Schuster* v. *New York State Crime Victims Board,* 502 U.S. 105 (1991).

[33] *Rasul* v. *Bush,* 542 U.S. 466 (2004).

[34] *Hamdi* v. *Rumsfeld,* 542 U.S. 507 (2004).

[35] Ibid.

[36] *Rumsfeld* v. *Padilla,* 542 U.S. 426 (2004).

[37] Ibid.

[38] *Missouri* v. *Seibert,* 542 U.S. 600 (2004).

[39] *Hiibel* v. *Sixth Judicial District Court of Nevada,* 542 U.S. 177 (2004).

[40] *Aetna Health* v. *Davila* and *Cigna Corporation* v. *Calad,* 542 U.S. 200 (2004).

[41] *Gonzales* v. *Raich,* No. 03-1454 (2005).

[42] *Kelo* v. *The City of New London* (2005)

[43] *Gonzales* v. *Oregon,* No. 04-623 (2006).

[44] *Georgia* v. *Randolph,* No. 04-1067 (2006).

[45] Ibid.

[46] "Justice Black and the Bill of Rights," interview broadcast over CBS television network, December 3, 1968, transcript in *Congressional Quarterly,* Weekly Report, January 3, 1969, p. 9.

[47] In Joseph W. Bishop, Jr., "The Warren Court Is Not Likely to Be Overruled," *New York Times Magazine,* September 7, 1969, p. 31.

[48] J. Anthony Lukas, *Nightmare: The Underside of the Nixon Years* (New York: Viking Press, 1976), p. 518. Associate Justice William H. Rehnquist disqualified himself and did not participate in the tapes decision, since he had served in the Justice Department under Nixon.

[49] Jackson, *The Supreme Court in the American System of Government,* p. 9.

[50] Walter F. Murphy, *Congress and the Court* (Chicago: University of Chicago Press, 1962), pp. 246–247.

[51] Dahl, "Decision-Making in a Democracy," pp. 171, 180.

[52] *Pollock* v. *Farmers' Loan and Trust Co.,* 158 U.S. 601 (1895).

[53] The Eleventh and Fourteenth Amendments to the Constitution also reversed specific Supreme Court rulings.

[54] *Grove City* v. *Bell,* 465 U.S. 555 (1984).

[55] *Washington Post,* May 23, 1993, pp. A1, A20.

[56] Bob Woodward and Scott Armstrong, *The Brethren: Inside the Supreme Court* (New York: Simon & Schuster, 1979).

[57] For two earlier analyses of conflict and decision making in the Supreme Court, see J. Woodford Howard, Jr., *Mr. Justice Murphy: A Political Biography* (Princeton, N.J.: Princeton University Press, 1968); and Walter F. Murphy, *Elements of Judicial Strategy* (Chicago: University of Chicago Press, 1964).

[58] Woodward and Armstrong, *The Brethren,* p. 284.

[59] Abraham, *The Judicial Process,* p. 187.

[60] David J. Danelski, "The Influence of the Chief Justice in the Decisional Process," in Walter F. Murphy and C. Herman Pritchett, eds., *Courts, Judges and Politics: An Introduction to the Judicial Process,* 3rd ed. (New York: Random House, 1979), pp. 695–703.

[61] In Danelski, "The Influence of the Chief Justice in the Decisional Process," p. 698.

[62] Woodward and Armstrong, *The Brethren,* pp. 187–188.

[63] *New York Times,* July 11, 1987, p. 18.

[64] Ibid.

[65] Ibid.

[66] Abraham, *The Judicial Process,* p. 146.

[67] Data provided by the Office of Statistics, Administrative Office of the United States Courts.

[68] *United States* v. *Tempia,* 16 USCMA 629 (1967).

[69] *Solorio* v. *United States,* 483 U.S. 435 (1987).

[70] *Parker* v. *Levy,* 417 U.S. 733 (1974); *Secretary of the Navy* v. *Avrech,* 418 U.S. 676 (1974).

[71] Abraham, *The Judicial Process,* p. 148.

[72] Brian J. Ostrom and Neal B. Kauder, *Examining the Work of State Courts, 1998: A National Perspective from the Court Statistics Project* (Williamsburg, Va.: National Center for State Courts, 1999), p. 12.

[73] U.S. Department of Justice, Office of Justice Programs, Bureau of Justice Statistics, *State Court Organization 1998,* pp. 34–49. Only one state, Montana, combines elections and the Missouri method.

[74] Glenn R. Winters and Robert E. Allard, "Judicial Selection and Tenure in the United States," in Harry W. Jones, ed., *The Courts, the Public, and the Law Explosion,* prepared for the American Assembly, Columbia University (Englewood Cliffs, N.J.: Prentice Hall, 1965), p. 157.

[75] *The Challenge of Crime in a Free Society,* report by the President's Commission on Law Enforcement and Administration of Justice (Washington, D.C.: U.S. Government Printing Office, 1967), p. 146.

[76] "Violence and Law Enforcement," in *To Establish Justice, To Insure Domestic Tranquility,* Final Report of the National Commission on the Causes and Prevention of Violence (Washington, D.C.: U.S. Government Printing Office, December 1969), pp. 143–144.

[77] Ibid., pp. 149–152, 155.

[78] Edward L. Barrett, Jr., "Criminal Justice: The Problem of Mass Production," in Jones, *The Courts, the Public, and the Law Explosion,* pp. 86–87.

[79]"Crime in the United States 2004," Uniform Crime Reports, Summary of the Federal Bureau of Investigation reporting program, p. 7, online at <http://www.fbi.gov/ucr/ucr.htm>.

[80] *Washington Post,* December 5, 1999, p. A3.

[81] *New York Times,* June 13, 2006, p. A.14.

[82] *The Challenge of Crime in a Free Society,* pp. 21–22.

[83] *Task Force Report: Crime and Its Impact—An Assessment,* The President's Commission on Law Enforcement and Administration of Justice (Washington, D.C.: U.S. Government Printing Office, 1967), pp. 93–94.

[84] *The Challenge of Crime in a Free Society,* p. 19.

[85]Richard Harris, *Justice: The Crisis of Law, Order, and Freedom in America* (New York: Dutton, 1970), pp. 27–28.

[86]"Crime in the United States 2004," Arrests, table 38.

[87]Harris, *Justice,* p. 44.

[88]U.S. Department of Justice, Bureau of Justice Statistics, "Firearms Purchase Applications Declined During 2000," July 1, 2001, online at <http://www.ojp.usdoj.gov/bjs/>.

[89] *USA Today,* December 1, 1999, p. 23A.

[90]U.S. Department of Justice, Bureau of Justice Statistics, "Background Checks for Firearm Transfers, 2004."

[91] *New York Times,* August 2, 2000, p. A11.

[92]Ibid.

[93]NBC News/*Wall Street Journal* poll, November 8–10, 2003, online at <http://www.pollingreport.com>.

[94]U.S. Department of Justice, Office of Justice Programs, Bureau of Justice Statistics, "Nation's Prison and Jail Population grew 2.6 percent during 12 Months that Ended June 30, 2005," released May 21, 2006.

[95] *Rhodes* v. *Chapman,* 452 U.S. 337 (1981).

[96] *Hudson* v. *Palmer,* 468 U.S. 517 (1984); *Block* v. *Rutherford,* 468 U.S. 576 (1984).

[97] *Keeney* v. *Tamayo-Reyes,* 504 U.S. 1 (1992).

[98] *Hudson* v. *McMillian,* 503 U.S. 1 (1992).

[99] *The Challenge of Crime in a Free Society,* p. 159.

[100] *Attica: The Official Report of the New York State Special Commission on Attica* (New York: Bantam Books, 1972), p. xii.

[101]The Officer Down Memorial Page, online at <http://www.odmp.org>.

[102]Gallup poll, September 17, 1968. The question asked of 1,507 people was, "Do you approve or disapprove of the way the Chicago police dealt with the young people who were registering their protest against the Vietnam war at the time of the Chicago Convention?" The nationwide findings were: approve, 56 percent; disapprove, 31 percent; no opinion, 13 percent.

[103]Daniel Walker, *Rights in Conflict, Report of the Chicago Study Team to the National Commission on the Causes and Prevention of Violence* (New York: Bantam Books, 1968), p. 5.

[104]For example, 76 percent of the people questioned in a telephone survey by the Columbia Broadcasting System said extremist groups should not be allowed to "organize protests" against the government; 55 percent said news media should not report stories that the government considers harmful to the national interest; and 58 percent thought that a suspect in a serious crime should be held in jail by police until they can get enough evidence to charge him or her with the crime. See The CBS News Poll, Survey Operations Department, CBS News Election Unit, March 20, 1970, pp. 1–6.

[105]Gallup poll, April 30–May 1, 1992.

[106] *Time,* September 11, 1995, pp. 38–41; *New York Times,* March 24, 1996, p. 35; and *The Philadelphia Inquirer,* January 21, 1998, p. A1.

[107] *Time,* September 27, 1999, p. 44.

[108]See, for example, James Q. Wilson, *Varieties of Police Behavior* (Cambridge, Mass.: Harvard University Press, 1968), pp. 7, 278.

[109] *New York Times,* June 24, 2004, p. A1.

[110]Federal Bureau of Investigation, "Frequently Asked Questions Overview," online at <http://www.fbi.gov/aboutus/faqs/faqsone.htm>.

[111]Federal Bureau of Investigation, "FBI Mission, History, and Organization," online at <http://www.fbi.gov/contact/legat/legat.htm?>.

[112]Data provided by the Federal Bureau of Investigation.

[113]David Wise, "The FBI's Greatest Hits," *Washington Post Magazine,* October 27, 1996, p. 15.

[114]For details of these and other abuses by the intelligence agencies, see U.S. Congress, Senate Select Committee to Study Governmental Operations with Respect to Intelligence Activities, *Intelligence Activities and the Rights of Americans, Book II,* 94th Cong., 2nd sess., Final Report (Washington, D.C.: U.S. Government Printing Office, 1976).

[115]As noted in Chapter 2, the Supreme Court has held that the "due process clause" of the Constitution requires the presumption that a criminal defendant is innocent until proven guilty "beyond a reasonable doubt." *Davis* v. *United States,* 160 U.S. 469 (1895); *Coffin* v. *United States,* 156 U.S. 432 (1895); *In re Samuel Winship,* 397 U.S. 358 (1970).

[116] *The Challenge of Crime in a Free Society,* p. 134.

[117] *Brady* v. *United States,* 396 U.S. 809 (1970).

[118] *Attica,* p. xiii.

[119]Ronald Goldfarb, *Ransom* (New York: Harper & Row, 1965), p. 1.

[120] *Duncan* v. *Louisiana,* 391 U.S. 145 (1968).

[121] *Baldwin* v. *New York,* 399 U.S. 66 (1970).

[122] *Johnson* v. *Louisiana,* 406 U.S. 356 (1972); *Apodaca* v. *Oregon,* 406 U.S. 404 (1972).

[123] *Williams* v. *Florida,* 399 U.S. 78 (1970).

[124] *Colgrove* v. *Battin,* 413 U.S. 149 (1973).

[125]Under the "three strikes" provision, the first two violent felony convictions may be for state or federal crimes, but the third must be a federal offense other than a drug conviction.

[126] *New York Times,* February 1, 2000, p. A20.

[127]Ibid. Ryan was convicted in federal court in 2006 of racketeering conspiracy for accepting payoffs and steering state contracts to associates as secretary of state and then as governor.

[128]Death Penalty Information Center, NAACP Legal Defense Fund, "Death Row USA", Spring 2004 (April 1, 2006).

[129]Ibid.

[130] *Washington Post,* June 22, 2000, p. A3.

[131] *Furman* v. *Georgia,* 408 U.S. 238 (1972).

[132] *Gregg* v. *Georgia,* 428 U.S. 153 (1976).

[133] *Woodson* v. *North Carolina,* 428 U.S. 280 (1976); *Roberts* v. *Louisiana,* 428 U.S. 325 (1976).

[134] *Thompson* v. *Oklahoma,* 487 U.S. 815 (1988).

[135]Death Penalty Information Center, online at <http://www.deathpenaltyinfo.org>.

[136]Robert Sherrill, "Death Row on Trial," *New York Times Magazine,* November 13, 1983, p. 80.

[137]The study, by Michael L. Radelet and Hugo Adam Bedau, was published in *Stanford Law Review,* November 1987.

[138]Ibid. Source: *New York Times,* May 3, 1989, p. A18.

[139] *Atkins* v. *Virginia,* 536 U.S. 304 (2002).

[140] *Roper* v. *Simmons,* No. 03-633 (March 1, 2005).

[141]Fred J. Cook, "The People v. The Mob; or, Who Rules New Jersey?" *New York Times Magazine,* February 1, 1970, p. 36.

[142] *New York Times,* January 7, 1970, p. 28.

[143] *The Challenge of Crime in a Free Society,* p. 191.

[144]Ibid., pp. 193–194.

[145]Ibid., p. 191.

[146]Donald R. Cressey, *Theft of the Nation* (New York: Harper & Row, 1969), pp. 252–253.

[147] *The Challenge of Crime in a Free Society,* p. 209.

[148]Woodward and Armstrong, *The Brethren,* p. 26.

[149] *Cipollone* v. *Liggett Group,* 505 U.S. 504 (1992).

[150]Cox, *The Warren Court,* p. 5.

[151]See, for example, Justice Black's opinion in *Chambers* v. *Florida,* 309 U.S. 227 (1940).

[152] *The Challenge of Crime in a Free Society,* p. 15.

[153]Jackson, *The Supreme Court in the American System of Government,* p. 61.

[154] *New York Times,* June 24, 1969, p. C24.

## Chapter 16

[1] *New York Times,* August 1, 2006, p. A13.

[2] *USAToday*/Gallup Poll, 6/21–23/04; 1/20–22/06, 7/21–23/06, online at <www.pollingreport.com/iraq.htm>.

[3] *New York Times,* September 21, 2001, p. A1.

[4]CNN/*USA Today*/Gallup poll, reported in the *New York Times,* September 24, 2001, p. B6.

[5] *Final Report of the National Commission on Terrorist Attacks Upon the United States* (New York: W. W. Norton, 2004), p. 261.

[6] *New York Times,* June 2, 2002, p. 1.

[7] "The National Security Strategy of the United States of America," September 17, 2002, online at <http://www.whitehouse.gov>.

[8] *New York Times,* October 8, 2002, p. A1; and Condoleezza Rice, *CNN Late Edition with Wolf Blitzer,* September 8, 2002.

[9] *New York Times,* February 6, 2003, p. A1.

[10] Interview with Barbara Walters on "20/20," *ABC News,* September 9, 2005.

[11] Department of Defense, "Iraq World Views," April 23, 2003, online at <http://www.defendamerica.mil/iraq/worldviews042303.html>.

[12] *Final Report of the National Commission on Terrorist Attacks Upon the United States,* p. 66.

[13] Roger Hilsman, *To Move a Nation* (Garden City, N.Y.: Doubleday, 1967), pp. 12–13, 541.

[14] Paul H. Nitze, "The Secretary and the Execution of Foreign Policy," in Don K. Price, ed., *The Secretary of State,* prepared for the American Assembly, Columbia University (Englewood Cliffs, N.J.: Prentice Hall, 1960), pp. 6–7.

[15] Robert F. Kennedy, *Thirteen Days* (New York: Norton, 1969), p. 44.

[16] *Washington Post,* June 29, 1996, p. A1. The Guatemala study was conducted by the president's Intelligence Oversight Board.

[17] Richard J. Barnet and Ronald E. Muller, *Global Reach: The Power of the Multinational Corporations* (New York: Simon & Schuster, 1974), p. 25.

[18] The Churchill Centre, Washington D.C., online at <http://www.winstonchurchill.org/i4a/pages/index.cfm?pageid5429>.

[19] Mr. X, "The Sources of Soviet Conduct," Foreign Affairs, July 1947, pp. 566–582. "Mr. X" was later revealed to be George F. Kennan.

[20] Harry S. Truman, *Memoirs by Harry S. Truman, vol. 2, Years of Trial and Hope* (Garden City, N.Y.: Doubleday, 1958), p. 106.

[21] Joseph S. Nye, Jr., and Robert O. Keohane, eds., *Transnational Relations and World Politics* (Cambridge, Mass.: Harvard University Press, 1972), pp. x–xi.

[22] Robert O. Keohane and Joseph S. Nye, *Power and Interdependence: World Politics in Transition* (Boston: Little, Brown, 1977), p. 9.

[23] A Gallup poll of June 1970 reported that 56 percent of the public considered that the United States had made "a mistake" in sending troops to Vietnam. As noted, the percentage of people who answered "yes" when asked "Do you think the United States made a mistake sending troops to fight in Vietnam?" rose above 50 percent for the first time in August 1968 and never dipped below that percentage thereafter.

[24] *New York Times,* March 15, 1983, p. A25.

[25] The total initial cost to the United States of the Persian Gulf War was $61.3 billion. However, allied countries, including Kuwait, Saudi Arabia, Japan, and Germany, reimbursed the United States almost $54 billion, so that the final cost to American taxpayers was reduced to $7.3 billion. See Department of Defense, *Conduct of the Persian Gulf War: Final Report to Congress,* April 1992, pp. P-2–P-3, online at <http://www.globalsecurity.org/military/library/report/1992/cpgw.pdf>.

[26] U.S. State Department, "Patterns of Global Terrorism," online at <http://www.state.gov/s/ct/rls/pgtrpt/2003/>. Figures are approximate; the State Department was forced to revise its estimate of terrorist incidents in 2003 after the total was discovered to be too low.

[27] Television and radio interview: "After Two Years—A Conversation with the President," December 17, 1962, in *Public Papers of the Presidents of the United States: John F. Kennedy, 1962* (Washington, D.C.: U.S. Government Printing Office, 1963), p. 889.

[28] U.S. Senate, Subcommittee on National Security Staffing and Operations, Committee on Government Operations, "Basic Issues," in *Administration of National Security* (Washington, D.C.: U.S. Government Printing Office, 1965), p. 7.

[29] Richard E. Neustadt, testimony to U.S. Senate, Subcommittee on National Security Staffing and Operations, Committee on Government Operations, March 25, 1963, in *Administration of National Security,* p. 76.

[30] Eric F. Goldman, *The Tragedy of Lyndon Johnson* (New York: Knopf, 1969), p. 383.

[31] David Wise, "Remember the Maddox!" *Esquire,* April 1968, p. 126. See also, Joseph C. Goulden, *Truth Is the First Casualty* (New York: Rand McNally, 1969).

[32] U.S. Senate, Committee on Foreign Relations, 90th Cong., 2nd sess., *Hearings, The Gulf of Tonkin: The 1964 Incidents* (Washington, D.C.: U.S. Government Printing Office, 1968), p. 54.

[33] Ibid., p. 91.

[34] U.S. Senate, Committee on Foreign Relations, 90th Cong., 1st sess., *Report on National Commitments* (Washington, D.C.: U.S. Government Printing Office, 1967), p. 14.

[35] *Congressional Quarterly,* Weekly Report, February 20, 1970, p. 518.

[36] George F. Kennan, *American Diplomacy* (Chicago: University of Chicago Press, 1951), pp. 91–92.

[37] Arthur M. Schlesinger, Jr., *A Thousand Days* (Boston: Houghton Mifflin, 1965), p. 406.

[38] U.S. State Department, "Department of State Organization Chart," online at <http://www.state.gov/documents/organization/8792.pdf>.

[39] Office of Personnel Management, *Fedscope,* December 2003, online at <http://www.fedscope.opm.gov>.

[40] U.S. Senate, Subcommittee on National Security Staffing and Operations, Committee on Government Operations, "Basic Issues," in *Administration of National Security,* p. 16.

[41] *New York Times,* April 21, 2006, p. A18.

[42] David Wise, *Nightmover: How Aldrich Ames Sold the CIA to the KGB for $4.6 Million* (New York: HarperCollins, 1995).

[43] See U.S. Senate, Select Committee to Study Governmental Operations with Respect to Intelligence Activities, 94th Cong., 1st sess., *Alleged Assassination Plots Involving Foreign Leaders, Interim Report* (Washington, D.C.: U.S. Government Printing Office, 1975). In addition to describing the efforts to assassinate Castro, the report also details CIA plots against Patrice Lumumba of the Congo, Rafael Trujillo of the Dominican Republic, President Salvador Allende and General René Schneider of Chile, President Ngo Dinh Diem of South Vietnam, President François Duvalier of Haiti, and President Achmed Sukarno of Indonesia.

[44] *New York Times,* December 22, 1974, p. 1.

[45] *Report to the President by the Commission on CIA Activities within the United States* (Washington, D.C.: U.S. Government Printing Office, 1975), p. 10.

[46] U.S. Senate, Select Committee to Study Governmental Operations with Respect to Intelligence Activities, 95th Cong., 2nd sess., *Foreign and Military Intelligence, Final Report* (Washington, D.C.: U.S. Government Printing Office, 1976), book 1, p. 128.

[47] *New York Times,* June 11, 1984, p. 1.

[48] *USA Today,* February 3, 2004, p. 8A.

[49] *Washington Post,* June 5, 2003, p. A31, and March 12, 1996, p. A11.

[50] David Wise and Thomas B. Ross, *The Invisible Government* (New York: Random House, 1964), p. 3.

[51] Hilsman, *To Move a Nation,* pp. 64–65.

[52] Allen Dulles, *The Craft of Intelligence* (New York: Harper & Row, 1963), p. 189.

[53] U.S. Senate, Select Committee to Study Governmental Operations with Respect to Intelligence Activities, *Foreign and Military Intelligence,* p. 46.

[54] Dulles, *The Craft of Intelligence,* pp. 48–51, 235–236.

[55] *Washington Post,* March 12, 1996, p. A11; and data from the Federation of American Scientists, online at <http://www.fas.org/irp/commission/budget>.

[56] *Washington Post,* April 7, 2006, p. A3.

[57] *USA Today,* May 11, 2006, p. 1A.

[58] See David Wise, *The American Police State* (New York: Random House, 1976).

[59] Congressional Research Service, "Foreign Aid: An Introductory Overview of U.S. Programs and Policy," pp. 30–31, April 15, 2004, online at <http://usinfo.state.gov/usa/infousa/trade/files/98-916.pdf>.

[60] *New York Times,* June 25, 1995, p. 6.

[61] "The UN in Brief," online at <http://www.un.org>; employment from "Who Works at the United Nations?" online at <http://www.un.org/geninfo/ir/ch6/ch6.htm>.

[62] Gabriel A. Almond, *The American People and Foreign Policy* (New York: Praeger, 1950), pp. 53, 4–6.

[63] James N. Rosenau, "Foreign Policy as an Issue-Area," in James N. Rosenau, ed., *Domestic Sources of Foreign Policy* (New York: Free Press, 1967), p. 49.

[64] Kenneth N. Waltz, "Electoral Punishment and Foreign Policy Crises," in Rosenau, ed., *Domestic Sources of Foreign Policy,* pp. 273, 283.

[65] "President Nixon's August 5, 1974 Statement" and "The June 23, 1972 Nixon-Haldeman Transcripts" in the *New York Times, The End of a Presidency* (New York: Bantam Books, 1974), pp. 324–353.

[66] Kenneth N. Waltz, *Foreign Policy and Democratic Politics* (Boston: Little, Brown, 1967), p. 86.

[67] *Washington Post,* September 17, 2004, p. A20.

[68] Speech by George W. Bush, Ridley Park, Pennsylvania, August 17, 2004, online at <http://www.whitehouse.gov/news/releases/2004/08/20040817-6.html>.

[69] The United States Department of Defense, news release, "Fiscal 2007 Department of Defense Budget Is Released," February 6, 2006.

[70] *New York Times,* June 8, 1984, p. 8.

[71] Burton M. Sapin, *The Making of United States Foreign Policy* (New York: Praeger, for The Brookings Institution, 1966), p. 136.

[72] The United States Department of Defense, "Civilian Personnel Reports," online at <http://www.dior.whs.mil/mmid/civilian/fy2004/August2004/August2004.htm>,

and The Center for Defense Information, "100 Companies Receiving the Largest Dollar Volume of Prime Contract Awards—Fiscal Year 2003," table 2, online at <http://www.cdi.org>.

[73] Kennedy, *Thirteen Days,* p. 48.

[74] *Rostker* v. *Goldberg,* 453 U.S. 57 (1981).

[75] Center for Defense Information, online at <http://www.cdi.org>.

[76] Herman Kahn, *On Thermonuclear War* (Princeton, N.J.: Princeton University Press, 1961), p. 21.

[77] Ralph E. Lapp, *Kill and Overkill* (New York: Basic Books, 1962), p. 10.

[78] *Seattle Times,* August 26, 1984, p. B2.

[79] *New York Times,* March 7, 2003, p. A7.

[80] Dwight D. Eisenhower, *The White House Years, Waging Peace 1956–1961* (New York: Doubleday, 1965), p. 616.

[81] Data from The Statistical Information Analysis Division, "Top Ten Companies Receiving the Largest Dollar Volume of Prime Contract Awards—Fiscal Year 2005," online at <http://siadapp.dior.whs.mil/procurement/historical_reports/statistics/p01/fy2005/top100.htm>

[82] Paul Kennedy, *The Rise and Fall of the Great Powers: Economic Change and Military Conflict from 1500 to 2000* (New York: Random House, 1987), p. xvi.

[83] Nick Kotz, *Wild Blue Yonder: Money, Politics, and the B-1 Bomber* (New York: Pantheon, 1988), p. 234.

[84] Ibid., p. 235.

[85] *New York Times,* August 30, 2004, p. A6.

[86] Gareth Porter and Janet Welsh Brown, *Global Environmental Politics* (Boulder, Colo.: Westview Press, 1991), p. 141.

## Chapter 17

[1] A *New York Times*/CBS News poll, June 23–27, 2004 reported that 60 percent of respondents considered the loss of American life and other costs of the war in Iraq to be "not worth it." In the same poll, 58 percent disapproved of Bush's handling of "the situation with Iraq." A CNN/*USA Today*/Gallup poll, June 21–23, 2004, found that 55 percent of the public thought the war in Iraq had made the U.S. "less safe" from terrorism; online at <http://pollingreport.com/iraq2.htm>.

[2] CNN/*USA Today*/Gallup poll, January 2–5, 2004. Respondents were asked, "What will be the most important issues that you will take into account when deciding whom to vote for?"; online at <http://www.pollingreport.com/prioriti.htm>.

[3] In May 2000, 54 percent of adult Americans reported that individually, or with a spouse, they had money invested in the stock market. CNN/*USA Today*/Gallup poll, May 16, 2000.

[4] The Commission on Presidential Debates, excerpt from the debate between Governor George W. Bush and Vice President Al Gore, St. Louis, Missouri, October 17, 2000, online at <http://www.debates.org/pages/his_2000.html#oct17>.

[5] *New York Times,* October 1, 1998, p. A.1.

[6] The words literally mean "to allow" (people) "to do" (what they please).

[7] Congressional Budget Office, "The Combined Effects of Major Changes in Federal Taxes and Spending Programs since 1981," Staff Memorandum, April 1984, table 5; and the *Washington Post,* July 26, 1984, p. A7.

[8] U.S. Bureau of the Census, Current Population Reports, *Money Income and Poverty Status of Families and Persons in the United States: 1983,* August 1984, p. 1; and the *New York Times,* July 26, 1984, p. A19.

[9] Debt total as of June 24, 2004, Bureau of Public Debt, "The Debt to the Penny," online at <http://www.publicdebt.treas.gov/opd/opdpenny.htm>.

[10] *Budget of the United States Government, Fiscal Year 2005* (Washington, D.C.: U.S. Government Printing Office, 2004), Federal Receipts, p. 239.

[11] From 1941 until 1991, economists used the term gross national product (GNP) as a measure of the nation's total output of goods and services. The GNP included production by American companies or individuals anywhere in the world. The GDP covers output within the borders of the United States.

[12] Adapted from U.S. Bureau of the Census, *Statistical Abstract of the United States: 2003,* p. 856. Data for 2002.

[13] *New York Times,* December 1, 1999, p. A1.

[14] Ibid.

[15] *USA Today,* August 28, 2000, p. 1B; and Center for Trade Policy Studies, "After 10 Years, NAFTA Continues to Pay Dividends," January 8, 2004, online at <http://www.cato.org/dailys/01-08-04.html>.

[16] Data from Ward's Communications, *2004 World Almanac,* p. 321.

[17] International Trade Administration, U.S. Department of Commerce, Office of Trade and Economic Analysis, U.S. Foreign Trade Data, "U.S. International Trade Summary 2000–2004," online at <http://www.ita.doc.gov/td/industry/otea/usftd/>.

[18] Ibid.

## Chapter 18

[1] *New York Times,* September 18, 2004, p. 1.

[2] *Time,* March 20, 1995, p. 24.

[3] Anthony King, "The American Polity in the Late 1970s: Building Coalitions in the Sand," in Anthony King, ed., *The New American Political System* (Washington, D.C.: American Enterprise Institute for Public Policy Research, 1978), p. 371.

[4] Sar A. Levitan and Robert Taggart, *The Promise of Greatness* (Cambridge, Mass.: Harvard University Press, 1976), pp. 283, 293.

[5] *Lochner* v. *New York,* 198 U.S. 45 (1905).

[6] Edward S. Herman, *Corporate Control, Corporate Power: A Twentieth Century Fund Study* (New York: Cambridge University Press, 1981), p. 177.

[7] Ibid., p. 185.

[8] *United States* v. *E. I. du Pont de Nemours and Co.,* 353 U.S. 586 (1957).

[9] *New York Times,* April 4, 2000, p. A1.

[10] *New York Times,* June 29, 2001, p. A1.

[11] John Kenneth Galbraith, *The New Industrial State* (Boston: Houghton Mifflin, 1967), p. 179.

[12] *New York Times,* May 4, 2000, p. C1.

[13] Global Policy Forum, "Top 200: The Rise of Global Corporate Power," *Corporate Watch,* June 2000, online at <http://www.igc.org/globalpolicy/socecon/tncs/top200.htm>.

[14] Charles E. Lindblom, *Politics and Markets: The World's Political-Economic Systems* (New York: Basic Books, 1977), pp. 163–164.

[15] E. E. Schattschneider, *The Semisovereign People* (New York: Holt, Rinehart and Winston, 1960), pp. 118, 121.

[16] Corporate Fraud Task Force, "First Year Report to the President," online at <http://www.usdoj.gov/dag/cftf/first_year_report.pdf>; and the *Washington Post,* October 20, 2004, p. E1.

[17] *New York Times,* April 4, 1999, section 5, p. 3.

[18] Congressional Quarterly, *Weekly Report,* May 4, 1996, p. 1243.

[19] Bureau of Labor Statistics, "Union Members Summary," January 21, 2004, online at <http://www.bls.gov/news.release/union2.nr0.htm>; and AFL-CIO, FAQ, online at <http://www.aflcio.org>.

[20] Bureau of Labor Statistics, "Union Members Summary."

[21] In 1970, four years after the Senate hearings, GM paid Nader $425,000 in an out-of-court settlement of his invasion-of-privacy suit. See the *New York Times,* August 14, 1970, p. 1.

[22] David Caplovitz, *The Poor Pay More* (New York: Free Press of Glencoe, 1963), pp. 84, 85.

[23] Clinton speech at the Democratic National Convention, New York City, *New York Times,* July 17, 1992, p. A14.

[24] Data provided by Social Security Administration, "Performance and Accountability Report, Fiscal Year 2003," online at <http://www.ssa.gov>; Bureau of Labor Statistics, "Employment Situation Summary, 9/3/04," online at <http://bls.gov/news.release/empsit.nr0.htm>; and U.S. Department of Labor, Employment and Training Administration, "Monthly Program and Financial Data," online at <http://www.doleta.gov>.

[25] Gilbert Y. Steiner, *Social Insecurity: The Politics of Welfare* (Chicago: Rand McNally, 1966), pp. 7–8.

[26] The percentages are composed of the tax for Social Security and a smaller tax for the Medicare program for the elderly.

[27] Social Security Administration, "Press Office Fact Sheet," online at <http://www.ssa.gov/pressoffice/basicfact.htm>.

[28] Data from Families USA, "Cost Overdose: Growth in Drug Spending for the Elderly, 1992–2010," July 2000, online at <http://www.familiesusa.org/site/DocServer/drugod.pdf?docID=726>.

[29] Daniel P. Moynihan, "One Step We Must Take," *Saturday Review of Literature,* May 23, 1970, p. 22.

[30] *New York Times,* October 20, 2003, p. A16.

[31] Ibid.

[32] Ibid.

[33] *1964 Congressional Quarterly Almanac,* p. 862.

[34] Michael Harrington, *The Other America* (New York: Macmillan, 1962), p. 4.

[35] Ben H. Bagdikian, *In the Midst of Plenty* (Boston: Beacon, 1964), pp. 6–7.

[36] U.S. Bureau of the Census, *Poverty Thresholds 2005,* online at <http://www.census.gov/hhes/poverty/threshld/thresh03.htm>.

[37] U.S. Bureau of the Census, *Income, Poverty, and Health Insurance Coverage in the United States: 2005,* p. 14, table 4.

[38] Daniel P. Moynihan, *Maximum Feasible Misunderstanding: Community Action in the War on Poverty* (New York: Free Press, 1969).

[39] *Philadelphia Inquirer,* July 31, 2000.

[40] Second Harvest, "Current Hunger and Poverty Statistics," online at <http://www.secondharvest.org/site_content.asp?s=59&p=1>.

[41] *New York Times,* May 2, 1984, p. 1.

[42] The Urban Institute, "Millions Still Face Homelessness in a Booming Economy," February 1, 2000, online at <http://www.urban.org/url.cfm?ID=900050>.

[43] Food and Nutrition Service, USDA, "Food Stamp Program," online at <http://www.fns.usda.gov/fsp/faqs.htm>.

[44] Adapted from the *Budget of the United States Government, Fiscal Year 2005* (Washington, D.C.: U.S. Government Printing Office, 2004), table 16.1.

[45] "A Citizen's Guide to the Federal Budget," *Budget of the United States Government, Fiscal Year 1997* (Washington, D.C.: U.S. Government Printing Office, 1996), p. 10.

[46] Data provided by the Health Care Financing Administration.

[47] *New York Times,* November 20, 2004, p. A1.

[48] *New York Times,* June 20, 2000, p. A1.

[49] U.S. Bureau of the Census, *Statistical Abstract of the United States: 2003,* online at <http://www.census.gov/prod/www/statistical-abstract-03.html>.

[50] *Washington Post,* September 5, 2004, p. C1.

[51] Senator E. L. Bartlett, Democrat of Alaska, in Don K. Price, *The Scientific Estate* (Cambridge, Mass.: Belknap Press of Harvard University Press, 1965), p. 57.

[52] Adapted from *Budget of the United States Government, Fiscal Year 2005* (Washington, D.C.: U.S. Government Printing Office, 2004), historical tables, 9.8, online at <http://www.gpoaccess.gov/usbudget/fy05/sheets/hist09z8.xls>.

[53] Price, *The Scientific Estate,* p. 12.

[54] *Washington Post,* September 15, 1992, p. A8.

[55] Ibid.

[56] *New York Times,* April 2, 1993, p. A22.

[57] U.S. Bureau of the Census, population clock, online at <http://www.census.gov/main/www/popclock.html>.

[58] Ibid.

[59] *New York Times,* May 21, 1996, p. A1.

[60] *Washington Post,* May 31, 1996, p. A3; October 2, 2004, p. A4; and *New York Times,* September 20, 2003, p. A4.

[61] *Washington Post,* April 18, 2000, p. A2.

[62] *New York Times,* December 19, 1999, p. A1.

[63] *Washington Post,* November 12, 1997, p. A1.

[64] Council on Environmental Quality, *Seventh Annual Report* (Washington, D.C.: U.S. Government Printing Office, 1976), p. 272.

[65] *New York Times,* May 26, 1992, p. A1.

[66] *Tennessee Valley Authority* v. *Hill et al.,* 437 U.S. 153 (1978).

[67] *New York Times,* August 15, 2003, p. A1.

[68] *USA Today,* November 2, 1982, p. A3.

[69] Energy Information Administration, Department of Energy, "Annual Energy Review," table 11.3, "World Primary Energy Consumption by Region, 1993–2002," online at <http://www.eia.doe.gov/emeu/aer/txt/ptb1103.html>.

[70] U.S. Nuclear Regulatory Commission, "Radioactive Waste: Production, Storage, Disposal," May 2002, online at <http://www.nrc.gov>.

[71] Benjamin I. Page, *Who Gets What from Government* (Berkeley: University of California Press, 1983), p. 19.

## Chapter 19

[1] U.S. Bureau of the Census, "U.S. Interim Projections by Age, Sex, Race, and Hispanic Origin," table 1a, online at <http://www.census.gov/ipc/www/usinterimproj/> March 18, 2004. Figures rounded.

[2] U.S. Bureau of the Census, "U.S. Interim Projections by Age, Sex, Race, and Hispanic Origin."

[3] U.S. Bureau of the Census, "World Population: 1950 to 2050," online at <http://www.census.gov/ipc/www/img/worldpop.gif>.

[4] U.S. Bureau of the Census, "Population by Metropolitan-Nonmetropolitan Residence, Sex, and Race and Hispanic Origin," March 1999, table 16. The terms "urban," "rural," "metropolitan," and "suburban" are subject to varying definitions. The federal government in 1983 divided the nation into Metropolitan Statistical Areas (MSAs), each of which contains at least one city of 50,000 people, or an urban area of that size and a total population of 100,000 (75,000 in New England). Suburbs are defined here as areas outside central cities but within the Census Bureau definition of a metropolitan area. Not all the millions of people in the suburbs, so defined, might feel that they live in suburbia; suburban population obviously depends on how one defines a "suburb."

[5] Adapted from U.S. Bureau of the Census, *Statistical Abstract of the United States: 2003,* p. 32, online at <http://www.census.gov/prod/www/statistical-abstract-03.html>.

[6] *New York Times,* December 31, 1998, p. A11, citing a survey by the National Governors Association and the National Association of State Budget Officers.

[7] *New York Times,* November 25, 2005, p. A1, and *Washington Post,* December 21, 2005, p. A2.

[8] *Washington Post,* August 2, 1996, p. A9.

[9] Ibid., quoting Frank Mecca, executive director of the California Welfare Directors Association.

[10] U.S. Bureau of the Census, *Statistical Abstract of the United States: 2003,* p. 276.

[11] Karl E. Taeuber, "Racial Segregation: The Persisting Dilemma," *Annals of the American Academy of Political and Social Science* (November 1975), p. 93.

[12] U.S. Bureau of the Census, *2000 Census of Population,* "Population by Metropolitan-Nonmetropolitan Residence, Sex, and Race and Hispanic Origin," table 20.1, online at <http://www.census.gov/population/www/socdemo/hispanic/ppl-171.html>.

[13] U.S. Bureau of the Census, *Statistical Abstract of the United States: 2003,* p. 285.

[14] Ibid.

[15] *The Book of the States,* 2004 edition, p. 331.

[16] James Q. Wilson, "Urban Problems in Perspective," in James Q. Wilson, ed., *The Metropolitan Enigma* (Washington, D.C.: U.S. Chamber of Commerce, 1967), p. 395.

[17] *Washington Post,* April 5, 2006, p. 276.

[18] *New York Times,* January 2, 2006, p. 93.

[19] Duane Lockard, *The Politics of State and Local Government,* 2nd ed. (New York: Macmillan, 1969), p. 85.

[20] Duane Lockard, *The Politics of State and Local Government,* 3rd ed. (New York: Macmillan, 1983), p. 94.

[21] *The Book of the States,* 2004 edition, p. 10.

[22] Ibid., p. 4.

[23] As of 2004, 18 states allowed their constitutions to be amended by some form of initiative. Data from Initiative and Referendum Institute, online at <http://www.iandrinstitute.org>.

[24] *New York Times,* October 16, 1992, p. A10.

[25] Initiative and Referendum Institute, University of Southern California, "Ballotwatch," online at <http://www.iandrinstitute.org/ballotwatch.htm>.

[26] *New York Times,* October 25, 2000, p. A1.

[27] Joseph F. Zimmerman, *The Recall: Tribunal of the People* (Westport, Conn.: Praeger, 1997), pp. 52–53.

[28] *The Book of the States,* 2004 edition, p. 7. Lynn Frazier, elected governor of North Dakota as the candidate of the Nonpartisan League (NPL), was recalled in 1921 in a dispute over a state bank that had been created to make loans to farmers.

[29] Larry Sabato, *Goodbye to Good-Time Charlie: The American Governorship Transformed,* 2nd ed. (Washington, D.C.: CQ Press, 1983), p. 201.

[30] Advisory Commission on Intergovernmental Relations, *Fiscal Balance in the American System,* vol. 1 (Washington, D.C.: U.S. Government Printing Office, October 1967), pp. 233–234.

[31] Thad L. Beyle, "Governors: The Middlemen and Women in Our Political System," in Virginia Gray and Herbert Jacob, eds., *Politics in the American States: A Comparative Analysis,* 6th ed. (Washington, D.C.: CQ Press, 1996), pp. 228–237.

[32] Ibid., p. 221.

[33] *The Book of the States,* 2004 edition, pp. 164–165.

[34] Beyle, "Governors: The Middlemen and Women in Our Political System," in Gray and Jacob, eds., *Politics in the American States,* p. 231.

[35] *The Book of the States,* 2004 edition, pp. 113–115. Data as of October 2003.

[36] Ibid., pp. 157–158.

[37] Quoted in the *Washington Post,* October 30, 2000, p. A2.

[38] *The Book of the States,* 2004 edition, pp. 78–80.

[39] Ibid., pp. 94–95.

[40] Samuel C. Patterson, "State Legislators and Legislatures" in Virginia Gray, Herbert Jacob, and Robert B. Albritton, eds., *Politics in the American States: A Comparative Analysis,* 5th ed., (Glenview, Ill.: Scott, Foresman, 1990), p. 176.

[41] *The Book of the States,* 2004 edition, p. 392.

[42] Ibid., p. 394.

[43] *Baker* v. *Carr,* 369 U.S. 186 (1962).

[44] *Reynolds* v. *Sims,* 377 U.S. 533 (1964).

[45] *New York Times,* February 14, 2000, p. A1.

[46] *U.S. Term Limits* v. *Thornton,* 115 S. Ct. 1842 (1995).

[47] John F. Bibby and Thomas M. Holbrook, "Parties and Elections," in Virginia Gray and Russell L. Hanson, eds., *Politics in the American States,* 8th ed. (Washington, D.C.: CQ Press, 2004), pp. 87–88. The measure of interparty competition used in this study is based entirely on elections for state offices between 1999 and 2002. The authors point out that the states are more competitive in presidential and congressional elections. In addition, they note, the study gave more weight to partisan control of state legislatures than of governorships. As a result, the study does not reflect Republican successes in gubernatorial elections in such once reliably Democratic states as Mississippi, Alabama, and Arkansas.

[48] Data provided by the International City/Council Management Association, online at <http://www.icma.org>.

[49] Ibid.

[50] Data from *Encarta Encyclopedia 2004,* CD-ROM, Microsoft, "municipal governments."

[51] Data provided by the International City/Council Management Association.

[52] U.S. Bureau of the Census, *Statistical Abstract of the United States: 2003,* p. 276.

[53] *New York Times,* June 21, 1970, p. 1.

[54] In William L. Riordon, *Plunkitt of Tammany Hall* (New York: Dutton, 1963), p. 21. (Originally published in 1905.)

[55] Jean Gottmann, *Megalopolis* (New York: Twentieth Century Fund, 1961), p. 4.

[56] Adapted from U.S. Bureau of the Census, *2000 Census of Population,* table 18.1.

[57] Lewis Mumford, *The City in History: Its Origins, Its Transformations, and Its Prospects* (New York: Harcourt Brace Jovanovich, 1961), pp. 3, 543–548.

[58] Edward C. Banfield, *The Unheavenly City* (Boston: Little, Brown, 1970), p. 5.

[59] Advisory Commission on Intergovernmental Relations, *Changing Public Attitudes on Governments and Taxes 1988,* table 38, p. 60. Data for 1986. The poll showed that 51 percent of respondents wanted governments to "keep taxes and services about where they are," while 31 percent favored a decrease, for a total of 82 percent; 9 percent favored increased services and taxes, and 9 percent had no opinion.

[60] Charles Tilly, "Race and Migration to the American City," in Wilson, ed., *The Metropolitan Enigma,* pp. 129–131.

[61] Ibid., p. 142.

[62] Congressional Quarterly, *Weekly Report,* August 8, 1992, p. 2354.

[63] Donald H. Haider, "Fiscal Scarcity: A New Urban Perspective," in Louis H. Masotti and Robert L. Lineberry, *The New Urban Politics* (Cambridge, Mass: Ballinger, 1976), p. 187.

[64] Ibid., p. 202.

[65] Ibid., p. 204.

[66] Ibid., p. 187.

[67] Data provided by National Law Center on Homelessness and Poverty in America.

[68] Speech, Robert F. Kennedy Memorial Journalism Awards dinner, Washington, D.C., June 19, 1969; notes taken by the author.

[69] President Nixon's message to Congress on community development, September 19, 1973, quoted in Congressional Quarterly, *Weekly Report,* September 22, 1973, p. 2522.

[70] *Village of Arlington Heights* v. *Metropolitan Development Corporation,* 429 U.S. 252 (1977).

[71] Michael N. Danielson, *The Politics of Exclusion* (New York: Columbia University Press, 1976), p. 83.

[72] Ibid., pp. 83–92.

[73] *National Journal,* April 9, 1988, p. 977.

[74] Mumford, *The City in History,* pp. 549–550.

[75] *New York Times,* January 3, 2004, p. A7.

[76] U.S. Bureau of the Census, *Poverty in the United States: 2002,* p. 6, online at <http://www.census.gov/prod/2003pubs/p60-222.pdf>.

[77] U.S. Bureau of the Census, Current Population Reports, *Poverty in the United States: 1990,* series P-60, no. 175, August 1991, p. 6.

[78] Floyd Hunter, *Community Power Structure* (Chapel Hill: University of North Carolina Press, 1953).

[79] Robert A. Dahl, *Who Governs?* (New Haven, Conn.: Yale University Press, 1961).

[80] Edward C. Banfield and James Q. Wilson, *City Politics* (Cambridge, Mass.: Harvard University Press, 1963), pp. 244–245.

[81] Paul E. Peterson, *City Limits* (Chicago: University of Chicago Press, 1981), p. 4.

[82] Ibid., p. 41.

[83] Ibid., pp. 167–183.

[84] Data provided by the National Conference of Black Mayors, online at <www.ncbm.org>.

[85] John J. Harrigan, *Political Change in the Metropolis* (Boston: Little, Brown, 1976), pp. 139–146.

[86] Wallace S. Sayre and Herbert Kaufman, *Governing New York City: Politics in the Metropolis* (New York: Norton, 1965), pp. 710–712.

[87] John P. Kotter and Paul R. Lawrence, *Mayors in Action: Five Approaches to Urban Governance* (New York: Wiley, 1974).

[88] Quoted in the *New York Times,* October 7, 1980, p. 1.

[89] Herbert J. Gans, *The Levittowners* (New York: Pantheon, 1967), p. 155.

[90] Peter H. Rossi, *Why Families Move* (New York: Free Press of Glencoe, 1955).

[91] Louis H. Masotti and Jeffrey K. Hadden, eds., *The Urbanization of the Suburbs* (Beverly Hills: Sage, 1973), p. 17.

[92] Gans, *The Levittowners,* p. 418.

[93] *New York Times,* July 7, 1992, p. A1.

[94] Alan K. Campbell and Donna E. Shalala, "Problems Unsolved, Solutions Untried: The Urban Crisis," in Alan K. Campbell, ed., *The States and the Urban Crisis* (Englewood Cliffs, N.J.: Prentice Hall, 1970), p. 21.

[95] Richard Lehne, "Suburban Foundations of the New Congress," *Annals of the American Academy of Political and Social Science* (November 1975), pp. 143, 144.

[96] Ibid., p. 150.

[97] Thomas P. Murphy and John Rehfuss, *Urban Politics in the Suburban Era* (Homewood, Ill.: Dorsey, 1976), pp. 29, 40, 42.

[98] Data provided by the Geography Division, U.S. Bureau of the Census.

[99] *USA Today,* February 9, 2004, p. 13A.

[100] Robert L. Bish and Vincent Ostrom, *Understanding Urban Government: Metropolitan Reform Reconsidered* (Washington, D.C.: American Enterprise Institute for Public Policy Research, 1973), p. 73.

[101] York Willbern, *The Withering Away of the City* (Tuscaloosa: University of Alabama Press, 1964), p. 33.

[102] Text of speech prepared for delivery to the Illinois Constitutional Convention, Springfield, Ill., May 13, 1970.

## Appendix

[1] Modified by the Fourteenth and Sixteenth amendments.

[2] Superseded by the Seventeenth Amendment.

[3] Modified by the Seventeenth Amendment.

[4] Superseded by the Twentieth Amendment.

[5] Modified by the Sixteenth Amendment.

[6] Superseded by the Twelfth Amendment.

[7] Modified by the Twenty-fifth Amendment.

[8] Modified by the Eleventh Amendment.

[9] Superseded by the Thirteenth Amendment.

[10] The first ten amendments were passed by Congress September 25, 1789. They were ratified by three-fourths of the states December 15, 1791.

[11] Date of ratification.

[12] Superseded by the Twentieth Amendment.

[13] Repealed by the Twenty-first Amendment.

# Glossary

**absolute position** The view advocated by Supreme Court Justices Hugo Black and William O. Douglas that there are provisions of the Bill of Rights that cannot be diluted by judicial decisions.

**administrative law** The rules and regulations made and applied by federal regulatory agencies and commissions.

**adversary system of justice** A judicial system in which the power of the state is balanced by the defendant's constitutional rights and by the presumption that a person is innocent until proven guilty beyond a reasonable doubt.

**affirmative action** Programs of government, universities, and businesses designed to favor minorities and remedy past discrimination.

**agenda setting** The power to determine which public policy questions will be debated or considered.

**Antiballistic Missile (ABM) Treaty** A 1972 treaty between the United States and the Soviet Union limiting the number of defensive missiles each country could build. In 2001 President George W. Bush withdrew the United States from the treaty.

**Antifederalists** Those who opposed ratification of the Constitution.

**appropriations bills** Bills passed by Congress to pay for the spending it has authorized.

**arraignment** The proceeding before a judge in which the formal charges of an indictment or information are read to an accused person, who may plead guilty or not guilty.

**Articles of Confederation (1781–1789)** The written framework for the government of the original 13 states before the Constitution was adopted. Under the Articles of Confederation, the national government was weak and dominated by the states. There was a unicameral legislature, but no national executive or judiciary.

**assignment committees** *See* **steering committees.**

**authorizations** Laws passed by Congress that recommend levels of funding for federal programs. *See* **appropriations bills.**

**backgrounder** A meeting in which government officials discuss policies and plans with reporters with the mutual understanding that the information can be attributed only to unnamed "officials" or sometimes not attributed to any source.

**bail** An amount of money "posted" with the courts as security in exchange for a defendant's freedom until the case comes to trial.

**balance of payments** The net balance or relationship between total income and total expenditures by the nation in its dealings with the rest of the world, including trade, loans, and investments.

**balance of trade** The relationship between the total cost of foreign goods imported to this country and sales of U.S. products overseas.

**balancing test** The view of the majority of the Supreme Court that First Amendment rights must be weighed against the competing needs of the community to preserve order.

**bandwagon effect** The possible tendency of some voters or convention delegates to support the candidate who is leading in the polls and seems likely to win.

**bicameral legislature** A two-house legislature.

**bill of attainder** A law aimed at a particular individual. Prohibited by the Constitution.

**Bill of Rights** The first 10 amendments to the Constitution, which set forth basic protections for individuals. (Some scholars define the Bill of Rights as only the first eight or nine amendments.)

**bipartisanship** A view that both major political parties should support the president on foreign policy issues.

**blanket primary** A primary in which any registered voter is able to vote for candidates from more than one party. A voter, for example, may vote for a Democrat for U.S. senator and for a Republican for governor. In 2000, the Supreme Court struck down the blanket primary in California, Washington state, and Alaska but left intact Louisiana's somewhat different "nonpartisan" version of the blanket primary.

**block grants** Federal grants to states and local communities that are for general use in a broad area, such as community development.

**"blog"** A web log; a website journal updated daily or frequently and often open to other Internet users who wish to post comments.

***Brown* v. *Board of Education of Topeka, Kansas*** Ruling by the Supreme Court in 1954 that racial segregation in public schools violates the Fourteenth Amendment's requirement of equal protection of the laws for all persons.

**budget deficit** The gap that occurs when the government's income in a fiscal year is less than its outlays.

**budget resolutions** Overall spending targets set by the Congress.

**budget surplus** The amount of money available when the government's income is greater than what it spends in a fiscal year.

**bureaucrats** Public administrators.

**cabinet** The president, the vice president, the heads of the major executive departments of the government, and certain other senior officials who may hold "cabinet rank."

**cabinet departments** The 15 cabinet departments are units of government under the president and major components of the federal bureaucracy.

**capitalism** An economic system of free enterprise with private ownership of the means of production.

**categorical grants** Federal grants to states and local communities earmarked for specific purposes, such as pollution control, schools, or hospitals. Also known as grants-in-aid.

**caucus** A group or a meeting of a group of a political party or organization in which such matters as selection of candidates, leaders, or positions on issues are decided.

**certiorari, writ of** A legal document issued by the Supreme Court agreeing to review a case. The overwhelming majority of cases presented to the Court come in the form of petitions for a writ of certiorari. The Court can choose which of the cases it wants to hear by denying or granting certiorari.

**charter colonies** Colonies in which freely elected legislatures chose the governor and the king could not veto laws.

**checks and balances** The provisions of the Constitution that divide power among three constitutionally equal and independent branches of government—legislative, executive, and judicial—in the hope of preventing any single branch from becoming too powerful.

**civil cases** Court cases that involve relations between individuals and organizations, such as a divorce action, or a suit for damages arising from an automobile accident or for violation of a business contract.

**civil disobedience** The conscious refusal to obey laws that are believed to be unjust, unconstitutional, or immoral.

**civil liberties** The fundamental rights of a free society that are protected by the Bill of Rights against the power of the government, such as freedom of speech, religion, press, and assembly.

**civil rights** The constitutional rights of all individuals, and especially of African Americans and other minorities, to enjoy full equality and equal protection of the laws.

**civil service** The civilian employees of the government and the administrative system in which they work.

**civilian supremacy** The principle of civilian control of the military, based on the clear constitutional power of the president as supreme commander of the armed forces.
**clear and present danger test** A test established by Supreme Court Justice Oliver Wendell Holmes, Jr., in 1919 to define the point at which speech loses the protection of the First Amendment.
**closed primary** A form of primary election in which only registered members of a political party or people declaring their affiliation with a party can vote.
**closed shop** A place of work in which only union members may be hired.
**cloture** A Senate procedure to cut off a filibuster by a vote of three-fifths (60 members) of the entire Senate.
**cluster sampling** A technique polling organizations use in which several people from the same neighborhood are interviewed.
**coalitions** Alliances of segments of the electorate, interest groups, and unorganized masses of voters who coalesce behind a political candidate or party.
**coattail effect** The ability of a major candidate, such as a presidential or gubernatorial candidate, to help carry into office lesser candidates from the same party who are also on the ballot.
**COINTELPRO** The "counterintelligence program" of the FBI that harassed American citizens and disrupted their organizations from 1956 to 1971 through a wide variety of clandestine techniques.
**Cold War (1945–1991)** The period after the Second World War marked by rivalry and tension between the two nuclear superpowers, the United States and the communist government of the Soviet Union. The Cold War ended when the Soviet government collapsed in 1991.
**collective security** A principle embraced by the United States during the Truman and Eisenhower administrations, under which the nation attempted to "contain" communism and entered into a series of military alliances with other countries for this purpose.
**commission plan** A form of city government under which a board of city commissioners is popularly elected (often on a nonpartisan ballot). The commissioners make policy as a city council, but they also run city departments as administrators.
**Committees of Correspondence** A political communications network established in 1772 by Samuel Adams to unite the colonists in their fight against British rule.
**Committee of the Whole** A device that allows the House of Representatives to conduct its business with fewer restrictions on debate and a quorum of only 100 members.
**common law** The cumulative body of judicial decisions, custom, and precedent, rather than law created by statute.
**concurrent powers** Powers of government exercised independently by both the federal and state governments, such as the power to tax.
**confederation** A group of independent states or nations that come together for a common purpose and whose central authority is usually limited to defense and foreign relations.
**conference committee** A committee composed of members of the House and Senate that tries to reconcile disagreements between the two branches of Congress over differing versions of a bill.
**conglomerates** Multi-interest and often multinational corporations that, under one corporate roof, may manufacture a wide variety of products.
**Connecticut Compromise** The plan adopted during the Constitutional Convention of 1787 providing for a House of Representatives based on population and a Senate with two members from each state. (Also known as the **Great Compromise.**)
**constituencies** Voters in a political district, or supporters of an elected official; or interest groups or client groups that are either directly regulated by the bureaucracy or vitally affected by its decisions.
**Constitution** The written framework for the government of the United States that establishes a strong national government of three branches—legislative, executive, and judicial—and provides for the control and operation of that government.
**constitutional amendment** A change to the Constitution proposed by a two-thirds vote of both houses of Congress or a constitutional convention, and ratified by legislatures or ratifying conventions in three-fourths of the states.
**containment** The foreign policy of the United States during the period after the Second World War, designed to contain the expansion of Soviet power.
**cooperative federalism** A view that the various levels of government in America are related parts of a single governmental system, characterized by cooperation and shared functions.
**council-manager plan** A form of city government under which a council, usually elected on a nonpartisan ticket, hires a professional city manager, who runs the city government and has power to hire and fire officials.
**court-packing plan** A plan proposed by President Franklin D. Roosevelt in 1937, which Congress rejected, to appoint additional, younger justices to the Supreme Court who would be more sympathetic to the New Deal.
**covert operations** Secret political action within other countries.
**creative federalism** A term coined by President Lyndon B. Johnson to describe his own view of the relationship between Washington and the states.
**credentials committee** The body of a political convention that decides which delegates should be seated, subject to approval of the entire convention.
**criminal cases** Court cases that concern crimes committed against the public order.
**criminal information** A formal accusation by a prosecutor, made under oath before a court, charging a person with a crime. Used in most state cases in place of a grand jury indictment to bring a person to trial.
**dark horse** A political candidate who is thought to have only an outside chance of gaining the nomination.
**deficit** The gap between the government's income and outlays.
**delegates** The men and women formally entitled to select the presidential nominees of the two major parties at their party's presidential nominating convention.
**demands** What people and groups want from the political system.
**democracy** Rule by the people.
**deregulation** The elimination or reduction of government regulation of industry.
**desegregation** The process of ending separation of people by race.
**détente** A relaxation of international tensions.
**deviating elections** Elections in which the majority party (according to party identification) is defeated in a temporary reversal.
**direct mail fund-raising** A technique to raise money directly from the public with the aid of computerized mailing lists.
**distribution** What occurs when government adopts a public policy that provides, or distributes, benefits to people or groups.
**distributive policy** A public policy that is meant to benefit everyone.
**double jeopardy** More than one prosecution for the same offense. Prohibited by the Constitution.
**downsizing** Corporate action to cut costs by the layoff or dismissal of large numbers of employees and executives.
***Dred Scott* decision** A ruling by the Supreme Court in 1857—reversed by the Fourteenth Amendment in 1868—that black Americans were not citizens under the Constitution.
**dual federalism** The concept—accepted until 1937—of the federal government and the states as competing power centers, with the Supreme Court as referee.
**due process of law** A phrase, contained in the Fifth and Fourteenth amendments, that protects the individual against the arbitrary power of the state. *Substantive due process* means that laws must be reasonable. *Procedural due process* means that laws must be administered in a fair manner.

**earmarks** Funds set aside in appropriations bills or tax legislation for specific projects, locations, or institutions.

**elastic clause** Article I, Section 8, of the Constitution, which allows Congress to make all laws that are "necessary and proper" to carry out the powers of the Constitution.

**elections** The procedure by which voters choose, usually among competing candidates, to determine who will hold public office. *See also* **deviating elections, maintaining elections,** and **realigning elections.**

**electoral college** The body composed of electors from the 50 states who formally have the power to elect the president and vice president of the United States. Each state has a number of electors and electoral votes equal to its number of senators and representatives in Congress.

**elite theory** The view that power in America is held by the few, not by the masses of people.

**eminent domain** The principle that the government, as provided in the Fifth Amendment, can take property for "public use" with "just compensation" to the owners.

**enabling act** A congressional act that allows the people of a territory desiring statehood to frame a state constitution.

**enterprise zones** Urban or rural areas in which businesses are encouraged to locate because of tax breaks and other incentives.

**entitlement programs** Programs mandated by law and not subject to annual review by Congress or the president.

**enumerated powers** Powers of government that are specifically granted to the three branches of the federal government under the Constitution.

**equal protection clause** The provision of the Fourteenth Amendment that seeks to guarantee equal treatment for all people.

**Equal Rights Amendment (ERA)** A proposed amendment to the Constitution, aimed at ending discrimination against women, that stated: "Equality of rights under the law shall not be denied or abridged by the United States or by any state on account of sex." The proposal was defeated in 1982.

**equal time provision** A provision of the Federal Communications Act that requires broadcasters to provide "equal time" to all legally qualified political candidates.

**equality** A concept that all people are of equal worth, even if not of equal ability.

**equity** A legal principle of fair dealing, which may provide preventive measures and legal remedies that are unavailable under existing common law and statutory law.

**establishment clause** The First Amendment provision that "Congress shall make no law respecting an establishment of religion."

**exclusionary rule** A doctrine established by the Supreme Court that, with some exceptions, bars the federal government from using illegally seized evidence in court.

**executive agencies** Units of government under the president, within the executive branch, that are not part of a cabinet department.

**executive agreements** International agreements between the president and foreign heads of state that, unlike treaties, do not require Senate approval.

**executive privilege** The claim by presidents of an inherent right to withhold information from Congress and the judiciary.

**ex parte contacts** One-sided contacts, such as an approach to a regulatory agency by a lawyer representing one side in a case.

**ex post facto law** A law that punishes an act that was not illegal at the time it was committed. Prohibited by the Constitution.

**exit polls** Polls taken as people leave voting places. In the past, television networks sometimes used these polls to predict election outcomes before the polls close. In 1992, the television networks agreed not to project the winner in a state until the majority of the polls had closed in that state.

**extradition** A constitutional provision allowing a state to request another state to return fugitives.

**fairness doctrine** A requirement by the Federal Communications Commission, abolished in 1987, that radio and television broadcasters present all sides of important public issues.

**Federal Election Campaign Act amendments of 1975** An act that attempted to regulate campaign finance by providing for public funding of presidential elections and by placing limits on campaign contributions.

**Federal Election Commission** A six-member commission created in 1974 to enforce campaign finance laws and administer public financing of presidential elections.

**federal system** *See* **federalism.**

**federalism** A system of government characterized by a constitutional sharing of power between a national government and regional units of government.

***Federalist, The*** A series of letters published in the late 1780s by Alexander Hamilton, James Madison, and John Jay to explain and help bring about ratification of the Constitution.

**Federalists** Those who supported the Constitution during the struggle over its ratification after the Constitutional Convention of 1787.

**feedback** The response of the rest of society to decisions made by the authorities of a political system.

**felonies** Serious crimes, such as murder, arson, or rape.

**filibuster** The process by which a single senator, or a group of senators, can sometimes talk a bill to death and prevent it from coming to a vote.

**First Amendment of the Constitution** Protects freedom of speech, freedom of the press, freedom of religion, and freedom of assembly.

**fiscal policy** Government regulation of the economy through its control over taxes and government spending.

**527 organizations** Groups named for the section of the Internal Revenue Service code under which they must report their expenditures. The tax-exempt groups were created to exploit a loophole in the law regulating campaign finance.

**flexible construction** The principle, established by Chief Justice John Marshall in 1819 in the case of *McCulloch* v. *Maryland*, that the Constitution must be interpreted flexibly to meet changing conditions.

**foreign policy** The sum of the goals, decisions, and actions that govern a nation's relations with the rest of the world.

**franking privilege** A system entitling members of Congress to send mail to constituents without charge by putting their frank, or mark, on the envelope. The law forbids using this privilege for soliciting money or votes, or for mass mailings 60 days before an election.

**free exercise clause** The First Amendment provision that Congress shall make no law "prohibiting the free exercise" of religion. The clause protects the right of individuals to worship or believe as they wish, or to hold no religious beliefs.

**Freedom of Information Act** A law passed in 1966 that requires federal executive branch and regulatory agencies to make information available to journalists, scholars, and the public unless it falls into one of several confidential categories.

**full faith and credit** A clause in Article IV of the Constitution, requiring each state to respect the laws, records, and court decisions of another state.

**gender gap** A difference, such as that in the 2000 elections, in the voting behavior of men and women.

**general purpose grants** Federal aid that states and localities may use mostly as they wish.

**gerrymandering** The drawing of the lines of congressional districts, or of any other political district, in order to favor one political party or group over another.

**globalization** A world economy characterized by the free movement of goods, capital, labor, and information across national borders.

**government** The individuals, institutions, and processes that make the rules for society and possess the power to enforce them.

**Goverment Accountability Office (GAO)** The agency that serves as a federal watchdog for waste or fraud in the bureaucracy and conducts investigations at the request of congressional committees.

**government corporations** Agencies that were at one time semiautonomous but that through legislation have been placed under presidential control since 1945.

**Grass roots lobbying** Efforts by interest groups to generate phone calls, faxes, e-mails, and letters in support of, or in opposition to, a bill or program.

**Great Compromise** The plan adopted during the Constitutional Convention of 1787 providing for a House of Representatives based on population and a Senate with two members from each state. (Also known as the **Connecticut Compromise.**)

**gross domestic product (GDP)** The yearly value of goods and services produced within a country.

**guaranteed annual income** A proposed alternate approach to welfare that would guarantee everyone a minimum income.

**habeas corpus, writ of** A writ designed to protect against illegal imprisonment by requiring that a person who is detained be brought before a judge for investigation.

**Hatch Act** A federal law passed by Congress in 1939 to restrict political activities by federal workers. The law prevents federal employees while on duty from taking an active part in party politics or campaigns and also bars federal employees from running for public office as a candidate of a political party.

**hold** The practice that allows senators to delay or even kill floor action on legislation, a nomination, or other matters by asking their party leaders not to schedule them.

**home rule** The power of some municipalities to modify their charters and run their affairs without approval by the state legislature.

**impeachment** Under the Constitution, the formal proceedings against the president or other federal officials or federal judges, who may be removed from office if convicted of "Treason, Bribery or other high Crimes and Misdemeanors."

**implementation** The action, or actions, taken by government to carry out a policy.

**implied powers** Powers of the national government that flow from its enumerated powers and the "elastic clause" of the Constitution.

**independent counsel** A special federal prosecutor appointed under the 1978 Ethics in Government Act in cases involving possible crimes by high officials. The law providing for independent counsels expired in 1999.

**independent expenditures** Funds spent for or against a candidate by committees not formally connected to the candidate's campaign and without coordination with the campaign.

**independent regulatory agencies** Government agencies that exercise quasi-judicial and quasi-legislative powers and are administratively independent of both the president and Congress (although politically independent of neither).

**Indiana ballot** Also known as the **party-column ballot.** Used in a majority of states, it lists the candidates of each party in a row or column, beside or under the party emblem. Allows for and encourages **straight-ticket voting.**

**indictment** A finding by a grand jury that there is enough evidence against an individual to warrant a criminal trial.

**information** *See* **criminal information.**

**inherent powers** Powers of government that the national government may exercise simply because it exists as a government, such as the right to conduct foreign relations.

**initiative** A method of amending state constitutions under which proposed constitutional amendments can be placed on the ballot if enough signatures are obtained on a petition. Almost half the states also employ the initiative on the ballot to allow voters to enact or repeal laws.

**injunction** An order from a court to prevent or require an action.

**inputs** The demands upon, and supports for, a political system.

**instructed delegate** A legislator who automatically mirrors the will of the majority of his or her constituents.

**interest groups** Private groups that attempt to influence the government to respond to the shared attitudes of their members.

**internationalism** The policy established after the Second World War that America must take an active leadership role in world affairs.

**interstate compacts** Agreements between or among states made with the approval of Congress.

**interventionism** A strand of American foreign policy that was visible by the end of the 19th century; it included "gunboat diplomacy" and other forms of military involvement by the United States in various parts of the world.

**Iran-contra scandal** The attempt by President Ronald Reagan's White House to trade arms for American hostages in the Middle East.

**iron triangle** A powerful alliance of mutual benefit among an agency or unit of the government, an interest group, and a committee or subcommittee of Congress. Also called a **triangle** or a **subgovernment.**

**isolationism** A policy of avoiding foreign involvement.

**issue networks** A loose grouping of people and organizations who seek to influence policy formation.

**Jim Crow laws** Laws that were designed to segregate black and white Americans and give legal recognition to discrimination.

**Joint Chiefs of Staff** The chair, the chiefs of staff of the three armed services, and, when Marine Corps matters are under consideration, the commandant of the marines. By law, the Joint Chiefs of Staff advise the president and the secretary of defense and are the chiefs of their respective military services.

**joint committees** Committees of Congress composed of both representatives and senators.

**judicial activism** A philosophy that Supreme Court justices and other judges should boldly apply the Constitution to social and political questions.

**judicial restraint** A philosophy that the Supreme Court should avoid constitutional questions when possible and uphold acts of Congress unless they clearly violate a specific section of the Constitution.

**judicial review** The power of the Supreme Court to declare acts of Congress or actions by the executive branch—or laws and actions at any level of local, state, and federal government—unconstitutional.

**jurisdiction** The kinds of cases that a court has the authority to decide.

**jus sanguinis** Right of blood. Under this principle, the citizenship of a child is determined by that of the parents.

**jus soli** Right of soil. Under this principle, citizenship is conferred by place of birth.

**kitchen cabinet** Informal advisers to the president who hold no official position on the White House staff.

**laissez-faire** The philosophy that government should intervene as little as possible in economic affairs.

**lame duck** A legislator or other official whose term of office extends beyond an election at which he or she has been defeated or did not run.

**legislative oversight** The power of Congress to examine and supervise the operations of the executive branch.

**legislative veto** A provision of law in which Congress asserts the power to nullify actions of the executive branch. In 1983 the Supreme Court ruled that the "legislative veto" was unconstitutional, but Congress continued to pass laws containing such provisions.

**liaison officers** Employees of government agencies whose job is to maintain good relations with Congress.

**line-item veto** The power of the president, struck down by the Supreme Court in 1998, to veto parts of appropriations bills. Most state governors have this power.

**literacy tests** Tests of a voter's ability to read and write, which were often used to keep recent immigrants and blacks from voting.

**lobbying** Communication with legislators or other government officials to try to influence their decisions.

**magistrates' courts** Courts in which justices of the peace, or magistrates, handle misdemeanors and minor offenses such as speeding, and perform civil marriages.

**Magna Carta** An historic British document, signed by King John in 1215, in which the nobles confirmed that the power of the king was not absolute.

**maintaining elections** Elections that reflect the basic party identification of the voters.

**major political party** A broadly based coalition that attempts to gain control of the government by winning elections in order to exercise power and reward its members.

**majority leader** A leader elected by the majority party in a legislative house.

**majority rule** A concept of government by the people in which everyone is free to vote, but normally whoever gets the most votes wins the election and represents all the people (including those who voted for the losing candidate).

***Mallory* rule** A rule established by the Supreme Court in *Mallory* v. *United States* (1957) requiring that a suspect in a federal case be arraigned without unnecessary delay.

***Marbury* v. *Madison*** The 1803 case in which the Supreme Court, by declaring a portion of an act of Congress unconstitutional, first firmly set forth and established the power of judicial review.

**marginal district** A legislative district in which the winning candidate receives less than 55 percent of the vote.

**Marshall Plan** A plan named for its creator, Secretary of State George C. Marshall, to provide billions of dollars of American aid to Western Europe to speed its economic and social recovery after the Second World War.

**Massachusetts ballot** Also known as the **office-column ballot.** This ballot groups candidates according to the office for which they are running.

**matching requirements** The federal government's requirement that state or local governments put up some of their own funds in order to be eligible for federal aid for a program.

**mayor-council plan** A form of city government under which power is divided between a mayor and an elected city council.

***McCulloch* v. *Maryland*** An important decision of the Supreme Court in 1819 that established the key concepts of implied powers, broad construction of the Constitution, and supremacy of the national government.

**Medicaid** A public assistance program established in 1965 to help pay hospital, doctor, and medical bills for people with low incomes.

**Medicare** A federal program established in 1965 to provide hospital and medical services to older people through the Social Security system.

**megalopolis** By definition, a very large city. The term has also been used to describe the cluster of metropolitan areas of the northeastern seaboard of the United States.

**merit commissions** Commissions set up to recommend candidates for federal district and circuit courts on the basis of merit.

**military-industrial complex** A term often used to describe the economic and political ties between the military establishment and the defense-aerospace industry.

**minor party** A political party other than one of the major parties; also known as a **third party.**

**minority leader** A leader elected by the minority party in a legislative house.

***Miranda* warnings** Warnings that police must give suspects to advise them of their constitutional rights. Under the Supreme Court decision in *Miranda* v. *Arizona* (1966), before suspects are questioned they must be warned that they have the right to remain silent, that any statements they make may be used against them, and that they have the right to a lawyer.

**misdemeanors** Minor criminal offenses, such as speeding.

**mixed (or modified) free enterprise system** An economic system, such as that of the United States, in which both private industry and government play important roles.

**monetary policy** Government regulation of the economy through its control over the supply of money and the cost and availability of credit.

**money supply** The quantity of money in circulation.

**monopoly** Control of a market by a single company.

**Monroe Doctrine** A declaration by President James Monroe in 1823 that warned European powers to keep out of the Western Hemisphere and pledged that the United States would not intervene in the internal affairs of Europe.

**muckrakers** A group of writers, journalists, and critics who exposed corporate malfeasance and political corruption in the first decade of the 20th century.

**national chair** The head of a national political party.

**national committee** Between conventions, the governing body of a major political party. Members of the national committee are chosen in the states and formally elected by the party's national convention.

**national convention** The formal source of all authority in each major political party. It nominates the party candidates for president and vice president, writes a platform, settles disputes, writes rules, and elects the members of the national committee.

**national debt** The total amount of money that the United States owes to its creditors.

**national presidential primary** A proposed new form of primary in which voters could directly choose the presidential candidates of the major parties.

**national security** A broad concept that may be defined in many ways, but the term is generally used to refer to the basic protection and defense of the nation.

**National Security Council (NSC)** A White House council created under the National Security Act of 1947 to advise the president and help coordinate American military and foreign policy.

**nationalism** Love of country and a desire for independence; it can also mean an excessive form of patriotism exploited by political leaders.

**natural rights** The belief that all people possess certain basic rights that may not be abridged by government.

**negative advertising** Political commercials that strongly attack a rival candidate.

**negative campaigning** Political campaigning in which the candidates appear to spend more time attacking each other than discussing policies and programs.

**new federalism** President Richard Nixon's effort to return federal tax money to state and local governments. The term was also adopted by President Ronald Reagan.

**New Jersey Plan** A plan offered at the Constitutional Convention of 1787 by William Paterson of New Jersey, and favored by the small states, which called for one vote for each state in the legislature, an executive of more than one person to be elected by Congress, and a Supreme Court to be appointed by the executive.

***New York Times* rule** A rule established by the Supreme Court in the case of *New York Times Company* v. *Sullivan* (1964), which makes it almost impossible to libel a public official unless the statement is made with "actual malice"—that is, unless it is deliberately or recklessly false. Also sometimes called the *Sullivan* rule.

**nuclear proliferation** The spread of nuclear weapons to more nations.

**office-column ballot** Also known as the **Massachusetts ballot,** groups candidates according to the office for which they are running—all the presidential candidates of all the parties appear in one column or row, for example.

**oligopoly** The concentration of economic power in the hands of a relatively few large companies.

**ombudsman** An official complaint taker who tries to help citizens who have been wronged by the actions of government agencies.

**open primary** A form of primary election in which any voter may participate and vote for a slate of candidates of one political party.
**original jurisdiction** The right of the Supreme Court, under the Constitution, to hear certain kinds of cases directly, such as cases involving foreign diplomats, or cases in which one of the 50 states is a party.
**out party** A major political party that functions as an opposition party because it does not control the presidency.
**outputs** The binding decisions that a political system makes, whether in the form of laws, regulations, or judicial decisions.
**party-column ballot** Also known as the **Indiana ballot,** lists the candidates of each party in a row or column, beside or under the party emblem. In most cases, the voter can make one mark at the top of the column, or pull one lever, and thus vote for all the party's candidates for various offices. This ballot encourages **straight-ticket voting.**
**party identification** Attraction to one political party by a voter.
**patronage** *See* **political patronage.**
**Pentagon Papers** A 47-volume study of the Vietnam War compiled by the Defense Department and leaked to the press by a former Pentagon official in 1971.
**periodic registration** A system of voter registration in which voters must register every year or at other stated intervals.
**permanent registration** A system of voter registration in which voters must register only once in their district.
**plea bargaining** A bargain in which a defendant in a criminal case agrees to plead guilty to a less serious charge than might be proved at a trial. In return, the prosecutor agrees to reduce the charges or recommend leniency.
**plum book** A listing of the non–civil-service jobs that an incoming president may fill.
**pluralism** A system in which many conflicting groups within the community have access to government officials and compete with one another in an effort to influence policy decisions.
**pocket veto** A power of the president to kill a bill by taking no action (if Congress adjourns during the 10-day period after the president receives the bill). Some court rulings have suggested that a president may exercise a pocket veto only when Congress adjourns for good at the end of a second session, and not during a recess.
**policy** A course of action decided upon by a government—or by any organization, group, or individual—that usually involves a choice among competing alternatives.
**political action committees (PACs)** Independent organizations, but more often the political arms of corporations, labor unions, or interest groups, established to contribute to candidates or to work for general political goals.
**political culture** A nation's set of fundamental beliefs about how government and politics should be conducted.
**political opinion** Opinions on political issues, such as a choice among candidates or parties.
**political participation** The involvement of citizens in the political process of a nation.
**political patronage** The practice of victorious politicians to reward their followers with jobs. Also known as the **spoils system.**
**political socialization** The process through which an individual acquires a set of political attitudes and forms opinions about political and social issues.
**politics** The pursuit and exercise of power.
**poll tax** A tax on voting abolished by the Twenty-fourth Amendment in 1964, long used by southern states to keep blacks (and, in some cases, poor whites) from participating in elections.
**pork-barrel legislation** Bills that benefit legislators' home districts, or powerful corporate contributors, with sometimes wasteful or unnecessary public works or other projects.
**power** The possession of control over others.
**power structure** A term popularized by sociologist Floyd Hunter to describe the community leaders who he said determined policy in Atlanta, Georgia. More broadly, the term is used to describe "power elites" generally.
**precedent** An earlier court case that serves as a justification for a decision in a later case. Also known as **stare decisis.**
**presidential primary** Method used by about three-quarters of the states in which voters in one or both parties express their preference for a presidential nominee and choose all or some convention delegates.
**primary groups** Groups that a person comes into face-to-face contact with in everyday life; for example, friends, office associates, or a local social club.
**prior restraint** The censoring of news stories by the government before publication.
**proportional representation** A system of multimember election districts that encourages the existence of many parties by allotting legislative seats to competing parties according to the percentage of votes that they win.
**Proposition 13** A constitutional amendment approved by California voters in 1978 that limits real estate taxes in the state to 1 percent of previous property values.
**proprietary colonies** Colonies in which the proprietors (who had obtained their patents from the king) named the governors, subject to the king's approval.
**psychological method** An approach in studying how voters decide that attempts to find out what is going on inside the minds of the voters and to measure their perceptions of parties, candidates, and issues.
**public administration** The term most political scientists prefer to describe the bureaucratic process—the business of making government work.
**public assistance** A welfare program that distributes public funds to people who are poor.
**public interest law firms** Law firms, often staffed by young lawyers, that represent consumers, minorities, and the poor.
**public opinion** The expression of attitudes about government and politics.
**public policy** A course of action chosen by government officials.
**quota sample** A method of polling, considered less reliable than a random sample, in which interviewers are instructed to question members of a particular group in proportion to their percentage in the population as a whole.
**random sample** A group of people, chosen by poll-takers, that is representative of the universe that is being polled.
**realigning elections** Elections that may lead to a basic shift in the party identification of the electorate.
**recall** A procedure that in certain circumstances permits voters to remove elected state or local officials from office before their terms have expired.
**recess appointment** The constitutional power of the president to make a temporary appointment when the Senate is not in session.
**recorded vote** A vote in the House of Representatives in which the position of each member is noted and published in the *Congressional Record.*
**redistributive policy** A public policy that takes something away from one person or group and gives it to another person or group.
**redistricting** The drawing of new boundary lines for legislative districts based on the results of a census of the population.
**reference groups** Groups whose views serve as guidelines to an individual's opinion. *See also* **primary groups** and **secondary groups.**
**referendum** A method available in most states that allows voters, in effect, to "veto" a bill passed by the legislature or to accept or reject a proposal, such as a bond issue, made by a government agency.
**regulatory federalism** The emergence of federal programs that set standards and requirements for the states through federal laws and regulations. The federal programs are then implemented by state and local governments.

**representative democracy** A democracy in which leaders are elected to speak for and represent the people. Also called a **republic.**

**republic** A form of government in which the people are sovereign but their power is exercised by their elected representatives. Also called a **representative democracy.**

**retrospective voting** Voting based on looking back and making judgments about the way things have gone and the kind of government experienced during a political leader's time in office.

**riders** Provisions tacked on to a piece of legislation that are not relevant to the bill.

**right to work laws** State legislation designed to outlaw the union shop, passed by 21 states acting under Section 14B of the federal Taft-Hartley Act.

***Roe* v. *Wade*** A 1973 Supreme Court decision affirming that no state may interfere with a woman's right to have an abortion during the first three months of pregnancy.

**roll-call vote** A method of voting in a legislature in which the positions of the members become a matter of public record.

**royal colonies** Colonies controlled by the British king through governors appointed by him and through the king's veto power over colonial laws.

**safe congressional district** As usually defined, a district in which the winner receives 55 percent or more of the vote.

**secondary groups** Organizations or groups, such as labor unions or fraternal, professional, or religious groups, that may influence an individual's opinion.

**Secret Service** The government agency that guards the president, the vice president, the major presidential and vice-presidential candidates, and their spouses.

**segregation** The separation of people by race.

**select committees** Committees created by Congress to conduct special investigations. Although normally temporary, some select committees become, in effect, permanent.

**selective incorporation** The process under which the Supreme Court has applied most of the provisions of the Bill of Rights to the states under the Fourteenth Amendment.

**senatorial courtesy** An unwritten custom by which individual senators who belong to the same political party as the president exercise an informal veto power over presidential appointments in their states.

**Senior Executive Service (SES)** A group of high-level administrators and managers at the top of the government bureaucracy. SES members have less job tenure but are eligible for substantial cash bonuses for merit.

**seniority system** A system, until modified and reformed in the 1970s, that automatically resulted in the selection as committee chair of those members of the majority party in Congress who had the longest continuous service on a committee.

**separate but equal** A doctrine established by the Supreme Court in 1896 under which "Jim Crow" segregation laws were held to be constitutional. Overruled by the Supreme Court in 1954 in ***Brown* v. *Board of Education of Topeka, Kansas.***

**separation of powers** The principle that each of the three branches of government is constitutionally equal to and independent of the others.

**shared powers** The fusing or overlapping of powers and functions among the separate branches of government.

**shield laws** Laws passed by state legislatures that are designed to protect reporters from being forced to reveal their news sources.

**smoke-filled room** A phrase that grew out of the 1920 Republican Convention in Chicago symbolizing the selection of a candidate by political bosses operating in secret.

**social regulation** Laws, rules, and government programs designed to protect individual rights and specific groups, as well as to benefit society as a whole in such areas as health, worker safety, consumer protection, and the environment.

**Social Security** A compulsory national insurance program, financed by taxes on employers and employees. The insurance falls into four categories: old-age and survivors insurance, disability insurance, Medicare, and unemployment insurance.

**sociological method** An approach in studying how the voters decide that focuses on the social and economic background of the voters, their income, social class, ethnic group, education, and similar factors.

**soft money** Until the law was changed in 2002, the term described unregulated campaign funds not subject to the limits of federal law because they went to party committees and not directly to candidates. The 2002 law banned contributions of soft money to national political parties.

**speaker of the House** The presiding officer and most powerful member of the House of Representatives. The speaker is technically elected by the full House but in practice is chosen by the majority party.

**special committees** Committees created by Congress to conduct special investigations.

**special prosecutor** An independent federal prosecutor appointed under the 1978 Ethics in Government Act in cases involving possible crimes by high officials. Later known formally as an "independent counsel." The law expired in 1999.

**special publics** A concept developed by political scientists to describe those segments of the public with views about particular issues.

**special rule** A rule from the House Rules Committee that limits the time to be allowed for floor discussion of a bill and the extent to which it may be amended.

**spoils system** The practice under which victorious politicians reward their followers with jobs.

**standing committees** The permanent committees of a legislature that consider bills and conduct hearings and investigations.

**stare decisis** A Latin phrase meaning "stand by past decisions," a principle that judges often use in deciding cases.

**statutory law** Law enacted by Congress, or by state legislatures or local legislative bodies.

**steering committees** Committees that appoint House members and Democratic senators to standing committees. (The Republican Committee on Committees appoints Republican senators.) Also known as assignment committees.

**straight-ticket voting** Voting for all candidates of a single party for all offices.

**Strategic Arms Limitation Talks (SALT)** Negotiations between the United States and the Soviet Union that resulted in the signing of two nuclear arms agreements in 1972, SALT I and the Anti-Ballistic Missile (ABM) Treaty, and the SALT II agreement in 1979. SALT II was not ratified by the U.S. Senate.

**Strategic Arms Reduction Treaty (START)** A treaty to reduce strategic nuclear arms, signed by the United States and the Soviet Union in 1991.

**strategic deterrence** A policy adopted by the United States after the Second World War that assumed that if enough nuclear weapons were deployed by the United States, an enemy would not attack for fear of being destroyed in retaliation.

**subcommittees** Small committees formed from the members of a larger committee.

**subgovernment** A powerful alliance of mutual benefit among an agency or unit of the government, an interest group, and a committee or subcommittee of Congress. Also called a **triangle** or **iron triangle.**

**subpoena** A written document issued by a court that orders a person to appear in court or to produce evidence.

**subsidy** A government grant of money.

**suffrage** The right to vote.

**supply-side economics** An economic philosophy that advocates both tax and budget cuts to increase incentives to produce in order to expand the total supply of the nation's goods and services.

**supports** The attitudes and actions of people that sustain and buttress the political system at all levels and allow it to continue to work.

**supremacy clause** Article VI, Paragraph 2, of the Constitution, which declares that the Constitution, and the laws and treaties of the United States made under it, are "the supreme Law of the Land" and prevail over any conflicting state constitutions or laws.

**suspension of the rules** A procedure permitted two days each week under the rules of the House of Representatives that allows many noncontroversial bills to be debated and passed by two-thirds of the members who are voting.

**system maintenance** The process of keeping a diverse, unwieldy institution, such as the House of Representatives, functioning.

**tariff** A federal tax on imports.

**third party** A minor party that is an alternative to the two major parties; for example, the Know-Nothings of the 1850s, a party that exploited fear of Irish immigrants and other "foreigners," or the Populists of the 1890s, a protest party of western farmers favoring "free silver."

**ticket-splitter** A voter who votes for candidates of more than one party in the same election.

**tombstone voters** Deceased voters whose names are fraudulently recorded as voting in an election.

**town meeting** An annual meeting held in the spring in many New England towns, at which the townspeople come together to elect a board of selectmen and to discuss local policy questions. The town meeting has become a symbol of participatory democracy.

**transnational relations** Contacts, coalitions, and interactions across national boundaries—such as personal contacts or business relationships—that are not controlled by the central foreign policy organs of governments.

**triangle** A powerful alliance of mutual benefit among an agency or unit of the government, an interest group, and a committee or subcommittee of Congress. Also called an **iron triangle** or a **subgovernment.**

**Truman Doctrine** As enunciated by President Harry S Truman, a doctrine declaring that American security and world peace depend on protection by the United States for the "free peoples of the world."

**trustee** Concept of the British statesman Edmund Burke that legislators should act according to their own consciences.

**unanimous consent** A time-saving procedure under which bills may be called up for consideration in the Senate unless one or more members object.

**unfunded mandates** Federal laws that require states to meet certain standards, but often provide no money to help the states comply. The practice was restricted by a law passed in 1995.

**unicameral legislature** A legislature with only one house.

**union shop** A place of work in which any person may be hired provided that he or she joins the union within a specified time.

**unitary system of government** A centralized system of government, such as that of France, where most of the important policy decisions are made by a central government.

**United Nations** A world organization founded in 1945 for the purpose of collectively keeping the peace and working for the betterment of humanity.

**universe** The total group from which poll-takers may select a random sample in order to measure public opinion.

**unreasonable searches and seizures** Searches prohibited by the Fourth Amendment, often because they take place without a search warrant issued by a court.

**USA Patriot Act** A controversial law overwhelmingly passed by Congress in October 2001, after the terrorist attacks of September 11 on the World Trade Center and the Pentagon. It greatly expanded the power of federal law enforcement authorities to move against suspected terrorists.

**vanishing marginals** An electoral trend in which the number of unsafe, marginal districts in House elections appears to be declining.

**veto** Disapproval of a bill by a chief executive, such as the president or a governor.

**Virginia Plan** A plan offered at the Constitutional Convention of 1787, and favored by the large states, that called for a two-house legislature, the lower house chosen by the people and the upper house chosen by the lower; and a national executive and a national judiciary chosen by the legislature.

**War Powers Resolution** A law passed by Congress in 1973 in an effort to set a time limit on the use of combat forces abroad by a president.

**Watergate scandal** The 1972 break-in at Democratic Party headquarters in the Watergate office building in Washington, D.C., by burglars working for the Republican president's reelection campaign. The scandal led to the resignation and pardon of President Richard Nixon in 1974.

**welfare state** A government like that of the United States that exercises responsibility for the welfare of its citizens in such areas as social security, housing, and education.

**whip** A legislative leader of each party who is responsible for rounding up party members for important votes.

**whistle-blowers** Government employees who publicly expose evidence of official waste or corruption that they have learned about in the course of their duties.

**winner-take-all primaries** Presidential primaries in which the victorious candidate could win all of a state's convention delegates, no matter how slim the margin of victory. The Democratic Party abandoned this type of primary in 1976. The Republican Party has continued to use winner-take-all primaries in many states.

**writ of certiorari** *See* **certiorari, writ of.**

**writ of habeas corpus** *See* **habeas corpus, writ of.**

# Credits

This page constitutes an extension of the copyright page. We have made every effort to trace the ownership of all copyrighted material and to secure permission from copyright holders. In the event of any question arising as to the use of any material, we will be pleased to make the necessary corrections in future printings. Thanks are due to the following authors, publishers, and agents for permission to use the material indicated.

The following images are used along with selected features throughout the chapters:

**Feature: Contents photo:** Frank Wing/Photodisc Green/Getty Images
**Feature: Myth vs. Reality photo:** Photodisc Blue/Getty Images
**Feature: The American Past photo:** Photodisc Blue/Getty Images
**Feature: Comparing Governments photo:** The Studio Dog/Photodisc Green/Getty Images
**Feature: Making a Difference photo:** Chabruken/Photodisc Green/Getty Images

The following pages present the entire contents of *New York Times* articles adapted for this text (see pages 59, 533, 592, 630, 658, 672, and 676).


The New York Times
May 8, 1992

## 1789 Amendment Is Ratified But Now the Debate Begins

By Richard L. Berke, Special to The New York Times

WASHINGTON, May 7. What could be the 27th Amendment to the Constitution was ratified by the necessary 38th state today. But it is unclear whether the measure, which won its first state ratification in 1789, will ever take effect.

The vote by the Michigan Legislature, on an Amendment to prevent Congress from voting itself an immediate pay raise, stunned members of Congress and stumped scholars, who debated whether a proposal written 203 years ago by James Madison could still become part of the Constitution.

In any case, the practical effect of the Amendment would be modest: simply requiring that any pay increase could not take effect until the next session. But as a historical curiosity, the Amendment stands as a barometer of public discontent through the centuries.

Over the years, surges of ratification votes were touched off by public rage over Congress voting itself bigger salaries. The final push came as legislatures in Alabama and Missouri on Tuesday, and Michigan and New Jersey today responded to voters' anger over the Senate's "midnight pay raise" of 1991.

The current burst of activity is a tribute in part to the doggedness of a Texas gadfly. After languishing in a political netherworld for more than two centuries, Madison's Amendment was resurrected 10 years ago by Gregory D. Watson, who at the time was a student of government at the University of Texas, who stumbled on it while doing research on a paper for school. Since then, he has been a one-man band, urging states to pass the Amendment.

More recently, the newest crop of spoon-banging members of the House of Representatives, elected in 1990, also took up the cause as something of a class project, eager to distance themselves from a branch of Government that the public has grown to resent.

"I always knew in my heart of hearts that without a deadline looming ominously overhead, that this day would come," said Mr. Watson, now a 30-year-old aide to a Democratic state legislator in Texas. "The American people want a Congress that is honest, that has integrity. This Amendment is one vehicle by which some degree of decorum can be restored."

### Adds Fuel to Debate

Adding fuel to the angry public debate over Congressional pay and perquisites, Michigan became the decisive 38th state to approve the Amendment. The vote by the state House was unanimous; the Michigan Senate had approved the Amendment in March.

The New Jersey Legislature had hoped to cast the decisive vote today, but ratified the Amendment after Michigan had already acted.

"Most things take a year around here, and others take 203," quipped Bill Martin, a Michigan state representative who helped lead the ratification drive. "I believe that the passage of this legislation has every thing to do with the reform attitude of Congress today."

In pressing for the Amendment, which was originally sent to states for ratification as part of the Bill of Rights, Madison uttered words that would not have raised a brow in the well of the House today.

"There is a seeming impropriety in leaving any set of men without control to put their hand into the public coffers, to take out money to put in their pockets," he said as he proposed the Amendment.

While many members of Congress did not dare speak against an Amendment that touches the sensitive issue of Congressional privilege, Representative Don Edwards, chairman of the Judiciary Committee's subcommittee on Constitutional rights, said the measure was unnecessary.

"To put specific things like this in our beautiful Constititution is disturbing," said Mr. Edwards, a California Democrat. "If James Madison had been interested in this provision, he would have put it in the Constitution. He was sitting there the whole time."

Mr. Edwards said the Amendment was duplicative of current law and that his colleagues were pushing for it as a way of "playing to the folks back home."

### Legal Questions

Beyond the political ramifications, legal scholars raised questions about the Amendment's legal standing—the thorniest, and most immediate, being whether an amendment could take effect 200 years after it was drafted. The first Congress put no deadlines on ratifying the Amendment, though in recent years amendments, like the Equal Rights Amendment, have been sent to the states with time limits for ratification.

Intended as the Second Amendment, Madison's proposal states: "No law varying the compensation for the services of the Senators and Representatives shall take effect, until an election of Representatives shall have intervened."

The closest precedent to the Madison Amendment came in 1939, when the Supreme Court ruled that it was up to Congress to decide whether a Constitutional amendment on child care that had been proposed 13 years earlier could still be ratified or had "lost its vitality through lapse of time." The Congress never acted in the case, so the Amendment did not become law.

### Constitutional Politics

Walter E. Dellinger 3d, a law professor at Duke University, cited the 1939 case as evidence that the Madison Amendment cannot automatically take effect. "This is an amendment proposed in a different era and which failed to be ratified long ago and therefore simply withered and died," he said. "To drag out a two-centuries-old amendment and play Constitutional politics with it is a trivial way to go about dealing with this issue."

Linda R. Monk, a Constitutional lawyer here, said it was "a gray area" whether the Amendment would take effect. "What if some states say,

'Wait a minute: This was 180 years ago that we O.K.'d this Amendment?' " she said.

The matter may not be resolved soon in a test case because, with the current climate on Capitol Hill, as Mr. Dellinger put it, "Congress is not about to pass a pay raise to take effect immediately."

In the meantime, the next step is for the Archivist of the United States to verify that the bills ratified in each state are the same. If so, he then can certify the Amendment and pass it to the President for signing. The Amendment would then take effect, though it would still be open to legal challenge.

Even if the Amendment takes effect, it will face other difficult legal questions.

In a comment that would be prove to be prophetic, Madison said that leaving members of Congress to regulate their own wages was "an indecent thing and might in time prove a dangerous one."

March 6, 1999, Saturday
National Desk

## Death Row Lessons and One Professor's Mission

By Pam Belluck

David Protess believes his career was shaped at age 7, growing up near Sheepshead Bay in Brooklyn. In that year, 1953, Julius and Ethel Rosenberg were executed.

"I saw the headline, 'Rosenbergs Fried,'" Mr. Protess said, recalling that he was the same age as one of the Rosenbergs' sons. "It seemed so unjust, and I'm not taking a position about whether they were guilty or not. What was unjust was that the state orphaned two young boys."

Now 52, Mr. Protess, a journalism professor at Northwestern University, examines death row cases, assigning them to his students and teaching them to pore over documents, re-enact crimes and interview witnesses.

It has brought him and a handful of students remarkable success.

In 1996, Mr. Protess and three students helped prove the innocence of four men who had spent 18 years in prison for a double murder in Ford Heights. Today, the men agreed to a $36 million settlement in a civil suit they filed against Cook County.

Last month, an investigation by Mr. Protess and six students led to the release of Anthony Porter, 43, who had spent 16 years on death row in the murder of a Chicago couple.

The state's principal witness recanted statements incriminating Mr. Porter. A woman implicated her estranged husband, Alstory Simon, a Milwaukee laborer. And Mr. Simon, interviewed by a private investigator working with Mr. Protess, confessed to the killings.

Mr. Porter, although not officially exonerated, is free while the authorities investigate the new findings.

Mr. Protess's pursuit of cases, his enthusiastic style, and the skills he teaches have earned him admirers among students, journalists and professors. Still, he gets questions about his passion in these cases.

"Do I bring a passion to my work?" he asked. "Yeah, I do. Sometimes that is controversial. I just believe that the higher calling of journalism is that after you find the truth, you can in fact right the wrong."

He added: "In some cases, the truth was they guy was guilty, and those students got an A."

Mr. Protess has tempered his approach somewhat since 1995, when he and 10 students tried to overturn the murder conviction of Gervies Davis. They testified at Mr. Davis's clemency hearing. On the day of the execution, Mr. Protess gathered students at his home with a grief counselor on standby for what he said "was really a wake." Mr. Davis called from prison and "I put him on the speaker phone so we could all hear him." Mr. Protess said.

After that execution, some people accused Mr. Protess of being more advocate than journalist.

He believes he should have done things differently. For example, instead of testifying, he should have required defense lawyers subpoena his research so he would not appear to be working for the defense.

"I think we became too personally involved," he said.

Mr. Protess, who has a doctorate in public policy, investigated cases for the Better Government Association, a private watchdog group, in the 1970s. Afterward, while teaching at Northwestern, he investigated wrongful convictions for Chicago Lawyer magazine, asking his students to help with the legwork. He now gets three to four requests a day from inmates and lawyers around the country.

He looks for cases with no incriminating physical evidence like blood or semen, no credible eyewitness, no reliable confession, and other "viable suspects."

In the Porter case there was no physical evidence and a shaky witness. One victim was in Mr. Porter's gang, which cast doubt on motive. The other victim's mother believed Mr. Porter was innocent because she last saw her daughter with Mr. Simon and his wife.

Mr. Protess emphasizes that his investigations are collaborative efforts.

Early on in Mr. Protess's course, the private investigator, Paul Ciolino, teaches about dicey neighborhoods. Mr. Protess makes students act out all interviews in advance.

"We rehearse everything, so that if there's a person in prison who hasn't talked about his crime for years, we practice how to get him talk," said Shawn Armbrust, a student on the Porter case.

Mr. Protess wants his students to learn investigative skills, but he also wants to solve cases. Sometimes he speaks to witnesses before students do. Sometimes he suggests a certain interview team, knowing students appear less threatening than a professional reporter or an investigator. On crucial interviews, he or Mr. Ciolino go along, because "the credibility of college students would be in question," he said.

Mr. Protess sat in a car while Ms. Armbrust and Cara Rubinsky, another student, went into Mr. Simon's home in Milwaukee. The students were to play "good cops" while Mr. Protess would come in later as the "bad cop."

When students found Mr. Simon's estranged wife, Inez Jackson, in Milwaukee, they told her there was a message from a relative in prison that their professor wanted to deliver personally. They did not reveal the relative's name because Mr. Protess feared that would prompt a detailed conversation in which he should take part.

Mr. Protess knows private investigators like Mr. Ciolino may use techniques that journalists would not. Mr. Ciolino tried to elicit Mr. Simon's confession by showing a videotape of a man who said he saw Mr. Simon commit the murders. The man, who worked for Mr. Ciolino, was only pretending to be an eyewitness.

Prosecutors have delayed exonerating Mr. Porter, saying they need to investigate the impact of the fake tape. Mr. Simon's lawyer is not saying his client did not kill the couple, only that it was self-defense.

Mr. Protess said he considered a tactic like Mr. Ciolino's tape inappropriate for journalists unless it was the only way to get information "in a story with life and death stakes." He said other methods were available in the Porter case.

Mr. Protess also involves members of the news media to get the story out. He allowed a CBS producer to follow the Porter investigation. And he often consults with a columnist at the Chicago Tribune.

Sometimes, Mr. Protess's approach spawns the criticism that he is controlling or didactic.

"There were some issues that we did not agree with him on, how to handle the case, and we would have to do it his way," said Laura Sullivan, a student on the Ford Heights case.

Ms. Sullivan, now a reporter with The Sun in Baltimore, added, "It's like your greatest defects are also your best assets. It's all those negative attributes that make him so good at what he does." After the Ford Heights case, Mr. Protess had a well-publicized spat with his students over a movie deal. Ms. Sullivan said the students felt that he pressured them to sign a contract. Mr. Protess said he was angry that the students pocketed their movie fees. He gave his to the wrongly convicted men. In retrospect, Mr. Protess, who is rejecting movie deals on the Porter case, said he could have been "more understanding' in conveying his views.

Mr. Protess has also learned to alter his dealings with prosecutors and defense lawyers, requiring both to subpoena information. When prosecutors interviewed them about Inez Jackson, Mr. Protess refused to disclose her address.

"I didn't want to have a bunch of cops running up there and interrogating her," he said. "They said, 'We're going to find her anyway.' We said, 'We don't think so.'"

The New York Times
July 4, 1996

# The Risks of Keeping a Promise; In Becoming an Icon, a Mill Owner Bets His Company

By Louis Uchitelle

LAWRENCE, Mass. In his 60's, Aaron M. Feuerstein, awakening at 5:30 a.m., began to devote the first hour of his day to memorizing passages from Scripture and Shakespeare. He worried that age would erode his memory and this early-morning ritual became his daily antidote. Perhaps prophetically, he gravitated to Lear and Hamlet, each with his tragic flaw.

Mr. Feuerstein—now 70, gaunt, white-haired, patriarchal—is strikingly theatrical himself as he paces restlessly in his office during an interview, grasping a thin silver-and-mahogany walking stick as if it were a sage's staff. Six months after a fire nearly destroyed his textile company, Malden Mills Industries, he has set himself up as a hero of corporate responsibility, insisting that his loyalty to his workers should be the model for all chief executives.

But in playing the role of model chief executive—lionized in the media for promising to re-employ all his workers once he rebuilt and for paying most of them in the interim—he is risking his company and his reputation. And therein, his wife worries, lies the potential for a modern-day tragedy.

There were certainly safer alternatives. He could have closed and walked away with tens of millions of dollars in fire insurance, giving up to rivals his company's flagship product, Polartec, a synthetic fabric much in demand for sporty outerwear. Or he could have reduced the risk by being far more parsimonious in his payments to his workers and less ambitious in rebuilding.

Mr. Feuerstein will have none of that. He is rebuilding in the grand style, installing huge quantities of the best machinery and restoring the fine details of 19th-century factory buildings—spending in two years what he normally invests in a decade. By relying on insurance to pay the entire bill and on the efficiency and inventiveness of loyal workers to make the investment pay off, he is gambling with the solvency of his company. If he fails, he could become a target of those who would hold him up as a faulty icon of the nascent corporate responsibility movement.

"Aaron never talks about these negatives," his wife, Louise, said. "He came from a family that gave him a lot of self-confidence. He has always had financial security, and that has made him a risk-taker. Me? I support him in all his decisions, but I am the worrier. I see the glass as more half empty than half full."

Mr. Feuerstein became a corporate folk hero overnight for his response to the devastating fire in December at Malden Mills, the company that his grandfather founded and that he now owns and runs as chairman. He guaranteed his 3,200 workers their jobs and said he would pay full wages for a while to those forced out of work while he rebuilt right here. At a moment when layoffs and job insecurity were a national preoccupation, he was praised, as People magazine put it, for being a "mensch"—Yiddish for a very decent human being.

But many experts argue that while his brand of worker and community loyalty, and his largesse, might be excellent business practice for a company like Malden, they are not particularly appropriate for many other corporations, especially those not enjoying Malden's rapid sales growth. "What he did is absolutely not a model for everyone," said David Weil, a Boston University economist and textile-industry expert, "anymore than downsizing is."

Mr. Feuerstein, however, embraced this larger role with the same certainty that King Lear displayed in mistakenly trusting his two older daughters. At first, Mr. Feuerstein said he had simply done the decent, ethical thing, and he still makes this point. As a deeply observant Orthodox Jew, he felt he could do no less. But by March another theme had taken center stage, and increasingly since then—on national television, in Washington and at the numerous ceremonies honoring him—he has argued that his commitment to his workers and to his community should be a prototype for the behavior of all chief executives.

"I feel that I am a symbol of the movement against downsizing and layoffs that will ultimately produce an answer," he said. "People see me as a turning of the tide."

Symbols, though, still have to pay their bills. Malden Mills is spending more than $300 million to rebuild quickly with new, sophisticated machinery and no certainty where it will get so much money. The sum includes $15 million to $20 million paid to 1,380 laid-off workers for periods of up to 90 days, to keep available, the insurer was told, "people vital to the operation."

The risk is evident in Malden Mills' balance sheet. Mr. Feuerstein and his executives are counting on fire insurance to cover the entire cost. So far, however, only $70 million has been collected, and Malden has quintupled its bank borrowing, to more than $100 million, to bridge the gap while it negotiates with its insurer. The outlays include skylights in one building over workers' shoulders, the extra cost of constructing a major new factory in 19th-century style, and higher pay for employees than the going rate in this area.

That is more debt than a company with $425 million in annual sales and $30 million or so in net income can easily support. But Howard L. Ackerman, the chief operating officer, is confident. "There is no reason why profits should not grow to between $40 and $60 million in a few years," he said, "and that would be absolutely enough to handle the bank debt."

But if the insurance company fails to come through, or if sales should fall, then Mr. Ackerman's profit projection would go awry and Malden Mills would be in trouble.

Mr. Feuerstein, voluble on so many subjects, glosses over the numbers. He dwells instead on other themes. For example, he has publicly accused Alfred J. Dunlap—who became a symbol of the heartless corporate chief just as Mr. Feuerstein took on the opposite mantle—of losing the "good will and loyalty" of his employees at the Scott Paper Company through mass layoffs. Mr. Dunlap counters that his action made the survivors more secure in their jobs.

Malden Mills is housed in a series of huge, high-windowed, century-old, rundown brick buildings that front on Broadway for several blocks and straddle the border between Lawrence and Methuen, just north of Boston. The round-faced black clocks on the main tower are stuck at 7:00 and 2:45, and a great pile of rubble, residue from the fire, obscures the steel girders of a new building rising on the site of the two that were destroyed. Passing through, Malden Mills seems like another bygone New England company.

From these unprepossessing buildings come textiles that Mr. Feuerstein describes as pure innovation, sprung from the minds, skills and enthusiasm of his workers. The reason Mr. Feuerstein feels so strongly about loyalty is that he views his workers as the company's creative force and its saving grace.

The textiles that account for more than half of Malden's sales are woolen-like synthetics, warm but lightweight, that are featured today in outerwear sold by L. L. Bean, Lands' End, Patagonia and other outfitters. They are not laboratory inventions, but the result of a unique way that Mr. Feuerstein's workers found of combining artificial yarns and of raising and shaving the pile, or surface, to simulate natural materials.

Malden Mills made big money for years in fake furs until fur, fake or real, lost to the environmental movement, forcing Mr. Feuerstein into a bankruptcy filing in 1982.

But even as fake fur went under, several of his longtime employees were developing the new fabric, sold mainly as Polartec today, that would save their boss and, as it turned out, themselves. They were innovative, and loyal, people like Douglas S. Lumb, 52, whose mother had been a Malden employee. Now chief of fabric development, Mr. Lumb joined Malden as a young man a few years after training at the nearby Lowell Textile Institute, now defunct.

"We were making fleeces in the early '80's for children's blankets," he said, displaying fabric swatches on a showroom table to illustrate his story. "The breakthrough came when we figured out how to make this cloth with different textured faces. Patagonia kept pushing us to do it even better, and finally we did. Lots of people can knit these goods, but very few can finish the facing. You are literally breaking yarns and individualizing the fibers."

The manufacturing is just as complex as the design. Slight temperature changes or shifts in air moisture show up suddenly as imperfections in the fabric. Operators like Adelina Santiago must respond quickly, as she did the other day, shutting her giant computerized machine when the vaguest white line, invisible to an untrained eye, appeared in the dark cloth rolling out at 50 yards a minute.

"I give to catching imperfections the same importance that I would give if this were my own business," she said. Ms. Santiago, a 42-year-old single mother, earns $11 an hour, having joined Malden Mills in 1994 after being laid off from a $15-an-hour job at the Raytheon Company, the nearby military contractor.

"Aaron did not have an obligation to reopen here, but he did," she said. "We felt pleased that he paid us while we were out, but that was not as important as knowing we would get our jobs back."

They are jobs that pay above-average wages. Even Paul Corey, leader of the union local at Malden, said that at wages averaging $12 an hour, Mr. Feuerstein spends $2 more than what is required to hire and hold dedicated workers in this area.

Mr. Feuerstein and his managers think the extra money is worth it. Downsizing might be acceptable as a last-ditch tactic to cut costs when sales are flat or falling, they say, but the challenge for Malden for the last few years has been to increase its staff to keep up with sales growth.

In 1992, for example, Mr. Feuerstein sought to go to a seven-day week from five, and 12-hour shifts from 8; he raised wages then to win the needed work-rule changes.

After the fire, the goal was to restart Polartec production quickly and not forfeit sales to a competitor. Rebuilding here, with an already skilled labor force, was the fastest way; all but 500 workers have been recalled. Ms. Santiago found herself back within a week to operate a machine hastily installed in a huge warehouse nearby. And the union, lifting seniority rules, let managers recall the most skilled workers first.

The publicity that has descended on Mr. Feuerstein has also been a bonanza. "Just to buy the amount of space we have gotten in newspaper coverage would have cost us $40 million," said Jeff Bowman, Malden's brand manager.

Most important, apparel companies are tagging their clothing more frequently with "Malden Mills" and "Polartec" labels. "They are like 'Made in America' tags," Mr. Bowman said. "People feel good about us because of Aaron."

Still, Mrs. Feuerstein worries. "Here is Aaron, as a national spokesman for worker loyalty, trying to save jobs, and what if he loses the company?" she said. "That would be a terrible thing."


The New York Times
October 16, 1997

## What about Mississippi?: A special report; Welfare Law Weighs Heavy In Delta, Where Jobs Are Few

By Jason DeParle

GREENVILLE, Miss. While President Clinton has flatly declared "the debate is over—we know now that welfare reform works," the hard-luck counties of the Mississippi Delta show the difficulties that can emerge when tough laws collide with a weak economy.

The welfare rolls have fallen sharply across this 200-mile stretch of cotton fields and catfish farms, as they have in most of the country. But with unemployment rates hovering at 10 percent or more, many of those leaving the rolls are failing to find jobs. Indeed, during one recent period, the families dropped for violating the new work rules outnumbered those placed in jobs by a margin of nearly two to one.

And the penalties in Mississippi are the nation's toughest. Those who miss appointments or decline work assignments surrender not only their entire cash grant, but all their family's food stamps and the medical insurance of adults. Across the Delta, mothers dropped from the welfare rolls are now turning to relatives, boyfriends or other Federal programs—most notably disability payments—or traveling long distances in search of work.

Maggie Miller lost her benefits and moved in with her sister, raising the number of children in the two-bedroom house to 15. Patricia Watson worked a day at a distant catfish-processing plant but quit after returning home to discover that her baby-sitter could not find her 6-year-old daughter.

Curley Barron threw up her hands and returned her niece and nephew to foster care. Busy caring for her ailing mother, she refused to join a work program and therefore lost the $435 in cash and food stamps she was receiving for the children's monthly support.

It was scenarios like these in places like this that critics of last year's landmark law feared. The landmark measure ended a 61-year-old guarantee of Federal aid and transferred money and authority to the states. While some states might make good use of their autonomy, the critics said, said, others would prove unwilling or unable to construct safety nets of their own. Mindful of this state's many last-place rankings on socioeconomic scales, they summarized their fears with a frequent refrain: "What about Mississippi?"

The same could be asked of other states, particularly in the South, that combine high poverty rates with low spending. But the poverty here has historically run highest, and the spending levels lowest. Mississippi's Republican Governor, Kirk Fordice, is known for the vehemence of his anti-government views. And with black families making up more than 80 percent of the caseload, the welfare reductions inevitably remind critics of the state's difficult racial past.

For all its unique regional features, the Mississippi Delta—the poorest region in the poorest state—may offer broader lessons for the nation's great welfare experiment.

Though many states are boasting of early success in a robust economy, they could find themselves in related struggles should their job markets falter.

Mississippi officials blame the old system for letting joblessness and teen-age parenthood become a subculture's norm, especially in the Delta, and almost everyone agrees that the program needed to change. Officials here say the tough new rules now properly discourage those who do not really need the help.

And not all the state is down-in-the-mouth like the Delta. The Gulf Coast and Tupelo are booming, and the statewide unemployment rate has averaged just 5.6 percent this year, only slightly higher than the national rate of 5.3 percent.

Mississippi also boasts a bureaucratic advantage over other states, like Arkansas and Louisiana, that are trying to put the welfare poor to work in rural, depressed areas. Unlike its neighbors, Mississippi has run experimental programs for several years, accumulating what officials call a wealth of important lessons.

Even in the Delta some women say the new work rules gave them the push they needed to find employment. "I thought it was going to be hard, but it wasn't," said Felicia Fields, 22, the new receptionist at Cunningham's Insurance in Greenville, who landed her position after a few weeks in a job-search class.

Still, the difficulty of converting "work" from a slogan to a program is particularly evident in a region like this, where jobs and child care are scarce, education levels are low, distances are great, and public transportation does not exist. Though the new watchword is self-sufficiency, the region's plantation economy was originally built on the opposite premise. Hugely profitable to a handful of white planters, it rested on a subjugated army of black sharecroppers kept dependent by design.

A poverty belt this large would prove vexing under any circumstances. But Mississippi's program also receives the nation's smallest Federal investment. The annual Federal subsidy of about $2,100 per family is just over half the national average of $4,100. And it is less than a third of the $7,200 per family taken in by the nation's most heavily subsidized state, Wisconsin. That is because under the new Federal program, called Temporary Assistance to Needy Families, Federal subsidies are tied to past state spending levels, and Mississippi's have been the nation's lowest. The state offers a mother with two children just $120 a month.

Donald R. Taylor, executive director of the state's Department of Human Services, said the program has all the money it needs. The Federal grant, though less than what other states receive, actually represents a per capita increase over what Mississippi has received in the past.

Mr. Taylor said the real problem resides with "the old system, which told the poor, 'We know you're not capable of making it; here are a few crumbs.'" After decades of policy failure, he said, "the problems we have stem more from behavioral poverty than material poverty."

But he speaks more cautiously about the 11 Delta counties, which account for a quarter of the state's caseload. He warns that some of the 8,000 welfare families there may just have to move to places that have jobs. "If you've seen

'The Grapes of Wrath,' that's what it was all about," he said. "But you've got some people in rural Mississippi who are tied to the land, and I can understand their reluctance."

"That area's going to be our biggest problem," he said.

### The Experiment: Starting Strong, Losing Steam

Mississippi began its welfare experiment in the fall of 1995, operating a trial program called Work First in six counties. The program, run with Federal permission, placed about 7,000 recipients in job-search classes. It offered substantial subsidies to businesses that hired them. And it withheld benefits from recipients who did not attend the classes or accept offers of employment.

About 42 percent of the participants found jobs. But only half of those—or 21 percent of the total—were still working after the program's 15th month. "The retention rate is a huge problem," said Bill Brister, a researcher at Millsaps College in Jackson, who evaluated the program.

Meanwhile, penalty rates were high. About 19 percent violated the rules and lost all cash and food stamps. (Most had their benefits restored within two months, after complying with the program's rules.) That is, almost as many people temporarily lost their benefits as landed and kept jobs.

And that ratio worsened as the program went on. That was especially the case in Greenville and surrounding Washington County, the only Delta county in the experiment. In the fifth quarter of the program, 72 families landed jobs, while 130 lost their benefits.

Larry Temple, the state official who ran the Work First program, attributed the fall-off to an autumn economic decline. "That's deer-hunting season—nobody's hiring then," he said. But the flagging results could also suggest that the program, having placed the most job-ready clients, might not succeed with the more troubled clients still on the rolls.

Mr. Temple, who recently took a top job with the Texas welfare program, describes the Mississippi experiment as "wildly successful," especially in reducing caseloads. The rolls in the Work First counties fell 19 percent in the first year, compared with 6 percent in the rest of the state, and new applications in the Work First counties fell by a remarkable 65 percent.

Pointing to those numbers, Mr. Temple said the burden of meeting a work requirement leads people to explore other options.

"For the first time in many years, we're getting down to a legitimate caseload," he said.

But he also acknowledged that people who land jobs "are not staying on to the degree we'd like." To address that problem, Mississippi has no longer provides job-placement services itself but hires private companies through competitive bids. And it pays them their full fee only if a client stays at work for six months.

The experiment ended last year with the passage of the Federal law giving new authority to the states. Given Mississippi's political climate, its detractors feared the state would lead a "race to the bottom" characterized by dwindling support of the poor. Mr. Fordice's distrust of government programs seems pronounced even by Mississippi standards, and he has a penchant for the provocative move.

He staged an upset victory in 1991 in part by running a stark anti-welfare commercial. He once threatened to call out the National Guard if the United States Supreme Court ruled the state's universities were illegally segregated. And he wore a necktie bearing a confederate flag to a recent hearing on minority set-asides.

So far, though, the critics' fears have been only half-realized. Mr. Fordice has essentially adhered to the outline set by Work First: with few exceptions, recipients must spend 35 hours a week in a job-search class or a work program, or face the loss of all their benefits. That alone makes the program one of the nation's toughest. But sobered by some of the lessons from Work First, the state did not take several steps that could have made it tougher still.

With Mississippi's economy strong, for instance, officials did not reduce state spending as critics feared they would. And, significantly, they did not shorten the Federal time limit, which restricts most recipients to five years of lifetime aid.

In a 1995 interview, Mr. Fordice insisted that two years would be "the absolute outside limit" the state would allow. But Mr. Temple said the experiment showed, "you can't get to everybody in that short a period—that was a great lesson learned."

### The Delta: A Long History Of Difficult Times

When it comes to the Delta, the state may need all the time it can get. The region has been suffering high rates of joblessness for at least a half-century, since farm mechanization displaced many thousands of uneducated laborers. They escaped in droves to the industrial cities of the North, leaving behind a string of impoverished hamlets. The poverty rate of 41 percent is nearly three times the national average, and nine of the region's 11 counties rank among the nation's 50 poorest.

Frank Howell, a researcher at Mississippi State University, recently examined the job prospects of welfare recipients in the five-county area surrounding Greenville, the Delta's most populous town. He projected the development of one new job for every 254 families leaving the rolls. "There's just a very bleak economic outlook," Mr. Howell said.

Still the rolls have shrunk under the tough new rules. In Washington County, they have fallen 26 percent in the last year alone, despite an average unemployment rate of 9.7 percent. And the pattern holds true for the five contiguous counties, where the unemployment rate has averaged 13.2 percent but caseloads have fallen by a fifth.

Many of the jobs that do exist are distant and difficult. Of the 27 Greenville women placed in jobs last month, 10 went to a single catfish plant, Springwater Farms, in Eudora, Ark. To get there, recipients make an hour-long commute on a school bus that leaves Greenville at 6:30 each morning.

Arriving at the plant, they don hairnets, earplugs and steel-lined safety gloves to work along the clattering saws and conveyer belts that process 100,000 catfish a day. Noting that turnover runs more than 300 percent a year, Donald Taylor, the plant's comptroller, acknowledged the unappealing nature of the minimum-wage work. "You work in the cold, you work in the wet—and of course you're around guts," he said.

But Mr. Taylor, who also hires welfare recipients from Arkansas and Louisiana, praised the Mississippi program for withholding benefits from those who quit. "If they can go back to Uncle Sam, you can't keep them in the plant," he said.

To raise the prospects of welfare clients, the state is offering deep subsidies to businesses. Employers pay just $1 an hour for the first six months, while the state provides $4.15 to bring clients up to the minimum wage. (The subsidy comes in part from money that would have gone toward welfare and food stamps.)

But the results have so far have proved disappointing. Of the 1,299 Work First clients in Washington County, only 61 got subsidized jobs and just 15 kept them—about 1 percent of the caseload. Many employers remain reluctant to deal with welfare recipients, and with unemployment rates so high, they can afford to be choosy.

Kevin Cunningham was wary about hiring Felicia Fields even at $1 an hour. Mr. Cunningham is a gregarious Greenville insurance agent with a tie clip shaped like a golf club. "This could be stereotyping on my part," he said, but he worried her friends might say, "Hey, Felicia works up there at Cunningham's office—she knows where the cash drawer is." And when Ms. Fields, who is black, arrived for work, Mr. Cunningham, who is white, said he warned her that "business language isn't Ebonics."

The comment points at the racial and class tensions that the work program must confront. Almost all the Delta's recipients are black, and most businesses are run by whites. In the case of Mr. Cunningham, he was reassured when he learned that Ms. Fields played the piano in church. And Ms. Fields said that working for Mr. Cunningham was "not as bad as dealing with the church people." The $190.46 she earns each week is more than twice the $309 package of welfare and food stamps she used to receive each month.

"And I can say I earned this money," she said.

### The Penalties: Habits and Duties Collide With Rules

Ms. Fields represents one of the region's easier cases: she has a high school diploma, just one child and a mother willing to baby-sit. Maggie Miller had eight children by six men, no diploma, no work history and no interest in the work program. She lost her check and moved in with her sister, Debbie, who is unmarried, pregnant and has seven children of her own.

Now Debbie Miller, 37, supports the combined family with $324 in food stamps, $484 in Supplemental Security Income for a disabled daughter, and $744 in Social Security benefits for two sons whose father has died. Plus, she added, "I got a man—somebody's helping me with the kids."

Barbara Petty, another difficult client, took a more promising step. Notorious in the Greenville office for her disdain for the work program, Ms. Petty, 34, buried her caseworker with medical excuses and complaints, and even appealed to her congressman. Finally, she just gave up, and surrendered the $96 she received each month for one of her children.

"It was just too much hassle to go through," Ms. Petty said, especially when her two other children received a total of $968 a month in supplemental security payments.

But then Ms. Petty did something that surprised even herself: she got a job, providing adult day care to an ailing man. "I wasn't looking for a job," she said. "But with all those hassles with the welfare, I started asking people, 'Do you need any help?' "

Mr. Temple, the former Mississippi official, points to cases like Ms. Petty's in arguing that the penalties are a key to making the program work. "They are tough," he said. "But they are for people who are absolutely refusing to go to work to feed their children."

But circumstances often fall into a gray zone. The attempt to work can sometimes conflict with the attempt to be a good parent, especially for single mothers traveling long distances with uncertain child care and transportation. The state is promising to reimburse recipients for their child care expenses. But many women still find baby-sitters unavailable or undependable during the hours they need.

Among those referred to the Springwater catfish plant was Patricia Watson, a 34-year-old divorced woman who adopted her niece, Jasmine, at birth. Since Ms. Watson had to catch the 6:30 bus, she entrusted a teen-age relative to take 6-year-old Jasmine to school and watch her afterward. When Ms. Watson returned late in the afternoon, the teen-ager had not even realized the child was missing. "I was scared to death," Ms. Watson said. "I said, 'Oh, Lord, somebody's walked off with my baby!' "

Ms. Watson began a house-by-house search, and discovered her daughter a half-hour later, playing with a friend down the block. She quit the plant, lost her welfare benefits and is relying on her mother for now.

A lost check brought more immediate upheaval to the family of Curley Barron. She was already caring for a mother with emphysema and a brother with a rare bone disease when she took in her brother's two children last year. The children—James, 9, and Joel, 7—had been placed in foster care after their mother developed a drug habit.

Ms. Barron, 44, began receiving $435 in cash and food stamps for the children's support. She was incensed when she received a notice last spring saying she would have to perform 35 hours a week of community service to maintain her benefits. "The kids were a ward of the state—they weren't mine," she said. "So I don't feel like I should have to go out and work for free, just for food stamps." Plus, Ms. Barron said, "I'm not going to neglect my mother."

Saying she could not support the children without the state aid, Ms. Barron returned them to foster care, where they are costing the state $510 a month—more than the cash and food stamps Ms. Barron received. She cannot qualify for payments as a foster parent unless she completes a licensing course. "It doesn't make any sense at all," she said. "I'm going to take care of them better than some stranger."

### The Outlook: In One Small Town, Future Holds Little

Pessimism about the Delta's prospects runs especially deep in Glendora, 90 minutes east of Greenville. The town made a cameo appearance in civil rights history as the place where a black teen-ager, Emmett Till, was beaten in 1955 after he was accused of whistling at a white woman. He was then killed, and his body was thrown in the Tallahatchie River.

"Not much has changed, except for the worse," grumbles the mayor, Johnny Thomas, speaking of the town's shrinking economy. Of the town's 88 households, Mr. Thomas speculates that all but three receive public assistance at some time of the year. Industry is all but nonexistent in Tallahatchie County, and the nearest place hiring is a poultry plant in Water Valley, about 70 miles away. Even by the standards of the region, "Tallahatchie's a challenge," said Jean-Marie Hill, who runs the state's job-placement program in the Delta. Mr. Thomas's main hope for the town now resides with a quixotic plan to build a plant that would slaughter and process goats.

On a recent afternoon, he assembled a half-dozen residents who had lost their benefits after declining work assignments in distant towns. One had moved in with a boyfriend. Another was getting food packages from a private agency. A third was living on her children's disability checks, after turning down a night job in a neighboring county.

Among those dropped from the rolls this year was Carrie Ann Bridges, a 26-year-old mother of four. "She had been cut off cause she wasn't working," said her father, Elijah Bridges. "She had to get a job." She found one on the second shift at the Water Valley plant, sharing the round-trip drive of three hours with her aunt, Geneva Bridges. The two were driving home after midnight in July when Carrie Ann fell asleep and drove into a ditch, killing them both.

Accidents happen everywhere, of course. But the long, late-night commute highlights the added challenges that work programs face in a region starved for jobs. Mr. Bridges now receives $72 each in Social Security payments for his daughter's four children, whose ages range from 11 to 1. A genial man who supports himself with seasonal work at a cotton gin, Mr. Bridges agreed the old welfare system needed to change. But he also warned, "some people really need the help."


The New York Times
January 26, 2001

## The Driveway? In Another State; A Blunder in 1642 Creates Headaches Today For Homeowners Who Straddle a Border

By Paul Zielbauer

SOUTHWICK, Mass., Jan. 24. Up here in the Notch, a tidy pocket of land where Connecticut borders Massachusetts on three sides, strange things happen to ordinary people.

Take Rocco Cianfarani, 64, a supermarket manager who thought he had built his wood-frame house squarely in Southwick. Because of modern-day confusion spawned by a 359-year-old surveying blunder that created the Notch, Mr. Cianfarani is now the owner of a Connecticut address, a Connecticut phone number and Connecticut tax bills he wants nothing to do with. And when he calls the police, Connecticut officers may or may not drive up his Massachusetts driveway.

"It's not funny," he said.

Norma Yourous, 82, is another Notch resident for whom the geographic divot whacked out of Connecticut's otherwise Cartesian northern border is an expensive fact of life. Unlike Mr. Cianfarani, Ms. Yourous officially lives in Southwick. But since she can walk to Granby, Conn., without leaving her backyard, she also pays Connecticut property taxes, which are higher than those in Massachusetts.

"That's just how it's always been," she said.

Then there are Janice and Thomas Carr, whose camper caught fire and was quickly devoured by the Notch 10 years ago. Because the Carrs technically live in Granby, Granby firefighters responded to their 911 call. But when they saw that the flaming camper was parked in a Massachusetts patch of the Carrs' property, the firefighters rolled up their hoses and urged the Carrs to call a fire department from that state.

Result: "The damn thing burned down," Mrs. Carr said.

It should surprise no one. Since April 14, 1642, the Notch has been a headache for residents, governors and, for a few decades anyway, even the English crown.

"It's an interesting puzzle, and tends to be an annoyance in some ways," said Patricia Odiorne, the archivist for the Southwick Historical Society who has studied the Notch and its quiddities. "You would think that they would have things squared away by now."

It all began back in the mid-17th century, when the Massachusetts colony dispatched two Boston surveyors to map its border with Connecticut. The two surveyors, Nathaniel Woodward and Solomon Saffery, started their work three miles south of the Charles River. From there, according to the Massachusetts charter, the colony's southern boundary was to run west to the Pacific Ocean.

Normally, surveyors would simply begin tacking westward, marking the state line as they went. But Woodward and Saffery were afraid of being slaughtered by Indian tribes in the untamed New England interior (now known as metropolitan Springfield, Mass.), so the two instead chose to sail around Cape Cod, down into Long Island Sound and up the Connecticut River, until they reached what they believed was the proper latitude.

In fact, they were about seven miles too far south. So they fudged the mistake, added a large dip in Massachusetts' southern boundary that took in 108,000 acres of what had been Connecticut, and kept moving west. Down in Hartford, officials quickly learned of the maneuver and demanded a new survey. Massachusetts ignored them. Thus began decades of Notch-related feuding.

It got so bad that twice, in 1708 and 1753, Massachusetts and Connecticut complained to Queen Anne and King George II in London about each other's nastiness. Christopher Collier, the state historian for Connecticut, stated the obvious: "This poisoned or embittered interstate relationships for a time."

Incredibly, 162 years passed before both states finally agreed on a compromise in 1804 that cemented the Notch's current smaller size and ended its role in the longest interstate boundary dispute in United States history.

Almost two centuries later, the acrimony along the border has mostly died down. Nowadays, pine trees outnumber people, and peace and quiet still defeat the most advanced cellular telephone signal.

"It's a good story," Mr. Collier said, shrugging. "The only thing is, it's not of great significance."

Southwick moved on. Between 1804 and today, the town became known more for its tremendous ice houses along the spring-fed Congamond Lakes and its place along the Farmington Canal than for its increasingly meaningless boundary squabble.

The ice houses, the largest in New England, were the pride of Southwick, employing hundreds of men who sent ice cakes to customers as far south as New York City, until electric refrigeration put them out of business.

The canal, long buried, opened in 1835 and stretched across 60 locks from Northampton, Mass., to New Haven, on the shores of Long Island Sound. It was a short-lived project; by 1847, the Connecticut General Assembly had approved a plan to fill in the canal to make way for a new railroad service.

But through the years and all the changes in technology and landscape, the Notch, albeit shrunken, remained. As did minor border squabbles.

Around 1900, for example, some of Southwick's children attended a school just inside the Connecticut line whose outhouse, however, was in Massachusetts. As a result, they crossed state lines to relieve themselves, said Donald A. Hamberg, 78, whose father, Harold H. Hamberg, attended the school. "Going to Massachusetts" became a derogatory jab that pupils from Connecticut aimed at their Southwick classmates.

The joke on Rocco Cianfarani, the grocery store manager, lives on today. When he built his house in 1962, he did not realize that though it is in Southwick, his mailbox—therefore his state citizenship and his higher tax rate—is in Granby. He remembers the day he discovered the stone state boundary marker in his backyard flower bed.

"If I knew what I know now when I bought the place, I would have never bought it," Mr. Cianfarani said last week, sitting in his kitchen with a cigarette.

It is nearly impossible to find any Southwick resident who longs to be from Connecticut. "Never, not for a second," was how Gilbert Arnold, 79, a retired Southwick tobacco grower, described the amount of time he has spent fantasizing about moving to Granby. "There's state pride on both sides," he said.

Occasionally, Connecticut fires back, usually with worn cartographic jokes about the Notch —"It keeps Massachusetts from sliding into the sea"—or political bravado.

In 1971, after Lt. Gov. T. Clark Hull was placed temporarily in charge of Connecticut while Gov. Thomas J. Meskill was away on business, he told reporters that his first priority as chief executive would be to rally the state militia, invade Massachusetts and "take back the Notch."

Why would anyone choose to live in the path of a possible militia attack? Well, there are the lake views and the scent of the pines. Mr. Cianfarani, for all his gripes, said he loves his land and loves the Notch, including the acre or so that made him into a reluctant Connecticut resident, probably for the rest of his life.

"I plan to get buried here," he said with a contented smile. Preferably, of course, on the Massachusetts side of his flower bed.


The New York Times
February 4, 1991

## Project Tenants See Island Of Safety Washing Away
By Don Terry

Herman Everett bounded down the stairs, his grandmother's voice filling the graffiti-smeared hallway behind him. "Be safe," she called. "Be safe."

In Mr. Everett's neighborhood these days, people don't usually say, "See you later" or "Have a nice day." They say, "Be safe."

Mr. Everett's neighborhood is the Martin Luther King Jr. Towers, a sprawling public housing project that rises from the faded Harlem checkerboard of tenements lived-in, tenements abandoned and lots now vacant but for the weeds and the rats. Trouble rings the world beyond his door like a tightening noose.

### Dangerous Status Symbol

A few days after Thanksgiving, as they walked through King Towers to a store out on Lenox Avenue, the 19-year-old Mr. Everett and two boyhood friends were attacked by an armed mugger who was after Mr. Everett's black shearling coat —the current dangerous-to-wear status symbol on the city's fast and hard streets.

Only Mr. Everett escaped unharmed. One of his friends, 18-year-old Desmond Lawrence, was wounded in the shoulder. The other, Bernard Richardson, a quiet young man of 20 with a wisp of a goatee, was shot in the back and killed.

Mr. Richardson lived and died a child of King Towers, neither the best nor the worst of the 324 public housing projects that have traditionally been islands of stability in New York's roughest areas, safety nets of shelter for the working poor. His father is a maintenance man, his mother a nurse's aide. Mr. Richardson himself worked in the print shop of a Wall Street insurance company.

And with Mr. Everett and their friends, he dreamed—of cars, college and, especially, escape. But if the projects are still a foothold toward the middle class—if that part of the American dream is still possible in New York—his death is testimony that the climb has grown longer and harder, as neighborhoods like King Towers begin to buckle under the surrounding poverty, homelessness and crime. The midtown skyline rising in the distance down Lenox Avenue might as well be another country.

"Bernard died right here in his own project," Mr. Everett said some weeks after the killing. "You're not safe anywhere. If you're not safe where you live at, where are you safe?"

Mr. Richardson had spent his entire life in the project. He still lived in his parents' apartment, with one of his two sisters and her small daughter.

Tall and powerfully built, Mr. Richardson was a devoted basketball player, and he looked it. But by all accounts, he was just beginning to grow up into the man he had already become; he had a gentleness slightly out of step with the streets.

"He could crush you with his hands, but he never had nothing to do with violence," said Michael Sagginario, Mr. Richardson's boss at the print shop since his junior year at Brandeis High School.

If anything, his friend Desmond Lawrence said, he was a bit of a homebody, often too busy or tired from work and school to spend much time with his friends. "He'd either be upstairs in the house or at work," Mr. Lawrence said. "I liked that. It showed responsibility."

Since graduating, though, Mr. Richardson had been breaking out some, tentatively shedding his shyness with women, hanging out on the corner of 115th Street and Lenox Avenue. One-fifteenth and Lenox, just beyond the fringe of King Towers, is a popular spot. Bored teen-agers with little to do gather there to flirt, show off new clothes and "snap on"—that is, tease—one another. Some young people also gather there to sell drugs.

### 'Risk Himself for Others'

And where there are drugs, there are bound to be guns. Mr. Everett recalled a party a week before the shooting: When somebody pulled out a pistol, Mr. Richardson quickly grabbed a girl, dragged her to the floor and shielded her from harm.

"He'd risk himself for others," Mr. Everett said. "This is a kid who deserves not to be forgotten," said his boss, Mr. Sagginario, who remembers how proud Mr. Richardson was of a small patch of white in his beard. He thought it made him look older.

"I said, 'Let's shave it off,'" Mr. Sagginario said. "He said, 'No. That's my trademark.' But the undertaker shaved it off. He took off his glasses, too. Bernard loved those glasses."

Another memory: When Mr. Richardson was in high school, he was confronted by two teen-agers who demanded his coat. Instead of fighting, he surrendered the coat and walked home in the snow.

For months before he died, Mr. Richardson's parents had been thinking about moving the family back down South. Mr. Richardson did not want to go; he loved the city.

One week after Thanksgiving, Bernie and Lula Richardson took their son home to South Carolina and buried him there.

### The Project: Safety Behind The Locks

King Towers hasn't always been King Towers. When it opened in 1951, the project was called the Foster Houses, after Stephen Foster, the pre-Civil War songwriter whose works—"My Old Kentucky Home," "Massa's in de Cold Ground" and "Old Black Joe"—were popularized by minstrel groups in blackface. But shortly after the assassination of the Rev. Dr. Martin Luther King Jr. in 1968, the residents demanded the name change, to honor the fallen civil rights leader and better reflect the project's population, which is, and has always been, predominantly black.

King Towers is the size of a small town—population 3,600 or so—fit into the three city blocks framed by Fifth and Lenox Avenues and 112th and 115th Streets. The grounds, worn but still not worn out, are a landscape of trees, grass and playgrounds insulated from the streets by 10 rust-colored buildings that rise 13 and 14 stories into the Harlem sky.

In the scarred annals of public housing in America, King Towers—like many of the New York City Housing Authority's projects—must be considered a measured success. King Towers is poor, but it is not one of those devastated places that have become the social scientists' standards of public-housing failure.

### Working-Class Residents

At King Towers, 30.4 percent of the families receive some form of welfare. For the most part, the people of King Towers are working men and women living ordinary lives despite the nightmare raging outside their doors. They are the New Yorkers who catch the early bus to work: the maintenance men, cleaning women and nurse's aides. They are the short-order cooks and low-level clerks. They wash the clothes and empty the bedpans.

After work, they rush home, a series of locks clicking behind them. Rarely are they caught on the street when darkness falls. Some even plot trips to the store as though mapping a route through a minefield.

"If you're going to ride the elevators alone at night," said Crystal Glover, a 31-year-old lifelong resident of the project, "you better go with Jesus."

Lena Everett, Herman Everett's grandmother, has lived in King Towers for two generations and more. She was a young mother and wife when she moved in. She is a great-grandmother and widow now.

### 150,000 Are Waiting

Public housing was built for families like the Everetts. Today, there are 150,000 of them on the Housing Authority's waiting list. The decent, affordable apartments offered an alternative to the crumbling Harlem tenements. For many tenants, moving to the projects meant having a regular source of hot water for the first time; for the upwardly mobile, it also meant a chance to save for a house of one's own.

"This was my first real apartment," Mrs. Everett said the other day, standing over a steaming pan of corn bread.

Mrs. Everett and her husband, Fred, raised four children and a grandson in King Towers. She worked in a small factory, making clocks. Her husband worked at a laundry for more than 30 years before he suffered a fatal heart attack while riding a bus to work in 1982; he was 55. Money was always scarce, she said, hands resting on her hips, but "nowhere will you find a time when we were on welfare."

"Don't get me wrong; I'm not knocking it," she said. "Welfare helps a lot of people in need. It's just not for me. But we got by. I think I must have a guardian angel somewhere."

She had never thought of living anywhere else—until recently.

"The streets around here have gone crazy," she said. "There are so many guns around and now they're killing for fun."

### The Statistics: The Outside Is Worse

In the cold, statistical light of day, life is still easier and safer inside King Towers than out.

"The tenants are more stable, even the ones on welfare," said Dr. Colin McCord, a Harlem Hospital physician who collaborated on a recent study of mortality in central Harlem. "It's a little-known fact that in New York City, public housing has been a great success."

In central Harlem as a whole, black men on average die earlier than any other group of New Yorkers, according to Dr. McCord's study. In fact, death comes earlier for men in central Harlem than in Bangladesh.

This bleak picture, though, is less bleak in the projects. In central Harlem, the doctors found, the overall death rate is 23.1 per 1,000; in Harlem's public housing it is 13.9. In central Harlem, the rate of drug-related deaths is 42.1 per 100,000; in the projects, it is 14.2.

Crime rates are lower, too, In 1989, according to the Housing Authority, there were 56.1 major crimes per 1,000 people in King Towers, compared to 108.5 over all in the 28th Precinct in central Harlem.

But the projects are being squeezed from without.

"The neighborhoods around them have declined dramatically in the last few years," said William Kornblum, a professor at the City University Graduate Center who has been studying King Towers and three other Harlem housing projects for more than a year. "The proliferation of guns in the community, especially outside the projects, has been so rapid over the last few years that it has created a situation that can only be called an emergency."

The chairwoman of the city's Housing Authority, Laura D. Blackburne, said that while buildings around the projects may be deteriorating, "we are not. We are maintaining our properties like a responsible landlord."

"What's wrong with King Towers," said Mr. Kornblum, "has to do with the decline of the social environment of the city and the society. There has been an enormous erosion of opportunities for people who are at the lower end of the scale. We have faltered in our commitment to create communities where everybody gets a share of the good life."

One result has been to turn young men into targets, mother love into despair and hope into skepticism.

Skepticism was running deep at the December meeting of the King Towers tenant association when a husky Housing Police lieutenant, John Odermatt, rolled up his sleeves and rose to speak.

He said that crime—burglary, assault, drug activity—was actually down in the development, that statistically "things are nowhere near as bad as a lot of people think."

When he had finished, Ruby Kitchen, the president of the tenant association, loudly cleared her throat.

"Excuse me," she said. "You know why your statistics are down? People aren't reporting crime. They're afraid. Nothing's changed."

Even the mailboxes seem dangerous.

The development is getting new, bigger mailboxes, and Mrs. Kitchen does not like them because they jut out into the building lobbies, providing a perfect hiding space for a child playing a game or a mugger waiting for a "vic."

"Somebody could hide behind it and shoot you, stab you or whatever," she said. "I was trained before how to come into the hallways, and now I have to learn another way."

### 'He Was a Good Kid'

Lieut. Kenneth Lindahl of the 28th Precinct has been in and out of King Towers since Richardson's death, searching for his killer.

"He was a good kid," the lieutenant said. "He came from a good home. Decent parents."

As he spoke, the lieutenant tiptoed through the debris scattered over a muddy vacant lot across the street from King Towers. He had another murder to investigate.

Lying at the foot of a spindly tree in a valley of abandoned buildings was a dead woman, her face battered and bloody. The woman, in her 30's, might have been dumped in the lot the night before. She had no identification or shoes.

A middle-aged woman approached the lieutenant's partner, Detective Joseph Rendine, and asked, "Can I see her? I haven't seen my daughter in six months. That might be her."

The detective showed her a snapshot of the dead woman and the mother walked away, relieved until the next body shows up.

So far, the police are not that much closer to solving the Richardson case, even though there were at least a half-dozen people standing nearby when he was shot.

"We've had cooperation in the past from the housing area," Lieutenant Lindahl said. "But sometimes people are afraid to come forward initially. It takes time. "

### The Killing: 'Like My Chest Was On Fire'

The sound of gunshots snapped Mrs. Everett awake shortly after 1 a.m. on Nov. 25. She rushed to her kitchen window but then relaxed, thinking to herself, "Thank God, Herman's in the house."

Then her 25-year-old daughter, Shawn, told her Herman and his friends had gone out to the store.

"I felt my heart fall right down to my feet," she said. "I stayed in that window, watching for him until I almost caught the flu."

A couple of hours earlier, Bernard Richardson had knocked on Mrs. Everett's door to visit with her grandson.

"Bernard was his usual quiet self," she recalled. "I asked him to have a seat. He smiled gently."

When she went to bed, the young men, including Mr. Lawrence and several others, were sprawled on her living-room floor playing video games.

Shortly after midnight, Mr. Richardson said he was hungry and wanted to go to the store across the project on 116th Street and Lenox Avenue.

"I said it was too late, but he was hungry," Mr. Everett said. "So we went after we finished playing video basketball."

Mr. Richardson slipped on his brown leather jacket. Mr. Everett put on his aunt's expensive black shearling coat.

"I told him before not to wear it," his aunt said."Why? Because it's dangerous."

Just after 1 a.m., the three friends left the apartment and began walking across the project. Mr. Lawrence, the youngest and smallest, wearing a coat that resembled a shearling but was not, was in the middle.

As they approached 40 West 115th Street, Mr. Lawrence heard music pouring out of an upstairs window. Then a young man, not much past his teens, stepped away from a group on the street and said, "Give me your shearlings."

The three friends ignored him and kept on walking. He did not have a gun in his hand. He was one "fool" against three guys, Mr. Lawrence said. He had to be crazy.

Again the man demanded the coats.

"I looked back, and that's when I saw the gun," Mr. Lawrence recalled. "Then I heard the shot. Then I fell to the ground. It was like a numbness in my arm. It was like my chest was on fire. Then I heard two or three more shots. I thought he was trying to kill me real bad."

The next shot hit Mr. Richardson in the back. Two more were aimed at Mr. Everett's head but missed.

And when it was over, the killer walked back into the project, leaving the coats.

Three hours later, a nurse walked into Mr. Lawrence's room at Harlem Hospital and told him his friend was dead.

"That put me in a daze," Mr. Lawrence said. "This world is crazy."

### Thoughts of Revenge

The other day, Mr. Everett sat in his grandmother's living room, doing homework.

"I think the reason he shot was he felt we disrespected him," Mr. Everett said. "Initially, I don't think he wanted to kill us. He just wanted to prove something to us. After he was shooting, I think he felt some sort of power. It felt good to him to be shooting.

"I've shot a gun before, on vacation down South. It does give you a sense of power. But I don't see killing anyone for no reason, especially now. I know how it feels to lose someone. I can't see myself causing somebody else that kind of pain.

"I know it's not healthy, but I want revenge," he said. "But I know there'd be a big chance that I'd get caught and go to jail. My future would be ruined. And thinking about my future is basically the only thing keeping me sane."

Since the slaying, Mr. Lawrence and Mr. Everett say, they have tried to concentrate on their futures. Both are taking accounting classes at night. Mr. Lawrence dreams of becoming a rap music producer or a writer. "I haven't made up my mind yet," he said.

For years, Mr. Everett wanted to become a defense lawyer. Now he is confused.

"I think I want to be a prosecutor," he said. "I want to get some of these criminals off the street. But I also know that there are a lot of innocent people in jail.

"As far as the criminal-justice system is concerned, I don't have much faith in it. Around here, people could be shooting for five minutes and the cops don't come. The cops only come in to pick up the pieces. Downtown doesn't seem to care about us.

"But it's like I feel very careless about my life. It's like I don't have a fear of dying no more."

### A Lone Voice

Two nights after the shooting, an old woman, her face slack with grief, lingered on the steps of the King Towers community center. She watched a group of boys playing basketball, puffs of breath hanging in the cold night air like ghosts.

"Did you hear?" she said, almost to herself, "we lost another one of our young men the other night."

She turned up her collar and began walking away, the thump of the bouncing ball echoing from the court.

"Be careful, honey," she called over her shoulder. "Our young men are dropping like flies and folks don't seem to care."


The New York Times
June 4, 1996

## She Pushed and a Pipeline Moved; A Dutchess County Woman Fought a Utility, and Shamed It

By William Glaberson

CLINTON CORNERS, N.Y., May 28. In the tradition of ordinary people who wage crusades against big business, Anne Marie Mueser may set a new standard of stubbornness. To fight a pipeline, she put aside just about everything for 10 years, including, she says, cleaning her rickety farmhouse and painting her dilapidated barn.

Her target was a company that built one of the largest utility projects in the Northeast in years, the Iroquois Pipeline, which brings Canadian natural gas through New York State and Connecticut to Long Island.

She was vindicated on May 23, when the Iroquois Pipeline Operating Company, its former president and three other former executives pleaded guilty to violating Federal environmental laws by failing to install required erosion-control devices. The company agreed to pay $22 million in fines in what prosecutors said was the biggest environmental settlement since the Exxon Valdez case.

The battle she started in 1987 and, for some reason, refused to give up, is one of those David-and-Goliath yarns that include dozens of boxes of evidence, angry farmers and suggestions about which actors to cast in the movie. The most dramatic scene would undoubtedly be the one in which just about everyone acknowledges that she is largely responsible for the humiliation of a big company.

Her opposition "certainly played a role" in Iroquois's decision to plead guilty to four felony violations of the Federal Clean Water Act, said an unhappy-sounding Gary B. Davis, a company spokesman.

"I think the resistance we've seen from communities and landowners, the high profile the project has seen, the unnecessary conflict, are a result of Anne's opposition," Mr. Davis said. "She has been the No. 1 most visible opponent of the pipeline since 1987."

Before, during and after construction of the pipeline in 1991 and 1992, she fought. After celebrities like Dustin Hoffman and Arthur Miller blocked a plan to build the pipeline through Litchfield County in Connecticut in 1986, she quickly defeated a plan to put it through her own property here in Dutchess County.

Then, she kept fighting. "The route into Dutchess County was designed purely for appeasing the rich and famous people in Connecticut," she said. "They didn't figure they would get me."

She fought in hearings, and in community meetings. She cross-examined witnesses. She slipped information to reporters. A writer with a doctorate in education from Yeshiva University in the Bronx, she mastered the bureaucratic language of regulators. She built a network of sources through a loose coalition of opponents called Gasp. ("It's what we did when we heard about Iroquois; it's not an acronym.")

She proposed other routes for the pipeline, to minimize environmental damage and take it out of sight. The route that passes about a half-mile from the old Dutchess County dairy farm given to her by her grandfather is called "Anne's Alternate."

She traveled to Canada and upstate New York to meet with disgruntled landowners along the pipe's 375-mile path. Without charging fees, she took on the causes of people who said the pipeline had wrecked their land. She helped critics who said that crews were spoiling hundreds of rivers and streams.

"She can make them jump; she knows exactly how to go about it," said Ricky K. Karpinski, a farmer from upstate Boonville, N.Y. Mr. Karpinski is still fighting Iroquois over damage to his land that he says was done by construction crews sent to repair earlier damage.

In 1991, Dr. Mueser put on construction boots and went to work for local pipeline contractors as a consultant to help them comply with environmental regulations. At one point, she took charge of rebuilding the stone walls in Dutchess County obliterated by bulldozers.

When Federal prosecutors began a four-year investigation of Iroquois's construction practices in 1992, she shipped them 53 cartons and three duffel bags of records. "We have been provided enormous amounts of information by her, which we have invariably found to be accurate and helpful," said Craig A. Benedict, the assistant United States attorney in charge of the prosecution.

Why did she spend 10 years fighting Iroquois after she had already driven the pipe off her own land?

Everyone has a theory. "At first it was because she didn't want it to be in her backyard," said Daniel Macey, executive editor of Gas Daily, an industry publication, who has reported on Iroquois for 10 years. "Then it became an obsession."

Mr. Benedict suggested that Dr. Mueser had been provoked by the way Iroquois executives underestimated her. "They treated her in some instances as an unworthy adversary, which has continued to kindle fires," he said.

Dr. Mueser, who is 54 and a single mother, said part of the answer was that she could afford to spend the time. The co-author of a guide for expectant mothers that has sold about 4 million copies ("While Waiting," St. Martin's Press), she said she had enough royalty payments to keep herself and her 15-year-old daughter in food and fax paper.

But, sitting behind a desk littered with newspapers, transcripts, old soda bottles and a box of dog food, she also suggested that some combination of tradition and mischief might have spurred her on.

When she was growing up in Riverdale in the Bronx, her father worked as a chemist at Con Edison. Eventually, his laboratory findings linked pollution from one of the utility's plants to damaged paint on cars near the plant. In the 1970's, she said, after executives pressed him to reach different findings, he retired.

That ending to his career, she said, reinforced her long-held suspicions of utility executives and their regulators. "I grew up with a healthy disrespect for the Public Service Commission," she said, "because Daddy always felt they did nothing for the public and they were in bed with the utilities. It's all a big sham."

But the Iroquois fight was fun, too, she said, leaning back in her musty study, where "Fight the Pipe" and "Impeach Pataki" signs decorate the walls. She chortled about the buttoned-down types she had tied in knots. "It was kind of interesting," she said, "being in a room full of $300-an-hour-plus suits and beating them at their own game."

It was so rewarding, she said, that she is now working on a book recounting her experiences, and emphasized what a great movie it would make. "You've got this middle-aged woman in Dutchess County who got a pipeline dumped in her backyard, and she said, 'Uh-uh,' and there are all these twists."

Despite the real-life melodrama from the pipeline, both Dr. Mueser and her daughter, Anna Maire, (pronounced AHN-a MOR-a) said there was a price to pay for a decade of activism. Anna Maire said pipeline business often crowded out other things, like arranging for overnight gatherings with grade-school friends. "It's been our life," she said.

For many of the critics and landowners affected by the pipeline, the guilty pleas on May 23 were the finale to a long fight. But some of those who know Dr. Mueser are not sure it will be her last chapter.

"There have been people who have opposed projects, and once their issues have been addressed, they move on," said Mr. Davis, the Iroquois spokesman. "In Anne's case, she's continually looking for issues. This is an integral part of her life now and I'm not sure she'll ever let it go."

For once, Dr. Mueser and Mr. Davis seemed to agree. Outside near the barn, she said the calm after the guilty pleas had given her some time to begin to get things in order in the barn and the house. "We're doing spring cleaning. I'd like to get my life back," Dr. Mueser said.

But then, she said, there are people like the Boonville farmer who are counting on her. "You know," she said, "there are the Ricky Karpinskis." By which, it seemed, she meant that she was not quite finished with the pipeline.

# Index

Italic page numbers indicate photographs, tables, and figures; boldface entries are key terms.

## 1976

**Electoral votes†**

**Carter (D) 297**
**Ford (R) 241**

†A Republican elector from the state of Washington cast his vote for Ronald Reagan, making the official count: Carter, 297; Ford, 240; Reagan, 1.

## 1980

**Electoral votes**

**Carter (D) 49**
**Reagan (R) 489**

## 1992

**Electoral votes**

**Clinton (D) 370**
**Bush (R) 168**

## 1996

**Electoral votes**

**Clinton (D) 379**
**Dole (R) 159**